Research Methods in Education

This rewritten and updated sixth edition of the long-running bestseller *Research Methods in Education* covers the whole range of methods currently employed by educational research at all stages. It has five main parts: the context of educational research, planning educational research, styles of educational research, strategies for data collection and researching and data analysis. The book contains references to a comprehensive dedicated web site of accompanying materials. It continues to be the standard text for students and lecturers undertaking, understanding and using educational research.

This sixth edition comprises new material including:

- complexity theory, ethics, sampling, sensitive educational research, researching powerful people, Internet-based research, interviewing and surveys
- expanded coverage of, and practical guidance in, experimental research, questionnaire design and administration
- an entirely new part, containing five new chapters covering qualitative and quantitative data analysis including content analysis, grounded theory, statistics and how to use them, effect size, and reporting data, all with practical examples
- detailed cross-referencing to a major educational resource web site designed specifically to run alongside this book.

Research Methods in Education, sixth edition, is essential reading for both the professional researcher and anyone involved in educational research.

Louis Cohen is Emeritus Professor of Education at Loughborough University, UK.

Lawrence Manion was former Principal Lecturer in Music at Didsbury School of Education, Manchester Metropolitan University, UK.

Keith Morrison is Professor of Education at the Inter-University Institute of Macau and formerly Senior Lecturer in Education at the University of Durham, UK.

Research Methods in Education

Sixth edition

Louis Cohen, Lawrence Manion and Keith Morrison

Routledge
Taylor & Francis Group

LONDON AND NEW YORK

First published 2007 by Routledge
2 Park Square, Milton Park, Abingdon, Oxon OX14 4RN

Simultaneously published in the USA and Canada
by Routledge
270 Madison Avenue, New York, NY 10016

Reprinted 2008 (twice), 2009, 2010

Routledge is an imprint of the Taylor & Francis Group, an informa business

© 2007 Louis Cohen, Lawrence Manion and Keith Morrison

Typeset in Goudy by Laserwords Private Limited, Chennai, India
Printed and bound in Great Britain by the MPG Books Group

British Library Cataloguing in Publication Data
A catalogue record for this book is available from the British Library

Library of Congress Cataloging-in-Publication Data
A catalog record for this book has been requested

ISBN 10: 0–415–37410–3 (hbk)
ISBN 10: 0–415–36878–2 (pbk)
ISBN 10: 0–203–02905–4 (ebk)

ISBN 13: 978–0–415–37410–1 (hbk)
ISBN 13: 978–0–415–36878–0 (pbk)
ISBN 13: 978–0–203–02905–3 (ebk)

For Lawrence Manion, a wise counsellor and a good friend

Contents

Boxes

Acknowledgements

Our thanks are due to the following publishers and authors for permission to include materials in the text:

Allyn & Bacon/Pearson Education, for material from Best, J. W. (1970) *Research in Education*.

Blackwell Publishers, for material from Dyer, C. (1995) *Beginning Research in Psychology*; Robson, C. (1993) *Real World Research*; Robson, C. (2002) *Real World Research* (second edition).

British Psychological Society, for material from Adams-Webber, J. R. (1970) Elicited versus provided constructs in repertory grid technique: a review, *British Journal of Medical Psychology*, 43, 349–54. Reproduced with permission from the *British Journal of Medical Psychology* © The British Psychological Society.

Campbell, D. T. and Stanley, J. C. *Experimental and Quasi-Experimental Designs for Research*. Copyright © 1963 by Houghton Mifflin Company.

Continuum Books, for material from Walford, G. (2001) *Doing Qualitative Educational Research*, pp. 30, 31, 36, 137.

Deakin University Press, Deakin, Australia, for words from Kemmis, S. and McTaggart, R. (1981) *The Action Research Planner*, and Kemmis, S. and McTaggart, R. (1992) *The Action Research Planner* (third edition) 8 and 21–8.

Elsevier, for material reprinted from *International Journal of Educational Research*, vol. 18(3), Edwards, D. Concepts, memory and the organisation of pedagogic discourse, pp. 205–25, copyright © 1993, with permission from Elsevier; *Social Method and Social Life*, M. Brenner (ed.), article by J. Brown and J. Sime: A methodology for accounts, p. 163, copyright © 1981, with permission from Elsevier.

Hughes, J. (1976), for material from *Sociological Analysis: Methods of Discovery*, Nelson Thornes, p. 34.

Lawrence Erlbaum Associates, for material from Murphy, J., John, M. and Brown, H. (eds) (1984) *Dialogues and Debates in Social Psychology*. London: Lawrence Erlbaum Associates.

McAleese, R. and Hamilton, D. (eds) (1978) *Understanding Classroom Life*. Slough: National Foundation for Educational Research.

Multilingual Matters Ltd, Clevedon, for figures from Parsons, E., Chalkley, B. and Jones, A. (1996) The role of Geographic Information Systems in the study of parental choice and secondary school catchments, *Evaluation and Research in Education*, 10(1), 23–34; for words from Stronach, I. and Morris, B (1994) Polemical notes on educational evaluation in an age of 'policy hysteria', *Evaluation and Research in Education*, 8(1), 5–19.

Patton, M. Q. (1980) *Qualitative Evaluation Methods*, p. 206, copyright © Sage Publications Inc., reprinted by permission of Sage Publications Inc.

Pearson Education Ltd, for material from Harris, N., Pearce, P. and Johnstone, S. (1992) *The Legal Context of Teaching*.

Penguin Group UK, for material from Armistead, N. (1974) *Reconstructing Social Psychology*.

Prentice-Hall, for material from Garfinkel, H. (1974) *Studies in Ethnomethodology*; Smith, R. W. (1978) *Strategies in Social Research*.

Princeton University Press, for material from Kierkegaard, S. (1974) *Concluding Unscientific Postscript*.

Reips, U.-D. (2002a) Internet-based psychological experimenting: five dos and don'ts. *Social Science Computer Review*, 20(3), 241–9; (2002b) Standards for Internet-based experimenting. *Experimental Psychology*, 49(4), 243–56.

Springer, for Hycner, R. H. (1985) Some guidelines for the phenomenological analysis of interview data, *Human Studies*, 8, 279–303, with kind permission of Springer Science and Business Media.

Stanford University Press, for material from Sears, R., Maccoby, E. and Levin, H. (1976) *Patterns of Child Rearing* (originally published 1957).

Taylor & Francis, for Brenner, M. and Marsh, P. (eds) (1978) *The Social Contexts of Method*; Burgess, R. (ed.) (1993) *Educational Research for Policy and Practice*, pp. 119 and 135; Burgess, R. (ed.) (1985) *Issues in Educational Research*, pp. 116–28 and 244–7; Burgess, R. (ed.) (1989) *The Ethics of Educational Research*, p. 194; Cuff, E. G. and Payne, G. (1979) *Perspectives in Sociology*, p. 4; Hammersley, M. and Atkinson, P. (1983) *Ethnography: Principles and Practice*, pp. 18, 19, 76; Hitchcock, G. and Hughes, D. (1995) *Research and the Teacher* (second edition), pp. 20–2, 41; Kincheloe, J. (2003) *Teachers as Researchers: Qualitative Inquiry as a Path to Empowerment* (second edition), pp. 138–9; McCormick, J. and Solman, R. (1992) Teachers' attributions of responsibility for occupational stress and satisfaction: an organisational perspective, *Educational Studies*, 18(92), 201–22; McNiff, J. (2002) *Action Research: Principles and Practice* (second edition), pp. 85–91; Medawar, P. (1972) *The Hope of Progress*; Oldroyd, G. (1986) *The Arch of Knowledge: An Introductory Study of the History of the Philosophy and Methodology of Science*; Plummer, K. (1983) *Documents of Life: An Introduction to the Problems and Literature of a Humanistic Method*; Rex, J. (1974) *Approaches to Sociology*; Simons, H. and Usher, R. (2000) *Situated Ethics in Educational Research*, pp. 1–2; Walford, G. (1994) *Researching the Powerful in Education*; Zuber-Skerritt, O. (1996) *New Directions in Action Research*, p. 99; Winter, R. (1982) Dilemma analysis: a contribution to methodology for action research, *Cambridge Journal of Education*, 12(3), 161–74.

University of Chicago Press, for brief quotations from Whyte, W. F. (1993) *Street Corner Society*, pp. 292, 301, 303; Merton, K. and Kendall, P. L. (1946) The focused interview. *American Journal of Sociology*, 51, 541–57.

Introduction

It is seven years since the fifth edition of *Research Methods in Education* was published and we are indebted to Routledge for the opportunity to produce a sixth edition. The book continues to be received very favourably worldwide and is the standard text for many courses in research methods.

The sixth edition contains much new material, including a completely new part on data analysis. This means that the book now covers all stages of educational research, from planning and design, through data collection to data analysis and reporting. While retaining the best features of the former edition, the reshaping, updating and new additions undertaken for this new volume now mean that the book covers a greater spread of issues than the previous editions. In particular, the following new material has been included:

Part One:

- feminist theory
- complexity theory and educational research.

Part Two:

- ethical codes and responsibilities to sponsors and the research community
- informed consent and deception
- sampling, confidence levels and confidence intervals, together with the calculation of sample sizes
- an entirely new chapter on planning and conducting sensitive educational research, including researching powerful people.

Part Three:

- further coverage of documentary research
- postal, interview and telephone surveys
- an entirely new chapter on Internet-based research and computer usage, covering Internet surveys, experiments, interviews, questionnaire design, evaluation of web sites, searching for materials, computer simulations and Geographical Information Systems
- very considerably expanded coverage of experimental research, reflecting the resurgence of interest in this method in evidence-based education.

Part Four:

- more detailed coverage of questionnaire design and administration, with practical guidance on these matters
- interviewing children and telephone interviewing.

Part Five:

- an entirely new part, containing five new chapters, covering qualitative and quantitative data analysis
- how to conduct a content analysis
- grounded theory and 'how to do it'
- how to present and report qualitative data
- computer usage in qualitative data analysis
- an introduction to statistics and statistical concepts
- hypotheses and how to test them
- variables and how to handle them
- effect size and how to calculate and interpret it
- practical 'hands on' advice for novice researchers, on which statistics to choose and how to use them, from the simplest statistics to high-level factor analysis and multiple regression, and from descriptive to inferential statistics
- advice on how to select appropriate statistics, with charts and diagrams to ease selection
- how to avoid selecting incorrect statistics, and what are the assumptions underlying the main kinds of statistics
- plentiful examples of statistics and how to interpret them, with worked examples that use SPSS output and processing (the Statistical

Package for the Social Sciences (SPSS) is the most widely used statistical package in the social sciences).

Additionally there are copious web site references in nearly every chapter, most of which provide free online materials. A signal feature of this edition is the inclusion of several worked examples, particularly in the chapters on data analysis in the new Part Five.

To accompany this volume, a companion web site provides a comprehensive range of materials to cover all aspects of research (including a full course on research methods on PowerPoint slides), exercises and examples, explanatory material and further notes, SPSS data files and SPSS manual for novice researchers, QSR data files and manual for qualitative data treatment, together with further statistics and statistical tables. (Qualitative Solutions and Research (QSR) is a company which had produced software such as N-Vivo for qualitative data analysis.) These are indicated in the book. A wealth of supporting materials is available on the web site.

We have refined the referencing, relocating several backup references to the Notes, thereby indicating in the main text the most prominent sources and key issues.

We hope that this volume will continue to constitute the first port of call for educational researchers.

Part One

The context of educational research

This part locates the research enterprise in several contexts. It commences with positivist and scientific contexts of research and then proceeds to show the strengths and weaknesses of such traditions for educational research. As an alternative paradigm, the cluster of approaches that can loosely be termed interpretive, naturalistic, phenomenological, interactionist and ethnographic are brought together and their strengths and weaknesses for educational research are examined. The rise of critical theory as a paradigm in which educational research is conducted has been spectacular and its implications for the research undertaking are addressed in several ways here, resonating with curriculum research and feminist research (this too has been expanded and updated). Indeed

critical theory links the conduct of educational research with politics and policy-making, and this is reflected in the discussions here of research and evaluation, arguing how much educational research has become evaluative in nature. A more recent trend has been the rise of complexity theory, originally from the natural sciences, but moving inexorably into social science research. This part introduces the field of complexity theory and steers readers to the accompanying web site for further details. That educational research serves a political agenda is seen in the later sections of this part. The intention here is to introduce readers to different research traditions, with the advice that 'fitness for purpose' must be the guiding principle: different research paradigms for different research purposes.

The nature of inquiry – Setting the field

Introduction

This chapter explores the context of educational research. It sets out several foundations on which different kinds of empirical research are constructed:

- scientific and positivistic methodologies
- naturalistic and interpretive methodologies
- methodologies from critical theory
- feminist educational research.

Our analysis takes an important notion from Hitchcock and Hughes (1995: 21) who suggest that ontological assumptions give rise to epistemological assumptions; these, in turn, give rise to methodological considerations; and these, in turn, give rise to issues of instrumentation and data collection. This view moves us beyond regarding research methods as simply a technical exercise and as concerned with understanding the world; this is informed by how we view our world(s), what we take understanding to be, and what we see as the purposes of understanding. The chapter also acknowledges that educational research, politics and decision-making are inextricably intertwined, and it draws attention to the politics of educational research and the implications that this has for undertaking research (e.g. the move towards applied and evaluative research and away from 'pure' research). Finally, we add a note about methodology.

The search for truth

People have long been concerned to come to grips with their environment and to understand the nature of the phenomena it presents to their senses. The means by which they set out to achieve these ends may be classified into three broad categories: *experience*, *reasoning* and *research* (Mouly 1978). Far from being independent and mutually exclusive, however, these categories must be seen as complementary and overlapping, features most readily in evidence where solutions to complex modern problems are sought.

In our endeavours to come to terms with the problems of day-to-day living, we are heavily dependent upon experience and authority. It must be remembered that as tools for uncovering ultimate truth they have decided limitations. The limitations of personal experience in the form of *common-sense knowing*, for instance, can quickly be exposed when compared with features of the scientific approach to problem-solving. Consider, for example, the striking differences in the way in which theories are used. Laypeople base them on haphazard events and use them in a loose and uncritical manner. When they are required to test them, they do so in a selective fashion, often choosing only that evidence that is consistent with their hunches and ignoring that which is counter to them. Scientists, by contrast, construct their theories carefully and systematically. Whatever hypotheses they formulate have to be tested empirically so that their explanations have a firm basis in fact. And there is the concept of *control* distinguishing the layperson's and the scientist's attitude to experience. Laypeople generally make no attempt to control any extraneous sources of influence when trying to explain an occurrence. Scientists, on the other hand, only too conscious of the multiplicity of causes for a given occurrence, resort to definite techniques and procedures to isolate and test the effect of one or more of the alleged causes. Finally, there is the difference of attitude to the relationships among phenomena. Laypeople's concerns with such relationships are loose, unsystematic and uncontrolled. The chance occurrence of two events in close proximity is sufficient reason to predicate a causal link between them. Scientists, however, display a much more serious professional concern with relationships and only as a result of rigorous experimentation will they postulate a relationship between two phenomena.

People attempt to comprehend the world around them by using three types of reasoning: *deductive reasoning*, *inductive reasoning* and the *combined inductive-deductive* approach. Deductive reasoning is based on the syllogism which was Aristotle's great contribution to formal logic. In its simplest form the syllogism consists of a major premise based on an a priori or self-evident proposition, a minor premise providing a particular instance, and a conclusion. Thus:

> All planets orbit the sun.
> The earth is a planet.
> Therefore the earth orbits the sun.

The assumption underlying the syllogism is that through a sequence of formal steps of logic, from the general to the particular, a valid conclusion can be deduced from a valid premise. Its chief limitation is that it can handle only certain kinds of statement. The syllogism formed the basis of systematic reasoning from the time of its inception until the Renaissance. Thereafter its effectiveness was diminished because it was no longer related to observation and experience and became merely a mental exercise. One of the consequences of this was that empirical evidence as the basis of proof was superseded by authority and the more authorities one could quote, the stronger one's position became. Naturally, with such abuse of its principal tool, science became sterile.

The history of reasoning was to undergo a dramatic change in the 1600s when Francis Bacon began to lay increasing stress on the observational basis of science. Being critical of the model of deductive reasoning on the grounds that its major premises were often preconceived notions which inevitably bias the conclusions, he proposed in its place the method of inductive reasoning by means of which the study of a number of individual cases would lead to an hypothesis and eventually to a generalization. Mouly (1978) explains it by suggesting that Bacon's basic premise was that, with sufficient data, even if one does not have a preconceived idea of their significance or meaning, nevertheless important relationships and laws would be discovered by the alert observer. Bacon's major contribution to science was thus that he was able to rescue it from the death-grip of the deductive method whose abuse had brought scientific progress to a standstill. He thus directed the attention of scientists to nature for solutions to people's problems, demanding empirical evidence for verification. Logic and authority in themselves were no longer regarded as conclusive means of proof and instead became sources of hypotheses about the world and its phenomena.

Bacon's inductive method was eventually followed by the inductive-deductive approach which combines Aristotelian deduction with Baconian induction. Here the researcher is involved in a back-and-forth process of induction (from observation to hypothesis) and deduction (from hypothesis to implications) (Mouly 1978). Hypotheses are tested rigorously and, if necessary, revised.

Although both deduction and induction have their weaknesses, their contributions to the development of science are enormous and fall into three categories:

- the suggestion of hypotheses
- the logical development of these hypotheses
- the clarification and interpretation of scientific findings and their synthesis into a conceptual framework.

A further means by which we set out to discover truth is *research*. This has been defined by Kerlinger (1970) as the systematic, controlled, empirical and critical investigation of hypothetical propositions about the presumed relations among natural phenomena. Research has three characteristics in particular which distinguish it from the first means of problem-solving identified earlier, namely, experience. First, whereas experience deals with events occurring in a haphazard manner, research is systematic and controlled, basing its operations on the inductive-deductive model outlined above. Second, research is empirical. The scientist turns to experience for validation. As Kerlinger (1970) puts it, subjective, personal belief has to have a reality check against objective, empirical facts and tests. And third, research is self-correcting. Not only does the scientific method have built-in mechanisms to protect scientists from error as far as is humanly possible, but also their procedures and results are open to public scrutiny by fellow professionals. Incorrect results in time will be found and either revised or discarded (Mouly 1978). Research is a combination of both experience and reasoning and must be regarded as the most successful approach to the discovery of truth, particularly as far as the natural sciences are concerned (Borg 1963).[1]

Educational research has absorbed several competing views of the social sciences – the established, traditional view and an interpretive view, and several others that we explore in this chapter – critical theory, feminist theory and complexity theory. The established, traditional view holds that the social sciences are essentially the same as the natural sciences and are therefore concerned with discovering natural and universal laws regulating and determining individual and social behaviour; the interpretive view, however, while sharing the rigour of the natural sciences and the same concern of traditional social science to describe and explain human behaviour, emphasizes how people differ from inanimate natural phenomena and, indeed, from each other. These contending views – and also their corresponding reflections in educational research – stem in the first instance from different conceptions of social reality and of individual and social behaviour. It will help our understanding of the issues to be developed subsequently if we examine these in a little more detail (see http://www.routledge.com/textbooks/9780415368780 – Chapter 1, file 1.1.ppt).

Two conceptions of social reality

The views of social science that we have just identified represent strikingly different ways of looking at social reality and are constructed on correspondingly different ways of interpreting it. We can perhaps most profitably approach these conceptions of the social world by examining the explicit and implicit assumptions underpinning them. Our analysis is based on the work of Burrell and Morgan (1979), who identified four sets of such assumptions.

First, there are assumptions of an ontological kind – assumptions which concern the very nature or essence of the social phenomena being investigated. Thus, the authors ask, is social reality external to individuals – imposing itself on their consciousness from without – or is it the product of individual consciousness? Is reality of an objective nature, or the result of individual cognition? Is it a given 'out there' in the world, or is it created by one's own mind? These questions spring directly from what philosophy terms the nominalist–realist debate. The former view holds that objects of thought are merely words and that there is no independently accessible thing constituting the meaning of a word. The realist position, however, contends that objects have an independent existence and are not dependent for it on the knower.

The second set of assumptions identified by Burrell and Morgan (1979) are of an epistemological kind. These concern the very bases of knowledge – its nature and forms, how it can be acquired, and how communicated to other human beings. How one aligns oneself in this particular debate profoundly affects how one will go about uncovering knowledge of social behaviour. The view that knowledge is hard, objective and tangible will demand of researchers an observer role, together with an allegiance to the methods of natural science; to see knowledge as personal, subjective and unique, however, imposes on researchers an involvement with their subjects and a rejection of the ways of the natural scientist. To subscribe to the former is to be positivist; to the latter, anti-positivist.

The third set of assumptions concern human nature and, in particular, the relationship between human beings and their environment. Since the human being is both its subject and object of study, the consequences for social science of assumptions of this kind are indeed far-reaching. Two images of human beings emerge from such assumptions – the one portrays them as responding mechanically and deterministically to their environment, i.e. as products of the environment, controlled like puppets; the other, as initiators of their own actions with free will and creativity, producing their own environments. The difference is between *determinism* and *voluntarism* respectively (Burrell and Morgan 1979).

It would follow from what we have said so far that the three sets of assumptions identified above have direct implications for the methodological concerns of researchers, since the contrasting ontologies, epistemologies and models of human beings will in turn demand different research methods. Investigators adopting an objectivist (or positivist) approach to the social world and who treat it like the world of natural phenomena as being hard, real and external to the individual will choose from a range of traditional options – surveys, experiments, and the like. Others favouring the more subjectivist (or anti-positivist) approach and who view the social world as being of a much softer, personal and humanly created kind will select from a comparable range of recent and emerging techniques – accounts, participant observation and personal constructs, for example.

Where one subscribes to the view that treats the social world like the natural world – as if it were a hard, external and objective reality – then scientific investigation will be directed at analysing the relationships and regularities between selected factors in that world. It will be predominantly quantitative and will be concerned with identifying and defining elements and discovering ways in which their relationships can be expressed. Hence, they argue, methodological issues, of fundamental importance, are thus the concepts themselves, their measurement and the identification of

underlying themes in a search for universal laws that explain and govern that which is being observed (Burrell and Morgan 1979). An approach characterized by procedures and methods designed to discover general laws may be referred to as *nomothetic*.

However, if one favours the alternative view of social reality which stresses the importance of the subjective experience of individuals in the creation of the social world, then the search for understanding focuses upon different issues and approaches them in different ways. The principal concern is with an understanding of the way in which the individual creates, modifies and interprets the world in which he or she finds himself or herself. The approach now takes on a qualitative as well as quantitative aspect. As Burrell and Morgan (1979) and Kirk and Miller (1986: 14) observe, emphasis here is placed on explanation and understanding of the unique and the particular individual case rather than the general and the universal; the interest is in a subjective, relativistic social world rather than an absolutist, external reality. In its emphasis on the particular and individual this approach to understanding individual behaviour may be termed *idiographic*.

In this review of Burrell and Morgan's analysis of the ontological, epistemological, human and methodological assumptions underlying two ways of conceiving social reality, we have laid the foundations for a more extended study of the two contrasting perspectives evident in the practices of researchers investigating human behaviour and, by adoption, educational problems. Box 1.1 summarizes these assumptions along a subjective–objective dimension. It identifies the four sets of assumptions by using terms we have adopted in the text and by which they are known in the literature of social philosophy.

Each of the two perspectives on the study of human behaviour outlined above has profound implications for research in classrooms and schools. The choice of problem, the formulation of questions to be answered, the characterization of pupils and teachers, methodological concerns, the kinds of data sought and their mode of treatment,

Box 1.1
The subjective–objective dimension

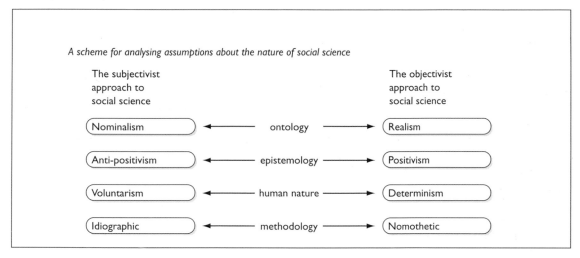

A scheme for analysing assumptions about the nature of social science

The subjectivist
approach to
social science

The objectivist
approach to
social science

Nominalism ◄——— ontology ———► Realism

Anti-positivism ◄——— epistemology ———► Positivism

Voluntarism ◄——— human nature ———► Determinism

Idiographic ◄——— methodology ———► Nomothetic

Source: Burrell and Morgan 1979

all are influenced by the viewpoint held. Some idea of the considerable practical implications of the contrasting views can be gained by examining Box 1.2 which compares them with respect to a number of critical issues within a broadly societal and organizational framework. Implications of the two perspectives for research into classrooms and schools will unfold in the course of the text.

Because of its significance for the epistemological basis of social science and its consequences for educational research, we devote much discussion in this chapter to the positivist and anti-positivist debate.

Positivism

Although positivism has been a recurrent theme in the history of western thought from the Ancient Greeks to the present day, it is historically associated with the nineteenth-century French philosopher, Auguste Comte, who was the first thinker to use the word for a philosophical position (Beck 1979). His positivism turns to observation and reason as means of understanding behaviour; explanation proceeds by way of scientific description. In

his study of the history of the philosophy and methodology of science, Oldroyd (1986) says:

> It was Comte who consciously 'invented' the new science of society and gave it the name to which we are accustomed . . . . For social phenomena were to be viewed in the light of physiological (or biological) laws and theories and investigated empirically, just like physical phenomena.
>
> (Oldroyd 1986)

Comte's position was to lead to a general doctrine of positivism which held that all genuine knowledge is based on sense experience and can be advanced only by means of observation and experiment. Following in the empiricist tradition, it limited inquiry and belief to what can be firmly established and in thus abandoning metaphysical and speculative attempts to gain knowledge by reason alone, the movement developed what has been described as a 'tough-minded orientation to facts and natural phenomena' (Beck 1979).

Although the term positivism is used by philosophers and social scientists, a residual meaning is always present and this derives from an acceptance of natural science as the paradigm of human knowledge (Duncan 1968). This includes

Box 1.2

Alternative bases for interpreting social reality

	Conceptions of social reality	
Dimensions of comparison	Objectivist	Subjectivist
Philosophical basis	Realism: the world exists and is knowable as it really is. Organizations are real entities with a life of their own.	Idealism: the world exists but different people construe it in very different ways. Organizations are invented social reality.
The role of social science	Discovering the universal laws of society and human conduct within it.	Discovering how different people interpret the world in which they live.
Basic units of social reality	The collectivity: society or organizations.	Individuals acting singly or together.
Methods of understanding	Identifying conditions or relationships which permit the collectivity to exist. Conceiving what these conditions and relationships are.	Interpretation of the subjective meanings which individuals place upon their action. Discovering the subjective rules for such action.
Theory	A rational edifice built by scientists to explain human behaviour.	Sets of meanings which people use to make sense of their world and behaviour within it.
Research	Experimental or quasi-experimental validation of theory.	The search for meaningful relationships and the discovery of their consequences for action.
Methodology	Abstraction of reality, especially through mathematical models and quantitative analysis.	The representation of reality for purposes of comparison. Analysis of language and meaning.
Society	Ordered. Governed by a uniform set of values and made possible only by those values.	Conflicted. Governed by the values of people with access to power.
Organizations	Goal oriented. Independent of people. Instruments of order in society serving both society and the individual.	Dependent upon people and their goals. Instruments of power which some people control and can use to attain ends which seem good to them.
Organizational pathologies	Organizations get out of kilter with social values and individual needs.	Given diverse human ends, there is always conflict among people acting to pursue them.
Prescription for change	Change the structure of the organization to meet social values and individual needs.	Find out what values are embodied in organizational action and whose they are. Change the people or change their values if you can.

Source: adapted from Barr Greenfield 1975

the following connected suppositions, identified by Giddens (1975). First, the methodological procedures of natural science may be directly applied to the social sciences. Positivism here implies a particular stance concerning the social scientist as an observer of social reality. Second, the end-product of investigations by social scientists can be formulated in terms parallel to those of natural science. This means that their analyses must be expressed in laws or law-like generalizations of the same kind that have been established in relation to natural phenomena. Positivism here involves a definite view of social scientists as analysts or interpreters of their subject matter. Positivism claims that science provides us with the clearest possible ideal of knowledge.

Where positivism is less successful, however, is in its application to the study of human behaviour where the immense complexity of human nature and the elusive and intangible quality of social phenomena contrast strikingly with the order and regularity of the natural world. This point is nowhere more apparent than in the contexts of classroom and school where the problems of teaching, learning and human interaction present the positivistic researcher with a mammoth challenge (see http://www.routledge.com/textbooks/ 9780415368780 – Chapter 1, file 1.2. ppt).

For further information on positivism within the history of the philosophy and methodology of science, see Oldroyd (1986). We now look more closely at some of its features.

The assumptions and nature of science

We begin with an examination of the tenets of scientific faith: the kinds of assumptions held by scientists, often implicitly, as they go about their daily work. First, there is the assumption of *determinism*. This means simply that events have causes, that events are determined by other circumstances; and science proceeds on the belief that these causal links can eventually be uncovered and understood, that the events are explicable in terms of their antecedents. Moreover, not only are events in the natural world determined by other circumstances, but also there is regularity about the way they are determined: the universe does not behave capriciously. It is the ultimate aim of scientists to formulate laws to account for the happenings in the world, thus giving them a firm basis for prediction and control.

The second assumption is that of *empiricism*. We have already touched upon this viewpoint, which holds that certain kinds of reliable knowledge can only derive from experience. In practice, this means scientifically that the tenability of a theory or hypothesis depends on the nature of the empirical evidence for its support. Empirical here means that which is verifiable by observation and

direct experience (Barratt 1971); and evidence, data yielding proof or strong confirmation, in probability terms, of a theory or hypothesis in a research setting.

Mouly (1978) identifies five steps in the process of empirical science:

1   *experience*: the starting point of scientific endeavour at the most elementary level
2   *classification*: the formal systematization of otherwise incomprehensible masses of data
3   *quantification*: a more sophisticated stage where precision of measurement allows more adequate analysis of phenomena by mathematical means
4   *discovery of relationships*: the identification and classification of functional relationships among phenomena
5   *approximation to the truth*: science proceeds by gradual approximation to the truth.

The third assumption underlying the work of the scientist is the principle of *parsimony*. The basic idea is that phenomena should be explained in the most economical way possible, as Einstein was known to remark – one should make matters as simple as possible, but no simpler! The first historical statement of the principle was by William of Occam when he said that explanatory principles (entities) should not be needlessly multiplied. It may, of course, be interpreted in various ways: that it is preferable to account for a phenomenon by two concepts rather than three; that a simple theory is to be preferred to a complex one.

The final assumption, that of *generality*, played an important part in both the deductive and inductive methods of reasoning. Indeed, historically speaking, it was the problematic relationship between the concrete particular and the abstract general that was to result in two competing theories of knowledge – the rational and the empirical. Beginning with observations of the particular, scientists set out to generalize their findings to the world at large. This is so because they are concerned ultimately with explanation. Of course, the concept of generality presents much less of a problem to natural scientists working chiefly with inanimate matter than to human scientists who, of necessity having to deal with samples of larger human populations, have to exercise great caution when generalizing their findings to the particular parent populations.

We come now to the core question: What is science? Kerlinger (1970) points out that in the scientific world itself two broad views of science may be found: the *static* and the *dynamic*. The *static* view, which has particular appeal for laypeople, is that science is an activity that contributes systematized information to the world. The work of the scientist is to uncover new facts and add them to the existing corpus of knowledge. Science is thus seen as an accumulated body of findings, the emphasis being chiefly on the present state of knowledge and adding to it.[2] The *dynamic* view, by contrast, conceives science more as an activity, as something that scientists *do*. According to this conception it is important to have an accumulated body of knowledge of course, but what really matter most are the discoveries that scientists make. The emphasis here, then, is more on the heuristic nature of science.

Contrasting views exist on the functions of science. We give a composite summary of these in Box 1.3. For the professional scientists, however, science is seen as a way of comprehending the world; as a means of explanation and understanding, of prediction and control. For them the ultimate aim of science is theory.

Theory has been defined by Kerlinger as 'a set of interrelated constructs [concepts], definitions, and propositions that presents a systematic view of phenomena by specifying relations among variables, with the purpose of explaining and predicting the phenomena' (Kerlinger 1970). In a sense, theory gathers together all the isolated bits of empirical data into a coherent conceptual framework of wider applicability. More than this, however, theory is itself a potential source of further information and discoveries. It is in this way a source of new hypotheses and hitherto unasked questions; it identifies critical areas for further investigation; it discloses gaps in our knowledge; and enables a researcher to postulate the existence of previously unknown phenomena.

Box 1.3
The functions of science

1 Its problem-seeking, question-asking, hunch-encouraging, hypotheses-producing function.
2 Its testing, checking, certifying function; its trying out and testing of hypotheses; its repetition and checking of experiments; its piling up of facts.
3 Its organizing, theorizing, structuring function; its search for larger and larger generalizations.
4 Its history-collecting, scholarly function.
5 Its technological side; instruments, methods, techniques.
6 Its administrative, executive and organizational side.
7 Its publicizing and educational functions.
8 Its applications to human use.
9 Its appreciation, enjoyment, celebration and glorification.

Source: Maslow 1954

Clearly there are several different types of theory, and each type of theory defines its own kinds of 'proof'. For example, Morrison (1995a) identifies *empirical theories*, *'grand' theories* and *'critical' theory*. Empirical theories and critical theories are discussed below. 'Grand theory' is a metanarrative, defining an area of study, being speculative, clarifying conceptual structures and frameworks, and creatively enlarging the way we consider behaviour and organizations (Layder 1994). It uses fundamental ontological and epistemological postulates which serve to define a field of inquiry (Hughes 1976). Here empirical material tends to be used by way of illustration rather than 'proof'. This is the stuff of some sociological theories, for example Marxism, consensus theory and functionalism. While sociologists may be excited by the totalizing and all-encompassing nature of such theories, they have been subject to considerable undermining. For example, Merton (1949), Coser and Rosenberg (1969), Doll (1993) and Layder (1994) contend that while they might possess the attraction of large philosophical systems of considerable – Byzantine – architectonic splendour and logical consistency, nevertheless they are scientifically sterile, irrelevant and out of touch with a world that is characterized by openness, fluidity, heterogeneity and fragmentation. This book does not endeavour to refer to this type of theory.

The status of theory varies quite considerably according to the discipline or area of knowledge in question. Some theories, as in the natural sciences, are characterized by a high degree of elegance and sophistication; others, perhaps like educational theory, are only at the early stages of formulation and are thus characterized by great unevenness. Popper (1968), Lakatos (1970),[3] Mouly (1978), Laudan (1990) and Rasmussen (1990) identify the following characteristics of an effective empirical theory:

- A theoretical system must permit deductions and generate laws that can be tested empirically; that is, it must provide the means for its confirmation or rejection. One can test the validity of a theory only through the validity of the propositions (hypotheses) that can be derived from it. If repeated attempts to disconfirm its various hypotheses fail, then greater confidence can be placed in its validity. This can go on indefinitely, until possibly some hypothesis proves untenable. This would constitute indirect evidence of the inadequacy of the theory and could lead to its rejection (or more commonly to its replacement by a more adequate theory that can incorporate the exception).
- Theory must be compatible with both observation and previously validated theories. It must be grounded in empirical data that have been verified and must rest on sound postulates and hypotheses. The better the theory, the more adequately it can explain the phenomena under consideration, and the more facts it can incorporate into a meaningful structure of ever-greater generalizability. There should be internal consistency between these facts. It should clarify the precise terms in which it seeks to explain, predict and generalize about empirical phenomena.
- Theories must be stated in simple terms; that theory is best that explains the most in the simplest way. This is the law of parsimony. A theory must explain the data adequately

and yet must not be so comprehensive as to be unwieldy. On the other hand, it must not overlook variables simply because they are difficult to explain.

- A theory should have considerable explanatory and predictive potential.
- A theory should be able to respond to observed anomalies.
- A theory should spawn a research enterprise (echoing Siegel's (1987) comment that one of the characteristics of an effective theory is its fertility).
- A theory should demonstrate precision and universality, and set the grounds for its own falsification and verification, identifying the nature and operation of a 'severe test' (Popper 1968). An effective empirical theory is tested in contexts which are different from those that gave rise to the theory, i.e. they should move beyond simply corroboration and induction and towards 'testing' (Laudan 1990). It should identify the type of evidence which is required to confirm or refute the theory.
- A theory must be operationalizable precisely.
- A test of the theory must be replicable.

Sometimes the word *model* is used instead of, or interchangeably with, *theory*. Both may be seen as explanatory devices or schemes having a broadly conceptual framework, though models are often characterized by the use of analogies to give a more graphic or visual representation of a particular phenomenon. Providing they are accurate and do not misrepresent the facts, models can be of great help in achieving clarity and focusing on key issues in the nature of phenomena.

Hitchcock and Hughes (1995) draw together the strands of the discussion so far when they describe a theory thus:

Theory is seen as being concerned with the development of systematic construction of knowledge of the social world. In doing this theory employs the use of concepts, systems, models, structures, beliefs and ideas, hypotheses (theories) in order to make statements about particular types of actions, events or activities, so as to make analyses of their causes, consequences and process. That is, to explain events in ways which are consistent with a particular philosophical rationale or, for example, a particular sociological or psychological perspective. Theories therefore aim to both propose and analyze sets of relations existing between a number of variables when certain regularities and continuities can be demonstrated via empirical enquiry.

(Hitchcock and Hughes 1995: 20–1)

Scientific theories must, by their very nature, be provisional. A theory can never be complete in the sense that it encompasses all that can be known or understood about the given phenomenon. As Mouly (1978) argues, one scientific theory is replaced by a superior, more sophisticated theory, as new knowledge is acquired.

In referring to theory and models, we have begun to touch upon the tools used by scientists in their work. We look now in more detail at two such tools which play a crucial role in science – the concept and the hypothesis.

The tools of science

Concepts express generalizations from particulars – anger, achievement, alienation, velocity, intelligence, democracy. Examining these examples more closely, we see that each is a word representing an idea: more accurately, a concept is the relationship between the word (or symbol) and an idea or conception. Whoever we are and whatever we do, we all make use of concepts. Naturally, some are shared and used by all groups of people within the same culture – child, love, justice, for example; others, however, have a restricted currency and are used only by certain groups, specialists, or members of professions – idioglossia, retroactive inhibition, anticipatory socialization.

Concepts enable us to impose some sort of meaning on the world; through them reality is given sense, order and coherence. They are the means by which we are able to come to terms with our experience. How we perceive the world, then, is highly dependent on the repertoire of concepts we can command. The more we have, the more sense data we can pick up and the surer will be our perceptual (and cognitive) grasp of

whatever is 'out there'. If our perceptions of the world are determined by the concepts available to us, it follows that people with differing sets of concepts will tend to view the 'same' objective reality differently – a doctor diagnosing an illness will draw upon a vastly different range of concepts from, say, the restricted and simplistic notions of the layperson in that context.

So, you may ask, where is all this leading? Simply to this: that social scientists have likewise developed, or appropriated by giving precise meaning to, a set of concepts which enable them to shape their perceptions of the world in a particular way, to represent that slice of reality which is their special study. And collectively, these concepts form part of their wider meaning system which permits them to give accounts of that reality, accounts which are rooted and validated in the direct experience of everyday life. These points may be exemplified by the concept of social class. Hughes (1976) says that it offers

a rule, a grid, even though vague at times, to use in talking about certain sorts of experience that have to do with economic position, life-style, life-chances, and so on. It serves to identify aspects of experience, and by relating the concept to other concepts we are able to construct theories about experience in a particular order or sphere.

(Hughes 1976: 34)

There are two important points to stress when considering scientific concepts. The first is that they do not exist independently of us: they are indeed our inventions enabling us to acquire some understanding at least of the apparent chaos of nature. The second is that they are limited in number and in this way contrast with the infinite number of phenomena they are required to explain.

A second tool of great importance to the scientist is the *hypothesis*. It is from this that much research proceeds, especially where cause-and-effect or concomitant relationships are being investigated. The hypothesis has been defined by Kerlinger (1970) as a conjectural statement of the relations between two or more variables, or 'an educated guess', though it is unlike an educated guess in that it is often the result of considerable study, reflective thinking and observation. Medawar (1972) writes of the hypothesis and its function thus:

> All advances of scientific understanding, at every level, begin with a speculative adventure, an imaginative preconception *of what might be true* – a preconception which always, and necessarily, goes a little way (sometimes a long way) beyond anything which we have logical or factual authority to believe in. It is the invention of a possible world, or of a tiny fraction of that world. The conjecture is then exposed to criticism to find out whether or not that imagined world is anything like the real one. Scientific reasoning is therefore at all levels an interaction between two episodes of thought – a dialogue between two voices, the one imaginative and the other critical; a dialogue, if you like, between the possible and the actual, between proposal and disposal, conjecture and criticism, between what might be true and what is in fact the case.
>
> (Medawar 1972)

Kerlinger (1970) has identified two criteria for 'good' hypotheses. The first is that hypotheses are statements about the relations between variables; and second, that hypotheses carry clear implications for testing the stated relations. To these he adds two ancillary criteria: that hypotheses disclose compatibility with current knowledge; and that they are expressed as economically as possible. Thus if we conjecture that social class background determines academic achievement, we have a relationship between one variable, social class, and another, academic achievement. And since both can be measured, the primary criteria specified by Kerlinger can be met. Neither do they violate the ancillary criteria proposed by Kerlinger (see also Box 1.4).

He further identifies four reasons for the importance of hypotheses as tools of research. First, they organize the efforts of researchers. The relationship expressed in the hypothesis indicates what they should do. They enable them to understand the problem with greater clarity and provide them with a framework for collecting, analysing and interpreting their data.

Box 1.4
The hypothesis

> Once one has a hypothesis to work on, the scientist can move forward; the hypothesis will guide the researcher on the selection of some observations rather than others and will suggest experiments. Scientists soon learn by experience the characteristics of a good hypothesis. A hypothesis that is so loose as to accommodate *any* phenomenon tells us precisely nothing; the more phenomena it prohibits, the more informative it is.
>
> A good hypothesis must also have *logical immediacy*, i.e. it must provide an explanation of whatever it is that needs to be explained and not an explanation of other phenomena. Logical immediacy in a hypothesis means that it can be tested by comparatively direct and practicable means. A large part of the *art of the soluble* is the art of devising hypotheses that can be tested by practicable experiments.

Source: adapted from Medawar 1981

Second, they are, in Kerlinger's words, the working instruments of theory. They can be deduced from theory or from other hypotheses. Third, they can be tested, empirically or experimentally, thus resulting in confirmation or rejection; and there is always the possibility that a hypothesis, once supported and established, may become a law. Fourth, hypotheses are powerful tools for the advancement of knowledge because, as Kerlinger (1970) explains, they enable us to get outside ourselves. Hypotheses and concepts play a crucial part in the scientific method and it is to this that we now turn our attention.

The scientific method

If the most distinctive feature of science is its empirical nature, the next most important characteristic is its set of procedures which show not only how findings have been arrived at, but are sufficiently clear for fellow-scientists to repeat them, i.e. to check them out with the same or other materials and thereby test the results. As Cuff and Payne (1979) say: 'A scientific approach necessarily involves standards and procedures for demonstrating the "empirical warrant" of its findings, showing the match or fit between its statements and what is happening or has happened in the world' (Cuff and Payne 1979: 4). These standards and procedures we will call for convenience 'the scientific method', though this can be somewhat misleading for the following reason: the combination of the definite article, adjective and singular noun conjures up in the minds of some people a single invariant approach to problem-solving, an approach frequently involving atoms or rats, and taking place within the confines of a laboratory. Yet there is much more to it than this. The term in fact cloaks a number of methods which vary in their degree of sophistication depending on their function and the particular stage of development a science has reached. Box 1.5 sets out the sequence of stages through which a science normally passes in its development or, perhaps more realistically, that are constantly present in its progress and on which scientists may draw depending on the kind of information they seek or the kind of problem confronting them. Of particular interest in our efforts to elucidate the term 'scientific method' are stages 2, 3 and 4. Stage 2 is a relatively uncomplicated point at which the researcher is content to observe and record facts and possibly arrive at some system of classification. Much research in the field of education, especially at classroom and school level, is conducted in this way, e.g. surveys and case studies. Stage 3 introduces a note of added sophistication as attempts are made to establish relationships between variables within a loose framework of inchoate theory. Stage 4 is the most sophisticated stage and often the one that many people equate exclusively with the scientific method. In order to arrive at causality, as distinct from mere measures of association, researchers here design experimental situations in which variables are manipulated to test their chosen hypotheses. This process moves from early, inchoate ideas, to more rigorous hypotheses, to empirical testing of those hypotheses, thence to confirmation or modification of the hypotheses (Kerlinger 1970).

With stages 3 and 4 of Box 1.5 in mind, we may say that the scientific method begins

Box 1.5
Stages in the development of a science

1 Definition of the science and identification of the phenomena that are to be subsumed under it.
2 Observational stage at which the relevant factors, variables or items are identified and labelled, and at which categories and taxonomies are developed.
3 Correlational research in which variables and parameters are related to one another and information is systematically integrated as theories begin to develop.
4 The systematic and controlled manipulation of variables to see if experiments will produce expected results, thus moving from correlation to causality.
5 The firm establishment of a body of theory as the outcomes of the earlier stages are accumulated. Depending on the nature of the phenomena under scrutiny, laws may be formulated and systematized.
6 The use of the established body of theory in the resolution of problems or as a source of further hypotheses.

consciously and deliberately by selecting from the total number of elements in a given situation. More recently Hitchcock and Hughes (1995: 23) suggest an eight-stage model of the scientific method that echoes Kerlinger. This is represented in Box 1.6.

The elements the researchers fasten on to will naturally be suitable for scientific formulation; this means simply that they will possess quantitative

Box 1.6
An eight-stage model of the scientific method

Stage 1: Hypotheses, hunches and guesses
Stage 2: Experiment designed; samples taken; variables isolated
Stage 3: Correlations observed; patterns identified
Stage 4: Hypotheses formed to explain regularities
Stage 5: Explanations and predictions tested; falsifiability
Stage 6: Laws developed or disconfirmation (hypothesis rejected)
Stage 7: Generalizations made
Stage 8: New theories.

aspects. Their principal working tool will be the hypothesis which, as we have seen, is a statement indicating a relationship (or its absence) between two or more of the chosen elements and stated in such a way as to carry clear implications for testing. Researchers then choose the most appropriate method and put their hypotheses to the test.

Criticisms of positivism and the scientific method

In spite of the scientific enterprise's proven success using positivism – especially in the field of natural science – its ontological and epistemological bases have been the focus of sustained and sometimes vehement criticism from some quarters. Beginning in the second half of the nineteenth century, the revolt against positivism occurred on a broad front, attracting some of the best intellectuals in Europe – philosophers, scientists, social critics and creative artists. Essentially, it has been a reaction against the world picture projected by science which, it is contended, undermines life and mind. The precise target of the anti-positivists' attack has been science's mechanistic and reductionist view of nature which, by definition, defines life in measurable terms rather than inner experience, and excludes notions of choice, freedom, individuality, and moral responsibility, regarding the universe as a living organism rather than as a machine (e.g. Nesfield-Cookson 1987).

Another challenge to the claims of positivism came from Søren Kierkegaard, the Danish philosopher, one of the originators of existentialism. Kierkegaard was concerned with individuals and their need to fulfil themselves to the highest level of development. This realization of a person's potential was for him the meaning of existence which he saw as 'concrete and individual, unique and irreducible, not amenable to conceptualization' (Beck 1979). Characteristic features of the age in which we live – democracy's trust in the crowd mentality, the ascendancy of reason, scientific and technological progress – all militate against the achievement of this end and contribute to the dehumanization of the individual. In his desire to free people from

their illusions, the illusion Kierkegaard was most concerned about was that of objectivity. By this he meant the imposition of rules of behaviour and thought, and the making of a person into an observer set on discovering general laws governing human behaviour. The capacity for subjectivity, he argued, should be regained. This he regarded as the ability to consider one's own relationship to whatever constitutes the focus of inquiry. The contrast he made between objectivity and subjectivity is brought out in the following passage:

> When the question of truth is raised in an objective manner, reflection is directed objectively to the truth as an object to which the knower is related. Reflection is not focused on the relationship, however, but upon the question of whether it is the truth to which the knower is related. If only the object to which he is related is the truth, the subject is accounted to be in the truth. When the question of truth is raised subjectively, reflection is directed subjectively to the nature of the individual's relationship; if only the mode of this relationship is in the truth, the individual is in the truth, even if he should happen to be thus related to what is not true.
>
> (Kierkegaard 1974: 178)

For Kierkegaard, 'subjectivity and concreteness of truth are together the light. Anyone who is committed to science, or to rule-governed morality, is benighted, and needs to be rescued from his state of darkness' (Warnock 1970).

Also concerned with the dehumanizing effects of the social sciences is Ions (1977). While acknowledging that they can take much credit for throwing light in dark corners, he expresses serious concern at the way in which quantification and computation, assisted by statistical theory and method, are used. He argues that quantification is a form of collectivism, but that this runs the risk of depersonalization. His objection is not directed at quantification *per se*, but at quantification when it becomes an end in itself – 'a branch of mathematics rather than a humane study seeking to explore and elucidate the gritty circumstances of the human condition' (Ions 1977). This echoes Horkheimer's (1972) powerful critique of positivism as the mathematization of concepts about nature.

Another forceful critic of the objective consciousness has been Roszak (1970; 1972), who argues that science, in its pursuit of objectivity, is a form of alienation from our true selves and from nature. The justification for any intellectual activity lies in the effect it has on increasing our awareness and degree of consciousness. This increase, some claim, has been retarded in our time by the excessive influence that the positivist paradigm has exerted on areas of our intellectual life. Holbrook (1977), for example, affording consciousness a central position in human existence and deeply concerned with what happens to it, condemns positivism and empiricism for their bankruptcy of the inner world, morality and subjectivity.

Hampden-Turner (1970) concludes that the social science view of human beings is biased in that it is conservative and ignores important qualities. This restricted image of humans, he contends, comes about because social scientists concentrate on the repetitive, predictable and invariant aspects of the person; on 'visible externalities' to the exclusion of the subjective world; and on the parts of the person in their endeavours to understand the whole.

Habermas (1972), in keeping with the Frankfurt School of critical theory (critical theory is discussed below), provides a corrosive critique of positivism, arguing that the scientific mentality has been elevated to an almost unassailable position – almost to the level of a religion (scientism) – as being the only epistemology of the west. In this view all knowledge becomes equated with scientific knowledge. This neglects hermeneutic, aesthetic, critical, moral, creative and other forms of knowledge. It reduces behaviour to technicism.

Positivism's concern for control and, thereby, its appeal to the passivity of behaviourism and for instrumental reason is a serious danger to the more open-ended, creative, humanitarian aspects of social behaviour. Habermas (1972; 1974) and Horkheimer (1972) argue that scientism silences an important debate about values, informed opinion, moral judgements and beliefs. Scientific explanation seems to be the only means of explaining behaviour, and, for them, this seriously diminishes the very characteristics that make humans human. It makes for a society without conscience. Positivism is unable to answer many interesting or important areas of life (Habermas 1972: 300). Indeed this is an echo of Wittgenstein's (1974) famous comment that when all possible scientific questions have been addressed they have left untouched the main problems of life.

Other criticisms are commonly levelled at positivistic social science from within its own ranks. One is that it fails to take account of our unique ability to interpret our experiences and represent them to ourselves. We can and do construct theories about ourselves and our world; moreover, we act on these theories. In failing to recognize this, positivistic social science is said to ignore the profound differences between itself and the natural sciences. Social science, unlike natural science, stands in a subject–subject rather than a subject–object relation to its field of study, and works in a pre-interpreted world in the sense that the meanings that subjects hold are part of their construction of the world (Giddens 1976).

The difficulty in which positivism finds itself is that it regards human behaviour as passive, essentially determined and controlled, thereby ignoring intention, individualism and freedom. This approach suffers from the same difficulties that inhere in behaviourism, which has scarcely recovered from Chomsky's (1959) withering criticism where he writes that a singular problem of behaviourism is our inability to infer causes from behaviour, to identify the stimulus that has brought about the response – the weakness of Skinner's stimulus–response theory. This problem with positivism also rehearses the familiar problem in social theory, namely the tension between agency and structure (Layder 1994): humans exercise agency – individual choice and intention – not necessarily in circumstances of their own choosing, but nevertheless they do not behave simply or deterministically like puppets.

Finally, the findings of positivistic social science are often said to be so banal and trivial that they are of little consequence to those for whom they are intended, namely, teachers, social workers, counsellors, personnel managers, and the like. The more effort, it seems, that researchers put into their scientific experimentation in the laboratory by restricting, simplifying and controlling variables, the more likely they are to end up with a 'pruned, synthetic version of the whole, a constructed play of puppets in a restricted environment.'[4]

These are formidable criticisms; but what alternatives are proposed by the detractors of positivistic social science?

Alternatives to positivistic social science: naturalistic approaches

Although the opponents of positivism within social science itself subscribe to a variety of schools of thought each with its own subtly different epistemological viewpoint, they are united by their common rejection of the belief that human behaviour is governed by general, universal laws and characterized by underlying regularities. Moreover, they would agree that the social world can be understood only from the standpoint of the individuals who are part of the ongoing action being investigated and that their model of a person is an autonomous one, not the plastic version favoured by positivist researchers. In rejecting the viewpoint of the detached, objective observer – a mandatory feature of traditional research – anti-positivists would argue that individuals' behaviour can only be understood by the researcher sharing their frame of reference: understanding of individuals' interpretations of the world around them has to come from the inside, not the outside. Social science is thus seen as a subjective rather than an objective undertaking, as a means of dealing with the direct experience of people in specific contexts, and where social scientists understand, explain and demystify social reality through the eyes of different participants; the participants themselves define the social reality (Beck 1979) (see http://www.routledge.com/textbooks/9780415368780 – Chapter 1, file 1.3. ppt).

The anti-positivist movement has influenced those constituent areas of social science of most concern to us, namely, psychology, social psychology and sociology. In the case of psychology, for instance, a school of humanistic psychology has emerged alongside the coexisting behaviouristic and psychoanalytic schools. Arising as a response to the challenge to combat the growing feelings of dehumanization which characterize many social and cultural milieux, it sets out to study and understand the person as a *whole* (Buhler and Allen 1972). Humanistic psychologists present a model of people that is positive, active and purposive, and at the same time stresses their own involvement with the life experience itself. They do not stand apart, introspective, hypothesizing. Their interest is directed at the intentional and creative aspects of the human being. The perspective adopted by humanistic psychologists is naturally reflected in their methodology. They are dedicated to studying the individual in preference to the group, and consequently prefer idiographic approaches to nomothetic ones. The implications of the movement's philosophy for the education of the human being have been drawn by Carl Rogers.[5]

Comparable developments within social psychology may be perceived in the 'science of persons' movement. It is argued here that we must use ourselves as a key to our understanding of others and conversely, our understanding of others as a way of finding out about ourselves, an anthropomorphic model of people. Since anthropomorphism means, literally, the attribution of human form and personality, the implied criticism is that social psychology as traditionally conceived has singularly failed, so far, to model people as they really are. As some wry commentators have pleaded, 'For scientific purposes, treat people as if they were human beings' (Harré and Secord 1972), which entails treating them as capable of monitoring and arranging their own actions, exercising their agency.

Social psychology's task is to understand people in the light of this anthropomorphic model. Proponents of this 'science of persons' approach place great store on the systematic and painstaking analysis of social episodes, i.e. behaviour in context.

In Box 1.7 we give an example of such an episode taken from a classroom study. Note how the particular incident would appear on an interaction analysis coding sheet of a researcher employing a positivistic approach. Note, too, how this slice of classroom life can be understood only by knowledge of the specific organizational background and context in which it is embedded.

The approach to analysing social episodes in terms of the 'actors' themselves is known as the 'ethogenic method'.[6] Unlike positivistic social psychology, which ignores or presumes its subjects' interpretations of situations, ethogenic social psychology, concentrates upon the ways in which persons construe their social world. By probing at their accounts of their actions, it endeavours to come up with an understanding of what those persons were doing in the particular episode.

As an alternative to positivist approaches, naturalistic, qualitative, interpretive approaches of various hue possess particular distinguishing features:

- People are deliberate and creative in their actions, they act intentionally and make meanings in and through their activities (Blumer 1969).
- People actively construct their social world – they are not the 'cultural dopes' or passive dolls of positivism (Garfinkel, 1967; Becker 1970).
- Situations are fluid and changing rather than fixed and static; events and behaviour evolve over time and are richly affected by context – they are 'situated activities'.
- Events and individuals are unique and largely non-generalizable.
- A view that the social world should be studied in its natural state, without the intervention of, or manipulation by, the researcher (Hammersley and Atkinson 1983).

Box 1.7
A classroom episode

Walker and Adelman describe an incident in the following manner:

In one lesson the teacher was listening to the boys read through short essays that they had written for homework on the subject of 'Prisons'. After one boy, Wilson, had finished reading out his rather obviously skimped piece of work, the teacher sighed and said, rather crossly:

   T: Wilson, we'll have to put you away if you don't change your ways, and do your homework. Is that all you've done?
   P: Strawberries, strawberries. (Laughter)

Now at first glance this is meaningless. An observer coding with Flanders Interaction Analysis Categories (FIAC) would write down:

   '7' (teacher criticizes) followed by a,
   '4' (teacher asks question) followed by a,
   '9' (pupil irritation) and finally a,
   '10' (silence or confusion) to describe the laughter

Such a string of codings, however reliable and valid, would not help anyone to *understand* why such an interruption was funny. Human curiosity makes us want to know *why* everyone laughs – and so, I would argue, the social scientist needs to know too. Walker and Adelman (1976), asked subsequently why 'strawberries' was a stimulus to laughter and were told that the teacher frequently said the pupils' work was 'like strawberries – good as far as it goes, but it doesn't last nearly long enough'. Here a casual comment made in the past has become an integral part of the shared meaning system of the class. It can be comprehended only by seeing the relationship as developing over time.

Source: adapted from Delamont 1976

- Fidelity to the phenomena being studied is fundamental.
- People interpret events, contexts and situations, and act on the bases of those events (echoing Thomas's (1928) famous dictum that if people define their situations as real then they are real in their consequences – if I believe there is a mouse under the table, I will act as though there is a mouse under the table, whether there is or not (Morrison 1998)).
- There are multiple interpretations of, and perspectives on, single events and situations.
- Reality is multilayered and complex.
- Many events are not reducible to simplistic interpretation, hence 'thick descriptions' (Geertz 1973b) are essential rather than reductionism, that is to say thick descriptions representing the complexity of situations are preferable to simplistic ones.
- We need to examine situations through the eyes of participants rather than the researcher.

The anti-positivist movement in sociology is represented by three schools of thought – phenomenology, ethnomethodology and symbolic interactionism. A common thread running through the three schools is a concern with phenomena, that is, the things we directly apprehend through our senses as we go about our daily lives, together with a consequent emphasis on qualitative as opposed to quantitative methodology. The differences between them and the significant roles each phenomenon plays in research in classrooms and schools are such as to warrant a more extended consideration of them in the discussion below.

A question of terminology: the normative and interpretive paradigms

So far we have introduced and used a variety of terms to describe the numerous branches and schools of thought embraced by the positivist and anti-positivist viewpoints. As a matter of convenience and as an aid to communication, we clarify at this point two generic terms conventionally used to describe these two perspectives and the categories subsumed under each, particularly as they refer to social psychology and sociology. The terms in question are 'normative' and 'interpretive'. The normative paradigm (or model) contains two major orienting ideas (Douglas 1973): first, that human behaviour is essentially rule-governed, and second, that it should be investigated by the methods of natural science. The interpretive paradigm, in contrast to its normative counterpart, is characterized by a concern for the individual. Whereas normative studies are positivist, all theories constructed within the context of the interpretive paradigm tend to be anti-positivist. As we have seen, the central endeavour in the context of the interpretive paradigm is to understand the subjective world of human experience. To retain the integrity of the phenomena being investigated, efforts are made to get inside the person and to understand from within. The imposition of external form and structure is resisted, since this reflects the viewpoint of the observer as opposed to that of the actor directly involved.

Two further differences between the two paradigms may be identified at this stage: the first concerns the concepts of 'behaviour' and 'action'; the second, the different conceptions of 'theory'. A key concept within the normative paradigm, behaviour refers to responses either to external environmental stimuli (another person, or the demands of society, for instance) or to internal stimuli (hunger, or the need to achieve, for example). In either case, the cause of the behaviour lies in the past. Interpretive approaches, on the other hand, focus on action. This may be thought of as behaviour-with-meaning; it is intentional behaviour and as such, future oriented. Actions are meaningful to us only in so far as we are able to ascertain the intentions of actors to share their experiences. A large number of our everyday interactions with one another rely on such shared experiences.

As regards theory, normative researchers try to devise general theories of human behaviour and to validate them through the use of increasingly complex research methodologies which, some believe, push them further and further from the experience and understanding of the everyday world and into a world of abstraction. For them, the basic reality is the collectivity; it is external to the actor and manifest in society, its institutions and its organizations. The role of theory is to say how reality hangs together in these forms or how it might be changed so as to be more effective. The researcher's ultimate aim is to establish a comprehensive 'rational edifice', a universal theory, to account for human and social behaviour.

But what of the interpretive researchers? They begin with individuals and set out to understand their interpretations of the world around them. Theory is emergent and must arise from particular situations; it should be 'grounded' in data generated by the research act (Glaser and Strauss 1967). Theory should not precede research but follow it. Investigators work directly with experience and understanding to build their theory on them. The data thus yielded will include the meanings and purposes of those people who are their source. Further, the theory so generated must make sense to those to whom it applies. The aim of scientific investigation for the interpretive researcher is to understand how this glossing of reality goes on at one time and in one place and compare it with what goes on in different times and places. Thus theory becomes sets of meanings which yield insight and understanding of people's behaviour. These theories are likely to be as diverse as the sets of human meanings and understandings that they are to explain. From an interpretive perspective the hope of a universal theory which characterizes the normative outlook gives way to multifaceted images of human behaviour as varied as the situations and contexts supporting them.

Phenomenology, ethnomethodology and symbolic interactionism

There are many variants of qualitative, naturalistic approaches (Jacob 1987; Hitchcock and Hughes 1995). Here we focus on three significant 'traditions' in this style of research – phenomenology, ethnomethodology and symbolic interactionism.

In its broadest meaning, phenomenology is a theoretical point of view that advocates the study of direct experience taken at face value; and one which sees behaviour as determined by the phenomena of experience rather than by external, objective and physically described reality (English and English 1958). Although phenomenologists differ among themselves on particular issues, there is fairly general agreement on the following points identified by Curtis (1978) which can be taken as distinguishing features of their philosophical viewpoint:

- a belief in the importance, and in a sense the primacy, of subjective consciousness
- an understanding of consciousness as active, as meaning bestowing
- a claim that there are certain essential structures to consciousness of which we gain direct knowledge by a certain kind of reflection: exactly what these structures are is a point about which phenomenologists have differed.

Various strands of development may be traced in the phenomenological movement: we shall briefly examine two of them – the transcendental phenomenology of Husserl, and existential phenomenology, of which Schutz is perhaps the most characteristic representative.

Husserl, regarded by many as the founder of phenomenology, was concerned with investigating the source of the foundation of science and with questioning the commonsense, 'taken-for-granted' assumptions of everyday life (see Burrell and Morgan 1979). To do this, he set about opening up a new direction in the analysis of consciousness. His catch-phrase was 'Back to the things!' which for him meant finding out how things appear directly to us rather than through the media of cultural and symbolic structures. In other words, we are asked to look beyond the details of everyday life to the essences underlying them. To do this, Husserl exhorts us to 'put the world in brackets' or free ourselves from our usual ways of perceiving the world. What is left over from this reduction is our consciousness of which there are three elements – the 'I' who thinks, the mental acts of this thinking subject, and the intentional objects of these mental acts. The aim, then, of this method of *epoché*, as Husserl called it, is the dismembering of the constitution of objects in such a way as to free us from all preconceptions about the world (see Warnock 1970).

Schutz was concerned with relating Husserl's ideas to the issues of sociology and to the scientific study of social behaviour. Of central concern to him was the problem of understanding the meaning structure of the world of everyday life. The origins of meaning he thus sought in the 'stream of consciousness' – basically an unbroken stream of lived experiences which have no meaning in themselves. One can impute meaning to them only retrospectively, by the process of turning back on oneself and looking at what has been going on. In other words, meaning can be accounted for in this way by the concept of reflexivity. For Schutz, the attribution of meaning reflexively is dependent on the people identifying the purpose or goal they seek (see Burrell and Morgan 1979).

According to Schutz, the way we understand the behaviour of others is dependent on a process of typification by means of which the observer makes use of concepts resembling 'ideal types' to make sense of what people do. These concepts are derived from our experience of everyday life and it is through them, claims Schutz, that we classify and organize our everyday world. As Burrell and Morgan (1979) observe, we learn these typifications through our biographical locations and social contexts. Our knowledge of the everyday world inheres in social order and this world itself is socially ordered.

The fund of everyday knowledge by means of which we are able to typify other people's behaviour and come to terms with social reality varies from situation to situation. We thus live in a world of multiple realities, and social actors move within and between these with ease (Burrell and Morgan 1979), abiding by the rules of the game for each of these worlds.

Like phenomenology, ethnomethodology is concerned with the world of everyday life. In the words of its proponent, Harold Garfinkel, it sets out

to treat practical activities, practical circumstances, and practical sociological reasonings as topics of empirical study, and by paying to the most commonplace activities of daily life the attention usually accorded extraordinary events, seeks to learn about them as phenomena in their own right.

'(Garfinkel 1967)

He maintains that students of the social world must doubt the reality of that world; and that in failing to view human behaviour more sceptically, sociologists have created an ordered social reality that bears little relationship to the real thing. He thereby challenges the basic sociological concept of order.

Ethnomethodology, then, is concerned with how people make sense of their everyday world. More especially, it is directed at the mechanisms by which participants achieve and sustain interaction in a social encounter – the assumptions they make, the conventions they utilize and the practices they adopt. Ethnomethodology thus seeks to understand social accomplishments in their own terms; it is concerned to understand them from within (see Burrell and Morgan 1979).

In identifying the taken-for-granted assumptions characterizing any social situation and the ways in which the people involved make their activities rationally accountable, ethnomethodologists use notions like 'indexicality' and 'reflexivity'. Indexicality refers to the ways in which actions and statements are related to the social contexts producing them; and to the way their meanings are shared by the participants but not necessarily stated explicitly. Indexical expressions are thus the designations imputed to a particular social occasion by the participants in order to locate the event in the sphere of reality. Reflexivity, on the other hand, refers to the way in which all accounts of social settings – descriptions, analyses, criticisms, etc. – and the social settings occasioning them are mutually interdependent.

It is convenient to distinguish between two types of ethnomethodologists: linguistic and situational. The linguistic ethnomethodologists focus upon the use of language and the ways in which conversations in everyday life are structured. Their analyses make much use of the unstated taken-for-granted meanings, the use of indexical expressions and the way in which conversations convey much more than is actually said. The situational ethnomethodologists cast their view over a wider range of social activity and seek to understand the ways in which people negotiate the social contexts in which they find themselves. They are concerned to understand how people make sense of and order their environment. As part of their empirical method, ethnomethodologists may consciously and deliberately disrupt or question the ordered taken-for-granted elements in everyday situations in order to reveal the underlying processes at work.

The substance of ethnomethodology thus largely comprises a set of specific techniques and approaches to be used in studying what Garfinkel (1967) has described as the 'awesome indexicality' of everyday life. It is geared to empirical study, and the stress which its practitioners place upon the uniqueness of the situation encountered, projects its essentially relativist standpoint. A commitment to the development of methodology and fieldwork has occupied first place in the interests of its adherents, so that related issues of ontology, epistemology and the nature of human beings have received less attention than perhaps they deserve.

Essentially, the notion of symbolic inter-actionism derives from the work of Mead (1934). Although subsequently to be associated with such noted researchers as Blumer, Hughes, Becker and Goffman, the term does not represent a unified perspective in that it does not embrace a common set of assumptions and concepts accepted by all who subscribe to the approach. For our purposes, however, it is possible to identify three basic postulates. These have been set out by Woods (1979) as follows. First, human beings act towards things on the basis of the meanings they have for them. Humans inhabit two different worlds: the 'natural' world wherein they are organisms of drives and instincts and where the external world exists independently of them, and the social world where the existence of symbols, like language, enables them to give meaning to objects. This attribution of meanings, this interpreting, is

what makes them distinctively human and social. Interactionists therefore focus on the world of subjective meanings and the symbols by which they are produced and represented. This means not making any prior assumptions about what is going on in an institution, and taking seriously, indeed giving priority to, inmates' own accounts. Thus, if pupils appear preoccupied for too much of the time – 'being bored', 'mucking about', 'having a laugh', etc. the interactionist is keen to explore the properties and dimensions of these processes.

Second, this attribution of meaning to objects through symbols is a continuous process. Action is not simply a consequence of psychological attributes such as drives, attitudes or personalities, or determined by external social facts such as social structure or roles, but results from a continuous process of meaning attribution which is always emerging in a state of flux and subject to change. The individual constructs, modifies, pieces together, weighs up the pros and cons and bargains.

Third, this process takes place in a social context. Individuals align their actions to those of others. They do this by 'taking the role of the other', by making indications to 'themselves' about the likely responses of 'others'. They construct how others wish or might act in certain circumstances, and how they themselves might act. They might try to 'manage' the impressions others have of them, put on a 'performance', try to influence others' 'definition of the situation'.

Instead of focusing on the individual, then, and his or her personality characteristics, or on how the social structure or social situation causes individual behaviour, symbolic interactionists direct their attention at the nature of interaction, the dynamic activities taking place between people. In focusing on the interaction itself as a unit of study, the symbolic interactionist creates a more active image of the human being and rejects the image of the passive, determined organism. Individuals interact; societies are made up of interacting individuals. People are constantly undergoing change in interaction and society is changing through interaction. Interaction implies human beings acting in relation to each other, taking each other into account, acting, perceiving, interpreting, acting again. Hence, a more dynamic and active human being emerges rather than an actor merely responding to others. Woods (1983: 15–16) summarizes key emphases of symbolic interaction thus:

- individuals as constructors of their own actions
- the various components of the self and how they interact; the indications made to self, meanings attributed, interpretive mechanisms, definitions of the situation; in short, the world of subjective meanings, and the symbols by which they are produced and represented
- the process of negotiation, by which meanings are continually being constructed
- the social context in which they occur and whence they derive
- by taking the 'role of the other' – a dynamic concept involving the construction of how others wish to or might act in a certain circumstance, and how individuals themselves might act – individuals align their actions to those of others.

A characteristic common to the phenomenological, ethnomethodological and symbolic interactionist perspectives, which makes them singularly attractive to the would-be educational researcher, is the way they fit naturally to the kind of concentrated action found in classrooms and schools. Yet another shared characteristic is the manner in which they are able to preserve the integrity of the situation where they are employed. Here the influence of the researcher in structuring, analysing and interpreting the situation is present to a much smaller degree than would be the case with a more traditionally oriented research approach.

Criticisms of the naturalistic and interpretive approaches

Critics have wasted little time in pointing out what they regard as weaknesses in these newer qualitative perspectives. They argue that while it is undeniable that our understanding of the actions of our fellow-beings necessarily requires knowledge of their intentions, this, surely, cannot be said to comprise *the* purpose of a social science. As Rex (1974) has observed:

> While patterns of social reactions and institutions may be the product of the actors' definitions of the situations there is also the possibility that those actors might be falsely conscious and that sociologists have an obligation to seek an objective perspective which is not necessarily that of any of the participating actors at all.... We need not be confined purely and simply to that...social reality which is made available to us by participant actors themselves.
>
> (Rex 1974)

While these more recent perspectives have presented models of people that are more in keeping with common experience, some argue that anti-positivists have gone too far in abandoning scientific procedures of verification and in giving up hope of discovering useful generalizations about behaviour (see Mead 1934). Are there not dangers in rejecting the approach of physics in favour of methods more akin to literature, biography and journalism? Some specific criticisms of the methodologies are well directed, for example Argyle (1978) questions whether, if carefully controlled interviews such as those used in social surveys are inaccurate, then the less controlled interviews carry even greater risks of inaccuracy. Indeed Bernstein (1974) suggests that subjective reports may be incomplete and misleading.

Bernstein's criticism is directed at the overriding concern of phenomenologists and ethnomethodologists with the meanings of situations and the ways in which these meanings are negotiated by the actors involved. What is overlooked about such negotiated meanings, observes Bernstein (1974), is that the very process whereby one interprets and defines a situation is itself a product of the circumstances in which one is placed. One important factor in such circumstances that must be considered is the power of others to impose their own definitions of situations upon participants. Doctors' consulting rooms and headteachers' studies are locations in which inequalities in power are regularly imposed upon unequal participants. The ability of certain individuals, groups, classes and authorities to persuade others to accept their definitions of situations demonstrates that while – as ethnomethodologists insist – social structure is a consequence of the ways in which we perceive social relations, it is clearly more than this. Conceiving of social structure as external to ourselves helps us take its self-evident effects upon our daily lives into our understanding of the social behaviour going on about us. Here is rehearsed the tension between agency and structure of social theorists (Layder 1994); the danger of interactionist and interpretive approaches is their relative neglect of the power of external – structural – forces to shape behaviour and events. There is a risk in interpretive approaches that they become hermetically sealed from the world outside the participants' theatre of activity – they put artificial boundaries around subjects' behaviour. Just as positivistic theories can be criticized for their macro-sociological persuasion, so interpretive and qualitative theories can be criticized for their narrowly micro-sociological perspectives.

Critical theory and critical educational research

Positivist and interpretive paradigms are essentially concerned with understanding phenomena through two different lenses. Positivism strives for objectivity, measurability, predictability, controllability, patterning, the construction of laws and rules of behaviour, and the ascription of causality; the interpretive paradigms strive to understand and interpret the world in terms of its actors. In the former observed phenomena are important; in the latter meanings and interpretations are paramount. Habermas (1984: 109–10), echoing Giddens (1976), describes this latter as a 'double hermeneutic', where people strive to interpret and operate in an already interpreted world. An emerging approach to educational research is the paradigm of *critical educational research*. This regards the two previous paradigms as presenting incomplete accounts of social behaviour by their neglect of the political and ideological contexts of much educational research. Positivistic and interpretive paradigms are seen as preoccupied

with technical and hermeneutic knowledge respectively (Gage 1989). The paradigm of critical educational research is heavily influenced by the early work of Habermas and, to a lesser extent, his predecessors in the Frankfurt School, most notably Adorno, Marcuse, Horkheimer and Fromm. Here the expressed intention is deliberately political – the emancipation of individuals and groups in an egalitarian society (see http://www.routledge.com/textbooks/ 9780415368780 – Chapter 1, file 1.4. ppt).

Critical theory is explicitly prescriptive and normative, entailing a view of what behaviour in a social democracy *should* entail (Fay 1987; Morrison 1995a). Its intention is not merely to give an account of society and behaviour but to realize a society that is based on equality and democracy for all its members. Its purpose is not merely to understand situations and phenomena but to change them. In particular it seeks to emancipate the disempowered, to redress inequality and to promote individual freedoms within a democratic society.

In this enterprise critical theory identifies the 'false' or 'fragmented' consciousness (Eagleton 1991) that has brought an individual or social group to relative powerlessness or, indeed, power, and it questions the legitimacy of this. It holds up to the lights of legitimacy and equality issues of repression, voice, ideology, power, participation, representation, inclusion and interests. It argues that much behaviour (including research behaviour) is the outcome of particular illegitimate, dominatory and repressive factors, illegitimate in the sense that they do not operate in the general interest – one person's or group's freedom and power is bought at the price of another's freedom and power. Hence critical theory seeks to uncover the *interests* at work in particular situations and to interrogate the legitimacy of those interests, identifying the extent to which they are legitimate in their service of equality and democracy. Its intention is *transformative*: to transform society and individuals to social democracy. In this respect the purpose of critical educational research is intensely practical, to bring about a more just, egalitarian society in which individual and collective freedoms are practised, and to eradicate the exercise and effects of illegitimate power. The pedigree of critical theory in Marxism, thus, is not difficult to discern. For critical theorists, researchers can no longer claim neutrality and ideological or political innocence.

Critical theory and critical educational research, then, have their substantive agenda – for example examining and interrogating: the relationships between school and society – how schools perpetuate or reduce inequality; the social construction of knowledge and curricula, who defines worthwhile knowledge, what ideological interests this serves, and how this reproduces inequality in society; how power is produced and reproduced through education; whose interests are served by education and how legitimate these are (e.g. the rich, white, middle-class males rather than poor, non-white females).

The significance of critical theory for research is immense, for it suggests that much social research is comparatively trivial in that it *accepts* rather than *questions* given agendas for research, compounded by the funding for research, which underlines the political dimension of research sponsorship (discussed later) (Norris 1990). Critical theorists would argue that the positivist and interpretive paradigms are essentially technicist, seeking to understand and render more efficient an existing situation, rather than to question or transform it.

Habermas (1972) offers a useful tripartite conceptualization of interests that catches the three paradigms of research in this chapter. He suggests that knowledge – and hence research knowledge – serves different interests. Interests, he argues, are socially constructed, and are 'knowledge-constitutive', because they shape and determine what counts as the objects and types of knowledge. Interests have an ideological function (Morrison 1995a), for example a 'technical interest' (discussed below) can have the effect of keeping the empowered in their empowered position and the disempowered in their powerlessness – i.e. reinforcing and perpetuating the status quo. An 'emancipatory interest' (discussed below) threatens the status quo. In this view knowledge – and research

knowledge – is not neutral (see also Mannheim 1936). What counts as worthwhile knowledge is determined by the social and positional power of the advocates of that knowledge. The link here between objects of study and communities of scholars echoes Kuhn's (1962) notions of paradigms and paradigm shifts, where the field of knowledge or paradigm is seen to be only as good as the evidence and the respect in which it is held by 'authorities'. Knowledge and definitions of knowledge reflect the interests of the community of scholars who operate in particular paradigms. Habermas (1972) constructs the definition of worthwhile knowledge and modes of understanding around three cognitive interests (see http://www.routledge.com/textbooks/9780415368780 – Chapter 1, file 1.5. ppt):

- prediction and control
- understanding and interpretation
- emancipation and freedom.

He names these the '*technical*', '*practical*' and '*emancipatory*' interests respectively. The technical interest characterizes the scientific, positivist method outlined earlier, with its emphasis on laws, rules, prediction and control of behaviour, with passive research objects – instrumental knowledge. The 'practical' interest, an attenuation of the positivism of the scientific method, is exemplified in the hermeneutic, interpretive methodologies outlined in the qualitative approaches earlier (e.g. symbolic interactionism). Here research methodologies seek to clarify, understand and interpret the communications of 'speaking and acting subjects' (Habermas 1974: 8).

Hermeneutics focuses on interaction and language; it seeks to understand situations through the eyes of the participants, echoing the *verstehen* approaches of Weber and premised on the view that reality is socially constructed (Berger and Luckmann 1967). Indeed Habermas (1988: 12) suggests that sociology must understand social facts in their cultural significance and as socially determined. Hermeneutics involves recapturing the *meanings* of interacting others, recovering and reconstructing the *intentions* of the other actors in a situation. Such an enterprise involves the analysis of *meaning in a social context* (Held 1980). Gadamer (1975: 273) argues that the hermeneutic sciences (e.g. qualitative approaches) involve the *fusion of horizons* between participants. Meanings rather than phenomena take on significance here.

The emancipatory interest subsumes the previous two paradigms; it requires them but goes beyond them (Habermas 1972: 211). It is concerned with *praxis* – action that is informed by reflection with the aim to emancipate (Kincheloe 1991: 177). The twin intentions of this interest are to expose the operation of power and to bring about social justice as domination and repression act to prevent the full existential realization of individual and social freedoms (Habermas 1979: 14). The task of this knowledge-constitutive interest, indeed of critical theory itself, is to restore to consciousness those suppressed, repressed and submerged determinants of unfree behaviour with a view to their dissolution (Habermas 1984: 194–5).

What we have in effect, then, in Habermas's early work is an attempt to conceptualize three research styles: the scientific, positivist style; the interpretive style; and the emancipatory, ideology critical style. Not only does critical theory have its own research agenda, but also it has its own research methodologies, in particular ideology critique and action research. With regard to ideology critique, a particular reading of ideology is being adopted here, as the *suppression of generalizable interests* (Habermas 1976: 113), where systems, groups and individuals operate in rationally indefensible ways because their power to act relies on the disempowering of other groups, i.e. that their principles of behaviour cannot be generalized.

Ideology – the values and practices emanating from particular dominant groups – is the means by which powerful groups promote and legitimize their particular – sectoral – interests at the expense of disempowered groups. Ideology critique exposes the operation of ideology in many spheres of education, the working out of vested interests under the mantle of the general good. The task of ideology critique is to uncover the vested interests at work which may be occurring consciously or subliminally, revealing to participants how they may be acting to perpetuate a system which keeps them either empowered or disempowered (Geuss 1981), i.e. which suppresses a generalizable interest. Explanations for situations might be other than those 'natural', taken for granted, explanations that the participants might offer or accept. Situations are not natural but problematic (Carr and Kemmis 1986). They are the outcomes or processes wherein interests and powers are protected and suppressed, and one task of ideology critique is to expose this (Grundy 1987). The interests at work are uncovered by ideology critique, which, itself, is premised on reflective practice (Morrison 1995a; 1995b; 1996a). Habermas (1972: 230) suggests that ideology critique through reflective practice can be addressed in four stages:

- *Stage* 1: a description and interpretation of the existing situation – a hermeneutic exercise that identifies and attempts to make sense of the current situation (echoing the *verstehen* approaches of the interpretive paradigm) (see http://www.routledge.com/textbooks/ 9780415368780 – Chapter 1, file 1.6. ppt).

- *Stage* 2: a penetration of the reasons that brought the existing situation to the form that it takes – the causes and purposes of a situation and an evaluation of their legitimacy, involving an analysis of interests and ideologies at work in a situation, their power and legitimacy (both in micro- and macro-sociological terms). Habermas's (1972) early work likens this to psychoanalysis as a means for bringing into the consciousness of 'patients' those repressed, distorted and oppressive conditions, experiences and factors that have prevented them from a full, complete and accurate understanding of their conditions, situations and behaviour, and that, on such exposure and examination, will be liberatory and emancipatory. Critique here reveals to individuals and groups how their views and practices might be ideological distortions that, in their effects, perpetuate a social order or situation that works against their democratic freedoms, interests and empowerment (see also Carr and Kemmis 1986: 138–9).

- *Stage* 3: an agenda for altering the situation – in order for moves to an egalitarian society to be furthered.
- *Stage* 4: an evaluation of the achievement of the situation in practice.

In the world of education Habermas's stages are paralleled by Smyth (1989) who, too, denotes a four-stage process:

- *description* (what am I doing?)
- *information* (what does it mean?)
- *confrontation* (how did I come to be like this?)
- *reconstruction* (how might I do things differently?)

It can be seen that ideology critique here has both a reflective, theoretical and a practical side to it; without reflection it is hollow and without practice it is empty.

As ideology is not mere theory but impacts directly on practice (Eagleton 1991) there is a strongly practical methodology implied by critical theory, which articulates with action research (Callawaert 1999). Action research (discussed in Chapter 14), as its name suggests, is about research that impacts on, and focuses on, practice. In its espousal of practitioner research, for example teachers in schools, participant observers and curriculum developers, action research recognizes the significance of *contexts* for practice – locational, ideological, historical, managerial, social. Furthermore it accords power to those who are operating in those contexts, for they are both the engines of research and of practice. In that sense the claim is made that action research is strongly empowering and emancipatory in that it gives practitioners a 'voice' (Carr and Kemmis 1986; Grundy 1987), participation in decision-making, and control over their environment and professional lives. Whether the strength of the claims for empowerment are as strong as their proponents would hold is another matter, for action research might be relatively powerless in the face of mandated changes in education. Here action research might be more concerned with the intervening in existing practice to ensure

that mandated change is addressed efficiently and effectively.

Morrison (1995a) suggests that critical theory, because it has a practical intent to transform and empower, can – and should – be examined and perhaps tested empirically. For example, critical theory claims to be empowering; that is a testable proposition. Indeed, in a departure from some of his earlier writing, in some of his later work Habermas (1990) acknowledges this; he argues for the need to find 'counter examples' (p. 6), to 'critical testing' (p. 7) and empirical verification (p. 117). He acknowledges that his views have only 'hypothetical status' (p. 32) that need to be checked against specific cases (p. 9). One could suggest, for instance, that the effectiveness of his critical theory can be examined by charting the extent to which equality, freedom, democracy, emancipation, empowerment have been realized by dint of his theory; the extent to which transformative practices have been addressed or occurred as a result of his theory; the extent to which subscribers to his theory have been able to assert their agency; the extent to which his theories have broken down the barriers of instrumental rationality. The operationalization and testing (or empirical investigation) of his theories clearly is a major undertaking, and one which Habermas has not done. In this respect critical theory, a theory that strives to improve practical living, runs the risk of becoming merely contemplative (see http://www.routledge.com/textbooks/9780415368780 – Chapter 1, file 1.7. ppt).

Criticisms of approaches from critical theory

There are several criticisms that have been voiced against critical approaches. Morrison (1995a) suggests that there is an artificial separation between Habermas's three interests – they are drawn far more sharply (Hesse 1982; Bernstein 1983: 33). For example, one has to bring hermeneutic knowledge to bear on positivist science and vice versa in order to make meaning of each other and in order to judge their own status. Further, the link between ideology critique and emancipation is neither clear nor proven, nor a logical necessity (Morrison 1995a: 67) – whether a person or society can become emancipated simply by the exercise of ideology critique or action research is an empirical rather than a logical matter (Morrison 1995a; Wardekker and Miedama 1997). Indeed one can become emancipated by means other than ideology critique; emancipated societies do not necessarily demonstrate or require an awareness of ideology critique. Moreover, it could be argued that the rationalistic appeal of ideology critique actually obstructs action designed to bring about emancipation. Roderick (1986: 65), for example, questions whether the espousal of ideology critique is itself as ideological as the approaches that it proscribes. Habermas, in his allegiance to the view of the social construction of knowledge through 'interests', is inviting the charge of relativism.

While the claim to there being three forms of knowledge has the epistemological attraction of simplicity, one has to question this very simplicity (e.g. Keat 1981: 67); there are a multitude of interests and ways of understanding the world and it is simply artificial to reduce these to three. Indeed it is unclear whether Habermas, in his three knowledge-constitutive interests, is dealing with a conceptual model, a political analysis, a set of generalities, a set of transhistorical principles, a set of temporally specific observations, or a set of loosely defined slogans (Morrison 1995a: 71) that survive only by dint of their ambiguity (Kolakowsi 1978). Lakomski (1999: 179–82) questions the acceptability of the consensus theory of truth on which Habermas's work is premised; she argues that Habermas's work is silent on social change, and is little more than speculation, a view echoed by Fendler's (1999) criticism of critical theory as inadequately problematizing subjectivity and ahistoricity.

More fundamental to a critique of this approach is the view that critical theory has a deliberate political agenda, and that the task of the researcher is not to be an ideologue or to have an agenda, but to be dispassionate, disinterested and objective (Morrison 1995a). Of course, critical theorists would argue that the call for researchers to be ideologically neutral is itself ideologically saturated with laissez-faire values which allow the status quo to be reproduced, i.e. that the call for researchers to be neutral and disinterested is just as value laden as is the call for them to intrude their own perspectives. The rights of the researcher to move beyond disinterestedness are clearly contentious, though the safeguard here is that the researcher's is only one voice in the community of scholars (Kemmis 1982). Critical theorists as researchers have been hoisted by their own petard, for if they are to become more than merely negative Jeremiahs and sceptics, berating a particular social order that is dominated by scientism and instrumental rationality (Eagleton 1991; Wardekker and Miedama 1997), then they have to generate a positive agenda, but in so doing they are violating the traditional objectivity of researchers. Because their focus is on an ideological agenda, they themselves cannot avoid acting ideologically (Morrison 1995a).

Claims have been made for the power of action research to empower participants as researchers (e.g. Carr and Kemmis 1986; Grundy 1987). This might be over-optimistic in a world in which power is often through statute; the reality of political power seldom extends to teachers. That teachers might be able to exercise some power in schools but that this has little effect on the workings of society at large was caught in Bernstein's (1970) famous comment that 'education cannot compensate for society'. Giving action researchers a small degree of power (to research their own situations) has little effect on the *real* locus of power and decision-making, which often lies outside the control of action researchers. Is action research genuinely and full-bloodedly empowering and emancipatory? Where is the evidence?

Critical theory and curriculum research

For research methods, the tenets of critical theory suggest their own substantive fields of enquiry and their own methods (e.g. ideology critique and action research). Beyond that the contribution to this text on empirical research methods is perhaps limited by the fact that the agenda of critical theory is highly particularistic, prescriptive and, as has been seen, problematical. Though it is an influential paradigm, it is influential in certain fields rather than in others. For example, its impact on curriculum research has been far-reaching.

It has been argued for many years that the most satisfactory account of the curriculum is given by a modernist, positivist reading of the development of education and society. This has its curricular expression in Tyler's (1949) famous and influential rationale for the curriculum in terms of four questions:

1   What educational purposes should the school seek to attain?
2   What educational experiences can be provided that are likely to attain these purposes?
3   How can these educational experiences be effectively organized?
4   How can we determine whether these purposes are being attained?

Underlying this rationale is a view that the curriculum is controlled (and controllable), ordered, predetermined, uniform, predictable and largely behaviourist in outcome – all elements of the positivist mentality that critical theory eschews. Tyler's rationale resonates sympathetically with a modernist, scientific, managerialist mentality of society and education that regards ideology and power as unproblematic, indeed it claims the putative political neutrality and objectivity of positivism (Doll 1993); it ignores the advances in psychology and psychopedagogy made by constructivism.

However, this view has been criticized for precisely these sympathies. Doll (1993) argues that it represents a *closed* system of planning and practice that sits uncomfortably with the notion of education as an *opening* process and with the view of postmodern society as open and diverse, multidimensional, fluid and with power less monolithic and more problematical. This view takes seriously the impact of chaos and complexity theory and derives from them some important features for contemporary curricula. These are

incorporated into a view of curricula as being *rich, relational, recursive* and *rigorous* (Doll 1993) with an emphasis on *emergence, process epistemology* and *constructivist psychology.*

Not all knowledge can be included in the curriculum; the curriculum is a selection of what is deemed to be worthwhile knowledge. The justification for that selection reveals the ideologies and power in decision-making in society and through the curriculum. Curriculum is an ideological selection from a range of possible knowledge. This resonates with Habermas's (1972) view that knowledge and its selection is neither neutral nor innocent.

Ideologies can be treated unpejoratively as sets of beliefs or, more sharply, as sets of beliefs emanating from powerful groups in society, designed to protect the interests of the dominant. If curricula are value-based then why is it that some values hold more sway than others? The link between values and power is strong. This theme asks not only *what* knowledge is important but also *whose* knowledge is important in curricula, *what and whose interests* such knowledge serves, and *how* the curriculum and pedagogy serve (or do not serve) differing interests. Knowledge is not neutral (as was the tacit view in modernist curricula). The curriculum is ideologically contestable terrain.

The study of the sociology of knowledge indicates how the powerful might retain their power through curricula and how knowledge and power are legitimized in curricula. The study of the sociology of knowledge suggests that the curriculum should be both subject to ideology critique and itself promote ideology critique in students. A research agenda for critical theorists, then, is how the curriculum perpetuates the societal status quo and how can it (and should it) promote equality in society.

The notion of ideology critique engages the early writings of Habermas (1972), in particular his theory of three knowledge-constitutive interests. His *technical interest* (in control and predictability) resonates with Tyler's (1949) model of the curriculum and reveals itself in technicist, instrumentalist and scientist views of curricula that are to be 'delivered' to passive recipients – the curriculum is simply another commodity in a consumer society in which differential cultural capital is inevitable. Habermas's *hermeneutic interest* (in understanding others' perspectives and views) resonates with a *process* view of the curriculum. His *emancipatory interest* (in promoting social emancipation, equality, democracy, freedoms and individual and collective empowerment) requires an exposure of the ideological interests at work in curricula in order that teachers and students can take control of their own lives for the collective, egalitarian good. Habermas's emancipatory interest denotes an inescapably political reading of the curriculum and the purposes of education – the movement away from authoritarianism and elitism and towards social democracy.

Habermas's work underpins and informs much contemporary and recent curriculum theory (e.g. Grundy 1987; Apple 1990; UNESCO 1996) and is a useful heuristic device for understanding the motives behind the heavy prescription of curriculum content in, for example, the United Kingdom, New Zealand, Hong Kong and France. For instance, one can argue that the National Curriculum of England and Wales is heavy on the technical and hermeneutic interests but very light on the emancipatory interest (Morrison 1995a) and that this (either deliberately or in its effects) supports – if not contributes to – the reproduction of social inequality. As Bernstein (1971: 47) argues: 'how a society selects, classifies, distributes, transmits and evaluates the educational knowledge it considers to be public, reflects both the distribution of power and the principles of social control'.

Several writers on curriculum theory (e.g. McLaren 1995; Leistyna *et al.* 1996) argue that power is a central, defining concept in matters of the curriculum. Here considerable importance is accorded to the political agenda of the curriculum, and the empowerment of individuals and societies is an inescapable consideration in the curriculum. One means of developing student and societal empowerment finds its expression in Habermas's (1972) emancipatory interest and critical pedagogy.

In the field of critical pedagogy the argument is advanced that educators must work with, and on, the lived experience that students bring to the pedagogical encounter rather than imposing a dominatory curriculum that reproduces social inequality. In this enterprise teachers are to transform the experience of domination in students and empower them to become 'emancipated' in a full democracy. Students' everyday experiences of oppression, of being 'silenced', of having their cultures and 'voices' excluded from curricula and decision-making are to be examined for the ideological messages that are contained in such acts. Raising awareness of such inequalities is an important step to overcoming them. Teachers and students together move forward in the progress towards 'individual autonomy within a just society' (Masschelein 1991: 97). In place of centrally prescribed and culturally biased curricula that students simply receive, critical pedagogy regards the curriculum as a form of cultural politics in which *participants in* (rather than *recipients of*) curricula question the cultural and dominatory messages contained in curricula and replace them with a 'language of possibility' and empowering, often community-related curricula. In this way curricula serve the 'socially critical' rather than the culturally and ideologically passive school.

One can discern a utopian and generalized tenor in some of this work, and applying critical theory to education can be criticized for its limited comments on practice. Indeed Miedama and Wardekker (1999: 68) go so far as to suggest that critical pedagogy has had its day, and that it was a stillborn child and that critical theory is a philosophy of science without a science (p. 75)! Nevertheless it is an important field for it recognizes and makes much of the fact that curricula and pedagogy are problematical and political.

A summary of the three paradigms

Box 1.8 summarizes some of the broad differences between the three approaches that we have made so far (see http://www.routledge.com/textbooks/ 9780415368780 – Chapter 1, file 1.8. ppt)

Box 1.8
Differing approaches to the study of behaviour

Normative	Interpretive	Critical
Society and the social system	The individual	Societies, groups and individuals
Medium/large-scale research	Small-scale research	Small-scale research
Impersonal, anonymous forces regulating behaviour	Human actions continuously recreating social life	Political, ideological factors, power and interests shaping behaviour
Model of natural sciences	Non-statistical	Ideology critique and action research
'Objectivity'	'Subjectivity'	Collectivity
Research conducted 'from the outside'	Personal involvement of the researcher	Participant researchers, researchers and facilitators
Generalizing from the specific	Interpreting the specific	Critiquing the specific
Explaining behaviour/seeking causes	Understanding actions/meanings rather than causes	Understanding, interrogating, critiquing, transforming actions and interests
Assuming the taken-for-granted	Investigating the taken-for-granted	
Macro-concepts: society, institutions, norms, positions, roles, expectations	Micro-concepts: individual perspective, personal constructs, negotiated meanings, definitions of situations	Interrogating and critiquing the taken for granted
Structuralists	Phenomenologists, symbolic interactionists, ethnomethodologists	Macro- and micro-concepts: political and ideological interests, operations of power
Technical interest	Practical interest	Critical theorists, action researchers, practitioner researchers
		Emancipatory interest

The emerging paradigm of complexity theory

An emerging fourth paradigm in educational research is that of complexity theory (Morrison 2002a). Complexity theory looks at the world in ways which break with simple cause-and-effect models, linear predictability, and a dissection approach to understanding phenomena, replacing them with organic, non-linear and holistic approaches (Santonus 1998: 3) in which relations within interconnected networks are the order of the day (Youngblood 1997: 27; Wheatley 1999: 10). Here key terms are feedback, recursion, emergence, connectedness and self-organization. Out go the simplistic views of linear causality, the ability to predict, control and manipulate, and in come uncertainty, networks and connection, self-organization, emergence over time through feedback and the relationships of the internal and external environments, and survival and development through adaptation and change.

Chaos and complexity theories argue against the linear, deterministic, patterned, universalizable, stable, atomized, modernistic, objective, mechanist, controlled, closed systems of law-like behaviour which may be operating in the laboratory but which do not operate in the social world of education. These features of chaos and complexity theories seriously undermine the value of experiments and positivist research in education (e.g. Gleick 1987; Waldrop 1992; Lewin 1993).

Complexity theory suggests that phenomena must be looked at holistically; to atomize phenomena into a restricted number of variables and then to focus only on certain factors is to miss the necessary dynamic interaction of several parts. More fundamentally, complexity theory suggests that the conventional units of analysis in educational research (as in other fields) should move away from, for example, individuals, institutions, communities and systems (cf. Lemke 2001). These should merge, so that the unit of analysis becomes a web or ecosystem (Capra 1996: 301), focused on, and arising from, a specific topic or centre of interest (a 'strange attractor'). Individuals, families, students, classes, schools, communities and societies exist in symbiosis; complexity theory tells us that their relationships are necessary, not contingent, and analytic, not synthetic. This is a challenging prospect for educational research, and complexity theory, a comparatively new perspective in educational research, offers considerable leverage into understanding societal, community, individual, and institutional change; it provides the nexus between macro- and micro-research in understanding and promoting change.

In addressing holism, complexity theory suggests the need for case study methodology, action research, and participatory forms of research, premised in many ways on interactionist, qualitative accounts, i.e. looking at situations through the eyes of as many participants or stakeholders as possible. This enables multiple causality, multiple perspectives and multiple effects to be charted. Self-organization, a key feature of complexity theory, argues for participatory, collaborative and multi-perspectival approaches to educational research. This is not to deny 'outsider' research; it is to suggest that, if it is conducted, outsider research has to take in as many perspectives as possible.

In educational research terms, complexity theory stands against simple linear methodologies based on linear views of causality, arguing for multiple causality and multidirectional causes and effects, as organisms (however defined: individuals, groups, communities) are networked and relate at a host of different levels and in a range of diverse ways. No longer can one be certain that a simple cause brings a simple or single effect, or that a single effect is the result of a single cause, or that the location of causes will be in single fields only, or that the location of effects will be in a limited number of fields.

Complexity theory not only questions the values of positivist research and experimentation, but also underlines the importance of educational research to catch the deliberate, intentional, agentic actions of participants and to adopt interactionist and constructivist perspectives. Addressing complexity theory's argument for self-organization, the call is for the teacher-as-researcher movement to be celebrated, and complexity theory suggests that research in education could concern itself with the symbiosis of internal and external researchers and research partnerships. Just as complexity theory suggests that there are multiple views of reality, so this accords not only with the need for several perspectives on a situation (using multi-methods), but resonates with those tenets of critical research that argue for different voices and views to be heard. Heterogeneity is the watchword. Complexity theory not only provides a powerful challenge to conventional approaches to educational research, but also suggests both a substantive agenda and a set of methodologies. It provides an emerging new paradigm for research (see http://www.routledge. com/textbooks/9780415368780 – Chapter 1,   file 1.1.doc).

Feminist research

It is perhaps no mere coincidence that feminist research should surface as a serious issue at the same time as ideology-critical paradigms for research; they are closely connected. Usher (1996: 124), although criticizing Habermas for his faith in family life as a haven from a heartless, exploitative world, nevertheless sets out several principles of feminist research that resonate with the ideology critique of the Frankfurt School:

- acknowledging the pervasive influence of gender as a category of analysis and organization
- deconstructing traditional commitments to truth, objectivity and neutrality
- adopting an approach to knowledge creation which recognizes that all theories are perspectival
- using a multiplicity of research methods
- acknowledging the interdisciplinary nature of feminist research
- involving the researcher and the people being researched

- deconstructing the theory–practice relationship.

Her suggestions build on earlier recognition of the significance of addressing the 'power issue' in research ('whose research', 'research for whom', 'research in whose interests') and the need to address the emancipatory element of educational research – that research should be empowering to all participants. The paradigm of critical theory questioned the putative objective, neutral, value-free, positivist, 'scientific' paradigm for the splitting of theory and practice and for its reproduction of asymmetries of power (reproducing power differentials in the research community and for treating participants/respondents instrumentally – as objects).

Robson (1993: 64) suggests seven sources of sexism in research:

- *androcentricity*: seeing the world through male eyes and applying male research paradigms to females
- *overgeneralization*: when a study generalizes from males to females
- *gender insensitivity*: ignoring sex as a possible variable
- *double standards*: using male criteria, measures and standards to judge the behaviour of women and vice versa (e.g. in terms of social status)
- *sex appropriateness*: e.g. that child-rearing is women's responsibility
- *familism*: treating the family, rather than the individual, as the unit of analysis
- *sexual dichotomism*: treating the sexes as distinct social groups when, in fact, they may share characteristics.

Feminist research, too, challenges the legitimacy of research that does not empower oppressed and otherwise invisible groups – women. Ezzy (2002: 20) writes of the need to replace a traditional masculine picture of science with an emancipatory commitment to knowledge that stems from a feminist perspective, since, 'if women's experience is analysed using only theories and observations from the standpoint of men, the resulting theories oppress women' (p. 23). Gender, as Ezzy (2002: 43) writes, is 'a category of experience'.

Positivist research served a given set of power relations, typically empowering the white, male-dominated research community at the expense of other groups whose voices were silenced. Feminist research seeks to demolish and replace this with a different substantive agenda – of empowerment, voice, emancipation, equality and representation for oppressed groups. In doing so, it recognizes the necessity for foregrounding issues of power, silencing and voicing, ideology critique and a questioning of the legitimacy of research that does not emancipate hitherto disempowered groups. In feminist research, women's consciousness of oppression, exploitation and disempowerment becomes a focus for research – the paradigm of ideology critique.

Far from treating educational research as objective and value-free, feminists argue that this is merely a smokescreen that serves the existing, disempowering status quo, and that the subject and value-laden nature of research must be surfaced, exposed and engaged (Haig 1999: 223). Supposedly value-free, neutral research perpetuates power differentials. Indeed Jayaratne and Stewart (1991) question the traditional, exploitative nature of much research in which the researchers receive all the rewards while the participants remain in their – typically powerless – situation, i.e. in which the status quo of oppression, under-privilege and inequality remain undisturbed. As Scott (1985: 80) writes: 'we may simply use other women's experiences to further our own aims and careers'. Cresswell (1998: 83), too, suggests that feminist research strives to establish collaborative and non-exploitative relationships. Indeed Scott (1985) questions how ethical it is for a woman researcher to interview those who are less privileged and more exploited than she herself is.

Changing this situation entails taking seriously issues of reflexivity, the effects of the research on the researched and the researchers, the breakdown of the positivist paradigm, and the raising of consciousness of the purposes and effects of the research. Ezzy (2002: 153) writes that 'the personal experience of the researcher is an integral part of the research process' and reinforces the point that objectivity is a false claim by researchers.

Ribbens and Edwards (1997) suggest that it is important to ask how researchers can produce work with reference to theoretical perspectives and formal traditions and requirements of public, academic knowledge while still remaining faithful to the experiences and accounts of research participants. Denzin (1989), Mies (1993), Haig (1999) and De Laine (2000) argue for several principles in feminist research:

- The asymmetry of gender relations and representation must be studied reflexively as constituting a fundamental aspect of social life (which includes educational research).
- Women's issues, their history, biography and biology, feature as a substantive agenda/focus in research – moving beyond mere perspectival/methodological issues to setting a research agenda.
- The raising of consciousness of oppression, exploitation, empowerment, equality, voice and representation is a methodological tool.
- The acceptability and notion of objectivity and objective research must be challenged.
- The substantive, value-laden dimensions and purposes of feminist research must be paramount.
- Research must empower women.
- Research need not be undertaken only by academic experts.
- Collective research is necessary: women need to collectivize their own individual histories if they are to appropriate these histories for emancipation.
- There is a commitment to revealing core processes and recurring features of women's oppression.
- There is an insistence on the inseparability of theory and practice.
- There is an insistence on the connections between the private and the public, between the domestic and the political.

- There is a concern with the construction and reproduction of gender and sexual difference.
- Narrow disciplinary boundaries are rejected.
- The artificial subject/researcher dualism is rejected.
- Positivism and objectivity as male mythology are rejected.
- There is an increased use of qualitative, introspective biographical research techniques.
- The gendered nature of social research and the development of anti-sexist research strategies are recognized.
- There is a review of the research process as consciousness and awareness raising and as fundamentally participatory.
- The primacy of women's personal subjective experience is recognized.
- Hierarchies in social research are rejected.
- The vertical, hierarchical relationships of researchers, research community and research objects, in which the research itself can become an instrument of domination and the reproduction and legitimation of power elites, have to be replaced by research that promotes the interests of dominated, oppressed, exploited groups.
- The equal status and reciprocal relationships between subjects and researchers are recognized.
- There is a need to change the status quo, not merely to understand or interpret it.
- The research must be a process of conscientization, not research solely by experts for experts, but to empower oppressed participants.

Indeed Webb et al. (2004) set out six principles for a feminist pedagogy in the teaching of research methodology:

- reformulating the professor–student relationship (from hierarchy to equality and sharing)
- ensuring empowerment (for a participatory democracy)
- building community (through collaborative learning)
- privileging the individual voice (not only the lecturer's)

- respecting diversity of personal experience (rooted, for example, in gender, race, ethnicity, class, sexual preference)
- challenging traditional views (e.g. the sociology of knowledge).

Gender shapes research agendas, the choice of topics and foci, the choice of data collection techniques and the relationships between researchers and researched. Several methodological principles flow from a 'rationale' for feminist research (Denzin 1989; Mies 1993; Haig 1997, 1999; De Laine 2000):

- The replacement of quantitative, positivist, objective research with qualitative, interpretive, ethnographic reflexive research, as objectivity in quantitative research is a smokescreen for masculine interests and agendas.
- Collaborative, collectivist research undertaken by collectives – often of women – combining researchers and researched in order to break subject–object and hierarchical, non-reciprocal relationships.
- The appeal to alleged value-free, neutral, indifferent and impartial research has to be replaced by conscious, deliberate partiality – through researchers identifying with participants.
- The use of ideology-critical approaches and paradigms for research.
- The spectator theory or contemplative theory of knowledge in which researchers research from ivory towers has to be replaced by a participatory approach – perhaps action research – in which all participants (including researchers) engage in the struggle for women's emancipation – a liberatory methodology.
- The need to change the status quo is the starting point for social research – if we want to know something we change it. (Mies (1993) cites the Chinese saying that if you want to know a pear then you must chew it!).
- The extended use of triangulation and multiple methods (including visual techniques such as video, photograph and film).
- The use of linguistic techniques such as conversational analysis.

- The use of textual analysis such as deconstruction of documents and texts about women.
- The use of meta-analysis to synthesize findings from individual studies (see Chapter 13).
- A move away from numerical surveys and a critical evaluation of them, including a critique of question wording.

Edwards and Mauthner (2002: 15, 27) characterize feminist research as that which concerns a critique of dominatory and value-free research, the surfacing and rejection of exploitative power hierarchies between the researcher and the participants, and the espousal of close – even intimate – relationships between the researcher and the researched. Positivist research is rejected as *per se* oppressive (Gillies and Alldred 2002: 34) and inherently unable to abide by its own principle of objectivity; it is a flawed epistemology. Research, and its underpinning epistemologies, are rooted in, and inseparable from interests (Habermas 1972).

The move is towards 'participatory action research' in which empowerment and emancipation are promoted and which is an involved and collaborative process (e.g. De Laine 2000: 109 ff.). Participation recognizes 'power imbalances and the need to engage oppressed people as agents of their own change' (Ezzy 2002: 44), while action research recognizes the value of 'using research findings to inform intervention decisions' (p. 44). As De Laine (2000: 16) writes: the call is 'for more participation and less observation, of *being with* and *for* the other, not *looking at*', with relations of reciprocity and equality rather than impersonality, exploitation and power/status differentials between researcher and participants.

The relationship between the researcher and participant, De Laine argues, must break a conventional patriarchy. The emphasis is on partnerships between researchers and participants, to the extent that researchers are themselves participants rather than outsiders and the participants shape the research process as co-researchers (De Laine 2000: 107), defining the problem, the methods, the data collection and analysis, interpretation and dissemination. The relationship between researchers and participants is one of equality, and outsider, objective, distant, positivist research relations are off the agenda; researchers are inextricably bound up in the lives of those they research. That this may bring difficulties in participant and researcher reactivity is a matter to be engaged rather than built out of the research.

Thapar-Björkert and Henry (2004) argue that the conventional, one-sided and unidirectional view of the researcher as powerful and the research participants as less powerful, with the researcher exploiting and manipulating the researched, could be a construction by western white researchers. They report research that indicates that power is exercised by the researched as well as the researchers, and is a much more fluid, shifting and negotiated matter than conventionally suggested, being dispersed through both the researcher and the researched. Indeed they show how the research participants can, and do, exercise considerable power over the researchers both before, during and after the research process. They provide a fascinating example of interviewing women in their homes in India, where, far from the home being a location of oppression, it was a site of their power and control.

With regard to methods of data collection, Oakley (1981) suggests that 'interviewing women' in the standardized, impersonal style which expects a response to a prescribed agenda and set of questions may be a 'contradiction in terms', as it implies an exploitative relationship. Rather, the subject–object relationship should be replaced by a guided dialogue. She criticizes the conventional notion of 'rapport' in conducting interviews (Oakley 1981: 35), arguing that they are instrumental, non-reciprocal and hierarchical, all of which are masculine traits. Rapport in this sense, she argues, is not genuine in that the researcher is using it for scientific rather than human ends (Oakley 1981: 55). Here researchers are 'faking friendship' for their own ends (Duncombe and Jessop 2002: 108), equating 'doing rapport' with trust, and, thereby, operating a very 'detached' form of friendship (p. 110). Similarly Thapar-Björkert and Henry (2004) suggest that attempts at friendship between researchers and participants are disingenuous, with 'purported solidarity' being a fraud perpetrated by well-intentioned feminists.

Duncombe and Jessop (2002: 111) ask a very searching question when they question whether, if interviewees are persuaded to take part in an interview by virtue of the researcher's demonstration of empathy and 'rapport', this is really giving informed consent. They suggest that informed consent, particularly in exploratory interviews, has to be continually renegotiated and care has to be taken by the interviewer not to be too intrusive. Personal testimonies, oral narratives and long interviews also figure highly in feminist approaches (De Laine 2000: 110; Thapar-Björkert and Henry 2004), not least in those that touch on sensitive issues. These, it is argued (Ezzy 2002: 45), enable women's voices to be heard, to be close to lived experiences, and avoid unwarranted assumptions about people's experiences.

The drive towards collective, egalitarian and emancipatory qualitative research is seen as necessary if women are to avoid colluding in their own oppression by undertaking positivist, uninvolved, dispassionate, objective research. Mies (1993: 67) argues that for women to undertake this latter form of research puts them into a schizophrenic position of having to adopt methods which contribute to their own subjugation and repression by ignoring their experience (however vicarious) of oppression and by forcing them to abide by the 'rules of the game' of the competitive, male-dominated academic world. In this view, argue Roman and Apple (1990: 59), it is not enough for women simply to embrace ethnographic forms of research, as this does not necessarily challenge the existing and constituting forces of oppression or asymmetries of power. Ethnographic research, they argue, has to be accompanied by ideology critique; indeed they argue that the transformative, empowering, emancipatory potential of research is a critical standard for evaluating that piece of research.

This latter point resonates with the call by Lather (1991) for researchers to be concerned with the political consequences of their research (e.g. consequential validity), not only the conduct of the research and data analysis itself.

Research must lead to change and improvement, particularly, in this context, for women (Gillies and Alldred 2002: 32). Research is a political activity with a political agenda (Gillies and Alldred 2002: 33; see also Lather 1991). Research and action – praxis – must combine 'knowledge *for*' as well as 'knowledge *what*' (Ezzy 2002: 47). As Marx reminds us in his *Theses on Feuerbach*: 'the philosophers have only interpreted the world, in various ways; the point, however, is to change it'. Gillies and Alldred (2002: 45), however, point out that 'many feminists have agonized over whether politicizing participants is necessarily helpful', as it raises awareness of constraints on their actions without being able to offer solutions or to challenge their structural causes. Research, thus politicized but unable to change conditions, may actually be disempowering and, indeed, patronizing in its simplistic call for enlightenment and emancipation. It could render women more vulnerable than before. Emancipation is a struggle.

Several of these views of feminist research and methodology are contested by other feminist researchers. For example, Jayaratne (1993: 109) argues for 'fitness for purpose', suggesting that exclusive focus on qualitative methodologies might not be appropriate either for the research purposes or, indeed, for advancing the feminist agenda (see also Scott 1985: 82-3). Jayaratne refutes the argument that quantitative methods are unsuitable for feminists because they neglect the emotions of the people under study. Indeed she argues for beating quantitative research on its own grounds (Jayaratne 1993: 121), suggesting the need for feminist quantitative data and methodologies in order to counter sexist quantitative data in the social sciences. She suggests that feminist researchers can accomplish this without 'selling out' to the positivist, male-dominated academic research community. Oakley (1998) suggests that the separation of women from quantitative methodology may have the unintended effect of perpetuating women as the 'other', and, thereby, discriminating against them.

De Laine (2000: 112) argues that shifting from quantitative to qualitative techniques may not solve many ethical problems in research, as these are endemic in any form of fieldwork. She argues that some feminist researchers may not wish to seek either less participation or more detachment, and that more detachment and less participation are not solutions to ethical dilemmas and 'morally responsible fieldwork' as these, too, bring their own ethical dilemmas, e.g. the risk of threat. She reports work (p. 113) that suggests that close relationships between researchers and participants may be construed as just as exploitative, if more disguised, as conventional researcher roles, and that they may bring considerable problems if data that were revealed in an intimate account between friends (researcher and participant) are then used in public research. The researcher is caught in a dilemma: if she is a true friend then this imposes constraints on the researcher, and yet if she is only pretending to be a friend, or limiting that friendship, then this provokes questions of honesty and personal integrity. Are research friendships real, ephemeral, or impression management used to gather data?

De Laine (2000: 115) suggests that it may be misguided to privilege qualitative research for its claim to non-exploitative relationships. While she acknowledges that quantitative approaches may perpetuate power differentials and exploitation, there is no guarantee that qualitative research will not do the same, only in a more disguised way. Qualitative approaches too, she suggests, can create and perpetuate unequal relations, not least simply because the researcher is in the field *qua* researcher rather than a friend; if it were not for the research then the researcher would not be present. Stacey (1988) suggests that the intimacy advocated for feminist ethnography may render exploitative relationships *more* rather than *less* likely. We refer readers to Chapter 5 on sensitive educational research for a further discussion of these issues.

Gillies and Alldred (2002: 43-6) suggest that action research, an area strongly supported in some quarters of feminist researchers, is, itself, problematic. It risks being an intervention in people's lives (i.e. a potential abuse of power), and the researcher typically plays a significant, if not central, role in initiating, facilitating, crystallizing and developing the meanings involved in, or stemming from, the research, i.e. the researcher is the one exercising power and influence.

Ezzy (2002: 44) reports that, just as there is no single feminist methodology, both quantitative and qualitative methods are entirely legitimate. Indeed, Kelly (1978) argues that a feminist commitment should enter research at the stages of formulating the research topic and interpreting the results, but it should be left out during the stages of data collection and conduct of the research.

Thapar-Björkert and Henry (2004) indicate that the researcher being an outsider might bring more advantages than if she were an insider. For example, being a white female researching non-white females may not be a handicap, as many non-white women might disclose information to white women that they would not disclose to a non-white person. Similarly, having interviewers and interviewees of the same racial and ethnic background does not mean that non-hierarchical relationships will still not be present. They also report that the categories of 'insider' and 'outsider' were much more fuzzy than exclusive. Researchers are both 'subject' and 'object', and those being researched are both 'observed' and 'observers'.

De Laine (2000: 110) suggests that there is a division among feminists between those who advocate closeness in relationships between researchers and subjects – a human researching fellow humans – and those who advocate 'respectful distance' between researchers and those being studied. Close relationships may turn into quasi-therapeutic situations rather than research (Duncombe and Jessop 2002: 111), yet it may be important to establish closeness in reaching deeper issues. Further, one has to question how far close relationships lead to reciprocal and mutual disclosure (p. 120). The debate is open: should the researcher share, be close and be prepared for more intimate social relations – a 'feminist ethic of care' (p. 111) – or keep those cool, outsider relations which might objectify those being researched? It is a moral as well as a methodological matter.

The issue runs deep: the suggestion is that emotions and feelings are integral to the research, rather than to be built out of the research in the interests of objectivity (Edwards and Mauthner 2002: 19). Emotions should not be seen as disruptive of research or as irrelevant (De Laine 2000: 151–2), but central to it, just as they are central to human life. Indeed emotional responses are essential in establishing the veracity of inquiries and data, and the 'feminist communitarian model' which De Laine (2000: 212–13) outlines values connectedness at several levels: emotions, emotionality and personal expressiveness, empathy. The egalitarian feminism that De Laine (2000: 108) and others advocate suggests a community of insiders in the same culture, in which empathy, reciprocity and egalitarianism are hallmarks.

Swantz (1996: 134) argues that there may be some self-deception by the researcher in adopting a dual role as a researcher and one who shares the situation and interests of the participants. She questions the extent to which the researcher may be able to be genuinely involved with the participants in other than a peripheral way and whether, simply because the researcher may have 'superior knowledge', a covert power differential may exist. De Laine (2000: 114) suggests that such superior knowledge may stem from the researcher's own background in anthropology or ethnography, or simply more education. The primary purpose of the researcher is research, and that is different from the primary purpose of the participants.

Further, the researcher's desire for identification and solidarity with her research subjects may be pious but unrealistic optimism, not least because she may not share the same race, ethnicity, background, life chances, experiences or colour as those being researched. Indeed Gillies and Alldred (2002: 39–40) raise the question of how far researchers can, or should, try to represent groups to which they themselves do not belong, not least those groups without power or voice, as this, itself, is a form of colonization and oppression. Affinity, they argue (p. 40), is no authoritative basis for representative research. Even the notion of affinity becomes suspect when it overlooks, or underplays, the significance of difference, thereby homogenizing groups and their particular experiences. In response to this, some feminist researchers (p. 40) suggest that researchers only have the warrant to confine themselves to their own immediate communities, though this is a contentious issue. There is value in speaking for others, not least for those who are silenced and marginalized, and in not speaking for others for fear of oppression and colonization. One has to question the acceptability and appropriateness of, and fidelity to, the feminist ethic, if one represents and uses others' stories (p. 41).

An example of a feminist approach to research is the Girls Into Science and Technology (GIST) action research project. This took place over three years, involving 2,000 students and their teachers in ten coeducational, comprehensive schools in one area of the United Kingdom, eight schools serving as the bases of the 'action', the remaining two acting as 'controls'. Several publications have documented the methodologies and findings of the GIST study (Kelly 1986; 1989a; 1989b; Kelly and Smail 1986; Whyte 1986), described by its co-director as 'simultaneous-integrated action research' (Kelly 1987) (i.e. integrating action and research). Kelly is open about the feminist orientation of the GIST project team, seeking deliberately to change girls' option choices and career aspirations, because the researchers saw that girls were disadvantaged by traditional sex-stereotypes. The researchers' actions, she suggests, were a small attempt to ameliorate women's subordinate social position (Kelly 1987).

Research and evaluation

The preceding discussion has suggested that research and politics are inextricably bound together. This can be taken further, as researchers in education will be advised to pay serious consideration to the politics of their research enterprise and the ways in which politics can steer research. For example, one can detect a trend in educational research towards more evaluative research, where, for example, a researcher's task is to evaluate the effectiveness (often of the implementation) of given policies and projects. This is particularly true in the

case of 'categorically funded' and commissioned research – research which is funded by policy-makers (e.g. governments, fund-awarding bodies) under any number of different headings that those policy-makers devise (Burgess 1993). On the one hand, this is laudable, for it targets research directly towards policy; on the other hand, it is dangerous in that it enables others to set the research agenda. Research ceases to become open-ended, pure research, and, instead, becomes the evaluation of *given* initiatives. Less politically charged, much research is evaluative, and indeed there are many similarities between research and evaluation. The two overlap but possess important differences. The problem of trying to identify differences between evaluation and research is compounded because not only do they share several of the same methodological characteristics but also one branch of research is called *evaluative research* or *applied research*. This is often kept separate from 'blue skies' research in that the latter is open-ended, exploratory, contributes something original to the substantive field and extends the frontiers of knowledge and theory whereas in the former the theory is *given* rather than *interrogated* or *tested*. One can detect many similarities between the two in that they both use methodologies and methods of social science research generally, covering, for example (see http://www.routledge.com/textbooks/ 9780415368780 – Chapter 1, file 1.9. ppt), the following:

- the need to clarify the *purposes* of the investigation
- the need to *operationalize* purposes and areas of investigation
- the need to address principles of *research design* that include:
  - formulating *operational questions*
  - deciding appropriate *methodologies*
  - deciding which *instruments* to use for data collection
  - deciding on the *sample* for the investigation
  - addressing *reliability* and *validity* in the investigation and instrumentation

- addressing *ethical* issues in conducting the investigation
- deciding on *data analysis* techniques
- deciding on *reporting* and *interpreting* results.

Indeed Norris (1990) argues that evaluation applies research methods to shed light on a problem of action (Norris 1990: 97); he suggests that evaluation can be viewed as an extension of research, because it shares its methodologies and methods, and because evaluators and researchers possess similar skills in conducting investigations (see http://www.routledge.com/textbooks/ 9780415368780 – Chapter 1, file 1.10. ppt). In many senses the eight features outlined above embrace many elements of the *scientific method*, which Smith and Glass (1987) set out in seven steps:

1   A *theory* about the phenomenon exists.
2   A *research problem* within the theory is detected and a *research question* is devised.
3   A *research hypothesis* is deduced (often about the relationship between constructs).
4   A *research design* is developed, *operationalizing* the research question and stating the *null hypothesis*.
5   The research is conducted.
6   The null hypothesis is tested based on the data gathered.
7   The original theory is revised or supported based on the results of the hypothesis testing.

Indeed, if steps 1 and 7 were removed then there would be nothing to distinguish between research and evaluation. Both researchers and evaluators pose questions and hypotheses, select samples, manipulate and measure variables, compute statistics and data, and state conclusions. Nevertheless there are important differences between evaluation and research that are not always obvious simply by looking at publications. Publications do not always make clear the background events that gave rise to the investigation, nor do they always make clear the uses of the material that they report, nor do they always make clear what the dissemination rights (Sanday 1993) are and who holds them. Several commentators set out some of the differences between evaluation and research. For example Smith and Glass (1987) offer eight main differences (see http://www.routledge.com/textbooks/ 9780415368780 – Chapter 1, file 1.11. ppt):

- *The intents and purposes of the investigation*: the researcher wants to advance the frontiers of knowledge of phenomena, to contribute to theory and to be able to make generalizations; the evaluator is less interested in contributing to theory or the general body of knowledge. Evaluation is more parochial than universal (Smith and Glass 1987: 33–4).
- *The scope of the investigation*: evaluation studies tend to be more comprehensive than research in the number and variety of aspects of a programme that are being studied (p. 34).
- *Values in the investigation*: research aspires to value neutrality, evaluations must represent multiple sets of values and include data on these values.
- *The origins of the study*: research has its origins and motivation in the researcher's curiosity and desire to know (p. 34). The researcher is answerable to colleagues and scientists (i.e. the research community) whereas the evaluator is answerable to the 'client'. The researcher is autonomous whereas the evaluator is answerable to clients and stakeholders. The researcher is motivated by a search for knowledge, the evaluator is motivated by the need to solve problems, allocate resources and make decisions. Research studies are public, evaluations are for a restricted audience.
- *The uses of the study*: the research is used to further knowledge, evaluations are used to inform decisions.
- *The timeliness of the study*: evaluations must be timely, research need not be. Evaluators' time scales are given, researchers' time scales need not be given.
- *Criteria for judging the study*: evaluations are judged by the criteria of utility and credibility, research is judged methodologically and by the contribution that it makes to the field (i.e. internal and external validity).

- *The agendas of the study*: an evaluator's agenda is given, a researcher's agenda is his or her own.

Norris (1990) reports an earlier piece of work by Glass and Worthen (1971) in which they identified eleven main differences between evaluation and research:

- *The motivation of the inquirer*: research is pursued largely to satisfy curiosity, evaluation is undertaken to contribute to the solution of a problem.
- *The objectives of the research*: research and evaluation seek different ends. Research seeks conclusions, evaluation leads to decisions.
- *Laws versus description*: research is the quest for laws (nomothetic), evaluation merely seeks to describe a particular thing (idiographic).
- *The role of explanation*: proper and useful evaluation can be conducted without producing an explanation of why the product or project is good or bad or of how it operates to produce its effects.
- *The autonomy of the inquiry*: evaluation is undertaken at the behest of a client, while researchers set their own problems.
- *Properties of the phenomena that are assessed*: evaluation seeks to assess social utility directly, research may yield evidence of social utility but often only indirectly.
- *Universality of the phenomena studied*: researchers work with constructs having a currency and scope of application that make the objects of evaluation seem parochial by comparison.
- *Salience of the value question*: in evaluation value questions are central and usually determine what information is sought.
- *Investigative techniques*: while there may be legitimate differences between research and evaluation methods, there are far more similarities than differences with regard to techniques and procedures for judging validity.
- *Criteria for assessing the activity*: the two most important criteria for judging the adequacy of research are internal and external validity, for evaluation they are utility and credibility.

- *Disciplinary base*: the researcher can afford to pursue inquiry within one discipline and the evaluator cannot.

A clue to some of the differences between evaluation and research can be seen in the definition of evaluation. Most definitions of evaluation include reference to several key features:

- answering specific, given questions
- gathering information
- making judgements
- taking decisions
- addressing the politics of a situation (Morrison 1993: 2).

(See http://www.routledge.com/textbooks/ 9780415368780 – Chapter 1, file 1.12. ppt.) Morrison (1993: 2) provides one definition of evaluation as: *the provision of information about specified issues upon which judgements are based and from which decisions for action are taken*. This view echoes MacDonald (1987) in his comments that the evaluator

> is faced with competing interest groups, with divergent definitions of the situation and conflicting informational needs . . . . He has to decide which decision-makers he will serve, what information will be of most use, when it is needed and how it can be obtained . . . . The resolution of these issues commits the evaluator to a political stance, an attitude to the government of education. No such commitment is required of the researcher. He stands outside the political process, and values his detachment from it. For him the production of new knowledge and its social use are separated. The evaluator is embroiled in the action, built into a political process which concerns the distribution of power, i.e. the allocation of resources and the determination of goals, roles and tasks . . . . When evaluation data influences power relationships the evaluator is compelled to weight carefully the consequences of his task specification . . . . The researcher is free to select his questions, and to seek answers to them. The evaluator, on the other hand, must never fall into the error of answering questions which no one but he is asking.
>
> (MacDonald 1987: 42)

MacDonald (1987) argues that evaluation is an inherently political enterprise. His much-used threefold typification of evaluations as autocratic, bureaucratic and democratic is premised on a political reading of evaluation (see also Chelinsky and Mulhauser (1993: 54) who refer to 'the inescapability of politics' in the world of evaluation). MacDonald (1987: 101), noting that 'educational research is becoming more evaluative in character', argues for research to be kept out of politics and for evaluation to square up to the political issues at stake:

> The danger therefore of conceptualizing evaluation as a branch of research is that evaluators become trapped in the restrictive tentacles of research respectability. Purity may be substituted for utility, trivial proofs for clumsy attempts to grasp complex significance. How much more productive it would be to define research as a branch of evaluation, a branch whose task it is to solve the technological problems encountered by the evaluator.
>
> (MacDonald 1987: 43)

However, the truth of the matter is far more blurred than these distinctions suggest. Two principal causes of this blurring lie in the *funding* and the *politics* of both evaluation and research. For example, the view of research as uncontaminated by everyday life is naïve and simplistic; Norris (1990: 99) argues that such an antiseptic view of research ignores the social context of educational research, some of which is located in the hierarchies of universities and research communities and the funding support provided for some research projects but not all by governments. His point has a pedigree that reaches back to Kuhn (1962), and is commenting on the politics of research funding and research utilization. Since the early 1980s one can detect a huge rise in 'categorical' funding of projects, i.e. defined, *given* projects (often by government or research sponsors) for which bids have to be placed. This may seem unsurprising if one is discussing research grants by government bodies, which are deliberately policy-oriented, though one can also detect in projects that have been granted by non-governmental organizations

(e.g. the UK Economic and Social Research Council) a move towards sponsoring policy-oriented projects rather than the 'blue-skies' research mentioned earlier. Indeed Burgess (1993: 1) argues that 'researchers are little more than contract workers...research in education must become policy relevant...research must come closer to the requirement of practitioners'.

This view is reinforced by several chapters in the collection edited by Anderson and Biddle (1991) which show that research and politics go together uncomfortably because researchers have different agendas and longer time scales than politicians and try to address the complexity of situations, whereas politicians, anxious for short-term survival want telescoped time scales, simple remedies and research that will be consonant with their political agendas. Indeed James (1993) argues that

> the power of research-based evaluation to provide evidence on which rational decisions can be expected to be made is quite limited. Policy-makers will always find reasons to ignore, or be highly selective of, evaluation findings if the information does not support the particular political agenda operating at the time when decisions have to be made.
>
> (James 1993: 135)

The politicization of research has resulted in funding bodies awarding research grants for categorical research that specify time scales and the terms of reference. Burgess's (1993) view also points to the constraints under which research is undertaken; if it is not concerned with policy issues then research tends not to be funded. One could support Burgess's view that research must have some impact on policy-making.

Not only is *research* becoming a political issue, but also this extends to the use being made of *evaluation* studies. It was argued above that evaluations are designed to provide useful data to inform decision-making. However, as evaluation has become more politicized so its uses (or non-uses) have become more politicized. Indeed Norris (1990) shows how politics frequently overrides evaluation or research evidence. Norris (1990: 135) writes that the announcement of the decision to extend the TVEI project was made without any evaluation reports having been received from evaluation teams in Leeds or the National Foundation for Educational Research. (The Technical and Vocational Education Initiative (TVEI) was a 1980s UK government-funded project frequently targeted to lower-attaining students.) This echoes James (1993) where she writes:

> The classic definition of the role of evaluation as providing information for decision-makers...is a fiction if this is taken to mean that policy-makers who commission evaluations are expected to make rational decisions based on the best (valid and reliable) information available to them.
>
> (James 1993: 119)

Where evaluations are commissioned and have heavily political implications, Stronach and Morris (1994) argue that the response to this is that evaluations become more 'conformative' (see http://www.routledge.com/textbooks/ 9780415368780 – Chapter 1, file 1.13. ppt), possessing several characteristics:

- Being short-term, taking project goals as given and supporting their realization.
- Ignoring the evaluation of longer-term learning outcomes, or anticipated economic or social consequences of the programme.
- Giving undue weight to the perceptions of programme participants who are responsible for the successful development and implementation of the programme; as a result, tending to 'over-report' change.
- Neglecting and 'under-reporting' the views of classroom practitioners, and programme critics.
- Adopting an atheoretical approach, and generally regarding the aggregation of opinion as the determination of overall significance.
- Involving a tight contractual relationship with the programme sponsors that either disbars public reporting, or encourages self-censorship in order to protect future funding prospects.
- Undertaking various forms of implicit advocacy for the programme in its reporting style.
- Creating and reinforcing a professional schizophrenia in the research and evaluation community, whereby individuals come to hold divergent public and private opinions, or offer criticisms in general rather than in particular, or quietly develop 'academic' critiques which are at variance with their contractual evaluation activities, alternating between 'critical' and 'conformative' selves.

The argument so far has been confined to large-scale projects that are influenced by and may or may not influence political decision-making. However, the argument need not remain there. Morrison (1993), for example, indicates how evaluations might influence the 'micro-politics of the school'. Hoyle (1986), for example, asks whether evaluation data are used to bring resources into, or take resources out of, a department or faculty. The issue does not relate only to evaluations, for school-based research, far from the emancipatory claims for it made by action researchers (e.g. Carr and Kemmis 1986; Grundy 1987), is often concerned more with finding out the most successful ways of organization, planning, teaching and assessment of a *given agenda* rather *than setting agendas* and following one's own research agendas. This is *problem-solving* rather than *problem-setting*. That evaluation and research are being drawn together by politics at both macro-level and micro-level is evidence of a growing interventionism by politics into education, thus reinforcing the hegemony of the government in power. Several points have been made here:

- There is considerable overlap between evaluation and research.
- There are some *conceptual* differences between evaluation and research, though, in practice, there is considerable blurring of the edges of the differences between the two.
- The funding and control of research and research agendas reflect the persuasions of political decision-makers.
- Evaluative research has increased in response to categorical funding of research projects.
- The attention being given to, and utilization of, evaluation varies according to the consonance between the findings and their political attractiveness to political decision-makers.

In this sense the views expressed earlier by MacDonald (1987) are now little more than an historical relic; there is very considerable blurring of the edges between evaluation and research because of the political intrusion into, and use of, these two types of study. One response to this can be seen in Burgess's (1993) view that a researcher needs to be able to meet the sponsor's requirements for evaluation while also generating research data (engaging the issues of the need to negotiate ownership of the data and intellectual property rights).

Research, politics and policy-making

The preceding discussion has suggested that there is an inescapable political dimension to educational research, both in the macro- and micro-political senses. In the macro-political sense this manifests itself in funding arrangements, where awards are made provided that the research is 'policy-related' (Burgess 1993) – guiding policy decisions, improving quality in areas of concern identified by policy-makers, facilitating the implementation of policy decisions, evaluating the effects of the implementation of policy. Burgess notes a shift here from a situation where the researcher specifies the topic of research and towards the sponsor specifying the focus of research. The issue of sponsoring research reaches beyond simply commissioning research towards the dissemination (or not) of research – who will receive or have access to the findings and how the findings will be used and reported. This, in turn, raises the fundamental issue of who owns and controls data, and who controls the release of research findings. Unfavourable reports might be withheld for a time, suppressed or selectively released! Research can be brought into the service of wider educational purposes – the politics of a local education authority, or indeed the politics of government agencies.

Though research and politics intertwine, the relationships between educational research, politics and policy-making are complex because research designs strive to address a complex social reality (Anderson and Biddle 1991); a piece of research does not feed simplistically or directly into a specific piece of policy-making. Rather, research generates a range of different types of knowledge – concepts, propositions, explanations, theories, strategies, evidence, methodologies (Caplan 1991). These feed subtly and often indirectly into the decision-making process, providing, for example, direct inputs, general guidance, a scientific gloss, orienting perspectives, generalizations and new insights. Basic and applied research have significant parts to play in this process.

The degree of influence exerted by research depends on careful dissemination; too little and its message is ignored, too much and data overload confounds decision-makers and makes them cynical – the syndrome of the boy who cried wolf (Knott and Wildavsky 1991). Hence researchers must give care to utilization by policy-makers (Weiss 1991a), reduce jargon, provide summaries, and improve links between the two cultures of researchers and policy-makers (Cook 1991) and, further, to the educational community. Researchers must cultivate ways of influencing policy, particularly when policy-makers can simply ignore research findings, commission their own research (Cohen and Garet 1991) or underfund research into social problems (Coleman 1991; Thomas 1991). Researchers must recognize their links with the power groups who decide policy. Research utilization takes many forms depending on its location in the process of policy-making, e.g. in research and development, problem solving, interactive and tactical models (Weiss 1991b). Researchers will have to judge the most appropriate forms of utilization of their research (Alkin et al. 1991).

The impact of research on policy-making depends on its degree of consonance with the political agendas of governments (Thomas 1991) and policy-makers anxious for their own political survival (Cook 1991) and the promotion of their social programmes. Research is used if it is politically acceptable. That the impact of research on policy is intensely and inescapably political is a truism (Horowitz and Katz 1991; Kamin 1991; Selleck 1991; Wineburg 1991). Research too easily becomes simply an 'affirmatory text' which 'exonerates the system' (Wineburg 1991) and is used by those who seek to hear in it only echoes of their own voices and wishes (Kogan and Atkin 1991).

There is a significant tension between researchers and policy-makers. The two parties have different, and often conflicting, interests, agendas, audiences, time scales, terminology, and concern for topicality (Levin 1991). These have huge implications for research styles. Policy-makers anxious for the quick fix of superficial facts, short-term solutions and simple remedies for complex and generalized social problems (Cartwright 1991; Cook 1991) – the Simple Impact model (Biddle and Anderson 1991; Weiss 1991a; 1991b) – find positivist methodologies attractive, often debasing the data through illegitimate summary. Moreover, policy-makers find much research uncertain in its effects (Cohen and Garet 1991; Kerlinger 1991), dealing in a *Weltanschauung* rather than specifics, and being too complex in its designs and of limited applicability (Finn 1991). This, reply the researchers, misrepresents the nature of their work (Shavelson and Berliner 1991) and belies the complex reality which they are trying to investigate (Blalock 1991). Capturing social complexity and serving political utility can run counter to each other.

The issue of the connection between research and politics – power and decision-making – is complex. On another dimension, the notion that research is inherently a political act because it is part of the political processes of society has not been lost on researchers. Usher and Scott (1996: 176) argue that positivist research has allowed a traditional conception of society to be preserved relatively unchallenged – the white, male, middle-class researcher – to the relative exclusion of 'others' as legitimate knowers. That this reaches into epistemological debate is evidenced in the issues of who defines the 'traditions of knowledge' and the disciplines of knowledge; the social construction of knowledge has to take into account the differential power of groups to define what is worthwhile research knowledge, what constitutes acceptable focuses and methodologies of research and how the findings will be used.

Methods and methodology

We return to our principal concern, methods and methodology in educational research. By methods, we mean that range of approaches used in educational research to gather data which are to be used as a basis for inference and interpretation, for explanation and prediction. Traditionally, the word refers to those techniques associated with the positivistic model – eliciting responses to predetermined questions, recording measurements, describing phenomena and performing experiments. For our purposes, we will extend the meaning to include not only the methods of normative research but also those associated with interpretive paradigms – participant observation, role-playing, non-directive interviewing, episodes and accounts. Although methods may also be taken to include the more specific features of the scientific enterprise such as forming concepts and hypotheses, building models and theories, and sampling procedures, we will limit ourselves principally to the more general techniques which researchers use.

If methods refer to techniques and procedures used in the process of data-gathering, the aim of methodology then is to describe approaches to, kinds and paradigms of research (Kaplan 1973). Kaplan suggests that the aim of methodology is to help us to understand, in the broadest possible terms, not the products of scientific inquiry but the process itself.

We, for our part, will attempt to present normative and interpretive perspectives in a complementary light and will try to lessen the tension that is sometimes generated between them. Merton and Kendall (1946)[7] express the same sentiment:

> Social scientists have come to abandon the spurious choice between qualitative and quantitative data: they are concerned rather with that combination of both which makes use of the most valuable features of each. The problem becomes one of determining *at*

which points they should adopt the one, and at which the other, approach.

(Merton and Kendall 1946)

The term *research* itself may take on a range of meanings and thereby be legitimately applied to a variety of contexts from, say, an investigation into the techniques of Dutch painters of the seventeenth century to the problem of finding more efficient means of improving traffic flow in major city centres. For our purposes, however, we will restrict its usages to those activities and undertakings aimed at developing a science of behaviour, the word *science* itself implying both normative and interpretive perspectives. Accordingly, when we speak of social research,

we have in mind the systematic and scholarly application of the principles of a science of behaviour to the problems of people within their social contexts and when we use the term educational research, we likewise have in mind the application of these same principles to the problems of teaching and learning within the formal educational framework and to the clarification of issues having direct or indirect bearing on these concepts.

The particular value of scientific research in education is that it will enable educators to develop the kind of sound knowledge base that characterizes other professions and disciplines; and one that will ensure education a maturity and sense of progression it at present lacks.

Part Two

Planning educational research

The planning of educational research is not an arbitrary matter; the research itself is an inescapably ethical enterprise. We place ethical issues at a very early point in the book to signal this. The research community and those using the findings have a right to expect that research be conducted rigorously, scrupulously and in an ethically defensible manner. All this necessitates careful planning, and this part introduces some key planning issues. In planning research, we need to consider the issues of sampling, reliability and validity at the very outset, and this part addresses these. These are complex issues, and we take readers through them systematically. In addition, a new chapter on sensitive educational research is included here, taking sensitivity not only in terms of content, but also in terms of process, purpose, outcome and usage. This new chapter also makes the point that often access itself is a sensitive matter, and this could be the major issue to be faced in planning research. This part sets out a range of planning possibilities so that the eventual selection of sampling procedures, versions of reliability and validity are made on the basis of *fitness for purpose*, and so that sensitivities in research are anticipated and addressed.

2 The ethics of educational and social research

Introduction

The awareness of ethical concerns in research is reflected in the growth of relevant literature and in the appearance of regulatory codes of research practice formulated by various agencies and professional bodies.[1] A major ethical dilemma is that which requires researchers to strike a balance between the demands placed on them as professional scientists in pursuit of truth, and their subjects' rights and values potentially threatened by the research. This is known as the 'costs/benefits ratio', the essence of which is outlined by Frankfort-Nachmias and Nachmias (1992) in Box 2.1, and is a concept we return to later in the chapter. Ethical problems for researchers can multiply surprisingly when they move from the general to the particular, and from the abstract to the concrete.

Ethical issues may stem from the kinds of problems investigated by social scientists and the methods they use to obtain valid and reliable data. This means that each stage in the research sequence raises ethical issues. They may arise from the nature of the research project itself (ethnic differences in intelligence, for example); the context for the research (a remand home); the procedures to be adopted (producing high levels of anxiety); methods of data collection (covert observation); the nature of the participants (emotionally disturbed adolescents); the type of data collected (highly personal and sensitive information); and what is to be done with the data (publishing in a manner that may cause participants embarrassment).

In this chapter we present a conspectus of the main issues that may confront researchers. Each research undertaking is an event *sui generis*, and the conduct of researchers cannot be, indeed should not be, forced into a procrustean system of ethics. When it comes to the resolution of a specific moral problem, each situation frequently offers a spectrum of possibilities (see http://www.routledge.com/textbooks/ 9780415368780 – Chapter 2, file 2.1. ppt).

In this chapter we review *seriatim* several issues in the ethical field. These can constitute a set of initial considerations that researchers should address in planning research:

- informed consent
- gaining access to and acceptance in the research setting
- the nature of ethics in social research generally
- sources of tension in the ethical debate, including non-maleficence, beneficence and human dignity, absolutist and relativist ethics
- problems and dilemmas confronting the researcher, including matters of privacy, anonymity, confidentiality, betrayal and deception
- ethical problems endemic in particular research methods
- ethics and evaluative research
- regulatory ethical frameworks, guidelines and codes of practice for research
- personal codes of practice
- sponsored research
- responsibilities to the research community.

While many of these issues concern procedural ethics, we have to recall that ethics concern right and wrong, good and bad, and so procedural ethics are not enough; one has to consider how the research purposes, contents, methods, reporting and outcomes abide by ethical principles and practices. Before this, however, we examine another fundamental concept which, along with the *costs/benefits ratio*, contributes to the

Box 2.1
The costs/benefits ratio

The *costs/benefits ratio* is a fundamental concept expressing the primary ethical dilemma in social research. In planning their proposed research, social scientists have to consider the likely social benefits of their endeavours against the personal costs to the individuals taking part. Possible benefits accruing from the research may take the form of crucial findings leading to significant advances in theoretical and applied knowledge. Failure to do the research may cost society the advantages of the research findings and ultimately the opportunity to improve the human condition. The costs to participants may include affronts to dignity, embarrassment, loss of trust in social relations, loss of autonomy and self-determination, and lowered self-esteem. On the other hand, the benefits to participants could take the form of satisfaction in having made a contribution to science and a greater personal understanding of the research area under scrutiny. The process of balancing benefits against possible costs is chiefly a subjective one and not at all easy. There are few or no absolutes and researchers have to make decisions about research content and procedures in accordance with professional and personal values. This costs/benefits *ratio* is the basic dilemma residual in a great deal of social research.

Source: adapted from Frankfort-Nachmias and Nachmias 1992

bedrock of ethical procedure – that of *informed consent*.

Informed consent

Much social research necessitates obtaining the consent and cooperation of subjects who are to assist in investigations and of significant others in the institutions or organizations providing the research facilities (see http://www.routledge.com/textbooks/9780415368780 – Chapter 2, file 2.2. ppt). While some cultures may not be stringent about informed consent, in others there are strict protocols for informed consent. Frankfort-Nachmias and Nachmias (1992) suggest that informed consent is particularly important if participants are going to be exposed to any stress, pain, invasion of privacy, or if they are going to lose

control over what happens (e.g. in drug research); such informed consent requires full information about the possible consequences and dangers.

The principle of informed consent arises from the subject's right to freedom and self-determination. Being free is a condition of living in a democracy, and when restrictions and limitations are placed on that freedom they must be justified and consented to, as in research. Consent thus protects and respects the right of self-determination and places some of the responsibility on the participant should anything go wrong in the research. As part of the right to self-determination, the subject has the right to refuse to take part, or to withdraw once the research has begun (see Frankfort-Nachmias and Nachmias 1992). Thus informed consent implies informed refusal.

Informed consent has been defined by Diener and Crandall (1978) as 'the procedures in which individuals choose whether to participate in an investigation after being informed of facts that would be likely to influence their decisions'. This definition involves four elements: competence, voluntarism, full information and comprehension.

Competence implies that responsible, mature individuals will make correct decisions if they are given the relevant information. It is incumbent on researchers to ensure they do not engage individuals incapable of making such decisions because of immaturity or some form of psychological impairment.

Voluntarism entails applying the principle of informed consent and thus ensuring that participants freely choose to take part (or not) in the research and guarantees that exposure to risks is undertaken knowingly and voluntarily. This element can be problematical, especially in the field of medical research where unknowing patients are used as guinea-pigs.

Full information implies that consent is fully informed, though in practice it is often impossible for researchers to inform subjects on everything, e.g. on the statistical treatment of data; and, as we shall see below, on those occasions when the researchers themselves do not know everything about the investigation. In such circumstances, the strategy of reasonably informed consent has to be applied. Box 2.2 illustrates a set of guidelines used in the United States that are based on the idea of *reasonably informed consent*.[2]

Comprehension refers to the fact that participants fully understand the nature of the research project, even when procedures are complicated and entail risks. Suggestions have been made to ensure that subjects fully comprehend the situation they are putting themselves into, e.g. by using highly educated subjects, by engaging a consultant to explain difficulties, or by building into the research scheme a time lag between the request for participation and decision time.

If these four elements are present, researchers can be assured that subjects' rights will have been given appropriate consideration. As Frankfort-Nachmias and Nachmias (1992) note, however, informed consent may not always be necessary (e.g. deception may be justified), but that, as a general rule, the greater risk, the more important it is to gain informed consent.

Ruane (2005: 21) also raises the question of 'how much information is enough'; she argues that this may be an unknown, not necessarily deliberately withheld. Further, just as providing information may bias the results (i.e. it is important for the integrity of the research *not* to disclose its purposes or contents, e.g. the Milgram experiments, see Chapter 21), she argues that it may actually confuse the respondents.

It must also be remembered that there are some research methods where it is impossible to seek informed consent. Covert observation, for example, as used in Patrick's (1973) study of a Glasgow gang (Chapter 11), or experimental techniques involving deception, as in Milgram's (1974) obedience-to-authority experiments (Chapter 21), would, by their very nature, rule out the option. And, of course, there may be occasions when problems arise even though consent has been obtained. Burgess (1989), for example, cites his own research in which teachers had been informed that research was taking place but in which it was not possible to specify exactly what data would be collected or how they would be used. It could be said, in this particular case, that individuals were not fully informed, that consent had not been obtained, and that privacy had been violated. As a general rule, however, informed consent is an important principle. It is this principle that will form the basis of an implicit contractual relationship between the researcher and the researched and will serve as a foundation on which subsequent ethical considerations can be structured.

From the remarks on informed consent so far, we may appear to be assuming relationships between peers – researcher and teachers, for example, or research professor and postgraduate students – and this assumption would seem to underpin many of the discussions of an ethical nature in the research literature generally. However, much educational research involves children who cannot be regarded as being on equal terms with the researcher and it is important to keep this in mind at all stages in the research process, including the point where informed consent is sought. In this connection we refer to the important work of Fine and Sandstrom (1988), whose ethnographic and participant observational studies of children and young people focus, among other issues, on this asymmetry with respect to the problems of obtaining informed consent from their young subjects and explaining the research in a comprehensible fashion. As a

Box 2.2
Guidelines for reasonably informed consent

1   A fair explanation of the procedures to be followed and their purposes.
2   A description of the attendant discomforts and risks reasonably to be expected.
3   A description of the benefits reasonably to be expected.
4   A disclosure of appropriate alternative procedures that might be advantageous to the participants.
5   An offer to answer any inquiries concerning the procedures.
6   An instruction that the person is free to withdraw consent and to discontinue participation in the project at any time without prejudice to the participant.

Source: US Department of Health, Education and Welfare *et al.* 1971

guiding principle, they advise that, while it is desirable to lessen the power differential between children and adult researchers, the difference will remain and its elimination may be ethically inadvisable.

There are other aspects of the problem of informed consent (or refusal) in relation to young, or very young, children. Seeking informed consent with regard to minors involves two stages. First, researchers consult and seek permission from those adults responsible for the prospective subjects, and second, they approach the young people themselves. The adults in question will be, for example, parents, teachers, tutors, psychiatrists, youth leaders, or team coaches, depending on the research context. The point of the research will be explained, questions invited, and permission to proceed to the next stage sought. Objections, for whatever reason, will be duly respected. Obtaining approval from relevant adults may be more difficult than in the case of the children, but, being sensitive to children's welfare, it is vital that researchers secure such approval. It may be useful if, in seeking the consent of children, researchers bear in mind the provisory comments below.

While seeking children's permission and cooperation is an automatic part of quantitative research (a child cannot unknowingly complete a simple questionnaire), the importance of informed consent in qualitative research is not always recognized. Speaking of participant observation, for example, Fine and Sandstrom (1988) say that researchers must provide a credible and meaningful explanation of their research intentions, especially in situations where they have little authority, and that children must be given a real and legitimate opportunity to say that they do not want to take part. The authors advise that where subjects do refuse, they should not be questioned, their actions should not be recorded, and they should not be included in any book or article (even under a pseudonym). Where they form part of a group, they may be included as part of a collectivity. Fine and Sandstrom (1988) consider that such rejections are sometimes a result of mistrust of the researcher. They suggest that at a later date, when the researcher has been able to establish greater rapport with the group, those who refused initially may be approached again, perhaps in private.

Two particular groups of children require special mention: very young children, and those not capable of making a decision. Researchers intending to work with pre-school or nursery children may dismiss the idea of seeking informed consent from their would-be subjects because of their age, but Fine and Sandstrom (1988) would recommend otherwise. Even though such children would not understand what research was, the authors advise that the children be given some explanation. For example, one to the effect that an adult will be watching and playing with them might be sufficient to provide a measure of informed consent consistent with the children's understanding. As Fine and Sandstrom comment:

> Our feeling is that children should be told as much as possible, even if some of them cannot understand the full explanation. Their age should not diminish their rights, although their level of understanding must be taken into account in the explanations that are shared with them.
>
> (Fine and Sandstrom 1988)

The second group consists of those children who are to be used in a research project and who may not meet Diener and Crandall's (1978) criterion of 'competence' (a group of psychologically impaired children, for example – the issue of 'advocacy' applies here). In such circumstances there may be institutional or local authority guidelines to follow. In the absence of these, the requirements of informed consent would be met by obtaining the permission of headteachers acting *in loco parentis* or who have had delegated to them the responsibility for providing informed consent by the parents.

Two cautions: first, where an extreme form of research is planned, parents would have to be fully informed in advance and their consent obtained; and second, whatever the nature of the research and whoever is involved, should a child show signs of discomfort or stress, the research should be terminated immediately. For further discussion on the care that needs to be exercised in working with children we refer readers to Graue and Walsh (1998); Greig and Taylor (1998); Holmes (1998).

Informed consent requires an explanation and description of several factors, including, for example:

- the purposes, contents and procedures of the research
- any foreseeable risks and negative outcomes, discomfort or consequences and how they will be handled
- benefits that might derive from the research
- incentives to participate and rewards from participating
- right to voluntary non-participation, withdrawal and rejoining the project
- rights and obligations to confidentiality and non-disclosure of the research, participants and outcomes
- disclosure of any alternative procedures that may be advantageous
- opportunities for participants to ask questions about any aspect of the research
- signed contracts for participation.

There are many more issues, and researchers will need to decide what to include in informed consent. Not least among these is the issue of volunteering. Participants may feel coerced to volunteer (e.g. by a school principal), or may not wish to offend a researcher by refusing to participate, or may succumb to peer pressure to volunteer (or not to volunteer), or may wish to volunteer for reasons other than the researcher's (e.g. to malign a school principal or senior colleagues, to gain resources for his or her department, or to gain approval from colleagues). Researchers have to ensure that volunteers have real freedom of choice if informed consent is to be fulfilled.

Access and acceptance

The relevance of the principle of informed consent becomes apparent at the initial stage of the research project – that of access to the institution or organization where the research is to be conducted, and acceptance by those whose permission one needs before embarking on the task. We highlight this stage of access

and acceptance in particular at this point because it offers the best opportunity for researchers to present their credentials as serious investigators and establish their own ethical position with respect to their proposed research.

Investigators cannot expect access to a nursery, school, college or university as a matter of right. They have to demonstrate that they are worthy, as researchers and human beings, of being accorded the facilities needed to carry out their investigations. The advice of Bell (1991: 37) is to gain permission early on, with fully informed consent gained, and indicating to participants the possible benefits of the research.

The first stage thus involves the gaining of official permission to undertake one's research in the target community. This will mean contacting, in person or in writing, an appropriate official and/or the chairperson of the governors if one is to work in a school, along with the headteacher or principal. At a later point, significant figures who will be responsible for, or assist in, the organization and administration of the research will also need to be contacted – the deputy head or senior teacher, for instance, and most certainly the class teacher if children are to be used in the research. Since the researcher's potential for intrusion and perhaps disruption is considerable, amicable relations with the class teacher in particular should be fostered as expeditiously as possible. If the investigation involves teachers as participants, propositions may have to be put to the stakeholders and conditions negotiated. Where the research is to take place in another kind of institution, e.g. a youth club or detention centre, the approach will be similar, although the organizational structure will be different.

Achieving goodwill and cooperation is especially important where the proposed research extends over a period of time: days, perhaps, in the case of an ethnographic study; months (or perhaps years) where longitudinal research is involved. Access does not present quite such a problem when, for example, a one-off survey requires respondents to give up half-an-hour of their time or when a researcher is normally a member of the organization where the research is taking place (an insider), though in the case of the latter, it is generally unwise to take co-operation for granted. Where research procedures are extensive and complicated, however, or where the design is developmental or longitudinal, or where researchers are not normally based in the target community, the problems of access are more involved and require greater preparation. Box 2.3 gives a flavour of the kinds of accessibility problems that can be experienced (Foster 1989).

Having identified the official and significant figures whose permission must be sought, and before actually meeting them, researchers will need to clarify in their own minds the precise nature and scope of their research. It is desirable that they have a total picture of what it all entails, even if the overall scheme is a provisional one (though we have to bear in mind that this may cause difficulties later). In this respect researchers could, for instance, identify the aims of the research; its practical applications, if any, the design, methods and procedures to be used, the nature and size of samples or groups, what tests are to be administered and how, what activities are to be observed, which subjects are to be interviewed, observational needs, the time involved, the degree of disruption envisaged; arrangements to guarantee confidentiality with respect to data (if this is necessary), the role of feedback and how findings can best be disseminated, the overall timetable within which the research is to be encompassed, and finally, whether assistance will be required in the organization and administration of the research.

By such planning and foresight, both researchers and institutions will have a good idea of the demands likely to be made on both subjects (be they children or teachers) and organizations. It is also a good opportunity to anticipate and resolve likely problems, especially those of a practical kind. A long, complicated questionnaire, for example, may place undue demands on the comprehension skills and attention spans of a particular class of 13 year olds, or a relatively inexperienced teacher could feel threatened by sustained research scrutiny. Once this kind of information has been sorted out and clarified, researchers will be in a stronger position to discuss their proposed plans in an informed, open and frank manner (though not necessarily too open, as we shall see) and may thereby more readily gain permission, acceptance and support. It must be remembered that hosts will have perceptions of researchers and their intentions and that these need to be positive. Researchers can best influence such perceptions by presenting themselves as competent, trustworthy and accommodating.

Once this preliminary information has been collected, researchers are duly prepared for the next stage: making actual contact in person, perhaps after an introductory letter, with appropriate people in the organization with a view to negotiating access. If the research is university-based, they will have the support of their university and supervisor. Festinger and Katz (1966) consider that there is real economy in going to the very top of the organization or system in question to obtain assent and cooperation. This is particularly so where the structure is clearly hierarchical and where lower levels are always dependent on their superiors. They consider it likely that the nature

Box 2.3
Close encounters of a researcher kind

My first entry into a staffroom at the college was the occasion of some shuffling and shifting of books and chairs so that I could be given a comfortable seat while the tutor talked to me from a standing position. As time progressed my presence was almost taken for granted and later, when events threatened the security of the tutors, I was ignored. No one enquired as to whether they could assist me and my own enquiries were met with cursory answers and confused looks, followed by the immediate disappearance of the individuals concerned, bearing a pile of papers. I learned not to make too many enquiries. Unfortunately, when individuals feel insecure, when their world is threatened with change that is beyond their control, they are likely to respond in an unpredictable manner to persons within their midst whose role is unclear, and the role of the researcher is rarely understood by those not engaged in research.

Source: Foster 1989: 194

of the research will be referred to the top of the organization sooner or later, and that there is a much better chance for a favourable decision if leaders are consulted at the outset. It may also be the case that heads will be more open-minded than those lower down, who, because of their insecurity, may be less cooperative.

Festinger and Katz (1996) also warn against using the easiest entrances into the organization when seeking permission. Researchers may perhaps seek to come in as allies of individuals or groups who have a special interest to exploit and who see research as a means to their ends, rather than entering the situation in the common interests of all parties, with findings equally available to all groups and persons (Festinger and Katz 1966). Investigators should thus seek as broad a basis for their support as possible. Other potential problems may be circumvented by making use of accepted channels of communication in the institution or organization. Festinger and Katz (1966) caution that if information is limited to a single channel then the study risks becoming identified with the interests that are associated with that channel.

Following contact, there will be a negotiation process. At this point researchers will give as much information about the aims, nature and procedures of the research as is appropriate. This is very important: information that may prejudice the results of the investigation may have to be withheld. Aronson and Carlsmith (1969), for instance, note that one cannot imagine researchers who are studying the effects of group pressure on conformity announcing their intentions in advance. On the other hand, researchers may find themselves on dangerous ground if they go to the extreme of maintaining a 'conspiracy of silence', because, as Festinger and Katz note, such a stance is hard to keep up if the research is extensive and lasts over several days or weeks, and trying to preserve secrecy might lead to an increase in the spread and wildness of rumours (Festinger and Katz 1966). If researchers do not want their potential hosts and/or subjects to know too much about specific hypotheses and objectives, then a simple way out is to present an explicit statement at a fairly general

Box 2.4
Conditions and guarantees proffered for a school-based research project

1	All participants must be given the chance to remain anonymous.
2	All data must be given strict confidentiality.
3	Interviewees should have the chance to verify statements at the stage of drafting the report (respondent validation).
4	Participants should be given a copy of the final report.
5	Permission for publication must be gained from the participants.
6	If possible, the research report should be of benefit to the school and participants.

Source: adapted from Bell 1991

level with one or two examples of items that are not crucial to the study as a whole. As most research entails some risks, especially where field studies are concerned, and as the presence of an observer scrutinizing various aspects of community or school life may not be relished by all in the group, investigators must at all times manifest a sensitive appreciation of their hosts' and subjects' position and reassure anyone who feels threatened by the work. Such reassurance could take the form of a statement of conditions and guarantees given by researchers at this negotiation stage. By way of illustration, Box 2.4 contains conditions laid down for the Open University students' school-based research project.

Ethical considerations pervade the whole process of research; these will be no more so than at the stage of access and acceptance, where appropriateness of topic, design, methods, guarantees of confidentiality, analysis and dissemination of findings must be negotiated with relative openness, sensitivity, honesty, accuracy and scientific impartiality. There can be no rigid rules in this context. It will be a case of formulating and abiding by one's own situated ethics. These will determine what is acceptable and what is not acceptable. As Hitchcock and Hughes (1995) say in this regard:

Individual circumstances must be the final arbiter. As far as possible it is better if the teacher can discuss the research with all parties involved. On other occasions it may be better for the teacher to develop a pilot study and uncover some of the problems in advance of the research proper. If it appears that the research is going to come into conflict with aspects of school policy, management styles, or individual personalities, it is better to confront the issues head on, consult relevant parties, and make rearrangements in the research design where possible or necessary.

(Hitchcock and Hughes 1995: 41)

Where a pilot study is not feasible it may be possible to arrange one or two scouting forays to assess possible problems and risks. By way of summary, we refer the reader to Box 2.5.

The field of ethics

Whatever the specific nature of their work, social researchers must take into account the effects of the research on participants, and act in such a way as to preserve their dignity as human beings: responsibility to participants. Such is ethical behaviour. Indeed, ethics has been defined as 'a matter of principled sensitivity to the rights of others, and that 'while truth is good, respect for human dignity is better' (Cavan 1977: 810).

Kimmel (1988) has pointed out that it is important we recognize that the distinction between ethical and unethical behaviour is not dichotomous, even though the normative code of prescribed ('ought') and proscribed ('ought not') behaviours, as represented by the ethical standards of a profession, seem to imply that it is. Judgements about whether behaviour conflicts with professional values lie on a *continuum* that ranges from the clearly ethical to the clearly unethical. The point here is that ethical principles are not absolute, generally speaking, though some maintain that they are as we shall see shortly, but must be interpreted in the light of the research context and of other values at stake.

Of course, a considerable amount of research does not cause pain or indignity to the participants, self-esteem is not necessarily undermined nor

confidences betrayed, and the social scientist may only infrequently be confronted with an unresolvable ethical dilemma. Where research is ethically sensitive, however, many factors may need to be taken into account and these may vary from situation to situation, for example: the age of those being researched; whether the subject matter of the research is a sensitive area; whether the aims of the research are in any way subversive (*vis-à-vis* subjects, teachers, or institution); the extent to which the researcher and researched can participate and collaborate in planning the research; how the data are to be processed, interpreted, and used. Laing (1967: 53) offers an interesting, cautionary view of data where he writes that they are 'not so much given as *taken* out of a constantly elusive matrix of happenings. We should speak of *capta* rather than data'.

Sources of tension

Non-maleficence, beneficence and human dignity

The first tension, as expressed by Aronson and Carlsmith (1969), is that which exists between two sets of related values held by society: a belief in the value of free scientific inquiry in pursuit of truth and knowledge, and a belief in the dignity of individuals and their right to those considerations that follow from it. It is this polarity that we referred to earlier as the costs/benefits ratio and by which 'greater consideration must be given to the risks to physical, psychological, humane, proprietary and cultural values than to the potential contribution of research to knowledge' (Social Sciences and Humanities Research Council of Canada 1981), i.e. the issue of 'non-maleficence' (where no harm is wished upon subjects or occurs) (see http://www.routledge.com/textbooks/ 9780415368780 – Chapter 2, file 2.3. ppt).

Non-maleficence (do not harm) is enshrined in the Hippocratic oath, in which the principle of *primum non nocere* (first of all, do no harm) is held as a guiding precept. So also with research. At first sight this seems uncontentious; of course we do not wish to bring harm to our research

Box 2.5
Negotiating access checklist

1   **Clear official channels by formally requesting permission to carry out your investigation as soon as you have an agreed project outline.**
    Some LEAs insist that requests to carry out research are channelled through the LEA office. Check what is required in your area.
2   **Speak to the people who will be asked to cooperate.**
    Getting the LEA or head's permission is one thing, but you need to have the support of the people who will be asked to give interviews or complete questionnaires.
3   **Submit the project outline to the head, if you are carrying out a study in your or another educational institution.**
    List people you would like to interview or to whom you wish to send questionnaires and state conditions under which the study will be conducted.
4   **Decide what you mean by anonymity and confidentiality.**
    Remember that if you are writing about 'the head of English' and there is only one head of English in the school, the person concerned is immediately recognizable.
5   **Decide whether participants will receive a copy of the report and/or see drafts or interview transcripts.**
    There are cost and time implications. Think carefully before you make promises.
6   **Inform participants what is to be done with the information they provide.**
    Your eyes and those of the examiner only? Shown to the head, the LEA etc.?
7   **Prepare an outline of intentions and conditions under which the study will be carried out to hand to the participants.**
    Even if you explain the purpose of the study the conditions and the guarantees, participants may forget.
8   **Be honest about the purpose of the study and about the conditions of the research.**
    If you say an interview will last ten minutes, you will break faith if it lasts an hour. If you are conducting the investigation as part of a degree or diploma course, say so.
9   **Remember that people who agree to help are doing you a favour.**
    Make sure you return papers and books in good order and on time. Letters of thanks should be sent, no matter how busy you are.
10 **Never assume 'it will be all right'. Negotiating access is an important stage in your investigation.**
    If you are an inside researcher, you will have to live with your mistakes, so take care.

Source: adapted from Bell 1991

subjects. However, what constitutes 'harm' is unclear: one person's harm is a society's benefit, and whether a little harm for a few is tolerable in the interests of a major benefit for all, or even for the person concerned, throws into relief the tension involved here. The question is whether the end justifies the means. As a general principle we would advocate the application of *primum non nocere* and, indeed, ethics regulatory boards, for example in universities perusing research proposals (discussed later), are guided heavily by this principle. However, there could be tensions here. What do you do if you discover that the headteacher has a serious alcohol problem or is having an affair with a parent? What do you do if your research shows teachers in the school

with very serious weaknesses, such that their contracts should be terminated in the interests of the students?

When researchers are confronted with dilemmas such as these (though they are likely to occur much less in education than in social psychology or medicine), it is generally considered that they resolve them in a manner that avoids the extremes of, on the one hand, giving up the idea of research and, on the other, ignoring the rights of the subjects. At all times, the welfare of subjects should be kept in mind, even if it involves compromising the impact of the research. Researchers should never lose sight of the obligations they owe to those who are helping, and should constantly be alert to alternative techniques should the ones they are employing at the time prove controversial. Indeed, this polarity between the research and the researched is reflected in the principles of the American Psychological Association which, as Zechmeister and Shaughnessy (1992) show, attempts to strike a balance between the rights of investigators to seek an understanding of human behaviour, and the rights and welfare of individuals who participate in the research. In the final reckoning, the decision to go ahead with a research project rests on a subjective evaluation of the costs both to the individual and society.

The corollary of non-maleficence is benefi-cence: what benefits will the research bring, and to whom? Many would-be participants could be persuaded to take part in research if it is made clear that it will, or may, bring personal, educa-tional and social benefits. For example, it may lead to the improvement of learning, increased fund-ing and resources for a particular curriculum area, improved approaches to the teaching of a subject, increased self-esteem for students, or additional teachers in a school. While it is sometimes worth including a statement of potential benefit when contacting schools and individuals, it may also be an actual requirement for ethics regulatory boards or sponsors.

The recipients of the benefit also have to be factored into the discussion here. A researcher may gain promotion, publications, a degree, research sponsorship and celebrity from a piece of research. However, the research might still leave the participants untouched, underprivileged, living and working in squalid and under-resourced conditions, under-supported, and with no material, educational or other improvements brought to the quality of their lives and work. On the one hand, it could be argued that research that did not lead to such benefits is unethical; on the other hand, it could be that the research helps to place the issue on the agenda of decision-makers and that, in the long run, it could contribute to a groundswell of opinion that, itself, brings change. While it may be fanciful to believe that a single piece of research will automatically lead to improvement, the ethical question raised here – who benefits? – suggests

that a selfish approach to the benefits of the research by the researcher is unethical.

This latter point requires researchers to do more than pay lip service to the notion of treating research participants as subjects rather than as objects to be used instrumentally – research fodder, so to speak – imbuing them with self-esteem and respect. One can treat people with respect but still the research may make no material difference to their lives. While it is surely impossible to argue against treating people with dignity and respect, it raises the issue of the obligations and commitments of the researcher. Let us say that the researcher has been working closely in a school for one or two years; surely that researcher has an obligation to improve the lives of those being researched, rather than simply gathering data instrumentally? To do the latter would be inhumane and deeply disrespectful. The issue is tension ridden: is the research *for* people and issues or *about* people and issues? We have to be clear about our answer to the question 'what will this research do for the participants and the wider community, not just for the researcher?'

Bailey (1994: 457) suggests that there are several approaches that can be used to avoid harming research subjects, including:

- using computer simulations
- finding a situation in which the negative effects of harm already exist, i.e. where the research does not have the responsibility for having produced these conditions
- applying only a very low level of potential harm, or for only a short period of time, so that any effects are minimal
- obtaining informed consent (providing details of the potential negative effects and securing participants' consent)
- justifying the research on the grounds that the small amount of harm caused is much less than the harm caused by the existing situation (which the research is trying to improve)
- using samples rather than complete popula-tions, so that fewer people are exposed to the harm

- maintaining the privacy of participants through the use of aggregated or anonymised data.

While some of these are uncontentious, others in this list are debatable, and researchers will need to be able to justify the decision that they reach.

Absolutist and relativist ethics

The second source of tension in this context is that generated by the competing absolutist and relativist positions. The absolutist view holds that clear, set principles should guide the researchers in their work and that these should determine what ought and what ought not to be done (see Box 2.6). To have taken a wholly absolutist stance, for example, in the case of the Stanford Prison Experiment (see Chapter 21), where the researchers studied interpersonal dynamics in a simulated prison, would have meant that the experiment should not have taken place at all or that it should have been terminated well before the sixth day. Zimbardo (1984) has stated that the absolutist ethical position, in which it is unjustified to induce any human suffering, would bring about the end of much psychological or medical research, regardless of its possible benefits to society.

Box 2.6
Absolute ethical principles in social research

Ethics embody individual and communal codes of conduct based upon a set of explicit or implicit principles and which may be abstract and impersonal or concrete and personal. Ethics can be 'absolute' and 'relative'. When behaviour is guided by absolute ethical standards, a higher-order moral principle is invoked which does not vary with regard to the situation in hand. Such absolutist ethics permit no degree of freedom for ends to justify means or for any beneficial or positive outcomes to justify occasions where the principle is suspended, altered or diluted, i.e. there are no special or extenuating circumstances which can be considered as justifying a departure from, or modification to, the ethical standard.

Source: adapted from Zimbardo 1984

By this absolute principle, the Stanford Prison Experiment must be regarded as unethical because the participants suffered considerably.

In absolutist principles – 'duty ethics of principles' (Edwards and Mauthner 2002: 20), a deontological model – research is governed by universal precepts such as justice, honesty and respect (among others). In the 'utilitarian ethics of consequences' (p. 20) ethical research is judged in terms of its consequences, e.g. increased knowledge, benefit for many.

Those who hold a relativist position would argue that there can be no absolute guidelines and that ethical considerations will arise from the very nature of the particular research being pursued at the time: situation determines behaviour. This underlines the significance of 'situated ethics' (Simons and Usher 2000), where overall guidelines may offer little help when confronted with a very specific situation.

There are some contexts, however, where neither the absolutist nor the relativist position is clear cut. Writing of the application of the principle of informed consent with respect to life history studies, Plummer (1983) says:

> Both sides have a weakness. If, for instance, as the absolutists usually insist, there should be informed consent, it may leave relatively privileged groups under-researched (since they will say 'no') and underprivileged groups over-researched (they have nothing to lose and say 'yes' in hope). If the individual conscience is the guide, as the relativists insist, the door is wide open for the unscrupulous – even immoral – researcher.
>
> (Plummer 1983)

He suggests that broad guidelines laid down by professional bodies which offer the researcher room for personal ethical choice are a way out of the problem. We consider these later in this chapter.

Voices of experience

Whatever the ethical stance one assumes and no matter what forethought one brings to bear on one's work, there will always be unknown, unforeseen problems and difficulties lying in wait (Kimmel 1988). Baumrind (1964), for example, warns of the possible failure on the researchers' part to perceive a positive indebtedness to their subjects for their services, perhaps, she suggests, because the detachment which investigators bring to their task prevents appreciation of subjects as individuals. This kind of omission can be averted if the experimenters are prepared to spend a few minutes with subjects afterwards in order to thank them for their participation, answer their questions, reassure them that they did well, and generally talk to them for a time. If the research involves subjects in a failure experience, isolation or loss of self-esteem, for example, researchers must ensure that the subjects do not leave the situation more humiliated, insecure and alienated than when they arrived. From the subject's point of view, procedures which involve loss of dignity, injury to self-esteem, or affect trust in rational authority are probably most harmful in the long run and may require the most carefully organized ways of recompensing the subject in some way if the researcher chooses to carry on with those methods.

With particularly sensitive areas, participants need to be fully informed of the dangers of serious after-effects. There is reason to believe that at least some of the obedient subjects in Milgram's (1963) experiments (see Chapter 21) came away from the experience with a lower self-esteem, having to live with the realization that they were willing to yield to destructive authority to the point of inflicting extreme pain on a fellow human being (Kelman 1967). It follows that researchers need to reflect attitudes of compassion, respect, gratitude and common sense without being too effusive. Subjects clearly have a right to expect that the researchers with whom they are interacting have some concern for the welfare of participants.

Further, the subject's sensibilities need also to be taken into account when the researcher comes to write up the research. It is unacceptable for researchers to show scant regard for subjects' feelings at the report stage. A related and not insignificant issue concerns the formal recognition of those who have assisted in the investigation, if such be the case. This means that whatever form the written account takes, be it a report, article, chapter or thesis, and no matter the readership for which it is intended, its authors must acknowledge and thank all who helped in the research, even to the extent of identifying by name those whose contribution was significant. This can be done in a foreword, introduction or footnote. All this is really a question of commonsensical ethics.

Ethical problems in educational research can often result from thoughtlessness, oversight or taking matters for granted. Again, researchers engaged in sponsored research may feel they do not have to deal with ethical issues, believing their sponsors to have them in hand. Likewise, each researcher in a collaborative venture may take it for granted, wrongly, that colleagues have the relevant ethical questions in mind, consequently appropriate precautions go by default. A student whose research is part of a course requirement and who is motivated wholly by self-interest, or academic researchers with professional advancement in mind, may overlook the 'oughts' and 'ought nots'.

A related issue here is that it is unethical for the researcher to be incompetent in the area of research. Competence may require training (Ticehurst and Veal 2000: 55). Indeed an ethical piece of research must demonstrate rigour in the design, conduct, analysis and reporting of the research (Morrison 1996b).

An ethical dilemma that is frequently discussed is in the experiment. Gorard (2001: 146) summarizes the issue as being that the design is discriminatory, in that the control group is being denied access to a potentially better treatment (e.g. curriculum, teaching style). Of course, the response to this is that, in a genuine experiment, we do not know which treatment is better, and that, indeed, this is the point of the experiment.

Ethical dilemmas

Robson (1993: 33) raises ten questionable practices in social research:

- involving people without their knowledge or consent

- coercing them to participate
- withholding information about the true nature of the research
- deceiving participants in other ways
- inducing them to commit acts diminishing their self-esteem
- violating rights of self-determination (e.g. in studies seeking to promote individual change)
- exposing participants to physical or mental stress
- invading their privacy
- withholding benefits from some participants (e.g. in comparison groups)
- not treating participants fairly, or with consideration, or with respect.

Interestingly, Robson (1993) calls these 'questionable practices' rather than areas to be proscribed, indicating that they are not black and white, right or wrong matters. They constitute the problem of ethical dilemmas.

At the beginning of this chapter, we spoke of the costs/benefits ratio. Frankfort-Nachmias and Nachmias (1992) express this as a conflict between two rights: the rights to conduct research in order to gain knowledge versus the rights of participants to self-determination, privacy and dignity. This constitutes the fundamental ethical dilemma of the social scientist for whom there are no absolute right or wrong answers. Which proposition is favoured, or how a balance between the two is struck will depend very much on the background, experience, and personal values of the individual researcher. We examine here other dilemmas that may confront investigators once they have come to some accommodation with this fundamental dilemma and decided to proceed with their research.

Privacy

For the most part, individual 'right to privacy' is usually contrasted with public 'right to know' (Pring 1984) and this has been defined in the *Ethical Guidelines for the Institutional Review Committee for Research with Human Subjects* as that which

extends to all information relating to a person's physical and mental condition, personal circumstances and social relationships which is not already in the public domain. It gives to the individual or collectivity the freedom to decide for themselves when and where, in what circumstances and to what extent their personal attitudes, opinions, habits, eccentricities, doubts and fears are to be communicated to or withheld from others.

(Social Sciences and Humanities Research Council of Canada 1981)

In the context of research, therefore, 'right to privacy' may easily be violated during the course of an investigation or denied after it has been completed. At either point the participant is vulnerable.

Privacy has been considered from three different perspectives by Diener and Crandall (1978). These are the sensitivity of the information being given, the setting being observed, and dissemination of information. Sensitivity of information refers to how personal or potentially threatening the information is that is being collected by the researcher. Certain kinds of information are more personal than others and may be more threatening. According to a report by the American Psychological Association (1973) for example, 'Religious preferences, sexual practices, income, racial prejudices, and other personal attributes such as intelligence, honesty, and courage are more sensitive items than "name, rank and serial number"'. Thus, the greater the sensitivity of the information, the more safeguards are called for to protect the privacy of the participants.

The setting being observed may vary from very private to completely public. The home, for example, is considered one of the most private settings and intrusions into people's homes without their consent are forbidden by law. Dissemination of information concerns the ability to match personal information with the identity of the research participants. Indeed, personal data are defined at law as those data which uniquely identify the individual providing them. When such information is publicized with names through the media, for example, privacy is seriously violated. The more people there are who can learn about the information, the more concern there must be about privacy (see Diener and Crandall 1978).

As is the case with most rights, privacy can be voluntarily relinquished. Research participants may choose to give up their right to privacy either by allowing a researcher access to sensitive topics or settings or by agreeing that the research report may identify them by name. The latter case at least would be an occasion where informed consent would need to be sought.

Generally speaking, if researchers intend to probe into the private aspects or affairs of individuals, their intentions should be made clear and explicit and informed consent should be sought from those who are to be observed or scrutinized in private contexts. Other methods to protect participants are anonymity and confidentiality and our examination of these follows.

Privacy is more than simple confidentiality (discussed below). The right to privacy means that a person has the right not to take part in the research, not to answer questions, not to be interviewed, not to have their home intruded into, not to answer telephone calls or emails, and to engage in private behaviour in their own private place without fear of being observed. It is *freedom from* as well as *freedom for*. This is frequently an issue with intrusive journalism. Hence researchers may have an obligation to inform participants of their rights to refuse to take part in any or all of the research, to obtain permission to conduct the research, to limit the time needed for participation and to limit the observation to public behaviour.

Anonymity

Frankfort-Nachmias and Nachmias (1992) underline the need for confidentiality of participants' identities, and that any violations of this should be made with the agreement of the participants. The essence of anonymity is that information provided by participants should in no way reveal their identity. The obverse of this is, as we saw earlier, personal data that uniquely identify their

supplier. A participant or subject is therefore considered anonymous when the researcher or another person cannot identify the participant or subject from the information provided. Where this situation holds, a participant's privacy is guaranteed, no matter how personal or sensitive the information is. Thus a respondent completing a questionnaire that bears absolutely no identifying marks – names, addresses, occupational details or coding symbols – is ensured complete and total anonymity. A subject agreeing to a face-to-face interview, on the other hand, can in no way expect anonymity. At most, the interviewer can promise confidentiality. Non-traceability is an important matter, and this extends to aggregating data in some cases, so that an individual's response is unknowable.

The principal means of ensuring anonymity, then, is not using the names of the participants or any other personal means of identification. Further ways of achieving anonymity have been listed by Frankfort-Nachmias and Nachmias (1992), for example, the use of aliases, the use of codes for identifying people (to keep the information on individuals separate from access to them) and the use of password-protected files.

These may work satisfactorily in most situations, but as Raffe and his colleagues (1989) have shown, there is sometimes the difficulty of maintaining an assurance of anonymity when, for example, combining data may uniquely identify an individual or institution or when there is access to incoming returns by support staff. Plummer (1983), likewise, refers to life studies in which names have been changed, places shifted, and fictional events added to prevent acquaintances of subjects discovering their identity. Although one can go a long way down this path, there is no absolute guarantee of total anonymity as far as life studies are concerned. In experimental research the experimenter is interested in 'human' behaviour rather than in the behaviour of specific individuals (Aronson and Carlsmith 1969). Consequently the researcher has absolutely no interest in linking the person as a unique, named individual to actual behaviour, and the research data can be transferred to coded, unnamed data sheets. As they comment, 'the very impersonality of the process is a great advantage ethically because it eliminates some of the negative consequences of the invasion of privacy' (Aronson and Carlsmith 1969).

Confidentiality

The second way of protecting a participant's right to privacy is through the promise of confidentiality. This means that although researchers know who has provided the information or are able to identify participants from the information given, they will in no way make the connection known publicly; the boundaries surrounding the shared secret will be protected. The essence of the matter is the extent to which investigators keep faith with those who have helped them. It is generally at the access stage or at the point where researchers collect their data that they make their position clear to the hosts and/or subjects. They will thus be quite explicit in explaining to subjects what the meaning and limits of confidentiality are in relation to the particular research project. On the whole, the more sensitive, intimate or discrediting the information, the greater is the obligation on the researcher's part to make sure that guarantees of confidentiality are carried out in spirit and letter. Promises must be kept.

Kimmel (1988) notes that some potential respondents in research on sensitive topics will refuse to cooperate when an assurance of confidentiality is weak, vague, not understood, or thought likely to be breached. He concludes that the usefulness of data in sensitive research areas may be seriously affected by the researcher's inability to provide a credible promise of confidentiality. Assurances do not appear to affect cooperation rates in innocuous studies perhaps because, as Kimmel suggests, there is expectation on the part of most potential respondents that confidentiality will be protected.

A number of techniques have been developed to allow public access to data and information without confidentiality being betrayed. These have been listed by Frankfort-Nachmias and Nachmias (1992) as follows:

- deletion of identifiers (for example, deleting the names, addresses or other means of identification from the data released on individuals)
- crude report categories (for example, releasing the year of birth rather than the specific date, profession but not the speciality within that profession, general information rather than specific)
- micro-aggregation (that is, the construction of 'average persons' from data on individuals and the release of these data, rather than data on individuals)
- error inoculation (deliberately introducing errors into individual records while leaving the aggregate data unchanged).

Cooper and Schindler (2001: 117) suggest that confidentiality can be protected by obtaining signed statements indicating non-disclosure of the research, restricting access to data which identify respondents, seeking the approval of the respondents before any disclosure about respondents takes place, non-disclosure of data (e.g. subsets that may be able to be combined to identify an individual).

Betrayal

The term 'betrayal' is usually applied to those occasions where data disclosed in confidence are revealed publicly in such a way as to cause embarrassment, anxiety or perhaps suffering to the subject or participant disclosing the information. It is a breach of trust, in contrast to confidentiality, and is often a consequence of selfish motives of either a personal or professional nature. As Plummer (1983) comments, 'in sociology, there is something slightly awry when a sociologist can enter a group and a person's life for a lengthy period, learn their most closely guarded secrets, and then expose all in a critical light to the public' (see http://www.routledge.com/textbooks/ 9780415368780 – Chapter 2, file 2.4. ppt).

One of the research methods that is perhaps most vulnerable to betrayal is action research. As Kelly (1989a) notes, this can produce several ethical problems. She says that if we treat teachers as collaborators in our day-to-day interactions, it may seem like betrayal of trust if these interactions are recorded and used as evidence. This is particularly the case where the evidence is negative. One way out, Kelly (1989a) suggests, could be to submit reports and evaluations of teachers' reactions to the teachers involved for comment, to get them to assess their own changing attitudes. She warns, however, that this might work well with teachers who have become converts, but is more problematic where teachers remain indifferent or hostile to the aims of the research project. How does one write an honest but critical report of teachers' attitudes, she asks, if one hopes to continue to work with those involved?

Similarly Morrison (2006) considers the case of a school that is under-performing, poorly managed or badly led. Does not the consumer, indeed the state, have a right or a duty respectively to know or address this, such action typically involving the exposure to the public of a school's shortcomings, and will this not damage individuals working in the school, the principal and the teachers? What 'fiduciary trust' (Mitchell 1993) not to harm individuals (the ethical issue of 'non-maleficence') does the researcher have to the school or to the public, and how can these two potentially contradictory demands be reconciled? Should the researcher expose the school's weaknesses, which almost certainly could damage individuals but which may be in the public interest, or, in the interests of *primum non nocere*, remain silent? The issue hinges on trust: the pursuit of truth and the pursuit of trust may run counter to each other (Kelly 1985: 147); indeed Kelly herself writes that 'I do not think we have yet found a satisfactory way of resolving this dilemma'.

Finch (1985) raises ethical issues in the consequences of reporting. In her research she worried that her reporting

> could well mean that I was further reinforcing those assumptions deeply embedded in our culture and political life that working class women (especially the urban poor) are inadequate mothers and too incompetent to be able to organize facilities that most normal women could manage.
>
> (Finch 1985: 117)

Indeed she uses the word 'betrayal' in her concern that she might be betraying the trust of the women with whom she had worked for three years, not least because they were in a far worse economic and personal state than she herself was (Finch 1985: 118).

Deception

The use of deception in social psychological and sociological research has attracted a certain amount of adverse publicity. Deception may lie in not telling people that they are being researched (in some people's eyes this is tantamount to spying), not telling the truth, telling lies, or compromising the truth. It may also lie in using people in a degrading or dehumanizing way (e.g. as a rat in an experiment). In social psychological research, the term is applied to that kind of experimental situation where the researcher knowingly conceals the true purpose and conditions of the research, or else positively misinforms the subjects, or exposes them to unduly painful, stressful or embarrassing experiences, without the subjects having knowledge of what is going on. The deception lies in not telling the whole truth. Bailey (1994: 463) gives a clear example here, where respondents may be asked to complete a postal questionnaire, and believe that they are being asked for information about length and type of postage, whereas, in fact, the study is designed to compare different kinds of questionnaire. He reports that 88 per cent of studies from a sample of 457 studies used deception (see http://www.routledge.com/textbooks/9780415368780 – Chapter 2, file 2.5. ppt).

Advocates of the method feel that if a deception experiment is the only way to discover something of real importance, the truth so discovered is worth the lies told in the process, so long as no harm comes to the subject (see Aronson *et al.* 1990). Deception may be justified on the grounds that the research serves the public good, and that the deception prevents any bias from entering the research, and also that it may protect the confidentiality of a third party (for example, a sponsor). The problem from the researcher's point of view is: 'What is the proper balance between the interests of science and the thoughtful, humane treatment of people who, innocently, provide the data?' In other words, the problem again hinges on the costs/benefits ratio.

The pervasiveness of the issue of deception becomes even more apparent when we remember that it is even built into many of our measurement devices, since it is important to keep the respondent ignorant of the personality and attitude dimensions that we wish to investigate. There are many problems that cannot be investigated without deception and, although there is some evidence that most subjects accept without resentment the fact of having been duped once they understand the necessity for it (e.g. the Milgram (1974) obedience-to-authority experiment: see Chapter 21), it is important to keep in the forefront of one's mind the question of whether the amount and type of deception is justified by the significance of the study and the unavailability of alternative procedures.

The use of deception resulting in particularly harmful consequences would be another occasion where ethical considerations would need to be given priority. An example here would be the study by Campbell *et al.* (1964) which created extremely stressful conditions by using drugs to induce temporary interruption of breathing (see Box 2.7).

Box 2.7
An extreme case of deception

In an experiment designed to study the establishment of a conditioned response in a situation that is traumatic but not painful, Campbell *et al.* (1964) induced – through the use of a drug – a temporary interruption of respiration in their subjects. The subjects' reports confirmed that this was a 'horrific' experience for them. All the subjects thought they were dying. The subjects, male alcoholic patients who had volunteered for the experiment when they were told that it was connected with a possible therapy for alcoholism, were not warned in advance about the effect of the drug, since this information would have reduced the traumatic impact of the experience.

Source: adapted from Kelman 1967

Kelman (1967) has suggested three ways of dealing with the problem of deception. First, it is important that we increase our active awareness that it exists as a problem. It is crucial that we always ask ourselves the question whether deception is necessary and justified. We must be wary of the tendency to dismiss the question as irrelevant and to accept deception as a matter of course. Active awareness is thus in itself part of the solution, for it makes the use of deception a focus for discussion, deliberation, investigation and choice.

The second way of approaching the problem concerns counteracting and minimizing the negative effects of deception. For example, subjects must be selected in a way that will exclude individuals who are especially vulnerable; any potentially harmful manipulation must be kept to a moderate level of intensity; researchers must be sensitive to danger signals in the reactions of subjects and be prepared to deal with crises when they arise; and at the conclusion of the research, they must take time not only to reassure subjects, but also to help them work through their feelings about the experience to whatever degree may be required. The principle that subjects ought not to leave the research situation with greater anxiety or lower levels of self-esteem than they came with is a good one to follow (the issue of non-maleficence again). Desirably, subjects should be enriched by the experience and should leave it with the feeling that they have learned something.

The primary way of counteracting negative effects of research employing deception is to ensure that adequate feedback is provided at the end of the research or research session. Feedback must be kept inviolable and in no circumstances should subjects be given false feedback or be misled into thinking they are receiving feedback when the researcher is in fact introducing another experimental manipulation. Debriefing may include the following (Cooper and Schindler 2001: 116):

- explaining any deception and the reasons for it
- describing the purposes, hypotheses, objectives and methods of the research

- sharing the results after the research
- ensuring follow-up psychological or medical attention after the research.

Even here, however, there are dangers. As Aronson and Carlsmith (1969) say:

> debriefing a subject is not simply a matter of exposing him to the truth. There is nothing magically curative about the truth; indeed ... if harshly presented, the truth can be more harmful than no explanation at all. There are vast differences in how this is accomplished, and it is precisely these differences that are of crucial importance in determining whether or not a subject is uncomfortable when he leaves the experimental room.
>
> (Aronson and Carlsmith 1969: 31)

They consider that the one essential aspect of the debriefing process is that researchers communicate their own sincerity as scientists seeking the truth and their own discomfort about the fact that they found it necessary to resort to deception in order to uncover the truth. As they say, 'No amount of postexperimental gentleness is as effective in relieving a subject's discomfort as an honest accounting of the experimenter's *own* discomfort in the situation' (Aronson and Carlsmith 1969: 31–2).

The third way of dealing with the problem of deception is to ensure that new procedures and novel techniques are developed. It is a question of tapping one's own creativity in the quest for alternative methods. It has been suggested that role-playing, or 'as-if' experiments, could prove a worthwhile avenue to explore – the 'role-playing versus deception' debate is raised in Chapter 21. By this method, as we shall see, the subject is asked to behave as if he or she were a particular person in a particular situation. Whatever form they take, however, new approaches will involve a radically different set of assumptions about the role of the subject in this type of research. They require us to *use* subjects' motivations rather than bypassing them. They may even call for increasing the sophistication of potential subjects, rather than maintaining their naivety.

Plummer (1983) informs us that even in an unlikely area like life history, deceptions of a lesser nature occur. Thus, for example, the general description given of research may leave out some key issues; indeed, to tell the subject what it is you are looking for may bias the outcome quite substantially. Further, different accounts of the research may have to be presented to different groups. He quotes an instance from his own research, a study of sexual minorities, which required various levels of release – for the subjects, for colleagues, for general enquiries, and for outside friends. None of these accounts actually lied, they merely emphasized a different aspect of the research.

In the social sciences, the dilemma of deception has played an important part in experimental social psychology where subjects are not told the true nature of the experiment. Another area where it is used is that of sociology, where researchers conceal their identities and 'con' their way into alien groups – the overt/covert debate (Mitchell 1993). Covert, or secret participation, refers to that kind of research where researchers spend an extended period of time in particular research settings, concealing the fact that they are researchers and pretending to play some other role.

Bulmer (1982) notes that there are no simple and universally agreed answers to the ethical issues that covert research produces. Erikson (1967), for example, suggests that sociologists have responsibilities to their subjects and that secret research can injure other people in ways that cannot be anticipated or compensated for afterwards, and that sociologists have responsibilities towards fellow sociologists. Douglas (1976), by contrast, argues that covert observation is necessary, useful and revealing. Bulmer (1982), too, concludes that the most compelling argument in favour of covert research is that it has produced good social science which would not have been possible without the method. It would be churlish, he adds, not to recognize that the use of covert methods has advanced our understanding of society.

Kimmel (1988) claims that few researchers feel that they can do without deception entirely, since the adoption of an overtly conservative approach could render the study of important research hardly worth the effort. A study of racial prejudice, for example, accurately labelled as such, would certainly affect the behaviour of the subjects taking part. Deception studies, he considers, differ so greatly that even the harshest critics would be hard pressed to state unequivocally that all deception has potentially harmful effects on participants or is wrong.

Ethics and research methods in education

Ethical problems arising from research methods used in educational contexts occur *passim* in Burgess's (1989) edited collection, *The Ethics of Educational Research* and in Simons and Usher's (2000) edited volume, *Situated Ethics in Educational Research*. Every contribution in these reflects the reality of the day-to-day problems, issues and dilemmas that the educational researcher and beginning researchers are likely to encounter. These two books show that the issues thrown up by the complexities of research methods in educational institutions and their ethical consequences are probably among the least anticipated, particularly among the more inexperienced researchers, not least the socio-political dimension of research. Newcomers to the field need to be aware of those kinds of research which, by their nature, lead from one problem to another. Indeed, the researcher will frequently find that methodological and ethical issues are inextricably interwoven in much of the research we have designated as qualitative or interpretative. As Hitchcock and Hughes (1989) note:

> Doing participant observation or interviewing one's peers raises ethical problems that are directly related to the nature of the research technique employed. The degree of openness or closure of the nature of the research and its aims is one that directly faces the teacher researcher.
>
> (Hitchcock and Hughes 1989)

They go on to pose the kinds of question that may arise in such a situation. 'Where for the researcher does formal observation end and informal observation begin?' 'Is it justifiable to be open with some teachers and closed with others?' 'How much can the researcher tell the pupils about a particular piece of research?' 'When is a casual conversation part of the research data and when is it not?' 'Is gossip legitimate data and can the researcher ethically use material that has been passed on in confidence?' As Hitchcock and Hughes (1989) conclude, the list of questions is endless yet they can be related to the nature of both the research technique involved and the social organization of the setting being investigated. The key to the successful resolution of such questions lies in establishing good relations. This will involve the development of a sense of rapport between researchers and their subjects that will lead to feelings of trust and confidence.

Fine and Sandstrom (1988) discuss in some detail the ethical and practical aspects of doing fieldwork with children. In particular they show how the ethical implications of participant observation research differ with the age of the children. Another feature of qualitative methods in this connection has been identified by Finch (1985: 116–17) who comments on the possible acute political and ethical dilemmas arising from how data are used, both by the researcher and others, and that researchers have a duty of trust placed in them by the participants to use privileged data appropriately, not least for improvement of the condition of the participants.

Kelly (1989a) suggests that the area in qualitative research where one's ethical antennae need to be especially sensitive is that of action research, and it is here that researchers, be they teachers or outsiders, must show particular awareness of the traps that lie in wait. These difficulties have been summed up by Hopkins (1985: 135) when he suggests that, as the researcher's actions are deeply embedded in the organization, it is important to work within these, and this throws into relief issues of confidentiality and personal respect.

Box 2.8 presents a set of principles specially formulated for action researchers by Kemmis and McTaggart (1981) and quoted by Hopkins (1985).

Box 2.8
Ethical principles for the guidance of action researchers

- *Observe protocol:* take care to ensure that the relevant persons, committees and authorities have been consulted, informed and that the necessary permission and approval have been obtained.
- *Involve participants:* encourage others who have a stake in the improvement you envisage to shape and form the work.
- *Negotiate with those affected:* not everyone will want to be directly involved; your work should take account of the responsibilities and wishes of others.
- *Report progress:* keep the work visible and remain open to suggestions so that unforeseen and unseen ramifications can be taken account of; colleagues must have the opportunity to lodge a protest to you.
- *Obtain explicit authorizations:* this applies where you wish to observe your professional colleagues, and where you wish to examine documentation.
- *Negotiate descriptions of people's work:* always allow those described to challenge your accounts on the grounds of fairness, relevance and accuracy.
- *Negotiate accounts of others' points of view* (e.g. in accounts of communication): always allow those involved in interviews, meetings and written exchanges to require amendments which enhance fairness, relevance and accuracy.
- *Obtain explicit authorization before using quotations:* this includes verbatim transcripts, attributed observations, excerpts of audio and video recordings, judgements, conclusions or recommendations in reports (written or to meetings).
- *Negotiate reports for various levels of release:* remember that different audiences require different kinds of reports; what is appropriate for an informal verbal report to a faculty meeting may not be appropriate for a staff meeting, a report to council, a journal article, a newspaper, a newsletter to parents; be conservative if you cannot control distribution.
- *Accept responsibility for maintaining confidentiality.*
- *Retain the right to report your work:* provided that those involved are satisfied with the fairness, accuracy and relevance of accounts which pertain to them, and that the accounts do not unnecessarily expose or embarrass those involved, then accounts should not be subject to veto or be sheltered by prohibitions of confidentiality.
- *Make your principles of procedure binding and known:* all of the people involved in your action research project must agree to the principles before the work begins; others must be aware of their rights in the process.

Source: adapted from Kemmis and McTaggart (1981) and quoted in Hopkins (1985: 134–6)

Ethics and evaluative research

Strike (1990), discussing the ethics of educational evaluation, offers two broad principles which may form the basis of further considerations in the field of evaluation. These are the principle of benefit maximization and the principle of equal respect. The former, the principle of benefit maximization, holds that the best decision is the one that results in the greatest benefit for most people. It is pragmatic in the sense that it judges the rightness of our actions by their consequences or, as Strike (1990) says, the best action is the one with the best results. The principle of utilitarianism requires us to identify the particular benefits we wish to maximize, to identify a suitable population for maximization, specify what is to count as maximization, and fully understand the consequences of our actions. The second principle, that of equal respect, demands that we respect the equal worth of all people. This requires us to treat people as ends rather than means, to regard them as free and rational, and to accept that they are entitled to the same basic rights as others.

Strike (1990) lists the following ethical principles which he regards as particularly important to evaluative research and which may be seen in the light of the two broad principles outlined above:

- *Due process:* evaluative procedures must ensure that judgements are reasonable: that known and accepted standards are consistently applied from case to case, that evidence is reasonable and that there are systematic and reasonable procedures for collecting and testing evidence.

- *Privacy:* this involves a right to control information about oneself, and protects people from unwarranted interference in their affairs. In evaluation, it requires that procedures are not overtly intrusive and that such evaluation pertains only to those aspects of a teacher's activity that are job related. It also protects the confidentiality of evaluation information.
- *Equality:* in the context of evaluation, this can best be understood as a prohibition against making decisions on irrelevant grounds, such as race, religion, gender, ethnicity or sexual orientation.
- *Public perspicuity:* this principle requires openness to the public concerning evaluative procedures, their purposes and their results.
- *Humaneness:* this principle requires that consideration is shown to the feelings and sensitivities of those in evaluative contexts.
- *Client benefit:* this principle requires that evaluative decisions are made in a way that respects the interests of students, parents and the public, in preference to those of educational institutions and their staff. This extends to treating participants as subjects rather than as 'research fodder'.
- *Academic freedom:* this requires that an atmosphere of intellectual openness is maintained in the classroom for both teachers and students. Evaluation should not be conducted in a way that chills this environment.
- *Respect for autonomy:* teachers are entitled to reasonable discretion in, and to exercise reasonable judgement about, their work. Evaluations should not be conducted so as to unreasonably restrict discretion and judgement.

Strike (1990) develops these principles in a more extended and systematic form in his contribution.

Research and regulation: ethical codes and review

Ethical regulation exists at several levels: legislation, ethics review committees to oversee research in universities and other institutions (these can constitute a major hurdle for those planning to undertake research), ethical codes of the professional bodies and associations as well as the personal ethics of individual researchers are all important regulatory mechanisms. All investigators, from undergraduates pursuing a course-based research project to professional researchers striving at the frontiers of knowledge, must take cognizance of the ethical codes and regulations governing their practice. Failure to meet these responsibilities on the part of researchers is perceived as undermining the whole scientific process and may lead to legal and financial penalties and liabilities for individuals and institutions.

Professional societies and associations have formulated codes of practice which express the consensus of values within a particular group and which help individual researchers in indicating what is desirable and what is to be avoided. Of course, this does not solve all problems, for there are few absolutes and in consequence ethical principles may be open to a wide range of interpretations. The establishment of comprehensive regulatory mechanisms is well founded in the United Kingdom, but it is perhaps in the field of information and data – how they are stored and the uses to which they are put, for example – that educational researchers are likely to find growing interest. This category would include, for instance, statistical data, data used as the basis for evaluation, curricular records, written records, transcripts, data sheets, personal documents, research data, computer files, and audio and video recordings.

As information technology establishes itself in a centre-stage position and as society has become increasingly dependent on information, the concept of information is important not only for what it is, but for what it can do. Numerous writers have pointed out the connection between information and power, for example Harris *et al.*'s (1992) comments on the power over individuals through the control of personal information and its relationship to power of professionalism in which submission to expert knowledge is required. Data misuse, therefore, or disclosure at the wrong time or to the wrong client or organ, can result in the most unfortunate consequences for an individual, group or institution. And matters are greatly exacerbated if it is the wrong information, or incomplete, or deliberately misleading.

In an increasingly information-rich world, it is essential that safeguards be established to protect it from misuse or abuse. The UK Data Protection Acts of 1984 and 1998 are designed to achieve such an end. These cover the principles of data protection, the responsibilities of data users, and the rights of data subjects. Data held for 'historical and research' purposes are exempted from the principle which gives individuals the right of access to personal data about themselves, provided the data are not made available in a form which identifies individuals. Research data also have partial exemption from two further principles, with the effect that such data may be held indefinitely and the use of the data for research purposes need not be disclosed at the time of data collection.

Of the two most important principles which do concern research data, one states that personal data (i.e. data that uniquely identify the person supplying them) shall be held only for specified and lawful purposes. The second principle states that appropriate security measures shall be taken against unauthorized access to, or alteration, disclosure or destruction of personal data and against accidental loss or destruction of personal data.

Most institutions of higher education have their own ethics committees, and these usually have their own codes of ethics against which they evaluate research proposals. In addition, some important codes of practice and guidelines are published by research associations, for example the British Educational Research Association (http://www.bera.ac.uk), the British Psychological Society (http://www.bps.org.uk), the British Sociological Association (http://www.britsoc.co.uk), the Social Research Association (http://www.the-sra.org.uk), the American Educational Research Association (http://www.aera.net), the American Psychological Association (http://www.apa.org) and the American Sociological Association (http://www.asanet.org). We advise readers to consult these in detail.

The British Psychological Society's *Code of Conduct, Ethical Principles and Guidelines* (2005) includes, among many others, sections on competence, obtaining consent, confidentiality and personal conduct. Its section on *Ethical Principles for Conducting Research with Human Participants* first discusses deception, debriefing, risk and implementation (pp. 6–7) and then moves to eleven main sections: introduction; general principles, including the guiding precept that 'the essential principle is that the investigation should be considered from the standpoint of all the participants; foreseeable threats to their psychological well-being, health, values or dignity should be eliminated' (p. 8); consent; deception; debriefing; withdrawal from the investigation; confidentiality; protection of participants; observational research; giving advice; and colleagues. Interestingly it does not insist on informed consent, rather expressing it as 'wherever possible, the investigator should inform all participants of the objectives of the investigation' (para. 3.1). Similarly it does not proscribe deception, indicating that 'it may be impossible to study some psychological processes without withholding information about the true object of the study or deliberately misleading the participants' (para. 4.3). However, it says that these need to be rigorously justified, and alternatives must have been explored and found to be unavailable.

The American Psychological Association's *Ethical Principles and Code of Conduct* (2002) states five general principles: beneficence and non-maleficence, fidelity and responsibility, integrity, justice, and respect for people's rights and dignity. These principles then become the basis for ten sections of 'ethical standards': resolving ethical issues; competence; human relations (including 'avoiding harm' 'exploitative relationships' and 'informed consent'); privacy and confidentiality; advertising and other public statements; record keeping and fees; education and training; research and publication; assessment; and therapy.

The American Sociological Association's *Code of Ethics and Policies and Procedures of the ASA Committee on Professional Ethics* (1999) has five general principles: professional competence; integrity; professional and scientific responsibility; respect for people's rights, dignity and diversity; and social responsibility. These are then devolved onto twenty *ethical standards*, including non-exploitation, confidentiality, informed consent, deception, offering inducements and many others.

The *Statement of Ethical Practice for the British Sociological Association* (2002) includes sections on: professional integrity; relations with and responsibilities towards research participants; relationships with research participants; covert research; anonymity, privacy and confidentiality; relations with and responsibilities towards sponsors and/or funders; carrying obligations, roles and rights; pre-empting outcomes and negotiations about research; and obligations to sponsors and/or funders during the research process.

The Social Research Association's *Ethical Guidelines* (2003) draws on European law (http://www.respectproject.org) and indicates four levels of obligations: to society; to funders and employers; to colleagues; and to subjects (including avoiding undue intrusion, obtaining informed consent, modifications to informed consent, protecting the interests of subjects, enabling participation, maintaining confidentiality of records, and preventing disclosure of identities).

The British Educational Research Association's *Ethical Guidelines* (2000) are devolved onto: responsibilities to the research profession; responsibility to the participants (including working with children, informed consent, rights to withdrawal); responsibility to the public; relationships with funding agencies; publication; intellectual ownership; relationship with host institution. Similarly, the *Ethical Standards of the American Educational Research Association* (2000) includes: responsibilities to the field; research populations, educational institutions, and the public (including working with children), informed consent, confidentiality, honesty ('deception is discouraged' and 'should be used only when clearly necessary', after which the reasons for the deception should be explained

(para. B3)), rights of withdrawal, exploitation for personal gain, sensitivity to local circumstances (e.g. culture, religion, gender), avoidance of negative consequences, dissemination, anonymity; intellectual ownership; editing, reviewing and appraising research; sponsors, policy-makers and other users of research; and students and student researchers.

Web sites of these research associations' ethical principles and guidelines can be found either on the home page of each association or as follows:

American Educational Research Association: http://www.aera.net/uploadedFiles/About_AERA/Ethical_Standards/Ethical Standards.pdf
American Psychological Association: http://www.apa.org/ethics/code2002.html
American Sociological Association: http://www.asanet.org/members/ecoderev.html
British Educational Research Association: http://www.bera.ac.uk
British Psychological Society: http://www.bps.org.uk/document-download-area/document-download$.cfm?file_uuid=6D0645CC-7E96-C67F-D75E2648E5580115&ext=pdf
British Sociological Association: http://www.britsoc.co.uk/new_site/user_doc/Statement%20of%20Ethical%20Practice.doc
Social Research Association: http://www.thesra.org.uk/ethics03.pdf

The difficulty and yet the strength with ethical codes is that they cannot and do not provide specific advice for what to do in specific situations. Ultimately, it is researchers themselves, their integrity and conscience, informed by an acute awareness of ethical issues, underpinned by guideline codes and regulated practice, which should decide what to do in a specific situation, and this should be justified, justifiable, thought through and defensible.

There is a certain degree of homogeneity between the codes and guidelines cited above. While they are helpful in providing guidance, they cannot tell the researcher what to do in every unique circumstance. The issue here is that ethics are 'situated' (Simons and Usher 2000). Indeed the authors state at the outset that

> while ethics has traditionally been seen as a set of general principles invariantly and validly applied to all situations . . . on the contrary, ethical principles are mediated within different research practices and thus take on different significances in relation to those practices.
>
> (Simons and Usher 2000: 1)

The authors state that this implies that situated ethics are 'immune to universalization', because

> researchers cannot avoid weighing up conflicting considerations and dilemmas which are located in the specificities of the research situation and where there is a need to make ethical decisions but where those decisions cannot be reached by appeal to unambiguous and univalent principles or codes.
>
> (Simons and Usher 2000: 2)

Indeed, it was observed earlier that many ethical codes and guidelines themselves avoid univalency and unambiguity, arguing, for example, that deception, covert research and the lack of informed consent may be justified. The need for polyvalency (multiple interpretations of what is worthwhile, acceptable and valuable) and situated ethics, Simons and Usher (2000: 11) argue, arises from the practicality of conducting research, the need for sensitivity to socio-political contexts and to be fair to disadvantaged groups, and to take account of the diversity and uniqueness of different research practices. What this suggests, then, is that, while codes and guidelines may be useful in raising issues and orienting researchers, they cannot decide what should and should not be done in a specific situation; that is for individual researchers and their informed conscience to decide.

Sponsored research

Sponsored research does not absolve the researcher from ethical behaviour. For example, it may be considered unethical for the sponsor to tell the researcher:

- how to conduct the research
- what results the researcher should look for and what findings should be suppressed
- what should and should not be reported
- to conceal who the sponsor is
- what are the purposes of the research.

On the other hand, sponsors do have the right to remain confidential; they may have the right to non-disclosure of who they are, and the purposes and findings of the research.

While sponsored research is usually contractual between the researcher and the sponsor, and between the researcher and the participants, and while the research may be for the sponsor alone and not for the public, this does not privilege the sponsor in dictating how the research should be conducted and what it should find; in short, 'fixing' the study.

Of course the researcher's responsibilities may lie only in conducting the study and providing the sponsor with a report; what happens to the report after that (e.g. whether it is released completely, selectively or not at all to the public or other parties within the sponsor's organization) is a matter for the sponsor. However, this does not absolve the researcher from decisions about the conduct of the study, and the researcher must retain the right to conduct the study as she or he thinks fit, informed by, but not decided by, the sponsor. The researcher's integrity must be absolute. It is often the case that researchers will negotiate publication rights with the sponsor in advance of the research and what confidentiality the researcher must respect.

The sponsor has a right to expect high quality, rigorous and usable research. The researcher should not succumb to pressure to

- betray the confidentiality of the respondents
- tamper with data, their analysis or presentation to meet a particular objective
- present selective and unrepresentative data and conclusions
- make recommendations that do not arise from the data themselves
- use the data for non-negotiated personal interests, agendas, purposes and advancement

• conduct a study in which personal research objectives influence the nature, contents and conduct of the research.

The researcher has obligations to the sponsor, but not to doctor or compromise the research.

Responsibilities to the research community

The researcher has responsibilities to the research community, for example not to jeopardize the reputation of the research community (e.g. the university) or spoil the opportunities for further research. Thus, a novice researcher working for a higher degree may approach a school directly, using a clumsy approach, with inadequate data collection instruments and a poor research design, and then proceed to publicize the results as though they are valid and reliable. This researcher does not deserve the degree; at the very least he or she should have sought and gained advice from the supervisor, modified the research as necessary, gained approval for the research, made suitably sensitive overtures to the school, and agreed rights of disclosure. Not to do so puts the researcher's institution at risk of being denied further access, of damaging the reputation of the institution, and, if word spreads, of being publicly vilified and denied the opportunity for further research to be conducted. In this case the novice researcher has behaved unethically (see http://www.routledge.com/textbooks/9780415368780 – Chapter 2, file 2.6. ppt).

Further, what responsibility to the research community does the researcher have? If a negative research report is released will schools retrench, preventing future research in schools from being undertaken? Negative research data, such as reported evidence on deliberate grade inflation by schools in order to preserve reputation (Morrison and Tang 2002), may not endear researchers to schools.

The researcher has a responsibility to colleagues to

• protect their safety (e.g. in conducting sensitive research or research in dangerous locations)
• protect their well-being

• protect their reputation
• enable further research to be conducted
• expect them to behave ethically
• ensure that they adhere to correct and agreed procedures
• protect the anonymity and confidentiality of sponsors if so agreed.

The researcher is a member of a research community, and this brings ethical responsibilities.

Conclusion

In this chapter we have attempted to acquaint readers with some of the ethical difficulties they are likely to experience in the conduct of such research. It is not possible to identify all potential ethical questions or adjudicate on what is correct researcher behaviour.[3] It is hoped that these pages will have induced in readers a certain disposition that will enable them to approach their own projects with a greater awareness and fuller understanding of the ethical dilemmas and moral issues lurking in the interstices of the research process. However inexperienced in these matters researchers are, they bring to social research a sense of rightness (Huizinga 1949) on which they can construct a set of rational principles appropriate to their own circumstances and based on personal, professional, and societal values (we stress the word 'rational' since reason is a prime ingredient of ethical thinking and it is the combination of reason and a sense of rightness that researchers must keep faith with if they are to bring a rich ethical quality to their work).

Although no code of practice can anticipate or resolve all problems, there is a six-fold advantage in fashioning a personal code of ethical practice. First, such a code establishes one as a member of the wider scientific community having a shared interest in its values and concerns. Second, a code of ethical practice makes researchers aware of their obligations to their subjects and also to those problem areas where there is a general consensus about what is acceptable and what is not. In this sense it has a clarificatory value. Third, when one's professional behaviour is guided by a principled code of ethics, then it is possible to consider that there may be alternative ways of doing the same thing, ways that are more ethical or less unethical should one be confronted by a moral challenge. Fourth, a balanced code can be an important organizing factor in researchers' perceptions of the research situation, and as such may assist them in their need to anticipate and prepare. Fifth, a code of practice validated by their own sense of rightness will help researchers to develop an intuitive sensitivity that will be particularly helpful to them in dealing with the unknown and the unexpected, especially where the more fluidic methods such as ethnography and participant observation are concerned. And sixth, a code of practice will bring discipline to researchers' awareness. Box 2.9 gives

a short ethical code, by way of example. It must be stressed, however, that bespoke items, i.e. those designed to meet the needs of a specific project, are preferable to standard ones. The items in Box 2.9 are illustrative, and in no way exhaustive.

In more detail, one can suggest that further considerations have to be borne in mind in planning, conducting and reporting educational research (Box 2.10).

Box 2.10 raises issues and suggestions, not solutions or decisions. These will have to be decided by each researcher in respect of the particular situation he or she faces. For a summary of ethical principles for social research see the accompanying web site (http://www.routledge.com/textbooks/9780415368780 – Chapter 2, file 2.1.doc).

Box 2.9
An ethical code: an illustration

1	It is important for the researcher to reveal fully his or her identity and background.
2	The purpose and procedures of the research should be fully explained to the subjects at the outset.
3	The research and its ethical consequences should be seen from the subjects' and institution's point of view.
4	Possible controversial findings need to be anticipated and, where they ensue, handled with great sensitivity.
5	The research should be as objective as possible: this will require careful thought being given to the design, conduct and reporting of research.
6	Informed consent should be sought from all participants: all agreements reached at this stage should be honoured.
7	Sometimes it is desirable to obtain informed consent in writing.
8	Subjects should have the option to refuse to take part and know this, and the right to terminate their involvement at any time and know this also.
9	Arrangements should be made during initial contacts to provide feedback for participants who request it: this may take the form of a written résumé of findings.
10	The dignity, privacy and interests of the participants should be respected and protected at all times.
11	Deceit should be used only when absolutely necessary.
12	When ethical dilemmas arise, the researcher may need to consult other researchers or teachers.

Source: adapted from Reynolds 1979

Box 2.10

Ethical principles for educational research (to be agreed *before* the research commences)

Responsibility to research

- The researcher should be competent and aware of what is involved in conducting research.
- The research must be conducted rigorously and with the correct procedures – avoid misuse of procedures at all stages.
- Report procedures accurately and publicly (rigour).
- Don't jeopardize future research(ers).
- Report clearly and make data available for checking.
- Tell the truth: do not tell lies or falsify data, avoid being unfairly selective (e.g. to support a case), do not misrepresent data.
- Maintain the integrity and autonomy of the research, e.g. avoid censorship of, or interference with, the research by sponsors or those who give permission for the research to be undertaken.

Responsibility to participants and audience(s)

- Gain fully informed consent where appropriate (usually in writing), in order to respect self-determination and autonomy; provide information on all aspects of the research and its possible consequences.
- Decide whether, and how, overt or covert research is required/justified.
- Decide whether, and how, deception is required/justified; be honest or justify dishonesty.
- Ensure non-maleficence (no harm, hurt or suffering to be caused to participants and those who might be affected by the research); be humane.
- Ensure beneficence (the research will bring benefit to the participants or will contribute to the welfare of participants).
- Ensure that participants do not leave the research worse off than when they started it.
- Respect people's rights and dignity and interests, and be respectful: research participants are subjects, not objects to be exploited. Treat people as subjects, not objects.
- Agree individuals' rights to privacy.
- Ensure participants have the right to withdraw at any time.
- Inform participants who will have access to the data/report, i.e. the audiences of the research, how public it will be, when it will become public, and how it will be disseminated; negotiate levels of release, i.e. who see which parts of the research.
- Ensure anonymity/confidentiality/non-traceability; if these are not possible then tell participants in advance.
- Indicate how anonymity will be addressed (e.g. by confidentiality, aggregation of data).
- Inform participants how data will be collected and how files/questionnaires/audio data/video data/computer files will be stored during the research and destroyed after use.
- Ensure sensitivity to people (e.g. age, ethnicity, gender, culture, religion, language, socio-economic status).
- Gain permission from all relevant parties (e.g. parents/guardians, school, principals etc.) for access.
- Respect vulnerability (e.g. in interviewing children or those without power).
- Agree respondent validation.
- Agree ownership of the data (and when ownership passes from participants to researcher).
- Allow time for review.
- Avoid causing unnecessary offence. Thank the participants.
- Ensure that participants and sponsors have the right to dissent or distance themselves from the research.
- Demonstrate social responsibility and obligations.
- Consider indemnification, liabilities and disclaimers.
- Don't abuse your position or power as a researcher.
- Don't use dangerous methods.

3 Planning educational research

Introduction

There is no single blueprint for planning research. Research design is governed by the notion of 'fitness for purpose'. The purposes of the research determine the methodology and design of the research. For example, if the purpose of the research is to map the field, or to make generalizable comments then a survey approach might be desirable, using some form of stratified sample; if the effects of a specific intervention are to be evaluated then an experimental or action research model may be appropriate; if an in-depth study of a particular situation or group is important then an ethnographic model might be suitable.

That said, it is possible, nevertheless, to identify a set of issues that researchers need to address, regardless of the specifics of their research. This chapter addresses this set of issues, to indicate those matters that need to be addressed in practice so that an area of research interest can become practicable and feasible. This chapter indicates how research might be operationalized, i.e. how a general set of research aims and purposes can be translated into a practical, researchable topic.

To change the 'rules of the game' in midstream once the research has commenced is a sure recipe for problems. The terms of the research and the mechanism of its operation must be ironed out in advance if it is to be credible, legitimate and practicable. Once they have been decided upon, the researcher is in a very positive position to undertake the research. The setting up of the research is a balancing act, for it requires the harmonizing of *planned possibilities* with *workable, coherent practice*, i.e. the resolution of the difference between what could be done/what one would like to do and what will actually work/what one can actually do, for, at the end of the day, research has to work. In planning research there are two phases – a divergent phase and a convergent phase. The divergent phase will open up a range of possible options facing the researcher, while the convergent phase will sift through these possibilities, see which ones are desirable, which ones are compatible with each other, which ones will actually work in the situation, and move towards an action plan that can realistically operate. This can be approached through the establishment of a framework of planning issues (see http://www.routledge.com/textbooks/ 9780415368780 – Chapter 3, file 3.1. ppt).

A framework for planning research

Clearly, the set of issues that constitute a framework for planning research will need to be interpreted differently for different styles of research, nevertheless it is useful to indicate what those issues might be (see Box 3.1).

A possible sequence of consideration is shown in the diagram.

Preparatory issues	→	Methodology	→	Sampling and instrumentation	→	Piloting	→	Timing and sequencing
Constraints, purposes, foci, ethics, research question, politics	→	Approaches, reliability and validity	→	Reliability and validity, pre-piloting	→		→	

Box 3.1
The elements of research design

1	A clear statement of the problem/need that has given rise to the research.
2	Constraints on the research (e.g. access, time, people, politics).
3	The general aims and purposes of the research.
4	The intended outcomes of the research: what the research will do and what is the 'deliverable' outcome.
5	How to operationalize research aims and purposes.
6	Generating research questions (specific, concrete questions to which concrete answers can be given) and hypotheses (if appropriate).
7	The foci of the research.
8	Identifying and setting in order the priorities for the research.
9	Approaching the research design.
10	Focusing the research.
11	Research methodology (approaches and research styles, e.g. survey; experimental; ethnographic/naturalistic; longitudinal; cross-sectional; historical; correlational; *ex post facto*).
12	Ethical issues and ownership of the research (e.g. informed consent; overt and covert research; anonymity; confidentiality; non-traceability; non-maleficence; beneficence; right to refuse/withdraw; respondent validation; research subjects; social responsibility; honesty and deception).
13	Politics of the research: who is the researcher; researching one's own institution; power and interests; advantage; insider and outsider research.
14	Audiences of the research.
15	Instrumentation, e.g. questionnaires; interviews; observation; tests; field notes; accounts; documents; personal constructs; role-play.
16	Sampling: size/access/representativeness; type: probability: random, systematic, stratified, cluster, stage, multi-phase; non-probability: convenience, quota, purposive, dimensional, snowball.
17	Piloting: technical matters: clarity, layout and appearance, timing, length, threat, ease/difficulty, intrusiveness; questions: validity, elimination of ambiguities, types of questions (e.g. multiple choice, open-ended, closed), response categories, identifying redundancies; pre-piloting: generating categories, grouping and classification.
18	Time frames and sequence (what will happen, when and with whom).
19	Resources required.
20	Validity: construct; content; concurrent; face; ecological; internal; external.
21	Reliability: consistency (replicability); equivalence (inter-rater, equivalent forms), predictability; precision; accuracy; honesty; authenticity; richness; dependability; depth; overcoming Hawthorne and halo effects; triangulation: time; space; theoretical; investigator; instruments.
22	Data analysis.
23	Verifying and validating the data.
24	Reporting and writing up the research.

Clearly this need not be the actual sequence; for example it may be necessary to consider access to a possible sample at the very outset of the research (see http://www.routledge.com/textbooks/ 9780415368780 – Chapter 3, file 3.2. ppt).

These issues can be arranged into four main areas (Morrison 1993):

- orienting decisions
- research design and methodology
- data analysis
- presenting and reporting the results.

Orienting decisions are those decisions which set the boundaries or the constraints on the research. For example, let us say that the overriding feature of the research is that it has to be completed within six months; this will exert an influence on the enterprise. On the one hand, it will 'focus the mind', requiring priorities to be settled and data to be provided in a relatively short time. On the other hand, this may reduce the variety of possibilities available to the researcher. Hence questions of time scale will affect:

- the research questions which might be answered feasibly and fairly (for example, some research questions might require a long data collection period)
- the number of data collection instruments used (for example, there might be only enough time for a few instruments to be used)
- the sources (people) to whom the researcher might go (for example, there might only be enough time to interview a handful of people)
- the number of foci which can be covered in the time (for example, for some foci it will take a long time to gather relevant data)
- the size and nature of the reporting (there might only be time to produce one interim report).

By clarifying the time scale a valuable note of realism is injected into the research, which enables questions of practicability to be answered.

Let us take another example. Suppose the overriding feature of the research is that the costs in terms of time, people and materials for carrying it out are to be negligible. This, too, will exert an effect on the research. On the one hand, it will inject a sense of realism into proposals, identifying what is and what is not manageable. On the other hand, it will reduce, again, the variety of possibilities which are available to the researcher. Questions of cost will affect:

- the research questions which might be feasibly and fairly answered (for example, some research questions might require interviewing, which is costly in time both to administer and transcribe, or expensive commercially produced data collection instruments (e.g. tests) and costly computer services, which may include purchasing software)
- the number of data collection instruments used (for example, some data collection instruments, e.g. postal questionnaires, are costly for reprographics and postage)
- the people to whom the researcher might go (for example, if teachers are to be released from teaching in order to be interviewed, then cover for their teaching may need to be found)

- the number of foci which can be covered in the time (for example, in uncovering relevant data, some foci might be costly in researcher's time)
- the size and nature of the reporting (for example, the number of written reports produced, the costs of convening meetings).

Certain time scales permit certain types of research, thus a short time scale permits answers to short-term issues, while long-term or large questions might require a long-term data collection period to cover a range of foci. Costs in terms of time, resources and people might affect the choice of data collection instruments. Time and cost will require the researcher to determine, for example, what will be the minimum representative sample of teachers or students in a school, as interviews are time-consuming and questionnaires are expensive to produce. These are only two examples of the real constraints on the research which must be addressed. Planning the research early on will enable the researcher to identify the boundaries within which the research must operate and what the constraints are on it.

Let us take another important set of questions: is the research feasible? Can it actually be done? Will the researchers have the necessary access to the schools, institutions and people? This issue becomes a major feature if the research is in any way sensitive (see Chapter 5).

With these preliminary comments, let us turn to the four main areas of the framework for planning research.

Orienting decisions

Decisions in this field are strategic; they set the general nature of the research, and there are several questions that researchers may need to consider:

- Who wants the research?
- Who will receive the research/who is it for?
- Who are the possible/likely audiences of the research?
- What powers do the recipients of the research have?
- What are the general aims and purposes of the research?

- What are the main priorities for and constraints on the research?
- Is access realistic?
- What are the time scales and time frames of the research?
- Who will own the research?
- At what point will the ownership of the research pass from the participants to the researcher and from the researcher to the recipients of the research?
- Who owns the data?
- What ethical issues are to be faced in undertaking the research?
- What resources (e.g. physical, material, temporal, human, administrative) are required for the research?

It can be seen that decisions here establish some key parameters of the research, including some political decisions (for example, on ownership and on the power of the recipients to take action on the basis of the research). At this stage the overall feasibility of the research will be addressed.

Research design and methodology

If the preceding orienting decisions are strategic then decisions in this field are tactical; they establish the practicalities of the research, assuming that, generally, it is feasible (i.e. that the orienting decisions have been taken). Decisions here include addressing such questions as:

- What are the specific purposes of the research?
- How are the general research purposes and aims operationalized into specific research questions?
- What are the specific research questions?
- What needs to be the focus of the research in order to answer the research questions?
- What is the main methodology of the research (e.g. a quantitative survey, qualitative research, an ethnographic study, an experiment, a case study, a piece of action research etc.)?
- How will validity and reliability be addressed?
- What kinds of data are required?
- From whom will data be acquired (i.e. sampling)?

- Where else will data be available (e.g. documentary sources)?
- How will the data be gathered (i.e. instrumentation)?
- Who will undertake the research?

How to operationalize research questions

The process of *operationalization* is critical for effective research. Operationalization means specifying a set of operations or behaviours that can be measured, addressed or manipulated. What is required here is translating a very general research aim or purpose into specific, concrete questions to which specific, concrete answers can be given. The process moves from the general to the particular, from the abstract to the concrete. Thus the researcher breaks down each general research purpose or general aim into more specific research purposes and constituent elements, continuing the process until specific, concrete questions have been reached to which specific answers can be provided. Two examples of this are provided below.

Let us imagine that the overall research aim is to ascertain the continuity between primary and secondary education (Morrison 1993: 31–3). This is very general, and needs to be translated into more specific terms. Hence the researcher might deconstruct the term 'continuity' into several components, for example experiences, syllabus content, teaching and learning styles, skills, concepts, organizational arrangements, aims and objectives, ethos, assessment. Given the vast scope of this the decision is taken to focus on continuity of pedagogy. This is then broken down into its component areas:

- the level of continuity of pedagogy
- the nature of continuity of pedagogy
- the degree of success of continuity of pedagogy
- the responsibility for continuity
- record keeping and documentation of continuity
- resources available to support continuity.

The researcher might take this further into investigating: the *nature* of the continuity (i.e. the provision of information about continuity); the *degree* of continuity (i.e. a measure against a given criterion); the *level of success of the continuity* (i.e. a judgement). An operationalized set of research questions, then, might be as follows:

- How much continuity of pedagogy is occurring across the transition stages in each curriculum area? What kind of evidence is required to answer this question? On what criteria will the level of continuity be decided?
- What pedagogical styles operate in each curriculum area? What are the most frequent and most preferred? What is the balance of pedagogical styles? How is pedagogy influenced by resources? To what extent is continuity planned and recorded? On what criteria will the nature of continuity be decided? What kind of evidence is required to answer this question?
- On what aspects of pedagogy does planning take place? By what criteria will the level of success of continuity be judged? Over how many students, teachers or curriculum areas will the incidence of continuity have to occur for it to be judged successful? What kind of evidence is required to answer this question?
- Is continuity occurring by accident or design? How will the extent of planned and unplanned continuity be gauged? What kind of evidence is required to answer this question?
- Who has responsibility for continuity at the transition points? What is being undertaken by these people?
- How are records kept on continuity in the schools? Who keeps these records? What is recorded? How frequently are the records updated and reviewed? What kind of evidence is required to answer this question?
- What resources are there to support continuity at the point of transition? How adequate are these resources? What kind of evidence is required to answer this question?

It can be seen that these questions, several in number, have moved the research from simply an expression of interest (or a general aim) into a series of issues that lend themselves to being investigated in concrete terms. This is precisely what we mean by *the process of operationalization*.

It is now possible to identify not only the specific questions to be posed, but also the instruments that might be needed to acquire data to answer them (e.g. semi-structured interviews, rating scales on questionnaires, or documentary analysis). By this process of operationalization we thus make a general purpose amenable to investigation, e.g. by measurement (Rose and Sullivan 1993: 6) or some other means. The number of operationalized research questions is large here, and may have to be reduced to maybe four or five at most, in order to render the research manageable (see http://www.routledge.com/textbooks/9780415368780 – Chapter 3, file 3.3. ppt).

An alternative way of operationalizing research questions takes the form of hypothesis raising and hypothesis testing. A 'good' hypothesis has several features. First, it is clear on whether it is directional or non-directional: a directional hypothesis states the kind or direction of difference or relationship between two conditions or two groups of participants (e.g. students' performance *increases* when they are intrinsically motivated). A non-directional hypothesis simply predicts that there will be a difference or relationship between two conditions or two groups of participants (e.g. there is a *difference* in students' performance according to their level of intrinsic motivation), without stating whether the difference, for example, is an increase or a decrease). (For statistical purposes, a directional hypothesis requires a one-tailed test whereas a non-directional hypothesis uses a two-tailed test, see Part Five.) Directional hypotheses are often used when past research, predictions, or theory suggest that the findings may go in a particular direction, whereas non-directional hypotheses are used when past research or theory is unclear or contradictory or where prediction is not possible, i.e. where the results are more open-ended.

Second, a 'good' hypothesis is written in a testable form, in a way that makes it clear how the researcher will design an experiment or survey to test the hypothesis, for example, *people perform a mathematics task better when there is silence in the room than when there is not*. The concept of *interference* by noise has been operationalized in order to produce a testable hypothesis.

Third, a 'good' hypothesis is written in a form that can yield measurable results. For example, in the hypothesis *people work better in quiet rather than noisy conditions* it is important to define the operations for 'work better', 'quiet' and 'noisy'. Here 'perform better' might mean 'obtain a higher score on the mathematics test', 'quiet' might mean 'silence', and 'noisy' might mean 'having music playing'. Hence the fully operationalized hypothesis might be *people obtain a higher score on a mathematics test when tested when there is silence rather than when there is music playing*. One can see here that the score is measurable and that there is zero noise, i.e. a measure of the noise level.

In conducting research using hypotheses one has to be prepared to use several hypotheses (Muijs 2004: 16) in order to catch the complexity of the phenomenon being researched, and not least because mediating variables have to be included in the research. For example, the degree of 'willing cooperation' (dependent variable) in an organization's staff is influenced by professional leadership (independent variable) and the personal leadership qualities of the leader (mediating variable: Mastrangelo *et al.* 2004) – which needs to be operationalized more specifically, of course.

There is also the need to consider the null hypothesis and the alternative hypothesis (discussed in Part Five) in research that is cast into a hypothesis testing model. The *null hypothesis* states that, for example, there is *no* relationship between two variables, or that there has been *no* difference in participants' scores on a pretest and a post-test of history, or that there is *no* difference between males and females in respect of their science examination results. The *alternative hypothesis* states, for example: there *is* a correlation between motivation and performance; there *is* a difference between males' and females' scores on science; there *is* a difference between the pretest and post-test scores on history. The alternative hypothesis is often supported when the null hypothesis is 'not supported', i.e. if the null hypothesis is not supported then the alternative hypothesis is. The two kinds of hypothesis are

usually written thus:

H_0 :   the null hypothesis

H_1 :   the alternative hypothesis.

We address the hypothesis testing approach fully in Part Five.

Distinguishing methods from methodologies

In planning research it is important to clarify a distinction that needs to be made between methodology and methods, approaches and instruments, styles of research and ways of collecting data. Several of the later chapters of this book are devoted to specific instruments for collecting data; for example:

- interviews
- questionnaires
- observation
- tests
- accounts
- biographies and case studies
- role-playing;
- simulations
- personal constructs.

The decision on which instrument (method) to use frequently follows from an important earlier decision on which kind (methodology) of research to undertake, for example:

- a survey
- an experiment
- an in-depth ethnography
- action research
- case study research
- testing and assessment.

Subsequent chapters of this book set out each of these research styles, their principles, rationales and purposes, and the instrumentation and data types that seem suitable for them. For conceptual clarity it is possible to set out some key features of these models (Box 3.2). It is intended that, when decisions have been reached on the stage of research design and methodology, a clear plan of action will have been prepared. To this

Box 3.2

Elements of research styles

Model	Purposes	Foci	Key terms	Characteristics
Survey	Gathering large-scale data in order to make generalizations	Opinions	Measuring	Describes and explains
		Scores	Testing	
		Outcomes	Representativeness	Represents wide population
		Conditions	Generalizability	
	Generating statistically manipulable data	Ratings		Gathers numerical data
				Much use of questionnaires and assessment/test data
	Gathering context-free data			
Experiment	Comparing under controlled conditions	Initial states, intervention and outcomes	Pretest and post-test	Control and experimental groups
	Making generalizations about efficacy	Randomized controlled trials	Identification, isolation and control of key variables	Treats situations like a laboratory
	Objective measurement of treatment		Generalizations	Causes due to experimental intervention
			Comparing	
	Establishing causality		Causality	Does not judge worth
				Simplistic
Ethnography	Portrayal of events in subjects' terms	Perceptions and views of participants	Subjectivity	Context specific
	Subjective and reporting of multiple perspectives	Issues as they emerge over time	Honesty, authenticity	Formative and emergent
			Non-generalizable	Responsive to emerging features
			Multiple perspectives	
	Description, understanding and explanation of a specific situation		Exploration and rich reporting of a specific context	Allows room for judgements and multiple perspectives
			Emergent issues	Wide database gathered over a long period of time
				Time-consuming to process data

continued

Chapter 3

Box 3.2
continued

Model	Purposes	Foci	Key terms	Characteristics
Action research	To plan, implement, review and evaluate an intervention designed to improve practice/solve local problem	Everyday practices Outcomes of interventions	Action Improvement Reflection Monitoring Evaluation Intervention Problem-solving Empowering Planning Reviewing	Context-specific Participants as researchers Reflection on practice
	To empower participants through research involvement and ideology critique	Participant empowerment		Interventionist – leading to solution of 'real' problems and meeting 'real' needs
	To develop reflective practice			Empowering for participants
	To promote equality democracy	Reflective practice		Collaborative
	To link practice and research	Social democracy and equality		Promoting praxis and equality
	To promote collaborative research	Decision-making		Stakeholder research
Case study	To portray, analyse and interpret the uniqueness of real individuals and situations through accessible accounts	Individuals and local situations Unique instances A single case	Individuality, uniqueness In-depth analysis and portrayal Interpretive and inferential analysis	In-depth, detailed data from wide data source Participant and non-participant observation
	To catch the complexity and situatedness of behaviour	Bounded phenomena and systems: • individual • group • roles • organizations • community	Subjective Descriptive Analytical Understanding specific situations	Non-interventionist Empathic Holistic treatment of phenomena
	To contribute to action and intervention		Sincerity Complexity Particularity	What can be learned from the particular case
	To present and represent reality – to give a sense of 'being there'			

continued

Box 3.2
continued

Model	Purposes	Foci	Key terms	Characteristics
Testing and assessment	To measure achievement and potential	Academic and non-academic, cognitive, affective and psychomotor	Reliability Validity Criterion-referencing Norm-referencing	Materials designed to provide scores that can be aggregated
	To diagnose strengths and weaknesses	domains – low-order to high-order	Domain-referencing Item-response Formative	Enables individuals and groups to be compared
	To assess performance and abilities	Performance, achievement, potential, abilities Personality characteristics	Summative Diagnostic Standardization Moderation	In-depth diagnosis Measures performance

end, considering models of research might be useful (Morrison 1993).

Data analysis

The prepared researcher will need to consider how the data will be analysed. This is very important, as it has a specific bearing on the form of the instrumentation. For example, a researcher will need to plan the layout and structure of a questionnaire survey very carefully in order to assist data entry for computer reading and analysis; an inappropriate layout may obstruct data entry and subsequent analysis by computer. The planning of data analysis will need to consider:

- What needs to be done with the data when they have been collected? How will they be processed and analysed?
- How will the results of the analysis be verified, cross-checked and validated?

Decisions will need to be taken with regard to the statistical tests that will be used in data analysis as this will affect the layout of research items (for example in a questionnaire), and the computer packages that are available for processing quantitative and qualitative data, e.g. SPSS and N-Vivo respectively. For statistical processing the researcher will need to ascertain the level of data being processed – nominal, ordinal, interval or ratio (discussed in Chapter 24). Part Five addresses issues of data analysis and which statistics to use:

the choice is not arbitrary (Siegel 1956; Cohen and Holliday 1996; Hopkins *et al.* 1996). For qualitative data analysis the researchers have at their disposal a range of techniques, for example:

- coding and content analysis of field notes (Miles and Huberman 1984)
- cognitive mapping (Jones 1987; Morrison 1993)
- seeking patterning of responses
- looking for causal pathways and connections (Miles and Huberman 1984)
- presenting cross-site analysis (Miles and Huberman 1984)
- case studies
- personal constructs
- narrative accounts
- action research analysis
- analytic induction (Denzin 1970b)
- constant comparison and grounded theory (Glaser and Strauss 1967)
- discourse analysis (Stillar 1998)
- biographies and life histories (Atkinson 1998).

The criteria for deciding which forms of data analysis to undertake are governed both by fitness for purpose and legitimacy – the form of data analysis must be appropriate for the kinds of data gathered. For example, it would be inappropriate to use certain statistics with certain kinds of numerical data (e.g. using means on nominal data), or to use causal pathways on unrelated cross-site analysis.

Presenting and reporting the results

As with the stage of planning data analysis, the prepared researcher will need to consider the form of the reporting of the research and its results, giving due attention to the needs of different audiences (for example, an academic audience may require different contents from a wider professional audience and, *a fortiori*, from a lay audience). Decisions here will need to consider:

- how to write up and report the research
- when to write up and report the research (e.g. ongoing or summative)
- how to present the results in tabular and/or written-out form
- how to present the results in non-verbal forms
- to whom to report (the necessary and possible audiences of the research)
- how frequently to report.

For examples of setting out a research report, see the accompanying web site (http://www.routledge.com/textbooks/9780415368780 – Chapter 3, file 3.1.doc).

A *planning matrix for research*

In planning a piece of research, the range of questions to be addressed can be set into a matrix. Box 3.3 provides such a matrix, in the left-hand column of which are the questions which figure in the four main areas set out so far:

- orienting decisions
- research design and methodology
- data analysis
- presenting and reporting the results.

Questions 1–10 are the orienting decisions, questions 11–22 concern the research design and methodology, questions 23–4 cover data analysis, and questions 25–30 deal with presenting and reporting the results. Within each of the 30 questions there are several sub-questions which research planners may need to address. For example, within question 5 ('What are the purposes of the research?') the researcher would have to differentiate major and minor purposes, explicit and maybe implicit purposes, whose purposes are being served by the research, and whose interests are being served by the research. An example of these sub-issues and problems is contained in the second column.

At this point the planner is still at the divergent phase of the research planning, dealing with *planned possibilities* (Morrison 1993: 19), opening up the research to all facets and interpretations. In the column headed 'decisions' the research planner is moving towards a convergent phase, where planned possibilities become visible within the terms of constraints available to the researcher. To do this the researcher has to move down the column marked 'decisions' to see how well the decision which is taken in regard to one issue/question fits in with the decisions in regard to other issues/questions. For one decision to fit with another, four factors must be present:

- All of the cells in the 'decisions' column must be coherent – they must not contradict each other.
- All of the cells in the 'decisions' column must be mutually supporting.
- All of the cells in the 'decisions' column must be practicable when taken separately.
- All of the cells in the 'decisions' column must be practicable when taken together.

Not all of the planned possibilities might be practicable when these four criteria are applied. It would be of very little use if the methods of data collection listed in the 'decisions' column of question 21 ('How will the data be gathered?') offered little opportunity to fulfil the needs of acquiring information to answer question 7 ('What must be the focus in order to answer the research questions?'), or if the methods of data collection were impracticable within the time scales available in question 4.

In the matrix of Box 3.3 the cells have been completed in a deliberately content-free way, i.e. the matrix as presented here does not deal with the specific, actual points which might emerge in a particular research proposal. If the matrix were to be used for planning an actual piece of research, then, instead of couching the wording of each

Box 3.3

A matrix for planning research

Orienting Decisions Question	Sub-issues and problems	Decisions
1 Who wants the research?	Is the research going to be useful? Who might wish to use the research? Are the data going to be public? What if different people want different things from the research? Can people refuse to participate?	Find out the controls over the research which can be exercised by respondents. What are the scope and audiences of the research. Determine the reporting mechanisms.
2 Who will receive the research?	Will participants be able to veto the release of parts of the research to specified audiences? Will participants be able to give the research to whomsoever they wish? Will participants be told to whom the research will go?	Determine the proposed internal and external audiences of the research. Determine the controls over the research which can be exercised by the participants. Determine the rights of the participants and the researcher to control the release of the research.
3 What powers do the recipients of the research have?	What use will be made of the research? How might the research be used for or against the participants? What might happen if the data fall into the 'wrong' hands? Will participants know in advance what use will and will not be made of the research?	Determine the rights of recipients to do what they wish with the research. Determine the respondents' rights to protection as a result of the research.
4 What are the time scales of the research?	Is there enough time to do all the research? How to decide what to be done within the time scale?	Determine the time scales and timing of the research.
5 What are the purposes of the research?	What are the formal and hidden agendas here? Whose purposes are being served by the research? Who decides the purposes of the research? How will different purposes be served in the research?	Determine all the possible uses of the research. Determine the powers of the respondents to control the uses made of the research. Decide on the form of reporting and the intended and possible audiences of the research.
6 What are the research questions?	Who decides what the questions will be? Do participants have rights to refuse to answer or take part? Can participants add their own questions?	Determine the participants' rights and powers to participate in the planning, form and conduct of the research. Decide the balance of all interests in the research.
7 What must be the focus in order to answer the research questions?	Is sufficient time available to focus on all the necessary aspects of the research? How will the priority foci be decided? Who decides the foci?	Determine all the aspects of the research, prioritize them, and agree on the minimum necessary areas of the research. Determine decision-making powers on the research.

continued

Box 3.3
continued

Question	Sub-issues and problems	Decisions
8 What costs are there – human, material, physical, administrative, temporal?	What support is available for the researcher? What materials are necessary?	Cost out the research.
9 Who owns the research?	Who controls the release of the report? What protections can be given to participants? Will participants be identified and identifiable/traceable? Who has the ultimate decision on what data are included?	Determine who controls the release of the report. Decide the rights and powers of the researcher. Decide the rights of veto. Decide how to protect those who may be identified/identifiable in the research.
10 At what point does the ownership pass from the respondent to the researcher and from the researcher to the recipients?	Who decides the ownership of the research? Can participants refuse to answer certain parts if they wish, or, if they have the option not to take part, must they opt out of everything? Can the researcher edit out certain responses?	Determine the ownership of the research at all stages of its progress. Decide the options available to the participants. Decide the rights of different parties in the research, e.g. respondents, researcher, recipients.

Research design and methodology

Question	Sub-issues and problems	Decisions
11 What are the specific purposes of the research?	How do these purposes derive from the overall aims of the research? Will some areas of the broad aims be covered, or will the specific research purposes have to be selective? What priorities are there?	Decide the specific research purposes and write them as concrete questions.
12 How are the general research purposes and aims operationalized into specific research questions?	Do the specific research questions together cover all the research purposes? Are the research questions sufficiently concrete as to suggest the kinds of answers and data required and the appropriate instrumentation and sampling? How to balance adequate coverage of research purposes with the risk of producing an unwieldy list of sub-questions?	Ensure that each main research purpose is translated into specific, concrete questions that, together, address the scope of the original research questions. Ensure that the questions are sufficiently specific as to suggest the most appropriate data types, kinds of answers required, sampling, and instrumentation. Decide how to ensure that any selectivity still represents the main fields of the research questions.
13 What are the specific research questions?	Do the specific research questions demonstrate construct and content validity?	Ensure that the coverage and operationalization of the specific questions addresses content and construct validity respectively.
14 What needs to be the focus of the research in order to answer the research questions?	How many foci are necessary? Are the foci clearly identifiable and operationalizable?	Decide the number of foci of the research questions. Ensure that the foci are clear and can be operationalized.

continued

Box 3.3
continued

Question	Sub-issues and problems	Decisions
15 What is the main methodology of the research?	How many methodologies are necessary? Are several methodologies compatible with each other? Will a single focus/research question require more than one methodology (e.g. for triangulation and concurrent validity)?	Decide the number, type and purposes of the methodologies to be used. Decide whether one or more methodologies is necessary to gain answers to specific research questions. Ensure that the most appropriate form of methodology is employed.
16 How will validity and reliability be addressed?	Will there be the opportunity for cross-checking? Will the depth and breadth required for content validity be feasible within the constraints of the research (e.g. time constraints, instrumentation)? In what senses are the research questions valid (e.g. construct validity)? Are the questions fair? How does the researcher know if people are telling the truth? What kinds of validity and reliability are to be addressed? How will the researcher take back the research to respondents for them to check that the interpretations are fair and acceptable? How will data be gathered consistently over time? How to ensure that each respondent is given the same opportunity to respond?	Determine the process of respondent validation of the data. Decide a necessary minimum of topics to be covered. Subject the plans to scrutiny by critical friends ('jury' validity). Pilot the research. Build in cross-checks on data. Address the appropriate forms of reliability and validity. Decide the questions to be asked and the methods used to ask them. Determine the balance of open and closed questions.
17 How will reflexivity be addressed?	How will reflexivity be recognized? Is reflexivity a problem? How can reflexivity be included in the research?	Determine the need to address reflexivity and to make this public. Determine how to address reflexivity in the research.
18 What kinds of data are required?	Does the research need words, numbers or both? Does the research need opinions, facts or both? Does the research seek to compare responses and results or simply to illuminate an issue?	Determine the most appropriate types of data for the foci and research questions. Balance objective and subjective data. Determine the purposes of collecting different types of data and the ways in which they can be processed.
19 From whom will data be acquired (i.e. sampling)?	Will there be adequate time to go to all the relevant parties? What kind of sample is required (e.g. probability/non-probability/random/ stratified etc.)? How to achieve a representative sample (if required)?	Determine the minimum and maximum sample. Decide on the criteria for sampling. Decide the kind of sample required. Decide the degree of representativeness of the sample. Decide how to follow up and not to follow up on the data gathered.

continued

Box 3.3
continued

Question	Sub-issues and problems	Decisions
20 Where else will data be available?	What documents and other written sources of data can be used? How to access and use confidential material? What will be the positive or negative effects on individuals of using certain documents?	Determine the necessary/desirable/ possible documentary sources. Decide access and publication rights and protection of sensitive data.
21 How will the data be gathered (i.e. instrumentation)?	What methods of data gathering are available and appropriate to yield data to answer the research questions? What methods of data gathering will be used? How to construct interview schedules/questionnaires/tests/observation schedules? What will be the effects of observing participants? How many methods should be used (e.g. to ensure reliability and validity)? Is it necessary or desirable to use more than one method of data collection on the same issue? Will many methods yield more reliable data? Will some methods be unsuitable for some people or for some issues?	Determine the most appropriate data collection instruments to gather data to answer the research questions. Pilot the instruments and refine them subsequently. Decide the strengths and weaknesses of different data collection instruments in the short and long term. Decide which methods are most suitable for which issues. Decide which issues will require more than one data collection instrument. Decide whether the same data collection methods will be used with all the participants.
22 Who will undertake the research?	Can different people plan and carry out different parts of the research?	Decide who will carry out the data collection, processing and reporting.

Data analysis

Question	Sub-issues and problems	Decisions
23 How will the data be analysed?	Are the data to be processed numerically or verbally? What computer packages are available to assist data processing and analysis? What statistical tests will be needed? How to perform a content analysis of word data? How to summarize and present word data? How to process all the different responses to open-ended questions? Will the data be presented person by person, issue by issue, aggregated to groups, or a combination of these? Does the research seek to make generalizations? Who will process the data?	Clarify the legitimate and illegitimate methods of data processing and analysis of quantitative and qualitative data. Decide which methods of data processing and analysis are most appropriate for which types of data and for which research questions. Check that the data processing and analysis will serve the research purposes. Determine the data protection issues if data are to be processed by 'outsiders' or particular 'insiders'.

continued

Box 3.3
continued

Question	Sub-issues and problems	Decisions
24 How to verify and validate the data and their interpretation?	What opportunities will there be for respondents to check the researcher's interpretation? At what stages of the research is validation necessary? What will happen if respondents disagree with the researcher's interpretation?	Determine the process of respondent validation during the research. Decide the reporting of multiple perspectives and interpretations. Decide respondents' rights to have their views expressed or to veto reporting.

Presenting and reporting the results

Question	Sub-issues and problems	Decisions
25 How to write up and report the research?	Who will write the report and for whom? How detailed must the report be? What must the report contain? What channels of dissemination of the research are to be used?	Ensure that the most appropriate form of reporting is used for the audiences. Keep the report as short, clear and complete as possible. Provide summaries if possible/fair. Ensure that the report enables fair critique and evaluation to be undertaken.
26 When to write up and report the research (e.g. ongoing or summative)?	How many times are appropriate for reporting? For whom are interim reports compiled? Which reports are public?	Decide the most appropriate timing, purposes and audiences of the reporting. Decide the status of the reporting (e.g. formal, informal, public, private).
27 How to present the results in tabular and/or written-out form?	How to ensure that everyone will understand the language or the statistics? How to respect the confidentiality of the participants? How to report multiple perspectives?	Decide the most appropriate form of reporting. Decide whether to provide a glossary of terms. Decide the format(s) of the reports. Decide the number and timing of the reports. Decide the protection of the individual's rights, balancing this with the public's rights to know.
28 How to present the results in non-verbal forms?	Will different parties require different reports? How to respect the confidentiality of the participants? How to report multiple perspectives?	Decide the most appropriate form of reporting. Decide the number and timing of the reports. Ensure that a written record is kept of oral reports. Decide the protection of the individual's rights, balancing this with the public's rights to know.
29 To whom to report (the necessary and possible audiences of the research)?	Do all participants receive a report? What will be the effects of not reporting to stakeholders?	Identify the stakeholders. Determine the least and most material to be made available to the stakeholders.
30 How frequently to report?	Is it necessary to provide interim reports? If interim reports are provided, how might this affect the future reports or the course of the research?	Decide on the timing and frequency of the reporting. Determine the formative and summative nature of the reports.

cell in generalized terms, it would be more useful if *specific, concrete* responses were given which addressed particular issues and concerns in the research proposal in question.

Many of these questions concern rights, responsibilities and the political uses (and abuses) of the research. This underlines the view that research is an inherently political and moral activity; it is not politically or morally neutral. The researcher has to be concerned with the uses as well as the conduct of the research.

Managing the planning of research

The preceding discussion has revealed the complexity of planning a piece of research, yet it should not be assumed that research will always go according to plan! For example, the mortality of the sample might be a feature (participants leaving during the research), or a poor response rate to questionnaires might be encountered, rendering subsequent analysis, reporting and generalization problematical; administrative support might not be forthcoming, or there might be serious slippage in the timing. This is not to say that a plan for the research should not be made; rather it is to suggest that it is dangerous to put absolute faith in it! For an example of what to include in a research proposal see the accompanying web site: (http://www.routledge.com/textbooks/9780415368780 – Chapter 3, file 3.2.doc).

To manage the complexity in planning outlined above a simple four-stage model can be proposed:

1 Identify the purposes of the research.
2 Identify and give priority to the constraints under which the research will take place.
3 Plan the possibilities for the research within these constraints.
4 Decide the research design.

Each stage contains several operations (see http://www.routledge.com/textbooks/9780415368780 – Chapter 3, file 3.4. ppt). Box 3.4 clarifies this four-stage model, drawing out the various operations contained in each stage.

It may be useful for research planners to consider which instruments will be used at which stage of the research and with which sectors of the sample population. Box 3.5 sets out a matrix of these for planning (see also Morrison 1993: 109), for example, of a small-scale piece of research.

A matrix approach such as this enables research planners to see at a glance their coverage of the sample and of the instruments used at particular points in time, making omissions clear, and promoting such questions as the following:

- Why are certain instruments used at certain times and not at others?
- Why are certain instruments used with certain people and not with others?
- Why do certain times in the research use more instruments than other times?
- Why is there such a heavy concentration of instruments at the end of the study?
- Why are certain groups involved in more instruments than other groups?
- Why are some groups apparently neglected (e.g. parents): is there a political dimension to the research?
- Why are questionnaires the main kinds of instrument to be used?
- Why are some instruments (e.g. observation, testing) not used at all?
- What makes the five stages separate?
- Are documents held only by certain parties (and, if so, might one suspect an 'institutional line' to be revealed in them)?
- Are some parties more difficult to contact than others (e.g. university teacher educators)?
- Are some parties more important to the research than others (e.g. the principals)?
- Why are some parties excluded from the sample (e.g. school governors, policy-makers, teachers' associations and unions)?
- What is the difference between the three groups of teachers?

Matrix planning is useful for exposing key features of the planning of research. Further matrices might be constructed to indicate other features of the research, for example:

- the timing of the identification of the sample
- the timing of the release of interim reports

Box 3.4

A planning sequence for research

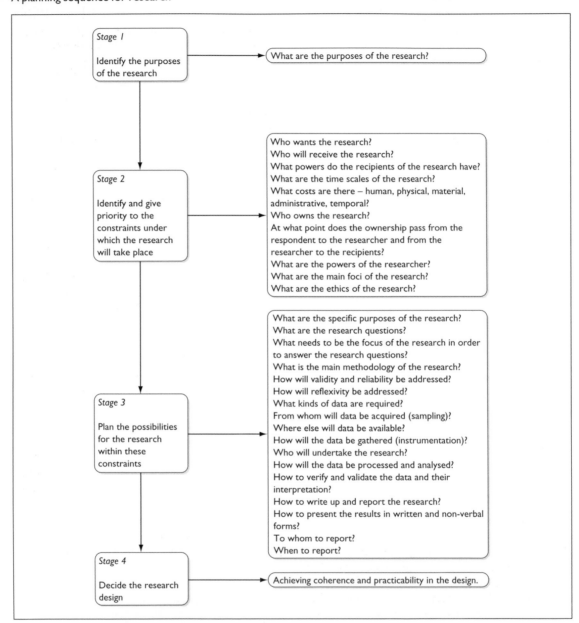

Box 3.5
A planning matrix for research

Time sample	Stage 1 (start)	Stage 2 (3 months)	Stage 3 (6 months)	Stage 4 (9 months)	Stage 5 (12 months)
Principal/ headteacher	Documents Interview Questionnaire 1	Interview	Documents Questionnaire 2	Interview	Documents Interview Questionnaire 3
Teacher group 1	Questionnaire 1		Questionnaire 2		Questionnaire 3
Teacher group 2	Questionnaire 1		Questionnaire 2		Questionnaire 3
Teacher group 3	Questionnaire 1		Questionnaire 2		Questionnaire 3
Students			Questionnaire 2		Interview
Parents	Questionnaire 1		Questionnaire 2		Questionnaire 3
University teacher educators	Interview Documents				Interview Documents

- the timing of the release of the final report
- the timing of pretests and post-tests (in an experimental style of research)
- the timing of intensive necessary resource support (e.g. reprographics)
- the timing of meetings of interested parties.

These examples cover timings only; other matrices might be developed to cover other combinations, for example: reporting by audiences; research team meetings by reporting; instrumentation by participants etc. They are useful summary devices.

A worked example

Let us say that a school is experiencing very low morale and a researcher has been brought in to investigate the school's organizational culture. The researcher has been given open access to the school and has five months from the start of the project to producing the report (for a fuller version of this see the accompanying web site, http://www.routledge.com/textbooks/ 9780415368780 – Chapter 3, file 3.3.doc). The researcher plans the research as follows:

Purposes

- To present an overall and in-depth picture of the organizational culture(s) and subcultures, including the prevailing cultures and subcultures, within the school.

- To provide an indication of the strength of the organizational culture(s).
- To make suggestions and recommendations about the organizational culture of, and its development at, the school.

Research questions

- What are the major and minor elements of organizational culture in the school?
- What are the organizational cultures and subcultures in the school?
- Which (sub)cultures are the most and least prevalent in the school, and in which parts of the school are these most and least prevalent?
- How strong and intense are the (sub)cultures in the school?
- What are the causes and effects of the (sub)cultures in the school?
- How can the (sub)cultures be improved in the school?

Focus

Three levels of organizational cultures will be examined:

- underlying values and assumptions
- espoused values and enacted behaviours
- artefacts.

Organizational culture concerns values, assumptions, beliefs, espoused theories and mental models, observed practices, areas of conflict and consensus, the formal and hidden messages contained in artefacts, messages, documents and language, the 'way we do things', the physical environment, relationships, power, control, communication, customs and rituals, stories, the reward system and motivation, the micro-politics of the school, involvement in decision-making, empowerment and exploitation/manipulation, leadership, commitment, and so on.

Methodology

Organizational culture is intangible yet its impact on a school's operations is very tangible. This suggests that, while quantitative measures may be used, they are likely only to yield comparatively superficial information about the school's culture. In order to probe beneath the surface of the school's culture, to examine the less overt aspects of the school's culture(s) and subcultures, it is important to combine quantitative and qualitative methodologies for data collection. A mixed methodology will be used for the empirical data collection, using numerical and verbal data, in order to gather rounded, reliable data. A survey approach will be used to gain an overall picture, and a more fine-grained analysis will be achieved through individual and group interviews and focus groups (Box 3.6).

Instrumentation

The data gathered will be largely perception based, and will involve gathering employees' views of the (sub)cultures. As the concept of organizational

Box 3.6
Understanding the levels of organizational culture

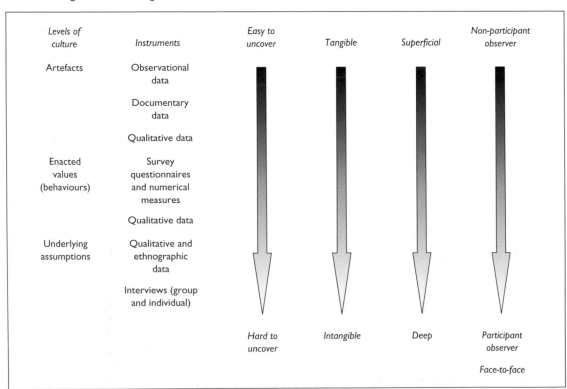

culture is derived, in part from ethnography and anthropology, the research will use qualitative and ethnographic methods.

One of the difficulties anticipated is that the less tangible aspects of the school might be the most difficult on which to collect data. Not only will people find it harder to articulate responses and constructs, but also they may be reluctant to reveal these in public. The more the project addresses intangible and unmeasurable elements, and the richer the data that are to be collected, the more there is a need for increased and sensitive interpersonal behaviour, face-to-face data collection methods and qualitative data.

There are several instruments for data collection: questionnaires, semi-structured interviews (individual and group), observational data and documentary data will constitute a necessary minimum, as follows:

Questionnaires

Questionnaire surveys, use commercially available instruments, each of which measures different aspects of school's culture, in particular:

- The Organizational Culture Questionnaire (Harrison and Stokes 1992) looks at overall cultures and provides a general picture in terms of *role*, *power*, *achievement* and *support* cultures, and examines the differences between existing and preferred cultures.
- The Organizational Culture Inventory (Cooke and Lafferty 1989) provides a comprehensive and reliable analysis of the presenting organizational cultures.

Questionnaires, using rating scales, will catch articulated, espoused, enacted, visible aspects of organizational culture, and will measure, for example, the extent of sharedness of culture, congruence between existing and ideal, strength and intensity of culture.

Semi-structured interviews

Semi-structured qualitative interviews for individuals and groups gather data on the more intangible aspects of the school's culture, e.g. values, assumptions, beliefs, wishes, problems. Interviews will be semi-structured, i.e. with a given agenda and open-ended questions. As face-to-face individual interviews might be intimidating for some groups, group interviews will be used. In all of the interviews the important part will be the supplementary question 'why'.

Observational data

Observational data will comment on the physical environment, and will then be followed up with interview material to discover participants' responses to, perceptions of, messages contained in and attitudes to the physical environment. Artefacts, clothing, shared and private spaces, furniture, notices, regulations etc. all give messages to participants.

Documentary data

Documentary analysis and additional stored data, reporting the formal matters in the school, will be examined for what they include and what they exclude.

Sampling

First, the questionnaire will be given to all employees who are willing to participate. Second, the semi-structured interviews will be conducted on a 'critical case' basis, i.e. with participants who are in key positions and who are 'knowledgeable people' about the activities and operations of the school.

There will be stratified sampling for the survey instruments, in order to examine how perceptions of the school's organizational culture vary according to the characteristics of the subsamples. This will enable the levels of congruence or disjunction between the responses of the various subgroups to be charted. Nominal characteristics of the sampling will be included, for example, age, level in the school, departments, sex, ethnicity, nationality, years of working in the school.

Parameters

The data will be collected on a 'one-shot' basis rather than longitudinally. A multi-method approach will be used for data collection.

Stages in the research

There are five stages in the research, as follows.

Stage 1: Development and operationalization

This stage includes:

- a review of literature and commercially produced instruments
- clarification of the research questions
- clarification of methodology and sampling.

Stage 2: Instrumentation and the piloting of the instruments

This stage includes:

- questionnaire development and piloting
- semi-structured interview schedules and piloting
- gathering of observational data
- analysis of documentary data.

Because of the limited number of senior staff, it will not be possible to conduct pilot interviews with them, as this will preclude them from the final data collection.

Stage 3: Data collection

This will proceed in the following sequence. First, administration of the questionnaire will be followed by analysis of questionnaire data to provide material for the interviews. Interviews will be conducted concurrently.

Stage 4: Data analysis and interpretation

Numerical data will be analysed using SPSS, which will also enable the responses from subgroups of the school to be separated for analysis. Qualitative data will be analysed using protocols of content analysis.

Stage 5: Reporting

A full report on the findings will include conclusions, implications and recommendations.

Ethics and ownership

Participation in the project will be on the basis of informed consent, and on a voluntary basis, with rights of withdrawal at any time. Given the size and scope of the cultural survey, it is likely that key people in the school will be able to be identified, even though the report is confidential. This will be made clear to the potential participants. Copies of the report will be available for all the employees. Data, once given to the researcher, are his or hers, and the researcher may not use them in any way which will publicly identify the school; the report is the property of the school.

Time frames

The project will be completed in five months:

- the first month for a review of the relevant literature
- the second month to develop the instrumentation and research design
- the third month to gather the data
- the fourth month to analyse the data
- the fifth month to complete the report.

The example indicates a systematic approach to the planning and conduct of the research, which springs from a perceived need in the school. It works within given constraints and makes clear what it will 'deliver'. Though the research does not specify hypotheses to be tested, nevertheless it would not be difficult to convert the research questions into hypotheses if this style of research were preferred.

Conclusion

The notion of 'fitness for purpose' reins in planning research; the research plan must suit the purposes of the research. If the reader is left feeling, at the end of this chapter, that the task of research is complex, then that is an important message, for rigour and thoughtful, thorough planning are necessary if the research is to be worthwhile and effective. For a checklist for evaluating research see the accompanying web site (http://www.routledge.com/textbooks/ 9780415368780 – Chapter 3, file 3.4.doc).

Chapter 3

4 Sampling

Introduction

The quality of a piece of research stands or falls not only by the appropriateness of methodology and instrumentation but also by the suitability of the sampling strategy that has been adopted (see also Morrison 1993: 112–17). Questions of sampling arise directly out of the issue of defining the population on which the research will focus. Researchers must take sampling decisions early in the overall planning of a piece of research. Factors such as expense, time, accessibility frequently prevent researchers from gaining information from the whole population. Therefore they often need to be able to obtain data from a smaller group or subset of the total population in such a way that the knowledge gained is representative of the total population (however defined) under study. This smaller group or subset is the *sample*. Experienced researchers start with the total population and work down to the sample. By contrast, less experienced researchers often work from the bottom up, that is, they determine the minimum number of respondents needed to conduct the research (Bailey 1978). However, unless they identify the total population in advance, it is virtually impossible for them to assess how representative the sample is that they have drawn.

Suppose that a class teacher has been released from her teaching commitments for one month in order to conduct some research into the abilities of 13-year-old students to undertake a set of science experiments; that the research is to draw on three secondary schools which contain 300 such students each, a total of 900 students, and that the method that the teacher has been asked to use for data collection is a semi-structured interview. Because of the time available to the teacher it would be impossible for her to interview all 900 students (the total population being all the cases). Therefore she has to be selective and to interview fewer than all 900 students. How will she decide that selection; how will she select which students to interview?

If she were to interview 200 of the students, would that be too many? If she were to interview just 20 of the students would that be too few? If she were to interview just the males or just the females, would that give her a fair picture? If she were to interview just those students whom the science teachers had decided were 'good at science', would that yield a true picture of the total population of 900 students? Perhaps it would be better for her to interview those students who were experiencing difficulty in science and who did not enjoy science, as well as those who were 'good at science'. Suppose that she turns up on the days of the interviews only to find that those students who do not enjoy science have decided to absent themselves from the science lesson. How can she reach those students?

Decisions and problems such as these face researchers in deciding the sampling strategy to be used. Judgements have to be made about four key factors in sampling:

- the sample size
- representativeness and parameters of the sample
- access to the sample
- the sampling strategy to be used.

The decisions here will determine the sampling strategy to be used (see http://www.routledge.com/textbooks/9780415368780 – Chapter 4, file 4.1.ppt). This assumes that a sample is actually required; there may be occasions on which the researcher can access the whole population rather than a sample.

The sample size

A question that often plagues novice researchers is just how large their samples for the research should be. There is no clear-cut answer, for the correct sample size depends on the purpose of the study and the nature of the population under scrutiny. However, it is possible to give some advice on this matter. Generally speaking, the larger the sample the better, as this not only gives greater reliability but also enables more sophisticated statistics to be used.

Thus, a sample size of thirty is held by many to be the minimum number of cases if researchers plan to use some form of statistical analysis on their data, though this is a very small number and we would advise very considerably more. Researchers need to think out in advance of any data collection the sorts of relationships that they wish to explore within subgroups of their eventual sample. The number of variables researchers set out to control in their analysis and the types of statistical tests that they wish to make must inform their decisions about sample size prior to the actual research undertaking. Typically an anticipated minimum of thirty cases per variable should be used as a 'rule of thumb', i.e. one must be assured of having a minimum of thirty cases for each variable (of course, the thirty cases for variable one could also be the same thirty as for variable two), though this is a very low estimate indeed. This number rises rapidly if different subgroups of the population are included in the sample (discussed below), which is frequently the case.

Further, depending on the kind of analysis to be performed, some statistical tests will require larger samples. For example, less us imagine that one wished to calculate the chi-square statistic,

a commonly used test (discussed in Part Five) with cross-tabulated data, for example looking at two subgroups of stakeholders in a primary school containing sixty 10-year-old pupils and twenty teachers and their responses to a question on a 5-point scale (see diagram below).

Here one can notice that the sample size is eighty cases, an apparently reasonably sized sample. However, six of the ten cells of responses (60 per cent) contain fewer than five cases. The chi-square statistic requires there to be five cases or more in 80 per cent of the cells (i.e. eight out of the ten cells). In this example only 40 per cent of the cells contained more than five cases, so even with a comparatively large sample, the statistical requirements for reliable data with a straightforward statistic such as chi-square have not been met. The message is clear, one needs to anticipate, as far as one is able, some possible distributions of the data and see if these will prevent appropriate statistical analysis; if the distributions look unlikely to enable reliable statistics to be calculated then one should increase the sample size, or exercise great caution in interpreting the data because of problems of reliability, or not use particular statistics, or, indeed, consider abandoning the exercise if the increase in sample size cannot be achieved.

The point here is that each variable may need to be ensured of a reasonably large sample size (a minimum of maybe six–ten cases). Indeed Gorard (2003: 63) suggests that one can start from the minimum number of cases required in each cell, multiply this by the number of cells, and then double the total. In the example above, with six cases in each cell, the minimum sample would be 120 ($6 \times 10 \times 2$), though, to be on the safe side, to try to ensure ten cases in each cell, a minimum

Variable: 10-year-old pupils should do one hour's homework each weekday evening					
	Strongly disagree	Disagree	Neither agree nor disagree	Agree	Strongly agree
10-year-old pupils in the school	25	20	3	8	4
Teachers in the school	6	4	2	4	4

sample of 200 might be better ($10 \times 10 \times 2$), though even this is no guarantee.

The issue arising out of the example here is also that one can observe considerable variation in the responses from the participants in the research. Gorard (2003: 62) suggests that if a phenomenon contains a lot of potential variability then this will increase the sample size. Surveying a variable such as intelligence quotient (IQ) for example, with a potential range from 70 to around 150, may require a larger sample rather than a smaller sample.

As well as the requirement of a minimum number of cases in order to examine relationships between subgroups, researchers must obtain the minimum sample size that will accurately represent the population being targeted. With respect to size, will a large sample guarantee representativeness? Not necessarily! In our first example, the researcher could have interviewed a total sample of 450 females and still not have represented the male population. Will a small size guarantee representativeness? Again, not necessarily! The latter falls into the trap of saying that 50 per cent of those who expressed an opinion said that they enjoyed science, when the 50 per cent was only one student, a researcher having interviewed only two students in all. Furthermore, too large a sample might become unwieldy and too small a sample might be unrepresentative (e.g. in the first example, the researcher might have wished to interview 450 students but this would have been unworkable in practice, or the researcher might have interviewed only ten students, which, in all likelihood, would have been unrepresentative of the total population of 900 students).

Where simple random sampling is used, the sample size needed to reflect the population value of a particular variable depends both on the size of the population and the amount of heterogeneity in the population (Bailey 1978). Generally, for populations of equal heterogeneity, the larger the population, the larger the sample that must be drawn. For populations of equal size, the greater the heterogeneity on a particular variable, the larger the sample that is needed. To the extent that a sample fails to represent accurately the

population involved, there is sampling error, discussed below.

Sample size is also determined to some extent by the style of the research. For example, a survey style usually requires a large sample, particularly if inferential statistics are to be calculated. In ethnographic or qualitative research it is more likely that the sample size will be small. Sample size might also be constrained by cost – in terms of time, money, stress, administrative support, the number of researchers, and resources. Borg and Gall (1979: 194–5) suggest that correlational research requires a sample size of no fewer than thirty cases, that causal-comparative and experimental methodologies require a sample size of no fewer than fifteen cases, and that survey research should have no fewer than 100 cases in each major subgroup and twenty–fifty in each minor subgroup.

Borg and Gall (1979: 186) advise that sample size has to begin with an estimation of the smallest number of cases in the smallest subgroup of the sample, and 'work up' from that, rather than vice versa. So, for example, if 5 per cent of the sample must be teenage boys, and this subsample must be thirty cases (e.g. for correlational research), then the total sample will be $30 \div 0.05 = 600$; if 15 per cent of the sample must be teenage girls and the subsample must be forty-five cases, then the total sample must be $45 \div 0.15 = 300$ cases.

The size of a probability (random) sample can be determined in two ways, either by the researcher exercising prudence and ensuring that the sample represents the wider features of the population with the minimum number of cases or by using a table which, from a mathematical formula, indicates the appropriate size of a random sample for a given number of the wider population (Morrison 1993: 117). One such example is provided by Krejcie and Morgan (1970), whose work suggests that if the researcher were devising a sample from a wider population of thirty or fewer (e.g. a class of students or a group of young children in a class) then she or he would be well advised to include the whole of the wider population as the sample.

Krejcie and Morgan (1970) indicate that the smaller the number of cases there are in the wider, whole population, the larger the proportion of that population must be which appears in the sample. The converse of this is true: the larger the number of cases there are in the wider, whole population, the smaller the proportion of that population can be which appears in the sample (see http://www.routledge.com/textbooks/9780415368780 – Chapter 4, file 4.2.ppt). They note that as the population increases the proportion of the population required in the sample diminishes and, indeed, remains constant at around 384 cases (Krejcie and Morgan 1970: 610). Hence, for example, a piece of research involving all the children in a small primary or elementary school (up to 100 students in all) might require between 80 per cent and 100 per cent of the school to be included in the sample, while a large secondary school of 1,200 students might require a sample of 25 per cent of the school in order to achieve randomness. As a rough guide in a random sample, the larger the sample, the greater is its chance of being representative.

In determining sample size for a probability sample one has to consider not only the population size but also the confidence level and confidence interval, two further pieces of terminology. The confidence level, usually expressed as a percentage (usually 95 per cent or 99 per cent), is an index of how sure we can be (95 per cent of the time or 99 per cent of the time) that the responses lie within a given variation range, a given confidence interval (e.g. ±3 per cent) (see http://www.routledge.com/textbooks/9780415368780 – Chapter 4, file 4.3.ppt). The confidence interval is that degree of variation or variation range (e.g. ±1 per cent, or ±2 per cent, or ±3 per cent) that one wishes to ensure. For example, the confidence interval in many opinion polls is ±3 per cent; this means that, if a voting survey indicates that a political party has 52 per cent of the votes then it could be as low as 49 per cent (52 − 3) or as high as 55 per cent (52 + 3). A confidence level of 95 per cent here would indicate that we could be sure of this result within this range (±3 per cent) for 95 per cent of the time.

If we want to have a very high confidence level (say 99 per cent of the time) then the sample size will be high. On the other hand, if we want a less stringent confidence level (say 90 per cent of the time), then the sample size will be smaller. Usually a compromise is reached, and researchers opt for a 95 per cent confidence level. Similarly, if we want a very small confidence interval (i.e. a limited range of variation, e.g. 3 per cent) then the sample size will be high, and if we are comfortable with a larger degree of variation (e.g. 5 per cent) then the sample size will be lower.

A full table of sample sizes for a probability sample is given in Box 4.1, with three confidence levels (90 per cent, 95 per cent and 99 per cent) and three confidence intervals (5 per cent, 4 per cent and 3 per cent).

We can see that the size of the sample reduces at an increasing rate as the population size increases; generally (but, clearly, not always) the larger the population, the smaller the proportion of the probability sample can be. Also, the higher the confidence level, the greater the sample, and the lower the confidence interval, the higher the sample. A conventional sampling strategy will be to use a 95 per cent confidence level and a 3 per cent confidence interval.

There are several web sites that offer sample size calculation services for random samples. One free site at the time of writing is from Creative Service Systems (http://www.surveysystem.com/sscalc.htm), and another is from Pearson NCS (http://www.pearsonncs.com/research/sample-calc.htm), in which the researcher inputs the desired confidence level, confidence interval and the population size, and the sample size is automatically calculated.

If different subgroups or strata (discussed below) are to be used then the requirements placed on the total sample also apply to each subgroup. For example, let us imagine that we are surveying a whole school of 1,000 students in a multiethnic school. The formulae above suggest that we need 278 students in our random sample, to ensure representativeness. However, let us imagine that we wished to stratify our groups into, for example, Chinese (100 students), Spanish (50 students), English (800 students) and American (50 students). From tables of random sample sizes we work out a random sample.

Box 4.1
Sample size, confidence levels and confidence intervals for random samples

Population	Confidence level 90 per cent			Confidence level 95 per cent			Confidence level 99 per cent		
	Confi-dence	Confi-dence	Confi-dence	Confi-dence	Confi-dence	Confi-dence	Confi-dence	Confi-dence	Confi-dence
30	27	28	29	28	29	29	29	29	30
50	42	45	47	44	46	48	46	48	49
75	59	64	68	63	67	70	67	70	72
100	73	81	88	79	86	91	87	91	95
120	83	94	104	91	100	108	102	108	113
150	97	111	125	108	120	132	122	131	139
200	115	136	158	132	150	168	154	168	180
250	130	157	188	151	176	203	182	201	220
300	143	176	215	168	200	234	207	233	258
350	153	192	239	183	221	264	229	262	294
400	162	206	262	196	240	291	250	289	329
450	170	219	282	207	257	317	268	314	362
500	176	230	301	217	273	340	285	337	393
600	187	249	335	234	300	384	315	380	453
650	192	257	350	241	312	404	328	400	481
700	196	265	364	248	323	423	341	418	507
800	203	278	389	260	343	457	363	452	558
900	209	289	411	269	360	468	382	482	605
1,000	214	298	431	278	375	516	399	509	648
1,100	218	307	448	285	388	542	414	534	689
1,200	222	314	464	291	400	565	427	556	727
1,300	225	321	478	297	411	586	439	577	762
1,400	228	326	491	301	420	606	450	596	796
1,500	230	331	503	306	429	624	460	613	827
2,000	240	351	549	322	462	696	498	683	959
2,500	246	364	581	333	484	749	524	733	1,061
5,000	258	392	657	357	536	879	586	859	1,347
7,500	263	403	687	365	556	934	610	911	1,480
10,000	265	408	703	370	566	964	622	939	1,556
20,000	269	417	729	377	583	1,013	642	986	1,688
30,000	270	419	738	379	588	1,030	649	1,002	1,737
40,000	270	421	742	381	591	1,039	653	1,011	1,762
50,000	271	422	745	381	593	1,045	655	1,016	1,778
100,000	272	424	751	383	597	1,056	659	1,026	1,810
150,000	272	424	752	383	598	1,060	661	1,030	1,821
200,000	272	424	753	383	598	1,061	661	1,031	1,826
250,000	272	425	754	384	599	1,063	662	1,033	1,830
500,000	272	425	755	384	600	1,065	663	1,035	1,837
1,000,000	272	425	756	384	600	1,066	663	1,036	1,840

	Population	*Sample*
Chinese	100	80
Spanish	50	44
English	800	260
American	50	44
Total	1,000	428

Our original sample size of 278 has now increased, very quickly, to 428. The message is very clear: the greater the number of strata (subgroups), the larger the sample will be. Much educational research concerns itself with strata rather than whole samples, so the issue is significant. One can rapidly generate the need for a very large sample. If subgroups are required then the same rules for calculating overall sample size apply to each of the subgroups.

Further, determining the size of the sample will also have to take account of non-response, attrition and respondent mortality, i.e. some participants will fail to return questionnaires, leave the research, return incomplete or spoiled questionnaires (e.g. missing out items, putting two ticks in a row of choices instead of only one). Hence it is advisable to overestimate rather than to underestimate the size of the sample required, to build in redundancy (Gorard 2003: 60). Unless one has guarantees of access, response and, perhaps, the researcher's own presence at the time of conducting the research (e.g. presence when questionnaires are being completed), then it might be advisable to estimate up to double the size of required sample in order to allow for such loss of clean and complete copies of questionnaires or responses.

In some circumstances, meeting the requirements of sample size can be done on an evolutionary basis. For example, let us imagine that you wish to sample 300 teachers, randomly selected. You succeed in gaining positive responses from 250 teachers to, for example, a telephone survey or a questionnaire survey, but you are 50 short of the required number. The matter can be resolved simply by adding another 50 to the random sample, and, if not all of these are successful, then adding some more until the required number is reached.

Borg and Gall (1979: 195) suggest that, as a general rule, sample sizes should be large where

- there are many variables
- only small differences or small relationships are expected or predicted
- the sample will be broken down into subgroups
- the sample is heterogeneous in terms of the variables under study
- reliable measures of the dependent variable are unavailable.

Oppenheim (1992: 44) adds to this the view that the nature of the scales to be used also exerts an influence on the sample size. For nominal data the sample sizes may well have to be larger than for interval and ratio data (i.e. a variant of the issue of the number of subgroups to be addressed, the greater the number of subgroups or possible categories, the larger the sample will have to be).

Borg and Gall (1979) set out a formula-driven approach to determining sample size (see also Moser and Kalton 1977; Ross and Rust 1997: 427–38), and they also suggest using correlational tables for correlational studies – available in most texts on statistics – as it were 'in reverse' to determine sample size (Borg and Gall 1979: 201), i.e. looking at the significance levels of correlation coefficients and then reading off the sample sizes usually required to demonstrate that level of significance. For example, a correlational significance level of 0.01 would require a sample size of 10 if the estimated coefficient of correlation is 0.65, or a sample size of 20 if the estimated correlation coefficient is 0.45, and a sample size of 100 if the estimated correlation coefficient is 0.20. Again, an inverse proportion can be seen – the larger the sample population, the smaller the estimated correlation coefficient can be to be deemed significant.

With both qualitative and quantitative data, the essential requirement is that the sample is representative of the population from which it is drawn. In a dissertation concerned with a life history (i.e. $n = 1$), the sample is the population!

Qualitative data

In a qualitative study of thirty highly able girls of similar socio-economic background following an A level Biology course, a sample of five or six may suffice the researcher who is prepared to obtain additional corroborative data by way of validation.

Where there is heterogeneity in the population, then a larger sample must be selected on some basis that respects that heterogeneity. Thus, from a staff of sixty secondary school teachers differentiated by gender, age, subject specialism, management or classroom responsibility, etc., it would be insufficient to construct a sample consisting of ten female classroom teachers of Arts and Humanities subjects.

Quantitative data

For quantitative data, a precise sample number can be calculated according to the *level of accuracy* and the *level of probability* that researchers require in their work. They can then report in their study the rationale and the basis of their research decisions (Blalock 1979).

By way of example, suppose a teacher/researcher wishes to sample opinions among 1,000 secondary school students. She intends to use a 10-point scale ranging from 1 = totally unsatisfactory to 10 = absolutely fabulous. She already has data from her own class of thirty students and suspects that the responses of other students will be broadly similar. Her own students rated the activity (an extracurricular event) as follows: mean score = 7.27; standard deviation = 1.98. In other words, her students were pretty much 'bunched' about a warm, positive appraisal on the 10-point scale. How many of the 1,000 students does she need to sample in order to gain an accurate (i.e. reliable) assessment of what the whole school ($n = 1,000$) thinks of the extracurricular event?

> *It all depends on what degree of accuracy and what level of probability she is willing to accept.*

A simple calculation from a formula by Blalock (1979: 215–18) shows that:

- if she is happy to be within + or − 0.5 of a scale point and accurate 19 times out of 20, then she requires a sample of 60 out of the 1,000;
- if she is happy to be within + or − 0.5 of a scale point and accurate 99 times out of 100, then she requires a sample of 104 out of the 1,000
- if she is happy to be within + or − 0.5 of a scale point and accurate 999 times out of 1,000, then she requires a sample of 170 out of the 1,000
- if she is a perfectionist and wishes to be within + or − 0.25 of a scale point and accurate 999 times out of 1,000, then she requires a sample of 679 out of the 1,000.

It is clear that sample size is a matter of judgement as well as mathematical precision; even formula-driven approaches make it clear that there are elements of prediction, standard error and human judgement involved in determining sample size.

Sampling error

If many samples are taken from the same population, it is unlikely that they will all have characteristics identical with each other or with the population; their means will be different. In brief, there will be sampling error (see Cohen and Holliday 1979, 1996). Sampling error is often taken to be the difference between the sample mean and the population mean. Sampling error is not necessarily the result of mistakes made in sampling procedures. Rather, variations may occur due to the chance selection of different individuals. For example, if we take a large number of samples from the population and measure the mean value of each sample, then the sample means will not be identical. Some will be relatively high, some relatively low, and many will cluster around an average or mean value of the samples. We show this diagrammatically in Box 4.2 (see http://www.routledge.com/textbooks/ 9780415368780 – Chapter 4, file 4.4.ppt).

Why should this occur? We can explain the phenomenon by reference to the Central Limit Theorem which is derived from the laws of probability. This states that if random large samples of equal size are repeatedly drawn from any population, then the mean of those samples will be approximately normally distributed. The distribution of sample means approaches the normal distribution as the size of the sample increases, regardless of the shape – normal or otherwise – of the parent population (Hopkins *et al.* 1996: 159, 388). Moreover, the average or mean of the sample means will be approximately the same as the population mean. Hopkins *et al.* (1996: 159–62) demonstrate this by reporting the use of computer simulation to examine the sampling distribution of means when computed 10,000 times (a method that we discuss in

Box 4.2
Distribution of sample means showing the spread of a selection of sample means around the population mean

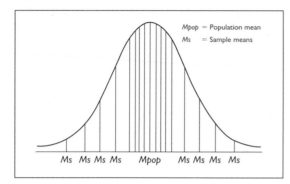

Mpop = Population mean
Ms   = Sample means

Ms Ms Ms Ms   Mpop   Ms Ms Ms Ms

Source: Cohen and Holliday 1979

Chapter 10). Rose and Sullivan (1993: 144) remind us that 95 per cent of all sample means fall between plus or minus 1.96 standard errors of the sample and population means, i.e. that we have a 95 per cent chance of having a single sample mean within these limits, that the sample mean will fall within the limits of the population mean.

By drawing a large number of samples of equal size from a population, we create a sampling distribution. We can calculate the error involved in such sampling (see http://www.routledge.com/textbooks/9780415368780 – Chapter 4, file 4.5.ppt). The standard deviation of the theoretical distribution of sample means is a measure of sampling error and is called the standard error of the mean (SE_M). Thus,

$$SE = \frac{SD_s}{\sqrt{N}}$$

where SD_S = the standard deviation of the sample and N = the number in the sample.

Strictly speaking, the formula for the standard error of the mean is:

$$SE = \frac{SD_{pop}}{\sqrt{N}}$$

where SD_{pop} = the standard deviation of the population.

However, as we are usually unable to ascertain the SD of the total population, the standard deviation of the sample is used instead. The standard error of the mean provides the best estimate of the sampling error. Clearly, the sampling error depends on the variability (i.e. the heterogeneity) in the population as measured by SD_{pop} as well as the sample size (N) (Rose and Sullivan 1993: 143). The smaller the SD_{pop} the smaller the sampling error; the larger the N, the smaller the sampling error. Where the SD_{pop} is very large, then N needs to be very large to counteract it. Where SD_{pop} is very small, then N, too, can be small and still give a reasonably small sampling error. As the sample size increases the sampling error decreases. Hopkins *et al.* (1996: 159) suggest that, unless there are some very unusual distributions, samples of twenty-five or greater usually yield a normal sampling distribution of the mean. For further analysis of steps that can be taken to cope with the estimation of sampling in surveys we refer the reader to Ross and Wilson (1997).

The standard error of proportions

We said earlier that one answer to 'How big a sample must I obtain?' is 'How accurate do I want my results to be?' This is well illustrated in the following example:

A school principal finds that the 25 students she talks to at random are reasonably in favour of a proposed change in the lunch break hours, 66 per cent being in favour and 34 per cent being against. How can she be sure that these proportions are truly representative of the whole school of 1,000 students?

A simple calculation of the standard error of proportions provides the principal with her answer.

$$SE = \sqrt{\frac{P \times Q}{N}}$$

where

P = the percentage in favour

Q = 100 per cent − P

N = the sample size

The formula assumes that each sample is drawn on a simple random basis. A small correction factor called the finite population correction (fpc) is generally applied as follows:

$$\text{SE of proportions} = \sqrt{\frac{(1-f)P \times Q}{N}}$$ where f is the

proportion included in the sample.

Where, for example, a sample is 100 out of 1,000, f is 0.1.

$$\text{SE of proportions} = \sqrt{\frac{(1-0.1)(66 \times 34)}{100}} = 4.49$$

With a sample of twenty-five, the SE = 9.4. In other words, the favourable vote can vary between 56.6 per cent and 75.4 per cent; likewise, the unfavourable vote can vary between 43.4 per cent and 24.6 per cent. Clearly, a voting possibility ranging from 56.6 per cent in favour to 43.4 per cent against is less decisive than 66 per cent as opposed to 34 per cent. Should the school principal enlarge her sample to include 100 students, then the SE becomes 4.5 and the variation in the range is reduced to 61.5 per cent−70.5 per cent in favour and 38.5 per cent−29.5 per cent against. Sampling the whole school's opinion (n = 1,000) reduces the SE to 1.5 and the ranges to 64.5 per cent−67.5 per cent in favour and 35.5 per cent−32.5 per cent against. It is easy to see why political opinion surveys are often based upon sample sizes of 1,000 to 1,500 (Gardner 1978).

What is being suggested here generally is that, in order to overcome problems of sampling error, in order to ensure that one can separate random effects and variation from non-random effects, and in order for the power of a statistic to be felt, one should opt for as large a sample as possible. As Gorard (2003: 62) says, 'power is an estimate of the ability of the test you are using to separate the effect size from random variation', and a large sample helps the researcher to achieve statistical power. Samples of fewer than thirty are dangerously small, as they allow the possibility of considerable standard error, and, for over around eighty cases, any increases to the sample size have little effect on the standard error.

The representativeness of the sample

The researcher will need to consider the extent to which it is important that the sample in fact represents the whole population in question (in the example above, the 1,000 students), if it is to be a valid sample. The researcher will need to be clear what it is that is being represented, i.e. to set the parameter characteristics of the wider population – the sampling frame – clearly and correctly. There is a popular example of how poor sampling may be unrepresentative and unhelpful for a researcher. A national newspaper reports that one person in every two suffers from backache; this headline stirs alarm in every doctor's surgery throughout the land. However, the newspaper fails to make clear the parameters of the study which gave rise to the headline. It turns out that the research took place in a damp part of the country where the incidence of backache might be expected to be higher than elsewhere, in a part of the country which contained a disproportionate number of elderly people, again who might be expected to have more backaches than a younger population, in an area of heavy industry where the working population might be expected to have more backache than in an area of lighter industry or service industries, and used only two doctors' records, overlooking the fact that many backache sufferers went to those doctors' surgeries because the two doctors concerned were known to be overly sympathetic to backache sufferers rather than responsibly suspicious.

These four variables – climate, age group, occupation and reported incidence – were seen to exert a disproportionate effect on the study, i.e. if the study were to have been carried out in an area where the climate, age group, occupation and reporting were to have been different, then the results might have been different. The newspaper report sensationally generalized beyond the parameters of the data, thereby overlooking the limited representativeness of the study.

It is important to consider adjusting the weightings of subgroups in the sample once the data have been collected. For example, in a secondary school where half of the students are male and half are female, consider pupils' responses to the question 'How far does your liking of the form teacher affect your attitude to work?'

| Variable: How far does your liking of the form teacher affect your attitude to school work? | | | | |
	Very little	A little	Some-what	Quite a lot	A very great deal
Male	10	20	30	25	15
Female	50	80	30	25	15
Total	60	100	60	50	30

Let us say that we are interested in the attitudes according to the gender of the respondents, as well as overall. In this example one could surmise that generally the results indicate that the liking of the form teacher has only a small to moderate effect on the students' attitude to work. However, we have to observe that twice as many girls as boys are included in the sample, and this is an unfair representation of the population of the school, which comprises 50 per cent girls and 50 per cent boys, i.e. girls are over-represented and boys are under-represented. If one equalizes the two sets of scores by gender to be closer to the school population (either by doubling the number of boys or halving the number of girls) then the results look very different.

| Variable: How far does your liking of the form teacher affect your attitude to school work? | | | | |
	Very little	A little	Some-what	Quite a lot	A very great deal
Male	20	40	60	50	30
Female	50	80	30	25	15
Total	70	120	90	75	45

In this latter case a much more positive picture is painted, indicating that the students regard their liking of the form teacher as a quite important feature in their attitude to school work. Here equalizing the sample to represent more fairly the population by weighting yields a different picture. Weighting the results is an important consideration.

The access to the sample

Access is a key issue and is an early factor that must be decided in research. Researchers will need to ensure that access is not only permitted but also, in fact, practicable. For example, if a researcher were to conduct research into truancy and unauthorized absence from school, and decided to interview a sample of truants, the research might never commence as the truants, by definition, would not be present! Similarly access to sensitive areas might be not only difficult but also problematical both legally and administratively, for example, access to child abuse victims, child abusers, disaffected students, drug addicts, school refusers, bullies and victims of bullying. In some sensitive areas access to a sample might be denied by the potential sample participants themselves, for example AIDS counsellors might be so seriously distressed by their work that they simply cannot face discussing with a researcher the subject matter of their traumatic work; it is distressing enough to do the job without living through it again with a researcher.

Access might also be denied by the potential sample participants themselves for very practical reasons, for example a doctor or a teacher simply might not have the time to spend with the researcher. Further, access might be denied by people who have something to protect, for example a school which has recently received a very poor inspection result or poor results on external examinations, or people who have made an important discovery or a new invention and who do not wish to disclose the secret of their success; the trade in intellectual property has rendered this a live issue for many researchers. There are very many reasons that might prevent access to the sample, and researchers cannot afford to neglect this potential source of difficulty in planning research.

In many cases access is guarded by 'gatekeepers' – people who can control researchers' access to those whom they really want to target. For school staff this might be, for example, headteachers, school governors, school secretaries, form teachers; for pupils this might be friends, gang members, parents, social workers and so on. It is critical for researchers to consider not only whether access is possible but also how access will be undertaken – to whom does one have to go, both formally and informally, to gain access to the target group.

Not only might access be difficult but also its corollary – release of information – might be problematic. For example, a researcher might gain access to a wealth of sensitive information and appropriate people, but there might be a restriction on the release of the data collection; in the field of education in the UK reports have been known to be suppressed, delayed or 'doctored'. It is not always enough to be able to 'get to' the sample, the problem might be to 'get the information out' to the wider public, particularly if it could be critical of powerful people.

The sampling strategy to be used

There are two main methods of sampling (Cohen and Holliday 1979; 1982; 1996; Schofield 1996). The researcher must decide whether to opt for a probability (also known as a random sample) or a non-probability sample (also known as a purposive sample). The difference between them is this: in a probability sample the chances of members of the wider population being selected for the sample are known, whereas in a non-probability sample the chances of members of the wider population being selected for the sample are unknown. In the former (probability sample) every member of the wider population has an equal chance of being included in the sample; inclusion or exclusion from the sample is a matter of chance and nothing else. In the latter (non-probability sample) some members of the wider population definitely will be excluded and others definitely included (i.e. every member of the wider population does not have an equal chance of being included in the sample). In this latter type the researcher has deliberately – purposely – selected a particular section of the wider population to include in or exclude from the sample.

Probability samples

A probability sample, because it draws randomly from the wider population, will be useful if the researcher wishes to be able to make generalizations, because it seeks representativeness of the wider population. It also permits two-tailed tests to be administered in statistical analysis of quantitative data. Probability sampling is popular in randomized controlled trials. On the other hand, a non-probability sample deliberately avoids representing the wider population; it seeks only to represent a particular group, a particular named section of the wider population, such as a class of students, a group of students who are taking a particular examination, a group of teachers (see http://www.routledge.com/textbooks/9780415368780 – Chapter 4, file 4.6.ppt).

A probability sample will have less risk of bias than a non-probability sample, whereas, by contrast, a non-probability sample, being unrepresentative of the whole population, may demonstrate skewness or bias. (For this type of sample a one-tailed test will be used in processing statistical data.) This is not to say that the former is bias free; there is still likely to be sampling error in a probability sample (discussed below), a feature that has to be acknowledged, for example opinion polls usually declare their error factors, e.g. ±3 per cent.

There are several types of probability samples: simple random samples; systematic samples; stratified samples; cluster samples; stage samples, and multi-phase samples. They all have a measure of randomness built into them and therefore have a degree of generalizability.

Simple random sampling

In simple random sampling, each member of the population under study has an equal chance of being selected and the probability of a member of the population being selected is unaffected by the selection of other members of the population, i.e. each selection is entirely independent of the next. The method involves selecting at random from a list of the population (a sampling frame) the required number of subjects for the sample. This can be done by drawing names out of a container until the required number is reached, or by using a table of random numbers set out in matrix form (these are reproduced in many books on quantitative research methods and statistics), and allocating these random numbers to participants or cases (e.g. Hopkins *et al.* 1996: 148–9). Because of probability and chance, the sample should contain subjects with characteristics similar to the population as a whole; some old, some young, some tall, some short, some fit, some unfit, some rich, some poor etc. One problem associated with this particular sampling method is that a complete list of the population is needed and this is not always readily available (see http://www.routledge.com/textbooks/9780415368780 – Chapter 4, file 4.7.ppt).

Systematic sampling

This method is a modified form of simple random sampling. It involves selecting subjects from a population list in a systematic rather than a random fashion. For example, if from a population of, say, 2,000, a sample of 100 is required, then every twentieth person can be selected. The starting point for the selection is chosen at random (see http://www.routledge.com/textbooks/9780415368780 – Chapter 4, file 4.8.ppt).

One can decide how frequently to make systematic sampling by a simple statistic – the total number of the wider population being represented divided by the sample size required:

$$f = \frac{N}{sn}$$

  f = frequency interval

  N = the total number of the wider population

  sn = the required number in the sample.

Let us say that the researcher is working with a school of 1,400 students; by looking at the table of sample size (Box 4.1) required for a random sample of these 1,400 students we see that 302 students are required to be in the sample. Hence

the frequency interval (f) is:

$$\frac{1,400}{302} = 4.635 \text{ (which rounds up to 5.0)}$$

Hence the researcher would pick out every fifth name on the list of cases.

Such a process, of course, assumes that the names on the list themselves have been listed in a random order. A list of females and males might list all the females first, before listing all the males; if there were 200 females on the list, the researcher might have reached the desired sample size before reaching that stage of the list which contained males, thereby distorting (skewing) the sample. Another example might be where the researcher decides to select every thirtieth person identified from a list of school students, but it happens that: (a) the school has just over thirty students in each class; (b) each class is listed from high ability to low ability students; (c) the school listing identifies the students by class.

In this case, although the sample is drawn from each class, it is not fairly representing the whole school population since it is drawing almost exclusively on the lower ability students. This is the issue of *periodicity* (Calder 1979). Not only is there the question of the order in which names are listed in systematic sampling, but also there is the issue that this process may violate one of the fundamental premises of probability sampling, namely that every person has an equal chance of being included in the sample. In the example above where every fifth name is selected, this guarantees that names 1–4, 6–9 etc. will be excluded, i.e. everybody does not have an equal chance to be chosen. The ways to minimize this problem are to ensure that the initial listing is selected randomly and that the starting point for systematic sampling is similarly selected randomly.

Stratified sampling

Stratified sampling involves dividing the population into homogenous groups, each group containing subjects with similar characteristics. For example, group A might contain males and group B, females. In order to obtain a sample representative of the whole population in terms of sex, a random selection of subjects from group A and group B must be taken. If needed, the exact proportion of males to females in the whole population can be reflected in the sample. The researcher will have to identify those characteristics of the wider population which must be included in the sample, i.e. to identify the parameters of the wider population. This is the essence of establishing the sampling frame (see http://www.routledge.com/textbooks/9780415368780 – Chapter 4, file 4.9.ppt).

To organize a stratified random sample is a simple two-stage process. First, identify those characteristics that appear in the wider population that must also appear in the sample, i.e. divide the wider population into homogenous and, if possible, discrete groups (strata), for example males and females. Second, randomly sample within these groups, the size of each group being determined either by the judgement of the researcher or by reference to Boxes 4.1 or 4.2.

The decision on which characteristics to include should strive for simplicity as far as possible, as the more factors there are, not only the more complicated the sampling becomes, but often the larger the sample will have to be to include representatives of all strata of the wider population.

A stratified random sample is, therefore, a useful blend of randomization and categorization, thereby enabling both a quantitative and qualitative piece of research to be undertaken. A quantitative piece of research will be able to use analytical and inferential statistics, while a qualitative piece of research will be able to target those groups in institutions or clusters of participants who will be able to be approached to participate in the research.

Cluster sampling

When the population is large and widely dispersed, gathering a simple random sample poses administrative problems. Suppose we want to survey students' fitness levels in a particularly large community or across a country. It would be completely impractical to select students randomly and spend an inordinate amount of time travelling about in order to test them. By cluster sampling, the researcher can select a specific number of schools and test all the students in those selected schools, i.e. a geographically close cluster is sampled (see http://www.routledge.com/textbooks/9780415368780 – Chapter 4, file 4.10.ppt).

One would have to be careful to ensure that cluster sampling does not build in bias. For example, let us imagine that we take a cluster sample of a city in an area of heavy industry or great poverty; this may not represent all kinds of cities or socio-economic groups, i.e. there may be similarities within the sample that do not catch the variability of the wider population. The issue here is one of representativeness; hence it might be safer to take several clusters and to sample lightly within each cluster, rather to take fewer clusters and sample heavily within each.

Cluster samples are widely used in small-scale research. In a cluster sample the parameters of the wider population are often drawn very sharply; a researcher, therefore, would have to comment on the generalizability of the findings. The researcher may also need to stratify within this cluster sample if useful data, i.e. those which are focused and which demonstrate discriminability, are to be acquired.

Stage sampling

Stage sampling is an extension of cluster sampling. It involves selecting the sample in stages, that is, taking samples from samples. Using the large community example in cluster sampling, one type of stage sampling might be to select a number of schools at random, and from within each of these schools, select a number of classes at random, and from within those classes select a number of students.

Morrison (1993: 121–2) provides an example of how to address stage sampling in practice. Let us say that a researcher wants to administer a questionnaire to all 16-year-old pupils in each of eleven secondary schools in one region. By contacting the eleven schools she finds that there are 2,000 16-year-olds on roll. Because of questions of confidentiality she is unable to find out the names of all the students so it is impossible to draw their names out of a container to achieve randomness (and even if she had the names, it would be a mind-numbing activity to write out 2,000 names to draw out of a container!). From looking at Box 4.1 she finds that, for a random sample of the 2,000 students, the sample size is 322 students. How can she proceed?

The first stage is to list the eleven schools on a piece of paper and then to write the names of the eleven schools on to small cards and place each card in a container. She draws out the first name of the school, puts a tally mark by the appropriate school on her list and returns the card to the container. The process is repeated 321 times, bringing the total to 322. The final totals might appear thus:

School   1 2 3 4 5 6 7 8 9 10 11 Total
Required no.
of students   22 31 32 24 29 20 35 28 32 38 31 322

For the second stage the researcher then approaches the eleven schools and asks each of them to select randomly the required number of students for each school. Randomness has been maintained in two stages and a large number (2,000) has been rendered manageable. The process at work here is to go from the general to the specific, the wide to the focused, the large to the small. Caution has to be exercised here, as the assumption is that the schools are of the same size and are large; that may not be the case in practice, in which case this strategy may be inadvisable.

Multi-phase sampling

In stage sampling there is a single unifying purpose throughout the sampling. In the previous example the purpose was to reach a particular group of students from a particular region. In a multi-phase sample the purposes change at each phase, for example, at phase one the selection of the sample might be based on the criterion of geography (e.g. students living in a particular region); phase two might be based on an economic criterion (e.g. schools whose budgets are administered in

markedly different ways); phase three might be based on a political criterion (e.g. schools whose students are drawn from areas with a tradition of support for a particular political party), and so on. What is evident here is that the sample population will change at each phase of the research (see http://www.routledge.com/textbooks/9780415368780 – Chapter 4, file 4.11.ppt).

Non-probability samples

The selectivity which is built into a non-probability sample derives from the researcher targeting a particular group, in the full knowledge that it does not represent the wider population; it simply represents itself. This is frequently the case in small-scale research, for example, as with one or two schools, two or three groups of students, or a particular group of teachers, where no attempt to generalize is desired; this is frequently the case for some ethnographic research, action research or case study research (see http://www.routledge.com/textbooks/9780415368780 – Chapter 4, file 4.12.ppt). Small-scale research often uses non-probability samples because, despite the disadvantages that arise from their non-representativeness, they are far less complicated to set up, are considerably less expensive, and can prove perfectly adequate where researchers do not intend to generalize their findings beyond the sample in question, or where they are simply piloting a questionnaire as a prelude to the main study.

Just as there are several types of probability sample, so there are several types of non-probability sample: convenience sampling, quota sampling, dimensional sampling, purposive sampling and snowball sampling. Each type of sample seeks only to represent itself or instances of itself in a similar population, rather than attempting to represent the whole, undifferentiated population.

Convenience sampling

Convenience sampling – or, as it is sometimes called, accidental or opportunity sampling – involves choosing the nearest individuals to serve as respondents and continuing that process until the required sample size has been obtained or those who happen to be available and accessible at the time. Captive audiences such as students or student teachers often serve as respondents based on convenience sampling. Researchers simply choose the sample from those to whom they have easy access. As it does not represent any group apart from itself, it does not seek to generalize about the wider population; for a convenience sample that is an irrelevance. The researcher, of course, must take pains to report this point – that the parameters of generalizability in this type of sample are negligible. A convenience sample may be the sampling strategy selected for a case study or a series of case studies (see http://www.routledge.com/textbooks/9780415368780 – Chapter 4, file 4.13.ppt).

Quota sampling

Quota sampling has been described as the non-probability equivalent of stratified sampling (Bailey 1978). Like a stratified sample, a quota sample strives to represent significant characteristics (strata) of the wider population; unlike stratified sampling it sets out to represent these in the proportions in which they can be found in the wider population. For example, suppose that the wider population (however defined) were composed of 55 per cent females and 45 per cent males, then the sample would have to contain 55 per cent females and 45 per cent males; if the population of a school contained 80 per cent of students up to and including the age of 16 and 20 per cent of students aged 17 and over, then the sample would have to contain 80 per cent of students up to the age of 16 and 20 per cent of students aged 17 and above. A quota sample, then, seeks to give proportional weighting to selected factors (strata) which reflects their weighting in which they can be found in the wider population (see http://www.routledge.com/textbooks/9780415368780 – Chapter 4, file 4.14.ppt). The researcher wishing to devise a quota sample can proceed in three stages:

1 Identify those characteristics (factors) which appear in the wider population which must also appear in the sample, i.e. divide the wider population into homogenous and, if possible, discrete groups (strata), for example, males and females, Asian, Chinese and African Caribbean.
2 Identify the proportions in which the selected characteristics appear in the wider population, expressed as a percentage.
3 Ensure that the percentaged proportions of the characteristics selected from the wider population appear in the sample.

Ensuring correct proportions in the sample may be difficult to achieve if the proportions in the wider community are unknown or if access to the sample is difficult; sometimes a pilot survey might be necessary in order to establish those proportions (and even then sampling error or a poor response rate might render the pilot data problematical).

It is straightforward to determine the minimum number required in a quota sample. Let us say that the total number of students in a school is 1,700, made up thus:

Performing arts	300 students
Natural sciences	300 students
Humanities	600 students
Business and Social Sciences	500 students

The proportions being 3:3:6:5, a minimum of 17 students might be required $(3 + 3 + 6 + 5)$ for the sample. Of course this would be a minimum only, and it might be desirable to go higher than this. The price of having too many characteristics (strata) in quota sampling is that the minimum number in the sample very rapidly could become very large, hence in quota sampling it is advisable to keep the numbers of strata to a minimum. The larger the number of strata, the larger the number in the sample will become, usually at a geometric rather than an arithmetic rate of progression.

Purposive sampling

In purposive sampling, often (but by no means exclusively) a feature of qualitative research, researchers handpick the cases to be included in the sample on the basis of their judgement of their typicality or possession of the particular characteristics being sought. In this way, they build up a sample that is satisfactory to their specific needs. As its name suggests, the sample has been chosen for a specific purpose, for example: a group of principals and senior managers of secondary schools is chosen as the research is studying the incidence of stress among senior managers; a group of disaffected students has been chosen because they might indicate most distinctly the factors which contribute to students' disaffection (they are *critical cases*, akin to 'critical events' discussed in Chapter 18, or *deviant cases* – those cases which go against the norm: (Anderson and Arsenault 1998: 124); one class of students has been selected to be tracked throughout a week in order to report on the curricular and pedagogic diet which is offered to them so that other teachers in the school might compare their own teaching to that reported. While it may satisfy the researcher's needs to take this type of sample, it does not pretend to represent the wider population; it is deliberately and unashamedly selective and biased (see http://www.routledge.com/textbooks/ 9780415368780 – Chapter 4, file 4.15.ppt).

In many cases purposive sampling is used in order to access 'knowledgeable people', i.e. those who have in-depth knowledge about particular issues, maybe by virtue of their professional role, power, access to networks, expertise or experience (Ball 1990). There is little benefit in seeking a random sample when most of the random sample may be largely ignorant of particular issues and unable to comment on matters of interest to the researcher, in which case a purposive sample is vital. Though they may not be representative and their comments may not be generalizable, this is not the primary concern in such sampling; rather the concern is to acquire in-depth information from those who are in a position to give it.

Another variant of purposive sampling is the *boosted* sample. Gorard (2003: 71) comments on the need to use a boosted sample in order to include those who may otherwise be excluded from, or under-represented in, a sample because there are so few of them. For example, one might have a very small number of special needs teachers or pupils in a primary school or nursery, or one might have a very small number of children from certain ethnic minorities in a school, such that they may not feature in a sample. In this case the researcher will deliberately seek to include a sufficient number of them to ensure appropriate statistical analysis or representation in the sample, adjusting any results from them, through weighting, to ensure that they are not over-represented in the final results. This is an endeavour, perhaps, to reach and meet the demands of social inclusion.

A further variant of purposive sampling is *negative case sampling*. Here the researcher deliberately seeks those people who might disconfirm the theories being advanced (the Popperian equivalent of falsifiability), thereby strengthening the theory if it survives such disconfirming cases. A softer version of negative case sampling is *maximum variation* sampling, selecting cases from as diverse a population as possible (Anderson and Arsenault 1998: 124) in order to ensure strength and richness to the data, their applicability and their interpretation. In this latter case, it is almost inevitable that the sample size will increase or be large.

Dimensional sampling

One way of reducing the problem of sample size in quota sampling is to opt for dimensional sampling. Dimensional sampling is a further refinement of quota sampling. It involves identifying various factors of interest in a population and obtaining at least one respondent of every combination of those factors. Thus, in a study of race relations, for example, researchers may wish to distinguish first, second and third generation immigrants. Their sampling plan might take the form of a multidimensional table with 'ethnic group' across the top and 'generation' down the side. A second example might be of a researcher who may be interested in studying disaffected students, girls and secondary-aged students and who may find a single disaffected secondary female student, i.e. a respondent who is the bearer of all of the sought characteristics (see http://www.routledge.com/textbooks/ 9780415368780 – Chapter 4, file 4.16.ppt).

Snowball sampling

In snowball sampling researchers identify a small number of individuals who have the characteristics in which they are interested. These people are then used as informants to identify, or put the researchers in touch with, others who qualify for inclusion and these, in turn, identify yet others – hence the term snowball sampling. This method is useful for sampling a population where access is difficult, maybe because it is a sensitive topic (e.g. teenage solvent abusers) or where communication networks are undeveloped (e.g. where a researcher wishes to interview stand-in 'supply' teachers – teachers who are brought in on an *ad-hoc* basis to cover for absent regular members of a school's teaching staff – but finds it difficult to acquire a list of these stand-in teachers), or where an outside researcher has difficulty in gaining access to schools (going through informal networks of friends/acquaintance and their friends and acquaintances and so on rather than through formal channels). The task for the researcher is to establish who are the critical or key informants with whom initial contact must be made (see http://www.routledge.com/textbooks/ 9780415368780 – Chapter 4, file 4.17.ppt).

Volunteer sampling

In cases where access is difficult, the researcher may have to rely on volunteers, for example, personal friends, or friends of friends, or participants who reply to a newspaper advertisement, or those who happen to be interested from a particular school, or those attending courses. Sometimes this is inevitable (Morrison 2006), as it is the only kind of sampling that is possible, and it may be better to have this kind of sampling than no research at all.

In these cases one has to be very cautious in making any claims for generalizability or representativeness, as volunteers may have a range of different motives for volunteering, e.g. wanting to help a friend, interest in the research, wanting to benefit society, an opportunity for revenge on a particular school or headteacher. Volunteers may be well intentioned, but they do not necessarily represent the wider population, and this would have to be made clear.

Theoretical sampling

This is a feature of grounded theory. In grounded theory the sample size is relatively immaterial, as one works with the data that one has. Indeed grounded theory would argue that the sample size could be infinitely large, or, as a fall-back position, large enough to saturate the categories and issues, such that new data will not cause the theory that has been generated to be modified.

Theoretical sampling requires the researcher to have sufficient data to be able to generate and 'ground' the theory in the research context, however defined, i.e. to create a theoretical explanation of what is happening in the situation, without having any data that do not fit the theory. Since the researcher will not know in advance how much, or what range of data will be required, it is difficult, to the point of either impossibility, exhaustion or time limitations, to know in advance the sample size required. The researcher proceeds in gathering more and more data until the theory remains unchanged or until the boundaries of the context of the study have been reached, until no modifications to the grounded theory are made in light of the constant comparison method. Theoretical saturation (Glaser and Strauss 1967: 61) occurs when no additional data are found that advance, modify, qualify, extend or add to the theory developed.

Glaser and Strauss (1967) write that

> theoretical sampling is the process of data collection for generating theory whereby the analyst jointly collects, codes, and analyzes his [*sic.*] data and decides what data to collect next and where to find them, in order to develop his theory as it emerges.
>
> (Glaser and Strauss 1967: 45)

The two key questions, for the grounded theorist using theoretical sampling are, first, to which groups does one turn next for data? Second, for what theoretical purposes does one seek further data? In response to the first, Glaser and Strauss (1967: 49) suggest that the decision is based on theoretical relevance, i.e. those groups that will assist in the generation of as many properties and categories as possible.

Hence the size of the data set may be fixed by the number of participants in the organization, or the number of people to whom one has access, but the researcher has to consider that the door may have to be left open for him/her to seek further data in order to ensure theoretical adequacy and to check what has been found so far with further data (Flick *et al.* 2004: 170). In this case it is not always possible to predict at the start of the research just how many, and who, the research will need for the sampling; it becomes an iterative process.

Non-probability samples also reflect the issue that sampling can be of *people* but it can also be of *issues*. Samples of people might be selected because the researcher is concerned to address specific issues, for example, those students who misbehave, those who are reluctant to go to school, those with a history of drug dealing, those who prefer extra-curricular to curricular activities. Here it is the issue that drives the sampling, and so the question becomes not only 'whom should I sample' but also 'what should I sample' (Mason 2002: 127–32). In turn this suggests that it is not only people who may be sampled, but texts, documents, records, settings, environments, events, objects, organizations, occurrences, activities and so on.

Planning a sampling strategy

There are several steps in planning the sampling strategy:

1 Decide whether you need a sample, or whether it is possible to have the whole population.
2 Identify the population, its important features (the sampling frame) and its size.
3 Identify the kind of sampling strategy you require (e.g. which variant of probability and non-probability sample you require).

4 Ensure that access to the sample is guaranteed. If not, be prepared to modify the sampling strategy (step 2).
5 For probability sampling, identify the confidence level and confidence intervals that you require.
   For non-probability sampling, identify the people whom you require in the sample.
6 Calculate the numbers required in the sample, allowing for non-response, incomplete or spoiled responses, attrition and sample mortality, i.e. build in redundancy.
7 Decide how to gain and manage access and contact (e.g. advertisement, letter, telephone, email, personal visit, personal contacts/friends).
8 Be prepared to weight (adjust) the data, once collected.

Conclusion

The message from this chapter is the same as for many of the others – that every element of the research should not be arbitrary but planned and deliberate, and that, as before, the criterion of planning must be *fitness for purpose*. The selection of a sampling strategy must be governed by the criterion of suitability. The choice of which strategy to adopt must be mindful of the purposes of the research, the time scales and constraints on the research, the methods of data collection, and the methodology of the research. The sampling chosen must be appropriate for all of these factors if validity is to be served.

To the question 'how large should my sample be?', the answer is complicated. This chapter has suggested that it all depends on:

- population size
- confidence level and confidence interval required
- accuracy required (the smallest sampling error sought)
- number of strata required
- number of variables included in the study
- variability of the factor under study

- the kind of sample (different kinds of sample within probability and non-probability sampling)
- representativeness of the sample
- allowances to be made for attrition and non-response

- need to keep proportionality in a proportionate sample.

That said, this chapter has urged researchers to use large rather than small samples, particularly in quantitative research.

Much educational research can be sensitive, in several senses, and researchers have to be acutely aware of a variety of delicate issues. This chapter sets out different ways in which educational research might be sensitive. It then takes two significant issues in the planning and conduct of sensitive research – sampling and access – and indicates why these twin concerns might be troublesome for researchers, and how they might be addressed. Our outline includes a discussion of gatekeepers and their roles. Sensitive research raises a range of difficult, sometimes intractable, ethical issues, and we set out some of these in the chapter. Investigations involving powerful people are taken as an instance of sensitive educational research, and this is used as a vehicle for examining several key problematic matters in this area. The chapter moves to a practical note, proffering advice on how to ask questions in sensitive research. Finally, the chapter sets out a range of key issues to be addressed in the planning, conduct and reporting of sensitive research.

What is sensitive research?

Sensitive research is that 'which potentially poses a substantial threat to those who are involved or have been involved in it' (Lee 1993: 4), or when those studied view the research as somehow undesirable (Van Meter 2000). Sensitivity can derive from many sources, including:

- Consequences for the participants (Sieber and Stanley 1988: 49).
- Consequences for other people, e.g. family members, associates, social groups and the wider community, research groups and institutions (Lee 1993: 5).

- Contents, e.g. taboo or emotionally charged areas of study (Farberow 1963), e.g. criminality, deviance, sex, race, bereavement, violence, politics, policing, human rights, drugs, poverty, illness, religion and the sacred, lifestyle, family, finance, physical appearance, power and vested interests (Lee 1993; Arditti 2002; Chambers 2003).
- Situational and contextual circumstances (Lee 1993).
- Intrusion into private spheres and deep personal experience (Lee and Renzetti 1993: 5), e.g. sexual behaviour, religious practices, death and bereavement, even income and age.
- Potential sanction, risk or threat of stigmatization, incrimination, costs or career loss to the researcher, participants or others, e.g. groups and communities (Lee and Renzetti 1993; Renzetti and Lee 1993; De Laine 2000), a particular issue for the researcher who studies human sexuality and who, consequently, suffers from 'stigma contagion', i.e. sharing the same stigma as those being studied (Lee 1993: 9).
- Impingement on political alignments (Lee 1993).
- Cultural and cross-cultural factors and inhibitions (Sieber 1992: 129).
- Fear of scrutiny and exposure (Payne *et al.* 1980);
- Threat to the researchers and to the family members and associates of those studied (Lee 1993); Lee (1993: 34) suggests that 'chilling' may take place, i.e. where researchers are 'deterred from producing or disseminating research' because they anticipate hostile reactions from colleagues, e.g. on race. 'Guilty knowledge' may bring personal and professional risk from colleagues; it

is threatening both to researchers and participants (De Laine 2000: 67, 84).

- Methodologies and conduct, e.g. when junior researchers conduct research on powerful people, when men interview women, when senior politicians are involved, or where access and disclosure are difficult (Simons 1989; Ball 1990; 1994a; Liebling and Shah 2001).

Sometimes all or nearly all of the issues listed above are present simultaneously. Indeed, in some situations the very activity of actually undertaking educational research *per se* may be sensitive. This has long been the situation in totalitarian regimes, where permission has typically had to be granted from senior government officers and departments in order to undertake educational research. Closed societies may permit educational research only on approved, typically non-sensitive and comparatively apolitical topics. As Lee (1993: 6) suggests: 'research for some groups . . . is quite literally an anathema'. The very *act* of doing the educational research, regardless of its purpose, focus, methodology or outcome, is itself a sensitive matter (Morrison 2006). In this situation the conduct of educational research may hinge on interpersonal relations, local politics and micro-politics. What start as being simply methodological issues can turn out to be ethical and political/micro-political minefields.

Lee (1993: 4) suggests that sensitive research falls into three main areas: intrusive threat (probing into areas which are 'private, stressful or sacred'); studies of deviance and social control, i.e. which could reveal information that could stigmatize or incriminate (threat of sanction); and political alignments, revealing the vested interests of 'powerful persons or institutions, or the exercise of coercion or domination', or extremes of wealth and status (Lee 1993). As Beynon (1988: 23) says, 'the rich and powerful have encouraged hagiography, not critical investigation'. Indeed, Lee (1993: 8) argues that there has been a tendency to 'study down' rather than 'study up', i.e. to direct attention to powerless rather than powerful groups, not least because these are easier and less sensitive

to investigate. Sensitive educational research can act as a voice for the weak, the oppressed, those without a voice or who are not listened to; equally it can focus on the powerful and those in high profile positions.

The three kinds of sensitivities indicated above may appear separately or in combination. The sensitivity concerns not only the topic itself, but also, perhaps more importantly, 'the relationship between that topic and the social context' within which the research is conducted (Lee 1993: 5). What appears innocent to the researcher may be highly sensitive to the researched or to other parties. Threat is a major source of sensitivity; indeed Lee (1993: 5) suggests that, rather than generating a list of sensitive topics, it is more fruitful to look at the conditions under which 'sensitivity' arises within the research process. Given this issue, the researcher will need to consider how sensitive the educational research will be, not only in terms of the subject matter itself, but also in terms of the several parties that have a stake in it, for example: headteachers and senior staff; parents; students; schools; governors; local politicians and policy-makers; the researcher(s) and research community; government officers; the community; social workers and school counsellors; sponsors and members of the public; members of the community being studied; and so on.

Sensitivity inheres not only in the educational topic under study, but also, much more significantly, in the social context in which the educational research takes place and on the likely consequences of that research on all parties. Doing research is not only a matter of designing a project and collecting, analysing and reporting data – that is the optimism of idealism or ignorance – but also a matter of interpersonal relations, potentially continual negotiation, delicate forging and sustaining of relationships, setback, modification and compromise. In an ideal world educational researchers would be able to plan and conduct their studies untrammelled; however, the ideal world, in the poet Yeats's words, is 'an image of air'. Sensitive educational research exposes this very clearly. While most educational research will incur sensitivities, the attraction of discussing sensitive research *per se* is that it highlights what these delicate issues might be and how they might be felt at their sharpest. We advise readers to consider most educational research as sensitive, to anticipate what those sensitivities might be, and what trade-offs might be necessary.

Sampling and access

Walford (2001: 33) argues that gaining access and becoming accepted is a slow process. Hammersley and Atkinson (1983: 54) suggest that gaining access not only is a practical matter but also provides insights into the 'social organisation of the setting'.

Lee (1993: 60) suggests that there are potentially serious difficulties in sampling and access in sensitive research, not least because of the problem of estimating the size of the population from which the sample is to be drawn, as members of particular groups, e.g. deviant or clandestine groups, will not want to disclose their associations. Similarly, like-minded groups may not wish to open themselves to public scrutiny. They may have much to lose by revealing their membership and, indeed, their activities may be illicit, critical of others, unpopular, threatening to their own professional security, deviant and less frequent than activities in other groups, making access to them a major obstacle. What if a researcher is researching truancy, or teenage pregnancy, or bullying, or solvent abuse among school students, or alcohol and medication use among teachers, or family relationship problems brought about by the stresses of teaching?

Lee (1993: 61) suggests several strategies to be used, either separately or in combination, for sampling 'special' populations (e.g. rare or deviant populations):

- *List sampling*: looking through public domain lists of, for example, the recently divorced (though such lists may be more helpful to social researchers than, specifically, educational researchers).
- *Multipurposing*: using an existing survey to reach populations of interest (though problems

of confidentiality may prevent this from being employed).

- *Screening*: targeting a particular location and canvassing within it (which may require much effort for little return).
- *Outcropping*: this involves going to a particular location where known members of the target group congregate or can be found (e.g. Humphreys' (1970) celebrated study of homosexual 'tearoom trade'); in education this may be a particular staffroom (for teachers), or meeting place for students. Outcropping risks bias, as there is no simple check for representativeness of the sample.
- *Servicing*: Lee (1993: 72) suggests that it may be possible to reach research participants by offering them some sort of service in return for their participation. Researchers must be certain that they really are able to provide the services promised. As Walford (2001: 36) writes: 'people don't buy products; they buy benefits', and researchers need to be clear on the benefits offered.
- *Professional informants*: Lee (1993: 73) suggests these could be, for example, police, doctors, priests, or other professionals. In education these may include social workers and counsellors. This may be unrealistic optimism, as these very people may be bound by terms of legal or ethical confidentiality or voluntary self-censorship (e.g. an AIDS counsellor, after a harrowing day at work, may not wish to continue talking to a stranger about AIDS counselling, or a social worker or counsellor may be constrained by professional confidentiality, or an exhausted teacher may not wish to talk about teaching difficulties). Further, Lee suggests that, even if such people agree to participate, they may not know the full story; Lee (1993: 73) gives the example of drug users whose contacts with the police may be very different from their contacts with doctors or social workers, or, the corollary of this, the police, doctors and social workers may not see the same group of drug users.
- *Advertising*: though this can potentially reach a wide population, it may be difficult to control

the nature of those who respond, in terms of representativeness or suitability.

- *Networking*: this is akin to snowball sampling, wherein one set of contacts puts the researcher in touch with more contacts, who puts the researcher in touch with yet more contacts and so on. This is a widely used technique, though Lee (1993: 66) reports that it is not always easy for contacts to be passed on, as initial informants may be unwilling to divulge members of a close-knit community. On the other hand, Morrison (2006) reports that networking is a popular technique where it is difficult to penetrate a formal organization such as a school, if the gatekeepers (those who can grant or prevent access to others, e.g. the headteacher or senior staff) refuse access. He reports the extensive use of informal networks by researchers, in order to contact friends and professional associates, and, in turn, their friends and professional associates, thereby sidestepping the formal lines of contact through schools.

Walford (2001: 36–47) sets out a four-step process of gaining access:

1 *Approach* (gaining entry, perhaps through a mutual friend or colleague – a link person). In this context Walford (2001) cautions that an initial letter should be used only to gain an initial interview or an appointment, or even to arrange to telephone the headteacher in order to arrange an interview, not to conduct the research or to gain access.

2 *Interest* (using a telephone call to arrange an initial interview). In this respect Walford (2001: 43) notes that headteachers like to talk, and so it is important to let them talk, even on the telephone when arranging an interview to discuss the research.

3 *Desire* (overcoming objections and stressing the benefits of the research). As Walford (2001: 44) wisely comments: 'after all, schools have purposes other than to act as research sites'. He makes the telling point that the research may actually benefit the school, but that the school may not realize this until it is

pointed out. For example, a headteacher may wish to confide in a researcher, teachers may benefit from discussions with a researcher, students may benefit from being asked about their learning.

4 *Sale* (where the participants agree to the research).

Whitty and Edwards (1994: 22) argue that in order to overcome problems of access, ingenuity and even the temptation to use subterfuge could be considered: 'denied co-operation initially by an independent school, we occasionally contacted some parents through their child's primary school and then told the independent schools we already were getting some information about their pupils'. They also add that it is sometimes necessary for researchers to indicate that they are 'on the same side' as those being researched.[1] Indeed they report that 'we were questioned often about our own views, and there were times when to be viewed suspiciously from one side proved helpful in gaining access to the other' (Whitty and Edwards 1994: 22). This harks back to Becker's (1968) advice to researchers to decide whose side they are on.

The use of snowball sampling builds in 'security' (Lee 1993), as the contacts are those who are known and trusted by the members of the 'snowball'. That said, this itself can lead to bias, as relationships between participants in the sample may consist of 'reciprocity and transitivity' (Lee 1993: 67), i.e. participants may have close relationships with one another and may not wish to break these. Thus homogeneity of the sample's attributes may result.

Such snowball sampling may alter the research, for example changing random, stratified or proportionate sampling into convenience sampling, thereby compromising generalizability or generating the need to gain generalizability by synthesizing many case studies. Nevertheless, it often comes to a choice between accepting non-probability strategies or doing nothing.

The issues of access to people in order to conduct sensitive research may require researchers to demonstrate a great deal of ingenuity and forethought in their planning. Investigators have to be adroit in anticipating problems of access, and set up their studies in ways that circumvent such problems, preventing them from arising in the first place, e.g. by exploring their own institutions or personal situations, even if this compromises generalizability. Such anticipatory behaviour can lead to a glut of case studies, action research and accounts of their own institutions, as these are the only kinds of research possible, given the problem of access.

Gatekeepers

Access might be gained through gatekeepers, that is, those who control access. Lee (1993: 123) suggests that 'social access crucially depends on establishing *interpersonal trust*. Gatekeepers play a significant role in research, particularly in ethnographic research (Miller and Bell 2002: 53). They control access and re-access (Miller and Bell 2002: 55). They may provide or block access; they may steer the course of a piece of research, 'shepherding the fieldworker in one direction or another' (Hammersley and Atkinson 1983: 65), or exercise surveillance over the research.

Gatekeepers may wish to avoid, contain, spread or control risk and therefore may bar access or make access conditional. Making research conditional may require researchers to change the nature of their original plans in terms of methodology, sampling, focus, dissemination, reliability and validity, reporting and control of data (Morrison 2006).

Morrison (2006) found that in conducting sensitive educational research there were problems of

- gaining access to schools and teachers
- gaining permission to conduct the research (e.g. from school principals)
- resentment by principals
- people vetting which data could be used
- finding enough willing participants for the sample
- schools/institutions/people not wishing to divulge information about themselves

- schools/institutions not wishing to be identifiable, even with protections guaranteed
- local political factors that impinge on the school/educational institution
- teachers'/participants' fear of being identified/traceable, even with protections guaranteed
- fear of participation by teachers (e.g. if they say critical matters about the school or others they could lose their contracts)
- unwillingness of teachers to be involved because of their workload
- the principal deciding on whether to involve the staff, without consultation with the staff
- schools' fear of criticism/loss of face or reputation
- the sensitivity of the research – the issues being investigated
- the power/position of the researcher (e.g. if the researcher is a junior or senior member of staff or an influential person in education).

Risk reduction may result in participants imposing conditions on research (e.g. on what information investigators may or may not use; to whom the data can be shown; what is 'public'; what is 'off the record' (and what should be done with off-the-record remarks). It may also lead to surveillance/'chaperoning' of the researcher while the study is being conducted on site (Lee 1993: 125).

Gatekeepers may want to 'inspect, modify or suppress the published products of the research' (Lee 1993: 128). They may also wish to use the research for their own ends, i.e. their involvement may not be selfless or disinterested, or they may wish for something in return, e.g. for the researcher to include in the study an area of interest to the gatekeeper, or to report directly – and maybe exclusively – to the gatekeeper. The researcher has to negotiate a potential minefield here, for example, not to be seen as an informer for the headteacher. As Walford (2001: 45) writes: 'headteachers [may] suggest that researchers observe certain teachers whom they want information about'. Researchers may need to reassure participants that their data will not be given to the headteacher.

On the other hand, Lee (1993: 127) suggests that the researcher may have to make a few concessions in order to be able to undertake the investigation, i.e. that it is better to do a little of the gatekeeper's bidding rather than not to be able to do the research at all.

In addition to gatekeepers the researcher may find a 'sponsor' in the group being studied. A sponsor may provide access, information and support. A celebrated example of this is in the figure of 'Doc' in Whyte's classic study of *Street Corner Society* (1993: the original study published in 1943). Here Doc, a leading gang figure in the Chicago street corner society, is quoted as saying (p. 292):

> You tell me what you want me to see, and we'll arrange it. When you want some information, I'll ask for it, and you listen. When you want to find out their philosophy of life, I'll start an argument and get it for you . . .. You won't have any trouble. You come in as a friend.
>
> (Whyte 1993: 292)

As Whyte writes:

> My relationship with Doc changed rapidly . . .. At first he was simply a key informant – and also my sponsor. As we spent more time together, I ceased to treat him as a passive informant. I discussed with him quite frankly what I was trying to do, what problems were puzzling me, and so on . . . so that Doc became, in a real sense, a collaborator in the research.
>
> (Whyte 1993: 301)

Whyte comments on how Doc was able to give him advice on how best to behave when meeting people as part of the research:

> Go easy on that 'who', 'what', 'why', 'when', 'where' stuff, Bill. You ask those questions and people will clam up on you. If people accept you, you can just hang around, and you'll learn the answers in the long run without even having to ask the questions'
>
> (Whyte 1993: 303)

Indeed Doc played a role in the writing of the research: 'As I wrote, I showed the various parts to Doc and went over them in detail. His criticisms were invaluable in my revision' (p. 341). In his

Box 5.1
Issues of sampling and access in sensitive research

- How to calculate the population and sample.
- How representative of the population the sample may or may not be.
- What kind of sample is desirable (e.g. random), but what kind may be the only sort that is practicable (e.g. snowball).
- How to use networks for reaching the sample, and what kinds of networks to utilize.
- How to research in a situation of threat to the participants (including the researcher).
- How to protect identities and threatened groups.
- How to contact the hard-to-reach.
- How to secure and sustain access.
- How to find and involve gatekeepers and sponsors.
- What to offer gatekeepers and sponsors.
- On what matters compromise may need to be negotiated.
- On what matters can there be no compromise.
- How to negotiate entry and sustained field relations.
- What services the researcher may provide.
- How to manage initial contacts with potential groups for study.

1993 edition, Whyte reflects on the study with the question as to whether he exploited Doc (p. 362); it is a salutary reminder of the essential reciprocity that might be involved in conducting sensitive research.

In addressing issues of sampling and access, there are several points that arise from the discussion (Box 5.1).

Much research stands or falls on the sampling. These points reinforce our view that, rather than barring the research altogether, compromises may have to be reached in sampling and access. It may be better to compromise rather than to abandon the research altogether.

Ethical issues in sensitive research

A difficulty arises in sensitive research in that researchers can be party to 'guilty knowledge' (De Laine 2000) and have 'dirty hands' (Klockars 1979) about deviant groups or members of a school who may be harbouring counter-attitudes to those prevailing in the school's declared mission. Pushed further, this means that researchers will need to decide the limits of tolerance, beyond which they will not venture. For example, in Patrick's (1973) study of a Glasgow gang, the researcher is witness to a murder. Should he report the matter to the police and, thereby, 'blow his cover', or remain silent in order to keep contact with the gang, thereby breaking the law, which requires a murder to be reported?

In interviewing students they may reveal sensitive matters about themselves, their family, their teachers, and the researcher will need to decide whether and how to act on this kind of information. What should the researcher do, for example, if, during the course of an interview with a teacher about the leadership of the headteacher, the interviewee indicates that the headteacher has had sexual relations with a parent, or has an alcohol problem? Does the researcher, in such cases, do nothing in order to gain research knowledge, or does the researcher act? What is in the public interest – the protection of an individual participant's private life, or the interests of the researcher? Indeed Lee (1993: 139) suggests that some participants may even deliberately engineer situations whereby the researcher gains 'guilty knowledge' in order to test the researcher's affinities: 'trust tests'.

Ethical issues are thrown into sharp relief in sensitive educational research. The question of covert research rises to the fore, as the study of deviant or sensitive situations may require the researcher to go under cover in order to obtain data. Covert research may overcome 'problems of reactivity' (Lee 1993: 143) wherein the research influences the behaviour of the participants (Hammersley and Atkinson 1983: 71). It may also enable the researcher to obtain insiders' true views, for, without the cover of those being researched not knowing that they are being researched, entry could easily be denied, and access to important areas of understanding could be lost. This is particularly so in the case of researching powerful people who may not wish to disclose information and who, therefore, may prevent or deny access. The ethical issue of informed consent, in this case, is violated in the interests of exposing matters that are in the public interest.

To the charge that this is akin to spying, Mitchell (1993: 46) makes it clear that there is a vast difference between covert research and spying:

- 'Spying is ideologically proactive, whereas research is ideologically naïve' (Mitchell 1993: 46). Spies, he argues, seek to further a particular value system or ideology; research seeks to understand rather than to persuade.
- Spies have a sense of mission and try to achieve certain instrumental ends, whereas research has no such specific mission.
- Spies believe that they are morally superior to their subjects, whereas researchers have no such feelings; indeed, with reflexivity being so important, they are sensitive to how their own role in the investigation may distort the research.
- Spies are supported by institutions which train them to behave in certain ways of subterfuge, whereas researchers have no such training.
- Spies are paid to do the work, whereas researchers often operate on a not-for-profit or individualistic basis.

On the other hand, not to gain informed consent could lead to participants feeling duped, very angry, used and exploited, when the results of the research are eventually published and they realize that they have been studied without their approval consent.[2] The researcher is seen as a predator (Lee 1993: 157), using the research 'as a vehicle for status, income or professional advancement which is denied to those studied'. As Lee (1993: 157) remarks, 'it is not unknown for residents in some ghetto areas of the United States to complain wryly that they have put dozens of students through graduate school'. Further, the researched may have no easy right of reply; feel misrepresented by the research; feel that they have been denied a voice; have wished not to be identified and their situation put into the public arena; feel that they have been exploited.

The cloak of anonymity is often vital in sensitive research, such that respondents are entirely untraceable. This raises the issue of 'deductive disclosure' (Boruch and Cecil 1979), wherein it is possible to identify individuals (people, schools, departments etc.) in question by reconstructing and combining data. Researchers should guard against this possibility. Where the details that are presented could enable identification of a person (e.g. in a study of a school there may be only one male teacher aged 50 who teaches biology, such that putting a name is unnecessary, as he will be identifiable), it may be incumbent on the researcher not to disclose such details, so that readers, even if they wished to reassemble the details in order to identify the respondent, are unable to do so.

The researcher may wish to preserve confidentiality, but may also wish to be able to gather data from individuals on more than one occasion. In this case a 'linked file' system (Lee 1993: 173) can be employed. Here three files are kept; in the first file the data are held and arbitrary numbers are assigned to each participant; the second file contains the list of respondents; the third file contains the list of information necessary to be able to link the arbitrarily assigned numbers from the first file to the names of the respondents in the second, and this third file is kept by a neutral 'broker', not the researcher. This procedure is akin to double-blind clinical experiments, in which the researcher does not know the names of those who are or are not receiving experimental medication or a placebo. That this may be easier in respect of quantitative rather than qualitative data is acknowledged by Lee (1993: 179).

Clearly, in some cases, it is impossible for individual people, schools and departments not to be identified, for example schools may be highly distinctive and, therefore, identifiable (Whitty and Edwards 1994: 22). In such cases clearance may need to be obtained for the disclosure of information. This is not as straightforward as it may seem. For example, a general principle of educational research is that no individuals should be harmed (non-maleficence), but what if a matter that is in the legitimate public interest (e.g. a school's failure to keep to proper accounting procedures) is brought to light? Should the researcher follow up the matter privately, publicly, or not at all? If it is followed up then certainly harm may come to the school's officers.

Ethical issues in the conduct of research are thrown into sharp relief against a backdrop of personal, institutional and societal politics, and the boundaries between public and private spheres are not only relative but also highly ambiguous. The ethical debate is heightened, for example concerning the potential tension between the individual's right to privacy versus the public's right to know and the concern not to damage or harm individuals versus the need to serve the public good. Because public and private spheres may merge, it is difficult, if not impossible, to resolve such tensions straightforwardly (cf. Day 1985; Lee 1993). As Walford (2001: 30) writes: 'the potential gain to public interest . . . was great. There would be some intrusion into the private lives of those involved, but this could be justified in research on . . . an important policy issue'. The end justified the means.

These issues are felt most sharply if the research risks revealing negative findings. To expose practices to research scrutiny may be like taking the plaster off an open wound. What responsibility to the research community does the researcher have? If a negative research report is released, will schools retrench, preventing future research in schools from being undertaken (a particular problem if the researcher wishes to return or wishes not to prevent further researchers from gaining access)? Whom is the researcher serving – the public, the schools, the research community? The sympathies of the researcher may be called into question here; politics and ethics may be uncomfortable bedfellows in such circumstances. Negative research data, such as the negative hidden curriculum of training for conformity in schools (Morrison 2005a) may not endear researchers to schools. This can risk stifling educational research – it is simply not worth the personal or public cost. As Simons (2000: 45) writes: 'the price is too high'.

Further, Mitchell (1993: 54) writes that 'timorous social scientists may excuse themselves from the risk of confronting powerful, privileged, and cohesive groups that wish to obscure their actions and interests from public scrutiny' (see also Lee 1993: 8). Researchers may not wish to take the risk of offending the powerful or of placing themselves in uncomfortable situations. As Simons and Usher (2000: 5) remark: 'politics and ethics are inextricably entwined'.

In private, students and teachers may criticize their own schools, for example, in terms of management, leadership, work overload and stress, but they may be reluctant to do so in public and, indeed, teachers who are on renewable contracts will not bite the hand that feeds them; they

may say nothing rather than criticize (Burgess 1993; Morrison 2001a; 2002b).

The field of ethics in sensitive research is different from ethics in everyday research in significance rather than range of focus. The same issues as must be faced in all educational research are addressed here, and we advise readers to review Chapter 2 on ethics. However, sensitive research highlights particular ethical issues very sharply; these are presented in Box 5.2.

These are only introductory issues. We refer the reader to Chapter 2 for further discussion of these and other ethical issues. The difficulty with ethical issues is that they are 'situated' (Simons and Usher 2000), i.e. contingent on specific local circumstances and situations. They have to be negotiated and worked out in relation to the specifics of the situation; universal guidelines may help but they don't usually solve the practical problems, they have to be interpreted locally.

Box 5.2
Ethical issues in sensitive research

- How does the researcher handle 'guilty knowledge' and 'dirty hands'?
- Whose side is the researcher on? Does this need to be disclosed? What if the researcher is not on the side of the researched?
- When is covert research justified?
- When is the lack of informed consent justified?
- Is covert research spying?
- How should the researcher overcome the charge of exploiting the participants (i.e. treating them as objects instead of as subjects of research)?
- How should the researcher address confidentiality and anonymity?
- How should the balance be struck between the individual's right to privacy and the public's right to know?
- What is really in the public interest?
- How to handle the situation where it is unavoidable to identify participants?
- What responsibility does the researcher have to the research community, some of whom may wish to conduct further research in the field?
- How does the researcher handle frightened or threatened groups who may reveal little?
- What protections are in the research, for whom, and from what?
- What obligations does the researcher have?

Researching powerful people

A branch of sensitive research concerns that which is conducted on, or with, powerful people, those in key positions, or elite institutions. In education, for example, this would include headteachers and senior teachers, politicians, senior civil servants, decision-makers, local authority officers and school governors. This is particularly the case in respect of research on policy and leadership issues (Walford 1994a: 3). Researching the powerful is an example of 'researching up' rather than the more conventional 'researching down' (e.g. researching children, teachers and student teachers).

What makes the research sensitive is that it is often dealing with key issues of policy generation and decision-making, or issues about which there is high-profile debate and contestation, as issues of a politically sensitive nature. Policy-related research is sensitive. This can be also one of the reasons why access is frequently refused. The powerful are those who exert control to secure what they want or can achieve, those with great responsibility and whose decisions have significant effects on large numbers of people.

Academic educational research on the powerful may be unlike other forms of educational research in that confidentiality may not be able to be assured. The participants are identifiable and public figures. This may produce 'problems of censorship and self-censorship' (Walford 1994c: 229). It also means that information given in confidence and 'off the record' unfortunately may have to remain so. The issue raised in researching the powerful is the disclosure of identities, particularly if it is unclear what has been said 'on the record' and 'off the record' (Fitz and Halpin 1994: 35–6).

Fitz and Halpin (1994) indicate that the government minister whom they interviewed stated, at the start of the interview, what was to be attributable. They also report that they used semi-structured interviews in their research of powerful people, valuing both the structure and the flexibility of this type of interview, and that they gained permission to record the interviews for later transcription, for the sake of a research record. They also used two interviewers for each session, one to conduct the main part of the interview and the other to take notes and ask supplementary questions; having two interviewers present also enabled a post-interview cross-check to be undertaken. Indeed having two questioners helped to negotiate the way through the interview in which advisers to the interviewee were also present, to monitor the proceedings and interject where deemed fitting, and to take notes (Fitz and Halpin 1994: 38, 44, 47).

Fitz and Halpin (1994: 40) comment on the considerable amount of gatekeeping that was present in researching the powerful, in terms of access to people (with officers guarding entrances and administrators deciding whether interviews will take place), places ('elite settings'), timing (and scarcity of time with busy respondents), 'conventions that screen off the routines of policy-making from the public and the academic gaze', conditional access and conduct of the research ('boundary maintenance') monitoring and availability (Fitz and Halpin 1994: 48–9). Gewirtz and Ozga (1994: 192–3) suggest that gatekeeping in researching the powerful can produce difficulties which include 'misrepresentation of the research intention, loss of researcher control, mediation of the research process, compromise and researcher dependence'.

Research with powerful people usually takes place on their territory, under their conditions and agendas (a 'distinctive civil service voice': Fitz and Halpin 1994: 42), working within discourses set by the powerful (and, in part, reproduced by the researchers), and with protocols concerning what may or may not be disclosed (e.g. under a government's Official Secrets Act or privileged information), within a world which may be unfamiliar and, thereby, disconcerting for researchers and with participants who may be overly assertive, and sometimes rendering the researcher as having to pretend to know less than he or she actually knows. As Fitz and Halpin (1994: 40) commented: 'we glimpsed an unfamiliar world that was only ever partially revealed', and one in which they did not always feel comfortable. Similarly, Ball (1994b: 113) suggests that 'we need to recognize ... the interview as an extension of the "play of power" rather than separate from it, merely a commentary upon it', and that, when interviewing powerful people 'the interview is both an ethnographic ... and a political event'. As Walford (1994c) remarks:

> Those in power are well used to their ideas being taken notice of. They are well able to deal with interviewers, to answer and avoid particular questions to suit their own ends, and to present their own role in events in a favourable light. They are aware of what academic research involves, and are familiar with being interviewed and having their words tape-recorded. In sum, their power in the educational world is echoed in the interview situation, and interviews pose little threat to their own positions.
>
> (Walford 1994c: 225)

McHugh (1994: 55) comments that access to powerful people may take place not only through formal channels but also through intermediaries who introduce researchers to them. Here his own vocation as a priest helped him to gain access to powerful Christian policy-makers and, as he was advised, 'if you say whom you have met, they'll know you are not a way-out person who will distort what they say' (McHugh 1994: 56). Access is a significant concern in researching the powerful, particularly if the issues being researched are controversial or contested. Walford (1994c: 222, 223) suggests that it can be eased through informal and personal 'behind the scenes' contacts: 'the more sponsorship that can be obtained, the better', be it institutional or personal. Access can be eased if the research is seen to be 'harmless' (Walford 1994c: 223); in this respect Walford reports that female researchers may be at an advantage in that they are viewed as more harmless and non-threatening. Walford also makes the point that 'persistence pays' (p. 224); as he writes elsewhere (Walford 2001: 31), 'access is a process and not a once-only decision'.

McHugh (1994) also reports the need for meticulous preparation for an interview with the powerful person, to understand the full picture and to be as fully informed as the interviewee, in terms of facts, information and terminology, so that it is an exchange between the informed rather than an airing of ignorance, i.e. to do one's homework. He also states the need for the interview questions to be thoroughly planned and prepared, with very careful framing of questions. McHugh (1994: 60, 62) suggests that during the interview it is important for the interviewer not only to be as flexible as possible, to follow the train of thought of the respondent, but also to be persistent if the interviewee does not address the issue. However, he reminds us that 'an interview is of course not a courtroom' (p. 62) and so tact, diplomacy and – importantly – empathy are essential. Diplomacy in great measure is necessary when tackling powerful people about issues that might reveal their failure or incompetence, and powerful people may wish to exercise control over which questions they answer. Preparation for the conduct as well as the content of the interview is vital.

There are difficulties in reporting sensitive research with the powerful, as charges of bias may be difficult to avoid, not least because research reports and publications are placed in the public domain. Walford (2001: 141) indicates the risk

of libel actions if public figures are named. He asks (1994b: 84) 'to what extent is it right to allow others to believe that you agree with them?', even if you do not? Should the researcher's own political, ideological or religious views be declared? As Mickelson (1994: 147) states: 'I was not completely candid when I interviewed these powerful people. I am far more genuine and candid when I am interviewing non-powerful people'. Deem (1994: 156) reports that she and her co-researcher encountered 'resistance and access problems in relation to our assumed ideological opposition to Conservative government education reforms', where access might be blocked 'on the grounds that ours was not a neutral study'.

Mickelson (1994: 147) takes this further in identifying an ethical dilemma when 'at times, the powerful have uttered abhorrent comments in the course of the interview'. Should the researcher say nothing, thereby tacitly condoning the speaker's comments, or speak out, thereby risking closing the interview? She contends that, in retrospect, she wished that she had challenged these views, and had been more assertive (Mickelson 1994: 148). Walford (2001) reports the example of an interview with a church minister whose views included ones with which he disagreed:

> AIDS is basically a homosexual disease ... and is doing a very effective job of ridding the population of undesirables. In Africa it's basically a non-existent disease in many places .... If you're a woolly woofter, you get what you deserve .... I would never employ a homosexual to teach at my school.
>
> (Walford 2001: 137)

In researching powerful people Mickelson (1994: 132) observes that they are rarely women, yet researchers are often women. This gender divide might prove problematic. Deem (1994: 157) reports that, as a woman, she encountered greater difficulty in conducting research than did her male colleague, even though, in fact, she held a more senior position than him. On the other hand, she reports that males tended to be more open with female than male researchers, as females researchers were regarded as less important. Gewirtz and Ozga (1994) report:

Box 5.3
Researching powerful people

- What renders the research sensitive.
- How to gain and sustain access to powerful people.
- How much the participants are likely to disclose or withhold.
- What is on and off the record.
- How to prepare for interviews with powerful people.
- How to probe and challenge powerful people.
- How to conduct interviews that balance the interviewer's agenda and the interviewee's agenda and frame of reference.
- How to reveal the researcher's own knowledge, preparation and understanding of the key issues.
- The status of the researcher vis-à-vis the participants.
- Who should conduct interviews with powerful people.
- How neutral and accepting the researcher should be with the participant.
- Whether to identify the participants in the reporting.
- How to balance the public's right to know and the individual's right to privacy.
- What is in the public interest.

we felt [as researchers] that we were viewed as women in very stereotypical ways, which included being seen as receptive and supportive, and that we were obliged to collude, to a degree, with that version of ourselves because it was productive of the project.

(Gewirtz and Ozga 1994: 196)

In approaching researching powerful people, then, it is wise to consider several issues. These are set out in Box 5.3.

Asking questions

In asking questions in research, Sudman and Bradburn (1982: 50–1) suggest that open questions may be preferable to closed questions and long questions may be preferable to short questions. Both of these enable respondents to answer in their own words, which might be more suitable for sensitive topics. Indeed they

suggest that while short questions may be useful for gathering information about attitudes, longer questions are more suitable for asking questions about behaviour, and can include examples to which respondents may wish to respond. Longer questions may reduce the under-reporting of the frequency of behaviour addressed in sensitive topics (for example, the use of alcohol or medication by stressed teachers). On the other hand, the researcher has to be cautious to avoid tiring, emotionally exhausting or stressing the participant by a long question or interview.

Lee (1993: 78) advocates using familiar words in questions as these can reduce a sense of threat in addressing sensitive matters and help the respondent to feel more relaxed. He also suggests the use of 'vignettes': 'short descriptions of a person or a social situation which contain precise references to what are thought to be the most important factors in the decision-making or judgement-making processes of respondents' (Lee 1993: 79). These can not only encapsulate concretely the issues under study, but also deflect attention away from personal sensitivities by projecting them onto another external object – the case or vignette – and the respondent can be asked to react to them personally, e.g. 'What would you do in this situation?'

Researchers investigating sensitive topics have to be acutely percipient of the situation themselves. For example, their non-verbal communication may be critical in interviews. They must, therefore, give no hint of judgement, support or condemnation. They must avoid counter-transference (projecting the researchers' own views, values, attitudes biases, background onto the situation). Interviewer effects are discussed in Chapter 16 in connection with sensitive research; these effects concern the characteristics of the researcher (e.g. sex, race, age, status, clothing, appearance, rapport, background, expertise, institutional affiliation, political affiliation, type of employment or vocation, e.g. a priest). Females may feel more comfortable being interviewed by a female; males may feel uncomfortable being interviewed by a female; powerful people may feel insulted by being interviewed by a lowly, novice research assistant. Interviewer effects also concern the expectations that the interviewers may have of the interview (Lee 1993: 99). For example, a researcher may feel apprehensive about, or uncomfortable with, an interview about a sensitive matter. Bradburn and Sudman (1979, in Lee 1993: 101) report that interviewers who did not anticipate difficulties in the interview achieved a 5–30 per cent higher level of reporting on sensitive topics than those who anticipated difficulties. This suggests the need for interviewer training.

Lee (1993: 102–14) suggests several issues to be addressed in conducting sensitive interviews:

- How to approach the topic (in order to prevent participants' inhibitions and to help them address the issue in their preferred way). Here the advice is to let the topic 'emerge gradually over the course of the interview' (Lee 1993: 103) and to establish trust and informed consent.

- How to deal with contradictions, complexities and emotions (which may require training and supervision of interviewers); how to adopt an accepting and non-judgemental stance, how to handle respondents who may not be people whom interviewers particularly like or with whom they agree).

- How to handle the operation of power and control in the interview: (a) where differences of power and status operate, where the interviewer has greater or lesser status than the respondent and where there is equal status between the interviewer and the respondent; (b) how to handle the situation where the interviewer wants information but is in no position to command that this be given and where the respondent may or may not wish to disclose information; (c) how to handle the situation wherein powerful people use the interview as an opportunity for lengthy and perhaps irrelevant self-indulgence; (d) how to handle the situation in which the interviewer, by the end of the session, has information that is sensitive and could give

the interviewer power over the respondent and make the respondent feel vulnerable; (e) what the interviewer should do with information that may act against the interests of the people who gave it (e.g. if some groups in society say that they are not clever enough to handle higher or further education); and (f) how to handle the conduct of the interview (e.g. conversational, formal, highly structured, highly directed).

- Handling the conditions under which the exchange takes place Lee (1993: 112) suggests that interviews on sensitive matters should 'have a one-off character', i.e. the respondent should feel that the interviewer and the interviewee may never meet again. This can secure trust, and can lead to greater disclosure than in a situation where a closer relationship between interviewer and interviewee exists. On the other hand, this does not support the development of a collaborative research relationship (Lee 1993: 113).

Much educational research is more or less sensitive; it is for the researcher to decide how to approach the issue of sensitivities and how to address their many forms, allegiances, ethics, access, politics and consequences.

Conclusion

In approaching educational research, our advice is to consider it to be far from a neat, clean, tidy, unproblematic and neutral process, but to regard it as shot through with actual and potential sensitivities. With this in mind we have resisted the temptation to provide a list of sensitive topics, as this could be simplistic and overlook the fundamental issue which is that it is the *social context* of the research that makes the research sensitive. What may appear to the researcher to be a bland and neutral study can raise deep sensitivities in the minds of the participants. We have argued that it is *these* that often render the research sensitive rather than the selection of topics of focus. Researchers have to consider the likely or possible effects of the research project, conduct, outcomes, reporting and dissemination not only on themselves but also on the participants, on those connected to the participants and on those affected by, or with a stakeholder interest in, the research (i.e. to consider 'consequential validity': the effects of the research). This suggests that it is wise to be cautious and to regard all educational research as potentially sensitive. There are several questions that can be asked by researchers, in their planning, conduct, reporting and dissemination of their studies, and we present these in Box 5.4.

These questions reinforce the importance of regarding ethics as 'situated' (Simons and Usher 2000), i.e. contingent on particular situations rather than largely on ethical codes and guidelines. In this respect sensitive educational research is like any other research, but sharper in the criticality of ethical issues. Also, behind many of these questions of sensitivity lurks the nagging issue of power: who has it, who does not, how it circulates around research situations (and with what consequences), and how it should be addressed. Sensitive educational research is often as much a power play as it is substantive. We advise researchers to regard most educational research as involving sensitivities; these need to be identified and addressed.

Box 5.4
Key questions in considering sensitive educational research

- What renders the research sensitive?
- What are the obligations of the researcher, to whom, and how will these be addressed? How do these obligations manifest themselves?
- What is the likely effect of this research (at all stages) to be on participants (individuals and groups), stakeholders, the researcher, the community? Who will be affected by the research, and how?
- Who is being discussed and addressed in the research?
- What rights of reply and control do participants have in the research?
- What are the ethical issues that are rendered more acute in the research?
- Over what matters in the planning, focus, conduct, sampling, instrumentation, methodology, reliability, analysis, reporting and dissemination might the researcher have to compromise in order to effect the research? On what can there be compromise? On what can there be no compromise?
- What securities, protections (and from what), liabilities and indemnifications are there in the research, and for whom? How can these be addressed?
- Who is the research for? Who are the beneficiaries of the research? Who are the winners and losers in the research (and about what issues)?
- What are the risks and benefits of the research, and for whom? What will the research 'deliver' and do?
- Should researchers declare their own values, and challenge those with which they disagree or consider to be abhorrent?
- What might be the consequences, repercussions and backlash from the research, and for whom?
- What sanctions might there be in connection with the research?
- What has to be secured in a contractual agreement, and what is deliberately left out?
- What guarantees must and should the researcher give to the participants?
- What procedures for monitoring and accountability must there be in the research?
- What must and must not, should and should not, may or may not, could or could not be disclosed in the research?
- Should the research be covert, overt, partially overt, partially covert, honest in its disclosure of intentions?
- Should participants be identifiable and identified? What if identification is unavoidable?
- How will access and sampling be secured and secure respectively?
- How will access be sustained over time?
- Who are the gatekeepers and how reliable are they?

6 Validity and reliability

There are many different types of validity and reliability. Threats to validity and reliability can never be erased completely; rather the effects of these threats can be attenuated by attention to validity and reliability throughout a piece of research.

This chapter discusses validity and reliability in quantitative and qualitative, naturalistic research. It suggests that both of these terms can be applied to these two types of research, though how validity and reliability are addressed in these two approaches varies. Finally validity and reliability are addressed, using different instruments for data collection. It is suggested that reliability is a necessary but insufficient condition for validity in research; reliability is a necessary precondition of validity, and validity may be a sufficient but not necessary condition for reliability. Brock-Utne (1996: 612) contends that the widely held view that reliability is the sole preserve of quantitative research has to be exploded, and this chapter demonstrates the significance of her view.

Defining validity

Validity is an important key to effective research. If a piece of research is invalid then it is worthless. Validity is thus a requirement for both quantitative and qualitative/naturalistic research (see http://www.routledge.com/textbooks/ 9780415368780 – Chapter 6, file 6.1. ppt).

While earlier versions of validity were based on the view that it was essentially a demonstration that a particular instrument in fact measures what it purports to measure, more recently validity has taken many forms. For example, in qualitative data validity might be addressed through the honesty, depth, richness and scope of the data achieved, the participants approached, the extent of triangulation and the disinterestedness or objectivity of the researcher (Winter 2000). In quantitative data validity might be improved through careful sampling, appropriate instrumentation and appropriate statistical treatments of the data. It is impossible for research to be 100 per cent valid; that is the optimism of perfection. Quantitative research possesses a measure of standard error which is inbuilt and which has to be acknowledged. In qualitative data the subjectivity of respondents, their opinions, attitudes and perspectives together contribute to a degree of bias. Validity, then, should be seen as a matter of degree rather than as an absolute state (Gronlund 1981). Hence at best we strive to minimize invalidity and maximize validity.

There are several different kinds of validity (see http://www.routledge.com/textbooks/ 9780415368780 – Chapter 6, file 6.2. ppt):

- content validity
- criterion-related validity
- construct validity
- internal validity
- external validity
- concurrent validity
- face validity
- jury validity
- predictive validity
- consequential validity
- systemic validity
- catalytic validity
- ecological validity
- cultural validity
- descriptive validity
- interpretive validity
- theoretical validity
- evaluative validity.

It is not our intention in this chapter to discuss all of these terms in depth. Rather the main types of validity will be addressed. The argument will be made that, while some of these terms are more comfortably the preserve of quantitative methodologies, this is not exclusively the case. Indeed, validity is the touchstone of all types of educational research. That said, it is important that validity in different research traditions is faithful to those traditions; it would be absurd to declare a piece of research invalid if it were not striving to meet certain kinds of validity, e.g. generalizability, replicability and controllability. Hence the researcher will need to locate discussions of validity within the research paradigm that is being used. This is not to suggest, however, that research should be paradigm-bound, that is a recipe for stagnation and conservatism. Nevertheless, validity must be faithful to its premises and positivist research has to be faithful to positivist principles, for example:

- controllability
- replicability
- predictability
- the derivation of laws and universal statements of behaviour
- context-freedom
- fragmentation and atomization of research
- randomization of samples
- observability.

By way of contrast, naturalistic research has several principles (Lincoln and Guba 1985; Bogdan and Biklen, 1992):

- The natural setting is the principal source of data.
- Context-boundedness and 'thick description' are important.
- Data are socially situated, and socially and culturally saturated.
- The researcher is part of the researched world.
- As we live in an already interpreted world, a doubly hermeneutic exercise (Giddens 1979) is necessary to understand others' understandings of the world; the paradox here is that the most

sufficiently complex instrument to understand human life is another human (Lave and Kvale 1995: 220), but that this risks human error in all its forms.

- There should be holism in the research.
- The researcher – rather than a research tool – is the key instrument of research.
- The data are descriptive.
- There is a concern for processes rather than simply with outcomes.
- Data are analysed inductively rather than using a priori categories.
- Data are presented in terms of the respondents rather than researchers.
- Seeing and reporting the situation should be through the eyes of participants – from the native's point of view (Geertz 1974).
- Respondent validation is important.
- Catching meaning and intention are essential.

Indeed Maxwell (1992) argues that qualitative researchers need to be cautious not to be working within the agenda of the positivists in arguing for the need for research to demonstrate concurrent, predictive, convergent, criterion-related, internal and external validity. The discussion below indicates that this need not be so. He argues, with Guba and Lincoln (1989), for the need to replace positivist notions of validity in qualitative research with the notion of authenticity. Maxwell (1992), echoing Mishler (1990), suggests that 'understanding' is a more suitable term than 'validity' in qualitative research. We, as researchers, are part of the world that we are researching, and we cannot be completely objective about that, hence other people's perspectives are equally as valid as our own, and the task of research is to uncover these. Validity, then, attaches to accounts, not to data or methods (Hammersley and Atkinson 1983); it is the meaning that subjects give to data and inferences drawn from the data that are important. 'Fidelity' (Blumenfeld-Jones 1995) requires the researcher to be as honest as possible to the self-reporting of the researched.

The claim is made (Agar 1993) that, in qualitative data collection, the intensive personal involvement and in-depth responses of individuals secure a sufficient level of validity and reliability. This claim is contested by Hammersley (1992: 144) and Silverman (1993: 153), who argue that these are insufficient grounds for validity and reliability, and that the individuals concerned have no privileged position on interpretation. (Of course, neither are actors 'cultural dopes' who need a sociologist or researcher to tell them what is 'really' happening!) Silverman (1993) argues that, while immediacy and authenticity make for interesting journalism, ethnography must have more rigorous notions of validity and reliability. This involves moving beyond selecting data simply to fit a preconceived or ideal conception of the phenomenon or because they are spectacularly interesting (Fielding and Fielding 1986). Data selected must be representative of the sample, the whole data set, the field, i.e. they must address content, construct and concurrent validity.

Hammersley (1992: 50–1) suggests that validity in qualitative research replaces certainty with confidence in our results, and that, as reality is independent of the claims made for it by researchers, our accounts will be only representations of that reality rather than reproductions of it.

Maxwell (1992) argues for five kinds of validity in qualitative methods that explore his notion of 'understanding':

- *Descriptive validity* (the factual accuracy of the account, that it is not made up, selective or distorted): in this respect validity subsumes reliability; it is akin to Blumenfeld-Jones's (1995) notion of 'truth' in research – what actually happened (objectively factual).
- *Interpretive validity* (the ability of the research to catch the meaning, interpretations, terms, intentions that situations and events, i.e. data, have for the participants/subjects themselves, in their terms): it is akin to Blumenfeld-Jones's (1995) notion of 'fidelity' – what it means to the researched person or group (subjectively meaningful); interpretive validity has no clear counterpart in experimental/positivist methodologies.

- *Theoretical validity* (the theoretical constructions that the researcher brings to the research, including those of the researched): theory here is regarded as explanation. Theoretical validity is the extent to which the research explains phenomena; in this respect is it akin to construct validity (discussed below); in theoretical validity the constructs are those of all the participants.
- *Generalizability* (the view that the theory generated may be useful in understanding other similar situations): generalizing here refers to generalizing *within* specific groups or communities, situations or circumstances validly and, beyond, to specific *outsider* communities, situations or circumstances (external validity); internal validity has greater significance here than external validity.
- *Evaluative validity* (the application of an evaluative, judgemental of that which is being researched, rather than a descriptive, explanatory or interpretive framework). Clearly this resonates with critical-theoretical perspectives, in that the researcher's own evaluative agenda might intrude.

Both qualitative and quantitative methods can address internal and external validity.

Internal validity

Internal validity seeks to demonstrate that the explanation of a particular event, issue or set of data which a piece of research provides can actually be sustained by the data. In some degree this concerns accuracy, which can be applied to quantitative and qualitative research. The findings must describe accurately the phenomena being researched.

In ethnographic research internal validity can be addressed in several ways (LeCompte and Preissle 1993: 338):

- using low-inference descriptors
- using multiple researchers
- using participant researchers
- using peer examination of data

- using mechanical means to record, store and retrieve data.

In ethnographic, qualitative research there are several overriding kinds of internal validity (LeCompte and Preissle 1993: 323–4):

- confidence in the data
- the authenticity of the data (the ability of the research to report a situation through the eyes of the participants)
- the cogency of the data
- the soundness of the research design
- the credibility of the data
- the auditability of the data
- the dependability of the data
- the confirmability of the data.

LeCompte and Preissle (1993) provide greater detail on the issue of authenticity, arguing for the following:

- *Fairness*: there should be a complete and balanced representation of the multiple realities in, and constructions of, a situation.
- *Ontological authenticity*: the research should provide a fresh and more sophisticated understanding of a situation, e.g. making the familiar strange, a significant feature in reducing 'cultural blindness' in a researcher, a problem which might be encountered in moving from being a participant to being an observer (Brock-Utne 1996: 610).
- *Educative authenticity*: the research should generate a new appreciation of these understandings.
- *Catalytic authenticity*: the research gives rise to specific courses of action.
- *Tactical authenticity*: the research should bring benefit to all involved – the ethical issue of 'beneficence'.

Hammersley (1992: 71) suggests that internal validity for qualitative data requires attention to

- plausibility and credibility
- the kinds and amounts of evidence required (such that the greater the claim that is being made, the more convincing the evidence has to be for that claim)

- clarity on the kinds of claim made from the research (e.g. definitional, descriptive, explanatory, theory generative).

Lincoln and Guba (1985: 219, 301) suggest that credibility in naturalistic inquiry can be addressed by

- *Prolonged engagement in the field*.
- *Persistent observation*: in order to establish the relevance of the characteristics for the focus.
- *Triangulation*: of methods, sources, investigators and theories.
- *Peer debriefing*: exposing oneself to a disinterested peer in a manner akin to cross-examination, in order to test honesty, working hypotheses and to identify the next steps in the research.
- *Negative case analysis*: in order to establish a theory that fits every case, revising hypotheses retrospectively.
- *Member checking*: respondent validation, to assess intentionality, to correct factual errors, to offer respondents the opportunity to add further information or to put information on record; to provide summaries and to check the adequacy of the analysis.

Whereas in positivist research history and maturation are viewed as threats to the validity of the research, ethnographic research simply assumes that this will happen; ethnographic research allows for change over time – it builds it in. Internal validity in ethnographic research is also addressed by the reduction of observer effects by having the observers sample both widely and staying in the situation for such a long time that their presence is taken for granted. Further, by tracking and storing information clearly, it is possible for the ethnographer to eliminate rival explanations of events and situations.

External validity

External validity refers to the degree to which the results can be generalized to the wider population, cases or situations. The issue of generalization is problematical. For positivist researchers generalizability is a *sine qua non*, while this is attenuated in naturalistic research. For one school of thought, generalizability through stripping out contextual variables is fundamental, while, for another, generalizations that say little about the context have little that is useful to say about human behaviour (Schofield 1990). For positivists variables have to be isolated and controlled, and samples randomized, while for ethnographers human behaviour is infinitely complex, irreducible, socially situated and unique.

Generalizability in naturalistic research is interpreted as comparability and transferability (Lincoln and Guba 1985; Eisenhart and Howe 1992: 647). These writers suggest that it is possible to assess the typicality of a situation – the participants and settings, to identify possible comparison groups, and to indicate how data might translate into different settings and cultures (see also LeCompte and Preissle 1993: 348). Schofield (1990: 200) suggests that it is important in qualitative research to provide a clear, detailed and in-depth description so that others can decide the extent to which findings from one piece of research are generalizable to another situation, i.e. to address the twin issues of *comparability* and *translatability*. Indeed, qualitative research can be generalizable (Schofield 1990: 209), by studying the typical (for its applicability to other situations – the issue of *transferability*: LeCompte and Preissle 1993: 324) and by performing multi-site studies (e.g. Miles and Huberman 1984), though it could be argued that this is injecting a degree of positivism into non-positivist research. Lincoln and Guba (1985: 316) caution the naturalistic researcher against this; they argue that it is not the researcher's task to provide an index of transferability; rather, they suggest, researchers should provide sufficiently rich data for the readers and users of research to determine whether transferability is possible. In this respect transferability requires thick description.

Bogdan and Biklen (1992: 45) argue that generalizability, construed differently from its usage in positivist methodologies, can be addressed in qualitative research. Positivist researchers, they argue, are more concerned to derive universal statements of general social processes rather than to provide accounts of the degree of commonality between various social settings (e.g. schools and classrooms). Bogdan and Biklen (1992) are more interested not with the issue of whether their findings are generalizable in the widest sense but with the question of the settings, people and situations to which they might be generalizable.

In naturalistic research threats to external validity include (Lincoln and Guba 1985: 189, 300):

- *selection effects:* where constructs selected in fact are only relevant to a certain group
- *setting effects:* where the results are largely a function of their context
- *history effects:* where the situations have been arrived at by unique circumstances and, therefore, are not comparable
- *construct effects:* where the constructs being used are peculiar to a certain group.

Content validity

To demonstrate this form of validity the instrument must show that it fairly and comprehensively covers the domain or items that it purports to cover. It is unlikely that each issue will be able to be addressed in its entirety simply because of the time available or respondents' motivation to complete, for example, a long questionnaire. If this is the case, then the researcher must ensure that the elements of the main issue to be covered in the research are both a fair representation of the wider issue under investigation (and its weighting) and that the elements chosen for the research sample are themselves addressed in depth and breadth. Careful sampling of items is required to ensure their representativeness. For example, if the researcher wished to see how well a group of students could spell 1,000 words in French but decided to have a sample of only 50 words for the spelling test, then that test would have to ensure that it represented the range of spellings in the 1,000 words – maybe by ensuring that the spelling rules had all been included or that possible spelling errors had been covered in the test in the proportions in which they occurred in the 1,000 words.

Construct validity

A construct is an abstract; this separates it from the previous types of validity which dealt in actualities – defined content. In this type of validity agreement is sought on the 'operationalized' forms of a construct, clarifying what we mean when we use this construct. Hence in this form of validity the articulation of the construct is important; is the researcher's understanding of this construct similar to that which is generally accepted to be the construct? For example, let us say that the researcher wished to assess a child's intelligence (assuming, for the sake of this example, that it is a unitary quality). The researcher could say that he or she construed intelligence to be demonstrated in the ability to sharpen a pencil. How acceptable a construction of intelligence is this? Is not intelligence something else (e.g. that which is demonstrated by a high result in an intelligence test)?

To establish construct validity the researcher would need to be assured that his or her *construction* of a particular issue agreed with other constructions of the same underlying issue, e.g. intelligence, creativity, anxiety, motivation. This can be achieved through correlations with other measures of the issue or by rooting the researcher's construction in a wide literature search which teases out the meaning of a particular construct (i.e. a theory of what that construct is) and its constituent elements. Demonstrating construct validity means not only confirming the construction with that given in relevant literature, but also looking for counter-examples which might falsify the researcher's construction. When the confirming and refuting evidence is balanced, the researcher is in a position to demonstrate construct validity, and can stipulate what he or she takes this construct to be. In the case of conflicting interpretations of a construct, the researcher might have to acknowledge that conflict and

then stipulate the interpretation that will be used.

In qualitative/ethnographic research construct validity must demonstrate that the categories that the researchers are using are meaningful *to the participants themselves* (Eisenhart and Howe 1992: 648), i.e. that they reflect the way in which the participants actually experience and construe the situations in the research, that they see the situation through the actors' eyes.

Campbell and Fiske (1959), Brock-Utne (1996) and Cooper and Schindler (2001) suggest that construct validity is addressed by convergent and discriminant techniques. *Convergent techniques* imply that different methods for researching the same construct should give a relatively high inter-correlation, while *discriminant techniques* suggest that using similar methods for researching different constructs should yield relatively low inter-correlations, i.e. that the construct in question is different from other potentially similar constructs. Such discriminant validity can also be yielded by factor analysis, which clusters together similar issues and separates them from others.

Ecological validity

In quantitative, positivist research variables are frequently isolated, controlled and manipulated in contrived settings. For qualitative, naturalistic research a fundamental premise is that the researcher deliberately does not try to manipulate variables or conditions, that the situations in the research occur naturally. The intention here is to give accurate portrayals of the realities of social situations in their own terms, in their natural or conventional settings. In education, ecological validity is particularly important and useful in charting how policies are actually happening 'at the chalk face' (Brock-Utne 1996: 617). For ecological validity to be demonstrated it is important to include and address in the research as many characteristics in, and factors of, a given situation as possible. The difficulty for this is that the more characteristics are included and described, the more difficult it is to abide by central ethical tenets of much research – non-traceability, anonymity and non-identifiability.

Cultural validity

A type of validity related to ecological validity is cultural validity (Morgan 1999). This is particularly an issue in cross-cultural, intercultural and comparative kinds of research, where the intention is to shape research so that it is appropriate to the culture of the researched, and where the researcher and the researched are members of different cultures. Cultural validity is defined as 'the degree to which a study is appropriate to the cultural setting where research is to be carried out' (Joy 2003: 1). Cultural validity, Morgan (1999) suggests, applies at all stages of the research, and affects its planning, implementation and dissemination. It involves a degree of sensitivity to the participants, cultures and circumstances being studied. Morgan (2005) writes that

> cultural validity entails an appreciation of the cultural values of those being researched. This could include: understanding possibly different target culture attitudes to research; identifying and understanding salient terms as used in the target culture; reviewing appropriate target language literature; choosing research instruments that are acceptable to the target participants; checking interpretations and translations of data with native speakers; and being aware of one's own cultural filters as a researcher.
>
> (Morgan 2005: 1)

Joy (2003: 1) presents twelve important questions that researchers in different cultural contexts may face, to ensure that research is culture-fair and culturally sensitive:

- Is the research question understandable and of importance to the target group?
- Is the researcher the appropriate person to conduct the research?
- Are the sources of the theories that the research is based on appropriate for the target culture?

- How do researchers in the target culture deal with the issues related to the research question (including their method and findings)?
- Are appropriate gatekeepers and informants chosen?
- Are the research design and research instruments ethical and appropriate according to the standards of the target culture?
- How do members of the target culture define the salient terms of the research?
- Are documents and other information translated in a culturally appropriate way?
- Are the possible results of the research of potential value and benefit to the target culture?
- Does interpretation of the results include the opinions and views of members of the target culture?
- Are the results made available to members of the target culture for review and comment?
- Does the researcher accurately and fairly communicate the results in their cultural context to people who are not members of the target culture?

Catalytic validity

Catalytic validity embraces the paradigm of critical theory discussed in Chapter 1. Put neutrally, catalytic validity simply strives to ensure that research leads to action. However, the story does not end there, for discussions of catalytic validity are substantive; like critical theory, catalytic validity suggests an agenda. Lather (1986, 1991) and Kincheloe and McLaren (1994) suggest that the agenda for catalytic validity is to help participants to understand their worlds in order to transform them. The agenda is explicitly political, for catalytic validity suggests the need to expose whose definitions of the situation are operating in the situation. Lincoln and Guba (1986) suggest that the criterion of 'fairness' should be applied to research, meaning that it should not only augment and improve the participants' experience of the world, but also improve the empowerment of the participants. In this respect the research might focus on what *might* be (the leading edge of innovations and future trends) and what *could* be (the ideal, possible futures) (Schofield 1990: 209).

Catalytic validity – a major feature in feminist research which, Usher (1996) suggests, needs to permeate all research – requires solidarity in the participants, an ability of the research to promote emancipation, autonomy and freedom within a just, egalitarian and democratic society (Masschelein 1991), to reveal the distortions, ideological deformations and limitations that reside in research, communication and social structures (see also LeCompte and Preissle 1993). Validity, it is argued (Mishler 1990; Scheurich 1996), is no longer an ahistorical given, but contestable, suggesting that the definitions of valid research reside in the academic communities of the powerful. Lather (1986) calls for research to be emancipatory and to empower those who are being researched, suggesting that catalytic validity, akin to Freire's (1970) notion of 'conscientization', should empower participants to understand and transform their oppressed situation.

Validity, it is proposed (Scheurich 1996), is but a mask that in fact polices and sets boundaries to what is considered to be acceptable research by powerful research communities; discourses of validity in reality are discourses of power to define worthwhile knowledge.

How defensible it is to suggest that researchers should have such ideological intents is, perhaps, a moot point, though not to address this area is to perpetuate inequality by omission and neglect. Catalytic validity reasserts the centrality of ethics in the research process, for it requires researchers to interrogate their allegiances, responsibilities and self-interestedness (Burgess 1989).

Consequential validity

Partially related to catalytic validity is consequential validity, which argues that the ways in which research data are used (the consequences of the research) are in keeping with the capability or intentions of the research, i.e. the consequences of the research do not exceed the capability of the research and the action-related consequences of the research are both legitimate and fulfilled. Clearly, once the research is in the public domain, the researcher has little or no control over the way in which it is used. However, and this is often a political matter, research should not be used in ways in which it was not intended to be used, for example by exceeding the capability of the research data to make claims, by acting on the research in ways that the research does not support (e.g. by using the research for illegitimate epistemic support), by making illegitimate claims by using the research in unacceptable ways (e.g. by selection, distortion) and by not acting on the research in ways that were agreed, i.e. errors of omission and commission.

A clear example of consequential validity is formative assessment. This is concerned with the extent to which students improve as a result of feedback given, hence if there is insufficient feedback for students to improve, or if students are unable to improve as a result of – a consequence of – the feedback, then the formative assessment has little consequential validity.

Criterion-related validity

This form of validity endeavours to relate the results of one particular instrument to another external criterion. Within this type of validity there are two principal forms: predictive validity and concurrent validity.

Predictive validity is achieved if the data acquired at the first round of research correlate highly with data acquired at a future date. For example, if the results of examinations taken by 16 year olds correlate highly with the examination results gained by the same students when aged 18, then we might wish to say that the first examination demonstrated strong predictive validity.

A variation on this theme is encountered in the notion of *concurrent validity*. To demonstrate this form of validity the data gathered from using one instrument must correlate highly with data gathered from using another instrument. For example, suppose it was decided to research a student's problem-solving ability. The researcher might observe the student working on a problem, or might talk to the student about how she is tackling the problem, or might ask the student to write down how she tackled the problem. Here the researcher has three different data-collecting instruments – observation, interview and documentation respectively. If the results all agreed – concurred – that, according to given criteria for problem-solving ability, the student demonstrated a good ability to solve a problem, then the researcher would be able to say with greater confidence (validity) that the student was good at problem-solving than if the researcher had arrived at that judgement simply from using one instrument.

Concurrent validity is very similar to its partner – predictive validity – in its core concept (i.e. agreement with a second measure); what differentiates concurrent and predictive validity is the absence of a time element in the former; concurrence can be demonstrated simultaneously with another instrument.

An important partner to concurrent validity, which is also a bridge into later discussions of reliability, is triangulation.

Triangulation

Triangulation may be defined as the use of two or more methods of data collection in the study of some aspect of human behaviour. The use of multiple methods, or the multi-method approach as it is sometimes called, contrasts with the ubiquitous but generally more vulnerable single-method approach that characterizes so much of research in the social sciences. In its original and literal sense, triangulation is a technique of physical measurement: maritime navigators, military strategists and surveyors, for example, use (or used to use) several locational markers in their endeavours to pinpoint a single spot or objective. By analogy, triangular techniques in the social sciences attempt to map out, or explain more fully, the richness and complexity of human behaviour by studying it from more than one standpoint and, in so doing, by making use of both quantitative and qualitative data. Triangulation is a powerful way of demonstrating concurrent validity, particularly in qualitative research (Campbell and Fiske 1959).

The advantages of the multi-method approach in social research are manifold and we examine two of them. First, whereas the single observation in fields such as medicine, chemistry and physics normally yields sufficient and unambiguous information on selected phenomena, it provides only a limited view of the complexity of human behaviour and of situations in which human beings interact. It has been observed that as research methods act as filters through which the environment is selectively experienced, they are never atheoretical or neutral in representing the world of experience (Smith 1975). Exclusive reliance on one method, therefore, may bias or distort the researcher's picture of the particular slice of reality being investigated. The researcher needs to be confident that the data generated are not simply artefacts of one specific method of collection (Lin 1976). Such confidence can be achieved, as far as nomothetic research is concerned, when different methods of data collection yield substantially the same results. (Where triangulation is used in interpretive research to investigate different actors' viewpoints, the same method, e.g. accounts, will naturally produce different sets of data.)

Further, the more the methods contrast with each other, the greater the researcher's confidence. If, for example, the outcomes of a questionnaire survey correspond to those of an observational study of the same phenomena, the more the researcher will be confident about the findings. Or, more extreme, where the results of a rigorous experimental investigation are replicated in, say, a role-playing exercise, the researcher will experience even greater assurance. If findings are artefacts of method, then the use of contrasting methods considerably reduces the chances of any consistent findings being attributable to similarities of method (Lin 1976).

We come now to a second advantage: some theorists have been sharply critical of the limited use to which existing methods of inquiry in the social sciences have been put. One writer, for example, comments:

> Much research has employed particular methods or techniques out of methodological parochialism or ethnocentrism. Methodologists often push particular pet methods either because those are the only ones they have familiarity with, or because they believe their method is superior to all others.
>
> (Smith 1975)

The use of triangular techniques, it is argued, will help to overcome the problem of 'method-boundedness', as it has been termed; indeed Gorard and Taylor (2004) demonstrate the value of combining qualitative and quantitative methods.

In its use of multiple methods, triangulation may utilize either normative or interpretive techniques; or it may draw on methods from both these approaches and use them in combination.

Referring us back to naturalistic inquiry, Lincoln and Guba (1985: 315) suggest that triangulation is intended as a check on data, while member checking, and elements of credibility, are to be used as a check on members' constructions of data.

Types of triangulation and their characteristics

We have just seen how triangulation is characterized by a multi-method approach to a problem in contrast to a single-method approach. Denzin (1970b) has, however, extended this view of triangulation to take in several other types as well as the multi-method kind which he terms 'methodological triangulation':

- *Time triangulation:* this type attempts to take into consideration the factors of change and process by utilizing cross-sectional and longitudinal designs. Kirk and Miller (1986) suggest that *diachronic reliability* seeks stability of observations over time, while *synchronic reliability* seeks similarity of data gathered in the same time.
- *Space triangulation:* this type attempts to overcome the parochialism of studies conducted in the same country or within the same subculture by making use of cross-cultural techniques.
- *Combined levels of triangulation:* this type uses more than one level of analysis from the three principal levels used in the social sciences, namely, the individual level, the interactive level (groups), and the level of collectivities (organizational, cultural or societal).
- *Theoretical triangulation:* this type draws upon alternative or competing theories in preference to utilizing one viewpoint only.
- *Investigator triangulation:* this type engages more than one observer, data are discovered independently by more than one observer (Silverman 1993: 99).
- *Methodological triangulation:* this type uses either the same method on different occasions, or different methods on the same object of study.

Many studies in the social sciences are conducted at one point only in time, thereby ignoring the effects of social change and process. Time triangulation goes some way to rectifying these omissions by making use of cross-sectional and longitudinal approaches. Cross-sectional studies collect data at one point in time; longitudinal studies collect data from the same group at different points in the time sequence. The use of panel studies and trend studies may also be mentioned in this connection. The former compare the same measurements for the same individuals in a sample at several different points in time; and the latter examine selected processes continually over time. The weaknesses of each of these methods can be strengthened by using a combined approach to a given problem.

Space triangulation attempts to overcome the limitations of studies conducted within one culture or subculture. As Smith (1975) says, 'Not only are the behavioural sciences culture-bound, they are sub-culture-bound. Yet many such scholarly works are written as if basic principles have been discovered which would hold true as tendencies in any society, anywhere, anytime'. Cross-cultural studies may involve the testing of theories among different people, as in Piagetian and Freudian psychology; or they may measure differences between populations by using several different measuring instruments. We have addressed cultural validity earlier.

Social scientists are concerned in their research with the individual, the group and society. These reflect the three levels of analysis adopted by researchers in their work. Those who are critical of much present-day research argue that some of it uses the wrong level of analysis, individual when it should be societal, for instance, or limits itself to one level only when a more meaningful picture would emerge by using more than one level. Smith (1975) extends this analysis and identifies seven possible levels: the aggregative or individual level, and six levels that are more global in that 'they characterize the collective as a whole, and do not derive from an accumulation of individual characteristics' (Smith 1975). The six levels include:

- *group analysis:* the interaction patterns of individuals and groups
- *organizational units of analysis:* units which have qualities not possessed by the individuals making them up
- *institutional analysis:* relationships within and across the legal, political, economic and familial institutions of society
- *ecological analysis:* concerned with spatial explanation
- *cultural analysis:* concerned with the norms, values, practices, traditions and ideologies of a culture
- *societal analysis:* concerned with gross factors such as urbanization, industrialization, education, wealth, etc.

Where possible, studies combining several levels of analysis are to be preferred. Researchers are sometimes taken to task for their rigid adherence to one particular theory or theoretical orientation to the exclusion of competing theories. Indeed Smith (1975) recommends the use of research to test competing theories.

Investigator triangulation refers to the use of more than one observer (or participant) in a research setting. Observers and participants working on their own each have their own observational styles and this is reflected in the resulting data. The careful use of two or more observers or participants independently, therefore, can lead to more valid and reliable data (Smith 1975), checking divergences between researchers leading to minimal divergence, i.e. reliability.

In this respect the notion of triangulation bridges issues of reliability and validity. We have already considered methodological triangulation earlier. Denzin (1970b) identifies two categories in his typology: 'within methods' triangulation and 'between methods' triangulation. Triangulation within methods concerns the replication of a study as a check on reliability and theory confirmation. Triangulation between methods involves the use of more than one method in the pursuit of a given objective. As a check on validity, the between methods approach embraces the notion of convergence between independent measures of the same objective (Campbell and Fiske 1959).

Of the six categories of triangulation in Denzin's typology, four are frequently used in education. These are: *time triangulation* with its longitudinal and cross-sectional studies; *space triangulation* as on the occasions when a number of schools in an area or across the country are investigated in some way; *investigator triangulation* as when two observers independently rate the same classroom phenomena; and *methodological triangulation*. Of these four, methodological triangulation is the one used most frequently and the one that possibly has the most to offer.

Triangular techniques are suitable when a more holistic view of educational outcomes is sought (e.g. Mortimore *et al.*'s (1988) search for school effectiveness), or where a complex phenomenon requires elucidation. Triangulation is useful when an established approach yields a limited and frequently distorted picture. Finally, triangulation can be a useful technique where a researcher is engaged in a case study, a particular example of complex phenomena (Adelman *et al.* 1980).

Triangulation is not without its critics. For example, Silverman (1985) suggests that the very notion of triangulation is positivistic, and that this is exposed most clearly in *data triangulation*, as it is presumed that a multiple data source (concurrent validity) is superior to a single data source or instrument. The assumption that a single unit can always be measured more than once violates the interactionist principles of emergence, fluidity, uniqueness and specificity (Denzin 1997: 320). Further, Patton (1980) suggests that even having multiple data sources, particularly of qualitative data, does not ensure consistency or replication. Fielding and Fielding (1986) hold that methodological triangulation does not necessarily increase validity, reduce bias or bring objectivity to research.

With regard to investigator triangulation, Lincoln and Guba (1985: 307) contend that it is erroneous to assume that one investigator will corroborate another, nor is this defensible, particularly in qualitative, reflexive inquiry. They extend their concern to include theory and methodological triangulation, arguing that the search for theory and methodological triangulation is epistemologically incoherent and empirically empty (see also Patton 1980). No two theories, it is argued, will ever yield a sufficiently complete explanation of the phenomenon being researched. These criticisms are trenchant, but they have been answered equally trenchantly by Denzin (1997).

Ensuring validity

It is very easy to slip into invalidity; it is both insidious and pernicious as it can enter at every stage of a piece of research. The attempt to build out invalidity is essential if the researcher is to be able to have confidence in the elements of the research plan, data acquisition, data processing analysis, interpretation and its ensuing judgement (see http://www.routledge.com/textbooks/9780415368780 – Chapter 6, file 6.3. ppt).

At the design stage, threats to validity can be minimized by:

- choosing an appropriate time scale
- ensuring that there are adequate resources for the required research to be undertaken
- selecting an appropriate methodology for answering the research questions
- selecting appropriate instrumentation for gathering the type of data required
- using an appropriate sample (e.g. one which is representative, not too small or too large)
- demonstrating internal, external, content, concurrent and construct validity and 'operationalizing' the constructs fairly
- ensuring reliability in terms of stability (consistency, equivalence, split-half analysis of test material)
- selecting appropriate foci to answer the research questions
- devising and using appropriate instruments: for example, to catch accurate, representative, relevant and comprehensive data (King *et al.* 1987); ensuring that readability levels are appropriate; avoiding any ambiguity of instructions, terms and questions; using instruments that will catch the complexity of issues; avoiding leading questions; ensuring that the level of test is appropriate – e.g. neither too easy nor too difficult; avoiding test items with little discriminability; avoiding making the instruments too short or too long; avoiding too many or too few items for each issue
- avoiding a biased choice of researcher or research team (e.g. insiders or outsiders as researchers).

There are several areas where invalidity or bias might creep into the research at the stage of data gathering; these can be minimized by:

- reducing the Hawthorne effect (see the accompanying web site: http://www.routledge.com/textbooks/9780415368780 – Chapter 6, file 6.1.doc)
- minimizing reactivity effects: respondents behaving differently when subjected to scrutiny or being placed in new situations, for example the interview situation – we distort people's lives in the way we go about studying them (Lave and Kvale 1995: 226)
- trying to avoid dropout rates among respondents
- taking steps to avoid non-return of questionnaires

- avoiding having too long or too short an interval between pretests and post-tests
- ensuring inter-rater reliability
- matching control and experimental groups fairly
- ensuring standardized procedures for gathering data or for administering tests
- building on the motivations of the respondents
- tailoring the instruments to the concentration span of the respondents and addressing other situational factors (e.g. health, environment, noise, distraction, threat)
- addressing factors concerning the researcher (particularly in an interview situation); for example, the attitude, gender, race, age, personality, dress, comments, replies, questioning technique, behaviour, style and non-verbal communication of the researcher.

At the stage of data analysis there are several areas where invalidity lurks; these might be minimized by:

- using respondent validation
- avoiding subjective interpretation of data (e.g. being too generous or too ungenerous in the award of marks), i.e. lack of standardization and moderation of results
- reducing the halo effect, where the researcher's knowledge of the person or knowledge of other data about the person or situation exerts an influence on subsequent judgements
- using appropriate statistical treatments for the level of data (e.g. avoiding applying techniques from interval scaling to ordinal data or using incorrect statistics for the type, size, complexity, sensitivity of data)
- recognizing spurious correlations and extraneous factors which may be affecting the data (i.e. tunnel vision)
- avoiding poor coding of qualitative data
- avoiding making inferences and generalizations beyond the capability of the data to support such statements
- avoiding the equating of correlations and causes
- avoiding selective use of data

- avoiding unfair aggregation of data (particularly of frequency tables)
- avoiding unfair telescoping of data (degrading the data)
- avoiding Type I and/or Type II errors (see http://www.routledge.com/textbooks/ 9780415368780 – Chapter 6, file 6.2.doc).

A Type I error is committed where the researcher rejects the null hypothesis when it is in fact true (akin to convicting an innocent person: Mitchell and Jolley 1988: 121); this can be addressed by setting a more rigorous level of significance (e.g. $\rho < 0.01$ rather than $\rho < 0.05$). A Type II error is committed where the null hypothesis is accepted when it is in fact not true (akin to finding a guilty person innocent: Mitchell and Jolley: 1988: 121). Boruch (1997: 211) suggests that a Type II error may occur if the measurement of a response to the intervention is insufficiently valid; the measurement of the intervention is insufficiently relevant; the statistical power of the experiment is too low; the wrong population was selected for the intervention.

A Type II error can be addressed by reducing the level of significance (e.g. $\rho < 0.20$ or $\rho < 0.30$ rather than $\rho < 0.05$). Of course, the more one reduces the chance of a Type I error, the more chance there is of committing a Type II error, and vice versa. In qualitative data a Type I error is committed when a statement is believed when it is, in fact, not true, and a Type II error is committed when a statement is rejected when it is in fact true.

At the stage of data reporting invalidity can show itself in several ways; the researcher must take steps to minimize this by, for example:

- avoiding using data selectively and unrepresentatively, for example, accentuating the positive and neglecting or ignoring the negative
- indicating the context and parameters of the research in the data collection and treatment, the degree of confidence which can be placed in the results, the degree of context-freedom or context-boundedness of the data (i.e. the level to which the results can be generalized)

...e data without misrepresenting its

...ims which are sustainable by the

- avoiding inaccurate or wrong reporting of data (i.e. technical errors or orthographic errors)
- ensuring that the research questions are answered; releasing research results neither too soon nor too late.

Having identified where invalidity lurks, the researcher can take steps to ensure that, as far as possible, invalidity has been minimized in all areas of the research.

Reliability in quantitative research

The meaning of reliability differs in quantitative and qualitative research (see http://www.routledge.com/textbooks/9780415368780 – Chapter 6, file 6.4 ppt). We explore these concepts separately in the next two sections. Reliability in quantitative research is essentially a synonym for dependability, consistency and replicability over time, over instruments and over groups of respondents. It is concerned with precision and accuracy; some features, e.g. height, can be measured precisely, while others, e.g. musical ability, cannot. For research to be reliable it must demonstrate that if it were to be carried out on a similar group of respondents in a similar context (however defined), then similar results would be found. There are three principal types of reliability: stability, equivalence and internal consistency (see http://www.routledge.com/textbooks/9780415368780 – Chapter 6, file 6.5. ppt).

Reliability as stability

In this form reliability is a measure of consistency over time and over similar samples. A reliable instrument for a piece of research will yield similar data from similar respondents over time. A leaking tap which each day leaks one litre is leaking reliably whereas a tap which leaks one litre some days and two litres on others is not. In the experimental and survey models of research this would mean that if a test and then a retest were undertaken within an appropriate time span, then similar results would be obtained. The researcher has to decide what an appropriate length of time is; too short a time and respondents may remember what they said or did in the first test situation, too long a time and there may be extraneous effects operating to distort the data (for example, maturation in students, outside influences on the students). A researcher seeking to demonstrate this type of reliability will have to choose an appropriate time scale between the test and retest. Correlation coefficients can be calculated for the reliability of pretests and post-tests, using formulae which are readily available in books on statistics and test construction.

In addition to stability over time, reliability as stability can also be stability over a similar sample. For example, we would assume that if we were to administer a test or a questionnaire simultaneously to two groups of students who were very closely matched on significant characteristics (e.g. age, gender, ability etc. – whatever characteristics are deemed to have a significant bearing, on the responses), then similar results (on a test) or responses (to a questionnaire) would be obtained. The correlation coefficient on this form of the test/retest method can be calculated either for the whole test (e.g. by using the Pearson statistic or a t-test) or for sections of the questionnaire (e.g. by using the Spearman or Pearson statistic as appropriate or a t-test). The statistical significance of the correlation coefficient can be found and should be 0.05 or higher if reliability is to be guaranteed. This form of reliability over a sample is particularly useful in piloting tests and questionnaires.

In using the test-retest method, care has to be taken to ensure (Cooper and Schindler 2001: 216) the following:

- The time period between the test and retest is not so long that situational factors may change.
- The time period between the test and retest is not so short that the participants will remember the first test.
- The participants may have become interested in the field and may have followed it up

themselves between the test and the retest times.

Reliability as equivalence

Within this type of reliability there are two main sorts. Reliability may be achieved first through using equivalent forms (also known as alternative forms) of a test or data-gathering instrument. If an equivalent form of the test or instrument is devised and yields similar results, then the instrument can be said to demonstrate this form of reliability. For example, the pretest and post-test in an experiment are predicated on this type of reliability, being alternate forms of instrument to measure the same issues. This type of reliability might also be demonstrated if the equivalent forms of a test or other instrument yield consistent results if applied simultaneously to matched samples (e.g. a control and experimental group or two random stratified samples in a survey). Here reliability can be measured through a t-test, through the demonstration of a high correlation coefficient and through the demonstration of similar means and standard deviations between two groups.

Second, reliability as equivalence may be achieved through inter-rater reliability. If more than one researcher is taking part in a piece of research then, human judgement being fallible, agreement between all researchers must be achieved, through ensuring that each researcher enters data in the same way. This would be particularly pertinent to a team of researchers gathering structured observational or semi-structured interview data where each member of the team would have to agree on which data would be entered in which categories. For observational data, reliability is addressed in the training sessions for researchers where they work on video material to ensure parity in how they enter the data.

At a simple level one can calculate the inter-rater agreement as a percentage:

$$\frac{\textit{Number of actual agreements}}{\textit{Number of possible agreements}} \times 100$$

Robson (2002: 341) sets out a more sophisticated way of measuring inter-rater reliability in coded

observational data, and his method can be used with other types of data.

Reliability as internal consistency

Whereas the test/retest method and the equivalent forms method of demonstrating reliability require the tests or instruments to be done twice, demonstrating internal consistency demands that the instrument or tests be run once only through the split-half method.

Let us imagine that a test is to be administered to a group of students. Here the test items are divided into two halves, ensuring that each half is matched in terms of item difficulty and content. Each half is marked separately. If the test is to demonstrate split-half reliability, then the marks obtained on each half should be correlated highly with the other. Any student's marks on the one half should match his or her marks on the other half. This can be calculated using the Spearman-Brown formula:

$$\text{Reliability} = \frac{2r}{1+r}$$

where r = the actual correlation between the halves of the instrument (see http://www.routledge.com/textbooks/9780415368780 – Chapter 6, file 6.6. ppt).

This calculation requires a correlation coefficient to be calculated, e.g. a Spearman rank order correlation or a Pearson product moment correlation.

Let us say that using the Spearman-Brown formula, the correlation coefficient is 0.85; in this case the formula for reliability is set out thus:

$$\text{Reliability} = \frac{2 \times 0.85}{1 + 0.85} = \frac{1.70}{1.85} = 0.919$$

Given that the maximum value of the coefficient is 1.00 we can see that the reliability of this instrument, calculated for the split-half form of reliability, is very high indeed.

This type of reliability assumes that the test administered can be split into two matched halves; many tests have a gradient of difficulty or different items of content in each half. If this is the case and, for example, the test contains twenty items, then the researcher, instead of splitting the test into two by assigning items one to ten to one half and items eleven to twenty to the second half, may assign all the even numbered items to one group and all the odd numbered items to another. This would move towards the two halves being matched in terms of content and cumulative degrees of difficulty.

An alternative measure of reliability as internal consistency is the Cronbach alpha, frequently referred to as the alpha coefficient of reliability, or simply the alpha. The Cronbach alpha provides a coefficient of inter-item correlations, that is, the correlation of each item with the sum of all the other relevant items, and is useful for multi-item scales. This is a measure of the internal consistency among the *items* (not, for example, the people). We address the alpha coefficient and its calculation in Part Five.

Reliability, thus construed, makes several assumptions, for example that instrumentation, data and findings should be controllable, predictable, consistent and replicable. This presupposes a particular style of research, typically within the positivist paradigm. Cooper and Schindler (2001: 218) suggest that, in this paradigm, reliability can be improved by minimizing any external sources of variation: standardizing and controlling the conditions under which the data collection and measurement take place; training the researchers in order to ensure consistency (inter-rater reliability); widening the number of items on a particular topic; excluding extreme responses from the data analysis (e.g. outliers, which can be done with SPSS).

Reliability in qualitative research

While we discuss reliability in qualitative research here, the suitability of the term for qualitative research is contested (e.g. Winter 2000; Stenbacka 2001; Golafshani 2003). Lincoln and Guba (1985) prefer to replace 'reliability' with terms such as 'credibility', 'neutrality', 'confirmability', 'dependability', 'consistency', 'applicability', 'trustworthiness' and 'transferability', in particular the notion of 'dependability'.

LeCompte and Preissle (1993: 332) suggest that the canons of reliability for quantitative research

may be simply unworkable for qualitative research. Quantitative research assumes the possibility of replication; if the same methods are used with the same sample then the results should be the same. Typically quantitative methods require a degree of control and manipulation of phenomena. This distorts the natural occurrence of phenomena (see earlier: ecological validity). Indeed the premises of naturalistic studies include the uniqueness and idiosyncrasy of situations, such that the study cannot be replicated – that is their strength rather than their weakness.

On the other hand, this is not to say that qualitative research need not strive for replication in generating, refining, comparing and validating constructs (see http://www.routledge.com/textbooks/9780415368780 – Chapter 6, file 6.7.ppt). Indeed LeCompte and Preissle (1993: 334) argue that such replication might include repeating

- the status position of the researcher
- the choice of informant/respondents
- the social situations and conditions
- the analytic constructs and premises that are used
- the methods of data collection and analysis.

Further, Denzin and Lincoln (1994) suggest that reliability as replicability in qualitative research can be addressed in several ways:

- *stability of observations:* whether the researcher would have made the same observations and interpretation of these if they had been observed at a different time or in a different place
- *parallel forms:* whether the researcher would have made the same observations and interpretations of what had been seen if he or she had paid attention to other phenomena during the observation
- *inter-rater reliability:* whether another observer with the same theoretical framework and observing the same phenomena would have interpreted them in the same way.

Clearly this is a contentious issue, for it is seeking to apply to qualitative research the canons of reliability of quantitative research. Purists might argue against the legitimacy, relevance or need for this in qualitative studies.

In qualitative research reliability can be regarded as a fit between what researchers record as data and what actually occurs in the natural setting that is being researched, i.e. a degree of accuracy and comprehensiveness of coverage (Bogdan and Biklen 1992: 48). This is not to strive for uniformity; two researchers who are studying a single setting may come up with very different findings but both sets of findings might be reliable. Indeed Kvale (1996: 181) suggests that, in interviewing, there might be as many different interpretations of the qualitative data as there are researchers. A clear example of this is the study of the Nissan automobile factory in the United Kingdom, where Wickens (1987) found a 'virtuous circle' of work organization practices that demonstrated flexibility, teamwork and quality consciousness, whereas the same practices were investigated by Garrahan and Stewart (1992), who found a 'vicious circle' of exploitation, surveillance and control respectively. Both versions of the same reality coexist because reality is multilayered. What is being argued for here is the notion of reliability through an eclectic use of instruments, researchers, perspectives and interpretations (echoing the comments earlier about triangulation) (see also Eisenhart and Howe 1992).

Brock-Utne (1996) argues that qualitative research, being holistic, strives to record the multiple interpretations of, intention in and meanings given to situations and events. Here the notion of reliability is construed as *dependability* (Lincoln and Guba 1985: 108–9; Anfara *et al.* 2002), recalling the earlier discussion on internal validity. For them, dependability involves member checks (respondent validation), debriefing by peers, triangulation, prolonged engagement in the field, persistent observations in the field, reflexive journals, negative case analysis, and independent audits (identifying acceptable processes of conducting the inquiry so that the results are consistent with the data). Audit trails enable the research to address the issue of confirmability of

results, in terms of process and product (Golafshani 2003: 601). These are a safeguard against the charge levelled against qualitative researchers, namely that they respond only to the 'loudest bangs or the brightest lights'.

Dependability raises the important issue of *respondent validation* (see also McCormick and James 1988). While dependability might suggest that researchers need to go back to respondents to check that their findings are dependable, researchers also need to be cautious in placing exclusive store on respondents, for, as Hammersley and Atkinson (1983) suggest, they are not in a privileged position to be sole commentators on their actions.

Bloor (1978) suggests three means by which respondent validation can be addressed:

- researchers attempt to predict what the participants' classifications of situations will be
- researchers prepare hypothetical cases and then predict respondents' likely responses to them
- researchers take back their research report to the respondents and record their reactions to that report.

The argument rehearses the paradigm wars discussed in the opening chapter: quantitative measures are criticized for combining sophistication and refinement of process with crudity of concept (Ruddock 1981) and for failing to distinguish between educational and statistical significance (Eisner 1985); qualitative methodologies, while possessing immediacy, flexibility, authenticity, richness and candour, are criticized for being impressionistic, biased, commonplace, insignificant, ungeneralizable, idiosyncratic, subjective and short-sighted (Ruddock 1981). This is an arid debate; rather the issue is one of fitness for purpose. For our purposes here we need to note that criteria of reliability in quantitative methodologies differ from those in qualitative methodologies. In qualitative methodologies reliability includes fidelity to real life, context- and situation-specificity, authenticity, comprehensiveness, detail, honesty, depth of response and meaningfulness to the respondents.

Validity and reliability in interviews

In interviews, inferences about validity are made too often on the basis of face validity (Cannell and Kahn 1968), that is, whether the questions asked look as if they are measuring what they claim to measure. One cause of invalidity is bias, defined as 'a systematic or persistent tendency to make errors in the same direction, that is, to overstate or understate the "true value" of an attribute' (Lansing *et al.* 1961). One way of validating interview measures is to compare the interview measure with another measure that has already been shown to be valid. This kind of comparison is known as 'convergent validity'. If the two measures agree, it can be assumed that the validity of the interview is comparable with the proven validity of the other measure.

Perhaps the most practical way of achieving greater validity is to minimize the amount of bias as much as possible. The sources of bias are the characteristics of the interviewer, the characteristics of the respondent, and the substantive content of the questions. More particularly, these will include:

- the attitudes, opinions and expectations of the interviewer
- a tendency for the interviewer to see the respondent in his or her own image
- a tendency for the interviewer to seek answers that support preconceived notions
- misperceptions on the part of the interviewer of what the respondent is saying
- misunderstandings on the part of the respondent of what is being asked.

Studies have also shown that race, religion, gender, sexual orientation, status, social class and age in certain contexts can be potent sources of bias, i.e. interviewer effects (Lee 1993; Scheurich 1995). Interviewers and interviewees alike bring their own, often unconscious, experiential and biographical baggage with them into the interview situation. Indeed Hitchcock and Hughes (1989) argue that because interviews are interpersonal, humans interacting with humans, it is inevitable that the researcher will have some influence on the interviewee and, thereby, on the data. Fielding and Fielding (1986: 12) make the telling comment that even the most sophisticated surveys only manipulate data that at some time had to be gained by asking people! Interviewer neutrality is a chimera (Denscombe 1995).

Lee (1993) indicates the problems of conducting interviews perhaps at their sharpest, where the researcher is researching sensitive subjects, i.e. research that might pose a significant threat to those involved (be they interviewers or interviewees). Here the interview might be seen as an intrusion into private worlds, or the interviewer might be regarded as someone who can impose sanctions on the interviewee, or as someone who can exploit the powerless; the interviewee is in the searchlight that is being held by the interviewer (see also Scheurich 1995). Indeed Gadd (2004) reports that an interviewee may reduce his or her willingness to 'open up' to an interviewer if the dynamics of the interview situation are too threatening, taking the role of the 'defended subject'. The issues also embrace *transference* and *counter-transference*, which have their basis in psychoanalysis. In transference the interviewees project onto the interviewer their feelings, fears, desires, needs and attitudes that derive from their own experiences (Scheurich 1995). In counter-transference the process is reversed.

One way of controlling for reliability is to have a highly structured interview, with the same format and sequence of words and questions for each respondent (Silverman 1993), though Scheurich (1995: 241–9) suggests that this is to misread the infinite complexity and open-endedness of social interaction. Controlling the wording is no guarantee of controlling the interview. Oppenheim (1992: 147) argues that wording is a particularly important factor in attitudinal questions rather than factual questions. He suggests that changes in wording, context and emphasis undermine reliability, because it ceases to be the same question for each respondent. Indeed he argues that error and bias can stem from alterations to wording, procedure, sequence, recording and rapport, and that training for interviewers is essential to minimize this. Silverman (1993) suggests that it is important for each interviewee to understand the question in the same way. He suggests that the reliability of interviews can be enhanced by: careful piloting of interview schedules; training of interviewers; inter-rater reliability in the coding of responses; and the extended use of closed questions.

On the other hand, Silverman (1993) argues for the importance of open-ended interviews, as this enables respondents to demonstrate their unique way of looking at the world – their definition of the situation. It recognizes that what is a suitable sequence of questions for one respondent might be less suitable for another, and open-ended questions enable important but unanticipated issues to be raised.

Oppenheim (1992: 96–7) suggests several causes of bias in interviewing:

- biased sampling (sometimes created by the researcher not adhering to sampling instructions)
- poor rapport between interviewer and interviewee
- changes to question wording (e.g. in attitudinal and factual questions)
- poor prompting and biased probing
- poor use and management of support materials (e.g. show cards)
- alterations to the sequence of questions
- inconsistent coding of responses
- selective or interpreted recording of data/ transcripts
- poor handling of difficult interviews.

One can add to this the issue of 'acquiescence' (Breakwell 2000: 254), the tendency that respondents may have to say 'yes', regardless of the question or, indeed, regardless of what they really feel or think.

There is also the issue of *leading questions*. A leading question is one which makes assumptions about interviewees or 'puts words into their mouths', where the question influences the answer, perhaps illegitimately. For example (Morrison 1993: 66–7) the question 'When did you stop complaining to the headteacher?' assumes that the interviewee had been a frequent com and the question 'How satisfied are you with the new Mathematics scheme?' assumes a degree of satisfaction with the scheme. The leading questions here might be rendered less leading by rephrasing, for example: 'How frequently do you have conversations with the headteacher?' and 'What is your opinion of the new Mathematics scheme?' respectively.

In discussing the issue of leading questions, we are not necessarily suggesting that there is not a place for them. Indeed Kvale (1996: 158) makes a powerful case *for* leading questions, arguing that they may be necessary in order to obtain information that the interviewer suspects the interviewee might be withholding. Here it might be important to put the 'burden of denial' onto the interviewee (e.g. 'When did you stop beating your wife?'). Leading questions, frequently used in police interviews, may be used for reliability checks with what the interviewee has already said, or may be deliberately used to elicit particular non-verbal behaviours that give an indication of the sensitivity of the interviewee's remarks.

Hence reducing bias becomes more than simply: careful formulation of questions so that the meaning is crystal clear; thorough training procedures so that an interviewer is more aware of the possible problems; probability sampling of respondents; and sometimes matching interviewer characteristics with those of the sample being interviewed. Oppenheim (1992: 148) argues, for example, that interviewers seeking attitudinal responses have to ensure that people with known characteristics are included in the sample – the criterion group. We need to recognize that the interview is a shared, negotiated and dynamic social moment.

The notion of power is significant in the interview situation, for the interview is not simply a data collection situation but a social and frequently a political situation. Literally the word 'inter-view' is a view *between* people, mutually, not the interviewer extracting data, one-way, from the interviewee. Power can reside with interviewer and interviewee alike (Thapar-Björkert and Henry 2004), though Scheurich (1995: 246) argues that, typically, more power resides with the interviewer: the interviewer generates the questions and the interviewee answers them; the interviewee is under scrutiny while the interviewer is not. Kvale (1996: 126), too, suggests that there are definite asymmetries of power as the interviewer tends to define the situation, the topics, and the course of the interview.

J. Cassell (cited in Lee 1993) suggests that elites and powerful people might feel demeaned or insulted when being interviewed by those with a lower status or less power. Further, those with power, resources and expertise might be anxious to maintain their reputation, and so will be more guarded in what they say, wrapping this up in well-chosen, articulate phrases. Lee (1993) comments on the asymmetries of power in several interview situations, with one party having more power and control over the interview than the other. Interviewers need to be aware of the potentially distorting effects of power, a significant feature of critical theory, as discussed in Chapter 1.

Neal (1995) draws attention to the feelings of powerlessness and anxieties about physical presentation and status on the part of interviewers when interviewing powerful people. This is particularly so for frequently lone, low-status research students interviewing powerful people; a low-status female research student might find that an interview with a male in a position of power (e.g. a university Vice-chancellor, a senior politician or a senior manager) might turn out to be very different from an interview with the same person if conducted by a male university professor where it is perceived by the interviewee to be more of a dialogue between equals (see also Gewirtz and Ozga 1993, 1994). Ball (1994b) comments that, when powerful people are being interviewed, interviews must be seen as an extension of the 'play of power' – with its game-like connotations. He suggests that powerful people control the agenda and course of the interview, and are usually very adept at this because they have both a personal and professional investment in being interviewed (see also Batteson and Ball 1995; Phillips 1998).

The effect of power can be felt even before the interview commences, notes Neal (1995),

where she instances being kept waiting, and subsequently being interrupted, being patronized, and being interviewed by the interviewee (see also Walford 1994d). Indeed Scheurich (1995) suggests that many powerful interviewees will rephrase or not answer the question. Connell et al. (1996) argue that a working-class female talking with a multinational director will be very different from a middle-class professor talking to the same person. Limerick et al. (1996) comment on occasions where interviewers have felt themselves to be passive, vulnerable, helpless and indeed manipulated. One way of overcoming this is to have two interviewers conducting each interview (Walford 1994c: 227). On the other hand, Hitchcock and Hughes (1989) observe that if the researchers are known to the interviewees and they are peers, however powerful, then a degree of reciprocity might be taking place, with interviewees giving answers that they think the researchers might want to hear.

The issue of power has not been lost on feminist research (e.g. Thapar-Björkert and Henry 2004), that is, research that emphasizes subjectivity, equality, reciprocity, collaboration, non-hierarchical relations and emancipatory potential (catalytic and consequential validity) (Neal 1995), echoing the comments about research that is influenced by the paradigm of critical theory. Here feminist research addresses a dilemma of interviews that are constructed in the dominant, male paradigm of pitching questions that demand answers from a passive respondent.

Limerick et al. (1996) suggest that, in fact, it is wiser to regard the interview as a gift, as interviewees have the power to withhold information, to choose the location of the interview, to choose how seriously to attend to the interview, how long it will last, when it will take place, what will be discussed – and in what and whose terms – what knowledge is important, even how the data will be analysed and used (see also Thapar-Björkert and Henry 2004). Echoing Foucault, they argue that power is fluid and is discursively constructed through the interview rather than being the province of either party.

Miller and Cannell (1997) identify some particular problems in conducting telephone interviews, where the reduction of the interview situation to just auditory sensory cues can be particularly problematical. There are sampling problems, as not everyone will have a telephone. Further, there are practical issues, for example, interviewees can retain only a certain amount of information in their short-term memory, so bombarding the interviewee with too many choices (the non-written form of 'show cards' of possible responses) becomes unworkable. Hence the reliability of responses is subject to the memory capabilities of the interviewee – how many scale points and descriptors, for example, can an interviewee retain about a single item? Further, the absence of non-verbal cues is significant, e.g. facial expression, gestures, posture, the significance of silences and pauses (Robinson 1982), as interviewees may be unclear about the meaning behind words and statements. This problem is compounded if the interviewer is unknown to the interviewee.

Miller and Cannell (1997) report important research evidence to support the significance of the non-verbal mediation of verbal dialogue. As discussed earlier, the interview is a social situation; in telephone interviews the absence of essential social elements could undermine the salient conduct of the interview, and hence its reliability and validity. Non-verbal paralinguistic cues affect the conduct, pacing and relationships in the interview and the support, threat and confidence felt by the interviewees. Telephone interviews can easily slide into becoming mechanical and cold. Further, the problem of loss of non-verbal cues is compounded by the asymmetries of power that often exist between interviewer and interviewee; the interviewer will need to take immediate steps to address these issues (e.g. by putting interviewees at their ease).

On the other hand, Nias (1991) and Miller and Cannell (1997) suggest that the very factor that interviews are not face-to-face may strengthen their reliability, as the interviewee might disclose information that may not be so readily forthcoming in a face-to-face, more intimate situation. Hence, telephone interviews have their strengths and weaknesses, and their use should be governed by the criterion of fitness for purpose. They tend to be shorter, more focused and useful for contacting busy people (Harvey 1988; Miller, 1995).

In his critique of the interview as a research tool, Kitwood (1977) draws attention to the conflict it generates between the traditional concepts of validity and reliability. Where increased reliability of the interview is brought about by greater control of its elements, this is achieved, he argues, at the cost of reduced validity. He explains:

> In proportion to the extent to which 'reliability' is enhanced by rationalization, 'validity' would decrease. For the main purpose of using an interview in research is that it is believed that in an interpersonal encounter people are more likely to disclose aspects of themselves, their thoughts, their feelings and values, than they would in a less human situation. At least for some purposes, it is necessary to generate a kind of conversation in which the 'respondent' feels at ease. In other words, the distinctively human element in the interview is necessary to its 'validity'. The more the interviewer becomes rational, calculating, and detached, the less likely the interview is to be perceived as a friendly transaction, and the more calculated the response also is likely to be.
>
> (Kitwood 1977)

Kitwood (1977) suggests that a solution to the problem of validity and reliability might lie in the direction of a 'judicious compromise'.

A cluster of problems surround the person being interviewed. Tuckman (1972), for example, has observed that, when formulating their questions, interviewers have to consider the extent to which a question might influence respondents to show themselves in a good light; or the extent to which a question might influence respondents to be unduly helpful by attempting to anticipate what the interviewer wants to hear; or the extent to which a question might be asking for information about respondents that they are not certain or likely to know themselves. Further, interviewing procedures are based on the assumption that the people interviewed have insight into the cause of their behaviour. Insight of this kind may be rarely achieved and, when it is, it is after long and difficult effort, usually in the context of repeated clinical interviews.

In educational circles interviewing might be a particular problem in working with children. Simons (1982) and McCormick and James (1988) comment on particular problems involved in interviewing children, for example:

- establishing trust
- overcoming reticence
- maintaining informality
- avoiding assuming that children 'know the answers'
- overcoming the problems of inarticulate children
- pitching the question at the right level
- choosing the right vocabulary
- being aware of the giving and receiving of non-verbal cues
- moving beyond the institutional response or receiving what children think the interviewer wants to hear
- avoiding the interviewer being seen as an authority, spy or plant
- keeping to the point
- breaking silences on taboo areas and those which are reinforced by peer-group pressure
- seeing children as being of lesser importance than adults (maybe in the sequence in which interviews are conducted, e.g. the headteacher, then the teaching staff, then the children).

These are not new matters. The studies by Labov in the 1960s showed how students reacted very strongly to contextual matters in an interview situation (Labov 1969). The language of children varied according to the ethnicity of the interviewee, the friendliness of the surroundings, the opportunity for the children to be interviewed with friends, the ease with which the scene was set for the interview, the demeanour of the adult (e.g. whether the adult was standing or sitting) and the nature of the topics covered. The differences were significant, varying from monosyllabic responses by children

in unfamiliar and uncongenial surroundings to extended responses in the more congenial and less threatening surroundings – more sympathetic to the children's everyday world. The language, argot and jargon (Edwards 1976), social and cultural factors of the interviewer and interviewee all exert a powerful influence on the interview situation.

The issue is also raised here (Lee 1993) of whether there should be a single interview that maintains the detachment of the researcher (perhaps particularly useful in addressing sensitive topics), or whether there should be repeated interviews to gain depth and to show fidelity to the collaborative nature of research (a feature, as was noted above, which is significant for feminist research: Oakley 1981).

Kvale (1996: 148–9) suggests that a skilled interviewer should:

- know the subject matter in order to conduct an informed conversation
- structure the interview well, so that each stage of the interview is clear to the participant
- be clear in the terminology and coverage of the material
- allow participants to take their time and answer in their own way
- be sensitive and empathic, using active listening and being sensitive to how something is said and the non-verbal communication involved
- be alert to those aspects of the interview which may hold significance for the participant
- keep to the point and the matter in hand, steering the interview where necessary in order to address this
- check the reliability, validity and consistency of responses by well-placed questioning
- be able to recall and refer to earlier statements made by the participant
- be able to clarify, confirm and modify the participants' comments with the participant.

Walford (1994c: 225) adds to this the need for interviewers to have done their homework when interviewing powerful people, as such people could well interrogate the interviewer – they will assume up-to-dateness, competence and knowledge in the interviewer. Powerful interviewees are usually busy people and will expect the interviewer to have read the material that is in the public domain.

The issues of reliability do not reside solely in the preparations for and conduct of the interview; they extend to the ways in which interviews are analysed. For example, Lee (1993) and Kvale (1996: 163) comment on the issue of 'transcriber selectivity'. Here transcripts of interviews, however detailed and full they might be, remain selective, since they are interpretations of social situations. They become decontextualized, abstracted, even if they record silences, intonation, non-verbal behaviour etc. The issue, then, is how useful they are to researchers overall rather than whether they are completely reliable.

One of the problems that has to be considered when open-ended questions are used in the interview is that of developing a satisfactory method of recording replies. One way is to summarize responses in the course of the interview. This has the disadvantage of breaking the continuity of the interview and may result in bias because the interviewer may unconsciously emphasize responses that agree with his or her expectations and fail to note those that do not. It is sometimes possible to summarize an individual's responses at the end of the interview. Although this preserves the continuity of the interview, it is likely to induce greater bias because the delay may lead to the interviewer forgetting some of the details. It is these forgotten details that are most likely to be the ones that disagree with the interviewer's own expectations.

Validity and reliability in experiments

As we have seen, the fundamental purpose of experimental design is to impose control over conditions that would otherwise cloud the true effects of the independent variables upon the dependent variables.

Clouding conditions that threaten to jeopardize the validity of experiments have been identified by Campbell and Stanley (1963), Bracht and Glass (1968) and Lewis-Beck (1993), conditions

that are of greater consequence to the validity of quasi-experiments (more typical in educational research) than to true experiments in which random assignment to treatments occurs and where both treatment and measurement can be more adequately controlled by the researcher. The following summaries adapted from Campbell and Stanley (1963), Bracht and Glass (1968) and Lewis-Beck (1993) distinguish between 'internal validity' and 'external validity'. Internal validity is concerned with the question, 'Do the experimental treatments, in fact, make a difference in the specific experiments under scrutiny?'. External validity, on the other hand, asks the question, 'Given these demonstrable effects, to what populations or settings can they be generalized?' (see http://www.routledge.com/textbooks/9780415368780 – Chapter 6, file 6.8. ppt).

Threats to internal validity

- *History:* Frequently in educational research, events other than the experimental treatments occur during the time between pretest and post-test observations. Such events produce effects that can mistakenly be attributed to differences in treatment.
- *Maturation:* Between any two observations subjects change in a variety of ways. Such changes can produce differences that are independent of the experimental treatments. The problem of maturation is more acute in protracted educational studies than in brief laboratory experiments.
- *Statistical regression:* Like maturation effects, regression effects increase systematically with the time interval between pretests and post-tests. Statistical regression occurs in educational (and other) research due to the unreliability of measuring instruments and to extraneous factors unique to each experimental group. Regression means, simply, that subjects scoring highest on a pretest are likely to score relatively lower on a post-test; conversely, those scoring lowest on a pretest are likely to score relatively higher on a post-test. In short, in pretest-post-test situations, there is

regression to the mean. Regression effects can lead the educational researcher mistakenly to attribute post-test gains and losses to low scoring and high scoring respectively.

- *Testing:* Pretests at the beginning of experiments can produce effects other than those due to the experimental treatments. Such effects can include sensitizing subjects to the true purposes of the experiment and practice effects which produce higher scores on post-test measures.

- *Instrumentation:* Unreliable tests or instruments can introduce serious errors into experiments. With human observers or judges or changes in instrumentation and calibration, error can result from changes in their skills and levels of concentration over the course of the experiment.

- *Selection:* Bias may be introduced as a result of differences in the selection of subjects for the comparison groups or when intact classes are employed as experimental or control groups. Selection bias, moreover, may interact with other factors (history, maturation, etc.) to cloud even further the effects of the comparative treatments.

- *Experimental mortality:* The loss of subjects through dropout often occurs in long-running experiments and may result in confounding the effects of the experimental variables, for whereas initially the groups may have been randomly selected, the residue that stays the course is likely to be different from the unbiased sample that began it.

- *Instrument reactivity:* The effects that the instruments of the study exert on the people in the study (see also Vulliamy *et al.* 1990).

- *Selection-maturation interaction:* This can occur where there is a confusion between the research design effects and the variable's effects.

Threats to external validity

Threats to external validity are likely to limit the degree to which generalizations can be made from the particular experimental conditions to other populations or settings. We summarize here a number of factors (adapted from Campbell and Stanley 1963; Bracht and Glass 1968; Hammersley and Atkinson 1983; Vulliamy 1990; Lewis-Beck 1993) that jeopardize external validity.

- *Failure to describe independent variables explicitly:* Unless independent variables are adequately described by the researcher, future replications of the experimental conditions are virtually impossible.

- *Lack of representativeness of available and target populations:* While those participating in the experiment may be representative of an available population, they may not be representative of the population to which the experimenter seeks to generalize the findings, i.e. poor sampling and/or randomization.

- *Hawthorne effect:* Medical research has long recognized the psychological effects that arise out of mere participation in drug experiments, and placebos and double-blind designs are commonly employed to counteract the biasing effects of participation. Similarly, so-called Hawthorne effects threaten to contaminate experimental treatments in educational research when subjects realize their role as guinea pigs.

- *Inadequate operationalizing of dependent variables:* Dependent variables that experimenters operationalize must have validity in the non-experimental setting to which they wish to generalize their findings. A paper and pencil questionnaire on career choice, for example, may have little validity in respect of the actual employment decisions made by undergraduates on leaving university.

- *Sensitization/reactivity to experimental conditions:* As with threats to internal validity, pretests may cause changes in the subjects' sensitivity to the experimental variables and thus cloud the true effects of the experimental treatment.

- *Interaction effects of extraneous factors and experimental treatments:* All of the above threats to external validity represent interactions of various clouding factors with treatments. As well as these, interaction effects may also arise as a result of any or all of those factors identified under the section on 'Threats to internal validity'.

- *Invalidity or unreliability of instruments*: The use of instruments which yield data in which confidence cannot be placed (see below on tests).
- *Ecological validity*, and its partner, the extent to which behaviour observed in one context can be generalized to another: Hammersley and Atkinson (1983: 10) comment on the serious problems that surround attempts to relating inferences from responses gained under experimental conditions, or from interviews, to everyday life.

By way of summary, we have seen that an experiment can be said to be internally valid to the extent that, within its own confines, its results are credible (Pilliner 1973); but for those results to be useful, they must be generalizable beyond the confines of the particular experiment. In a word, they must be externally valid also: see also Morrison (2001b) for a critique of randomized controlled experiments and the problems of generalizability. Pilliner (1973) points to a lopsided relationship between internal and external validity. Without internal validity an experiment cannot possibly be externally valid. But the converse does not necessarily follow; an internally valid experiment may or may not have external validity. Thus, the most carefully designed experiment involving a sample of Welsh-speaking children is not necessarily generalizable to a target population which includes non-Welsh-speaking subjects.

It follows, then, that the way to good experimentation in schools, or indeed any other organizational setting, lies in maximizing both internal and external validity.

Validity and reliability in questionnaires

Validity of postal questionnaires can be seen from two viewpoints (Belson 1986). First, whether respondents who complete questionnaires do so accurately, honestly and correctly; and second, whether those who fail to return their questionnaires would have given the same distribution of answers as did the returnees. The question of accuracy can be checked by means of the intensive interview method, a technique consisting of twelve principal tactics that include familiarization, temporal reconstruction, probing and challenging. The interested reader should consult Belson (1986: 35-8).

The problem of non-response – the issue of 'volunteer bias' as Belson (1986) calls it – can, in part, be checked on and controlled for, particularly when the postal questionnaire is sent out on a continuous basis. It involves follow-up contact with non-respondents by means of interviewers trained to secure interviews with such people. A comparison is then made between the replies of respondents and non-respondents. Further, Hudson and Miller (1997) suggest several strategies for maximizing the response rate to postal questionnaires (and, thereby, to increase reliability). They involve:

- including stamped addressed envelopes
- organizing multiple rounds of follow-up to request returns (maybe up to three follow-ups)
- stressing the importance and benefits of the questionnaire
- stressing the importance of, and benefits to, the client group being targeted (particularly if it is a minority group that is struggling to have a voice)
- providing interim data from returns to non-returners to involve and engage them in the research
- checking addresses and changing them if necessary
- following up questionnaires with a personal telephone call
- tailoring follow-up requests to individuals (with indications to them that they are personally known and/or important to the research – including providing respondents with clues by giving some personal information to show that they are known) rather than blanket generalized letters
- detailing features of the questionnaire itself (ease of completion, time to be spent,

sensitivity of the questions asked, length of the questionnaire)

- issuing invitations to a follow-up interview (face-to-face or by telephone)
- providing encouragement to participate by a friendly third party
- understanding the nature of the sample population in depth, so that effective targeting strategies can be used.

The advantages of the questionnaire over interviews, for instance, are: it tends to be more reliable; because it is anonymous, it encourages greater honesty (though, of course, dishonesty and falsification might not be able to be discovered in a questionnaire); it is more economical than the interview in terms of time and money; and there is the possibility that it can be mailed. Its disadvantages, on the other hand, are: there is often too low a percentage of returns; the interviewer is unable to answer questions concerning both the purpose of the interview and any misunderstandings experienced by the interviewee, for it sometimes happens in the case of the latter that the same questions have different meanings for different people; if only closed items are used, the questionnaire may lack coverage or authenticity; if only open items are used, respondents may be unwilling to write their answers for one reason or another; questionnaires present problems to people of limited literacy; and an interview can be conducted at an appropriate speed whereas questionnaires are often filled in hurriedly. There is a need, therefore, to pilot questionnaires and refine their contents, wording, length, etc. as appropriate for the sample being targeted.

One central issue in considering the reliability and validity of questionnaire surveys is that of sampling. An unrepresentative, skewed sample, one that is too small or too large can easily distort the data, and indeed, in the case of very small samples, prohibit statistical analysis (Morrison 1993). The issue of sampling was covered in Chapter 4.

Validity and reliability in observations

There are questions about two types of validity in observation-based research. In effect, comments about the subjective and idiosyncratic nature of the participant observation study are about its external validity. How do we know that the results of this one piece of research are applicable to other situations? Fears that observers' judgements will be affected by their close involvement in the group relate to the internal validity of the method. How do we know that the results of this one piece of research represent the real thing, the genuine product? In Chapter 4 on sampling, we refer to a number of techniques (quota sampling, snowball sampling, purposive sampling) that researchers employ as a way of checking on the representativeness of the events that they observe and of cross-checking their interpretations of the meanings of those events.

In addition to external validity, participant observation also has to be rigorous in its internal validity checks. There are several threats to validity and reliability here, for example:

- the researcher, in exploring the present, may be unaware of important antecedent events
- informants may be unrepresentative of the sample in the study
- the presence of the observer might bring about different behaviours (reactivity and ecological validity)
- the researcher might 'go native', becoming too attached to the group to see it sufficiently dispassionately.

To address this Denzin (1970a) suggests triangulation of data sources and methodologies. Chapter 18 discusses the principal ways of overcoming problems of reliability and validity in observational research in naturalistic inquiry. In essence it is suggested that the notion of 'trustworthiness' (Lincoln and Guba 1985) replaces more conventional views of reliability and validity, and that this notion is devolved on issues of *credibility*, *confirmability*, *transferability* and *dependability*. Chapter 18 indicates how these areas can be addressed.

If observational research is much more structured in its nature, yielding quantitative data, then the conventions of intra- and inter-rater reliability apply. Here steps are taken to ensure that observers enter data into the appropriate categories consistently (i.e. intra- and inter-rater reliability) and accurately. Further, to ensure validity, a pilot must have been conducted to ensure that the observational categories themselves are appropriate, exhaustive, discrete, unambiguous and effectively operationalize the purposes of the research.

Validity and reliability in tests

The researcher will have to judge the place and significance of test data, not forgetting the problem of the Hawthorne effect operating negatively or positively on students who have to undertake the tests. There is a range of issues which might affect the reliability of the test – for example, the time of day, the time of the school year, the temperature in the test room, the perceived importance of the test, the degree of formality of the test situation, 'examination nerves', the amount of guessing of answers by the students (the calculation of *standard error* which the test demonstrates feature here), the way that the test is administered, the way that the test is marked, the degree of closure or openness of test items. Hence the researcher who is considering using testing as a way of acquiring research data must ensure that it is appropriate, valid and reliable (Linn 1993; Borsboom *et al.* 2004).

Wolf (1994) suggests four main factors that might affect reliability: the range of the group that is being tested, the group's level of proficiency, the length of the measure (the longer the test the greater the chance of errors), and the way in which reliability is calculated. Fitz-Gibbon (1997: 36) argues that, other things being equal, longer tests are more reliable than shorter tests. Additionally there are several ways in which reliability might be compromised in tests. Feldt and Brennan (1993) suggest four types of threat to reliability:

- *individuals:* their motivation, concentration, forgetfulness, health, carelessness, guessing, their related skills (e.g. reading ability, their usedness to solving the type of problem set, the effects of practice)

- *situational factors:* the psychological and physical conditions for the test – the context
- *test marker factors:* idiosyncrasy and subjectivity
- *instrument variables:* poor domain sampling, errors in sampling tasks, the realism of the tasks and relatedness to the experience of the testees, poor question items, the assumption or extent of unidimensionality in item response theory, length of the test, mechanical errors, scoring errors, computer errors.

Sources of unreliability

There are several threats to reliability in tests and examinations, particularly tests of performance and achievement, for example (Cunningham 1998; Airasian 2001), with respect to *examiners* and *markers*:

- *errors in marking:* e.g. attributing, adding and transfer of marks
- *inter-rater reliability:* different markers giving different marks for the same or similar pieces of work
- *inconsistency in the marker:* e.g. being harsh in the early stages of the marking and lenient in the later stages of the marking of many scripts
- *variations in the award of grades:* for work that is close to grade boundaries, some markers may place the score in a higher or lower category than other markers
- *the Halo effect:* a student who is judged to do well or badly in one assessment is given undeserved favourable or unfavourable assessment respectively in other areas.

With reference to the *students* and *teachers* themselves, there are several sources of unreliability:

- Motivation and interest in the task have a considerable effect on performance. Clearly, students need to be motivated if they are going to make a serious attempt at any test that they are required to undertake, where motivation is *intrinsic* (doing something for its own sake) or *extrinsic* (doing something for an external reason, e.g. obtaining a certificate or employment or entry into higher education). The results of a test completed in a desultory fashion by resentful pupils are hardly likely to supply the students' teacher with reliable information about the students' capabilities (Wiggins 1998). Motivation to participate in test-taking sessions is strongest when students have been helped to see its purpose, and where the examiner maintains a warm, purposeful attitude toward them during the testing session (Airasian 2001).

- The relationship (positive to negative) between the assessor and the testee exerts an influence on the assessment. This takes on increasing significance in teacher assessment, where the students know the teachers personally and professionally – and vice versa – and where the assessment situation involves face-to-face contact between the teacher and the student. Both *test-takers* and *test-givers* mutually influence one another during examinations, oral assessments and the like (Harlen 1994). During the test situation, students respond to such characteristics of the evaluator as the person's sex, age and personality.

- The conditions – physical, emotional, social – exert an influence on the assessment, particularly if they are unfamiliar. Wherever possible, students should take tests in familiar settings, preferably in their own classrooms under normal school conditions. Distractions in the form of extraneous noise, walking about the room by the examiner and intrusions into the room, all have significant impact upon the scores of the test-takers, particularly when they are younger pupils (Gipps 1994). An important factor in reducing students' anxiety and tension during an examination is the extent to which they are quite clear about what exactly they are required to do. Simple instructions, clearly and calmly given by the examiner, can significantly lower the general level of tension in the test-room. Teachers who intend to conduct testing sessions may find it beneficial in this respect to rehearse the instructions they wish to give to pupils *before* the actual testing session. Ideally, test instructions should be simple, direct and as brief as possible.

- The Hawthorne effect, wherein, in this context, simply informing students that this is an assessment situation will be enough to disturb their performance – for the better or the worse (either case not being a fair reflection of their usual abilities).

- Distractions, including superfluous information, will have an effect.

- Students respond to the tester in terms of their perceptions of what he/she expects of them (Haladyna 1997; Tombari and Borich 1999; Stiggins, 2001).

- The time of the day, week, month will exert an influence on performance. Some students are fresher in the morning and more capable of concentration (Stiggins 2001).

- Students are not always clear on what they think is being asked in the question; they may know the right answer but not infer that this is what is required in the question.

- The students may vary from one question to another – a student may have performed better with a different set of questions which tested the same matters. Black (1998) argues that two questions which, to the expert, may seem to be asking the same thing but in different ways, to the students might well be seen as completely different questions.

- Students (and teachers) practise test-like materials, which, even though scores are raised, might make them better at taking tests but the results might not indicate increased performance.

- A student may be able to perform a specific skill in a test but not be able to select or perform it in the wider context of learning.

- Cultural, ethnic and gender background affect how meaningful an assessment task or activity is to students, and meaningfulness affects their performance.

- Students' personalities may make a difference to their test performance.

- Students' learning strategies and styles may make a difference to their test performance.

- Marking practices are not always reliable, markers may be being too generous, marking by effort and ability rather than performance.
- The context in which the task is presented affects performance: some students can perform the task in everyday life but not under test conditions.

With regard to the *test items* themselves, there may be problems (e.g. test bias):

- The task itself may be multidimensional, for example, testing 'reading' may require several components and constructs. Students can execute a Mathematics operation in the Mathematics class but they cannot perform the same operation in, for example, a Physics class; students will disregard English grammar in a Science class but observe it in an English class. This raises the issue of the number of contexts in which the behaviour must be demonstrated before a criterion is deemed to have been achieved (Cohen *et al.* 2004). The question of transferability of knowledge and skills is also raised in this connection. The *context* of the task affects the student's performance.
- The validity of the items may be in question.
- The language of the assessment and the assessor exerts an influence on the testee, for example if the assessment is carried out in the testee's second language or in a 'middle-class' code (Haladyna 1997).
- The readability level of the task can exert an influence on the test, e.g. a difficulty in reading might distract from the purpose of a test which is of the use of a mathematical algorithm.
- The size and complexity of numbers or operations in a test (e.g. of Mathematics) might distract the testee who actually understands the operations and concepts.
- The number and type of operations and stages to a task: the students might know how to perform each element, but when they are presented in combination the size of the task can be overwhelming.
- The form and presentation of questions affects the results, giving variability in students' performances.

- A single error early on in a complex sequence may confound the later stages of the sequence (within a question or across a set of questions), even though the student might have been able to perform the later stages of the sequence, thereby preventing the student from gaining credit for all she or he can, in fact, do.
- Questions might favour boys more than girls or vice versa.
- Essay questions favour boys if they concern impersonal topics and girls if they concern personal and interpersonal topics (Haladyna 1997; Wedeen *et al.* 2002).
- Boys perform better than girls on multiple choice questions and girls perform better than boys on essay-type questions (perhaps because boys are more willing than girls to guess in multiple-choice items), and girls perform better in written work than boys.
- Questions and assessment may be culture-bound: what is comprehensible in one culture may be incomprehensible in another.
- The test may be so long, in order to ensure coverage, that boredom and loss of concentration may impair reliability.

Hence specific contextual factors can exert a significant influence on learning and this has to be recognised in conducting assessments, to render an assessment as unthreatening and natural as possible.

Harlen (1994: 140-2) suggests that inconsistency and unreliability in teacher-based and school-based assessment may derive from differences in:

- interpreting the assessment purposes, tasks and contents, by teachers or assessors
- the actual task set, or the contexts and circumstances surrounding the tasks (e.g. time and place)
- how much help is given to the test-takers during the test
- the degree of specificity in the marking criteria
- the application of the marking criteria and the grading or marking system that accompanies it

- how much additional information about the student or situation is being referred to in the assessment.

Harlen (1994) advocates the use of a range of moderation strategies, both before and after the tests, including:

- statistical reference/scaling tests
- inspection of samples (by post or by visit)
- group moderation of grades
- post-hoc adjustment of marks
- accreditation of institutions
- visits of verifiers
- agreement panels
- defining marking criteria
- exemplification
- group moderation meetings.

While moderation procedures are essentially post-hoc adjustments to scores, agreement trials and practice-marking can be undertaken before the administration of a test, which is particularly important if there are large numbers of scripts or several markers.

The issue here is that the results as well as the instruments should be reliable. Reliability is also addressed by:

- calculating coefficients of reliability, split-half techniques, the Kuder-Richardson formula, parallel/equivalent forms of a test, test/retest methods, the alpha coefficient
- calculating and controlling the standard error of measurement
- increasing the sample size (to maximize the range and spread of scores in a norm-referenced test), though criterion-referenced tests recognize that scores may bunch around the high level (in mastery learning for example), i.e. that the range of scores might be limited, thereby lowering the correlation coefficients that can be calculated
- increasing the number of observations made and items included in the test (in order to increase the range of scores)
- ensuring effective domain sampling of items in tests based on item response theory (a

particular issue in Computer Adaptive Testing see chapter 19: Thissen 1990)
- ensuring effective levels of item discriminability and item difficulty.

Reliability has to be not only achieved but also seen to be achieved, particularly in 'high stakes' testing (where a lot hangs on the results of the test, e.g. entrance to higher education or employment). Hence the procedures for ensuring reliability must be transparent. The difficulty here is that the more one moves towards reliability as defined above, the more the test will become objective, the more students will be measured as though they are inanimate objects, and the more the test will become decontextualized.

An alternative form of reliability, which is premissed on a more constructivist psychology, emphasizes the significance of context, the importance of subjectivity and the need to engage and involve the testee more fully than a simple test. This rehearses the tension between positivism and more interpretive approaches outlined in Chapter 1 of this book. Objective tests, as described in this chapter, lean strongly towards the positivist paradigm, while more phenomenological and interpretive paradigms of social science research will emphasize the importance of settings, of individual perceptions, of attitudes, in short, of 'authentic' testing (e.g. by using non-contrived, non-artificial forms of test data, for example portfolios, documents, course work, tasks that are stronger in realism and more 'hands on'). Though this latter adopts a view which is closer to assessment rather than narrowly 'testing', nevertheless the two overlap, both can yield marks, grades and awards, both can be formative as well as summative, both can be criterion-referenced.

With regard to validity, it is important to note here that an effective test will adequately ensure the following:

- *Content validity* (e.g. adequate and representative coverage of programme and test objectives in the test items, a key feature of domain sampling): this is achieved by ensuring that the content of the test fairly samples the class or fields of the situations or subject matter in question. Content validity is achieved by making professional judgements about the relevance and sampling of the contents of the test to a particular domain. It is concerned with coverage and representativeness rather than with patterns of response or scores. It is a matter of judgement rather than measurement (Kerlinger 1986). Content validity will need to ensure several features of a test (Wolf 1994): (a) test coverage (the extent to which the test covers the relevant field); (b) test relevance (the extent to which the test items are taught through, or are relevant to, a particular programme); (c) programme coverage (the extent to which the programme covers the overall field in question).

- *Criterion-related validity* is where a high correlation coefficient exists between the scores on the test and the scores on other accepted tests of the same performance: this is achieved by comparing the scores on the test with one or more variables (criteria) from other measures or tests that are considered to measure the same factor. Wolf (1994) argues that a major problem facing test devisers addressing criterion-related validity is the selection of the suitable criterion measure. He cites the example of the difficulty of selecting a suitable criterion of academic achievement in a test of academic aptitude. The criterion must be: relevant (and agreed to be relevant); free from bias (i.e. where external factors that might contaminate the criterion are removed); reliable – precise and accurate; capable of being measured or achieved.
- *Construct validity* (e.g. the clear relatedness of a test item to its proposed construct/unobservable quality or trait, demonstrated by both empirical data and logical analysis and debate, i.e. the extent to which particular constructs or concepts can give an account for performance on the test): this is achieved by ensuring that performance on the test is fairly explained by particular appropriate constructs or concepts. As with content validity, it is not based on test scores, but is more a matter of whether the test items are indicators of the underlying, latent construct in question.

In this respect construct validity also subsumes content and criterion-related validity. It is argued (Loevinger 1957) that, in fact, construct validity is the queen of the types of validity because it is subsumptive and because it concerns constructs or explanations rather than methodological factors. Construct validity is threatened by under-representation of the construct, i.e. the test is too narrow and neglects significant facets of a construct, and by the inclusion of irrelevancies – excess reliable variance.

- *Concurrent validity* is where the results of the test concur with results on other tests or instruments that are testing/assessing the same construct/performance – similar to predictive validity but without the time dimension. Concurrent validity can occur simultaneously with another instrument rather than after some time has elapsed.
- *Face validity* is where, superficially, the test appears – at face value – to test what it is designed to test.
- *Jury validity* is an important element in construct validity, where it is important to agree on the conceptions and operationalization of an unobservable construct.
- *Predictive validity* is where results on a test accurately predict subsequent performance – akin to criterion-related validity.
- *Consequential validity* is where the inferences that can be made from a test are sound.
- *Systemic validity* (Frederiksen and Collins 1989) is where programme activities both enhance test performance and enhance performance of the construct that is being addressed in the objective. Cunningham (1998) gives an example of systemic validity where, if the test and the objective of vocabulary performance leads to testees increasing their vocabulary, then systemic validity has been addressed.

To ensure test validity, then, the test must demonstrate fitness for purpose as well as addressing the several types of validity outlined above. The most difficult for researchers to address, perhaps, is construct validity, for it argues for agreement on the definition and operationalization of an unseen, half-guessed-at construct or phenomenon. The community of scholars has a role to play here. For a full discussion of validity see Messick (1993). To conclude this chapter, we turn briefly to consider validity and reliability in life history accounts.

Validity and reliability in life histories

Three central issues underpin the quality of data generated by life history methodology. They are to do with representativeness, validity and reliability. Plummer draws attention to a frequent criticism of life history research, namely that its cases are atypical rather than representative. To avoid this charge, he urges intending researchers to, 'work out and explicitly state the life history's relationship to a wider population' (Plummer 1983) by way of appraising the subject on a continuum of representativeness and non-representativeness.

Reliability in life history research hinges upon the identification of sources of bias and the application of techniques to reduce them. Bias arises from the informant, the researcher, and the interactional encounter itself. Box 6.1, adapted from Plummer (1983), provides a checklist of some aspects of bias arising from these principal sources.

Several validity checks are available to intending researchers. Plummer (1983) identifies the following:

- The subject of the life history may present an autocritique of it, having read the entire product.
- A comparison may be made with similar written sources by way of identifying points of major divergence or similarity.
- A comparison may be made with official records by way of imposing accuracy checks on the life history.

Box 6.1
Principal sources of bias in life history research

Source: *Informant*
Is misinformation (unintended) given?
Has there been evasion?
Is there evidence of direct lying and deception?
Is a 'front' being presented?
What may the informant 'take for granted' and hence not reveal?
How far is the informant 'pleasing you'?
How much has been forgotten?
How much may be self-deception?
Source: *Researcher*
Attitudes of researcher: age, gender, class, race, religion, politics etc.
Demeanour of researcher: dress, speech, body language etc.
Personality of researcher: anxiety, need for approval, hostility, warmth etc.
Scientific role of researcher: theory held (etc.), researcher expectancy
Source: *The interaction*
The encounter needs to be examined. Is bias coming from:
The physical setting – 'social space'?
The prior interaction?
Non-verbal communication?
Vocal behaviour?

Source: adapted from Plummer 1983: Table 5.2, p. 103

- A comparison may be made by interviewing other informants.

Essentially, the validity of any life history lies in its ability to represent the informant's subjective reality, that is to say, his or her definition of the situation.

Part Three

Styles of educational research

It is important to distinguish between design, methodology and instrumentation. Too often methods are confused with methodology and methodology is confused with design. Part Two provided an introduction to design issues and this part examines different styles, kinds of, and approaches to, research, separating them from methods – instruments for data collection. We identify eight main styles of educational research in this section, including a new chapter on the developing field of Internet-based research and computer usage. Although we recognize that these are by no means exhaustive, we suggest that they cover the major styles of research methodology. These take in quantitative as well as qualitative research, together with small-scale and large-scale approaches. As with the previous parts, the key here is the application of the notion of *fitness for purpose*. We do not advocate slavish adherence to a single methodology in research; indeed combining methodologies may be appropriate for the research in hand. The intention here is to shed light on the different styles of research, locating them in the paradigms of research introduced in Part One.

Elements of naturalistic inquiry

The social and educational world is a messy place, full of contradictions, richness, complexity, connectedness, conjunctions and disjunctions. It is multilayered, and not easily susceptible to the atomization process inherent in much numerical research. It has to be studied in total rather than in fragments if a true understanding is to be reached. Chapter 1 indicated that several approaches to educational research are contained in the paradigm of qualitative, naturalistic and ethnographic research. The characteristics of that paradigm (Boas 1943; Blumer 1969; Lincoln and Guba 1985; Woods 1992; LeCompte and Preissle 1993) include the following:

- Humans actively construct their own meanings of situations.
- Meaning arises out of social situations and is handled through interpretive processes (see http://www.routledge.com/textbooks/ 9780415368780 – Chapter 7, file 7.1. ppt).
- Behaviour and, thereby, data are socially situated, context-related, context-dependent and context-rich. To understand a situation researchers need to understand the context because situations affect behaviour and perspectives and vice versa.
- Realities are multiple, constructed and holistic.
- Knower and known are interactive and inseparable.
- Only time-bound and context-bound working hypotheses (idiographic statements) are possible.
- All entities are in a state of mutual simultaneous shaping, so that it is impossible to distinguish causes from effects.

- Inquiry is value-bound.
- Inquiries are influenced by inquirer values as expressed in the choice of a problem, evaluand or policy option, and in the framing, bounding and focusing of that problem, evaluand or policy option.
- Inquiry is influenced by the choice of the paradigm that guides the investigation into the problem.
- Inquiry is influenced by the choice of the substantive theory utilized to guide the collection and analysis of data and in the interpretation of findings.
- Inquiry is influenced by the values that inhere in the context.
- Inquiry is either value-resident (reinforcing or congruent) or value-dissonant (conflicting). Problem, evaluand, or policy option, paradigm, theory and context must exhibit congruence (value-resonance) if the inquiry is to produce meaningful results.
- Research must include 'thick descriptions' (Geertz 1973b) of the contextualized behaviour.
- The attribution of meaning is continuous and evolving over time.
- People are deliberate, intentional and creative in their actions.
- History and biography intersect – we create our own futures but not necessarily in situations of our own choosing.
- Social research needs to examine situations through the eyes of the participants – the task of ethnographies, as Malinowski (1922: 25) observed, is 'to grasp the point of view of the native [sic], his [sic] view of the world and in relation to his life'.

- Researchers are the instruments of the research (Eisner 1991).
- Researchers generate rather than test hypotheses.
- Researchers do not know in advance what they will see or what they will look for.
- Humans are anticipatory beings.
- Human phenomena seem to require even more conditional stipulations than do other kinds.
- Meanings and understandings replace proof.
- Generalizability is interpreted as generalizability to identifiable, specific settings and subjects rather than universally.
- Situations are unique.
- The processes of research and behaviour are as important as the outcomes.
- People, situations, events and objects have meaning conferred upon them rather than possessing their own intrinsic meaning.
- Social research should be conducted in natural, uncontrived, real world settings with as little intrusiveness as possible by the researcher.
- Social reality, experiences and social phenomena are capable of multiple, sometimes contradictory interpretations and are available to us through social interaction.
- All factors, rather than a limited number of variables, have to be taken into account.
- Data are analysed inductively, with constructs deriving from the data during the research.
- Theory generation is derivative – grounded (Glaser and Strauss 1967) – the data suggest the theory rather than vice versa.

Lincoln and Guba (1985: 39–43) tease out the implications of these axioms:

- Studies must be set in their natural settings as context is heavily implicated in meaning.
- Humans are the research instrument.
- Utilization of tacit knowledge is inescapable.
- Qualitative methods sit more comfortably than quantitative methods with the notion of the human-as-instrument.
- Purposive sampling enables the full scope of issues to be explored.
- Data analysis is inductive rather than a priori and deductive.

- Theory emerges rather than is pre-ordinate. A priori theory is replaced by grounded theory.
- Research designs emerge over time (and as the sampling changes over time).
- The outcomes of the research are negotiated.
- The natural mode of reporting is the case study.
- Nomothetic interpretation is replaced by idiographic interpretation.
- Applications are tentative and pragmatic.
- The focus of the study determines its boundaries.
- Trustworthiness and its components replace more conventional views of reliability and validity.

LeCompte and Preissle (1993) suggest that ethnographic research is a process involving methods of inquiry, an outcome and a resultant record of the inquiry. The intention of the research is to create as vivid a reconstruction as possible of the culture or groups being studied (p. 235). There are several purposes of qualitative research, for example, description and reporting, the creation of key concepts, theory generation and testing. LeCompte and Preissle (1993) indicate several key elements of ethnographic approaches:

- Phenomenological data are elicited (LeCompte and Preissle 1993: 3).
- The world view of the participants is investigated and represented – their 'definition of the situation' (Thomas 1923).
- Meanings are accorded to phenomena by both the researcher and the participants; the process of research, therefore, is hermeneutic, uncovering meanings (LeCompte and Preissle 1993: 31–2).
- The constructs of the participants are used to structure the investigation.
- Empirical data are gathered in their naturalistic setting (unlike laboratories or in controlled settings as in other forms of research, where variables are manipulated).
- Observational techniques are used extensively (both participant and non-participant) to acquire data on real-life settings.

- The research is holistic, that is, it seeks a description and interpretation of 'total phenomena'.
- There is a move from description and data to inference, explanation, suggestions of causation, and theory generation.
- Methods are 'multimodal' and the ethnographer is a 'methodological omnivore' (LeCompte and Preissle 1993: 232).

Hitchcock and Hughes (1989: 52–3) suggest that ethnographies involve

- the production of descriptive cultural knowledge of a group
- the description of activities in relation to a particular cultural context from the point of view of the members of that group themselves
- the production of a list of features constitutive of membership in a group or culture
- the description and analysis of patterns of social interaction
- the provision as far as possible of 'insider accounts'
- the development of theory.

Lofland (1971) suggests that naturalistic methods are intended to address three major questions:

- What are the characteristics of a social phenomenon?
- What are the causes of the social phenomenon?
- What are the consequences of the social phenomenon?

In this one can observe: the environment; people and their relationships; behaviour, actions and activities; verbal behaviour; psychological stances; histories; physical objects (Baker 1994: 241–4).

There are several key differences between the naturalistic approach and that of the positivists to whom we made reference in Chapter 1. LeCompte and Preissle (1993: 39–44) suggest that ethnographic approaches are concerned more with description rather than prediction, induction rather than deduction, generation rather than verification of theory, construction rather than enumeration, and subjectivities rather

than objective knowledge. With regard to the latter the authors distinguish between *emic* approaches (as in the term 'phonemic', where the concern is to catch the subjective meanings placed on situations by participants) and *etic* approaches (as in the term 'phonetic', where the intention is to identify and understand the objective or researcher's meaning and constructions of a situation) (LeCompte and Preissle 1993: 45).

Woods (1992: 381), however, argues that some differences between quantitative and qualitative research have been exaggerated. He proposes, for example, that the 1970s witnessed an unproductive dichotomy between the two, the former being seen as strictly in the hypothetico-deductive mode (testing theories) and the latter being seen as the inductive method used for generating theory. He suggests that the epistemological contrast between the two is overstated, as qualitative techniques can be used both for generating and testing theories.

Indeed Dobbert and Kurth-Schai (1992: 94–5) urge not only that ethnographic approaches become more systematic but also that they study and address regularities in social behaviour and social structure. The task of ethnographers is to balance a commitment to catch the diversity, variability, creativity, individuality, uniqueness and spontaneity of social interactions (e.g. by 'thick descriptions': Geertz 1973b) with a commitment to the task of social science to seek regularities, order and patterns within such diversity. As Durkheim (1950) noted, there are 'social facts'.

Following this line, it is possible, therefore, to suggest that ethnographic research can address issues of generalizability – a tenet of positivist research – interpreted as 'comparability' and 'translatability' (LeCompte and Preissle 1993: 47). For comparability the characteristics of the group that is being studied need to be made explicit so that readers can compare them with other similar or dissimilar groups. For translatability the analytic categories used in the research as well as the characteristics of the groups are made explicit so that meaningful comparisons can be made with other groups and disciplines.

Spindler and Spindler (1992: 72–4) put forward several hallmarks of effective ethnographies:

- Observations have contextual relevance, both in the immediate setting in which behaviour is observed and in further contexts beyond.
- Hypotheses emerge *in situ* as the study develops in the observed setting.
- Observation is prolonged and often repetitive. Events and series of events are observed more than once to establish reliability in the observational data.
- Inferences from observation and various forms of ethnographic inquiry are used to address insiders' views of reality.
- A major part of the ethnographic task is to elicit sociocultural knowledge from participants, rendering social behaviour comprehensible.
- Instruments, schedules, codes, agenda for interviews, questionnaires, etc. should be generated *in situ*, and should derive from observation and ethnographic inquiry.
- A transcultural, comparative perspective is usually present, although often it is an unstated assumption, and cultural variation (over space and time) is natural.
- Some sociocultural knowledge that affects behaviour and communication under study is tacit/implicit, and may not be known even to participants or known ambiguously to others. It follows that one task for an ethnography is to make explicit to readers what is tacit/implicit to informants.
- The ethnographic interviewer should not frame or predetermine responses by the kinds of questions that are asked, because the informants themselves have the emic, native cultural knowledge.
- In order to collect as much live data as possible, any technical device may be used.
- The ethnographer's presence should be declared and his or her personal, social and interactional position in the situation should be described.

With 'mutual shaping and interaction' between researchers and participants taking place (Lincoln and Guba 1985: 155), researchers become, as it were, the 'human instrument' in the research, building on their tacit knowledge in addition to their propositional knowledge, using methods that sit comfortably with human inquiry, e.g. observations, interviews, documentary analysis and 'unobtrusive' methods (Lincoln and Guba 1985: 187). The advantage of the 'human instrument' is his or her adaptability, responsiveness, knowledge, ability to handle sensitive matters, ability to see the whole picture, ability to clarify and summarize, to explore, to analyse, to examine atypical or idiosyncratic responses (Lincoln and Guba 1985: 193–4).

The main *kinds* of naturalistic inquiry are (Arsenault and Anderson 1998: 121; Flick 2004):

- *case study:* an investigation into a specific instance or phenomenon in its real-life context
- *comparative studies:* where several cases are compared on the basis of key areas of interest
- *retrospective studies:* which focus on biographies of participants or which ask participants to look back on events and issues
- *snapshots:* analyses of particular situations, events or phenomena at a single point in time
- *longitudinal studies:* which investigate issues or people over time
- *ethnography:* a portrayal and explanation of social groups and situations in their real-life contexts
- *grounded theory:* developing theories to explain phenomena, the theories emerging from the data rather than being prefigured or predetermined
- *biography:* individual or collective
- *phenomenology:* seeing things as they really are and establishing the meanings of things through illumination and explanation rather than through taxonomic approaches or abstractions, and developing theories through the dialogic relationships of researcher to researched.

The main *methods* for data collection in naturalistic inquiry (Hammersley and Atkinson 1983) are as follows:

- participant observation
- interviews and conversations

- documents and field notes
- accounts
- notes and memos.

Planning naturalistic research

In many ways the issues in naturalistic research are not exclusive; they apply to other forms of research, for example identifying the problem and research purposes; deciding the focus of the study; selecting the research design and instrumentation; addressing validity and reliability; ethical issues; approaching data analysis and interpretation. These are common to all research. More specifically Wolcott (1992: 19) suggests that naturalistic researchers should address the stages of watching, asking and reviewing, or, as he puts it, experiencing, enquiring and examining. In naturalistic inquiry it is possible to formulate a more detailed set of stages that can be followed (Hitchcock and Hughes 1989: 57–71; Bogdan and Biklen 1992; LeCompte and Preissle 1993). These eleven stages are presented below and are subsequently dealt with later on in this chapter (see http://www.routledge.com/textbooks/9780415368780 – Chapter 7, file 7.2. ppt):

1 Locating a field of study.
2 Addressing ethical issues.
3 Deciding the sampling.
4 Finding a role and managing entry into the context.
5 Finding informants.
6 Developing and maintaining relations in the field.
7 Data collection *in situ*.
8 Data collection outside the field.
9 Data analysis.
10 Leaving the field.
11 Writing the report.

These stages are shot through with a range of issues that will affect the research:

- Personal issues: the disciplinary sympathies of the researcher, researcher subjectivities and characteristics. Hitchcock and Hughes (1989: 56) indicate that there are several serious strains in conducting fieldwork because the researcher's own emotions, attitudes, beliefs, values, characteristics enter the research; indeed, the more this happens the less will be the likelihood of gaining the participants' perspectives and meanings.
- The kinds of participation that the researcher will undertake.
- Issues of advocacy: where the researcher may be expected to identify with the same emotions, concerns and crises as the members of the group being studied and wishes to advance their cause, often a feature that arises at the beginning and the end of the research when the researcher is considered to be a legitimate spokesperson for the group.
- Role relationships.
- Boundary maintenance in the research.
- The maintenance of the balance between distance and involvement.
- Ethical issues.
- Reflexivity.

Reflexivity recognizes that researchers are inescapably part of the social world that they are researching (Hammersley and Atkinson 1983: 14) and, indeed, that this social world is an already interpreted world by the actors, undermining the notion of objective reality. Researchers are in the world and of the world. They bring their own biographies to the research situation and participants behave in particular ways in their presence. Reflexivity suggests that researchers should acknowledge and disclose their own selves in the research, seeking to understand their part in, or influence on, the research. Rather than trying to eliminate researcher effects (which is impossible, as researchers are part of the world that they are investigating), researchers should hold themselves up to the light, echoing Cooley's (1902) notion of the 'looking glass self'. As Hammersley and Atkinson (1983) say:

> He or she [the researcher] is the research instrument *par excellence*. The fact that behaviour and attitudes are often not stable across contexts and that the researcher may play a part in shaping the context becomes central to the analysis. . . . The theories we

develop to explain the behaviour of the people we study should also, where relevant, be applied to our own activities as researchers.

(Hammersley and Atkinson 1983: 18–19)

Highly reflexive researchers will be acutely aware of the ways in which their selectivity, perception, background and inductive processes and paradigms shape the research. They are research instruments. McCormick and James (1988: 191) argue that combating reactivity through reflexivity requires researchers to monitor closely and continually their own interactions with participants, their own reaction, roles, biases, and any other matters that might affect the research. This is addressed more fully in Chapter 5 on validity, encompassing issues of triangulation and respondent validity.

Lincoln and Guba (1985: 226–47) set out ten elements in research design for naturalistic studies:

1 Determining a focus for the inquiry.
2 Determining the fit of paradigm to focus.
3 Determining the fit of the inquiry paradigm to the substantive theory selected to guide the inquiry.
4 Determining where and from whom data will be collected.
5 Determining successive phases of the inquiry.
6 Determining instrumentation.
7 Planning data collection and recording modes.
8 Planning data analysis procedures.
9 Planning the logistics:
   • prior logistical considerations for the project as a whole
   • the logistics of field excursions prior to going into the field
   • the logistics of field excursions while in the field
   • the logistics of activities following field excursions
   • the logistics of closure and termination
10 Planning for trustworthiness.

These elements can be set out into a sequential, staged approach to planning naturalistic research (see, for example, Schatzman and Strauss 1973; Delamont 1992). Spradley (1979) sets out the stages of: selecting a problem; collecting cultural data; analysing cultural data; formulating ethnographic hypotheses; writing the ethnography. We offer a fuller, eleven-stage model later in the chapter.

Like other styles of research, naturalistic and qualitative methods will need to formulate research questions which should be clear and unambiguous but open to change as the research develops. Strauss (1987) terms these 'generative questions': they stimulate the line of investigation, suggest initial hypotheses and areas for data collection, yet they do not foreclose the possibility of modification as the research develops. A balance has to be struck between having research questions that are so broad that they do not steer the research in any particular direction, and so narrow that they block new avenues of inquiry (Flick 2004: 150).

Miles and Huberman (1994) identify two types of qualitative research design: loose and tight. Loose research designs have broadly defined concepts and areas of study, and, indeed, are open to changes of methodology. These are suitable, they suggest, when the researchers are experienced and when the research is investigating new fields or developing new constructs, akin to the flexibility and openness of theoretical sampling of Glaser and Strauss (1967). By contrast, a tight research design has narrowly restricted research questions and predetermined procedures, with limited flexibility. These, the authors suggest, are useful when the researchers are inexperienced, when the research is intended to look at particular specified issues, constructs, groups or individuals, or when the research brief is explicit.

Even though, in naturalistic research, issues and theories emerge from the data, this does not preclude the value of having research questions. Flick (1998: 51) suggests three types of research questions in qualitative research, namely those that are concerned, first, with describing states, their causes and how these states are sustained; second, with describing processes of change and consequences of those states; third, with how suitable they are for supporting or not supporting hypotheses and assumptions or for generating new hypotheses and assumptions (the 'generative questions' referred to above).

Should one have a hypothesis in qualitative research?

We mentioned in Chapter 1 that positivist approaches typically test pre-formulated hypotheses and that a distinguishing feature of naturalistic and qualitative approaches is its reluctance to enter the hypothetico-deductive paradigm (e.g. Meinefeld 2004: 153), not least because there is a recognition that the researcher influences the research and because the research is much more open and emergent in qualitative approaches. Indeed Meinefeld (2004), citing classic studies like Whyte's (1955) *Street Corner Society*, suggests that it is impossible to predetermine hypotheses, whether one would wish to or not, as prior knowledge cannot be presumed. Glaser and Strauss (1967) suggest that researchers should deliberately free themselves from all prior knowledge, even suggesting that it is impossible to read up in advance, as it is not clear what reading will turn out to be relevant – the data speak for themselves. Theory is the end point of the research, not its starting point.

One has to be mindful that the researcher's own background interest, knowledge, and biography precede the research and that though initial hypotheses may not be foregrounded in qualitative research, nevertheless the initial establishment of the research presupposes a particular area of interest, i.e. the research and data for focus are not theory-free; knowledge is not theory-free. Indeed Glaser and Strauss (1967) acknowledge that they brought their own prior knowledge to their research on dying.

The resolution of this apparent contradiction – the call to reject an initial hypothesis in qualitative research, yet a recognition that all research commences with some prior knowledge or theory that gives rise to the research, however embryonic – may lie in several fields. These include: an openness to data (Meinefeld 2004: 156–7); a preparedness to modify one's initial presuppositions and position; a declaration of the

extent to which the researcher's prior knowledge may be influencing the research (i.e. reflexivity); a recognition of the tentative nature of one's hypothesis; a willingness to use the research to generate a hypothesis; and, as a more extreme position, an acknowledgment that having a hypothesis may be just as much a part of qualitative research as it is of quantitative research.

Features and stages of a qualitative study

An effective qualitative study has several features (Cresswell 1998: 20–2), and these can be addressed in evaluating qualitative research:

- The study uses rigorous procedures and multiple methods for data collection.
- The study is framed within the assumptions and nature of qualitative research.
- Enquiry is a major feature, and can follow one or more different traditions (e.g. biography, ethnography, phenomenology, case study, grounded theory).
- The project commences with a single focus on an issue or problem rather than a hypothesis or the supposition of a causal relationship of variables. Relationships may emerge later, but that is open.
- Criteria for verification are set out, and rigour is practised in writing up the report.
- Verisimilitude is required, such that readers can imagine being in the situation.
- Data are analysed at different levels; they are multilayered.
- The writing engages the reader and is replete with unexpected insights, while maintaining believability and accuracy.

Stage 1: Locating a field of study

Bogdan and Biklen (1992: 2) suggest that research questions in qualitative research are not framed by simply operationalizing variables as in the positivist paradigm. Rather, research questions are formulated *in situ* and in response to situations observed, i.e. that topics are investigated in all their complexity, in the naturalistic context. The field, as Arsenault and Anderson (1998: 125) state, 'is used generically in qualitative research and quite simply refers to where the phenomenon exists'.

In some qualitative studies, the selection of the research field will be informed by the research purposes, the need for the research, what gave rise to the research, the problem to be addressed, and the research questions and sub-questions. In other qualitative studies these elements may only emerge after the researcher has been immersed for some time in the research site itself.

Stage 2: Addressing ethical issues

Deyle *et al.* (1992: 623) identify several critical ethical issues that need to be addressed in approaching the research:

How does one present oneself in the field? As whom does one present oneself? How ethically defensible is it to pretend to be somebody that you are not in order to gain knowledge that you would otherwise not be able to acquire, and to obtain and preserve access to places which otherwise you would be unable to secure or sustain.

The issues here are several. First, there is the matter of *informed consent* (to participate and for disclosure), whether and how to gain participant assent (see also LeCompte and Preissle 1993: 66). This uncovers another consideration, namely *covert* or *overt* research. On the one hand, there is a powerful argument for informed consent. However, the more participants know about the research the less naturally they may behave (LeCompte and Preissle 1993: 108), and naturalism is self-evidently a key criterion of the naturalistic paradigm.

Mitchell (1993) catches the dilemma for researchers in deciding whether to undertake overt or covert research. The issue of informed consent, he argues, can lead to the selection of particular forms of research – those where researchers can control the phenomena under investigation – thereby excluding other kinds of research where subjects behave in less controllable, predictable, prescribed ways, indeed where subjects may come in and out of the research over time.

He argues that in the real social world, access to important areas of research is prohibited if informed consent has to be sought, for example in researching those on the margins of society or the disadvantaged. It is to the participants' own advantage that secrecy is maintained as, if secrecy is not upheld, important work may not be done and 'weightier secrets' (Mitchell 1993: 54) may be kept which are of legitimate public concern and in the participants' own interests. Mitchell makes a powerful case for secrecy, arguing that informed consent may excuse social scientists from the risk of confronting powerful, privileged and cohesive groups who wish to protect themselves from public scrutiny. Secrecy and informed consent are moot points. Researchers, then, have to consider their loyalties and responsibilities (LeCompte and Preissle 1993: 106), for example what is the public's right to know and what is the individual's right to privacy (Morrison 1993; De Laine 2000: 13).

In addition to the issue of overt or covert research, LeCompte and Preissle (1993) indicate that the problems of *risk* and *vulnerability* to subjects must be addressed; steps must be taken to prevent risk or harm to participants (non-maleficence – the principle of *primum non nocere*). Bogdan and Biklen (1992: 54) extend this to include issues of embarrassment as well as harm to those taking part. The question of vulnerability is present at its strongest when participants in the research have their freedom to choose limited, e.g. by dint of their age, by health, by social constraints, by dint of their life style (e.g. engaging in criminality), social acceptability, experience of being victims (e.g. of abuse, of violent crime) (Bogdan and Biklen 1992:107). As the authors comment, participants rarely initiate research, so it is the responsibility of the researcher to protect them. Relationships between researcher and the researched are rarely symmetrical in terms of power; it is often the case that those with more power, information and resources research those with less.

A standard protection is often the guarantee of *confidentiality*, withholding participants' real names and other identifying characteristics. Bogdan and Biklen (1992: 106) contrast this with anonymity, where identity is withheld because it is genuinely unknown. The issues are raised of identifiability and traceability. Further, participants might be able to identify themselves in the research report though others may not be able to identify them. A related factor here is the *ownership* of the data and the results, the control of the release of data (and to whom, and when) and what rights respondents have to veto the research results. Patrick (1973) indicates this point at its sharpest: as an ethnographer of a Glasgow gang, he was witness to a murder. The dilemma was clear – to report the matter (and thereby, also to blow his cover, consequently endangering his own life) or to stay as a covert researcher.

Bogdan and Biklen (1992: 54) add to this discussion the need to respect participants as subjects, not simply as research objects to be used and then discarded. Mason (2002: 41) suggests that it is important for researchers to consider the parties, bodies, practices that might be interested in, or affected by, the research and the implications of the answer to these questions for the conduct, reporting and dissemination of the inquiry. We address ethics in Chapters 2 and 5 and we advise readers to refer to these chapters.

Stage 3: Deciding the sampling

In an ideal world the researcher would be able to study a group in its entirety. This was the case in Goffman's (1968) work on 'total institutions', such as hospitals, prisons and police forces. It was also the practice of anthropologists who were able to explore specific isolated communities or tribes. That is rarely possible nowadays because such groups are no longer isolated or insular. Hence the researcher is faced with the issue of sampling, that is, deciding which people it will be possible to select to represent the wider group (however defined). The researcher has to decide the groups for which the research questions are appropriate, the contexts which are important for the research, the time periods that will be needed, and the possible artefacts of interest to the investigator. In other words decisions are necessary on the sampling of people, contexts,

issues, time frames, artefacts and data sources. This takes the discussion beyond conventional notions of sampling.

In several forms of research sampling is fixed at the start of the study, though there may be attrition of the sample through 'mortality' (e.g. people leaving the study). Mortality is seen as problematic. Ethnographic research regards this as natural rather than irksome. People come into and go from the study. This impacts on the decision whether to have a synchronic investigation occurring at a single point in time, or a diachronic study where events and behaviour are monitored over time to allow for change, development and evolving situations. In ethnographic inquiry sampling is recursive and *ad hoc* rather than fixed at the outset; it changes and develops over time. Let us consider how this might happen.

LeCompte and Preissle (1993: 82–3) point out that ethnographic methods rule out statistical sampling, for a variety of reasons:

- The characteristics of the wider population are unknown.
- There are no straightforward boundary markers (categories or strata) in the group.
- Generalizability, a goal of statistical methods, is not necessarily a goal of ethnography.
- Characteristics of a sample may not be evenly distributed across the sample.
- Only one or two subsets of a characteristic of a total sample may be important.
- Researchers may not have access to the whole population.
- Some members of a subset may not be drawn from the population from which the sampling is intended to be drawn.

Hence other types of sampling are required. A criterion-based selection requires the researcher to specify in advance a set of attributes, factors, characteristics or criteria that the study must address. The task then is to ensure that these appear in the sample selected (the equivalent of a stratified sample). There are other forms of sampling (discussed in Chapter 4) that are useful in ethnographic research (Bogdan and Biklen 1992: 70; LeCompte and Preissle 1993: 69–83), such as:

- *convenience sampling:* opportunistic sampling, selecting from whoever happens to be available
- *critical-case sampling:* e.g. people who display the issue or set of characteristics in their entirety or in a way that is highly significant for their behaviour
- *identifying the norm of a characteristic:* then the extremes of that characteristic are located, and the bearers of that extreme characteristic are selected
- *typical case-sampling:* a profile of attributes or characteristics that are possessed by an 'average', typical person or case is identified, and the sample is selected from these conventional people or cases
- *unique-case sampling:* cases that are rare, unique or unusual on one or more criteria are identified, and sampling takes places within these; here whatever other characteristics or attributes a person might share with others, a particular attribute or characteristic sets that person apart
- *reputational-case sampling:* a variant of extreme-case and unique-case sampling, where a researcher chooses a sample on the recommendation of experts in the field
- *snowball sampling:* using the first interviewee to suggest or recommend other interviewees.

Patton (1980) identifies several types of sampling that are useful in naturalistic research, including

- *sampling extreme/deviant cases:* in order to gain information about unusual cases that may be particularly troublesome or enlightening
- *sampling typical cases:* in order to avoid rejecting information on the grounds that it has been gained from special or deviant cases
- *snowball sampling:* one participant provides access to a further participant and so on
- *maximum variation sampling:* in order to document the range of unique changes that have emerged, often in response to the different conditions to which participants have had to adapt; useful if the aim of the research is to investigate the variations, range and patterns in

a particular phenomenon or phenomena (Ezzy 2002: 74)
- *sampling according to intensity:* depending on which features of interest are displayed or occur
- *sampling critical cases:* in order to permit maximum applicability to others; if the information holds true for critical cases (e.g. cases where all of the factors sought are present), then it is likely to hold true for others
- *sampling politically important or sensitive cases:* to draw attention to the case
- *convenience sampling:* saves time and money and spares the researcher the effort of finding less amenable participants.

One can add to this list types of sample from Miles and Huberman (1994: 28):

- *homogeneous sampling:* focuses on groups with similar characteristics
- *theoretical sampling:* in grounded theory, discussed below, where participants are selected for their ability to contribute to the developing/emergent theory
- *confirming and disconfirming cases:* akin to the extreme and deviant cases indicated by Patton (1980), in order to look for exceptions to the rule, which may lead to the modification of the rule
- *random purposeful sampling:* when the potential sample is too large, a smaller subsample can be used which still maintains some generalizability
- *stratified purposeful sampling:* to identify subgroups and strata
- *criterion sampling:* all those who meet some stated criteria for membership of the group or class under study
- *opportunistic sampling:* to take advantage of unanticipated events, leads, ideas, issues.

Miles and Huberman (1994) make the point that these strategies can be used in combination as well as in isolation, and that using them in combination contributes to triangulation.

We discuss below two other categories of sample: 'primary informants' and 'secondary informants'

(Morse 1994: 228), those who completely fulfil a set of selection criteria and those who fill a selection of those criteria respectively.

Lincoln and Guba (1985: 201–2) suggest an important difference between conventional and naturalistic research designs. In the former the intention is to focus on similarities and to be able to make generalizations, whereas in the latter the objective is informational, to provide such a wealth of detail that the uniqueness and individuality of each case can be represented. To the charge that naturalistic inquiry, thereby, cannot yield generalizations because of sampling flaws, the writers argue that this is necessarily though trivially true. In a word, it is unimportant.

Patton (1980: 184) takes a slightly more cavalier approach to sampling, suggesting that 'there are no rules for sample size in qualitative inquiry', with the size of the sample depending on what one wishes to know, the purposes of the research, what will be useful and credible, and what can be done within the resources available, e.g. time, money, people, support – important considerations for the novice researcher.

Ezzy (2002: 74) underlines the notion of 'theoretical sampling' from Glaser and Strauss (1967) in his comment that, unlike other forms of research, qualitative inquiries may not always commence with the full knowledge of whom to sample, but that the sample is determined on an ongoing, emergent basis. Theoretical sampling starts with data and then, having reviewed these, the researcher decides where to go next in order to develop the emerging theory (Glaser and Strauss 1967: 45). We discuss this more fully in Chapter 23.

Individuals and groups are selected for their potential – or hoped for – ability to offer new insights into the emerging theory, i.e. they are chosen on the basis of their significant contribution to theory generation and development. As the theory develops, so the researcher decides whom to approach to request their participation. Theoretical sampling does not claim to know the population characteristics or to represent known populations in advance, and

sample size is not defined in advance; sampling is only concluded when theoretical saturation (discussed below) is reached.

Ezzy (2002: 74–5) gives as an example of theoretical sampling his own work on unemployment where he developed a theory that levels of distress experienced by unemployed people were influenced by their levels of financial distress. He interviewed unemployed low-income and high-income groups with and without debt, to determine their levels of distress. He reported that levels of distress were not caused so much by absolute levels of income but levels of income in relation to levels of debt.

In the educational field one could imagine theoretical sampling in an example thus: interviewing teachers about their morale might give rise to a theory that teacher morale is negatively affected by disruptive student behaviour in schools. This might suggest the need to sample teachers working with many disruptive students in difficult schools, as a 'critical case sampling'. However, the study finds that some of the teachers working in these circumstances have high morale, not least because they have come to expect disruptive behaviour from students with so many problems, and so are not surprised or threatened by it, and because the staff in these schools provide tremendous support for each other in difficult circumstances – they all know what it is like to have to work with challenging students.

So the study decides to focus on teachers working in schools with far fewer disruptive students. The researcher discovers that it is these teachers who experience far lower morale, and hypothesizes that this is because this latter group of teachers has higher expectations of student behaviour, such that having only one or two students who do not conform to these expectations deflates staff morale significantly, and because disruptive behaviour is regarded in these schools as teacher weakness, and there is little or no mutual support. The researcher's theory, then, is refined, to suggest that teacher morale is affected more by teacher expectations than by disruptive behaviour, so the researcher adopts a 'maximum variation sampling' of teachers in a range of schools, to investigate how expectations and morale are related to disruptive behaviour. In this case the sampling emerges as the research proceeds and the theory emerges; this is theoretical sampling, the 'royal way for qualitative studies' (Flick 2004: 151). Schatzman and Strauss (1973: 38 ff.) suggest that sampling within theoretical sampling may change according to time, place, individuals and events.

The above procedure accords with Glaser and Strauss's (1967) view that sampling involves continuously gathering data until practical factors (boundaries) put an end to data collection, or until no amendments have to be made to the theory in light of further data – their stage of 'theoretical saturation' – where the theory fits the data even when new data are gathered. Theoretical saturation is described by Glaser and Strauss (1967: 61) as being reached when 'no additional data are being found whereby the sociologist can develop properties of the category'. That said, the researcher has to be cautious to avoid premature cessation of data collection; it would be too easy to close off research with limited data, when, in fact, further sampling and data collection might lead to a reformulation of the theory.

An extension of theoretical sampling is 'analytic induction', a process advanced by Znaniecki (1934). Here the researcher starts with a theory (that may have emerged from the data, as in grounded theory) and then deliberately proceeds to look for deviant or discrepant cases, to provide a robust defence of the theory. This accords with Popper's notion of a rigorous scientific theory having to stand up to falsifiability tests. In analytic induction, the researcher deliberately seeks data which potentially could falsify the theory, thereby giving strength to the final theory.

We are suggesting here that, in qualitative research, sampling cannot always be decided in advance on a 'once and for all' basis. It may have to continue through the stages of data collection, analysis and reporting. This reflects the circular process of qualitative research, in which data collection, analysis, interpretation and reporting and sampling do not necessarily have to proceed in a linear fashion; the process is recursive and iterative. Sampling is not decided *a priori* – in advance – but may be decided, amended, added to, increased and extended as the research progresses.

Stage 4: Finding a role and managing entry into the context

This involves matters of access and permission, establishing a reason for being there, developing a role and a persona, identifying the gatekeepers who facilitate entry and access to the group being investigated (see LeCompte and Preissle 1993: 100 and 111). The issue here is complex, for the researcher will be both a member of the group and yet studying that group, so it is a delicate matter to negotiate a role that will enable the investigator to be both participant and observer. LeCompte and Preissle (1993: 112) comment that the most important elements in securing access are the willingness of researchers to be flexible and their sensitivity to nuances of behaviour and response in the participants. As De Laine (2000: 41) remarks: 'demonstrated ability to get on with people in the setting and a willingness to share experience in ongoing activities are important criteria of access'.

Wolff (2004: 195–6) suggests that there are two fundamental questions to be addressed in considering access and entry into the field:

- How can researchers succeed in making contact and securing cooperation from informants?
- How can researchers position themselves in the field so as to secure the necessary time, space and social relations to be able to carry out the research?

Flick (1998: 57) summarizes Wolff's (2004) work in identifying several issues in entering institutions for the purpose of conducting research:

- Research is always an intrusion and intervention into a social system, and, so, disrupts the system to be studied, such that the system reacts, often defensively.
- There is a 'mutual opacity' between the social system under study and the research project,

which is not reduced by information exchange between the system under study and the researcher; rather this increases the complexity of the situation and, hence, 'immune reactions'.

- Rather than striving for mutual understanding at the point of entry, it is more advisable to strive for an agreement as a process.
- While it is necessary to agree storage rights for data, this may contribute to increasing the complexity of the agreement to be reached.
- The field under study becomes clear only when one has entered it.
- The research project usually has nothing to offer the social system; hence no great promises for benefit or services can be made by the researcher, yet there may be no real reason why the social system should reject the researcher.

As Flick (1998: 57) remarks, the research will disturb the system and disrupt routines without being able to offer any real benefit for the institution.

The issue of managing relations is critical for the qualitative researcher. We discuss issues of access, gatekeepers and informants in Chapter 4. The researcher is seen as coming 'without history' (Wolff 2004: 198), a 'professional stranger' (Flick 1998: 59), one who has to be accepted, become familiar and yet remain distant from those being studied. Indeed Flick (1998: 60) suggests four roles of the researcher: stranger, visitor, insider and initiate. The first two essentially maintain the outsider role, while the latter two attempt to reach into the institution from an insider's perspective. These latter two become difficult to manage if one is dealing with sensitive issues (see Chapter 5). This typology resonates with the four roles typically cited for observers, as shown in the diagram below.

Role negotiation, balance and trust are significant and difficult. For example, if one were to research a school, what role should one adopt:

a teacher, a researcher, an inspector, a friend, a manager, a provider of a particular service (e.g. extracurricular activities), a counsellor, a social worker, a resource provider, a librarian, a cleaner, a server in the school shop or canteen, and so on? The issue is that one has to try to select a role that will provide access to as wide a range of people as possible, preserve neutrality (not being seen as on anybody's side), and enable confidences to be secured.

Role conflict, strain and ambiguity are to be expected in qualitative research. For example, De Laine (2002: 29) comments on the potential conflicts between the researcher *qua* researcher, therapist, friend. She indicates that diverse role positions are rarely possible to plan in advance, and are an inevitable part of fieldwork, giving rise to ethical and moral problems for the researcher, and, in turn, requiring ongoing negotiation and resolution.

Roles change over time. Walford (2001: 62) reports a staged process wherein the researcher's role moved through five phases: newcomer, provisional acceptance, categorical acceptance, personal acceptance and imminent migrant. Walford (2001: 71) also reports that it is almost to be expected that managing different roles not only throws the researcher into questioning his/her ability to handle the situation, but also brings considerable emotional and psychological stress, anxiety and feelings of inadequacy. This is thrown into sharp relief when researchers have to conceal information, take on different roles in order to gain access, retain neutrality, compromise personal beliefs and values, and handle situations where they are seeking information from others but not divulging information about themselves. Walford (2001) suggests that researchers may have little opportunity to negotiate roles and manoeuvre roles, as they are restricted by the expectations of those being researched.

Outsider			Insider
Detached observer	Observer as participant	Participant as observer	Complete participant

A related issue is the timing of the point of entry, so that researchers can commence the research at appropriate junctures (e.g. before the start of a programme, at the start of a programme, during a programme, at the end of a programme, after the end of a programme). The issue goes further than this, for the ethnographer will need to ensure acceptance into the group, which will be a matter of dress, demeanour, persona, age, colour, ethnicity, empathy and identification with the group, language, accent, argot and jargon, willingness to become involved and to take on the group's values and behaviour etc. (see Patrick's (1973) fascinating study of a Glasgow gang). The researcher, then, has to be aware of the significance of 'impression management' (Hammersley and Atkinson 1983: 78 ff.). In covert research these factors take on added significance, as one slip could blow one's cover (Patrick 1973).

Lofland (1971) suggests that the field researcher should attempt to adopt the role of the 'acceptable incompetent', balancing intrusion with knowing when to remain apart. Such balancing is an ongoing process. Hammersley and Atkinson (1983: 97–9) suggest that researchers have to handle the management of 'marginality': they are in the organization but not of it. They comment that 'the ethnographer must be intellectually poised between "familiarity" and "strangeness", while socially he or she is poised between "stranger" and "friend".' They also comment that this management of several roles, not least the management of marginality, can engender 'a continual sense of insecurity' (Hammersley and Atkinson 1983: 100).

Gaining access and entry, as we argue in Chapter 5, should be regarded as a process (Walford 2001: 31) that unfolds over time, rather than a once and for all matter. Walford charts the several setbacks, delays and modifications that occur and have to be expected in gaining entry to qualitative research sites.

Stage 5: Finding informants

Finding informants involves identifying those people who have the knowledge about the society or group being studied. This places researchers in a difficult position, for they have to be able to evaluate key informants, to decide:

- whose accounts are more important than others
- which informants are competent to pass comments
- which are reliable
- what the statuses of the informants are
- how representative are the key informants (of the range of people, of issues, of situations, of views, of status, of roles, of the group)
- how to see the informants in different settings
- how knowledgeable informants actually are – do they have intimate and expert understanding of the situation
- how central to the organization or situation the informant is (e.g. marginal or central)
- how to meet and select informants
- how critical the informants are as gatekeepers to other informants, opening up or restricting entry to people (Hammersley and Atkinson 1983: 73)
- the relationship between the informant and others in the group or situation being studied.

Selecting informants and engaging with them is problematical; LeCompte and Preissle (1993: 95), for example, suggest that the first informants that an ethnographer meets might be self-selected people who are marginal to the group, have a low status, and who, therefore, might be seeking to enhance their own prestige by being involved with the research. Indeed, Lincoln and Guba (1985: 252) argue that the researcher must be careful to use informants rather than informers, the latter possibly having 'an axe to grind'. Researchers who are working with gatekeepers, they argue, will be engaged in a constant process of bargaining and negotiation.

A 'good' informant, Morse (1994: 228) declares, is one who has the necessary knowledge, information and experience of the issue being researched, is capable of reflecting on that knowledge and experience, has time to be involved in the project, is willing to be involved in the project, and, indeed, can provide access to other informants. An informant who fulfils all of these criteria is termed a 'primary informant'. Morse (1994) also cautions that not all these features may be present in the informants, but that they may still be useful for the research, though the researcher would have to decide how much time to spend with these 'secondary' informants.

Stage 6: Developing and maintaining relations in the field

This involves addressing interpersonal and practical issues, for example:

- building participants' confidence in the researcher
- developing rapport, trust, sensitivity and discretion
- handling people and issues with which the researcher disagrees or finds objectionable or repulsive
- being attentive and empathizing
- being discreet
- deciding how long to stay.

Spindler and Spindler (1992: 65) suggest that ethnographic validity is attained by having the researcher *in situ* long enough to see things happening repeatedly rather than just once, that is to say, observing regularities.

LeCompte and Preissle (1993: 89) suggest that fieldwork, particularly because it is conducted face-to-face, raises problems and questions that are less significant in research that is conducted at a distance, including:

- how to communicate meaningfully with participants
- how they and the researcher might be affected by the emotions evoked in one another, and how to handle these
- differences and similarities between the researcher and the participants (e.g. personal characteristics, power, resources), and how these might affect relationships between parties and the course of the investigation
- the researcher's responsibilities to the participants (*qua* researcher and member of their community), even if the period of residence in the community is short

- how to balance responsibilities to the community with responsibilities to other interested parties.

Critically important in this area is the maintenance of trust and rapport (De Laine 2000: 41), showing interest, assuring confidentiality (where appropriate) and avoiding being judgemental. She adds to these the ability to tolerate ambiguity, to keep self-doubt in check, to withstand insecurity, and to be flexible and accommodating (De Laine 2000: 97). Such features are not able to be encapsulated in formal agreements, but they are the lifeblood of effective qualitative enquiry. They are process matters.

The issue here is that the data collection process is itself socially situated; it is neither a clean, antiseptic activity nor always a straightforward negotiation.

Stage 7: Data collection *in situ*

The qualitative researcher is able to use a variety of techniques for gathering information. There is no single prescription for which data collection instruments to use; rather the issue here is of 'fitness for purpose' because, as was mentioned earlier, the ethnographer is a methodological omnivore! That said, there are several types of data collection instruments that are used more widely in qualitative research than others. The researcher can use field notes, participant observation, journal notes, interviews, diaries, life histories, artefacts, documents, video recordings, audio recordings etc. Several of these are discussed elsewhere in this book. Lincoln and Guba (1985: 199) distinguish between 'obtrusive' (e.g. interviews, observation, non-verbal language) and 'unobtrusive' methods (e.g. documents and records), on the basis of whether another human typically is present at the point of data collection.

Field notes can be written both *in situ* and away from the situation. They contain the results of observations. The nature of observation in ethnographic research is discussed fully in Chapter 17. Accompanying observation techniques is the use of interviews, documentary analysis and life histories. These are discussed separately in Chapters 7, 15 and 16. The popularly used interview technique employed in qualitative research is the semi-structured interview, where a schedule is prepared that is sufficiently open-ended to enable the contents to be reordered, digressions and expansions made, new avenues to be included, and further probing to be undertaken. Carspecken (1996: 159–60) describes how such interviews can range from the interrogator giving bland encouragements, 'non-leading' leads, active listening and low-inference paraphrasing to medium- and high-inference paraphrasing. In interviews the researcher might wish to further explore some matters arising from observations. In naturalistic research the canons of validity in interviews include: honesty, depth of response, richness of response, and commitment of the interviewee (Oppenheim 1992).

Lincoln and Guba (1985: 268–70) propose several purposes for interviewing, including: *present constructions* of events, feelings, persons, organizations, activities, motivations, concerns, claims, etc.; *reconstructions* of past experiences; *projections* into the future; *verifying, amending and extending data.*

Further, Silverman (1993: 92–3) adds that interviews in qualitative research are useful for: gathering facts; accessing beliefs about facts; identifying feelings and motives; commenting on the standards of actions (what could be done about situations); exploring present or previous behaviour; eliciting reasons and explanations.

Lincoln and Guba (1985) emphasize that the planning of the conduct of the interview is important, including the background preparation, the opening of the interview, its pacing and timing, keeping the conversation going and eliciting knowledge, and rounding off and ending the interview. Clearly, it is important that careful consideration be given to the several stages of the interview. For example, at the planning stage, attention will need to be given to the number (per person), duration, timing, frequency, setting/location, number of people in a single interview situation (e.g. individual or group interviews) and respondent styles (LeCompte and

Preissle 1993: 177). At the implementation stage the conduct of the interview will be important, for example, responding to interviewees, prompting, probing, supporting, empathizing, clarifying, crystallizing, exemplifying, summarizing, avoiding censure, accepting. At the analysis stage there will be several important considerations, for example (LeCompte and Preissle 1993: 195): the ease and clarity of communication of meaning; the interest levels of the participants; the clarity of the question and the response; the precision (and communication of this) of the interviewer; how the interviewer handles questionable responses (e.g. fabrications, untruths, claims made).

The qualitative interview tends to move away from a prestructured, standardized form towards an open-ended or semi-structured arrangement (see Chapter 16), which enables respondents to project their own ways of defining the world. It permits flexibility rather than fixity of sequence of discussions, allowing participants to raise and pursue issues and matters that might not have been included in a pre-devised schedule (Denzin 1970b; Silverman 1993).

In addition to interviews, Lincoln and Guba (1985) discuss data collection from non-human sources, including:

- *Documents and records* (e.g. archival records, private records): these have the attraction of being always available, often at low cost, and being factual. On the other hand, they may be unrepresentative, they may be selective, lack objectivity, be of unknown validity, and may possibly be deliberately deceptive (see Finnegan 1996).
- *Unobtrusive informational residues:* these include artefacts, physical traces, and a variety of other records. While they frequently have face validity, and while they may be simple and direct, gained by non-interventional means (hence reducing the problems of reactivity), they may also be very heavily inferential, difficult to interpret, and may contain elements whose relevance is questionable.

Qualitative data collection is not hidebound to a few named strategies; it is marked by eclecticism and fitness for purpose. It is not to say that 'anything goes' but 'use what is appropriate' is sound advice. Mason (2002: 33–4) advocates the integration of methods, for several reasons:

- to explore different elements or parts of a phenomenon, ensuring that the researcher knows how they interrelate
- to answer different research questions
- to answer the same research question but in different ways and from different perspectives
- to give greater or lesser depth and breadth to analysis
- to triangulate (corroborate) by seeking different data about the same phenomenon.

Mason (2002: 35) argues that integration can take many forms. She suggests that it is necessary for researchers to consider whether the data are to complement each other, to be combined, grouped and aggregated, and to contribute to an overall picture. She also argues that it is important for the data to complement each other ontologically, to be ontologically consistent, i.e. whether they are 'based on similar, complementary or comparable assumptions about the nature of social entities and phenomena'. Added to this Mason (2002: 36) suggests that integration must be in an epistemological sense, i.e. where the data emanate from the same, or at least complementary, epistemologies, whether they are based on 'similar, complementary or comparable assumptions about what can legitimately constitute knowledge of evidence'. Finally Mason (2002: 36) argues that integration must occur at the level of explanation. By this she means that the data from different courses and methods must be able to be combined into a coherent, convincing and relevant explanation and argument.

Stage 8: Data collection outside the field

In order to make comparisons and to suggest explanations for phenomena, researchers might find it useful to go beyond the confines of the groups in which they occur. That this is a thorny issue is indicated in the following example. Two students are arguing very violently and physically in a school. At one level it is simply a fight between two people. However, this is a common occurrence between these two students as they are neighbours outside school and they don't enjoy positive amicable relations as their families are frequently feuding. The two households have been placed next door to each other by the local authority because if has taken a decision to keep together families who are very poor at paying for local housing rent (i.e. a 'sink' estate). The local authority has taken this decision because of a government policy to keep together disadvantaged groups so that targeted action and interventions can be more effective, thus meeting the needs of whole communities as well as individuals.

The issue here is: how far out of a micro-situation does the researcher need to go to understand that micro-situation? This is an imprecise matter but it is not insignificant in educational research: for example, it underpinned: (a) the celebrated work by Bowles and Gintis (1976) on schooling in capitalist America, in which the authors suggested that the hidden curricula of schools were preparing students for differential occupational futures that perpetuated an inegalitarian capitalist system, (b) research on the self-fulfilling prophecy (Hurn 1978), (c) work by Pollard (1985: 110) on the social world of the primary school, where everyday interactions in school were preparing students for the individualism, competition, achievement orientation, hierarchies and self-reliance that characterize mass private consumption in wider society, (d) Delamont's (1981) advocacy that educationists should study similar but different institutions to schools (e.g. hospitals and other 'total' institutions) in order to make the familiar strange (see also Erickson 1973).

Stage 9: Data analysis

Although we devote two chapters specifically to qualitative data analysis later in this book (Chapters 22 and 23), there are some preliminary remarks that we make here, by way of fidelity to the eleven-stage process of qualitative research outlined earlier in the chapter. Data analysis involves organizing, accounting for, and explaining the data; in short, making sense of data in terms of participants' definitions of the situation, noting patterns, themes, categories and regularities. Typically in qualitative research, data analysis commences during the data collection process. There are several reasons for this, and these are discussed below.

At a practical level, qualitative research rapidly amasses huge amounts of data, and early analysis reduces the problem of data overload by selecting out significant features for future focus. Miles and Huberman (1984) suggest that careful data display is an important element of data reduction and selection. 'Progressive focusing', according to Parlett and Hamilton (1976), starts with the researcher taking a wide-angle lens to gather data, and then, by sifting, sorting, reviewing and reflecting on them, the salient features of the situation emerge. These are then used as the agenda for subsequent focusing. The process is like funnelling from the wide to the narrow.

At a theoretical level a major feature of qualitative research is that analysis commences early on in the data collection process so that theory generation can be undertaken (LeCompte and Preissle 1993: 238). LeCompte and Preissle (1993: 237–53) advise that researchers should set out the main outlines of the phenomena that are under investigation. They then should assemble chunks or groups of data, putting them together to make a coherent whole (e.g. through writing summaries of what has been found). Then they should painstakingly take apart their field notes, matching, contrasting, aggregating, comparing and ordering notes made. The intention is to move from description to explanation and theory generation.

For clarity, the process of data analysis can be portrayed in a sequence of seven steps which are set out here and addressed in subsequent pages.

> **Step 1:** Establish units of analysis of the data, indicating how these units are similar to and different from each other
> **Step 2:** Create a 'domain analysis'

Step 3: Establish relationships and linkages between the domains
Step 4: Making speculative inferences
Step 5: Summarizing
Step 6: Seeking negative and discrepant cases
Step 7: Theory generation

Step 1: *Establish units of analysis of the data, indicating how these units are similar to and different from each other.* The criterion here is that each unit of analysis (category – conceptual, actual, classification element, cluster, issue) should be as discrete as possible while retaining fidelity to the integrity of the whole, i.e. that each unit must be a fair rather than a distorted representation of the context and other data. The creation of units of analysis can be done by ascribing *codes* to the data (Miles and Huberman 1984). This is akin to the process of 'unitizing' (Lincoln and Guba 1985: 203).

Step 2: *Create a 'domain analysis'.* A domain analysis involves grouping together items and units into related clusters, themes and patterns, a domain being a category which contains several other categories. We address domain analysis in more detail in Chapter 23.

Step 3: *Establish relationships and linkages between the domains.* This process ensures that the data, their richness and 'context-groundedness' are retained. Linkages can be found by identifying confirming cases, by seeking 'underlying associations' (LeCompte and Preissle 1993: 246) and connections between data subsets.

Step 4: *Making speculative inferences.* This is an important stage, for it moves the research from description to inference. It requires the researcher, on the basis of the evidence, to posit some explanations for the situation, some key elements and possibly even their causes. It is the process of hypothesis generation or the setting of working hypotheses that feeds into theory generation.

Step 5: *Summarizing.* This involves the researcher in writing a preliminary summary of the main features, key issues, key concepts, constructs and ideas encountered so far in the research. We address summarizing in more detail in Chapter 23.

Step 6: *Seeking negative and discrepant cases.* In theory generation it is important to seek not only confirming cases but to weigh the significance of disconfirming cases. LeCompte and Preissle (1993: 270) suggest that because interpretations of the data are grounded in the data themselves, results that fail to support an original hypothesis are neither discarded nor discredited; rather, it is the hypotheses themselves that must be modified to accommodate these data. Indeed Erickson (1992: 208) identifies progressive problem-solving as one key aspect of ethnographic research and data analysis. LeCompte and Preissle (1993: 250–1) define a negative case as an exemplar which disconfirms or refutes the working hypothesis, rule or explanation so far. It is the qualitative researcher's equivalent of the positivist's null hypothesis. The theory that is being developed becomes more robust if it addresses negative cases, for it sets the boundaries to the theory; it modifies the theory, it sets parameters to the applicability of the theory.

Discrepant cases are not so much exceptions to the rule (as in negative cases) as variants of the rule (LeCompte and Preissle 1993: 251). The discrepant case leads to the modification or elaboration of the construct, rule or emerging hypothesis. Discrepant case analysis requires the researcher to seek out cases for which the rule, construct, or explanation cannot account or with which they will not fit, i.e. they are neither exceptions nor contradictions, they are simply different!

Step 7: *Theory generation.* Here the theory derives from the data – it is grounded in the data and emerges from it. As Lincoln and Guba (1985: 205) argue, grounded theory must fit the situation that is being researched. Grounded theory is an iterative process, moving backwards and forwards between data and theory until the theory fits the data. This breaks the linearity of much conventional research (Flick 1998: 41, 43) in which hypotheses are formulated, sampling is

decided, data are collected and then analysed and hypotheses are supported or not supported. In grounded theory a circular and recursive process is adopted, wherein modifications are made to the theory in light of data, more data are sought to investigate emergent issues (theoretical sampling), and hypotheses and theories emerge from the data.

Lincoln and Guba (1985: 354–5) urge the researcher to be mindful of several issues in analysing and interpreting the data, including:

- data overload
- the problem of acting on first impressions only
- the availability of people and information (e.g. how representative these are and how to know if missing people and data might be important)
- the dangers of only seeking confirming rather than disconfirming instances
- the reliability and consistency of the data and confidence that can be placed in the results.

These are significant issues in addressing reliability, trustworthiness and validity in the research (see the discussions of reliability and validity in Chapter 5). The essence of this approach, that theory emerges from and is grounded in data, is not without its critics. For example, Silverman (1993: 47) suggests that it fails to acknowledge the implicit theories which guide research in its early stages (i.e. data are not theory neutral but theory saturated) and that it might be strong on providing categorizations without necessarily explanatory potential. These are caveats that should feed into the process of reflexivity in qualitative research, perhaps.

Stage 10: Leaving the field

The issue here is how to conclude the research, how to terminate the roles adopted, how (and whether) to bring to an end the relationships that have built up over the course of the research, and how to disengage from the field in ways that bring as little disruption to the group or situation as possible (LeCompte and Preissle 1993: 101). De

Laine (2000: 142) remarks that some participants may want to maintain contact after the research is over, and not to do this might create, for them, a sense of disappointment, exploitation or even betrayal. One has to consider the after-effects of leaving and take care to ensure that nobody comes to harm or is worse off from the research, even if it is impossible to ensure that they have benefited from it.

Stage 11: Writing the report

In research literature there is a move away from the *conduct* of the research and towards the *reporting* of the research. It is often the case that the main vehicle for writing naturalistic research is the case study (see Chapter 11), whose 'trustworthiness' (Lincoln and Guba 1985: 189) is defined in terms of credibility, transferability, dependability and confirmability – discussed in Chapter 6. Case studies are useful in that they can provide the thick descriptions that are useful in ethnographic research, and can catch and portray to the reader what it is like to be involved in the situation (p. 214). As Lincoln and Guba (1985: 359) comment, the case study is the ideal instrument for *emic* inquiry. It also builds in and builds on the tacit knowledge that the writer and reader bring to the report, and, thereby, takes seriously their notion of the 'human instrument' in research, indicating the interactions of researcher and participants.

Lincoln and Guba (1985: 365–6) provide several guidelines for writing case studies:

- The writing should strive to be informal and to capture informality.
- As far as possible the writing should report facts except in those sections where interpretation, evaluation and inference are made explicit.
- In drafting the report it is more advisable to opt for over-inclusion rather than under-inclusion.
- The ethical conventions of report writing must be honoured, e.g. anonymity, non-traceability.
- The case study writer should make clear the data that give rise to the report, so the readers have a means of checking back for reliability and validity and inferences.
- A fixed completion date should be specified.

Spradley (1979) suggests nine practical steps that can be followed in writing an ethnography:

1 Select the audience.
2 Select the thesis.
3 Make a list of topics and create an outline of the ethnography.
4 Write a rough draft of each section of the ethnography.
5 Revise the outline and create subheadings.
6 Edit the draft.
7 Write an introduction and a conclusion.
8 Reread the data and report to identify examples.
9 Write the final version.

Clearly there are several other aspects of case study reporting that need to be addressed. These are set out in Chapter 11.

Critical ethnography

An emerging branch of ethnography that resonates with the critical paradigm outlined in Chapter 1 is the field of critical ethnography. Here not only is qualitative, anthropological, participant, observer-based research undertaken, but also its theoretical basis lies in critical theory (Quantz 1992: 448; Carspecken 1996). As was outlined in Chapter 1, this paradigm is concerned with the exposure of oppression and inequality in society with a view to emancipating individuals and groups towards collective empowerment. In this respect research is an inherently political enterprise. Carspecken (1996: 4 ff.) suggests several key premises of critical ethnography:

- Research and thinking are mediated by power relations.
- These power relations are socially and historically located.
- Facts and values are inseparable.

- Relationships between objects and concepts are fluid and mediated by the social relations of production.
- Language is central to perception.
- Certain groups in society exert more power than others.
- Inequality and oppression are inherent in capitalist relations of production and consumption.
- Ideological domination is strongest when oppressed groups see their situation as inevitable, natural or necessary.
- Forms of oppression mediate each other and must be considered together (e.g. race, gender, class).

Quantz (1992: 473–4) argues that research is inescapably value-laden in that it serves some interests, and that in critical ethnography researchers must expose these interests and move participants towards emancipation and freedom. The focus and process of research are thus political at heart, concerning issues of power, domination, voice and empowerment. In critical ethnography the cultures, groups and individuals being studied are located in contexts of power and interests. These contexts have to be exposed, their legitimacy interrogated, and the value base of the research itself exposed. Reflexivity is high in critical ethnography. What separates critical ethnography from other forms of ethnography is that, in the former, questions of legitimacy, power, values in society and domination and oppression are foregrounded.

How does the critical ethnographer proceed?

Carspecken and Apple (1992: 512–14) and Carspecken (1996: 41–2) identify five stages in critical ethnography, as described below.

Stage 1: Compiling the primary record through the collection of monological data

At this stage researchers are comparatively passive and unobtrusive – participant observers.

The task here is to acquire *objective* data and it is 'monological' in the sense that it concerns only the researchers writing their own notes to themselves. Lincoln and Guba (1985) suggest that validity checks at this stage will include

- using multiple devices for recording together with multiple observers
- using a flexible observation schedule in order to minimize biases
- remaining in the situation for a long time in order to overcome the Hawthorne effect
- using low-inference terminology and descriptions
- using peer-debriefing
- using respondent validation.

Echoing Habermas's (1979; 1982; 1984) work on validity claims, validity here includes truth (the veracity of the utterance), legitimacy (rightness and appropriateness of the speaker), comprehensibility (that the utterance is comprehensible) and sincerity (of the speaker's intentions). Carspecken (1996: 104–5) takes this further in suggesting several categories of reference in objective validity: that the act is comprehensible, socially legitimate and appropriate; that the actor has a particular identity and particular intentions or feelings when the action takes place; that objective, contextual factors are acknowledged.

Stage 2: Preliminary reconstructive analysis

Reconstructive analysis attempts to uncover the taken-for-granted components of meaning or abstractions that participants have of a situation. Such analysis is intended to identify the value systems, norms, key concepts that are guiding and underpinning situations. Carspecken (1996: 42) suggests that the researcher goes back over the primary record from Stage 1 to examine patterns of interaction, power relations, roles, sequences of events, and meanings accorded to situations. He asserts that what distinguishes this stage as 'reconstructive' is that cultural themes, social and system factors that are not usually articulated by the participants themselves are, in fact, reconstructed and articulated, making the undiscursive into discourse. In moving to higher level abstractions this stage can utilize high level coding (see the discussion of coding in this chapter).

In critical ethnography Carspecken (1996: 141) delineates several ways of ensuring validity at this stage:

- Use interviews and group discussions with the subjects themselves.
- Conduct member checks on the reconstruction in order to equalize power relations.
- Use peer debriefing (a peer is asked to review the data to suggest if the researcher is being too selective, e.g. of individuals, of data, of inference) to check biases or absences in reconstructions.
- Employ prolonged engagement to heighten the researcher's capacity to assume the insider's perspective.
- Use 'strip analysis' – checking themes and segments of extracted data with the primary data, for consistency.
- Use negative case analysis.

Stage 3: Dialogical data collection

Here data are generated by, and discussed with, the participants (Carspecken and Apple 1992). The authors argue that this is not-naturalistic in that the participants are being asked to reflect on their own situations, circumstances and lives and to begin to theorize about their lives. This is a crucial stage because it enables the participants to have a voice, to democratize the research. It may be that this stage produces new data that challenge the preceding two stages.

In introducing greater subjectivity by participants into the research at this stage Carspecken (1996: 164–5) proffers several validity checks, e.g. consistency checks on interviews that have been recorded; repeated interviews with participants; matching observation with what participants say is happening or has happened; avoiding leading questions at interview, reinforced by having peer debriefers check on this; respondent validation; asking participants to use their own terms in describing naturalistic contexts, and encouraging them to explain these terms.

Stage 4: Discovering system relations

This stage relates the group being studied to other factors that impinge on that group, e.g. local community groups, local sites that produce cultural products. At this stage Carspecken (1996: 202) notes that validity checks will include maintaining the validity requirements of the earlier stages, seeking a match between the researcher's analysis and the commentaries that are provided by the participants and other researchers, and using peer debriefers and respondent validation.

Stage 5: Using system relations to explain findings

This stage seeks to examine and explain the findings in light of macro-social theories (Carspecken 1996: 202). In part, this is a matching exercise to fit the research findings within a social theory.

In critical ethnography, therefore, the move is from describing a situation, to understanding it, to questioning it, and to changing it. This parallels the stages of ideology critique set out in Chapter 1:

> **Stage 1:** a description of the existing situation – a hermeneutic exercise
> **Stage 2:** a penetration of the reasons that brought the situation to the form that it takes
> **Stage 3:** an agenda for altering the situation
> **Stage 4:** an evaluation of the achievement of the new situation.

Some problems with ethnographic and naturalistic approaches

There are several difficulties in ethnographic and natural approaches (see http://www.routledge.com/textbooks/9780415368780 – Chapter 7, file

7.3. ppt). These might affect the reliability and validity of the research, and include the following.

1 *The definition of the situation:* the participants are being asked for their definition of the situation, yet they have no monopoly on wisdom. They may be 'falsely conscious' (unaware of the 'real' situation), deliberately distorting or falsifying information, or being highly selective. The issues of reliability and validity here are addressed in Chapter 6 (see the discussions of triangulation).

2 *Reactivity:* the Hawthorne effect – the presence of the researcher alters the situation as participants may wish to avoid, impress, direct, deny, or influence the researcher. Again, this is discussed in Chapter 6. Typically the problem of reactivity is addressed by careful negotiation in the field, remaining in the field for a considerable time, ensuring as far as possible a careful presentation of the researcher's self.

3 *The halo effect:* where existing or given information about the situation or participants might be used to be selective in subsequent data collection, or may bring about a particular reading of a subsequent situation (the research equivalent of the self-fulfilling prophecy). This is an issue of reliability, and can be addressed by the use of a wide, triangulated database and the assistance of an external observer. The *halo effect* commonly refers to the researcher's belief in the goodness of participants (the participants have haloes around their heads!), such that the more negative aspects of their behaviour or personality are neglected or overlooked. By contrast, the *horns effect* refers to the researcher's belief in the badness of the participants (the participants have devils' horns on their heads!), such that the more positive aspects of their behaviour or personality are neglected or overlooked.

4 The *implicit conservatism* of the interpretive methodology. The kind of research described in this chapter, with the possible exception of critical ethnography, accepts the perspective of the participants and corroborates the status quo. It is focused on the past and the present rather than on the future.

5 There is the difficulty of focusing on the *familiar*, participants (and, maybe researchers too) being so close to the situation that they neglect certain, often tacit, aspects of it. The task, therefore, is to make the familiar strange. Delamont (1981) suggests that this can be done by:

   • studying unusual examples of the same issue (e.g. atypical classrooms, timetabling or organizations of schools)
   • studying examples in other cultures
   • studying other situations that might have a bearing on the situation in hand (e.g. if studying schools it might be useful to look at other similar-but-different organizations, for instance hospitals or prisons)
   • taking a significant issue and focusing on it deliberately, e.g. gendered behaviour.

6 The *open-endedness and diversity* of the situations studied. Hammersley (1993) counsels that the drive towards focusing on specific contexts and situations might overemphasize the difference between contexts and situations rather than their gross similarity, their routine features. Researchers, he argues, should be as aware of regularities as of differences.

7 The *neglect of wider social contexts and constraints*. Studying situations that emphasize how highly context-bound they are, might neglect broader currents and contexts – micro-level research risks putting boundaries that exclude important macro-level factors. Wider macro-contexts cannot be ruled out of individual situations.

8 The issue of *generalizability*. If situations are unique and non-generalizable, as many naturalistic principles would suggest, how is the issue of generalizability going to be addressed? To which contexts will the findings apply, and what is the role and nature of replication studies?

9   How to write up *multiple realities* and explanations? How will a representative view be reached? What if the researcher sees things that are not seen by the participants?

10 Who *owns* the data, the report, and who has control over the release of the data?

Naturalistic and ethnographic research, then, are important but problematical research methods in education. Their widespread use signals their increasing acceptance as legitimate and important styles of research.

8 Historical and documentary research

Introduction

Mouly (1978) states that while historical research cannot meet some of the tests of the scientific method interpreted in the specific sense of its use in the physical sciences (it cannot depend, for instance, on direct observation or experimentation, but must make use of reports that cannot be repeated), it qualifies as a scientific endeavour from the standpoint of its subscription to the same principles and the same general scholarship that characterize all scientific research.

Historical research has been defined as the systematic and objective location, evaluation and synthesis of evidence in order to establish facts and draw conclusions about past events (Borg (1963). It is an act of reconstruction undertaken in a spirit of critical inquiry designed to achieve a faithful representation of a previous age. In seeking data from the personal experiences and observations of others, from documents and records, researchers often have to contend with inadequate information so that their reconstructions tend to be sketches rather than portraits. Indeed, the difficulty of obtaining adequate data makes historical research one of the most taxing kinds of inquiry to conduct satisfactorily.[1] Reconstruction implies an holistic perspective in that the method of inquiry characterizing historical research attempts to 'encompass and then explain the whole realm of man's [sic] past in a perspective that greatly accents his social, cultural, economic, and intellectual development' (Hill and Kerber 1967).

Ultimately, historical research is concerned with a broad view of the conditions and not necessarily the specifics which bring them about, although such a synthesis is rarely achieved without intense debate or controversy, especially on matters of detail. The act of historical research involves the identification and limitation of a problem or an area of study; sometimes the formulation of an hypothesis (or set of questions); the collection, organization, verification, validation, analysis and selection of data; testing the hypothesis (or answering the questions) where appropriate; and writing a research report. This sequence leads to a new understanding of the past and its relevance to the present and future.

The values of historical research have been categorized by Hill and Kerber (1967) as follows:

- It enables solutions to contemporary problems to be sought in the past.
- It throws light on present and future trends.
- It stresses the relative importance and the effects of the various interactions that are to be found within all cultures.
- It allows for the revaluation of data in relation to selected hypotheses, theories and generalizations that are presently held about the past.

As the writers point out, the ability of history to employ the past to predict the future, and to use the present to explain the past, gives it a dual and unique quality which makes it especially useful for all sorts of scholarly study and research.[2]

The particular value of historical research in the field of education is unquestioned. Although one of the most difficult areas in which to undertake research, the outcomes of inquiry into this domain can bring great benefit to educationalists and the community at large. It can, for example, yield insights into some educational problems that could not be achieved by any other means. Further, the historical study of an educational idea or institution can do much to help us understand how our present educational system has come about; and this kind of understanding can in turn help to establish a sound basis for further progress of change. Historical research in education can also show how and why educational theories and practices developed. It enables educationalists to use former practices to evaluate newer, emerging ones. Recurrent trends can be more easily identified and assessed from an historical standpoint – witness, for example, the various guises in which progressivism in education has appeared. And it can contribute to a fuller understanding of the relationship between politics and education, between school and society, between local and central government, and between teacher and pupil.

Historical research in education may concern itself with an individual, a group, a movement, an idea or an institution. As Best (1970) points out, however, not one of these objects of historical interest and observation can be considered in isolation. No one person can be subjected to historical investigation without some consideration of his or her contribution to the ideas, movements or institutions of a particular time or place. These elements are always interrelated. The focus merely determines the point of emphasis towards which historical researchers direct their attention. Box 8.1 illustrates some of these relationships from the history of education. For example, no matter whether the historian chooses to study the Jesuit order, religious teaching orders, the

Counter-Reformation or Ignatius Loyola, each of the other elements appears as a prominent influence or result, and an indispensable part of the narrative.

For an example of historical research see Thomas (1992) and Gaukroger and Schwartz (1997).

Choice of subject

As with other methods we consider in this book, historical research may be structured by a flexible sequence of stages, beginning with the selection and evaluation of a problem or area of study. Then follows the definition of the problem in more precise terms, the selection of suitable sources of data, collection, classification and processing of the data, and finally, the evaluation and synthesis of the data into a balanced and objective account of the subject under investigation. There are, however, some important differences between the method of historical research and other research methods used in education. The principal difference has been highlighted by Borg (1963), who suggests that in historical research, it is important for the student to define carefully the problem and appraise its appropriateness before moving into earnest into the project, as many problems may not be suitable for historical research methods, while, on the other hand, other problems may have little or no chance of yielding any significant results either because of the dearth of relevant data or because the problem is trivial.

Box 8.1
Some historical interrelations between men, movements and institutions

Men	Movements	Institutions Type	Specific
Ignatius Loyola	Counter-Reformation	Religious teaching order	Society of Jesus, 1534
Benjamin Franklin	Scientific movement; Education for life	Academy	Philadelphia Academy, 1751
John Dewey	Experimentalism Progressive education	Experimental school	University of Chicago Elementary School, 1896

Source: adapted from Best 1970

One can see from Borg's observations that the choice of a problem can sometimes be a daunting business for the potential researcher. Once a topic has been selected, however, and its potential and significance for historical research evaluated, the next stage is to define it more precisely, or, perhaps more pertinently, delimit it so that a more potent analysis will result. Too broad or too vague a statement can result in the final report lacking direction or impact. Best (1970) expresses it like this: 'The experienced historian realizes that research must be a penetrating analysis of a limited problem, rather than the superficial examination of a broad area. The weapon of research is the rifle not the shotgun'. Various prescriptions exist for helping to define historical topics. Gottschalk (1951) recommends that four questions should be asked in identifying a topic:

- Where do the events take place?
- Who are the people involved?
- When do the events occur?
- What kinds of human activity are involved?

As Travers (1969) suggests, the scope of a topic can be modified by adjusting the focus of any one of the four categories; the geographical area involved can be increased or decreased; more or fewer people can be included in the topic; the time span involved can be increased or decreased; and the human activity category can be broadened or narrowed. It sometimes happens that a piece of historical research can only begin with a rough idea of what the topic involves; and that delimitation of it can take place only after the pertinent material has been assembled.

In hand with the careful specification of the problem goes the need, where this is appropriate, for an equally specific and testable hypothesis (sometimes a sequence of questions may be substituted). As in empirical research, the hypothesis gives direction and focus to data collection and analysis in historical research, overcoming the risk of aimless and simple accretion of facts, i.e. a hypothesis informs the search for, and selection of, data, a particular problem if many data exist in the field. It imposes a selection, a structure on what would otherwise

be an overwhelming mass of information. Borg (1963) observes that this requires the careful focusing, delimiting and operationalization of the hypothesis.

Hill and Kerber (1967) have pointed out that the evaluation and formulation of a problem associated with historical research often involve the personality of the researcher to a greater extent than do other basic types of research. They suggest that personal factors of the investigator such as interest, motivation, historical curiosity, and educational background for the interpretation of historical facts tend to influence the selection of the problem to a great extent.

Data collection

One of the principal differences between historical research and other forms of research is that historical research must deal with data that already exist. Hockett (1955) argues that, as history is not a science which uses *direct* observation as in chemistry or biology, the historian, like the archaeologist, has to interpret past events by the traces which have been left. Of course, the historian has to base judgements on evidence, weighing, evaluating and judging the truth of the evidence of others' observations until the hypothesis explains all the relevant evidence.

Sources of data in historical research may be classified into two main groups: *primary sources*, which are the life-blood of historical research, and *secondary sources*, which may be used in the absence of, or to supplement, primary data.

Primary sources of data have been described as those items that are original to the problem under study and may be thought of as being in two categories. First, the remains or relics of a given period: although such remains and artefacts as skeletons, fossils, weapons, tools, utensils, buildings, pictures, furniture, coins and objets d'art were not meant to transmit information to subsequent eras, nevertheless they may be useful sources providing sound evidence about the past. Second, those items that have had a direct physical relationship with the events being reconstructed: this category would include not only the written and oral testimony provided by actual participants in, or witnesses of, an event, but also the participants themselves. Documents considered as primary sources include manuscripts, charters, laws, archives of official minutes or records, files, letters, memoranda, memoirs, biography, official publications, wills, newspapers and magazines, maps, diagrams, catalogues, films, paintings, inscriptions, recordings, transcriptions, log books and research reports. All these are, intentionally or unintentionally, capable of transmitting a first-hand account of an event and are therefore considered as sources of primary data. Historical research in education draws chiefly on the kind of sources identified in this second category.

Secondary sources are those that do not bear a direct physical relationship to the event being studied. They are made up of data that cannot be described as original. A secondary source would thus be one in which the person describing the event was not actually present but who obtained descriptions from another person or source. These may or may not have been primary sources. Other instances of secondary sources used in historical research include: quoted material, textbooks, encyclopedias, other reproductions of material or information, prints of paintings or replicas of art objects. Best (1970) points out that secondary sources of data are usually of limited worth because of the errors that result when information is passed on from one person to another.

Various commentators stress the importance of using primary sources of data where possible (Hill and Kerber 1967). The value, too, of secondary sources should not be minimized. There are numerous occasions where a secondary source can contribute significantly to more valid and reliable historical research than would otherwise be the case.

One further point: the review of the literature in other forms of educational research is regarded as a preparatory stage to gathering data and serves to acquaint researchers with previous research on the topics they are studying (Travers 1969). It thus enables them to continue in a tradition, to place their work in context, and to learn from earlier endeavours. The function of the review of the literature in historical research, however, is different in that it provides the data for research; the researchers' acceptance or otherwise of their hypotheses will depend on their selection of information from the review and the interpretation they put on it. Borg (1963) has identified other differences: one is that the historical researcher will have to peruse longer documents than the empirical researcher who normally studies articles very much more succinct and precise. Further, documents required in historical research often date back much further than those in empirical research. And one final point: documents in education often consist of unpublished material and are therefore less accessible than reports of empirical studies in professional journals.

For a detailed consideration of the specific problems of documentary research, the reader is referred to the articles by Platt (1981) where she considers those of authenticity, availability of documents, sampling problems, inference and interpretation.

Evaluation

Because workers in the field of historical research gather much of their data and information from records and documents, these must be carefully evaluated so as to attest their worth for the purposes of the particular study. Evaluation of historical data and information is often referred to as historical criticism and the reliable data yielded by the process are known as historical evidence. Historical evidence has thus been described as that body of validated facts and information which can be accepted as trustworthy, as a valid basis for the testing and interpretation of hypotheses. Historical criticism is usually undertaken in two stages: first, the authenticity of the source is appraised; and second, the accuracy or worth of the data is evaluated. The two processes are known as external and internal criticism respectively, and since they each present problems of evaluation they merit further inspection.

External criticism

External criticism is concerned with establishing the authenticity or genuineness of data. It is therefore aimed at the document (or other source) itself rather than the statements it contains; with analytic forms of the data rather than the interpretation or meaning of them in relation to the study. It therefore sets out to uncover frauds, forgeries, hoaxes, inventions or distortions. To this end, the tasks of establishing the age or authorship of a document may involve tests of factors such as signatures, handwriting, script, type, style, spelling and place-names. Further, was the knowledge it purports to transmit available at the time and is it consistent with what is known about the author or period from another source? Increasingly sophisticated analyses of physical factors can also yield clues establishing authenticity or otherwise: physical and chemical tests of ink, paper, parchment, cloth and other materials, for example. Investigations in the field of educational history are less likely to encounter deliberate forgeries than in, say, political or social history, though it is possible to find that official documents, correspondence and autobiographies have been 'ghosted', that is, prepared by a person other than the alleged author or signer.

Internal criticism

Having established the authenticity of the document, the researcher's next task is to evaluate the accuracy and worth of the data contained therein. While they may be genuine, they may not necessarily disclose the most faithful picture. In their concern to establish the meaning and reliability of data, investigators are confronted with a more difficult problem than external criticism because they have to establish the credibility of the author of the documents. Travers (1969) has listed those characteristics commonly considered in making evaluations of writers. Were they trained or untrained observers of the events? In other words, how competent were they? What were their relationships to the events? To what extent were they under pressure, from fear or vanity, say, to distort or omit facts? What were the intents of the writers of the documents? To what extent were they experts at recording those particular events? Were the habits of the authors such that they might interfere with the accuracy of recordings? Were they too antagonistic or too sympathetic to give true pictures? How long after the event did they record their testimonies? And were they able to remember accurately? Finally, are they in agreement with other independent witnesses?

Many documents in the history of education tend to be neutral in character, though it is possible that some may be in error because of these kinds of observer characteristics. A particular problem arising from the questions posed by Travers (1969) is that of bias. This can be particularly acute where life histories are being studied. The chief concern here, as Plummer (1983) reminds us, resides in examining possible sources of bias which prevent researchers from finding out what is wanted and using techniques to minimize the possible sources of bias.

Researchers generally recognize three sources of bias: those arising from the subject being interviewed, those arising from themselves as researchers and those arising from the subject–researcher interaction (Travers 1969).

Writing the research report

Once the data have been gathered and subjected to external criticism for authenticity and to internal criticism for accuracy, the researcher is next confronted with the task of piecing together an account of the events embraced by the research problem. This stage is known as the process of synthesis. It is probably the most difficult phase in the project and calls for considerable imagination and resourcefulness. The resulting pattern is then applied to the testing of the hypothesis.

The writing of the final report is equally demanding and calls for creativity and high standards of objective and systematic analysis.

Best (1970) has listed the kinds of problems occurring in the various types of historical research projects submitted by students. These include:

- Defining the problem too broadly.
- The tendency to use easy-to-find secondary sources of data rather than sufficient primary sources, which are harder to locate but usually more trustworthy.
- Inadequate historical criticism of data, due to failure to establish authenticity of sources and trustworthiness of data. For example, there is often a tendency to accept a statement as necessarily true when several observers agree. It is possible that one may have influenced the others, or that all were influenced by the same inaccurate source of information.
- Poor logical analysis resulting from:
  - oversimplification – failure to recognize the fact that causes of events are more often multiple and complex than single and simple
  - overgeneralization on the basis of insufficient evidence, and false reasoning by analogy, basing conclusions upon superficial similarities of situations
  - failure to interpret words and expression in the light of their accepted meaning in an earlier period
  - failure to distinguish between significant facts in a situation and those that are irrelevant or unimportant.
- Expression of personal bias, as revealed by statements lifted out of context for purposes of persuasion, assuming too generous or uncritical an attitude towards a person or idea (or being too unfriendly or critical), excessive admiration for the past (sometimes known as the 'old oaken bucket' delusion), or an equally unrealistic admiration for the new or contemporary, assuming that all change represents progress.
- Poor reporting in a style that is dull and colourless, too flowery or flippant, too persuasive or of the 'soap-box' type, or lacking in proper usage.

Borg and Gall (1979: 400) suggest several mistakes that can be made in conducting historical research:

- selecting a topic for which historical sources are slight, inaccessible or non-existent
- being over-reliant on secondary sources
- failing to subject the historical sources to internal or external validity/criticism checks
- lacking reflexivity and the researcher's selectivity and bias in using sources
- importing concepts from other disciplines
- making illegitimate inferences of causality and monocausality
- generalizing beyond acceptable limits of the data
- listing facts without appropriate thematization.

In addition to these, Sutherland (1969) has brilliantly illustrated two further common errors among historians of education. These are, first, projecting current battles backwards onto an historical background which leads to distortion, and second, 'description in a vacuum' which fails to illustrate the relationship of the educational system to the structure of society.

To conclude on a more positive note, Mouly (1978) itemizes five basic criteria for evaluating historical research:

- *Problem:* Has the problem been clearly defined? It is difficult enough to conduct historical research adequately without adding to the confusion by starting out with a nebulous problem. Is the problem capable of solution? Is it within the competence of the investigator?
- *Data:* Are data of a primary nature available in sufficient completeness to provide a solution, or has there been an overdependence on secondary or unverifiable sources?
- *Analysis:* Has the dependability of the data been adequately established? Has the relevance of the data been adequately explored?
- *Interpretation:* Does the author display adequate mastery of his data and insight into the relative significance? Does he display adequate historical perspective? Does he maintain his objectivity or does he allow personal bias to distort the evidence? Are his hypotheses plausible? Have they been adequately tested? Does he take a sufficiently broad view of the

total situation? Does he see the relationship between his data and other 'historical facts'?

- *Presentation:* Does the style of writing attract as well as inform? Does the report make a contribution on the basis of newly discovered data or new interpretation, or is it simply 'uninspired hack-work'? Does it reflect scholarliness?

The use of quantitative methods

By far the greater part of research in historical studies is qualitative in nature. This is so because the proper subject-matter of historical research consists to a great extent of verbal and other symbolic material emanating from a society's or a culture's past. The basic skills required of the researcher to analyse this kind of qualitative or symbolic material involve collecting, classifying, ordering, synthesizing, evaluating and interpreting. At the basis of all these acts lies sound personal judgement. In the comparatively recent past, however, attempts have been made to apply the quantitative methods of the scientist to the solution of historical problems (Travers 1969). Of these methods, the one having greatest relevance to historical research is that of content analysis, the basic goal of which is to take a verbal, non-quantitative document and transform it into quantitative data (Bailey 1978). We discuss content analysis in greater detail in Chapter 23.

Content analysis itself has been defined as a multipurpose research method developed specifically for investigating a broad spectrum of problems in which the content of communication serves as a basis of inference, from word counts to categorization. Approaches to content analysis are careful to identify appropriate categories and units of analysis, both of which will reflect the nature of the document being analysed and the purpose of the research. Categories are normally determined after initial inspection of the document and will cover the main areas of content.

We can readily see how the technique of content analysis may be applied to selected aspects of historical research in education. It could be used, for instance, in the analysis of educational documents. In addition to elucidating the content of the document, the method may throw additional light on the source of the communication, its author, and on its intended recipients, those to whom the message is directed. Further, an analysis of this kind would tell us more about the social context and the kinds of factors stressed or ignored, and of the influence of political factors, for instance. It follows from this that content analysis may form the basis of comparative or cross-cultural studies. Another usage that comes readily to mind would be an examination of the content of textbooks at different points in recent history as a means of indicating, say, cultural differences, cultural censorship or cultural change. The purposes of content analysis have been identified by Holsti (1968):

- to describe trends in communication content
- to relate known characteristics of sources to messages they produce
- to audit communication content against standards
- to analyse techniques of persuasion
- to analyse style
- to relate known attributes of the audience to messages produced for them
- to describe patterns of communication.

Different examples of the use of content analysis in historical contexts are provided by Thomas and Znaniecki (1918)[3] and Bradburn and Berlew (1961). A further example of content analysis in historical settings is McClelland *et al.*'s (1953) study of the relationship between the need to achieve (*n'ach*, for short) among members of a society and the economic growth of the particular society in question. Finally, for a more detailed and technical consideration of the use of quantitative methods in historical research, a study which looks at the classifying and arranging of historical data and reviews basic descriptive statistics, we refer the reader to Floud (1979).

Life histories

Thomas and Znaniecki's monumental study, *The Polish Peasant in Europe and America* (1918), serves as an appropriate introduction to this section, for their detailed account of the life and times of Wladek Wisniewski is commonly held to be the first sociological life history.

The life history, according to Plummer (1983), is frequently a full-length book about one person's life in his or her own words. Often, Plummer observes, it is gathered over a number of years, the researcher providing gentle guidance to the subject, encouraging him or her either to write down episodes of life or to tape-record them. And often as not, these materials will be backed up with intensive observations of the subject's life, with interviews of the subject's friends and acquaintances and with close scrutiny of relevant documents such as letters, diaries and photographs. Essentially, the life history is an 'interactive and co-operative technique directly involving the researcher' (Plummer 1983).

Accounts of the perspectives and interpretations of people in a variety of educational settings are both significant and pertinent,[4] for they provide valuable 'insights into the ways in which educational personnel come to terms with the constraints and conditions in which they work' (Goodson 1983). Life histories, Goodson argues, 'have the potential to make a far-reaching contribution to the problem of understanding the links between "personal troubles" and "public issues", a task that lies at the very heart of the sociological enterprise'. Their importance, he asserts, 'is best confirmed by the fact that teachers continually, most often unsolicited, import life history data into their accounts of classroom events' (Goodson 1983).

Miller (1999) demonstrates that biographical research is a distinctive way of conceptualizing social activity. He provides outlines of the three main approaches to analysis, that is to say:

- the *realist*, focusing upon grounded-theory techniques
- the *neo-positivist*, employing more structured interviews

- the *narrative*, using the interplay between interviewer and interviewee to actively construct life histories.

Denzin (1999) suggests that there are several varieties of biographical research methods including:

- biography
- autobiography
- story
- discourse
- narrative writing
- personal history
- oral history
- case history
- life history
- personal experience
- case study.

This is addressed further by Connelly and Clandinin (1999) who indicate several approaches to narrative inquiry:

- oral history
- stories
- annals and chronicles
- photographs
- memory boxes
- interviews
- journals
- autobiography
- letters
- conversations
- documents.

In exploring the appropriateness of life history techniques to a particular research project, and with ever-present constraints of time, facilities and finance in mind, it is useful to distinguish life histories both by type and mode of presentation, both factors bearing directly upon the scope and feasibility of the research endeavour. Box 8.2 draws on an outline by Hitchcock and Hughes (1989). Readers may wish to refer to the descriptions of types and modes of presentation contained in Box 8.2 in assessing the differing demands that are made on intending researchers as they gather, analyse and present their data. Whether

Chapter 8

Box 8.2
A typology of life histories and their modes of presentation

Types

Retrospective life history
A reconstruction of past events from the present feelings and interpretations of the individual concerned.

Contemporaneous life history
A description of an individual's daily life in progress, here and now.

Modes of presentation

Naturalistic
A first-person life history in which the life story is largely in the words of the individual subject, supported by a brief introduction, commentary and conclusion on the part of the researcher.

Thematically edited
Subject's words are retained intact but are presented by the researcher in terms of a series of themes, topics or headings, often in chapter-by-chapter format.

Interpreted and edited
The researcher's influence is most marked in his or her version of a subject's life story which the researcher has sifted, distilled, edited and interpreted.

Source: adapted from Hitchcock and Hughes 1989

retrospective or contemporaneous, a life history involves five broad research processes. These have been identified and described by Plummer (1983).

Preparation

This involves the researcher both in selecting an appropriate problem and devising relevant research techniques. Questions to be asked at this stage are first, 'Who is to be the object of the study?' – the great person, the common person, the volunteer, the selected, the coerced? Second, 'What makes a good informant?' Plummer (1983) draws attention to key factors such as accessibility of place and availability of time, and the awareness of the potential informant of his or her particular cultural milieu. A good informant is able and willing to establish and maintain a close, intimate relationship with the researcher. It is axiomatic that common sympathies and mutual respect are prerequisites for the sustenance and success of a life history project. Third, 'What needs clarifying in the early stages of the research?' The motivations of the researcher need to be made explicit to the intended subject. So too, the question of remuneration for the subject's services should be clarified from the outset. The issue of anonymity

must also be addressed, for unlike other research methodologies, life histories reveal intimate details (names, places, events) and provide scant cover from prying eyes. The earlier stages of the project also provide opportunities for discussing with the research subject the precise nature of the life history study, the logistics of interview situations and modes of data recording.

Data collection

Central to the success of a life history is the researcher's ability to use a variety of interview techniques (see also Chapter 16). As the occasion demands, these may range from relatively structured interviews that serve as general guides from the outset of the study, to informal, unstructured interviews reminiscent of non-directive counselling approaches espoused by Carl Rogers (1945) and his followers. In the case of the latter, Plummer (1983) draws attention to the importance of empathy and 'non-possessive warmth' on the part of the interviewer-researcher. A third interviewing strategy involves a judicious mixture of participant observation (see Chapter 18) and casual chatting, supplemented by note-taking.

Data storage

Typically, life histories generate enormous amounts of data. Intending researchers must make early decisions about the use of tape-recordings, the how, what and when of their transcription and editing, and the development of coding and filing devices if they are to avoid being totally swamped by the materials created. Readers are referred to the discussion in Chapter 7 and to Fiedler's (1978) extensive account of methods appropriate to field studies in natural settings.

Data analysis

Three central issues underpin the quality of data generated by life history methodology. They are to do with representativeness, reliability and validity (see also Chapters 4 and 6). Plummer (1983) draws attention to a frequent criticism of life history research, namely that its cases are atypical rather than representative. To avoid this charge, he urges intending researchers to 'work out and explicitly state the life history's relationship to a wider population' (Plummer 1983) by way of appraising the subject on a continuum of representativeness and non-representativeness.

Reliability in life history research hinges upon the identification of sources of bias and the application of techniques to reduce them. Bias arises from the informant, the researcher and the interactional encounter itself: see Box 8.2. Several validity checks are available to intending researchers. Plummer (1983) identifies the following:

- The subject of the life history may present an autocritique of it, having read the entire product.
- A comparison may be made with similar written sources by way of identifying points of major divergence or similarity.
- A comparison may be made with official records by way of imposing accuracy checks on the life history.
- A comparison may be made by interviewing other informants.

Essentially, the validity of any life history lies in its ability to represent the informant's subjective reality, that is to say, his or her definition of the situation. Detailed personal accounts and life histories can be interrogated thematically (e.g. the work of Thomas and Znaniecki 1918). Indeed the use of biographies, autobiographies, fictional accounts or newspaper journalism raises the question of what counts as legitimate research data. Perhaps such accounts may be better used to provide sensitizing concepts and contexts rather than as mainstream research data. The issue concerns reliability and validity; we address these matters below and in Chapter 6.

Data presentation

Plummer (1983) provides three points of direction for the researcher intent upon writing a life history. First, have a clear view of who you are writing for and what you wish to accomplish by writing the account. Are you aiming to produce a case history or a case study? Case histories 'tell a good story for its own sake' (Plummer 1983). Case studies, by contrast, use personal documents for wider theoretical purposes such as the verification and/or the generation of theory. Second, having established the purpose of the life history, decide how far you should intrude upon your assembled data. Intrusion occurs both through editing and interpreting. Editing ('cutting', sequencing, disguising names, places etc.) is almost a *sine qua non* of any life history study. Paraphrasing Plummer, editing involves getting your subject's own words, grasping them from the inside and turning them into a structured and coherent statement that uses the subject's words in places and your own, as researcher, in others, but retains their authentic meaning at all times. Third, as far as the mechanics of writing a life history are concerned, practise writing regularly. Writing, Plummer observes, needs working at, and daily drafting, revising and redrafting is necessary. For an example of life history methodology and research see Evetts (1991).

Documentary research

There are copious documentary sources of data in research and, although these are helpful for the researcher, a range of considerations has to be brought to bear on their use. For example, some social worlds, cultures and events are 'literate', i.e. documents are plentiful and are part of the everyday world of the participants, while other cultures may be less so. This affects the status of the documents. Further, while some documents may have been written deliberately for research, most have not; some are written by researchers for researchers but, again, most are not. Indeed most have been written for a purpose, agenda, an audience other than researchers, and this raises questions about their reliability and validity. Documents are useful in rendering more visible the phenomena under study (Prior 2003: 87). However, they have to be taken in conjunction with a whole range of other factors occurring at the same time. Prior (2003: 173) cites the analogy of the inert opera libretto, which cannot be read on its own, but has to be understood in the context of the whole action, drama, music and performance of the opera; it is only one part of the jigsaw (see http://www.routledge.com/textbooks/9780415368780 – Chapter 8, file 8.1. ppt).

Documents take a multitude of forms, including, for example:

- field notes
- diaries and journals
- records
- biographies
- autobiographies
- formal records
- timesheets/timetables
- technical documents
- minutes of meetings
- samples of students' work
- memos and emails
- reports and statistics
- correspondence
- plans
- pamphlets and advertisements
- prospectuses and directories
- archives
- stories
- annals and chronicles
- photographs and artefacts
- conversations and speeches
- policy documents
- primary and secondary sources
- newspaper articles
- books and articles
- public records.

This is only an initial list and, indeed, one can see that no written source is ruled out in documentary analysis.

Documentary analysis has several attractions (Bailey 1994: 294–6). It can enable the researcher to reach inaccessible persons or subjects, as in the case in historical research. Further, like non-participant or indirect observation, there is little or no reactivity on the part of the writer, particularly if the document was not written with the intention of being research data. Documentary study is also useful in longitudinal analysis, as it may show how situations have evolved over time. Some documents enable large samples to be addressed (e.g. registers of births, marriages and deaths, census returns, obituaries in newspapers and suchlike). Documents, many written 'live' and *in situ*, may catch the dynamic situation at the time of writing. Some documents, particularly if they are very personal (e.g. letters and diaries) may catch personal details and feeling ('confessions': Bailey 1994: 296) that would not otherwise surface. If documents are held in a central location, e.g. a library, collection or archive, savings of cost and time may be made. Finally, many documents in the public domain may have been written by skilled professionals and may contain more valuable information and insights than those written by relatively uninformed amateurs.

On the other hand, documents bring difficulties (Bailey 1994: 296–8). They may be highly biased and selective, as they were not intended to be regarded as research data but were written for a different purpose, audience and context. They, themselves, may be interpretations of events rather than objective accounts. Indeed, attrition and 'selective survival', together with selective interpretation by the writer, may mean that they may present an incomplete record of the situation under concern. Some documents, though they exist, may not be available to the researcher, hence limiting the study. Where documents do exist, they may come in so many different forms that a standard analytical format (e.g. content analysis, discussed in Chapter 23) may be impossible. Further, the documents must be studied in their context, in order to understand their significance at the time. A simple example serves to make our point: one hundred pounds sterling may seem a small amount at the present time, but when a document was written say 200 years previously, it would represent a great deal of money.

In approaching documentary research, a comprehensive, perhaps formidable, series of questions has to be addressed (see http://www.routledge.com/textbooks/9780415368780 – Chapter 8, file 8.2. ppt):

The context of the document

- What is the document?
- Where has the document come from?
- When was the document written?
- What kind of document is it?
- What is the document about?
- What is the focus of the document?
- What was the original intention and purposes (explicit and/or latent) of the document?
- What were the reasons for, or causes of, the document? Why was it written?
- What were the political and social contexts surrounding the document?
- What were the intended outcomes of the document?
- How was the document used/intended to be used?
- How was the document actually used?
- What were the effects/outcomes of the document?
- How did the document function in the phenomenon or situation being researched?
- What other documents fed into the production of, or were being used at the same time as, the document in question?

- What was the original agenda that the document served?
- Who were the original intended audiences of the document?
- What is, and was, the status of the document?
- What was the original context of the document?
- What are the style and register of the document?
- What does the document both include and exclude?
- What does the document's author(s) take for granted in the reader(s)?

The writer of the document

- Who wrote the document?
- What can be inferred about the writer?
- What were the interests of the writer?
- What were the status/position/knowledgeability of the author(s)?
- What does the document say about its author(s)?

The researcher and the document

- How should the document be read?
- Who owns/owned the document (e.g. the researcher, others)?
- Does the researcher personally know the author(s) of the document, i.e. what is the relationship between the researcher and the author(s)?
- Was the researcher present in the events reported (raising the issue of researcher effects)?
- How close to, or detached from, the participants was/is the researcher?
- What (additional) information does the researcher and the audience need to know in order to make sense of the document?
- How can, should or should not the document be used in the research?
- How does the document structure the researcher?
- How can the document be best analysed?
- In reading the document, what does it tell you about yourself as a reader/researcher?

- What are you, the reader/researcher bringing to the document in trying to make sense of it?
- What alternative interpretations of the document are possible and tenable? How is the chosen interpretation justified?
- What are the problems of reliability and validity in your reading of the document?
- What is the place of the document in the overall research project?

Questions are being raised here about the reliability and validity of the documents (see http://www.routledge.com/textbooks/9780415368780 – Chapter 8, file 8.3. ppt). They are social products, located in specific contexts, and, as such, have to be interrogated and interpreted rather than simply accepted. They are often selective, deliberately excluding certain details or information and serving purposes and audiences other than the researcher. Documents lie on several continua, for example:

Formal/official	↔	Informal/lay
Published	↔	Unpublished
Public domain	↔	Private papers
Anonymous	↔	Authored
Facts	↔	Beliefs
Professional	↔	Lay
For circulation	↔	Not for circulation

Placing documents along these several continua can assist the researcher in answering the preceding long list of questions.

Reliability and validity in documentary analysis

Validity may be strong in first person documents or in documents that were written for a specific purpose (Bailey 1994: 317). However, that purpose may not coincide with that of research, thereby undermining its validity for research purposes. We mentioned earlier the problem of bias, selectivity, being written for an audience and purposes different from those of the researcher, attrition and selective survival; all these undermine validity. In historical research great care is paid to authenticity and provenance, and documents may be subject to chemical analysis here (e.g. of inks, paper, parchment and so on) in order to detect forgeries. Bailey (1994: 318) suggests that face validity and construct validity in documents may be stronger and more sufficient than other forms of validity, though corroboration with other documents should be undertaken wherever possible.

With regard to reliability, while subjectivity may feature highly in certain documents, reliability by corroboration may also be pursued. The standards and criteria of reliability have to be declared by the researcher. Scott (1990) suggests four criteria for validity and reliability in using documents: authenticity; credibility (including accuracy, legitimacy and sincerity); representativeness (including availability and which documents have survived the passage of time); and meaning (actual and interpreted).

It is often difficult to disentangle fact from interpretation in a document and the research that is conducted using it (see http://www.routledge.com/textbooks/9780415368780 – Chapter 8, file 8.4. ppt). Understanding documents is a hermeneutic exercise, at several stages. Giddens (1979) remarked that researchers have to live with a 'double hermeneutic', that is, they interpret a world that is already interpreted by the participants, a pre-interpreted world. Actors or participants interpret or ascribe meaning to the world and then the researcher interprets or ascribes meaning to these interpretations. However, for the user of documents, the matter extends further. Documents record live events, so written data on social events become second hand because they translate the researcher's/writer's interpretation/inference of the world into another medium – from action to writing: a triple hermeneutic. Documents are part of the world and the action on which they are commenting. Then the reader places his or her interpretation/inference on the document, a quadruple hermeneutic. At each of these four stages interpretation, inference and bias and, thereby, unreliability could enter the scene. As Connelly and Clandinin (1997: 84) remark, converting field text into a research text is a process of (increasing) interpretation. Field texts and documents, they suggest, are close to the actual experience under study, whereas research texts are at a remove; that distance lets in unreliability and invalidity. While acknowledgement of this by the researcher, and the researcher's identification of the criteria for judging the research, may go some way towards addressing this issue (i.e. reflexivity), nevertheless it may not solve the problem, only articulate it.

The issue is that the researcher has to exercise extreme caution in using documents. As well as having a life of their own, documents are interpretations of events. As Prior (2003: 26) suggests, the content of documents may not be the most important feature of the document, and documents are 'situated products'. They are the drivers, media (channels), mediators (filters) and outcomes of social interaction (a clear exemplification of Giddens' theory of structuration). Understanding their context is crucial to understanding the document. Documents are multilevelled and have to be interpreted at their many levels; they need to be contextualized.

For a detailed analysis of several aspects of documents in research we refer readers to Prior (2003). For examples of documents, we refer the reader to the accompanying web site pages (http://www.routledge.com/textbooks/9780415368780 – Chapter 8, file 8.1.doc; http://www.routledge.com/textbooks/9780415368780 – Chapter 8, file 8.2.doc).

9 Surveys, longitudinal, cross-sectional and trend studies

Introduction

Many educational research methods are descriptive; that is, they set out to describe and to interpret what is. Descriptive research, according to Best, is concerned with:

> conditions or relationships that exist; practices that prevail; beliefs, points of views, or attitudes that are held; processes that are going on; effects that are being felt; or trends that are developing. At times, descriptive research is concerned with how *what is* or *what exists* is related to some preceding event that has influenced or affected a present condition or event.
>
> (Best 1970)

Such studies look at individuals, groups, institutions, methods and materials in order to describe, compare, contrast, classify, analyse and interpret the entities and the events that constitute their various fields of inquiry.

We deal here with several types of descriptive survey research, including longitudinal, cross-sectional and trend or prediction studies. This chapter should be read in conjunction with the chapters on sampling, questionnaires, interviews and data analysis techniques. Many researchers reading this book will probably be studying for higher degrees within a fixed and maybe short time frame, which may render longitudinal study out of the question for them. Nevertheless longitudinal study is an important type of research, and we introduce it here. More likely, researchers for higher degrees will find cross-sectional survey research appropriate, and it is widely used in higher degree research (see http://www.routledge.com/textbooks/9780415368780 – Chapter 9, file 9.1.ppt).

Collectively longitudinal, cross-sectional and trend or prediction studies are sometimes termed developmental research because they are concerned both to describe what the present relationships are among variables in a given situation and to account for changes occurring in those relationships over time. The term 'developmental' is primarily biological, having to do with the organization and the life processes of living things. The concept has been appropriated and applied to diverse educational, historical, sociological and psychological phenomena. In education, developmental studies often retain the original biological orientation of the term, having to do with the acquisition of motor and perceptual skills in young children. However, the designation 'developmental' has wider application in education, for example, in connection with Piaget's studies of qualitative changes occurring in children's thinking, and Kohlberg's work on moral development.

Typically, surveys gather data at a particular point in time with the intention of describing the nature of existing conditions, or identifying standards against which existing conditions can be compared, or determining the relationships that exist between specific events. Thus, surveys may vary in their levels of complexity from those that provide simple frequency counts to those that present relational analysis.

Surveys may be further differentiated in terms of their scope. A study of contemporary developments in post-secondary education, for example, might encompass the whole of western Europe; a study of subject choice, on the other hand, might be confined to one secondary school. The complexity and scope of surveys in education can be illustrated by reference to familiar examples. The surveys undertaken for the Plowden Committee on primary school children (Central Advisory Council for Education 1967) collected a wealth of information on children, teachers and parents and used sophisticated analytical techniques to predict pupil attainment. By contrast, the small-scale survey of Jackson and Marsden (1962) involved a detailed study of the backgrounds and values of 88 working-class adults who had achieved success through selective secondary education. Similarly, a study of training in multicultural perspectives by Bimrose and Bayne (1995) used only 28 participants in the survey research.

A survey has several characteristics and several claimed attractions; typically it is used to scan a wide field of issues, populations, programmes etc. in order to measure or describe any generalized features. It is useful (Morrison, 1993: 38–40) in that it usually:

- gathers data on a one-shot basis and hence is economical and efficient
- represents a wide target population (hence there is a need for careful sampling, see Chapter 4)
- generates numerical data
- provides descriptive, inferential and explanatory information
- manipulates key factors and variables to derive frequencies (e.g. the numbers registering a particular opinion or test score)
- gathers standardized information (i.e. using the same instruments and questions for all participants)
- ascertains correlations (e.g. to find out if there is any relationship between gender and scores)
- presents material which is uncluttered by specific contextual factors
- captures data from multiple choice, closed questions, test scores or observation schedules
- supports or refutes hypotheses about the target population
- generates accurate instruments through their piloting and revision

- makes generalizations about, and observes patterns of response in, the targets of focus
- gathers data which can be processed statistically
- usually relies on large-scale data gathering from a wide population in order to enable generalizations to be made about given factors or variables.

Examples of surveys are as follows:[1]

- opinion polls, which refute the notion that only opinion polls can catch opinions
- test scores (e.g. the results of testing students nationally or locally)
- students' preferences for particular courses (e.g. humanities, sciences)
- reading surveys (e.g. Southgate et al.'s (1981) example of teaching practices in the United Kingdom).

Web sites for the National Child Development Study (NCDS) can be found at:

> http://www.cls.ioe.ac.uk/Ncds/
> nibntro.htm
> http://www.cls.ioe./ac.uk.Ncds/
> narchive.htm
> http://www.mimas.ac.uk/surveys.
> ncds/
> http://www.mimas.ac.uk/surveys.
> ncds/ncds_info.html

Web sites for the Centre for Longitudinal Studies (CLS) can be found at:

> http://www.cls.ioe.ac.uk/Bcs70/
> bhome.htm
> http://www.cls.ioe.ac.uk/Bcs70.
> bintro.htm

Surveys in education often use test results, self-completion questionnaires and attitude scales. A researcher using this model typically will be seeking to gather large-scale data from as representative a sample population as possible in order to say with a measure of statistical confidence that certain observed characteristics occur with a degree of regularity, or that certain factors cluster together (see Chapter 25) or that they correlate with each other (correlation and covariance), or that they change over time and location (e.g. results of test scores used to ascertain the 'value-added' dimension of education, maybe using regression analysis and analysis of residuals to determine the difference between a predicted and an observed score), or regression analysis to use data from one variable to predict an outcome on another variable.

Surveys can be *exploratory*, in which no assumptions or models are postulated, and in which relationships and patterns are explored (e.g. through correlation, regression, stepwise regression and factor analysis). They can also be *confirmatory*, in which a model, causal relationship or hypothesis is tested (see the discussion of exploratory and confirmatory analysis in Part Five). Surveys can be descriptive or analytic (e.g. to examine relationships). Descriptive surveys simply describe data on variables of interest, while analytic surveys operate with hypothesized predictor or explanatory variables that are tested for their influence on dependent variables.

Most surveys will combine nominal data on participants' backgrounds and relevant personal details with other scales (e.g. attitude scales, data from ordinal, interval and ratio measures). Surveys are useful for gathering factual information, data on attitudes and preferences, beliefs and predictions, behaviour and experiences – both past and present (Weisberg *et al.* 1996).

The attractions of a survey lie in its appeal to generalizability or universality within given parameters, its ability to make statements which are supported by large data banks and its ability to establish the degree of confidence which can be placed in a set of findings.

On the other hand, if a researcher is concerned to catch local, institutional or small scale factors and variables – to portray the specificity of a situation, its uniqueness and particular complexity, its interpersonal dynamics, and to provide explanations of why a situation occurred or why a person or group of people returned a particular set of results or behaved in a particular way in a situation, or how a programme changes and develops over time, then a survey approach

is probably unsuitable. Its degree of explanatory potential or fine detail is limited; it is lost to broad-brush generalizations which are free of temporal, spatial or local contexts, i.e. its appeal largely rests on the basis of positivism. The individual instance is sacrificed to the aggregated response (which has the attraction of anonymity, non-traceability and confidentiality for respondents).

Surveys typically, though by no means exclusively, rely on large-scale data, e.g. from questionnaires, test scores, attendance rates, results of public examinations etc., all of which enable comparisons to be made over time or between groups. This is not to say that surveys cannot be undertaken on a small-scale basis, as indeed they can; rather it is to say that the generalizability of such small-scale data will be slight. In surveys the researcher is usually very clearly an outsider, indeed questions of reliability must attach themselves to researchers conducting survey research on their own subjects, such as participants in a course that they have been running (e.g. Bimrose and Bayne 1995; Morrison 1997). Further, it is critical that attention is paid to rigorous sampling, otherwise the basis of the survey's applicability to wider contexts is seriously undermined. Non-probability samples tend to be avoided in surveys if generalizability is sought; probability sampling will tend to lead to generalizability of the data collected.

Some preliminary considerations

Three prerequisites to the design of any survey are: the specification of the exact purpose of the inquiry; the population on which it is to focus; and the resources that are available. Hoinville and Jowell's (1978) consideration of each of these key factors in survey planning can be illustrated in relation to the design of an educational inquiry.

The purpose of the inquiry

First, a survey's general purpose must be translated into a specific central aim. Thus, 'to explore teachers' views about in-service work' is somewhat nebulous, whereas 'to obtain a detailed description of primary and secondary teachers' priorities in the provision of in-service education courses' is reasonably specific.

Having decided upon and specified the primary objective of the survey, the second phase of the planning involves the identification and itemizing of subsidiary topics that relate to its central purpose. In our example, subsidiary issues might well include: the types of courses required; the content of courses; the location of courses; the timing of courses; the design of courses; and the financing of courses.

The third phase follows the identification and itemization of subsidiary topics and involves formulating specific information requirements relating to each of these issues. For example, with respect to the type of courses required, detailed information would be needed about the duration of courses (one meeting, several meetings, a week, a month, a term or a year), the status of courses (non-award bearing, award bearing, with certificate, diploma, degree granted by college or university), the orientation of courses (theoretically oriented involving lectures, readings, etc., or practically oriented involving workshops and the production of curriculum materials).

As these details unfold, note Hoinville and Jowell (1978), consideration would have to be given to the most appropriate ways of collecting items of information (interviews with selected teachers, postal questionnaires to selected schools, etc.).

The population upon which the survey is focused

The second prerequisite to survey design, the specification of the population to which the inquiry is addressed, affects decisions that researchers must make both about sampling and resources. In our hypothetical survey of in-service requirements, for example, we might specify the population as 'those primary and secondary teachers employed in schools within a thirty-mile radius of Loughborough University'. In this case, the population is readily identifiable and, given sufficient resources to contact every member of the

designated group, sampling decisions do not arise. Things are rarely so straightforward, however. Often the criteria by which populations are specified ('severely challenged', 'under-achievers', 'intending teachers' or 'highly anxious') are difficult to operationalize. Populations, moreover, vary considerably in their accessibility; pupils and student teachers are relatively easy to survey, gypsy children and headteachers are more elusive. More importantly, in a large survey researchers usually draw a sample from the population to be studied; rarely do they attempt to contact every member. We deal with the question of sampling shortly.

The resources available

The third important factor in designing and planning a survey is the financial cost. Sample surveys are labour-intensive (see Davidson 1970), the largest single expenditure being the fieldwork, where costs arise out of the interviewing time, travel time and transport claims of the interviewers themselves. There are additional demands on the survey budget. Training and supervising the panel of interviewers can often be as expensive as the costs incurred during the time that they actually spend in the field. Questionnaire construction, piloting, printing, posting, coding, together with computer programme – all eat into financial resources.

Proposals from intending education researchers seeking governmental or private funding are often weakest in the amount of time and thought devoted to a detailed planning of the financial implications of the projected inquiries. (In this chapter we confine ourselves from this point to a discussion of surveys based on self-completion questionnaires. A full account of the interview as a research technique is given in Chapter 16.)

Planning a survey

Whether the survey is large scale and undertaken by some governmental bureau or small scale and carried out by the lone researcher, the collection of information typically involves one or more of the following data-gathering techniques:

structured or semi-structured interviews, self-completion or postal questionnaires, telephone interviews, Internet surveys, standardized tests of attainment or performance, and attitude scales. Typically, too, surveys proceed through well-defined stages, though not every stage outlined in Box 9.1 is required for the successful completion of a survey (see http://www.routledge.com/textbooks/9780415368780 – Chapter 9, file 9.2.ppt).

The process moves from the general to the specific. A general research topic is broken down into complementary issues and questions, and, for each component, questions are set. As will be discussed in questionnaires (Chapter 15), it is important, in the interests of reliability and validity, to have several items or questions for each component issue, as this does justice to the all-round nature of the topic. Sapsford (1999: 34–40) suggests that there are four main considerations in planning a survey:

- *Problem definition:* deciding what kinds and contents of answers are required; what hypotheses there are to be tested; what variables there are to explore
- *Sample selection:* what is the target population; how can access and representativeness be assured; what other samples will need to be drawn for the purpose of comparison
- *Design of measurements:* what will be measured, and how (i.e. what metrics will be used – see Chapter 15 on questionnaires); what variables will be required; how reliability and validity will be assured
- *Concern for participants:* protection of confidentiality and anonymity; avoidance of pain to the respondents; avoiding harm to those who might be affected by the results; avoiding over-intrusive questions; avoiding coercion; informed consent (see Chapter 2 on ethics).

A fourteen-stage process of planning a survey can be considered:

1 Define the objectives.
2 Decide the kind of survey required (e.g. longitudinal, cross-section, trend study, cohort study).
3 Formulate research questions or hypotheses (if appropriate): the null hypothesis and alternative hypothesis.
4 Decide the issues on which to focus.
5 Decide the information that is needed to address the issues.
6 Decide the sampling required.
7 Decide the instrumentation and the metrics required.
8 Generate the data collection instruments.
9 Decide how the data will be collected (e.g. postal survey, interviews).
10 Pilot the instruments and refine them.
11 Train the interviewers (if appropriate).
12 Collect the data.
13 Analyse the data.
14 Report the results.

Rosier (1997) suggests that the planning of a survey will need to include clarification of:

- The research questions to which answers need to be provided.
- The conceptual framework of the survey, specifying in precise terms the concepts that will be used and explored.
- Operationalizing the research questions (e.g. into hypotheses).
- The instruments to be used for data collection, e.g. to chart or measure background characteristics of the sample (often nominal data), academic achievements (e.g. examination results, degrees awarded), attitudes and opinions (often using ordinal data from rating scales) and behaviour (using observational techniques).
- Sampling strategies and subgroups within the sample (unless the whole population is being surveyed, e.g. through census returns or nationally aggregated test scores etc.).
- Pre-piloting the survey.
- Piloting the survey.
- Data collection practicalities and conduct (e.g. permissions, funding, ethical considerations, response rates).
- Data preparation (e.g. coding, data entry for computer analysis, checking and verification).

Box 9.1

Stages in the planning of a survey

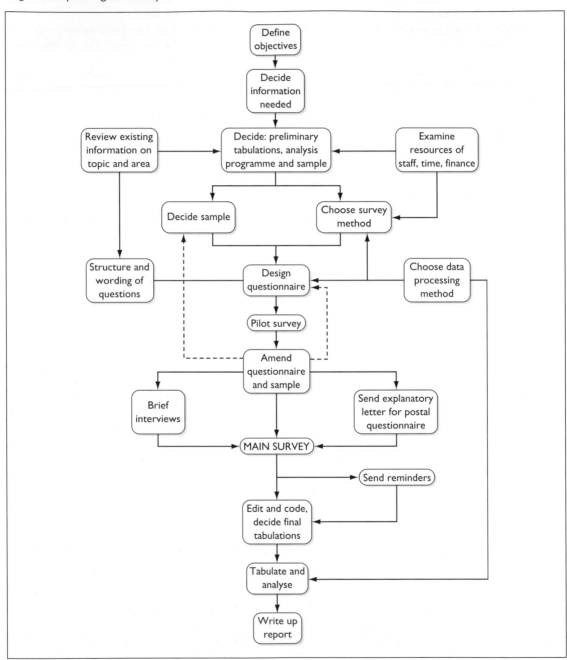

Source: adapted from Davidson 1970

- Data analysis (e.g. statistical processes, construction of variables and factor analysis, inferential statistics).
- Reporting the findings (answering the research questions).

It is important to pilot and pre-pilot a survey. The difference between the pre-pilot and the pilot is significant. Whereas the pre-pilot is usually a series of open-ended questions that are used to generate categories for closed, typically multiple choice questions, the pilot is used to test the actual survey instrument itself (see Chapter 15).

A rigorous survey, then, formulates clear, specific objectives and research questions, ensures that the instrumentation, sampling, and data types are appropriate to yield answers to the research questions, ensures that as high a level of sophistication of data analysis is undertaken as the data will sustain (but no more!).

Survey sampling

Sampling is a key feature of a survey approach, and we advise readers to look closely at Chapter 4 on sampling. Because questions about sampling arise directly from the second of our preliminary considerations, that is, defining the population upon which the survey is to focus, researchers must take sampling decisions early in the overall planning of a survey (see Box 9.1). We have already seen that due to factors of expense, time and accessibility, it is not always possible or practical to obtain measures from a population. Researchers endeavour therefore to collect information from a smaller group or subset of the population in such a way that the knowledge gained is representative of the total population under study. This smaller group or subset is a 'sample'. Notice how competent researchers start with the total population and work down to the sample. By contrast, novices work from the bottom up, that is, they determine the minimum number of respondents needed to conduct a successful survey. However, unless they identify the total population in advance, it is virtually impossible for them to assess how representative the sample

is that they have drawn. There are two methods of sampling. One yields probability samples in which, as the term implies, the probability of selection of each respondent is known. The other yields non-probability samples, in which the probability of selection is unknown.

As Chapter 4 tells us, probability samples include:

- simple random samples
- systematic samples
- stratified samples
- cluster samples
- stage samples
- multi-phase samples.

Their appeal is to the generalizability of the data that are gathered. Non-probability samples include:

- convenience sampling
- quota sampling
- dimensional sampling
- purposive sampling
- snowball sampling.

These kinds of sample do not seek to generalize from the data collected. Each type of sample seeks only to represent itself. The researcher will need to decide the sampling strategy to be used on the basis of fitness for purpose, in parallel with considerations of, for example, the representativeness of the sample, the desire to generalize, the access to the sample, and the size of the sample. Chapter 4 covers all these, and other, aspects of sampling.

Longitudinal, cross-sectional and trend studies

The term 'longitudinal' is used to describe a variety of studies that are conducted over a period of time. Often, as we have seen, the word 'developmental' is employed in connection with longitudinal studies that deal specifically with aspects of human growth.

A clear distinction is drawn between longitudinal and cross-sectional studies.[2] The longitudinal study gathers data over an extended period of time;

a short-term investigation may take several weeks or months; a long-term study can extend over many years. Where successive measures are taken at different points in time from the same respondents, the term 'follow-up study' or 'cohort study' is used in the British literature, the equivalent term in the United States being the 'panel study'. The term 'cohort' is a group of people with some common characteristic. A cohort study is sometimes differentiated from a panel study. In a cohort study a specific population is tracked over a specific period of time but selective sampling within that sample occurs (Borg and Gall 1979: 291). This means that some members of a cohort may not be included each time. By contrast, in a panel study each same individual is tracked over time.

Where different respondents are studied at different points in time, the study is called 'cross-sectional'. Where a few selected factors are studied continuously over time, the term 'trend study' is employed. One example of regular or repeated cross-sectional social surveys is the General Household Survey, in which the same questions are asked every year though they are put to a different sample of the population each time. The British Social Attitudes Survey is an example of a repeated cross-sectional survey, using some 3,600 respondents.

A famous example of a longitudinal (cohort) study is the National Child Development Study, which started in 1958. The British General Household Panel Survey interviewed individuals from a representative sample each year in the 1990s. Another example is the British Family Expenditure Survey. These latter two are cross-sectional in that they tell us about the population at a given point in time, and hence provide aggregated data.

By contrast, longitudinal studies can also provide individual level data, by focusing on the same individuals over time (e.g. the Household Panel Studies) which follow individuals and families over time (Ruspini 2002: 4). Paul Lazarsfeld introduced the concept of a panel in the 1940s (Lazarsfeld 1940), attempting to identify causal patterns and the difficulties in tracing causal patterns (Ruspini 2002: 13).

Longitudinal studies

Longitudinal studies can use repeated cross-sectional studies, which are 'carried out regularly, each time using a largely different sample or a completely new sample' (Ruspini 2002: 3), or use the same sample over time. They enable researchers to: 'analyse the duration of social phenomena' (Ruspini 2002: 24); highlight similarities, differences and changes over time in respect of one or more variables or participants (within and between participants); identify long-term ('sleeper') effects; and explain changes in terms of stable characteristics, e.g. sex, or variable characteristics, such as income. The appeal of longitudinal research is its ability to establish causality and to make inferences. Ruspini adds to these the ability of longitudinal research to 'construct more complicated behavioural models than purely cross-sectional or time-series data' (p. 26); they catch the complexity of human behaviour. Further, longitudinal studies can combine numerical and qualitative data.

Cohort studies and trend studies are *prospective* longitudinal methods, in that they are ongoing in their collection of information about individuals or their monitoring of specific events. *Retrospective* longitudinal studies, on the other hand, focus upon individuals who have reached some defined end-point or state. For example, a group of young people may be the researcher's particular interest (intending social workers, convicted drug offenders or university dropouts, for example), and the questions which the researcher will address are likely to include ones such as: 'Is there anything about the previous experience of these individuals that can account for their present situation?' Retrospective longitudinal studies will specify the period over which to be retrospective, e.g. one year, five years.

Retrospective analysis is not confined to longitudinal studies alone. For example, Rose and Sullivan (1993: 185) and Ruane (2005: 87) suggest that cross-sectional studies can use retrospective factual questions, e.g. previous occupations, dates of birth within the family, dates of marriage, divorce, though Rose and Sullivan (1993: 185) advise against collecting other types of retrospective data in cross-sectional studies, as the quality of the data diminishes the further back one asks respondents to recall previous states or even facts.

Cross-sectional studies

A cross-sectional study is one that produces a 'snapshot' of a population at a particular point in time. The epitome of the cross-sectional study is a national census in which a representative sample of the population consisting of individuals of different ages, different occupations, different educational and income levels, and residing in different parts of the country, is interviewed on the same day. More typically in education, cross-sectional studies involve indirect measures of the nature and rate of changes in the physical and intellectual development of samples of children drawn from representative age levels. The single 'snapshot' of the cross-sectional study provides researchers with data for either a retrospective or a prospective enquiry.

A cross-sectional study can also bear several hallmarks of a longitudinal study of parallel groups (e.g. age groups) which are drawn simultaneously from the population. For example, drawing students aged 5, 7, 9 and 11 at a single point in time would bear some characteristics of a longitudinal study in that developments over age groups could be seen, although, of course, it would not have the same weight as a longitudinal study conducted on the same age group over time. This is the case for international studies of educational achievement, requiring samples to be drawn from the same population (Lietz and Keeves, 1997: 122) and for factors that might influence changes in the dependent variables to remain constant across the age groups. Cross-sectional studies, catching a frozen moment in time, may be ineffective for studying change. If changes are to be addressed through cross-sectional surveys, then this suggests the need for repeated applications of the survey, or by the use of trend analysis.

Trend studies

Trend studies focus on factors rather than people, and these factors are studied over time. New samples are drawn at each stage of the data collection, but focusing on the same factors. By taking different samples the problem of reactivity is avoided (see below: 'pretest sensitization'), that is earlier surveys affecting the behaviour of participants in the later surveys. This is particularly useful if the research is being conducted on sensitive issues, as raising a sensitive issue early on in research may change an individual's behaviour, which could affect the responses in a later round of data collection. By drawing a different sample each time this problem is overcome.

Trend or prediction studies have an obvious importance to educational administrators or planners. Like cohort studies, they may be of relatively short or long duration. Essentially, the trend study examines recorded data to establish patterns of change that have already occurred in order to predict what will be likely to occur in the future. In trend studies two or more cross-sectional studies are undertaken with identical age groups at more than one point in time in order to make comparisons over time (e.g. the Scholastic Aptitude and Achievement tests in the United States) (Keeves, 1997b: 141) and the National Assessment of Educational Progress results (Lietz and Keeves, 1997: 122). A major difficulty researchers face in conducting trend analyses is the intrusion of unpredictable factors that invalidate forecasts formulated on past data. For this reason, short-term trend studies tend to be more accurate than long-term analyses. Trend studies do not include the same respondents over time, so the possibility exists for variation in data due to the different respondents rather than the change in trends. Gorard (2001: 87) suggests that this problem can be attenuated by a 'rolling sample' in which a proportion of the original sample is retained in the second wave of data collection, and a proportion of this sample is retained in the third wave, and so on.

The distinctions we have drawn between the various terms used in developmental research are illustrated in Box 9.2.

Box 9.2
Types of developmental research

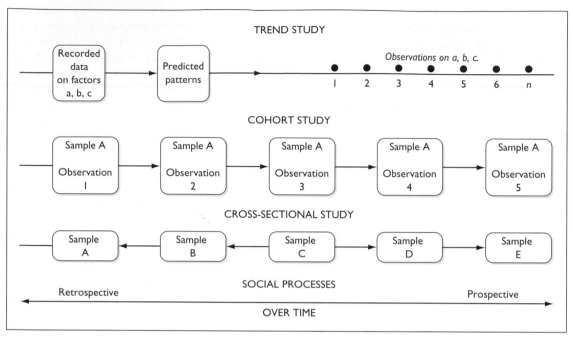

Strengths and weaknesses of longitudinal, cohort and cross-sectional studies

Longitudinal studies of the cohort analysis type have an important place in the research armoury of educational investigators. Longitudinal studies have considerable potential for yielding rich data that can trace changes over time, and with great accuracy (Gorard 2001: 86). On the other hand, they suffer from problems of attrition (participants leaving the research over time, a particular problem in panel studies which research the same individuals over time), and they can be expensive to conduct in terms of time and money (Ruspini, 2002: 71). Gorard (2001) reports a study of careers and identities that had an initial response rate of between 60 and 70 per cent in the first round, and then risked dropping to 25 per cent by the third round, becoming increasingly more middle class in each wave of the study. Gorard (2001) also discusses a Youth Cohort Study in which only 45 per cent of the respondents took part

in all three waves of the data collection. Ruspini (2002: 72) identifies an attrition rate of 78 per cent in the three waves of the European Community Household Panel survey of the United Kingdom in 1997.

Ruspini (2002) also indicates how a small measurement error in a longitudinal study may be compounded over time. She gives the example of an error in income occurring at a point in time that could lead to 'false transitions' appearing over time in regard to poverty and unemployment (Ruspini 2002: 72).

Further, long-term studies, Gorard (2001: 86) avers, face 'a threat to internal validity' that stems from the need 'to test and retest the same individuals'. Dooley (2001: 120) terms this 'pretest sensitisation'; it is also termed 'panel conditioning' or 'time-in sample bias' (Ruspini, 2002: 73). Here the first interview in an interview survey can cause changes in the second interview, i.e. the first interview may set up a self-fulfilling prophecy that is recorded in the second interview. Dooley

(2001) gives the example of a health survey in the first round of data collection, which may raise participants' awareness of the dangers of smoking, such that they reduce or give up smoking by the time the second round takes place. Trend studies overcome this problem by drawing different populations at each stage of the data collection in the research.

Dooley (2001) also raises the issue of the difficulties caused by changes in the research staff over time in longitudinal surveys. Changes in interviewee response, he suggests, may be due to having different researchers rather than to the respondents themselves. Even using the same instruments, different researchers may use them differently (e.g. in interviewing behaviour).

To add to these matters, Ruspini (2002: 73) suggests that longitudinal data are affected by:

- history: events occurring may change the observations of a group under study
- maturation: participants mature at different speeds and in different ways
- testing: test sensitization may occur – participants learn from exposure to repeated testing/interviews
- the timing of cause and effect: some causes may produce virtually instantaneous effects and others may take a long time for the effects to show
- the direction of causality not always being clear or singular.

A major concern in longitudinal studies concerns the comparability of data over time. For example, though public examinations in schools may remain constant over time, the contents and format of those examinations do not. (This rehearses the argument that public examinations like A levels are becoming easier over time.) This issue concerns the need to ensure consistency in the data collection instruments over time. Further, if comparability of data in a longitudinal study is to be addressed then this means that the initial rounds of data collection, in the earliest stage of the research, will need to anticipate and include all the variables that will be addressed over time.

Longitudinal studies are more prone to attrition than cross-sectional studies, and are more expensive to conduct in terms of time and cost. On the other hand, whereas trend studies change their populations, thereby disabling micro-level – individual level – analysis from being conducted, longitudinal analysis enables such individual-level analysis to be performed. Indeed, whereas cross-sectional designs (even if they are repeated cross-sectional designs) may be unsuitable for studying developmental patterns and causality within cohorts, in longitudinal analysis this is a strength. Longitudinal data can supply 'satisfactory answers to questions concerning the dynamics and the determinants of individual behaviour' (Ruspini 2002: 71), issues which are not easily addressed in cross-sectional designs.

Retrospective longitudinal studies rely on the memories of the participants. These may be faulty, and the further back one's memory reaches, the greater is the danger of distortion or inability to recall. Memory is affected by, for example (Ruspini, 2002: 97):

- the time that has elapsed since the event took place
- the significance of the event for the participant
- the amount of information required for the study – the greater the amount, the harder it is to provide
- the contamination/interference effect of other memories of a similar event (i.e. the inability to separate similar events)
- the emotional content or the social desirability of the content
- the psychological condition of the participant at interview.

Further, participants will look at past events through the lens of hindsight and subsequent events rather than what those events meant at the time. Further, it is not always easy for these participants to recall their emotional state at the time in question. Factually speaking, it may not be possible to gather data from some time past, as they simply do not exist, e.g. medical records, data on income, or they cannot be found or recovered.

Cohort studies of human growth and development conducted on representative samples of populations are uniquely able to identify typical patterns of development and to reveal factors operating on those samples which elude other research designs. They permit researchers to examine individual variations in characteristics or traits, and to produce individual growth curves. Cohort studies, too, are particularly appropriate when investigators attempt to establish causal relationships, for this task involves identifying changes in certain characteristics that result in changes in others.

Cross-sectional designs are inappropriate in causal research as they cannot sustain causal analysis unless they are repeated over time. Cohort analysis is especially useful in sociological research because it can show how changing properties of individuals fit together into changing properties of social systems as a whole. For example, the study of staff morale and its association with the emerging organizational climate of a newly opened school would lend itself to this type of developmental research. A further strength of cohort studies in schools is that they provide longitudinal records whose value derives in part from the known fallibility of any single test or assessment (see Davie 1972). Finally, time, always a limiting factor in experimental and interview settings, is generally more readily available in cohort studies, allowing the researcher greater opportunity to observe trends and to distinguish 'real' changes from chance occurrences (see Bailey 1978).

In longitudinal, cohort and trend studies there is the risk that characteristics of the respondents may affect the results (Robson 1993: 128). For example, their memory, knowledge, motivation and personality may affect their responses and, indeed, they may withhold information, particularly if it is sensitive.

Longitudinal research indicates the influence of biological factors over time (e.g. human development), environmental influences and intervention influences (Keeves 1997b: 139) and their interactions. Addressing these, the appeal of longitudinal analysis is that it enables causal analysis to be undertaken. Time series studies in longitudinal research also enable

emergent patterns to be observed over time, by examining a given range of variables over time, in addition to other factors. This permits individual and group profiles to be examined over time and development, indicating similarities and differences within and between individuals and groups in respect of given variables. As longitudinal studies do not concern themselves with time-specific influences, only those naturally occurring influences are included (Keeves 1997b: 142).

Longitudinal studies suffer several disadvantages (though the gravity of these weaknesses is challenged by supporters of cohort analysis). The disadvantages are, first, that they are time-consuming and expensive, because the researcher is obliged to wait for growth data to accumulate. Second, there is the difficulty of sample mortality. Inevitably during the course of a long-term cohort study, subjects drop out, are lost or refuse further cooperation. Such attrition makes it unlikely that those who remain in the study are as representative of the population as the sample that was originally drawn. Sometimes attempts are made to lessen the effects of sample mortality by introducing aspects of cross-sectional study design, that is, 'topping up' the original cohort sample size at each time of retesting with the same number of respondents drawn from the same population. The problem here is that differences arising in the data from one survey to the next may then be accounted for by differences in the persons surveyed rather than by genuine changes or trends.

A third difficulty has been termed 'control effect' (sometimes referred to as measurement effect). Often, repeated interviewing results in an undesired and confusing effect on the actions or attitudes under study, influencing the behaviour of subjects, sensitizing them to matters that have hitherto passed unnoticed, or stimulating them to communication with others on unwanted topics (see Riley 1963). Fourth, cohort studies can suffer from the interaction of biological, environmental and intervention influences (Keeves 1997b: 139). Finally, cohort studies in education pose considerable problems of organization due to the continuous changes that occur in pupils, staff, teaching methods and the like. Such changes make it highly unlikely that a study will be completed in the way that it was originally planned.

Cohort studies, as we have seen, are particularly appropriate in research on human growth and development. Why then are so many studies in this area cross-sectional in design? The reason is that they have a number of advantages over cohort studies; they are less expensive; they produce findings more quickly; they are less likely to suffer from control effects; and they are more likely to secure the cooperation of respondents on a 'one-off' basis. Generally, cross-sectional designs are able to include more subjects than are cohort designs.

The strengths of cohort analysis are the weaknesses of the cross-sectional design. The cross-sectional study is a less effective method for the researcher who is concerned to identify individual variations in growth or to establish causal relationships between variables. Sampling in the cross-sectional study is complicated because different subjects are involved at each age level and may not be comparable. Further problems arising out of selection effects and the obscuring

of irregularities in growth weaken the cross-sectional study so much that one observer dismisses the method as a highly unsatisfactory way of obtaining developmental data except for the crudest purposes. Douglas (1976), who pioneered the first national cohort study to be undertaken in any country, makes a spirited defence of the method against the common criticisms that are levelled against it – that it is expensive and time-consuming. His account of the advantages of cohort analysis over cross-sectional designs is summarized in Box 9.3.

Cross-sectional studies require attention to be given to sampling, to ensure that the information on which the sample was based is comprehensive (Lietz and Keeves 1997: 124). Further, there is a risk that some potential participants may decline to take part, thereby weakening the sample, or that some respondents may not answer specific questions or, wittingly or unwittingly, give incorrect answers. Measurement error may also occur if the instrument is faulty, for example, choosing inappropriate metrics or scales.

The comparative strengths and weaknesses of longitudinal studies (including retrospective

Box 9.3

Advantages of cohort over cross-sectional designs

1   Some types of information, for example, on attitudes or assessment of potential ability, are only meaningful if collected contemporaneously. Other types are more complete or more accurate if collected during the course of a longitudinal survey, though they are likely to have some value even if collected retrospectively, for example, length of schooling, job history, geographical movement.

2   In cohort studies, no duplication of information occurs, whereas in cross-sectional studies the same type of background information has to be collected on each occasion. This increases the interviewing costs.

3   The omission of even a single variable, later found to be important, from a cross-sectional study is a disaster, whereas it is usually possible in a cohort study to fill the gap, even if only partially, in a subsequent interview.

4   A cohort study allows the accumulation of a much larger number of variables, extending over a much wider area of knowledge than would be possible in a cross-sectional study. This is of course because the collection can be spread over many interviews. Moreover, information may be obtained at the most appropriate time, for example, information on job entry may be obtained when it occurs even if this varies from one member of the sample to another.

5   Starting with a birth cohort removes later problems of sampling and allows the extensive use of subsamples. It also eases problems of estimating bias and reliability.

6   Longitudinal studies are free of one of the major obstacles to causal analysis, namely, the re-interpretation of remembered information so that it conforms with conventional views on causation. It also provides the means to assess the direction of effect.

Source: adapted from Douglas 1976

studies), cross-section analysis and trend studies are summarized in Box 9.4 (see also Rose and Sullivan 1993: 184–8).

Several of the strengths and weaknesses of retrospective longitudinal studies share the same characteristics as those of *ex post facto* research, discussed in Chapter 12.

Postal, interview and telephone surveys

Although we introduce some important features of approaches to data collection here, we advise readers to consult Chapters 10, 15 and 16 on Internet-based research, questionnaire design and interviews respectively.

Postal surveys

Robson (1993) indicates strengths and difficulties with postal and interview surveys. Postal surveys can reach a large number of people, gather data at comparatively low cost and quite quickly, and can give assurances of confidentiality (Bailey 1994: 148). Similarly they can be completed at the respondents' own convenience and in their preferred surroundings and own time; this will enable them to check information if necessary (e.g. personal documents) and think about the responses. As standardized wording is used, there is a useful degree of comparability across the responses, and, as no interviewer is present, there is no risk of interviewer bias. Further, postal questionnaires enable widely scattered populations to be reached.

On the other hand, postal surveys typically suffer from a poor response rate, and, because one does not have any information about the non-respondents, one does not know whether the sample is representative of the wider population. Further, respondents may not take the care required to complete the survey carefully and, indeed, may misunderstand the questions. There is no way of checking this. Bailey (1994: 149) suggests that the very issues that make postal surveys attractive might also render them less appealing, for example:

- the standardization of wording
- the inability to catch anything other than a verbal response
- the lack of control over the environment in which the survey questionnaire is completed
- the lack of control over the order in which the questions are read and answered
- the risk that some questions will not be answered
- the inability to record spontaneous answers
- the difficulty in separating non-response from bad response (the former being where intended respondents receive the survey but do not reply to it, and the latter being where intended recipients do not receive the survey, e.g. because they have moved house)
- the need for simplicity in format as there is no interviewer present to guide the respondent through a more complex format.

Interview surveys

Whereas postal surveys are self-administered, interview surveys are supervised, and, hence potentially prone to fewer difficulties. Interview methods of gathering survey data are useful in that the presence of the interviewer can help clarify queries from the respondents and can stimulate the respondent to give full answers to an on-the-spot supervisor rather than an anonymous researcher known through an introductory letter (Robson 1993). Indeed, there is evidence that face-to-face encounters improve response rates. Furthermore, as interviews can be flexible, questioners are able both to probe and explain more fully (Bailey 1994: 174). Interviews are also useful when respondents have problems with reading and writing. Using non-verbal behaviour to encourage respondents to participate is also possible. Moreover, with interviews there are greater opportunities to control the environment in which the survey is conducted, particularly in respect of privacy, noise and external distractions.

The potential for trust and cooperation between the interviewer and the respondent is

Box 9.4

The characteristics, strengths and weaknesses of longitudinal, cross-sectional, trend analysis, and retrospective longitudinal studies

Study type	Features	Strengths	Weaknesses
Longitudinal studies (cohort/panel studies)	1 Single sample over extended period of time. 2 Enables the same individuals to be compared over time (diachronic analysis). 3 Micro-level analysis.	1 Useful for establishing causal relationships and for making reliable inferences. 2 Shows how changing properties of individuals fit into systemic change. 3 Operates within the known limits of instrumentation employed. 4 Separates real trends from chance occurrence. 5 Brings the benefits of extended time frames. 6 Useful for charting growth and development. 7 Gathers data contemporaneously rather than retrospectively, thereby avoiding the problems of selective or false memory. 8 Economical in that a picture of the sample is built up over time. 9 In-depth and comprehensive coverage of a wide range of variables, both initial and emergent – individual specific effects and population heterogeneity. 10 Enables change to be analysed at the *individual/micro* level. 11 Enables the dynamics of change to be caught, the flows into and out of particular states and the transitions between states. 12 Individual level data are more accurate than macro-level, cross-sectional data. 13 Sampling error reduced as the study remains with the same sample over time. 14 Enables clear recommendations for intervention to be made.	1 Time-consuming – it takes a long time for the studies to be conducted and the results to emerge. 2 Problems of sample mortality heighten over time and diminish initial representativeness. 3 Control effects – repeated interviewing of the same sample influences their behaviour. 4 Intervening effects attenuate the initial research plan. 5 Problem of securing participation as it involves repeated contact. 6 Data, being rich at an individual level, are typically complex to analyse.

continued

Box 9.4
continued

Study type	Features	Strengths	Weaknesses
Cross-sectional studies	1 Snapshot of different samples at one or more points in time (synchronic analysis). 2 Large-scale and representative sampling. 3 Macro-level analysis. 4 Enables different groups to be compared. 5 Can be retrospective and/or prospective.	1 Comparatively quick to conduct. 2 Comparatively cheap to administer. 3 Limited control effects as subjects only participate once. 4 Stronger likelihood of participation as it is for a single time. 5 Charts aggregated patterns. 6 Useful for charting population-wide features at one or more single points in time. 7 Enable researchers to identify the proportions of people in particular groups or states. 8 Large samples enable inferential statistics to be used, e.g. to compare subgroups within the sample.	1 Do not permit analysis of causal relationships. 2 Unable to chart individual variations in development or changes, and their significance. 3 Sampling not entirely comparable at each round of data collection as different samples are used. 4 Can be time-consuming as background details of each sample have to be collected each time. 5 Omission of a single variable can undermine the results significantly. 6 Unable to chart changing social processes over time. 7 They only permit analysis of overall, *net* change at the macro-level through aggregated data.
Trend analysis	1 Selected factors studied continuously over time. 2 Uses recorded data to predict future trends.	1 Maintains clarity of focus throughout the duration of the study. 2 Enables prediction and projection on the basis of identified and monitored variables and assumptions.	1 Neglects influence of unpredicted factors. 2 Past trends are not always a good predictor of future trends. 3 Formula-driven, i.e. could be too conservative or initial assumptions might be erroneous. 4 Neglects the implications of chaos and complexity theory, e.g. that long-range forecasting is dangerous. 5 The criteria for prediction may be imprecise.

continued

Box 9.4
continued

Study type	Features	Strengths	Weaknesses
Retrospective longitudinal studies	1 Retrospective analysis of history of a sample. 2 Individual- and micro-level data.	1 Useful for establishing causal relationships. 2 Clear focus (e.g. how did this particular end state or set of circumstances come to be?). 3 Enables data to be assembled that are not susceptible to experimental analysis.	1 Remembered information might be faulty, selective and inaccurate. 2 People might forget, suppress or fail to remember certain factors. 3 Individuals might interpret their own past behaviour in light of their subsequent events, i.e. the interpretations are not contemporaneous with the actual events. 4 The roots and causes of the end state may be multiple, diverse, complex, unidentified and unstraightforward to unravel. 5 Simple causality is unlikely. 6 A cause may be an effect and vice versa. 7 It is difficult to separate real from perceived or putative causes. 8 It is seldom easily falsifiable or confirmable.

strong in face-to-face encounters (Dooley 2001: 122). Further, interviewers can either ensure that the sequence of the survey protocol is strictly adhered to or they can tailor the order of responses to individual participants, making certain, incidentally, that all questions are answered. Interview surveys, moreover, can guarantee that it is the respondent alone who answers the questions, whereas in postal surveys the researcher never knows what help or comments are solicited from or given by other parties. Bailey (1994) adds that the opportunity for spontaneous behaviour and responses is also possible in interview surveys. Further, interviews can use more complex structures than postal questionnaires, the researcher being on hand to take participants through the schedule.

On the other hand, the very features that make interview methods attractive may also make them problematic. For example, interview survey methods may be affected by the characteristics of the interviewer (e.g. sex, race, ethnicity, personality, skills, social status, clothing and appearance). They may also be affected by the conduct of the interview itself (e.g. rapport between the interviewer and the interviewee), and interviewees may be reluctant to disclose some information if they feel that the interview will not be anonymous or if sensitive information is being requested. The flexibility which the interview gives also contributes to the potential lack of standardization of the interview survey, and this may render consistency and, thereby, reliability, a problem. Further, interview surveys are costly in time for the researcher and the interviewee, and, as they are conducted at a fixed time, they may prevent the interviewee from consulting records that may be important to answer the questions. Further, they may require the interviewer to travel long distances to reach interviewees, which can be expensive both in time and travel costs (Bailey 1994: 175). If interviews are intended to be conducted in the participants' own homes, then participants may be unwilling to admit strangers. Moreover, neighbourhoods may be dangerous for some researchers to visit (e.g. a white researcher with a clipboard going into a non-white area of great deprivation, or a black researcher going into a conservative white area).

Telephone surveys

Telephone surveys, it is claimed (Dooley 2001: 122), have the advantage of reducing costs in time and travel, for where a potential respondent is not at home a call-back costs only a few coins and the time to redial. Re-visits to often distant locations, on the other hand, can incur considerable expense in time and travel. Furthermore, if the intended participant is unable or unwilling to respond, then it is a relatively easy matter to maintain the required sample size by calling a replacement. Again, where respondents are unable or unwilling to answer all the questions required, then their partial replies may be discarded and further substitutes sought from the sample listing. It is easy to see why telephone interviews must always have a much longer list of potential respondents in order to attain the required sample size.

On the other hand, not everyone has a telephone (e.g. the poor, the young, the less educated) and this may lead to a skewed sample. Nor, for that matter, is everyone available for interview, particularly if they work. Furthermore, many people are ex-directory, i.e. their numbers are withheld from public scrutiny. In addition, Dooley (2001: 123) reports that others – the younger, unmarried and higher occupational status groups – use answering machines that may screen out and delete researchers' calls. These could also lead to a skewed sample.

Even when the telephone is answered, the person responding may not be the most suitable one to take the call; she or he may not know the answer to the questions or have access to the kind of information required. For example, in an inquiry about household budgets, the respondent may simply be ignorant about a family's income or expenditure on particular items. A child may answer the call or an elderly person who may not be the householder. Interviewers will need to prepare a set of preliminary, screening questions or arrange a call-back time when a more appropriate person can be interviewed.

Telephone interviewing has its own strengths and weaknesses. For example, more often than not a respondent's sex will be clear from their voice, so particular questions may be inappropriate. On the other hand, it is unwise to have several multiple choices in a telephone interview, as respondents will simply forget the categories available, there being no written prompts to which the respondent can refer.

Similarly, order effects can be high: items appearing early in the interview exert an influence on responses to later ones, while items appearing early in a list of responses may be given greater consideration than those occurring later, a matter not confined to telephone surveys but to questionnaires in general. Dooley (2001: 136) indicates that 17 per cent difference in agreement was recorded to a general statement question when it appeared *before* rather than *after* a specific statement. He cites further research demonstrating that responses to particular questions are affected by questions surrounding them. His advice is to ask *general* questions before *specific* ones. Otherwise, the general questions are influenced by earlier responses to specific questions. Once again, this is a matter not confined to telephone surveys but to questionnaires in general.

Further, if the questioning becomes too sensitive, respondents may simply hang up in the middle of the survey interview, tell lies or withhold information. Dooley (2001: 123) reports that, in comparison to face-to-face interviews, telephone respondents tend to produce more missing data, to be more evasive, more acquiescent (i.e. they tend to agree more with statements) and more extreme in their responses (e.g. opting for the extreme ends of rating scales).

Because telephone interviews lack the sensory stimulation of visual or face-to-face interviews or written instructions and presentation, it is unwise to plan a long telephone survey call. Ten to fifteen minutes is often the maximum time tolerable to most respondents and, indeed, fifteen minutes for many may be too long. This means that careful piloting will need to take place in order to include those items, and only those items, that are necessary for the research. The risk to reliability and validity is considerable, as the number of items may be fewer than in other forms of data collection.

Improving response rates in a survey

A major difficulty in survey research is securing a sufficiently high response rate to give credibility and reliability to the data. In some postal research, response rates can be as low as 20–30 per cent, and this compromises the reliability of the data very considerably. There is a difference between the *intended* and the *achieved* sample (Fogelman 2002: 105). Punch (2003: 43) suggests that it is important to plan for poor response rates (e.g. by increasing the sample size) rather than trying to adjust sampling *post hoc*. He also suggests that access to the sample needs to be researched before the survey commences, maybe pre-notifying potential participants if that is deemed desirable. He argues that a poor response level may also be due to the careless omission of details of how and when the questionnaire will be returned or collected. This is a matter that needs to be made clear in the questionnaire itself. In the case of a postal survey a stamped addressed envelope should always be included.

Further, the design, layout and presentation of the survey may also exert an influence on response rate. It is important to include a brief covering letter that explains the research clearly and introduces the researcher. The timing of the survey is important, for example schools will not welcome researchers or surveys in examination periods or at special occasions, e.g. Christmas or inspection times (Fogelman 2002: 106). Finally, it is important to plan the follow-up to surveys, to ensure that non-respondents are called again and reminded of the request to complete the survey.

There are several possible ways of increasing response rates to mailed surveys, including, for example:

- arranging follow-ups and polite reminders (e.g. by mail, email, telephone call)
- sending advance notification of the survey (e.g. by telephone, post or email)
- supplying pre-paid return stamped addressed envelopes
- acknowledging institutional affiliation, survey sponsorship or support from a high-status agent
- offering financial incentives (though increasing the financial incentive to a high figure does not bring commensurate returns in response rates)
- giving rewards for return
- ensuring surveys are easy to read
- making instructions about responses and return very clear
- flattering the participants without being seen to flatter them
- providing information about the research through a covering letter and/or advance notification
- making the survey look very unlike junk mail
- delivering the questionnaire personally rather than through the mail.

Cooper and Schindler (2001: 314–15) report that the following factors make little or no appreciable difference to response rates:

- personalizing the introductory letter
- making promises of anonymity
- considering questionnaire length: it is not always the case that a short questionnaire produces more returns than a long questionnaire, but researchers will need to consider the effect of a long survey questionnaire on the respondents – they may feel positive or negative about it, or set it aside temporarily and forget to return it later
- attending to size, reproduction and colour of the questionnaire
- giving deadline dates for return (it was found that these did not increase response rate but did accelerate the return of questionnaires).

It is important to consider why respondents may not reply to requests to participate in surveys. These might include, for example:

- the pressure of competing activities on the time of the respondent
- potential embarrassment at their own ignorance if respondents feel unable to answer a question
- ignorance of the topic/no background in the topic
- dislike of the contents or subject matter of the interview
- fear of possible consequences of the survey to himself/herself or others
- lack of clarity in the instructions
- fear or dislike of being interviewed
- sensitivity of the topic, or potentially insulting or threatening topic
- betrayal of confidences
- losing the return envelope or return address
- the wrong person may open the mail, and fail to pass it on to the most appropriate person.

On the other hand, potential respondents may be persuaded to participate depending on, for example:

- the status and prestige of the institution or researcher carrying out the research
- the perceived benefit of the research
- the perceived importance of the topic
- personal interest in the research
- interest in being interviewed, i.e. the interview experience
- personal liking for, or empathy with, the researcher
- feelings of duty to the public and sense of civic responsibility
- loneliness or boredom (nothing else to do)
- sense of self-importance.

We advise readers to consult Chapter 15 on questionnaires.

Event history analysis

Recent developments in longitudinal studies include the use of 'event history analysis' (e.g. von Eye 1990; Rose and Sullivan 1993: 189–90; Plewis 1997; Ruspini 2002). Event history analysis 'offers a record of the events that have punctuated the life-course of a group of subjects' (Ruspini 2002: 5). Such 'life-courses' are determined by individual trajectories and transitions: paths taken and changes within, and to, paths. An event is a punctuation or change point. Similarities exist between event history analysis and longitudinal analysis in their retrospective nature, taking participants back through time to identify change moments and events in their lives. Event history analysis differs from longitudinal and cross-sectional analysis in that specific time points for data collection are not fixed. What drives the analysis is not the time frame for data collection, but the timing of the event itself. Whereas longitudinal analysis deals with discrete and given time periods (e.g. every six months), event history analysis is timed by whenever the event occurs. In fixed time frames it is not always straightforward to ascertain what happened *during* a time period.

Event history analysis also uses a set of statistical techniques whose key concepts include: *a risk set* (a set of participants who have yet to experience a particular event or situation); a *survivor function* or *survivor curve* (the decline in the size of risk over time); the *hazard* or *hazard rate* (the rate at which particular events occur, or the risk of a particular event occurring at a particular time). The notion of 'survival' owes its pedigree to the origins of event history analysis, in which the survival time that elapsed was measured between an animal being giving a drug and the death of that animal. Further terms include 'transition rate', 'risk function', 'mortality rate' and 'transition intensity'.

Event history analysis suggests that it is possible to consider the dependent variable in (e.g. marriage, employment changes, redundancy, further and higher education, moving house, death) as predictable within certain time frames for individuals. The rationale for this derives from life-table analysis used by demographers to calculate survival and mortality rates in a given population over time. For example, if x number of the population are alive at time t, then it may be possible to predict the survival rate of that population at time $t + 1$. In a sense it is akin to a prediction study. Life-table studies are straightforward in that they are concerned with specific, non-repeatable events (e.g. death); in this case the calculation of life expectancy does not rely on distinguishing various causes of death (Rose and Sullivan 1993: 189). However, in event history analysis the parameters become much more complex as multiple factors come into the equation, requiring some form of multivariate analysis to be undertaken.

In event history analysis the task is to calculate the 'hazard rate' – the probability of a dependent variable occurring to an individual within a specified time frame. The approach is mathematical, using log-linear analysis to compute the relative size of each of several factors (independent variables), e.g. by calculating coefficients in cross-tabulations, that will have an effect on the hazard rate, the likelihood of an event occurring to an individual within a specific time frame (Rose and Sullivan 1993: 190).[3]

Event history analysis also addresses the problem of attrition, as members leave a study over time. Plewis (1997: 117) suggests that many longitudinal studies suffer from sample loss over time, and attempts to address the issue of *censoring* – the adjustments necessary in a study in order to take account of the accretion of missing data. *Right censoring* occurs when we know when a particular event commences but not when it finishes; *left censoring* occurs when we know of the existence of a particular event or situation, but not when it began. Plewis (1997: 118) suggests that censored events and episodes (where attrition has taken place) last longer than uncensored events and episodes, and, hence, hazard rates that are based on uncensored observations will usually be too high. Event history is a valuable and increasingly used technique for research.

Introduction

The rise of the Internet has not only opened the door to developing conventional research techniques such as surveys, questionnaires, experiments and interviews, but also enabled researchers to use literature search-and-retrieval techniques to locate and return materials from the web at an exponential rate in terms of size and rapidity. Here we review some of the most commonly used features in using the Internet as a research facility, commenting particularly on surveys and their related questionnaires, experiments and interviews, and using the Internet for locating research materials.

Internet-based surveys

Using the Internet for the conduct of surveys is becoming commonplace in many branches of social science. Although Internet-based surveys have many features in common with paper-based surveys, they also have their own particular features.

Internet-based surveys have moved from being in the form of emails to emails-plus-attachments of the questionnaire itself, to emails directing potential respondents to a web site, or simply to web sites. While emails have the attraction of immediacy, the potential for web-based surveys to include graphics has been too great for many researchers to resist. Often a combination of the two is used: emails direct potential participants to a web site at which the survey questionnaire is located in HTML form. Although email surveys tend to attract greater response than web-based surveys, web-based surveys have the potential to reach greater numbers of participants, so

web-based surveys are advisable; emails can be used as an addition, to contact participants to advise them to go to a particular web site.

Some principles for constructing Internet-based surveys

Dillman et al. (1998a; 1998b; 1999) set out several principles of web-based surveys. Some of these are technical and some are presentational. For example, in terms of technical matters, they found that the difference between simple and 'fancy' [sic] versions of questionnaires (the former with few graphics, the latter with many, using sophisticated software) could be as much as three times the size of the file to be downloaded (317 k in contrast to 959 k), with a time of downloading of 225 seconds for the plain version and 682 seconds for the 'fancy' version. They found that either respondents with slow browsers or limited power spent longer in downloading the file or, indeed, the machine crashed before the file was downloaded. They also found that recipients of plain versions were more likely to complete a questionnaire than those receiving fancy versions (93.1 per cent and 82.1 per cent respectively), as it took less time to complete the plain version. Utilizing advanced page layout features does not translate into higher completion rates, indeed more advanced page layout reduced completion rates. This echoes the work of Fricker and Schonlau (2002) who report studies that indicate a 43 per cent response rate to an email survey compared to a 71 per cent response rate for the same mailed paper questionnaire. Indeed they report that it is only with specialized samples (e.g. undergraduates) that higher response rates can be obtained in an Internet survey. The different kinds of software packages are discussed at http://www.tucows.com/, which lists and reviews a range of packages, while http://www.my3q.com/misc/register/register.phtml provides free online survey software.

For presentational matters Dillman and his colleagues (1998a; 1999) make the point that in a paper-based survey the eyes and the hands are focused on the same area, while in a web-based survey the eyes are focused on the screen while the hands are either on the keyboard or on the mouse, and so completion is more difficult. This is one reason to avoid asking respondents to type in many responses to open-ended questions, and replacing these with radio buttons or clicking on a mouse that automatically inserts a tick into a box (Witte et al. 1999: 139). Further, some respondents may have less developed computer skills than others. They suggest a mixed mode of operation (paper-based together with web-based versions of the same questionnaire). The researchers also found that 'check-all-that-apply' lists of factors to be addressed had questionable reliability, as respondents would tend to complete those items at the top of the list and ignore the remainder. Hence they recommend avoiding the use of check-all-that-apply questions in a web-based survey.

Similarly they advocate keeping the introduction to the questionnaire short (no more than one screen), informative (e.g. of how to move on) and avoiding giving a long list of instructions. Further, as the first question in a survey tends to raise in respondents' minds a particular mind-set, care is needed on setting the first question, to entice participants and not to put them off participating. (e.g. not too difficult, not too easy, interesting, straightforward to complete, avoiding drop-down boxes and scrolling). Dillman et al. (1998a; 1998b; 1999) make specific recommendations about the layout of the screen, for example keeping the response categories close to the question for ease of following, using features like brightness, large fonts and spacing for clarity in the early parts of the survey. They also suggest following the natural movement of the eyes from the top left (the most important part of the screen, hence the part in which the question is located) to the bottom right quadrants of the screen (the least important part of

the screen, which might contain the researcher's logo). They comment that the natural movement of the eye is to read prose unevenly, with the risk of missing critical words, and that this is particularly true on long lines, hence they advocate keeping lines and sentences short (e.g. by inserting a hard break in the text or to use table-editing features, locating the text in a table frame). Taking this further, they also advocate the use of some marker to indicate to the respondent where he or she has reached in the questionnaire (e.g. a progress bar or a table that indicates what proportion of the questionnaire has been completed so far).

Respondents may not be familiar with web-based questionnaires, e.g. with radio buttons, scroll bars, the use of the mouse, the use of drop-down menus, where to insert open-ended responses, and the survey designer must not overestimate the capability of the respondent to use the software, though Roztocki and Lahri (2002) suggest that there is no relationship between perceived level of computer literacy and preference for web-based surveys. Indeed their use may have to be explained in the survey itself. Dillman et al. (1999) suggest that the problem of differential expertise in computer usage can be addressed in three ways:

- having the instructions for how to complete the item next to the item itself (not all placed together at the start of the questionnaire)
- asking the respondents at the beginning about their level of computer expertise, and, if they are more expert, offering them the questionnaire with certain instructions omitted and, if they are less experienced, directing them to instructions and further assistance
- having a 'floating window' that accompanies each screen and which can be maximized for further instructions.

Some web-based surveys prevent respondents from proceeding until they have completed all the items on the screen in question. While this might ensure coverage, it can also anger respondents – such that they give up and abandon the survey – or prevent them from having a deliberate non-response (e.g. if they do not wish to reveal particular information, or if, in fact, the question does not apply to them, or if they do not know the answer). Hence the advice of Dillman *et al.* (1999) is to avoid this practice. One way to address this matter is to give respondents the opportunity to answer an item with 'prefer not to answer' or 'don't know'. The point that relates to this is that it is much easier for participants in a web-based survey to abandon the survey – a simple click of a button – so more attention has to be given to keeping them participating than in a paper-based survey.

Redline *et al.* (2002) suggest that branching instructions (e.g. 'skip to item 13', 'go to item 10'; 'if "yes" go to item 12, if "no" then continue') can create problems in web-based surveys, as respondents may skip over items and series of questions that they should have addressed. This concerns the location of the instruction (e.g. to the right of the item, underneath the item, to the right of the answer box). Locating the instruction too far to the right of the answer box (e.g. more than nine characters of text to the right) can mean that it is outside the foveal view (2 degrees) of the respondent's vision and, hence, can be overlooked. Further, they report that having a branching instruction in the same font size and colour as the rest of the text can result in it being regarded as unimportant, not least because respondents frequently expect the completion of a form to be easier than it actually is. Hence they advocate making the instruction easier to detect by locating it within the natural field of vision of the reader, printing it in a large font to make it bolder, and using a different colour. They report that, for the most part, branching instruction errors occur because they are overlooked and respondents are unaware of them rather than deliberately disregarding them (Redline *et al.* 2002: 18).

The researchers also investigated a range of other variables that impacted on the success of using branching programmes, and reported the following:

- The number of words in the question has an impact on the respondent: the greater the number of words the less is the likelihood of correct branching processing by the reader, as the respondent is too absorbed with the question rather than with the instructions.

- Using large fonts, strategies and verbal design to draw attention to branching instructions leads to greater observance of these instructions.

- The number of answer categories can exert an effect on the respondent: more than seven categories and the respondent may make errors and also overlook branching instructions.

- Having to read branching instructions at the same time as looking at answer categories results in overlooking the branching instructions.

- Locating the branching instruction next to the final category of a series of answer boxes is a much safer guarantee of it being observed than placing it further up a list; this may mean changing the order of the list of response categories, so that the final category naturally leads to the branching instruction.

- Branching instructions should be placed where they are to be used and where they can be seen.

- Response-order effects operate in surveys, such that respondents in a self-administered survey tend to choose earlier items in a list rather than later items in a list (the primacy effect), thereby erroneously acting on branching instructions that appear with later items in a list.

- Questions with alternating branches (i.e. more than one branch) may be forgotten by the time they need to be acted upon after respondents have completed an item.

- If every answer has a branch then respondents may overlook the instructions for branching as all the branches appear to be similar.

- If respondents are required to write an open-ended response this may cause them to overlook a branching instruction as they are so absorbed in composing their own response and the branching instruction may be out of their field of vision when writing in their answer.

- Items that are located at the bottom of a page are more likely to elicit a non-response than items further up a page, hence if branching instructions are located near the bottom of a page they are more likely to be overlooked; placing branching instructions at the bottom of the page should be avoided.

- If the branching instructions are located too far from the answer box then they may be overlooked.

These pieces of advice from the research not only can be applied to online survey questionnaires but also are useful in the construction of paper-based survey questionnaires.

Dillman *et al.* (1999) and Dillman and Bowker (2000: 10–11) suggest that successful web-based surveys should take account of the inability of some respondents to access and respond to web questionnaires that include advanced programming features (e.g. that may require software that the respondents do not have or which download very slowly) and should also match the expectations of the respondents in completing the questionnaire design and layout.

Dillman and colleagues suggest several 'principles' for designing web-based questionnaires:

- Start the web questionnaire with a welcome screen that will motivate the respondents to continue, which makes it clear that it is easy to complete and gives clear instructions on how to proceed.
- Provide a PIN (personal identification number) in order to limit access to those people sought in the sample.
- Ensure that the first question can be seen in its entirety on the first screen, and is easy to understand and complete.
- Ensure that the layout of each question is as close as possible to a paper format, as respondents may be familiar with this.
- Ensure that the use of colour keeps the figure/ground consistency and readability, so that it is easy to navigate through the questionnaire and navigational flow is unimpeded, and so that the measurement properties of questions are clear and sustained.
- Avoid differences in the visual appearance of questions that may happen as a result of different computers, configurations, operating

systems, screen displays (e.g. partial and wrap-around text) and browsers.

- Keep the line length short, to fit in with the screen size.
- Minimize the use of drop-down boxes, and direct respondents to them where they occur.
- Give clear instructions for how to move through the questionnaire using the computer.
- Make instructions for skipping parts very clear.
- Keep instructions for computer actions to be taken at the point where the action is needed, rather than placing them all at the start of the questionnaire.
- Avoid requiring respondents to answer each question before being able to move on to the next question.
- Ensure that questionnaires scroll easily from question to question, unless order effects are important.
- If multiple choices are presented, try to keep them to a single screen; if this is not possible then consider double columns, providing navigational instructions.
- Provide graphical symbols or words to indicate where the respondent has reached in the questionnaire.
- Avoid the kinds of questions that cause problems in paper questionnaires (e.g. tick-all-those-that-apply kinds of questions).

Some advantages of Internet-based surveys

The most widely used data collection instrument for Internet surveys is the questionnaire. There are several claimed advantages to using an Internet questionnaire in comparison to a paper questionnaire (e.g. Watt 1997; Dillman *et al.* 1999; Dillman and Bowker 2000; Roztocki and Lahri 2002):

- It reduces costs (e.g. of postage, paper, printing, keying in data, processing data, interviewer costs).
- It reduces the time take to distribute, gather and process data (data entered onto a web-based survey can be processed automatically as soon as they are entered by the respondent

rather than being keyed in later by the researcher).

- It enables a wider and much larger population to be accessed.
- It enables researchers to reach difficult populations under the cover of anonymity and non-traceability.
- It may have novelty value (though this decreases over time).
- Respondents can complete the questionnaire from home (rather than, for example, in the workplace), i.e. in self-chosen and familiar settings.
- Respondents can complete it at a time to suit themselves, thereby minimizing organizational constraints on the part of the researcher or the respondents.
- Respondents can complete the survey over time (i.e. they do not need to do it all at one sitting).
- Reduction of researcher effects.
- Responses in web-based surveys show fewer missing entries than paper-based surveys.
- Human error is reduced in entering and processing online data.
- Additional features may make the survey attractive (e.g. graphics, colour, fonts, and so on).
- Greater generalizability may be obtained as Internet users come from a wide and diverse population.
- Because of volunteer participation (i.e. an absence of coercion), greater authenticity of responses may be obtained.

With regard to costs, Watt (1997) alerts us to the fact that cost savings always make a difference in comparison to a telephone survey, but that an Internet-based survey is only slightly cheaper than a mail survey unless that web-based survey gathers data from more than around 500 participants, as the costs in terms of development and design time are considerable. With over 500 participants, the Internet-based survey makes considerable cost savings. Further, Fricker and Schonlau (2002) suggest that the claims that Internet-based surveys are cheaper and faster are not always borne out by the evidence, and that, if Internet survey development, programming, testing and modification time, initial contact time and follow-up time to ensure an increased response rate are factored in, then the savings may not be as strong as the claims made. That said, they do acknowledge that as Internet surveys develop they are likely to meet these claims. Reips (2002a, 2002b) suggests that although there may be costs in terms of laboratory space, equipment and administration, these have to be offset by development costs. The jury is still out on overall time cost savings.

Key issues in Internet-based surveys

On the other hand, Internet-based surveys are not without their problems. Some of these are indicated in Box 10.1, together with possible solutions (Coomber 1997; Dillman *et al.* 1999; Frick *et al.* 1999; Witmer *et al.* 1999; Dillman and Bowker 2000; Solomon 2001; Reips 2002a, 2002b; Dillman *et al.* 2003; Hewson *et al.* 2003; Smyth *et al.* 2004).

As suggested in these lists, the importance of the visual aspect of questionnaires is heightened in Internet surveys (Smyth *et al.* 2004), and this affects the layout of questions, instructions and response lists, the grouping of items, the colours used, the spacing of response categories, the formatting of responses (e.g. writing in words or ticking boxes). Smyth *et al.* (2004) report that respondents use 'preattentive processing' when approaching Internet surveys, i.e. they try to take in and understand the whole scene (or screen) before attending to specific items, hence visual features are important, e.g. emboldened words, large fonts, colours, brightness, section headings, spacing, placing boxes around items. This rests on Gestalt psychology that abides by the principles of

- *proximity* (we tend to group together those items that are physically close to each other)
- *similarity* (we tend to group together those items that appear alike
- *prägnanz* (figures or items with simplicity, regularity and symmetry are more easily perceived and remembered).

Box 10.1

Problems and solutions in Internet-based surveys

Problem: sampling	Possible solution
Some subsample groups may be under-represented in the respondents.	Adjust the results by weighting the sample responses (see the comments on a 'boosted sample' and 'weighting' in Chapter 4).
There may be coverage error (not everyone has a non-zero chance of being included).	Disclose the sample characteristics in reporting.
Non-response and volunteer bias.	Follow-up messages posted on web sites and electronic discussion groups. Use emails to contact potential participants. Require the respondents to submit their replies screen by screen: this enables the researcher not only to use some data from incomplete responses, but also to identify in detail patterns of non-response, i.e. responding is not an all-or-nothing affair (either submit the whole questionnaire or none of it) but can be partial (a respondent may answer some questions but not others).

Problem: ethics	Possible solution
Respondents may wish to keep their identity from the researcher, and an email address identifies the respondent (in the case of sensitive research, e.g. on child abuse or drug abuse, this may involve criminal proceedings if the identity of the respondent is known or able to be tracked by criminal investigators who break into the site). Non-traceability of respondents may be problematic.	Direct respondents to a web site rather than to using email correspondence. Provide advice on using non-traceable connections to access and return the survey (e.g. an Internet café, a library, a university). Advise the respondent to print off the survey and return it by post to a given address. Avoid asking respondents to enter a password or to give an email address. Prevent access to unprotected directories and confidential data.
Respondents may not know anything about the researcher, or if it is a bona fide piece of research and not simply a marketing ploy.	Include the researcher's affiliation (e.g. university), with a logo if possible.
Informed consent.	Ensure that it is easy for respondents to withdraw at any time (e.g. include a 'Withdraw' button at the foot of each screen).

Problem: technical – hardware and software	Possible solution
The configuration of the questionnaire may vary from one machine to another (because of web browsers, connection, hardware, software) and can lead to dropout.	Opt for simplicity. Test the survey on different computer systems/browsers to ensure consistency. Avoid surveys that require real time completion.
The screen as set out by the survey designer may not appear the same as that which appears on the respondent's screen.	Opt for simplicity. Use a commercial survey software system for generating the questionnaire. Avoid high-level programmes.

continued

Box 10.1
continued

Problem: technical – hardware and software	Possible solution
Slow network connections or limited bandwidth can slow down loading.	Keep the use of graphics to a minimum. Advise on the possible time it takes to load.
Respondents may not have the same software, or the same version of the software as the sender, rendering downloading of the questionnaire either impossible or distorting the received graphics.	Avoid the use of graphics and more advanced software programmes.
Graphics may be corrupted/incompatible between the sender and the user, i.e. between one kind of machine, user platform and software and another. Hardware may differ between sender and receiver.	Opt for simplicity. Use commercially available web-based surveying systems and packages. Use image files (e.g. jpeg, .gif) to reduce loading time. Avoid pop-ups if possible as they reduce response rate.
The greater the use of graphics and plug-ins (e.g. using Java and Applets), the longer it takes to download, and, particularly – though not exclusively – if respondents do not have broadband access then time-consuming downloads could result in either the respondent giving up and cancelling the download, or creating a bad mood in the respondent.	Keep software requirements as low-tech as possible. Avoid questionnaires that use sophisticated computer graphics.
There may be slow loading times due to Internet congestion.	Avoid sophisticated graphics and 'fancy' presentations as these take longer to download.
The physical distance between points on an attitude scale may spread out because of configuration differences between machines.	Indicate how best the questionnaire may be viewed (e.g. 800×400).
The construction procedures for wrap-around text may vary between computers.	Keep lines of text short.
Email questionnaires may distort the layout of the questionnaire (some email software uses HTML, others do not).	Avoid sending a questionnaire directly using email; rather, post it on a web site (e.g. so that respondents visit a web site and then click a box for immediate transfer to the questionnaire). Consider using an email to direct participants to a web site (e.g. the email includes the web site which can be reached by clicking in the address contained in the email). Use an email that includes an attachment which contains the more graphically sophisticated survey instrument itself.

continued

Box 10.1
continued

Problem: respondents	Possible solution
Respondents may be unfamiliar or inexperienced with the Internet and the media.	Keep the questionnaire simple and easy to complete.
Respondents may send multiple copies of their completed questionnaire from the same or different addresses.	Have a security device that tracks and limits (as far as possible) respondents who may be returning the same questionnaire on more than one occasion. Use passwords (though this, itself, may create problems of identifiability). Collect personal identification items. Check for internal consistency across submissions.
There may be more than one respondent to a single questionnaire (the same problem as in, for example, a postal questionnaire).	Include questions to cross-check the consistency of replies to similar items.
Respondents may not be used to pull-down menus.	Provide clear instructions.
The language of email surveys can risk offending potential participants ('flaming').	Check the language used to avoid angering the participants.
Respondents' difficulty in navigating the pages of the online survey.	Keep instructions to the page in question. Make the instructions for branching very clear (font size, colour etc.).

Problem: layout and presentation	Possible solution
A page of paper is longer than it is wide, but a screen is wider than it is long, and a screen is smaller than a page, i.e. layout becomes a matter of concern.	Remember that screen-based surveys take a greater number of screens than their equivalent number of pages in a paper copy. Sectionalize the questionnaire so that each section fills the screen, and does not take more than one screen.
The layout of the text and instructions assumes greater importance than for paper questionnaires.	Opt for clarity and simplicity.
The layout uses a lot of grids and matrices.	Avoid grids and matrices: they are a major source of non-response.
The order of items affects response rates.	Locate requests for personal information at the beginning of the survey. Include 'warm-ups' and early 'high hurdles' to avoid dropout.

continued

Box 10.1
continued

Problem: layout and presentation	Possible solution
Respondents may be bombarded with too much information in an introductory message.	Place the advertisement for the survey on user groups as well as the general public, inviting participants to contact such-and-such a person or web site for further information and the questionnaire itself, i.e. separate the questionnaire from the advertisement for or introduction to the questionnaire.
Respondents may be overloaded with instructions at the beginning of the survey.	Avoid placing all the instructions at the start of the questionnaire, but keep specific instructions for specific questions.
Respondents may be overloaded with information at the beginning of the survey.	Keep the initial information brief and embed further information deeper in the survey.
Respondents may have to take multiple actions in order to answer each question (e.g. clicking on an answer, moving the scroll bar, clicking for the next screen, clicking to submit a screen of information).	Keep the number of actions required in order to move on to a minimum.
Respondents may not be able to see all the option choices without scrolling down the screen.	Ensure that the whole item and options are contained on a single screen.
Respondents may not understand instructions.	Provide a helpline, email address or contact details of the researcher. Pilot the instrument.
Instructions about options may be unclear.	Use radio buttons for single choice items, and try to keep layout similar to a paper layout.
Respondents only read part of each question before going to the response category.	Keep instructions and words to a necessary minimum.
Problem: reliability	**Possible solution**
Respondents may alter the instrument itself. The researcher relinquishes a greater amount of control to the respondents than in conventional questionnaires.	Include technological safeguards to prevent alteration and have procedures to identify altered instruments.
Respondents may be forced to answer every question even when they consider some response categories inappropriate.	Pilot the survey. Include options such as 'don't know' and 'do not wish to answer' and avoid forcing respondents to reply before they can move on.
Respondents may not be telling the truth – they may misrepresent themselves.	Include questions to cross-check replies (to try to reduce the problem of respondents not telling the truth).

continued

Box 10.1
continued

Problem: dropout	Possible solution
Respondents may lose interest after a while and abandon the survey, thereby losing all the survey data.	Have a device that requires respondents to send their replies screen by screen (e.g. a 'Submit' button at the foot of each screen) section by section, or item by item. Put each question or each section on a separate screen, with 'submit' at the end of each screen. Adopt a 'one-item-one-screen' technique.
Respondents may not know how long the questionnaire is, and so may lose interest.	Include a device for indicating how far through the questionnaire the respondent has reached: a progress bar at the bottom or the side of the survey.
Internet surveys take longer to complete than paper-based surveys.	Keep the Internet survey as short, clear and easy to complete as possible.
People do not want to take part, and it is easier for someone to quit or cancel an Internet-based survey than a paper-based survey (simply a click of a button).	Increase incentives to participate (e.g. financial incentives, lottery tickets, if they are permitted in the country).
Diminishing returns (the survey response drops off quite quickly). Newsgroup postings and electronic discussion group data are removed, relegated or archived after a period of time (e.g. a week), and readers do not read lower down the lists of postings.	Ensure that the web site is re-posted each week during the data collection period.
Non-participation may be high (i.e. potential participants may not choose to start, in contrast to those who start and who subsequently drop out).	Increase incentives to participate. Locate personal informational questions at the start of the survey.
Error messages (e.g. if an item has not been completed) cause frustration and may cause respondents to abandon the questionnaire.	Avoid error messages if possible, but, if not possible, provide clear reasons why the error was made and how to rectify it.

Smyth *et al.* (2004: 21) also suggest that the use of headings and separation of sections take on added significance in Internet-based surveys. They report that separating items into two sections with headings had a 'dramatic effect' on responses, as respondents felt compelled to answer both subgroups (70 per cent gave an answer in both subgroups whereas only 41 per cent did so when there were no headings or sectionalization). They also found that separating a vertical list of items into subgroups and columns (double-banking) was not a 'desirable construction practice' and should be avoided if possible. They report that asking respondents for some open-ended responses (e.g. writing their subject specialisms) can be more efficient than having them track down a long list of subjects to find the one that applies to them, though this can be mitigated by placing simple lists in alphabetical order. Finally they found that placing very short guides underneath the write-in box rather than at its side (e.g. dd/mm/yy for 'day/month/year', and using 'yy' for 'year' rather than 'yyyy') increased response rates, and that placing instructions very close to the answer box improved response rates.

Dillman *et al.* (2003: 23) also found that having respondents use a yes/no format (a 'forced choice') for responding resulted in increased numbers of affirmative answers, even though this requires more cognitive processing than non-forced choice questions (e.g. 'tick[check]-all-that-apply' questions). This is because respondents may not wish to answer questions in the outright negative (Dillman *et al.* 2003: 10); even if they do not really have an opinion or they are neutral or the item does not really apply to them, they may choose a 'yes' rather than a 'no' category. They may leave a blank rather than indicating a 'no'. The percentage of affirmative responses was higher in a paper-based survey than in an Internet-based survey (11.3 per cent and 6.5 per cent respectively) (Dillman *et al.* 2003: 22).

Similarly, as mentioned earlier, Dillman *et al.* (2003) report that respondents tend to select items higher up a list than lower down a list of options (the primacy effect), opting for the 'satisficing' principle (they are satisfied with a minimum sufficient response, selecting the first reasonable response in a list and then moving on rather than working their way down the list to find the optimal response), suggesting that item order is a significant feature, making a difference of over 39 per cent to responses (Dillman *et al.* 2003: 7). This is particularly so, the authors aver, when respondents are asked for opinions and beliefs rather than topics seeking factual information. They also suggest that the more difficult the item is, the more respondents will move towards 'satisficing'. Dillman *et al.* (2003: 22) found that 'satisficing' and the primacy effect were stronger in Internet surveys than paper-based surveys, and that changing 'check-all-that-apply' to forced responses (yes/no) did not eliminate response order effects.

Dillman *et al.* (2003: 6) also report that the order of response items can have an effect on responses, citing as an example a study that found that asking college students whether their male or female teachers were more empathetic was affected by whether the 'male' option was placed before or after the 'female' option: 'respondents evaluated their female teachers more positively when they were asked to compare them to their male teachers than when they were asked to compare their male teachers to their female teachers'. Respondents compare the second item in light of the first item in a list rather than considering the items separately.

Internet-based surveys are subject to the same ethical rules as paper-based surveys. These include, for example, informed consent and confidentiality. While the former may be straightforward to ensure, the issue of confidentiality on the Internet is more troublesome for researchers. For example, on the one hand, an email survey can be quick and uncomplicated, it can also reveal the identity and traceability of the respondent. As Witmer *et al.* (1999: 147) remark, this could stall a project. Security (e.g. through passwords and PINs) is one possible solution, although this, too, can create problems in that respondents may feel that they are being identified and tracked, and, indeed, some surveys may deposit unwelcome 'cookies' onto the respondent's computer, for future contact.

Sampling in Internet-based surveys

Sampling bias is a major concern for Internet-based surveys (Coomber 1997; Roztocki and Lahri 2002). Hewson *et al.* (2003: 27) suggest that 'Internet-mediated research is immediately subject to serious problems concerning sampling representativeness and validity of data', e.g. that the Internet researcher tends to tap into middle-class and well-educated populations, mainly from the United States, or undergraduate and college students. Survey 2000 (Witte *et al.* 1999) found that 92.5 per cent of respondents were white. However, the view of over-representation of some and under-representation of others is being increasingly challenged (Smith and Leigh 1997;

Witte *et al.* 1999; Hewson *et al.* 2003), with results showing that samples taken from users and non-users of the Internet did not differ in terms of income, education, sexual orientation, marital status, ethnicity and religious belief. However, they did differ in terms of age, with the Internet samples containing a wider age range than non-Internet samples, and in terms of sex, with the Internet samples containing more males. Hewson *et al.* (2003) report overall a greater diversity of sample characteristics in Internet-based samples, though they caution that this is inconclusive, and that the sample characteristics of Internet samples, like non-Internet samples, depend on the sampling strategy used. Stewart and Yalonis (2001) suggest that one can overcome the possible bias in sampling through simple stratification techniques.

A major problem in sampling for Internet surveys is estimating the size and nature of the population from which the sample is drawn: a key feature of sampling strategy. Researchers have no clear knowledge of the population characteristics or size, and indeed the same applies to the sample. The number of Internet users is not a simple function of the number of computers or the number of servers (e.g. many users can employ a single computer or server), though at the time of writing, a figure of over 500 million users has been suggested (Hewson *et al.* 2003: 36). Further, it is difficult to know how many or what kind of people saw a particular survey on a web site (e.g. more males than females), i.e. the sampling frame is unclear. Moreover, certain sectors of the population may still be excluded from the Internet, for example: those not wishing to, or unable to (e.g. because of cost or availability), gain access to the Internet. The situation is changing rapidly. In 1997 it was reported (Coomber 1997) that Internet users tended to be white, relatively affluent and relatively well-educated males from the developed world; more recent studies (e.g. Hewson *et al.* 2003) suggest that the Internet is attracting a much more diverse population that is closer to the general population.

There are further concerns about the sampling on Internet-based surveys. Internet-based surveys are based largely on volunteer samples, obtained through general posting on the web (e.g. an advertisement giving details and directing volunteers to a site for further information), or, more popular in the social sciences, through announcements to specific newsgroups and interest groups on the web, e.g. contacting user groups (e.g. through the SchoolNet). Lists of different kinds of user (USENET) groups, newsgroups and electronic discussion groups (e.g. Listservs) can be found on the web. Several search engines exist that seek and return web mailing lists, such as: http://www.liszt.com (categorized by subject); Catalist (the official catalogue of LISTSERV lists at http://www.lsoft.com/catalist.html); Mailbase (http://www.mailbase.ac.uk), which is a major collection of over 2,500 lists concerning the academic community in the United Kingdom; and Meta-List.net (http://www.meta-list.net), which searches a database of nearly a quarter of a million mailing lists. Dochartaigh (2002) provides useful material on web searching for educational and social researchers.

The issue here is that the researcher is using non-probability, volunteer sampling, and this may decrease the generalizability of the findings (though, of course, this may be no more a problem on Internet-based surveys than on other surveys). Opportunity samples (e.g. of undergraduate or postgraduate students using the web, or of particular groups) may restrict the generalizability of the research, but this may be no more than in conventional research, and may not be a problem so long as it is acknowledged. The issue of volunteer samples runs deeper, for volunteers may differ from non-volunteers in terms of personality (e.g. they may be more extravert or concerned for self-actualization: Bargh *et al.* 2002) and may self-select themselves into, or out of, a survey, again restricting the generalizability of the results.

One method to try to overcome the problem of volunteer bias is to strive for extremely large samples, or to record the number of hits on a web site, though these are crude indices. Another method of securing the participation of non-volunteers in an Internet survey is to contact them by email (assuming that their email addresses are known), e.g. a class of students, a group of teachers. However, email addresses themselves do not give the researcher any indication of the sample characteristics (e.g. age, sex, nationality etc).

Watt (1997) suggests that there are three types of Internet sample:

- an *unrestricted* sample: anyone can complete the questionnaire, but it may have limited representativeness
- a *screened* sample: quotas are placed on the subsample categories and types (e.g. gender, income, job responsibility etc.)
- a *recruited* sample: respondents complete a preliminary classification questionnaire and then, based on the data provided in them, are recruited or not.

Response rate for an Internet survey is typically lower than for a paper-based survey, as is the rate of completion of the whole survey (Reips 2002a). Witmer *et al.* (1999: 147) report that for a paper-based survey the response could be as high as 50 per cent and as low as 20 per cent; for an Internet survey it could be as low as 10 per cent or even lower. Dillman *et al.* (1998b) report a study that found that 84 per cent of a sample completed a particular paper-based survey, while only 68 per cent of a sample completed the same survey online. Solomon (2001) reported that response rates to an Internet-based survey are lower than for their equivalent mail surveys. However, this issue is compounded because in an Internet-based survey, there is no real knowledge of the population or the sample, unless only specific people have been approached (e.g. through email). In the same study Witmer *et al.* found that short versions of an Internet-based questionnaire did not produce a significantly higher response rate than the long version (p. 155). Solomon (2001) suggests that response rates can be improved through the use of personalized email, follow-up reminders, the use of simple formats and pre-notification of the intent to survey.

Reips (2002a) provides some useful guidelines for increasing response rates on an Internet survey. He suggests that response rates can be increased by utilizing the multiple site entry technique, i.e. having several web sites and postings on several discussion groups that link potential participants or web surfers to the web site containing the questionnaire. Reips (2002a: 249) also suggests utilizing a 'high hurdle' technique, where 'motivationally adverse factors are announced or concentrated as close to the beginning' as possible, so that any potential dropouts will self-select at the start rather than during the data collection. A 'high hurdle' technique, he suggests, comprises:

- *Seriousness:* inform the participants that the research is serious and rigorous.
- *Personalization:* ask for an email address or contact details and personal information.
- *Impression of control:* inform participants that their identity is traceable.
- *Patience: loading time:* use image files to reduce loading time of Web pages.
- *Patience: long texts:* place most of the text in the first page, and successively reduce the amount on each subsequent page.
- *Duration:* inform participants how long the survey will take.
- *Privacy:* inform the participants that some personal information will be sought.
- *Preconditions:* indicate the requirements for particular software.
- *Technical pretests:* conduct tests of compatibility of software.
- *Rewards:* indicate that any rewards/incentives are contingent on full completion of the survey.

Of course, some of these strategies could backfire on the researcher (e.g. the disclosure of personal and traceable details), but the principle here is that it is better for the participant not to take part in the first place rather than to drop out during the process. Indeed Frick *et al.* (1999) found that early dropout was not increased by asking for personal information at the beginning. In relation to online experiments they found that 'the tendency of leaving the experiment when personal information is requested is higher after the experiment has already been finished' (Frick *et al.* 1999: 4), i.e. it is better to ask for personal information at the beginning.

Reips (2002a) also advocates the use of 'warm-up' techniques in Internet-based research in conjunction with the 'high hurdle' technique (see also Frick *et al.* 1999). He suggests that most dropouts occur earlier rather than later in data collection, or, indeed, at the very beginning (non-participation) and that most such initial dropouts occur because participants are overloaded with information early on. Rather, he suggests, it is preferable to introduce some simple-to-complete items earlier on to build up an idea of how to respond to the later items and to try out practice materials. Frick *et al.* (1999) report that offering financial incentives may be useful in reducing dropouts, ensuring that respondents continue an online survey to completion (up to twice as likely to ensure completion), and that they may be useful if intrinsic motivation is insufficient to guarantee completion.

Internet-based experiments

A growing field in psychological research is the use of the Internet for experiments (e.g. http://www.psych.unizh.ch/genpsy/Ulf/Lab/webExpPsyLab.html). Hewson *et al.* (2003) classify these into four principal types:

> those that present static printed materials (for example, printed text or graphics); second are those that make use of non-printed materials (for example, video or sound); third are reaction-time experiments; and fourth are experiments that involve some form of interpersonal interaction.
>
> (Hewson *et al.* 2003: 48)

The first kind of experiment is akin to a survey in that it sends formulated material to respondents (e.g. graphically presented material) by email or by web page, and the intervention will be to send different groups different materials. Here all the cautions and comments that were made about Internet-based surveys apply, particularly those problems of download times, different browsers and platforms. However, the matter of download time applies more strongly to the second type

of Internet-based experiments that use video clips or sound, and some software packages will reproduce higher quality than others, even though the original that is transmitted is the same for everyone. This can be addressed by ensuring that the material runs at its optimum even on the slowest computer (Hewson *et al.* 2003: 49) or by stating the minimum hardware required for the experiment to be run successfully.

Reaction-time experiments, those that require very precise timing (e.g. to milliseconds) are difficult in remote situations, as different platforms and Internet connection speeds and congestion on the Internet through having multiple users at busy times can render standardization virtually impossible. One solution to this is to have the experiment downloaded and then run offline before loading it back onto the computer and sending it.

The fourth type involves interaction, and is akin to Internet interviewing (discussed below), facilitated by chat rooms. However, this is solely a written medium and so intonation, inflection, hesitancies, non-verbal cues, extra-linguistic and paralinguistic factors are ruled out of this medium. It is, in a sense, incomplete, although the increasing availability and use of simple screen-top video cameras is mitigating this. Indeed this latter development renders observational studies an increasing possibility in the Internet age.

Reips (2002a) reports that in comparison to laboratory experiments, Internet-based experiments experienced greater problems of dropout, that the dropout rate in an Internet experiment was very varied (from 1 per cent to 87 per cent, and that dropout could be reduced by offering incentives, e.g. payments or lottery tickets, bringing a difference of as much as 31 per cent to dropout rates. Dropout on Internet-based research was due to a range of factors, for example motivation, how interesting the experiment was, not least of which was the non-compulsory nature of the experiment (in contrast, for example, to the compulsory nature of experiments undertaken by university student participants as part of their degree studies). The discussion of the 'high hurdle' technique earlier is applicable to experiments here. Reips (2002b:

245–6) also reports that greater variance in results is likely in an Internet-based experiment than in a conventional experiment due to technical matters (e.g. network connection speed, computer speed, multiple software running in parallel).

On the other hand, Reips (2002b: 247) also reports that Internet-based experiments have an attraction over laboratory and conventional experiments:

- They have greater generalizability because of their wider sampling.
- They demonstrate greater ecological validity as typically they are conducted in settings that are familiar to the participants and at times suitable to the participant ('the experiment comes to the participant, not vice versa'), though, of course, the obverse of this is that the researcher has no control over the experimental setting (Reips 2002b: 250).
- They have a high degree of voluntariness, such that more authentic behaviours can be observed.

How correct these claims are is an empirical matter. For example, the use of sophisticated software packages (e.g. Java) can reduce experimenter control as these packages may interact with other programming languages. Indeed Schwarz and Reips (2001) report that the use of Javascript led to a 13 per cent higher dropout rate in an experiment compared to an identical experiment that did not use Javascript. Further, multiple returns by a single participant could confound reliability (discussed above in connection with survey methods).

Reips (2002a, 2002b) provides a series of 'dos' and 'don'ts' in Internet experimenting. In terms of 'dos' he gives five main points:

- Use dropout as a dependent variable.
- Use dropout to detect motivational confounding (i.e. to identify boredom and motivation levels in experiments).
- Place questions for personal information at the beginning of the Internet study. Reips (2002b) suggests that asking for personal information may assist in keeping participants

in an experiment, and that this is part of the 'high hurdle' technique, where dropouts self-select out of the study, rather than dropping out during the study.

- Use techniques that help ensure quality in data collection over the Internet (e.g. the 'high hurdle' and 'warm-up' techniques discussed earlier, subsampling to detect and ensure consistency of results, using single passwords to ensure data integrity, providing contact information, reducing dropout).
- Use Internet-based tools and services to develop and announce your study (using commercially produced software to ensure that technical and presentational problems are overcome). There are also web sites (e.g. the American Psychological Society) that announce experiments.

In terms of 'don'ts' Reips gives five main points:

- Do not allow external access to unprotected directories. This can violate ethical and legal requirements, as it provides access to confidential data. It also might allow the participants to have access to the structure of the experiment, thereby contaminating the experiment.
- Do not allow public display of confidential participant data through URLs (uniform resource locators, a problem if respondents use the GET protocol, which is a way of requesting an html page, whether or not one uses query parameters), as this, again, violates ethical codes.
- Do not accidentally reveal the experiment's structure (as this could affect participant behaviour). This might be done through including the experiment's details on a related file or a file in the same directory.
- Do not ignore the technical variance inherent in the Internet (configuration details, browsers, platforms, bandwidth and software might all distort the experiment, as discussed above).
- Do not bias results through improper use of form elements, such as measurement errors, where omitting particular categories (e.g.

'neutral', 'do not want to respond', 'neither agree nor disagree') could distort the results.

Indeed, the points made in connection with Internet surveys and questionnaires apply equally to Internet experiments, and readers are advised to review these.

Reips (2000b) points out that it is a misconception to regard an Internet-based experiment as the same as a laboratory experiment, as

- Internet participants could choose to leave the experiment at any time
- they can conduct the experiment at any time and in their own settings
- they are often conducted with larger samples than conventional experiments
- they rely on technical matters, network connections, and the computer competence of the participants
- they are more public than most conventional experiments.

On the other hand, he also cautions against regarding the Internet-based experiment as completely different from the laboratory experiment, as

- many laboratory experiments also rely on computers
- fundamental ideas are the same for laboratory and Internet-based surveys
- similar results have been produced by both means.

Reips (200b) suggests several issues in conducting Internet-based experiments:

- Consider a web-based software tool to develop the experimental materials.
- Pilot the experiment on different platforms for clarity of instructions and availability on different platforms.
- Decide the level of sophistication of HMTL scripting and whether to use HTML or non-HTML.
- Check the experiments for configuration errors and variance on different computers.

- Place the experiment on several web sites and services.
- Run the experiment online and offline to make comparisons.
- Use the 'warm-up' and 'high hurdle' techniques, asking filter questions (e.g. about the seriousness of the participant, their background and expertise, language skills).
- Use dropout to ascertain whether there is motivational confounding.
- Check for obvious naming of files and conditions (to reduce the possibility of unwanted access to files).
- Consider using passwords and procedures (e.g. consistency checks) to reduce the possibility of multiple submissions.
- Keep an experimental log of data for any subsequent analysis and verification of results.
- Analyse and report dropout.
- Keep the experimental details on the Internet, to give a positive impression of the experiment.

At the time of writing, the Internet-based experiment is currently more a child of psychology than of education. However, given the rise of evidence-based practice in education, and the advocacy of randomized controlled trials in education, this form of experimentation is set to become more widely used in education.

Details of the development of Internet-based experimental software can be found at:

http://www.genpsylab.unizch/wextor/index.html
http://psych.hanover.edu.APS/exponnet.html
http://www.genpsy.unizch/Ulf.Lab/webexplist.html.

Internet-based interviews

The opportunity that Internet interviews present for interviewing respondents is immense. For example, online interviews which are entirely real-time and synchronous through chat rooms, can be anonymous for both parties if so desired, and the opportunity to contact respondents at mutually convenient times is enhanced. For example, at the time of writing, Skype.com provides a real-time, extremely inexpensive means of direct conversation via the Internet, either from computer to computer or from computer to a fixed line. Because of these or other features, the Internet may also enable researchers to contact hard-to-reach groups and individuals (e.g. in the case of conducting research on sensitive topics). On the other hand, as mentioned above, the reduction of the interview to purely a written exchange can mitigate some of the essential features of an interview as discussed in Chapter 16: the need to regard interviews as a full social encounter.

Chat rooms provide the opportunity for split screens and shared screens, thereby displaying the ongoing dialogue between participants. If chat rooms are not to be used, then email provides an alternative, which presents an opportunity for ongoing discussion that is dependent on the (usually fast) speed of the email facility. These approaches may lack the spontaneity and richness of conventional interviews, but they also have the attractions afforded by anonymity and the absence of a face-to-face encounter (though the use of video cameras located above computer screens can also be added to the interview). The quality of the image may be poor and may not be synchronous with the speaker – there often being a slight delay, broken images or movement in a series of freeze-frame rather than continuous imaging. Internet interviewing can also go offline, with respondents writing their own responses to questions and sending them at different times, though, to some extent, this merges the interview with the questionnaire survey, the only difference perhaps being in the degree of flexibility of questions (contents, nature, emerging issues and follow-up) in online interviews in comparison to questionnaires. Internet interviews simply require both parties to agree a time to log on to the computer in order to conduct the interview, and, if required or possible, to set up the video camera.

Searching for research materials on the Internet

The storage and retrieval of research data on the Internet play an important role not only in keeping researchers abreast of developments across the world, but also in providing access to data which can inform literature searches to establish construct and content validity in their own research. Indeed, some kinds of research are essentially large-scale literature searches (e.g. the research papers published in the journal *Review of Educational Research*). Online journals, abstracts and titles enable researchers to keep up with the cutting edge of research and to conduct a literature search of relevant material on their chosen topic. Web sites and email correspondence enable networks and information to be shared. For example, researchers wishing to gain instantaneous global access to literature and recent developments in research associations can reach Australia, East Asia, the United Kingdom and United States in a matter of seconds through such web sites as the following:

American Educational Research Association: http://www.aera.net

American Educational Research Association (again): http://www.lalc.k12.ca.us/catalog/providers/185.html

Australian Council for Educational Research: http://www.acer.edu.au/index2.html

British Educational Research Association: http://www.bera.ac.uk

Chinese American Educational Research Association: http://www.ttu.eedu/~edupsy/regis.html

Curriculum, Evaluation and Management Centre (UK: among the largest monitoring centres of its kind in the world): http://www.cemcentre.org

Economic and Social Research Council (UK) http://www.esrc.ac.uk

Educators' Reference Desk (the source of ERIC in the United States, publications of the American Educational Research Association): http://www.eduref.org/

European Educational Research Association: http://www.eera.ac.uk/index.html

Hong Kong Educational Research Association: http://www.fed.cuhk.edu.hk/~hkera

Mid-South Educational Research Association (a very large regional association in the United States): http://www.msstate.edu/org/msera/msera.html

National Foundation for Educational Research (UK) http://www.nfer.ac.uk
Scottish Council for Research in Education: http://scre.ac.uk
Scottish Council for Research in Education's links to electronic journals: http://www.scre.ac.uk/is/webjournals.html
Washington Educational Research Association (USA): http://www.wera-web.org/index.html

Researchers wishing to access online journal indices and references for published research results (rather than to specific research associations as in the web sites above) have a variety of web sites which they can visit, for example:

http://www.leeds.ac.uk/bei (to gain access to the British Education Index)
http://brs.leeds.ac.uk/~beiwww/beid.html (the web site for online searching of the British Educational Research Association's archive)
http://www.eera.ac.uk/links5.html (the web site of the European Educational Research Association that links to free online journals)
http://www.routledge.com:9996/routledge/journal/er.html (the web site of Routledge, an international publisher that provides information on all its research articles)
http://www.carfax.co.uk (a service provided by a UK publisher to gain access to the Scholarly Articles Research Alerting network in the United Kingdom)
http://www.sagepub.co.uk (Sage Publications)
http://www.tandf.co.uk/era/ (Educational Research Abstracts Online, an alerting service from the publisher Taylor & Francis)
http://www.journals.routledge.com (Routledge journals)
http://bubl.ac.uk (a UK national information service, provided for the higher education community)
http://www.scout.cs.wisc.edu/archive (Scout Report Archives, which locates and provides short descriptions of several thousand resource sites)
http://www.sosig.ac.uk and http://www.sosog.esrc.ac.uk (the Social Science Information Gateway, providing access to worldwide resources and information)
http://sosig.ac.uk/social_science_general/social_science_methodology) (the Social Science

Information Gateway's sections on research methods, both quantitative and qualitative)
http://www.carfax.co.uk/ber-ad.htm (the web site of the *British Educational Research Journal*)
http://www.unesco.org/general.eng.infoserv (the UNESCO web site that provides material for social science researchers)
http://www.statistics.gov.uk (the UK government's official statistics site)
http://wos.mimas.ac.uk (the web site of the Web of Science, that, among other functions, provides access to the Social Science Citation Index, the Science Citation Index and the Arts and Humanities Citation Index)
http://www.essex.ac.uk (the web site of the data archive at the University of Essex).

With regard to searching libraries, there are several useful web sites:

http://www.lights.com/webcats (provides researchers with links to library catalogues organized by the type of library and its location)
http://www.loc.gov (the United States Library of Congress)
http://www.lcweb.loc.gov/z3950 (links to US libraries)
http://www.libdex.com/ (the Library Index web site, linking to 18,000 libraries)
http://www.copac.ac.uk.copac (this enables researchers to search major UK libraries)
http://www.bl.uk (the British Library online catalogue)
http://vlib.org/ (the Virtual Library, and provides online resources).

For checking what is in print, http://www.booksinprint.com provides a comprehensive listing of current books in print, while http://www.bibliofind.com is a site of old, out-of-print and rare books. The web site http://www.lights.com links researchers to some 6,000 publishers.

Most journals provide access to abstracts free online, though access to the full article is usually by subscription only. Providers of online journals include, for example (in alphabetical order):

Bath Information and Data Services (BIDS): http://www.bids.ac.uk
EBSCO: http://www.ebsco.com
Elsevier: http://www.elsevier.com
Emerald: http://www.emeraldinsight.com
FirstSearch: http://www.oclc.org
Ingenta: http://www.ingenta.com
JSTOR: http://www.jstor.org
Kluweronline: http://www.kluweronline.com
Northern Light: http://www.northernlight.com
ProQuest: http://www.proquest.com and http://www.bellhowell,infolearning.com.proquest
ProQuest Digital Dissertations: http://www.bib.umi.com/dissertations
Science Direct: http://www.sciencedirect.com
Swets: http://www.swetsnet.nl and http://www.swetsnet.com
Uncover Web: http://www.Uncweb.carl.org
Web of Science: http://www.isinet.com

For theses, Aslib Index to Theses is useful (http://www.theses.com) and the Networked Digital Library of Theses and Dissertations can be located at http://www.theses.org. Some major government web sites also have a free alerting service (e.g. Ofsted).

Researchers who do not know a web site address have at their disposal a variety of search engines to locate it. At the time of writing some widely used engines are:

Google: http://www.google.com
MSN Search: http://www.msn.com
AOL Search: http://www.search.aol.com
Netscape Navigator: http://www.netscape.com
Fast Search: http://www.alltheweb.com
Internet Explorer: http://www.microsoft.com
AltaVista: http://www.altavista.com
Direct Hit: http://www.directhit.com
Excite: http://www.Excite.com
Ask Jeeves: http://www.askjeeves.com
Lycos: http://www.Lycos.com
Go To: http://www.go2.com
Yahoo: http://www.yahoo.com
HotBot: http://www.hotbot.com
Northern Light: http://www.northernlight.com
Metacrawler: http://www.metacrawler.com.

There are very many more. All of these search engines enable researchers to conduct searches by keywords. Some of these are parallel search engines (which will search several single search engines at a time) and some are file search engines (which will search files across the world).

Finding research information, where not available from databases and indices on CD-Roms, is often done through the Internet by trial-and-error and serendipity, identifying the key words singly or in combination (between double inverted commas). The system of 'bookmarking' web sites enables rapid retrieval of these web sites for future reference; this is perhaps essential, as some Internet connections are slow, and a vast amount of material on it is, at best, unhelpful!

http://www.nap.edu/category.html?id=ed (the web site of the National Academies Press, Education section, providing free online materials)
http://www.educationindex.com/ and http://www.shawmultimedia.com/links2.html (centres for the provision of free educational materials and related web sites)
http://lii.org/ (the librarians' index to the Internet)
http://www.ncrel.org/ (the web site of the North Central Regional Educational Laboratories, an organization providing a range of educational resources)
http://www.sedl.org/ (the web site of the Southwest Educational Development Laboratory, an organization providing a range of educational resources).

Evaluating web sites

The use of the Internet for educational research will require an ability to evaluate web sites. The Internet is a vast store of disorganized and largely unvetted material, and researchers will need to be able to ascertain quite quickly how far the web-based material is appropriate. There are several criteria for evaluating web sites, including the following (e.g. Tweddle et al. 1998; Rodrigues and Rodrigues, 2000):

- the *purpose* of the site, as this will enable users to establish its relevance and appropriateness

- *authority* and *authenticity* of the material, which should both be authoritative and declare its sources
- *content* of the material – its up-to-dateness, relevance and coverage
- *credibility* and *legitimacy* of the material (e.g. is it from a respected source or institution)
- *correctness*, *accuracy*, *completeness* and *fairness* of the material
- *objectivity* and *rigour* of the material being presented and/or discussed.

In evaluating educational research materials on the web, researchers and teachers can ask themselves several questions (Hartley *et al.* 1997):

- Is the author identified?
- Does the author establish her/his expertise in the area, and institutional affiliation?
- Is the organization reputable?
- Is the material referenced; does the author indicate how the material was gathered?
- What is the role that this web site is designed to play (e.g. to provide information, to persuade)?
- Is the material up-to-date?
- Is the material free from biases, personal opinions and offence?
- How do we know that the author is authoritative on this web site?

It is important for the researcher to keep full bibliographic data of the web site material used, including the date in which it was retrieved and the web site address.

Computer simulations

Computer simulations and virtual technology have significant contributions to make to educational research. Simulations have two main components: a *system* in which the researcher is interested and that lends itself to being modelled or simulated, and a *model* of that system (Wilcox 1997). The system comprises any set of interrelated features, while the model, that is, the analogue of the system, is often mathematical.

Wilcox (1997) has indicated two forms of simulation. In *deterministic simulations* all the mathematical and logical relationships between the components of a system are known and fixed. In *stochastic simulations*, typically the main types used in educational research, at least one variable is random. A simulation is a model of the real world in which the relevant factors in the research can be included and manipulated. A model may operationalize a theory and convert it into a computer programme (see Gilbert and Troitzsch 2005: 3), making explicit its assumptions.

Gilbert and Troitzsch (2005: 6) suggest that the prime purposes of computer simulations are for discovery, proof and experiment. Beyond simply prediction, computer simulations enable an *understanding* and *explanation* to be gained of how processes operate and unfold over time, and the results of these. This explodes the value of *prediction* as a test of a theory; rather it argues that the test of a theory should be its explanatory and hermeneutic power, rather than its predictive value. Indeed computer simulations may be useful in developing rather than testing theories.

Computer simulations, by enabling the researcher to control and manipulate the variables and components, are useful in addressing 'what if' questions, e.g. 'What happens if I change this parameter or that parameter?'; 'What if the person behaves in such-and-such a way?'; 'What happens if I change such-and-such a feature of the environment?' The relevant elements are put into the simulation and are then manipulated – set to different parameters – to see what happens and what results.

Computers can handle very rapidly data that would take humans several years to process. Simulations based on mathematical modelling (e.g. multiple iterations of the same formula) provide researchers with a way of imitating behaviours and systems, and extrapolating what might happen if the system runs over time or if the same mathematical calculations are repeated over and over again, where data are fed back – formatively – into the next round of calculation of the same formula. Hopkins *et al.* (1996: 159-62) report such a case in proving the Central Limit Theorem (discussed in Chapter 4), where the process of calculation of means was repeated 10,000 times. Such modelling has its roots in chaos theory and complexity theory.

For Laplace and Newton, the universe was rationalistic, deterministic and of clockwork order; effects were functions of causes, small causes (minimal initial conditions) produced small effects (minimal and predictable) and large causes (multiple initial conditions) produced large (multiple) effects. Predictability, causality, patterning, universality and 'grand' overarching theories, linearity, continuity, stability, objectivity, all contributed to the view of the universe as an ordered and internally harmonistic mechanism in an albeit complex equilibrium, a rational, closed and deterministic system susceptible to comparatively straightforward scientific discovery and laws.

From the 1960s this view has been increasingly challenged with the rise of theories of chaos and complexity. Central to these theories are several principles (e.g. Gleick 1987; Morrison 1998, 2002a):

- Small-scale changes in initial conditions can produce massive and unpredictable changes in outcome (e.g. a butterfly's wing beat in the Caribbean can produce a hurricane in the United States).
- Very similar conditions can produce very dissimilar outcomes (e.g. using simple mathematical equations: Stewart 1990).
- Regularity, conformity and linear relationships between elements break down to irregularity, diversity and nonlinear relationships between elements.
- Even if differential equations are very simple, the behaviour of the system that they are modelling may not be simple.
- Effects are not straightforward continuous functions of causes.
- The universe is largely unpredictable.
- If something works once there is no guarantee that it will work in the same way a second time.
- Determinism is replaced by indeterminism; deterministic, linear and stable systems are replaced by 'dynamical', changing, evolving systems and non-linear explanations of phenomena.

- Continuity is replaced by discontinuity, turbulence and irreversible transformation.
- Grand, universal, all-encompassing theories and large-scale explanations provide inadequate accounts of localized and specific phenomena.
- Long-term prediction is impossible.

More recently theories of chaos have been extended to complexity theory (Waldrop 1992; Lewin 1993) in analysing systems, with components at one level acting as the building blocks for components at another. A complex system comprises independent elements which, themselves, might be made up of complex systems. These interact and give rise to patterned behaviour in the system as a whole. Order is not totally predetermined and fixed, but the universe (however defined) is creative, emergent (through iteration, learning, feedback, recursion and self-organization), evolutionary and changing, transformative and turbulent. Order emerges in complex systems that are founded on simple rules (perhaps formulae) for interacting organisms (Kauffman 1995: 24).

Through feedback, recursion, perturbance, autocatalysis, connectedness and self-organization, higher and greater levels of complexity are differentiated, new forms arise from lower levels of complexity and existing forms. These complex forms derive from often comparatively simple sets of rules – local rules and behaviours generating complex global order and diversity (Waldrop 1992: 16–17; Lewin 1993: 38). Dynamical systems (Peak and Frame 1994: 122) are a product of initial conditions and often simple rules for change. General laws can govern adaptive, dynamical processes (Kauffman 1995: 27). There are laws of emergent order, and complex behaviours and systems do not need to have complex roots (Waldrop 1992: 270). Importantly, given these simple rules, behaviour and systems can be modelled in computer simulations.

It is important to note that the foundations of computer simulations lie in complexity theory, as this provides a response to the charge laid at computer simulations, that they oversimplify the real world. Complexity theory argues that, in many respects, the real world, though highly complex, is built on comparatively simple rules that give rise to such complexity (see also Gilbert and Troitzsch 2005: 10).

Simulations have been used in the natural sciences and economic forecasting for several decades. For example, Lewin (1993) and Waldrop (1992), in the study of the rise and fall of species and their behaviour, indicate how the consecutive iteration – repeated calculation – of simple formulae to express the iteration of a limited number of variables (initial conditions), wherein the data from one round of calculations are used in the next round of calculation of the same formula and so on (i.e. building in continuous feedback), can give rise to a huge diversity of outcomes (e.g. of species, of behaviour) such that it beggars simple prediction or simple cause-and-effect relationships. Waldrop (1992: 241–2) provides a fascinating example of this in the early computer simulation program Boids, where just three initial conditions are built into a mathematical formula that catches the actuality of the diverse patterns of flight of a flock of birds. These are, first, the boids (birds) strive to keep a minimum distance from other objects (including other boids); second, the boids strive to keep to the same speed as other boids; third, each boid strives to move towards the centre of the flock.

Some of the key features of simulations are:

- The computer can model and imitate the behaviour of systems and their major attributes.
- Computer use can help us to understand the system that is being imitated by testing the simulation in a range of simulated, imitated environments (e.g. enabling researchers to see 'what happens if' the system is allowed to run its course or if variables are manipulated, i.e. to be able to predict).
- The mathematical formula models and inter-prets – represents and processes – key features of the reality rather than catching and manip-ulating the fine grain of reality.
- Mathematical relationships are assumed to be

acting over and over again deterministically in controlled, bounded and clearly defined situations, on occasions giving rise to unanticipated, emergent and unexpected, wide-ranging outcomes (Tymms 1996: 124).
- Feedback and multiple, continuous iteration are acceptable procedures for understanding the emergence of phenomena and behaviours.
- Complex and wide-ranging phenomena and behaviours derive from the repeated interplay of initial conditions/variables.
- Deterministic laws (the repeated calculation of a formula) lead to unpredictable outcomes.

In the field of education what is being suggested is that schools and classrooms, while being complex, non-linear, dynamical systems, can be understood in terms of the working out of simple mathematical modelling. This may be at the level of analogy only (see Morrison 2002a), but, as Tymms (1996: 130) remarks, if the analogue fits the reality then researchers have a powerful tool for understanding such complexity in terms of the interplay of key variables or initial conditions and a set of simple rules. Further, if the construct validity of such initial conditions or key variables can be demonstrated then researchers have a powerful means of predicting what might happen over time.

Three immediate applications of simulations have been in the field of educational change (Ridgway 1998), school effectiveness (Tymms 1996), and understanding education systems. In the former, Ridgway (1998) argues that the complexity of the change process might be best understood as a complex, emergent system (see also Fullan 1999).

In the second, Tymms (1996) indicates the limitations of linear (input and output) or multilevel modelling to understand or explain why schools are effective or why there is such a range of variation between and within schools. He puts forward the case for using simulations based on mathematical modelling to account for such diversity and variation between schools; as he argues in his provocative statement: 'the world is too complicated for words' (Tymms 1996: 131) (of course, similarly, for qualitative researchers the world may be too complicated for numbers!). Tymms indicates the limitations of existing school effectiveness research that is based on linear premises, however sophisticated. Instead, pouring cold water on much present school effectiveness research, he argues:

> simulation models would suggest that even if it were possible to arrange for exactly the same classes to have exactly the same teacher for two years in the same classroom living through the same two years that the outcomes would not be the same.
>
> (Tymms 1996: 132–3)

For him, it is little surprise that school effectiveness research has failed to account effectively for variance between schools, because such research is based on the wrong principles. Rather, he argues, such variance is the natural outcome of the interplay of key – common – variables.

In the third example, Gilbert and Troitzsch (2005: 117–23) report a study of post-war gender desegregation in German high schools and high school teachers. The model, using the MIMOSE program, used 4,500 teachers in 150 schools of three types, and shows the closeness of the computer model to the real-life situation observed: a validation of the simulation. The module uses only three assumptions: first, all the teachers who leave their jobs are replaced with an equal probability/opportunity to be chosen, by men and women (p. 117); second, men remain in their jobs for twice as long as women; third, new women take up posts in a individual school with a given probability which varies according to the proportion of its women teachers.

This chapter will not discuss the stages of developing computer simulations (e.g. identifying the question, defining the target for modelling, conducting initial observations to establish the parameters and key features, establishing the assumptions underpinning the simulation, verification of the implementation of the simulation, validation of the simulation (its correspondence to the real-world situation that it is modelling), and sensitivity analysis of the simulation's responsiveness to initial conditions and changes to parameters (Gilbert and Troitzsch 2005: 18–19). Nor will it discuss the different kinds of simulations (e.g. system dynamics, microsimulation, queuing models, multilevel models, cellular automata, multi-agent models, learning models). We refer readers to Gilbert and Troitzsch (2005) for fuller analyses of computer simulation and their different types.

Advantages and disadvantages of computer simulations

Bailey (1994: 322–4) suggests that simulations have advantages such as:

- *economy*: they are cheaper to run than the real-life situation
- *visibility*: they can make a phenomenon more accessible and clear to the researcher
- *control*: the researcher has more control over the simulation than in the real-life situation
- *safety*: researchers can work on situations that may be too dangerous, sensitive, ethically questionable or difficult in real life natural situations.

Computer simulations are powerful in that, as well as enabling researchers to *predict* the future (e.g. in economic forecasting), simulations also enable them to *understand* and explore a phenomenon. Simulations can act as a substitute for human expertise, sometimes enabling non-experts to conduct research that, prior to the advent of computers, would have been the exclusive preserve of experts: Gilbert and Troitzsch (2005: 5) cite the example of geologists, chemists and doctors. Gilbert and Troitzsch also suggest that computer simulations are useful for *training* purposes (e.g. pilots) and, indeed, for *entertainment*. However, Gilbert and Troitzsch (2005: 5) underline the prime importance of computer simulations as being *discovery* and *formalization* of theory (i.e. clarity, coherence, operationalization, inclusion of elements, and completeness of a theory).

On the other hand, Bailey (1994: 324–5) reports several reservations about computer simulations:

- *artificiality:* they mimic life, rather than being the real thing
- *cost:* e.g. for the purchase of computer simulations
- *training of participants:* many computer simulations require considerable training
- *quantitative problems:* software, not just the computer simulation itself, may require programming expertise.

There are several potential concerns about, and criticisms of, computer simulations. To the charges that they artificially represent the world and that they are a *reductio ad absurdum*, it can be stated that researchers, like theorists, strive to construct the best fit with reality, to provide the most comprehensive explanation, and that the closer the analogy – the simulation – fits reality, the better (Tymms 1996: 130). That is an argument for refining rather than abandoning simulations. We only need to know key elements to be able to construct an abstraction, we do not need complete, fine-grain detail.

To the charges that a computer simulation is no better than the assumptions on which it is built, and that a computer can only do what it is programmed to do (rendering human agency and freedom insignificant), it can be stated that: simulations can reveal behaviours that occur 'behind the backs' of social actors – there are social facts (Durkheim 1956) and patterns; simulations can tell us what we do not know (Simon 1996) – we may know premises and starting points but not where they might lead to or what they imply; we do not need to know all the workings of the system to be able to explain it, only those parts that are essential for the model.

Other concerns can be voiced about simulations, for example:

- Complexity and chaos theory that underpin many mathematical simulations might explain diverse, variable outcomes (as in school effectiveness research), but how do they enable developers to intervene to promote improvement, e.g. in schools – explanation here is retrospective rather than prospective (Morrison 2002a); this charge is refutable in the possibility of researchers to manipulate the parameters of the variables and to see what happens when they do this.
- How does one ascertain the key initial conditions to build into the simulation (i.e. construct validity) and how do simulations from these lead to prescriptions for practice?
- How acceptable is it to regard systems as the recurring iteration and reiteration of the same formula/model?
- In understanding chaotic complexity (in the scientific sense), how can researchers work back from this to identify the first principles or elements or initial conditions that are important – the complex outcomes might be due to the interaction of completely different sets of initial conditions. This is akin to Chomsky's (1959) withering critique of Skinner's behaviourism – it is impossible to infer a particular stimulus from an observation of behaviour, we cannot infer a cause from an observation or putative effect.
- Simulations work out and assume only the interplay of initial conditions, thereby neglecting the introduction of additional factors 'on the way', i.e. the process is too deterministic (that said, there are computer simulations in which the computer 'learns' during the simulation).
- What is being argued here is only common sense, that the interaction of people produces unpredicted and unpredictable behaviour. That is also its greatest attraction – it celebrates agency.
- Planned interventions might work at first but ultimately do not work (a reiteration, perhaps, of the Hawthorne effect); all we can predict is that we cannot predict.
- Manipulating human variables is technicist.

- There is more to behaviour than the repeated iteration of the same mathematical model.
- There will always be a world of difference between the real world and the simulated world other than at an unhelpfully simplistic level.
- The agentic, moral and reflexive behaviour of humans is not as simple as the often instinctive behaviour of other forms of life or what happens to inanimate phenomena that have been studied in computer simulations (e.g. birds and ants, and piles of sand respectively).
- As with other numerical approaches, simulations might combine refinement of process with crudity of concept (Ruddock 1981: 49).
- If reality operates 'behind the backs' of players, where does responsibility for agentic actions lie? How does free will operate in a computer simulation?
- While random elements can be introduced into computer simulations, this means that the simulation must be run several times in order to establish robustness with different values and the sensitivity of the simulation to changes.
- Reducing the world to numbers, however sophisticated, is quite simply wrong-headed; the world is too complicated for numbers.

These criticisms are serious, and indicate that this field of research has much to do to gain legitimacy. The issue of agency is important, as it could be argued to be weaker in computer simulations than in real life, though Wooldridge and Jennings (1995), while acknowledging this, suggest that agents in computer systems have characteristics built into them, such as autonomy, proactivity, reactivity and social ability.

The criticisms are not to dismiss computer simulations; rather it is to seek their advance. These reservations – at conceptual and practical levels – do not argue against simulations but, rather, for their development and refinement. They promise much and in areas of the sciences apart from education have already yielded much of value. For further information on complexity theory and simulations we suggest that readers visit web sites such as:

http://www.santafe.edu (the web site of the Santa Fe Institute – a major institute for the study of complexity theory)
http://www.brint.com/Systems.htm (a web site that provides an index of material on complexity theory)
www.complexity-society.com (the UK Complexity Society)
http://emergence.org/ (web site of the journal *Emergence: Complexity and Organization*)
http://journal-ci.csse.monash.edu. au// (web site of the journal *Complexity International*)
http://www.udel.edu/aeracc/sites. html (links to web sites on complexity theory)
http://www.answers.com/complex %20systems%20theory (links to web sites on complexity theory).

Conclusion

Simulation methods provide a means of alleviating a number of problems inherent in laboratory experiments. At the same time, they permit the retention of some of their virtues. Simulations, notes Palys (1978), share with the laboratory experiment the characteristic that the experimenter has complete manipulative control over every aspect of the situation. At the same time, the subjects' humanity is left intact in that they are given a realistic situation in which to act in whatever way they think appropriate. The inclusion of the time dimension is another important contribution of the simulation, allowing the subject to take an active role in interacting with the environment, and the experimenter the opportunity of observing a social system in action with its feedback loops, multidirectional causal connections and so forth. Finally, Palys observes, the high involvement normally associated with participation in simulations shows that the self-consciousness usually associated with the laboratory experiment is more easily dissipated.

Geographical Information Systems

While not exactly a simulation, the computer-based Geographical Information Systems are becoming increasingly used in educational research, for example in discussing patterns of student recruitment and school choice. Educational policy frequently has geographical implications and dimensions, e.g. catchment areas, school closures, open enrolment and school choice, the distribution of resources and financial expenditure, the distribution of assessment scores and examination results. Geographical Information Systems is a computer-based system for capturing, storing, validating, analysing and displaying spatial data, both large scale and small scale, integrating several types of data from different sources (Worrall 1990; Parsons *et al.* 1996; Gorard *et al.* 2002). This is useful for teasing out the implications and outcomes of policy initiatives, for example: 'What is the effect of parental choice on school catchments?'; 'What is the spread of examination scores in a particular region?'; 'How effective is the provision of secondary schools for a given population?'; 'How can a transport system be made more effective for taking students to and from school?'; 'What is the evidence for the creation of 'magnet' and 'sink' schools in a particular city?'. Examples of the data presented here are given in Boxes 10.2 and 10.3.

Clearly the political sensitivity and significance of these kinds of data are immense, indicating how research can inform policy-making and its effects very directly. Parsons *et al.* (1996) provide a straightforward, fully referenced introduction to this field of research in education, and they present case studies of catchment areas and examination performance, the redistribution of school catchments, and the pattern of movements in catchments.

Readers wishing to research Geographical Information Systems (GIS) on the Internet can access several sites by keying in 'education research Geographical Information Systems' on a search engine for the Internet or by visiting the following web sites:

Box 10.2

Geographical Information Systems in secondary schools

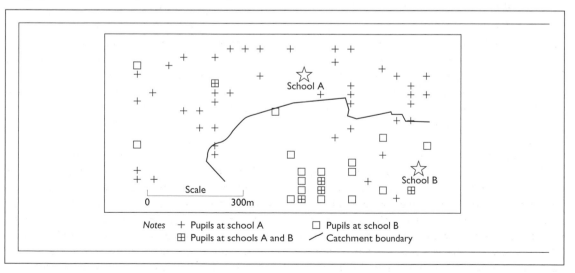

Source: Parsons *et al.* 1996

Box 10.3

Location of home postcodes using Geographical Information Systems

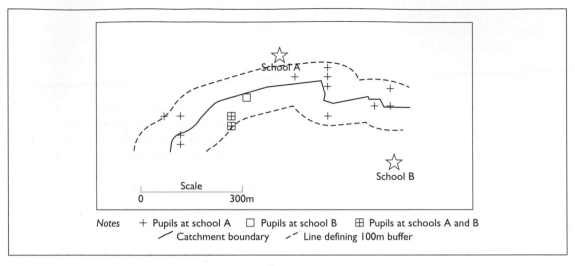

Source: Parsons *et al.* 1996

http://www.geo.ed.ac.uk/home/giswww.html (a GIS World Wide Web resource list)

http://www.tec.army.mil/gis/ (includes Education links)

http://www.census.gov/geo/www/gis_gateway.html (GIS resources from the US census bureau)

http://www.geo.uni-bonn.de/members/haack/gisinfo.html (European link server)

http://unr.edu/homepage/daved/gislinks.html (GIS resources over the Internet)

▌▌ Case studies

What is a case study?

A case study is a specific instance that is frequently designed to illustrate a more general principle (Nisbet and Watt 1984: 72), it is 'the study of an instance in action' (Adelman *et al.* 1980) (see http://www.routledge.com/textbooks/ 9780415368780 – Chapter 11, file 11.1. ppt). The single instance is of a bounded system, for example a child, a clique, a class, a school, a community. It provides a unique example of real people in real situations, enabling readers to understand ideas more clearly than simply by presenting them with abstract theories or principles. Indeed a case study can enable readers to understand how ideas and abstract principles can fit together (Nisbet and Watt 1984: 72–3). Case studies can penetrate situations in ways that are not always susceptible to numerical analysis. As Robson (2002: 183) remarks, case studies opt for analytic rather than statistical generalization, that is they develop a theory which can help researchers to understand other similar cases, phenomena or situations.

Case studies can establish cause and effect, indeed one of their strengths is that they observe effects in real contexts, recognizing that context is a powerful determinant of both causes and effects. As Nisbet and Watt (1984: 78) remark, the whole is more than the sum of its parts. Sturman (1999: 103) argues that a distinguishing feature of case studies is that human systems have a wholeness or integrity to them rather than being a loose connection of traits, necessitating in-depth investigation. Further, contexts are unique and dynamic, hence case studies investigate and report the complex dynamic and unfolding interactions of events, human relationships and other factors in a unique instance. Hitchcock and Hughes (1995: 316) suggest that case studies are distinguished less by the methodologies that they employ than by the subjects/objects of their inquiry (though, as indicated below, there is frequently a resonance between case studies and interpretive methodologies). Hitchcock and Hughes (1995: 322) further suggest that the case study approach is particularly valuable when the researcher has little control over events. They consider (p. 317) that a case study has several hallmarks:

- It is concerned with a rich and vivid description of events relevant to the case.
- It provides a chronological narrative of events relevant to the case.
- It blends a description of events with the analysis of them.
- It focuses on individual actors or groups of actors, and seeks to understand their perceptions of events.
- It highlights specific events that are relevant to the case.
- The researcher is integrally involved in the case.
- An attempt is made to portray the richness of the case in writing up the report.

Case studies are set in temporal, geographical, organizational, institutional and other contexts that enable boundaries to be drawn around the case; they can be defined with reference to characteristics defined by individuals and groups involved; and they can be defined by participants' roles and functions in the case (Hitchcock and Hughes 1995: 319) (see http://www. routledge.com/textbooks/9780415368780 – Chapter 11, file 11.2. ppt).

Case studies

- will have temporal characteristics which help to define their nature
- have geographical parameters allowing for their definition
- will have boundaries which allow for definition
- may be defined by an individual in a particular context, at a point in time
- may be defined by the characteristics of the group
- may be defined by role or function
- may be shaped by organizational or institutional arrangements.

Case studies strive to portray 'what it is like' to be in a particular situation, to catch the close up reality and 'thick description' (Geertz 1973b) of participants' lived experiences of, thoughts about and feelings for a situation. They involve looking at a case or phenomenon in its real-life context, usually employing many types of data (Robson 2002: 178). They are descriptive and detailed, with a narrow focus, combining subjective and objective data (Dyer 1995: 48–9). It is important in case studies for events and situations to be allowed to speak for themselves, rather than to be largely interpreted, evaluated or judged by the researcher. In this respect the case study is akin to the television documentary.

This is not to say that case studies are unsystematic or merely illustrative; case study data are gathered systematically and rigorously. Indeed Nisbet and Watt (1984: 91) specifically counsel case study researchers to avoid:

- *journalism*: picking out more striking features of the case, thereby distorting the full account in order to emphasize these more sensational aspects
- *selective reporting*: selecting only that evidence which will support a particular conclusion, thereby misrepresenting the whole case
- *an anecdotal style*: degenerating into an endless series of low-level banal and tedious illustrations that take over from in-depth, rigorous analysis; one is reminded of Stake's (1978) wry comment that 'our scrapbooks are full of enlargements of enlargements', alluding to the tendency of some case studies to overemphasize detail to the detriment of seeing the whole picture

- *pomposity*: striving to derive or generate profound theories from low-level data, or by wrapping up accounts in high-sounding verbiage
- *blandness*: unquestioningly accepting only the respondents' views, or including only those aspects of the case study on which people agree rather than areas on which they might disagree.

Case studies can make theoretical statements, but, like other forms of research and human sciences, these must be supported by the evidence presented. This requires the nature of generalization in case study to be clarified. Generalization can take various forms, for example:

- from the single instance to the class of instances that it represents (for example, a single-sex selective school might act as a case study to catch significant features of other single-sex selective schools)
- from features of the single case to a multiplicity of classes with the same features
- from the single features of part of the case to the whole of that case.

Simons (1996) has argued that case study needs to address six paradoxes; it needs to:

- reject the subject–object dichotomy, regarding all participants equally
- recognize the contribution that a genuine creative encounter can make to new forms of understanding education
- regard different ways of seeing as new ways of knowing
- approximate the ways of the artist
- free the mind of traditional analysis
- embrace these paradoxes, with an overriding interest in people.

There are several types of case study. Yin (1984) identifies three such types in terms of their outcomes: exploratory (as a pilot to other studies or research questions); descriptive (providing narrative accounts); explanatory (testing theories). Exploratory case studies that act as a pilot can be used to generate hypotheses that are tested in larger scale surveys, experiments or other forms of research, e.g. observational. However, Adelman *et al.* (1980) caution against using case studies solely as preliminaries to other studies, e.g. as pre-experimental or pre-survey; rather, they argue, case studies exist in their own right as a significant and legitimate research method (see http://www.routledge.com/textbooks/9780415368780 – Chapter 11, file 11.3. ppt).

Yin's (1984) classification accords with Merriam (1988) who identifies three types: descriptive (narrative accounts); interpretative (developing conceptual categories inductively in order to examine initial assumptions); evaluative (explaining and judging). Merriam (1988) also categorizes four common domains or kinds of case study: ethnographic, historical, psychological and sociological. Sturman (1999: 107), echoing Stenhouse (1985), identifies four kinds of case study: an ethnographic case study – single in-depth study; action research case study; evaluative case study; and educational case study. Stake (1994) identifies three main types of case study: intrinsic case studies (studies that are undertaken in order to understand the particular case in question); instrumental case studies (examining a particular case in order to gain insight into an issue or a theory); collective case studies (groups of individual studies that are undertaken to gain a fuller picture). Because case studies provide fine-grain detail they can also be used to complement other, more coarsely grained – often large-scale – kinds of research. Case study material in this sense can provide powerful human-scale data on macro-political decision-making, fusing theory and practice, for example the work of Ball (1990), Bowe *et al.* (1992) and Ball (1994a) on the impact of government policy on specific schools.

Robson (2002: 181–2) suggests that there are an individual case study; a set of individual case studies; a social group study; studies of organizations and institutions; studies of events, roles and relationships. All of these, he argues, find expression in the case study method. Robson (2002) adds to these the distinction between a

critical case study and an extreme or unique case. The former, he argues, is

> when your theoretical understanding is such that there is a clear, unambiguous and non-trivial set of circumstances where predicted outcomes will be found. Finding a case which fits, and demonstrating what has been predicted, can give a powerful boost to knowledge and understanding.
>
> (Robson 2002: 182)

One can add to the critical case study the issue that the case in question might possess all, or most, of the characteristics or features that one is investigating, more fully or distinctly than under 'normal' circumstances, for example, a case study of student disruptive behaviour might go on in a *very* disruptive class, with students who are very seriously disturbed or challenging, rather than going into a class where the level of disruption is not so marked.

By contrast, Robson (2002: 182) argues that the extreme and the unique case can provide a valuable 'test bed'. Extremes include, he argues, the situation in which 'if it can work here it will work anywhere', or choosing an ideal set of circumstances in which to try out a new approach or project, maybe to gain a fuller insight into how it operates before taking it to a wider audience (e.g. the research and development model).

Case studies have several claimed strengths and weaknesses. These are summarized in Box 11.1 (Adelman *et al.* 1980) and Box 11.2 (Nisbet and Watt 1984) (see http://www.routledge.com/textbooks/9780415368780 – Chapter 11, file 11.4. ppt).

Shaughnessy *et al.* (2003: 290–9) suggest that case studies often lack a high degree of control, and treatments are rarely controlled systematically, yet they are applied simultaneously, and with little control over extraneous variables. This, they argue, renders it difficult to make inferences to draw cause-and-effect conclusions from case studies, and there is potential for bias in some case studies as the therapist is both the participant and observer and, in that role, may overstate or understate the case. Case studies, they argue, may be impressionistic, and self-reporting may be biased (by the participant or the observer). Further, they

Box 11.1
Possible advantages of case study

Case studies have a number of advantages that make them attractive to educational evaluators or researchers. Thus:

- Case study data, paradoxically, are 'strong in reality' but difficult to organize. In contrast, other research data are often 'weak in reality' but susceptible to ready organization. This strength in reality is because case studies are down-to-earth and attention-holding, in harmony with the reader's own experience, and thus provide a 'natural' basis for generalization.
- Case studies allow generalizations either about an instance or from an instance to a class. Their peculiar strength lies in their attention to the subtlety and complexity of the case in its own right.
- Case studies recognize the complexity and 'embeddedness' of social truths. By carefully attending to social situations, case studies can represent something of the discrepancies or conflicts between the viewpoints held by participants. The best case studies are capable of offering some support to alternative interpretations.
- Case studies, considered as products, may form an archive of descriptive material sufficiently rich to admit subsequent reinterpretation. Given the variety and complexity of educational purposes and environments, there is an obvious value in having a data source for researchers and users whose purposes may be different from our own.
- Case studies are 'a step to action'. They begin in a world of action and contribute to it. Their insights may be directly interpreted and put to use; for staff or individual self-development, for within-institutional feedback; for formative evaluation; and in educational policy-making.
- Case studies present research or evaluation data in a more publicly accessible form than other kinds of research report, although this virtue is to some extent bought at the expense of their length. The language and the form of the presentation is (we hope) less esoteric and less dependent on specialized interpretation than conventional research reports. The case study is capable of serving multiple audiences. It reduces the dependence of the reader upon unstated implicit assumptions and makes the research process itself accessible. Case studies, therefore, may contribute towards the 'democratization' of decision-making (and knowledge itself). At its best, they allow readers to judge the implications of a study for themselves.

Source: adapted from Adelman *et al.* 1980

Box 11.2
Strengths and weaknesses of case study

Strengths

- The results are more easily understood by a wide audience (including non-academics) as they are frequently written in everyday, non-professional language.
- They are immediately intelligible; they speak for themselves.
- They catch unique features that may otherwise be lost in larger scale data (e.g. surveys); these unique features might hold the key to understanding the situation.
- They are strong on reality.
- They provide insights into other, similar situations and cases, thereby assisting interpretation of other similar cases.
- They can be undertaken by a single researcher without needing a full research team.
- They can embrace and build in unanticipated events and uncontrolled variables.

Weaknesses

- The results may not be generalizable except where other readers/researchers see their application.
- They are not easily open to cross-checking, hence they may be selective, biased, personal and subjective.
- They are prone to problems of observer bias, despite attempts made to address reflexivity.

Source: Nisbet and Watt 1984

argue that bias may be a problem if the case study relies on an individual's memory.

Dyer (1995: 50–2) remarks that, reading a case study, one has to be aware that a process of selection has already taken place, and only the author knows what has been selected in or out, and on what criteria; indeed, the participants themselves may not know what selection has taken place. Dyer (1995: 48–9) observes that case studies combine knowledge and inference, and it is often difficult to separate these; the researcher has to be clear on which of these feature in the case study data.

From the preceding analysis it is clear that case studies frequently follow the interpretive tradition of research – seeing the situation through the eyes of participants – rather than the quantitative paradigm, though this need not always be the case. Its sympathy to the interpretive paradigm has rendered case study an object of criticism. Consider, for example, Smith (1991: 375), who argues that not only is the case study method the logically weakest method of knowing but also studying individual cases, careers and communities is a thing of the past, and that attention should be focused on patterns and laws in historical research.

This is prejudice and ideology rather than critique, but signifies the problem of respectability and legitimacy that case study has to conquer among certain academics. Like other research methods, case study has to demonstrate reliability and validity. This can be difficult, for given the uniqueness of situations, they may be, by definition, inconsistent with other case studies or unable to demonstrate this positivist view of reliability. Even though case studies do not have to demonstrate this form of reliability, nevertheless there are important questions to be faced in undertaking case studies, for example (Adelman *et al.* 1980; Nisbet and Watt 1984; Hitchcock and Hughes 1995) (see http://www.routledge.com/textbooks/9780415368780 – Chapter 11, file 11.5. ppt):

- What exactly is a case?
- How are cases identified and selected?
- What kind of case study is this (what is its purpose)?
- What is reliable evidence?
- What is objective evidence?
- What is an appropriate selection to include from the wealth of generated data?
- What is a fair and accurate account?
- Under what circumstances is it fair to take an exceptional case (or a critical event – see the discussion of observation in Chapter 18)?
- What kind of sampling is most appropriate?
- To what extent is triangulation required and how will this be addressed?
- What is the nature of the validation process in case studies?
- How will the balance be struck between uniqueness and generalization?
- What is the most appropriate form of writing up and reporting the case study?
- What ethical issues are exposed in undertaking a case study?

A key issue in case study research is the selection of information. Although it is frequently useful to record typical, representative occurrences, the researcher need not always adhere to criteria of representativeness. It may be that infrequent, unrepresentative but critical incidents or events occur that are crucial to the understanding of the case. For example, a subject might only demonstrate a particular behaviour once, but it is so important as not to be ruled out simply because it occurred once; sometimes a single event might occur which sheds a hugely important insight into a person or situation (see the discussion of critical incidents in Chapter 18); it can be a key to understanding a situation (Flanagan 1949).

For example, it may be that a psychological case study might happen upon a single instance of child abuse earlier in an adult's life, but the effects of this were so profound as to constitute a turning point in understanding that adult. A child might suddenly pass a single comment that indicates complete frustration with or complete fear of a teacher, yet it is too important to overlook. Case studies, in not having to seek frequencies of occurrences, can replace quantity with quality and intensity, separating the *significant few* from the *insignificant many* instances of behaviour. Significance rather than frequency is a hallmark of case studies, offering the researcher an insight into the real dynamics of situations and people.

Examples of kinds of case study

Unlike the experimenter who manipulates variables to determine their causal significance or the surveyor who asks standardized questions of large, representative samples of individuals, the case study researcher typically observes the characteristics of an individual unit – a child, a clique, a class, a school or a community. The purpose of such observation is to probe deeply and to analyse intensively the multifarious phenomena that constitute the life cycle of the unit with a view to establishing generalizations about the wider population to which that unit belongs.

Antipathy among researchers towards the statistical – experimental paradigm has created something of a boom industry in case study research. Delinquents (Patrick 1973), dropouts (Parker 1974), drug-users (Young 1971) and schools (King 1979) attest to the wide use of the case study in contemporary social science and educational research. Such wide use is marked by an equally diverse range of techniques employed in the collection and analysis of both qualitative and quantitative data. Whatever the problem or the approach, at the heart of every case study lies a method of observation.

In Box 11.3 we set out a typology of observation studies on the basis of which our six examples are selected (for further explication of these examples, see the accompanying web site: http://www.routledge.com/textbooks/ 9780415368780 – Chapter 11, file 11.1.doc).

Acker's (1990) study is an ethnographic account that is based on several hundred hours of participant observation material, while Boulton's (1992) work, by contrast, is based on highly structured, non-participant observation conducted over five years. The study by Wild *et al.* (1992) used participant observation, loosely structured interviews that yielded simple frequency counts. Blease and Cohen's (1990) study of coping with computers used highly structured observation schedules, undertaken by non-participant observers, with the express intention of obtaining precise, quantitative data on the classroom use of a computer programme. This was part of a longitudinal study in primary classrooms, and yielded typical profiles of individual behaviour and group interaction in students' usage of the computer programme. Antonsen's (1988)) study was of a single child undergoing psychotherapy at a child psychiatric unit, and uses unstructured observation within the artificial setting of a psychiatric clinic and is a record of the therapist's non-directive approach. Finally Houghton's (1991) study uses data from structured sets of test materials together with focused interviews with those with whom this international student had contact. Together these case studies provide a valuable insight into the range and types of case study (see http://www.routledge.com/textbooks/ 9780415368780 – Chapter 11, file 11.6. ppt).

There are two principal types of observation – participant observation and non-participant observation. In the former, observers engage in the very activities they set out to observe. Often, their 'cover' is so complete that as far as the other participants are concerned, they are simply one of the group. In the case of Patrick (1973) for example, born and bred in Glasgow, his researcher role remained hidden from the members of the Glasgow gang in whose activities he participated for a period of four months. Such complete anonymity is not always possible, however. Thus in Parker's (1974) study of downtown Liverpool adolescents, it was generally known that the researcher was waiting to take up a post at the university. In the mean time, 'knocking around' during the day with the lads and frequenting their pub at night rapidly established that he was 'OK'. The researcher was, in his own terms, 'a drinker, a hanger-arounder' who could be relied on to keep quiet in illegal matters.

Cover is not necessarily a prerequisite of participant observation. In an intensive study of a small group of working-class boys during their last two years at school and their first months in employment, Willis (1977) attended all the different subject classes at school – 'not as a teacher, but as a member of the class' – and worked alongside each boy in industry for a short period (see http://www.routledge.com/textbooks/ 9780415368780 – Chapter 11, file 11.7. ppt).

Non-participant observers, on the other hand, stand aloof from the group activities they are investigating and eschew group membership – no great difficulty for King (1979), an adult observer in infant classrooms. King (1979) recalls how he firmly established his non-participant status with young children by recognizing that they regarded any adult as another teacher or surrogate teacher. Hence he would stand up to maintain social distance, and deliberately decline to show immediate interest, and avoided eye contact.

The best illustration of the non-participant observer role is perhaps the case of the researcher sitting at the back of a classroom coding up every three seconds the verbal exchanges between teacher and pupils by means of a structured set of observational categories.

Often the type of observation undertaken by the researcher is associated with the type of setting in which the research takes place. In Box 11.3 we identify a continuum of settings ranging from the 'artificial' environments of the counsellor's and the therapist's clinics (cells 5 and 6) to the 'natural' environments of school classrooms, staffrooms and playgrounds (cells 1 and 2). Because our continuum is crude and arbitrary we are at liberty to locate studies of an information technology audit and computer usage (cells 3 and 4) somewhere between the 'artificial' and the 'natural' poles.

Although in theory each of the six examples of case studies in Box 11.3 could have been undertaken either as a participant or as a non-participant observation study, a number of factors intrude to make one or other of the observational strategies the dominant mode of inquiry in a particular type of setting. Bailey (1994: 247) explains that it is hard for a researcher who wishes to undertake covert research not to act as a participant in a natural setting, as, if the researcher does not appear to be participating, then why is he/she there? Hence, in many natural settings the researchers will be participants. This is in contrast to laboratory or artificial settings, in which non-participant observation (e.g. through video recording) may take place.

What we are saying is that the unstructured, ethnographic account of teachers' work (cell 1)

Box 11.3

A typology of observation studies

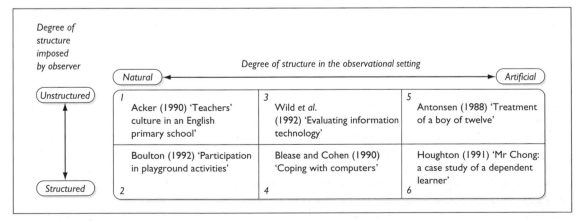

Source: adapted from Bailey 1978

is the most typical method of observation in the natural surroundings of the school in which that study was conducted. Similarly, the structured inventories of study habits and personality employed in the study of Mr Chong (cell 6) reflect a common approach in the artificial setting of a counsellor's office.

Why participant observation?

The natural scientist, Schutz (1962) points out, explores a field that means nothing to the molecules, atoms and electrons therein. By contrast, the subject matter of the world in which the educational researcher is interested is composed of people and is essentially meaningful to them. That world is subjectively structured, possessing particular meanings for its inhabitants. The task of the educational investigator is very often to explain the means by which an orderly social world is established and maintained in terms of its shared meanings. How do participant observation techniques assist the researcher in this task? Bailey (1994: 243–4) identifies some inherent advantages in the participant observation approach:

- Observation studies are superior to experiments and surveys when data are being collected on non-verbal behaviour.
- In observation studies, investigators are able to discern ongoing behaviour as it occurs and are able to make appropriate notes about its salient features.
- Because case study observations take place over an extended period of time, researchers can develop more intimate and informal relationships with those they are observing, generally in more natural environments than those in which experiments and surveys are conducted.
- Case study observations are less reactive than other types of data-gathering methods. For example, in laboratory-based experiments and in surveys that depend upon verbal responses to structured questions, bias can be introduced in the very data that researchers are attempting to study.

Recording observations

I filled thirty-two notebooks with about half a million words of notes made during nearly six hundred hours [of observation].

(King 1979)

The recording of observations is a frequent source of concern to inexperienced case study researchers. How much ought to be recorded? In what form should the recordings be made? What does one do with the mass of recorded data? Lofland (1971) gives a number of useful suggestions about collecting field notes:

- Record the notes as quickly as possible after observation, since the quantity of information forgotten is very slight over a short period of time but accelerates quickly as more time passes.
- Discipline yourself to write notes quickly and reconcile yourself to the fact that although it may seem ironic, recording of field notes can be expected to take as long as is spent in actual observation.
- Dictating rather than writing is acceptable if one can afford it, but writing has the advantage of stimulating thought.
- Typing field notes is vastly preferable to handwriting because it is faster and easier to read, especially when making multiple copies.
- It is advisable to make at least two copies of field notes and preferable to type on a master for reproduction. One original copy is retained for reference and other copies can be used as rough draught to be cut up, reorganized and rewritten.
- The notes ought to be full enough adequately to summon up for one again, months later, a reasonably vivid picture of any described event. This probably means that one ought to be writing up, at the very minimum, at least a couple of single-space typed pages for every hour of observation.

The sort of note-taking recommended by Lofland (1971) and actually undertaken by King (1979) and Wolcott (1973) in their ethnographic accounts grows out of the nature of the unstructured observation study. Note-taking, confessed Wolcott (1973), helped him fight the acute boredom that he sometimes felt when observing the interminable meetings that are the daily lot of the school principal. Occasionally, however, a series of events would occur so quickly that Wolcott (1973) had time only to make cursory notes which he supplemented later with fuller accounts. One useful tip from this experienced ethnographer is worth noting: never resume your observations until the notes from the preceding observation are complete. There is nothing to be gained merely by your presence as an observer. Until your observations and impressions from one visit are a matter of record, there is little point in returning to the classroom or school and reducing the impact of one set of events by superimposing another and more recent set. Indeed, when to record one's data is but one of a number of practical problems identified by Walker (1980), which are listed in Box 11.4.

Planning a case study

In planning a case study there are several issues that researchers may find useful to consider (e.g. Adelman *et al.* 1980) (see http://www. routledge.com/textbooks/9780415368780 – Chapter 11, file 11.8. ppt):

- The particular circumstances of the case, including: the possible disruption to individual participants that participation might entail; negotiating access to people; negotiating ownership of the data; negotiating release of the data.
- The conduct of the study, including: the use of primary and secondary sources; the opportunities to check data; triangulation (including peer examination of the findings, respondent validation and reflexivity); data collection methods – in the interpretive paradigm, case studies tend to use certain data collection methods, e.g. semi-structured and open interviews, observation, narrative accounts and documents, diaries, maybe also tests, rather than other methods, e.g. surveys, experiments. Nisbet and Watt (1984) suggest that,

Box 11.4
The case study and problems of selection

Among the issues confronting the researcher at the outset of the case study are the problems of selection. The following questions indicate some of the obstacles in this respect:

- How do you get from the initial idea to the working design (from the idea to a specification, to usable data)?
- What do you lose in the process?
- What unwanted concerns do you take on board as a result?
- How do you find a site which provides the best location for the design?
- How do you locate, identify and approach key informants?
- How they see you creates a context within which you see them. How can you handle such social complexities?
- How do you record evidence? When? How much?
- How do you file and categorize it?
- How much time do you give to thinking and reflecting about what you are doing?
- At what points do you show your subject what you are doing?
- At what points do you give them control over who sees what?
- Who sees the reports first?

Source: adapted from Walker 1980

in conducting interviews, it may be wiser to interview senior people later rather than earlier so that the most effective use of discussion time can be made, the interviewer having been put into the picture fully before the interview. Finally, the conduct of research involves data analysis, theory generation where appropriate, and writing the report. Nisbet and Watt (1984) suggest that it is important to separate conclusions from the evidence, with the essential evidence included in the main text, and to balance illustration with analysis and generalization.

- The consequences of the research (for participants). This might include the anonymizing of the research in order to protect participants, though such anonymization might suggest that a primary goal of case study is generalization rather than the portrayal of a unique case, i.e. it might go against a central feature of case study. Anonymizing reports might render them anodyne, and Adelman *et al.* (1980) suggest that the distortion that is involved in such anonymization – to render cases unrecognizable might be too high a price to pay for going public.

Nisbet and Watt (1984: 78) suggest three main stages in undertaking a case study. Because case studies catch the dynamics of unfolding situations it is advisable to commence with a very wide field of focus, an open phase, without selectivity or prejudgement. Thereafter progressive focusing enables a narrower field of focus to be established, identifying key foci for subsequent study and data collection. At the third stage a draft interpretation is prepared which needs to be checked with respondents before appearing in the final form. Nisbet and Watt (1984: 79) advise against the generation of hypotheses too early in a case study; rather, they suggest, it is important to gather data openly. Respondent validation can be particularly useful as respondents might suggest a better way of expressing the issue or may wish to add or qualify points.

There is a risk in respondent validation, however, that they may disagree with an interpretation. Nisbet and Watt (1984: 81) indicate the need to have negotiated rights to veto. They also recommend that researchers promise that respondents can see those sections of the report that refer to them (subject to controls for confidentiality, e.g. of others in the case study), and take full account of suggestions and responses made by respondents and, where possible, to modify the account. In the case of disagreement between researchers and respondents, researchers should promise to publish respondents' comments and criticisms alongside the researchers' report.

Sturman (1997) places on a set of continua the nature of data collection, types and analysis techniques in case study research. These are presented in summary form (Box 11.5) (see http://

Box 11.5
Continua of data collection, types and analysis in case study research

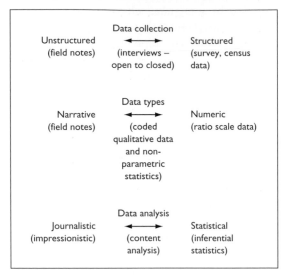

Source: adapted from Sturman 1997

www.routledge.com/textbooks/9780415368780 – Chapter 11, file 11.9. ppt).

At one pole we have unstructured, typically qualitative data, while at the other we have structured, typically quantitative data. Researchers using case study approaches will need to decide which methods of data collection, which type of data and techniques of analysis to employ.

Writing up a case study

The writing up of a case study abides by the twin notions of 'fitness for purpose' and 'fitness for audience'. Robson (2002: 512–13) suggests six forms of organizing the writing-up of a case study:

- In the *suspense structure* the author presents the main findings (e.g. an executive summary) in the opening part of the report and then devotes the remainder of the report to providing evidence, analysis, explanations, justifications (e.g. for what is selected in or out, what conclusions are drawn, what alternative explanations are rejected), and argument that leads to the overall picture or conclusion.

- In the *narrative report* a prose account is provided, interspersed with relevant figures, tables, emergent issues, analysis and conclusion.
- In the *comparative structure* the same case is examined through two or more lenses (e.g. explanatory, descriptive, theoretical) in order either to provide a rich, all-round account of the case, or to enable the reader to have sufficient information from which to judge which of the explanations, descriptions or theories best fit(s) the data.
- In the *chronological structure* a simple sequence or chronology is used as the organizational principle, thereby enabling not only cause and effect to be addressed, but also possessing the strength of an ongoing story. Adding to Robson's (2002) comments, the chronology can be sectionalized as appropriate (e.g. key events or key time frames), and intersperse commentaries on, interpretations of and explanations for, and summaries of emerging issues as events unfold (e.g. akin to 'memoing' in ethnographic research). The chronology becomes an organizing principle, but different kinds of contents are included at each stage of the chronological sequence.
- In the *theory-generating structure*, the structure follows a set of theoretical constructs or a case that is being made. Here, Robson (2002) suggests, each succeeding section of the case study contributes to, or constitutes, an element of a developing 'theoretical formulation', providing a link in the chain of argument, leading eventually to the overall theoretical formulation.
- In the *unsequenced structures* the sequence, e.g. chronological, issue-based, event-based, theory based, is unimportant. Robson (2002) suggests that this approach renders it difficult for the reader to know which areas are important or unimportant, or whether there are any omissions. It risks the caprice of the writer.

Some case studies are of a single situation – a single child, a single social group, a single class, a single school. Here any of the above six approaches may be appropriate. Some case studies require an unfolding of events, some case studies operate under a 'snapshot' approach (e.g. of several schools, or classes, or groups at a particular point in time). In the former it may be important to preserve the chronology, whereas in the latter such a chronology may be irrelevant. Some case studies are divided into two main parts (e.g. Willis 1977): the data reporting and then the analysis/interpretation/explanation.

Conclusion

The different strategies we have illustrated in our six examples of case studies in a variety of educational settings suggest that participant observation is best thought of as a generic term that describes a methodological approach rather than one specific method.[1] What our examples have shown is that the representativeness of a particular sample often relates to the observational strategy open to the researcher. Generally speaking, the larger the sample, the more representative it is, and the more likely that the observer's role is of a participant nature.

For examples of case studies, see the accompanying web site (http://www.routledge.com/ textbooks/9780415368780 – Chapter 11, file 11.2.doc, http://www.routledge.com/textbooks/ 9780415368780 – Chapter 11, file 11.3.doc and http://www.routledge.com/textbooks/ 9780415368780 – Chapter 11, file 11.4 doc).

12 *Ex post facto* research

Introduction

When translated literally, *ex post facto* means 'from what is done afterwards'. In the context of social and educational research the phrase means 'after the fact' or 'retrospectively' and refers to those studies which investigate possible cause-and-effect relationships by observing an existing condition or state of affairs and searching back in time for plausible causal factors. In effect, researchers ask themselves what factors seem to be associated with certain occurrences, or conditions, or aspects of behaviour. *Ex post facto* research, then, is a method of teasing out possible antecedents of events that have happened and cannot, therefore, be controlled, engineered or manipulated by the investigator (Cooper and Schindler 2001: 136). Researchers can report only what has happened or what is happening, by trying to hold factors constant by careful attention to the sampling.

The following example will illustrate the basic idea. Imagine a situation in which there has been a dramatic increase in the number of fatal road accidents in a particular locality. An expert is called in to investigate. Naturally, there is no way in which she can study the actual accidents because they have happened; nor can she turn to technology for a video replay of the incidents. What she can do, however, is attempt a reconstruction by studying the statistics, examining the accident spots, and taking note of the statements given by victims and witnesses. In this way the expert will be in a position to identify possible determinants of the accidents. These may include excessive speed, poor road conditions, careless driving, frustration, inefficient vehicles, the effects of drugs or alcohol and so on. On the basis of her examination, the expert can formulate hypotheses as to the likely causes and submit them to the appropriate authority in the form of recommendations. These may include improving road conditions, or lowering the speed limit, or increasing police surveillance, for instance. The point of interest to us is that in identifying the causes retrospectively, the expert adopts an *ex post facto* perspective.

Ex post facto research is a method that can also be used instead of an experiment, to test hypotheses about cause and effect in situations where it is unethical to control or manipulate the dependent variable. For example, let us say that we wished to test the hypothesis that family violence caused poor school performance. Here, ethically speaking, we should not expose a student to family violence. However, one could put students into two groups, matched carefully on a range of factors, with one group comprising those who have experienced family violence and the other whose domestic circumstances are more acceptable. If the hypothesis is supportable then the researcher should be able to discover a difference in school performance between the two groups when the other variables are matched or held as constant as possible.

Kerlinger (1970) has defined *ex post facto* research as that in which the independent variable or variables have already occurred and in which the researcher starts with the observation of a dependent variable or variables. The researcher then studies the independent variable or variables in retrospect for their possible relationship to, and effects on, the dependent variable or variables. The researcher is thus examining retrospectively the effects of a naturally occurring event on a subsequent outcome with a view to establishing a causal link between them. Some instances of *ex post facto* designs correspond to experimental research in reverse, for instead of taking groups that are equivalent and subjecting them to different treatments so as to bring about differences in the dependent variables to be measured, an *ex post facto* experiment begins with groups that are already different in some respect and searches in retrospect for the factor that brought about the difference. Indeed Spector (1993: 42) suggests that *ex post facto* research is a procedure that is intended to transform a non-experimental research design into a pseudo-experimental form.

One can discern two approaches to *ex post facto* research. In the first approach one commences with subjects who differ on an *independent* variable (for example their years of study in mathematics) and then study how they differ on the *dependent* variable, e.g. a mathematics test. In a second approach, one can commence with subjects who differ on the *dependent* variable (for example their performance in a mathematics test) and discover how they differ on a range of independent variables, e.g. their years of study, their liking for the subject, the amount of homework they do in mathematics. The *ex post facto* research here seeks to discover the causes of a particular outcome (mathematics test performance) by comparing those students in whom the outcome is high (high marks on the mathematics test) with students whose outcome is low (low marks on the mathematics test), after the independent variable has occurred.

An example of an *ex post facto piece* of research can be presented. It has been observed that staff at a very large secondary school have been absent on days when they teach difficult classes. An *ex post facto* piece of research was conducted to try to establish the causes of this. Staff absences on days when teaching difficult secondary classes were noted, as shown in the diagram.

	Days when teaching difficult secondary classes	
Absences	Yes	No
High	26	30
Low	22	50
Total	48	80
	Overall total: 128	

Here the question of time was important: were the staff absent only on days when they were teaching difficult classes or at other times? Were there other variables that could be factored into the study, for example age groups? Hence the study was refined further, collecting more data, as shown.

	Days when teaching difficult secondary classes		Days when not teaching difficult secondary classes	
Age	High absence	Low absence	High absence	Low absence
>30 years old	30	6	16	10
30–50 years old	4	4	4	20
>50 years old	2	2	2	28
Total	36	12	22	58
		Overall total: 128		

This shows that age was also a factor as well as days when teaching difficult secondary classes: younger people are likely to be absent. Most teachers who were absent were under 30 years of age. Within age groups, it is also clear that young teachers have a higher incidence of excessive absence when teaching difficult secondary classes than teachers of the same (young) age group when they are not teaching difficult secondary classes.

Of course, a further check here would be to compare the absence rates of the same teachers when they do and do not teach difficult classes.

Co-relational and criterion groups designs

Two kinds of design may be identified in *ex post facto* research – the co-relational study and the criterion group study. The former is sometimes termed 'causal research' and the latter, 'causal-comparative research'. A co-relational (or causal) study is concerned with identifying the antecedents of a present condition. As its name suggests, it involves the collection of two sets of data, one of which will be retrospective, with a view to determining the relationship between them. The basic design of such an experiment may be represented thus:[1]

$$\boxed{X \qquad O}$$

A study by Borkowsky (1970) was based upon this kind of design. He attempted to show a relationship between the quality of a music teacher's undergraduate training (X) and his subsequent effectiveness as a teacher of his subject (O). Measures of the quality of a music teacher's college training can include grades in specific courses, overall grade average and self-ratings, etc. Teacher effectiveness can be assessed by indices of pupil performance, pupil knowledge, pupil attitudes and judgement of experts, etc. Correlations between all measures were obtained to determine the relationship. At most, this study could show that a relationship existed, after the fact, between the quality of teacher preparation and subsequent teacher effectiveness. Where a strong relationship is found between the independent and dependent variables, three possible interpretations are open to the researcher:

- that the variable X has caused O.
- that the variable O has caused X
- that some third unidentified, and therefore unmeasured, variable has caused X and O.

It is often the case that a researcher cannot tell which of these is correct.

The value of co-relational or causal studies lies chiefly in their exploratory or suggestive character for, as we have seen, while they are not always adequate in themselves for establishing causal relationships among variables, they are a useful first step in this direction in that they do yield measures of association.

In the criterion-group (or causal-comparative) approach, the investigator sets out to discover possible causes for a phenomenon being studied, by comparing the subjects in which the variable is present with similar subjects in whom it is absent. The basic design in this kind of study may be represented thus:

$$\boxed{X \begin{array}{c} O_1 \\ \\ O_2 \end{array}}$$

If, for example, a researcher chose such a design to investigate factors contributing to teacher effectiveness, the criterion group O_1 the effective teachers, and its counterpart O_2, a group *not* showing the characteristics of the criterion group, are identified by measuring the differential effects of the groups on classes of children. The researcher may then examine X, some variable or event, such as the background, training, skills and personality of the groups, to discover what might 'cause' only some teachers to be effective.

Criterion-group or causal-comparative studies may be seen as bridging the gap between descriptive research methods on the one hand and true experimental research on the other.

Characteristics of ex post facto research

In *ex post facto* research the researcher takes the effect (or dependent variable) and examines the data retrospectively to establish causes, relationships or associations, and their meanings.

Other characteristics of *ex post facto* research become apparent when it is contrasted with true experimental research. Kerlinger (1970) describes the *modus operandi* of the experimental researcher. ('If *x*, then *y*' in Kerlinger's (1970) usage. We have substituted X for *x* and O for *y* to fit in with Campbell's and Stanley's (1963) conventions throughout the chapter.) Kerlinger (1970) hypothesizes: if X, then O; if frustration, then aggression. Depending on circumstances and his own predilections in research design, he uses some method to manipulate X. He then observes O to see if concomitant variation, the variation expected or predicted from the variation in X, occurs. If it does, this is evidence for the validity of the proposition, X-O, meaning 'If X, then O'. Note that the scientist here predicts from a controlled X to O. To help him achieve control, he can use the principle of randomization and active manipulation of X and can assume, other things being equal, that O is varying as a result of the manipulation of X.

In *ex post facto* designs, on the other hand, O is observed. Then a retrospective search for X ensues. An X is found that is plausible and agrees with the hypothesis. Due to lack of control of X and other possible Xs, the truth of the hypothesized relation between X and O cannot be asserted with the confidence of the experimental researcher. Basically, then, *ex post facto* investigations have, so to speak, a built-in weakness: lack of control of the independent variable or variables. As Spector (1993: 43) suggests, it is impossible to isolate and control every possible variable, or to know with absolute certainty which are the most crucial variables.

This brief comparison highlights the most important difference between the two designs – control. In the experimental situation, investigators at least have manipulative control; they have as a minimum one active variable. If an experiment is a 'true' experiment, they can also exercise control by randomization. They can assign subjects to groups randomly; or, at the very least, they can assign treatments to groups at random. In the *ex post facto* research situation, this control of the independent variable is not possible, and, perhaps more important, neither is randomization. Investigators must take things as they are and try to disentangle them, though having said this, they can make use of selected procedures that will give them an element of control in this research. These we shall touch upon shortly.

By their very nature, *ex post facto* experiments can provide support for any number of different, perhaps even contradictory, hypotheses; they are so completely flexible that it is largely a matter of postulating hypotheses according to one's personal preference. The investigator begins with certain data and looks for an interpretation consistent with them; often, however, a number of interpretations may be at hand. Consider again the hypothetical increase in road accidents in a given town. A retrospective search for causes will disclose half a dozen plausible ones. Experimental studies, by contrast, begin with a specific interpretation and then determine whether it is congruent with externally derived data. Frequently, causal relationships seem to be established on nothing more substantial than the premise that any related event occurring prior to the phenomenon under study is assumed

to be its cause – the classical *post hoc, ergo propter hoc* fallacy.[2] Overlooked is the fact that even when we do find a relationship between two variables, we must recognize the possibility that both are individual results of a common third factor rather than the first being necessarily the cause of the second. As we have seen earlier, there is also the real possibility of reverse causation, e.g. that a heart condition promotes obesity rather than the other way around, or that they encourage each other. The point is that the evidence simply *illustrates* the hypothesis; it does not test it, since hypotheses cannot be tested on the same data from which they were derived. The relationship noted may actually exist, but it is not necessarily the only relationship, or perhaps the crucial one. Before we can accept that smoking is the primary cause of lung cancer, we have to rule out alternative hypotheses.

Further, a researcher may find that watching television correlates with poor school performance. Now, it may be there is a causal effect here: watching television causes poor school performance; or there may be reverse causality: poor school performance causes students to watch more television. However, there may be a third explanation: students who, for whatever reason (e.g. ability, motivation), do not do well at school also like watching television; it may be the third variable (the independent variable of ability or motivation) that is causing the other two outcomes (watching a lot of television or poor school performance).

We must not conclude from what has just been said that *ex post facto* studies are of little value; many of our important investigations in education and psychology are *ex post facto* designs. There is often no choice in the matter: an investigator cannot cause one group to become failures, delinquent, suicidal, brain-damaged or dropouts. Research must of necessity rely on existing groups. On the other hand, the inability of *ex post facto* designs to incorporate the basic need for control (e.g. through manipulation or randomization) makes them vulnerable from a scientific point of view and the possibility of their being misleading should be clearly acknowledged. *Ex post facto* designs are probably better conceived more circumspectly, not as experiments with the greater certainty that these denote, but more as surveys, useful as sources of hypotheses to be tested by more conventional experimental means at a later date.

Occasions when appropriate

Ex post facto designs are appropriate in circumstances where the more powerful experimental method is not possible. These arise when, for example, it is not possible to select, control and manipulate the factors necessary to study cause-and-effect relationships directly; or when the control of all variables except a single independent variable may be unrealistic and artificial, preventing the normal interaction with other influential variables; or when laboratory controls for many research purposes would be impractical, costly or ethically undesirable.

Ex post facto research is particularly suitable in social, educational and – to a lesser extent – psychological contexts where the independent variable or variables lie outside the researcher's control. Examples of the method abound in these areas: the research on cigarette-smoking and lung cancer, for instance; or studies of teacher characteristics; or studies examining the relationship between political and religious affiliation and attitudes; or investigations into the relationship between school achievement and independent variables such as social class, race, sex and intelligence. Many of these may be divided into large-scale or small-scale *ex post facto* studies, for example, Stables' (1990) large-scale study of differences between students from mixed and single-sex schools and Arnold and Atkins's (1991) small-scale study of the social and emotional adjustment of hearing-impaired students.

Advantages and disadvantages of ex post facto research

Among the advantages of the approach are the following:

- *Ex post facto* research meets an important need of the researcher where the more rigorous

experimental approach is not possible. In the case of the alleged relationship between smoking and lung cancer, for instance, this cannot be tested experimentally (at least as far as human beings are concerned).

- The method yields useful information concerning the nature of phenomena – what goes with what and under what conditions. In this way, *ex post facto* research is a valuable exploratory tool.
- Improvements in statistical techniques and general methodology have made *ex post facto* designs more defensible.
- In some ways and in certain situations the method is more useful than the experimental method, especially where the setting up of the latter would introduce a note of artificiality into research proceedings.
- *Ex post facto* research is particularly appropriate when simple cause-and-effect relationships are being explored.
- The method can give a sense of direction and provide a fruitful source of hypotheses that can subsequently be tested by the more rigorous experimental method.

Among the limitations and weaknesses of *ex post facto* designs the following may be mentioned:

- There is the problem of lack of control in that the researcher is unable to manipulate the independent variable or to randomize her subjects.
- One cannot know for certain whether the causative factor has been included or even identified.
- It may be that no single factor is the cause.
- A particular outcome may result from different causes on different occasions.
- When a relationship has been discovered, there is the problem of deciding which is the cause and which the effect; the possibility of reverse causation must be considered.
- The relationship of two factors does not establish cause and effect.
- Classifying into dichotomous groups can be problematic.

- There is the difficulty of interpretation and the danger of the post-hoc assumption being made, that is, believing that because X precedes O, X causes O.
- It often bases its conclusions on too limited a sample or number of occurrences.
- It frequently fails to single out the really significant factor or factors, and fails to recognize that events have multiple rather than single causes.
- As a method it is regarded by some as too flexible.
- It lacks nullifiability and confirmation.
- The sample size might shrink massively with multiple matchings (Spector 1993: 43).

Designing an ex post facto *investigation*

We earlier referred to the two basic designs embraced by *ex post facto* research – the correlational (or causal) model and the criterion group (or causal-comparative) model. As we saw, the causal model attempts to identify the antecedent of a present condition and may be represented thus:

Independent variable	Dependent variable
X	O

Although one variable in an *ex post facto* study cannot be confidently said to depend upon the other as would be the case in a truly experimental investigation, it is nevertheless usual to designate one of the variables as independent (X) and the other as dependent (O). The left to right dimension indicates the temporal order, though having established this, we must not overlook the possibility of reverse causality.

In a typical investigation of this kind, then, two sets of data relating to the independent and dependent variables respectively will be gathered. As indicated earlier in the chapter, the data on the independent variable (X) will be retrospective in character and as such will be prone to the kinds of weakness, limitations and distortions to which all historical evidence is subject. Let us now translate the design into a hypothetical situation. Imagine a

secondary school in which it is hypothesized that low staff morale (O) has come about as a direct result of reorganization some two years earlier, say. A number of key factors distinguishing the new organization from the previous one can be readily identified. Collectively these could represent or contain the independent variable X and data on them could be accumulated retrospectively. They could include, for example, the introduction of mixed ability and team teaching, curricular innovation, loss of teacher status, decline in student motivation, modifications to the school catchment area, or the appointment of a new headteacher. These could then be checked against a measure of prevailing teachers' attitudes (O), thus providing the researcher with some leads at least as to possible causes of current discontent.

The second model, the causal-comparative, may be represented schematically as shown.

Group	Independent variable	Dependent variable
E	X	O_1
C		O_2

Using this model, the investigator hypothesizes the independent variable and then compares two groups, an experimental group (E) which has been exposed to the presumed independent variable X and a control group (C) which has not. (The dashed line in the model shows that the comparison groups E and C are not equated by random assignment). Alternatively, the investigator may examine two groups that are different in some way or ways and then try to account for the difference or differences by investigating possible antecedents. These two examples reflect two types of approach to causal-comparative research: the 'cause-to-effect' kind and the 'effect-to-cause' kind.

The basic design of causal-comparative investigations is similar to an experimentally designed study. The chief difference resides in the nature of the independent variable, X. In a truly experimental situation, this will be under the control of the investigator and may therefore be described as manipulable. In the causal-comparative model (and also the causal model), however, the independent variable is beyond her control, having already occurred. It may therefore be described in this design as non-manipulable.

Procedures in ex post facto *research*

Ex post facto research is concerned with discovering relationships among variables in one's data; and we have seen how this may be accomplished by using either a causal or causal-comparative model. We now examine the steps involved in implementing a piece of *ex post facto* research. We may begin by identifying the problem area to be investigated. This stage will be followed by a clear and precise statement of the hypothesis to be tested or questions to be answered. The next step will be to make explicit the assumptions on which the hypothesis and subsequent procedures will be based. A review of the research literature will follow. This will enable the investigator to ascertain the kinds of issues, problems, obstacles and findings disclosed by previous studies in the area. There will then follow the planning of the actual investigation and this will consist of three broad stages – identification of the population and samples; the selection and construction of techniques for collecting data; and the establishment of categories for classifying the data. The final stage will involve the description, analysis and interpretation of the findings.

It was noted earlier that the principal weakness of *ex post facto* research is the absence of control over the independent variable influencing the dependent variable in the case of causal designs or affecting observed differences between dependent variables in the case of causal-comparative designs. Although *ex post facto* researchers are denied not only this kind of control but also the principle of randomization, they can nevertheless utilize procedures that provide some measure of control in their investigation; it is to some of these that we now turn.

One of the commonest means of introducing control into this type of research is that of matching the subjects in the experimental and control groups where the design is causal-comparative. Ary *et al.* (1972) indicate that matched pair designs (see Chapter 13) are careful to match the participants on important and relevant characteristics that may have a bearing on the research.

There are difficulties with this procedure, however, for it assumes that the investigator knows what the relevant factors are, that is, the factors that may be related to the dependent variable. Further, there is the possibility of losing those subjects who cannot be matched, thus reducing one's sample.

As an alternative procedure for introducing a degree of control into *ex post facto* research, Ary and his colleagues (1972) suggest building the extraneous independent variables into the design and then using an analysis of variance technique. For example, if intelligence is a relevant extraneous variable but it is not possible to control it through matching or other means, then it could be added to the research as another independent variable, with the participants being classified in terms of intelligence levels. Through analysis of variance techniques the dependent variable measures would then be analysed and this would reveal the main and interaction effects of intelligence, indicating any statistically significant differences between the groups on the dependent variable, even though no causal relationship between intelligence and the dependent variable could be assumed.

Yet another procedure which may be adopted for introducing a measure of control into *ex post facto* design is that of selecting samples that are as homogeneous as possible on a given variable. For example, Ary *et al.* (1972) suggest that if intelligence were a relevant extraneous variable, its effects could be controlled by including participants from only one intelligence level. This would disentangle the independent variable from other variables with which it is commonly associated, so that any effects found could be associated justifiably with the independent variable.

Finally, control may be introduced into an *ex post facto* investigation by stating and testing any alternative hypotheses that might be plausible explanations for the empirical outcomes of the study. A researcher has thus to beware of accepting the first likely explanation of relationships in an *ex post facto* study as necessarily the only or final one. A well-known instance to which reference has already been made is the presumed relationship between cigarette smoking and lung cancer. Health officials have been quick to seize on the explanation that smoking causes lung cancer. Tobacco firms, however, have put forward an alternative hypothesis – that both smoking and lung cancer are possibly the result of a third, as yet unspecified, factor, i.e. the possibility that both the independent and dependent variables are simply two separate results of a single common cause cannot be ignored.

13 Experiments, quasi-experiments, single-case research and meta-analysis

Introduction

The issue of *causality* and, hence, predictability has exercised the minds of researchers considerably (Smith 1991: 177). One response has been in the operation of *control*, and it finds its apotheosis in the experimental design. If rival causes or explanations can be eliminated from a study then clear causality can be established; the model can *explain* outcomes. Smith (1991: 177) claims the high ground for the experimental approach, arguing that it is the *only* method that directly concerns itself with causality; this, clearly is contestable, as we make clear in Part Three of this book.

In Chapter 12, we described *ex post facto* research as experimentation in reverse in that *ex post facto* studies start with groups that are already different with regard to certain characteristics and then proceed to search, in retrospect, for the factors that brought about those differences. We then went on to cite Kerlinger's description of the experimental researcher's approach:

> If *x*, then *y*; if frustration, then aggression ... the researcher uses some method to measure *x* and then observes *y* to see if concomitant variation occurs.
>
> (Kerlinger 1970)

The essential feature of experimental research is that investigators deliberately control and manipulate the conditions which determine the events in which they are interested, introduce an intervention and measure the difference that it makes. An experiment involves making a change in the value of one variable – called the independent variable – and observing the effect of that change on another variable – called the dependent variable. Using a fixed design, experimental research can be *confirmatory*, seeking to support or not to support a null hypothesis, or *exploratory*, discovering the effects of certain variables. An independent variable is the input variable, whereas the dependent variable is the outcome variable – the result; for example, Kgaile and Morrison (2006) indicate seven independent variables that have an effect on the result (the effectiveness of the school) (Box 13.1).

In an experiment the post-test measures the dependent variable, and the independent variables are isolated and controlled carefully.

Imagine that we have been transported to a laboratory to investigate the properties of a new wonder-fertilizer that farmers could use on their cereal crops, let us say wheat (Morrison 1993: 44–5). The scientist would take the bag of wheat seed and randomly split it into two equal parts. One part would be grown under normal existing conditions – controlled and measured amounts of soil, warmth, water and light and no other factors. This would be called the control group. The other part would be grown under the same conditions – the same controlled and measured amounts of soil, warmth, water and light as the control group, *but*, additionally, the new wonder-fertilizer. Then, four months later, the two groups are examined and their growth measured. The control group has grown half a metre and each ear of wheat is in place but the seeds are small. The experimental group, by contrast, has grown half a metre as well but has significantly more seeds on each ear, the seeds are larger, fuller and more robust.

Box 13.1
Independent and dependent variables

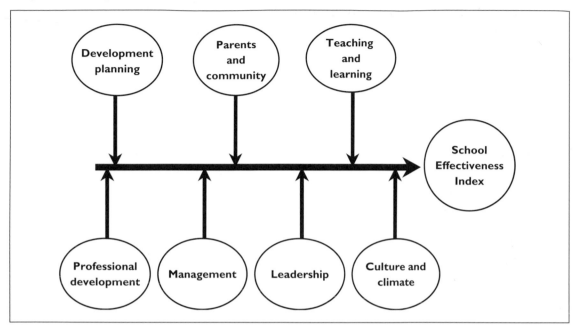

Source: Kgaile and Morrison 2006

The scientist concludes that, because both groups came into contact with nothing other than measured amounts of soil, warmth, water and light, then it could not have been anything else but the new wonder-fertilizer that caused the experimental group to flourish so well. The key factors in the experiment were the following:

- the random allocation of the whole bag of wheat into two matched groups (the control and the experimental group), involving the initial measurement of the size of the wheat to ensure that it was the same for both groups (i.e. the pretest)
- the identification of key variables (soil, warmth, water, and light)
- the control of the key variables (the same amounts to each group)
- the exclusion of any other variables
- the giving of the special treatment (the intervention) to the experimental group while

holding every other variable constant for the two groups
- the final measurement of yield and growth to compare the control and experimental groups and to look at differences from the pretest results (the post-test)
- the comparison of one group with another
- the stage of generalization – that this new wonder-fertilizer improves yield and growth under a given set of conditions.

This model, premised on notions of isolation and control of variables in order to establish causality, may be appropriate for a laboratory, though whether, in fact, a social situation either ever *could become* the antiseptic, artificial world of the laboratory or *should become* such a world is both an empirical and a moral question respectively. Further, the ethical dilemmas of treating humans as manipulable, controllable and inanimate are considerable (see Chapter 2). However, let us pursue the experimental model further.

Frequently in learning experiments in classroom settings, the independent variable is a stimulus of some kind, a new method in arithmetical computation for example, and the dependent variable is a response, the time taken to do twenty sums using the new method. Most empirical studies in educational settings, however, are quasi-experimental rather than experimental. The single most important difference between the quasi-experiment and the true experiment is that in the former case, the researcher undertakes his study with groups that are intact, that is to say, the groups have been constituted by means other than random selection. In this chapter we identify the essential features of true experimental and quasi-experimental designs, our intention being to introduce the reader to the meaning and purpose of control in educational experimentation.

In experiments, researchers can remain relatively aloof from the participants, bringing a degree of objectivity to the research (Robson 2002: 98). Observer effects can distort the experiment, for example researchers may record inconsistently, or inaccurately, or selectively, or, less consciously, they may be having an effect on the experiment. Further, participant effects might distort the experiment (see the discussion of the Hawthorne effect in Chapter 6); the fact of simply being in an experiment, rather than what the experiment is doing, might be sufficient to alter participants' behaviour.

In medical experiments these twin concerns are addressed by giving placebos to certain participants, to monitor any changes, and experiments are blind or double blind. In blind experiments, participants are not told whether they are in a control group or an experimental group, though which they are is known to the researcher. In a double blind experiment not even the researcher knows whether a participant is in the control of experimental group – that knowledge resides with a third party. These are intended to reduce the subtle effects of participants knowing whether they are in a control or experimental group. In educational research it is easier to conduct a blind experiment rather than a double blind experiment, and it is even possible not to tell participants that they are in an experiment at all, or to tell them that the experiment is about X when, in fact, it is about Y, i.e. to 'put them off the scent'. This form of deception needs to be justified; a common justification is that it enables the experiment to be conducted under more natural conditions, without participants altering their everyday behaviour.

Designs in educational experimentation

There are several different kinds of experimental design, for example:

- the *controlled experiment* in laboratory conditions (the 'true' experiment): two or more groups
- the *field or quasi-experiment* in the natural setting rather than the laboratory, but where variables are isolated, controlled and manipulated.
- the *natural experiment* in which it is not possible to isolate and control variables.

We consider these in this chapter (see http://www.routledge.com/textbooks/9780415368780 – Chapter 13, file 13.1. ppt). The laboratory experiment (the classic true experiment) is conducted in a specially contrived, artificial environment, so that variables can be isolated, controlled and manipulated (as in the example of the wheat seeds above). The field experiment is similar to the laboratory experiment in that variables are isolated, controlled and manipulated, but the setting is the real world rather than the artificially constructed world of the laboratory.

Sometimes it is not possible, desirable or ethical to set up a laboratory or field experiment. For example, let us imagine that we wanted to investigate the trauma effects on people in road traffic accidents. We could not require a participant to run under a bus, or another to stand in the way of a moving lorry, or another to be hit by a motorcycle, and so on. Instead we might examine hospital records to see the trauma effects of victims of bus accidents, lorry accidents and motorcycle accidents, and see which group seem to have sustained the greatest traumas. It may be that the lorry accident victims had the greatest trauma, followed by the motorcycle victims, followed by the bus victims. Now, although it is not possible to say with 100 per cent certainty what caused the trauma, one could make an intelligent guess that those involved in lorry accidents suffer the worst injuries. Here we look at the outcomes and work backwards to examine possible causes. We cannot isolate, control or manipulate variables, but nevertheless we can come to some likely defensible conclusions.

In the outline of research designs that follows we use symbols and conventions from Campbell and Stanley (1963):

- X represents the exposure of a group to an experimental variable or event, the effects of which are to be measured.
- O refers to the process of observation or measurement.
- Xs and Os in a given row are applied to the same persons.
- Left to right order indicates temporal sequence.
- Xs and Os vertical to one another are simultaneous.
- R indicates random assignment to separate treatment groups.
- Parallel rows unseparated by dashes represent comparison groups equated by randomization, while those separated by a dashed line represent groups not equated by random assignment.

True experimental designs

There are several variants of the 'true' experimental design, and we consider many of these below (see http://www.routledge.com/textbooks/9780415368780 – Chapter 13, file 13.2. ppt):

- the pretest-post-test control and experimental group design
- the two control groups and one experimental group pretest-post-test design
- the post-test control and experimental group design

- the post-test two experimental groups design
- the pretest-post-test two treatment design
- the matched pairs design
- the factorial design
- the parametric design
- repeated measures designs.

The laboratory experiment typically has to identify and control a large number of variables, and this may not be possible. Further, the laboratory environment itself can have an effect on the experiment, or it may take some time for a particular intervention to manifest its effects (e.g. a particular reading intervention may have little immediate effect but may have a delayed effect in promoting a liking for reading in adult life, or may have a cumulative effect over time).

A 'true' experiment includes several key features:

- one or more control groups
- one or more experimental groups
- random allocation to control and experimental groups
- pretest of the groups to ensure parity
- post-test of the groups to see the effects on the dependent variable
- one or more interventions to the experimental group(s)
- isolation, control and manipulation of independent variables
- non-contamination between the control and experimental groups.

If an experiment does not possess all of these features then it is a quasi-experiment: it may look *as if* it is an experiment ('quasi' means 'as if') but it is not a true experiment, only a variant on it.

An alternative to the laboratory experiment is the quasi-experiment or field experiment, including:

- the one-group pretest-post-test
- the non-equivalent control group design
- the time series design.

We consider these below. Field experiments have less control over experimental conditions or extraneous variables than a laboratory experiment and, hence, inferring causality is more contestable, but they have the attraction of taking place in a natural setting. Extraneous variables may include, for example:

- *participant factors*: they may differ on important characteristics between the control and experimental groups
- *intervention factors*: the intervention may not be exactly the same for all participants, varying, for example, in sequence, duration, degree of intervention and assistance, and other practices and contents
- *situational factors*: the experimental conditions may differ.

These can lead to experimental error, in which the results may not be due to the independent variables in question.

The pretest-post-test control and experimental group design

A complete exposition of experimental designs is beyond the scope of this chapter. In the brief outline that follows, we have selected one design from the comprehensive treatment of the subject by Campbell and Stanley (1963) in order to identify the essential features of what they term a 'true experimental' and what Kerlinger (1970) refers to as a 'good' design. Along with its variants, the chosen design is commonly used in educational experimentation (see http://www.routledge.com/textbooks/9780415368780 – Chapter 13, file 13.3. ppt).

The pretest-post-test control group design can be represented as:

Experimental	RO_1	X	O_2
Control	RO_3		O_4

Kerlinger (1970) observes that, in theory, random assignment to E and C conditions controls all possible independent variables. In practice, of course, it is only when enough subjects are included in the experiment that the principle of randomization has a chance to operate as a powerful control. However, the effects of

Box 13.2
The effects of randomization

Select twenty cards from a pack, ten red and ten black. Shuffle and deal into two ten-card piles. Now count the number of red cards and black cards in either pile and record the results. Repeat the whole sequence many times, recording the results each time.

You will soon convince yourself that the most likely distribution of reds and blacks in a pile is five in each: the next most likely, six red (or black) and four black (or red); and so on. You will be lucky (or unlucky for the purposes of the demonstration!) to achieve one pile of red and the other entirely of black cards. The probability of this happening is 1 in 92,378. On the other hand, the probability of obtaining a 'mix' of not more than six of one colour and four of the other is about 82 in 100.

If you now imagine the red cards to stand for the 'better' ten children and the black cards for the 'poorer' ten children in a class of twenty, you will conclude that the operation of the laws of chance alone will almost probably give you close equivalent 'mixes' of 'better' and 'poorer' children in the experimental and control groups.

Source: adapted from Pilliner 1973

randomization even with a small number of subjects is well illustrated in Box 13.2.

Randomization, then, ensures the greater likelihood of equivalence, that is, the apportioning out between the experimental and control groups of any other factors or characteristics of the subjects which might conceivably affect the experimental variables in which the researcher is interested. If the groups are made equivalent, then any so-called 'clouding' effects should be present in both groups.

So strong is this simple and elegant true experimental design, that all the threats to internal validity identified in Chapter 6 are, according to Campbell and Stanley (1963), controlled in the pretest-post-test control group design. The causal effect of an intervention can be calculated in three steps:

1 Subtract the pretest score from the post-test score for the experimental group to yield score 1.

2   Subtract the pretest score from the post-test score for the control group to yield score 2.
3   Subtract score 2 from score 1.

Using Campbell's and Stanley's terminology, the effect of the experimental intervention is:

$$(O_2 - RO_1) - (O_4 - RO_3)$$

If the result is negative then the causal effect was negative.

One problem that has been identified with this particular experimental design is the interaction effect of testing. Good (1963) explains that whereas the various threats to the validity of the experiments listed in Chapter 6 can be thought of as main effects, manifesting themselves in mean differences independently of the presence of other variables, interaction effects, as their name implies, are joint effects and may occur even when no main effects are present. For example, an interaction effect may occur as a result of the pretest measure sensitizing the subjects to the experimental variable.[1] Interaction effects can be controlled for by adding to the pretest-post-test control group design two more groups that do not experience the pretest measures. The result is a four-group design, as suggested by Solomon (1949) below. Later in the chapter, we describe an educational study which built into a pretest-post-test group design a further control group to take account of the possibility of pretest sensitization.

Randomization, Smith (1991: 215) explains, produces equivalence over a whole range of variables, whereas matching produces equivalence over only a few named variables. The use of randomized controlled trials (RCTs), a method used in medicine, is a putative way of establishing causality and generalizability (though, in medicine, the sample sizes for some RCTs is necessarily so small – there being limited sufferers from a particular complaint – that randomization is seriously compromised).

A powerful advocacy of RCTs for planning and evaluation is provided by Boruch (1997). Indeed he argues that the problem of poor experimental controls has led to highly questionable claims being made about the success of programmes (Boruch 1997: 69). Examples of the use of RCTs can be seen in Maynard and Chalmers (1997).

The randomized controlled trial is the 'gold standard' of many educational researchers, as it purports to establish controllability, causality and generalizability (Coe et al. 2000; Curriculum, Evaluation and Management Centre 2000). How far this is true is contested (Morrison 2001b). For example, complexity theory replaces simple causality with an emphasis on networks, linkages, holism, feedback, relationships and interactivity in context (Cohen and Stewart 1995), emergence, dynamical systems, self-organization and an open system (rather than the closed world of the experimental laboratory). Even if we could conduct an experiment, its applicability to ongoing, emerging, interactive, relational, changing, open situations, in practice, may be limited (Morrison 2001b). It is misconceived to hold variables constant in a dynamical, evolving, fluid, open situation.

Further, the laboratory is a contrived, unreal and artificial world. Schools and classrooms are not the antiseptic, reductionist, analysed-out or analysable-out world of the laboratory. Indeed the successionist conceptualization of causality (Harré 1972), wherein researchers make inferences about causality on the basis of observation, must admit its limitations. One cannot infer causes from effects or multiple causes from multiple effects. Generalizability from the laboratory to the classroom is dangerous, yet with field experiments, with their loss of control of variables, generalizability might be equally dangerous.

Classical experimental methods, abiding by the need for replicability and predictability, may not be particularly fruitful since, in complex phenomena, results are never clearly replicable or predictable: we never step into the same river twice. In linear thinking small causes bring small effects and large causes bring large effects, but in complexity theory small causes can bring huge effects and huge causes may have little or no effect. Further, to atomize phenomena into measurable variables and then to focus only on certain ones of these is to miss synergy and the spirit of the whole. Measurement, however acute, may tell us little of value about a phenomenon; I can measure every physical variable of a person but the nature of the person, what makes that person who she or he is, eludes atomization and measurement. Randomized controlled trials belong to a discredited view of science as positivism.

Though we address ethical concerns in Chapter 2, it is important here to note the common reservation that is voiced about the two-group experiment (e.g. Gorard 2001: 146), which is to question how ethical it is to deny a control group access to a treatment or intervention in order to suit the researcher (to which the counter-argument is, as in medicine, that the researcher does not know whether the intervention (e.g. the new drug) will work or whether it will bring harmful results, and, indeed, the purpose of the experiment is to discover this).

The two control groups and one experimental group pretest-post-test design

This is the Solomon (1949) design, intended to identify the interaction effect that may occur if the subject deduces the desired result from looking at the pretest and the post-test. It is the same as the randomized controlled trial above, except that there are two control groups instead of one. In the standard randomized controlled trial any change in the experimental group can be due to the intervention or the pretest, and any change in the control group can be due to the pretest. In the Solomon variant the second control group receives the intervention but no pretest. This can be modelled thus:

Experimental RO_1 X O_2

Control$_1$ RO_3 O_4
Control$_2$ X O_5

Thus any change in this second control group can be due only to the intervention. We refer readers to Bailey (1994: 231–4) for a full explication of this technique and its variants (see

http://www.routledge.com/textbooks/ 9780415368780 – Chapter 13, file 13.4. ppt).

The post-test control and experimental group design

Here participants are randomly assigned to a control group and an experimental group, but there is no pretest. The experimental group receives the intervention and the two groups are given only a post-test (see http://www.routledge.com/ textbooks/9780415368780 – Chapter 13, file 13.5. ppt). The design is:

Experimental R_1 X O_1
Control R_2 O_2

The post-test two experimental groups design

Here participants are randomly assigned to each of two experimental groups. Experimental group 1 receives intervention 1 and experimental group 2 receives intervention 2. Only post-tests are conducted on the two groups (see http://www.routledge.com/ textbooks/9780415368780 – Chapter 13, file 13.6. ppt). The design is:

Experimental$_1$ R_1 X_1 O_1
Experimental$_2$ R_2 X_2 O_2

The pretest-post-test two treatment design

Here participants are randomly allocated to each of two experimental groups. Experimental group 1 receives intervention 1 and experimental group 2 receives intervention 2. Pretests and post-tests are conducted to measure changes in individuals in the two groups (see http://www.routledge.com/textbooks/ 9780415368780 – Chapter 13, file 13.7. ppt). The design is:

Experimental$_1$ RO_1 X_1 O_2
Experimental$_2$ RO_3 X_2 O_4

The true experiment can also be conducted with one control group and two or more experimental groups. (see http://www.routledge.com/

textbooks/9780415368780 – Chapter 13, file 13.8. ppt). So, for example, the designs might be:

Experimental$_1$	RO_1	X_1	O_2
Experimental$_2$	RO_3	X_2	O_4
Control	RO_5		O_6

This can be extended to the post-test control and experimental group design and the post-test two experimental groups design, and the pretest-post-test two treatment design.

The matched pairs design

As the name suggests, here participants are allocated to control and experimental groups randomly, but the basis of the allocation is that one member of the control group is matched to a member of the experimental group on the several independent variables considered important for the study (e.g. those independent variables that are considered to have an influence on the dependent variable, such as sex, age, ability). So, first, pairs of participants are selected who are matched in terms of the independent variable under consideration (e.g. whose scores on a particular measure are the same or similar), and then each of the pair is randomly assigned to the control or experimental group. Randomization takes place at the pair rather than the group level. Although, as its name suggests, this ensures effective matching of control and experimental groups, in practice it may not be easy to find sufficiently close matching, particularly in a field experiment, although finding such a close match in a field experiment may increase the control of the experiment considerably. Matched pairs designs are useful if the researcher cannot be certain that individual differences will not obscure treatment effects, as it enables these individual differences to be controlled.

Borg and Gall (1979: 547) set out a useful series of steps in the planning and conduct of an experiment:

1   Carry out a measure of the dependent variable.
2   Assign participants to matched pairs, based on the scores and measures established from Step 1.
3   Randomly assign one person from each pair to the control group and the other to the experimental group.
4   Administer the experimental treatment/intervention to the experimental group and, if appropriate, a placebo to the control group. Ensure that the control group is not subject to the intervention.
5   Carry out a measure of the dependent variable with both groups and compare/measure them in order to determine the effect and its size on the dependent variable.

Borg and Gall indicate that difficulties arise in the close matching of the sample of the control and experimental groups. This involves careful identification of the variables on which the matching must take place. Borg and Gall (1979: 547) suggest that matching on a number of variables that correlate with the dependent variable is more likely to reduce errors than matching on a single variable. The problem, of course, is that the greater the number of variables that have to be matched, the harder it is actually to find the sample of people who are matched. Hence the balance must be struck between having too few variables such that error can occur, and having so many variables that it is impossible to draw a sample. Instead of matched pairs, random allocation is possible, and this is discussed below.

Mitchell and Jolley (1988: 103) pose three important questions that researchers need to consider when comparing two groups:

• Are the two groups equal at the commencement of the experiment?
• Would the two groups have grown apart naturally, regardless of the intervention?
• To what extent has initial measurement error of the two groups been a contributory factor in differences between scores?

Borg and Gall (1979) draw attention to the need to specify the degree of exactitude (or variance) of the match. For example, if the subjects were to be matched on, say, linguistic ability as measured in a standardized test, it is important to define the limits of variability that will be used to define the matching (e.g. ± 3 points). As before, the greater the degree of precision in the matching here, the closer will be the match, but the greater the degree of precision the harder it will be to find an exactly matched sample.

One way of addressing this issue is to place all the subjects in rank order on the basis of the scores or measures of the dependent variable. Then the first two subjects become one matched pair (which one is allocated to the control group and which to the experimental group is done randomly, e.g. by tossing a coin), the next two subjects become the next matched pair, then the next two subjects become the next matched pair, and so on until the sample is drawn. Here the loss of precision is counterbalanced by the avoidance of the loss of subjects.

The alternative to matching that has been discussed earlier in the chapter is randomization. Smith (1991: 215) suggests that matching is most widely used in quasi-experimental and non-experimental research, and is a far inferior means of ruling out alternative causal explanations than randomization.

The factorial design

In an experiment there may be two or more independent variables acting on the dependent variable. For example, performance in an examination may be a consequence of availability of resources (independent variable one: limited availability, moderate availability, high availability) and motivation for the subject studied (independent variable two: little motivation, moderate motivation, high motivation). Each independent variable is studied at each of its levels (in the example here it is three levels for each independent variable) (see http://www.routledge.com/textbooks/9780415368780 – Chapter 13, file 13.9.ppt). Participants are randomly assigned to groups that cover all the possible combinations of levels of each independent variable, as shown in the model.

INDEPENDENT VARIABLE	LEVEL ONE	LEVEL TWO	LEVEL THREE
Availability of resources	Limited availability (1)	Moderate availability (2)	High availability (3)
Motivation for the subject studied	Little motivation (4)	Moderate motivation (5)	High motivation (6)

Here the possible combinations are: 1 + 4, 1 + 5, 1 + 6, 2 + 4, 2 + 5, 2 + 6, 3 + 4, 3 + 5 and 3 + 6. This yields 9 groups (3 × 3 combinations). Pretests and post-tests or post-tests only can be conducted. It might show, for example, that limited availability of resources and little motivation had a statistically significant influence on examination performance, whereas moderate and high availability of resources did not, or that high availability and high motivation had a statistically significant effect on performance, whereas high motivation and limited availability did not, and so on.

This example assumes that there are the same number of levels for each independent variable; this may not be the case. One variable may have, say, two levels, another three levels, and another four levels. Here the possible combinations are 2 × 3 × 4 = 24 levels and, therefore, 24 experimental groups. One can see that factorial designs quickly generate several groups of participants. A common example is a 2 × 2 design, in which two independent variables each have two values (i.e. four groups). Here experimental group 1 receives the intervention with independent variable 1 at level 1 and independent variable 2 at level 1; experimental group 2 receives the intervention with independent variable 1 at level 1 and independent variable 2 at level 2; experimental group 3 receives the intervention with independent variable 1 at level 2 and independent variable 2 at level 1; experimental group 4 receives the intervention with independent variable 1 at level 2 and independent variable 2 at level 2.

Factorial designs also have to take account of the interaction of the independent variables. For example, one factor (independent variable) may be 'sex' and the other 'age' (Box 13.3). The researcher may be investigating their effects on motivation for learning mathematics (see http://www.routledge.com/textbooks/9780415368780 – Chapter 13, file 13.10. ppt).

Here one can see that the difference in motivation for mathematics is not constant between males and females, but that it varies according to the age of the participants. There is an interaction effect between age and sex, such that the effect of sex depends on age. A factorial design is useful for examining interaction effects.

At their simplest, factorial designs may have two levels of an independent variable, e.g. its presence or absence, but, as has been seen here, it can become more complex. That complexity is bought at the price of increasing exponentially the number of groups required.

The parametric design

Here participants are randomly assigned to groups whose parameters are fixed in terms of the levels of the independent variable that each receives. For example, let us imagine that an experiment is conducted to improve the reading abilities of poor, average, good, and outstanding readers (four levels of the independent variable 'reading ability'). Four experimental groups are set up to receive the intervention, thus: experimental group one (poor readers); experimental group two (average readers), experimental group three (good readers and experimental group four (outstanding readers). The control group (group five) would receive no intervention. The researcher could chart the differential effects of the intervention on the groups, and thus have a more sensitive indication of its effects than if there was only one experimental group containing a wide range of reading abilities; the researcher would know which group was most and least affected by the intervention. Parametric designs are useful if an independent variable is considered to have different levels or a range of values which may have a bearing on the outcome (confirmatory research) or if the researcher wishes to discover whether different levels of an independent variable have an effect on the outcome (exploratory research).

Repeated measures designs

Here participants in the experimental groups are tested under two or more experimental conditions. So, for example, a member of the experimental group may receive more than one 'intervention', which may or may not include a control condition. This is a variant of the matched pairs

Box 13.3
Interaction effects in an experiment

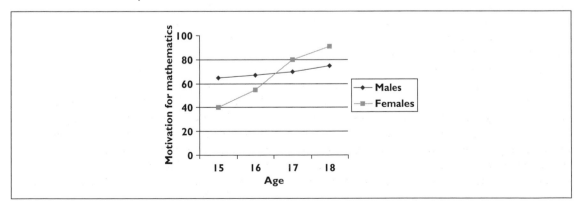

design, and offers considerable control potential, as it is exactly the same person receiving different interventions. (see http://www.routledge.com/textbooks/9780415368780 – Chapter 13, file 13.11. ppt). Order effects raise their heads here: the order in which the interventions are sequenced may have an effect on the outcome; the first intervention may have an influence – a carry-over effect – on the second, and the second intervention may have an influence on the third and so on. Further, early interventions may have a greater effect than later interventions. To overcome this it is possible to randomize the order of the interventions and assign participants randomly to different sequences, though this may not ensure a balanced sequence. Rather, a deliberate ordering may have to be planned, for example, in a three-intervention experiment:

- Group 1 receives intervention 1 followed by intervention 2, followed by intervention 3.
- Group 2 receives intervention 2 followed by intervention 3, followed by intervention 1.
- Group 3 receives intervention 3 followed by intervention 1, followed by intervention 2.
- Group 4 receives intervention 1 followed by intervention 3, followed by intervention 2.
- Group 5 receives intervention 2 followed by intervention 1, followed by intervention 3.
- Group 6 receives intervention 3 followed by intervention 2, followed by intervention 1.

Repeated measures designs are useful if it is considered that order effects are either unimportant or unlikely, or if the researcher cannot be certain that individual differences will not obscure treatment effects, as it enables these individual differences to be controlled.

A quasi-experimental design: the non-equivalent control group design

Often in educational research, it is simply not possible for investigators to undertake true experiments, e.g. in random assignation of participants to control or experimental groups. Quasi-experiments are the stuff of field experimentation, i.e. outside the laboratory (see http://

www.routledge.com/textbooks/9780415368780 – Chapter 13, file 13.12. ppt). At best, they may be able to employ something approaching a true experimental design in which they have control over what Campbell and Stanley (1963) refer to as 'the who and to whom of measurement' but lack control over 'the when and to whom of exposure', or the randomization of exposures – essential if true experimentation is to take place. These situations are quasi-experimental and the methodologies employed by researchers are termed quasi-experimental designs. (Kerlinger (1970) refers to quasi-experimental situations as 'compromise designs', an apt description when applied to much educational research where the random selection or random assignment of schools and classrooms is quite impracticable.)

Quasi-experiments come in several forms, for example:

- Pre-experimental designs: the one group pretest-post-test design; the one group post-tests only design; the post-tests only non-equivalent design.
- Pretest-post-test non-equivalent group design.
- One-group time series.

We consider these below.

A pre-experimental design: the one group pretest-post-test

Very often, reports about the value of a new teaching method or interest aroused by some curriculum innovation or other reveal that a researcher has measured a group on a dependent variable (O_1), for example, attitudes towards minority groups, and then introduced an experimental manipulation (X), perhaps a ten-week curriculum project designed to increase tolerance of ethnic minorities. Following the experimental treatment, the researcher has again measured group attitudes (O_2) and proceeded to account for differences between pretest and post-test scores by reference to the effects of X.

The one group pretest-post-test design can be represented as:

Experimental O_1 X O_2

Suppose that just such a project has been undertaken and that the researcher finds that O_2 scores indicate greater tolerance of ethnic minorities than O_1 scores. How justified is the researcher in attributing the cause of $O_1 - O_2$ differences to the experimental treatment (X), that is, the term's project work? At first glance the assumption of causality seems reasonable enough. The situation is not that simple, however. Compare for a moment the circumstances represented in our hypothetical educational example with those which typically obtain in experiments in the physical sciences. Physicists who apply heat to a metal bar can confidently attribute the observed expansion to the rise in temperature that they have introduced because within the confines of the laboratory they have excluded (i.e. controlled) all other extraneous sources of variation (Pilliner 1973).

The same degree of control can never be attained in educational experimentation. At this point readers may care to reflect upon some possible influences other than the ten-week curriculum project that might account for the $O_1 - O_2$ differences in our hypothetical educational example.

They may conclude that factors to do with the pupils, the teacher, the school, the classroom organization, the curriculum materials and their presentation, the way that the subjects' attitudes were measured, to say nothing of the thousand and one other events that occurred in and about the school during the course of the term's work, might all have exerted some influence upon the observed differences in attitude. These kinds of extraneous variables which are outside the experimenters control in one-group pretest-post-test designs threaten to invalidate their research efforts. We later identify a number of such threats to the validity of educational experimentation.

A pre-experimental design: the one group post-tests only design

Here an experimental group receives the intervention and then takes the post-test. Although this has some features of an experiment

(an intervention and a post-test), the lack of a pretest, of a control group, of random allocation, and of controls, renders this a flawed methodology.

A pre-experimental design: the post-tests only non-equivalent groups design

Again, although this appears to be akin to an experiment, the lack of a pretest, of matched groups, of random allocation, and of controls, renders this a flawed methodology.

A quasi-experimental design: the pretest-post-test non-equivalent group design

One of the most commonly used quasi-experimental designs in educational research can be represented as:

Experimental	O_1	X	O_2
- - - - - - - - - -			
Control	O_3		O_4

The dashed line separating the parallel rows in the diagram of the non-equivalent control group indicates that the experimental and control groups have not been equated by randomization – hence the term 'non-equivalent'. The addition of a control group makes the present design a decided improvement over the one group pretest-post-test design, for to the degree that experimenters can make E and C groups as equivalent as possible, they can avoid the equivocality of interpretations that plague the pre-experimental design discussed earlier. The equivalence of groups can be strengthened by matching, followed by random assignment to E and C treatments.

Where matching is not possible, the researcher is advised to use samples from the same population or samples that are as alike as possible (Kerlinger 1970). Where intact groups differ substantially, however, matching is unsatisfactory due to regression effects which lead to different group means on post-test measures. Campbell and Stanley (1963) put it this way:

> If [in the non-equivalent control group design] the means of the groups are substantially different, then

the process of matching not only fails to provide the intended equation but in addition insures the occurrence of unwanted regression effects. It becomes predictably certain that the two groups will differ on their post-test scores altogether independently of any effects of X, and that this difference will vary directly with the difference between the total populations from which the selection was made and inversely with the test-retest correlation.

(Campbell and Stanley 1963: 49)

The one-group time series

Here the one group is the experimental group, and it is given more than one pretest and more than one post-test. The time series uses repeated tests or observations both before and after the treatment, which, in effect, enables the participants to become their own controls, which reduces the effects of reactivity. Time series allow for trends to be observed, and avoid reliance on only one single pretesting and post-testing data collection point. This enables trends to be observed such as no effect at all (e.g. continuing an existing upward, downward or even trend), a clear effect (e.g. a sustained rise or drop in performance), delayed effects (e.g. some time after the intervention has occurred). Time series studies have the potential to increase reliability.

Single-case research: ABAB design

At the beginning of Chapter 11, we described case study researchers as typically engaged in observing the characteristics of an individual unit, be it a child, a classroom, a school, or a whole community. We went on to contrast case study researchers with experimenters whom we described as typically concerned with the manipulation of variables in order to determine their causal significance. That distinction, as we shall see, is only partly true.

Increasingly, in recent years, single-case research as an experimental methodology has extended to such diverse fields as clinical psychology, medicine, education, social work, psychiatry and counselling. Most of the single-case studies carried out in these (and other) areas share the following characteristics:

- They involve the continuous assessment of some aspect of human behaviour over a period of time, requiring on the part of the researcher the administration of measures on multiple occasions within separate phases of a study.
- They involve 'intervention effects' which are replicated in the same subject(s) over time.

Continuous assessment measures are used as a basis for drawing inferences about the effectiveness of intervention procedures.

The characteristics of single-case research studies are discussed by Kazdin (1982) in terms of ABAB designs, the basic experimental format in most single-case researches. ABAB designs, Kazdin observes, consist of a family of procedures in which observations of performance are made over time for a given client or group of clients. Over the course of the investigation, changes are made in the experimental conditions to which the client is exposed. The basic rationale of the ABAB design is illustrated in Box 13.4. What it does is this. It examines the effects of an intervention by alternating the baseline condition (the A phase), when no intervention is in effect, with the intervention condition (the B phase). The A and B phases are then repeated to complete the four phases. As Kazdin (1982) says, the effects of the intervention are clear if performance improves during the first intervention phase, reverts to or approaches original baseline levels of performance when the treatment is withdrawn, and improves again when treatment is recommenced in the second intervention phase.

An example of the application of the ABAB design in an educational setting is provided by Dietz (1977) whose single-case study sought to measure the effect that a teacher could have upon the disruptive behaviour of an adolescent boy whose persistent talking disturbed his fellow classmates in a special education class.

In order to decrease the unwelcome behaviour, a reinforcement programme was devised in which the boy could earn extra time with the teacher by decreasing the number of times he called out. The boy was told that when he made three (or fewer) interruptions during any fifty-five-minute

Box 13.4
The ABAB design

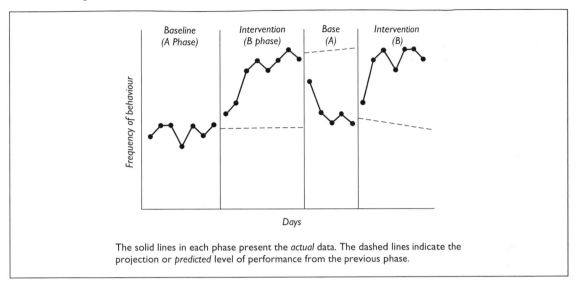

The solid lines in each phase present the *actual* data. The dashed lines indicate the projection or *predicted* level of performance from the previous phase.

Source: adapted from Kazdin 1982

class period the teacher would spend extra time working with him. In the technical language of behaviour modification theory, the pupil would receive reinforcing consequences when he was able to show a low rate of disruptive behaviour (in Box 13.5 this is referred to as 'differential reinforcement of low rates' or DRL).

When the boy was able to desist from talking aloud on fewer than three occasions during any timetabled period, he was rewarded by the teacher spending fifteen minutes with him helping him with his learning tasks. The pattern of results displayed in Box 13.5 shows the considerable changes that occurred in the boy's behaviour when the intervention procedures were carried out and the substantial increases in disruptions towards baseline levels when the teacher's rewarding strategies were withdrawn. Finally, when the intervention was reinstated, the boy's behaviour is seen to improve again.

The single-case research design is uniquely able to provide an experimental technique for evaluating interventions for the individual subject. Moreover, such interventions can be directed towards the particular subject or group and replicated over time or across behaviours, situations, or persons. Single-case research offers an alternative strategy to the more usual methodologies based on between-group designs. There are, however, a number of problems that arise in connection with the use of single-case designs having to do with ambiguities introduced by trends and variations in baseline phase data and with the generality of results from single-case research. The interested reader is directed to Kazdin (1982), Borg (1981) and Vasta (1979).[2]

Procedures in conducting experimental research

An experimental investigation must follow a set of logical procedures. Those that we now enumerate, however, should be treated with some circumspection. It is extraordinarily difficult (and foolhardy) to lay down clear-cut rules as guides to experimental research. At best, we can identify an ideal route to be followed, knowing full well that educational research rarely proceeds in such a systematic fashion.[3]

Box 13.5

An ABAB design in an educational setting

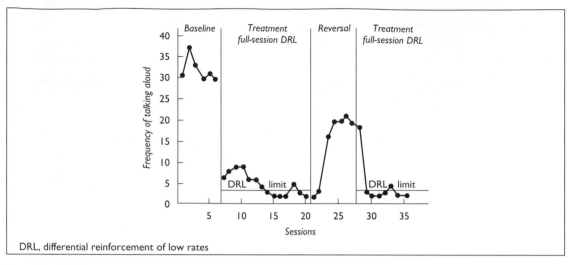

DRL, differential reinforcement of low rates

Source: Kazdin 1982

First, researchers must identify and define the research problem as precisely as possible, always supposing that the problem is amenable to experimental methods.

Second, researchers must formulate hypotheses that they wish to test. This involves making predictions about relationships between specific variables and at the same time making decisions about other variables that are to be excluded from the experiment by means of controls. Variables, remember, must have two properties. The first property is that variables must be measurable. Physical fitness, for example, is not directly measurable until it has been operationally defined. Making the variable 'physical fitness' operational means simply defining it by letting something else that is measurable stand for it – a gymnastics test, perhaps. The second property is that the proxy variable must be a valid indicator of the hypothetical variable in which one is interested. That is to say, a gymnastics test probably is a reasonable proxy for physical fitness; height, on the other hand, most certainly is not. Excluding variables from the experiment is inevitable, given constraints of time and money. It follows therefore that one must set up priorities among the variables in which one is interested so that the most important of them can be varied experimentally while others are held constant.

Third, researchers must select appropriate levels at which to test the independent variables. By way of example, suppose an educational psychologist wishes to find out whether longer or shorter periods of reading make for reading attainment in school settings (see Simon 1978). The psychologist will hardly select five-hour and five-minute periods as appropriate levels; rather, she is more likely to choose thirty-minute and sixty-minute levels, in order to compare with the usual timetabled periods of forty-five minutes' duration. In other words, the experimenter will vary the stimuli at such levels as are of practical interest in the real-life situation. Pursuing the example of reading attainment somewhat further, our hypothetical experimenter will be wise to vary the stimuli in large enough intervals so as to obtain measurable results. Comparing reading periods of forty-four minutes, or forty-six minutes, with timetabled reading lessons of forty-five minutes is scarcely likely to result in observable differences in attainment.

Fourth, researchers must decide which kind of experiment they will adopt, perhaps from the varieties set out in this chapter.

Fifth, in planning the design of the experiment, researchers must take account of the population to which they wish to generalize their results. This involves making decisions over sample sizes and sampling methods. Sampling decisions are bound up with questions of funds, staffing and the amount of time available for experimentation.

Sixth, with problems of validity in mind, researchers must select instruments, choose tests and decide upon appropriate methods of analysis.

Seventh, before embarking upon the actual experiment, researchers must pilot test the experimental procedures to identify possible snags in connection with any aspect of the investigation. This is of crucial importance.

Eighth, during the experiment itself, researchers must endeavour to follow tested and agreed-on procedures to the letter. The standardization of instructions, the exact timing of experimental sequences, the meticulous recording and checking of observations – these are the hallmark of the competent researcher.

With their data collected, researchers face the most important part of the whole enterprise. Processing data, analysing results and drafting reports are all extremely demanding activities, both in intellectual effort and time. Often this last part of the experimental research is given too little time in the overall planning of the investigation. Experienced researchers rarely make such a mistake; computer program faults and a dozen more unanticipated disasters teach the hard lesson of leaving ample time for the analysis and interpretation of experimental findings.

A ten-step model for the conduct of the experiment can be suggested (see http://www.routledge.com/textbooks/9780415368780 – Chapter 13, file 13.13. ppt):

1 Identify the purpose of the experiment.
2 Select the relevant variables.
3 Specify the level(s) of the intervention (e.g. low, medium, high intervention).
4 Control the experimental conditions and environment.
5 Select the appropriate experimental design.
6 Administer the pretest.
7 Assign the participants to the group(s).
8 Conduct the intervention.
9 Conduct the post-test.
10 Analyse the results.

The sequence of steps 6 and 7 can be reversed; the intention in putting them in the present sequence is to ensure that the two groups are randomly allocated and matched. In experiments and fixed designs, data are aggregated rather than related to specific individuals, and data look for averages, the range of results, and their variation. In calculating differences or similarity between groups at the stages of the pretest and the post-test, the t-test for independent samples is often used.

Examples from educational research

Example 1: a pre-experimental design

A pre-experimental design was used in a study involving the 1991–92 postgraduate diploma in education group following a course of training to equip them to teach social studies in senior secondary schools in Botswana. The researcher wished to find out whether the programme of studies he had devised would effect changes in the students' orientations towards social studies teaching. To that end, he employed a research instrument, the Barth/Shermis Studies Preference Scale (BSSPS), which has had wide use in differing cultures including the United States, Egypt and Nigeria, and whose construction meets commonly required criteria concerning validity and internal consistency reliability.

The BSSPS consists of forty-five Likert-type items (Chapter 15), providing measures of what purport to be three social studies traditions or philosophical orientations, the oldest of which, Citizenship Transmission, involves indoctrination of the young in the basic values of a society. The second orientation, the Social Science, is held to relate to the acquisition of knowledge-gathering skills based on the mastery of social science concepts and processes. The third tradition, Reflective Inquiry, is said to derive from John Dewey's pragmatism with its emphasis on the process of inquiry. Forty-eight postgraduate diploma students were administered the BSSPS during the first session of their one-year course of study. At the end of the programme, the BSSPS was again completed in order to determine whether changes had occurred in students' philosophical orientations. Briefly, the 'preferred orientation' in the pretest and post-test was the criterion measure, the two orientations least preferred being ignored. Broadly speaking, students tended to move from a majority holding a Citizenship Transmission orientation at the beginning of the course to a greater affirmation of the Social Science and the Reflective Inquiry traditions. Using the symbols and conventions adopted earlier to represent research designs, we can illustrate the Botswana study as:

Experimental O_1 X O_2

The briefest consideration reveals inadequacies in the design. Indeed, Campbell and Stanley (1963) describe the one group pretest-post-test design as 'a "bad example" to illustrate several of the confounded extraneous variables that can jeopardize internal validity. These variables offer plausible hypotheses explaining an $O_1 - O_2$ difference, rival to the hypothesis that caused the difference' (Campbell and Stanley 1963). The investigator is rightly cautious in his conclusions: 'it is possible to say that the social studies course *might* be responsible for this phenomenon, although other extraneous variables might be operating' (Adeyemi 1992, emphasis added). Somewhat ingenuously he puts his finger on one potential explanation, that the changes could have occurred among his intending teachers because the shift from 'inculcation to rational decision-making was in line with the recommendation of the Nine Year Social Studies Syllabus issued by the Botswana Ministry of Education in 1989' (Adeyemi 1992).

Example 2: a quasi-experimental design

Mason *et al.*'s (1992) longitudinal study took place between 1984 and 1992. Its principal aim was to test whether the explicit teaching of linguistic features of GCSE textbooks, coursework and

examinations would produce an improvement in performance across the secondary curriculum. The title of their report, 'Illuminating English: how explicit language teaching improved public examination results in a comprehensive school', suggests that the authors were persuaded that they had achieved their objective. In light of the experimental design selected for the research, readers may ask themselves whether or not the results are as unequivocal as reported.

The design adopted in the Shevington study (Shevington is the location of the experiment in north-west England) may be represented as:

Experimental O_1 X O_2
- - - - - - - - - -
Control O_3 O_4

This is, of course, the non-equivalent control group design outlined earlier in this chapter in which parallel rows separated by dashed lines represent groups that have not been equated by random assignment.

In brief, the researchers adopted a methodology akin to teaching English as a foreign language and applied this to Years 7–9 (for pupils aged 11–14) in Shevington Comprehensive School and two neighbouring schools, monitoring the pupils at every stage and comparing their performance with control groups drawn both from Shevington and the two other schools. Inevitably, because experimental and control groups were not randomly allocated, there were significant differences in the performance of some groups on pre-treatment measures such as the York Language Aptitude Test. Moreover, because no standardized reading tests of sufficient difficulty were available as post-treatment measures, tests had to be devised by the researchers, who provide no details as to their validity or reliability. These difficulties notwithstanding, pupils in the experimental groups taking public examinations in 1990 and 1991 showed substantial gains in respect of the percentage increases of those obtaining GCSE Grades A–C. The researchers note that during the three years 1989 to 1991, 'no other significant change in the policy, teaching staff or organization of the school took place which could account for this dramatic improvement of 50 per cent' (Mason *et al.* 1992).

Although the Shevington researchers attempted to exercise control over extraneous variables, readers may well ask whether threats to internal and external validity such as those alluded to earlier were sufficiently met as to allow such a categorical conclusion as 'the pupils . . . achieved greater success in public examinations as a result of taking part in the project' (Mason *et al.* 1992).

Example 3: a 'true' experimental design

Another investigation (Bhadwal and Panda 1991) concerned with effecting improvements in pupils' performance as a consequence of changing teaching strategies used a more robust experimental design. In rural India, the researchers drew a sample of seventy-eight pupils, matched by socio-economic backgrounds and non-verbal IQs, from three primary schools that were themselves matched by location, physical facilities, teachers' qualifications and skills, school evaluation procedures and degree of parental involvement. Twenty-six pupils were randomly selected to comprise the experimental group, the remaining fifty-two being equally divided into two control groups. Before the introduction of the changed teaching strategies to the experimental group, all three groups completed questionnaires on their study habits and attitudes. These instruments were specifically designed for use with younger children and were subjected to the usual item analyses, test-retest and split-half reliability inspections. Bhadwal and Panda's research design can be represented as:

Experimental	RO_1	X	RO_2
First control	RO_3		RO_4
Second control	RO_5		RO_6

Recalling Kerlinger's (1970) discussion of a 'good' experimental design, the version of the pretest-post-test control design employed here (unlike the design used in Example 2 above) resorted to randomization which, in theory, controls all possible independent variables. Kerlinger (1970) adds, however, '*in practice*, it is only when enough

subjects are included in the experiment that the principle of randomization has a chance to operate as a powerful control'. It is doubtful whether twenty-six pupils in each of the three groups in Bhadwal and Panda's (1991) study constituted 'enough subjects'.

In addition to the matching procedures in drawing up the sample, and the random allocation of pupils to experimental and control groups, the researchers also used analysis of covariance, as a further means of controlling for initial differences between E and C groups on their pretest mean scores on the independent variables, study habits and attitudes.

The experimental programme involved improving teaching skills, classroom organization, teaching aids, pupil participation, remedial help, peer-tutoring and continuous evaluation. In addition, provision was also made in the experimental group for ensuring parental involvement and extra reading materials. It would be startling if such a package of teaching aids and curriculum strategies did not effect significant changes in their recipients and such was the case in the experimental results. The Experimental Group made highly significant gains in respect of its level of study habits as compared with Control Group 2 where students did not show a marked change. What did surprise the investigators, we suspect, was the significant increase in levels of study habits in Control Group 1. Maybe, they opined, this unexpected result occurred because Control Group 1 pupils were tested immediately prior to the beginning of their annual examinations. On the other hand, they conceded, some unaccountable variables might have been operating. There is, surely, a lesson here for all researchers! (For a set of examples of problematic experiments see http://www.routledge.com/textbooks/9780415368780 – Chapter 13, file 13.1.doc).

Evidence-based educational research and meta-analysis

Evidence-based research

In an age of evidence-based education (Thomas and Pring 2004), meta-analysis is an increasingly used method of investigation, bringing together different studies to provide evidence to inform policy-making and planning. Meta-analysis is a research strategy in itself. That this is happening significantly is demonstrated in the establishment of the EPPI-Centre (Evidence for Policy and Practice Information and Co-ordinating Centre) at the University of London (http://eppi.ioe.ac.uk/EPPIWeb/home.aspx), the Social, Psychological, Educational and Criminological Controlled Trials Register (SPECTR), later transferred to the Campbell Collaboration (http://www.campbellcollaboration.org), a parallel to the Cochrane Collaboration in medicine (http://www.cochrane.org/index0.htm), which undertakes systematic reviews and meta-analyses of, typically, experimental evidence in medicine, and the Curriculum, Evaluation and Management (CEM) centre at the University of Durham (http://www.cemcentre.org). 'Evidence' here typically comes from randomized controlled trials of one hue or another (Tymms 1999; Coe et al. 2000; Thomas and Pring 2004: 95), with their emphasis on careful sampling, control of variables, both extraneous and included, and measurements of effect size. The cumulative evidence from collected RCTs is intended to provide a reliable body of knowledge on which to base policy and practice (Coe et al. 2000). Such accumulated data, it is claimed, deliver evidence of 'what works', although Morrison (2001b) suggests that this claim is suspect.

The roots of evidence-based practice lie in medicine, where the advocacy by Cochrane (1972) for randomized controlled trials together with their systematic review and documentation led to the foundation of the Cochrane Collaboration (Maynard and Chalmers 1997), which is now worldwide. The careful, quantitative-based research studies that can contribute to the accretion of an evidential base is seen to be a powerful counter to the often untried and under-tested schemes that are injected into practice.

More recently evidence-based education has entered the worlds of social policy, social work (MacDonald 1997) and education (Fitz-Gibbon 1997). At the forefront of educational research in this area are Fitz-Gibbon (1996; 1997; 1999) and Tymms (1996), who, at the Curriculum, Evaluation and Management Centre at the University of Durham, have established one of the world's largest monitoring centres in education. Fitz-Gibbon's work is critical of multilevel modelling and, instead, suggests how indicator systems can be used with experimental methods to provide clear evidence of causality and a ready answer to her own question, 'How do we know what works?' (Fitz-Gibbon 1999: 33).

Echoing Anderson and Biddle (1991), Fitz-Gibbon suggests that *policy-makers* shun evidence in the development of policy and that *practitioners*, in the hurly-burly of everyday activity, call upon tacit knowledge rather than the knowledge which is derived from RCTs. However, in a compelling argument (Fitz-Gibbon 1997: 35–6), she suggests that evidence-based approaches are necessary in order to challenge the imposition of unproven practices, solve problems and avoid harmful procedures, and create improvement that leads to more effective learning. Further, such evidence, she contends, should examine effect sizes rather than statistical significance.

While the nature of information in evidence-based education might be contested by researchers whose sympathies (for whatever reason) lie outside randomized controlled trials, the message from Fitz-Gibbon will not go away: the educational community needs evidence on which to base its judgements and actions. The development of indicator systems worldwide attests to the importance of this, be it through assessment and examination data, inspection findings, national and international comparisons of achievement, or target setting. Rather than being a shot in the dark, evidence-based education suggests that policy formation should be informed, and policy decision-making should be based on the best information to date rather than on hunch, ideology or political will. It is bordering on the unethical to implement untried and untested recommendations in educational practice, just as it is unethical to use untested products and procedures on hospital patients without their consent.

Meta-analysis

The study by Bhadwal and Panda (1991) is typical of research undertaken to explore the effectiveness of classroom methods. Often as not, such studies fail to reach the light of day, particularly when they form part of the research requirements for a higher degree. Meta-analysis is, simply, the analysis of other analyses. It involves aggregating and combining the results of comparable studies into a coherent account to discover main effects. This is often done statistically, though qualitative analysis is also advocated. Among the advantages of using meta-analysis, Fitz-Gibbon (1985) cites the following:

- Humble, small-scale reports which have simply been gathering dust may now become useful.
- Small-scale research conducted by individual students and lecturers will be valuable since meta-analysis provides a way of coordinating results drawn from many studies without having to coordinate the studies themselves.
- For historians, a whole new genre of studies is created – the study of how *effect sizes* vary over time, relating this to historical changes.

(Fitz-Gibbon 1985: 46)

McGaw (1997: 371) suggests that *quantitative* meta-analysis replaces intuition, which is frequently reported narratively (Wood 1995: 389), as a means of synthesizing different research studies transparently and explicitly (a *desideratum* in many synthetic studies: Jackson 1980), particularly when they differ very substantially. Narrative reviews, suggest Jackson (1980), Cook *et al.* (1992: 13) and Wood (1995: 390), are prone to:

- lack comprehensiveness, being selective and only going to subsets of studies
- misrepresentation and crude representation of research findings
- over-reliance on significance tests as a means of supporting hypotheses, thereby overlooking the point that sample size exerts a major effect on significance levels, and overlooking effect size

- reviewers' failure to recognize that random sampling error can play a part in creating variations in findings among studies
- overlook differing and conflicting research findings
- reviewers' failure to examine critically the evidence, methods and conclusions of previous reviews
- overlook the extent to which findings from research are mediated by the characteristics of the sample
- overlook the importance of intervening variables in research
- unreplicability because the procedures for integrating the research findings have not been made explicit.

Since the late 1970s a quantitative method for synthesizing research results has been developed by Glass and colleagues (Glass and Smith 1978; Glass *et al.* 1981) and others (e.g. Hedges and Olkin 1985; Hedges 1990; Rosenthal 1991) to supersede narrative intuition. Meta-analysis, essentially the 'analysis of analysis', is a means of quantitatively identifying generalizations from a range of separate and disparate studies, and discovering inadequacies in existing research such that new emphases for future research can be proposed. It is simple to use and easy to understand, though the statistical treatment that underpins it is somewhat complex. It involves the quantification and synthesis of findings from separate studies on some common measure, usually an aggregate of effect size estimates, together with an analysis of the relationship between effect size and other features of the studies being synthesized. Statistical treatments are applied to attenuate the effects of other contaminating factors, e.g. sampling error, measurement errors, and range restriction. Research findings are coded into substantive categories for generalizations to be made (Glass *et al.* 1981), such that consistency of findings is discovered that, through the traditional means of intuition and narrative review, would have been missed.

Fitz-Gibbon (1985: 45) explains the technique by suggesting that in *meta-analysis* the effects of variables are examined in terms of their *effect size*, that is to say, in terms of *how much* difference they make rather than only in terms of whether or not the effects are statistically significant at some arbitrary level such as 5 per cent. Because, with *effect sizes*, it becomes easier to concentrate on the educational significance of a finding rather than trying to assess its importance by its statistical significance, we may finally see statistical significance kept in its place as just one of many possible threats to internal validity. The move towards elevating effect size over significance levels is very important (see also Chapter 24), and signals an emphasis on 'fitness for purpose' (the size of the effect having to be suitable for the researcher's purposes) over arbitrary cut-off points in significance levels as determinants of utility.

The term 'meta-analysis' originated in 1976 (Glass 1976) and early forms of meta-analysis used calculations of combined probabilities and frequencies with which results fell into defined categories (e.g. statistically significant at given levels), although problems of different sample sizes confounded rigour (e.g. large samples would yield significance in trivial effects, while important data from small samples would not be discovered because they failed to reach statistical significance) (Light and Smith 1971; Glass *et al.* 1981; McGaw 1997: 371). Glass (1976) and Glass *et al.* (1981) suggested three levels of analysis:

- primary analysis of the data
- secondary analysis, a re-analysis using different statistics
- meta-analysis analysing results of several studies statistically in order to integrate the findings.

Glass *et al.* (1981) and Hunter *et al.* (1982) suggest eight steps in the procedure:

1   Identify the variables for focus (independent and dependent).
2   Identify all the studies which feature the variables in which the researcher is interested.
3   Code each study for those characteristics that might be predictors of outcomes and effect sizes. (e.g. age of participants, gender, ethnicity, duration of the intervention).

4   Estimate the effect sizes through calculation for each pair of variables (dependent and independent variable) (see Glass 1977), weighting the effect-size by the sample size.
5   Calculate the mean and the standard deviation of effect-sizes across the studies, i.e. the variance across the studies.
6   Determine the effects of sampling errors, measurement errors and range of restriction.
7   If a large proportion of the variance is attributable to the issues in Step 6, then the average effect-size can be considered an accurate estimate of relationships between variables.
8   If a large proportion of the variance is not attributable to the issues in Step 6, then review those characteristics of interest which correlate with the study effects.

Cook *et al.* (1992: 7–12) set out a five step model for an integrative review as a research process, covering:

1   Problem formulation, where a high quality meta-analysis must be rigorous in its attention to the design, conduct and analysis of the review.
2   Data collection, where sampling of studies for review has to demonstrate fitness for purpose.
3   Data retrieval and analysis, where threats to validity in non-experimental research – of which integrative review is an example – are addressed. Validity here must demonstrate fitness for purpose, reliability in coding, and attention to the methodological rigour of the original pieces of research.
4   Analysis and interpretation, where the accumulated findings of several pieces of research should be regarded as complex data points that have to be interpreted by meticulous statistical analysis.

Fitz-Gibbon (1984: 141–2) sets out four steps in conducting a meta-analysis:

1   Finding studies (e.g. published, unpublished, reviews) from which effect sizes can be computed.

2   Coding the study characteristics (e.g. date, publication status, design characteristics, quality of design, status of researcher).
3   Measuring the effect sizes (e.g. locating the experimental group as a z-score in the control group distribution) so that outcomes can be measured on a common scale, controlling for 'lumpy data' (non-independent data from a large data set).
4   Correlating effect sizes with context variables (e.g. to identify differences between well-controlled and poorly-controlled studies).

Effect size (e.g. Cohen's d and eta squared) are the preferred statistics over statistical significance in meta-analyses, and we discuss this in Part Five. Effect size is a measure of the degree to which a phenomenon is present or the degree to which a null hypothesis is not supported. Wood (1995: 393) suggests that effect-size can be calculated by dividing the significance level by the sample size. Glass *et al.* (1981: 29, 102) calculate the effect size as:

(Mean of experimental group – mean of control group)
Standard deviation of the control group

Hedges (1981) and Hunter *et al.* (1982) suggest alternative equations to take account of differential weightings due to sample size variations. The two most frequently used indices of effect sizes are standardized mean differences and correlations (Hunter *et al.* 1982: 373), though non-parametric statistics, e.g. the median, can be used. Lipsey (1992: 93–100) sets out a series of statistical tests for working on effect sizes, effect size means and homogeneity. It is clear from this that Glass and others assume that meta-analysis can be undertaken only for a particular kind of research – the experimental type – rather than for all types of research; this might limit its applicability.

Glass *et al.* (1981) suggest that meta-analysis is particularly useful when it uses unpublished dissertations, as these often contain weaker correlations than those reported in published research, and hence act as a brake on misleading, more spectacular generalizations. Meta-analysis, it is claimed (Cooper and Rosenthal 1980), is a means

of avoiding Type II errors (failing to find effects that really exist), synthesizing research findings more rigorously and systematically, and generating hypotheses for future research. However, Hedges and Olkin (1980) and Cook *et al.* (1992: 297) show that Type II errors become more likely as the number of studies included in the sample increases.

Further, Rosenthal (1991) has indicated a method for avoiding Type I errors (finding an effect that, in fact, does not exist) that is based on establishing how many unpublished studies that average a null result would need to be undertaken to offset the group of published statistically significant studies. For one example he shows a ratio of 277:1 of unpublished to published research, thereby indicating the limited bias in published research.

Meta-analysis is not without its critics (e.g. Wolf 1986; Elliott 2001; Thomas and Pring 2004). Wolf (1986: 14–17) suggests six main areas:

- It is difficult to draw logical conclusions from studies that use different interventions, measurements, definitions of variables, and participants.
- Results from poorly designed studies take their place alongside results from higher quality studies.
- Published research is favoured over unpublished research.
- Multiple results from a single study are used, making the overall meta-analysis appear more reliable than it is, since the results are not independent.
- Interaction effects are overlooked in favour of main effects.
- Meta-analysis may have 'mischievous consequences' (Wolf 1986: 16) because its apparent objectivity and precision may disguise procedural invalidity in the studies.

Wolf (1986) provides a robust response to these criticisms, both theoretically and empirically. Wolf (1986: 55–6) also suggests a ten-step sequence for carrying out meta-analyses rigorously:

1   Make clear the criteria for inclusion and exclusion of studies.

2   Search for unpublished studies.
3   Develop coding categories that cover the widest range of studies identified.
4   Look for interaction effects and examine multiple independent and dependent variables separately.
5   Test for heterogeneity of results and the effects of outliers, graphing distributions of results.
6   Check for inter-rater coding reliability.
7   Use indicators of effect size rather than statistical significance.
8   Calculate unadjusted (raw) and weighted tests and effects sizes in order to examine the influence of sample size on the results found.
9   Combine qualitative and quantitative reviewing methods.
10 Report the limitations of the meta-analyses conducted.

One can add to this the need to specify the research questions being asked, the conceptual frameworks being used, the review protocols being followed, the search and retrieval strategies being used, and the ways in which the syntheses of the findings from several studies are brought together (Thomas and Pring 2004: 54–5).

Gorard (2001: 72–3) suggests a four-step model for conducting meta-analysis:

1   Collect all the appropriate studies for inclusion.
2   Weight each study 'according to its size and quality'.
3   List the outcome measures used.
4   Select a method for aggregation, based on the nature of the data collected (e.g. counting those studies in which an effect appeared and those in which an effect did not appear, or calculating the average effect size across the studies).

Evans and Benefield (2001: 533–7) set out six principles for undertaking systematic reviews of evidence:

• A clear specification of the research question which is being addressed.

• A systematic, comprehensive and exhaustive search for relevant studies.
• The specification and application of clear criteria for the inclusion and exclusion of studies, including data extraction criteria: published; unpublished; citation details; language; keywords; funding support; type of study (e.g. process or outcome-focused, prospective or retrospective); nature of the intervention; sample characteristics; planning and processes of the study; outcome evaluation.
• Evaluations of the quality of the methodology used in each study (e.g. the kind of experiment and sample; reporting of outcome measures).
• The specification of strategies for reducing bias in selecting and reviewing studies.
• Transparency in the methodology adopted for reviewing the studies.

Gorard (2001) acknowledges that subjectivity can enter into meta-analysis. Since so much depends upon the quality of the results that are to be synthesized, there is the danger that adherents may simply multiply the inadequacies of the database and the limits of the sample (e.g. trying to compare the incomparable). Hunter *et al.* (1982) suggest that sampling error and the influence of other factors has to be addressed, and that it should account for less than 75 per cent of the variance in observed effect sizes if the results are to be acceptable and able to be coded into categories. The issue is clear here: coding categories have to declare their level of precision, their reliability (e.g. inter-coder reliability – the equivalent of inter-rater reliability, see Chapter 6) and validity (McGaw 1997: 376–7).

To the charge that selection bias will be as strong in meta-analysis – which embraces both published and unpublished research – as in solely published research, Glass *et al.* (1981: 226–9) argue that it is necessary to counter gross claims made in published research with more cautious claims found in unpublished research.

Because the quantitative mode of (many) studies demands only a few common variables to be measured in each case, explains Tripp (1985), cumulation of the studies tends to increase sample size much more than it increases the complexity of the data in terms of the number of variables. Meta-analysis risks attempting to synthesize studies which are insufficiently similar to each other to permit this with any legitimacy (Glass *et al.* 1981: 22; McGaw 1997: 372) other than at an unhelpful level of generality. The analogy here might be to try to keep together oil and water as 'liquids'; meta-analysts would argue that differences between studies and their relationships to findings can be coded and addressed in meta-analysis. Eysenck (1978) suggests that early meta-evaluation studies mixed apples with oranges. Morrison (2001b) asks:

> How can we be certain that meta-analysis is fair if the hypotheses for the separate experiments were not identical, if the hypotheses were not operationalizations of the identical constructs, if the conduct of the separate RCTs (e.g. time frames, interventions and programmes, controls, constitution of the groups, characteristics of the participants, measures used) were not identical?
>
> (Morrison 2001b: 78)

Although Glass *et al.* (1981: 218–20) address these kinds of charges, it remains the case (McGaw 1997) that there is a risk in meta-analysis of dealing indiscriminately with a large and sometimes incoherent body of research literature.

It is unclear, too, how meta-analysis differentiates between 'good' and 'bad' research – e.g. between methodologically rigorous and poorly constructed research (Cook *et al.* 1992: 297). Smith and Glass (1977) and Levačić and Glatter (2000) suggest that it is possible to use study findings, regardless of their methodological quality, though Glass and Smith (1978) and Slavin (1984a, 1984b), in a study of the effects of class size, indicate that methodological quality does make a difference. Glass *et al.* (1981: 220–6) effectively address the charge of using data from 'poor' studies, arguing, among other points, that

many weak studies can add up to a strong conclusion, and that the differences in the size of experimental effects between high-validity and low-validity studies are surprisingly small (Glass *et al.* 1981: 221, 226).

Further, Wood (1995: 296) suggests that meta-analysis oversimplifies results by concentrating on overall effects to the neglect of the interaction of intervening variables. To the charge that, because meta-analyses are frequently conducted on large data sets where multiple results derive from the same study (i.e. that the data are non-independent) and are therefore unreliable, Glass *et al.* (1981: 153–216) indicate how this can be addressed by using sophisticated data analysis techniques. Finally, a practical concern is the time required not only to use the easily discoverable studies (typically large-scale published studies) but also to include the smaller-scale unpublished studies; the effect of neglecting the latter might be to build in bias in the meta-analysis.

It is the traditional pursuit of generalizations from each quantitative study which has most hampered the development of a database adequate to reflect the complexity of the social nature of education. The cumulative effects of 'good' and 'bad' experimental studies is graphically illustrated in Box 13.6.

An example of meta-analysis in educational research

Glass and Smith (1978) and Glass *et al.* (1981: 35–44) identified 77 empirical studies of the relationship between class size and pupil learning. These studies yielded 725 comparisons of the achievements of smaller and larger classes, the comparisons resting on data accumulated from nearly 900,000 pupils of all ages and aptitudes studying all manner of school subjects. Using regression analysis, the 725 comparisons were integrated into a single curve showing the relationship between class size and achievement in general. This curve revealed a definite inverse relationship between class size and pupil learning.

Box 13.6

Class size and learning in well-controlled and poorly controlled studies

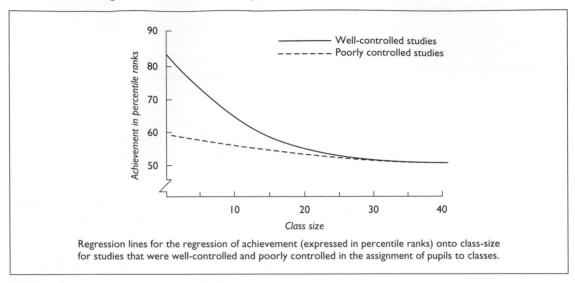

Regression lines for the regression of achievement (expressed in percentile ranks) onto class-size for studies that were well-controlled and poorly controlled in the assignment of pupils to classes.

Source: adapted from Glass and Smith 1978

When the researchers derived similar curves for a variety of circumstances that they hypothesized would alter the basic relationship (for example, grade level, subject taught, pupil ability etc.), virtually none of these special circumstances altered the basic relationship. Only one factor substantially affected the curve – whether the original study controlled adequately in the experimental sense for initial differences among pupils and teachers in smaller and larger classes. Adequate and inadequate control curves are set out in Box 13.6.[4]

14 Action research

Introduction

Action research is a powerful tool for change and improvement at the local level. Indeed, Kurt Lewin's own work (one of action research's founding fathers) was deliberately intended to change the life chances of disadvantaged groups in terms of housing, employment, prejudice, socialization and training. Its combination of *action* and *research* has contributed to its attraction to researchers, teachers and the academic and educational community alike.

The scope of action research as a method is impressive. It can be used in almost any setting where a problem involving people, tasks and procedures cries out for solution, or where some change of feature results in a more desirable outcome. It can be undertaken by the individual teacher, a group of teachers working cooperatively within one school, or a teacher or teachers working alongside a researcher or researchers in a sustained relationship, possibly with other interested parties like advisers, university departments and sponsors on the periphery (Holly and Whitehead 1986). Action research can be used in a variety of areas, for example:

- *teaching methods:* replacing a traditional method by a discovery method
- *learning strategies:* adopting an integrated approach to learning in preference to a single-subject style of teaching and learning
- *evaluative procedures:* improving one's methods of continuous assessment
- *attitudes and values:* encouraging more positive attitudes to work, or modifying pupils' value systems with regard to some aspect of life
- *continuing professional development of teachers:* improving teaching skills, developing new

methods of learning, increasing powers of analysis, of heightening self-awareness
- *management and control:* the gradual introduction of the techniques of behaviour modification
- *administration:* increasing the efficiency of some aspect of the administrative side of school life.

These examples do not mean, however, that action research can be typified straightforwardly; that is to distort its complex and multifaceted nature. Indeed Kemmis (1997) suggests that there are several schools of action research.

Defining action research

The different conceptions of action research can be revealed in some typical definitions of action research, for example Hopkins (1985: 32) suggests that the combination of action and research renders that action a form of disciplined inquiry, in which a personal attempt is made to understand, improve and reform practice. Ebbutt (1985: 156), too, regards action research as a systematic study that combines action and reflection with the intention of improving practice. Cohen and Manion (1994: 186) define it as 'a small-scale intervention in the functioning of the real world and a close examination of the effects of such an intervention' (see http://www.routledge.com/textbooks/9780415368780 – Chapter 14, file 14.1. ppt). The rigour of action research is attested by another of its founding fathers, Corey (1953: 6), who argues that it is a process in which practitioners study problems *scientifically* (our italics) so that they can evaluate, improve and steer decision-making and practice. Indeed Kemmis and McTaggart (1992: 10) argue that 'to do action research is to plan, act, observe and reflect more carefully, more systematically, and more rigorously than one usually does in everyday life'.

A more philosophical stance on action research, that echoes the work of Habermas, is taken by Carr and Kemmis (1986: 162), who regard it as a form of 'self-reflective enquiry' by participants, which is undertaken in order to improve their understanding of their practices in context with a view to maximizing social justice. McNiff (2002: 17) suggests that action researchers support the view that people can 'create their own identities' and that they should allow others to do the same. Grundy (1987: 142) regards action research as concerned with improving the 'social conditions of existence'. Kemmis and McTaggart (1992) suggest that:

> Action research is concerned equally with changing *individuals*, on the one hand, and, on the other, the *culture* of the groups, institutions and societies to which they belong. The culture of a group can be defined in terms of the characteristic substance and forms of the language and discourses, activities and practices, and social relationships and organization which constitute the interactions of the group.
>
> (Kemmis and McTaggart 1992: 16)

Action research is designed to bridge the gap between research and practice (Somekh 1995: 340), thereby striving to overcome the perceived persistent failure of research to impact on, or improve, practice (see also Rapoport 1970: 499; McCormick and James 1988: 339). Stenhouse (1979) suggests that action research should contribute not only to practice but to a theory of education and teaching which is accessible to other teachers, making educational practice more reflective (Elliott 1991: 54).

Action research combines diagnosis, action and reflection (McNiff 2002: 15), focusing on practical issues that have been identified by participants and which are somehow both problematic yet capable of being changed (Elliott 1978: 355–6). Zuber-Skerritt (1996b: 83) suggests that 'the aims of any action research project or programme are to bring about practical improvement, innovation, change or development of social practice, and

the practitioners' better understanding of their practices'.

The several strands of action research are drawn together by Kemmis and McTaggart (1988) in their all-encompassing definition:

> Action research is a form of *collective* self-reflective enquiry undertaken by participants in social situations in order to improve the rationality and justice of the own social or educational practices, as well as their understanding of these practices and the situations in which these practices are carried out. ... The approach is only action research when it is *collaborative*, though it is important to realize that the action research of the group is achieved through the *critically examined action* of individual group members.
>
> (Kemmis and McTaggart 1988: 5)

Kemmis and McTaggart (1992: 21–2) distinguish action research from the everyday actions of teachers:

- It is *not* the usual thinking teachers do when they think about their teaching. Action research is more systematic and collaborative in collecting evidence on which to base rigorous group reflection.
- It is *not* simply problem-solving. Action research involves problem-posing, not just problem-solving. It does not start from a view of 'problems' as pathologies. It is motivated by a quest to improve and understand the world by changing it and learning how to improve it from the effects of the changes made.
- It is *not* research done on other people. Action research is research by particular people on their own work, to help them improve what they do, including how they work with and for others. ...
- Action research is *not* 'the scientific method' applied to teaching. There is not just one view of 'the scientific method'; there are many.

Noffke and Zeichner (1987) make several claims for action research with teachers, namely that it

- brings about changes in their definitions of their professional skills and roles
- increases their feelings of self-worth and confidence

- increases their awareness of classroom issues
- improves their dispositions toward reflection
- changes their values and beliefs
- improves the congruence between practical theories and practices
- broadens their views on teaching, schooling and society.

A significant feature here is that action research lays claim to the professional development of teachers; action research for professional development is a frequently heard maxim (e.g. Nixon 1981; Oja and Smulyan 1989; Somekh 1995: 343; Winter 1996). It is 'situated learning'; learning *in* the workplace and *about* the workplace (Collins and Duguid 1989). The claims for action research, then, are several. Arising from these claims and definitions are several principles.

Principles and characteristics of action research

Hult and Lennung (1980) and McKernan (1991: 32–3) suggest that action research

- makes for practical problem-solving as well as expanding scientific knowledge
- enhances the competencies of participants
- is collaborative
- is undertaken directly *in situ*
- uses feedback from data in an ongoing cyclical process
- seeks to understand particular complex social situations
- seeks to understand the processes of change within social systems
- is undertaken within an agreed framework of ethics
- seeks to improve the quality of human actions
- focuses on those problems that are of immediate concern to practitioners
- is participatory
- frequently uses case study
- tends to avoid the paradigm of research that isolates and controls variables
- is formative, such that the definition of the problem, the aims and methodology may alter during the process of action research

- includes evaluation and reflection
- is methodologically eclectic
- contributes to a science of education
- strives to render the research usable and shareable by participants
- is dialogical and celebrates discourse
- has a critical purpose in some forms
- strives to be emancipatory.

Zuber-Skerritt (1996b) suggests that action research is:

> *critical* (and self-critical) collaborative inquiry by *reflective* practitioners being *accountable* and making results of their enquiry public *self-evaluating* their practice and engaged in *participatory* problem-solving and continuing professional development.
> (Zuber-Skerritt 1996b: 85)

This latter view is echoed in Winter's (1996: 13–14) six key principles of action research:

- *reflexive critique*, which is the process of becoming aware of our own perceptual biases
- *dialectical critique*, which is a way of understanding the relationships between the elements that make up various phenomena in our context
- *collaboration*, which is intended to mean that everyone's view is taken as a contribution to understanding the situation
- *risking disturbance*, which is an understanding of our own taken-for-granted processes and willingness to submit them to critique
- *creating plural structures*, which involves developing various accounts and critiques, rather than a single authoritative interpretation
- *theory and practice internalized*, which is seeing theory and practice as two interdependent yet complementary phases of the change process.

The several features that the definitions at the start of this chapter have in common suggest that action research has key principles. These are summarized by Kemmis and McTaggart (1992: 22–5):

- Action research is an approach to *improving education* by *changing* it and learning from the consequences of changes.

- Action research is *participatory*: it is research through which people work towards the improvement of *their own practices* (and only secondarily on other people's practices).
- Action research develops through *the self-reflective spiral*: a spiral of cycles of *planning*, *acting* (implementing plans), *observing* (systematically), *reflecting* ... and then re-planning, further implementation, observing and reflecting. ...
- Action research is *collaborative*: it involves those responsible for action in improving that action. ...
- Action research establishes *self-critical communities* of people participating and collaborating in all phases of the research process: the planning, the action, the observation and the reflection; it aims to build communities of people committed to *enlightening* themselves about the relationship between circumstance, action and consequence in their own situation, and *emancipating* themselves from the institutional and personal constraints which limit their power to live their own legitimate educational and social values.
- Action research is a *systematic learning process* in which people act deliberately, though remaining open to surprises and responsive to opportunities. ...
- Action research involves people in *theorizing* about their practices – being *inquisitive* about circumstances, action and consequences and coming to *understand* the relationships between circumstances, actions and consequences in their own lives. ...
- Action research requires that people put their practices, ideas and assumptions about institutions to the *test* by gathering *compelling evidence* which could convince them that their previous practices, ideas and assumptions were wrong or wrong-headed.
- Action research is open-minded about what counts as evidence (or data) – it involves not only *keeping records* which describe what is happening as accurately as possible ... but also *collecting and analysing our own judgements,*

reactions and impressions about what is going on.
- Action research involves keeping a *personal journal* in which we record our progress and our reflections about two parallel sets of learning: our learnings about the practices we are studying ... and our learnings about the process (the practice) of studying them. ...
- Action research is a *political process* because it involves us in making changes that will affect others. ...
- Action research involves people in making *critical analyses* of the situations (classrooms, schools, systems) in which they work: these situations are *structured* institutionally. ...
- Action research *starts small*, by working through changes which even a single person (myself) can try, and works towards extensive changes – even critiques of ideas or institutions which in turn might lead to more general reforms of classroom, school or system-wide policies and practices.
- Action research starts with *small cycles* of planning, acting, observing and reflecting which can help to define issues, ideas and assumptions more clearly so that those involved can define more *power questions* for themselves as their work progresses.
- Action research starts with *small groups* of collaborators at the start, but widens the community of participating action researchers so that it gradually includes more and more of those involved and affected by the practices in question.
- Action research allows us to build *records* of our improvements: records of our changing *activities and practices*, records of the changes in the *language and discourse* in which we describe, explain and justify our practices, records of the changes in the *social relationships and forms of organization* which characterize and constrain our practices, and records of the development in mastery of *action research*.
- Action research allows us to give a *reasoned justification* of our educational work to others because we can show how the evidence we

have gathered and the critical reflection we have done have helped us to create a *developed, tested and critically-examined rationale* for what we are doing.

Although these principles find widespread support in the literature on action research, they require some comment. For example, there is a strong emphasis in these principles on action research as a cooperative, collaborative activity (e.g. Hill and Kerber 1967). Kemmis and McTaggart (1992: 6) locate this in the work of Lewin himself, commenting on his commitment to group decision-making. They argue, for example, that

those affected by planned changes have the primary responsibility for deciding on courses of critically informed action which seem likely to lead to improvement, and for evaluating the results of strategies tried out in practice ... *action research is a group activity* [and] *action research is not individualistic.* [To] lapse into individualism is to destroy the critical dynamic of the group.

(Kemmis and McTaggart 1992: 15, italics in original)

The view of action research solely as a group activity, however, might be too restricting. It is possible for action research to be an individualistic matter as well, relating action research to the 'teacher-as-researcher' movement (Stenhouse 1975). Whitehead (1985: 98) explicitly writes about action research in individualistic terms, and we can take this to suggest that a teacher can ask herself or himself : 'What do I see as my problem?' 'What do I see as a possible solution?' 'How can I direct the solution?' 'How can I evaluate the outcomes and take subsequent action?'

The adherence to action research as a group activity derives from several sources. *Pragmatically*, Oja and Smulyan (1989: 14), in arguing for collaborative action research, suggest that teachers are more likely to change their behaviours and attitudes if they have been involved in the research that demonstrates not only the need for such change but also that it can be done – the issue of 'ownership' and 'involvement' that finds its parallel in management literature that suggests that those closest to the problem are

in the best position to identify it and work towards its solution (e.g. Morrison 1998).

Ideologically, there is a view that those experiencing the issue should be involved in decision-making, itself hardly surprising given Lewin's own work with disadvantaged and marginalized groups, i.e. groups with little voice. That there is a coupling of the ideological and political debate here has been brought more up to date with the work of Freire (1970) and Torres (1992: 56) in Latin America, the latter setting out several principles of participatory action research:

- It commences with explicit social and political intentions that articulate with the dominated and poor classes and groups in society.
- It must involve popular participation in the research process, i.e. it must have a social basis.
- It regards knowledge as an agent of social transformation as a whole, thereby constituting a powerful critique of those views of knowledge (theory) as somehow separate from practice.
- Its epistemological base is rooted in critical theory and its critique of the subject/object relations in research.
- It must raise the consciousness of individuals, groups and nations.

Participatory action research does not mean that all participants need be doing the same. This recognizes a role for the researcher as facilitator, guide, formulator and summarizer of knowledge, raiser of issues (e.g. the possible consequences of actions, the awareness of structural conditions) (Weiskopf and Laske 1996: 132–3).

What is being argued here is that action research is a democratic activity (Grundy 1987: 142). This form of democracy is participatory (rather than, for example, representative), a key feature of critical theory (discussed below; see also Aronowitz and Giroux 1986; Giroux 1989). It is not merely a form of change theory, but addresses fundamental issues of power and power relationships, for, in according power to participants, action research is seen as an empowering activity. Elliott (1991: 54) argues that such empowerment has to be at a collective rather than individual level as individuals do not operate is isolation from each other, but they are shaped by organizational and structural forces.

The issue is important, for it begins to separate action research into different camps (Kemmis 1997: 177). On the one hand, are long-time advocates of action research such as Elliott (1978; 1991) who are in the tradition of Joseph Schwab and Donald Schön and who emphasize reflective practice; this is a particularly powerful field of curriculum research with notions of the teacher-as-researcher (Stenhouse 1975) and the reflective practitioner (Schön 1983; 1987). On the other hand are advocates in the 'critical' action research model, e.g. Carr and Kemmis (1986).

Action research as critical praxis

Much of the writing in this field of action research draws on the Frankfurt School of critical theory (discussed in Chapter 1), in particular the work of Habermas. Indeed Weiskopf and Laske (1996: 123) locate action research, in the German tradition, squarely as a 'critical social science'. Using Habermas's (1972, 1974) early writing on knowledge-constitutive interests, a threefold typification of action research can be constructed; the classification was set out in Chapter 1.

Grundy (1987: 154) argues that 'technical' action research is designed to render an existing situation more efficient and effective. In this respect it is akin to Argyris's (1990) notion of 'single-loop learning', being functional, often short term and technical. It is akin to Schön's (1987) notion of 'reflection-in-action' (Morrison 1995a). Elliott (1991: 55) suggests that this view is limiting for action research since it is too individualistic and neglects wider curriculum structures, regarding teachers in isolation from wider factors.

By contrast, 'practical' action research is designed to promote teachers' professionalism by drawing on their informed judgement (Grundy 1987: 154). This underpins the 'teacher-as-researcher' movement, inspired by Stenhouse (1975). It is akin to Schön's (1987) 'reflection-on-action' and is a hermeneutic activity of understanding and interpreting social situations

with a view to their improvement. Echoing this, Kincheloe (2003: 42) suggests that action research rejects positivistic views of rationality, objectivity, truth and methodology, preferring hermeneutic understanding and emancipatory practice. As Kincheloe (2003: 108) says, the teacher-as-researcher movement is a political enterprise rather than the accretion of trivial cookbook remedies – a technical exercise.

Emancipatory action research has an explicit agenda which is as political as is it educational. Grundy (1987) provides a useful introduction to this view. She argues that emancipatory action research seeks to develop in participants their understandings of illegitimate structural and interpersonal constraints that are preventing the exercise of their autonomy and freedom (Grundy 1987: 146–7). These constraints, she argues, are based on illegitimate repression, domination and control. When participants develop a consciousness of these constraints, she suggests, they begin to move from unfreedom and constraint to freedom, autonomy and social justice.

Kincheloe (2003: 138–9) suggests a seven-step process of emancipatory action research:

1   Constructing a system of meaning.
2   Understanding dominant research methods and their effects.
3   Selecting what to study.
4   Acquiring a variety of research strategies.
5   Making sense of information collected.
6   Gaining awareness of the tacit theories and assumptions which guide practice.
7   Viewing teaching as an emancipatory, praxis-based act.

'Praxis' here is defined as action informed through reflection, and with emancipation as its goal.

Action research, then, empowers individuals and social groups to take control over their lives within a framework of the promotion, rather than the suppression of generalizable interests (Habermas 1976). It commences with a challenge to the illegitimate operation of power, hence in some respects (albeit more politicized because it embraces the dimension of power) it is akin to Argyris's (1990) notion of 'double-loop learning' in that it requires participants to question and challenge given value systems. For Grundy (1987), praxis fuses theory and practice within an egalitarian social order, and action research is designed with the political agenda of improvement towards a more just, egalitarian society. This accords to some extent with Lewin's (1946) view that action research leads to equality and cooperation, an end to exploitation and the furtherance of democracy (see also Hopkins 1985: 32; Carr and Kemmis 1986: 163). Zuber-Skerritt (1996a: 3) suggests that

> emancipatory action research ... is collaborative, critical and self-critical inquiry by practitioners ... into a major problem or issue or concern in their own practice. They own the problem and feel responsible and accountable for solving it through teamwork and through following a cyclical process of :
>
> 1 strategic *planning*;
> 2 *action*, i.e. implementing the plan;
> 3 *observation*, evaluation and self-evaluation;
> 4 critical and self-critical *reflection* on the results of points 1–3 and making decisions for the next cycle of action research.
>
> (Zuber-Skerritt 1996a: 3)

Action research, Zuber-Skerrit (1996a: 5) argues, is *emancipatory* when it aims not only at technical and practical improvement and the participants' better understanding, along with transformation and change within the existing boundaries and conditions, but also at changing the system itself or those conditions which impede desired improvement in the system/organization. There is no hierarchy, but open and 'symmetrical communication'.

The emancipatory interest takes very seriously the notion of action researchers as participants in a community of equals. This, in turn, is premised on the later work of Habermas (1984; 1987; 1990) in his notion of the 'ideal speech situation'. Here:

- Action research is construed as reflective practice with a political agenda.
- All participants (and action research is participatory) are equal 'players'.

- Action research is necessarily dialogical – interpersonal – rather than monological (individual).
- Communication is an intrinsic element, with communication being among the community of equals: Grundy and Kemmis (1988: 87) term this 'symmetrical communication'.
- Because it is a community of equals, action research is necessarily democratic and promotes democracy.
- The search is for consensus (and consensus requires more than one participant), hence it requires collaboration and participation.

In this sense emancipatory action research fulfils the requirements of action research set out by Kemmis and McTaggart (1992) above, indeed it could be argued that *only* emancipatory action research (in the threefold typology) has the potential to do this.

Kemmis (1997: 177) suggests that the distinction between the two camps (the reflective practitioners and the critical theorists) lies in their interpretation of action research. For the former, action research is an improvement to professional practice at the local, perhaps classroom level, within the capacities of individuals and the situations in which they are working; for the latter, action research is part of a broader agenda of changing education, changing schooling and changing society.

A key term in action research is 'empowerment'; for the former camp, empowerment is largely a matter of the professional sphere of operations, achieving professional autonomy through professional development. For the latter, empowerment concerns taking control over one's life within a just, egalitarian, democratic society. Whether the latter is realizable or utopian is a matter of critique of this view. Where is the evidence that critical action research either empowers groups or alters the macro-structures of society? Is critical action research socially transformative? At best the jury is out; at worst the jury simply has gone away as capitalism overrides egalitarianism world-wide. The point at issue here is the extent to which the notion of emancipatory action research has attempted to hijack the action research agenda, and whether, in so doing (if it has), it has wrested action research away from practitioners and into the hands of theorists and the academic research community only.

More specifically, several criticisms have been levelled at this interpretation of emancipatory action research (Gibson 1985; Morrison 1995a; 1995b; Somekh 1995; Grundy 1996; McTaggart 1996; Melrose 1996; Webb 1996; Weiskopf and Laske 1996; Kemmis 1997), including the following views:

- It is utopian and unrealizable.
- It is too controlling and prescriptive, seeking to capture and contain action research within a particular mould – it moves towards conformity.
- It adopts a narrow and particularistic view of emancipation and action research, and how to undertake the latter.
- It undermines the significance of the individual teacher-as-researcher in favour of self-critical communities: Kemmis and McTaggart (1992: 152) pose the question 'Why *must* action research consist of a *group* process?'.
- The threefold typification of action research is untenable.
- It assumes that rational consensus is achievable, that rational debate will empower all participants (i.e. it understates the issue of power, wherein the most informed are already the most powerful). Grundy (1996: 111) argues that the better argument derives from the one with the most evidence and reasons, and that these are more available to the powerful, thereby rendering the conditions of equality suspect.
- It overstates the desirability of consensus-oriented research (which neglects the complexity of power).
- Power cannot be dispersed or rearranged simply by rationality.
- Action research as critical theory reduces its practical impact and confines it to the commodification of knowledge in the academy.
- It is uncritical and self-contradicting.

- It will promote conformity through slavish adherence to its orthodoxies.
- It is naïve in its understanding of groups and celebrates groups over individuals, particularly the 'in-groups' rather than the 'out-groups'.
- It privileges its own view of science (rejecting objectivity) and lacks modesty.
- It privileges the authority of critical theory.
- It is elitist while purporting to serve egalitarianism.
- It assumes an undifferentiated view of action research.
- It is attempting to colonize and redirect action research.

This seemingly devastating critique serves to remind the reader that critical action research, even though it has caught the high ground of recent coverage, is highly problematical. It is just as controlling as those controlling agendas that it seeks to attack (Morrison 1995b). Indeed Melrose (1996: 52) suggests that, because critical research is, itself, value laden it abandons neutrality; it has an explicit social agenda that, under the guise of examining values, ethics, morals and politics that are operating in a particular situation, is actually aimed at transforming the status quo.

For a simple introductory exercise for understanding action research see the accompanying web site (http://www.routledge.com/textbooks/9780415368780 – Chapter 14, file 14.1.doc).

Procedures for action research

There are several ways in which the steps of action research have been analysed. One can suggest that action research can be cast into two simple stages: a diagnostic stage in which the problems are analysed and the hypotheses developed; and a therapeutic stage in which the hypotheses are tested by a consciously directed intervention or experiment *in situ*. Lewin (1946; 1948) codified the action research process into four main stages: planning, acting, observing and reflecting.

He suggests that action research commences with a general idea and data are sought about the presenting situation. The successful outcome of this examination is the production of a plan of action to reach an identified objective, together with a decision on the first steps to be taken. Lewin acknowledges that this might involve modifying the original plan or idea. The next stage of implementation is accompanied by ongoing fact-finding to monitor and evaluate the intervention, i.e. to act as a formative evaluation. This feeds forward into a revised plan and set of procedures for implementation, themselves accompanied by monitoring and evaluation. Lewin (1948: 205) suggests that such 'rational social management' can be conceived of as a spiral of planning, action and fact-finding about the outcomes of the actions taken.

The legacy of Lewin's work, though contested (e.g. McTaggart 1996: 248), is powerful in the steps of action research set out by Kemmis and McTaggart (1981):

> In practice, the process begins with a *general idea* that some kind of improvement or change is desirable. In deciding just where to begin in making improvements, one decides on a *field of action* ... where the battle (not the whole war) should be fought. It is a decision on where it is possible to have an impact. The general idea prompts a '*reconnaissance*' of the circumstances of the field, and fact-finding about them. Having decided on the field and made a preliminary reconnaissance, the action researcher decides on a *general plan* of action. Breaking the general plan down into achievable steps, the action researcher settles on the *first action step*. Before taking this first step the action researcher becomes more circumspect, and devises a way of *monitoring* the effects of the first action step. When it is possible to maintain fact-finding by monitoring the action, the first step is taken. As the step is implemented, new data start coming in and the effect of the action can be described and *evaluated*. The general plan is then revised in the light of the new information about the field of action and the second action step can be planned along with appropriate monitoring procedures. The second step is then implemented, monitored and evaluated; and the spiral of action, monitoring, evaluation and replanning continues.
>
> (Kemmis and McTaggart 1981: 2)

McKernan (1991: 17) suggests that Lewin's model of action research is a series of spirals, each of which incorporates a cycle of analysis, reconnaissance, reconceptualization of the problem, planning of the intervention, implementation of the plan, evaluation of the effectiveness of the intervention. Ebbutt (1985) adds to this the view that feedback within and between each cycle is important, facilitating reflection. This is reinforced in the model of action research by Altricher and Gstettner (1993: 343) where, though they have four steps – (1): finding a starting point, (2) clarifying the situation, (3) developing action strategies and putting them into practice, (4) making teachers' knowledge public – they suggest that steps (2) and (3) need not be sequential, thereby avoiding the artificial divide that might exist between data collection, analysis and interpretation.

Zuber-Skerritt (1996b: 84) sets emancipatory (critical) action research into a cyclical process of: '(1) strategic planning, (2) implementing the plan (action), (3) observation, evaluation and self-evaluation, (4) critical and self-critical reflection on the results of (1) – (3) and making decisions for the next cycle of research'. In an imaginative application of action research to organizational change theory she takes the famous work of Lewin (1952) on forcefield analysis and change theory (unfreezing → moving → refreezing) and the work of Beer *et al.* (1990) on task alignment, and sets them into an action research sequence that clarifies the steps of action research very usefully (Box 14.1).

McNiff (2002: 71) sets out an eight-step model of the action research process (see http://www.routledge.com/textbooks/9780415368780 – Chapter 14, file 14.2. ppt):

1 Review your current practice.
2 Identify an aspect that you wish to improve.
3 Imagine a way forward in this.
4 Try it out.
5 Monitor and reflect on what happens.
6 Modify the plan in the light of what has been found, what has happened, and continue.
7 Evaluate the modified action.

Box 14.1

A model of emancipatory action research for organizational change

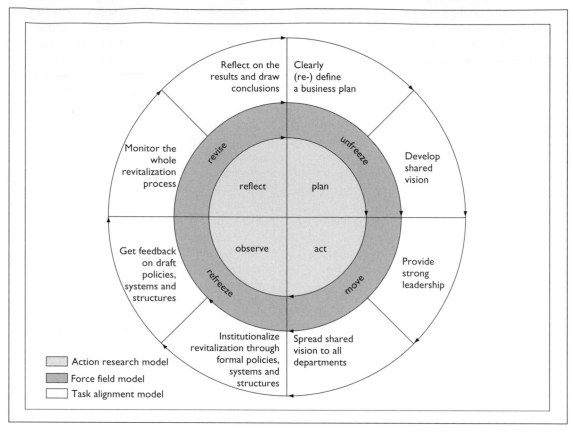

Source: Zuber-Skerritt 1996b: 99

8 Continue until you are satisfied with that aspect of your work (e.g. repeat the cycle).

Sagor (2005: 4) sets out a straightforward four-step model of action research:

1 Clarify vision and targets.
2 Articulate appropriate theory.
3 Implement action and collect data.
4 Reflect on the data and plan informed action.

Another approach is to set out a seven-step model:

1 Decide and agree one common problem that you are experiencing or need that must be addressed.
2 Identify some causes of the problem (need).

3 Brainstorm a range of possible practical solutions to the problem, to address the real problem and the real cause(s).
4 From the range of possible practical solutions decide one of the solutions to the problem, perhaps what you consider to be the most suitable or best solution to the problem. Plan how to put the solution into practice.
5 Identify some 'success criteria' by which you will be able to judge whether the solution has worked to solve the problem, i.e. how will you know whether the proposed solution, when it is put into practice, has been successful. Identify some practical criteria that will tell you how successful the project has been.

6   Put the plan into action; monitor, adjust and evaluate what is taking place.

7   Evaluate the outcome to see how well it has addressed and solved the problem or need, using the success criteria identified in Step 5.

8   Review and plan what needs to be done in light of the evaluation.

The key features of action research here are:

- It works on, and tries to solve real, practitioner-identified problems of everyday practice.
- It is collaborative and builds in teacher involvement.
- It seeks causes and tries to work on those causes.
- The solutions are suggested by the practitioners involved.
- It involves a divergent phase and a convergent phase.
- It plans an intervention by the practitioners themselves.
- It implements the intervention.
- It evaluates the success of the intervention in solving the identified problem.

In our earlier editions we set out an eight-stage process of action research that attempts to draw together the several strands and steps of the action research undertaking. The first stage will involve the identification, evaluation and formulation of the problem perceived as critical in an everyday teaching situation. 'Problem' should be interpreted loosely here so that it could refer to the need to introduce innovation into some aspect of a school's established programme.

The second stage involves preliminary discussion and negotiations among the interested parties – teachers, researchers, advisers, sponsors, possibly – which may culminate in a draft proposal. This may include a statement of the questions to be answered (e.g. 'Under what conditions can curriculum change be best effected?' 'What are the limiting factors in bringing about effective curriculum change?' 'What strong points of action research can be employed to bring about curriculum change?'). The researchers in their capacity as consultants (or sometimes as programme initiators) may draw upon their expertise to bring the problem more into focus, possibly determining causal factors or recommending alternative lines of approach to established ones. This is often the crucial stage for the venture as it is at this point that the seeds of success or failure are planted, for, generally speaking, unless the objectives, purposes and assumptions are made perfectly clear to all concerned, and unless the role of key concepts is stressed (e.g. feedback), the enterprise can easily miscarry.

The third stage may in some circumstances involve a review of the research literature to find out what can be learned from comparable studies, their objectives, procedures and problems encountered.

The fourth stage may involve a modification or redefinition of the initial statement of the problem in the first stage. It may now emerge in the form of a testable hypothesis, or as a set of guiding objectives. Sometimes change agents deliberately decide against the use of objectives on the grounds that they have a constraining effect on the process itself. It is also at this stage that assumptions underlying the project are made explicit (e.g. in order to effect curriculum changes, the attitudes, values, skills and objectives of the teachers involved must be changed).

The fifth stage may be concerned with the selection of research procedures – sampling, administration, choice of materials, methods of teaching and learning, allocation of resources and tasks, deployment of staff and so on.

The sixth stage will be concerned with the choice of the evaluation procedures to be used and will need to take into consideration that evaluation in this context will be continuous.

The seventh stage embraces the implementation of the project itself (over varying periods of time). It will include the conditions and methods of data collection (e.g. fortnightly meetings, the keeping of records, interim reports, final reports, the submission of self-evaluation and group-evaluation reports, etc.), the monitoring of tasks and the transmission of feedback to the research team, and the classification and analysis of data.

The eighth and final stage will involve the interpretation of the data; inferences to be drawn;

and overall evaluation of the project (see Woods 1989). Discussions on the findings will take place in the light of previously agreed evaluative criteria. Errors, mistakes and problems will be considered. A general summing-up may follow this in which the outcomes of the project are reviewed, recommendations made, and arrangements for dissemination of results to interested parties decided.

As we stressed, this is a basic framework; much activity of an incidental and possibly *ad hoc* nature will take place in and around it. This may comprise discussions among teachers, researchers and pupils; regular meetings among teachers or schools to discuss progress and problems, and to exchange information; possibly regional conferences; and related activities, all enhanced by the range of current hardware and software.

Hopkins (1985), McNiff (1988), Edwards (1990) and McNiff *et al.* (1996) offer much practical advice on the conduct of action research, including 'getting started', operationalization, planning, monitoring and documenting the intervention, collecting data and making sense of them, using case studies, evaluating the action research, ethical issues and reporting. We urge readers to go to these helpful sources. These are essentially both introductory sources and manuals for practice. McNiff (2002: 85–91) provides useful advice for novice action researchers:

- Stay small, stay focused.
- Identify a clear research question.
- Be realistic about what you can do; be aware that wider change begins with you.
- Plan carefully.
- Set a realistic time scale.
- Involve others (as participants, observers, validators – including critical friends – potential researchers).
- Ensure good ethical practice.
- Concentrate on learning, not on the outcomes of action.
- The focus of the research is you, in company with others.
- Beware of happy endings.
- Be aware of political issues.

McNiff (2002: 98) makes the point that it is important to set evaluative criteria. Without success criteria it is impossible for the researcher to know whether, or how far, the action research has been successful. Action researchers could ask themselves, 'How will we know whether we have been successful?'

Kemmis and McTaggart (1992: 25-7) offer a useful series of observations for beginning action research:

- Get an action research group together and *participate* yourself – be a model learner about action research.
- Be content to start to work with a *small group*.
- *Get organized.*
- *Start small.*
- *Establish a time line.*
- Arrange for *supportive work-in-progress discussions* in the action research group.
- Be tolerant and supportive – expect people to learn from experience.
- Be persistent about monitoring.
- Plan for a long haul on the bigger issues of changing classroom practices and school structures.
- Work to involve (in the research process) those who are involved (in the action), so that they share responsibility for the whole action research process.
- Remember that *how you think about things* – the language and understandings that shape your action – may need changing just as much as the specifics of what you do.
- *Register progress* not only with the participant group but also with the whole staff and other interested people.
- If necessary arrange *legitimizing rituals* – involving consultants or other outsiders.
- Make time to *write* throughout your project.
- Be explicit about what you have achieved by *reporting progress.*
- Throughout, keep in mind *the distinction between education and schooling.*
- Throughout, ask yourself whether your action research project is helping you (and those with whom you work) to improve the extent to

which you are *living your educational values.* (italics in original)

It is clear from this list that action research is a blend of practical and theoretical concerns; it is both action and research.

In conducting action research the participants can be both methodologically eclectic and can use a variety of instruments for data collection: questionnaires, diaries, interviews, case studies, observational data, experimental design, field notes, photography, audio and video recording, sociometry, rating scales, biographies and accounts, documents and records, in short the full *gamut* of techniques (for a discussion of these see Hopkins 1985; McKernan 1991; see also Chapters 7–21 in our own book here).

Additionally a useful way of managing to gain a focus within a group of action researchers is through the use of Nominal Group Technique (Morrison 1993). The administration is straightforward and is useful for gathering information in a single instance. In this approach one member of the group provides the group with a series of questions, statements or issues. A four-stage model can be adopted:

1   A short time is provided for individuals to write down without interruption or discussion with anybody else their own answers, views, reflections and opinions in response to questions/statements/issues provided by the group leader (e.g. problems of teaching or organizing such-and-such, or an identification of issues in the organization of a piece of the curriculum etc.).

2   The responses are entered onto a sheet of paper which is then displayed for others to view. The leader invites *individual* comments on the displayed responses to the questions/statements/issue, but no group discussion, i.e. the data collection is still at an individual level, and then notes these comments on the display sheet on which the responses have been collected. The process of inviting individual comments/contributions which are then displayed for everyone to

see is repeated until no more comments are received.

3   At this point the leader asks the respondents to identify *clusters* of displayed comments and responses, i.e. to put some structure, order and priority into the displayed items. It is here that control of proceedings moves from the leader to the participants. A group discussion takes place since a process of clarification of meanings and organizing issues and responses into coherent and cohesive bundles is required which then moves to the identification of priorities.

4   Finally the leader invites any further group discussion about the material and its organization.

The process of the Nominal Group Technique enables individual responses to be included within a group response, i.e. the individual's contribution to the group delineation of significant issues is maintained. This technique is very useful in gathering data from individuals and putting them into some order which is shared by the group (and action research is largely, though not exclusively, a group matter), e.g. of priority, of similarity and difference, of generality and specificity. It also enables individual disagreements to be registered and to be built into the group responses and identification of significant issues to emerge. Further, it gives equal status to all respondents in the situation, for example, the voice of the new entrant to the teaching profession is given equal consideration to the voice of the headteacher of several years' experience. The attraction of this process is that it balances writing with discussion, a divergent phase with a convergent phase, space for individual comments and contributions to group interaction. It is a useful device for developing collegiality. All participants have a voice and are heard.

The written partner to the Nominal Group Technique is the Delphi technique. This has the advantage that it does not *require* participants to meet together as a whole group. This is particularly useful in institutions where time is precious and where it is difficult to arrange a whole group meeting. The process of data collection resembles that of the Nominal Group Technique in many respects: it can be set out in a three-stage process:

1   The leader asks participants to respond to a series of questions and statements in writing. This may be done on an individual basis or on a small group basis – which enables it to be used flexibly, e.g. within a department, within an age phase.

2   The leader collects the written responses and collates them into clusters of issues and responses (maybe providing some numerical data on frequency of response). This analysis is then passed back to the respondents for comment, further discussion and identification of issues, responses and priorities. At this stage the respondents are presented with a *group response* (which may reflect similarities or record differences) and the respondents are asked to react to this *group response*. By adopting this procedure the individual has the opportunity to agree with the group response (i.e. to move from a possibly small private individual disagreement to a general group agreement) or to indicate a more substantial disagreement with the group response.

3   This process is repeated as many times as it is necessary. In saying this, however, the leader will need to identify the most appropriate place to stop the recirculation of responses. This might be done at a group meeting which, it is envisaged, will be the plenary session for the participants, i.e. an endpoint of data collection will be in a whole group forum.

By presenting the group response back to the participants, there is a general progression in the technique towards a polarizing of responses, i.e. a clear identification of areas of consensus and dissensus (and emancipatory action research strives for consensus). The Delphi technique brings advantages of clarity, privacy, voice and collegiality. In doing so it engages the issues of confidentiality, anonymity and disclosure of relevant information while protecting participants' rights to privacy. It is a very useful means of undertaking behind-the-scenes data collection which can then be brought to a whole group meeting; the price that this exacts is that the leader has much more work to do in collecting, synthesizing, collating, summarizing, prioritizing and recirculating data than in the Nominal Group Technique, which is immediate. As participatory techniques both the Nominal Group Technique and Delphi techniques are valuable for data collection and analysis in action research.

Reflexivity in action research

The analysis so far has made much of the issue of reflection, be it reflection-in-action, reflection-on-action, or critical reflection (Morrison 1995a). Reflection, it has been argued, occurs at every stage of action research. Beyond this, the notion of *reflexivity* is central to action research, because the researchers are also the participants and practitioners in the action research – they are part of the social world that they are studying (Hammersley and Atkinson 1983: 14). Hall (1996: 29) suggests that reflexivity is an integral element and epistemological basis of emancipatory action research because it takes as its basis the view of the construction of knowledge in which data are authentic and reflect the experiences of all participants, democratic relations exist between all participants in the research, and the researcher's views (which may be theory-laden) do not hold precedence over the views of participants.

What is being required in the notion of reflexivity is a self-conscious awareness of the effects that the participants-as-practitioners-and-researchers are having on the research process, how their values, attitudes, perceptions, opinions, actions, feelings etc. are feeding into the situation being studied (akin, perhaps, to the notion of counter-transference in counselling). The participants-as-practitioners-and-researchers need to apply to themselves the same critical scrutiny that they are applying to others and to the research. This issue is discussed in Chapter 7.

Some practical and theoretical matters

Much has been made in this chapter of the democratic principles that underpin a considerable amount of action research. The ramifications of this are several. For example, there must be a free flow of information between participants and communication must be extensive (Elliott 1978: 356) and communication must be open, unconstrained and unconstraining – the force of the better argument in Habermas's 'ideal speech situation'. That this might be problematic in some organizations has been noted by Holly (1984: 100), as action research and schools are often structured differently, schools being hierarchical, formal and bureaucratic while action research is collegial, informal, open, collaborative and crosses formal boundaries. In turn this suggests that, for action research to be successful, the conditions of collegiality have to be present, for example (Morrison 1998: 157-8):

- participatory approaches to decision-making
- democratic and consensual decision-making
- shared values, beliefs and goals
- equal rights of participation in discussion
- equal rights to determine policy
- equal voting rights on decisions
- the deployment of subgroups who are accountable to the whole group
- shared responsibility and open accountability
- an extended view of expertise
- judgements and decisions based on the power of the argument rather than the positions power of the advocates
- shared ownership of decisions and practices.

It is interesting, perhaps, that these features, de-rived from management theory, can apply so well to action research – action research nests comfortably within certain management styles. Indeed Zuber-Skerritt (1996b: 90) suggests that the main barriers to emancipatory action research are:

- single-loop learning (rather than double-loop learning: Argyris 1990)
- overdependence on experts or seniors to the extent that independent thought and expression are stifled

- an orientation to efficiency rather than to research and development (one might add here 'rather than to reflection and problem posing')
- a preoccupation with operational rather than strategic thinking and practice.

Zuber-Skerritt (1996a: 17) suggests four practical problems that action researchers might face:

- How can we formulate a method of work which is sufficiently economical as regards the amount of data gathering and data processing for a practitioner to undertake it alongside a normal workload, over a limited time scale?
- How can action research techniques be sufficiently specific that they enable a small-scale investigation by a practitioner to lead to genuinely new insights, and avoid being accused of being either too minimal to be valid, or too elaborate to be feasible?
- How can these methods, given the above, be readily available and accessible to anyone who wishes to practise them, building on the competencies which practitioners already possess?
- How can these methods contribute a genuine improvement of understanding and skill, beyond prior competence, in return for the time and energy expended – that is, a more rigorous process than that which characterizes positivist research?

Zuber-Skerritt (1996a) also suggests that the issue of the audience of action research reports is problematic:

The answer to the question 'who are action research reports written for?' is that there are three audiences – each of equal importance. One audience comprises those colleagues with whom we have collaborated in carrying out the research reported. . . . It is important to give equal importance to the second audience. These are interested colleagues in other institutions, or in other areas of the same institution, for whom the underlying structure of the work presented may be similar to situations in which they work. . . . But the third, and perhaps most important audience, is ourselves. The process of writing involves clarifying and exploring ideas and interpretations.

(Zuber-Skerritt 1996a: 26)

We have already seen that the participants in a change situation may be either a teacher, a group of teachers working internally, or else teachers and researchers working on a collaborative basis. It is this last category, where action research brings together two professional bodies each with its own objectives and values, that we shall consider further at this point because of its inherent problematic nature. Both parties share the same interest in an educational problem, yet their respective orientations to it differ. It has been observed (e.g. Halsey 1972) that research values precision, control, replication and attempts to generalize from specific events. Teaching, on the other hand, is concerned with action, with doing things, and translates generalizations into specific acts. The incompatibility between action and research in these respects, therefore, can be a source of problems (Marris and Rein 1967).

Another issue of some consequence concerns headteachers' and teachers' attitudes to the possibility of change as a result of action research. Hutchinson and Whitehouse (1986), for example, having monitored teachers' efforts to form collaborative groups within their schools, discovered one source of difficulty to be resistance not only from heads but also, and in their view more importantly, from some teachers themselves to the action researcher's efforts to have them scrutinize individual and social practice, possibly with a view to changing it, e.g. in line with the headteacher's policies.

Finally, Winter (1982) draws attention to the problem of interpreting data in action research. He writes:

The action research/case study tradition does have a methodology for the *creation* of data, but not (as yet) for the interpretation of data. We are shown how the descriptive journal, the observer's field notes, and the open-ended interview are utilized to create accounts of events which will *confront* the practitioner's current pragmatic assumptions and

definitions; we are shown the potential value of this process (in terms of increasing teachers' sensitivity) and the problem it poses for individual and collective professional equilibrium. What we are *not* shown is *how* the teacher can or should handle the data thus collected.

(Winter 1982)

The problem for Winter (1982) is how to carry out an interpretive analysis of restricted data, that is, data which can make no claim to be generally representative. In other words, the problem of validity cannot be sidestepped by arguing that the contexts are unique.

Conclusion

Action research has been seen as a significant vehicle for empowering teachers, though this chapter has questioned the extent of this. As a research device it combines six notions:

- a straightforward cycle of identifying a problem, planning an intervention, implementing the intervention, evaluating the outcome
- reflective practice
- political emancipation
- critical theory
- professional development
- participatory practitioner research.

It is a flexible, situationally responsive methodology that offers rigour, authenticity and voice. That said, this chapter has tried to expose both the attractions and problematic areas of action research. In its thrust towards integrating action and research one has to question whether this is an optimistic way of ensuring that research impacts on practice for improvement, or whether it is a recessive hybrid.

There are several important web sites for action research:

1 *Action Research International* (journal): http://www.scu.edu.au/schools/gcm/ar/ari/arihome.html
2 Action research net: http://www.actionresearch.net

3   Action research resources: http://carbon.cudenver. edu/~mryder/itc_data/act_res.html

4   Action research resources: http://www.scu. edu.au/schools/gcm/ar/arhome.html

5   *ARexpeditions* (journal): http://www.arexpeditions. montana.edu/docs/about.html

6   CEL centre for action research: http://www.celt.stir. ac.uk/resources/research/action-research-resources.html

7   Centre for Action Research in Professional Practice (CARPP): http://www.bath.ac.uk/carpp/

8   Centre for Applied Research in Education (CARE): http://www.uea.ac.uk/care/

9   *Educational Action Research* (journal): http://www. triangle.co.uk/ear/

10   Other home pages: http://www.bath.ac.uk/~edsajw /otherpages.shtml

11   Parnet (Participative Action Research Network at Cornell University): http://www.parnet.org/

12   University of Colorado action research site: http://carbon.cudenver.edu/~mryder/reflect/ act_res.html

Chapter 14

Part Four

Strategies for data collection and researching

This part of the book moves to a closer-grained account of instruments for collecting data, how they can be used, and how they can be constructed. We identify seven main kinds of data collection instruments, with many variants included in each. We have expanded on our discussion of these from the previous editions, particularly in respect of questionnaire design and interviews. The intention of this part is to enable researchers to decide on the most appropriate instruments for data collection, and to design such instruments. The strengths and weaknesses of these instruments are set out, so that decisions on their suitability and the criterion of *fitness for purpose* can be addressed. Hence this part not only introduces underlying principles of instruments, but also offers sound, tested, practical advice for their usage. This is intended to enable researchers to gather useful and usable data.

15 Questionnaires

Introduction

The field of questionnaire design is vast. This chapter provides a straightforward introduction to its key elements, indicating the main issues to be addressed, some important problematical considerations and how they can be resolved. The chapter follows a sequence in designing a questionnaire that, it is hoped, will be useful for researchers. The serial order is:

- ethical issues
- approaching the planning of a questionnaire
  - operationalizing the questionnaire
  - structured, semi-structured and unstructured questionnaires
- types of questionnaire items
  - closed and open questions compared
  - scales of data
  - the dangers of assuming knowledge or viewpoints
  - dichotomous questions
  - multiple choice questions
  - rank ordering
  - rating scales
  - constant sum questions
  - ratio data questions
  - open-ended questions
  - matrix questions
  - contingency questions, filters and branches
- asking sensitive questions
- avoiding pitfalls in question writing
- sequencing the questions
- questionnaires containing few verbal items
- the layout of the questionnaire
- covering letters or sheets and follow-up letters
- piloting the questionnaire
- practical considerations in questionnaire design

- administering questionnaires
  - self-administered questionnaires
  - postal questionnaires
- processing questionnaire data.

It is suggested that researchers may find it useful to work through these issues in sequence, though, clearly, a degree of recursion is desirable.

The questionnaire is a widely used and useful instrument for collecting survey information, providing structured, often numerical data, being able to be administered without the presence of the researcher, and often being comparatively straightforward to analyse (Wilson and McLean 1994). These attractions have to be counterbalanced by the time taken to develop, pilot and refine the questionnaire, by the possible unsophistication and limited scope of the data that are collected, and from the likely limited flexibility of response (though, as Wilson and McLean (1994: 3) observe, this can frequently be an attraction). The researcher will have to judge the appropriateness of using a questionnaire for data collection, and, if so, what kind of questionnaire it should be.

Ethical issues

The questionnaire will always be an intrusion into the life of the respondent, be it in terms of time taken to complete the instrument, the level of threat or sensitivity of the questions, or the possible invasion of privacy. Questionnaire respondents are not passive data providers for researchers; they are subjects not objects of research. There are several sequiturs that flow from this.

Respondents cannot be coerced into completing a questionnaire. They might be strongly encouraged, but the decision whether to become involved and when to withdraw from the research is entirely theirs. Their involvement in the research is likely to be a function of the following factors:

- Their *informed consent* (see Chapter 2 on the ethics of educational research).
- Their *rights to withdraw* at any stage or *not to complete* particular items in the questionnaire.
- The potential of the research to improve their situation (the issue of *beneficence*).
- The guarantees that the research will not harm them (the issue of *non-maleficence*).
- The guarantees of *confidentiality*, *anonymity* and *non-traceability* in the research.
- The degree of *threat* or *sensitivity* of the questions, which may lead to respondents' over-reporting or under-reporting (Sudman and Bradburn 1982: 32 and Chapter 3).
- Factors in the questionnaire itself (e.g. its coverage of issues, its ability to catch what respondents want to say rather than to promote the researcher's agenda), i.e. the avoidance of bias and the assurance of validity and reliability in the questionnaire – the issues of *methodological rigour and fairness*. Methodological rigour is an ethical not simply a technical matter (Morrison 1996c), and respondents have a right to expect reliability and validity.
- The *reactions* of the respondent, for example, respondents will react if they consider an item to be offensive, intrusive, misleading, biased, misguided, irritating, inconsiderate, impertinent or abstruse.

These factors impact on every stage of the use of a questionnaire, to suggest that attention has to be given to the questionnaire itself, the approaches that are made to the respondents, the explanations that are given to the respondents, the data analysis and the data reporting.

Approaching the planning of a questionnaire

At this preliminary stage of design, it can sometimes be helpful to use a flow chart technique to plan the sequencing of questions. In this way, researchers are able to anticipate the type and range of responses that their questions are likely to elicit. In Box 15.1 we illustrate a flow chart employed in a commercial survey based upon an interview schedule, although the application of the method to a self-completion questionnaire is self-evident.

On a more positive note, Sellitz and her associates (1976) have provided a fairly exhaustive guide to researchers in constructing their questionnaires which we summarize in Box 15.2 (see http://www.routledge.com/textbooks/9780415368780 – Chapter 15, file 15.1. ppt).

These are introductory issues, and the remainder of this chapter takes each of these and unpacks them in greater detail. Additionally, one can set out a staged sequence for planning a questionnaire, thus:

1 Decide the purposes/objectives of the questionnaire.
2 Decide the population and the sample (as questions about their characteristics will need to be included on the questionnaire under 'personal details').
3 Generate the topics/constructs/concepts/issues to be addressed and data required in order to meet the objectives of the research (this can be done from literature, or a pre-pilot, for example, focus groups and semi-structured interviews).
4 Decide the kinds of measures/scales/questions /responses required.
5 Write the questionnaire items.
6 Check that each issue from (3) has been addressed, using several items for each issue.
7 Pilot the questionnaire and refine items as a consequence.
8 Administer the final questionnaire.

Within these stages there are several sub-components, and this chapter addresses these.

Operationalizing the questionnaire

The process of operationalizing a questionnaire is to take a general purpose or set of purposes and turn these into concrete, researchable fields about which actual data can be gathered. First, a questionnaire's general purposes must be clarified

Box 15.1
A flow chart technique for question planning

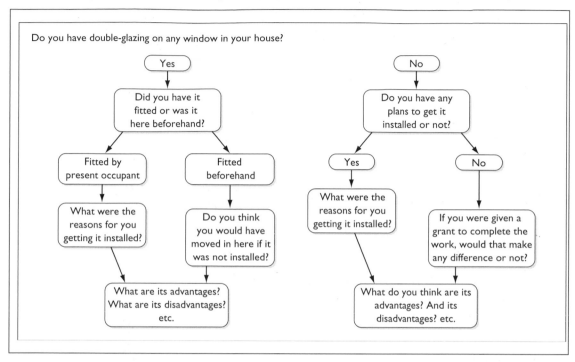

Source: Social and Community Planning Research 1972

and then translated into a specific, concrete aim or set of aims. Thus, 'to explore teachers' views about in-service work' is somewhat nebulous, whereas 'to obtain a detailed description of primary and secondary teachers' priorities in the provision of in-service education courses' is reasonably specific.

Having decided upon and specified the primary objective of the questionnaire, the second phase of the planning involves the identification and itemizing of subsidiary topics that relate to its central purpose. In our example, subsidiary issues might well include the types of courses required, the content of courses, the location of courses, the timing of courses, the design of courses, and the financing of courses.

The third phase follows the identification and itemization of subsidiary topics and involves formulating specific information requirements relating to each of these issues. For example, with

respect to the type of courses required, detailed information would be needed about the duration of courses (one meeting, several meetings, a week, a month, a term or a year), the status of courses (non-award bearing, award bearing, with certificate, diploma, degree granted by college or university), the orientation of courses (theoretically oriented involving lectures, readings, etc., or practically oriented involving workshops and the production of curriculum materials).

What we have in the example, then, is a move from a generalized area of interest or purpose to a very specific set of features about which direct data can be gathered. Wilson and McLean (1994: 8–9) suggest an alternative approach which is to identify the research problem, then to clarify the relevant concepts or constructs, then to identify what kinds of measures (if appropriate) or empirical indicators there are of these, i.e. the kinds of data required to give the researcher relevant evidence about the

Box 15.2

A guide for questionnaire construction

A *Decisions about question content*

1 Is the question necessary? Just how will it be useful?
2 Are several questions needed on the subject matter of this question?
3 Do respondents have the information necessary to answer the question?
4 Does the question need to be more concrete, specific and closely related to the respondent's personal experience?
5 Is the question content sufficiently general and free from spurious concreteness and specificity?
6 Do the replies express general attitudes and only seem to be as specific as they sound?
7 Is the question content biased or loaded in one direction, without accompanying questions to balance the emphasis?
8 Will the respondents give the information that is asked for?

B *Decisions about question wording*

1 Can the question be misunderstood? Does it contain difficult or unclear phraseology?
2 Does the question adequately express the alternative with respect to the point?
3 Is the question misleading because of unstated assumptions or unseen implications?
4 Is the wording biased? Is it emotionally loaded or slanted towards a particular kind of answer?
5 Is the question wording likely to be objectionable to the respondent in any way?
6 Would a more personalized wording of the question produce better results?
7 Can the question be better asked in a more direct or a more indirect form?

C *Decisions about form of response to the question*

1 Can the question best be asked in a form calling for check answer (or short answer of a word or two, or a number), free answer or check answer with follow-up answer?
2 If a check answer is used, which is the best type for this question – dichotomous, multiple-choice ('cafeteria' question), or scale?
3 If a checklist is used, does it cover adequately all the significant alternatives without overlapping and in a defensible order? Is it of reasonable length? Is the wording of items impartial and balanced?
4 Is the form of response easy, definite, uniform and adequate for the purpose?

D *Decisions about the place of the question in the sequence*

1 Is the answer to the question likely to be influenced by the content of preceding questions?
2 Is the question led up to in a natural way? Is it in correct psychological order?
3 Does the question come too early or too late from the point of view of arousing interest and receiving sufficient attention, avoiding resistance, and so on?

Source: Sellitz *et al.* 1976

concepts or constructs, e.g. their presence, their intensity, their main features and dimensions, their key elements etc.

What unites these two approaches is their recognition of the need to ensure that the questionnaire:

- is clear on its purposes
- is clear on what needs to be included or covered in the questionnaire in order to meet the purposes
- is exhaustive in its coverage of the elements of inclusion
- asks the most appropriate *kinds* of question (discussed below)

- elicits the most appropriate *kinds* of data to answer the research purposes and sub-questions
- asks for empirical data.

Structured, semi-structured and unstructured questionnaires

Although there is a large range of types of questionnaire, there is a simple rule of thumb: the larger the size of the sample, the more structured, closed and numerical the questionnaire may have to be, and the smaller the size of the sample, the less structured, more open and word-based the questionnaire may be.

The researcher can select several types of questionnaire, from highly structured to unstructured.

If a closed and structured questionnaire is used, enabling patterns to be observed and comparisons to be made, then the questionnaire will need to be piloted and refined so that the final version contains as full a range of possible responses as can be reasonably foreseen. Such a questionnaire is heavy on time early in the research; however, once the questionnaire has been set up, then the mode of analysis might be comparatively rapid. For example, it may take two or three months to devise a survey questionnaire, pilot it, refine it and set it out in a format that will enable the data to be processed and statistics to be calculated. However, the trade-off from this is that the data analysis can be undertaken fairly rapidly. We already know the response categories, the nature of the data and the statistics to be used; it is simply a matter of processing the data – often using computer analysis.

It is perhaps misleading to describe a questionnaire as being 'unstructured', as the whole devising of a questionnaire requires respondents to adhere to some form of given structure. That said, between a completely open questionnaire that is akin to an open invitation to 'write what one wants' and a completely closed, completely structured questionnaire, there is the powerful tool of the semi-structured questionnaire. Here a series of questions, statements or items are presented and the respondents are asked to answer, respond to or comment on them in a way that they think best. There is a clear structure, sequence and focus, but the format is open-ended, enabling respondents to reply in their own terms. The semi-structured questionnaire sets the agenda but does not presuppose the nature of the response.

Types of questionnaire items

Closed and open questions compared

There are several kinds of question and response modes in questionnaires, including, for example, dichotomous questions, multiple choice questions, rating scales, constant sum questions, ratio data and open-ended questions. These are considered below (see also Wilson 1996). Closed questions prescribe the range of responses from which the respondent may choose. Highly structured, closed questions are useful in that they can generate frequencies of response amenable to statistical treatment and analysis. They also enable comparisons to be made across groups in the sample (Oppenheim 1992: 115). They are quicker to code up and analyse than word-based data (Bailey 1994: 118) and, often, they are directly to the point and deliberately more focused than open-ended questions. Indeed it would be almost impossible, as well as unnecessary, to try to process vast quantities of word-based data in a short time frame.

If a site-specific case study is required, then qualitative, less structured, word-based and open-ended questionnaires may be more appropriate as they can capture the specificity of a particular situation. Where measurement is sought then a quantitative approach is required; where rich and personal data are sought, then a word-based qualitative approach might be more suitable. Open-ended questions are useful if the possible answers are unknown or the questionnaire is exploratory (Bailey 1994: 120), or if there are so many possible categories of response that a closed question would contain an extremely long list of options. They also enable respondents to answer as much as they wish, and are particularly suitable for investigating complex issues, to which simple answers cannot be provided. Open questions may be useful for generating items that will subsequently become the stuff of closed questions in a subsequent questionnaire (i.e. a pre-pilot).

In general closed questions (dichotomous, multiple choice, constant sum and rating scales) are quick to complete and straightforward to code (e.g. for computer analysis), and do not discriminate unduly on the basis of how articulate respondents are (Wilson and McLean 1994: 21). On the other hand, they do not enable respondents to add any remarks, qualifications and explanations to the categories, and there is a risk that the categories might not be exhaustive and that there might be bias in them (Oppenheim 1992: 115).

Open questions enable participants to write a free account in their own terms, to explain and qualify their responses and avoid the limitations of pre-set categories of response. On the other hand, open questions can lead to irrelevant and redundant information; they may be too open-ended for the respondent to know what *kind* of information is being sought; they may require much more time from the respondent to enter a response (thereby leading to refusal to complete the item), and they may make the questionnaire appear long and discouraging. With regard to analysis, the data are not easily compared across participants, and the responses are difficult to code and to classify (see http://www.routledge.com/textbooks/9780415368780 – Chapter 15, file 15.2. ppt).

We consider in more detail below the different kinds of closed and open questions.

Scales of data

The questionnaire designer will need to choose the metric – the scale of data – to be adopted. This concerns numerical data, and we advise readers to turn to Part Five for an analysis of the different scales of data that can be gathered (nominal, ordinal, interval and ratio) and the different statistics that can be used for analysis. Nominal data indicate categories; ordinal data indicate order ('high' to 'low', 'first' to 'last', 'smallest' to 'largest', 'strongly disagree' to 'strongly agree', 'not at all' to 'a very great deal'); ratio data indicate continuous values and a true zero (e.g. marks in a test, number of attendances per year) (see http://www.routledge.com/textbooks/9780415368780 – Chapter 15, file 15.3. ppt). These are presented thus:

Question type	Level of data
Dichotomous questions	Nominal
Multiple choice questions	Nominal
Rank ordering	Ordinal
Rating scales	Ordinal
Constant sum questions	Ordinal
Ratio data questions	Ratio
Open-ended questions	Word-based data

The dangers of assuming knowledge or viewpoints

There is often an assumption that respondents will have the information or have an opinion about the matters in which researchers are interested. This is a dangerous assumption. It is particularly a problem when administering questionnaires to children, who may write anything rather than nothing. This means that the opportunity should be provided for respondents to indicate that they have no opinion, or that they don't know the answer to a particular question, or to state that they feel the question does not apply to them. This is frequently a matter in surveys of customer satisfaction in social science, where respondents are asked, for example, to answer a host of questions about the services provided by utility companies (electricity, gas, water, telephone) about which they have no strong feelings, and, in fact, they are only interested in whether the service is uninterrupted, reliable, cheap, easy to pay for, and that their complaints are solved.

There is also the issue of choice of vocabulary and the concepts and information behind them. It is essential that, regardless of the type of question asked, the language and the concepts behind the language should be within the grasp of the respondents. Simply because the researcher is interested in, and has a background in, a particular topic is no guarantee that the respondents will be like minded. The effect of the questionnaire on the respondent has to be considered carefully.

Dichotomous questions

A highly structured questionnaire will ask closed questions. These can take several forms. *Dichotomous* questions require a 'yes'/'no' response, e.g. 'Have you ever had to appear in court?', 'Do you prefer didactic methods to child-centred methods?' (see http://www.routledge.com/textbooks/9780415368780 – Chapter 15, file 15.4. ppt). The layout of a dichotomous question can be thus:

Sex(please tick) :   Male ☐   Female ☐

The dichotomous question is useful, for it compels respondents to come off the fence on an issue. It provides a clear, unequivocal response. Further, it is possible to code responses quickly, there being only two categories of response. A dichotomous question is also useful as a funnelling or sorting device for subsequent questions, for example: 'If you answered "yes" to question X, please go to question Y; if you answered "no" to question X, please go to question Z' (see the section below on contingency questions). Sudman and Bradburn (1982: 89) suggest that if dichotomous questions are being used, then it is desirable to use several to gain data on the same topic, in order to reduce the problems of respondents' 'guessing' answers.

On the other hand, the researcher must ask, for instance, whether a 'yes'/'no' response actually provides any useful information. Requiring respondents to make a 'yes'/'no' decision may be inappropriate; it might be more appropriate to have a range of responses, for example in a rating scale. There may be comparatively few complex or subtle questions which can be answered with a simple 'yes' or 'no'. A 'yes' or a 'no' may be inappropriate for a situation whose complexity is better served by a series of questions which catch that complexity. Further, Youngman (1984: 163) suggests that it is a natural human tendency to agree with a statement rather than to disagree with it; this suggests that a simple dichotomous question might build in respondent bias. Indeed people may be more reluctant to agree with a negative statement than to disagree with a positive question (Weems *et al.* 2003).

In addition to dichotomous questions ('yes'/'no' questions) a piece of research might ask for information about dichotomous variables, for example gender (male/female), type of school (elementary/secondary), type of course (vocational/non-vocational). In these cases only one of two responses can be selected. This enables nominal data to be gathered, which can then be processed using the chi-square statistic, the binomial test, the G-test and cross-tabulations (see Cohen and Holliday (1996) for examples). Dichotomous questions are treated as nominal data (see Part Five).

Multiple choice questions

To try to gain some purchase on complexity, the researcher can move towards *multiple choice questions*, where the range of choices is designed to capture the likely range of responses to given statements (see http://www.routledge.com/textbooks/9780415368780 – Chapter 15, file 15.5. ppt). For example, the researcher might ask a series of questions about a new chemistry scheme in the school; a statement precedes a set of responses thus:

The New Intermediate Chemistry Education (NICE) is:

(a) a waste of time
(b) an extra burden on teachers
(c) not appropriate to our school
(d) a useful complementary scheme
(e) a useful core scheme throughout the school
(f) well-presented and practicable.

The categories would have to be discrete (i.e. having no overlap and being mutually exclusive) and would have to exhaust the possible range of responses. Guidance would have to be given on the completion of the multiple-choice, clarifying, for example, whether respondents are able to tick only *one* response (a *single answer* mode) or *several* responses (*multiple answer* mode) from the list. Like dichotomous questions, multiple choice questions can be quickly coded and quickly aggregated to give frequencies of response. If that is appropriate for the research, then this might be a useful instrument.

The layout of a multiple choice question can be thus:

Number of years in teaching   1–5 ☐   6–14 ☐
                               15–24 ☐   25+ ☐

Which age group do you teach at present (you may tick more than one)?

Infant   ☐
Primary   ☐
Secondary (excluding sixth form)   ☐
Sixth form only   ☐

Just as dichotomous questions have their parallel in dichotomous variables, so multiple choice questions have their parallel in *multiple elements of a variable*. For example, the researcher may be asking to which form a student belongs – there being up to, say, forty forms in a large school, or the researcher may be asking which post-16 course a student is following (e.g. academic, vocational, manual, non-manual). In these cases only one response may be selected. As with the dichotomous variable, the listing of several categories or elements of a variable (e.g. form membership and course followed) enables nominal data to be collected and processed using the chi-square statistic, the G-test and cross-tabulations (Cohen and Holliday 1996). Multiple choice questions are treated as nominal data (see Part Five).

It may be important to include in the multiple choices those that will enable respondents to select the response that most closely represents their view, hence a pilot is needed to ensure that the categories are comprehensive, exhaustive and representative. On the other hand, the researcher may be interested in certain features only, and it is these that would figure in the response categories only.

The multiple choice questionnaire seldom gives more than a crude statistic, for words are inherently ambiguous. In the example above of chemistry, the notion of 'useful' is unclear, as are 'appropriate', 'practicable' and 'burden'. Respondents could interpret these words differently in their own contexts, thereby rendering the data ambiguous. One respondent might see the utility of the chemistry scheme in one area and thereby say that it is useful – ticking (d). Another respondent might see the same utility in that same one area but, because it is only useful in that single area, may see this as a flaw and therefore not tick category (d). With an anonymous questionnaire this difference would be impossible to detect.

This is the heart of the problem of questionnaires – that different respondents interpret the same words differently. 'Anchor statements' can be provided to allow a degree of discrimination in response (e.g. 'strongly agree', 'agree' etc.) but there is no guarantee that respondents will always interpret them in the way that is intended. In the example above this might not be a problem as the researcher might only be seeking an index of utility – without wishing to know the areas of utility or the reasons for that utility. The evaluator might be wishing only for a crude statistic (which might be very useful statistically in making a decisive judgement about a programme). In this case this rough and ready statistic might be perfectly acceptable.

One can see in the example of chemistry above not only ambiguity in the wording but also a very incomplete set of response categories which is hardly capable of representing all aspects of the chemistry scheme. That this might be politically expedient cannot be overlooked, for if the choice of responses is limited, then those responses might enable bias to be built into the research. For example, if the responses were limited to statements about the *utility* of the chemistry scheme, then the evaluator would have little difficulty in establishing that the scheme was useful. By avoiding the inclusion of negative statements or the opportunity to record a negative response the research will surely be biased. The issue of the wording of questions has been discussed earlier.

Multiple choice items are also prone to problems of word order and statement order. For example, Dillman *et al.* (2003: 6) report a study of German students who were asked to compare their high school teachers in terms of whether male or female teachers were more empathetic. They found that respondents rated their female teachers more highly than their male teachers when asked to compare female teachers to male teachers than when they were asked to compare their male teachers to their female teachers. Similarly they report a study in which tennis was found to be less exciting than football when the tennis option was presented before the football option, and more exciting when the football option was placed before the tennis option. These studies suggest that respondents tend to judge later items in terms of the earlier items, rather than vice versa and that they overlook features specific to later items if these are not contained in the earlier items. This is an instance of the 'primacy effect' or 'order effect', wherein items earlier in a list are given greater weight than items lower in the list. Order effects are resilient to efforts to minimize them, and primacy effects are particularly strong in Internet questionnaires (Dillman *et al.* 2003: 22).

Rank ordering

The rank order question is akin to the multiple choice question in that it identifies options from which respondents can choose, yet it moves beyond multiple choice items in that it asks respondents to identify priorities. This enables a *relative* degree of preference, priority, intensity etc. to be charted (see http://www.routledge.com/textbooks/9780415368780 – Chapter 15, file 15.6. ppt). In the rank ordering exercise a list of factors is set out and the respondent is required to place them in a rank order, for example:

Please indicate your priorities by placing numbers in the boxes to indicate the ordering of your views, 1 = the highest priority, 2 = the second highest, and so on.

The proposed amendments to the mathematics scheme might be successful if the following factors are addressed:

- the appropriate material resources are in school □
- the amendments are made clear to all teachers □
- the amendments are supported by the mathematics team □
- the necessary staff development is assured □
- there are subsequent improvements to student achievement □
- the proposals have the agreement of all teachers □
- they improve student motivation □
- parents approve of the amendments □
- they will raise the achievements of the brighter students □
- the work becomes more geared to problem-solving □

In this example ten items are listed. While this might be enticing for the researcher, enabling fine distinctions possibly to be made in priorities, it might be asking too much of the respondents to make such distinctions. They genuinely might not be able to differentiate their responses, or they simply might not feel strongly enough to make such distinctions. The inclusion of too long a list might be overwhelming. Indeed Wilson and McLean (1994: 26) suggest that it is unrealistic to ask respondents to arrange priorities where there are more than five ranks that have been requested. In the case of the list of ten points above, the researcher might approach this problem in one of two ways. The list in the questionnaire item can be reduced to five items only, in which case the *range* and comprehensiveness of responses that fairly catches what the respondent feels is significantly reduced. Alternatively, the list of ten items can be retained, but the request can be made to the respondents only to rank their first five priorities, in which case the range is retained and the task is not overwhelming (though the problem of sorting the data for analysis is increased).

An example of a shorter list might be:

Please place these in rank order of the most to the least important, by putting the position (1–5) against each of the following statements, number 1 being the most important and number 5 being the least important:

Students should enjoy school   [ ]
Teachers should set less homework   [ ]
Students should have more choice of subjects in school   [ ]
Teachers should use more collaborative methods [ ]
Students should be tested more, so that they work harder   [ ]

Rankings are useful in indicating *degrees* of response. In this respect they are like rating scales, discussed below. Ranking questions are treated as ordinal data (see Part Five for a discussion of ordinal data).

Rating scales

One way in which degrees of response, intensity of response, and the move away from dichotomous questions have been managed can be seen in the notion of *rating scales* – Likert scales, semantic differential scales, Thurstone scales and Guttman scaling. These are very useful devices for the researcher, as they build in a degree of sensitivity and differentiation of response while still generating numbers. This chapter will focus on the first two of these, though readers will find the others discussed in Oppenheim (1992) (see http://www.routledge.com/textbooks/9780415368780 – Chapter 15, file 15.7. ppt). A Likert scale (named after its deviser, Rensis Likert 1932) provides a range of responses to a given question or statement, for example:

> How important do you consider work placements to be for secondary school students?
>
> 1 = not at all
> 2 = very little
> 3 = a little
> 4 = quite a lot
> 5 = a very great deal
>
> All students should have access to free higher education.
>
> 1 = strongly disagree
> 2 = disagree
> 3 = neither agree nor disagree
> 4 = agree
> 5 = strongly agree

Such a scale could be set out thus:

> Please complete the following by placing a tick in one space only, as follows:
>
> 1 = strongly disagree; 2 = disagree;
>
> 3 = neither agree nor disagree;
>
> 4 = agree; 5 = strongly agree
>
>   1   2   3   4   5
> Senior school staff [ ] [ ] [ ] [ ] [ ]
> should teach more

In these examples the categories need to be discrete and to exhaust the range of possible responses which respondents may wish to give. Notwithstanding the problems of interpretation which arise as in the previous example – one respondent's 'agree' may be another's 'strongly agree', one respondent's 'very little' might be another's 'a little' – the greater subtlety of response which is built into a rating scale renders this a very attractive and widely used instrument in research.

These two examples both indicate an important feature of an attitude scaling instrument, namely the assumption of *unidimensionality* in the scale; the scale should be measuring only one thing at a time (Oppenheim 1992: 187–8). Indeed this is a cornerstone of Likert's (1932) own thinking.

It is a very straightforward matter to convert a dichotomous question into a multiple choice question. For example, instead of asking the 'do you?', 'have you?', 'are you?', 'can you?' type questions in a dichotomous format, a simple addition to wording will convert it into a much more subtle rating scale, by substituting the words 'to what extent?', 'how far?', 'how much?', 'how often?' etc.

A semantic differential is a variation of a rating scale which operates by putting an adjective at one end of a scale and its opposite at the other, for example:

> How informative do you consider the new set of history textbooks to be?
>
>   1 2 3 4 5 6 7
> Useful – – – – – – – Useless

Respondents indicate their opinion by circling or putting a mark on that position on the scale which most represents what they feel. Researchers devise their own terms and their polar opposites, for example:

Approachable	....	Unapproachable
Generous	....	Mean
Friendly	....	Hostile
Caring	....	Uncaring
Attentive	....	Inattentive
Hard-working	....	Lazy

Osgood *et al.* (1957), the pioneers of this technique, suggest that semantic differential scales are useful in three contexts: *evaluative* (e.g. valuable-valueless, useful-useless, good-bad); *potency* (e.g. large-small, weak-strong, light-heavy); and *activity* (e.g. quick-slow; active-passive, dynamic-lethargic).

There are several commonly used categories in rating scales, for example:

> Strongly disagree/disagree/neither agree nor disagree/agree/strongly agree
> Very seldom/occasionally/quite often/very often

Very little/a little/somewhat/a lot/a very great deal
Never/almost never/sometimes/often/very often
Not at all important/unimportant/neither important nor unimportant/important/very important
Very true of me/a little bit true of me/don't know/not really true of me/very untrue of me
Strongly agree/agree/uncertain/disagree/strongly agree

To these could be added the category 'don't know' or 'have no opinion'. Rating scales are widely used in research, and rightly so, for they combine the opportunity for a flexible response with the ability to determine frequencies, correlations and other forms of quantitative analysis. They afford the researcher the freedom to fuse measurement with opinion, quantity and quality.

Though rating scales are powerful and useful in research, the investigator, nevertheless, needs to be aware of their limitations. For example, the researcher may infer a degree of sensitivity and subtlety from the data that they cannot bear. There are other cautionary factors about rating scales, be they Likert scales or semantic differential scales:

- There is no assumption of equal intervals between the categories, hence a rating of 4 indicates neither that it is twice as powerful as 2 nor that it is twice as strongly felt; one cannot infer that the intensity of feeling in the Likert scale between 'strongly agree' and 'disagree' somehow matches the intensity of feeling between 'strongly disagree' and 'agree'. These are illegitimate inferences. The problem of equal intervals has been addressed in Thurstone scales (Thurstone and Chave 1929; Oppenheim 1992: 190–5).
- We have no check on whether respondents are telling the truth. Some may be deliberately falsifying their replies.
- We have no way of knowing if the respondent might have wished to add any other comments about the issue under investigation. It might have been the case that there was something far more pressing about the issue than the rating scale included but which was condemned to silence for want of a category. A straightforward way to circumvent this issue is to run

a pilot and also to include a category entitled 'other (please state)'.

- Most of us would not wish to be called extremists; we often prefer to appear like each other in many respects. For rating scales this means that we might wish to avoid the two extreme poles at each end of the continuum of the rating scales, reducing the number of positions in the scales to a choice of three (in a 5-point scale). That means that *in fact* there could be very little choice for us. The way round this is to create a larger scale than a 5-point scale, for example a 7-point scale. To go beyond a 7-point scale is to invite a degree of detail and precision which might be inappropriate for the item in question, particularly if the argument set out above is accepted, that one respondent's scale point 3 might be another's scale point 4.
- There is a tendency for participants to opt for the mid-point of a 5-point or 7-point scale (the central tendency). This is notably an issue in East Asian respondents, where the 'doctrine of the mean' is advocated in Confucian culture. One option to overcome this is to use an even number scaling system, as there is no mid-point. On the other hand, it could be argued that if respondents wish to sit on the fence and choose a mid-point, then they should be given the option to do so.
- On the scales so far there have been mid-points; on the 5-point scale it is category 3, and on the 7-point scale it is category 4. The use of an odd number of points on a scale enables this to occur. However, choosing an even number of scale points, for example a 6-point scale, might *require* a decision on rating to be indicated.

For example, suppose a new staffing structure has been introduced into a school and the headteacher is seeking some guidance on its effectiveness. A 6-point rating scale might ask respondents to indicate their response to the statement:

The new staffing structure in the school has enabled teamwork to be managed within a clear model of line management.

(Circle one number)

                1 2 3 4 5 6
Strongly   –   –   –   –   –   Strongly
agree   disagree

Let us say that one member of staff circled 1, eight staff circled 2, twelve staff circled 3, nine staff circled 4, two staff circled 5, and seven staff circled 6. There being no mid-point on this continuum, the researcher could infer that those respondents who circled 1, 2 or 3 were in some measure of agreement, while those respondents who circled 4, 5 or 6 were in some measure of disagreement. That would be very useful for, say, a headteacher, in publicly displaying agreement, there being twenty-one staff $(1 + 8 + 12)$ agreeing with the statement and eighteen $(9 + 2 + 7)$ displaying a measure of disagreement. However, one could point out that the measure of 'strongly disagree' attracted seven staff – a very strong feeling – which was not true for the 'strongly agree' category, which attracted only one member of staff. The extremity of the voting has been lost in a crude aggregation.

Further, if the researcher were to aggregate the scoring around the two mid-point categories (3 and 4) there would be twenty-one members of staff represented, leaving nine $(1 + 8)$ from categories 1 and 2 and nine $(2 + 7)$ from categories 5 and 6; adding together categories 1, 2, 5 and 6, a total of eighteen is reached, which is less than the twenty-one total of the two categories 3 and 4. It seems on this scenario that it is far from clear that there was agreement with the statement from the staff; indeed taking the high incidence of 'strongly disagree', it could be argued that those staff who were perhaps ambivalent (categories 3 and 4), coupled with those who registered a 'strongly disagree', indicate not agreement but disagreement with the statement.

The interpretation of data has to be handled very carefully; ordering data to suit a researcher's own purposes might be very alluring but quite illegitimate. The golden rule here is that crude data can yield only crude interpretation; subtle statistics require subtle data. The interpretation of data must not distort the data unfairly. Rating scale questions are treated as ordinal data (see Part Five), using modal scores and non-parametric data analysis, though one can find very many examples where this rule has been violated, and non-parametric data have been treated as parametric data. This is unacceptable.

It has been suggested that the attraction of rating scales is that they provide more opportunity than dichotomous questions for rendering data more sensitive and responsive to respondents. This makes rating scales particularly useful for tapping attitudes, perceptions and opinions. The need for a pilot study to devise and refine categories, making them exhaustive and discrete, has been suggested as a necessary part of this type of data collection.

Questionnaires that are going to yield numerical or word-based data can be analysed using computer programmes (for example SPSS or Ethnograph respectively). If the researcher intends to process the data using a computer package it is essential that the layout and coding system of the questionnaire are appropriate for that particular computer package. Instructions for layout in order to facilitate data entry are contained in manuals that accompany such packages.

Rating scales are more sensitive instruments than dichotomous scales. Nevertheless, they are limited in their usefulness to researchers by their fixity of response caused by the need to select from a given choice. A questionnaire might be tailored even more to respondents by including *open-ended* questions to which they can reply in their own terms and own opinions. We consider these later.

Constant sum questions

In this type of question respondents are asked to distribute a given number of marks (points) between a range of items (see http://www.routledge.com/textbooks/9780415368780 – Chapter 15, file 15.8. ppt). For example:

> Please distribute a total of 10 points among the sentences that you think most closely describe your behaviour. You may distribute these freely: they may be spread out, or awarded to only a few statements, or all allocated to a single sentence if you wish.

I can take advantage of new opportunities   [ ]
I can work effectively with all kinds of people   [ ]
Generating new ideas is one of my strengths   [ ]
I can usually tell what is likely to work in practice   [ ]
I am able to see tasks through to the very end   [ ]
I am prepared to be unpopular for the good of the school   [ ]

This enables priorities to be identified, comparing highs and lows, and for equality of choices to be indicated, and, importantly, for this to be done in the respondents' own terms. It requires respondents to make comparative judgements and choices across a range of items. For example, we may wish to distribute 10 points for aspects of an individual's personality:

Talkative   [ ]
Cooperative   [ ]
Hard-working   [ ]
Lazy   [ ]
Motivated   [ ]
Attentive   [ ]

This means that the respondent has to consider the *relative* weight of each of the given aspects before coming to a decision about how to award the marks. To accomplish this means that the all-round nature of the person, in the terms provided, has to be considered, to see, on balance, which aspect is stronger when compared to another.[1]

The difficulty with this approach is to decide how many marks can be distributed (a round number, for example 10, makes subsequent calculation easily comprehensible) and how many statements/items to include, e.g. whether to have the same number of statements as there are marks, or more or fewer statements than the total of marks. Having too few statements/items does not do justice to the complexity of the issue, and having too many statements/items may mean that it is difficult for respondents to decide how to distribute their marks. Having too few marks available may be unhelpful, but, by contrast, having too many marks and too many statements/items can lead to simple computational errors by respondents. Our advice is to keep the number of marks to ten and the number of statements to around six to eight.

Constant sum data are ordinal, and this means that non-parametric analysis can be performed on the data (see Part Five).

Ratio data questions

We discuss ratio data in Part Five and we refer the reader to the discussion and definition there (see http://www.routledge.com/textbooks/9780415368780 – Chapter 15, file 15.9. ppt). For our purposes here we suggest that ratio data questions deal with continuous variables where there is a true zero, for example:

How much money do you have in the bank?   —
How many times have you been late for school?   —
How many marks did you score in the mathematics test?   —
How old are you (in years)?   —

Here no fixed answer or category is provided, and the respondent puts in the numerical answer that fits his/her exact figure, i.e. the accuracy is higher, much higher than in *categories* of data. This enables averages (means), standard deviations, range, and high-level statistics to be calculated, e.g. regression, factor analysis, structural equation modelling (see Part Five).

An alternative form of ratio scaling is where the respondent has to award marks out of, say, ten, for a particular item. This is a device that has been used in business and commerce for measuring service quality and customer satisfaction, and is being used in education by Kgaile and Morrison (2006); see for example Box 15.3.

This kind of scaling is often used in telephone interviews, as it is easy for respondents to understand. The argument could be advanced that this is a sophisticated form of rating scale, but the terminology used in the instruction clearly suggests that it asks for ratio scale data.

Open-ended questions

The open-ended question is a very attractive device for smaller scale research or for those

Box 15.3
A 10-point marking scale in a questionnaire

Please give a mark from 1 to 10 for the following statements, with 10 being excellent and 1 being very poor. Please circle the appropriate number for each statement.

Teaching and learning

	Very poor								Excellent	
1 The attention given to teaching and learning at the school	1	2	3	4	5	6	7	8	9	10
2 The quality of the lesson preparation	1	2	3	4	5	6	7	8	9	10
3 How well learners are cared for, guided and supported	1	2	3	4	5	6	7	8	9	10
4 How effectively teachers challenge and engage learners	1	2	3	4	5	6	7	8	9	10
5 The educators' use of assessment for maximizing learners' learning	1	2	3	4	5	6	7	8	9	10
6 How well students apply themselves to learning	1	2	3	4	5	6	7	8	9	10
7 Discussion and review by educators of the quality of teaching and learning	1	2	3	4	5	6	7	8	9	10

sections of a questionnaire that invite an honest, personal comment from respondents in addition to ticking numbers and boxes (see http://www.routledge.com/textbooks/9780415368780 – Chapter 15, file 15.10. ppt). The questionnaire simply puts the open-ended questions and leaves a space (or draws lines) for a free response. It is the open-ended responses that might contain the 'gems' of information that otherwise might not be caught in the questionnaire. Further, it puts the responsibility for and ownership of the data much more firmly into respondents' hands.

It is useful for the researcher to provide some support for respondents, so that they know the kind of reply being sought. For example, an open question that includes a prompt could be:

Please indicate the most important factors that reduce staff participation in decision-making.

Please comment on the strengths and weaknesses of the mathematics course.

Please indicate areas for improvement in the teaching of foreign languages in the school.

This is not to say that the open-ended question might well not frame the answer, just as the stem of a rating scale question might frame the response given. However, an open-ended question can catch the authenticity, richness, depth of response, honesty and candour which, as is argued elsewhere in this book, are the hallmarks of qualitative data.

Oppenheim (1992: 56–7) suggests that a sentence-completion item is a useful adjunct to an open-ended question, for example:

Please complete the following sentence in your own words:

An effective teacher...

or

The main things that I find annoying with disruptive students are...

Open-endedness also carries problems of data handling. For example, if one tries to convert opinions into numbers (e.g. so many people indicated some degree of satisfaction with the new principal's management plan), then it could be argued that the questionnaire should have used rating scales in the first place. Further, it might well be that the researcher is in danger of violating one principle of word-based data, which is that they are not validly susceptible to aggregation, i.e. that it is trying to bring to word-based data the principles of numerical data, borrowing from one paradigm (quantitative, positivist methodology) to inform another paradigm (qualitative, interpretive methodology).

Further, if a genuinely open-ended question is being asked, it is perhaps unlikely that responses will bear such a degree of similarity to each other so as to enable them to be aggregated too tightly. Open-ended questions make it difficult for the researcher to make comparisons between respondents, as there may be little in common to compare. Moreover, to complete an open-ended questionnaire takes much longer than placing a tick in a rating scale response box; not only will time be a constraint here, but there is an assumption that respondents will be sufficiently or equally capable of articulating their thoughts and committing them to paper.

In practical terms, Redline *et al.* (2002) report that using open-ended questions can lead to respondents overlooking instructions, as they are occupied with the more demanding task of writing in their own words than reading instructions.

Despite these cautions, the space provided for an open-ended response is a window of opportunity for the respondent to shed light on an issue or course. Thus, an open-ended questionnaire has much to recommend it.

Matrix questions

Matrix questions are not types of questions but concern the layout of questions. Matrix questions enable the same kind of response to be given to several questions, for example 'strongly disagree' to 'strongly agree'. The matrix layout helps to save space, for example:

Please complete the following by placing a tick in one space only, as follows:
1 = not at all; 2 = very little; 3 = a moderate amount; 4 = quite a lot; 5 = a very great deal
How much do you use the following for assessment purposes?

	1	2	3	4	5
(a) commercially published tests	[ ]	[ ]	[ ]	[ ]	[ ]
(b) your own made-up tests	[ ]	[ ]	[ ]	[ ]	[ ]
(c) students' projects	[ ]	[ ]	[ ]	[ ]	[ ]
(d) essays	[ ]	[ ]	[ ]	[ ]	[ ]
(e) samples of students' work	[ ]	[ ]	[ ]	[ ]	[ ]

Here five questions have been asked in only five lines, excluding, of course, the instructions and explanations of the anchor statements. Such a layout is economical of space.

A second example indicates how a matrix design can save a considerable amount of space in a questionnaire. Here the size of potential problems in conducting a piece of research is asked for, and data on how much these problems were soluble are requested. For the first issue (the size of the problem), 1 = no problem, 2 = a small problem, 3 = a moderate problem, 4 = a large problem, 5 = a very large problem. For the second issue (how much the problem was solved), 1 = not solved at all, 2 = solved only a very little, 3 = solved a moderate amount, 4 = solved a lot, 5 = completely solved (see Box 15.4).

Here thirty questions (15 × 2) have been able to be covered in just a short amount of space.

Laying out the questionnaire like this enables the respondent to fill in the questionnaire rapidly. On the other hand, it risks creating a mind set in the respondent (a 'response set': Baker 1994: 181) in that the respondent may simply go down the questionnaire columns and write the same number each time (e.g. all number 3) or, in a rating scale, tick all number 3. Such response sets can be detected by looking at patterns of replies and eliminating response sets from subsequent analysis.

The conventional way of minimizing response sets has been by reversing the meaning of some of the questions so that the respondents will need to read them carefully. However, Weems *et al.* (2003) argue that using positively and negatively worded items within a scale is not measuring the same underlying traits. They report that some respondents will tend to disagree with a negatively worded item, that the reliability levels of negatively worded items are lower than for positively worded items, and that negatively worded items receive greater non-response than positively worded items. Indeed Weems *et al.* (2003) argue against mixed-item formats, and supplement this by reporting that inappropriately worded items can induce an artificially extreme response which, in turn, compromises the reliability of the data. Mixing

Box 15.4
Potential problems in conducting research

	Size of the problem (1–5)	How much the problem was solved (1–5)
1 Gaining access to schools and teachers		
2 Gaining permission to conduct the research (e.g. from principals)		
3 Resentment by principals		
4 People vetting what could be used		
5 Finding enough willing participants for your sample		
6 Schools suffering from 'too much research' by outsiders and insiders		
7 Schools or people not wishing to divulge information about themselves		
8 Schools not wishing to be identifiable, even with protections guaranteed		
9 Local political factors that impinge on the school		
10 Teachers' fear of being identified/traceable, even with protections guaranteed		
11 Fear of participation by teachers (e.g. if they say critical matters about the school or others they could lose their contracts)		
12 Unwillingness of teachers to be involved because of their workload		
13 The principal deciding on whether to involve the staff, without consultation with the staff		
14 Schools' or institutions' fear of criticism or loss of face		
15 The sensitivity of the research: the issues being investigated		

negatively and positively worded items in the same scale, they argue, compromises both validity and reliability. Indeed they suggest that respondents may not read negatively worded items as carefully as positively worded items.

Contingency questions, filters and branches

Contingency questions depend on responses to earlier questions, for example: 'if your answer to question (1) was "yes" please go to question (4)'. The earlier question acts as a filter for the later question, and the later question is contingent on the earlier, and is a branch of the earlier question. Some questionnaires will write in words the number of the question to which to go (e.g. 'please go to question 6'); others will place an arrow to indicate the next question to be answered if your answer to the first question was such-and-such.

Contingency and filter questions may be useful for the researcher, but they can be confusing for

the respondent as it is not always clear how to proceed through the sequence of questions and where to go once a particular branch has been completed. Redline *et al.* (2002) found that respondents tend to ignore, misread and incorrectly follow branching instructions, such that item non-response occurs for follow-up questions that are applicable only to certain subsamples, and respondents skip over, and therefore fail to follow-up on those questions that they should have completed. Redline *et al.* (2002) found that the increased complexity of the questionnaire brought about by branching instructions negatively influenced its correct completion.

Redline *et al.* (2002: 7) report that the number of words in the question affected the respondents' ability to follow branching instructions – the greater the number of words in the question, the greater was the likelihood of the respondents overlooking the branching instructions. Redline *et al.* (2002: 19) report that up to seven items, and no more, could be retained in the short-term memory. This has implications for the number of items in a list of telephone interviews, where there is no visual recall or checking possible. Similarly, the greater was the number of answer categories, the greater was the likelihood of making errors, e.g. overlooking branching instructions. They report that respondents tend to see branching instructions when they are placed by the last category, particularly if they have chosen that last category.

Further, Redline *et al.* (2002: 8) note that sandwiching branching instructions between items that do not branch is likely to lead to errors of omission and commission being made: omitting to answer all the questions and answering the wrong questions. Further, locating the instructions for branching some distance away from the preceding answer box can also lead to errors in following the instructions. Redline *et al.* (2002: 17) report that 'altering the visual and verbal design of branching instructions had a substantial impact on how well respondents read, comprehend, and act upon the branching instructions'. It follows from this that the *clear location* and *visual impact* of instructions are important for successful completion of branching instructions. Most respondents, they acknowledge, did not deliberately ignore branching instructions; they simply were unaware of them.

The implications of the findings from Redline *et al.* (2002) is that instructions should be placed where they are to be used and where they can be seen.

We would advise judicious and limited use of filtering and branching devices. It is particularly important to avoid having participants turning pages forwards and backwards in a questionnaire in order to follow the sequence of questions that have had filters and branches following from them. It is a particular problem in Internet surveys where the screen size is much smaller than the length of a printed page. One way of overcoming the problem of branches is to sectionalize the questionnaire, keeping together conceptually close items and keeping the branches within that section.

Asking sensitive questions

Sudman and Bradburn (1982: ch. 3) draw attention to the important issue of including sensitive items in a questionnaire. While the anonymity of a questionnaire and, frequently, the lack of face-to-face contact between the researcher and the respondents in a questionnaire might facilitate responses to sensitive material, the issues of sensitivity and threat cannot be avoided, as they might lead to under-reporting (non-disclosure and withholding data) or over-reporting (exaggeration) by participants. Some respondents may be unwilling to disclose sensitive information, particularly if it could harm themselves or others. Why should they share private matters (e.g. about family life and opinions of school managers and colleagues) with a complete stranger (Cooper and Schindler 2001: 341)? Even details of age, income, educational background, qualifications, and opinions can be regarded as private and/or sensitive matters.

Sudman and Bradburn (1982: 55–6) identify several important considerations in addressing potentially threatening or sensitive issues, for example socially undesirable behaviour (e.g. drug abuse, sexual offences, violent behaviour, criminality, illnesses, employment and unemployment, physical features, sexual activity, behaviour and sexuality, gambling, drinking, family details, political beliefs, social taboos). They suggest the following strategies:

- Open rather than closed questions might be more suitable to elicit information about socially undesirable behaviour, particularly frequencies.
- Long rather than short questions might be more suitable for eliciting information about socially undesirable behaviour, particularly frequencies.
- Using familiar words might increase the number of reported frequencies of socially undesirable behaviour.
- Using data gathered from informants, where possible, can enhance the likelihood of obtaining reports of threatening behaviour.

- Deliberately loading the question so that overstatements of socially desirable behaviour and understatements of socially undesirable behaviour are reduced might be a useful means of eliciting information.
- With regard to socially undesirable behaviour, it might be advisable first to ask whether the respondent has engaged in that behaviour previously, and then move to asking about his or her current behaviour. By contrast, when asking about socially acceptable behaviour the reverse might be true, i.e. asking about current behaviour before asking about everyday behaviour.
- In order to defuse threat, it might be useful to locate the sensitive topic within a discussion of other more or less sensitive matters, in order to suggest to respondents that this issue might not be too important.
- Use alternative ways of asking standard questions, for example sorting cards, or putting questions in sealed envelopes, or repeating questions over time (this has to be handled sensitively, so that respondents do not feel that they are being 'checked'), and in order to increase reliability.
- Ask respondents to keep diaries in order to increase validity and reliability.
- At the end of an interview ask respondents their views on the sensitivity of the topics that have been discussed.
- If possible, find ways of validating the data.

Indeed, Sudman and Bradburn (1982: 86) suggest that, as the questions become more threatening and sensitive, it is wise to expect greater bias and unreliability. They draw attention to the fact that several nominal, demographic details might be considered threatening by respondents (Sudman and Bradburn 1982: 208). This has implications for their location within the questionnaire (discussed below). The issue here is that sensitivity and threat are to be viewed through the eyes of respondents rather than the questionnaire designer; what might appear innocuous to the researcher might be highly sensitive or offensive to participants. We refer readers to Chapter 5 on sensitive educational research.

Avoiding pitfalls in question writing

Although there are several kinds of questions that can be used, there are some caveats about the framing of questions in a questionnaire (see http://www.routledge.com/textbooks/9780415368780 – Chapter 15, file 15.11. ppt):

- Avoid leading questions, that is, questions that are worded (or their response categories presented) in such a way as to suggest to respondents that there is only one acceptable answer, and that other responses might or might not gain approval or disapproval respectively. For example:

  > Do you prefer abstract, academic-type courses, or down-to-earth, practical courses that have some pay-off in your day-to-day teaching?

  The guidance here is to check the 'loadedness' or possible pejorative overtones of terms or verbs.

- Avoid highbrow questions even with sophisticated respondents. For example:

  > What particular aspects of the current positivistic/interpretive debate would you like to see reflected in a course of developmental psychology aimed at a teacher audience?

  Where the sample being surveyed is representative of the whole adult population, misunderstandings of what researchers take to be clear, unambiguous language are commonplace. Therefore it is important to use clear and simple language.

- Avoid complex questions. For example:

  > Would you prefer a short, non-award-bearing course (3, 4 or 5 sessions) with part-day release (e.g. Wednesday afternoons) and one evening per week attendance with financial reimbursement for travel, or a longer, non-award-bearing course (6, 7 or 8 sessions) with full-day release, or the whole course designed on part-day release without evening attendance?

- Avoid irritating questions or instructions. For example:

  Have you ever attended an in-service course of any kind during your entire teaching career?
  If you are over forty, and have never attended an in-service course, put one tick in the box marked *NEVER* and another in the box marked *OLD*.

- Avoid questions that use negatives and double negatives (Oppenheim 1992: 128). For example:

  How strongly do you feel that no teacher should enrol on the in-service, award-bearing course who has not completed at least two years' full-time teaching?

  Or:

  Do you feel that without a parent/teacher association teachers are unable to express their views to parents clearly?

  In this case, if you feel that a parent/teacher association *is* essential for teachers to express their views, do you vote 'yes' or 'no'? The hesitancy involved in reaching such a decision, and the possible required re-reading of the question could cause the respondent simply to leave it blank and move on to the next question. The problem is the double negative, 'without' and 'unable', which creates confusion.

- Avoid too many open-ended questions on self-completion questionnaires. Because self-completion questionnaires cannot probe respondents to find out just what they mean by particular responses, open-ended questions are a less satisfactory way of eliciting information. (This caution does not hold in the interview situation, however.) Open-ended questions, moreover, are too demanding of most respondents' time. Nothing can be more off-putting than the following format:

  Use pages 5, 6 and 7 respectively to respond to each of the questions about your attitudes to in-service courses in general and your beliefs about their value in the professional life of the serving teacher.

- Avoid extremes in rating scales, e.g. 'never', 'always', 'totally', 'not at all' unless there is a good reason to include them. Most respondents are reluctant to use such extreme categories (Anderson and Arsenault 2001: 174).

- Avoid pressuring/biasing by association, for example: 'Do you agree with your headteacher that boys are more troublesome than girls?'. In this case the reference to the headteacher should simply be excised.

- Avoid statements with which people tend either to disagree or agree (i.e. that have built-in skewedness (the 'base-rate' problem, in which natural biases in the population affect the sample results).

Finally, avoid ambiguous questions or questions that could be interpreted differently from the way that is intended. The problem of ambiguity in words is intractable; at best it can be minimized rather than eliminated altogether. The most innocent of questions is replete with ambiguity (Youngman 1984: 158–9; Morrison 1993: 71–2). Take the following examples:

Does your child regularly do homework?

What does 'regularly' mean – once a day; once a year; once a term; once a week?

How many students are there in the school?

What does this mean: on roll; on roll but absent; marked as present but out of school on a field trip; at this precise moment or this week (there being a difference in attendance between a Monday and a Friday), or between the first term of an academic year and the last term of the academic year for secondary school students as some of them will have left school to go into employment and others will be at home revising for examinations or have completed them?

How many computers do you have in school?

What does this mean: present but broken; including those out of school being repaired; the property of the school or staffs' and students' own computers; on average or exactly in school today?

Have you had a French lesson this week?

What constitutes a 'week': the start of the school week (i.e. from Monday to a Friday), since last Sunday (or Saturday, depending on one's religion) or, if the question were put on a Wednesday, since last Wednesday; how representative of all weeks is this week – there being public examinations in the school for some of the week?

How old are you?
15–20
20–30
30–40
40–50
50–60

The categories are not discrete; will an old-looking 40 year old flatter himself and put himself in the 30–40 category, or will an immature 20-year old seek the maturity of being put into the 20–30 category? The rule in questionnaire design is to avoid any overlap of categories.

Vocational education is available only to the lower ability students but it should be open to every student.

This is, in fact, a double question. What does the respondent do who agrees with the first part of the sentence -'vocational education is available only to the lower ability students' – but disagrees with the latter part of the sentence, or vice versa? The rule in questionnaire design is to ask only one question at a time.

Although it is impossible to legislate for the respondents' interpretation of wording, the researcher, of course, has to adopt a common-sense approach to this, recognizing the inherent ambiguity but nevertheless still feeling that it is possible to live with this indeterminacy.

An ideal questionnaire possesses the same properties as a good law, being clear, unambiguous and practicable, reducing potential errors in participants and data analysts, being motivating for participants and ensuring as far as possible that respondents are telling the truth (Davidson 1970).

The golden rule is to keep questions as short and as simple as possible.

Sequencing the questions

To some extent the order of questions in a schedule is a function of the target sample (e.g. how they will react to certain questions), the purposes of the questionnaire (e.g. to gather facts or opinions), the sensitivity of the research (e.g. how personal and potentially disturbing the issues are that will be addressed), and the overall balance of the questionnaire (e.g. where best to place sensitive questions in relation to less threatening questions, and how many of each to include).

The ordering of the questionnaire is important, for early questions may set the tone or the mind-set of the respondent to later questions. For example, a questionnaire that makes a respondent irritated or angry early on is unlikely to have managed to enable that respondent's irritation or anger to subside by the end of the questionnaire. As Oppenheim (1992: 121) remarks, one covert purpose of each question is to ensure that the respondent will continue to cooperate.

Further, a respondent might 'read the signs' in the questionnaire, seeking similarities and resonances between statements so that responses to early statements will affect responses to later statements and vice versa. While multiple items may act as a cross-check, this very process might be irritating for some respondents.

Krosnick and Alwin (1987) found a 'primacy effect' (discussed earlier), i.e. respondents tend to choose items that appear earlier in a list rather than items that appear later in a list. This is particularly important for branching instructions, where the instruction, because it appears at the bottom of the list, could easily be overlooked. Krosnick (1999) also found that the more difficult a question is, the greater is the likelihood of 'satisficing', i.e. choosing the first reasonable response option in a list, rather than working through a list methodically to find the most appropriate response category.

The key principle, perhaps, is to avoid creating a mood-set or a mind-set early on in the questionnaire. For this reason it is important to commence the questionnaire with non-threatening questions that respondents can readily answer. After that it might be possible to move towards more personalized questions.

Completing a questionnaire can be seen as a learning process in which respondents become more at home with the task as they proceed. Initial questions should therefore be simple, have high interest value, and encourage participation. This will build up the confidence and motivation of the respondent. The middle section of the questionnaire should contain the difficult questions; the last few questions should be of high interest in order to encourage respondents to return the completed schedule.

A common sequence of a questionnaire is as follows:

- Commence with unthreatening factual questions (that, perhaps, will give the researcher some nominal data about the sample, e.g. age group, sex, occupation, years in post, qualifications etc.).
- Move to closed questions (e.g. dichotomous, multiple choice, rating scales, constant sum questions) about given statements or questions, eliciting responses that require opinions, attitudes, perceptions, views.
- Then move to more open-ended questions (or, maybe, to intersperse these with more closed questions) that seek responses on opinions, attitudes, perceptions and views, together with reasons for the responses given. These responses and reasons might include sensitive or more personal data.

The move is from objective facts to subjective attitudes and opinions through justifications and to sensitive, personalized data. Clearly the ordering is neither as discrete nor as straightforward as this. For example, an apparently innocuous question about age might be offensive to some respondents, a question about income is unlikely to go down well with somebody who has just become unemployed, and a question about religious belief might be seen as an unwarranted intrusion into private matters.

Indeed, many questionnaires keep questions about personal details until the very end.

The issue here is that the questionnaire designer has to anticipate the sensitivity of the topics in terms of the respondents, and this has a large sociocultural dimension. What is being argued here is that the *logical* ordering of a questionnaire has to be mediated by its *psychological* ordering. The instrument has to be viewed through the eyes of the respondent as well as the designer.

In addition to the *overall* sequencing of the questionnaire, Oppenheim (1992: ch. 7) suggests that the sequence *within* sections of the questionnaire is important. He indicates that the questionnaire designer can use *funnels* and *filters* within the question. A funnelling process moves from the general to the specific, asking questions about the general context or issues and then moving toward specific points within that. A filter is used to include and exclude certain respondents, i.e. to decide if certain questions are relevant or irrelevant to them, and to instruct respondents about how to proceed (e.g. which items to jump to or proceed to). For example, if respondents indicate a 'yes; or a 'no' to a certain question, then this might exempt them from certain other questions in that section or subsequently.

Questionnaires containing few verbal items

The discussion so far has assumed that questionnaires are entirely word-based. This might be off-putting for many respondents, particularly children. In these circumstances a questionnaire might include visual information and ask participants to respond to this (e.g. pictures, cartoons, diagrams) or might include some projective visual techniques (e.g. to draw a picture or diagram, to join two related pictures with a line, to write the words or what someone is saying or thinking in a 'bubble' picture), to tell the story of a sequence of pictures together with personal reactions to it. The issue here is that in tailoring the format of the questionnaire to the characteristics of the sample, a very wide embrace might be necessary to take in non-word-based techniques. This is not only a matter of *appeal* to respondents, but, perhaps more significantly, is a matter of *accessibility* of the questionnaire to the respondents, i.e. a matter of reliability and validity.

The layout of the questionnaire

The appearance of the questionnaire is vitally important. It must look easy, attractive and interesting rather than complicated, unclear, forbidding and boring. A compressed layout is uninviting and it clutters everything together; a larger questionnaire with plenty of space for questions and answers is more encouraging to respondents. Verma and Mallick (1999: 120) suggest the use of high quality paper if funding permits.

Dillman *et al.* (1999) found that respondents tend to expect less of a form-filling task than is actually required. They expect to read a question, read the response, make a mark, and move on to the next question, but in many questionnaires it is more complicated than this. The rule is simple: keep it as uncomplicated as possible.

It is important, perhaps, for respondents to be introduced to the purposes of each section of a questionnaire, so that they can become involved in it and maybe identify with it. If space permits, it is useful to tell the respondent the purposes and focuses of the sections of the questionnaire, and the reasons for the inclusion of the items.

Clarity of wording and simplicity of design are essential. Clear instructions should guide respondents: 'Put a tick', for example, invites participation, whereas complicated instructions and complex procedures intimidate respondents. Putting ticks in boxes by way of answering a questionnaire is familiar to most respondents, whereas requests to circle precoded numbers at the right-hand side of the questionnaire can be a source of confusion and error. In some cases it might also be useful to include an example of how to fill in the questionnaire (e.g. ticking a box, circling a statement), though, clearly, care must be exercised to avoid leading the respondents to answering questions in a particular way by dint of the example provided (e.g. by

suggesting what might be a desired answer to the subsequent questions). Verma and Mallick (1999: 121) suggest the use of emboldening to draw the respondent's attention to significant features.

Ensure that short, clear instructions accompany each section of the questionnaire. Repeating instructions as often as necessary is good practice in a postal questionnaire. Since everything hinges on respondents knowing exactly what is required of them, clear, unambiguous instructions, boldly and attractively displayed, are essential.

Clarity and presentation also impact on the numbering of the questions. For example a four-page questionnaire might contain sixty questions, broken down into four sections. It might be off-putting to respondents to number each question (1–60) as the list will seem interminably long, whereas to number each section 1–4 makes the questionnaire look manageable. Hence it is useful, in the interests of clarity and logic, to break down the questionnaire into subsections with section headings. This will also indicate the overall logic and coherence of the questionnaire to the respondents, enabling them to 'find their way' through the questionnaire. It might be useful to preface each subsection with a brief introduction that tells them the purpose of that section.

The practice of sectionalizing and sublettering questions (e.g. Q9 (a) (b) (c)...) is a useful technique for grouping together questions about a specific issue. It is also a way of making the questionnaire look smaller than it actually is!

This previous point also requires the question-naire designer to make it clear if respondents are exempted from completing certain questions or sections of the questionnaire (discussed earlier in the section on filters). If so, then it is vital that the sections or questions are numbered so that the respondent knows exactly where to move to next. Here the instruction might be, for example: 'If you have answered "yes" to question 10 please go to question 15, otherwise continue with question 11', or, for example: 'If you are the school principal please answer this section, otherwise proceed to section 3'.

Arrange the contents of the questionnaire in such a way as to maximize cooperation. For example, include questions that are likely to be of general interest. Make sure that questions that appear early in the format do not suggest to respondents that the enquiry is not intended for them. Intersperse attitude questions throughout the schedule to allow respondents to air their views rather than merely describe their behaviour. Such questions relieve boredom and frustration as well as providing valuable information in the process.

Coloured pages can help to clarify the overall structure of the questionnaire and the use of different colours for instructions can assist respondents.

It is important to include in the questionnaire, perhaps at the beginning, assurances of confidentiality, anonymity and non-traceability, for example by indicating that respondents need not give their name, that the data will be aggregated, that individuals will not be able to be identified through the use of categories or details of their location etc. (i.e. that it will not be possible to put together a traceable picture of the respondents through the compiling of nominal, descriptive data about them). In some cases, however, the questionnaire might ask respondents to put their names so that they can be traced for follow-up interviews in the research (Verma and Mallick 1999: 121); here the guarantee of eventual anonymity and non-traceability will still need to be given.

Redline *et al.* (2002) indicate that the placing of the response categories to the immediate right of the text increases the chance of it being answered (the visual *location*), and making the material more salient (e.g. through emboldening and capitalization) can increase the chances of it being addressed (the *visibility* issue). This is particularly important for branching questions and instructions.

Redline *et al.* (2002) also note that questions placed at the bottom of a page tend to receive more non-response than questions placed further up on the page. Indeed they found that putting instructions at the bottom of the page, particularly if they apply to items on the next page, can easily lead to those instructions being overlooked. It is important, then, to consider what should go at the

bottom of the page, perhaps the inclusion of less important items at that point. Redline *et al.* (2002) suggest that questions with branching instructions should not be placed at the bottom of a page.

Finally, a brief note at the very end of the questionnaire can: ask respondents to check that no answer has been inadvertently missed out; solicit an early return of the completed schedule; thank respondents for their participation and cooperation, and offer to send a short abstract of the major findings when the analysis is completed.

Covering letters or sheets and follow-up letters

The purpose of the covering letter or sheet is to indicate the aim of the research, to convey to respondents its importance, to assure them of confidentiality, and to encourage their replies. The covering letter or sheet should:

- provide a title to the research
- introduce the researcher, her/his name, address, organization, contact telephone/fax/email address, together with an invitation to feel free to contact the researcher for further clarification or details
- indicate the purposes of the research
- indicate the importance and benefits of the research
- indicate why the respondent has been selected for receipt of the questionnaire
- indicate any professional backing, endorsement or sponsorship of, or permission for, the research (e.g. university, professional associations, government departments: the use of a logo can be helpful here)
- set out how to return the questionnaire (e.g. in the accompanying stamped, addressed envelope, in a collection box in a particular institution, to a named person; whether the questionnaire will be collected – and when, where and by whom)
- indicate the address to which to return the questionnaire
- indicate what to do if questions or uncertainties arise

- indicate a return-by date
- indicate any incentives for completing the questionnaire
- provide assurances of confidentiality, anonymity and non-traceability
- indication of how the results will and will not be disseminated, and to whom
- thank respondents in advance for their co-operation.

Verma and Mallick (1999: 122) suggest that, where possible, it is useful to personalize the letter, avoiding 'Dear colleague', 'Dear Madam/Ms/Sir' etc., and replacing these with exact names.

With these intentions in mind, the following practices are to be recommended:

- The appeal in the covering letter must be tailored to suit the particular audience. Thus, a survey of teachers might stress the importance of the study to the profession as a whole.
- Neither the use of prestigious signatories, nor appeals to altruism, nor the addition of handwritten postscripts affect response levels to postal questionnaires.
- The name of the sponsor or the organization conducting the survey should appear on the letterhead as well as in the body of the covering letter.
- A direct reference should be made to the confidentiality of respondents' answers and the purposes of any serial numbers and codings should be explained.
- A pre-survey letter advising respondents of the forthcoming questionnaire has been shown to have substantial effect on response rates.

A short covering letter is most effective; aim at no more than one page. An example of a covering letter for teachers and senior staff might be as follows:

Dear Colleague,

IMPROVING SCHOOL EFFECTIVENESS

We are asking you to take part in a project to improve school effectiveness, by completing this short research questionnaire. The project is part of your school development, support management and monitoring of school effectiveness, and the project will facilitate a change management programme that will be tailor-made for the school. This questionnaire is seeking to identify the nature, strengths and weaknesses of different aspects of your school, particularly in respect of those aspects of the school over which the school itself has some control. It would be greatly appreciated if you would be involved in this process by completing the sheets attached, and returning them to me. Please **be as truthful as possible** in completing the questionnaire.

You do not need to write your name, and no individuals will be identified or traced from this, i.e. confidentiality and anonymity are assured. If you wish to discuss any aspects of the review or this document please do not hesitate to contact me. I hope that you will feel able to take part in this project.

Thank you.

Signed

Contact details (address, fax, telephone, email)

Another example might be:

Dear Colleague,

PROJECT ON CONDUCTING EDUCATIONAL RESEARCH

I am conducting a small-scale piece of research into issues facing researchers undertaking investigations in education. The topic is very much under-researched in education, and that is why I intend to explore the area.

I am asking you to be involved as you yourself have conducted empirical work as part of a Master's or doctorate degree. No one knows the practical problems facing the educational researcher better than you.

The enclosed questionnaire forms part of my investigation. May I invite you to spend a short time in its completion?

If you are willing to be involved, please complete the questionnaire and return it to XXX by the end of

November. You may either place it in the collection box at the General Office at my institution or send it by post (stamped addressed envelope enclosed), or by fax or email attachment.

The questionnaire will take around fifteen minutes to complete. It employs rating scales and asks for your comments and a few personal details. You *do not need to write your name*, and you will not be able to be identified or traced. ANONYMITY AND NON-TRACEABILITY ARE ASSURED. When completed, I intend to publish my results in an education journal.

If you wish to discuss any aspects of the study then please do not hesitate to contact me.

I very much hope that you will feel able to participate. May I thank you, in advance, for your valuable cooperation.

Yours sincerely,

Signed

Contact details (address, fax, telephone, email)

For a further example of a questionnaire see the accompanying web site (http://www.routledge.com/textbooks/9780415368780 – Chapter 15, file 15.1.doc).

Piloting the questionnaire

It bears repeating that the wording of questionnaires is of paramount importance and that pretesting is crucial to their success (see http://www.routledge.com/textbooks/9780415368780 – Chapter 15, file 15.12. ppt). A pilot has several functions, principally to increase the reliability, validity and practicability of the questionnaire (Oppenheim 1992; Morrison 1993: Wilson and McLean 1994: 47):

- to check the clarity of the questionnaire items, instructions and layout
- to gain feedback on the validity of the questionnaire items, the operationalization of the constructs and the purposes of the research

- to eliminate ambiguities or difficulties in wording
- to check readability levels for the target audience
- to gain feedback on the *type* of question and its format (e.g. rating scale, multiple choice, open, closed etc.)
- to gain feedback on response categories for closed questions and multiple choice items, and for the appropriateness of specific questions or stems of questions
- to identify omissions, redundant and irrelevant items
- to gain feedback on leading questions
- to gain feedback on the attractiveness and appearance of the questionnaire
- to gain feedback on the layout, sectionalizing, numbering and itemization of the questionnaire
- to check the time taken to complete the questionnaire
- to check whether the questionnaire is too long or too short, too easy or too difficult
- to generate categories from open-ended responses to use as categories for closed response-modes (e.g. rating scale items)
- to identify how motivating/non-motivating /sensitive/threatening/intrusive/offensive items might be
- to identify redundant questions (e.g. those questions which consistently gain a total 'yes' or 'no' response: Youngman 1984: 172), i.e. those questions with little discriminability
- to identify which items are too easy, too difficult, too complex or too remote from the respondents' experience
- to identify commonly misunderstood or non-completed items (e.g. by studying common patterns of unexpected response and non-response (Verma and Mallick 1999: 120))
- to try out the coding/classification system for data analysis.

In short, as Oppenheim (1992: 48) remarks, *everything* about the questionnaire should be piloted; nothing should be excluded, not even the type face or the quality of the paper.

The above outline describes a particular kind of pilot: one that does not focus on data, but on matters of coverage and format, gaining feedback from a limited number of respondents and experts on the items set out above.

There is a second type of pilot. This is one which starts with a long list of items and, through statistical analysis and feedback, reduces those items (Kgaile and Morrison 2006). For example, a researcher may generate an initial list of, for example, 120 items to be included in a questionnaire, and wish to know which items to excise. A pilot is conducted on a sizeable and representative number of respondents (e.g. 50–100) and this generates real data – numerical responses. These data can be analysed for the following factors:

- *Reliability:* those items with low reliability (Cronbach's alpha for internal consistency: see Part Five) can be removed.
- *Collinearity:* if items correlate very strongly with others then a decision can be taken to remove one or more of them, provided, of course, that this does not result in the loss of important areas of the research (i.e. human judgement would have to prevail over statistical analysis).
- *Multiple regression:* those items with low betas (see Part Five) can be removed, provided, of course, that this does not result in the loss of important areas of the research (i.e. human judgement would have to prevail over statistical analysis).
- *Factor analysis:* to identify clusters of key variables and to identify redundant items (see Part Five).

As a result of such analysis, the items for removal can be identified, and this can result in a questionnaire of manageable proportions. It is important to have a good-sized and representative sample here in order to generate reliable data for statistical analysis; too few respondents to this type of pilot and this may result in important items being excluded from the final questionnaire.

Practical considerations in questionnaire design

Taking the issues discussed so far in questionnaire design, a range of practical implications for designing a questionnaire can be highlighted:

- Operationalize the purposes of the questionnaire carefully.
- Be prepared to have a pre-pilot to generate items for a pilot questionnaire, and then be ready to modify the pilot questionnaire for the final version.
- If the pilot includes many items, and the intention is to reduce the number of items through statistical analysis or feedback, then be prepared to have a second round of piloting, after the first pilot has been modified.
- Decide on the most appropriate *type* of question – dichotomous, multiple choice, rank orderings, rating scales, constant sum, ratio, closed, open.
- Ensure that every issue has been explored exhaustively and comprehensively; decide on the content and explore it in depth and breadth.
- Use several items to measure a specific attribute, concept or issue.
- Ensure that the data acquired will answer the research questions.
- Ask more closed than open questions for ease of analysis (particularly in a large sample).
- Balance comprehensiveness and exhaustive coverage of issues with the demotivating factor of having respondents complete several pages of a questionnaire.
- Ask only one thing at a time in a question. Use single sentences per item wherever possible.
- Keep response categories simple.
- Avoid jargon.
- Keep statements in the present tense wherever possible.
- Strive to be unambiguous and clear in the wording.
- Be simple, clear and brief wherever possible.
- Clarify the kinds of responses required in open questions.

- Balance brevity with politeness (Oppenheim 1992: 122). It might be advantageous to replace a blunt phrase like 'marital status' with a gentler 'Please indicate whether you are married, living with a partner, or single ....' or 'I would be grateful if would tell me if you are married, living with a partner, or single'.
- Ensure a balance of questions that ask for facts and opinions (this is especially true if statistical correlations and cross-tabulations are required).
- Avoid leading questions.
- Try to avoid threatening questions.
- Do not assume that respondents know the answers, or have information to answer the questions, or will always tell the truth (wittingly or not). Therefore include 'don't know', 'not applicable', 'unsure', 'neither agree nor disagree' and 'not relevant' categories.
- Avoid making the questions too hard.
- Balance the number of negative questions with the number of positive questions (Black 1999: 229).
- Consider the readability levels of the questionnaire and the reading and writing abilities of the respondents (which may lead the researcher to conduct the questionnaire as a structured interview).
- Put sensitive questions later in the questionnaire in order to avoid creating a mental set in the mind of respondents, but not so late in the questionnaire that boredom and lack of concentration have set it.
- Intersperse sensitive questions with non-sensitive questions.
- Be very clear on the layout of the questionnaire so that it is unambiguous and attractive (this is particularly the case if a computer program is going to be used for data analysis).
- Avoid, where possible, splitting an item over more than one page, as the respondent may think that the item from the previous page is finished.
- Ensure that the respondent knows how to enter a reply to each question, e.g. by underlining, circling, ticking, writing;

- provide the instructions for introducing, completing and returning (or collection of) the questionnaire (provide a stamped addressed envelope if it is to be a postal questionnaire).
- Pilot the questionnaire, using a group of respondents who are drawn from the possible sample but who will not receive the final, refined version.
- With the data analysis in mind, plan so that the appropriate scales and kinds of data (e.g. nominal, ordinal, interval and ratio) are used.
- Decide how to avoid falsification of responses (e.g. introduce a checking mechanism into the questionnaire responses to another question on the same topic or issue).
- Be satisfied if you receive a 50 per cent response to the questionnaire; decide what you will do with missing data and what is the significance of the missing data (that might have implications for the strata of a stratified sample targeted in the questionnaire), and why the questionnaires have not been completed and returned. For example, were the questions too threatening or was the questionnaire too long? (This might have been signalled in the pilot).
- Include a covering explanation, thanking the potential respondent for anticipated cooperation, indicating the purposes of the research, how anonymity and confidentiality will be addressed, who you are and what position you hold, and who will be party to the final report.
- If the questionnaire is going to be administered by someone other than the researcher, ensure that instructions for administration are provided and that they are clear.

A key issue that permeates this lengthy list is for the researcher to pay considerable attention to respondents; to see the questionnaire through their eyes, and envisage how they will regard it (e.g. from hostility to suspicion to apathy to grudging compliance to welcome; from easy to difficult, from motivating to boring, from straightforward to complex etc.).

Administering questionnaires

Questionnaires can be administered in several ways, including:

- self-administration
- post
- face-to-face interview
- telephone
- Internet.

Here we discuss only self-administered and postal questionnaires. Chapter 16 covers administration by face-to-face interview and by telephone, and Chapter 10 covers administration by the Internet. We also refer readers to Chapter 9 on surveys, to the section on conducting surveys by interview.

Self-administered questionnaires

There are two types of self-administered questionnaire: those that are completed in the presence of the researcher and those that are filled in when the researcher is absent (e.g. at home, in the workplace).

Self-administered questionnaires in the presence of the researcher

The presence of the researcher is helpful in that it enables any queries or uncertainties to be addressed immediately with the questionnaire designer. Further, it typically ensures a good response rate (e.g. undertaken with teachers at a staff meeting or with students in one or more classes). It also ensures that all the questions are completed (the researcher can check these before finally receiving the questionnaire) and filled in correctly (e.g. no rating scale items that have more than one entry per item, and no missed items). It means that the questionnaires are completed rapidly and on one occasion, i.e. it can gather data from many respondents simultaneously.

On the other hand, having the researcher present may be threatening and exert a sense of compulsion, where respondents may feel uncomfortable about completing the questionnaire, and may not want to complete it or even start it. Respondents may also want extra time to think about and complete the questionnaire, maybe at home, and they are denied the opportunity to do this.

Having the researcher present also places pressure on the researcher to attend at an agreed time and in an agreed place, and this may be time-consuming and require the researcher to travel extensively, thereby extending the time frame for data collection. Travel costs for conducting the research with dispersed samples could also be expensive.

Self-administered questionnaires without the presence of the researcher

The absence of the researcher is helpful in that it enables respondents to complete the questionnaire in private, to devote as much time as they wish to its completion, to be in familiar surroundings, and to avoid the potential threat or pressure to participate caused by the researcher's presence. It can be inexpensive to operate, and is more anonymous than having the researcher present. This latter point, in turn, can render the data more or less honest: it is perhaps harder to tell lies or not to tell the whole truth in the presence of the researcher, and it is also easier to be very honest and revealing about sensitive matters without presence of the researcher.

The down side, however, is that the researcher is not there to address any queries or problems that respondents may have, and they may omit items or give up rather than try to contact the researcher. Respondents may also wrongly interpret and, consequently, answer questions inaccurately. They may present an untrue picture to the researcher, for example answering what they would like a situation to be rather than what the actual situation is, or painting a falsely negative or positive picture of the situation or themselves. Indeed, the researcher has no control over the environment in which the questionnaire is completed, e.g. time of day, noise distractions, presence of others with whom to discuss the questions and responses, seriousness given to the completion of the questionnaire, or even whether it is completed by the intended person.

Postal questionnaires

Frequently, the postal questionnaire is the best form of survey in an educational inquiry. Take, for example, the researcher intent on investigating the adoption and use made of a new curriculum series in secondary schools. An interview survey based upon some sampling of the population of schools would be both expensive and time-consuming. A postal questionnaire, on the other hand, would have several distinct advantages. Moreover, given the usual constraints over finance and resources, it might well prove the only viable way of carrying through such an inquiry.

What evidence we have about the advantages and disadvantages of postal surveys derives from settings other than educational. Many of the findings, however, have relevance to the educational researcher. Here, we focus upon some of the ways in which educational researchers can maximize the response level that they obtain when using postal surveys.

A number of myths about postal questionnaires are not borne out by the evidence (see Hoinville and Jowell 1978). Response levels to postal surveys are not invariably less than those obtained by interview procedures; frequently they equal, and in some cases surpass, those achieved in interviews. Nor does the questionnaire necessarily have to be short in order to obtain a satisfactory response level. With sophisticated respondents, for example, a short questionnaire might appear to trivialize complex issues with which they are familiar. Hoinville and Jowell (1978) identify a number of factors in securing a good response rate to a postal questionnaire.

Initial mailing

- Use good-quality envelopes, typed and addressed to a named person wherever possible.

- Use first-class – rapid – postage services, with stamped rather than franked envelopes wherever possible.
- Enclose a first-class stamped envelope for the respondent's reply.
- In surveys of the general population, Thursday is the best day for mailing out; in surveys of organizations, Monday or Tuesday are recommended.
- Avoid at all costs a December survey (questionnaires will be lost in the welter of Christmas postings in the western world).

Follow-up letter

Of the four factors that Hoinville and Jowell (1978) discuss in connection with maximizing response levels, the follow-up letter has been shown to be the most productive. The following points should be borne in mind in preparing reminder letters:

- All of the rules that apply to the covering letter apply even more strongly to the follow-up letter.
- The follow-up should re-emphasize the importance of the study and the value of the respondent's participation.
- The use of the second person singular, the conveying of an air of disappointment at non-response and some surprise at non-cooperation have been shown to be effective ploys.
- Nowhere should the follow-up give the impression that non-response is normal or that numerous non-responses have occurred in the particular study.
- The follow-up letter must be accompanied by a further copy of the questionnaire together with a first-class stamped addressed envelope for its return.
- Second and third reminder letters suffer from the law of diminishing returns, so how many follow-ups are recommended and what success rates do they achieve? It is difficult to generalize, but the following points are worth bearing in mind. A well-planned postal survey should obtain at least a 40 per cent response rate and with the judicious use of reminders,

a 70 per cent to 80 per cent response level should be possible. A preliminary pilot survey is invaluable in that it can indicate the general level of response to be expected. The main survey should generally achieve at least as high as and normally a higher level of return than the pilot inquiry. The Office of Population Censuses and Surveys recommends the use of three reminders which, they say, can increase the original return by as much as 30 per cent in surveys of the general public. A typical pattern of responses to the three follow-ups is as follows:

- Original dispatch   40 per cent
- First follow-up   +20 per cent
- Second follow-up   +10 per cent
- Third follow-up   +5 per cent
- Total   75 per cent

Bailey (1994: 163–9) shows that follow-ups can be both by mail and by telephone. If a follow-up letter is sent, then this should be around three weeks after the initial mailing. A second follow-up is also advisable, and this should take place one week after the first follow up. Bailey (1994: 165) reports research that indicates that a second follow-up can elicit up to a 95.6 per cent response rate compared to a 74.8 per cent response with no follow-up. A telephone call *in advance* of the questionnaire can also help in boosting response rates (by up to 8 per cent).

Incentives

An important factor in maximizing response rates is the use of incentives. Although such usage is comparatively rare in British surveys, it can substantially reduce non-response rates particularly when the chosen incentives accompany the initial mailing rather than being mailed subsequently as rewards for the return of completed schedules. The explanation of the effectiveness of this particular ploy appears to lie in the sense of obligation that is created in the recipient. Care is needed in selecting the most appropriate type of incentive. It should clearly be seen as a token rather than a payment for the respondent's efforts and, according to Hoinville and Jowell (1978), should be as neutral as possible. In this respect, they suggest that books of postage stamps or ballpoint pens are cheap, easily packaged in the questionnaire envelopes, and appropriate to the task required of the respondent.

The preparation of a flow chart can help the researcher to plan the timing and the sequencing of the various parts of a postal survey. One such flow chart suggested by Hoinville and Jowell (1978) is shown in Box 15.5. The researcher might wish to add a chronological chart alongside it to help plan the exact timing of the events shown here.

Validity

Our discussion, so far, has concentrated on ways of increasing the response rate of postal questionnaires; we have said nothing yet about the validity of this particular technique.

Validity of postal questionnaires can be seen from two viewpoints according to Belson (1986). First, whether respondents who complete questionnaires do so accurately, and second, whether those who fail to return their questionnaires would have given the same distribution of answers as did the returnees.

The question of accuracy can be checked by means of the intensive interview method, a technique consisting of twelve principal tactics that include familiarization, temporal reconstruction, probing and challenging. The interested reader should consult Belson (1986: 35–8).

The problem of non-response (the issue of 'volunteer bias' as Belson calls it) can, in part, be checked on and controlled for, particularly when the postal questionnaire is sent out on a continuous basis. It involves follow-up contact with non-respondents by means of interviewers trained to secure interviews with such people. A comparison is then made between the replies of respondents and non-respondents.

Processing questionnaire data

Let us assume that researchers have followed the advice we have given about the planning

Box 15.5
A flow chart for the planning of a postal survey

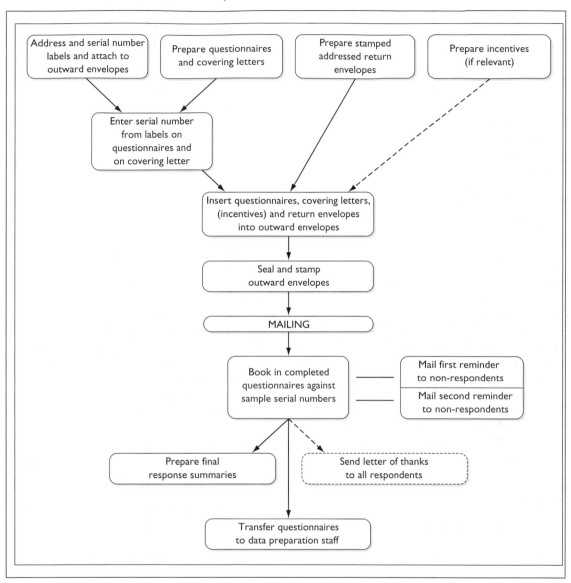

Source: Hoinville and Jowell 1978

of postal questionnaires and have secured a high response rate to their surveys. Their task is now to reduce the mass of data they have obtained to a form suitable for analysis. 'Data reduction', as the process is called, generally consists of coding data in preparation for analysis – by hand in the case of small surveys; by computers when numbers are larger. First, however, prior to coding, the questionnaires have to be checked. This task is referred to as *editing*.

Editing questionnaires is intended to identify and eliminate errors made by respondents. (In addition to the clerical editing that we discuss in this section, editing checks are also performed by the computer. For an account of computer-run structure checks and valid coding range checks, see Hoinville and Jowell (1978: 150–5). Moser and Kalton (1977) point to three central tasks in editing:

- *Completeness:* a check is made that there is an answer to every question. In most surveys, interviewers are required to record an answer to every question (a 'not applicable' category always being available). Missing answers can sometimes be cross-checked from other sections of the survey. At worst, respondents can be contacted again to supply the missing information.
- *Accuracy:* as far as is possible, a check is made that all questions are answered accurately. Inaccuracies arise out of carelessness on the part of either interviewers or respondents. Sometimes a deliberate attempt is made to mislead. A tick in the wrong box, a ring round the wrong code, an error in simple arithmetic – all can reduce the validity of the data unless they are picked up in the editing process.
- *Uniformity:* a check is made that interviewers have interpreted instructions and questions uniformly. Sometimes the failure to give explicit instructions over the interpretation of respondents' replies leads to interviewers recording the same answer in a variety of answer codes instead of one. A check on uniformity can help eradicate this source of error.

The primary task of data reduction is *coding*, that is, assigning a code number to each answer to a survey question. Of course, not all answers to survey questions can be reduced to code numbers. Many open-ended questions, for example, are not reducible in this way for computer analysis. Coding can be built into the construction of the questionnaire itself. In this case, we talk of precoded answers. Where coding is developed after the questionnaire has been administered and answered by respondents, we refer to post-coded answers. Precoding is appropriate for closed-ended questions – male 1, female 2, for example; or single 1, married 2, separated 3, divorced 4. For questions such as those whose answer categories are known in advance, a coding frame is generally developed before the interviewing commences so that it can be printed into the questionnaire itself. For open-ended questions (Why did you choose this particular in-service course rather than XYZ?), a coding frame has to be devised after the completion of the questionnaire. This is best done by taking a random sample of the questionnaires (10 per cent or more, time permitting) and generating a frequency tally of the range of responses as a preliminary to coding classification. Having devised the coding frame, the researcher can make a further check on its validity by using it to code up a further sample of the questionnaires. It is vital to get coding frames right from the outset – extending them or making alterations at a later point in the study is both expensive and wearisome.

There are several computer packages that will process questionnaire survey data. At the time of writing one such is SphinxSurvey. This package, like others of its type, assists researchers in the design, administration and processing of questionnaires, either for paper-based or for on-screen administration. Responses can be entered rapidly, and data can be examined automatically, producing graphs and tables, as well as a wide range of statistics (the Plus edition offers lexical analysis of open-ended text, and the Lexica Edition has additional functions for qualitative data analysis). A web site for previewing a demonstration of this programme can be found at http://www.scolari.co.uk and is typical of several of its kind.

While coding is usually undertaken by the researcher, Sudman and Bradburn (1982: 149) also make the case for coding by the respondents themselves, to increase validity. This is particularly valuable in open-ended questionnaire items, though, of course, it does assume not only the willingness of respondents to become involved *post hoc* but also that the researcher can identify and trace the respondents, which, as was indicated earlier, is an ethical matter.

16 Interviews

Introduction

The use of the interview in research marks a move away from seeing human subjects as simply manipulable and data as somehow external to individuals, and towards regarding knowledge as generated between humans, often through conversations (Kvale 1996: 11). Regarding an interview, as Kvale (1996: 14) remarks, as an *inter-view*, an interchange of views between two or more people on a topic of mutual interest, sees the centrality of human interaction for knowledge production, and emphasizes the social situatedness of research data. As we suggested in Chapter 2, knowledge should be seen as constructed between participants, generating *data* rather than *capta* (Laing 1967: 53). As such, the interview is not exclusively either subjective or objective, it is intersubjective (Laing 1967: 66). Interviews enable participants – be they interviewers or interviewees – to discuss their interpretations of the world in which they live, and to express how they regard situations from their own point of view. In these senses the interview is not simply concerned with collecting data about life: it is part of life itself, its human embeddedness is inescapable.

The interview is a flexible tool for data collection, enabling multi-sensory channels to be used: verbal, non-verbal, spoken and heard. The order of the interview may be controlled while still giving space for spontaneity, and the interviewer can press not only for complete answers but also for responses about complex and deep issues. In short, the interview is a powerful implement for researchers. On the other hand, the researcher using interviews has to be aware that they are expensive in time, they are open to interviewer bias, they may be inconvenient for respondents,

issues of interviewee fatigue may hamper the interview, and anonymity may be difficult. We explore these several issues in this chapter.

An interview is not an ordinary, everyday conversation (Dyer 1995: 56–8). For example, in contrast to an everyday conversation, it has a specific purpose, it is often question-based, with the questions being asked by the interviewer; the interviewer alone may express ignorance (and not the interviewee), and the responses must be as explicit and often as detailed as possible. The interview is a constructed rather than naturally occurring situation, and this renders it different from an everyday conversation; therefore the researcher has an obligation to set up, and abide by, the different 'rules of the game' in an interview.

Conceptions of the interview

Kitwood (1977) lucidly contrasts three conceptions of an interview. The first conception is that of a potential means of pure information transfer. He explains that

> if the interviewer does his job well (establishes rapport, asks questions in an acceptable manner, etc.), and if the respondent is sincere and well-motivated, accurate data may be obtained. Of course all kinds of bias are liable to creep in, but with skill these can largely be eliminated. In its fullest expression, this view accords closely with that of the psychometricians, who apparently believe that there is a relatively permanent, consistent, 'core' to the personality, about which a person will give information under certain conditions. Such features as lying, or the tendency to give a socially desirable response, are to be eliminated where possible.
>
> (Kitwood 1977)

This conception of the interview appears to be widely held.

A second conception of the interview is that of a transaction which inevitably has bias, that needs to be recognized and controlled. According to this viewpoint, Kitwood (1977) explains that 'each participant in an interview will define the situation in a particular way. This fact can be best handled by building controls into the research design, for example by having a range of interviewers with different biases.' The interview is best understood in terms of a theory of motivation which recognizes a range of non-rational factors governing human behaviour, like emotions, unconscious needs and interpersonal influences. Kitwood (1977) points out that both these views of the interview regard the inherent features of interpersonal transactions as if they were 'potential obstacles to sound research, and therefore to be removed, controlled, or at least harnessed in some way'.

The third conception of the interview sees it as an encounter necessarily sharing many of the features of everyday life (see, for example, Box 16.1). Kitwood (1977) suggests that what is required, according to this view, is not a technique for dealing with bias, but a theory of everyday life that takes account of the relevant features of interviews. These may include role-playing, stereotyping, perception and understanding. As Walford (2001: 90) remarks, 'interviewers and interviewees co-construct the interview'. The interview is a social encounter, not simply a site for information exchange, and researchers would be well advised to keep this in the forefront of their minds when conducting an interview.

One of the strongest advocates of this latter viewpoint is Cicourel (1964), who lists five of the unavoidable features of the interview situation that would normally be regarded as problematic:

- There are many factors which inevitably differ from one interview to another, such as mutual trust, social distance and the interviewer's control.

Box 16.1
Attributes of ethnographers as interviewers

Trust
There would have to be a relationship between the interviewer and interviewee that transcended the research, that promoted a bond of friendship, a feeling of togetherness and joint pursuit of a common mission rising above personal egos.

Curiosity
There would have to be a desire to know, to learn people's views and perceptions of the facts, to hear their stories, discover their feelings. This is the motive force, and it has to be a burning one, that drives researchers to tackle and overcome the many difficulties involved in setting up and conducting successful interviews.

Naturalness
As with observation one endeavours to be unobtrusive in order to witness events as they are, untainted by one's presence and actions, so in interviews the aim is to secure what is within the minds of interviewees, uncoloured and unaffected by the interviewer.

Source: adapted from Woods 1986

- The respondent may well feel uneasy and adopt avoidance tactics if the questioning is too deep.
- Both interviewer and respondent are bound to hold back part of what it is in their power to state.
- Many of the meanings that are clear to one will be relatively opaque to the other, even when the intention is genuine communication.
- It is impossible, just as in everyday life, to bring every aspect of the encounter within rational control.

The message that proponents of this view would express is that no matter how hard interviewers may try to be systematic and objective, the constraints of everyday life will be a part of whatever interpersonal transactions they initiate. Kitwood (1977) concludes:

The solution is to have as explicit a theory as possible to take the various factors into account. For those who hold this view, there are not good interviews and bad in the conventional sense. There are simply social encounters; goodness and badness are predicates applicable, rather, to the theories within which the phenomena are explained.

(Kitwood 1977)

Indeed Barker and Johnson (1998: 230) argue that the interview is a particular medium for enacting or displaying people's knowledge of cultural forms, as questions, far from being neutral, are couched in the cultural repertoires of all participants, indicating how people make sense of their social world and of each other.[1]

Purposes of the interview

The purposes of the interview in the wider context of life are many and varied, for example:

- to evaluate or assess a person in some respect
- to select or promote an employee
- to effect therapeutic change, as in the psychiatric interview
- to test or develop hypotheses
- to gather data, as in surveys or experimental situations
- to sample respondents' opinions, as in doorstep interviews.

Although in each of these situations the respective roles of the interviewer and interviewee may vary and the motives for taking part may differ, a common denominator is the transaction that takes place between seeking information on the part of one and supplying information on the part of the other.

As a distinctive research technique, the interview may serve three purposes. First, it may be used as the principal means of gathering information having direct bearing on the research objectives. As Tuckman (1972) describes it:

> By providing access to what is 'inside a person's head', [it] makes it possible to measure what a person knows (knowledge or information), what a person likes or dislikes (values and preferences), and what a person thinks (attitudes and beliefs).

(Tuckman 1972)

Second, it may be used to test hypotheses or to suggest new ones; or as an explanatory device to help identify variables and relationships. Third, the interview may be used in conjunction with other methods in a research undertaking. In this connection, Kerlinger (1970) suggests that it might be used to follow up unexpected results, for example, or to validate other methods, or to go deeper into the motivations of respondents and their reasons for responding as they do.

As our interests lie primarily in reviewing research methods and techniques, we will subsequently limit ourselves to the use of the interview as a specific research tool. Interviews in this sense range from the formal interview in which set questions are asked and the answers recorded on a standardized schedule through less formal interviews in which the interviewer is free to modify the sequence of questions, change the wording, explain them or add to them to the completely informal interview where the interviewer may have a number of key issues which he or she raises in conversational style instead of having a set questionnaire. Beyond this point is located the non-directive interview in which the interviewer takes on a subordinate role.

The research interview has been defined as 'a two-person conversation initiated by the interviewer for the specific purpose of obtaining research-relevant information, and focused by him on content specified by research objectives of systematic description, prediction, or explanation' (Cannell and Kahn 1968). It is an unusual method in that it involves the gathering of data through direct verbal interaction between individuals. In this sense it differs from the questionnaire where the respondent is required to record in some way her responses to set questions.

As the interview has some things in common with the self-administered questionnaire, it is frequently compared with it. Each has advantages over the other in certain respects. The advantages of the questionnaire, for instance, are that it tends to be more reliable because it is anonymous, it encourages greater honesty, it is more economical than the interview in terms of time and money and there is the possibility that it may be mailed. Its disadvantages, on the other hand, are that there is often too low a percentage of returns, the interviewer is able to answer questions concerning both the purpose of the interview and any misunderstandings experienced by the interviewee, for it sometimes happens in the case of the latter that the same questions have different meanings for different people. If only closed items are used, the questionnaire will be subject to the weaknesses already discussed; if only open items are used, respondents may be unwilling to write their answers for one reason or another. Questionnaires also present problems to people of limited literacy, and an interview can be conducted at an appropriate speed whereas questionnaires are often filled in hurriedly.

By way of interest, we illustrate the relative merits of the interview and the questionnaire in Box 16.2. It has been pointed out that the direct interaction of the interview is the source of both its advantages and disadvantages as a research technique (Borg 1963). One advantage, for example, is that it allows for greater depth than is the case with other methods of data collection. A disadvantage, on the other hand, is that it is prone to subjectivity and bias on the part of the interviewer.

Oppenheim (1992: 81–2) suggests that interviews have a higher response rate than questionnaires because respondents become more involved and, hence, motivated; they enable more to be said about the research than is usually mentioned in a covering letter to a questionnaire, and they are better than questionnaires for handling more difficult and open-ended questions.

Types of interview

The number of types of interview given is frequently a function of the sources one reads! For example, LeCompte and Preissle (1993) give six types: standardized interviews; in-depth interviews; ethnographic interviews; elite interviews; life history interviews; focus groups. Bogdan and Biklen (1992) add: semi-structured interviews; group interviews. Lincoln and Guba (1985) add: structured interviews. Oppenheim (1992: 65) adds: exploratory interviews.

Patton (1980: 206) outlines four types: informal conversational interviews; interview guide approaches; standardized open-ended interviews;

Box 16.2
Summary of relative merits of interview versus questionnaire

Consideration	Interview	Questionnaire
Personal need to collect data	Requires interviewers	Requires a secretary
Major expense	Payment to interviewers	Postage and printing
Opportunities for response-keying (personalization)	Extensive	Limited
Opportunities for asking	Extensive	Limited
Opportunities for probing	Possible	Difficult
Relative magnitude of data reduction	Great (because of coding)	Mainly limited to rostering
Typically, the number of respondents who can be reached	Limited	Extensive
Rate of return	Good	Poor
Sources of error	Interviewer, instrument, coding, sample	Limited to instrument and sample
Overall reliability	Quite limited	Fair
Emphasis on writing skill	Limited	Extensive

Source: Tuckman 1972

closed quantitative interviews. Patton (1980) sets these out clearly (Box 16.3).

How is the researcher to comprehend the range of these various types? Kvale (1996: 126–7) sets the several forms of interview along a series of continua, arguing that interviews differ in the openness of their purpose, their degree of structure, the extent to which they are exploratory or

Box 16.3
Strengths and weaknesses of different types of interview

Type of interview	Characteristics	Strengths	Weaknesses
Informal conversational interview	Questions emerge from the immediate context and are asked in the natural course of things; there is no predetermination of question topics or wording.	Increases the salience and relevance of questions; interviews are built on and emerge from observations; the interview can be matched to individuals and circumstances.	Different information collected from different people with different questions. Less systematic and comprehensive if certain questions don't arise 'naturally'. Data organization and analysis can be quite difficult.
Interview guide approach	Topics and issues to be covered are specified in advance, in outline form; interviewer decides sequence and working of questions in the course of the interview.	The outline increases the comprehensiveness of the data and makes data collection somewhat systematic for each respondent. Logical gaps in data can be anticipated and closed. Interviews remain fairly conversational and situational.	Important and salient topics may be inadvertently omitted. Interviewer flexibility in sequencing and wording questions can result in substantially different responses, thus reducing the comparability of responses.
Standardized open-ended interviews	The exact wording and sequence of questions are determined in advance. All interviewees are asked the same basic questions in the same order.	Respondents answer the same questions, thus increasing comparability of responses; data are complete for each person on the topics addressed in the interview. Reduces interviewer effects and bias when several interviewers are used. Permits decision-makers to see and review the instrumentation used in the evaluation. Facilitates organization and analysis of the data.	Little flexibility in relating the interview to particular individuals and circumstances; standardized wording of questions may constrain and limit naturalness and relevance of questions and answers.
Closed quantitative interviews	Questions and response categories are determined in advance. Responses are fixed; respondent chooses from among these fixed responses.	Data analysis is simple; responses can be directly compared and easily aggregated; many short questions can be asked in a short time.	Respondents must fit their experiences and feelings into the researcher's categories; may be perceived as impersonal, irrelevant, and mechanistic. Can distort what respondents really mean or experienced by so completely limiting their response choices.

Source: Patton 1980: 206

hypothesis-testing, whether they seek description or interpretation, or whether they are largely cognitive-focused or emotion-focused. A major difference appears to lie in the degree of structure in the interview, which, itself, reflects the purposes of the interview, for example, to generate numbers of respondents' feelings about a given issue or to indicate unique, alternative feelings about a particular matter. Lincoln and Guba (1985: 269) suggest that the structured interview is useful when researchers are aware of what they do not know and therefore are in a position to frame questions that will supply the knowledge required, whereas the unstructured interview is useful when researchers are not aware of what they do not know, and therefore, rely on the respondents to tell them!

The issue here is of 'fitness for purpose'; the more one wishes to gain comparable data – across people, across sites – the more standardized and quantitative one's interview tends to become; the more one wishes to acquire unique, non-standardized, personalized information about how individuals view the world, the more one veers towards qualitative, open-ended, unstructured interviewing. Indeed, this is true not simply of interviews but of their written counterpart – questionnaires. Oppenheim (1992: 86) indicates that standardization should refer to *stimulus equivalence*, i.e. that every respondent should *understand* the interview question in the same way, rather than replicating the exact wording, as some respondents might have difficulty with, or interpret very differently, and perhaps irrelevantly, particular questions. (He also adds that as soon as the wording of a question is altered, however minimally, it becomes, in effect, a different question!)

Oppenheim (1992: 65) suggests that *exploratory* interviews are designed to be essentially heuristic and seek to develop hypotheses rather than to collect facts and numbers. He notes that these frequently cover emotionally loaded topics and, hence, require skill on the part of the interviewer to handle the interview situation, enabling respondents to talk freely and emotionally and to have candour, richness, depth, authenticity and honesty about their experiences.

Morrison (1993: 34–6) sets out five continua of different ways of conceptualizing interviews. At one end of the first continuum are numbers, statistics, objective facts, quantitative data; at the other end are transcripts of conversations, comments, subjective accounts, essentially word-based qualitative data.

At one end of the second continuum are closed questions, multiple choice questions where respondents have to select from a given, predetermined range of responses that particular response which most accurately represents what they wish to have recorded for them; at the other end of the continuum are much more open-ended questions which do not require the selection from a given range of responses – respondents can answer the questions in their own way and in their own words, i.e. the research is responsive to participants' own frames of reference and response.

At one end of the third continuum is a desire to measure responses, to compare one set of responses with another, to correlate responses, to see how many people said this, how many rated a particular item as such-and-such; at the other end of the continuum is a desire to capture the uniqueness of a particular situation, person or programme – what makes it different from others, i.e. to record the quality of a situation or response.

At one end of the fourth continuum is a desire for formality and the precision of numbers and prescribed categories of response where the researcher knows in advance what is being sought; at the other end is a more responsive, informal intent where what is being sought is more uncertain and indeterminate – we know what we are looking for only when we have found it! The researcher goes into the situation and responds to what emerges.

At one end of the fifth continuum is the attempt to find regularities – of response, opinions etc. – in order to begin to make generalizations from the data, to describe what is happening; at the other end is the attempt to portray and catch uniqueness, the quality of a response, the complexity of a situation, to understand why respondents say what they say, and all of this in their own terms.

One can cluster the sets of poles of the five continua thus:

Quantitative approaches	Qualitative approaches
numbers	words
predetermined, given	open-ended, responsive
measuring	capturing uniqueness
short-term, intermittent	long-term, continuous
comparing	capturing particularity
correlating	valuing quality
frequencies	individuality
formality	informality
looking at	looking for
regularities	uniqueness
description	explanation
objective facts	subjective facts
describing	interpreting
looking in from the outside	looking from the inside
structured	unstructured
statistical	ethnographic, illuminative

The left-hand column is much more formal and pre-planned to a high level of detail, while the right-hand column is far less formal and the fine detail emerges only once the researcher is *in situ*. Interviews in the left-hand column are front-loaded, that is, they require all the categories and multiple choice questions to be worked out in advance. This usually requires a pilot to try out the material and refine it. Once the detail of this planning is completed, the analysis of the data is relatively straightforward because the categories for analysing the data have been worked out in advance, hence data analysis is rapid.

The right-hand column is much more end-loaded, that is, it is quicker to commence and gather data because the categories do not have to be worked out in advance, they emerge once the data have been collected. However, in order to discover the issues that emerge and to organize the data presentation, the analysis of the data takes considerably longer.

Kvale (1996: 30) sets out key characteristics of qualitative research interviews, which should do the following:

- Engage, understand and interpret the key feature of the lifeworlds of the participants.

- Use natural language to gather and understand qualitative knowledge.
- Be able to reveal and explore the nuanced descriptions of the lifeworlds of the participants.
- Elicit descriptions of specific situations and actions, rather than generalities.
- Adopt a deliberate openness to new data and phenomena, rather than being too pre-structured.
- Focus on specific ideas and themes, i.e. have direction, but avoid being too tightly structured.
- Accept the ambiguity and contradictions of situations where they occur in participants, if this is a fair reflection of the ambiguous and contradictory situation in which they find themselves.
- Accept that the interview may provoke new insights and changes in the participants themselves.
- Regard interviews as an interpersonal encounter, with all that this entails.
- Be a positive and enriching experience for all participants.

There are four main kinds of interview that we discuss here that may be used specifically as research tools: the structured interview, the unstructured interview, the non-directive interview and the focused interview. The *structured interview* is one in which the content and procedures are organized in advance. This means that the sequence and wording of the questions are determined by means of a schedule and the interviewer is left little freedom to make modifications. Where some leeway is granted to the interviewer, it too is specified in advance. It is therefore characterized by being a closed situation. In contrast to it in this respect, the *unstructured interview* is an open situation, having greater flexibility and freedom. As Kerlinger (1970) notes, although the research purposes govern the questions asked, their content, sequence and wording are entirely in the hands of the interviewer. This does not mean, however, that the unstructured interview is a more casual affair, for in its own way it also has to be carefully planned.

The *non-directive interview* as a research technique derives from the therapeutic or psychiatric interview. The principal features of it are the minimal direction or control exhibited by the interviewer and the freedom the respondent has to express her subjective feelings as fully and as spontaneously as she chooses or is able. Moser and Kalton (1977: 297) argue that respondents should be encouraged to talk about the subject under investigation (e.g. themselves) and to be free to guide the interview, with few set questions or pre-figured frameworks. The interviewer should prompt and probe, pressing for clarity and elucidation, rephrasing and summarizing where necessary and checking for confirmation of this, particularly if the issues are complex or vague.

The need to introduce rather more interviewer control into the non-directive situation led to the development of the *focused interview*. The distinctive feature of this type is that it focuses on a respondent's subjective responses to a known situation in which he or she has been involved and which has been analysed by the interviewer prior to the interview. The interviewer is thereby able to use the data from the interview to substantiate or reject previously formulated hypotheses. As Merton and Kendall (1946) explain,

> In the usual depth interview, one can urge informants to reminisce on their experiences. In the focused interview, however, the interviewer can, when expedient, play a more active role: he can introduce more explicit verbal cues to the stimulus pattern or even *represent* it. In either case this usually activates a concrete report of responses by informants.
>
> (Merton and Kendall 1946)

We shall be examining both the non-directive interview and the focused interview in more detail later in the chapter.

Planning interview-based research procedures

Kvale (1996: 88) sets out seven stages of an interview investigation that can be used to plan this type of research: thematizing, designing, interviewing, transcribing, analysing, verifying and reporting. We use these to structure our comments here about the planning of interview-based research.

Thematizing

The preliminary stage of an interview study will be the point where the purpose of the research is decided. It may begin by outlining the theoretical basis of the study, its broad aims, its practical value and the reasons why the interview approach was chosen. There may then follow the translation of the general goals of the research into more detailed and specific objectives. This is the most important step, for only careful formulation of objectives at this point will eventually produce the right kind of data necessary for satisfactory answers to the research problem.

Designing

There follows the preparation of the interview schedule itself. This involves translating the research objectives into the questions that will make up the main body of the schedule. This needs to be done in such a way that the questions adequately reflect what it is the researcher is trying to find out. It is quite usual to begin this task by writing down the variables to be dealt with in the study. As one commentator says, 'The first step in constructing interview questions is to *specify your variables by name*. Your variables are what you are trying to measure. They tell you where to begin' (Tuckman 1972).

Before the actual interview items are prepared, it is desirable to give some thought to the question format and the response mode. The choice of question format, for instance, depends on a consideration of one or more of the following factors:

- the objectives of the interview
- the nature of the subject matter
- whether the interviewer is dealing in facts, opinions or attitudes
- whether specificity or depth is sought

- the respondent's level of education
- the kind of information the respondent can be expected to have
- whether or not the respondent's thought needs to be structured; some assessment of his or her motivational level
- the extent of the interviewer's own insight into the respondent's situation
- the kind of relationship the interviewer can expect to develop with the respondent.

Having given prior thought to these matters, the researcher is in a position to decide whether to use open and/or closed questions, direct and/or indirect questions, specific and/or non-specific questions, and so on.

Construction of schedules

Three kinds of items are used in the construction of schedules used in research interviews (see Kerlinger 1970). First, 'fixed-alternative' items allow the respondent to choose from two or more alternatives. The most frequently used is the dichotomous item which offers two alternatives only: 'yes-no' or 'agree-disagree', for instance. Sometimes a third alternative such as 'undecided' or 'don't know' is also offered (see http://www.routledge.com/textbooks/ 9780415368780 – Chapter 16, file 16.1.doc).

> *Example:* Do you feel it is against the interests of a school to have to make public its examination results?
> Yes
> No
> Don't know

Kerlinger (1970) has identified the chief advantages and disadvantages of fixed-alternative items. They have, for example, the advantage of achieving greater uniformity of measurement and therefore greater reliability, of making the respondents answer in a manner fitting the response category, and of being more easily coded.

Disadvantages include their superficiality; the possibility of irritating respondents who find none of the alternatives suitable; and the possibility of forcing responses that are inappropriate, either because the alternative chosen conceals ignorance on the part of the respondent or because he or she may choose an alternative that does not accurately represent the true facts. These weaknesses can be overcome, however, if the items are written with care, mixed with open-ended ones, and used in conjunction with probes on the part of the interviewer.

Second, 'open-ended items' have been succinctly defined by Kerlinger (1970) as 'those that supply a frame of reference for respondents' answers, but put a minimum of restraint on the answers and their expression'. Other than the subject of the question, which is determined by the nature of the problem under investigation, there are no other restrictions on either the content or the manner of the interviewee's reply.

> *Example:* What kind of television programmes do you most prefer to watch?

Open-ended questions have a number of advantages: they are flexible; they allow the interviewer to probe so that she may go into more depth if she chooses, or to clear up any misunderstandings; they enable the interviewer to test the limits of the respondent's knowledge; they encourage cooperation and help establish rapport; and they allow the interviewer to make a truer assessment of what the respondent really believes. Open-ended situations can also result in unexpected or unanticipated answers which may suggest hitherto unthought-of relationships or hypotheses. A particular kind of open-ended question is the 'funnel' to which reference has been made earlier. This starts, the reader will recall, with a broad question or statement and then narrows down to more specific ones. Kerlinger (1970) quotes an example from the study by Sears *et al.* (1957):

> All babies cry, of course. Some mothers feel that if you pick up a baby every time it cries, you will spoil it. Others think you should never let a baby cry for very long. How do you feel about this? What did you do about it? How about the middle of the night?
>
> (Sears *et al.* 1957)

Third, the 'scale' is, as we have already seen, a set of verbal items to each of which the interviewee responds by indicating degrees of agreement or disagreement. The individual's response is thus located on a scale of fixed alternatives. The use of this technique along with open-ended questions is a comparatively recent development and means that scale scores can be checked against data elicited by the open-ended questions.

> *Example*: Attendance at school after the age of 14 should be voluntary:
> Strongly agree Agree Undecided Disagree Strongly disagree

It is possible to use one of a number of scales in this context: attitude scales, rank-order scales, rating scales, and so on. We touch upon this subject again subsequently.

In devising questions for the interview, attention has to be given to the following (Arksey and Knight 1999: 93–5):

- the vocabulary to be used (keeping it simple)
- the avoidance of prejudicial language
- the avoidance of ambiguity and imprecision
- leading questions (a decision has to be taken whether it is justified to use them)
- the avoidance of double-barrelled questions (asking more than one point at a time)
- questions that make assumptions (e.g. Do you go to work in your car?)
- hypothetical or speculative questions
- sensitive or personal questions (whether to ask or avoid them)
- assuming that the respondent has the required knowledge/information
- recall (how easy it will be for the respondent to recall memories).

Question formats

We now look at the kinds of questions and modes of response associated with interviewing. First, the matter of question format: how is a question to be phrased or organized (see Wilson 1996)? Tuckman (1972) has listed four such formats that an interviewer may draw upon. Questions may, for example, take a direct or indirect form. Thus an interviewer could ask a teacher whether she likes teaching: this would be a direct question. Or else an interviewer could adopt an indirect approach by asking for the respondent's views on education in general and the ways schools function. From the answers proffered, the interviewer could make inferences about the teacher's opinions concerning her own job. Tuckman (1972) suggests that by making the purpose of questions less obvious, the indirect approach is more likely to produce frank and open responses.

There are also those kinds of questions which deal with either a general or specific issue. To ask children what they thought of the teaching methods of the staff as a whole would be a general or non-specific question. To ask children what they thought of their teacher as a teacher would be a specific question. There is also the sequence of questions designated the funnel in which the movement is from the general and non-specific to the more specific. Tuckman (1972) comments: 'Specific questions, like direct ones, may cause a respondent to become cautious or guarded and give less-than-honest answers. Non-specific questions may lead circuitously to the desired information but with less alarm by the respondents.'

A further distinction is that between questions inviting factual answers and those inviting opinions. To ask people what political party they support would be a factual question. To ask them what they think of the current government's foreign policy would be an opinion question. Both fact and opinion questions can yield less than the truth, however: the former do not always produce factual answers; nor do the latter necessarily elicit honest opinions. In both instances, inaccuracy and bias may be minimized by careful structuring of the questions.

There are several ways of categorizing questions, for example (Spradley 1979; Patton 1980):

- descriptive questions
- experience questions
- behaviour questions
- knowledge questions
- construct-forming questions

- contrast questions (asking respondents to contrast one thing with another)
- feeling questions
- sensory questions
- background questions
- demographic questions.

These concern the *substance* of the question. Kvale (1996: 133–5) adds to these what might be termed the *process* questions, i.e. questions that

- introduce a topic or interview
- follow-up on a topic or idea
- probe for further information or response
- ask respondents to specify and provide examples
- directly ask for information
- indirectly ask for information
- interpret respondents' replies.

We may also note that interviewees may be presented with either a question or a statement. In the case of the latter they will be asked for their response to it in one form or another.

Example question: Do you think homework should be compulsory for all children between 11 and 16?

Example statement: Homework should be compulsory for all children between 11 and 16 years old.
Agree   Disagree   Don't know

Response modes

If there are varied ways of asking questions, it follows there will be several ways in which they may be answered. It is to the different response modes that we now turn. In all, Tuckman (1972) lists seven such modes.

The first of these is the *unstructured response*. This allows respondents to give their answer in whatever way they choose.

Example: Why did you not go to university?

A *structured response*, by contrast, would limit them in some way.

Example: Can you give me two reasons for not going to university?

Although the interviewer has little control over the unstructured response, it does ensure that respondents have the freedom to give their own answer as fully as they choose rather than being constrained in some way by the nature of the question. The chief disadvantage of the unstructured response concerns the matter of quantification. Data yielded in the unstructured response are more difficult to code and quantify than data in the structured response.

A *fill-in response* mode requires the respondent to supply rather than choose a response, though the response is often limited to a word or phrase.

Example: What is your present occupation?
or
How long have you lived at your present address?

The differences between the fill-in response and the unstructured response is one of degree.

A *tabular response* is similar to a fill-in response though more structured. It may demand words, figures or phrases, for example:

University	Subject	Degree	Dates	
			From	To

It is thus a convenient and short-hand way of recording complex information.

A *scaled response* is one structured by means of a series of gradations. Respondents are required to record their response to a given statement by selecting from a number of alternatives.

Example: What are your chances of reaching a top managerial position within the next five years?
Excellent   Good   Fair   Poor   Very Poor

Tuckman (1972) draws our attention to the fact that, unlike an unstructured response which has to be coded to be useful as data, a scaled response is collected in the form of usable and analysable data.

A *ranking response* is one in which a respondent is required to rank-order a series of words, phrases or statements according to a particular criterion.

Example: Rank order the following people in terms of their usefulness to you as sources of advice and guidance on problems you have encountered in the classroom. Use numbers 1 to 5, with 1 representing the person most useful.

Education tutor

Subject tutor

Class teacher

Headteacher

Other student

Ranked data can be analysed by adding up the rank of each response across the respondents, thus resulting in an overall rank order of alternatives.

A *checklist response* requires that respondents select one of the alternatives presented to them. In that they do not represent points on a continuum, they are nominal categories.

> *Example:* I get most satisfaction in college from:
> the social life
> studying on my own
> attending lectures
> college societies
> giving a paper at a seminar

This kind of response tends to yield less information than the other kinds considered.

Finally, the *categorical response* mode is similar to the checklist but simpler in that it offers respondents only two possibilities.

> *Example:* Material progress results in greater happiness for people
> True   False
> *or*
> In the event of another war, would you be prepared to fight for your country?
> Yes   No

Summing the numbers of respondents with the same responses yields a nominal measure.

As a general rule, the kind of information sought and the means of its acquisition will determine the choice of response mode. Data analysis, then, ought properly to be considered alongside the choice of response mode so that the interviewer can be confident that the data will serve her purposes and analysis of them can be duly prepared.

Box 16.4

The selection of response mode

Response mode	Type of data	Chief advantages	Chief disadvantages
Fill-in	Nominal	Less biasing; greater response flexibility	More difficult to score
Scaled	Interval	Easy to score	Time consuming; can be biasing
Ranking	Ordinal	Easy to score; forces discrimination	Difficult to complete
Checklist or categorical	Nominal (may be interval when totalled)	Easy to score; easy to respond	Provides less data and fewer options

Source: Tuckman 1972

Box 16.4 summarizes the relationship between response mode and type of data.

Once the variables to be measured or studied have been identified, questions can be constructed so as to reflect them. If, for example, one of the variables was to be a new social education project that had recently been attempted with 15 year olds in a comprehensive school, one obvious question would be: 'How do you think the project has affected the pupils?' Or, less directly, 'Do you think the children have been given too much or too little responsibility?' It is important to bear in mind that more than one question format and more than one response mode may be employed when building up a schedule. The final mixture will depend on the kinds of factors mentioned earlier – the objectives of the research, and so on.

Where an interview schedule is to be used as part of a field survey in which a number of trained interviewers are to be used, it will of course be necessary to include in it appropriate instructions for both interviewer and interviewees.

The framing of questions for a semi-structured interview will also need to consider *prompts* and *probes* (Morrison 1993: 66). Prompts enable the interviewer to clarify topics or questions, while probes enable the interviewer to ask respondents to extend, elaborate, add to, provide detail for, clarify or qualify their response, thereby addressing richness, depth of response, comprehensiveness and honesty that are some of the hallmarks of successful interviewing (see also Patton 1980: 238). A probe may be simply the follow-up 'why' question. It could comprise simply repeating the question, repeating the answer in a questioning tone, showing interest and understanding, asking for clarification or an example or further explication, or, indeed simply pausing.

Hence an interview schedule for a semi-structured interview (i.e. where topics and open-ended questions are written but the exact sequence and wording does not have to be followed with each respondent) might include the following:

- the topic to be discussed
- the specific possible questions to be put for each topic
- the issues within each topic to be discussed, together with possible questions for each issue
- a series of prompts and probes for each topic, issue and question.

It would be incomplete to end this section without some comment on sampling in addition to question type, for the design of the interview has to consider who is being interviewed. 'How many interviews do I need to conduct?' is a frequent question of novice researchers, asking both about the numbers of people and the number of interviews with each person. The advice here echoes that of Kvale (1996: 101) that one conducts interviews with as many people as necessary in order to gain the information sought. There is no simple rule of thumb, as this depends on the purpose of the interview, for example, whether it is to make generalizations, to provide in-depth, individual data, to gain a range of responses. Although the reader is directed to Chapter 4 on sampling for fuller treatment of these matters, the

issue here is that the interviewer must ensure that the interviewees selected will be able to furnish the researcher with the information, i.e. that they possess the information.

Interviewing

Setting up and conducting the interview will make up the next stage in the procedure. Where interviewers are initiating the research themselves, they will clearly select their own respondents; where interviewers are engaged by another agent, then they will probably be given a list of people to contact. Tuckman (1972) has succinctly reviewed the procedures to adopt at the interview itself. He writes that the interviewer should inform the participant of the nature or purpose of the interview, being honest yet without risking biasing responses, and should strive to put the participant at ease. The conduct of the interview should be explained (what happens, and how, and the structure and organization of the interview), how responses may be recorded (and to seek permission if this is to happen), and these procedures should be observed throughout. During the interview the biases and values of the interviewer should not be revealed, and the interviewer should avoid being judgemental. The interviewer may have to steer respondents if they are rambling off the point, without being impolite.

It is crucial to keep uppermost in one's mind the fact that the interview is a social, interpersonal encounter, not merely a data collection exercise. Indeed Kvale (1996: 125) suggests that an interview follows an unwritten script for interactions, the rules for which only surface when they are transgressed. Hence the interviewer must be at pains to conduct the interview carefully and sensitively. Kvale (1996: 147) adds that, as the researcher is the research instrument, the effective interviewer is not only knowledgeable about the subject matter but also an expert in interaction and communication. The interviewer will need to establish an appropriate atmosphere such that the participant can feel secure to talk freely. This operates at several levels.

For example, there is the need to address the *cognitive* aspect of the interview, ensuring that the interviewer is sufficiently knowledgeable about the subject matter that she or he can conduct the interview in an informed manner, and that the interviewee does not feel threatened by lack of knowledge. That this is a particular problem when interviewing children has been documented by Simons (1982) and Lewis (1992), who indicate that children will tend to say anything rather than nothing at all, thereby limiting the possible reliability of the data. The interviewer must also be vigilant to the fact that respondents may not always be what they seem; they may be providing misinformation, telling lies, evading the issue, putting on a front (Walford 2001: 91), settling scores, and being malicious.

Further, the ethical dimension of the interview needs to be borne in mind, ensuring, for example, informed consent, guarantees of confidentiality, beneficence and non-maleficence (i.e. that the interview may be to the advantage of the respondent and will not harm him or her). The issues of ethics also needs to take account of what is to count as data, for example, it is often after the cassette recorder or video camera has been switched off that the 'gems' of the interview are revealed, or people may wish to say something 'off the record'; the status of this kind of information needs to be clarified before the interview commences. The ethical aspects of interviewing are discussed later in the chapter.

Then there is a need to address the *interpersonal, interactional, communicative and emotional* aspects of the interview. For example, the interviewer and interviewee communicate non-verbally, by facial and bodily expression. Something as slight as a shift in position in a chair might convey whether the researcher is interested, angry, bored, agreeing, disagreeing and so on. Here the interviewer has to be adept at 'active listening'.

Further, the onus is on the interviewer to establish and maintain a good rapport with the interviewee. This concerns being clear, polite, non-threatening, friendly and personable, to the point, but without being too assertive. It also involves being respectful, e.g. some respondents may or may not wish to be called by their first name, family name or title; being dressed too casually may not inspire confidence. Rapport also requires the interviewer to communicate very clearly and positively the purpose, likely duration, nature and conduct and contents of the interview, to give the respondent the opportunity to ask questions, to be sensitive to any emotions in the respondent, to avoid giving any signs of annoyance, criticism or impatience, and to leave the respondent feeling better than, or at least no worse than, she or he felt at the start of the interview. This requires the interviewer to put himself/herself in the shoes of the respondent, and to be sensitive to how it must feel to be interviewed. Rapport does not mean 'liking' the respondent (Dyer 1995: 62); it means handling the situation sensitively and professionally.

The interviewer is also responsible for considering the *dynamics* of the situation, for example, how to keep the conversation going, how to motivate participants to discuss their thoughts, feelings and experiences, how to overcome the problems of the likely asymmetries of power in the interview (where the interviewer typically defines the situation, the topic, the conduct, the introduction, the course of the interview, and the closing of the interview) (Kvale 1996: 126). As Kvale suggests, the interview is not usually a reciprocal interaction between two equal participants. That said, it is important to keep the interview moving forward, and how to achieve this needs to be anticipated by the interviewer, for example by being clear on what one wishes to find out, asking those questions that will elicit the kinds of data sought, giving appropriate verbal and non-verbal feedback to the respondent during the interview. It extends even to considering when the interviewer should keep silent (Kvale 1996: 135).

The 'directiveness' of the interviewer has been scaled by Whyte (1982), where a 6-point scale of directiveness and responding was devised (1 = the least directive, and 6 = the most directive):

1   Making encouraging noises.
2   Reflecting on remarks made by the informant.

3   Probing on the last remark made by the informant.
4   Probing an idea preceding the last remark by the informant.
5   Probing an idea expressed earlier in the interview.
6   Introducing a new topic.

This is not to say that the interviewer should avoid being too directive or not directive enough; indeed, on occasions a confrontational style might yield much more useful data than a non-confrontational style. Further, it may be in the interests of the research if the interview is sometimes quite tightly controlled, as this might facilitate the subsequent analysis of the data. For example, if the subsequent analysis will seek to categorize and classify the responses, then it might be useful for the interviewer to clarify meaning and even suggest classifications during the interview (see Kvale 1996: 130).

Patton (1980: 210) suggests that it is important to maintain the interviewee's motivation, hence the interviewer must keep boredom at bay, for example by keeping to a minimum demographic and background questions. The issue of the *interpersonal* and *interactional* elements reaches further, for the language of all speakers has to be considered, for example, translating the academic language of the researcher into the everyday, more easy-going and colloquial language of the interviewee, in order to generate rich descriptions and authentic data. Patton (1980: 225) goes on to underline the importance of clarity in questioning, and suggests that this entails the interviewer finding out what terms the interviewees use about the matter in hand, what terms they use among themselves, and avoiding the use of academic jargon. The issue here is not only that the language of the interviewer must be understandable to interviewees but also that it must be part of their frame of reference, such that they feel comfortable with it.

This can be pursued even further, suggesting that the age, gender, race, class, dress, language of the interviewers and interviewees will all exert an influence on the interview itself. Bailey (1994:

183) reports that many interviewers are female, middle-class, white-collar workers, yet those they interview may have none of these characteristics. Bailey (1994: 180–2) reports that having women interviewers elicited a greater percentage of honest responses than having male interviewers, that having white interviewers interviewing black respondents yielded different results from having black interviewers interview black respondents. He also suggests that having interviewers avoiding specific identity with particular groups or countercultures in their dress (e.g. rings, pins etc.) should be eschewed (p. 185) as this can bias the interview; rather some unobtrusive clothing should be worn so as to legitimize the role of the interviewer by fitting in with the respondents' expectations of an interviewer's appearance. One can add here that people in power may expect to be interviewed by interviewers in powerful positions and it is more likely that an interview with a powerful person may be granted to a higher status interviewer. This is discussed fully in Chapter 5.

The *sequence* and *framing* of the interview questions will also need to be considered, for example, ensuring that easier and less threatening, non-controversial questions are addressed earlier in the interview in order to put respondents at their ease (see Patton 1980: 210–11). This might mean that the 'what' questions precede the more searching and difficult 'how' and 'why' questions, though, as Patton (1980: 211) reminds us, knowledge questions – 'what'-type questions – can be threatening. The interviewer's questions should be straightforward and brief, even though the responses need not be (Kvale 1996: 132). The interviewer will also need to consider the *kinds* of questions to be put to interviewees, discussed earlier.

There are several problems in the actual conduct of an interview that can be anticipated and, possibly, prevented, ensuring that the interview proceeds comfortably, for example (see Field and Morse 1989):

• avoiding interruptions from outside (e.g. telephone calls, people knocking on the door)
• minimizing distractions

- minimizing the risk of 'stage fright' in interviewees and interviewers
- avoiding asking embarrassing or awkward questions
- jumping from one topic to another
- giving advice or opinions (rather than active listening)
- summarizing too early or closing off an interview too soon
- being too superficial
- handling sensitive matters (e.g. legal matters, personal matters, emotional matters).

Arksey and Knight (1999: 53) suggest that the interviewer should

- appear to be interested
- keep to the interview schedule in a structured interview
- avoid giving signs of approval or disapproval of responses received
- be prepared to repeat questions at the respondent's request
- be prepared to move on to another question without irritation, if the respondent indicates unwillingness or inability to answer the question
- ensure that he/she (i.e. the interviewer) understands a response, checking if necessary (e.g. 'Am I right in thinking that you mean . . .')
- if a response is inadequate, but the interviewer feels that the respondent may have more to say, thank the respondent and add 'and could you please tell me . . . .'
- give the respondent time to answer (i.e. avoid answering the question for the respondent).

There is also the issue of how to record the interview as it proceeds. For example, an audiotape recorder might be unobtrusive but might constrain the respondent; a videotape might yield more accurate data but might be even more constraining, with its connotation of surveillance. Merton *et al.* (1956) comment on the tendency of taping to 'cool things down'. It might be less threatening not to have any mechanical means of recording the interview, in which case the reliability of the data might rely on the memory of the interviewer. An alternative might be to have the interviewer make notes *during* the interview, but this could be highly off-putting for some respondents. The issue here is that there is a trade-off between the need to catch as much data as possible and yet to avoid having so threatening an environment that it impedes the potential of the interview situation.

What is being suggested here is that the interview, as a social encounter, has to take account of, and plan for, the whole range of other possibly non-cognitive factors that form part of everyday conduct. The 'ideal' interview, then, meets several 'quality criteria' (Kvale 1996: 145):

- The extent of spontaneous, rich, specific, and relevant answers from the interviewee.
- The shorter the interviewer's questions and the longer the subject's answers, the better.
- The degree to which the interviewer follows up and clarifies the meanings of the relevant aspects of the answers.
- The ideal interview is to a large extent interpreted throughout the interview.
- The interviewer attempts to verify his or her interpretations of the subject's answers in the course of the interview.
- The interview is 'self-communicating' – it is a story contained in itself that hardly requires much extra description and explanation.

People may refuse to be interviewed (Bailey 1994: 186–7; Cooper and Schindler 2001: 301), e.g. they may

- not give a reason for refusing
- be hostile to what they see as intrusion
- hold anti-authoritarian feelings
- feel that surveys are a waste of time
- speak a foreign language
- take an instant dislike to the interviewer
- say that they are too busy
- feel embarrassed or ignorant
- dislike the topic under review
- be afraid of the consequences of participating
- may feel inadequate or that they do not know the right answer.

The onus is on the interviewer to try to overcome these factors, while recognizing, of course, that they may be legitimate, in which case no further attempt can be made to conduct the interview. It is important for the interviewer to render the interview as a positive, pleasant and beneficial experience, and to convince participants of their own worth and the importance of the topic. If there is a significant difference between the interviewer and the respondent (e.g. gender, age, ethnicity, race, social status, class), then it might be advisable to have another interviewer try to conduct the interview.

So far the assumption has been that there is only one interviewer present at the interview. There is an argument for having more than one interviewer present, not only so that one can transcribe or observe features that might be overlooked by the other interviewer while the other is engaging the respondent (and these roles have to be signaled clearly to the respondent at the interview), but also to share the interviewing. Joint interviews can provide two versions of the interview – a cross-check – and one can complement the other with additional points, leading to a more complete and reliable record. It also enables one interviewer to observe non-verbal features such as the power and status differentials and social dynamics, and, if there is more than one respondent present at the interview, the relationships between the respondents, e.g. how they support, influence, complement, agree and disagree with each other or, indeed, contradict each other, the power plays at work, and so on.

On the other hand, having more than one interviewer present is not without its difficulties. For example, the roles of the two interviewers may be unclear to the respondents (and it is the job of the interviewers to make this clear), or it may be intimidating to have more than one interviewer present. Researchers will need to weigh carefully the strengths and weaknesses of having more than one interviewer present, and what their roles will be.

Box 16.5 provides a list of guidelines for conduct during the interview.

Interviewers have to be sensitive to their own effect on the interview. For example (Cooper and Schindler 2001: 307), they may fail to secure full cooperation or keep to procedures, they may establish an inappropriate environment (physical, cognitive, interpersonal), they may be exerting undue influence or pressure on the respondent, or they may be selective in recording the data; we consider the issue of reliability in Chapter 6.

It is important for the interviewer to explain to the respondent the purpose, scope, nature and conduct of the interview, the use to be made of the data, ethical issues, the likely duration of the interview, i.e. to explain fully the 'rules of the game' so that the interviewee is left in no doubt as to what will happen during and after the interview. It is important for the interviewer to introduce herself/himself properly and fully to the respondent (maybe even providing identification). The interviewer has to set the scene appropriately, for example, to say that there are no right and wrong answers, that some of the topics may be deep but that they are not designed to be a test, to invite questions and interruptions, and to clear permission for recording. During the interview it is important, also, for the interviewee to speak more than the interviewer, for the interviewer to listen attentively and to be seen by the respondent to be listening attentively, and for the interviewer to be seen to be enjoying, or be at ease with, the interview.

Transcribing

This is a crucial step in interviewing, for there is the potential for massive data loss, distortion and the reduction of complexity. It has been suggested throughout that the interview is a social encounter, not merely a data collection exercise; the problem with much transcription is that it becomes solely a record of data rather than a record of a social encounter. Indeed this problem might have begun at the data collection stage, for example, and audiotape is selective, it filters out important contextual factors, neglecting the visual and non-verbal aspects of the interview (Mishler 1986). Indeed, it is frequently the non-verbal communication that gives more information than the verbal

Box 16.5

Guidelines for the conduct of interviews

- Interviews are an interpersonal matter.
- Avoid saying 'I want to know . . .'; the interviewee is doing you a favour, not being interrogated.
- How to follow up on questions/answers.
- How to keep people on track and how to keep the interview moving forward.
- How to show respect.
- How to divide your attention as interviewer and to share out the interviewees' responses – giving them all a chance to speak in a group interview.
- Do you ask everyone in a group interview to give a response to a question?
- If there is more than one interviewer, what are the roles of the 'silent' interviewer, and do the interviewees know the roles of the interviewers?
- Who is looking at whom.
- If you need to look at your watch, then maybe comment on this publicly.
- Try not to refer to your interview schedule; if you need to refer to it then comment on this publicly (e.g. 'Let me just check that I have covered the points that I wanted').
- Avoid using your pen as a threatening weapon, pointing it at the interviewee.
- Consider your non-verbal communication, eye contact, signs of anxiety, showing respect.
- Give people time to think – don't interrupt if there is silence.
- How to pass over from one interviewer to another and from one interviewee to another if there is more than one interviewer or interviewee.
- How to give feedback and acceptance to the interviewees.
- Should you write responses down – what messages does this give?
- Put yourself in the shoes of the interviewee.
- What are the effects of losing eye contact or of maintaining it for too long?
- Think of your body posture – not too laid back and not too menacing.
- How to interpret and handle silence.
- Avoid looking away from the respondent if possible.
- Avoid interrupting the respondent.
- Avoid judging the respondent or his/her response.
- The interviewer should summarize and crystallize issues and build on them – that is a way of showing respect.
- How to give signs of acceptance of what people are saying, and how to avoid being judgemental.
- Take care of timing – not too long to be boring.
- Give interviewees the final chance to add any comments, and thank them at the end.
- Plan how to hand over the questions to the next interviewer.
- How to arrange the chairs and tables – do you have tables: they may be a barrier or a protection?
- Identify who controls the data, and when the control of the data passes from the interviewee to the interviewer.
- What to do with 'off the record' data?
- Take time to 'manage' the interview and keep interviewees aware of what is happening and where it is going.
- Vary the volume/tone of your voice.
- Avoid giving your own view or opinion; be neutral.
- Who is working harder – the interviewer or the interviewee?
- Who is saying more – the interviewer or the interviewee?
- If there is more than one interviewer, how to avoid one interviewer undermining another.
- Think of prompts and probes.
- How to respond to people who say little?
- Consider the social (and physical) distance between the interviewer and interviewee(s).
- Consider the layout of the furniture – circle/oval/straight line or what?
- Have a clear introduction which makes it clear how the interview will be conducted and how the interviewees can respond (e.g. turn taking).

continued

Box 16.5
continued

- Make sure you summarize and crystallize every so often.
- How to handle interviewees who know more about the topic than you do?
- Do you have males interviewing females and vice versa (think of age/gender/race etc. of interviewers and interviewees)?
- Give some feedback to respondents every so often.
- What is the interview doing that cannot be done in a questionnaire?
- If there are status differentials then don't try to alter them in the space of an interview.
- Plan what to do if the interviewee turns the tables and tries to be the interviewer.
- Plan what to do with aggressive or angry interviewees.
- Plan what to do if powerful interviewees don't answer your questions: maybe you need to admit that you haven't understood very well, and ask for clarification, i.e. that it is your fault.
- Be very prepared, so that you don't need to look at your schedule.
- Know your subject matter well.
- If people speak fast then try to slow down everything.
- As an interviewer, you have the responsibility for making sure the interview runs well.

communication. Morrison (1993: 63) recounts the incident of an autocratic headteacher extolling the virtues of collegiality and democratic decision-making while shaking her head vigorously from side to side and pressing the flat of her hand in a downwards motion away from herself as if to silence discussion! To replace audio recording with video-recording might make for richer data and catch non-verbal communication, but this then becomes very time-consuming to analyse.

Transcriptions inevitably lose data from the original encounter. This problem is compounded, for a transcription represents the translation from one set of rule systems (oral and interpersonal) to another very remote rule system (written language). As Kvale (1996: 166) suggests, the prefix *trans* indicates a change of state or form; transcription is selective transformation. Therefore it is unrealistic to pretend that the data on transcripts are anything but *already interpreted* data. As Kvale (1996: 167) remarks, the transcript can become an opaque screen between the researcher and the original live interview situation.

Hence there can be no single 'correct' transcription; rather the issue becomes whether, to what extent, and how a transcription is useful for the research. Transcriptions are decontextualized, abstracted from time and space, from the dynamics of the situation, from the live form, and from the social, interactive, dynamic and fluid dimensions of their source; they are frozen.

The words in transcripts are not necessarily as solid as they were in the social setting of the interview. Scheurich (1995: 240) suggests that even conventional procedures for achieving reliability are inadequate here, for holding constant the questions, the interviewer, the interviewee, the time and place does not guarantee stable, unambiguous data. Indeed Mishler (1991: 260) suggests that data and the relationship between meaning and language are contextually situated; they are unstable, changing and capable of endless reinterpretation.

We are not arguing against transcriptions, rather we are cautioning against the researcher believing that they tell everything that took place in the interview. This might require the researcher to ensure that different *kinds* of data are recorded in the transcript of the audiotape, for example:

- what was being said
- the tone of voice of the speaker(s) (e.g. harsh, kindly, encouraging)
- the inflection of the voice (e.g. rising or falling, a question or a statement, a cadence or a pause,

a summarizing or exploratory tone, opening or closing a line of enquiry)

- emphases placed by the speaker
- pauses (short to long) and silences (short to long)
- interruptions
- the mood of the speaker(s) (e.g. excited, angry, resigned, bored, enthusiastic, committed, happy, grudging)
- the speed of the talk (fast to slow, hurried or unhurried, hesitant to confident)
- how many people were speaking simultaneously
- whether a speaker was speaking continuously or in short phrases
- who is speaking to whom
- indecipherable speech
- any other events that were taking place at the same time that the researcher can recall.

If the transcript is of videotape, then this enables the researcher to comment on all of the non-verbal communication that was taking place in addition to the features noted from the audiotape. The issue here is that it is often inadequate to transcribe only spoken words; other data are important. Of course, as soon as other data are noted, this becomes a matter of interpretation (what is a long pause, what is a short pause, was the respondent happy or was it just a 'front', what gave rise to such-and-such a question or response, why did the speaker suddenly burst into tears). As Kvale (1996: 183) notes, interviewees' statements are not simply collected by the interviewer, they are, in reality, co-authored.

Analysing

Once data from the interview have been collected, the next stage involves analysing them, often by some form of coding or scoring. In qualitative data the data analysis here is almost inevitably interpretive, hence the data analysis is less a completely accurate representation (as in the numerical, positivist tradition) but more of a reflexive, reactive interaction between the researcher and the decontextualized data that are already interpretations of a social encounter. The great tension in data analysis is between maintaining a sense of the holism of the interview and the tendency for analysis to atomize and fragment the data – to separate them into constituent elements, thereby losing the synergy of the whole, and in interviews often the whole is greater than the sum of the parts. There are several stages in analysis, for example:

- generating natural units of meaning
- classifying, categorizing and ordering these units of meaning
- structuring narratives to describe the interview contents
- interpreting the interview data.

These are comparatively generalized stages. Miles and Huberman (1994) suggest twelve tactics for generating meaning from transcribed and interview data:

- counting frequencies of occurrence (of ideas, themes, pieces of data, words)
- noting patterns and themes (Gestalts), which may stem from repeated themes and causes or explanations or constructs
- seeing plausibility: trying to make good sense of data, using informed intuition to reach a conclusion
- clustering: setting items into categories, types, behaviours and classifications
- making metaphors: using figurative and connotative language rather than literal and denotative language, bringing data to life, thereby reducing data, making patterns, decentring the data, and connecting data with theory
- splitting variables to elaborate, differentiate and 'unpack' ideas, i.e. to move away from the drive towards integration and the blurring of data
- subsuming particulars into the general, akin to Glaser's (1978) notion of 'constant comparison' (see Chapter 6 in this book) – a move towards clarifying key concepts

- factoring: bringing a large number of variables under a smaller number of (frequently) unobserved hypothetical variables
- identifying and noting relations between variables
- finding intervening variables: looking for other variables that appear to be 'getting in the way' of accounting for what one would expect to be strong relationships between variables
- building a logical chain of evidence: noting causality and making inferences
- making conceptual/theoretical coherence: moving from metaphors to constructs to theories to explain the phenomena.

This progression, though perhaps positivist in its tone, is a useful way of moving from the specific to the general in data analysis. Running through the suggestions from Miles and Huberman (1994) is the importance that they attach to coding of responses in interviews, partially as a way of reducing what is typically data overload from qualitative data.

Coding has been defined by Kerlinger (1970) as the translation of question responses and respondent information to specific categories for the purpose of analysis. As we have seen, many questions are precoded, that is, each response can be immediately and directly converted into a score in an objective way. Rating scales and checklists are examples of precoded questions. Coding is the ascription of a category label to a piece of data, with the category label either decided in advance or in response to the data that have been collected.

We discuss coding more fully in Chapter 23, and we refer the reader to that discussion.

Content analysis involves reading and judgement; Brenner et al. (1985) set out thirteen steps in undertaking a content analysis of open-ended data:

1 Briefing: understanding the problem and its context in detail.
2 Sampling: of people, including the types of sample sought (see Chapter 4).
3 Associating: with other work that has been done.
4 Developing a hypothesis.

5 Testing the hypothesis.
6 Immersing in the data collected, to pick up all the clues.
7 Categorizing: in which the categories and their labels must reflect the purpose of the research, be exhaustive and be mutually exclusive.
8 Incubating: reflecting on data and developing interpretations and meanings.
9 Synthesizing: involving a review of the rationale for coding and an identification of the emerging patterns and themes.
10 Culling: condensing, excising and even reinterpreting the data so that they can be written up intelligibly.
11 Interpreting: making meaning of the data.
12 Writing: including giving clear guidance on the incidence of occurrence; proving an indication of direction and intentionality of feelings; being aware of what is not said as well as what it said – silences; indicating salience to the readers and respondents (Brenner et al. 1985: 140–3).
13 Rethinking.

This process, Brenner et al. (1985: 144) suggest, requires researchers to address thirteen factors:

1 Understand the research brief thoroughly.
2 Evaluate the relevance of the sample for the research project.
3 Associate their own experiences with the problem, looking for clues from the past.
4 Develop testable hypotheses as the basis for the content analysis (the authors name this the 'Concept Book').
5 Test the hypotheses throughout the interviewing and analysis process.
6 Stay immersed in the data throughout the study.
7 Categorize the data in the Concept Book, creating labels and codes.
8 Incubate the data before writing up.
9 Synthesize the data in the Concept Book, looking for key concepts.
10 Cull the data, being selective is important because it is impossible to report everything that happened.

11 Interpret the data, identifying its meaning and implication.

12 Write up the report.

13 Rethink and rewrite: have the research objectives been met?

Hycner (1985) sets out procedures that can be followed when phenomenologically analysing interview data. We saw in Chapter 1 that the phenomenologist advocates the study of direct experience taken at face value and sees behaviour as determined by the phenomena of experience rather than by external, objective and physically described reality. Hycner (1985) points out that there is a reluctance on the part of phenomenologists to focus too much on specific steps in research methods for fear that they will become reified. The steps suggested by Hycner, however, offer a possible way of analysing data which allays such fears. As he himself explains, his guidelines 'have arisen out of a number of years of teaching phenomenological research classes to graduate psychology students and trying to be true to the phenomenon of interview data while also providing concrete guidelines' (Hycner 1985). In summary, the fifteen guidelines are as follows:

- *Transcription:* having the interview tape transcribed, noting not only the literal statements but also non-verbal and paralinguistic communication.
- *Bracketing and phenomenological reduction:* for Hycner this means 'suspending (bracketing) as much as possible the researcher's meaning and interpretations and entering into the world of the unique individual who was interviewed' (Hycner 1985). The researcher thus sets out to understand what the interviewee is saying rather than what she expects that person to say.
- *Listening to the interview for a sense of the whole:* this involves listening to the entire tape several times and reading the transcription a number of times in order to provide a context for the emergence of specific units of meaning and themes later on.
- *Delineating units of general meaning:* this entails a thorough scrutiny of both verbal and non-verbal gestures to elicit the participant's meaning. 'It is a crystallization and condensation of what the participant has said, still using as much as possible the literal words of the participant' (Hycner 1985). (See Box 16.6 for Hycner's own example. This is the second page of transcription describing an experience of wonderment and awe. On the previous page, the participant discussed the background where he and his girlfriend were up in the mountains on vacation. The scene being described is the beginning of an experience of wonder.)

- *Delineating units of meaning relevant to the research question:* once the units of general meaning have been noted, they are then reduced to units of meaning relevant to the research question. In the case of Hycner's study, the original eighteen general units (see Box 16.6) are reduced to thirteen units of meaning relevant to the research question (see Box 16.7).
- *Training independent judges to verify the units of relevant meaning:* findings can be verified by using other researchers to carry out the above procedures. Hycner's own experience in working with graduate students well trained in this type of research is that there are rarely significant differences in the findings.
- *Eliminating redundancies:* at this stage, the researcher checks the lists of relevant meaning and eliminates those clearly redundant to others previously listed.
- *Clustering units of relevant meaning:* the researcher now tries to determine if any of the units of relevant meaning naturally cluster together; whether there seems to be some common theme or essence that unites several discrete units of relevant meaning. Box 16.8 gives an example of clustering units of relevant meaning.
- *Determining themes from clusters of meaning:* the researcher examines all the clusters of meaning to determine if there is one (or more) central theme(s) which expresses the essence of these clusters.
- *Writing a summary of each individual interview:* it is useful at this point, Hycner (1985) suggests,

Box 16.6
Delineating units of general meaning

[1]I was looking at Mary and [2]all of a sudden I knew [3]I was looking at her like I never looked at anybody in my whole life – and [4]my eyes were sort of just kind of staring at her and the reason that [5]I realized that it was tremendous was that she said to me – what are you doing – [6]and I just said I'm looking at you – [7]and so we just sat there and she[8] sort of watched me look at her – and [9]she was getting kind of uncomfortable [10]and yet also kept saying – what's going on [11]but not really wanting to hear – [12]just letting me – have enough sensitivity to let me experience it – [13] a lot was going on – [14]I didn't realize what – what it was – [15]I was just sort of sitting there – [16]*I couldn't move* – [17]I didn't want to move – [18]I just want to continue looking at her.	[1]Was looking at Mary [2]suddenly he knew [3]He was looking at her like he never looked at anybody in his whole life [4]His eyes were just staring at her [5]Realized it was tremendous when she said 'What are you doing?' [6]He just said, 'I'm looking at you.' [7]Both just sat there [8]She sort of watched him look at her [9]She was getting kind of uncomfortable [10]She kept saying 'What's going on?' [11]She didn't seem to want a response [12]She had enough sensitivity to let him experience it [13]A lot was going on [14]He didn't realize what was going on [15]He continued to just sit there [16]He *couldn't move* [17]Didn't want to move [18]Just wanted to continue looking at her.

Source: Hycner 1985

to go back to the interview transcription and write up a summary of the interview incorporating the themes that have been elicited from the data.

Box 16.7
Units of relevant meaning

[1]Was looking at Mary
[2]Suddenly he knew
[3]He was looking at her like he never looked at anybody in his whole life
[4]His eyes were just staring at her
[5]Realized it was tremendous when she said 'What are you doing?'
[6]He just said, 'I'm looking at you.'
[7]Both just sat there
[12]She had enough sensitivity to let him experience it
[13]A lot was going on
[14]He didn't realize what was going on
[15]He continued to just sit there
[16]He *couldn't move* – [17]Didn't want to move
[18]Just wanted to continue looking at her

Source: Hycner 1985

- *Return to the participant with the summary and themes, conducting a second interview:* this is a check to see whether the essence of the first interview has been accurately and fully captured.
- *Modifying themes and summary:* with the new data from the second interview, the researcher looks at all the data as a whole and modifies or adds themes as necessary.
- *Identifying general and unique themes for all the interviews:* the researcher now looks for the themes common to most or all of the interviews as well as the individual variations. The first step is to note if there are themes common to all or most of the interviews. The second step is to note when there are themes that are unique to a single interview or a minority of the interviews.
- *Contextualization of themes:* at this point it is helpful to place these themes back within the overall contexts or horizons from which these themes emerged.
- *Composite summary:* Hycner (1985) considers it useful to write up a composite summary of all the interviews that would accurately capture

Box 16.8
Clusters of relevant meaning

I. *The tremendousness of the looking at Mary*
    A Looking at Mary in a way totally different than he
       had ever looked at anyone in his life. [1,3]
    B His eyes were just staring. [4]
    C Realized it was tremendous when she said 'What
       are you doing?'[5]
    D Was (just) looking at her. [6]
    E A lot was going on. [13]
    F Just wanted to continue looking at her. [16]

II *Realization*
    A A sudden realization[2] (Almost like it breaks in).
    B Realized how tremendous it was (through her
       question). [5]
    C A lot was going on and he didn't realize what was
       going on[13,14] (rhythm of awareness).

III *Continuation of what was happening*
    A Both just (continued) to sit there.[7]
    B He continued to sit. [15]

IV *Inability to move*
    A *Couldn't move*[16] (issue of volition).
    B Didn't want to move[17] (didn't desire to move).

V *Interpersonal dimension*
    A Was looking at Mary in a way he had never looked
       at anyone in his whole life. [1,3]
    B Her question elicited the realization of how
       tremendous it was. [5]
    C He just said 'I'm looking at you.' [6]
    D Both just sat there. [7]

Source: Hycner 1985

the essence of the phenomenon being investigated. 'Such a composite summary describes the "world" in general, as experienced by the participants. At the end of such a summary the researcher might want to note significant individual differences' (Hycner 1985).

Issues arising from this procedure are discussed in some detail in the second part of Hycner's (1985) article.

Verifying

Chapter 5 has discussed at length the issues of reliability, validity and generalizability of the data from interviews, and so these issues will not be repeated here. The reader is advised to explore not only that section of Chapter 5, but also the whole chapter. Kvale (1996: 237) makes the point that validation must take place at all seven stages of the interview-based investigation, set out earlier in this chapter. For example:

- the theoretical foundation of the research must be rigorous and there must be a logical link between such theory and the research questions
- all aspects of the research design must be sound and rigorous
- the data must be accurate, reliable and valid (with consistency and reliability checks undertaken)
- the translation of the data from an oral to a written medium must demonstrate fidelity to the key features of the interview situation
- data analysis must demonstrate fidelity to the data
- validation procedures should be in place and used
- the reporting should be fair and seen to be fair by readers.

One main issue here is that there is no single canon of validity; rather the notion of fitness for purpose within an ethically defensible framework should be adopted, giving rise to different kinds of validity for different kinds of interview-based research (e.g. structured to unstructured, qualitative to quantitative, nomothetic to idiographic, generalizable to unique, descriptive to explanatory, positivist to ethnographic, preordinate to responsive).

Reporting

The nature of the reporting will be decided to some extent by the nature of the interviewing. For example, a standardized, structured interview may yield numerical data that may be reported succinctly in tables and graphs, while a qualitative, word-based, open-ended interview will yield word-based accounts that take up considerably more space.

Kvale (1996: 263–6) suggests several elements of a report:

- an introduction that includes the main themes and contents
- an outline of the methodology and methods (from designing to interviewing, transcription and analysis)
- the results (the data analysis, interpretation and verification)
- a discussion.

If the report is largely numerical then figures and tables might be appropriate; if the interview is more faithfully represented in words rather than numbers then this presents the researcher with the issue of how to present particular quotations. Here Kvale (1996: 266) suggests that direct quotations should illuminate and relate to the general text while maintaining a balance with the main text, be contextualized and be accompanied by a commentary and interpretation, be particularly clear, useful, and the 'best' of the data (the 'gems'!), should include an indication of how they have been edited and be incorporated into a natural written style of the report.

For sample interview data, see the accompanying web site (http://www.routledge.com/textbooks/9780415368780 – Chapter 16, file 16.2.doc and http://www.routledge.com/textbooks/9780415368780 – Chapter 16, file 16.3.doc).

Group interviewing

One technique within the methodology of interviewing to have grown in popularity is that of group interviewing. Watts and Ebbutt (1987), for example, have considered the advantages and disadvantages of group interviewing as a means of collecting data in educational research. The advantages the authors identify include the potential for discussions to develop, thus yielding a wide range of responses. They explain, 'such interviews are useful . . . where a group of people have been working together for some time or common purpose, or where it is seen as important that everyone concerned is aware of what others in the group are saying' (Watts and Ebbutt 1987). The group interview can generate a wider range of responses than in individual interviews. Bogdan and Biklen (1992: 100) add that group interviews might be useful for gaining an insight into what might be pursued in subsequent individual interviews. There are practical and organizational advantages, too. Prearranged groups can be used for the purpose in question by teachers with minimum disruption. Group interviews are often quicker than individual interviews and hence are timesaving. The group interview can also bring together people with varied opinions, or as representatives of different collectivities.

Arksey and Knight (1999: 76) suggest that having more than one interviewee present can provide two versions of events – a cross-check – and one can complement the other with additional points, leading to a more complete and reliable record. It is also possible to detect how the participants support, influence, complement, agree and disagree with each other, and the relationships between them. On the other hand, one respondent may dominate the interview (particularly if one respondent is male and another female: Arksey and Knight 1999: 76). Further, Arksey and Knight suggest that antagonisms may be stirred up at the interview, individuals may be reticent in front of others, particularly if they are colleagues or if the matter is sensitive. They also suggest that a 'public line' may be offered instead of a more honest, personal response, and, indeed, that participants may collude in withholding information. Watts and Ebbutt (1987) note that group interviews are of little use in allowing personal matters to emerge, or in circumstances where the researcher has to aim a series of follow-up questions at one specific member of the group. As they explain, 'the dynamic of a group denies access to this sort of data' (Watts and Ebbutt 1987). Group interviews may produce 'group think', discouraging individuals who hold a different view from speaking out in front of the other group members. Further, Lewis (1992) comments on the problem of coding up the responses of group interviews. For further guidance on this topic and the procedures involved, we refer the reader to Simons (1982), Hedges (1985), Watts and Ebbutt (1987), Breakwell (1990), Spencer and Flin (1990), Lewis (1992) and Arksey and Knight (1999).

Several issues have to be addressed in the conduct of a group interview, for example:

- How to divide your attention as interviewer and to share out the interviewees' responses – giving them all a chance to speak in a group interview.
- Do you ask everyone in a group interview to give a response to a question?
- How to handle people who are too quiet, too noisy, who monopolize the conversation, who argue and disagree with each other?
- What happens if people become angry with you or with each other?
- How to make people be quiet or stop talking while being polite?
- How to handle differences in how talkative people are?
- How to arrange turn-taking (if appropriate)?
- Do you ask named individuals questions?
- How can you have individuals answer without forcing them?
- How to handle a range of very different responses to the same question?
- Why have you brought together the particular people in the group?
- Do you want people to answer in a particular sequence?
- What to do if the more experienced people always answer first in a group interview?
- As an interviewer, be vigilant to pick up on people who are trying to speak.

It must be borne in mind when conducting group interviews that the unit of analysis is the view of the whole group and not the individual member; a collective group response is being sought, even if there are individual differences or a range of responses within the group. This ensures that no individual is either unnecessarily marginalized or subject to blame or being ostracized for holding a different view.

Group interviews are also very useful when interviewing children, and it is to this that we now turn.

Interviewing children

It is important to understand the world of children through their own eyes rather than the lens of the adult. Children differ from adults in cognitive and linguistic development, attention and concentration span, ability to recall, life experiences, what they consider to be important, status and power (Arksey and Knight 1999: 116). All of these have a bearing on the interview. Arksey and Knight (1999: 116–18) also indicate that it is important to establish trust with children, to put the child at ease quickly and to help him/her to feel confident, to avoid overreacting (e.g. if the child is distracted), to make the interview non-threatening and enjoyable, to use straightforward language and child's language, to ask questions that are appropriate for the age of the child, to keep to the 'here and now', to avoid using 'why', 'when' and 'how' questions with very young children (e.g. below 5 years old), to ensure that children can understand abstract questions (often for older children), to allow time to think, and to combine methods and activities in an interview (e.g. drawing, playing, writing, speaking, playing a game, using pictures, newspapers, toys or photographs).

Group interviewing can be useful with children, as it encourages interaction between the group rather than simply a response to an adult's question. Group interviews of children might also be less intimidating for them than individual interviews. Eder and Fingerson (2003: 34) suggest that a power and status dynamic is heavily implicated in interviewing children; they have little in comparison to the adult. Indeed Thorne (1994) uses the term 'kids' rather than 'children', as the former is the term used by the children themselves, whereas 'children', she argues, is a term used exclusively by adults, denoting subordinacy (cf. Eder and Fingerson 2003: 34). Mayall (1999) suggests regarding children as a 'minority group', in that they lack power and control over their own lives. If this is the case, then it is important to take steps to ensure that children are given a voice and an interview setting in which they feel comfortable. Group interviewing is such a setting, taking place in as close to a natural surrounding as possible; indeed Eder and Fingerson (2003: 45) report the successful use of a high-status child as the interviewer with a group of children.

Group interviewing with children enables them to challenge each other and participate in a way that may not happen in a one-to-one, adult–child interview and using language that the children themselves use. For example, Lewis (1992) found that 10 year olds' understanding of severe learning difficulties was enhanced in group interview situations, the children challenging and extending each other's ideas and introducing new ideas into the discussion. Further, having the interview as part of a more routine, everyday activity can also help to make it less unnatural, as can making the interview more like a game (e.g. by using props such as toys and pictures). For example, it could be part of a 'show and tell' or 'circle time' session, or part of group discussion time. The issue here is to try to make the interview as informal as possible. Of course, sometimes it may be more useful to formalize the session, so that children have a sense of how important the situation is, and they can respond to this positively. It can be respectful to have an informal or, indeed, a formal interview; the former maybe for younger children and the latter for older children.

While group interviews may be useful with many children, it is also the case that individual interviews with children may also be valuable. For example, Eder and Fingerson (2003: 43–4) report the value of individual interviews with adolescents, particularly about sensitive matters, for example relationships, family, body issues, sexuality, love. Indeed they report examples where individual interview yielded different results from group interviews with the same people about the same topics, and where the individuals valued greatly the opportunity for a one-to-one conversation.

Interviews with children should try to employ open-ended questions, to avoid a single answer type of response. Another strategy is to use a projection technique. Here, instead of asking direct questions, the interviewer can show a picture or set of pictures, and then ask the children for their responses. For example, a child may first comment on the people's race in the pictures, followed by their sex, suggesting that race may be more important in their mind than their sex. This avoids a direct question and may reduce the possibility of a biased answer – where the respondent may be looking for cues as to how to respond. Other projection techniques include the use of dolls or puppets, photographs of a particular scene which the respondents have to comment upon (e.g. what is happening? What should be done here?), and the 'guess who' technique (Wragg 2002: 157) (which people might fit a particular description).

Simons (1982), Lewis (1992), Bailey (1994: 447–9) and Breakwell (2000: 245–6), however, chart some difficulties in interviewing children, for example how to

- overcome children being easily distracted (e.g. some interviewers provide toys or pictures, and these distract the children)
- avoid the researcher being seen as an authority figure (e.g. a teacher, a parent or an adult in a powerful position)
- understand what children mean and what they say (particularly with very young children)
- gather a lot of information in a short time, children's attention span being limited
- have children reveal what they really think and feel rather than what they think the researcher wants to hear
- avoid the situation being seen by the child as a test
- keep the interview relevant
- overcome young children's unwillingness to contradict an adult or assert themselves
- interview inarticulate, hesitant and nervous children
- get the children's teacher away from the children
- respond to the child who says something then immediately wishes she hadn't said it
- elicit genuine responses from children rather than simply responses to the interview situation

- get beyond the institutional, headteacher's or 'expected' response
- keep children to the point
- avoid children being too extreme or destructive of each other's views
- pitch language at the appropriate level
- avoid the interview being an arduous bore
- overcome children's poor memories
- avoid children being too focused on particular features or situations
- avoid the situation where the child will say 'yes' to anything ('acquiescence bias') addressed, for example, by avoiding 'yes/no' questions in favour of open-ended questions
- overcome the situation of the child saying anything in order to please
- overcome the proclivity of some children to say that they 'don't know', or simply shrug their shoulders and remain silent
- overcome the problem that some children will say anything rather than feel they do not have 'the answer'
- overcome the problem that some children dominate the conversation
- avoid the problem of children feeling very exposed in front of their friends
- avoid children feeling uncomfortable or threatened (addressed, perhaps, by placing children with their friends)
- avoid children telling lies.

Clearly these problems are not exclusive to children; they apply equally well to some adult group interviews. Group interviews require skilful chairing and attention to the physical layout of the room so that everyone can see everyone else. Group size is also an issue; too few and it can put pressure on individuals, too large and the group fragments and loses focus. Lewis (1992) summarizes research to indicate that a group of around six or seven is an optimum size, though it can be smaller for younger children. The duration of an interview may not be for longer than, at most, fifteen minutes, and it might be useful to ensure that distractions are kept to a minimum. Simple language to the point and without ambiguity (e.g. avoiding metaphors) is important.

Focus groups

As an adjunct to group interviews, the use of focus groups is growing in educational research, albeit more slowly than, for instance, in business and political circles. Focus groups are a form of group interview, though not in the sense of a backwards and forwards between interviewer and group. Rather, the reliance is on the interaction within the group who discuss a topic supplied by the researcher (Morgan 1988: 9), yielding a collective rather than an individual view. Hence the participants interact with each other rather than with the interviewer, such that the views of the participants can emerge – the participants' rather than the researcher's agenda can predominate. It is from the *interaction* of the group that the data emerge. Focus groups are contrived settings, bringing together a specifically chosen sector of the population to discuss a particular given theme or topic, where the interaction with the group leads to data and outcomes. Their contrived nature is both their strength and their weakness: they are unnatural settings yet they are very focused on a particular issue and, therefore, will yield insights that might not otherwise have been available in a straightforward interview; they are economical on time, producing a large amount of data in a short period of time, but they tend to produce less data than interviews with the same number of individuals on a one-to-one basis (Morgan 1988: 19).

Focus groups (Krueger 1988; Morgan 1988: Bailey 1994: 192–3; Robson 2002: 284–5) are useful for

- orienting to a particular field of focus
- developing themes, topic and schedules flexibly for subsequent interviews and/or questionnaires
- generating hypotheses that derive from the insights and data from the group
- generating and evaluating data from different subgroups of a population
- gathering qualitative data
- generating data quickly and at low cost
- gathering data on attitudes, values and opinions

- empowering participants to speak out, and in their own words
- encouraging groups, rather than individuals, to voice opinions
- encouraging non-literate participants
- providing greater coverage of issues than would be possible in a survey
- gathering feedback from previous studies.

Focus groups might be useful to triangulate with more traditional forms of interviewing, questionnaire, observation etc. There are several issues to be addressed in running focus groups (Morgan 1988: 41–8):

- Deciding the number of focus groups for a single topic (one group is insufficient, as the researcher will be unable to know whether the outcome is unique to the behaviour of the group).
- Deciding the size of the group (too small, and intra-group dynamics exert a disproportionate effect; too large, and the group becomes unwieldy and hard to manage; it fragments). Morgan (1988: 43) suggests between four and twelve people per group.
- Allowing for people not turning up on the day. Morgan (1988: 44) suggests the need to over-recruit by as much as 20 per cent.
- Taking extreme care with the sampling, so that *every* participant is the bearer of the particular characteristic required or that the group has homogeneity of background in the required area, otherwise the discussion will lose focus or become unrepresentative. Sampling is a major key to the success of focus groups.
- Ensuring that participants have something to say and feel comfortable enough to say it.
- Chairing the meeting so that a balance is struck between being too directive and veering off the point, i.e. keeping the meeting open-ended but to the point.

Unlike group interviewing with children, discussed above, focus groups operate more successfully if they are composed of relative strangers rather than friends unless friendship, of course, is an important criterion for the focus (e.g. that the group will discuss something that is usually discussed only among friends).

Focus groups are not without their drawbacks. For example, they tend not to yield numerical, quantifiable or generalizable data; the data may be difficult to analyse succinctly; the number of people involved tends to be small; they may yield less information than a survey; and the group dynamics may lead to non-participation by some members and dominance by others (e.g. status differentials may operate), the number of topics to be covered may be limited; intra-group disagreement and even conflicts may arise; inarticulate members may be denied a voice; the data may lack overall reliability.

Although its potential is considerable, the focus group, as a particular kind of group interviewing, still has to find its way into educational circles to the extent that it has in other areas of life. Focus groups require skilful facilitation and management by the researcher.

The non-directive interview and the focused interview

Originating from psychiatric and therapeutic fields with which it is most readily associated, the non-directive interview is characterized by a situation in which the respondents are responsible for initiating and directing the course of the encounter and for the attitudes they express in it, in contrast to the structured or research interview we have already considered, where the dominating role assumed by the interviewer results in 'an asymmetry of commitment' (Kitwood 1977). It has been shown to be a particularly valuable technique because it gets at the deeper attitudes and perceptions of the person being interviewed in such a way as to leave them free from interviewer bias. We shall examine briefly the characteristics of the therapeutic interview and then consider its usefulness as a research tool in the social and educational sciences.

The non-directive interview as it is currently understood grew out of the pioneering work of Freud and subsequent modifications to his approach by later analysts. His basic discovery was that if one can arrange a special set of conditions and have patients talk about their difficulties in a certain way, behaviour changes of many kinds can be accomplished. The technique developed was used to elicit highly personal data from patients in such a way as to increase their self-awareness and improve their skills in self-analysis. By these means they became better able to help themselves. As Madge (1965) observes, it is these techniques which have greatly influenced contemporary interviewing techniques, especially those of a more penetrating and less quantitative kind.

The present-day therapeutic interview has its most persuasive advocate in Carl Rogers, who has on different occasions testified to its efficacy. Basing his analysis on his own clinical studies, he has identified a sequence of characteristic stages in the therapeutic process, beginning with the client's decision to seek help. The client is met by a counsellor who is friendly and receptive, but not didactic. The next stage is signalled when the client begins to give vent to hostile, critical and destructive feelings, which the counsellor accepts, recognizes and clarifies. Subsequently, and invariably, these antagonistic impulses are used up and give way to the first expressions of positive feeling. The counsellor likewise accepts these until suddenly and spontaneously 'insight and self-understanding come bubbling through' (Rogers 1942). With insight comes the realization of possible courses of action and also the power to make decisions. It is in translating these into practical terms that clients free themselves from dependence on the counsellor.

Rogers (1945) subsequently identified a number of qualities in interviewers which he deemed essential: that interviewers base their work on attitudes of acceptance and permissiveness; that interviewers respect clients' responsibility for their own situation; that interviewers permit clients to explain their problem in their own way; and that interviewers do nothing that would in any way arouse the client's defences.

Such then are the principal characteristics of the non-directive interview technique in a therapeutic setting. But what of its usefulness as a purely research technique in societal and educational contexts? There are a number of features of the therapeutic interview which are peculiar to it and may well be inappropriate in other settings: for example, as we have seen, the interview is initiated by the respondent, whose motivation is to obtain relief from a particular symptom; the interviewer is primarily a source of help, not a procurer of information; the actual interview is part of the therapeutic experience; the purpose of the interview is to change the behaviour and inner life of the person and its success is defined in these terms; and there is no restriction on the topics discussed.

A researcher has a different order of priorities, however, and what appear as advantages in a therapeutic context may be decided limitations when the technique is used for research purposes, even though she may be sympathetic to the spirit of the non-directive interview. As Madge (1965) explains, increasingly there are those

> who wish to retain the good qualities of the non-directive technique and at the same time are keen to evolve a method that is economical and precise enough to leave a residue of results rather than merely a posse of cured souls.
>
> (Madge 1965)

One attempt to meet this need is to be found in a programme reported by Merton and Kendall (1946) in which the *focused interview* was developed. While seeking to follow closely the principle of non-direction, the method did introduce rather more interviewer control in the kinds of questions used and sought also to limit the discussion to certain parts of the respondent's experience.

The focused interview differs from other types of research interview in certain respects. These have been identified by Merton and Kendall (1946) as follows:

- The persons interviewed are known to have been involved in a particular situation: they may, for example, have watched a TV programme, or seen a film, or read a book or article or been a participant in a social situation.

- By means of the techniques of content analysis, elements in the situation which the researcher deems significant have previously been analysed by him or her. The researcher has thus arrived at a set of hypotheses relating to the meaning and effects of the specified elements.
- Using this analysis as a basis, the investigator constructs an interview guide. This identifies the major areas of inquiry and the hypotheses which determine the relevant data to be obtained in the interview.
- The actual interview is focused on the subjective experiences of the people who have been exposed to the situation. Their responses enable the researcher both to test the validity of the hypotheses, and to ascertain unanticipated responses to the situation, thus giving rise to further hypotheses.

From this it can be seen that the distinctive feature of the focused interview is the prior analysis by the researcher of the situation in which subjects have been involved. The advantages of this procedure have been cogently explained by Merton and Kendall:

> Fore-knowledge of the situation obviously reduces the task confronting the investigator, since the interview need not be devoted to discovering the objective nature of the situation. Equipped in advance with a content analysis, the interviewer can readily distinguish the objective facts of the case from the subjective definitions of the situation. He thus becomes alert to the entire field of 'selective response'. When the interviewer, through his familiarity with the objective situation, is able to recognize symbolic or functional silences, 'distortions', avoidances, or blockings, he is the more prepared to explore their implications.
>
> (Merton and Kendall 1946)

In the quest for what Merton and Kendall (1946) term 'significant data', the interviewer must develop the ability to evaluate continuously the interview while it is in progress. To this end, they established a set of criteria by which productive and unproductive interview material can be distinguished. Briefly, these are as follows:

- *Non-direction*: interviewer guidance should be minimal.
- *Specificity*: respondents' definitions of the situation should find full and specific expression.
- *Range and scope*: the interview should maximize the range of evocative stimuli and responses reported by the subject.
- *Depth and personal context*: the interview should bring out the affective and value-laden implications of the subjects' responses, to determine whether the experience had central or peripheral significance. It should elicit the relevant personal context, the idiosyncratic associations, beliefs and ideas.

Telephone interviewing

The use of telephone interviewing has long been recognized as an important method of data collection and is common practice in survey research, though, as Arksey and Knight (1999: 79) comment, telephone interviews do not feel like interviews, as both parties are deprived of several channels of communication and the establishment of a positive relationship (e.g. non-verbal), and we explore this here. Dicker and Gilbert (1988), Nias (1991), Oppenheim (1992) Borg and Gall (1996), Shaughnessy *et al.* (2003) and Shuy (2003) suggest several attractions to telephone interviewing:

- It is sometimes cheaper and quicker than face-to-face interviewing.
- It enables researchers to select respondents from a much more dispersed population than if they have to travel to meet the interviewees.
- Travel costs are omitted.
- It is particularly useful for brief surveys.
- It may protect the anonymity of respondents more than a personal interview.
- It is useful for gaining rapid responses to a structured questionnaire.
- Monitoring and quality control are undertaken more easily since interviews are undertaken

and administered centrally, indeed there are greater guarantees that the researcher actually carries out the interview as required.

- Interviewer effects are reduced.
- There is greater uniformity in the conduct of the interview and the standardization of questions.
- There is greater interviewer control of the interview.
- The results tend to be quantitative.
- They are quicker to administer than face-to-face interviews because respondents will only usually be prepared to speak on the telephone for, at most, fifteen minutes.
- Call-back costs are so slight as to make frequent call-backs possible, enhancing reliability and contact.
- Many groups, particularly of busy people, can be reached at times more convenient to them than if a visit were to be made.
- They are safer to undertake than, for example, having to visit dangerous neighbourhoods.
- They can be used to collect sensitive data, as possible feelings of threat of face-to-face questions about awkward, embarrassing or difficult matters are absent.
- It does not rely on the literacy of the respondent (as, for example, in questionnaires).
- The use of the telephone may put a little pressure on the respondent to respond, and it is usually the interviewer rather than the interviewee who terminates the call.
- Response rate is higher than, for example, questionnaires.

Clearly this issue is not as cut-and-dried as the claims made for it, as there are several potential problems with telephone interviewing, for example (see also Chapter 6):

- It is very easy for respondents simply to hang up on the caller.
- Motivation to participate may be lower than for a personal interview.
- There is a chance of skewed sampling, as not all of the population have a telephone (often those lower income households – perhaps the very people that the researcher wishes to target)

or can hear (e.g. elderly people and second language speakers in addition to those with hearing difficulties).

- There is a lower response rate at weekends.
- The standardized format of telephone interviews may prevent thoughtful or deep answers from being provided.
- Some people have a deep dislike of telephones, which sometimes extends to a phobia, and this inhibits their responses or willingness to participate.
- Respondents may not disclose information because of uncertainty about actual (even though promised) confidentiality.
- Respondents may come to snap judgements without the adequate or deeper reflection necessary for a full answer to serious issues.
- Respondents may not wish to spend a long time on the telephone, so telephone interviews tend to be briefer than other forms of interview.
- Concentration spans are shorter than in a face-to-face interview.
- The interviewer has to remain bright and focused, listen very carefully and respond – it is tiring.
- Questions tend to be closed, fixed and simple.
- There is a limit on the complexity of the questions that can be put.
- Response categories must be very simple or else respondents will forget what they are.
- Many respondents (up to 25 per cent, according to Oppenheim 1992: 97) will be 'ex-directory' and so their numbers will not be available in telephone directories.
- Respondents may withhold important information or tell lies, as the non-verbal behaviour that frequently accompanies this is not witnessed by the interviewer.
- It is often more difficult for complete strangers to communicate by telephone than face-to-face, particularly as non-verbal cues are absent.
- Respondents are naturally suspicious (e.g. of the caller trying to sell a product).
- One telephone might be shared by several people.
- Some respondents feel that telephone interviews afford less opportunity for them to

question or rebut the points made by the interviewer.

- There may be distractions for the respondent (e.g. a television may be switched on, children may be crying, dogs barking, others may be present).
- Responses are difficult to write down or record during the interview.

That said, Sykes and Hoinville (1985) and also Borg and Gall (1996) suggest that telephone interviewing reaches nearly the same proportion of many target populations as 'standard' interviews, that it obtains nearly the same rate of response, and produces comparable information to 'standard' interviews, sometimes at a fraction of the cost. The response rate issue is contested: Weisberg *et al.* (1996: 122) and Shuy (2003: 181) report lower response rates to telephone interviews.

Harvey (1988), Oppenheim (1992) and Miller (1995) consider that, first, telephone interviews need careful arrangements for timing and duration (typically that they are shorter and quicker than face-to-face interviews) – a preliminary call may be necessary to fix a time when a longer call can be made. Second, the interviewer will need to have ready careful prompts and probes, including more than usual closed questions and less complex questions, in case the respondent 'dries up' on the telephone. Third, both interviewer and interviewee need to be prepared in advance of the interview if its potential is to be realized. Fourth, sampling requires careful consideration, using, for example, random numbers or some form of stratified sample. In general, however, many of the issues from 'standard' forms of interviewing apply equally well to telephone interviewing (see also Chapter 4).

Face-to-face interviews may be more suitable than telephone interviews (Weisberg *et al.* 1996: 122; Shuy 2003: 179–82) in the following circumstances:

- The interviewer wishes to address complex issues or sensitive questions.
- A natural context might yield greater accuracy.
- Deeper and self-generated answers are sought (i.e. where the question does not frame the answer too strongly).

- Issues requiring probing, deep reflection and, thereby, a longer time is sought.
- Greater equality of power between interviewer and respondent is sought.
- Older, second language speakers and hearing-impaired respondents are being interviewed.
- Marginalized respondents are being sought.

It is not uncommon for telephone interviewing to be outsourced, and this might be an advantage or a disadvantage. On the one hand, it takes pressure off the researcher, not only because of the time involved but also because a fifteen-minute telephone interview might be more exhausting than a fifteen-minute face-to-face interview, there being more social and non-verbal cues in face-to-face interaction. On the other hand, in outsourced telephone interviews care has to be taken on standardization of the conduct of the interview, the content of questions, the entry of responses and indeed, to check that the interviews have been done and response not simply fabricated.

In conducting telephone interviews it is important to consider several issues:

- Will the people have the information that you require? Who will you need to speak to on the telephone? If the person answering the call is not the most suitable person then you need to talk to somebody else.
- There is a need to pilot the interview schedule and to prepare and train the telephonists, and to discover the difficult/sensitive/annoying/personal questions, the questions over which the respondents hesitate and answer very easily; the questions that will need prompts and explanations.
- Keep to the same, simple response categories for several questions, so that the respondents become used to these and keep in the same mind set for responding.
- Keep personal details, if any, until the end of the interview, in order to reduce a sense of threat.
- Keep to no more than, at the most, thirty-five questions, and to no more than, at the most, fifteen minutes, and preferably ten minutes.

- Clear with the respondents at the start of the interview that they have the time to answer and that they have the information sought (i.e. that they are suitable respondents). If they are not the most suitable respondents then ask if there is someone present in the premises who can answer the questions, or try to arrange callback times when the most suitable person can be reached. Ask to speak to the most suitable person.
- Keep the terminology simple and to the point, avoiding jargon and confusion.
- You should be able to tell the gender of the respondent by his or her voice, i.e. there may be no need to ask that particular question.
- Keep the response categories very simple and use them consistently (e.g. a mark out of 10, 'strongly agree' to 'strongly disagree', a 1–5 scale etc.).
- Rather than asking direct personal questions (unless you are confident of an answer), e.g. about age, income, ask about groups, such as which age group do they fall into (and give the age groups) or of income brackets (and give them).

Telephone interviewing is a useful but tricky art.

Ethical issues in interviewing

Interviews have an ethical dimension; they concern interpersonal interaction and produce information about the human condition. Although one can identify three main areas of ethical issues here – informed consent, confidentiality, and the consequences of the interviews – these need to be unpacked a little, as each is not unproblematic (Kvale 1996: 111–20). For instance, who should give the informed consent (e.g. participants, their superiors), and for whom and what? How much information should be given, and to whom? What is legitimate private and public knowledge? How might the research help or harm the interviewees? Does the interviewer have a duty to point out the possible harmful consequences of the research data or will this illegitimately steer the interview?

It is difficult to lay down hard and fast ethical rules, as, by definition, ethical matters are contestable. Nevertheless it is possible to raise some ethical questions to which answers need to be given before the interviews commence:

- Has the informed consent of the interviewees been gained?
- Has this been obtained in writing or orally?
- How much information should be given in advance of the study?
- How can adequate information be provided if the study is exploratory?
- Have the possible consequences of the research been made clear to the participants?
- Has care been taken to prevent any harmful effects of the research to the participants (and to others)?
- To what extent do any potential benefits outweigh the potential harm done by the research, and how justifiable is this for conducting the research?
- How will the research benefit the participants?
- Who will benefit from the research?
- To what extent is there reciprocity between what participants give to and receive from the research?
- Have confidentiality, anonymity, non-identifiability and non-traceability been guaranteed? Should participants' identities be disguised?
- How does the Data Protection Act (1984) operate in interview situations?
- Who will have access to the data?
- What has been done to ensure that the interview is conducted in an appropriate, non-stressful, non-threatening, manner?
- How will the data and transcriptions be verified, and by whom?
- Who will see the results of the research? Will some parts be withheld? Who own the data? At what stage does ownership of the data pass from interviewees to interviewers? Are there rights of veto for what appears? To whom should sensitive data be made available (e.g. should interview data on child abuse or drugs taking be made available with or without consent to parents and the police)?
- How far should the researcher's own agenda

and views predominate? What if the researcher makes a different interpretation from the interviewee? Should the interviewees be told, even if they have not asked for these interpretations?

These issues, by no means an exhaustive list, are not exclusive to the research interview, though they are highly applicable here. For further reading on ethical issues we refer readers to Chapter 2.

The personal safety of interviewers must also be addressed: it may be important, for example, for the interviewer to be accompanied, to leave details of where he or she is going, to take a friend, to show identification, to take a mobile phone, to reconnoitre the neighbourhood, to learn how to behave with fierce dogs, to use the most suitable transport. It is perhaps a sad indictment on society that these considerations have to be addressed, but they do.

17 Accounts

Introduction

The rationale of much of this chapter is located in the interpretive, ethnographic paradigm which strives to view situations through the eyes of participants, to catch their intentionality and their interpretations of frequently complex situations, their meaning systems and the dynamics of the interaction as it unfolds. This is akin to the notion of 'thick description' from Geertz (1973b). This chapter proceeds in several stages: first, we set out the characteristics of the ethogenic approach; second, we set out procedures in eliciting, analysing and authenticating accounts; third, we provide an introduction to handling qualitative accounts and their related fields of network analysis and discourse analysis; fourth, we provide an introduction to handling quantitative and qualitative accounts; finally, we review the strengths and weaknesses of ethogenic approaches. We recognize that the field of language and language use is vast, and to try to do justice to it here is the 'optimism of ignorance' (Edwards 1976). Rather, we attempt to indicate some important ways in which researchers can use accounts in collecting data for their research.

Although each of us sees the world from our own point of view, we have a way of speaking about our experiences which we share with those around us. Explaining our behaviour towards one another can be thought of as accounting for our actions in order to make them intelligible and justifiable to our fellowmen. Thus, saying 'I'm terribly sorry, I didn't mean to bump into you', is a simple case of the explication of social meaning, for by locating the bump outside any planned sequence and neutralizing it by making it intelligible in such a way that it is not warrantable, it ceases to be offensive in that situation (Harré 1978).

Accounting for actions in those larger slices of life called social episodes is the central concern of a participatory psychology which focuses upon actors' intentions, their beliefs about what sorts of behaviour will enable them to reach their goals, and their awareness of the rules that govern those behaviours. Studies carried out within this framework have been termed 'ethogenic', an adjective which expresses a view of the human being as a person, that is, a plan-making, self-monitoring agent, aware of goals and deliberately considering the best ways to achieve them. Ethogenic studies represent another approach to the study of social behaviour and their methods stand in bold contrast to those commonly employed in much of the educational research which we describe in Chapter 1. Before discussing the elicitation and analysis of accounts we need to outline the ethogenic approach in more detail. This we do by reference to the work of one of its foremost exponents, Rom Harré (1974; 1976; 1977a; 1977b; 1978).

The ethogenic approach

Harré (1978) identifies five main principles in the ethogenic approach. They are set out in Box 17.1.

Characteristics of accounts and episodes

The discussion of accounts and episodes that now follows develops some of the ideas contained in the principles of the ethogenic approach outlined above.

We have already noted that accounts must be seen within the context of social episodes. The

Chapter 17

Box 17.1
Principles in the ethogenic approach

- An explicit distinction is drawn between *synchronic analysis*, that is, the analysis of social practices and institutions as they exist at any one time, and *diachronic analysis*, the study of the stages and the processes by which social practices and institutions are created and abandoned, change and are changed. Neither type of analysis can be expected to lead directly to the discovery of universal social psychological principles or laws.
- In social interactions, it is assumed that action takes place through endowing intersubjective entities with meaning; the ethogenic approach therefore concentrates upon the *meaning system*, that is, the whole sequence by which a social act is achieved in an episode. Consider, for example, the action of a kiss in the particular episodes of leaving a friend's house, the passing-out parade at St Cyr and the meeting in the garden of Gethsemane.
- The ethogenic approach is concerned with speech which accompanies action. That speech is intended to make the action intelligible and justifiable in occurring at the time and the place it did in the whole sequence of unfolding and coordinated action. Such speech is *accounting*. In so far as accounts are socially meaningful, it is possible to derive *accounts of accounts*.
- The ethogenic approach is founded upon the belief that human beings tend to be the kind of person their language, their traditions, their tacit and explicit knowledge tell them they are.
- The skills that are employed in ethogenic studies therefore make use of commonsense understandings of the social world. As such the activities of the poet and the playwright offer the ethogenic researcher a better model than those of the physical scientist.

Source: adapted from Harré 1978

idea of an episode is a fairly general one. The concept itself may be defined as any coherent fragment of social life. Being a natural division of life, an episode will often have a recognizable beginning and end, and the sequence of actions that constitute it will have some meaning for the participants. Episodes may thus vary in duration and reflect innumerable aspects of life. A student entering primary school aged 7 and leaving at 11 would be an extended episode. A two-minute television interview with a political celebrity would be another. The contents of an episode which interest the ethogenic researcher include not only the perceived behaviour such as gesture and speech, but also the thoughts, the feelings and the intentions of those taking part. And the 'speech' that accounts for those thoughts, feelings and intentions must be conceived of in the widest connotation of the word. Thus, accounts may be personal records of the events we experience in our day-to-day lives, our conversations with neighbours, our letters to friends, our entries in diaries. Accounts serve to explain our past, present and future oriented actions.

Providing that accounts are authentic, it is argued, there is no reason why they should not be used as scientific tools in explaining people's actions.

Procedures in eliciting, analysing and authenticating accounts: an example

The account-gathering method proposed by Brown and Sime (1977) is summarized in Box 17.2. It involves attention to informants, the account-gathering situation, the transformation of accounts and researchers' accounts, and sets out control procedures for each of these elements.

Problems of eliciting, analysing and authenticating accounts are further illustrated in the following outlines of two educational studies. The first is concerned with valuing among older boys and girls; the second is to do with the activities of pupils and teachers in using computers in primary classrooms.

Kitwood (1977) developed an experience-sampling method, that is, a qualitative technique for gathering and analysing accounts based upon tape-recorded interviews that were themselves

Box 17.2
Account gathering

Research strategy Informants	*Control procedure*
• Definition of episode and role groups representing domain of interest • Identification of exemplars • Selection of individual informants	• Rationale for choice of episode and role groups • Degree of involvement of potential informants • Contact with individuals to establish motive for participation, competence and performance
Account gathering situation	
• Establishing venue • Recording the account • Controlling relevance of account • Authenticating account • Establishing role of interviewer and interviewee • Post account authentication	• Contextual effects of venue • Appropriateness and accuracy in documenting account • Accounts agenda • Negotiation and internal consistency • Degree of direction • Corroboration
Transformation of accounts	
• Provision of working documents • Data reduction techniques	• Transcription reliability; coder reliability • Appropriateness of statistical and content analyses
Researchers' accounts	
• Account of the account: summary, overview, interpretation	• Description of research operations, explanatory scheme and theoretical background

Source: Brown and Sime 1981: 163

prompted by the fifteen situations listed in Box 17.3.

Because the experience-sampling method avoids interrogation, the material which emerges is less organized than that obtained from a tightly structured interview. Successful handling of individual accounts therefore requires the researcher to know the interview content extremely well and to work toward the gradual emergence of tentative interpretive schemata which he then modifies, confirms or falsifies as the research continues. Kitwood identifies eight methods for dealing with the tape-recorded accounts. The first four methods are fairly close to the approach adopted in handling questionnaires, and the rest are more in tune with the ethogenic principles that we identified earlier:

- *The total pattern of choice*: the frequency of choice of various items permits some surface generalizations about the participants, taken as a group. The most revealing analyses may be those of the least and most popular items.
- *Similarities and differences*: using the same technique as in the first method, it is possible to investigate similarities and differences within the total sample of accounts according to some characteristic(s) of the participants such as age, sex, level of educational attainment, etc.
- *Grouping items together*: it may be convenient for some purposes to fuse together categories that cover similar subject matter. For example, items 1, 5 and 14 in Box 17.3 relate to conflict; items 4, 7 and 15 relate to personal growth and change.

Chapter 17

Box 17.3
Experience sampling method

Below are listed fifteen types of situation which most people have been in at some time. Try to think of something that has happened in your life in the past year or so, or perhaps something that keeps on happening, which fits into each of the descriptions. Then choose the ten of them which deal with the things that seem to you to be most important, which cover your main interests and concerns, and the different parts of your life. When we meet we will talk together about the situations you have chosen. Try beforehand to remember as clearly as you can what happened, what you and others did, and how you yourself felt and thought. Be as definite as you can. If you like, write a few notes to help you keep the situation in mind.

1   When there was a misunderstanding between you and someone else (or several others) . . .
2   When you got on really well with people . . .
3   When you had to make an important decision . . .
4   When you discovered something new about yourself . . .
5   When you felt angry, annoyed or resentful . . .
6   When you did what was expected of you . . .
7   When your life changed direction in some way . . .
8   When you felt you had done something well . . .
9   When you were right on your own, with hardly anyone taking your side . . .
10   When you 'got away with it', or were not found out . . .
11   When you made a serious mistake . . .
12   When you felt afterwards that you had done right . . .
13   When you were disappointed with yourself . . .
14   When you had a serious clash or disagreement with another person . . .
15   When you began to take seriously something that had not mattered much to you before . . .

Source: adapted from Kitwood 1977

- *Categorization of content:* the content of a particular item is inspected for the total sample and an attempt is then made to develop some categories into which all the material will fit. The analysis is most effective when two or more researchers work in collaboration, each initially proposing a category system independently and then exchanging views to negotiate a final category system.
- *Tracing a theme:* this type of analysis transcends the rather artificial boundaries which the items themselves imply. It aims to collect as much data as possible relevant to a particular topic regardless of where it occurs in the interview material. The method is exacting because it requires very detailed knowledge of content and may entail going through taped interviews several times. Data so collected may be further analysed along the lines suggested in the fourth method above.

- *The study of omissions:* the researcher may well have expectations about the kind of issues likely to occur in the interviews. When some of these are absent, that fact may be highly significant. The absence of an anticipated topic should be explored to discover the correct explanation of its omission.
- *Reconstruction of a social life-world:* this method can be applied to the accounts of a number of people who have part of their lives in common, for example, a group of friends who go around together. The aim is to attempt some kind of reconstruction of the world which the participants share in analysing the fragmentary material obtained in an interview. The researcher seeks to understand the dominant modes of orienting to reality, the conceptions of purpose and the limits to what is perceived.

- *Generating and testing hypotheses*: new hypotheses may occur to the researcher during the analysis of the tape-recordings. It is possible to do more than simply advance these as a result of tentative impressions; one can loosely apply the hypothetico-deductive method to the data. This involves putting the hypothesis forward as clearly as possible, working out what the verifiable inferences from it would logically be, and testing these against the account data. Where these data are too fragmentary, the researcher may then consider what kind of evidence and method of obtaining it would be necessary for more thorough hypothesis testing. Subsequent sets of interviews forming part of the same piece of research might then be used to obtain relevant data.

In the light of the weaknesses in account gathering and analysis (discussed later), Kitwood's (1977) suggestions of safeguards are worth mentioning. First, he calls for cross-checking between researchers as a precaution against consistent but unrecognized bias in the interviews themselves. Second, he recommends member tests, that is, taking hypotheses and unresolved problems back to the participants themselves or to people in similar situations to them for their comments. Only in this way can researchers be sure that they understand the participants' own grounds for action. Since there is always the possibility that an obliging participant will readily confirm the researcher's own speculations, every effort should be made to convey to the participant that one wants to know the truth as he or she sees it, and that one is as glad to be proved wrong as right.

A study by Blease and Cohen (1990) used cross-checking as a way of validating the classroom observation records of co-researchers, and member tests to authenticate both quantitative and qualitative data derived from teacher and pupil informants. Thus, in the case of cross-checking, the classroom observation schedules of research assistants and researchers were compared and discussed, to arrive at definitive accounts of the range and duration of specific computer activities occurring within observation sessions. Member tests arose when interpretations of interview data were taken back to participating teachers for their comments. Similarly, pupils' scores on certain self-concept scales were discussed individually with respondents in order to ascertain why children awarded themselves high or low marks in respect of a range of skills in using computer programs.

Network analyses of qualitative data

Another technique that has been successfully employed in the analysis of qualitative data is described by its originators as 'systematic network analysis' (Bliss *et al.* 1983). Drawing upon developments in artificial intelligence, Bliss and her colleagues employed the concept of 'relational network' to represent the content and structuring of a person's knowledge of a particular domain.

Essentially, network analysis involves the development of an elaborate system of categories by way of classifying qualitative data and preserving the essential complexity and subtlety of the materials under investigation. A notational technique is employed to generate network-like structures that show the interdependencies of the categories as they are developed. Network mapping is akin to cognitive mapping,[1] an example of which can be seen in the work of Bliss *et al.* (1983).

What makes a good network?

Bliss *et al.* (1983) point out that there cannot be one overall account of criteria for judging the merits of a particular network. They do, however, attempt to identify a number of factors that ought to feature in any discussion of the standards by which a network might fairly be judged as adequate.

First, any system of description needs to be valid and reliable: valid in the sense that it is appropriate in kind and, within that kind, sufficiently complete and faithful, reliable in the sense that there exists an acceptable level of agreement between people as to how to use the network system to describe data.

Second, there are properties that a network description should possess such as clarity, completeness and self-consistency. These relate to a further criterion of 'network utility', the sufficiency of detail contained in a particular network. A third property that a network should possess is termed 'learnability'. Communicating the terms of the analysis to others, say the authors, is of central importance. It follows therefore that much hinges on whether networks are relatively easy or hard to teach to others. A fourth aspect of network acceptability has to do with its 'testability'. Bliss *et al.* (1983) identify two forms of testability, the first having to do with testing a network as a 'theory' against data, the second with testing data against a 'theory' or expectation via a network.

Finally, the terms 'expressiveness' and 'persuasiveness' refer to qualities of language used in developing the network structure. And here, the authors proffer the following advice: 'Helpful as the choice of an expressive coding mood or neat use of indentation or brackets may be, *the code actually says no more than the network distinguishes*' (Bliss *et al.* 1983, our italics).

To conclude, network analysis would seem to have a useful role to play in educational research by providing a technique for dealing with the bulk and the complexity of the accounts that are typically generated in qualitative studies.

Discourse analysis

Discourse researchers explore the organization of ordinary talk and everyday explanations and the social actions performed in them. Collecting, transcribing and analysing discourse data constitutes a kind of psychological 'natural history' of the phenomena in which discourse analysts are interested (Edwards and Potter 1993). Discourses can be regarded as sets of linguistic material that are coherent in organization and content and enable people to construct meaning in social contexts. The emphasis on the *construction* of meaning indicates the action perspective of discourse analysis (Coyle 1995: 245).

Further, the focus on discourse and speech acts links this style of research to Habermas's critical theory set out at the start of this book. Habermas argues that utterances are never simply sentences (Habermas 1970: 368) that are disembodied from context, but, rather, their meaning derives from the intersubjective contexts in which they are set. A speech situation has a double structure, the propositional content (the locutionary aspect – what is being said) and the performatory content (the illocutionary and perlocutionary aspect – what is being done or achieved through the utterance). For Habermas (1979; 1984) each utterance has to abide by the criteria of legitimacy, truth, rightness, sincerity and comprehensibility. His concept of the 'ideal speech situation' argues that speech – and, for our purposes here – discourse, should seek to be empowering and not subject to repression or ideological distortion. His ideal speech situation is governed by several principles, not the least of which are mutual understanding between participants, freedom to enter a discourse, an equal opportunity to use speech acts, discussion to be free from domination, the movement towards consensus resulting from the discussion alone and the force of the argument alone (rather than the position power of speakers). For Habermas, then, discourse analysis would seek to uncover, through ideology critique (see Chapter 1), the repressive forces which 'systematically distort' communication. For our purposes, we can take from Habermas the need to expose and interrogate the dominatory influences that thread not only through the discourses which researchers are studying, but also the discourses that the research itself produces.

Various developments in discourse analysis have made important contributions to our understanding of children's thinking, challenging views (still common in educational circles) of 'the child as a lone organism, constructing a succession of general models of the world as each new stage is mastered' (Edwards 1991). Rather than treating children's language as representative of an inner cognitive world to be explored experimentally by controlling for a host of intruding variables, discourse analysts treat that language as action, as 'situated discursive practice'.

By way of example, Edwards (1993) explores discourse data emanating from a visit to a greenhouse by 5-year-old pupils and their teacher, to see plants being propagated and grown. His analysis shows how children take understandings of adults' meanings from the words they hear and the situations in which those words are used. And in turn, adults (in this case, the teacher) take from pupils' talk, not only what they might mean but also what they could and should mean. What Edwards describes as 'the discursive appropriation of ideas' (Edwards 1991) is illustrated in Box 17.4.

Discourse analysis requires a careful reading and interpretation of textual material, with interpretation being supported by the linguistic evidence. The inferential and interactional aspects of discourse and discourse analysis suggest the need for the researcher to be highly sensitive to the nuances of language (Coyle 1995: 247). In discourse analysis, as in qualitative data analysis generally (Miles and Huberman 1984), the researcher can use coding at an early stage of analysis, assigning codes to the textual material being studied (Parker 1992; Potter and Wetherall 1987). This enables the researcher to discover patterns and broad areas in the discourse. With this achieved the researcher can then re-examine the text to discover intentions, functions and consequences of the discourse (examining the speech act functions of the discourse, e.g. to impart information, to persuade, to accuse, to censure, to encourage etc.). By seeking *alternative explanations* and the *degree of variability* in the discourse, it is possible to rule out rival interpretations and arrive

Box 17.4

Concepts in children's talk

81	Sally	Cuttings can grow to plants.
82	Teacher	[*writing*] 'Cuttings can grow–,' instead of saying 'to
83		plants you can say 'grow, = ⌈ *in :* ⌉ to plants.'
84	Sally	= You wrote Chris ⌊ tina. ⌋
85	Teacher	Oops. Thank you. I'll do this again. 'Cuttings can
86		grow into plants'. That's also good. What is a cutting,
87		Christina?
88	Christina	A cutting is, umm, I don't know.
89	Teacher	Who knows what a cutting is besides Sally? Sam.
90	Sam	It's when you cut off a–, it's when you cut off a piece
91		of a plant.
92	Teacher	Exactly, and when you cut off a piece of a plant, what do
93		you then do with it to make it grow? If you leave
94		⌈ it–, ⌉
95	X	⌊ Put it in soil. ⌋
96	Teacher	Well, sometimes you can put it in soil.
97	Y	And ⌈ plant it, ⌉
98	Teacher	⌊ But what –, ⌋ wait, what else could you put it in?
99	Sam	Put it in a pot?
100	Teacher	Pot, with soil, or…? There's another way.
101	Sally	I know another way. =
102	Teacher	= Wait. Sam, do you know? No? =
103	Sam	= Dirt.
104	Teacher	No, it doesn't have to do with s –, it's not a solid, it's
105		a liquid. What ⌈ liquid -, ⌉
106	Meredith	⌊ Water. ⌋
107	Teacher	Right. […]

Source: Edwards 1993

at a fair reading of what was actually taking place in the discourse in its social context.

The application of discourse analysis to our understanding of classroom learning processes is well exemplified in a study by Edwards and Mercer (1987). Rather than taking the classroom talk as evidence of children's thought processes, the researchers explore it as

> contextualized dialogue with the teacher. The discourse itself is the educational reality and the issue becomes that of examining how teacher and children construct a shared account, a common interpretative framework for curriculum knowledge and for what happens in the classroom.
>
> (Edwards 1991)

Overriding asymmetries between teachers and pupils, Edwards (1991) concludes, both cognitive (in terms of knowledge) and interactive (in terms of power), impose different discursive patterns and functions. Indeed Edwards (1980) suggests that teachers control classroom talk very effectively, reproducing asymmetries of power in the classroom by telling the students when to talk, what to talk about, and how well they have talked.

Discourse analysis has been criticized for its lack of systematicity (Coyle 1995: 256), for its emphasis on the linguistic construction of a social reality, and the impact of the analysis in shifting attention away from what is being analysed and towards the analysis itself, i.e. the risk of losing the independence of phenomena. Discourse analysis risks reifying discourse. One must not lose sight of the fact that the discourse analysis itself is a text, a discourse that in turn can be analysed for its meaning and inferences, rendering the need for reflexivity to be high (Ashmore 1989).[2]

Edwards and Westgate (1987) show what substantial strides have been made in recent years in the development of approaches to the investigation of classroom dialogue. Some methods encourage participants to talk; others wait for talk to emerge and sophisticated audio/video techniques record the result by whatever method it is achieved. Thus captured, dialogue is reviewed, discussed and reflected upon; moreover, that reviewing, discussing and reflecting

is usually undertaken by researchers. It is they, generally, who read 'between the lines' and 'within the gaps' of classroom talk by way of interpreting the intentionality of the participating discussants (O'Neill and McMahon 1990).

Analysing social episodes

A major problem in the investigation of that natural unit of social behaviour, the 'social episode', has been the ambiguity that surrounds the concept itself and the lack of an acceptable taxonomy by which to classify an interaction sequence on the basis of empirically quantifiable characteristics. Several quantitative studies have been undertaken in this field. For example, McQuitty (1957), Magnusson (1971) and Ekehammer and Magnusson (1973) use factor analysis and linkage analysis respectively, while Peevers and Secord (1973), Secord and Peevers (1974) and Forgas (1976; 1978) use multidimensional scaling and cluster analysis.

Account gathering in educational research: an example

The 'free commentary' method that Secord and Peevers (1974) recommend as a way of probing for explanations of people's behaviour lies at the very heart of the ethnographer's skills. In the example of ethnographic research that now follows, one can detect the attempt of the researcher to get below the surface data and to search for the deeper, hidden patterns that are only revealed when attention is directed to the ways that group members interpret the flow of events in their lives.

Heath: 'Questioning at home and at school'

Heath's (1982) study of misunderstandings existing between black children and their white teachers in classrooms in the south of the United States brought to light teachers' assumptions that pupils would respond to language routines and the uses of language in building knowledge and skills just as other children (including their own) did. Specifically, Heath (1982) sought to understand why these particular children did *not* respond just as others did. Her research involved eliciting explanations from both the children's parents and teachers. 'We don't talk to our children like you folks do', the parents observed when questioned about their children's behaviour. Those children, it seemed to Heath, were not regarded as information givers or as appropriate conversational partners for adults. That is not to say that the children were excluded from language participation. They did, in fact, participate in a language that Heath describes as rich in styles, speakers and topics. Rather, it seemed to the researcher that the teachers' characteristic mode of questioning was 'to pull attributes of things out of context, particularly out of the context of books and name them – queens, elves, police, red apples' (Heath 1982). The parents did *not* ask these kinds of questions of their children, and the children themselves had their own ways of deflecting such questions, as the example in Box 17.5 well illustrates.

Heath (1982) elicited both parents' and teachers' accounts of the children's behaviour and their apparent communication 'problems' (see Box 17.6). Her account of accounts arose out of periods of participation and observation in classrooms and in some of the teachers' homes.

In particular, she focused upon the ways in which 'the children learned to use language to satisfy their needs, ask questions, transmit information, and convince those around them that they were competent communicators' (Heath 1982). This involved her in a much wider and more intensive study of the total fabric of life in Trackton, the southern community in which the research was located. She comments that she was able to collect data from a wide range of contexts and situations, tracking children longitudinally and in several contexts, taking care to record language used and the social contexts of the language, and the communicative competence of participants.[3]

Problems in gathering and analysing accounts

The importance of the meaning of events and actions to those who are involved in them is now generally recognized in social research. The implications of the ethogenic stance in terms of actual research techniques, however, remain problematic. Menzel (1978) discusses a number of ambiguities and shortcomings in the ethogenic approach, arising out of the multiplicity of meanings that may be held for the same behaviour. Most behaviour, Menzel (1978) observes, can be assigned meanings and more than one of these may very well be valid simultaneously. It is fallacious

Box 17.5
'Ain't nobody can talk about things being about theirselves'

This comment by a 9-year-old boy was directed to his teacher when she persisted in interrogating him about the story he had just completed in his reading group.

Teacher:	What is the story about?
Children:	(silence)
Teacher:	Uh . . . Let's . . . Who is it the story talks about?
Children:	(silence)
Teacher:	*Who* is *the* main character? . . . What *kind* of story is it?
Child:	Ain't nobody can talk about things being about theirselves.

The boy was saying 'There's no way anybody can talk (and ask) about things being about themselves'.

Source: adapted from Heath 1982

Box 17.6
Parents and teachers: divergent viewpoints on children's communicative competence

---

Parents
The teachers won't listen. My kid, he too scared to talk, 'cause nobody play by the rules he know. At home, I can't shut 'im up.

Miss Davis, she complain 'bout Ned not answerin' back. He say she asks dumb questions she already know 'bout.

Teachers
They don't seem to be able to answer even the simplest questions.

I would almost think some of them have a hearing problem; it is as though they don't hear me ask a question. I get blank stares to my questions. Yet when I am making statements or telling stories which interest them, they always seem to hear me.

The simplest questions are the ones they can't answer in the classroom; yet on the playground, they can explain a rule for a ballgame or describe a particular kind of bait with no problem. Therefore, I know they can't be as dumb as they seem in my class.

I sometimes feel that when I look at them and ask a question I'm staring at a wall I can't break through. There's something there; yet in spite of all the questions I ask, I'm never sure I've gotten through to what's inside that wall.

Source: adapted from Heath 1982

---

therefore, he argues, to insist upon determining 'the' meaning of an act. Nor can it be said that the task of interpreting an act is done when one has identified one meaning of it, or the one meaning that the researcher is pleased to designate as the true one.

A second problem that Menzel (1978) raises is to do with actors' meanings as sources of bias. How central a place, he asks, ought to be given to actors' meanings in formulating explanations of events? Should the researcher exclusively and invariably be guided by these considerations? To do so would be to ignore a whole range of potential explanations which few researchers would wish to see excluded from consideration.

These are far-reaching, difficult issues though by no means intractable. What solutions does Menzel (1978) propose? First, we must specify 'to whom' when asking what acts and situations mean. Second, researchers must make choices and take responsibility in the assignment of meanings to acts; moreover, problem formulations must respect the meaning of the act to us, the researchers. Third, explanations should respect the meanings of acts to the actors themselves but need not invariably be centred around these meanings.

Menzel's (1978) plea is for the usefulness of an outside observer's account of a social episode alongside the explanations that participants themselves may give of that event. A similar argument is implicit in McIntyre and Macleod's (1978) justification of objective, systematic observation in classroom settings. Their case is set out in Box 17.7.

Strengths of the ethogenic approach

The advantages of the ethogenic approach to the educational researcher lie in the distinctive insights that are made available to her through the analysis of accounts of social episodes. The benefits to be derived from the exploration of accounts are best seen by contrasting the ethogenic approach with a more traditional educational technique such as the survey that we discussed in Chapter 9.

There is a good deal of truth in the assertion of the ethogenically oriented researcher that approaches that employ survey techniques such as the questionnaire take for granted the very things that should be treated as problematic in an educational study. Too often, the phenomena that ought to be the focus of attention are taken

Box 17.7
Justification of objective systematic observation in classroom settings

When Smith looks at Jones and says, 'Jones, why does the blue substance spread through the liquid?' (probably with a particular kind of voice inflection), and then silently looks at Jones (probably with a particular kind of facial expression), the observer can unambiguously categorize the event as 'Smith asks Jones a question seeking an explanation of diffusion in a liquid.' Now Smith might describe the event as 'giving Jones a chance to show he knows something', and Jones might describe the event as 'Smith trying to get at me'; but if either of them denied the validity of the observer's description, they would be simply wrong, because the observer would be describing at least part of what the behaviour which occurred means in English in Britain. No assumptions are made here about the effectiveness of classroom communication; but the assumption is made that... communication is dependent on the system of conventional meanings available within the wider culture. More fundamentally, this interpretation implies that the systematic observer is concerned with an objective reality (or, if one prefers, a shared intersubjective reality) of classroom events. This is not to suggest that the subjective meanings of events to participants are not important, but only that these are not accessible to the observer and that *there is an objective reality to classroom activity which does not depend on these meanings* [our emphasis].

Source: McIntyre and Macleod 1978

as given, that is, they are treated as the starting point of the research rather than becoming the centre of the researcher's interest and effort to discover how the phenomena arose or came to be important in the first place. Numerous educational studies, for example, have identified the incidence and the duration of disciplinary infractions in school; only relatively recently, however, has the meaning of classroom disorder, as opposed to its frequency and type, been subjected to intensive investigation. Unlike the survey, which is a cross-sectional technique that takes its data at a single point in time, the ethogenic study employs an ongoing observational approach that focuses upon processes rather than products. Thus it is the process of becoming deviant in school which would capture the attention of the ethogenic researcher rather than the frequency and type of misbehaviour among k types of ability in children located in n kinds of school.

A note on stories

A comparatively neglected area in educational research is the field of stories and storytelling. Bauman (1986: 3) suggests that stories are oral literature whose meanings, forms and functions are situationally rooted in cultural contexts,

scenes and events which give meaning to action. This recalls Bruner (1986) who, echoing the interpretive mode of educational research, regards much action as 'storied text', with actors making meaning of their situations through narrative. Stories have a legitimate place as an inquiry method in educational research (Parsons and Lyons 1979) and, indeed, Jones (1990), Crow (1992), Dunning (1993) and Thody (1997) place them on a par with interviews as sources of evidence for research. Thody (1997: 331) suggests that, as an extension to interviews, stories – like biographies – are rich in authentic, live data; they are, she avers, an 'unparalleled method of reaching practitioners' mindsets'. Thody (1997: 333–4) provides a fascinating report on stories as data sources for educational management research as well as for gathering data from young children.

Thody (1997: 331) indicates how stories can be analysed, using, for example, conventional techniques such as categorizing and coding of content; thematization; concept building. In this respect stories have their place alongside other sources of primary and secondary documentary evidence (e.g. case studies, biographies). They can be used in *ex post facto* research, historical research, as accounts or in action research; in short they are part of the everyday battery of research instruments that are available to the researcher. The rise in the use of oral history as a legitimate research technique in social research can be seen here to apply to educational research. Although they might be problematic in that verification is difficult (unless other people were present to verify events reported), stories, being rich in the subjective involvement of the storyteller, offer an opportunity for the researcher to gather authentic, rich and 'respectable' data (Bauman 1986).

Chapter 17

18 Observation

Introduction

The distinctive feature of observation as a research process is that it offers an investigator the opportunity to gather 'live' data from naturally occurring social situations. In this way, the researcher can look directly at what is taking place *in situ* rather than relying on second-hand accounts. The use of immediate awareness, or direct cognition, as a principal mode of research thus has the potential to yield more valid or authentic data than would otherwise be the case with mediated or inferential methods. And this is observation's unique strength. There are other attractions in its favour: as Robson (2002: 310) says, what people do may differ from what they say they do, and observation provides a reality check; observation also enables a researcher to look afresh at everyday behaviour that otherwise might be taken for granted, expected or go unnoticed (Cooper and Schindler 2001: 374); and the approach with its carefully prepared recording schedules avoids problems caused when there is a time gap between the act of observation and the recording of the event – selective or faulty memory, for example. Finally, on a procedural point, some participants may prefer the presence of an observer to an intrusive, time-consuming interview or questionnaire.

Observation can be of *facts*, such as the number of books in a classroom, the number of students in a class, the number of students who visit the school library in a given period. It can also focus on *events* as they happen in a classroom, for example, the amount of teacher and student talk, the amount of off-task conversation and the amount of group collaborative work. Further, it can focus on *behaviours* or qualities, such as the friendliness of the teacher, the degree of aggressive behaviour or the extent of unsociable behaviour among students.

One can detect here a putative continuum from the observation of uncontestable facts to the researcher's interpretation and judgement of situations, which are then recorded as observations. What counts as evidence becomes cloudy immediately in observation, because what we observe depends on when, where and for how long we look, how many observers there are, and how we look. It also depends on what is taken to be evidence of, or a proxy for, an underlying, latent construct. What counts as acceptable evidence of unsociable behaviour in the example above requires an operational definition that is valid and reliable. Observers need to decide 'of what is the observation evidence', for example: is the degree of wear and tear on a book in the school library an indication of its popularity, or carelessness by its readers, or of destructive behaviour by students? One cannot infer cause from effect, intention from observation, stimulus from response.

Observational data are sensitive to contexts and demonstrate strong ecological validity (Moyles 2002). This enables researchers to understand the context of programmes, to be open-ended and inductive, to see things that might otherwise be unconsciously missed, to discover things that participants might not freely talk about in interview situations, to move beyond perception-based data (e.g. opinions in interviews) and to access personal knowledge. Because observed incidents are less predictable there is a certain freshness to this form of data collection that is often denied in other forms, e.g. a questionnaire or a test.

Observations (Morrison 1993: 80) enable the researcher to gather data on:

- the *physical setting* (e.g. the physical environment and its organization)
- the *human setting* (e.g. the organization of people, the characteristics and make up of the groups or individuals being observed, for instance, gender, class)
- the *interactional setting* (e.g. the interactions that are taking place, formal, informal, planned, unplanned, verbal, non-verbal etc.)
- the *programme setting* (e.g. the resources and their organization, pedagogic styles, curricula and their organization).

Additionally, observational data may be useful for recording non-verbal behaviour, behaviour in natural or contrived settings, and longitudinal analysis (Bailey 1994: 244). On the other hand, the lack of control in observing in natural settings may render observation less useful, coupled with difficulties in measurement, problems of small samples, difficulties of gaining access and negotiating entry, and difficulties in maintaining anonymity (Bailey 1994: 245–6). Observation can be a powerful research tool, but it is not without its difficulties, and this chapter exposes and addresses these.

Patton (1990: 202) suggests that observational data should enable the researcher to enter and understand the situation that is being described. The kind of observations available to the researcher lie on a continuum from unstructured to structured, responsive to pre-ordinate. A *highly structured* observation will know in advance what it is looking for (i.e. pre-ordinate observation) and will have its observation categories worked out in advance. A *semi-structured observation* will have an agenda of issues but will gather data to illuminate these issues in a far less predetermined or systematic manner. An *unstructured observation* will be far less clear on what it is looking for and will therefore have to go into a situation and observe what is taking place before deciding on its significance for the research. In a nutshell, a structured observation will already have its hypotheses decided and will use the observational data to conform or refute these hypotheses. On the other hand, a semi-structured and, more particularly, an unstructured observation, will be hypothesis-generating rather than hypothesis-testing. The semi-structured and unstructured observations will review observational data before suggesting an explanation for the phenomena being observed.

Though it is possible to argue that all research is some form of participant observation since we cannot study the world without being part of it (Adler and Adler 1994), nevertheless Gold (1958) offers a well-known classification of researcher roles in observation, that lie on a continuum. At one end is the *complete participant*, moving to the *participant-as-observer*, thence to the *observer-as-participant*, and finally to the *complete observer* (see http://www.routledge.com/textbooks/ 9780415368780 – Chapter 18, file 18.1.ppt). The move is from complete participation to complete detachment. The mid-points of this continuum strive to balance involvement with detachment, closeness with distance, familiarity with strangeness. The role of the complete observer is typified in the one-way mirror, the video-cassette, the audio-cassette and the photograph, while complete participation involves researchers taking on membership roles (overt or covert) (see http://www.routledge.com/textbooks/ 9780415368780 – Chapter 18, file 18.2.ppt).

Traditionally observation has been characterized as non-interventionist (Adler and Adler 1994: 378), where researchers do not seek to manipulate the situation or subjects, they do not pose questions for the subjects, nor do they deliberately create 'new provocations' (Adler and Adler 1994: 378). Quantitative research tends to have a small field of focus, fragmenting the observed into minute chunks that can subsequently be aggregated into a variable. Qualitative research, on the other hand, draws the researcher into the phenomenological complexity of participants' worlds; here situations unfold, and connections, causes and correlations can be observed as they occur over time. The qualitative researcher aims to catch the dynamic nature of events, to see intentionality, to seek trends and patterns over time.

If we know in advance what we wish to observe, i.e. if the observation is concerned to chart the *incidence*, *presence* and *frequency* of elements and maybe wishes to compare one situation with another, then it may be more efficient in terms of time to go into a situation with a prepared observation schedule. If, on the other hand, we want to go into a situation and let the elements of the situation speak for themselves, perhaps with no concern with how one situation compares with another, then it may be more appropriate to opt for a less structured observation.

The former, structured observation, takes much time to prepare but the data analysis is fairly rapid, the categories having already been established, while the latter, less structured approach, is quicker to prepare but the data take much longer to analyse. The former approach operates within the agenda of the researcher and hence might neglect aspects of the four settings above if they do not appear on the observation schedule, i.e. it looks selectively at situations. On the other hand, the latter operates within the agenda of the participants, i.e. it is responsive to what it finds and therefore, by definition, is honest to the situation as it unfolds. Here selectivity derives from the *situation* rather than from the *researcher* in the sense that key issues emerge from the observation rather than the researcher knowing in advance what those key issues will be. Structured observation is useful for testing hypotheses, while unstructured observation provides a rich description of a situation which, in turn, can lead to the subsequent generation of hypotheses.

Flick (1998: 137) suggests that observation has to be considered along five dimensions:

- structured, systematic and quantitative observation versus unstructured and unsystematic and qualitative observation
- participant observation versus non-participant observation
- overt versus covert observation
- observation in natural settings versus observation in unnatural, artificial settings (e.g. a 'laboratory' or contrived situation)
- self-observation versus observation of others.

Cooper and Schindler (2001: 375) suggest that observation can be considered along three dimensions:

- whether the observation is direct or indirect: the former requiring the presence of the observer, the latter requiring recording devices (e.g. video cameras)
- whether the presence of the observer is known or unknown (overt or covert research), whether the researcher is concealed (e.g. through a one-way mirror or hidden camera) or partially concealed, i.e. the researcher is seen but not known to be a researcher (e.g. the researcher takes up a visible role in the school)
- the role taken by the observer (participant to non-participant observation, discussed below).

We address these throughout the chapter.

Structured observation

A structured observation is very systematic and enables the researcher to generate numerical data from the observations. Numerical data, in turn, facilitate the making of comparisons between settings and situations, and frequencies, patterns and trends to be noted or calculated. The observer adopts a passive, non-intrusive role, merely noting down the incidence of the factors being studied. Observations are entered on an observational schedule. An example of this is shown in Box 18.1 (see http://www.routledge.com/textbooks/9780415368780 – Chapter 18, file 18.3.ppt). This is an example of a schedule used to monitor student and teacher conversations over a ten-minute period. The upper seven categories indicate who is speaking to whom, while the lower four categories indicate the nature of the talk. Looking at the example of the observation schedule, several points can be noted:

- The categories for the observation are discrete, i.e. there is no overlap between them. For this to be the case requires a pilot to have been developed and tested in order to iron out any problems of overlap of categories.

Box 18.1
A structured observation schedule

Student to student	/	/	/	/															
Student to students					/	/													
Student to teacher											/	/	/	/					
Students to teacher							/	/	/	/	/								
Teacher to student															√	√			
Teacher to students																	/	/	/
Student to self																			
Task in hand					√	√					√	√	√	√	√	√	√	√	√
Previous task							√	√	√	√	√								
Future task																			
Non-task	√	√	√	√															

/ = participants in the conversation
√ = nature of the conversation

- Each column represents a thirty-second time interval, i.e. the movement from left to right represents the chronology of the sequence, and the researcher has to enter data in the appropriate cell of the matrix every thirty seconds (see below: instantaneous sampling).
- Because there are so many categories that have to be scanned at speed (every thirty seconds), the researcher will need to practise completing the schedule until he or she becomes proficient and consistent in entering data (i.e. that the observed behaviours, settings etc. are entered into the same categories consistently), achieving reliability. This can be done either through practising with video material or through practising in a live situation with participants who will not subsequently be included in the research. If there is to be more than one researcher then it may be necessary to provide training sessions so that the team of researchers proficiently, efficiently and consistently enter the same sort of data in the same categories, i.e. that there is inter-rater reliability.
- The researcher will need to decide what entry is to be made in the appropriate category, for example: a tick (√), a forward slash (/), a backward slash (\), a numeral (1, 2, 3 etc.), a letter (a, b, c etc.), a tally mark (|). Whatever code or set of codes is used, it must be understood by all the researchers (if there is a team) and must be simple and quick to enter (i.e. symbols rather than words). Bearing in mind that every thirty seconds one or more entries must be made in each column, the researcher will need to become proficient in fast and accurate data entry of the appropriate codes.[1]

The need to pilot a structured observation schedule, as in the example, cannot be overemphasized. Categories must be mutually exclusive and must be comprehensive. The researcher, then, will need to decide

- the foci of the observation (e.g. people as well as events)
- the frequency of the observations (e.g. every thirty seconds, every minute, every two minutes)
- the length of the observation period (e.g. one hour, twenty minutes)
- what counts as evidence (e.g. how a behaviour is defined and operationalized)
- the nature of the entry (the coding system).

The criterion of 'fitness for purpose' is used for making decisions on these four matters. Structured observation will take much time in preparation but the analysis of the data should be rapid as the categories for analysis will have been built into the schedule itself. So, for example, if close, detailed scrutiny is required then the time intervals will be very short, and if less detail is required then the intervals may be longer.

Dyer (1995: 181–4) suggests that structured observation must address several key principles:

- The choice of the environment, such that there will be opportunities for the behaviour to be observed to be actually occurring – the availability and frequency of the behaviour of interest to the observer: a key feature if unusual or special behaviour is sought.
- The need for clear and unambiguous measures, particularly if a latent characteristic or construct is being operationalized.
- A manageable number of variables: a sufficient number for validity to be demonstrated, yet not so many as to render data entry unreliable.
- Overt or covert observation.
- Continuous, time-series or random observation.
- The different categories of behaviour to be observed.
- The number of people to be observed.
- The number of variables on which data must be gathered.
- The kind of observation schedule to be used.

Dyer (1995: 186) provides a checklist for planning a structured observation (Box 18.2).

There are five principal ways of entering data onto a structured observation schedule: event sampling, instantaneous sampling, interval recording, rating scales and duration recording.

Event sampling

Event sampling, also known as a sign system, requires a tally mark to be entered against each statement each time it is observed, for example (see http://www.routledge.com/textbooks/9780415368780 – Chapter 18, file 18.4.ppt):

teacher shouts at child	/////
child shouts at teacher	///
parent shouts at teacher	//
teacher shouts at parent	//

The researcher will need to devise statements that yield the data that answer the research questions. This method is useful for finding out the frequencies or incidence of observed situations or behaviours, so that comparisons can be made; we can tell, for example, that the teacher does most shouting and that the parent shouts least of all. However, while these data enable us to chart the incidence of observed situations or behaviours, the difficulty with them is that we are unable to determine the chronological order in which they occurred. For example, two different stories could be told from these data if the sequence of events were known. If the data were presented in a chronology, one story could be seen as follows, where the numbers 1–7 are the different periods over time (e.g. every thirty seconds):

	1	2	3	4	5	6	7
teacher shouts at child		/	/	/	/		/
child shouts at teacher	/	/					/
parent shouts at teacher		/				/	
teacher shouts at parent						/	/

Imagine the scene: a parent and child arrive late for school one morning and the child slips into the classroom; an event quickly occurs which prompts the child to shout at the teacher, the exasperated teacher is very cross when thus provoked by the child; the teacher shouts at the child, who then brings in the parent (who has not yet left the premises); the parent shouts at the teacher for unreasonable behaviour and the teacher shouts back at the child. It seems in this version that the teacher shouts only when provoked by the child or parent.

If the same number of tally marks were distributed in a different order, a very different story might emerge, for example:

	1	2	3	4	5	6	7
teacher shouts at child	/	/	/	/		/	
child shouts at teacher						/	/	/
parent shouts at teacher						/	/
teacher shouts at parent				/	/		

In this scene it is the teacher who is the instigator of the shouting, shouting at the child and then at the parent; the child and the parent

Box 18.2
Non-participant observation: a checklist of design tasks

The preliminary tasks

Have you

- Clearly described the research problem?
- Stated the precise aim of the research?
- Developed an explanation which either links your research to a theory or says why the observations should be made?
- Stated the hypotheses (if any) to be tested?
- Identified the appropriate test statistic (if needed)?

The observational system

Have you

- Identified the type(s) of behaviour to be observed ?
- Developed clear and objective definitions of each category of behaviour?
- Checked that the categories are complete, and cover all the target behaviours?
- Checked that each category is clearly distinct from the others?
- Checked that the differences between each category are easily seen in the observing situation?

The observational process

Have you

- Identified an appropriate location to make your observations?
- Decided which data sampling procedure to use?
- Decided whether to use overt or covert observation?
- Decided whether to use one or more observers to collect information?

And finally . . .

Have you

- Designed the data collection sheet?
- Reviewed the ethical standards of the investigation?
- Run a pilot study and made any necessary amendments to the observation system, or procedure?
- If more than one observer has been used, made a preliminary assessment of inter-observer reliability?

Source: Dyer 1995: 186

shout back only when they have been provoked (see http://www.routledge.com/textbooks/9780415368780 – Chapter 18, file 18.5.ppt).

Instantaneous sampling

If it is important to know the chronology of events, then it is necessary to use instantaneous sampling, sometimes called time sampling. Here researchers enter what they observe at standard intervals of time, for example every twenty seconds, every minute. On the stroke of that interval the researcher notes what is happening at that precise moment and enters it into the appropriate category on the schedule. For example, imagine that the sampling will take place every thirty seconds; numbers 1–7 represent each thirty-second interval thus:

	1	2	3	4	5	6	7
teacher smiles at child	/	/	/	/			
child smiles at teacher			/	/	/	/	
teacher smiles at parent	/	/	/	/			
parent smiles at teacher			/	/	/	/	

In this scene the researcher notes down what is happening on the thirty-second point and notices from these precise moments that the teacher initiates the smiling but that all parties seem to be doing quite a lot of smiling, with the parent and the child doing the same amount of smiling each (see http://www.routledge.com/textbooks/ 9780415368780 – Chapter 18, file 18.6.ppt). Instantaneous sampling involves recording what is happening on the instant and entering it on the appropriate category. The chronology of events is preserved.

Interval recording

This method charts the chronology of events to some extent and, like instantaneous sampling, requires the data to be entered in the appropriate category at fixed intervals. However, instead of charting what is happening on the instant, it charts what has happened during the preceding interval. So, for example, if recording were to take place every thirty seconds, then the researcher would note down in the appropriate category what had happened during the preceding thirty seconds. While this enables frequencies to be calculated, simple patterns to be observed and an approximate sequence of events to be noted, because it charts what has taken place in the preceding interval of time, some elements of the chronology might be lost. For example, if three events took place in the preceding thirty seconds of the example, then the order of the three events would be lost; we would know simply that they had occurred.

Wilkinson (2000: 236) distinguishes between *whole* interval recording and *partial* interval recording. In the former, behaviour is recorded only if it lasts for the whole of the interval; in the latter, behaviour is recorded if it occupies only a part of the interval in question. In the case of the partial interval recording, the researcher will need to specify how to record this.

Rating scales

In this method the researcher is asked to make some judgement about the events being observed, and to enter responses into a rating scale (see http://www.routledge.com/textbooks/ 9780415368780 – Chapter 18, file 18.7.ppt). For example, Wragg (1994) suggests that observed teaching behaviour might be entered onto rating scales by placing the observed behaviour onto a continuum:

	1	2	3	4	5	
Warm						Aloof
Stimulating						Dull
Businesslike						Slipshod

An observer might wish to enter a rating according to a 5-point scale of observed behaviour, for example:

1 = not at all 2 = very little 3 = a little 4 = a lot 5 = a very great deal

	1	2	3	4	5
Child seeks teacher's attention					
Teacher praises the child					
Teacher intervenes to stop misbehaviour					

What is required here is for the researcher to move from low inference (simply reporting observations) to a higher degree of inference (making judgements about events observed). This might introduce a degree of unreliability into the observation, for example through the halo effect, the central tendency wherein observers will avoid extreme categories, or recency – where observers are influenced by more recent events than less recent events. That said, this might be a helpful summary way of gathering observational data.

Duration recording

So far we have concerned ourselves with single events and their recording. This is very suitable for single and usually short-lived behaviours. However, sometimes certain behaviours last a long time and would over-run the interval categories or event categories described above, i.e. it is continuous behaviour rather than a single event. For example, a child may remove her shoes only once, but she may continue to be without her shoes for a twenty-minute period; a child may delay starting to do any writing for ten minutes, again a single behaviour but which continues for longer than each of the intervals in interval or instantaneous recording; a child may have a single tantrum which continues for twenty minutes, and so on. What we need is an indication of the *duration* of a particular behaviour. The observation is driven by the event, not the frequency of the observation. This means that the observer needs to structure the recording schedule to indicate the total duration of a single continuous behaviour.

For all the kinds of schedules discussed above, a decision will have to have been agreed in advance on how to enter data. Consistency of entering by a single and multiple observers will need to be found on what counts as evidence, when, where and how to observe, and how many people on whom to focus. For example, how will the observation schedule distinguish between one person being observed demonstrating the same behaviour twelve times (1 person × 12) and many people demonstrating the same behaviour fewer times (e.g. 2 people × 6 times each, or 4 people × 3 times each), i.e. is the focus to be on *people* or on *behaviour*?

While structured observation can provide useful numerical data (e.g. Galton and Simon 1980; Bennett *et al.* 1984), there are several concerns which must be addressed in this form of observation, for example:

- The method is behaviourist, excluding any mention of the intentions or motivations of the people being observed.
- The individual's subjectivity is lost to an aggregated score.
- There is an assumption that the observed behaviour provides evidence of underlying feelings, i.e. that concepts or constructs can be crudely measured in observed occurrences.

This last point is important, for it goes to the very heart of the notion of validity, since it requires researchers to satisfy themselves that it is valid to infer that a particular behaviour indicates a particular state of mind or particular intention or motivation. The desire to operationalize concepts and constructs can easily lead researchers to provide simple indicators of complex concepts.

Further, structured observation neglects the significance of contexts – temporal and spatial – thereby overlooking the fact that behaviours may be context specific. In their concern for the overt and the observable, researchers may overlook unintended outcomes which may have significance; they may be unable to show how significant are the behaviours of the participants being observed in their own terms. If we accept that behaviour is developmental, that interactions evolve over time and, therefore, are, by definition, fluid, then the three methods of structured observation outlined above appear to take a series of 'freeze-frame' snapshots of behaviour, thereby violating the principle of fluidity of action. Captured for an instant in time, it is difficult to infer a particular meaning to one or more events (Stubbs and Delamont 1976), just as it is impossible to say with any certainty what is taking place when we study a single photograph or a set of photographs of a particular event. Put simply, if structured observation is to hold water, then the researcher may need to gather additional data from other sources to inform the interpretation of observational data.

This latter point is a matter not only for structured observation but, equally, for unstructured observation, for what is being suggested here is the notion that *triangulation* (of methods, of observers, of time and space) can assist the researcher to generate reliable evidence. There is a risk that observations will be selective, and the effects of this can be attenuated by triangulation. One way of gathering more reliable data (for example about a particular student or group of students) is by *tracking* them through the course of a day or a week, following them from place to place, event to event. It is part of teaching folklore that students will behave very differently for one teacher than for another, and a full picture of students' behaviour might require the observer to see the students in different contexts.

Critical incidents

There will be times when reliability as consistency in observations is not always necessary. For example, a student might demonstrate a particular behaviour only once, but it is so important as not to be ruled out simply because it occurred once. One has to commit only a single murder to be branded a murderer! Sometimes one event can occur which reveals an extremely important insight into a person or situation. Critical incidents (Flanagan 1949) and critical events (Wragg 1994) are particular events or occurrences that might typify or illuminate very starkly a particular feature of a teacher's behaviour or teaching style for example. Wragg (1994: 64) writes that these are events that appear to the observer to have more interest than other ones, and therefore warrant greater detail and recording than other events; they have an important insight to offer. For example, a child might unexpectedly behave very aggressively when asked to work with another child – that might reveal an insight into the child's social tolerance; a teacher might suddenly overreact when a student produces a substandard piece of work – the straw that breaks the camel's back – that might indicate a level of frustration tolerance or intolerance and the effects of that threshold of tolerance being reached. These events are critical in that they may be non-routine but very revealing; they offer the researcher an insight that would not be available by routine observation. They are frequently unusual events.[2]

Naturalistic and participant observation

There are degrees of participation in observation (LeCompte and Preissle 1993: 93–4). The 'complete participant' is a researcher who takes on an insider role in the group being studied, and maybe who does not even declare that he or she is a researcher (discussed later in comments about the ethics of covert research). The 'participant-as-observer', as its name suggests, is part of the social life of participants and documents and records what is happening for research purposes. The 'observer-as-participant', like the participant-as-observer, is known as a researcher to the group, and maybe has less extensive contact with the group. With the 'complete observer' participants do not realize that they are being observed (e.g. using a one-way mirror), hence this is another form of covert research. Hammersley and Atkinson (1983: 93–5) suggest that comparative involvement may come in the forms of the complete participant and the participant-as-observer, with a degree of subjectivity and sympathy, while comparative detachment may come in the forms of the observer-as-participant and the complete observer, where objectivity and distance are key characteristics. Both complete participation and complete detachment are as limiting as each other. As a complete participant the researcher dare not go outside the confines of the group for fear of revealing his or her identity (in covert research), and as a complete observer there is no contact with the observed, so inference is dangerous. That said, both complete participation and complete detachment minimize reactivity, though in the former there is the risk of 'going native' – where the researcher adopts the values, norms and behaviours of the group, i.e. ceases to be a researcher and becomes a member of the group.

Participant observation may be particularly useful in studying small groups, or for events and processes that last only a short time or are frequent, for activities that lend themselves to being observed, for researchers who wish to reach inside a situation and have a long time available to them to 'get under the skin' of behaviour or organizations (as in an ethnography), and when the prime interest is in gathering detailed information about what is happening (i.e. is descriptive).

In participant observational studies the researcher stays with the participants for a substantial period of time to reduce reactivity effects (the effects of the researcher on the researched, changing the behaviour of the latter), recording what is happening, while taking a role in that situation. In schools this might be taking on some particular activities, sharing supervisions, participating in school life, recording impressions, conversations, observations, comments, behaviour, events and activities and the views of all participants in a situation. Participant observation is often combined with other forms of data collection that, together, elicit the participants' definitions of the situation and their organizing constructs in accounting for situations and behaviour. By staying in a situation over a long period the researcher is also able to see how events evolve over time, catching the dynamics of situations, the people, personalities, contexts, resources, roles etc. Morrison (1993: 88) argues that by 'being immersed in a particular context over time not only will the salient features of the situation emerge and present themselves but a more holistic view will be gathered of the interrelationships of factors'. Such immersion facilitates the generation of 'thick descriptions', particularly of social processes and interaction, which lend themselves to accurate explanation and interpretation of events rather than relying on the researcher's own inferences. The data derived from participant observation are 'strong on reality'.

Components of 'thick descriptions' involve recording (Carspecken 1996: 47), for example: speech acts; non-verbal communication; descriptions in low-inference vocabulary; careful and frequent recording of the time and timing of events; the observer's comments that are placed into categories; detailed contextual data.

Observations are recorded in field notes; these can be written at several levels (see http://www.routledge.com/textbooks/9780415368780 – Chapter 18, file 18.8.ppt). At the level of *description* (Spradley 1980; Bogdan and Biklen 1992: 120–1; LeCompte and Preissle 1993: 224), observations can take the following forms:

- quick, fragmentary jottings of key words/symbols
- transcriptions and more detailed observations written out fully
- descriptions that, when assembled and written out, form a comprehensive and comprehensible account of what has happened
- pen portraits of participants
- reconstructions of conversations

- descriptions of the physical settings of events
- descriptions of events, behaviour and activities
- a description of the researcher's activities and behaviour.

Lincoln and Guba (1985: 273) suggest a variety of elements or types of observations that include:

- ongoing notes, either verbatim or categorized *in situ*
- logs or diaries of field experiences (similar to field notes though usually written some time after the observations have been made)
- notes that are made on specific, predetermined themes (e.g. that have arisen from grounded theory)
- 'chronologs', where each separate behavioural episode is noted, together with the time at which it occurred, or recording an observation at regular time intervals, e.g. every two or three minutes
- context maps: maps, sketches, diagrams or some graphic display of the context (usually physical) within which the observation takes place, such graphics enabling movements to be charted
- entries on predetermined schedules (including rating scales, checklists and structured observation charts), using taxonomic or categoric systems, where the categories derive from previous observational or interview data
- sociometric diagrams indicating social relationships, e.g. isolates (whom nobody chooses), stars (whom everyone chooses) and dyads (who choose each other)
- debriefing questionnaires from respondents that are devised for, and by, the observer only, to be used for reminding the observer of main types of information and events once she or he has left the scene
- data from debriefing sessions with other researchers, again as an aide-memoire.

LeCompte and Preissle (1993: 199–200) provide a useful set of guidelines for directing observations of specific activities, events or scenes, suggesting that they should include answers to the following questions:

- Who is in the group/scene/activity – who is taking part?
- How many people are there, their identities and their characteristics?
- How do participants come to be members of the group/event/activity?
- What is taking place?
- How routine, regular, patterned, irregular and repetitive are the behaviours observed?
- What resources are being used in the scene?
- How are activities being described, justified, explained, organized, labelled?
- How do different participants behave towards each other?
- What are the statuses and roles of the participants?
- Who is making decisions, and for whom?
- What is being said, and by whom?
- What is being discussed frequently/infrequently?
- What appear to be the significant issues that are being discussed?
- What non-verbal communication is taking place?
- Who is talking and who is listening?
- Where does the event take place?
- When does the event take place?
- How long does the event take?
- How is time used in the event?
- How are the individual elements of the event connected?
- How are change and stability managed?
- What rules govern the social organization of, and behaviour in, the event?
- Why is this event occurring, and occurring in the way that it is?
- What meanings are participants attributing to what is happening?
- What are the history, goals and values of the group in question?

That this list is long (and by no means exhaustive) reflects the complexity of even the apparently most mundane activity!

Lofland (1971) suggests that there are six main categories of information in participant observation:

- *acts:* specific actions
- *activities:* last a longer time, for instance, a week, a term, months (e.g. attendance at school, membership of a club)
- *meanings:* how participants explain the causes of, meanings of, and purposes of particular events and actions
- *participation:* what the participants do (e.g. membership of a family group, school groups, peer group, clubs and societies, extra-curricular groups)
- *relationships:* observed in the several settings and contexts in which the observation is undertaken
- *settings:* descriptions of the settings of the actions and behaviours observed.

Spradley (1980) suggests a checklist of the content of field notes:

- *space:* the physical setting
- *actors:* the people in the situation
- *activities:* the sets of related acts that are taking place
- *objects:* the artefacts and physical things that are there
- *acts:* the specific actions that participants are doing
- *events:* the sets of activities that are taking place
- *time:* the sequence of acts, activities and events
- *goals:* what people are trying to achieve
- *feelings:* what people feel and how they express this.

Moyles (2002: 181) suggests that researchers need to record the physical and contextual setting of the observation, the participants (e.g. number, who they are, who comes and goes, what they do and what are their roles), the time of day of the observation, the layout of the setting (e.g. seating arrangements, arrangement of desks), the chronology of the events observed, and any critical incidents that happened.

At the level of *reflection*, field notes might include (Bogdan and Biklen 1992: 122):

- reflections on the descriptions and analyses that have been done

- reflections on the methods used in the observations and data collection and analysis
- ethical issues, tensions, problems and dilemmas
- the reactions of the observer to what has been observed and recorded – attitude, emotion, analysis etc.
- points of clarification that have been and/or need to be made
- possible lines of further inquiry.

Lincoln and Guba (1985: 327) indicate three main types of item that might be included in a journal:

- a daily schedule, including practical matters (e.g. logistics)
- a personal diary, for reflection, speculation and catharsis
- notes on and a log of methodology.

In deciding on what to focus, Wilkinson (2000: 228) suggests an important distinction between observing *molecular* and *molar* units of behaviour. Small units of behaviour are molecular, for example gestures, non-verbal behaviour, short actions, short phrases of a conversation. While these yield very specific data, they risk being taken out of context, such that their meanings and, thereby, their validity, are reduced. By contrast, the molar approach deals in large units of behaviour, the size of which is determined by the theoretical interests of the researcher. The researcher must ensure that the units of focus are valid indicators of the issues of concern to the researcher.

From all this we suggest that the data should be comprehensive enough to enable the reader to reproduce the analysis that was performed. It should focus on the observable and make explicit the inferential, and that the construction of abstractions and generalizations might commence early but should not starve the researcher of novel channels of inquiry (Sacks 1992).

Observations include both oral and visual data. In addition to the observer writing down details in field notes, a powerful recording device is through audio-visual recording (Erickson 1992: 209–10). Comprehensive audio-visual recording can overcome the partialness of the observer's view of a single event and can overcome the tendency towards recording only the frequently occurring events. Audio-visual data collection has the capacity for completeness of analysis and comprehensiveness of material, reducing the dependence on prior interpretations by the researcher. Of course, one has to be cautious here, for installing video cameras might create the problem of reactivity. If fixed they might be as selective as participant observers, and even if movable, they might still be highly selective (Morrison 1993: 91).

The context of observation is important (Silverman 1993: 146). Indeed Spradley (1979) and Kirk and Miller (1986) suggest that observers should keep four sets of observational data to include:

- notes made *in situ*
- expanded notes that are made as soon as possible after the initial observations
- journal notes to record issues, ideas, difficulties etc. that arise during the fieldwork
- a developing, tentative running record of ongoing analysis and interpretation.

The intention here is to introduce some systematization into observations in order to increase their reliability. In this respect Silverman (1993) reminds us of the important distinction between *etic* and *emic* analysis. *Etic* analysis uses the conceptual framework of the researcher, while *emic* approaches use the conceptual frameworks of those being researched. Structured observation uses *etic* approaches, with predefined frameworks that are adhered to unswervingly, while *emic* approaches sit comfortably within qualitative approaches, where the definitions of the situations are captured through the eyes of the observed.

Participant observation studies are not without their critics. The accounts that typically emerge from participant observations echo the criticisms of qualitative data outlined earlier, being described as subjective, biased, impressionistic, idiosyncratic and lacking in the precise quantifiable measures that are the hallmark of survey research and experimentation. While it is probably true that nothing can give better insight into the life of a gang of juvenile delinquents than going to live with them for an extended period of time, critics of participant observation studies will point to the dangers of 'going native' as a result of playing a role within such a group. How do we know that observers do not lose their perspective and become blind to the peculiarities that they are supposed to be investigating?

Adler and Adler (1994: 380) suggest several stages in an observation. Commencing with the selection of a setting on which to focus, the observer then seeks a means of gaining entry to the situation (for example, taking on a role in it). Having gained entry the observer can then commence the observation proper, be it structured or unstructured, focused or unfocused. If quantitative observation is being used then data are gathered to be analysed *post hoc*; if more ethnographic techniques are being used then *progressive focusing* requires the observer to undertake analysis *during* the period of observation itself (discussed earlier).

The question that researchers frequently ask is 'How much observation should I do?' or 'When do I stop observation?' Of course, there is no hard and fast rule here, although it may be appropriate to stop when 'theoretical saturation' has been reached (Adler and Adler 1994: 380), i.e. when the situations that are being observed appear to be repeating data that have already been collected. Of course, it may be important to carry on collecting data at this point, to indicate overall frequencies of observed behaviour, enabling the researcher to find the most to the least common behaviours observed over time. Further, the greater the number of observations, the greater the reliability of the data might be, enabling emergent categories to be verified. What is being addressed here is the reliability of the observations (see the earlier discussion of triangulation).

Natural and artificial settings for observation

Most observations by educational researchers will be undertaken in natural settings: schools, classrooms, playgrounds, lessons and suchlike. In studies of a psychological flavour it may be that a contrived, artificial setting is set up in order to give greater observational power to the observers. In Chapter 21 we describe two classic studies in the field of social psychology, both of which use contrived settings – the Milgram study of obedience and the Stanford Prison experiment. Similarly psychological researchers may wish to construct a classroom with a one-way mirror in order to observe children's behaviour without the presence of the observer. This raises the ethical issue of overt and covert research. The advantage of a contrived, artificial setting is the degree of control that the researcher can exert over the situation – typically as large a degree of control as in a laboratory experiment. To the charge that this is an unrealistic situation and that humans should neither be controlled nor manipulated, we refer the reader to the ethical issues addressed in Chapter 2.

One can place settings for observation along a continuum from structured to unstructured and from natural to artificial (Box 18.3). Settings may be classified by the degree of structure that is imposed on the environment by the observer/researcher, and by the degree of structure inherent in the environment itself (Cooper and Schindler 2001: 378).

Clearly the researcher will need to be guided by the notion of 'fitness for purpose' in the type of setting and the amount of structure imposed. There is fuzziness between the boundaries here. Structured settings may be useful in testing hypotheses while unstructured settings may be useful for generating hypotheses.

Ethical considerations

Although observation frequently claims neutrality by being non-interventionist, there are several ethical considerations that surround it. There is a well-documented literature on the dilemma surrounding overt and covert observation. Whereas in overt research the subjects know that they are being observed, in covert research they do not. On the one hand, this latter form of research

Box 18.3
Structured, unstructured, natural and artificial settings for observation

	Natural setting	Artificial setting
Structured	Structured field studies (e.g. Sears et al.'s (1965) study of *Identification and Child Rearing*)	Completely structured laboratory (e.g. the Stanford Prison Experiment, the Milgram experiment on obedience, see Chapter 21) and experiments with one-way mirrors or video recordings
Unstructured	Completely unstructured field study (e.g. Whyte's (1949) celebrated study of *Street Corner Society*) and ethnographic studies	Unstructured laboratory (e.g. Axline's (1964) celebrated study of *Dibs: In Search of Self*) and observations with one-way mirrors or video recordings

appears to violate the principle of informed consent, invades the privacy of subjects and private space, treats the participants instrumentally – as research objects – and places the researcher in a position of misrepresenting her/his role (Mitchell 1993), or rather, of denying it. However, on the other hand, Mitchell (1993) argues that there are some forms of knowledge that are legitimately in the public domain but access to which is available only to the covert researcher (see, for example, the fascinating account of the lookout 'watch queen' in the homosexual community (Humphreys 1975)). Covert research might be necessary to gain access to marginalized and stigmatized groups, or groups who would not willingly accede to the requests of a researcher to become involved in research. This might include those groups in sensitive positions, for example drug users and suppliers, HIV sufferers, political activists, child abusers, police informants and racially motivated attackers. Mitchell (1993)

makes a powerful case for covert research, arguing that not to undertake covert research is to deny access to powerful groups who operate under the protection of silence, to neglect research on sensitive but important topics, and to reduce research to mealy-mouthed avoidance of difficult but strongly held issues and beliefs, i.e. to capitulate when the going gets rough! In a series of examples from research undertaken covertly, he makes the case that not to have undertaken this kind of research would be to deny the public access to areas of legitimate concern, the agendas of the powerful (who can manipulate silence and denial of access to their advantage) and the public knowledge of poorly understood groups or situations.

Covert research can also be justified on the grounds that it overcomes problems of reactivity, in particular if the researcher believes that individuals would change their natural behaviour if they knew that they were being observed.

That covert research can be threatening is well documented, from Patrick's (1973) study of a Glasgow gang, where the researcher had to take extreme care not to blow his cover when witness to a murder, to Mitchell's (1993) account of the careful negotiation of role required to undertake covert research into a group of 'millennialists' – ultra-right-wing armed political groups in the United States who were bound by codes of secrecy, and to his research on mountaineers, where membership of the group involved initiation into the rigours and pains of mountaineering (the researcher had to become a fully-fledged mountaineer himself to gain acceptance by the group).

The ethical dilemmas are numerous, charting the tension between invasion and protection of privacy and the public's legitimate 'right to know', between informed consent and its violation in the interests of a wider public, between observation as a superficial, perhaps titillating, spectator sport and as important social research. At issue is the dilemma that arises between protecting the individual and protecting the wider public, posing the question 'whose beneficence?' – whom does the research serve, whom does the research protect, is the greater good the protection and interests of the individual or the protection and interests of the wider public, will the research harm already damaged or vulnerable people, will the research improve their lot, will the research have to treat the researched instrumentally in the interests of gathering otherwise unobtainable yet valuable research data? The researcher has inescapable moral obligations to consider and, while codes of ethical conduct abound, each case might have to be judged on its own merits.

Further, the issue of non-intervention is, itself, problematical. While the claim for observation as being non-interventionist was made at the start of this chapter, the issue is not as clean cut as this, for researchers inhabit the world that they are researching, and their influence may not be neutral (the Hawthorne and halo effects discussed in Chapter 5). This is clearly an issue in, for example, school inspections, where the presence of an inspector in the classroom exerts a powerful influence on what takes place; it is disingenuous to pretend otherwise. Observer effects can be considerable.

Moreover, the non-interventionist observer has to consider her/his position very closely. In the example of Patrick's (1973) witness to a murder above, should the researcher have blown his cover and reported the murder? What if not acting on the witnessed murder might have yielded access to further sensitive data? Should a researcher investigating drug or child abuse report the first incident or hang back in order to gain access to further, more sensitive data? Should a witness to abuse simply report it or take action about it? If observers see incidents of racial abuse or bullying, should they maintain their non-interventionist position? Is the observer merely a journalist, providing data for others to judge? When does non-intervention become morally reprehensible? These are issues for which one cannot turn to codes of conduct for a clear adjudication.

Some cautionary comments

Many observation situations carry the risk of bias (e.g. Wilkinson 2000: 228; Moyles 2002: 179;

Robson 2002: 324–5; Shaughnessy *et al*. 2003: 116–17), for example by:

- *Selective attention of the observer:* what we see is a function of where we look, what we look at, how we look, when we look, what we think we see, whom we look at, what is in our minds at the time of observation; what are our own interests and experiences.
- *Reactivity:* participants may change their behaviour if they know that they are being observed, e.g. they may try harder in class, they may feel more anxious, they may behave much better or much worse than normal, they may behave in ways in which they think the researcher wishes or in ways for which the researcher tacitly signals approval: 'demand characteristics' (Shaughnessy *et al*. 2003: 113).
- *Attention deficit:* what if the observer is distracted, or looks away and misses an event?
- *Validity of constructs:* decisions have to taken on what counts as valid evidence for a judgement. For example, is a smile a relaxed smile, a nervous smile, a friendly smile, a hostile smile? Does looking at a person's non-verbal gestures count as a valid indicator of interaction? Are the labels and indicators used to describe the behaviour of interest valid indicators of that behaviour?
- *Selective data entry:* what we record is sometimes affected by our personal judgement rather than the phenomenon itself; we sometimes interpret the situation and then record our interpretation rather than the phenomenon.
- *Selective memory:* if we write up our observations after the event our memory neglects and selects data, sometimes overlooking the need to record the contextual details of the observation; notes should be written either during or immediately after the observation.
- *Interpersonal matters and counter-transference:* our interpretations are affected by our judgements and preferences – what we like and what we don't like about people and their behaviour, together with the relationships that we may have developed with those being

observed and the context of the situation; researchers have to deliberately distance themselves from the situation and address reflexivity.

- *Expectancy effects*: the observer knows the hypotheses to be tested, or the findings of similar studies, or has expectations of finding certain behaviours, and these may influence her/his observations.

- *Decisions on how to record*: the same person in a group under observation may be demonstrating the behaviour repeatedly, but nobody else in the group may be demonstrating that behaviour: there is a need to record how many different people show the behaviour.

- *Number of observers*: different observers of the same situation may be looking in different directions, and so there may be inconsistency in the results. Therefore there is a need for training, for consistency, for clear definition of what constitutes the behaviour, of entry/judgement, and for kinds of recording.

- *The problem of inference*: observations can record only what happens, and it may be dangerous, without any other evidence, e.g. triangulation to infer the reasons, intentions and causes and purposes that lie behind actors' behaviours. One cannot always judge intention from observation: for example, a child may intend to be friendly, but it may be construed by an inexperienced observer as selfishness; a teacher may wish to be helpful but the researcher may interpret it as threatening. It is dangerous to infer a stimulus from a response, an intention from an observation.

The issues here concern validity and reliability. With regard to the validity of the observation, researchers have to ensure that the indicators of the construct under investigation are fair and operationalized, for example, so that there is agreement on what counts as constituting qualities such as 'friendly', 'happy', 'aggressive', 'sociable' and 'unapproachable'. The matter of what to observe is problematic. For example, do you focus only on certain people rather than the whole group, on certain events and at certain times rather than others, on molar or molecular units? Do you provide a close-grained, close-up observation or a holistic, wider-focused and wider-ranging observation, i.e. do you use a zoom lens and obtain high definition of a limited scope, or a wide-angle lens and obtain a full field but lacking in detail, or somewhere between the two? How do you decide on what to focus?

Expectancy effects can be overcome by ensuring that the observers do not know the purpose of the research, the 'double-blind' approach.

With regard to reliability, the indicators have to be applied fully, consistently and securely, with no variation in interpretation. Not only is this a matter for one observer – consistency in his or her observation and recording – but also it is a matter if there are several observers. A formula for calculating the degree of agreement (as a percentage) between observers can be used thus:

$$\frac{Number\ of\ times\ two\ observers\ agree}{Number\ of\ possible\ opportunities\ to\ agree} \times 100$$

In measuring inter-rater reliability one should strive for a high percentage (over 90 per cent minimum). Other measures of inter-rater reliability use correlations, and here coefficients of > 0.90 (i.e. over 90 per cent) should be sought (Shaughnessy *et al.* 2003: 111).

To ensure the researcher's or researchers' reliability, it is likely that training is required, so that, for example, researchers

- use the same operational definitions
- record the same observations in the same way
- have good concentration
- can focus on detail
- can be unobtrusive but attentive
- have the necessary experience to make informed judgements from the observational data.

These qualities are essential in order to avoid fatigue, 'observer drift' (Cooper and Schindler 2001: 380) and halo effects, all of which can reduce the reliability of the data.

With regard to the issue of reactivity, one suggestion is to adopt covert observation, though this raises ethical issues which have been addressed in Chapter 2. Another suggestion is to adopt habituation, i.e. the researcher remains in the situation for such a long time that participants not only become used to his or her presence but also revert to their natural behaviour.

Lofland (1971: 104–6) suggests that, to overcome problems of reliability in the research, it is also important for the observer to write up notes as soon after the event as possible, to write quickly yet to expect to take a long time to write notes, to consider dictating notes (though writing may stimulate more thought), to use a word-processing facility as it aids later analysis through software packages, and to make two copies: one of the original data and another for manipulation and analysis (e.g. cutting and pasting data).

Conclusion

Observation methods are powerful tools for gaining insight into situations.[3] As with other data collection techniques, they are beset by issues of validity and reliability. Even low inference observation, perhaps the safest form of observation, is itself highly selective, just as perception is selective. Higher forms of inference, while moving towards establishing causality, rely on greater levels of interpretation by the observer, wherein the observer makes judgements about intentionality and motivation. In this respect it has been suggested that additional methods of gathering data might be employed, to provide corroboration and triangulation, in short, to ensure that reliable inferences are derived from reliable data.

In planning observations one has to consider the following:

- When, where, how and what to observe.
- How much degree of structure is necessary in the observation.
- The duration of the observation period, which must be suitable for the behaviour to occur and be observed.
- The timing of the observation period (e.g. morning, afternoon, evening).

- The context of the observation (a meeting, a lesson, a development workshop, a senior management briefing etc.).
- The nature of the observation (structured, semi-structured, open, molar, molecular etc.).
- The need for there to be an opportunity to observe, for example to ensure that there is the presence of the people to be observed or the behaviour to be observed.
- The merging of subjective and objective observation, even in a structured observation: an observation schedule can become highly subjective when it is being completed, as interpretation, selection and counter-transference may enter the observation, and operational definitions may not always be sufficiently clear.
- The value of covert participant observation in order to reduce reactivity.
- Threats to reliability and validity.
- The need to operationalize the observation so that what counts as evidence is consistent, unambiguous and valid, for example, what constitutes a particular quality (e.g. anti-social behaviour: what counts as antisocial behaviour – one person's 'sociable' is another's 'unsociable' and vice versa).
- The need to choose the appropriate kind of structured observation and recording (e.g. event sampling, instantaneous sampling, whole interval/partial interval recording, duration recording, dichotomous/rating scale recording).
- How to go under cover, or whether informed consent is necessary.
- Whether deception is justified.
- Which role(s) to adopt on the continuum of complete participant, to participant-as-observer, to observer-as-participant, to complete observer.

Observation can be a very useful research tool. However, it exacts its price: it may take a long time to catch the required behaviour or phenomenon, it can be costly in time and effort, and it is prone to difficulties of interpreting or inferring what the data mean. This chapter has outlined several different types of observation and the premises that underlie them, the selection of the method to be used depending on 'fitness for purpose'. Overriding the issues of which specific method of observation to use, this chapter has suggested that observation places the observer into the moral domain, that it is insufficient simply to describe observation as a non-intrusive, non-interventionist technique and thereby to abrogate responsibility for the

participants involved. Like other forms of data collection in the human sciences, observation is not a morally neutral enterprise. Observers, like other researchers, have obligations to participants as well as to the research community.

For examples of observational data see the accompanying web site (http://www.routledge.com/textbooks/9780415368780 – Chapter 18, file 18.1. doc and http://www.routledge.com/textbooks/9780415368780 – Chapter 18, file 18.2 doc).

19 Tests

Introduction

Since the spelling test of Rice (1897), the fatigue test of Ebbinghaus (1897) and the intelligence scale of Binet (1905), the growth of tests has proceeded at an extraordinary pace in terms of volume, variety, scope and sophistication. The field of testing is so extensive that the comments that follow must needs be of an introductory nature and the reader seeking a deeper understanding will need to refer to specialist texts and sources on the subject. Limitations of space permit no more than a brief outline of a small number of key issues to do with tests and testing.

In tests, researchers have at their disposal a powerful method of data collection, an impressive array of tests for gathering data of a numerical rather than verbal kind. In considering testing for gathering research data, several issues need to be borne in mind, not the least of which is why tests are being used at all:

- What are we testing (e.g. achievement, aptitude, attitude, personality, intelligence, social adjustment etc.)?
- Are we dealing with parametric or non-parametric tests?
- Are they norm-referenced or criterion-referenced?
- Are they available commercially for researchers to use or will researchers have to develop home-produced tests?
- Do the test scores derive from a pretest and post-test in the experimental method?
- Are they group or individual tests?
- Do they involve self-reporting or are they administered tests?

Let us unpack some of these issues.

What are we testing?

There is a myriad of tests, to cover all aspects of a student's life and for all ages (young children to old adults), for example: aptitude, attainment, personality, social adjustment, attitudes and values, stress and burnout, performance, projective tests, potential, ability, achievement, diagnosis of difficulties, intelligence, verbal and non-verbal reasoning, higher order thinking, performance in school subjects, introversion and extraversion, self-esteem, locus of control, depression and anxiety, reading readiness, university entrance tests, interest inventories, language proficiency tests, motivation and interest, sensory and perceptual tests, special abilities and disabilities, and many others. *The Mental Measurement Yearbooks* and *Tests in Print* are useful sources of published tests, as well as specific publishers such as Harcourt Assessment and John Wiley. The American Psychological Association also produces on its web site *Finding Information about Psychological Tests* (http://www.apa.org/science/faq-findtests.html) and the British Psychological Society (http://www.bps.org.uk, http://www.psychtesting.org.uk and http://www.bps.org.uk/the-society/psych_testing/psych_testing_home.cfm) produces lists of tests and suppliers. Standard texts that detail copious tests, suppliers and web sites include Gronlund and Linn (1990), Kline (2000), Loewenthal (2001) and Aiken (2003).

Parametric and non-parametric tests

Parametric tests are designed to represent the wide population, e.g. of a country or age group. They make assumptions about the wider population and the characteristics of that wider population, i.e. the parameters of abilities are known. They assume the following (Morrison 1993):

- There is a normal curve of distribution of scores in the population: the bell-shaped symmetry of the Gaussian curve of distribution seen, for example, in standardized scores of IQ or the measurement of people's height or the distribution of achievement on reading tests in the population as a whole.
- There are continuous and equal intervals between the test scores and, with tests that have a true zero (see Chapter 24), the opportunity for a score of, say, 80 per cent to be double that of 40 per cent; this differs from the ordinal scaling of rating scales discussed earlier in connection with questionnaire design where equal intervals between each score could not be assumed.

Parametric tests will usually be published tests which are commercially available and which have been piloted and standardized on a large and representative sample of the whole population. They usually arrive complete with the backup data on sampling, reliability and validity statistics which have been computed in the devising of the tests. Working with these tests enables the researcher to use statistics applicable to interval and ratio levels of data.

Non-parametric tests make few or no assumptions about the distribution of the population (the parameters of the scores) or the characteristics of that population. The tests do not assume a regular bell-shaped curve of distribution in the wider population; indeed the wider population is perhaps irrelevant as these tests are designed for a given specific population – a class in school, a chemistry group, a primary school year group. Because they make no assumptions about the wider population, the researcher must work with non-parametric statistics appropriate to nominal and ordinal levels of data. Parametric tests, with a true zero and marks awarded, are the stock-in-trade of classroom teachers – the spelling test, the mathematics test, the end-of-year examination, the mock-examination.

The attraction of non-parametric statistics is their utility for small samples because they do not make any assumptions about how normal, even and regular the distributions of scores will be. Furthermore, computation of statistics for non-parametric tests is less complicated than that for parametric tests. Non-parametric tests have the advantage of being tailored to particular institutional, departmental and individual circumstances. They offer teachers a valuable opportunity for quick, relevant and focused feedback on student performance.

Parametric tests are more powerful than non-parametric tests because they not only derive from standardized scores but also enable the researcher to compare sub-populations with a whole population (e.g. to compare the results of one school or local education authority with the whole country, for instance in comparing students' performance in norm-referenced or criterion-referenced tests against a national average score in that same test). They enable the researcher to use powerful statistics in data processing (see Chapters 24–26), and to make *inferences* about the results. Because non-parametric tests make no assumptions about the wider population a different set of statistics is available to the researcher (see Chapter 24). These can be used in very specific situations – one class of students, one year group, one style of teaching, one curriculum area – and hence are valuable to teachers.

Norm-referenced, criterion-referenced and domain-referenced tests

A *norm-referenced test* compares students' achievements relative to other students' achievements, for example a national test of mathematical performance or a test of intelligence which has been standardized on a large and representative sample of students between the ages of 6 and 16. A *criterion-referenced test* does not compare student with student but, rather, requires the student to fulfil a given set of criteria, a predefined and absolute standard or outcome (Cunningham 1998). For example, a driving test is usually criterion-referenced since to pass it requires the ability to meet certain test items – reversing round a corner, undertaking an emergency stop, avoiding a crash, etc. – *regardless* of how many others have or have not passed the driving test. Similarly many tests of playing a musical instrument require specified performances, such as the ability to play a particular scale or arpeggio, the ability to play a Bach fugue without hesitation or technical error. If the student meets the criteria, then he or she passes the examination.

A criterion-referenced test provides the researcher with information about exactly what a student has learned, what he or she can do, whereas a norm-referenced test can only provide the researcher with information on how well one student has achieved in comparison with another, enabling rank orderings of performance and achievement to be constructed. Hence a major feature of the norm-referenced test is its ability to discriminate between students and their achievements – a well-constructed norm-referenced test enables differences in achievement to be measured acutely, i.e. to provide variability or a great range of scores. For a criterion-referenced test this is less of a problem: the intention here is to indicate whether students have achieved a set of given criteria, regardless of how many others might or might not have achieved them, hence variability or range is less important here.

More recently an outgrowth of criterion-referenced testing has seen the rise of *domain-referenced tests* (Gipps 1994: 81). Here considerable significance is accorded to the careful and detailed specification of the content or the domain which will be assessed. The domain is the particular field or area of the subject that is being tested, for example, light in science, two-part counterpoint in music, parts of speech in English language. The domain is set out very clearly and very fully, such that the full depth and breadth of the content are established. Test items are then selected from this very full field, with careful attention to sampling procedures so that representativeness of the wider field is ensured in the test items. The student's achievements on that test are computed to yield a proportion of the maximum score possible, and this, in turn, is used as an index of the proportion of the overall domain that she has grasped. So, for example, if a domain has 1,000 items and the test has 50 items, and the student scores 30 marks from the possible 50, then it is inferred that she has grasped 60 per cent ($\{30 \div 50\} \times 100$) of the domain of 1,000 items. Here inferences are being made from a limited number of items to the student's achievements in the whole domain; this requires careful and representative sampling procedures for test items.

Commercially produced tests and researcher-produced tests

There is a battery of tests in the public domain which cover a vast range of topics and that can be used for evaluative purposes (references were indicated earlier). Most schools will have used published tests at one time or another. There are several attractions to using published tests:

- They are objective.
- They have been piloted and refined.
- They have been standardized across a named population (e.g. a region of the country, the whole country, a particular age group or various age groups) so that they represent a wide population.
- They declare how reliable and valid they are (mentioned in the statistical details which are usually contained in the manual of instructions for administering the test).
- They tend to be parametric tests, hence enabling sophisticated statistics to be calculated.
- They come complete with instructions for administration.
- They are often straightforward and quick to administer and to mark.
- Guides to the interpretation of the data are usually included in the manual.
- Researchers are spared the task of having to devise, pilot and refine their own test.

On the other hand, Howitt and Cramer (2005) suggest that commercially produced tests are expensive to purchase and to administer; they are often targeted to special, rather than to general populations (e.g. in psychological testing), and they may not be exactly suited to the purpose required. Further, several commercially produced tests have restricted release or availability, hence the researcher might have to register with a particular association or be given clearance to use the test or to have copies of it. For example, Harcourt Assessment and McGraw-Hill publishers not only hold the rights to a world-wide battery of tests of all kinds but also require registration before releasing tests. In this example Harcourt Assessment also has different levels of clearance, so that certain parties or researchers may not be eligible to have a test released to them because they do not fulfil particular criteria for eligibility.

Published tests by definition are not tailored to institutional or local contexts or needs; indeed their claim to objectivity is made on the grounds that they are deliberately supra-institutional. The researcher wishing to use published tests must be certain that the purposes, objectives and content of the published tests match the purposes, objectives and content of the evaluation. For example, a published diagnostic test might not fit the needs of the evaluation to have an achievement test; a test of achievement might not have the predictive quality that the researcher seeks in an aptitude test, a published reading test might not address the areas of reading that the researcher is wishing to cover, a verbal reading test written in English might contain language that is difficult for a student whose first language is not English. These are important considerations. A much-cited text on evaluating the utility for researchers of commercially available tests is produced by the American Psychological Association (1999) in the *Standards for Educational and Psychological Testing* (http://www.apa.org/science/standards.html).

The golden rule for deciding to use a published test is that it must demonstrate *fitness for purpose*. If it fails to demonstrate this, then tests will have to be devised by the researcher. The attraction of this latter point is that such a 'home-grown' test will be tailored to the local and institutional context very tightly, i.e. that the purposes, objectives and content of the test will be deliberately fitted to the *specific* needs of the researcher in a specific, given context. In discussing fitness for

purpose, Cronbach (1949) and Gronlund and Linn (1990) set out a range of criteria against which a commercially produced test can be evaluated for its suitability for specific research purposes.

Against these advantages of course there are several important considerations in devising a 'home-grown' test. Not only might it be time-consuming to devise, pilot, refine and then administer the test but also, because much of it will probably be non-parametric, there will be a more limited range of statistics that may be applied to the data than in the case of parametric tests.

The scope of tests and testing is far-reaching; no areas of educational activity are untouched by them. *Achievement tests*, largely summative in nature, measure achieved performance in a given content area. *Aptitude tests* are intended to predict capability, achievement potential, learning potential and future achievements. However, the assumption that these two constructs – achievement and aptitude – are separate has to be questioned (Cunningham 1998); indeed, it is often the case that a test of aptitude for, say, geography at a particular age or stage will be measured by using an achievement test at that age or stage. Cunningham (1998) has suggested that an achievement test might include more straightforward measures of basic skills, whereas aptitude tests might put these in combination, for example combining reasoning (often abstract) and particular knowledge; thus achievement and aptitude tests differ according to what they are testing.

Not only do the tests differ according to what they measure, but also, since both can be used predictively, they differ according to what they might be able to predict. For example, because an achievement test is more specific and often tied to a specific content area, it will be useful as a predictor of future performance in that content area but will be largely unable to predict future performance out of that content area. An aptitude test tends to test more generalized abilities (e.g. aspects of 'intelligence', skills and abilities that are common to several areas of knowledge or curricula), hence it is able to be used as a more generalized predictor of achievement. Achievement tests, Gronlund (1985) suggests, are more linked to school experiences whereas aptitude tests encompass out-of-school learning and wider experiences and abilities. However, Cunningham (1998), in arguing that there is a considerable overlap between the two types, is suggesting that the difference is largely cosmetic. An achievement test tends to be much more specific and linked to instructional programmes and cognate areas than an aptitude test, which looks for more general aptitudes (Hanna 1993) (e.g. intelligence or intelligences: Gardner 1993).

Constructing a test

In devising a test the researcher will have to consider:

- the *purposes* of the test (for answering evaluation questions and ensuring that it tests what it is supposed to be testing, e.g. the achievement of the objectives of a piece of the curriculum)
- the *type* of test (e.g. diagnostic, achievement, aptitude, criterion-referenced, norm-referenced)
- the *objectives* of the test (cast in very specific terms so that the content of the test items can be seen to relate to specific objectives of a programme or curriculum)
- the *content* of the test (what is being tested and what the test items are)
- the *construction* of the test, involving *item analysis* in order to clarify the *item discriminability* and *item difficulty* of the test (see below)
- the *format* of the test: its layout, instructions, method of working and of completion (e.g. oral instructions to clarify what students will need to write, or a written set of instructions to introduce a practical piece of work)
- the nature of the *piloting* of the test
- the *validity and reliability* of the test
- the provision of a *manual of instructions* for the administration, marking and data treatment of the test (this is particularly important if the test is not to be administered by the researcher or if the test is to be administered by several

different people, so that reliability is ensured by having a standard procedure).

In planning a test the researcher can proceed thus:

1 Identify the purposes of the test.
2 Identify the test specifications.
3 Select the contents of the test.
4 Consider the form of the test.
5 Write the test item.
6 Consider the layout of the test.
7 Consider the timing of the test.
8 Plan the scoring of the test.

Identify the purposes of the test

The purposes of a test are several, for example to *diagnose* a student's strengths, weaknesses and difficulties, to measure *achievement*, to measure *aptitude* and *potential*, to identify *readiness* for a programme. Gronlund and Linn (1990) term this 'placement testing' and it is usually in a form of pretest, normally designed to discover whether students have the essential prerequisites to begin a programme (e.g. in terms of knowledge, skills, understandings). These types of tests occur at different stages. For example, the placement test is conducted prior to the commencement of a programme, and will identify starting abilities and achievements – the initial or 'entry' abilities in a student. If the placement test is designed to assign students to tracks, sets or teaching groups (i.e. to place them into administrative or teaching groupings), then the entry test might be criterion-referenced or norm-referenced; if it is designed to measure detailed starting points, knowledge, abilities and skills, then the test might be more criterion-referenced as it requires a high level of detail. It has its equivalent in 'baseline assessment' and is an important feature if one is to measure the 'value-added' component of teaching and learning: one can only assess how much a set of educational experiences has added value to the student if one knows that student's starting point and starting abilities and achievements.

- *Formative testing* is undertaken during a programme, and is designed to monitor students' progress during that programme, to measure achievement of sections of the programme, and to diagnose strengths and weaknesses. It is typically criterion-referenced.

- *Diagnostic testing* is an in-depth test to discover particular strengths, weaknesses and difficulties that a student is experiencing, and is designed to expose causes and specific areas of weakness or strength. This often requires the test to include several items about the same feature, so that, for example, several types of difficulty in a student's understanding will be exposed; the diagnostic test will need to construct test items that will focus on each of a range of very specific difficulties that students might be experiencing, in order to identify the exact problems that they are having from a range of possible problems. Clearly this type of test is criterion-referenced.

- *Summative testing* is the test given at the end of the programme, and is designed to measure achievement, outcomes, or 'mastery'. This might be criterion-referenced or norm-referenced, depending to some extent on the use to which the results will be put (e.g. to award certificates or grades, to identify achievement of specific objectives).

Identify the test specifications

The test specifications include:

- which programme objectives and student learning outcomes will be addressed

- which content areas will be addressed
- the relative weightings, balance and coverage of items
- the total number of items in the test
- the number of questions required to address a particular element of a programme or learning outcomes
- the exact items in the test.

To ensure validity in a test it is essential to ensure that the objectives of the test are fairly addressed in the test items. Objectives, it is argued (Mager 1962; Wiles and Bondi 1984), should

- be specific and be expressed with an appropriate degree of precision
- represent intended learning outcomes
- identify the actual and observable behaviour that will demonstrate achievement
- include an active verb
- be unitary (focusing on one item per objective).

One way of ensuring that the objectives are fairly addressed in test items can be done through a matrix frame that indicates the *coverage* of content areas, the coverage of *objectives* of the programme, and the *relative weighting* of the items on the test. Such a matrix is set out in Box 19.1 taking the example from a secondary school history syllabus.

Box 19.1 indicates the main areas of the programme to be covered in the test (*content areas*); then it indicates which objectives or detailed content areas will be covered (1a–3c) – these numbers refer to the identified specifications in the

Box 19.1
A matrix of test items

Content areas	Objective/area of programme content			Objective/area of programme content			Objective/area programme content			
Aspects of the Second World War	1a	1b	1c	2a	2b	2c	3a	3b	3c	Total
The build-up to the Second World War	1	2		2	1	1	1	1	1	10
The invasion of Poland	2	1	1	3	2	2	3	3	3	20
The invasion of France	3	4	5	4	4	3	4	4	4	35
The Allied invasion	3	2	3	3	4	3	3	2	2	25
The end of the conflict	2	1		1	1	1	2	2		10
Total	11	10	9	13	12	10	13	12	10	100

syllabus; then it indicates the marks/percentages to be awarded for each area. This indicates several points:

- The least emphasis is given to the build-up to and end of the war (10 marks each in the 'total' column).
- The greatest emphasis is given to the invasion of France (35 marks in the 'total' column).
- There is fairly even coverage of the objectives specified (the figures in the 'total' row only vary from 9 to 13).
- Greatest coverage is given to objectives 2a and 3a, and least coverage is given to objective 1c.
- Some content areas are not covered in the test items (the blanks in the matrix).

Hence we have here a test scheme that indicates relative weightings, coverage of objectives and content, and the relation between these two latter elements. Gronlund and Linn (1990) suggest that relative weightings should be addressed by first assigning percentages at the foot of each column, then by assigning percentages at the end of each row, and then completing each cell of the matrix within these specifications. This ensures that appropriate sampling and coverage of the items are achieved. The example of the matrix refers to specific objectives as column headings; of course these could be replaced by factual knowledge, conceptual knowledge and principles, and skills for each of the column headings. Alternatively they could be replaced with specific aspects of an activity, for example (Cohen et al. 2004: 339): designing a crane, making the crane, testing the

crane, evaluating the results, improving the design. Indeed these latter could become content (row) headings, as shown in Box 19.2. Here one can see that practical skills will carry fewer marks than recording skills (the column totals), and that making and evaluating carry equal marks (the row totals).

This exercise also enables some indication to be gained on the number of items to be included in the test, for instance in the example of the history test the matrix is $9 \times 6 = 54$ possible items, and in the crane activity example the matrix is $5 \times 4 = 20$ possible items. Of course, there could be considerable variation in this, for example more test items could be inserted if it were deemed desirable to test one cell of the matrix with more than one item (possible for cross-checking), or indeed there could be fewer items if it were possible to have a single test item that serves more than one cell of the matrix. The difficulty in matrix construction is that it can easily become a runaway activity, generating very many test items and, hence, leading to an unworkably long test – typically the greater the degree of specificity required, the greater the number of test items there will be. One skill in test construction is to be able to have a single test item that provides valid and reliable data for more than a single factor.

Having undertaken the test specifications, the researcher should have achieved clarity on the exact test items that test certain aspects of achievement of objectives, programmes, contents etc., the coverage and balance of coverage of the test items and the relative weightings of the test items.

Box 19.2
Compiling elements of test items

Content area	Identifying key concepts and principles	Practical skills	Evaluative skills	Recording results	Total
Designing a crane	2	1	1	3	7
Making the crane	2	5	2	3	12
Testing the crane	3	3	1	4	11
Evaluating the results	3		5	4	12
Improving the design	2	2	3	1	8
Total	12	11	12	15	50

Select the contents of the test

Here the test is subject to *item analysis*. Gronlund and Linn (1990) suggest that an item analysis will need to consider:

- the suitability of the format of each item for the (learning) objective (appropriateness)
- the ability of each item to enable students to demonstrate their performance of the (learning) objective (relevance)
- the clarity of the task for each item
- the straightforwardness of the task
- the unambiguity of the outcome of each item, and agreement on what that outcome should be
- the cultural fairness of each item
- the independence of each item (i.e. where the influence of other items of the test is minimal and where successful completion of one item is not dependent on successful completion of another)
- the adequacy of coverage of each (learning) objective by the items of the test.

In moving to test construction the researcher will need to consider how each element to be tested will be *operationalized*:

- what indicators and kinds of evidence of achievement of the objective will be required
- what indicators of high, moderate and low achievement there will be
- what will the students be doing when they are working on each element of the test
- what the outcome of the test will be (e.g. a written response, a tick in a box of multiple choice items, an essay, a diagram, a computation).

Indeed the Task Group on Assessment and Testing (1988) in the UK suggest that attention will have to be given to the *presentation, operation* and *response* modes of a test:

- how the task will be introduced (e.g. oral, written, pictorial, computer, practical demonstration)
- what the students will be doing when they are working on the test (e.g. mental computation, practical work, oral work, written)
- what the outcome will be – how they will show achievement and present the outcomes (e.g. choosing one item from a multiple choice question, writing a short response, open-ended writing, oral, practical outcome, computer output).

Operationalizing a test from objectives can proceed by stages:

- Identify the objectives/outcomes/elements to be covered.
- Break down the objectives/outcomes/elements into constituent components or elements.
- Select the components that will feature in the test, such that, if possible, they will represent the larger field (i.e. domain referencing, if required).
- Recast the components in terms of specific, practical, observable behaviours, activities and practices that fairly represent and cover that component.
- Specify the kinds of data required to provide information on the achievement of the criteria.
- Specify the success criteria (performance indicators) in practical terms, working out marks and grades to be awarded and how weightings will be addressed.
- Write each item of the test.
- Conduct a pilot to refine the language/readability and presentation of the items, to gauge item discriminability, item difficulty and distractors (discussed below), and to address validity and reliability.

Item analysis, Gronlund and Linn (1990: 255) suggest, is designed to ensure that the items function as they are intended, for example, that criterion-referenced items fairly cover the fields and criteria and that norm-referenced items demonstrate *item discriminability* (discussed below); the level of difficulty of the items is appropriate (see below: *item difficulty*); the test is reliable (free of distractors – unnecessary information and irrelevant cues, see below: *distractors*) (see Millman and Greene (1993). An item analysis will consider the accuracy levels available in the answer, the item difficulty, the importance of the knowledge or skill being tested, the match of the item to the programme, and the number of items to be included.

The basis of item analysis can be seen in *item response theory* (see Hambleton 1993). Item response theory (IRT) is based on the principle that it is possible to measure single, specific latent traits, abilities, attributes that, themselves, are not observable, i.e. to determine observable quantities of unobservable quantities. The theory assumes a relationship between a person's possession or level of a particular attribute, trait or ability and his or her response to a test item. IRT is also based on the view that it is possible:

- to identify objective levels of difficulty of an item, e.g. the Rasch model (Wainer and Mislevy 1990)
- to devise items that will be able to discriminate effectively between individuals
- to describe an item independently of any particular sample of people who might be responding to it, i.e. is not group dependent (i.e. the item difficulty and item discriminability are independent of the sample)
- to describe a testee's proficiency in terms of his or her achievement of an item of a known difficulty level
- to describe a person independently of any sample of items that has been administered to that person (i.e. a testee's ability does not depend on the particular sample of test items)
- to specify and predict the properties of a test before it has been administered;
- for traits to be unidimensional (single traits are specifiable, e.g. verbal ability, mathematical proficiency) and to account for test outcomes and performance
- for a set of items to measure a common trait or ability
- for a testee's response to any one test item not to affect his or her response to another test item
- that the probability of the correct response to an item does not depend on the number of testees who might be at the same level of ability

- that it is possible to identify objective levels of difficulty of an item
- that a statistic can be calculated that indicates the precision of the measured ability for each testee, and that this statistic depends on the ability of the testee and the number and properties of the test items.

In constructing a test the researcher will need to undertake an item analysis to clarify the item discriminability and item difficulty of each item of the test. *Item discriminability* refers to the potential of the item in question to be answered correctly by those students who have a lot of the particular quality that the item is designed to measure and to be answered incorrectly by those students who have less of the particular quality that the same item is designed to measure. In other words, how effective is the test item in showing up differences between a group of students? Does the item enable us to discriminate between students' abilities in a given field? An item with high discriminability will enable the researcher to see a potentially wide variety of scores on that item; an item with low discriminability will show scores on that item poorly differentiated. Clearly a high measure of discriminability is desirable, and items with low discriminability should be discarded.

Suppose the researcher wishes to construct a test of mathematics for eventual use with 30 students in a particular school (or with class A in a particular school). The researcher devises a test and *pilots* it in a different school or in class B respectively, administering the test to 30 students of the same age (i.e. the researcher matches the sample of the pilot school or class to the sample in the school which eventually will be used). The scores of the 30 pilot children are then split into three groups of 10 students each (high, medium and low scores). It would be reasonable to assume that there will be more correct answers to a particular item among the high scorers than among the low scorers. For each item compute the following:

$$\frac{A - B}{\frac{1}{2}(N)}$$

where

A = the number of *correct* scores from the high
   scoring group
B = the number of *correct* scores from the low
   scoring group
N = the *total* number of students in the two
   groups.

Suppose all 10 students from the high scoring group answered the item correctly and 2 students from the low scoring group answered the item correctly. The formula would work out thus:

$$\frac{8}{\frac{1}{2}(10 + 10)} = 0.80 \ (\textit{index of discriminability})$$

The maximum index of discriminability is 1.00. Any item whose index of discriminability is less than 0.67, i.e. is too undiscriminating, should be reviewed first to find out whether this is due to ambiguity in the wording or possible clues in the wording. If this is not the case, then whether the researcher uses an item with an index lower than 0.67 is a matter of judgement. It would appear, then, that the item in the example would be appropriate to use in a test. For a further discussion of item discriminability see Linn (1993) and Aiken (2003).

One can use the discriminability index to examine the effectiveness of *distractors*. This is based on the premise that an effective distractor should attract more students from a low scoring group than from a high scoring group. Consider the following example, where low and high scoring groups are identified:

	A	B	C
Top 10 students	10	0	2
Bottom 10 students	8	0	10

In example A, the item discriminates positively in that it attracts more correct responses (10) from the top 10 students than the bottom 10 (8) and hence is a poor distractor; here, also, the discriminability index is 0.20, hence is a poor discriminator and is also a poor distractor. Example B is an ineffective distractor because nobody was included from either group. Example C is an effective distractor because it includes far more students from the bottom

10 students (10) than the higher group (2). However, in this case any ambiguities must be ruled out before the discriminating power can be improved.

Distractors are the stuff of multiple choice items, where incorrect alternatives are offered, and students have to select the correct alternatives. Here a simple frequency count of the number of times a particular alternative is selected will provide information on the effectiveness of the distractor: if it is selected many times then it is working effectively; if it is seldom or never selected then it is not working effectively and it should be replaced.

If we wish to calculate the *item difficulty* of a test, we can use the following formula:

$$\frac{A}{N} \times 100$$

where

A = the number of students who answered the
   item correctly;
N = the *total* number of students who attempted
   the item.

Hence if 12 students out of a class of 20 answered the item correctly, then the formula would work out thus:

$$\frac{12}{20} \times 100 = 60 \ \text{per cent}$$

The maximum index of difficulty is 100 per cent. Items falling below 33 per cent and above 67 per cent are likely to be too difficult and too easy respectively. It would appear, then, that this item would be appropriate to use in a test. Here, again, whether the researcher uses an item with an index of difficulty below or above the cut-off points is a matter of judgement. In a norm-referenced test the item difficulty should be around 50 per cent (Frisbie 1981). For further discussion of item difficulty see Linn (1993) and Hanna (1993).

Given that the researcher can know the degree of item discriminability and difficulty only once the test has been undertaken, there is an unavoidable need to pilot home-grown tests. Items with limited discriminability and limited difficulty must be weeded out and replaced, those items with the greatest discriminability and the most appropriate degrees of difficulty can be retained; this can be undertaken only once data from a pilot have been analysed.

Item discriminability and item difficulty take on differential significance in norm-referenced and criterion-referenced tests. In a norm-referenced test we wish to compare students with each other, hence item discriminability is very important. In a criterion-referenced test, on the other hand, it is not important *per se* to be able to compare or discriminate between students' performance. For example, it may be the case that we wish to discover whether a group of students has learnt a particular body of knowledge, that is the objective, rather than, say, finding out how many have learned it better than others. Hence it may be that a criterion-referenced test has very low discriminability if all the students achieve very well or achieve very poorly, but the discriminability is less important than the fact than the students have or have not learnt the material. A norm-referenced test would regard such a poorly discriminating item as unsuitable for inclusion, whereas a criterion-referenced test would regard such an item as providing useful information (on success or failure).

With regard to item difficulty, in a criterion-referenced test the level of difficulty is that which is appropriate to the task or objective. Hence if an objective is easily achieved then the test item should be easily achieved; if the objective is difficult then the test item should be correspondingly difficult. This means that, unlike a norm-referenced test where an item might be reworked in order to increase its discriminability index, this is less of an issue in criterion-referencing. Of course, this is not to deny the value of undertaking an item difficulty analysis, rather it is to question the centrality of such a concern. Gronlund and Linn (1990: 265) suggest that where instruction has been effective the item difficulty index of a criterion-referenced test will be high.

In addressing the item discriminability, item difficulty and distractor effect of particular test items, it is advisable, of course, to pilot these tests and to be cautious about placing too great a store on indices of difficulty and discriminability that are computed from small samples.

In constructing a test with item analysis, item discriminability, item difficulty and distractor effects in mind, it is important also to consider the actual requirements of the test (Nuttall 1987; Cresswell and Houston 1991):

- Are all the items in the test equally difficult?
- Which items are easy, moderately hard, hard or very hard?
- What kinds of task is each item addressing: is it a practice item (repeating known knowledge), an application item (applying known knowledge, or a synthesis item (bringing together and integrating diverse areas of knowledge)?
- If not, what makes some items more difficult than the rest?
- Are the items sufficiently within the experience of the students?
- How motivated will students be by the contents of each item (i.e. how relevant will they perceive the item to be, how interesting is it)?

The contents of the test will also need to take account of the notion of *fitness for purpose*, for example in the types of test items. Here the researcher will need to consider whether the kinds of data to demonstrate ability, understanding and achievement will be best demonstrated in, for example (Lewis 1974; Cohen *et al.* 2004: ch. 16):

- an open essay
- a factual and heavily directed essay
- short answer questions
- divergent thinking items
- completion items
- multiple-choice items (with one correct answer or more than one correct answer)
- matching pairs of items or statements
- inserting missing words
- incomplete sentences or incomplete, un-labelled diagrams

- true/false statements
- open-ended questions where students are given guidance on how much to write (e.g. 300 words, a sentence, a paragraph)
- closed questions.

These items can test recall, knowledge, comprehension, application, analysis, synthesis and evaluation, i.e. different orders of thinking. These take their rationale from Bloom (1956) on hierarchies of thinking – from low order (comprehension, application), through middle order thinking (analysis, synthesis) to higher order thinking (evaluation, judgement, criticism). Clearly the selection of the form of the test item will be based on the principle of gaining the maximum amount of information in the most economical way. This is evidenced in the use of machine-scorable multiple choice completion tests, where optical mark readers and scanners can enter and process large-scale data rapidly.

In considering the contents of a test the test writer must also consider the *scale* for some kinds of test. The notion of a scale (a graded system of classification) can be created in two main ways (Howitt and Cramer 2005: 203):

- A list of items whose measurements go from the lowest to highest (e.g. an IQ test, a measure of sexism, a measure of aggressiveness), such that it is possible to judge where a student has reached on the scale by seeing the maximum level reached on the items;
- The method of 'summated scores' (Howitt and Cramer 2005: 203) in which a pool of items is created, and the student's score is the total score gained by summing the marks for all the items.

Further, many psychological tests used in educational research will be *unidimensional*, that is, the items all measure a single element or dimension. Howitt and Cramer (2005: 204) liken this to weighing 30 people using 10 bathroom scales, in which one would expect a high intercorrelation to be found between the bathroom scales. Other tests may be *multidimensional*, i.e. where two or more factors or dimensions are being measured in the same test. Howitt and Cramer

(2005: 204) liken this to weighing 30 people using 10 bathroom scales and then measuring their heights using 5 different tape measures. Here one would expect a high intercorrelation to be found between the bathroom scale measures, a high intercorrelation to be found between the measurements from the tape measures, and a low intercorrelation to be found between the bathroom scale measures and the measurements from the tape measures, because they are measuring different things or dimensions.

Test constructors, then, need to be clear whether they are using a unidimensional or a multidimensional scale. Many texts, while advocating the purity of using a unidimensional test that measures a single construct or concept, also recognize the efficacy, practicality and efficiency in using multidimensional tests. For example, though one might regard intelligence casually as a unidimensional factor, in fact a stronger measure of intelligence would be obtained by regarding it as a multidimensional construct, thereby requiring multidimensional scaling. Of course, some items on a test are automatically unidimensional, for example age, hours spent on homework.

Further, the selection of the items needs to be considered in order to have the highest reliability. Let us say that we have ten items that measure students' negative examination stress. Each item is intended to measure stress, for example:

Item 1: Loss of sleep at examination time.
Item 2: Anxiety at examination time.
Item 3: Irritability at examination time.
Item 4: Depression at examination time.
Item 5: Tearfulness at examination time.
Item 6: Unwillingness to do household chores at examination time.
Item 7: Mood swings at examination time.
Item 8: Increased consumption of coffee at examination time.
Item 9: Positive attitude and cheerfulness at examination time.
Item 10: Eager anticipation of the examination.

You run a reliability test (see Chapter 24 on SPSS reliability) of internal consistency and find strong intercorrelations between items 1–5 (e.g. around

0.85), negative correlations between items 9 and 10 and all the other items (e.g. −0.79), and a very low intercorrelation between items 6 and 8 and all the others (e.g. 0.26). Item-to-total correlations (one kind of item analysis in which the item in question is correlated with the sum of the other items) vary here. What do you do? You can retain items 1–5. For items 9 and 10 you can reverse the scoring (as these items looked at positive rather than negative aspects), and for items 6 and 8 you can consider excluding them from the test, as they appear to be measuring something else. Such item analysis is designed to include items that measure the same construct and to exclude items that do not. We refer readers to Howitt and Cramer (2005: Ch. 12) for further discussion of this.

An alternative approach to deciding which items to retain or exclude from the list of ten items above is to use factor analysis (see Chapter 25), a method facilitated greatly by SPSS. Factor analysis will group together a cluster of similar items and keep that cluster separate from clusters of other items. So, for our example above, the factor analysis could have found, by way of illustration, three factors:

- positive feelings (items 9 and 10)
- negative psychological states (items 2, 3, 4, 5, 7)
- physical, behavioural changes (items 1, 6, 8).

By looking at the factor loadings (see Chapter 25) the researcher would have to decide which were the most appropriate factors to retain, and, thereby, which items to include and exclude. As a general rule, items with low factor loadings (e.g. ≤ 0.3) should be considered for exclusion, as they do not contribute sufficiently to the factor. Factor analysis will indicate, also, whether the construct is unidimensional or multidimensional (if there is only one factor it is probably unidimensional).

Consider the form of the test

Much of the discussion in this chapter assumes that the test is of the pen-and-paper variety. Clearly this need not be the case; for example, tests can be written, oral, practical, interactive, computer-based, dramatic, diagrammatic, pictorial, photographic, involve the use of audio and video material, presentational and role-play, simulations. Oral tests, for example, can be conducted if the researcher feels that reading and writing will obstruct the true purpose of the test (i.e. it becomes a reading and writing test rather than, say, a test of mathematics). This does not negate the issues discussed in this chapter, for the form of the test will still need to consider, for example, reliability and validity, difficulty, discriminability, marking and grading, item analysis, timing. Indeed several of these factors take on an added significance in non-written forms of testing; for example, reliability is a major issue in judging live musical performance or the performance of a gymnastics routine – where a 'one-off' event is likely. Furthermore, reliability and validity are significant issues in group performance or group exercises – where group dynamics may prevent a testee's true abilities from being demonstrated. Clearly the researcher will need to consider whether the test will be undertaken individually, or in a group, and what form it will take.

Write the test item

The test will need to address the intended and unintended clues and cues that might be provided in it, for example (Morris *et al.* 1987):

- The number of blanks might indicate the number of words required.
- The number of dots might indicate the number of letters required.
- The length of blanks might indicate the length of response required.
- The space left for completion will give cues about how much to write.
- Blanks in different parts of a sentence will be assisted by the reader having read the other parts of the sentence (anaphoric and cataphoric reading cues).

Hanna (1993: 139–41) and Cunningham (1998) provide several guidelines for constructing short-answer items to overcome some of these problems:

- Make the blanks close to the end of the sentence.
- Keep the blanks the same length.
- Ensure that there can be only a single correct answer.
- Avoid putting several blanks close to each other (in a sentence or paragraph) such that the overall meaning is obscured.
- Only make blanks of key words or concepts, rather than of trivial words.
- Avoid addressing only trivial matters.
- Ensure that students know exactly the kind and specificity of the answer required.
- Specify the units in which a numerical answer is to be given.
- Use short-answers for testing knowledge recall.

With regard to multiple choice items there are several potential problems:

- the number of choices in a single multiple choice item and whether there is one or more right answer(s)
- the number and realism of the distractors in a multiple choice item (e.g. there might be many distractors but many of them are too obvious to be chosen – there may be several redundant items)
- the sequence of items and their effects on each other
- the location of the correct response(s) in a multiple choice item.

Gronlund and Linn (1990), Hanna (1993: 161–75), Cunningham (1998) and Aiken (2003) set out several suggestions for constructing effective multiple choice test items:

- ensure that they catch significant knowledge and learning rather than low-level recall of facts
- frame the nature of the issue in the stem of the item, ensuring that the stem is meaningful in itself (e.g. replace the general 'sheep': (a) are graminivorous, (b) are cloven footed, (c) usually give birth to one or two calves at a time' with 'how many lambs are normally born to a sheep at one time?')
- ensure that the stem includes as much of the item as possible, with no irrelevancies
- avoid negative stems to the item
- keep the readability levels low
- ensure clarity and unambiguity
- ensure that all the options are plausible so that guessing of the only possible option is avoided
- avoid the possibility of students making the correct choice through incorrect reasoning
- include some novelty to the item if it is being used to measure understanding
- ensure that there can only be a single correct option (if a single answer is required) and that it is unambiguously the right response
- avoid syntactical and grammatical clues by making all options syntactically and grammatically parallel and by avoiding matching the phrasing of a stem with similar phrasing in the response
- avoid including in the stem clues as to which may be the correct response
- ensure that the length of each response item is the same (e.g. to avoid one long correct answer from standing out)
- keep each option separate, avoiding options which are included in each other
- ensure that the correct option is positioned differently for each item (e.g. so that it is not always option 2)
- avoid using options like 'all of the above' or 'none of the above'
- avoid answers from one item being used to cue answers to another item – keep items separate.

The response categories of tests need to be considered, and we refer readers to our discussion of this topic in Chapter 15 on questionnaires (e.g. Likert scales, Guttman scales, semantic differential scales, Thurstone scales).

Morris *et al.* (1987: 161), Gronlund and Linn (1990), Hanna (1993: 147), Cunningham (1998) and Aiken (2003) also indicate particular problems in true–false questions:

- ambiguity of meaning
- some items might be partly true or partly false

- items that polarize – being too easy or too hard
- most items might be true or false under certain conditions
- it may not be clear to the student whether facts or opinions are being sought
- as this is dichotomous, students have an even chance of guessing the correct answer
- an imbalance of true to false statements
- some items might contain 'absolutes' which give powerful clues, e.g. 'always', 'never', 'all', 'none'.

To overcome these problems the authors suggest several points that can be addressed:

- avoid generalized statements (as they are usually false)
- avoid trivial questions
- avoid negatives and double negatives in statements
- avoid over-long and over-complex statements
- ensure that items are rooted in facts
- ensure that statements can be only true or false
- write statements in everyday language
- decide where it is appropriate to use 'degrees' – 'generally', 'usually', 'often' – as these are capable of interpretation
- avoid ambiguities
- ensure that each statement contains only one idea
- if an opinion is to be sought then ensure that it is attributable to a named source
- ensure that true statements and false statements are equal in length and number.

Morris *et al.* (1987), Hanna (1993: 150–2), Cunningham (1998) and Aiken (2003) also indicate particular potential difficulties in matching items:

- It might be very clear to a student which items in a list simply *cannot* be matched to items in the other list (e.g. by dint of content, grammar, concepts), thereby enabling the student to complete the matching by elimination rather than understanding.
- One item in one list might be able to be matched to several items in the other.

- The lists might contain unequal numbers of items, thereby introducing distractors – rendering the selection as much a multiple choice item as a matching exercise.

The authors suggest that difficulties in matching items can be addressed thus:

- ensure that the items for matching are homogeneous – similar – over the whole test (to render guessing more difficult)
- avoid constructing matching items to answers that can be worked out by elimination (e.g. by ensuring that: (a) there are different numbers of items in each column so that there are more options to be matched than there are items; (b) students can avoid being able to reduce the field of options as they increase the number of items that they have matched; (c) the same option may be used more than once)
- decide whether to mix the two columns of matched items (i.e. ensure, if desired, that each column includes both items and options)
- sequence the options for matching so that they are logical and easy to follow (e.g. by number, by chronology)
- avoid over-long columns and keep the columns on a single page
- make the statements in the options columns as brief as possible
- avoid ambiguity by ensuring that there is a clearly suitable option that stands out from its rivals
- make it clear what the nature of the relationship should be between the item and the option (on what terms they relate to each other)
- number the items and letter the options.

With regard to essay questions, there are several advantages that can be claimed. For example, an essay, as an open form of testing, enables complex learning outcomes to be measured, it enables the student to integrate, apply and synthesize knowledge, to demonstrate the ability for expression and self-expression, and to demonstrate higher order and divergent cognitive processes. Further, it is comparatively easy to construct an essay title. On the other hand, essays have been criticized for yielding unreliable data (Gronlund and Linn 1990; Cunningham 1998), for being prone to unreliable (inconsistent and variable) scoring and neglectful of intended learning outcomes and prone to marker bias and preference (being too intuitive, subjective, holistic, and time-consuming to mark). To overcome these difficulties the authors suggest the following:

- The essay question must be restricted to those learning outcomes that are unable to be measured more objectively.
- The essay question must ensure that it is clearly linked to desired learning outcomes and that it is clear what behaviours the students must demonstrate.
- The essay question must indicate the field and tasks very clearly (e.g. 'compare', 'justify', 'critique', 'summarize', 'classify', 'analyse', 'clarify', 'examine', 'apply', 'evaluate', 'synthesize', 'contrast', 'explain', 'illustrate').
- Time limits are set for each essay.
- Options are avoided, or, if options are to be given, ensure that, if students have a list of titles from which to choose, each title is equally difficult and equally capable of enabling the student to demonstrate achievement, understanding etc.
- Marking criteria are prepared and are explicit, indicating what must be included in the answers and the points to be awarded for such inclusions or ratings to be scored for the extent to which certain criteria have been met.
- Decisions are agreed on how to address and score irrelevancies, inaccuracies, poor grammar and spelling.
- The work is double marked, blind, and, where appropriate, without the marker knowing (the name of) the essay writer.

Clearly these are issues of reliability (see Chapter 6). The issue here is that layout can exert a profound effect on the test.

Consider the layout of the test

Deciding on the layout will include the following factors (Gronlund and Linn 1990; Hanna 1993; Linn 1993; Cunningham 1998):

- the nature, length and clarity of the instructions, for example what to do, how long to take, how much to do, how many items to attempt, what kind of response is required (e.g. a single word, a sentence, a paragraph, a formula, a number, a statement etc.), how and where to enter the response, where to show the 'working out' of a problem, where to start new answers (e.g. in a separate booklet)
- is one answer only required to a multiple choice item, or is more than one answer required
- spread out the instructions through the test, avoiding overloading students with too much information at first, and providing instructions for each section as they come to it
- what marks are to be awarded for which parts of the test
- minimizing ambiguity and taking care over the readability of the items
- the progression from the easy to the more difficult items of the test (i.e. the location and sequence of items)
- the visual layout of the page, for example avoiding overloading students with visual material or words
- the grouping of items – keeping together items that have the same contents or the same format
- the setting out of the answer sheets or locations so that they can be entered onto computers and read by optical mark readers and scanners (if appropriate).

The layout of the text should be such that it supports the completion of the test and that this is done as efficiently and as effectively as possible for the student.

Consider the timing of the test

The timing refers to two areas: when the test will take place (the day of the week, month, time of day) and the time allowances to be given to the test and its component items. With regard to the former, in part this is a matter of reliability, for the time of day or week etc. might influence how alert, motivated or capable a student might be. With regard to the latter, the researcher will need to decide what time restrictions are being imposed and why; for example, is the pressure of a time constraint desirable – to show what a student can do under time pressure – or an unnecessary impediment, putting a time boundary around something that need not be bounded (was Van Gogh put under a time pressure to produce paintings of sunflowers?) (see also Kohn 2000).

Although it is vital that students know what the overall time allowance is for the test, clearly it might be helpful to indicate notional time allowances for different elements of the test; if these are aligned to the relative weightings of the test (see the discussions of weighting and scoring) they enable students to decide where to place emphasis in the test – they may want to concentrate their time on the high scoring elements of the test. Further, if the items of the test have exact time allowances, this enables a degree of standardization to be built into the test, and this may be useful if the results are going to be used to compare individuals or groups.

Plan the scoring of the test

The awarding of scores for different items of the test is a clear indication of the relative significance of each item – the weightings of each item are addressed in their scoring. It is important to ensure that easier parts of the test attract fewer marks than more difficult parts of it, otherwise a student's results might be artificially inflated by answering many easy questions and fewer more difficult questions (Gronlund and Linn 1990). Additionally, there are several attractions to making the scoring of tests as detailed and specific as possible (Cresswell and Houston 1991; Gipps 1994; Aiken 2003), awarding specific points for each item and sub-item, for example:

- It enables partial completion of the task to be recognized – students gain marks in proportion

to how much of the task they have completed successfully (an important feature of domain-referencing).
- It enables a student to compensate for doing badly in some parts of a test by doing well in other parts of the test.
- It enables weightings to be made explicit to the students.
- It enables the rewards for successful completion of parts of a test to reflect considerations such as the length of the item, the time required to complete it, its level of difficulty, its level of importance.
- It facilitates moderation because it is clear and specific.
- It enables comparisons to be made across groups by item.
- It enables reliability indices to be calculated (see discussions of reliability).
- Scores can be aggregated and converted into grades straightforwardly.

Ebel (1979) argues that the more marks that are available to indicate different levels of achievement (e.g. for the awarding of grades), the greater the reliability of the grades will be, although clearly this could make the test longer. Scoring will also need to be prepared to handle issues of poor spelling, grammar and punctuation – is it to be penalized, and how will consistency be assured here? Further, how will issues of omission be treated, e.g. if a student omits the units of measurement (miles per hour, dollars or pounds, meters or centimetres)?

Related to the scoring of the test is the issue of reporting the results. If the scoring of a test is specific then this enables variety in reporting to be addressed, for example, results may be reported item by item, section by section, or whole test by whole test. This degree of flexibility might be useful for the researcher, as it will enable particular strengths and weaknesses in groups of students to be exposed.

The desirability of some of the above points is open to question. For example, it could be argued that the strength of criterion-referencing is precisely its specificity, and that to aggregate data (e.g. to assign grades) is to lose the very purpose of the criterion-referencing (Gipps 1994: 85). For example, if a student is awarded a grade E for spelling in English, and a grade A for imaginative writing, this could be aggregated into a C grade as an overall grade of the student's English language competence, but what does this C grade mean? It is meaningless, it has no frame of reference or clear criteria, it loses the useful specificity of the A and E grades, it is a compromise that actually tells us nothing. Further, aggregating such grades assumes equal levels of difficulty of all items.

Of course, raw scores are still open to interpretation – which is a matter of judgement rather than exactitude or precision (Wiliam 1996). For example, if a test is designed to assess 'mastery' of a subject, then the researcher is faced with the issue of deciding what constitutes 'mastery' – is it an absolute (i.e. very high score) or are there gradations, and if the latter, then where do these gradations fall? For published tests the scoring is standardized and already made clear, as are the conversions of scores into, for example, percentiles and grades.

Underpinning the discussion of scoring is the need to make it unequivocally clear exactly what the marking criteria are – what will and will not score points. This requires a clarification of whether there is a 'checklist' of features that must be present in a student's answer.

Clearly criterion-referenced tests will have to declare their lowest boundary – a cut-off point – below which the student has been deemed to fail to meet the criteria. A compromise can be seen in those criterion-referenced tests that award different grades for different levels of performance of the same task, necessitating the clarification of different cut-off points in the examination. A common example of this can be seen in the GCSE examinations for secondary school pupils in the United Kingdom, where students can achieve a grade between A and F for a criterion-related examination.

The determination of cut-off points has been addressed by Nedelsky (1954), Angoff (1971), Ebel (1979) and Linn (1993). Angoff (1971) suggests a method for dichotomously scored items. Here judges are asked to identify the proportion of minimally acceptable persons who would answer each item correctly. The sum of these proportions would then be taken to represent the minimally acceptable score. An elaborated version of this principle comes from Ebel (1979). Here a difficulty by relevance matrix is constructed for all the items. Difficulty might be assigned three levels (e.g. easy, medium and hard) and relevance might be assigned three levels (e.g. highly relevant, moderately relevant, barely relevant). When each and every test item has been assigned to the cells of the matrix, the judges estimate the proportion of items in each cell that minimally acceptable persons would answer correctly, with the standard for each judge being the weighted average of the proportions in each cell (which are determined by the number of items in each cell). In this method judges have to consider two factors – relevance and difficulty (unlike Angoff (1971), where only difficulty featured). What characterizes these approaches is the trust that they place in experts in making judgements about levels (e.g. of difficulty, or relevance, or proportions of successful achievement), that is they are based on fallible human subjectivity.

Ebel (1979) argues that one principle in assignation of grades is that they should represent equal intervals on the score scales. Reference is made to median scores and standard deviations, median scores because it is meaningless to assume an absolute zero on scoring, and standard deviations as the unit of convenient size for inclusion of scores for each grade (see also Cohen and Holliday 1996). One procedure is thus:

- Calculate the median and standard deviation of the scores.
- Determine the lower score limits of the mark intervals using the median and the standard deviation as the unit of size for each grade.

However, the issue of cut-off scores is complicated by the fact that they may vary according to the different purposes and uses of scores (e.g. for diagnosis, for certification, for selection, for programme evaluation, as these purposes will affect the number of cut-off points and grades, and the precision of detail required. For a full analysis of determining cut-off grades see Linn (1993).

The issue of scoring takes in a range of factors, for example: grade norms, age norms, percentile norms and standard score norms (e.g. z-scores, T-scores, stanine scores, percentiles). These are beyond the scope of this book to discuss, but readers are referred to Cronbach (1970), Gronlund and Linn (1990), Cohen and Holliday (1996), Hopkins *et al.* (1996).

Devising a pretest and post-test

The construction and administration of tests is an essential part of the experimental model of research, where a pretest and a post-test have to be devised for the control and experimental groups. The pretest and post-test must adhere to several guidelines:

- The pretest may have questions which differ in form or wording from the post-test, though the two tests must test the same content, i.e. they will be alternate forms of a test for the same groups.
- The pretest must be the same for the control and experimental groups.
- The post-test must be the same for both groups.
- Care must be taken in the construction of a post-test to avoid making the test easier to complete by one group than another.
- The level of difficulty must be the same in both tests.

Test data feature centrally in the experimental model of research; additionally they may feature as part of a questionnaire, interview and documentary material.

Reliability and validity of tests

Chapter 6 covers issues of reliability and validity. Suffice it here to say that reliability concerns the degree of confidence that can be placed in the results and the data, which is often a matter of statistical calculation and subsequent test redesigning. Validity, on the other hand, concerns the extent to which the test tests what it is supposed to test. This devolves on content, construct, face, criterion-related and concurrent validity.

Ethical issues in preparing for tests

A major source of unreliability of test data derives from the extent and ways in which students have been prepared for the test. These can be located on a continuum from direct and specific preparation, through indirect and general preparation, to no preparation at all. With the growing demand for test data (e.g. for selection, for certification, for grading, for employment, for tracking, for entry to higher education, for accountability, for judging schools and teachers) there is a perhaps understandable pressure to prepare students for tests. This is the 'high-stakes' aspect of testing (Harlen 1994), where much hinges on the test results. At one level this can be seen in the backwash effect of examinations on curricula and syllabuses; at another level it can lead to the direct preparation of students for specific examinations. Preparation can take many forms (Mehrens and Kaminski 1989; Gipps 1994):

- ensuring coverage, among other programme contents and objectives, of the objectives and programme that will be tested
- restricting the coverage of the programme content and objectives to only those that will be tested
- preparing students with 'exam technique'
- practising with past or similar papers
- directly matching the teaching to specific test items, where each piece of teaching and contents is the same as each test item
- practising on an exactly parallel form of the test
- telling students in advance what will appear on the test
- practising on and preparing the identical test itself (e.g. giving out test papers in advance) without teacher input
- practising on and preparing the identical test itself (e.g. giving out the test papers in advance), with the teacher working through the items, maybe providing sample answers.

How ethical it would be to undertake the final four of these is perhaps questionable, or indeed any apart from the first on the list. Are they cheating or legitimate test preparation? Should one teach to a test; is not to do so a dereliction of duty (e.g. in criterion- and domain-referenced tests) or giving students an unfair advantage and thus reducing the reliability of the test as a true and fair measure of ability or achievement? In high-stakes assessment (e.g. for public accountability and to compare schools and teachers) there is even the issue of not entering for tests students whose performance will be low (see, for example, Haladyna *et al.* 1991). There is a risk of a correlation between the 'stakes' and the degree of unethical practice – the greater the stakes, the greater the incidence of unethical practice. Unethical practice, observes Gipps (1994), occurs where scores are inflated but reliable inference on performance or achievement is not, and where different groups of students are prepared differentially for tests, i.e. giving some students an unfair advantage over others. To overcome such problems, she suggests, it is ethical and legitimate for teachers to teach to a broader domain than the test, that teachers should not teach directly to the test, and the situation should only be that better instruction rather than test preparation is acceptable (Cunningham 1998).

One can add to this list of considerations (Cronbach 1970; Hanna 1993; Cunningham 1998) the following views:

- Tests must be valid and reliable (see Chapter 6).
- The administration, marking and use of the test should be undertaken only by suitably competent/qualified people (i.e. people and projects should be vetted).
- Access to test materials should be controlled, thus test items should not be reproduced apart from selections in professional publication; the tests should be released only to suitably qualified professionals in connection with specific professionally acceptable projects.
- Tests should benefit the testee (beneficence).
- Clear marking and grading protocols should

exist (the issue of transparency is discussed in Chapter 6).
- Test results are reported only in a way that cannot be misinterpreted.
- The privacy and dignity of individuals should be respected (e.g. confidentiality, anonymity, non-traceability).
- Individuals should not be harmed by the test or its results (non-maleficence).
- Informed consent to participate in the test should be sought.

Computerized adaptive testing

Computerized adaptive testing (Wainer 1990; Aiken 2003: 50–2) is the decision on which particular test items to administer, which is based on the subjects' responses to previous items. It is particularly useful for large-scale testing, where a wide range of ability can be expected. Here a test must be devised that enables the tester to cover this wide range of ability; hence it must include some easy to some difficult items – too easy and it does not enable a range of high ability to be charted (testees simply getting all the answers right), too difficult and it does not enable a range of low ability to be charted (testees simply getting all the answers wrong). We find out very little about a testee if we ask a battery of questions which are too easy or too difficult. Further, it is more efficient and reliable if a test can avoid the problem for high ability testees of having to work through a mass of easy items in order to reach the more difficult items and for low ability testees of having to try to guess the answers to more difficult items. Hence it is useful to have a test that is flexible and that can be adapted to the testees. For example, if a testee found an item too hard the next item could adapt to this and be easier, and, conversely, if a testee was successful on an item the next item could be harder.

Wainer (1990) indicates that in an adaptive test the first item is pitched in the middle of the assumed ability range; if the testee answers it correctly then it is followed by a more difficult item, and if the testee answers it incorrectly then it is followed by an easier item. Computers here provide an ideal opportunity to address the flexibility, discriminability and efficiency of testing. Aiken (2003: 51) suggests that computer adaptive testing can reduce the number of test items present to around 50 per cent of those used in conventional tests. Testees can work at their own pace, they need not be discouraged but can be challenged, the test is scored instantly to provide feedback to the testee, a greater range of items can be included in the test and a greater degree of precision and reliability of measurement can be achieved; indeed, test security can be increased and the problem of understanding answer sheets is avoided.

Clearly the use of computer adaptive testing has several putative attractions. On the other hand, it requires different skills from traditional tests, and these might compromise the reliability of the test, for example:

- The mental processes required to work with a computer screen and computer program differ from those required for a pen and paper test.
- Motivation and anxiety levels increase or decrease when testees work with computers.
- The physical environment might exert a significant difference, e.g. lighting, glare from the screen, noise from machines, loading and running the software.
- Reliability shifts from an index of the variability of the test to an index of the standard error of the testee's performance. The usual formula for calculating standard error assumes that error variance is the same for all scores, whereas in item response theory it is assumed that error variance depends on each testee's ability – the conventional statistic of error variance calculates a single average variance of summed scores, whereas in item response theory this is at best very crude, and at worst misleading as variation is a function of ability rather than test variation and cannot fairly be summed (see Thissen (1990) for an analysis of how to address this issue).
- Having so many test items increases the chance of inclusion of poor items.

Computer adaptive testing requires a large item pool for each area of content domain to be developed (Flaugher 1990), with sufficient numbers, variety and spread of difficulty. All items must measure a single aptitude or dimension, and the items must be independent of each other, i.e. a person's response to an item should not depend on that person's response to another item. The items have to be pretested and validated, their difficulty and discriminability calculated, the effect of distractors reduced, the capability of the test to address unidimensionality and/or multidimensionality to be clarified, and the rules for selecting items to be enacted.

20 Personal constructs

Introduction

Personal constructs are the basic units of analysis in a complete and formally stated theory of personality proposed by George Kelly in his book *The Psychology of Personal Constructs* (1955). Kelly's own clinical experiences led him to the view that there is no objective, absolute truth and that events are meaningful only in relation to the ways that are construed by individuals. Kelly's primary focus is on the way individuals perceive their environment, the way they interpret what they perceive in terms of their existing mental structure, and the way in which, as a consequence, they behave towards it. In *The Psychology of Personal Constructs*, Kelly proposes a view of people actively engaged in making sense of and extending their experience of the world. Personal constructs are the dimensions that we use to conceptualize aspects of our day-to-day world, and, as Kelly writes, people differ from each other in their construction of events. The constructs that we create are used by us to forecast events and rehearse situations before their actual occurrence, and are sometimes organized into groups which embody subordinate and superordinate relationships. According to Kelly, we take on the role of scientist seeking to predict and control the course of events in which we are caught up. For Kelly, the ultimate explanation of human behaviour 'lies in scanning man's [*sic*.] undertakings, the questions he asks, the lines of inquiry he initiates and the strategies he employs' (Kelly 1969). Education, in Kelly's view, is necessarily experimental. Its ultimate goal is individual fulfilment and the maximizing of individual potential, capitalizing on the need of each individual to question and explore.

The central tenets of Kelly's theory are set out in terms of a fundamental postulate and a number of corollaries. It is not proposed here to undertake a detailed discussion of his theoretical propositions. Useful commentaries are available in Bannister (1970) and Ryle (1975) (see also http://www.brint.com/PCT.htm), while a thorough overview is provided by Fay Fransella's (2004) *International Handbook of Personal Construct Psychology* (see also Fransella 2005). Here we look at the method suggested by Kelly of eliciting constructs and assessing the mathematical relationships between them, that is, repertory grid technique.

Characteristics of the method

Kelly (1955) proposes that each person has access to a limited number of 'constructs' by means of which he or she evaluates the phenomena that constitute her world. These phenomena – people, events, objects, ideas, institutions and so on – are known as 'elements'. Kelly further suggests that the constructs that each of us employs may be thought of as bipolar, that is, capable of being defined in terms of polar adjectives (good–bad) or polar phrases (makes me feel happy–makes me feel sad).

A number of different forms of repertory grid technique have been developed since Kelly's first formulation. All have the two essential characteristics in common that we have already identified, that is, *constructs* – the dimensions used by a person in conceptualizing aspects of his or her world – and *elements* – the stimulus objects that a person evaluates in terms of the constructs she employs. In Box 20.1, we illustrate the empirical technique suggested by

Box 20.1
Eliciting constructs and constructing a repertory grid

A person is asked to name a number of people who are significant to him. These might be, for example, mother, father, wife, friend, employer, religious representative. These constitute the *elements* in the repertory grid.

The subject is then asked to arrange the elements into groups of threes in such a manner that two are similar in some way but at the same time different from the third. The ways in which the elements may be alike or different are the *constructs*, generally expressed in bipolar form (quiet–talkative; mean–generous; warm–cold). The way in which two of the elements are similar is called the *similarity pole* of the construct; and the way in which two of the elements are different from the third, the *contrast pole* of the construct.

A grid can now be constructed by asking the subject to place each element at either the *similarity* or the *contrast* pole of each construct. Let x = one pole of the construct, and blank = the other. The result can be set out as follows:

Constructs	Elements					
	A	B	C	D	E	F
I quiet–talkative	x	x	x			x
2 mean–generous	x			x	x	
3 warm–cold			x			x

It is now possible to derive different kinds of information from the grid. By studying each *row*, for example, we can get some idea of how a person defines each construct in terms of significant people in his life. From each *column*, we have a personality profile of each of the significant people in terms of the constructs selected by the subjects. More sophisticated treatments of grid data are discussed in examples presented in the text.

Source: adapted from Kelly 1969

Kelly for eliciting constructs and identifying their relationship with elements in the form of a repertory grid.

Since Kelly's (1955) original account of what he called 'The Role Construct Repertory Grid Test', several variations of repertory grid have been developed and used in different areas of research. It is the flexibility and adaptability of repertory grid technique that have made it such an attractive tool to researchers in psychiatric, counselling and, more recently, educational settings. We now review a number of developments in the form and the use of the technique. Alban-Metcalf (1997: 318) suggests that the use of repertory grids is largely twofold: in their 'static' form they elicit perceptions that people hold of others at a single point in time; in their 'dynamic' form, repeated application of the method indicates changes in perception over time; the latter is useful for charting development and change.

For an example of a repertory grid and triadic elicitation exercise see the accompanying web site (http://www.routledge.com/textbooks/9780415368780 – Chapter 20, file 20.1.doc).

'Elicited' versus 'provided' constructs

A central assumption of this 'standard' form of repertory grid is that it enables the researcher to elicit constructs that subjects customarily use in interpreting and predicting the behaviour of those people who are important in their lives. Kelly's method of eliciting personal constructs required the subject to complete a number of cards, 'each showing the name of a person in [his/her] life'. Similarly, in identifying elements, the subject was asked, 'Is there an important way in which two of [the elements] – any two – differ from the third?', i.e. 'triadic elicitation' (see, for example, Nash 1976). This insistence upon important persons and important ways that they are alike or differ, where both constructs and elements are nominated by the subjects themselves, is central to personal construct theory. Kelly gives it precise expression in his individuality corollary – 'Persons differ from each other in their construction of events.'

Several forms of repertory grid technique now in common use represent a significant departure from Kelly's individuality corollary in that they provide constructs to subjects rather than elicit constructs from them.

One justification for the use of provided constructs is implicit in Ryle's commentary on the individuality corollary: 'Kelly paid rather little attention to developmental and social processes', Ryle (1975) observes, 'his own concern was with the personal and not the social'. Ryle (1975) believes that the individuality corollary would be strengthened by the additional statement that 'persons *resemble* each other in their construction of events'.

Can the practice of providing constructs to subjects be reconciled with the individuality corollary assumptions? A review of a substantial body of research suggests a qualified 'yes':

> [While] it seems clear in the light of research that individuals prefer to use their own elicited constructs rather than provided dimensions to describe themselves and others ... the results of several studies suggest that normal subjects, at least, exhibit approximately the same degree of differentiation in using carefully selected supplied lists of adjectives as when they employ their own elicited personal constructs.
>
> (Adams-Webber 1970)

However, see Fransella and Bannister (1977) on elicited versus supplied constructs as a 'grid-generated' problem.

Bannister and Mair (1968) support the use of supplied constructs in experiments where hypotheses have been formulated and in those involving group comparisons. The use of elicited constructs alongside supplied ones can serve as a useful check on the meaningfulness of those that are provided, substantially lower inter-correlations between elicited and supplied constructs suggesting, perhaps, the lack of relevance of those provided by the researcher. The danger with supplied constructs, Bannister and Mair (1968) argue, is that researchers may assume that the polar adjectives or phrases they provide are the verbal equivalents of the psychological dimensions in which they are interested.

Allotting elements to constructs

When a subject is allowed to classify as many or as few elements at the similarity or the contrast pole, the result is often a very lopsided construct with consequent dangers of distortion in the estimation of construct relationships. Bannister and Mair (1968) suggest two methods for dealing with this problem which we illustrate in Box 20.2. The first, the 'split-half form', requires the subject

to place half the elements at the similarity pole of each construct, by instructing the subject to decide which element most markedly shows the characteristics specified by each of the constructs. Those elements that are left are allocated to the contrast pole. As Bannister (1970) observes, this technique may result in the discarding of constructs (for example, male–female) which cannot be summarily allocated. A second method, the 'rank order form', as its name suggests, requires the subject to rank the elements from the one which most markedly exhibits the particular characteristic (shown by the similarity pole description) to the one which least exhibits it. As the second example in Box 20.2 shows, a rank order correlation coefficient can be used to estimate the extent to which there is similarity in the allotment of elements on any two constructs. Following Bannister (1970), a 'construct relationship' score can be calculated by squaring the correlation coefficient and multiplying by 100. (Because correlations are not linearly related they cannot be used as scores.) The construct relationship score gives an estimate of the percentage variance that the two constructs share in common in terms of the rankings on the two grids.

A third method of allotting elements is the 'rating form'. Here, the subject is required to judge each element on a 7-point or a 5-point scale, for example, absolutely beautiful (7) to absolutely ugly (1). Commenting on the advantages of the rating form, Bannister and Mair (1968) note that it offers the subject greater latitude in distinguishing between elements than that provided for in the original form proposed by Kelly. At the same time the degree of differentiation asked of the subject may not be as great as that demanded in the ranking method. As with the rank order method, the rating form approach also allows the use of most correlation techniques. The rating form is the third example illustrated in Box 20.2.

Alban-Metcalf (1997: 317) suggests that there are two principles that govern the selection of elements in the repertory grid technique. The first is that the elements must be relevant to that part of the construct system that is being

Box 20.2
Allotting elements to constructs: three methods

Example 1: Split-half form

Elements | | | | | | | | | | Constructs

1	2	3	4	5	6	7	8	9	10	
×		×	×		×		×			1 fast–slow
	×	×		×		×			×	2 late–early
		×	×		×			×	×	3 dangerous–safe

Since the subject is forced to allocate half of the elements to one pole, the chance expectancy of matchings occurring on 10 elements when two constructs are compared is 5. Deviation scores can be computed from chance level. Thus 5 matchings = 0; in constructs 1 and 2, matchings = −3; in constructs 1 and 3, matchings = +1; and in constructs 2 and 3, matchings = −1. The probability of particular matching scores being obtained can be had by reference to statistical tables.

Example 2: Rank-order form

Elements | | | | | | | | | | Constructs

1	2	3	4	5	6	7	8	9	10	
10	1	2	5	8	7	3	4	9	6	1 fast–slow
9	4	10	1	6	8	5	2	3	7	2 late–early
7	9	5	6	10	2	1	4	8	3	3 dangerous–safe

Spearman's rho (r_s)   Relationship scores
Constructs 1 and 2 = .15 $(0.15)^2 \times 100 = +23$
Constructs 1 and 3 = .24 $(0.24)^2 \times 100 = +58$
Constructs 2 and 3 = −.16 $(-0.16)^2 \times 100 = -26$

Example 3: Rating form

Elements | | | | | | | | | | Constructs

1	2	3	4	5	6	7	8	9	10	
4	4	2	1	4	3	5	1	5	2	1 fast
1	1	3	5	1	3	2	2	5	5	2 late
5	1	3	2	2	1	4	5	1	2	3 dangerous

A 5-point rating scale is shown in which, in this example, single poles of the constructs are rated as follows:

Not at
all like   Average   Very much
                                                                                                            like
1   2   3   4   5

Bannister and Mair (1968: 63–5) suggest several methods for calculating relationships between constructs from the rating form. For a detailed discussion of measures of construct relationships, see Fransella and Bannister (1977: 60–72).

Source: adapted from Bannister and Mair 1968

investigated, and the second is that the selected elements must be representative. The greater the number of elements (typically between 10 and 25) or constructs that are elicited, the greater is the chance of representativeness. Constructs can be psychological (e.g. anxious), physical (e.g. tall), situational (e.g. from this neighbourhood), and behavioural (e.g. is good at sport).

Laddering and pyramid constructions

The technique known as laddering arises out of Hinkle's (1965) important revision of the theory of personal constructs and the method employed in his research. Hinkle's concern was for the location of any construct within an individual's construct system, arguing that a construct has differential implications within a given hierarchical context. Here a construct is selected by the interviewer, and the respondent is asked which pole applies to a particular, given element (Alban-Metcalf 1997: 316). The constructs that are elicited form a sequence that has a logic for the individual and that can be arranged in a hierarchical manner of subordinate and superordinate constructs (Alban-Metcalf 1997: 317). That is 'laddering up', where there is a progression from subordinate to superordinate constructs. The reverse process (superordinate to subordinate) is 'laddering down', asking, for example, how the respondent knows that such and such a construct applies to a particular person.

Hinkle (1965) went on to develop an Implication Grid or Impgrid, in which the subject is required to compare each of his constructs with every other to see which implies the other. The question 'Why?' is asked over and over again to identify the position of any construct in an individual's hierarchical construct system. Box 20.3 illustrates Hinkle's laddering technique with an example from educational research reported by Fransella (1975).

In pyramid construction respondents are asked to think of a particular 'element', a person, and then to specify an attribute which is characteristic of that person. Then the respondent is asked to identify a person who displays the opposite characteristic. This sets out the two poles of the construct. Finally, laddering down of each of the opposite poles is undertaken, thereby constructing a pyramid of relationships between the constructs (Alban-Metcalf 1997: 317). For further discussion of laddering we refer the reader to Butt (1995).

Grid administration and analysis

The example of grid administration and analysis outlined below employs the split-half method of allocating elements to constructs and a form of 'anchor analysis' devised by Bannister (1970). We assume that 16 elements and 15 constructs have already been elicited by means of a technique such as the one illustrated in Box 20.1.

Procedures in grid administration

Draw up a grid measuring 16 (elements) by 15 (constructs) as in Box 20.1, writing along the top the names of the elements, but first inserting the additional element, 'self'. Alongside the rows write in the construct poles.

You now have a grid in which each intersection or cell is defined by a particular column (element) and a particular row (construct). The administration takes the form of allocating every element on every construct. If, for example, your first construct is 'kind–cruel', allocate each element in turn on that dimension, putting a cross in the appropriate box if you consider that person (element) kind, or leaving it blank if you consider that person cruel. Make sure that half of the elements are designated kind and half cruel.

Proceed in this way for each construct in turn, always placing a cross where the construct pole to the left of the grid applies, and leaving it blank if the construct pole to the right is applicable. Every element must be allocated in this way, and half of the elements must always be allocated to the left-hand pole.

Procedures in grid analysis

The grid may be regarded as a reflection of conceptual structure in which constructs are

Box 20.3

Laddering

Constructs		A	B	C	D	E	F	G	H
	Elements teachers								
masculine		2	1	5	4	3	6	8	7
serious		6	2	1	3	8	4	5	7
good teacher									
authoritarian									
sexy									
old									
gets on with others									
lonely									
like me in character									
like I hope to become									

A matrix of rankings for a repertory grid with teachers as elements

You may decide to stop when you have elicited seven or eight constructs from the teacher elements. But you could go on to 'ladder' two or three of them. This process of laddering is in effect asking yourself (or someone else) to abstract from one conceptual level to another. You could ladder from *man–woman*, but it might be easier to start off with *serious–light-hearted*. Ask yourself which you would prefer to be – *serious* or *light-hearted*. You might reply *light-hearted*. Now pose the question 'why'. Why would you rather be a *light-hearted* person than a *serious* person? Perhaps the answer would be that *light-hearted* people *get on better with others* than do *serious* people. Ask yourself 'why' again. Why do you want to be the sort of person who gets on better with others? Perhaps it transpires that you think that people who do not get on well with others are *lonely*. In this way you elicit more constructs but ones that stand on the shoulders of those previously elicited. Whatever constructs you have obtained can be put into the grid.

Source: adapted from Fransella 1975

linked by virtue of their being applied to the same persons (elements). This linkage is measured by a process of matching construct rows.

To estimate the linkage between Constructs 1 and 2 in Box 20.4, for example, count the number of matches between corresponding boxes in each row. A match is counted where the same element has been designated with a cross (or a blank) on both constructs. So, for Constructs 1 and 2 in Box 20.4, we count six such matches. By chance we would expect eight (out of sixteen) matches, and we may subtract this from the observed value to arrive at an estimate of such deviation from chance.

Box 20.4

Elements

Construct	Self	1	2	3	4	5	6	7	8	9	10	11	12	13	14	15	Construct
KIND	X		X				X	X			X	X	X			X	CRUEL
CONFIDENT	X	X		X	X		X			X		X		X			UNSURE

Box 20.5
Difference score for constructs

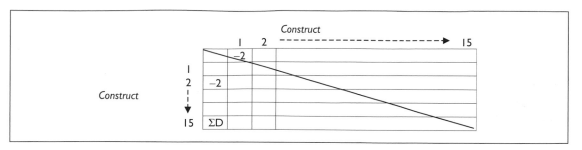

Constructs	Match	Difference score
1–2	6	$6 - 8 = -2$

By matching Construct 1 against all remaining constructs (3…15), we get a score for each comparison. Beginning then with Construct 2, and comparing this with every other construct (3…15), and so on, every construct on the grid is matched with every other one and a difference score for each obtained. This is recorded in matrix form, with the reflected half of the table also filled in (see difference score for Constructs 1–2 in Box 20.5). The sign of the difference score is retained. It indicates the direction of the linkage. A positive sign shows that the constructs are positively associated, a negative sign that they are negatively associated.

Now add up (without noting sign) the sum of the difference scores for each column (construct) in the matrix. The construct with the largest difference score is the one which, statistically, accounts for the greatest amount of variance in the grid. Note this down. Now look in the body of the matrix for that construct which has the largest non-significant association with the one which you have just noted (in the case of a 16-element grid as in Box 20.4, this will be a difference score of ± 3 or less). This second construct can be regarded as a dimension which is orthogonal to the first, and together they may form the axes for mapping the person's psychological space.

If we imagine the construct with the highest difference score to be 'kind–cruel' and the highest non-significant associated construct to be 'confident–unsure', then every other construct in the grid may be plotted with reference to these two axes. The coordinates for the map are provided by the difference scores relating to the matching of each construct with the two used to form the axes of the graph. In this way a pictorial representation of the individual's 'personal construct space' can be obtained, and inferences made from the spatial relationships between plotted constructs (see Box 20.6).

By rotating the original grid 90 degrees and carrying out the same matching procedure on the columns (figures), a similar map may be obtained for the people (figures) included in the grid. Grid matrices can be subjected to analyses of varying degrees of complexity. We have illustrated one of the simplest ways

Box 20.6
Grid matrix

	+8	Kind	
Confident			Unsure
-8		0	+8
	-8	Cruel	

of calculating relationships between constructs in Box 20.5. For the statistically minded researcher, a variety of programs exist for Grid Analysis (http://www.brint.com/PCT.htm). A fuller discussion of metric factor analysis is given in Fransella and Bannister (1977: 73–81) and Pope and Keen (1981: 77–91).

Non-metric methods of grid analysis make no assumptions about the linearity of relationships between the variables and the factors. Moreover, where the researcher is primarily interested in the relationships between elements, multidimensional scaling may prove a more useful approach to the data than principal components analysis.

The choice of one method rather than another must ultimately rest both upon what is statistically correct and what is psychologically desirable. The danger in the use of advanced computer programs, as Fransella and Bannister (1977) point out, is being caught up in the numbers game. Their plea is that grid users should have at least an intuitive grasp of the processes being so competently executed by their computers.

Strengths of repertory grid technique

It is in the application of interpretive perspectives in social research, where the investigator seeks to understand the meaning of events to those participating, that repertory grid technique offers exciting possibilities. It is particularly able to provide the researcher with an abundance and a richness of interpretable material. Repertory grid is, of course, especially suitable for the exploration of relationships between an individual's personal constructs as the studies of Foster (1992) and Neimeyer (1992), for example, show. Foster (1992) employed a Grids Review and Organizing Workbook (GROW), a structured exercise based on personal construct theory, to help a 16-year-old boy articulate constructs relevant to his career goals. Neimeyer's (1992) career counselling used a Vocational Reptest with a 19-year-old female student who compared and contrasted various vocational elements (occupations), laddering techniques being employed to determine construct

hierarchies. Repertory grid is equally adaptable to the problem of identifying changes in individuals that occur as a result of some educational experience. By way of example, Burke *et al.* (1992)[1] identified changes in the constructs of a cohort of technical teacher trainees during the course of their two-year studies leading to qualified status.

In modified formats (the 'dyad' and the 'double dyad') repertory grid has employed relationships between people as elements, rather than people themselves, and demonstrated the increased sensitivity of this type of grid in identifying problems of adjustment in such diverse fields as family counselling (Alexander and Neimeyer 1989) and sports psychology (Feixas *et al.* 1989).

Finally, repertory grid can be used in studying the changing nature of construing and the patterning of relationships between constructs in groups of children from relatively young ages as the work of Salmon (1969), Applebee (1976) and Epting (1988) have shown.

Difficulties in the use of repertory grid technique

Fransella and Bannister (1977) point to a number of difficulties in the development and use of grid technique, the most important of which is, perhaps, the widening gulf between technical advances in grid forms and analyses and the theoretical basis from which these are derived. There is, it seems, a rapidly expanding grid industry (see, for example http://www.brint.com/PCT.htm).

A second difficulty relates to the question of bipolarity in those forms of the grid in which customarily only one pole of the construct is used. Researchers may make unwarranted inferences about constructs' polar opposites. Yorke's (1978) illustration of the possibility of the researcher obtaining 'bent' constructs suggests the usefulness of the opposite method (Epting *et al.* 1971) in ensuring the bipolarity of elicited constructs.

A third caution is urged with respect to the elicitation and laddering of constructs. Laddering, note Fransella and Bannister (1977), is an art, not a science. Great care must be taken not to impose constructs. Above all, researchers must learn to listen to their subjects.

A number of practical problems commonly experienced in rating grids are identified by Yorke (1978):

- Variable perception of elements of low personal relevance.
- Varying the context in which the elements are perceived during the administration of the grid.
- Halo effect intruding into the ratings where the subject sees the grid matrix building up.
- Accidental reversal of the rating scale (mentally switching from 5 = high to 1 = high, perhaps because '5 points' and 'first' are both ways of describing high quality). This can happen both within and between constructs, and is particularly likely where a negative or implicitly negative property is ascribed to the pair during triadic elicitation.
- Failure to follow the rules of the rating procedure. For example, where the pair has had to be rated at the high end of a 5-point scale, triads have been found in a single grid rated as 5, 4, 4; 1, 1, 2; 1, 2, 4 which must call into question the constructs and their relationship with the elements.

More fundamental criticism of repertory grid, however, argues that it exhibits a nomothetic positivism that is discordant with the very theory on which it is based. Whatever the method of rating, ranking or dichotomous allocation of elements on constructs, is there not an implicit assumption, asks Yorke (1978), that the construct is stable across all of the elements being rated? Similar to scales of measurement in the physical sciences, elements are assigned to positions on a fixed scale of meaning as though the researcher were dealing with length or weight. But meaning, Yorke (1978) reminds us, is 'anchored in the shifting sands of semantics'. This he ably demonstrates by means of a hypothetical problem of rating four people on the construct 'generous–mean'. Yorke shows that it would require a finely wrought grid of enormous proportions to do justice to the nuances of meaning that could be elicited in respect of the chosen construct. The charge that the rating of elements on constructs and the subsequent statistical analyses retain a positivistic core in what purports to be a non-positivistic methodology is difficult to refute.

Finally, increasing sophistication in computer-based analyses of repertory grid forms leads inevitably to a burgeoning number of concepts by which to describe the complexity of what can be found within matrices. It would be ironic, would it not, Fransella and Bannister (1977) ask, if repertory grid technique were to become absorbed into the traditions of psychological testing and employed in terms of the assumptions which underpin such testing. From measures to traits is but a short step, they warn.

Some examples of the use of repertory grid in educational research

Three examples of the use of personal constructs in education have to do with course evaluation, albeit two less directly than the other. The first study employs the triadic sorting procedure that Kelly (1955) suggested in his original work; the second illustrates the use of sophisticated interactive software in the elicitation and analysis of personal constructs; and the third concerns the changing roles of primary headteachers. Kremer-Hayon's (1991) study sought to answer two questions: first, 'What are the personal constructs by which headteachers relate to their staff?' and second, 'To what extent can those constructs be made more "professional"?' The subjects of her research were thirty junior school headteachers participating in an in-service university programme about school organization and management, educational leadership and curriculum development. The broad aim of the course was to improve the professional functioning of its participants. Headteachers' personal constructs were elicited through the triadic sorting procedure in the following way:

1   Participants were provided with ten cards which they numbered 1 to 10. On each card

they wrote the name of a member of staff with whom they worked at school.

2   They were then required to arrange the cards in threes, according to arbitrarily selected numbers provided by the researcher.

3   Finally, they were asked to suggest one way in which two of the three named teachers in any one triad were similar and one way in which the third member was different.

During the course of the two-year in-service programme, the triadic sorting procedure was undertaken on three occasions: Phase 1 at the beginning of the first year, Phase 2 at the beginning of the second year, and Phase 3 two months later, after participants had engaged in a workshop aimed at enriching and broadening their perspectives as a result of analysing personal constructs elicited during Phases 1 and 2.

The analysis of the personal construct data generated categories derived directly from the headteachers' sortings. Categories were counted separately for each and for all headteachers, thus yielding personal and group profiles. This part of the analysis was undertaken by two judges working independently, who had previously attained 85 per cent agreement on equivalent data. In classifying categories as 'professional' Kremer-Hayon (1991) drew on a research literature which included the following attributes of a profession: 'a specific body of knowledge and expertise, teaching skill, theory and research, accountability, commitment, code of ethics, solidarity and autonomy'. Descriptors were further differentiated as 'cognitive' and 'affective'. By way of example, the first three attributes of professionalism listed above (specific body of knowledge, teaching skills and theory and research) were taken to connote cognitive aspects; the next four, affective. Thus, the data were classified into the following categories:

- professional features (cognitive and affective)
- general features (cognitive and affective)
- background data (professional and non-professional)
- miscellaneous.

Kremer-Hayon (1991) reports that, at the start of the in-service programme, the group of headteachers referred to their teachers by general and affective, rather than professional and cognitive descriptors, and that the overall group profile at Phase 1 appeared to be non-professional and affective. However, this changed at the start of the second year when the use of professional descriptors increased. By the end of the workshop (Phase 3), a substantial change towards a professional direction was noted.

Kremer-Hayon (1991) concludes that the growth in the number of descriptors pertaining to professional features bears some promise for professional staff development.

The research report of Fisher et al. (1991) arose out of an evaluation of a two-year diploma course in a college of further and higher education. Repertory Grid was chosen as a particularly suitable means of helping students chart their way through the course of study and reveal to them aspects of their personal and professional growth. At the same time, it was felt that Repertory Grid would provide tutors and course directors with important feedback about teaching, examining and general management of the course as a whole.

'Flexigrid', the interactive software used in the study, was chosen to overcome what Fisher et al. (1991) identify as the major problem of grid production and subsequent exploration of emerging issues – the factor of time. During the diploma course, five three-hour sessions were set aside for training and the elicitation of grids. Students were issued with a booklet containing exact instructions on using the computer. They were asked to identify six items they felt important in connection with their diploma course. These six elements, along with the constructs arising from the triads selected by the software, were entered into the computer. Students worked singly using the software and then discussed their individual findings in pairs, having already been trained how to interpret the 'maps' that appeared on the printouts. Individuals' and partners' interpretations were then entered in the students' booklets. Tape-recorders were made available for recording conversations between pairs. The analysis of the data in the research report derives from a series of computer printouts accompanied by detailed student commentaries, together with field notes made by the researchers and two sets of taped discussions.

From a scrutiny of all diploma student grids and commentaries, Fisher *et al.* (1991) drew the following conclusions about students' changing reactions to their studies as the course progressed:

- The overriding student concerns were to do with anxiety and stress connected with the completion of assignments; such concerns, moreover, linked directly to the role of assessors.

- Extrinsic factors took over from intrinsic ones, that is to say, finishing the course became more important than its intrinsic value.

- Tutorial support was seen to provide a cushion against excessive stress and fear of failure. There was some evidence that tutors had not been particularly successful at defusing problems to do with external gradings.

The researchers were satisfied with the potential of 'Flexigrid' as a tool for course evaluation. Particularly pleasing was the high level of internal validity shown by the congruence of results from the focused grids and the content analysis of students' commentaries.

In the third example Jones (1999) used repertory grids alongside interviews and participant observation to elicit headteachers' views of their roles and agenda in changing times. While the study found an increase in their management activities (one construct), it also found that not only did their changing role *not* lead to their deprofessionalization but also their core values were rooted in their values in, and views of, education (a second construct). The superordinate constructs for the primary headteachers were child-centred and management, in that order, i.e. the management systems were there to serve the child-centred values and vision. Constructs elicited included, for example: child-centred problem-solving, implementation policy, evaluation, involving other agencies, problem-solving and paperwork.

For further examples of repertory grid technique we refer the reader to: Harré and Rosser's (1975) account of ethogenically-oriented research into the rules governing disorderly behaviour among secondary school leavers, which parallels both the spirit and the approach of an extension of Repertory Grid described by Ravenette (1977); a study of student teachers' perceptions of the teaching practice situation (Osborne 1977) which uses 13×13 matrices to elicit elements (significant role incumbents) and provides an example of Smith's and Leach's (1972) use of hierarchical structures in repertory grids; Fournier's (1997) account of patterns of career development in graduates; Ewens *et al.*'s (2000) account of evaluating interprofessional education; and McLoughlin's (2002) study of students' conceptual frameworks in science.

Grid technique and audio/video lesson recording

Parsons *et al.* (1983) show how grid technique and audio/video recordings of teachers' work in classrooms can be used to make explicit the 'implicit models' that teachers have of how children learn.

Fourteen children were randomly selected and, on the basis of individual photographs, triadic comparisons were made to elicit constructs concerning one teacher's ideas about the similarities and differences in the manner in which these children learned. In addition, extensive observations of the teacher's classroom behaviour were undertaken under naturalistic conditions and verbatim recordings (audio and video) were made for future review and discussion between the teacher and the researchers at the end of each recording session. Parsons *et al.* (1983) stress that the whole study was carried out in a spirit of mutual inquiry, the researchers and the teacher joining together in using the analysis of the repertory grid as a source of counter or confirmatory accounts in the gradual identification of her implicit view of children's learning.

What very soon became evident in these ongoing complementary analyses was the clear distinction that Mrs C (the teacher) held for high and low achievers. The analysis of the children in class as shown in the videotapes revealed that not only did high and low achievers sit in separate groups but also the teacher's whole approach to these two groupings differed. With high achievers, the teacher often used a 'working with' approach, i.e. verbalizing what children had done, with their help. However, with low achievers, Mrs C would more often ask 'why' they had approached problems in the particular manner chosen, and then wait for an answer (Parsons *et al.* 1983).

Focused grids, non-verbal grids, exchange grids and sociogrids

A number of developments have been reported in the use of computer programs in repertory grid research. We briefly identify these as follows:

- Focusing a grid assists in the interpretation of raw grid data. Each element is compared with every other element and the ordering of elements in the grid is changed so that those most alike are clustered most closely together. A similar rearrangement is made in respect of each construct.
- Physical objects can be used as elements and grid elicitation is then carried out in non-verbal terms. Thomas (1978) claims that this approach enhances the exploration of sensory and perceptual experiences.
- Exchange grids are procedures developed to enhance the quality of conversational exchanges. Basically, one person's construing provides the format for an empty grid which is offered to another person for completion. The empty grid consists of the first person's verbal descriptions from which his ratings have been deleted. The second person is then invited to test his comprehending of the first person's point of view by filling in the grid as he believes the other has already completed it. Various computer programs ('Pairs', 'Cores' and 'Difference') are available to assist analysis

of the processes of negotiation elicited in exchange grids.

- In the 'Pairs' analysis, all constructs in one grid are compared with all constructs in the other grid and a measure of commonality in construing is determined. 'Pairs' analysis leads on to 'Sociogrids' in which the pattern of relationships between the grids of one group can be identified. In turn, 'Sociogrids' can provide a mode grid for the whole group or a number of mode grids identifying cliques. 'Socionets' which reveal the pattern of shared construing can also be derived.
- The software program FOCUS provides order cluster analysis, dendrograms, constructs and elements.
- Concept mapping using repertory grids, with computer assistance (e.g. CMap) is developing and its use reported by McLoughlin (2002).
- Principal components analysis, cluster analysis and dendritic analysis can be performed with the software Enquire within as well as more widely known software such as SPSS. WebGrid for data analysis can be found at: http://ksi.cpsc.ucalgary.ca/articles/WWW4WG/WG.html, http://repgrid.com/pcp/, http://tiger.cpsc.ucalgary.ca/ and http://repgrid.com/reports/. Further software is reported at: http://www.psyctc.org/grids/ and http://www.brint.com/PCT.htm#tools. OMNIGRID is reported at: http://www.psyctc.org/grids/omnigrid.htm.

With these brief examples, the reader will catch something of the flavour of what can be achieved using the various manifestations of repertory grid techniques in the field of educational research.[2] Further software analysis is reported in http://www.brint.com/PCT.htm. An introduction to the field can be found at http://www.enquirewithin.co.nz/theoryof.htm. The Personal Construct Psychology References Database can be found at http://www.psyc.uow.edu.au/pcp/citedb/. Further material is available from http://www.pcp-net.de/info/, and online papers are available at http://www.pcp-net.de/info/online.html. The European Personal Construct Association can be found at http://www.pcp-net.org/epca/. The e-journal Personal Construct Theory and Practice may be found at http://www.pcp-net.org/journal/.

21 | **Role-playing**

Introduction

Much current discussion of role-playing has occurred within the context of a protracted debate over the use of deception in experimental social psychology. Inevitably therefore, the following account of role-playing as a research tool involves some detailed comment on the 'deception' versus 'honesty' controversy. But role-playing has a much longer history of use in the social sciences than as a substitute for deceit. It has been employed for decades in assessing personality, in business training and in psychotherapy (Ginsburg 1978).[1] In this latter connection, role-playing was introduced to the United States as a therapeutic procedure by Jacob Moreno in the 1930s. His group therapy sessions were called 'psychodrama', and in various forms they spread to the group dynamics movement which was developing in the United States in the 1950s. Current interest in encounter sessions and sensitivity training can be traced back to the impact of Moreno's pioneering work in role-taking and role-enactment.

The focus of this chapter is on the use of role-playing as a technique of educational research, and on simulations. Role-playing is defined as participation in simulated social situations that are intended to throw light upon the role/rule contexts governing 'real life' social episodes. The present discussion aims to extend some of the ideas set out in Chapter 17 which dealt with account gathering and analysis. We begin by itemizing a number of role-playing methods that have been reported in the literature.

Various role-play methods have been identified by Hamilton (1976) and differentiated in terms of a passive–active distinction. Thus, an individual may role-play merely by reading a description of

a social episode and filling in a questionnaire about it; on the other hand, a person may role-play by being required to improvise a characterization and perform it in front of an audience. This passive–active continuum, Hamilton notes, glosses over three important analytical distinctions.

First, the individual may be asked simply to imagine a situation or actually to perform it. Hamilton (1976) terms this an 'imaginary-performed' situation. Second, in connection with performed role-play, he distinguishes between structured and unstructured activities, the difference depending upon whether the individual is restricted by the experimenter to present forms or lines. This Hamilton calls a 'scripted-improvised' distinction. Third, the participant's activities may be verbal responses, usually of the paper and pencil variety, or behavioural, involving something much more akin to acting. This distinction is termed 'verbal-behavioural'. Turning next to the content of role-play, Hamilton (1976) distinguishes between relatively involving or uninvolving contents, that is, where subjects are required to act or to imagine themselves in a situation or, alternatively, to react as they believe another person would in those circumstances, the basic issue here being what person the subject is supposed to portray. Furthermore, in connection with the role in which the person is placed, Hamilton differentiates between studies that assign the individual to the role of laboratory subject and those that place the person in any other role. Finally, the content of the role-play is seen to include the context of the acted or the imagined performance, that is, the elaborateness of the scenario, the involvement of other actors, and the presence or absence of an audience. The

Box 21.1
Dimensions of role-play methods

Set	Form imaginary versus performed	Content *Person:* self versus other
Action	scripted versus improvised	*Role:* subject versus another role
Dependent variables	verbal versus behavioural	*Context:* scenario other actors audience

Source: adapted from Hamilton 1976

various dimensions of role-play methods identified by Hamilton are set out in Box 21.1.

To illustrate the extremes of the range in the role-playing methods identified in Box 21.1 we have selected two studies, the first of which is passive, imaginary and verbal, typical of the way in which role-playing is often introduced to pupils; the second is active, performed and behavioural, involving an elaborate scenario and the participation of numerous other actors.

In a lesson designed to develop empathizing skills (Rogers and Atwood 1974), a number of magazine pictures were selected. The pictures included easily observed clues that served as the basis for inferring an emotion or a situation. Some pictures showed only the face of an individual, others depicted one or more persons in a particular social setting. The pictures exhibited a variety of emotions such as anger, fear, compassion, anxiety and joy. Students were asked to look carefully at a particular picture and then to respond to questions such as the following:

- How do you think the individual(s) is (are) feeling?
- Why do you think this is? (Encourage students to be specific about observations from which they infer emotions. Distinguish between observations and inferences.)
- Might the person(s) be feeling a different emotion than the one you inferred? Give an example.

- Have you ever felt this way? Why?
- What do you think might happen next to this person?
- If you inferred an unpleasant emotion, what possible action might the person(s) take in order to feel better?

The second example of a role-playing study is the well-known Stanford Prison experiment carried out by Haney *et al.* (1973), a brief overview of which is given in Box 21.2. Enthusiasts of role-playing as a research methodology cite experiments such as the Stanford Prison study to support their claim that where realism and spontaneity can be introduced into role-play, then such experimental conditions do, in fact, simulate both symbolically and phenomenologically the real-life analogues that they purport to represent. Advocates of role-play would concur with the conclusions of Haney and his associates that the simulated prison developed into a psychologically compelling prison environment and they, too, would infer that the dramatic differences in the behaviour of prisoners and guards arose out of their location in different positions within the institutional structure of the prison and the social psychological conditions that prevailed there, rather than from personality differences between the two groups of subjects (see Banuazizi and Movahedi 1975).

On the other hand, the passive, imaginary role-play required of subjects taking part in the lesson cited in the first example has been the focus of much of the criticism levelled at role-playing as a research technique. Ginsburg (1978) summarizes the argument against role-playing as a device for generating scientific knowledge:

- Role-playing is unreal with respect to the variables under study in that subjects report what they *would do*, and that is taken as though they did do it.
- The behaviour displayed is not spontaneous even in the more active forms of role-playing.
- The verbal reports in role-playing are very susceptible to artefactual influence such as social desirability.

Box 21.2
The Stanford Prison experiment

The study was conducted in the summer of 1971 in a mock prison constructed in the basement of the psychology building at Stanford University. The subjects were selected from a pool of 75 respondents to a newspaper advertisement asking for paid volunteers to participate in a psychological study of prison life. On a random basis half of the subjects were assigned to the role of guard and half to the role of prisoner. Prior to the experiment subjects were asked to sign a form, agreeing to play either the prisoner or the guard role for a maximum of two weeks. Those assigned to the prisoner role should expect to be under surveillance, to be harassed, but not to be physically abused. In return, subjects would be adequately fed, clothed and housed and would receive 15 dollars per day for the duration of the experiment.

The outcome of the study was quite dramatic. In less than two days after the initiation of the experiment, violence and rebellion broke out. The prisoners ripped off their clothing and their identification numbers and barricaded themselves inside the cells while shouting and cursing at the guards. The guards, in turn, began to harass, humiliate and intimidate the prisoners. They used sophisticated psychological techniques to break the solidarity among the inmates and to create a sense of distrust among them. In less than 36 hours one of the prisoners showed severe symptoms of emotional disturbance, uncontrollable crying and screaming and was released. On the third day, a rumour developed about a mass escape plot. The guards increased their harassment, intimidation and brutality towards the prisoners. On the fourth day, two prisoners showed symptoms of severe emotional disturbance and were released. On the fifth day, the prisoners showed symptoms of individual and group disintegration. They had become mostly passive and docile, suffering from an acute loss of contact with reality. The guards, on the other hand, had kept up their harassment, some behaving sadistically. Because of the unexpectedly intense reactions generated by the mock prison experience, the experimenters terminated the study at the end of the sixth day.

Source: adapted from Banuazizi and Movahedi 1975

- Role-playing procedures are not sensitive to complex interactions whereas deception designs are.

In general, Ginsburg (1978) concludes, critics of role-playing view science as involving the discovery of natural truths and they contend that role-playing simply cannot substitute for deception – a sad but unavoidable state of affairs.

Role-playing versus deception: the argument

As we shall shortly see, those who support role-playing as a legitimate scientific technique for systematic research into human social behaviour reject such criticisms by offering role-playing alternatives to deception studies of phenomena such as destructive obedience to authority and to conventional research in, for example, the area of attitude formation and change.

The objections to the use of deception in experimental research are articulated as follows:

- Lying, cheating and deceiving contradict the norms that we typically try to apply in our everyday social interactions. The use of deception in the study of interpersonal relations is equally reprehensible. In a word, deception is unethical.

- The use of deception is epistemologically unsound because it rests upon the acceptance of a less than adequate model of the subject as a person. Deception studies generally try to exclude the human capacities of the subject for choice and self-presentation. They tend therefore to focus upon 'incidental' social behaviour, that is, behaviours that are outside of the subject's field of choice, intention and self-presentation that typically constitute the main focus of social activity among human actors (see Forward et al. 1976).

- The use of deception is methodologically unsound. Deception research depends upon a continuing supply of subjects who are naive to the intentions of the researchers. But word soon gets round and potential subjects come to expect that they will be deceived. It is a fair guess that most subjects are suspicious and distrustful of psychological research despite the best intentions of deception researchers.

Finally, advocates of role-playing methods deplore the common practice of comparing the outcomes of role-playing replications against the standard of their deception study equivalents as a means of evaluating the relative validity of the two methods. The results of role-playing and deception, it is argued, are not directly comparable since role-playing introduces a far wider range of human behaviour into experiments (see Forward *et al.* 1976). If comparisons are to be made, then role-playing results should provide the yardstick against which deception study data are measured and not the other way round as is generally the case. We invite readers to follow this last piece of advice and to judge the well-known experiments of Milgram (1974) on destructive obedience to authority against their role-playing replications by Mixon (1972; 1974). A more sustained discussion of ethical problems involved in deception is given in Chapter 2.

Role-playing versus deception: the evidence

Milgram's obedience-to-authority experiments

In a series of studies from 1963 to 1974, Milgram carried out numerous variations on a basic obedience experiment which involved individuals acting, one at a time, as 'teachers' of another subject (who was, in reality, a confederate of the experimenter). 'Teachers' were required to administer electric shocks of increasing severity every time the learner failed to make a correct response to a verbal learning task. Over the years, Milgram involved over 1,000 subjects in the experiment – subjects, incidentally, who were drawn from all walks of life rather than from undergraduate psychology classes. Summarizing his findings, Milgram (1974) reported that typically some 67 per cent of his teachers delivered the maximum electric shock to the learner despite the fact that such a degree of severity was clearly labelled as highly dangerous to the physical well-being of the person on the receiving end. Milgram's (1974) explanation of

destructive obedience to authority is summarized by Brown and Herrnstein (1975).

Mixon's (1974) starting point was a disaffection for the deceit that played such an important part in generating emotional stress in Milgram's subjects, and a desire to explore alternative approaches to the study of destructive obedience to authority. Since Milgram's dependent variable was a rule-governed action, Mixon (1974) reasoned the rule-governed behaviour of Milgram's subjects could have been uniform or predictable. But it was not. Why, then, did some of Milgram's subjects obey and some defy the experimenter's instructions? The situation, Mixon (1974) notes, seemed perfectly clear to most commentators; the command to administer an electric shock appeared to be obviously immoral and all subjects should therefore have disobeyed the experimenter. If defiance was so obviously called for when looking at the experiment from the outside, why, asks Mixon, was it not obvious to those taking part on the inside? Mixon found a complete script of Milgram's experiment and proceeded to transform it into an active role-playing exercise.

Mixon (1974) wrote that previous interpretations of the Milgram data had rested on the assumption that obedient subjects helplessly performed what was clearly an immoral act. Although this situation seemed clear from the outside, yet to the actors it was not. In Mixon's role-playing version the actors could not understand why the experimenter behaved as if feedback from the 'victim' was unimportant, as such feedback was suggesting that something serious had happened and that the experiment had gone badly wrong, yet the experimenter was behaving as if nothing was wrong, thereby contradicting the clear evidence that suggested that the 'victim' was in serious trouble. When Mixon used the 'all-or-none' method he found that when it became perfectly clear that the experimenter believed the 'victim' was being seriously harmed, all the actors tried to defy the experimenter's commands. The 'all-or-none' analysis suggests that people will obey apparently inhumane commands in an experiment so long as there seem to be no good reasons to think that the experimental safeguards have broken down. Mixon also wrote that when the experimental situation is confusing, as was the case in the Milgram study, then some people will obey and some will defy experimental commands. We leave readers to compare Mixon's explanations with Milgram's account set out by Brown and Herrnstein (1975).

In summary, sophisticated role-playing methods such as those used by Mixon (1974) offer exciting possibilities to the educational researcher. They avoid the disadvantages of deception designs yet are able to incorporate many of the standard features of experiments such as constructing experimental conditions across factors of interest (in the Mixon studies for example, using scripts that vary the states of given role/rule contexts), randomly assigning actors to conditions as a way of randomizing out individual differences, using repeated-measures designs, and standardizing scripts and procedures to allow for replication of studies (Forward *et al.* 1976).

Despite what has just been said about the possibilities of incorporating experimental role-playing methodologies in exploratory rather than experimental settings, Harré and Secord (1972) distinguish between 'exploration' and 'experiment' as follows. Whereas the experiment is employed to test the authenticity of what is known, exploration serves quite a different purpose, as here the scientist, having no clear idea of what may occur, seeks to find out, i.e. the scientist knows where to go but not what he or she will find out or what to expect. The research does not confirm or refute a hypothesis.

Increasingly, exploratory (as opposed to experimental) research into human social behaviour is turning to role-playing methodologies. The reason is plain enough. Where the primary objective of such research is the identification and elucidation of the role/rule frameworks governing social interaction, informed rather than deceived subjects are essential if the necessary data on how they genuinely think and feel are to be made available to the researcher. Contrast the position of the fully participating, informed subject in such research with that of the deceived subject under the more usual experimental conditions.

It can be argued that many of the more pressing social problems that society faces today arise out of our current ignorance of the role/rule frameworks governing human interactions in diverse social settings. If this is the case, then role-playing techniques could offer the possibility of a greater insight into the natural episodes of human behaviour that they seek to elucidate than the burgeoning amount of experimental data already at hand. The danger may lie in too much being expected of role-playing as a key to such knowledge. Ginsburg (1978) offers a timely warning. Role-playing, he urges, should be seen as a complement to conventional experiments, survey research and field observations. That is, it is an important addition to our investigative armamentarium, not a replacement.

Role-playing in educational settings

Role-playing, gaming and computer simulation are three strands of development in simulation studies. The distinction between these three types of simulation – role-playing, games and computers – is by no means clear-cut; for example, simulation games often contain role-playing activities and may be designed with computer back-up services to expedite their procedures (see Taylor and Walford 1972).

In this section we focus particularly upon role-playing aspects of simulation, beginning with some brief observations on the purposes of role-playing in classroom settings and some practical suggestions directed towards the less experienced practitioners of role-playing methods. Later in the chapter we look at simulations.

The uses of role-playing

The uses of role-playing are classified by Van Ments (1978) as follows:

- *Developing sensitivity and awareness*: the definitions of positions such as mother, teacher, police officer and priest, for example, explicitly or implicitly incorporate various role characteristics which often lead to the stereotyping of position occupants. Role-playing provides a means of exploring such stereotypes and developing a deeper understanding of the point of view and feelings of someone who finds herself in a particular role.

- *Experiencing the pressures which create roles:* role-playing provides study material for group members on the ways in which roles are created in, for example, a committee. It enables subjects to explore the interactions of formal structure and individual personalities in role-taking.
- *Testing out for oneself possible modes of behaviour:* in effect, this is the rehearsal syndrome: the trying out in one's mind in advance of some new situation that one has to face. Role-playing can be used for a wide variety of situations where the subject, for one reason or another, needs to learn to cope with the rituals and conventions of social intercourse and to practise them so that they can be repeated under stress.
- *Simulating a situation for others (and possibly oneself) to learn from:* here, the role-player provides materials for others to use and work upon. In the simplest situation, there is just one role-player acting out a specific role. In more complex situations such as the Stanford Prison study discussed in Box 21.2, role-playing is used to provide an environment structured on the interactions of numerous role incumbents. Teachers wishing to use role-play in classroom settings might find the sequence from Van Ments (1983) useful. He suggests commencing with setting objectives and deciding how to integrate role-play into the teaching programme, then determining any external constraints on the situation, followed by listing critical factors in the problem to be explored. After this decisions are taken on the type and structure of the role-play, and then writing the briefs or the materials. Following this the session is run, with a subsequent debriefing and follow-up.

Setting objectives

The first observation made by Van Ments (1983) is that teachers must begin by asking themselves what exactly their intentions are in teaching by means of role-play. Is it, for example, to teach facts, or concepts, or skills, or awareness, or sensitivity? Depending on the specific nature of the teacher's objective, role-play can be fitted into the timetable in several ways. Van Ments (1983) identifies the following:

- as an introduction to the subject
- as a means of supplementing or following on from a point that is being explored
- as the focal point of a course or a unit of work
- as a break from the routine of the classroom or the workshop
- as a way of summarizing or integrating diverse subject matter
- as a way of reviewing or revising a topic
- as a means of assessing work.

Determining external constraints

Role-play can be extremely time-consuming. It is vital therefore that from the outset, teachers should be aware of the following factors that may inhibit or even preclude the running of a role-play (see Van Ments 1978):

- suitable room or space (size, layout, furniture, etc.)
- sufficient time for warm-up, running the actual role-play and debriefing
- availability of assistance to help run the session.

Critical factors

The teacher, Van Ments (1983) advises, must look at the critical issues involved in the problem area encompassed by the role-play and decide who has the power to influence those issues as well as who is affected by the decisions to be taken. By way of example, Box 21.3 identifies some of the principal protagonists in a role-play session to do with young people smoking.

Choosing or writing the role-play

The choice lies with teachers either to buy or to borrow a ready-made role-play or

Box 21.3

Critical factors in a role-play: smoking and young people

Roles involved:	Young people, parents, teachers, doctors, youth leaders, shopkeeper, cigarette manufacturer.
Critical issues:	Responsibility for health, cost of illness, freedom of action, taxation revenue, advertising, effects on others.
Key communication channels:	Advertisements, school contacts, family, friends.

Source: adapted from Van Ments 1983

to write their own. In practice, Van Ments (1983) observes, most role-plays are written for specific needs and with the intention of fitting into a particular course programme. Existing role-plays can, of course, be adapted by teachers to their own particular circumstances and needs. On balance it is probably better to write the role-play oneself in order to ensure that the background is familiar to the intended participants; they can then see its relevance to the specific problem that concern them.

Running the role-play

The counsel of perfection is always to pilot test the role-play material that one is going to use, preferably with a similar audience. In reality, pilot testing can be as time-consuming as the play itself and may therefore be totally impracticable given timetable pressures. But however difficult the circumstances, any form of piloting, says Van Ments (1983), is better than none at all, even if it is simply a matter of talking procedures through with one or two colleagues.

Once the materials are prepared, then the role-play follows its own sequence: introduction, warm-up, running and ending. One final word of caution. It is particularly important to time the ending of the role-play in such a way as to fit into the whole programme. One method of ensuring this is to write the mechanism for ending into the role-play itself. Thus: 'You must have reached agreement on all five points before 11.30 a.m. when you have to attend a meeting of the board of directors.'

Debriefing

Debriefing is more than simply checking that the right lesson has been learnt and feeding this information back to the teacher. Rather, Van Ments (1983) reminds us, it is a two-way process, during which the consequences of actions arising in the role-play can be analysed and conclusions drawn (as in the Milgram experiment). It is at this point in the role-play sequence when mistakes and misunderstandings can be rectified. Most important of all, it is from well-conducted debriefing sessions that the teacher can draw out the implications of what the pupils have been experiencing and can then plan the continuation of their learning about the topic at hand.

Follow-up

To conclude, Van Ments (1983) notes the importance of the follow-up session in the teacher's planning of the ways in which the role-play exercise will lead naturally into the next learning activity. Thus, when the role-play session has attempted to teach a skill or rehearse a novel situation, then it may be logical to repeat it until the requisite degree of competence has been reached. Conversely, if the purpose of the exercise has been to raise questions, then a follow-up session should be arranged to answer them. 'Whatever the objectives of using role-play, one must always consider the connection between it and the next learning activity' (Van Ments 1983). Above all else, avoid leaving the role-play activity in a vacuum.

Strengths and weaknesses of role-playing and other simulation exercises

Taylor and Walford (1972) identify two prominent themes in their discussion of some of the possible advantages and disadvantages in the use of classroom simulation exercises. They are, first, the claimed enhancement of pupil motivation, and second, the role of simulation in the provision of relevant learning materials. The motivational advantages of simulation are said to include:

- a heightened interest and excitement in learning
- a sustained level of freshness and novelty arising out of the dynamic nature of simulation tasks
- a transformation in the traditional pupil–teacher subordinate–superordinate relationship
- the fact that simulation is a universal behavioural mode.

As to the learning gains arising out of the use of simulation, Taylor and Walford (1972) identify:

- the learning that is afforded at diverse levels (cognitive, social and emotional)
- the decision-making experiences that participants acquire
- an increased role awareness
- the ability of simulation to provide a vehicle for free interdisciplinary communication
- the success with which the concrete approach afforded by simulation exercises bridges the gap between 'schoolwork' and 'the real world'.

What reservations are there in connection with simulation exercises? Taylor and Walford (1972) identify the following:

- Simulations, however interesting and attractive, are time-demanding activities and ought therefore to justify fully the restricted timetabling allotted to competing educational approaches.
- Many computer simulation exercises can be expensive.
- Simulation materials may pose problems of logistics, operation and general acceptance as

legitimate educational techniques particularly by parent associations.

Simulations catch some of the elements of the real world, but in a controlled, possibly safe environment, enabling the researcher to understand phenomena as well as to predict, and enabling a situation to be looked at holistically rather than as a simple composite of variables (the whole is greater than the sum of the parts). As Robson (2002: 363) suggests, they act as a half-way house between the unnatural world of the laboratory and the real, natural outside world.

Our discussion of the strengths and weaknesses of role-playing has focused upon its application in pupil groups. To illustrate Taylor and Walford's (1972) point that simulation is a universal behavioural mode, Robson and Collier's (1991) example of a role-play with students in further education is useful.

Role-playing in an educational setting: an example

Our example of role-play in an educational setting illustrates the fourth use of this approach that Van Ments (1983) identifies, namely, simulating a situation from which others may learn. As part of a study of secondary school pupils' perceptions of teacher racism, Naylor (1995) produced four five-minute video presentations of actual classroom events reconstructed for the purposes of the research. The films were scripted and role-played by twenty-one comprehensive school pupils, each video focusing on the behaviour of a white, female teacher towards pupils of visible ethnic minority groups. A gifted teacher of drama elicited performances from the pupils and faithfully interpreted their directions in her portrayal of their devised teachers' roles. The four parts she played consisted of a supply teacher of Geography, a teacher of French, a teacher of English and a Mathematics teacher.

In an opportunity sample drawn throughout England, Naylor (1995) showed the videos to over 1,000 adolescents differentiated by age, sex, ability and ethnicity. Pupils' written responses to the four videos were scored 0 to 5 on the Kohlberg-type scale set out in Box 21.4. The analysis of scripts from a stratified sample of some 480 pupils suggested that older, high-ability girls of visible ethnic minority group membership were most perceptive of teacher racism and younger, low-ability boys of indigenous white group membership, least perceptive. For further examples of role-play in an educational setting see Robson and Collier (1991) and Bolton and Heathcote (1999).

Evaluating role-playing and other simulation exercises

Because the use of simulation methods in classroom settings is growing, there is increasing need to evaluate claims concerning the advantages and effectiveness of these approaches against more traditional methods. Yet here lies a major problem. To date, as Megarry (1978) observes, a high proportion of evaluation effort has been directed towards the comparative experiment involving empirical comparisons between simulation-type exercises and more traditional teaching techniques in terms of specified learning pay-offs. However, there are weaknesses to this experimental method of evaluation (Megarry 1978) in that it misses the complex, multiple and only partly known inputs and outputs, the outputs may not be a consequence of the inputs, there are significant interaction effects which are important rather than being seen as contaminating 'noise' as in the experimental approach.

What alternatives are there to the traditional type of evaluative effort? Megarry (1978) lists the following promising approaches to simulation evaluation:

- using narrative reports
- using checklists gathered from students' recollections of outstanding positive and negative learning experiences
- encouraging players to relate ideas and concepts learned in games to other areas of their lives
- using the instructional interview, a form of tutorial carried out earlier with an individual learner or a small group in which materials

Box 21.4
Categorization of responses to four video extracts

Level (Score)	Description
0	No response or nothing which is intelligibly about the 'ways in which people treat one another' in the extract. Alternatively this level of response may be wrong in terms of fact and/or in interpretation.
1	No reference to racism (i.e. unfairness towards visible ethnic minority pupils) either by the teacher or by pupils, either implicitly or explicitly.
2	Either some reference to pupils' racism (see level 1 above) but not to the teacher's, or, reference to racism is left unspecified as to its perpetrator. Such reference is likely to be implied and may relate to one or more examples drawn from the extract without any generalization or synthesizing statement(s). The account is at a superficial level of analysis, understanding and explanation.
3	There is some reference to the teacher's racist behaviour and actions. Such reference is, however, implied rather than openly stated. There may also be implied condemnation of the teacher's racist behaviour or actions. There will not be any generalized statement(s) about the teacher's racism supported with examples drawn from the extract.
4	At this level the account will explicitly discuss and illustrate the teacher's racism but the analysis will show a superficial knowledge and understanding of the deeper issues.
5	At this level the account will explicitly discuss the teacher's racism as a generalization and this will be well illustrated with examples drawn from the extract. One or more of these examples may well be of the less obvious and more subtle types of racist behaviour or action portrayed in the extract.

Source: Naylor 1995

and methods are tested by an instructor who is versed not only in the use of the materials, but also in the ways in which pupils learn.

Notice how each of the above evaluative techniques is primarily concerned with the process rather than the product of simulation.

As was mentioned in Chapter 10, role-play (like simulation methods) can reduce several problems inherent in laboratory experiments while retaining some of their virtues. As in the laboratory experiment, the experimenter has complete manipulative control over every aspect of the situation. At the same time, the subjects' humanity is left intact in that they are given a realistic situation in which to act in whatever way they think appropriate. Further, the high involvement normally associated with participation in simulations shows that the self-consciousness usually associated with the laboratory experiment is more easily dissipated.

Part Five

Data analysis

This is an entirely new part in this edition, and comprises five chapters on data analysis, of which two are on qualitative data analysis, two are on quantitative data analysis, and one is on choosing the more suitable statistical tests. These chapters are accompanied by extensive materials and references to the companion web site, and we advise readers to go to these. The chapters on qualitative data analysis take readers from first principles to more complex issues of content analysis and grounded theory, making the point that texts – data – are multilayered and open to a variety of interpretations. We indicate in practical terms how researchers can analyse and present qualitative data, including an introduction to the principles that are the foundation to such approaches. In quantitative data we assume that researchers not only will have no experience of statistics but also may be frightened off by them! Hence we take readers by the hand from very first principles to more complex statistical processes. We take care to explain the foundations, principles and concepts underlying the statistical procedures, and deliberately avoid introducing formulae and numbers, except where they are helpful. To accompany the chapters on statistical treatments of numerical data we use SPSS analysis, and the web site includes an easy-to-use manual to introduce novice researchers to SPSS. For both the qualitative and quantitative data analysis we provide practical advice – including sample phrases and choice of words – on how to report results and findings.

22 Approaches to qualitative data analysis

Introduction

Qualitative data analysis involves organizing, accounting for and explaining the data; in short, making sense of data in terms of the participants' definitions of the situation, noting patterns, themes, categories and regularities. This chapter discusses several forms of qualitative data analysis. Chapter 23 focuses more specifically on content analysis and grounded theory. We deal here with different approaches to qualitative data analysis.

There is no one single or correct way to analyse and present qualitative data; how one does it should abide by the issue of *fitness for purpose*. Further, qualitative data analysis, as we shall see here, is often heavy on interpretation, and one has to note that there are frequently multiple interpretations to be made of qualitative data – that is their glory and their headache! In abiding by the principle of *fitness for purpose*, the researcher must be clear what he or she wants the data analysis to do as this will determine the kind of analysis that is undertaken. The researcher can set out, for example:

- to describe
- to portray
- to summarize
- to interpret
- to discover patterns
- to generate themes
- to understand individuals and idiographic features
- to understand groups and nomothetic features (e.g. frequencies, norms, patterns, 'laws')
- to raise issues
- to prove or demonstrate
- to explain and seek causality
- to explore

- to test
- to discover commonalities, differences and similarities
- to examine the application and operation of the same issues in different contexts.

The significance of deciding the purpose is that it will determine the kind of analysis performed on the data. This, in turn, will influence the way in which the analysis is written up. The data analysis will also be influenced by the kind of qualitative study that is being undertaken. For example, a biography and a case study may be most suitably written as descriptive narrative, often chronologically, with issues raised throughout. An ethnography may be written as narrative or stories, with issues raised, but not necessarily conforming to a chronology of events, and including description, analysis, interpretation and explanation of the key features of a group or culture. A grounded theory and content analysis will proceed through a systematic series of analyses, including coding and categorization, until theory emerges that explains the phenomena being studied or which can be used for predictive purposes.

The analysis will also be influenced by the number of data sets and people from whom data have been collected. Qualitative data often focus on smaller numbers of people than quantitative data, yet the data tend to be detailed and rich. Researchers will need to decide, for example, whether to present data individual by individual, and then, if desired, to amalgamate key issues emerging across the individuals, or whether to proceed by working within a largely predetermined analytical frame of issues that crosses the individuals concerned. Some qualitative studies (e.g. Ball 1990; 1994a; Bowe *et al.* 1992) deliberately focus on individuals and the responses of significant players in a particular scenario, often quoting verbatim responses in the final account; others are content to summarize issues without necessarily identifying exactly from whom the specific data were derived. Later on here we discuss methods to be used with respect to people and issues.

Some studies include a lot of verbatim conversations; others use fewer verbatim data. Some researchers feel that it is important to keep the flavour of the original data, so they report direct phrases and sentences, not only because they are often more illuminative and direct than the researchers' own words, but also because they feel that it is important to be faithful to the exact words used. Indeed, as reported in the example later, direct conversations can be immensely rich in data and detail. Ball (1990) and Bowe *et al.* (1992) use a lot of verbatim data, not least because those whom they interviewed were powerful people and justice needed to be done to the exact words that they used. By contrast Walford (2001: 92), commenting on the 'fetish of transcription', admits that he 'rarely fully transcribed more than a few interviews for any of [his] research studies', not least because of the time that it took for transcription (Walford suggests a ratio of five to one – five hours to transcribe one hour of interviews, though it can take much longer than this).

At a practical level, qualitative research rapidly amasses huge amounts of data, and early analysis reduces the problem of data overload by selecting out significant features for future focus. Miles and Huberman (1984) suggest that careful data display is an important element of data reduction and selection. 'Progressive focusing', according to Parlett and Hamilton (1976), starts with the researcher taking a wide angle lens to gather data, and then, by sifting, sorting, reviewing and reflecting on them, the salient features of the situation emerge. These are then used as the agenda for subsequent focusing. The process is akin to funnelling from the wide to the narrow.

At a theoretical level, a major feature of qualitative research is that analysis often begins early on in the data collection process so that theory generation can be undertaken (LeCompte and Preissle 1993: 238). Researchers should set out the main outlines of the phenomena that are under investigation. They should then assemble blocks or groups of data, putting them together to make a coherent whole (e.g. through writing summaries of what has been found). Then they should painstakingly take apart their field notes, matching, contrasting, aggregating, comparing and ordering notes made. The intention is to move from description to explanation and theory generation (LeCompte and Preissle 1993: 237–53).

Tabulating data

We outline several examples of data analysis and presentation in this chapter and the next. The first of these illustrates simple summary and clear, tabulated data presentation and commentary. It derives from a doctorate thesis.

Chinese children learning English: an example of analysing and presenting interview data

The interview data are presented question by question. In what follows, where the data for respondents in each age phase are similar they are grouped into a single set of responses by row; where there are dissimilar responses they are kept separate. The left-hand column in each table indicates the number of the respondent (1–12) and the level which the respondent taught (e.g. P1, F3 etc.), so, for example, '1–3: P 1' means the responses of respondents 1–3, who taught P1 classes; the right-hand column indicates the responses. In many cases it can be seen that respondents *all* gave similar responses in terms of the actual items mentioned and the coverage of items specified. A brief summary comment is provided after each table.

The data here derive from a doctorate thesis concerning the problems that school children experience in learning English in China. The data set reproduced is incomplete and has been selected for illustrative purposes only. Note that the data are not verbatim, but have already been summarized by the researcher, i.e. what is presented here is not the first stage of the data analysis, as the first stage would be transcription.

The coding is as follows:
P1–P6 = Primary forms (1–6), P1 = Year One, P2 = Year Two etc.
F1–F5 = Secondary forms (1–5), F1 = Form One (first year of secondary school), F2 = Form Two (second year of secondary school etc.)

The numbers preceding each letter in the left-hand column refer to the number ascribed to the teacher (Box 22.1). There were twelve teachers in all, six from primary and six from secondary schools.

English teaching and learning at school have not really achieved their intended purposes. Students are poor at understanding written or spoken English, speaking, reading, listening and writing; this limits their abilities, regardless of the number of years of learning English; low-level memorization model leads to superficial learning; teaching and learning are poor; students can enter university, even though their standard is poor, as there are many universities to take students; students do not require English to gain employment.

Comment: the primary English teachers had a wider range of views than the secondary teachers; there was greater unanimity between the primary teachers in comparison with the secondary teachers; all the Form Three secondary teachers were unanimous in their comments, and all the Form Five secondary teachers had different views.

Box 22.2 indicates that the strengths of English teaching were that students start to learn English very young, and schools had autonomy over the design of syllabuses. The weaknesses in English teaching were that insufficient emphasis was placed on understanding, students were too young to learn English, and syllabuses were unrealistic in their demands, being too rich, leading teachers to a 'spoon-feeding' mentality in their teaching. Also undue pressure was put on teachers and

Box 22.1

The effectiveness of English teaching

Q6: The effectiveness of English teaching

1-3: P1
- Students neither understood written or spoken English nor were able to speak or write very well.
- Although students started learning English at a very young age, their standard was still very low as they could not really understand or use English.

4-6: P6
- Students could not speak, read or write English well.
- Students had a low standard as they could not read, write or speak English.
- They used memorization to learn and thus their English knowledge was very superficial and confined to limited vocabulary.

7-9: F3
- On the whole, students' standard was low. English teaching and learning was not very successful.
- Even with a poor knowledge of English students still managed to get jobs.
- This was not an international city; English was not really that important even if students did not learn well.

10: F5   English teaching and learning were not very effective as students were not working hard and they resorted to memorization to learn English. However, students managed to get into universities.
11: F5   Students had learned at least some basic knowledge about English.
12: F5   It was effective to some extent as some students became English teachers themselves, having finished their university education.

Box 22.2

The strengths and weaknesses of English language teaching

Q7: Strengths and weaknesses of English language teaching

1: P1	Students started learning English at a very young age and they should be good at it. However, this could also be a disadvantage as students were too young to learn English and to understand what they were taught
2-6: P6	These respondents all commented that individual schools had great autonomy over syllabus design.
7-9: F3	Consequently, some syllabus contents were too rich to be covered within the limited time span. Therefore, it
10-12: F5	was hard to make adjustments, although students could not cope with the learning requirements. This put pressure on both teachers and students. Worse still, some schools made students learn other foreign languages apart from English, and that made the learning of English more difficult.

---

students because of the demands of the syllabus and English had to compete with other languages for curriculum space. Hence students did not learn well, despite years of learning English.

Comment: apart from one primary teacher, the other eleven teachers, drawn from both primary and secondary schools, were unanimous in the comments they gave.

It was clear that high class size (between 30 and 50 students, rising to 60) and tight syllabuses exerted a significant impact on teaching methods and restrictions of class activities, because of control issues (Box 22.3). The nature of this influence is to adopt largely didactic and grammar-translation methods, with little extended recourse to using or 'thinking in' English. Teaching utilized some group activity, but this was very limited. Teachers used Chinese to explain English.

Comment: all the teachers here were unanimous in their comments which fell mainly into two sets of points.

Students contributed significantly to their own success or failure in learning English (Box 22.4). They were shy, afraid of making mistakes and of losing face, and had little interest in learning at all, let alone English; they were overloaded with other subjects, a situation exacerbated by their poor time management; they held negative attitudes to the bookish nature of learning English and its unrelatedness to other curriculum subjects, had too many other distractions and had limited abilities in English; they had little incentive to learn fast as they could repeat courses, gave little priority to English, had poor foundations for learning English and had limited motivation or positive attitudes to learning English; they were given limited direction

Box 22.3

Teaching methods

Q9: Teaching methods

1-3: P1	• All respondents replied that teaching was mostly conducted on a didactic approach though they
4-6: P6	utilized visual aids and group activities to arouse students' interest, as they had a very tight syllabus to
7-9: F3	cover within the fixed number of periods. This method also gave them more control over the class,
10-12: F5	which was necessary as classes were usually big, between 30 and 50 and could rise to 60.
	• Whenever these teachers taught grammar, they relied heavily on the grammar-translation method. They used mostly Chinese (could be as much as 80 per cent) to explain grammar, as that would make it easier for students to understand the explanation.

Chapter 22

Box 22.4
Student-related factors

Q11: Student-related factors

1-3: P1
4-6: P6
- Students were shy and were afraid of losing face when they made mistakes in front of the class.
- Students basically had no interest in learning anything, especially a foreign language.
- Students had too many subjects to learn, and learning English was too bookish.
- There were too many other distractions such as surfing the Internet or going out with friends.

7: F3
- Students could not relate learning English to other things they learned at school, so they had no interest.
- Students' language learning ability was poor and they feared learning English.
- Students were allowed to repeat programmes, so they could become lazy and indifferent.

8: F3
- Students spent too much time surfing the Internet.
- Students put more time into science rather than language subjects.

9: F3
- Students' foundation was weak.

10-12: F5
- Students lacked enthusiasm and 'proper' learning attitudes.
- Students had poor time management.
- Students were afraid of losing face when they made mistakes in front of the class. They were shy as well.
- Students had no direction in their learning and they had no plan for their future. Therefore, they did not learn well, especially a foreign language.
- Students had many opportunities to enter universities, despite having a low standard of English.

---

in their learning and had limited incentive to learn English well, as universities required only a low standard of English.

Comment: there was a great variety of comments here. There were degrees of agreement: the teachers of the younger primary children agreed with each other; the teachers of the older primary children agreed with each other; and the teachers of the older secondary children agreed with each other. The teachers of the younger secondary children raised different points from each other. However, the four groups of teachers (younger primary, older primary, younger secondary and older secondary) raised different points from each other.

For an example of the layout of tabulated word-based data and supporting analysis see the accompanying web site (http://www.routledge.com/textbooks/9780415368780 – Chapter 22, file 22.1.doc).

Summary of the interview data

The issues that emerge from the interview data are striking in several ways. What characterizes the data is the widespread agreement of the respondents on the issues. For example:

- There was absolute unanimity in the responses to questions 9, 12.
- There was very considerable, though not absolute, unanimity on question 11.
- In addition to the unanimity already observed, there was additional unanimity among the primary teachers in respect of question 11.
- In addition to the considerable, though not absolute, unanimity already observed, there was much unanimity among the primary teachers concerning question 6.

Such a degree of unanimity gives considerable power to the results, even though, because of the sampling used, they cannot be said to be representative of the wider population. However, the sample of experienced teachers was deliberately selected to provide an informed overview of the key issues to be faced. It must be remembered that, though the unanimity is useful, the main purpose of the interview data was to identify key issues, regardless of unanimity, convergence or frequency of mention. That the respondents articulated similar issues, however, signals that these may be important elements.

Further, the issues themselves are seen to lie in a huge diversity of fields, such that there is no single or simplistic set of problems or solutions. Hence, to complement the considerable unanimity of voice is a similar consensus in identifying the scope of the problem, yet the range of the problems is vast. Both singly and together, the issues of English language teaching, learning and achievement in Macau are complex. The messages are clear in respect of Form Five students and their English teaching and learning. First, English performance is weak in all its aspects – reading, writing, speaking and listening – but it is particularly weak in speaking and writing. Second, local cultural factors exert an influence on learning English:

- Students do not wish to lose face in public (and the Chinese emphasis on gaining and maintaining face is powerful).
- Students are shy and afraid of making mistakes.
- The pressure of examination success is universal and severe.
- The local culture is not English; it is Chinese and, if anything else, is Portuguese rather than English, although this latter is very limited; there is little need for people to speak or use English at present;

In some quarters, knowledge of English culture is seen to be an important element in learning English; this was refuted by the teachers in this sample. The third main message is that English is seen instrumentally, but this message has to be qualified, as many students gain employment and university entrance even though their English is weak. The fact of English being an international language has limited effect on student motivation or achievement.

Finally, poor teaching and learning are significant contributors to poor performance, in several areas:

- There is great emphasis on drill, rote learning and memorization.
- There is a predominance of passive rather than active learning, with teaching as the delivery of facts rather than the promotion of learning and understanding.
- Traditional didactic methods are used.
- There is reliance on a very limited range of teaching and learning styles.
- The limited subject and pedagogical knowledge of English teachers are compounded by the lack of adequate initial and post-initial teacher education.
- Frequently the careful laying of foundations of English teaching and learning is absent.
- Students use so much Chinese during English lessons that they have little chance to think in English – they translate rather than think in English.

From the interview data it can be seen that the size of the problems and issues to be faced in English language teaching and learning is vast. In this example, tables are carefully laid out to draw together similar sets of responses. The tables enable the reader to see, at a glance, where similarities and differences lie between the two groups of respondents. Note also that after each table there is a summary of the main points to which the researcher wishes to draw the reader's attention, and that these comprise both substantive and overall comments (e.g. on the topic in hand and on the similarities and differences between the groups of respondents respectively). Finally, note that an overall summary of 'key messages' has been provided at the end of all the tables and their commentaries. This is a very abridged and selective example, and justice has not been done to the whole of the data that the original researcher used. Nevertheless the point is clearly illustrated here that summarizing and presenting data in tabular form can address the twin issues of qualitative research: data reduction through careful data display and commentary.

Five ways of organizing and presenting data analysis

We present five ways of organizing and presenting analysis as follows: the first two methods are by *people*, and the next two methods are by *issue*, and the final method is by *instrument*.

One can observe in the example of teaching English in Macau that the data have been organized and presented by respondents, in response to particular issues. Indeed, where the respondents said the same, they have been organized by groups of respondents in relation to a given issue. The groups of respondents were also organized by their membership of different strata in a stratified sample: teachers of younger primary children, older primary children, younger secondary children and older secondary children. This is only *one* way of organizing a qualitative data analysis – by *groups*. The advantage of this method is that it automatically groups the data and enables themes, patterns and similar to be seen at a glance. While this is a useful method for summarizing similar responses, the collective responses of an individual participant are dispersed across many categories and groups of people, and the integrity and coherence of the individual respondent risks being lost to a collective summary. Further, this method is often used in relation to a single-instrument approach, otherwise it becomes unwieldy (for example, trying to put together the data derived from qualitative questionnaires, interviews and observations could be very cumbersome in this approach). So, researchers may find it helpful to use this approach instrument by instrument.

A *second* way of organizing the data analysis is by *individuals*. Here the total responses of a single participant are presented, and then the analysis moves on to the next individual. This preserves the coherence and integrity of the individual's response and enables a whole picture of that person to be presented, which may be important for the researcher. However, this integrity exacts its price, in that, unless the researcher is interested only in individual responses, it often requires him or her then to put together the issues arising *across* the individuals (a second level of analysis) in order to look for themes, shared responses, patterns of response, agreement and disagreement, to compare individuals and issues that each of them has raised, i.e. to summarize the data.

While approaches that are concerned with people strive to be faithful to those involved in terms of the completeness of the picture of them *qua* people, unless case study approaches are deemed to be driving the research, they are usually accompanied by a second round of analysis, which is of the issues that arise from the people, and it is to the matter of issues that we turn now.

A *third* way of organizing data is to present all the data that are relevant to a particular *issue*. This is the method that was used in the example of Chinese students learning English. While it is economical in making comparisons across respondents (the issue of data reduction through careful data display, mentioned earlier), again the wholeness, coherence and integrity of each individual respondent risks being lost.

The derivation of the issue for which data are gathered needs to be clarified. For example, it could be that the issue has been decided *pre-ordinately*, in advance of the data collection. Then all the relevant data for that issue are simply collected together into that single basket – the issue in question. While this is an economical approach to handling, summarizing and presenting data, it raises three main concerns:

- The integrity and wholeness of each individual can be lost, such that comparisons across the whole picture from each individual is almost impossible.
- The data can become decontextualized. This may occur in two ways: first, in terms of their place in the emerging sequence and content of the interview or the questionnaire (e.g. some data may require an understanding of what preceded a particular comment or set of comments), and second, in terms of the overall picture of the relatedness of the issues, as this approach can fragment the data into relatively discrete chunks, thereby losing their interconnectedness.
- Having had its framework and areas of interest already decided pre-ordinately, the analysis

may be unresponsive to additional relevant factors that could emerge *responsively* in the data. It is akin to lowering a magnet onto data – the magnet picks up relevant data for the issue in question but it also leaves behind data not deemed relevant and these risk being lost. The researcher, therefore, has to trawl through the residual data to see if there are other important issues that have emerged that have not been caught in the pre-ordinate selection of categories and issues for attention.

The researcher, therefore, has to be mindful of the strengths and weaknesses not only of pre-ordinate categorization (and, by implication, include responsive categorization), but also the researcher must decide whether it is or is not important to consider the whole set of responses of an individual, i.e. to decide whether the data analysis is driven by people/respondents or by issues.

A *fourth* method of organizing the analysis is by *research question*. This is a very useful way of organizing data, as it draws together all the relevant data for the exact issue of concern to the researcher, and preserves the coherence of the material. It returns the reader to the driving concerns of the research, thereby 'closing the loop' on the research questions that typically were raised in the early part of an inquiry. In this approach all the relevant data from various data streams (interviews, observations, questionnaires etc.) are collated to provide a collective answer to a research question. There is usually a degree of systematization here, in that, for example, the numerical data for a particular research question will be presented, followed by the qualitative data, or vice versa. This enables patterns, relationships, comparisons and qualifications across data types to be explored conveniently and clearly.

A *fifth* method of organizing the data is by *instrument*. Typically this approach is often used in conjunction with another approach, e.g. by issue or by people. Here the results of each instrument are presented, e.g. all the interview data are presented and organized, and then all the data from questionnaires are presented, followed by all the documentary data and field notes, and so on. While this approach retains fidelity to the coherence of the instrument and enables the reader to see clearly which data derive from which instrument, one has to observe that the instrument is often only a means to an end, and that further analysis will be required to analyse the *content* of the responses – by issue and by people. Hence if it is important to know from which instrument the data are derived then this is a useful method; however, if that is not important then this could be adding an unnecessary level of analysis to the data. Further, connections between data could be lost if the data are presented instrument by instrument rather than across instruments.

In analysing qualitative data, a major tension may arise from using contrasting holistic and fragmentary/atomistic modes of analysis. The example of teaching English in Macau is clearly atomistic, breaking down the analysis into smaller sections and units. It could be argued that this violates the wholeness of the respondents' evidence, and there is some truth to this, though one has to ask whether this is a problem or not. Sectionalizing and fragmenting the analysis can make for easy reading. On the other hand, holistic approaches to qualitative data presentation will want to catch the wholeness of individuals and groups, and this may lead to a more narrative, almost case study or story style of reporting with issues emerging as they arise during the narrative! Neither approach is better than the other; researchers need to decide how to present data with respect to their aims and intended readership.

Systematic approaches to data analysis

Data analysis can be very systematic. Becker and Geer (1960) indicate how this might proceed:

- comparing different groups simultaneously and over time
- matching the responses given in interviews to observed behaviour
- analysing deviant and negative cases
- calculating frequencies of occurrences and responses

- assembling and providing sufficient data that keeps separate raw data from analysis.

In qualitative data the analysis here is almost inevitably interpretive, hence the data analysis is less a completely accurate representation (as in the numerical, positivist tradition) but more of a reflexive, reactive interaction between the researcher and the decontextualized data that are already interpretations of a social encounter. Indeed reflexivity is an important feature of qualitative data analysis, and we discuss this separately (Chapter 7). The issue here is that the researcher brings to the data his or her own preconceptions, interests, biases, preferences, biography, background and agenda. As Walford (2001: 98) writes: 'all research is researching yourself'. In practical terms it means that the researcher may be selective in his or her focus, or that the research may be influenced by the subjective features of the researcher. Robson (1993: 374–5) and Lincoln and Guba (1985: 354–5) suggest that these can include:

- data overload (humans may be unable to handle large amounts of data)
- first impressions (early data analysis may affect later data collection and analysis)
- availability of people (e.g. how representative these are and how to know if missing people and data might be important)
- information availability (easily accessible information may receive greater attention than hard-to-obtain data)
- positive instances (researchers may over-emphasize confirming data and underemphasize disconfirming data).
- internal consistency (the unusual, unexpected or novel may be under-treated).
- uneven reliability (the researcher may overlook the fact that some sources are more reliable or unreliable than others).
- missing data (that issues for which there is incomplete data may be overlooked or neglected)
- revision of hypotheses (researchers may over-react or under-react to new data)

- confidence in judgement (researchers may have greater confidence in their final judgements than is tenable)
- co-occurrence may be mistaken for association
- inconsistency (subsequent analyses of the same data may yield different results); a notable example of this is Bennett (1976) and Aitkin et al. (1981).

The issue here is that great caution and self-awareness must be exercised by the researcher in conducting qualitative data analysis, for the analysis and the findings may say more about the researcher than about the data. For example, it is the researcher who sets the codes and categories for analysis, be they pre-ordinate or responsive (decided in advance of or in response to the data analysis respectively). It is the researcher's agenda that drives the research and the researcher who chooses the methodology.

As the researcher analyses data, he or she will have ideas, insights, comments, reflections to make on data. These can be noted down in memos and, indeed, these can become data themselves in the process of reflexivity (though they should be kept separate from the primary data themselves). Glaser (1978) and Robson (1993: 387) argue that memos are not data in themselves but help the process of data analysis. This is debatable: if reflexivity is part of the data analysis process then memos may become legitimate secondary data in the process or journey of data analysis. Many computer packages for qualitative data analysis (discussed later) have a facility not only for the researcher to write a memo, but also to attach it to a particular piece of datum. There is no single nature or format of a memo; it can include subjective thoughts about the data, with ideas, theories, reflections, comments, opinions, personal responses, suggestions for future and new lines of research, reminders, observations, evaluations, critiques, judgements, conclusions, explanations, considerations, implications, speculations, predictions, hunches, theories, connections, relationships between codes and categories, insights and so on. Memos can be reflections on the past, present and the future, thereby beginning to examine the issue of causality. There is no required minimum or maximum length, though memos should be dated not only for ease of reference but also for a marking of the development of the researcher as well as of the research.

Memos are an important part of the self-conscious reflection on the data and have considerable potential to inform the data collection, analysis and theorizing processes. They should be written whenever they strike the researcher as important – during and after analysis. They can be written any time; indeed some researchers deliberately carry a pen and paper with them wherever they go, so that ideas that occur can be written down before they are forgotten.

The great tension in data analysis is between maintaining a sense of the holism of the data – the text – and the tendency for analysis to atomize and fragment the data – to separate them into constituent elements, thereby losing the synergy of the whole, and often the whole is greater than the sum of the parts. There are several stages in analysis, for example:

- generating natural units of meaning
- classifying, categorizing and ordering these units of meaning
- structuring narratives to describe the contents
- interpreting the data.

These are comparatively generalized stages. Miles and Huberman (1994) suggest twelve tactics for generating meaning from transcribed data:

- counting frequencies of occurrence (of ideas, themes, pieces of data, words)
- noting patterns and themes (Gestalts), which may stem from repeated themes and causes or explanations or constructs
- seeing plausibility: trying to make good sense of data, using informed intuition to reach a conclusion
- clustering: setting items into categories, types, behaviours and classifications
- making metaphors: using figurative and connotative language rather than literal and denotative language, bringing data to

life, thereby reducing data, making patterns, decentring the data, and connecting data with theory
- splitting variables to elaborate, differentiate and 'unpack' ideas, i.e. to move away from the drive towards integration and the blurring of data
- subsuming particulars into the general (akin to Glaser's (1978) notion of 'constant comparison': see Chapter 23 in this book) – a move towards clarifying key concepts
- factoring: bringing a large number of variables under a smaller number of (frequently) unobserved hypothetical variables
- identifying and noting relations between variables
- finding intervening variables: looking for other variables that appear to be 'getting in the way' of accounting for what one would expect to be strong relationships between variables
- building a logical chain of evidence: noting causality and making inferences
- making conceptual/theoretical coherence: moving from metaphors to constructs, to theories to explain the phenomena.

This progression, though perhaps positivist in its tone, is a useful way of moving from the specific to the general in data analysis. Running through the suggestions from Miles and Huberman (1994) is the importance that they attach to coding of data, partially as a way of reducing what is typically data overload from qualitative data. Miles and Huberman (1994) suggest that analysis through coding can be performed both within-site and cross-site, enabling causal chains, networks and matrices to be established, all of these addressing what they see as the major issue of reducing data overload through careful data display.

Content analysis involves reading and judgement; Brenner et al. (1985) set out several steps in undertaking a content analysis of open-ended data:

- *briefing*: understanding the problem and its context in detail
- *sampling*: of people, including the types of sample sought (see Chapter 4)

- *Associating:* with other work that has been done
- *Hypothesis development*
- *hypothesis testing*
- *Immersion:* in the data collected, to pick up all the clues
- *Categorizing:* in which the categories and their labels must reflect the purpose of the research, be exhaustive and be mutually exclusive
- *Incubation:* e.g. reflecting on data and developing interpretations and meanings
- *Synthesis:* involving a review of the rationale for coding and an identification of the emerging patterns and themes
- *Culling:* condensing, excising and even reinterpreting the data so that they can be written up intelligibly
- *Interpretation:* making meaning of the data
- *Writing:* including giving clear guidance on the incidence of occurrence; proving an indication of direction and intentionality of feelings; being aware of what is not said as well as what is said – silences; indicating salience (to the readers and respondents)
- *Rethinking.*

Content analysis is addressed more fully in Chapter 23. This process, Brenner *et al.* (1985: 144) suggest, requires researchers to address several factors:

- Understand the research brief thoroughly.
- Evaluate the relevance of the sample for the research project.
- Associate their own experiences with the problem, looking for clues from the past.
- Develop testable hypotheses as the basis for the content analysis (Brenner *et al.* 1985 name this the 'Concept Book').
- Test the hypotheses throughout the interviewing and analysis process.
- Stay immersed in the data throughout the study.
- Categorize the data in the Concept Book, creating labels and codes.
- Incubate the data before writing up.
- Synthesize the data in the Concept Book, looking for key concepts.

- Cull the data; being selective is important because it is impossible to report everything that happened.
- Interpret the data, identifying its meaning and implication.
- Write up the report.
- Rethink and rewrite: have the research objectives been met?

Hycner (1985) sets out procedures that can be followed when phenomenologically analysing interview data. We saw in Chapter 1 that the phenomenologist advocates the study of direct experience taken at face value and sees behaviour as determined by the phenomena of experience rather than by external, objective and physically described reality. Hycner (1985) points out that there is a reluctance on the part of phenomenologists to focus too much on specific steps in research methods for fear that they will become reified. The steps suggested by Hycner, however, offer a possible way of analysing data which allays such fears. As he himself explains, his guidelines 'have arisen out of a number of years of teaching phenomenological research classes to graduate psychology students and trying to be true to the phenomenon of interview data while also providing concrete guidelines' (Hycner 1985). In summary, the guidelines are as follows:

- *Transcription:* having the interview tape transcribed, noting not only the literal statements but also non-verbal and paralinguistic communication.
- *Bracketing and phenomenological reduction:* this means 'suspending (bracketing) as much as possible the researcher's meaning and interpretations and entering into the world of the unique individual who was interviewed' (Hycner 1985). The researcher thus sets out to understand what the interviewee is saying rather than what the researcher expects that person to say.
- *Listening to the interview for a sense of the whole:* this involves listening to the entire tape several times and reading the transcription a number of times in order to provide a context for the

emergence of specific units of meaning and themes later on.

- *Delineating units of general meaning:* this entails a thorough scrutiny of both verbal and non-verbal gestures to elicit the participant's meaning. 'It is a crystallization and condensation of what the participant has said, still using as much as possible the literal words of the participant' (Hycner 1985).
- *Delineating units of meaning relevant to the research question:* once the units of general meaning have been noted, they are then reduced to units of meaning relevant to the research question.
- *Training independent judges to verify the units of relevant meaning:* findings can be verified by using other researchers to carry out the above procedures. Hycner's own experience in working with graduate students well trained in this type of research is that there are rarely significant differences in the findings.
- *Eliminating redundancies:* at this stage, the researcher checks the lists of relevant meaning and eliminates those clearly redundant to others previously listed.
- *Clustering units of relevant meaning:* the researcher now tries to determine if any of the units of relevant meaning naturally cluster together; whether there seems to be some common theme or essence that unites several discrete units of relevant meaning.
- *Determining themes from clusters of meaning:* the researcher examines all the clusters of meaning to determine if there is one (or more) central theme(s) which expresses the essence of these clusters.
- *Writing a summary of each individual interview:* it is useful at this point, Hycner suggests, to go back to the interview transcription and write up a summary of the interview incorporating the themes that have been elicited from the data.
- *Return to the participant with the summary and themes, conducting a second interview:* this is a check to see whether the essence of the first interview has been accurately and fully captured.

- *Modifying themes and summary:* with the new data from the second interview, the researcher looks at all the data as a whole and modifies them or adds themes as necessary.
- *Identifying general and unique themes for all the interviews:* the researcher now looks for the themes common to most or all of the interviews as well as the individual variations. The first step is to note if there are themes common to all or most of the interviews. The second step is to note when there are themes that are unique to a single interview or a minority of the interviews.
- *Contextualization of themes:* at this point it is helpful to place these themes back within the overall contexts or horizons from which they emerged.
- *Composite summary:* Hycner (1985) considers it useful to write up a composite summary of all the interviews which would accurately capture the essence of the phenomenon being investigated. 'Such a composite summary describes the "world" in general, as experienced by the participants. At the end of such a summary the researcher might want to note significant individual differences' (Hycner 1985).

Methodological tools for analysing qualitative data

There are several procedural tools for analysing qualitative data. LeCompte and Preissle (1993: 253) see analytic induction, constant comparison, typological analysis and enumeration as valuable techniques for the qualitative researcher to use in analysing data and generating theory.

Analytic induction

Analytic induction is a term and process that was introduced by Znaniecki (1934) in deliberate opposition to statistical methods of data analysis. LeCompte and Preissle (1993: 254) suggest that the process is akin to the several steps set out above, in that data are scanned to generate categories of phenomena, relationships between these categories are sought and working typologies and summaries are written on the basis of the data examined. These are then refined by subsequent cases and analysis; negative and discrepant cases are deliberately sought to modify, enlarge or restrict the original explanation or theory. Denzin (1970b: 192) uses the term 'analytical induction' to describe the broad strategy of participant observation that is set out below:

- A rough definition of the phenomenon to be explained is formulated.
- A hypothetical explanation of that phenomenon is formulated.
- One case is studied in the light of the hypothesis, with the object of determining whether or not the hypothesis fits the facts in that case.
- If the hypothesis does not fit the facts, either the hypothesis is reformulated or the phenomenon to be explained is redefined, so that the case is excluded.
- Practical certainty may be attained after a small number of cases has been examined, but the discovery of negative cases disproves the explanation and requires a reformulation.
- This procedure of examining cases, redefining the phenomenon, and reformulating the hypothesis is continued until a universal relationship is established, each negative case calling for a redefinition of a reformulation.

A more deliberate seeking of disconfirming cases is advocated by Bogdan and Biklen (1992: 72) where they enumerate five main elements in analytic induction:

- In the early stages of the research a rough definition and explanation of the particular phenomenon is developed.
- This definition and explanation is examined in the light of the data that are being collected during the research.
- If the definition and/or explanation that have been generated need modification in the light of new data (e.g. if the data do not fit the explanation or definition) then this is undertaken.

- A deliberate attempt is made to find cases that may not fit into the explanation or definition.
- The process of redefinition and reformulation is repeated until the explanation is reached that embraces all the data, and until a generalized relationship has been established, which will also embrace the negative cases.

Constant comparison

In constant comparison the researcher compares newly acquired data with existing data and categories and theories that have been devised and which are emerging, in order to achieve a perfect fit between these and the data. Hence negative cases or data which challenge these existing categories or theories lead to their modification until they can fully accommodate all the data. We discuss this technique more fully in Chapter 23, as it is a major feature of qualitative techniques for data analysis.

Typological analysis

Typological analysis is essentially a classificatory process (LeCompte and Preissle 1993: 257) wherein data are put into groups, subsets or categories on the basis of some clear criterion (e.g. acts, behaviour, meanings, nature of participation, relationships, settings, activities). It is the process of *secondary coding* (Miles and Huberman 1984) where descriptive codes are then drawn together and put into subsets. Typologies are a set of phenomena that represent subtypes of a more general set or category (Lofland 1970). Lazarsfeld and Barton (1951) suggest that a typology can be developed in terms of an underlying dimension or key characteristic. In creating typologies Lofland (1970) insists that the researcher must deliberately assemble all the data on how a participant addresses a particular issue – what strategies are being employed; disaggregate and separate out the variations between the ranges of instances of strategies; classify these into sets and subsets; and present them in an ordered, named and numbered way for the reader.

Enumeration

The process of enumeration is one in which categories and the frequencies of codes, units of analysis, terms, words or ideas are counted. This enables incidence to be recorded, and, indeed statistical analysis of the frequencies to be undertaken (e.g. Monge and Contractor 2003). This is a method used in conventional forms of content analysis, and we address this topic in Chapter 23.

This chapter has suggested several approaches to analysing and presenting qualitative data. It should be read in conjunction with Chapter 23, as they complement each other.

There are many web sites that contain useful materials on qualitative data analysis, for example:

http://cwx.prenhall.com/bookbind/pubbooks/
creswell/chapter9/destinations1/deluxe-content.html
http://labweb.education.wisc.edu/cni916/
http://qualitative-research.net/fqs
http://sagepub.co.uk/journals.aspx?pid=105751
http://soc.surrey.ac.uk/sru/sru.htm
http://tandf.co.uk/journals/online/0951-8398.asp
http://ualberta.ca/~iiqm
http://www.auckland.ac.nz/msis/isworld
http://www.car.us.edu

http://www.esds.ac.uk/qualidata/support/
teaching.asp
http://www.nova.edu/ssss/QR/text.html
http://www.nova.edu/ssss/QR/web.html
http://www.nova.edu/ssss?QR/qualres.html
http://www.nova.edu/ssss?QR/qualres.index.html
http://www.qualitative-research.net/fqs/fqs-e/
rubriken-e.htm
http://www.qualitativeresearch.uga.edu/QualPage/
http://www.ringsurf.com/netring?ring=
QualitativeResearch;action=list
http://www.soc.surrey.ac.uk/caqdas
http://www.socresonline.org.uk/socresonline/1/1/
4.html
http://www.socresonline.org.uk/socresonline/2/2/
1.html
http://www.sosig.ac.uk/roads/subject-listing/
World-cat/qualmeth.html
http://www.textanalysis.info
http://www.ualberta.ca/%7Eiiqm/iiqmHomePages/
resources.html
http://www.umich.edu/~qualnet/resources.htm
http://onlineqda.hud.ac.uk

Many of these provide links to a host of other web sites providing guidance and resources for qualitative data analysis.

23 Content analysis and grounded theory

Introduction

This chapter addresses two main forms of qualitative data analysis: content analysis and grounded theory, and provides two worked examples. Many qualitative data analysts undertake forms of content analysis. One of the enduring problems of qualitative data analysis is the reduction of copious amounts of written data to manageable and comprehensible proportions. Data reduction is a key element of qualitative analysis, performed in a way that attempts to respect the *quality* of the qualitative data. One common procedure for achieving this is content analysis, a process by which the 'many words of texts are classified into much fewer categories' (Weber 1990: 15). The goal is to reduce the material in different ways (Flick 1998: 192). Categories are usually derived from theoretical constructs or areas of interest devised in advance of the analysis (pre-ordinate categorization) rather than developed from the material itself, though these may be modified, of course, by reference to the empirical data.

What is content analysis?

The term 'content analysis' is often used sloppily. In effect, it simply defines the process of summarizing and reporting written data – the main contents of data and their messages. More strictly speaking, it defines a strict and systematic set of procedures for the rigorous analysis, examination and verification of the contents of written data (Flick 1998: 192; Mayring 2004: 266). Krippendorp (2004: 18) defines it as 'a research technique for making replicable and valid inferences from texts (or other meaningful matter) to the contexts of their use'. Texts are defined as

any written communicative materials which are intended to be read, interpreted and understood by people other than the analysts (Krippendorp 2004: 30).

Originally deriving from analysis of mass media and public speeches, the use of content analysis has spread to examination of any form of communicative material, both structured and unstructured. It may be 'applied to substantive problems at the intersection of culture, social structure, and social interaction; used to generate dependent variables in experimental designs; and used to study groups as microcosms of society' (Weber 1990: 11). Content analysis can be undertaken with any written material, from documents to interview transcriptions, from media products to personal interviews. It is often used to analyse large quantities of text, facilitated by the systematic, rule-governed nature of content analysis, not least because this enables computer-assisted analysis to be undertaken.

Content analysis has several attractions. It is an unobtrusive technique (Krippendorp 2004: 40) in that one can observe without being observed (Robson 1993: 280). It focuses on language and linguistic features, meaning in context, is systematic and verifiable (e.g. in its use of codes and categories), as the rules for analysis are explicit, transparent and public (Mayring 2004: 267–9). Further, as the data are in a permanent form (texts), verification through reanalysis and replication is possible.

Many researchers see content analysis as an alternative to numerical analysis of qualitative data. But this is not so, although it is widely used as a device for extracting numerical data from word-based data. Indeed Anderson and Arsenault (1998: 101–2) suggest that content analysis can describe the *relative frequency* and importance of certain topics as well as to evaluate bias, prejudice or propaganda in print materials.

Weber (1990: 9) sees the purposes of content analysis as including the coding of open-ended questions in surveys, the revealing of the focus of individual, group, institutional and societal matters, and the description of patterns and trends in communicative content. The latter suggestion indicates the role of statistical techniques in content analysis; indeed Weber (1990: 10) suggests that the highest quality content-analytic studies use both quantitative and qualitative analysis of texts (texts defined as any form of written communication).

Content analysis takes texts and analyses, reduces and interrogates them into summary form through the use of both pre-existing categories and emergent themes in order to generate or test a theory. It uses systematic, replicable, observable and rule-governed forms of analysis in a theory-dependent system for the application of those categories.

Krippendorp (2004: 22–4) suggests that there are several features of texts that relate to a definition of content analysis, including the fact that texts have no objective reader-independent qualities; rather they have multiple meanings and can sustain multiple readings and interpretations. There is no one meaning waiting to be discovered or described in them. Indeed, the meanings in texts may be personal and are located in specific contexts, discourses, and purposes, and, hence, meanings have to be drawn in context. Content analysis, then, describes the manifest characteristics of communication (Krippendorp 2004: 46) (asking who is saying what to whom, and how), infers the antecedents of the communication (the reasons for, and purposes behind, the communication, and the context of communication: Mayring 2004: 267), and infers the consequences of the communication (its effects). Krippendorp (2004: 75–7) suggests that content analysis is at its most successful when it can break down 'linguistically constituted facts' into four classes: attributions, social relationships, public behaviours and institutional realities.

How does content analysis work?

Ezzy (2002: 83) suggests that content analysis starts with a sample of texts (the units), defines the units of analysis (e.g. words, sentences) and the categories to be used for analysis, reviews the texts in order to code them and place them into categories, and then counts and logs the occurrences of words, codes and categories. From here statistical analysis and quantitative methods are applied, leading to an interpretation of the results. Put simply, content analysis involves coding, categorizing (creating meaningful categories into which the units of analysis – words, phrases, sentences etc. – can be placed), comparing (categories and making links between them), and concluding – drawing theoretical conclusions from the text.

Anderson and Arsenault (1998: 102) indicate the quantitative nature of content analysis when they state that 'at its simplest level, content analysis involves counting concepts, words or occurrences in documents and reporting them in tabular form'. This succinct statement catches essential features of the process of content analysis:

- breaking down text into units of analysis
- undertaking statistical analysis of the units
- presenting the analysis in as economical a form as possible.

This masks some other important features of content analysis, including, for example, examination of the interconnectedness of units of analysis (categories), the emergent nature of themes and the testing, development and generation of theory. The whole process of content analysis can follow eleven steps.

Step 1: Define the research questions to be addressed by the content analysis

This will also include what one wants from the texts to be content-analysed. The research questions will be informed by, indeed may be derived from, the theory to be tested.

Step 2: Define the population from which units of text are to be sampled

The population here refers not only to people but also, and mainly, to text – the domains of the analysis. For example, is it to be newspapers, programmes, interview transcripts, textbooks, conversations, public domain documents, examination scripts, emails, online conversations and so on?

Step 3: Define the sample to be included

Here the rules for sampling people can apply equally well to documents. One has to decide whether to opt for a probability or non-probability sample of documents, a stratified sample (and, if so, the kind of strata to be used), random sampling, convenience sampling, domain sampling, cluster sampling, purposive, systematic, time sampling, snowball and so on (see Chapter 4). Robson (1993: 275–9) indicates the careful delineation of the sampling strategy here, for example, such-and-such a set of documents, such-and-such a time frame (e.g. of newspapers), such-and-such a number of television programmes or interviews. The key issues of sampling apply to the sampling of texts: representativeness, access, size of the sample and generalizability of the results.

Krippendorp (2004: 145) indicates that there may be 'nested recording units', where one unit is nested within another, for example, with regard to newspapers that have been sampled it may be thus:

> the issues of a newspaper sampled; the articles in an issue of a newspaper sampled; the paragraphs in an article in an issue of a newspaper sampled; the propositions constituting a paragraph in an article in an issue of a newspaper sampled.
>
> (Krippendorp 2004: 145)

This is the equivalent of stage sampling, discussed in Chapter 4.

Step 4: Define the context of the generation of the document

This will examine, for example: how the material was generated (Flick 1998: 193); who was involved; who was present; where the documents come from; how the material was recorded and/or edited; whether the person was willing to, able to, and did tell the truth; whether the data are accurately reported (Robson 1993: 273); whether the data are corroborated; the authenticity and credibility of the documents; the context of the generation of the document; the selection and evaluation of the evidence contained in the document.

Step 5: Define the units of analysis

This can be at very many levels, for example, a word, phrase, sentence, paragraph, whole text, people and themes. Robson (1993: 276) includes here, for newspaper analysis, the number of stories on a topic, column inches, size of headline, number of stories on a page, position of stories within a newspaper, the number and type of pictures. His suggestions indicate the careful thought that needs to go into the selection of the units of analysis. Different levels of analysis will raise different issues of reliability, and these are discussed later. It is assumed that the units of analysis will be classifiable into the same category text with the same or similar meaning in the context of the text itself (semantic validity) (Krippendorp 2004: 296), although this can be problematic (discussed later). The description of units of analysis will also include the units of measurement and enumeration.

The *coding unit* defines the smallest element of material that can be analysed, while the *contextual unit* defines the largest textual unit that may appear in a single category.

Krippendorp (2004: 99–101) distinguishes three kinds of units. *Sampling units* are those units that are included in, or excluded from, an analysis; they are units of selection. *Recording/coding units* are units that are contained within sampling units and are smaller than sampling units, thereby avoiding the complexity that characterises sampling units; they are units of description. *Context units* are 'units of textual matter that set limits on the information to be considered in the description of recording units'; they are units that 'delineate the scope of information that coders need to consult in characterising the recording units' (Krippendorp 2004: 101, 103).

Krippendorp (2004) continues by suggesting a further five kinds of sampling units: *physical* (e.g. time, place, size); *syntactical* (words, grammar, sentences, paragraphs, chapters, series etc.); *categorical* (members of a category have something in common); *propositional* (delineating particular constructions or propositions); and *thematic* (putting texts into themes and combinations of categories). The issue of categories signals the next step. The criterion here is that each unit of analysis (category – conceptual, actual, classification element, cluster, issue) should be as discrete as possible while retaining fidelity to the integrity of the whole, i.e. that each unit must be a fair rather than a distorted representation of the context and other data. The creation of units of analysis can be done by ascribing *codes* to the data (Miles and Huberman 1984). This is akin to the process of 'unitizing' (Lincoln and Guba 1985: 203).

Step 6: Decide the codes to be used in the analysis

Codes can be at different levels of specificity and generality when defining content and concepts. There may be some codes which subsume others, thereby creating a hierarchy of subsumption – subordination and superordination – in effect creating a tree diagram of codes. Some codes are very general; others are more specific. Codes are astringent, pulling together a wealth of material into some order and structure. They keep words as words; they maintain context specificity. Codes may be *descriptive* and might include (Bogdan and Biklen 1992: 167–72): situation codes; perspectives held by subjects; ways of thinking about people and objects; process codes; activity codes; event codes; strategy codes; relationship and social structure codes; methods codes. However, to be faithful to the data, the codes themselves derive from the data responsively rather than being created pre-ordinately. Hence the researcher will go through the data ascribing codes to each piece of datum. A code is a word or abbreviation

sufficiently close to that which it is describing for the researcher to see at a glance what it means (in this respect it is unlike a number). For example, the code 'trust' might refer to a person's trustworthiness; the code ' power' might refer to the status or power of the person in the group.

Miles and Huberman (1984) advise that codes should be kept as discrete as possible and that coding should start earlier rather than later as late coding enfeebles the analysis, although there is a risk that early coding might influence too strongly any later codes. It is possible, they suggest, for as many as ninety codes to be held in the working memory while going through data, although clearly, there is a process of iteration and reiteration whereby some codes that are used in the early stages of coding might be modified subsequently and vice versa, necessitating the researcher to go through a data set more than once to ensure consistency, refinement, modification and exhaustiveness of coding (some codes might become redundant, others might need to be broken down into finer codes). By coding up the data the researcher is able to detect frequencies (which codes are occurring most commonly) and patterns (which codes occur together).

Hammersley and Atkinson (1983: 177–8) propose that the first activity here is to read and reread the data to become thoroughly familiar with them, noting also any interesting patterns, any surprising, puzzling or unexpected features, any apparent inconsistencies or contradictions (e.g. between groups, within and between individuals and groups, between what people say and what they do).

Step 7: Construct the categories for analysis

Categories are the main groupings of constructs or key features of the text, showing links between units of analysis. For example, a text concerning teacher stress could have groupings such as 'causes of teacher stress', 'the nature of teacher stress', 'ways of coping with stress' and 'the effects of stress'. The researcher will have to decide whether to have mutually exclusive categories (preferable but difficult), how broad or narrow each category will be, the order or level of generality of a category (some categories may be very general and subsume other more specific categories, in which case analysis should only operate at the same level of each category rather than having the same analysis which combines and uses different levels of categories). Categories are inferred by the researcher, whereas specific words or units of analysis are less inferential; the more one moves towards inference, the more reliability may be compromised, and the more the researcher's agenda may impose itself on the data.

Categories will need to be exhaustive in order to address content validity; indeed Robson (1993: 277) argues that a content analysis 'is no better than its system of categories' and that these can include: subject matter; direction (how a matter is treated – positively or negatively); values; goals; method used to achieve goals; traits (characteristics used to describe people); actors (who is being discussed); authority (in whose name the statements are being made); location; conflict (sources and levels); and endings (how conflicts are resolved).

This stage (i.e. constructing the categories) is sometimes termed the creation of a 'domain analysis'. This involves grouping the units into domains, clusters, groups, patterns, themes and coherent sets to form domains. A domain is any symbolic category that includes other categories (Spradley 1979: 100). At this stage it might be useful for the researcher to recode the data into domain codes, or to review the codes used to see how they naturally fall into clusters, perhaps creating overarching codes for each cluster. Hammersley and Atkinson (1983) show how items can be assigned to more than one category and, indeed, see this as desirable as it maintains the richness of the data. This is akin to the process of 'categorization' (Lincoln and Guba 1985), putting 'unitized' data to provide descriptive and inferential information. Unitization is the process of putting data into meaning units for analysis, examining data, and identifying what those units are. A meaning unit is simply a piece of datum which the researcher

considers to be important; it may be as small as a word or phrase, or as large as a paragraph, groups of paragraphs, or, indeed, a whole text, provided that it has meaning in itself.

Spradley (1979) suggests that establishing domains can be achieved by four analytic tasks:

- selecting a sample of verbatim interview and field notes
- looking for the names of things
- identifying possible terms from the sample
- searching through additional notes for other items to include.

He identifies six steps to achieve these tasks:

- select a single semantic relationship
- prepare a domain analysis sheet
- select a sample of statements from respondents
- search for possible cover terms and include those that fit the semantic relationship identified
- formulate structural questions for each domain identified
- list all the hypothesized domains.

Domain analysis, then, strives to discover relationships between symbols (Spradley 1979: 157).

Like codes, categories can be at different levels of specificity and generality. Some categories are general and overarching; others are less so. Typically codes are much more specific than categories. This indicates the difference between *nodes* and *codes*. A code is a label for a piece of text; a node is a category into which different codes fall or are collected. A node can be a concept, idea, process, group of people, place or, indeed, any other grouping that the researcher wishes it to be; it is an organizing category. Whereas codes describe specific textual moments, nodes draw together codes into a categorical framework, making connections between coded segments and concepts. It is rather like saying that a text can be regarded as a book, with the chapters being the nodes and the paragraphs being the codes, or the content pages being the nodes and the index being the codes. Nodes can be related in several ways, for example: one concept can define another; they can be logically related; and they can be empirically related (found to accompany each other) (Krippendorp 2004: 296).

One has to be aware that the construction of codes and categories might steer the research and its findings, i.e. that the researcher may enter too far into the research process. For example, a researcher may have been examining the extra-curricular activities of a school and discovered that the benefits of these are to be found in non-cognitive and non-academic spheres rather than in academic spheres, but this may be fallacious. It could be that it was the codes and categories themselves rather than the data in the minds of the respondents that caused this separation of cognitive/academic spheres and issues from the non-cognitive/non-academic, and that if the researcher had specifically asked about or established codes and categories which established the connection between the academic and non-academic, then the researcher would have found more than he or she did. This is the danger of using codes and categories to predefine the data analysis.

Step 8: Conduct the coding and categorizing of the data

Once the codes and categories have been decided, the analysis can be undertaken. This concerns the actual ascription of codes and categories to the text. Coding has been defined by Kerlinger (1970) as the translation of question responses and respondent information to specific categories for the purpose of analysis. As we have seen, many questions are precoded, that is, each response can be immediately and directly converted into a score in an objective way. Rating scales and checklists are examples of precoded questions. Coding is the ascription of a category label to a piece of data; which is either decided in advance or in response to the data that have been collected.

Mayring (2004: 268–9) suggests that *summarizing content analysis* reduces the material to manageable proportions while maintaining fidelity to essential contents, and that *inductive category formation* proceeds through summarizing content analysis by inductively generating categories from the text material. This is in contrast to *explicit content analysis*, the opposite of summarizing content analysis, which seeks to add in further information in the search for intelligible text analysis and category location. The former reduces contextual detail, the latter retains it. *Structuring content analysis* filters out parts of the text in order to construct a cross-section of the material using specified pre-ordinate criteria.

It is important to decide whether to code simply for the existence or the incidence of the concept. This is important, as it would mean that, in the case of the former – existence – the frequency of a concept would be lost, and frequency may give an indication of the significance of a concept in the text. Further, the coding will need to decide whether it should code only the exact words or those with a similar meaning. The former will probably result in significant data loss, as words are not often repeated in comparison to the concepts that they signify; the latter may risk losing the nuanced sensitivity of particular words and phrases. Indeed some speechmakers may deliberately use ambiguous words or those with more than one meaning.

In coding a piece of transcription the researcher goes through the data systematically, typically line by line, and writes a descriptive code by the side of each piece of datum, for example:

Text	Code
The students will undertake problem-solving in science	PROB
I prefer to teach mixed ability classes	MIXABIL

One can see that the codes here are abbreviations, enabling the researcher to understand immediately the issue that they denote because they resemble that issue (rather than, for example, ascribing a number as a code for each piece of datum, where the number provides no clue as to what the datum or category concerns). Where they are not abbreviations, Miles and Huberman (1994) suggest that the coding label should bear sufficient resemblance to the original data so that the researcher can know, by looking at the code, what the original piece of datum concerned.

There are several computer packages that can help the coder here (e.g. ETHNOGRAPH, N-Vivo), though they require the original transcript to be entered onto the computer. One such, Code-A-Text, is particularly useful for analysing dialogues both quantitatively and qualitatively (the system also accepts sound and video input).

Having performed the first round of coding, the researcher is able to detect patterns, themes and begin to make generalizations (e.g. by counting the frequencies of codes). The researcher can also group codes into more general clusters, each with a code, i.e. begin the move towards factoring the data.

Miles and Huberman (1994) suggest that it is possible to keep as many as ninety codes in the working memory at any one time, though they make the point that data might be recoded on a second or third reading, as codes that were used early on might have to be refined in light of codes that are used later, either to make the codes more discriminating or to conflate codes that are unnecessarily specific. Codes, they argue, should enable the researcher to catch the complexity and comprehensiveness of the data.

Perhaps the biggest problem concerns the coding and scoring of open-ended questions. Two solutions are possible here. Even though a response is open-ended, an interviewer, for example, may precode the interview schedule so that while an interviewee is responding freely, the interviewer is assigning the content of the responses, or parts of it, to predetermined coding categories. Classifications of this kind may be developed during pilot studies.

Alternatively, data may be postcoded. Having recorded the interviewee's response, for example, either by summarizing it during or after the interview itself, or verbatim by tape-recorder, the researcher may subject it to content analysis and apply it to one of the available scoring procedures – scaling, scoring, rank scoring, response counting, etc.

Step 9: Conduct the data analysis

Once the data have been coded and categorized, the researcher can count the frequency of each code or word in the text, and the number of words in each category. This is the process of retrieval, which may be in multiple modes, for example words, codes, nodes and categories. Some words may be in more than one category, for example where one category is an overarching category and another is a subcategory. To ensure reliability, Weber (1990: 21–4) suggests that it is advisable at first to work on small samples of text rather than the whole text, to test out the coding and categorization, and make amendments where necessary. The complete texts should be analysed, as this preserves their semantic coherence.

Words and single codes on their own have limited power, and so it is important to move to associations between words and codes, i.e. to look at categories and relationships between categories. Establishing relationships and linkages between the domains ensures that the data, their richness and 'context-groundedness' are retained. Linkages can be found by identifying confirming cases, by seeking 'underlying associations' (LeCompte and Preissle 1993: 246) and connections between data subsets.

Weber (1990: 54) suggests that it is preferable to retrieve text based on categories rather than single words, as categories tend to retrieve more than single words, drawing on synonyms and conceptually close meanings. One can make category counts as well as word counts. Indeed, one can specify at what level the counting can be conducted, for example, words, phrases, codes, categories and themes.

The implication here is that the frequency of words, codes, nodes and categories provides an indication of their significance. This may or may not be true, since subsequent mentions of a word or category may be difficult in certain texts (e.g. speeches). Frequency does not equal importance, and not saying something (withholding comment) may be as important as saying something. Content analysis analyses only what is present rather than what is missing or unsaid (Anderson and Arsenault 1998: 104). Further, as Weber (1990) says:

> pronouns may replace nouns the further on one goes
> through a passage; continuing raising of the issue may

cause redundancy as it may be counter-productive repetition; constraints on text length may inhibit reference to the theme; some topics may require much more effort to raise than others.

(Weber 1990: 73)

The researcher can summarize the inferences from the text, look for patterns, regularities and relationships between segments of the text, and test hypotheses. The summarizing of categories and data is an explicit aim of statistical techniques, for these permit trends, frequencies, priorities and relationships to be calculated. At the stage of data analysis there are several approaches and methods that can be used. Krippendorp (2004: 48–53) suggests that these can include:

- *extrapolations:* trends, patterns and differences
- *standards:* evaluations and judgements
- *indices:* e.g. of relationships, frequencies of occurrence and co-occurrence, number of favourable and unfavourable items
- *linguistic re-presentations.*

Once frequencies have been calculated, statistical analysis can proceed, using, for example:

- *factor analysis:* to group the kinds of response
- *tabulation:* of frequencies and percentages
- *cross-tabulation:* presenting a matrix where the words or codes are the column headings and the nominal variables (e.g. the newspaper, the year, the gender) are the row headings
- *correlation:* to identify the strength and direction of association between words, between codes and between categories
- *graphical representation:* for example to report the incidence of particular words, concepts, categories over time or over texts
- *regression:* to determine the value of one variable/word/code/category in relationship to another – a form of association that gives exact values and the gradient or slope of the goodness of fit line of relationship – the regression line
- *multiple regression:* to calculate the weighting of independents on dependent variables
- *structural equation modelling and LISREL analysis:* to determine the multiple directions of causality and the weightings of different

associations in a pathway analysis of causal relations

- *dendrograms:* tree diagrams to show the relationship and connection between categories and codes, codes and nodes.

The calculation and presentation of statistics is discussed in Chapters 24–26. At this stage the argument here suggests that what starts as qualitative data – words – can be converted into numerical data for analysis.

If a less quantitative form of analysis is required then this does not preclude a qualitative version of the statistical procedures indicated here. For example, one can establish linkages and relationships between concepts and categories, examining their strength and direction (how strongly they are associated and whether the association is positive or negative respectively). Many computer packages will perform the qualitative equivalent of statistical procedures.

It is also useful to try to pursue the identification of core categories (see the later discussion of grounded theory). A core category is that which has the greatest explanatory potential and to which the other categories and subcategories seem to be repeatedly and closely related (Strauss 1987: 11). Robson (1993: 401) suggests that drawing conclusions from qualitative data can be undertaken by counting, patterning (noting recurrent themes or patterns), clustering (of people, issues, events etc. which have similar features), relating variables, building causal networks, and relating findings to theoretical frameworks.

While conducting qualitative data analysis using numerical approaches or paradigms may be criticized for being positivistic, one should note that one of the founders of grounded theory (Glaser 1996) is on record as saying that not only did grounded theory develop out of a desire to apply a quantitative paradigm to qualitative data, but also paradigmal purity was unacceptable in the real world of qualitative data analysis, in which *fitness for purpose* should be the guide. Further, one can note that Miles and Huberman (1984) strongly advocate the graphic display of data as an economical means of reducing qualitative data. Such graphics might serve both to indicate causal relationships as well as simply summarizing data.

Step 10: Summarizing

By this stage the investigator will be in a position to write a summary of the main features of the situation that have been researched so far. The summary will identify key factors, key issues, key concepts and key areas for subsequent investigation. It is a watershed stage during the data collection, as it pinpoints major themes, issues and problems that have arisen, so far, from the data (responsively) and suggests avenues for further investigation. The concepts used will be a combination of those derived from the data themselves and those inferred by the researcher (Hammersley and Atkinson 1983: 178).

At this point, the researcher will have gone through the preliminary stages of theory generation. Patton (1980) sets these out for qualitative data:

- finding a focus for the research and analysis
- organizing, processing, ordering and checking data
- writing a qualitative description or analysis
- inductively developing categories, typologies and labels
- analysing the categories to identify where further clarification and cross-clarification are needed
- expressing and typifying these categories through metaphors (see also Pitman and Maxwell 1992: 747)
- making inferences and speculations about relationships, causes and effects.

Bogdan and Biklen (1992: 154–63) identify several important factors that researchers need to address at this stage, including forcing oneself to take decisions that will focus and narrow the study and decide what kind of study it will be; developing analytical questions; using previous observational data to inform subsequent data collection; writing reflexive notes and memos about observations, ideas, what is being learned; trying out ideas

with subjects; analysing relevant literature while conducting the field research; generating concepts, metaphors and analogies and visual devices to clarify the research.

Step 11: Making speculative inferences

This is an important stage, for it moves the research from description to inference. It requires the researcher, on the basis of the evidence, to posit some explanations for the situation, some key elements and possibly even their causes. It is the process of hypothesis generation or the setting of working hypotheses that feeds into theory generation.

The stage of theory generation is linked to grounded theory, and we turn to this later in the chapter. Here we provide an example of content analysis that does not use statistical analysis but which nevertheless demonstrates the systematic approach to analysing data that is at the heart of content analysis.

A worked example of content analysis

In this example the researcher has already transcribed data concerning stress in the workplace from, let us say, a limited number of accounts and interviews with a few teachers, and these have already been summarized into key points. It is imagined that each account or interview has been written up onto a separate file (e.g. computer file), and now they are all being put together into a single data set for analysis. What we have are already-interpreted, rather than verbatim, data.

Stage 1: Extract the interpretive comments that have been written on the data

By the side of each, a code/category/descriptor word has been inserted (in capital letters) i.e. the summary data have already been collected together into 33 summary sentences.

- Stress is caused by deflated expectation, i.e. stress is caused by annoyance with other people not pulling their weight or not behaving as desired, or teachers letting themselves down. **CAUSE**

- Stress is caused by having to make greater demands on personal time to meet professional concerns. So, no personal time/space is a cause of stress. Stress is caused by having to compromise one's plans/desires. **CAUSE**

- Stress comes from having to manage several demands simultaneously, **CAUSE**, but the very fact that they are simultaneous means that they can't be managed at once, so stress is built into the problem of coping – it's an insoluble situation. **NATURE**

- Stress from one source brings additional stress which leads to loss of sleep – a sign that things are reaching a breaking point. **OUTCOME**

- Stress is a function of the importance attached to activities/issues by the person involved. **NATURE** Stress is caused when one's own integrity/values are not only challenged but also called into question. **CAUSE**

- Stress comes from 'frustration' – frustration leads to stress leads to frustration leads to stress etc. – a vicious circle. **NATURE**

- When the best laid plans go wrong this can be stressful. **CAUSE**

- The vicious circle of stress induces sleep irregularity which, in turn, induces stress. **NATURE**

- Reducing stress often works on symptoms rather than causes – may be the only thing possible, **CAUSE**, given that the stressors will not go away, but it allows the stress to fester. **CAUSE**

- The effects of stress are physical which, in turn, causes more stress – another vicious circle. **OUTCOMES**

- Stress comes from lowering enthusiasm/commitment/aspiration/expectation. **CAUSE**

- Pressure of work lowers aspiration which lowers stress. **CAUSE**

- Stress reduction is achieved through companionship. **HANDLING**

- Stress is caused by things out of one's control. **CAUSE**

- Stress comes through handling troublesome students. **CAUSE**

- Stress occurs because of a failure of management/leadership. **CAUSE**

- Stress comes through absence of fulfilment. **CAUSE**

- Stress rarely happens on its own, it is usually in combination – like a rolling snowball, it is cumulative. **NATURE**

- Stress is caused by worsening professional conditions that are out of the control of the participant. **CAUSE** Stress comes through loss of control and autonomy. **CAUSE**

- Stress through worsening professional conditions is exponential in its effects. **NATURE**

- Stress is caused when professional standards are felt to be compromised. **CAUSE**

- Stress occurs because matters are not resolved. **CAUSE**

- Stress comes through professional compromise which is out of an individual's control. **CAUSE**

- The rate of stress is a function of its size – a big bomb causes instant damage. **NATURE**

- Stress is caused by having no escape valve; it is bottled up and causes more stress, like a kettle with no escape valve, it will stress the metal and then blow up. **CAUSE**

- Stress comes through overload and frustration – a loss of control. Stress occurs when people cannot control the circumstances with which they have to work. **CAUSE**

- Stress occurs through overload. **CAUSE**

- Stress comes from seeing one's former work being undone by others' incompetence. **CAUSE**

- Stress occurs because nothing has been possible to reduce the level of stress. So, if the boil of stress is not lanced, it grows and grows. **CAUSE NATURE**

- Stress can be handled through relaxation and exercise. **HANDLING**

- Trying to relieve stress through self-damaging behaviour includes taking alcohol and smoking. **HANDLING NATURE**

- Stress is a function of the importance attached to activities by the participants involved. **NATURE**

- The closer the relationship to people who cause stress, the greater the stress. **NATURE**

The data have been coded very coarsely, in terms of three or four main categories. It may have been possible to have coded the data far more specifically, e.g. each specific cause has its code, indeed one school of thought would argue that it is important to generate the specific codes first. One can code for words (and, thereafter, the frequency of words) or meanings – it is sometimes dangerous to go for words rather than meanings, as people say the same things in different ways.

Stage 2: Sort data into key headings/areas

The codes that have been used fall into four main areas:

- causes of stress
- nature of stress
- outcomes of stress
- handling stress.

Stage 3: List the topics within each key area/heading and put frequencies in which items are mentioned

For each main area the relevant data are presented together, and a tally mark (/) is placed against the number of times that the issue has been mentioned by the teachers.

Causes of stress

- deflated expectation/aspiration /
- annoyance /
- others not pulling weight /
- others letting themselves down /
- professional demands, e.g. troublesome students /
- demands on personal time from professional tasks /
- difficulties of the job /
- loss of personal time and space /
- compromising oneself or one's professional standards and integrity ///
- plans go wrong /

- stress itself causes more stress /
- inability to reduce causes of stress /
- lowering enthusiasm/commitment/aspiration /
- pressure of work /
- things out of one's control //
- failure of management or leadership /
- absence of fulfilment /
- worsening professional conditions /
- loss of control and autonomy //
- inability to resolve situation /
- having no escape valve /
- overload at work /
- seeing one's work undone by others /

Nature of stress

- Stress is a function of the importance attached to activities issues by the participants. /
- Stress is inbuilt when too many simultaneous demands are made, i.e. it is insoluble. /
- It is cumulative (like a snowball) until it reaches a breaking point. /
- Stress is a vicious circle. //
- The effects of stress are exponential. /
- The rate of stress is a function of its size. /
- If stress has no escape valve then that causes more stress. //
- Handling stress can lead to self-damaging behaviour (smoking or alcohol). /
- Stress is a function of the importance attached to activities-issues by the participants. /
- The closer the relationship to people who cause stress, the greater the stress. /

Outcomes of stress

- loss of sleep or physical reaction //
- effects of stress themselves causing more stress /
- self-damaging behaviour /

Handling stress

- physical action or exercise /
- companionship /
- alcohol and smoking /

Stage 4: Go through the list generated in stage 3 and put the issues into groups (avoiding category overlap)

Here the grouped data are reanalysed and re-presented according to possible groupings of issues under the four main heading (causes, nature, outcomes and handling of stress).

Causes of stress

Personal factors

- deflated expectation or aspiration /
- annoyance /
- demands on personal time from professional tasks /
- loss of personal time and space /
- stress itself causes more stress /
- inability to reduce causes of stress /
- lowering enthusiasm, commitment or aspiration /
- things out of one's control //
- absence of fulfilment /
- loss of control and autonomy //
- inability to resolve situation /
- having no escape valve /

Interpersonal factors

- annoyance /
- others not pulling weight /
- others letting themselves down /
- compromising oneself or one's professional standards and integrity ///
- seeing one's work undone by others /

Management

- pressure of work /
- things out of one's control //
- failure of management or leadership /
- worsening professional conditions /
- seeing one's work undone by others /

Professional matters

- others not pulling weight /
- professional demands, e.g. troublesome students /

- demands on personal time from professional tasks /
- difficulties of the job /
- compromising oneself or one's professional standards and integrity ///
- plans go wrong /
- pressure of work /
- worsening professional conditions /
- loss of control and autonomy //
- overload at work /

Nature of stress

Objective

- It is a function of the importance attached to activities-issues by the participants. /
- Stress is inbuilt when too many simultaneous demands are made, i.e. it is insoluble. /
- It is cumulative (like a snowball) until it reaches a breaking point. /
- Stress is a vicious circle. //
- The effects of stress are exponential. /
- The rate of stress is a function of its size. /
- If stress has no escape valve then that causes more stress. //
- Handling stress can lead to self-damaging behaviour (smoking or alcohol). /

Subjective

- Stress is a function of the importance attached to activities-issues by the participants. /
- The closer the relationship to people who cause stress, the greater the stress. /

Outcomes of stress

Physiological

- loss of sleep /

Physical

- physical reactions //
- increased smoking /
- increased alcohol /

Psychological

- annoyance /

Handling stress

Physical

- physical action or exercise /

Social

- social solidarity, particularly with close people ///
- companionship /

Stage 5: Comment on the groups or results in stage 4 and review their messages

Once the previous stage has been completed, the researcher is then in a position to draw attention to general and specific points, for example:

- There is a huge number of causes of stress (give numbers).
- There are very few outlets for stress, so it is inevitable, perhaps, that stress will accumulate.
- Causes of stress are more rooted in personal factors than any others – management, professional etc. (give frequencies here).
- The demands of the job tend to cause less stress that other factors (e.g. management), i.e. people go into the job knowing what to expect, but the problem lies elsewhere, with management (give frequencies).
- Loss of control is a significant factor (give frequencies).
- Challenges to people and personal integrity/ self-esteem are very stressful (give frequencies).
- The nature of stress is complex, with several interacting components (give frequencies).
- Stress is omnipresent.
- Not dealing with stress compounds the problem; dealing with stress compounds the problem.
- The subjective aspects of the nature of stress are as important as its objective nature (give frequencies).
- The outcomes of stress tend to be personal rather than outside the person (e.g. systemic or system-disturbing) (give frequencies).
- The outcomes of stress are almost exclusively negative rather than positive (give frequencies).

- The outcomes of stress tend to be felt non-cognitively, e.g. emotionally and psychologically, rather than cognitively (give frequencies).
- There are few ways of handling stress (frequencies), i.e. opportunities for stress reduction are limited.

The stages of this analysed example embody several of the issues raised in the preceding discussion of content analysis, although the example here does not undertake word counts or statistical analysis, and, being fair to content analysis, this could – some would argue even 'should' – be a further kind of analysis. What has happened in this analysis raises several important issues:

- The researcher has looked *within* and *across* categories and groupings for patterns, themes, generalizations, as well as exceptions, unusual observations etc.
- The researcher has had to decide whether frequencies are important, or whether an issue is important even if it is mentioned only once or a few times.
- The researcher has looked for, and reported, disconfirming as well as confirming evidence for statements.
- The final stage of the analysis is that of theory generation, to account for what is being explained about stress. It might also be important, in further analysis, to try to find causal relationships here: what causes what and the directions of causality; it may also be useful to construct diagrams (with arrows) to show the directions, strength and positive/negative nature of stress.

Computer usage in content analysis

LeCompte and Preissle (1993) provide a summary of ways in which information technology can be utilized in supporting qualitative research (see also Tesch 1990). As can be seen from the list below, its uses are diverse. Data have to be processed, and as word data are laborious to process, and as several powerful packages for data analysis and processing exist, researchers will find it useful to make full use of computing facilities. These can be used to do the following (LeCompte and Preissle 1993: 280–1):

- store and check (e.g. proofread) data
- collate and segment data and to make numerous copies of data
- enable memoing to take place, together with details of the circumstances in which the memos were written
- conduct a search for words or phrases in the data and to retrieve text
- attach identification labels to units of text (e.g. questionnaire responses), so that subsequent sorting can be undertaken
- annotate and append text
- partition data into units that have been determined either by the researcher or in response to the natural language itself
- enable preliminary coding of data to be undertaken
- sort, resort, collate, classify and reclassify pieces of data to facilitate constant comparison and to refine schemas of classification
- code memos and bring them into the same schema of classification
- assemble, reassemble and recall data into categories
- undertake frequency counts (e.g. of words, phrases, codes)
- cross-check data to see if they can be coded into more than one category, enabling linkages between categories to be discovered
- establish the incidence of data that are contained in more than one category
- retrieve coded and noded data segments from subsets (e.g. by sex) in order to compare and contrast data
- search for pieces of data that appear in a certain (e.g. chronological) sequence
- establish linkages between coding categories
- display relationships of categories (e.g. hierarchical, temporal, relational, subsumptive, superordinate)
- quote data in the final report.

Kelle (1995) suggests that computers are particularly effective at coping with the often-encountered problem of data overload and retrieval in qualitative research. Computers, it is argued, enable the researcher to use codes, memos, hypertext systems, selective retrieval, co-occurring codes, and to perform quantitative counts of qualitative data types (see also Seidel and Kelle 1995). In turn, this enables linkages of elements to be undertaken, the building of networks and, ultimately, theory generation to be undertaken (Seidel and Kelle 1995). Indeed Lonkila (1995) indicates how computers can assist in the generation of grounded theory through coding, constant comparison, linkages, memoing, annotations and appending, use of diagrams, verification and, ultimately, theory building. In this process Kelle and Laurie (1995: 27) suggest that computer-aided methods can enhance validity (by the management of samples) and reliability (by retrieving all the data on a given topic, thereby ensuring trustworthiness of the data).

A major feature of computer use is in the coding and compilation of data (for example, Kelle 1995: 62–104). Lonkila (1995) identifies several kinds of codes. *Open coding* generates categories and defines their properties and dimensions. *Axial coding* works within one category, making connections between subgroups of that category and between one category and another. This might be in terms of the phenomena that are being studied, the causal conditions that lead to the phenomena, the context of the phenomena and their intervening conditions, and the actions and interactions of, and consequences for, the actors in situations. *Selective coding* identifies the core categories of text data, integrating them to form a theory. Seidel and Kelle (1995) suggest that codes can denote a text, passage or fact, and can be used to construct data networks.

There are several computer packages for qualitative data (see Kelle 1995), for example: AQUAD; ATLAS/ti; HyperQuad2; Hyper-RESEARCH; Hypersoft; Kwaliton; Martin; MAXqda; WINMAX; QSR.NUD.IST; Nvivo; QUALPRO; Textbase Alpha, ETHNOGRAPH, ATLAS.ti, Code-A-Text, Decision Explorer,

Diction. Some of these are reviewed by Prein *et al.* (1995: 190–209). These do not actually perform the analysis (in contrast to packages for quantitative data analysis) but facilitate and assist it. As Kelle (2004: 277) remarks, they do not analyse text so much as organize and structure text for subsequent analysis.

These programs have the attraction of coping with large quantities of text-based material rapidly and without any risk of human error in computation and retrieval, and releasing researchers from some mechanical tasks. With respect to words, phrases, codes, nodes and categories they can:

- search for and return text, codes, nodes and categories
- filter text
- return counts
- present the grouped data according to the selection criterion desired, both within and across texts
- perform the qualitative equivalent of statistical analyses, such as:
  - Boolean searches (intersections of text which have been coded by more than one code or node, using 'and', 'not' and 'or'; looking for overlaps and co-occurrences)
  - proximity searches (looking at clustering of data and related contextual data either side of a node or code)
  - restrictions, trees, cross-tabs (including and excluding documents for searching, looking for codes subsumed by a particular node, and looking for nodes which subsume others)
- construct dendrograms (tree structures) of related nodes and codes
- present data in sequences and locate the text in surrounding material in order to provide the necessary context
- select text on combined criteria (e.g. joint occurrences, collocations)
- enable analyses of similarities, differences and relationships between texts and passages of text
- annotate text and enable memos to be written about text.

Additionally, dictionaries and concordances of terms can be employed to facilitate coding, searching, retrieval and presentation.

Since the rules for coding and categories are public and rule-governed, computer analysis can be particularly useful for searching, retrieving and grouping text, both in terms of specific words and in terms of words with similar meanings. Single words and word counts can overlook the importance of context. Hence computer software packages have been developed that look at Key-Words-In-Context. Most software packages have advanced functions for memoing, i.e. writing commentaries to accompany text that are not part of the original text but which may or may not be marked as incorporated material into the textual analysis. Additionally many software packages include an annotation function, which lets the researcher annotate and append text, and the annotation is kept in the text but marked as an annotation.

Computers do not do away with 'the human touch', as humans are still needed to decide and generate the codes and categories, to verify and interpret the data. Similarly 'there are strict limits to algorithmic interpretations of texts' (Kelle 2004: 277), as texts contain more than that which can be examined mechanically. Further, Kelle (2004: 283) suggests that there may be problems where assumptions behind the software may not accord with those of the researchers or correspond to the researcher's purposes, and that the software does not enable the range and richness of analytic techniques that are associated with qualitative research. Kelle (2004) argues that software may be more closely aligned to the technique of grounded theory than to other techniques (e.g. hermeneutics, discourse analysis) (Coffey *et al.* 1996), that it may drive the analysis rather than vice versa (Fielding and Lee 1998), and that it has a preoccupation with coding categories (Seidel and Kelle 1995). One could also argue that software does not give the same added value that one finds in quantitative data analysis, in that the textual input is a highly laborious process and that it does not *perform* the analysis but only *supports* the researcher doing the analysis by organizing data and recording codes and nodes etc.

Reliability in content analysis

There are several issues to be addressed in considering the reliability of texts and their content analysis, indeed, in analysing qualitative data using a variety of means, for example:

- Witting and unwitting evidence (Robson 1993: 273): witting evidence is that which was intended to be imparted; unwitting evidence is that which can be inferred from the text, and which may not be intended by the imparter.
- The text may not have been written with the researcher in mind and may have been written for a very different purpose from that of the research (a common matter in documentary research); hence the researcher will need to know or be able to infer the intentions of the text.
- The documents may be limited, selective, partial, biased, non-neutral and incomplete because they were intended for a different purpose other than that of research (an issue of validity as well as of reliability).
- It may be difficult to infer the direction of causality in the documents – they may have been the cause or the consequence of a particular situation.
- Classification of text may be inconsistent (a problem sometimes mitigated by computer analysis), because of human error, coder variability (within and between coders), and ambiguity in the coding rules (Weber 1990: 17).
- Texts may not be corroborated or able to be corroborated.
- Words are inherently ambiguous and polyvalent (the problem of homographs): for example, what does the word 'school' mean: a building; a group of people; a particular movement of artists (e.g. the impressionist school); a department (a medical school); a noun; a verb (to drill, to induct, to educate, to train, to control, to attend an institution); a period of instructional time ('they stayed after school to play sports'); a modifier (e.g. a school day); a sphere of activity (e.g. 'the school of hard knocks'); a collection of people adhering to a particular set of principles (e.g. the utilitarian school); a style of life (e.g. 'a gentleman from the old school'); a group assembled for a particular purpose (e.g. a gambling school), and so on. This is a particular problem for computer programs which may analyse words devoid of their meaning.
- Coding and categorizing may lose the nuanced richness of specific words and their connotations.
- Category definitions and themes may be ambiguous, as they are inferential.
- Some words may be included in the same overall category but they may have more or less significance in that category (and a system of weighting the words may be unreliable).
- Words that are grouped together into a similar category may have different connotations and their usage may be more nuanced than the categories recognize.
- Categories may reflect the researcher's agenda and imposition of meaning more than the text may sustain or the producers of the text (e.g. interviewees) may have intended.
- Aggregation may compromise reliability. Whereas sentences, phrases and words and whole documents may have the highest reliability in analysis, paragraphs and larger but incomplete portions of text have lower reliability (Weber 1990: 39).
- A document may deliberately exclude something for mention, overstate an issue or understate an issue (Weber 1990: 73).

At a wider level, the limits of content analysis are suggested by Ezzy (2002: 84), who argues that, due to the pre-ordinate nature of coding and categorizing, content analysis is useful for testing or confirming a pre-existing theory rather than for building a new one, though this perhaps understates the ways in which content analysis can be used to generate new theory, not least through a grounded theory approach (discussed later). In many cases content analysts know in advance what they are looking for in text, and perhaps what the categories for analysis will be. Ezzy (2002: 85) suggests that this restricts the extent to which the analytical categories can be responsive to the data, thereby confining the data analysis to the agenda of the researcher rather than the 'other'. In this way it enables pre-existing theory to be tested. Indeed Mayring (2004: 269) argues that if the research question is very open or if the study is exploratory, then more open procedures than content analysis, e.g. grounded theory, may be preferable.

However, inductive approaches may be ruled out of the early stages of a content analysis, but this does not keep them out of the later stages, as themes and interpretations may emerge inductively from the data and the researcher, rather than only or necessarily from the categories or pre-existing theories themselves. Hence to suggest that content analysis denies induction or is confined to the testing of pre-existing theory (Ezzy 2002: 85) is uncharitable; it is to misrepresent the flexibility of content analysis. Indeed Flick (1998) suggests that pre-existing categories may need to be modified if they do not fit the data.

Grounded theory

Theory generation in qualitative data can be emergent, and grounded theory is an important method of theory generation. It is more inductive than content analysis, as the theories emerge from, rather than exist before, the data. Strauss and Corbin (1994: 273) remark: 'grounded theory is a general methodology for developing theory that is grounded in data systematically gathered and analysed'. For a summary sheet of grounded theory principles see the accompanying web site (http://www.routledge.com/textbooks/ 9780415368780 – Chapter 23, file 23.1 doc.). There are several features of this definition:

- Theory is *emergent* rather than predefined and tested.
- Theory emerges from the *data* rather than vice versa.
- Theory generation is a consequence of, and partner to, *systematic* data collection and analysis.
- Patterns and theories are implicit in data, waiting to be discovered.

Glaser (1996) suggests that 'grounded theory is the systematic generation of a theory from data'; it is an inductive process in which everything is integrated and in which data pattern themselves rather than having the researcher pattern them, as actions are integrated and interrelated with other actions. Glaser and Strauss's (1967) seminal work rejects simple linear causality and the decontextualization of data, and argues that the world which participants inhabit is multivalent, multivariate and connected. As Glaser (1996) says, 'the world doesn't occur in a vacuum' and the researcher has to take account of the interconnectedness of actions. In everyday life, actions are interconnected and people make connections naturally; it is part of everyday living, and hence grounded theory catches the naturalistic element of research and formulates it into a systematic methodology. In seeking to catch the complexity and interconnectedness of everyday actions grounded theory is faithful to how people act; it takes account of apparent inconsistencies, contradictions, discontinuities and relatedness in actions. As Glaser (1996) says, 'grounded theory is appealing because it tends to get at exactly what's going on.' Flick (1998: 41) writes that 'the aim is not to reduce complexity by breaking it down into variables but rather to increase complexity by including context'.

Grounded theory is a systematic theory, using systematized methods (discussed below) of theoretical sampling, coding constant comparison, the identification of a core variable, and saturation. Grounded theory is not averse to quantitative methods, it arose out of them (Glaser 1996) in terms of trying to bring to qualitative data some of the analytic methods applied in statistical techniques (e.g. multivariate analysis). In grounded theory the researcher discovers what is relevant; indeed Glaser and Strauss's (1967) work is entitled *The Discovery of Grounded Theory*.

However, where it parts company with much quantitative, positivist research is in its view of theory. In positivist research the theory pre-exists its testing and the researcher deduces from the data whether the theory is robust and can be confirmed. The data are 'forced' into a fit with the theory. Grounded theory, on the other hand, does not force data to fit with a predetermined theory (Glaser and Strauss 1967: 3); indeed the difference between inductive and deductive research is less clear than it appears to be at first sight. For example, before one can deduce, one has to generate theory and categories inductively.

Grounded theory starts with data, which are then analysed and reviewed to enable the theory to be generated from them; it is rooted in the data and little else. Here the theory derives from the data – it is grounded in the data and emerges from it. As Lincoln and Guba (1985: 205) argue, grounded theory must fit the situation that is being researched.

Glaser (1996) writes that 'forcing methodologies were too ascendant', not least in positivist research and that grounded theory had to reject forcing or constraining the nature of a research investigation by pre-existing theories. As grounded theory sets aside any preconceived ideas, letting the data themselves give rise to the theory, certain abilities are required of the researcher, for example:

- tolerance and openness to data and what is emerging
- tolerance of confusion and regression (feeling stupid when the theory does not become immediately obvious)
- resistance to premature formulation of theory
- ability to pay close attention to data
- willingness to engage in the process of theory generation rather than theory testing; it is an experiential methodology
- ability to work with emergent categories rather than preconceived or received categories.

As theory is not predetermined, the role of targeted pre-reading is not as strong as in other kinds of research (e.g. using literature reviews to generate issues for the research), indeed it may be dangerous as it may prematurely close off or determine what one sees in data; it may cause one to read data through given lenses rather than anew. As one does not know what one will find, one cannot be sure what one should read before undertaking grounded theory. One should read widely, both within and outside the field, rather than narrowly and in too focused a direction.

There are several elements of grounded theory that contribute to its systematic nature, and it is to these that we now turn.

Theoretical sampling

In theoretical sampling, data are collected on an ongoing, iterative basis, and the researcher keeps on adding to the sample until there is enough data to describe what is going on in the context or situation under study and until 'theoretical saturation' is reached (discussed below). As one cannot know in advance when this point will be reached, one cannot determine the sample size or representativeness until one is actually doing the research. In theoretical sampling, data collection continues until sufficient data have been gathered to create a theoretical explanation of what is happening and what constitutes its key features. It is not a question of representativeness, but, rather, a question of allowing the theory to emerge. Theoretical sampling, as Glaser and Strauss (1967) write, is

> the process of data collection for generating theory whereby the analyst jointly collects, codes, and analyses his [sic.] data and decides what data to collect next and where to find them, in order to develop his theory as it emerges. This process of data collection is *controlled* by the emerging theory.
> (Glaser and Strauss 1967: 45)

They write that 'the basic criterion governing the selection of comparison groups for discovering theory is their *theoretical relevance* for furthering the development of emerging categories' (Glaser and Strauss 1967: 49) rather than, for example, conventional sampling strategies.

Coding

Coding is

> the process of disassembling and reassembling the data. Data are disassembled when they are broken apart into lines, paragraphs or sections. These

fragments are then rearranged, through coding, to produce a new understanding that explores similarities, differences, across a number of different cases. The early part of coding should be confusing, with a mass of apparently unrelated material. However, as coding progresses and themes emerge, the analysis becomes more organized and structured.

(Ezzy 2002: 94)

In grounded theory there are three types of coding: *open*, *axial* and *selective* coding, the intention of which is to deconstruct the data into manageable chunks in order to facilitate an understanding of the phenomenon in question. *Open coding* involves exploring the data and identifying units of analysis to code for meanings, feelings, actions, events and so on. The researcher codes up the data, creating new codes and categories and subcategories where necessary, and integrating codes where relevant until the coding is complete. *Axial coding* seeks to make links between categories and codes, 'to integrate codes around the axes of central categories' (Ezzy 2002: 91); the essence of axial coding is the interconnectedness of categories (Cresswell 1998: 57). Hence codes are explored, their interrelationships are examined, and codes and categories are compared to existing theory. *Selective coding* involves identifying a core code; the relationship between that core code and other codes is made clear (Ezzy 2002: 93), and the coding scheme is compared with pre-existing theory. Cresswell (1998: 57) writes that 'in selective coding, the researcher identifies a "story line" and writes a story that integrates the categories in the axial coding model'.

As coding proceeds the researcher develops concepts and makes connections between them. Flick *et al.* (2004: 19) argue that 'repeated coding of data leads to denser concept-based relationships and hence to a theory', i.e. that the richness of the data is included in the theoretical formulation.

Constant comparison

The application of open, axial and selective coding adopts the method of constant comparison. In constant comparison the researcher compares the new data with existing data and categories, so that the categories achieve a perfect fit with the data. If there is a poor fit between data and categories, or indeed between theory and data, then the categories and theories have to be modified until all the data are accounted for. New and emergent categories are developed in order to be able to incorporate and accommodate data in a good fit, with no discrepant cases. Glaser and Strauss (1967: 102) write that 'the purpose of the constant comparative method of joint coding and analysis is to generate theory . . . *by using explicit coding and analytic procedures*'. That theory is not intended to 'ascertain universality or the proof of suggested causes or other properties. Since no proof is involved, the constant comparison method . . . requires only saturation of data – not consideration of *all* available data'.

In constant comparison, then, discrepant, negative and disconfirming cases are important in assisting the categories and emergent (grounded) theory to fit all the data. Constant comparison is the process 'by which the properties and categories across the data are compared continuously until no more variation occurs' (Glaser 1996), i.e. saturation is reached. In constant comparison data are compared across a range of situations, times, groups of people, and through a range of methods. The process resonates with the methodological notion of triangulation. Glaser and Strauss (1967: 105–13) suggest that the constant comparison method involves four stages: comparing incidents and data that are applicable to each category; integrating these categories and their properties; bounding the theory; setting out the theory. The first stage here involves coding of incidents and comparing them with previous incidents in the same and different groups and with other data that are in the same category. The second stage involves memoing and further coding. Here 'the constant comparative units change from comparison of incident with incident to comparison of incident with properties of the category that resulted from initial comparisons of incidents' (Glaser and Strauss 1967: 108). The third stage – of delimitation – occurs at the levels of the theory and the categories and in which the major modifications reduce as underlying uniformities and properties are discovered and in which theoretical saturation takes place. The final stage – of writing theory – occurs when the researcher has gathered and generated coded data, memos, and a theory, and this is then written in full.

By going through the previous sections of data, particularly the search for confirming, negative and discrepant cases, the researcher is able to keep a 'running total' of these cases for a particular theory. The researcher also generates alternative theories for the phenomena under investigation and performs the same count of confirming, negative and discrepant cases. Lincoln and Guba (1985: 253) argue that the theory with the greatest incidence of confirming cases and the lowest incidence of negative and discrepant cases is the most robust.

Constant comparison, LeCompte and Preissle (1993: 256) suggest, combines the elements of inductive category coding (discussed above) with simultaneously comparing these with the other events and social incidents that have been observed and coded over time and location. This enables social phenomena to be compared across categories, where necessary giving rise to new dimensions, codes and categories. Glaser (1978) indicates that constant comparison can proceed from the moment of starting to collect data, to seeking key issues and categories, to discovering recurrent events or activities in the data that become categories of focus, to expanding the range of categories. This process can continue during the writing-up process, which should be ongoing, so that a model or explanation of the phenomena can emerge that accounts for fundamental social processes and relationships.

The core variables and saturation

Through the use of constant comparison a core variable is identified: that variable which accounts for most of the data and to which as much as possible is related; that variable around which most data are focused. As Flick

et al. (2004: 19) suggest: 'the successive integration of concepts leads to one or more key categories and thereby to the core of the emerging theory'.

Saturation is reached when no new insights, codes or categories are produced even when new data are added, and when all of the data are accounted for in the core categories and subcategories (Glaser and Strauss 1967: 61). As Ezzy (2002: 93) remarks: 'saturation is achieved when the coding that has already been completed adequately supports and fills out the emerging theory'. Of course one can never know for certain that the categories are saturated, as there are limits to induction, i.e. fresh data may come along that refute the existing theory. The partner of saturation is theoretical completeness, when the theory is able to explain the data fully and satisfactorily.

Developing grounded theory

As a consequence of theoretical sampling, coding, constant comparison, the identification of the core variable, and the saturation of data, categories and codes, the grounded theory (of whatever is being theorized) emerges from the data in an unforced manner, accounting for all of the data. How adequate the derived theory is can be evaluated against several criteria. Glaser and Strauss (1967: 237) suggest four main criteria:

- The closeness of the *fit* between the theory and the data.
- How readily *understandable* the theory is by the lay persons working in the field, i.e. that it makes sense to them.
- The ability of the theory to be *general* to a 'multitude of diverse daily situations within the substantive area, not just to a specific type of situation'.
- The theory must allow 'partial *control* over the structure and process of daily situations as they change through time', i.e. it must 'enable the person who uses it to have enough control in everyday situations to make its application worth trying' (Glaser and Strauss 1967: 245).

Strauss and Corbin (1994: 253–6) suggest several criteria for evaluating the theory:

- How adequately and powerfully the theory accounts for the main concerns of the data.
- The relevance and utility of the theory for the participants should be considered.
- The closeness of the fit of the theory to the data and phenomenon being studied, and under what conditions the theory holds true, should be examined.
- What is the fit of the axial coding to the categories and codes?
- Is the theory able to embrace negative and discrepant cases?
- What is the fit of the theory to literature?
- How was the original sample selected? On what basis?
- What major categories emerged?
- What were some of the events, incidents, actions and so on (as indicators) that pointed to some of the major categories?
- On the basis of what categories did theoretical sampling proceed? Was it representative of the categories?
- What were some of the hypotheses pertaining to conceptual relations (that is, among categories), and on what ground were they formulated and tested?
- Were there instances when hypotheses did not hold up against what was actually seen? How were these discrepancies accounted for? How did they affect the hypotheses?
- How and why was the core category selected (sudden, gradual, difficult, easy)? On what grounds?
- Were concepts generated and systematically related?
- Were there many conceptual linkages, and were the categories well developed?
- Was much variation built into the theory? Were the broader conditions built into its explanation?
- Were change or movement taken into account in the development of the theory?

The essence of this approach, that theory emerges from and is grounded in data, is not without

its critics. For example, Silverman (1993: 47) suggests that it fails to acknowledge the implicit theories that guide research in its early stages (i.e. data are not theory neutral but theory saturated) and that it might be strong on providing categorizations without necessarily explanatory potential. These are caveats that should feed into the process of reflexivity in qualitative research.

Interpretation in qualitative data analysis: multilayered texts

Words carry many meanings; they are nuanced and highly context-sensitive. In qualitative data analysis it is often the case that interpretation and analysis are fused and, indeed, concurrent. It is naïve to suppose that the qualitative data analyst can separate analysis from interpretation, because words themselves are interpretations and are to be interpreted. Further, texts themselves carry many levels of meaning, and the qualitative researcher has to strive to catch these different levels or layers. The issues of projection and counter-transference are important: the researcher's analysis may say as much about the researcher as about the text being analysed, both in the selection of the levels of analysis and the imputation of intention and function of discourses in the text. The following example may expose the issues here (Cummings 1985). It is a transcript of a short conversation in an infant classroom which contains the potential for several levels of analysis.

A worked example: discussion in an infant classroom

This is a class of 27 5–6-year-old children, with the children seated on a carpet and the teacher seated on a chair. A new set of class books has arrived for the children's free use. After a few days the teacher feels that the class and the teacher should look at them together.

1	T	Right. Let's have a look at this book – 'cause these are – smashing books. Are you enjoying them?
2	CC	Yes//Yes//Yes.
3	T	What's it called this one? Can anyone tell me?
4	CC	Splosh//.
5	C	//Splish//
6	CC	//Splosh//
7	T	Splosh not splish. It's got an 'o' in the middle. Splosh.
8	CC	Splish splosh//
9	C	//Splosh//
10	T	Splosh it says. (Reading) A dog, a pig, a cow, a bear, a monkey, a donkey, all in the –
11	T & CC	Air
12	T	((Showing pictures)) There's the dog and the pig and the cow and the bear and the monkey and the donkey all in the air. What are they in the air in?
13	CC	( )//
14	T	//Put up your hand if you know. Vicky. ((Buzz of children trying to get in))
15	C	The cow's popped it
16	Vicky	//A hot air balloon.
17	T	A hot air balloon
18	C (as 15)	The cow's popped it.
19	T	What's the cow popped it with?
20	CC	Horn//horn//ear//horn//his horn.
21	T	His horn – it's not his *ear* is it – his ears//
22	CC	((Laughing))//
23	T	are down here. It's his horn that's sticking up.
24	CC	((Laughing))
25	T	What does this mean then? ((showing stylized drawings of air escaping))
26	C	Air's coming out//
27	C	//Air//
28	T	The air coming out of the balloon isn't it. Can you *really* see the air coming out of a balloon?
29	CC	No. No. No.
30	T	No – very often in cartoons it look like that doesn't it.
31	C	I can see gas coming out of my mouth when I () on the windows.
32	T	*When* can you see it?
33	C	When it's steamed up.
34	T	Yes. And if//
35	C	//When it's cold.
36	T	When it's cold. When you hhh//
37	C	//When your breath – when your breath turns over and it steams on the – steams on the window.
38	T	Yes//
39	C	And it//
40	T	But only when it's –
41	CC	Cold.
42	T	Cold. Only when it's cold.
43	C	I saw a airship.
44	T	Did you. When? Where?
45	C	On the park.
46	T	Really.
47	CC	I have//I saw//Mrs Cummings
48	T	Shh – Yes, Luke.
49	Luke	When we – when the airship was aft- when it was finished and the Pope was on we took the telly outside – and – we took the telly outside – and – and we saw – we saw the good old airship.
50	T	Did you.
51	Luke	An air balloon as well.
52	T	It's not good *old* airship – it's Goodyear – the Goodyear airship.
53	CC	Good year//Mrs Cummings
54	T	Good year. Yes.
55	C	I seed the airship. ((Many children talking at once))
56	T	Just a moment because I can't hear Luke because other people are chattering. You'll have your turn in a minute.
57	Luke	I said Mummy, what's that thing with the 'X' on the back and she didn't answer me but when I () it off () an air balloon.

continued

58	T	Yes. It was an airship. Yes. Actually I think we saw it at school one day last summer, didn't we.
59	CC	Yes.
60	T	We all went outside and had a look at it. It was going through the sky.
61	CC	( ) //
62	Luke	Mrs Cummings//
63	C	( )
64	T	Uuhm – Ben
65	Ben	I remember that time when it came ( ) over the school.
66	T	Did you. Y-//
67	Ben	//( ) the same one came over my house when I went home.
68	T	Yes. Paul.
69	Paul	I went to a airship where they did//
70	Luke	//It flew over my house ( ) //
71	T	//Just a moment Paul because Luke is now interrupting. We listened to him very carefully. Now it's his turn to listen to us.
72	Paul	I went to see a airship where they take off and when I – when I got there I saw ( ) going around.
73	T	Oh . . . What keeps an airship up in the air?
74	CC	Air//air//gas//
75	Luke	Mrs Cummings.
76	T	Air or gas. Yes. If it's air, it's got to be *hot* air to keep it up – or gas. Now put your hands down for a minute and we'll have a look at the rest of the book. ((Reading)) Help said Pig. There he is saying help. ((There is a cartoon-like 'bubble' from his mouth with 'help' written in)) Help said –
77	CC	Monkey
78	T	Help said donkey. It's gone wonky.
79	CC	h-h-h ((untranscribable talk from several children))
80	T	Look as though it had gone wonky once before. What makes me say that?
81	C	Because – because there's – something on the balloon.

82	T	Mmm. There's already a patch on it isn't there to cover a hole ((reading)) A bear, a cow, a pig, a dog, a donkey and a monkey *all – in – a –* and this is the word you got wrong before – all in a –
83	C	Bog
84	T	Bog – Who said it said dog at the end and it shouldn't?
85	James	Me.
86	T	*James!* James, what does it start with?
87	James	'b' for 'bog.
88	T	'b'. It only goes to show how important it is to get them the right way round//
89	C	//Toilet//
90	T	No. I don't think it means toilet.
91	CC	((Laughter))
92	T	I don't think they're in a toilet.
93	CC	((Laughter))
94	T	What's a bog when it isn't a toilet?
95	Gavin	My brother call it the bog.
96	T	Yes. Lots of people do – call a toilet a bog but I don't think that's what this means.
97	Paul	(fall in) something when – when it sticks to you.
98	T	Yes, you're quite right Paul. It's somewhere that's very sticky. If you fall in its very sticky//
99	C	( )
100	T	It's not glue
101	C	It's called a swamp.
102	T	Swamp is another word for it, good boy – but it's not glue, it's usually mud or somewhere. It's usually somewhere – somewhere in the countryside that's very wet. ((Many children talking))
103	C	Mrs Cummings what ( )
104	T	Just a moment you are forgetting to listen. You *are* remembering to think and to talk but you're forgetting to listen and take your turn. Now Olga.
105	Olga	Once my daddy –

Let us explore the levels of analysis here. If we ask 'What is being learned here by the children?' there are several kinds of response. At a formal level, first, there is a *curricular* response: the children are learning a little bit of language (reading, speaking, listening, vocabulary, spelling, letter orientation (e.g. 'bog' and 'dog'), science (condensation, hot and cold, hot air rising, hot air and gas-filled balloons) and soil (a muddy swamp). That concerns the academic curriculum, as it were. However, at a second level the children are learning other aspects of development, not just academic but personal, social, emotional and interpersonal, for example turn-taking, cooperation, shared enjoyment, listening to each other, contributing to a collective activity, taking risks with language (the risqué joke about the word 'bog' with its double-entendre of a swamp and an impolite term for a toilet).

At a third level one can notice language rights in the classroom. Here the text usefully provides numbered lines to assist analysis and to preserve the chronology of events. One can observe the following, using a closer textual analysis:

- A great deal of the conversation follows the sequence of teacher→student→teacher→ student and so on (e.g. lines 28–48).
- It is rare for the sequence to be broken, for instance teacher→student→student (e.g. lines 3–7 and 14–16).
- Where the sequence is broken, it is at the teacher's behest, and with individual children only (lines 48–52, 64–9, 84–8, 94–8).
- Where the conventional sequence is broken without the teacher's blessing the teacher intervenes to restore the sequence or to control the proceedings (lines 54–6, 70–1, 103–4).
- It appears that many of the 27 children are not joining in very much – the teacher only talks directly to, or encourages to talk, a few named children individually: Vicky, Luke, Ben, Paul, James and Olga.
- There are almost no instances of children *initiating* conversations (e.g. lines 43, 65, 101); most of the conversations are in *response* to the teacher's initiation (e.g. lines 3, 11, 20, 25, 28, 32, 34, 36 etc.).
- The teacher follows up on a child's initiation only when it suits her purposes (lines 43–6).
- Nearly everything goes through, or comes from the teacher who mediates everything.
- Where a child says something that the teacher likes or is in the teacher's agenda for the lesson then that child is praised (e.g. lines 34, 42, 54, 58, 76 and 96, 98 (the word 'yes'), 102) and the teacher repeats the child's correct answer (e.g. lines 16–17, 20–1, 29–30, 35–6, 41–2).
- The teacher feeds the children with clues as to the expected answer (lines 10–11, 40–1, 76–7, 82–3).
- Where the conversation risks being out of the teacher's control the teacher becomes much more explicit in the classroom rules (e.g. lines 56, 71, 104).
- When the teacher decides that it is time to move on to get through her agenda she closes off further discussion and moves on (line 76).
- The teacher is prepared to share a joke (lines 90–93) to maintain a good relationship but then moves the conversation on (line 94).
- Most of the conversation, in speech act terms, is perlocutionary (achieving the teacher's intended aim of the lesson) rather than illocutionary (an open-ended and free-range, multidirectional discussion where the outcome is unpredictable).
- The teacher talks a lot more than the children.

At a fourth level, one can begin to theorize from the materials here. It could be argued, for example, that the text discloses the overt and covert operations of power, to suggest, in fact, that what the children are learning very effectively is the hidden curriculum in which power is a major feature, for instance:

- The teacher has the power to decide who will talk, when they will talk, what they will talk about and how well they have talked (cf. Edwards 1980).
- The teacher has the power to control a mass of children (27 children sitting on the floor while

she, the teacher, sits on a chair, i.e. physically above them).

- The teacher controls and disciplines *through* her control of the conversation and its flow, and, when this does not work (e.g. lines 56, 71, 104) then her control and power become more overt and naked. What we have here is an example of Bernstein's (1975) 'invisible pedagogy', for example, where the control of the teacher over the child is implicit rather than explicit; where, ideally, the teacher arranges the *context* which the children are expected to rearrange and explore; where there is a reduced emphasis upon the transmission and acquisition of specific skills.

- What we have here is a clear example of the importance of the children learning the hidden curriculum of classrooms (Jackson 1968), wherein they have to learn how to cope with power and authority, praise, denial, delay, membership of a crowd, loss of individuality, rules, routines and socially acceptable behaviour. As Jackson (1968) says, if children are to do well in school then it is equally, if not more important that they learn, and abide by, the hidden curriculum rather than the formal curriculum.

- What we have here is also an example of Giddens's (1976; 1984) structuration theory, wherein the conversation in the classroom is the cause, the medium and the outcome of the perpetuation of the status quo of power asymmetries and differentials in the classroom, reinforcing the teacher's control, power and authority.

- The teacher has been placed in a difficult position by being the sole adult with 27 children, and so her behaviour, motivated perhaps benevolently, is, in fact a coping or survival strategy to handle and manage the discipline with large numbers of young and demanding children – crowd control.

- The children are learning to be compliant and that their role is to obey, and that if they are obedient to a given agenda then they will be rewarded.

- The 'core variable' (in terms of grounded theory') is power: the teacher is acting to promote and sustain her power; when it can be asserted and reinforced through an invisible pedagogy then it is covert; when this does not work it becomes overt.

Now, one has to ask whether, at the fourth level, the researcher is reading too much into the text, over-interpreting it, driven by her own personal hang-ups or negative experiences of power and authority, and over-concerned with the issue of discipline, projecting too much of herself onto the data interpretation. Maybe the teacher is simply teaching the children socially acceptable behaviour and moving the conversation on productively, exercising her professional task sensitively and skilfully, building in the children's contributions, and her behaviour has actually nothing to do with power. Further, one can observe at level four that several theories are being promulgated to try to explain the messages in the text, and one has to observe the fertility of a simple piece of transcription to support several grounded or pre-ordinate/pre-existing theories. The difficult question here is, 'Which interpretation is correct?' Here there is no single answer; they are all perhaps correct.

The classroom transcription records only what is said. People will deliberately withhold information; some children will give way to more vocal children, and others may be off task. What we have here is only one medium that has been recorded. Even though the transcription tries to note a few other features (e.g. children talking simultaneously), it does not catch all the events in the classroom. How do we know, for example, whether most children are bored, or if some are asleep, or some are fighting, or some are reading another book and so on? All we have here is a selection from what is taking place, and the selection is made on what is transcribable.

One can see in this example that the text is multilayered. At issue here is the levels of analysis that are required, or legitimate, and how analysis is intermingled with interpretation. In qualitative research, analysis and interpretation frequently merge. This raises the issues of validity and reliability. What we have here is a problem of the 'double hermeneutic' – as researchers we are members of the world that we are researching, so we cannot be neutral; we live in an already-interpreted world. More extensively Morrison (2003) suggests that the problem extends beyond this. Look at the example above:

- The teacher and the children act on the basis of their interpretations of the situation (their 'definitions of the situation').
- The lived actions are converted from one medium (observations, actions and live events) to another (written) by choosing to opt only for transcription – an interpretation of their interpretation.
- The researcher then interprets the written data (a third hermeneutic) and writes an unavoidably selective account (a fourth – quadruple – hermeneutic – an interpretation of an interpretation of an interpretation of an interpretation!).
- The reader then brings his/her own biography and background to interpret the researcher's written interpretation (a fifth – quintuple – hermeneutic).

Given the successive interpretations it is difficult not to suggest that reliability and validity can easily be compromised in qualitative research. Reflexivity as the disclosure of one's possible biased interpretations does little to reduce them – I can state my possible biases and interpretations but that does not necessarily stop them from being selective and biased. This suggests, perhaps, the limits of reflexivity. In connection with increasing reliability and validity, reflexivity is not enough.

The accompanying web site contains an introductory manual for using QSR NUD.IST (the principles of which apply to N-Vivo: see http://www.routledge.com/textbooks/9780415368780 – Chapter 23, file 23.2 doc). The web site also contains a full set of Word-based data files specifically prepared for QSR, concerning a single project of assessment and testing (see http://www.routledge.com/textbooks/9780415368780 – Chapter 23, files qsr23.13 through to qsr23.23). These have also been saved into Word documents (see http://www.routledge.com/textbooks/9780415368780 – Chapter 23, file 23.3.doc through to file 23.13.doc). A listing of the documents of qualitative data that are prepared is available on the accompanying web site (http://www.routledge.com/textbooks/9780415368780 – Chapter 23, file QSR FILES ON THE WEB SITE).

24 Quantitative data analysis

Introduction

The prospect of analysing numerical data sends shivers down the spines of many novice researchers who not only baulk at the thought of statistics but also hold fundamental objections to what they see as 'the mathematisation of nature' (Horkheimer 1972). Most concepts in education, some will assert, are simply not reducible to numerical analysis. Statistics, they will object, combine refinement of process with crudity of concept.

We do not hold with any of this. Quantitative data analysis has no greater or lesser importance than qualitative analysis. Its use is entirely dependent on *fitness for purpose*. Arbitrary dismissal of numerical analysis is mere ideology or prejudice.

Quantitative data analysis is a powerful research form, emanating in part from the positivist tradition. It is often associated with large-scale research, but can also serve smaller scale investigations, with case studies, action research, correlational research and experiments. In the following chapters we will show how numerical data can be reported and introduce some of the most widely used statistics that can be employed in their analysis.

Numerical analysis can be performed using software, for example the Statistical Package for Social Sciences (SPSS, Minitab, Excel). Software packages apply statistical formulae and carry out computations. With this in mind, we avoid extended outlines of statistical formulae though we do provide details where considered useful. Our primary aim is to explain the concepts that underpin statistical analyses and to do this in as user-friendly a way as possible. Lest our approach should raise purist eyebrows, we provide extended treatments in greater detail, signaled where appropriate by web site references. Our outline commentary is closely linked to SPSS, the most widely used statistical package for social sciences. An introductory SPSS manual to this volume is located in the accompanying web site (including printouts of data analysis) together with comments on what they show (see http://www.routledge.com/textbooks/ 9780415368780 – Chapter 24, file SPSS whole manual 24.1); the manual is also segmented into sections, and these are referred to throughout this chapter. It is often the case that such outputs can clarify issues more straightforwardly than extended prose. We also include a guide to all the SPSS files held on the web site (see http://www.routledge.com/textbooks/ 9780415368780 – Chapter 24, file SPSS files on the web site).

We begin by identifying some key concepts in numerical analysis (scales of data, parametric and non-parametric data, descriptive and inferential statistics, dependent and independent variables). We then address the concept of statistical significance. We finally conclude with a brief outline of some simple statistics. Throughout this chapter and the next we indicate how to report analysis; these are collected together in a single file on the accompanying web site (http://www.routledge.com/textbooks/ 9780415368780 – Chapter 24, file 24.1.doc).

Material in the accompanying web site also refers to statistical tables (see http://www. routledge.com/textbooks/9780415368780 – Chapter 24, file Appendices of Statistical Tables).

Scales of data

Before one can advance very far in the field of data analysis one needs to distinguish the kinds of numbers with which one is dealing. This takes us to the commonly reported issue of scales or levels of data, and four are identified, each of which, in the order given below, subsumes its predecessor.

The *nominal* scale simply denotes categories, 1 means such-and-such a category, 2 means another and so on, for example, '1' might denote males, '2' might denote females. The categories are mutually exclusive and have no numerical meaning. For example, consider numbers on a football shirt: we cannot say that the player wearing number 4 is twice as anything as a player wearing a number 2, nor half as anything as a player wearing a number 8; the number 4 simply identifies a category, and, indeed nominal data are frequently termed categorical data. The data classify, but have no order. Nominal data include items such as sex, age group (e.g. 30–35, 36–40), subject taught, type of school, socio-economic status. Nominal data denote discrete variables, entirely separate categories, e.g. according females the number 1 category and males the number 2 category (there cannot be a 1.25 or a 1.99 position). The figure is simply a conveniently short label (see http://www.routledge.com/textbooks/9780415368780 – Chapter 24, file 24.1.ppt).

The *ordinal* scale not only classifies but also introduces an order into the data. These might be rating scales where, for example, 'strongly agree' is stronger than 'agree', or 'a very great deal' is stronger than 'very little'. It is possible to place items in an order, weakest to strongest, smallest to biggest, lowest to highest, least to most and so on, but there is still an absence of a metric – a measure using calibrated or equal intervals. Therefore one cannot assume that the distance between each point of the scale is equal, i.e. the distance between 'very little' and 'a little' may not be the same as the distance between 'a lot' and 'a very great deal' on a rating scale. One could not say, for example, that, in a 5-point rating scale (1 = strongly disagree; 2 = disagree; 3 = neither agree nor disagree; 4 = agree; 5 = strongly agree)

point 4 is in twice as much agreement as point 2, or that point 1 is in five times more disagreement than point 5. However, one could place them in an order: 'not at all', 'very little', 'a little', 'quite a lot', 'a very great deal', or 'strongly disagree', 'disagree', 'neither agree nor disagree', 'agree', 'strongly agree', i.e. it is possible to rank the data according to rules of 'lesser than' of 'greater than', in relation to whatever the value is included on the rating scale. Ordinal data include items such as rating scales and Likert scales, and are frequently used in asking for opinions and attitudes.

The *interval* scale introduces a metric – a regular and equal interval between each data point – as well as keeping the features of the previous two scales, classification and order. This lets us know 'precisely how far apart are the individuals, the objects or the events that form the focus of our inquiry' (Cohen and Holliday 1996: 9). As there is an exact and same interval between each data point, interval level data are sometimes called *equal-interval scales* (e.g. the distance between 3 degrees Celsius and 4 degrees Celsius is the same as the distance between 98 degrees Celsius and 99 degrees Celsius). However, in interval data, there is no true zero. Let us give two examples. In Fahrenheit degrees the freezing point of water is 32 degrees, not zero, so we cannot say, for example, that 100 degrees Fahrenheit is twice as hot as 50 degrees Fahrenheit, because the measurement of Fahrenheit did not start at zero. In fact twice as hot as 50 degrees Fahrenheit is 68 degrees Fahrenheit $((\{50 - 32\} \times 2) + 32)$. Let us give another example. Many IQ tests commence their scoring at point 70, i.e. the lowest score possible is 70. We cannot say that a person with an IQ of 150 has twice the measured intelligence as a person with an IQ of 75 because the starting point is 70; a person with an IQ of 150 has twice the measured intelligence as a person with an IQ of 110, as one has to subtract the initial starting point of 70 $(\{150 - 70\} \div 2)$. In practice, the interval scale is rarely used, and the statistics that one can use with this scale are, to all extents and purposes, the same as for the fourth scale: the ratio scale.

The *ratio* scale embraces the main features of the previous three scales – classification, order and an equal interval metric – but adds a fourth, powerful feature: a true zero. This enables the researcher to determine proportions easily – 'twice as many as', 'half as many as', 'three times the amount of' and so on. Because there is an absolute zero, all of the arithmetical processes of addition, subtraction, multiplication and division are possible. Measures of distance, money in the bank, population, time spent on homework, years teaching, income, Celsius temperature, marks on a test and so on are all ratio measures as they are capable of having a 'true' zero quantity. If I have one thousand dollars in the bank then it is twice as much as if I had five hundred dollars in the bank; if I score 90 per cent in an examination then it is twice as many as if I had scored 45 per cent. The opportunity to use ratios and all four arithmetical processes renders this the most powerful level of data. Interval and ratio data are continuous variables that can take on any value within a particular, given range. Interval and ratio data typically use more powerful statistics than nominal and ordinal data.

The delineation of these four scales of data is important, as the consideration of which statistical test to use is dependent on the scale of data: it is incorrect to apply statistics which can only be used at a higher scale of data to data at a lower scale. For example, one should not apply averages (means) to nominal data, nor use t-tests and analysis of variances (discussed later) to ordinal data. Which statistical tests can be used with which data are set out clearly later. To close this section we record Wright's (2003: 127) view that the scale of measurement is not inherent to a particular variable, but something that researchers 'bestow on it based on our theories of that variable. It is a belief we hold about a variable'. What is being suggested here is that we have to justify classifying a variable as nominal, ordinal, interval or ratio, and not just assume that it is self-evident.

Parametric and non-parametric data

Non-parametric data are those which make no assumptions about the population, usually because the characteristics of the popula- tion are unknown (see http://www.routledge.com/

textbooks/9780415368780 – Chapter 24, file 24.2.ppt). Parametric data assume knowledge of the characteristics of the population, in order for inferences to be able to be made securely; they often assume a normal, Gaussian curve of distribution, as in reading scores, for example (though Wright (2003: 128) suggests that normal distributions are actually rare in psychology). In practice this distinction means this: nominal and ordinal data are considered to be non-parametric, while interval and ratio data are considered to be parametric data. The distinction, as for the four scales of data, is important, as the consideration of which statistical test to use is dependent on the kinds of data: it is incorrect to apply parametric statistics to non-parametric data, although it is possible to apply non-parametric statistics to parametric data (it is not widely done, however, as the statistics are usually less powerful). Non-parametric data are often derived from questionnaires and surveys (though these can also gain parametric data), while parametric data tend to be derived from experiments and tests (e.g. examination scores). (For the power efficiency of a statistical test see the accompanying web site (http://www.routledge.com/textbooks/ 9780415368780 – Chapter 24, file 'The power efficiency of a test').

Descriptive and inferential statistics

Descriptive statistics do exactly what they say: they describe and present data, for example, in terms of summary frequencies (see http:// www.routledge.com/textbooks/9780415368780 – Chapter 24, file 24.3.ppt). This will include, for example:

- the mode (the score obtained by the greatest number of people)
- the mean (the average score) (see http://www. routledge.com/textbooks/9780415368780 – Chapter 24, file 24.4.ppt)
- the median (the score obtained by the middle person in a ranked group of people, i.e. it has an equal number of scores above it and below it)
- minimum and maximum scores

- the range (the distance between the highest and the lowest scores)
- the variance (a measure of how far scores are from the mean, calculated as the average of the squared deviations of individual scores from the mean)
- the standard deviation (SD: a measure of the dispersal or range of scores, calculated as the square root of the variance)
- the standard error (SE: the standard deviation of sample means)
- the skewness (how far the data are asymmetrical in relation to a 'normal' curve of distribution)
- kurtosis (how steep or flat is the shape of a graph or distribution of data; a measure of how peaked a distribution is and how steep is the slope or spread of data around the peak).

Such statistics make no inferences or predictions, they simply report what has been found, in a variety of ways.

Inferential statistics, by contrast, strive to make inferences and predictions based on the data gathered. These will include, for example, hypothesis testing, correlations, regression and multiple regression, difference testing (e.g. t-tests and analysis of variance, factor analysis, and structural equation modelling. Sometimes simple frequencies and descriptive statistics may speak for themselves, and the careful portrayal of descriptive data may be important. However, often it is the inferential statistics that are more valuable for researchers, and typically these are more powerful.

One-tailed and two-tailed tests

In using statistics, researchers are sometimes confronted with the decision whether to use a one-tailed or a two-tailed test. Which to use is a function of the kind of result one might predict. In a one-tailed test one predicts, for example, that one group will score more highly than the other, whereas in a two-tailed test one makes no such prediction. The one-tailed test is a stronger test than the two-tailed test as it makes assumptions about the population and the direction of the outcome (i.e. that one group will score more highly than another), and hence, if supported, is more powerful than a two-tailed test. A one-tailed test will be used with a directional hypothesis (e.g. 'Students who do homework *without* the TV on produce *better* results than those who do homework with the TV playing'). A two-tailed test will be used with a non-directional hypothesis (e.g. 'There is a *difference* between homework done in noisy or silent conditions'). The directional hypothesis indicates 'more' or 'less', whereas the non-directional hypothesis indicates only difference, and not where the difference may lie.

Dependent and independent variables

Research often concerns relationships between variables (a variable can be considered as a construct, operationalized construct or particular property in which the researcher is interested). An independent variable is an input variable, that which causes, in part or in total, a particular outcome; it is a stimulus that influences a response, an antecedent or a factor which may be modified (e.g. under experimental or other conditions) to affect an outcome. A dependent variable, on the other hand, is the outcome variable, that which is caused, in total or in part, by the input, antecedent variable. It is the effect, consequence of, or response to, an independent variable. This is a fundamental concept in many statistics.

For example, we may wish to see if doing more homework increases students' performance in, say, mathematics. We increase the homework and measure the result and, we notice, for example, that the performance increases on the mathematics test. The independent variable has produced a measured outcome. Or has it? Maybe: (a) the threat of the mathematics test increased the students' concentration, motivation and diligence in class; (b) the students liked mathematics and the mathematics teacher, and this caused them to work harder, not the mathematics test itself; (c) the students had a good night's sleep before the mathematics test and, hence, were refreshed and alert; (d) the students' performance in the mathematics test, in fact, influenced how much homework they did – the higher the marks, the more they were motivated to doing mathematics homework; (e) the increase in homework increased the students' motivation for mathematics and this, in turn may have caused the increase in the mathematics test; (f) the students were told that if they did not perform well on the test then they would be punished, in proportion to how poorly they scored.

What one can observe here is important. In respect of (a), there are other *extraneous* variables which have to be factored into the causal relationship (i.e. in addition to the homework). In respect of (b), the assumed relationship is not really present; behind the coincidence of the rise in homework and the rise in the test result is a stronger causal relationship of the liking of the subject and the teacher which caused the students to work hard, a by-product of which was the rise in test scores. In respect of (c), an *intervening* variable was at work (a variable which affected the process of the test but which was not directly observed, measured or manipulated). In respect of (d) and (e), in fact the test caused the increase in homework, and not vice versa, i.e. the direction of causality was reversed. In respect of (f), the amount of increase was negatively correlated with the amount of punishment: the greater the mark, the lesser the punishment. In fact, what may be happening here is that causality may be less in a linear model and more multidirectional and multirelated, more like a web than a line.

This example indicates a range of issues in the discussion of dependent and independent variables:

- The direction of causality is not always clear: an independent variable may, in turn, become a dependent variable and vice versa.
- The direction of causality may be bidirectional.
- Assumptions of association may not be assumptions of causality.
- There may be a range of other factors that have a bearing on an outcome.
- There may be causes (independent variables) behind the identified causes (independent variables) that have a bearing on the dependent variable.
- The independent variable may cause something else, and it is the something else that causes the outcome (dependent variable).
- Causality may be non-linear rather than linear.
- The direction of the relationship may be negative rather than positive.
- The strength/magnitude of the relationship may be unclear.

Many statistics operate with dependent and independent variables (e.g. experiments using t-tests and analysis of variance, regression and multiple regression); others do not (e.g. correlational statistics, factor analysis). If one uses tests which require independent and dependent variables, great caution has to be exercised in assuming which is or is not the dependent or independent variable, and whether causality is as simple as the test assumes. Further, many statistical tests are based on linear relationships (e.g. correlation, regression and multiple regression, factor analysis) when, in fact, the relationships may not be linear (some software programs, e.g. SPSS, have the capability for handling non-linear relationships). The researcher has to make a fundamental decision about whether, in fact, the relationships are linear or non-linear, and select the appropriate statistical tests with these considerations in mind.

To draw these points together, the researcher will need to consider:

- What scales of data are there?
- Are the data parametric or non-parametric?
- Are descriptive or inferential statistics required?
- Do dependent and independent variables need to be identified?
- Are the relationships considered to be linear or non-linear?

The prepared researcher will need to consider the mode of data analysis that will be employed. This is very important as it has a specific bearing on the form of the instrumentation. For example, a researcher will need to plan the layout and structure of a questionnaire survey very carefully in order to assist data entry for computer reading and analysis; an inappropriate layout may obstruct data entry and subsequent analysis by computer. The planning of data analysis will need to consider:

- What needs to be done with the data when they have been collected – how will they be processed and analysed?
- How will the results of the analysis be verified, cross-checked and validated?

Decisions will need to be taken with regard to the statistical tests that will be used in data analysis as this will affect the layout of research items (for example in a questionnaire), and the computer packages that are available for processing quantitative and qualitative data, e.g. SPSS and NUD.IST respectively.

Reliability

We need to know how reliable is our instrument for data collection. Reliability in quantitative analysis takes two main forms, both of which are measures of internal consistency: the split-half technique and the alpha coefficient. Both calculate a coefficient of reliability that can lie between 0 and 1. The split-half reliability has been discussed in an earlier chapter. The formula given is:

$$r = \frac{2r}{1 + r}$$

where r = the actual correlation between the halves of the instrument (this requires the instrument to be able to be divided into two matched halves in terms of content and difficulty). So, for example, if the correlation coefficient between the two halves is 0.85 then the formula would be worked out thus:

$$r = \frac{2(0.85)}{1 + 0.85} = \frac{1.70}{1.85} = 0.919$$

Hence the split-half reliability coefficient is 0.919, which is very high. SPSS automatically calculates split-half reliability at the click of a button.

An alternative calculation of reliability as internal consistency can be found in Cronbach's alpha, frequently referred to simply as the alpha coefficient of reliability. The Cronbach alpha provides a coefficient of inter-item correlations, that is, the correlation of each item with the sum of all the other items. This is a measure of the internal consistency among the *items* (not, for example, the people). It is the average correlation among all the items in question, and is used for multi-item scales. SPSS calculates Cronbach's alpha at the click of a button; the formula for alpha is:

$$alpha = \frac{nr_{ii}}{1 + (n - 1)r_{ii}}$$

where n = the number of items in the test or survey (e.g. questionnaire) and r_{ii} = the average of all the inter-item correlations. Let us imagine that the number of items in the survey is ten, and that the average correlation is 0.738. The alpha correlation can be calculated thus:

$$alpha = \frac{nr_{ii}}{1 + (n - 1)r_{ii}} = \frac{10(.738)}{1 + (10 - 1).738}$$

$$= \frac{7.38}{7.64} = 0.97$$

This yields an alpha coefficient of 0.97, which is very high. The alpha coefficients are set out in Table 1 of the Appendices of Statistical Tables. For the split-half coefficient and the alpha coefficient the following guidelines can be used:

>0.90	very highly reliable
0.80–0.90	highly reliable
0.70–0.79	reliable
0.60–0.69	marginally/minimally reliable
<0.60	unacceptably low reliability

Bryman and Cramer (1990: 71) suggest that the reliability level is acceptable at 0.8, although others suggest that it is acceptable if it 0.67 or above.[1] (See http://www.routledge.com/textbooks/9780415368780 – Chapter 24, file SPSS Manual 24.2.)

Exploratory data analysis: frequencies, percentages and cross-tabulations

This is a form of analysis which is responsive to the data being presented, and is most closely concerned with seeing what the data themselves suggest, akin to a detective following a line of evidence. The data are usually descriptive. Here much is made of visual techniques of data presentation. Hence frequencies and percentages, and forms of graphical presentation are often used. A host of graphical forms of data presentation are available in software packages, including, for example:

- frequency and percentage tables (see http://www.routledge.com/textbooks/9780415368780 – Chapter 24, file SPSS Manual 24.3)
- bar charts (for nominal and ordinal data)
- histograms (for continuous – interval and ratio – data)
- line graphs
- pie charts
- high and low charts
- scatterplots
- stem and leaf displays
- box plots (box and whisker plots).

With most of these forms of data display there are various permutations of the ways in which data are displayed within the type of chart or graph chosen. While graphs and charts may look appealing, it is often the case that they tell the reader no more than could be seen in a simple table of figures, which take up less space in a report. Pie charts, bar charts and histograms are particularly prone to this problem, and the data in them could be placed more succinctly into tables. Clearly the issue of fitness for audience is important here: some readers may find charts more accessible and able to be understood than tables of figures, and this is important. Other charts and graphs can add greater value than tables, for example, line graphs, box plots and scatterplots with regression lines, and we would suggest that these are helpful. Here is not the place to debate the strengths and weaknesses of each type, although there are some guides here:

- Bar charts are useful for presenting categorical and discrete data, highest and lowest.

- Avoid using a third dimension (e.g. depth) in a graph when it is unnecessary; a third dimension to a graph must provide additional information.
- Histograms are useful for presenting continuous data.
- Line graphs are useful for showing trends, particularly in continuous data, for one or more variables at a time.
- Multiple line graphs are useful for showing trends in continuous data on several variables in the same graph.
- Pie charts and bar charts are useful for showing proportions.
- Interdependence can be shown through cross-tabulations (discussed below).
- Box plots are useful for showing the distribution of values for several variables in a single chart, together with their range and medians.
- Stacked bar charts are useful for showing the frequencies of different groups within a specific variable for two or more variables in the same chart.
- Scatterplots are useful for showing the relationship between two variables or several sets of two or more variables on the same chart.

At a simple level one can present data in terms of frequencies and percentages (a piece of datum about a course evaluation) (Box 24.1).

From this simple table (Box 24.1) we can tell that:

- 191 people completed the item.

Box 24.1

Frequencies and percentages for a course evaluation

The course was too hard			
		Frequency	Percentage
Valid	Not at all	24	12.6
	Very little	49	25.7
	A little	98	51.3
	Quite a lot	16	8.4
	A very great deal	4	2.1
Total		191	100.0

- Most respondents thought that the course was 'a little' too hard (with a response number of 98, i.e. 51.3 percent); the modal score is that category or score which is given by the highest number of respondents.
- The results were skewed, with only 10.5 per cent being in the categories 'quite a lot' and 'a very great deal'.
- More people thought that the course was 'not at all too hard' than thought that the course was 'quite a lot' or 'a very great deal' too hard.
- Overall the course appears to have been slightly too difficult but not much more.

Let us imagine that we wished to explore this piece of datum further. We may wish to discover, for example, the voting on this item by males and females. This can be presented in a simple cross-tabulation, following the convention of placing the nominal data (male and female) in rows and the ordinal data (the 5-point scale) in the columns. A cross-tabulation is simply a presentational device, whereby one variable is presented in relation to another, with the relevant data inserted into each cell (automatically generated by software packages, such as SPSS) (Box 24.2) (see http://www.routledge.com/textbooks/ 9780415368780 – Chapter 24, file 24.5.ppt).

Box 24.2 shows that, of the total sample, nearly three times more females (38.2 per cent) than males (13.1 per cent) thought that the course was 'a little' too hard, between two-thirds and three-quarters more females (19.9 per cent) than males (5.8 per cent) thought that the course was a 'very little' too hard, and around three times more males (1.6 per cent) than females (0.5 per cent) thought that the course was 'a very great deal' too hard. However, one also has to observe that the size of the two subsamples was uneven. Around three-quarters of the sample were female (73.8 per cent) and around one-quarter (26.2 per cent) was male.

There are two ways to overcome the problem of uneven subsample sizes. One is to adjust the sample, in this case by multiplying up the subsample of males by an exact figure in order to make the two subsamples the same size (141/50 = 2.82). Another way is to examine the data by each row rather than by the overall totals, i.e. to examine the proportion of males voting such and such, and, separately, the proportion of females voting for the same categories of the variable (Box 24.3).

If you think that these two calculations and recalculations are complicated or difficult (overall-percentaged totals and row-percentaged totals), then be reassured: many software packages, e.g. SPSS (the example used here) will do this at one keystroke.

In this second table (Box 24.3) one can observe that:

- There was consistency in the voting by males and females in terms of the categories 'a little' and 'quite a lot'.

Box 24.2
Cross-tabulation by totals

		Not at all	Very little	A little	Quite a lot	A very great deal	Total
Male	Count	7	11	25	4	3	50
	% of total	3.7%	5.8%	13.1%	2.1%	1.6%	26.2%
Female	Count	17	38	73	12	1	141
	% of total	8.9%	19.9%	38.2%	6.3%	0.5%	73.8%
Total	Count	24	49	98	16	4	191
	% of total	12.6%	25.7%	51.3%	8.4%	2.1%	100.0%

Sex* The course was too hard: cross-tabulation — The course was too hard

Box 24.3
Cross-tabulation by row totals

		Sex* The course was too hard: cross-tabulation					
		The course was too hard					
		Not at all	Very little	A little	Quite a lot	A very great deal	Total
Male	Count	7	11	25	4	3	50
	% within sex	14.0%	22.0%	50%	8.0%	6.0%	100%
Female	Count	17	38	73	12	1	141
	% within sex	12.1%	27.0%	52%	8.5%	0.7%	100%
Total	Count	24	49	98	16	4	191
	% within sex	12.6%	25.7%	51%	8.4%	2.1%	100%

- More males (6 per cent) than females (0.7 per cent) thought that the course was 'a very great deal' too hard.
- A slightly higher percentage of females (91.1 per cent: {12.1 per cent + 27 per cent + 52 per cent}) than males (86 per cent: {14 per cent + 22 per cent + 50 per cent}) indicated, overall, that the course was not too hard.
- The overall pattern of voting by males and females was similar, i.e. for both males and females the strong to weak categories in terms of voting percentages were identical.

We would suggest that this second table is more helpful than the first table, as, by including the row percentages, it renders fairer the comparison between the two groups: males and females. Further, we would suggest that it is usually preferable to give *both* the actual frequencies and percentages, but to make the comparisons by percentages. We say this, because it is important for the reader to know the actual numbers used. For example, in the first table (Box 24.2), if we were simply to be given the percentage of males voting that the course was a 'very great deal' too hard (1.6. per cent), as course planners we might worry about this. However, when we realize that 1.6 per cent is actually only 3 out of 141 people then we might be less worried. Had the 1.6 per cent represented, say, 50 people of a sample, then this

would have given us cause for concern. Percentages on their own can mask the real numbers, and the reader needs to know the real numbers.

It is possible to comment on particular cells of a cross-tabulated matrix in order to draw attention to certain factors (e.g. the very high 52 per cent in comparison to its neighbour 8.5 per cent in the voting of females in Box 24.3). It is also useful, on occasions, to combine data from more than one cell, as we have done in the example above. For example, if we combine the data from the males in the categories 'quite a lot' and 'a very great deal' (8 per cent + 6 per cent = 14 per cent) we can observe that, not only is this equal to the category 'not at all', but also it contains fewer cases than any of the other single categories for the males, i.e. the combined category shows that the voting for the problem of the course being too difficult is still very slight.

Combining categories can be useful in showing the general trends or tendencies in the data. For example, in the tables (Boxes 24.1 to 24.3), combining 'not at all', 'very little' and 'a little', all of these measures indicate that it is only a very small problem of the course being too hard, i.e. generally speaking the course was not too hard.

Combining categories can also be useful in rating scales of agreement to disagreement. For example, consider the following results in relation to a survey of 200 people on a particular item (Box 24.4).

Box 24.4

Rating scale of agreement and disagreement

Strongly disagree	Disagree	Neither agree nor disagree	Agree	Strongly agree
30	40	70	20	40
15%	20%	35%	10%	20%

Box 24.5

Satisfaction with a course

	Satisfaction with course			
	Low (1–3)	Medium (4–5)	High (6–7)	Total
Male	60 (41.4%)	70 (48.3%)	15 (10.3%)	145 (100%)
Female	35 (43.7%)	15 (18.8%)	30 (37.5%)	80 (100%)
Total	95 (42.2%)	85 (37.8%)	45 (20%)	225 (100%)

There are several ways of interpreting Box 24.4, for example, more people 'strongly agreed' (20 per cent) than 'strongly disagreed' (15 per cent), or the modal score was for the central neutral category (a central tendency) of 'neither agree nor disagree'. However, one can go further. If one wishes to ascertain an overall indication of disagreement and agreement then adding together the two disagreement categories yields 35 per cent (15 per cent + 20 per cent) and adding together the two agreement categories yields 30 per cent (10 per cent + 20 per cent), i.e. there was more disagreement than agreement, despite the fact that more respondents 'strongly agreed' than 'strongly disagreed', i.e. the *strength* of agreement and disagreement has been lost. By adding together the two disagreement and agreement categories it gives us a general rather than a detailed picture; this may be useful for our purposes. However, if we do this then we also have to draw attention to the fact that the total of the two disagreement categories (35 per cent) is the same as the total in the category 'neither agree nor disagree', in which case one could suggest that the modal category of 'neither agree nor disagree' has been superseded by bimodality, with disagreement being one modal score and 'neither agree nor disagree' being the other.

Combining categories can be useful although it is not without its problems, for example let us consider three tables (Boxes 24.5 to 24.7). The first presents the overall results of an imaginary course evaluation, in which three levels of satisfaction have been registered (low, medium, high) (Box 24.5).

Here one can observe that the modal category is 'low' (95 votes, 42.2 per cent)) and the lowest category is 'high' (45 votes, 20 per cent), i.e. overall the respondents are dissatisfied with the course. The females seem to be more satisfied with the course than the males, if the category 'high' is used as an indicator, and the males seem to be more moderately satisfied with the course than the females. However, if one combines categories (low and medium) then a different story could be told (Box 24.6).

By looking at the percentages, here it appears that the females are more satisfied with the course overall than males, and that the males are more dissatisfied with the course than females. However, if one were to combine categories differently

Box 24.6

Combined categories of rating scales

	Satisfaction with course		
	Low (1–5)	High (6–7)	Total
Male	130 (89.7%)	15 (10.3%)	145 (100%)
Female	50 (62.5%)	30 (37.5%)	80 (100%)
Total	180 (76.1%)	45 (23.9%)	225 (100%)
Difference	+27.2%	−27.2%	

Box 24.7

Representing combined categories of rating scales

	Satisfaction with course		
	Low (1–3)	High (4–7)	Total
Male	60	85	145
	(41.4%)	(58.6%)	(100%)
Female	35	45	80
	(43.7%)	(56.3%)	(100%)
Total	95	130	225
	(42.6%)	(57.4%)	(100%)
Difference	−2.1%	+1.9%	

(medium and high) then a different story could be told (Box 24.7).

By looking at the percentages, here it appears that there is not much difference between the males and the females, and that both males and females are highly satisfied with the course. At issue here is the notion of combining categories, or collapsing tables, and we advocate great caution in doing this. Sometimes it can provide greater clarity, and sometimes it can distort the picture. In the example it is wiser to keep with the

original table rather than collapsing it into fewer categories.

In examining data we can look to see how evenly or widely the data are distributed. For example, a line graph shows how respondents voted on how well learners are guided and supported in their learning, awarding marks out of ten for the voting, with a sample size of 400 respondents (Box 24.8).

One can see here that the data are skewed, with more votes being received at the top end of the scale. There is a long tail going to the negative end of the scores, so, even though the highest scores are given at the top end of the scale, we say that this table has a negative skew because there is a long tail down.

By contrast, let us look at a graph of how much staff take on voluntarily roles in the school, with 150 votes received and awarding marks out of 10 (Box 24.9).

Here one can observe a long tail going toward the upper end of the scores, and the bulk of the scores being in the lower range. Even though most of the scores are in the lower range, because the long tail is towards the upper end of the scale this is termed a positive skew. The skewness of the data is an important feature to observe in data, and to which to draw attention.

Box 24.8

How well learners are cared for, guided and supported

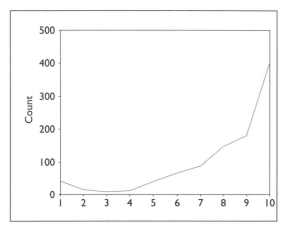

Box 24.9

Staff voluntarily taking on coordination roles

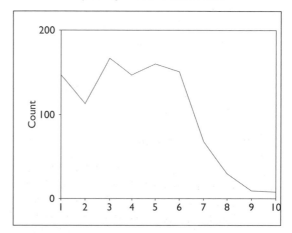

Box 24.10
Distribution of test scores

		Test scores	
		Frequency	Valid per cent
Valid	2	1	0.1
	3	223	22.3
	4	276	27.6
	5	32	3.2
	6	69	6.9
	7	149	14.9
	8	185	18.5
	9	39	3.9
	10	26	2.6
Total		1,000	100.0

If we have interval and ratio data then, in addition to the modal scores and cross-tabulations, we can calculate the mean (the average) and the standard deviation. Let us imagine that we have the test scores for 1,000 students, on a test that was marked out of 10 (Box 24.10).

Here we can calculate that the average score was 5.48. We can also calculate the *standard deviation*, which is a standardized measure of the dispersal of the scores, i.e. how far away from the mean/average each score is (see http://www.routledge.com/textbooks/9780415368780 – Chapter 24, file 24.6.ppt). It is calculated, in its most simplified form (there being more than one way of calculating it), as:

$$SD = \sqrt{\frac{\sum d^2}{N-1}}$$

where

d^2 = the deviation of the score from the mean

(average), squared

Σ = the sum of

N = the number of cases

A low standard deviation indicates that the scores cluster together, while a high standard deviation indicates that the scores are widely dispersed. This is calculated automatically by software packages such as SPSS at the simple click of a single button.

In the example here the standard deviation in the example of scores was 2.134. What does this tell us? First, it suggests that the marks were not very high (an average of 5.48). Second, it tells us that there was quite a variation in the scores. Third, one can see that the scores were unevenly spread, indeed there was a high cluster of scores around the categories of 3 and 4, and another high cluster of scores around the categories 7 and 8. This is where a line graph could be useful in representing the scores, as it shows two peaks clearly (Box 24.11).

It is important to report the standard deviation. For example, let us consider the following. Look at these three sets of numbers:

(1)   1   2   3   4   20   mean = 6
(2)   1   2   6   10   11   mean = 6
(3)   5   6   6   6   7   mean = 6

If we were to plot these points onto three separate graphs we would see very different results (Boxes 24.12 to 24.14) (see http://www.routledge.com/textbooks/9780415368780 – Chapter 24, file 24.7.ppt).

Box 24.11
A line graph of test scores

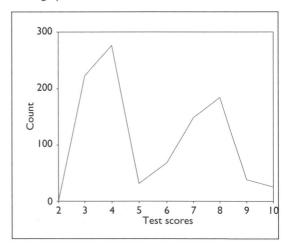

Box 24.12

Distribution around a mean with an outlier

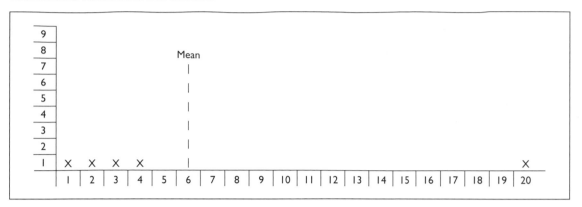

Box 24.12 shows the mean being heavily affected by the single score of 20 (an 'outlier' – an extreme score a long way from the others); in fact all the other four scores are some distance below the mean. The score of 20 is exerting a disproportionate effect on the data and on the mean, raising it. Some statistical packages (e.g. SPSS) can take out outliers. If the data are widely spread then it may be more suitable not to use the mean but to use the median score; SPSS performs this automatically at a click of a button. The median is the midpoint score of a range of data; half of the scores fall above it and half below it. If there is an even number of observations

then the median is the average of the two middle scores.

Box 24.13 shows one score actually on the mean but the remainder some distance away from it. The scores are widely dispersed and the shape of the graph is flat (a platykurtic distribution).

Box 24.14 shows the scores clustering very tightly around the mean, with a very peaked shape to the graph (a leptokurtic distribution).

The point at stake is this: it is not enough simply to calculate and report the mean; for a fuller picture of the data we need to look at the dispersal of scores. For this we require the statistic of the standard deviation, as this will indicate

Box 24.13

A platykurtic distribution of scores

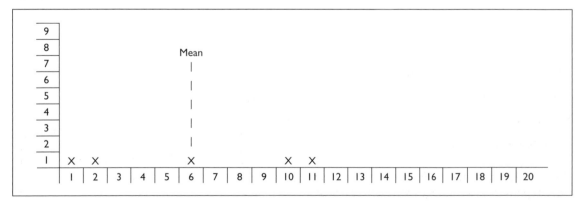

Box 24.14

A leptokurtic distribution of scores

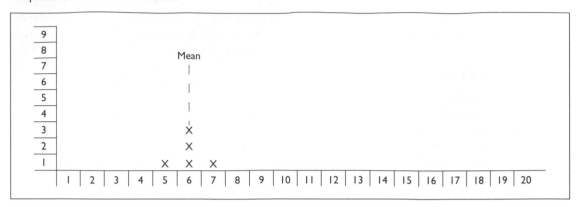

the range and degree of dispersal of the data, though the standard deviation is susceptible to the disproportionate effects of outliers. Some scores will be widely dispersed (the first graph), others will be evenly dispersed (the second graph), and others will be bunched together (the third graph). A high standard deviation will indicate a wide dispersal of scores, a low standard deviation will indicate clustering or bunching together of scores.

As a general rule, the mean is a useful statistic if the data are not skewed (i.e. if they are not bunched at one end or another of a curve of distribution) or if there are no outliers that may be exerting a disproportionate effect. One has to recall that the mean, as a statistical calculation only, can sometimes yield some strange results, for example fractions of a person!

The median is useful for ordinal data, but, to be meaningful, there have to be many scores rather than just a few. The median overcomes the problem of outliers, and hence is useful for skewed results. The modal score is useful for all scales of data, particularly nominal and ordinal data, i.e. discrete, rather than continuous data, and it is unaffected by outliers, though it is not strong if there are many values and many scores which occur with similar frequency (i.e. if there are only a few points on a rating scale).

A probability test for use with Likert-type examples is given on the accompanying web site (http://www.routledge.com/textbooks/ 9780415368780 – Chapter 24, file 24.2.doc).

Summary

What can we do with simple frequencies in exploratory data analysis? The answer to this question depends on the scales of data that we have (nominal, ordinal, interval and ratio). For all four scales we can calculate frequencies and percentages, and we can consider presenting these in a variety of forms. We can also calculate the mode and present cross-tabulations. We can consider combining categories and collapsing tables into smaller tables, providing that the sensitivity of the original data has not been lost. We can calculate the median score, which is particularly useful if the data are spread widely or if there are outliers. For interval and ratio data we can also calculate the mean and the standard deviation; the mean yields an average and the standard deviation indicates the range of dispersal of scores around that average, i.e. to see whether the data are widely dispersed (e.g. in a platykurtic distribution, or close together with a distinct peak (in a leptokurtic distribution). In examining frequencies and percentages one also has to investigate whether the data are skewed, i.e. over-represented at one end of a scale and under-represented at the other end. A positive skew has a long tail at the positive end and the majority of the data at the negative end, and a negative skew has a long tail at the negative end and the majority of the data at the positive end.

Statistical significance

Much statistical analysis hinges on the notion of statistical significance. Kirk (1999: 337) indicates that 'a statistically significant result is one for which chance is an unlikely explanation'. Research in a hypothetico-deductive mode often commences with one or more hypotheses. This is the essence of hypothesis testing in quantitative research. Typically hypotheses fall into two types. The *null hypothesis*, a major type of hypothesis states that, for example, there is *no* relationship between two variables, or that there has been *no* change in participants between a pretest and a post-test, or that there is *no* difference between three school districts in respect of their examination results, or that there is *no* difference between the voting of males and females on such-and-such a factor. The null hypothesis sits comfortably with the Popperian notion of the hallmark of a science being its essential falsifiability.

The point here is that by casting the hypothesis in a null form the burden of proof is placed on the researcher *not* to confirm that null hypothesis. The task is akin to a jury starting with a presumption of innocence and having to prove guilt beyond reasonable doubt. Not only is it often easier simply to support a straightforward positive hypothesis, but also, more seriously, even if that positive hypothesis is supported, there may be insufficient grounds for accepting that hypothesis, as the finding may be consistent with other hypotheses. For example, let us imagine that our hypothesis is that a coin is weighted and, therefore, unfair. We flip the coin 100 times, and find that 60 times out of 100 it comes out as heads. It would be easy to jump to the conclusion that the coin is weighted, but, equally easily, other reasons may account for the result. Of course, if the coin were to come out as heads 99 times out of 100 then perhaps there would be greater truth in

the hypothesis. The null hypothesis is a stronger version of evidence, not only requiring that the negative hypothesis be 'not supported', but also indicating a cut-off point only above which the null hypothesis is 'not supported', and below which the null hypothesis is supported. In our coin example it may be required to find that heads comes up 95 times out of 100 or 99 times out of 100, or even 999 times out of 1,000, to say, with increasing confidence in respect of these three sets of figures, that the null hypothesis is not supported (see http://www.routledge.com/textbooks/9780415368780 – Chapter 24, file 24.8.ppt).

We use terminology carefully here. Some researchers state that the null hypothesis is 'rejected'; others say that it is 'confirmed' or 'not confirmed'; other say that it is 'accepted' or 'not accepted'. We prefer the terminology of 'supported' or 'not supported'. This is not mere semantics or pedantry; rather it signals caution. Rejecting a null hypothesis is not the same as 'not confirming' or 'not supporting' that null hypothesis, rejection implying an absolute and universal state which the research will probably not be able to demonstrate, being bounded within strict parameters and not being applicable to all cases. Further, 'confirming' and 'not confirming', like 'rejecting', is too strong, absolute and universal a set of terms for what is, after all, research that is bounded and within delineated boundaries. Similarly, one cannot 'accept' a null hypothesis as a null hypothesis can never be proved unequivocally.

A second type of hypothesis is termed the *alternative hypothesis*. Whereas the null hypothesis states that there is *no* such-and-such (e.g. change, relationship, difference), the alternative hypothesis state that there *is* such-and-such, for example: there *is* a change in behaviour of the school students; there *is* a difference between students' scores on mathematics and science; there *is* a difference between the examination results of five school districts; there *is* a difference between the pretest and post-test results of such-and-such a class. This weaker form of hypothesis is often supported when the null hypothesis is 'not supported', i.e. if the null hypothesis is not supported then the alternative hypothesis is.

The two kinds of hypothesis are usually written thus:

H_0 :   the null hypothesis

H_1 :   the alternative hypothesis

Sometimes the alternative hypothesis is written as H_A. So, for example, the researcher could have null hypotheses and alternative hypotheses thus:

H_0:   There is no difference between the results of the control group and experimental group in the post-test of mathematics.

or   There is no statistically significant difference between males and females in the results of the English examination.

or   There is no statistically significant correlation between the importance given to a subject and the amount of support given to it by the headteacher.

H_1:   There is a statistically significant difference between the control group and experimental groups in the post-test of mathematics.

or   There is a statistically significant difference between males and females in the results of the English examination.

or   There is a statistically significant positive correlation between examination scores in mathematics and science.

The null hypothesis is the stronger hypothesis, requiring rigorous evidence *not* to support it. The alternative hypothesis is, perhaps, a fall-back position, taken up when the first – null – hypothesis is not confirmed. The latter is the logical opposite of the former. One should commence with the former and cast the research in the form of a null hypothesis, turning to the latter only in the case of finding the null hypothesis not to be supported.

Let us take an example from correlational research to unpack further the notion of statistical significance. A correlation enables a researcher to ascertain whether, and to what extent, there is a degree of association between two variables (this is discussed much more fully later in this chapter). Let us imagine that we observe that many people with large hands also have large feet and that people with small hands also have small feet (see Morrison 1993: 136–40). We decide to conduct an investigation to see if there is any correlation or degree of association between the size of feet and the size of hands, or whether it is just chance that some people have large hands and large feet. We measure the hands and the feet of 100 people and observe that 99 times out of 100 people with large feet also have large hands. Convinced that we have discovered an important relationship, we run the test on 1,000 people, and find that the relationship holds true in 999 cases out of 1,000. That seems to be more than mere coincidence; it would seem that we could say with some certainty that if a person has large hands then he or she will also have large feet. How do we know when we can make that assertion? When do we know that we can have confidence in this prediction?

For statistical purposes, if we observe this relationship occurring 95 times out of 100, i.e. that chance accounts for only 5 per cent of the difference, then we could say with some confidence that there seems to be a high degree of association between the two variables hands and feet; it would occur by chance in 5 people in every 100, reported as the 0.05 level of significance (0.05 being five-hundredths). If we observe this relationship occurring 99 times out of every 100 (as in the example of hands and feet), i.e. that chance accounts for only 1 per cent of the difference, then we could say with even greater confidence that there seems to be a very high degree of association between the two variables; it would occur by chance once in every 100, reported as the 0.01 level of significance (0.01 being one-hundredth). If we observe this relationship occurring 999 times out of every 1,000 (as in the example of hands and feet), i.e. that chance accounts for only 0.1 per cent of the difference, then we could say with even greater confidence that there seems to be a very high degree of association between the two variables; it would not occur only once in every 1,000, reported as the 0.001 level of significance (0.001 being one-hundredth).

We begin with a null hypothesis, which states that there is no relationship between the size of hands and the size of feet. The task is not to support the hypothesis, i.e. the burden of responsibility is not to support the null hypothesis. If we can show that the hypothesis is not supported for 95 per cent or 99 per cent or 99.9 per cent of the population, then we have demonstrated that there is a statistically significant relationship between the size of hands and the size of feet at the 0.05, 0.01 and 0.001 levels of significance respectively. These three levels of significance – the 0.05, 0.01 and 0.001 levels – are the levels at which statistical significance is frequently taken to have been demonstrated, usually the first two of these three levels. The researcher would say that the null hypothesis (that there is no statistically significant relationship between the two variables) has not been supported and that the level of significance observed (ρ) is at the 0.05, 0.01 or 0.001 level. Note here that we have used the terms 'statistically significant', and not simply 'significant'; this is important, for we are using the term in a specialized way.

Let us take a second example. Let us say that we have devised a scale of 1–8 which can be used to measure the sizes of hands and feet. Using the scale we make the following calculations for eight people, and set out the results thus (see http://www.routledge.com/textbooks/9780415368780 – Chapter 24, file 24.9.ppt):

	Hand size	Foot size
Subject A	1	1
Subject B	2	2
Subject C	3	3
Subject D	4	4
Subject E	5	5
Subject F	6	6
Subject G	7	7
Subject H	8	8

We can observe a perfect correlation between the size of the hands and the size of feet, from the person who has a size 1 hand and a size 1 foot to the person who has a size 8 hand and also a size 8 foot. There is a perfect positive correlation (as one variable increases, e.g. hand size, so the other variable – foot size – increases, and as one variable decreases so does the other). We can

use the mathematical formula for calculating the Spearman correlation (this is calculated automatically in SPSS):

$$r = 1 - \frac{6 \sum d^2}{N(N^2 - 1)}$$

where d = the difference between each pair of scores, Σ = the sum of, and N = the size of the population. We calculate that this perfect correlation yields an index of association – a coefficient of correlation – which is +1.00.

Suppose that this time we carry out the investigation on a second group of eight people and report the following results:

	Hand size	Foot size
Subject A	1	8
Subject B	2	7
Subject C	3	6
Subject D	4	5
Subject E	5	4
Subject F	6	3
Subject G	7	2
Subject H	8	1

This time the person with a size 1 hand has a size 8 foot and the person with the size 8 hand has a size 1 foot. There is a perfect negative correlation (as one variable increases, e.g. hand size, the other variable – foot size – decreases, and as one variable decreases, the other increases). Using the same mathematical formula we calculate that this perfect negative correlation yields an index of association – a coefficient of correlation – which is −1.00.

Now, clearly it is very rare to find a perfect positive or a perfect negative correlation; the truth of the matter is that looking for correlations will yield coefficients of correlation which lie somewhere between −1.00 and +1.00. How do we know whether the coefficients of correlation are statistically significant or not? (See http://www.routledge.com/textbooks/9780415368780 – Chapter 24, file 24.10.ppt.)

Let us say that we take a third sample of eight people and undertake an investigation into their hand and foot size. We enter the data case by case (Subject A to Subject H), indicating their rank order for hand size and then for foot size. This time the relationship is less clear because the rank ordering is more mixed, for example, Subject A has a hand size of 2 and 1 for foot size, Subject B has a hand size of 1 and a foot size of 2 etc.:

	Hand size	Foot size
Subject A	2	1
Subject B	1	2
Subject C	3	3
Subject D	5	4
Subject E	4	5
Subject F	7	6
Subject G	6	7
Subject H	8	8

Using the mathematical formula for calculating the correlation statistic, we find that the coefficient of correlation for the eight people is 0.7857. Is it statistically significant? From a table of significance (Tables 2 and 3 in the Appendices of Statistical Tables), we read off whether the coefficient is statistically significant or not for a specific number of cases, for example:

Number of cases	Level of significance	
	0.05	0.01
6	0.93	0.96
7	0.825	0.92
8	0.78	0.875
9	0.71	0.83
10	0.65	0.795
20	0.455	0.595
30	0.36	0.47

We see that for eight cases in an investigation the correlation coefficient has to be 0.78 or higher, if it is to be significant at the 0.05 level, and 0.875 or higher, if it is to be significant at the 0.01 level of significance. As the correlation coefficient in the example of the third experiment with eight subjects is 0.7857 we can see that it is higher than that required for significance at the 0.05 level (0.78) but not as high as that required for significance at the 0.01 level (0.875). We are safe, then, in stating that the degree of association between the hand and foot sizes does not support the null hypothesis and demonstrates statistical significance at the 0.05 level.

The first example above of hands and feet is very neat because it has 100 people in the sample. If we have more or less than 100 people how do we know if a relationship between two factors is statistically significant? Let us say that we have data on 30 people; in this case, because sample size is so small, we might hesitate to say that there is a strong association between the size of hands and size of feet if we observe it occurring in 27 people (i.e. 90 per cent of the population). On the other hand, let us say that we have a sample of 1,000 people and we observe the association in 700 of them. In this case, even though only 70 per cent of the sample demonstrate the association of hand and foot size, we might say that because the sample size is so large we can have greater confidence in the data than in the case of the small sample.

Statistical significance varies according to the size of the number in the sample (as can be seen also in the section of the table of significance reproduced above) (see http://www.routledge.com/textbooks/9780415368780 – Chapter 24, file 24.11.ppt). In order to be able to determine significance we need to have two facts in our possession: the size of the sample and, in correlational research, the coefficient of correlation or, in other kinds of research, the appropriate coefficients or data (there are many kinds, depending on the test being used). Here, as the selection from the table of significance reproduced above shows, the coefficient of correlation can decrease and still be statistically significant as long as the sample size increases. (This resonates with Krejcie's and Morgan's (1970) principles for sampling, observed in Chapter 4, namely as the population increases the sample size increases at a diminishing rate in addressing randomness.) This is a major source of debate for critics of statistical significance, who argue that it is almost impossible *not* to find statistical significance when dealing with large samples, as the coefficients can be very low and still attain statistical significance.

To ascertain statistical significance from a table, then, is a matter of reading off the significance level from a table of significance according to the sample size, or processing data on a computer program to yield the appropriate statistic. In the selection from the table of significance for the third example above concerning hand and foot size, the first column indicates the number of people in the sample and the other two columns indicate significance at the two levels. Hence, if we have 30 people in the sample then, for the correlation to be statistically significant at the 0.05 level, we would need a correlation coefficient of 0.36, whereas, if there were only 10 people in the sample, we would need a correlation coefficient of 0.65 for the correlation to be statistically significant at the same 0.05 level. Most statistical packages (e.g. SPSS) automatically calculate the level of statistical significance, indeed SPSS automatically asterisks each case of statistical significance at the 0.05 and 0.01 levels or smaller. We discuss correlational analysis in more detail later in this chapter, and we refer the reader to that discussion.

Hypothesis testing

The example that we have given above from correlational analysis illustrates a wider issue of hypothesis testing. This follows four stages.

Stage 1

In quantitative research, as mentioned above, we commence with a null hypothesis, for example:

- There is *no* statistical significance in the distribution of the data in a contingency table (cross-tabulation).
- There is *no* statistically significant correlation between two factors.
- There is *no* statistically significant difference between the means of two groups.
- There is *no* statistically significant difference between the means of a group in a pretest and a post-test.
- There is *no* statistically significant difference between the means of three or more groups.
- There is *no* statistically significant difference between two subsamples.
- There is *no* statistically significant difference between three or more subsamples.

- There is *no* significant prediction capability between one independent variable X and dependent variable Y.
- There is *no* significant prediction capability between two or more independent variables X, Y, Z . . . and dependent variable A.

The task of the researcher is to support or not to support the null hypothesis.

Stage 2

Having set the null hypothesis, the researcher then sets the level of significance (α) that will be used to support or not to support the null hypothesis; this is the alpha (α) level. The level of alpha is determined by the researcher. Typically it is 0.05, i.e. for 95 per cent of the time the null hypothesis is not supported. In writing this we could say 'Let $\alpha = 0.05$'. If one wished to be more robust then one would set a higher alpha level ($\alpha = 0.01$ or $\alpha = 0.001$). This is the level of risk that one wishes to take in supporting or not supporting the null hypothesis.

Stage 3

Having set the null hypothesis and the level at which it will be supported or not supported, one then computes the data in whatever form is appropriate for the research in question (e.g. measures of association, measures of difference, regression and prediction measures).

Stage 4

Having analysed the data, one is then in a position to support or not to support the null hypothesis, and this is what would be reported.

It is important to distinguish two types of hypothesis (Wright 2003: 132): a *causal* hypothesis and an *associative* hypothesis. As its name suggests, a causal hypothesis suggests that input X will affect outcome Y, as in, for example, an experimental design. An associative hypothesis describes how variables may relate to each other, not necessarily in a causal manner (e.g. in correlational analysis).

Box 24.15
Type I and Type II errors

Decision	H_0 true	H_0 false
Support H_0	Correct	Type II error (β)
Do not support H_0	Type I error α	Correct

One has to be careful not to describe an associative hypothesis (e.g. gender) as a causal hypothesis, as gender may not be actually having a causal effect.

In hypothesis testing one has to avoid Type I and Type II errors. A Type I error occurs when one does not support the null hypothesis when it is in fact true. This is a particular problem as the sample increases, as the chances of finding a significant association increase, irrespective of whether a true association exists (Rose and Sullivan 1993: 168), requiring the researcher, therefore, to set a higher alpha (α) limit (e.g. 0.01 or 0.001) for statistical significance to be achieved). A Type II error occurs when one supports the null hypothesis when it is in fact not true (often the case if the levels of significance are set too stringently, i.e. requiring the researcher to lower the alpha (α) level of significance (e.g. 0.1 or 0.2) required). Type 1 and Type II can be represented as in Box 24.15.

Effect size

One has to be cautious in using statistical significance. Statistical significance is not the same as educational significance. For example, I might find a statistically significant correlation between the amount of time spent on mathematics and the amount of time spent in watching television. This may be completely unimportant. Similarly I might find that there is no statistically significant difference between males and females in their liking of physics. However, close inspection might reveal that there is a difference. Say, for example, that more males than females like physics, but that the difference does not reach the 'cut-off' point of the 0.05 level of significance; maybe it is 0.065. To say that there is no difference, or simply to support

the null hypothesis here might be inadvisable. There are two issues here: first, the cut-off level of significance is comparatively arbitrary, although high; second, one should not ignore coefficients that fall below the conventional cut-off points. This leads us into a discussion of effect size as an alternative to significance levels.

Statistical significance on its own has come to be seen as an unacceptable index of effect; (Thompson 1994; 1996; 1998; 2001; 2002; Fitz-Gibbon 1997: 43; Rozeboom 1997: 335; Thompson and Snyder 1997; Wilkinson and the Task Force on Statistical Inference, APA Board of Scientific Affairs 1999; Olejnik and Algina 2000; Capraro and Capraro 2002; Wright 2003; Kline 2004) because it depends on both sample size and the coefficient (e.g. of correlation). Statistical significance can be attained *either* by having a large coefficient together with a small sample *or* having a small coefficient together with a large sample. The problem is that one is not able to deduce which is the determining effect from a study using statistical significance (Coe 2000: 9). It is important to be able to tell whether it is the sample size or the coefficient that is making the difference. The effect size can do this.

What is required either to accompany or to replace statistical significance is information about *effect size* (American Psychological Association 1994: 18; 2001; Wilkinson and the Task Force on Statistical Inference, APA Board of Scientific Affairs 1999; Kline 2004). Indeed effect size is seen as much more important than significance, and many international journals either have abandoned statistical significance reporting in favour of effect size, or have insisted that statistical significance be accompanied by indications of effect size (Olejnik and Algina 2000; Capraro and Capraro 2002; Thompson 2002). Statistical significance is seen as arbitrary in its cut-off points and unhelpful – a 'corrupt form of the scientific method' (Carver 1978), an obstacle rather than a facilitator in educational research. It commands slavish adherence rather than addressing the subtle, sensitive and helpful notion of effect size (see Fitz-Gibbon 1997: 118). Indeed commonsense should tell the researcher that a differential measure of effect size is more useful than the blunt edge of statistical significance.

An effect size is

> simply a way of quantifying the difference between two groups. For example, if one group has had an 'experimental treatment' and the other has not (the 'control'), then the Effect Size is a measure of the effectiveness of the treatment.
>
> (Coe 2000: 1)

It tells the reader 'how big the effect is, something that the p value [statistical significance] does not do' (Wright 2003: 125). An effect size (Thompson 2002: 25) 'characterizes the degree to which sample results diverge from the null hypothesis'; it operates through the use of standard deviations.

Wood (1995: 393) suggests that effect size can be calculated by dividing the significance level by the sample size. Glass *et al.* (1981: 29, 102) calculate the effect size as:

$$\frac{\text{(mean of experimental group – mean of control group)}}{\text{standard deviation of the control group}}$$

Coe (2000: 7), while acknowledging that there is a debate on whether to use the standard deviation of the experimental or control group as the denominator, suggests that that of the control group is preferable as it provides 'the best estimate of standard deviation, since it consists of a representative group of the population who have not been affected by the experimental intervention'. However, Coe (2000) also suggests that it is perhaps preferable to use a 'pooled' estimate of standard deviation, as this is more accurate than that provided by the control group alone. To calculate the pooled deviation he suggests that the formula should be:

$$SD_{pooled} = \sqrt{\frac{(N_E - 1)SD_E^2 + (N_C - 1)SD_C^2}{N_E + N_C - 2}}$$

where N_E = number in the experimental group, N_C = number in the control group, SD_E = standard deviation of the experimental group and SD_C = standard deviation of the control group.

The formula for the pooled deviation then becomes (Muijs 2004: 136):

$$\frac{\text{(mean of experimental group – mean of control group)}}{\text{pooled standard deviation}}$$

where the pooled standard deviation = (standard deviation of group 1 + standard deviation of group 2).

There are several different calculations of effect size, for example (Richardson 1996; Capraro and Capraro 2002: 771): r^2, adjusted R^2, η^2, ω^2, Cramer's V, Kendall's W, Cohen's d, and Eta. Different kinds of statistical treatments use different effect size calculations. For example, the formula given by Muijs (2004) here yields the statistic termed Cohen's d. Further details of this, together with a facility which calculates it automatically, can be found at http://www.uccs.edu/~lbecker/psy590/escalc3.htm.

An effect size can lie between 0 to 1 (some formulae yield an effect size that is larger than 1 – see Coe 2000). In using Cohen's d:

0–0.20	= weak effect
0.21–0.50	= modest effect
0.51–1.00	= moderate effect
>1.00	= strong effect

In correlational data the coefficient of correlation is used as the effect size in conjunction with details of the direction of the association (i.e. a positive or negative correlation). The coefficient of correlation (effect size) is interpreted thus:

< 0 + / − 0.1	weak
< 0 + / − 0.3	modest
< 0 + / − 0.5	moderate
< 0 + / − 0.8	strong
≥ +/− 0.8	very strong

We provide more detail on interpreting correlation coefficients later in this chapter. However, Thompson (2001; 2002) argues forcibly against simplistic interpretations of effect size as 'small', 'medium' and 'large', as to do this commits the same folly of fixed benchmarks as that of statistical significance. He writes that 'if people interpret effect sizes with the same rigidity that $\alpha = .05$ has been used in statistical testing, we would merely be being stupid in another metric' (Thompson 2001: 82–3). Rather, he avers, it is important to avoid fixed benchmarks (i.e. cut-off points), and relate the effect sizes found to those of prior studies, confidence intervals and power analyses. Wright (2003: 125) also suggests that it is important to report the units of measurement of the effect size, for example in the units of measure of the original variables as well in standardized units (e.g. standard deviations), the latter being useful if different scales of measures are being used for the different variables.

We discussed *confidence intervals* in Chapter 4. It is the amount of the 'true population value of the parameter' (Wright 2003: 126), e.g. 90 per cent of the population, 95 per cent of the population, 99 per cent of the population. A confidence interval is reported as $1 - \alpha$, i.e. the level of likelihood that a score falls within a pre-specified range of scores (e.g. 95 per cent, 99 per cent likelihood). Software for calculating confidence intervals for many measures can be found at http://glass.ed.asu/stats/analysis/.

The *power of a test* is 'an estimate of the ability of the test to separate the effect size from random variation' (Gorard 2001: 14), the 'probability of rejecting a specific effect size for a specific sample size at a particular α level (i.e. the critical level to reject H_0) (Wright 2003: 126). Wright (2003) suggests that it should be a minimum of 80 per cent and to be typically with an α level at 5 per cent. Software for calculating power analysis can be found at http://www.psycho.uni_duesseldorf.de/aap/projects/gpower.

In calculating the effect size (Eta squared) for independent samples in a t-test (discussed later) the following formula can be used.

$$\text{Eta squared} = \frac{t^2}{t^2 + (N_1 + N_2 - 2)}$$

Here $t =$ the t-value (calculated by SPSS); $N_1 =$ the number in the sample of group one and $N_2 =$ the number in the sample of group 2. Let us take an example of the results of an evaluation item in which the two groups are leaders/senior management team (SMT) of schools, and teachers, (Boxes 24.16 and 24.17).

Here the t-value is 1.923, N_1 is 347 and N_2 is 653. Hence the formula is:

$$\frac{t^2}{t^2 + (N_1 + N_2 - 2)} = \frac{1.923^2}{1.923^2 + (347 + 653 - 2)}$$
$$= \frac{3.698}{3.698 + 998} = 0.0037$$

The guidance here from Cohen (1988) is that $0.01 =$ a very small effect; $0.06 =$ a moderate effect; and $0.14 =$ a very large effect. Here the result of 0.003 is a tiny effect, i.e. only 0.3 per cent of the variance in the variable 'How well learners are cared for, guided and supported' is explained by whether one is a leader/SMT member or a teacher.

For a paired sample t-test (discussed later) the effect size (Eta squared) is calculated by the following formula:

$$\text{Eta squared} = \frac{t^2}{t^2 + (N_1 - 1)}$$

Let us imagine that the same group of students had scored marks out of 100 in 'Maths' and 'Science' (Boxes 24.18 and 24.19).

Box 24.16
Mean and standard deviation in an effect size

	Group statistics				
	Who are you	N	Mean	SD	SE mean
How well learners are cared for, guided and supported	Leader/SMT member	347	8.37	2.085	0.112
	Teachers	653	8.07	2.462	0.096

Box 24.17
The Levene test for equality of variances

| | | Levene's test for equality of variances | | t-test for equality of means | | | | | 95 % confidence interval of the difference | |
		F	Sig.	t	df	Sig. (2-tailed)	Mean difference	SE difference	Lower	Upper
How well learners are cared for, guided and supported	Equal variances assumed	8.344	0.004	1.923	998	0.055	0.30	0.155	−0.006	0.603
	Equal variances not assumed			2.022	811.922	0.044	0.30	0.148	0.009	0.589

Independent samples test

The effect size can be worked out thus (using SPSS):

$$\frac{t^2}{t^2 + (N_1 - 1)} = \frac{16.588^2}{16.588^2 + (1000 - 1)}$$

$$= \frac{275.162}{275.162 + 999} = 0.216$$

In this example the effect size is 0.216, a very large effect, i.e. there was a very substantial difference between the scores of the two groups.

For analysis of variance (discussed later) the effect size is calculated thus:

$$\text{Eta squared} = \frac{\text{Sum of squares between groups}}{\text{Total sum of squares}}$$

In SPSS this is given as 'partial eta squared'. For example, let us imagine that we wish to compute the effect size of the difference between four groups of schools on mathematics performance in a public examination. The four groups of schools are: rural primary; rural secondary; urban primary; urban secondary. Analysis of variance yields the result shown in Box 24.20.

Working through the formula yields the following:

$$\frac{\text{Sum of squares between groups}}{\text{Total sum of squares}} = \frac{7078.619}{344344.8} = 0.021$$

Box 24.18
Mean and standard deviation in a paired sample test

Paired samples statistics

		Mean	N	SD	SE mean
Pair 1	Maths	81.71	1,000	23.412	0.740
	Science	67.26	1,000	27.369	0.865

The figure of 0.021 indicates a small effect size, i.e. that there is a small difference between the four groups in their mathematics performance (note that this is a much smaller difference than that indicated by the significance level of 0.006, which suggests a statistically highly significant difference between the four groups of schools).

In regression analysis (discussed later) the effect size of the predictor variables is given by the beta weightings. In interpreting effect size here Muijs (2004: 194) gives the following guidance:

0–0.1	weak effect
0.1–0.3	modest effect
0.3–0.5	moderate effect
>0.5	strong effect

Hedges (1981) and Hunter *et al.* (1982) suggest alternative equations to take account of

Box 24.19
Difference test for a paired sample

Paired samples test

Paired differences

		Mean	SD	SE mean	95 % confidence interval of the difference		t	df	Sig. (2-tailed)
					Lower	Upper			
Pair 1	Maths-Science	14.45	27.547	0.871	12.74	16.16	16.588	999	0.000

Box 24.20
Effect size in analysis of variance

ANOVA

Maths

	Sum of squares	df	Mean square	F	Sig.
Between groups	7078.619	3	2359.540	4.205	0.006
Within groups	337266.2	601	561.175		
Total	344344.8	604			

differential weightings due to sample size variations. The two most frequently used indices of effect sizes are standardized mean differences and correlations (Hunter *et al.* 1982: 373), although non-parametric statistics, e.g. the median, can be used. Lipsey (1992: 93–100) sets out a series of statistical tests for working on effect sizes, effect size means and homogeneity.

Muijs (2004: 126) indicates that a measure of effect size for cross-tabulations, instead of chi-square, should be *phi*, which is the square root of the calculated value of chi-square divided by the overall valid sample size. He gives an example: 'if chi-square = 14.810 and the sample size is 885 then phi = 14.810/885 = 0.0167 and then take the square root of this = 0.129'.

Effect sizes are susceptible to a range of influences. These include (Coe 2000):

- *Restricted range:* the smaller the range of scores, the greater is the possibility of a higher effect size, therefore it is important to use the standard

deviation of the whole population (and not just one group), i.e. a pooled standard deviation, in calculating the effect size. It is important to report the possible restricted range or sampling here (e.g. a group of highly able students rather than, for example, the whole ability range).
- *Non-normal distributions:* effect size usually assumes a normal distribution, so any non-normal distributions would have to be reported.
- *Measurement reliability:* the reliability (accuracy, stability and robustness) of the instrument being used (e.g. the longer the test, or the more items that are used to measure a factor, the more reliable it could be).

There are downloadable software programs available that will calculate effect size simply by the researcher keying in minimal amounts of data, for example:

- The Effect Size Generator by Grant Devilly: http://www.swin.edu.au/victims

- The Effect Size Calculator by Marley Watkins (including the calculation of Cohen's d and Hedges' unbiased d) (see also http://www. routledge.com/textbooks/9780415368780 – Chapter 24, file SPSS Manual 24.4).

More information on effect sizes can be found at: http://www.latrobe.edu.au/psy/esci and http://cemcentre.org/ebeuk/research/effectsize/ ESbrief.htm. (Kline 2004; Leech and Onwuegbuzie 2004).

The chi-square test

Difference testing is an important feature in understanding data and we address it more fully later. We can conduct a statistical test to investigate difference; it is the chi-square test (χ^2) (pronounced 'kigh', as in 'high'). We start with the null hypothesis that states that there is *no* statistically significant difference between, say, males and females in their liking for mathematics, and the onus on the data is *not* to support this. We then set the level of significance (α) that we wish to use for supporting or not supporting the null hypothesis; for example we could say 'Let $\alpha = 0.05$'.

The chi-square test measures the difference between a statistically generated expected result and an actual result to see if there is a statistically significant difference between them, i.e. to see if the frequencies observed are significant; it is a measure of 'goodness of fit' between an expected and an actual result or set of results (see http://www.routledge.com/textbooks/ 9780415368780 – Chapter 24, file 24.12.ppt). The expected result is based on a statistical process discussed below. The chi-square statistic addresses the notion of statistical significance, itself based on notions of probability. Here is not the place to go into the mathematics of the test, not least because computer packages automatically calculate the results. That said, the formula for calculating chi-square is

$$\chi^2 = \sum \frac{(O-E)^2}{E}$$

where

O = observed frequencies

E = expected frequencies

Σ = the sum of

In the hypothetical example above, say that the computer package (SPSS) tells us that the significance level is 0.016, i.e. the distribution of the data is not simply due to chance. We recall that the conventionally accepted minimum level of significance is usually 0.05, and the significance level of our data here is smaller than that, i.e. it is statistically significant. Hence we can suggest that the difference between the voting of the males and females is statistically significant and not just due to chance, i.e. there is a meaningful difference between the two groups. Hence the null hypothesis is not supported and the alternative hypothesis, that there is a statistically significant difference between the voting of the two groups, is supported.

One can report the results of the chi-square test thus, for example:

> When the chi-square statistic was calculated for the distribution of males and females on their liking for mathematics, a statistically significant difference was found between the males and the females ($\chi^2 = 14.51$, df = 2, $\rho = 0.01$).

The chi-square statistic is usually used with nominal data, and our example illustrates this. For a chi-square statistic, data are set into a contingency table, an example of which can be seen in Box 24.21, a 2 × 3 contingency table, i.e. two horizontal rows and three columns (contingency tables may contain more than this number of variables). The example in this figure presents data concerning sixty students' entry into science, arts and humanities, in a college, and whether the students are male or female (Morrison 1993: 132–4). The lower of the two figures in each cell is the number of actual students who have opted for the particular subjects (sciences, arts, humanities). The upper of the two figures in each cell is what might be expected purely by chance to be the number of

Box 24.21

A 2 × 3 contingency table for chi-square

	Science subjects	Arts subjects	Humanities subjects	
Males	7.6 14	8 4	8.4 6	24
Females	11.4 5	12 16	12.6 15	36
	19	20	21	60

students opting for each of the particular subjects. The figure is arrived at by statistical computation, hence the decimal fractions for the figures. What is of interest to the researcher is whether the actual distribution of subject choice by males and females differs significantly from that which could occur by chance variation in the population of college entrants (Box 24.21).

The researcher begins with the null hypothesis that there is no statistically significant difference between the actual results noted and what might be expected to occur by chance in the wider population. When the chi-square statistic is calculated, if the observed, actual distribution differs from that which might be expected to occur by chance alone, then the researcher has to determine whether that difference is statistically significant, i.e. not to support the null hypothesis.

In our example of sixty students' choices, the chi-square formula yields a final chi-square value of 14.64. This we refer to the tables of the distribution of chi-square (see Table 4 in The Appendices of Statistical Tables) to determine whether the derived chi-square value indicates a statistically significant difference from that occurring by chance. Part of the chi-square distribution table is shown here.

Degrees of freedom	Level of significance	
	0.05	0.01
3	7.81	11.34
4	9.49	13.28
5	11.07	15.09
6	12.59	16.81

The researcher will see that the 'degrees of freedom' (a mathematical construct that is related

to the number of restrictions that have been placed on the data) have to be identified. In many cases, to establish the degrees of freedom, one simply takes 1 away from the total number of rows of the contingency table and 1 away from the total number of columns and adds them; in this case it is $(2-1) + (3-1) = 3$ degrees of freedom. Degrees of freedom are discussed in the next section. (Other formulae for ascertaining degrees of freedom hold that the number is the total number of cells minus one – this is the method set out later in this chapter.) The researcher looks along the table from the entry for the three degrees of freedom and notes that the derived chi-square value calculated (14.64) is statistically significant at the 0.01 level, i.e. is higher than the required 11.34, indicating that the results obtained – the distributions of the actual data – could not have occurred simply by chance. The null hypothesis is not supported at the 0.01 level of significance. Interpreting the specific numbers of the contingency table (Box 24.21) in educational rather than statistical terms, noting the low incidence of females in the science subjects and the high incidence of females in the arts and humanities subjects, and the high incidence of males in the science subjects and the low incidence of males in the arts and humanities, the researcher would say that this distribution is statistically significant – suggesting, perhaps, that the college needs to consider action possibly to encourage females into science subjects and males into arts and humanities.

The chi-square test is one of the most widely used tests, and is applicable to nominal data in particular. More powerful tests are available for ordinal, interval and ratio data, and we discuss these separately. However, one has to be cautious of the limitations of the chi-square test. Look at the example in Box 24.22.

If one were to perform the chi-square test on this table then one would have to be extremely cautious. The chi-square statistic assumes that no more than 20 per cent of the total number of cells contain fewer than five cases. In the example here we have one cell with four cases, another with three, and another with only one case, i.e.

Box 24.22

A 2 × 5 contingency table for chi-square

	Music	Physics	Maths	German	Spanish		
Males	7	11	25	4	3	50	
	14.0%	22.0%	50%	8.0%	6%	100%	
Females	17	38	73	12	1	141	
	12.1%	27.0%	52%	8.5%	0.7%	100%	
Total	24	49	98	16	4	191	
	12.6%	25.7%	51%	8.4%	2.1%	100%	

three cells out of the ten (two rows – males and females – with five cells in each for each of the rating categories). This means that 30 per cent of the cells contain fewer than five cases; even though a computer will calculate a chi-square statistic, it means that the result is unreliable. This highlights the point made in Chapter 4 about sampling, that the subsample size has to be large. For example, if each category here were to contain five cases then it would mean that the minimum sample size would be fifty (10 × 5), assuming that the data are evenly spread. In the example here, even though the sample size is much larger (191) it still does not guarantee that the 20 per cent rule will be observed, as the data are unevenly spread.

Because of the need to ensure that at least 80 per cent of the cells of a chi-square contingency table contain more than five cases if confidence is to be placed in the results, it may not be feasible to calculate the chi-square statistic if only a small sample is being used. Hence the researcher would tend to use this statistic for larger-scale survey data. Other tests could be used if the problem of low cell frequencies obtains, e.g. the binomial test and, more widely used, the Fisher exact test (Cohen and Holliday 1996: 218–20). The required minimum number of cases in each cell renders the chi-square statistic problematic, and, apart from with nominal data, there are alternative statistics that can be calculated and which overcome this problem (e.g. the Mann-Whitney, Wilcoxon, Kruskal-Wallis and Friedman tests for non-parametric – ordinal – data, and the t-test and analysis of variance test for parametric – interval and ratio – data) (see http://www.routledge.com/textbooks/

9780415368780 – Chapter 24, file SPSS Manual 24.5).

Methods of analysing data cast into 2 × 2 contingency tables by means of the chi-square test are generally well covered in research methods books. Increasingly, however, educational data are classified in multiple rather than two-dimensional formats. Everitt (1977) provides a useful account of methods for analysing multidimensional tables.

Two significance tests for very small samples are give in the accompanying web site: http://www.routledge.com/textbooks/9780415368780 – Chapter 24, file 24.3.doc.

Degrees of freedom

The chi-square statistic introduces the term *degrees of freedom*. Gorard (2001: 233) suggests that 'the degrees of freedom is the number of scores we need to know before we can calculate the rest'. Cohen and Holliday (1996) explain the term clearly:

Suppose we have to select any five numbers. We have complete freedom of choice as to what the numbers are. So, we have five degrees of freedom. Suppose however we are then told that the five numbers must have a total value of 25. We will have complete freedom of choice to select four numbers but the fifth will be dependent on the other four. Let's say that the first four numbers we select are 7, 8, 9, and 10, which total 34, then if the total value of the five numbers is to be 25, the fifth number must be −9.

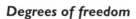

$$7 + 8 + 9 + 10 - 9 = 25$$

A restriction has been placed on one of the observations; only four are free to vary; the fifth has lost its freedom. In our example then df = 4, that is $N - 1 = 5 - 1 = 4$.

Suppose now that we are told to select any five numbers, the first two of which have to total 9, and the total value of all five has to be 25. One restriction is apparent when we wish the total of the first two numbers to be 9. Another restriction is apparent in the requirement that all five numbers must total 25. In other words we have lost two degrees of freedom in our example. It leaves us with df = 3, that is, $N - 2 = 5 - 2 = 3$.

(Cohen and Holliday 1996: 113)

For a cross-tabulation (a contingency table), degrees of freedom refer to the freedom with which the researcher is able to assign values to the cells, given fixed marginal totals, usually given as (number of rows − 1) + (number of columns − 1). There are many variants of this, and readers will need to consult more detailed texts to explore this issue. We do not dwell on degrees of freedom here, as it is automatically calculated and addressed in subsequent calculations by most statistical software packages such as SPSS.

Measuring association

Much educational research is concerned with establishing interrelationships among variables. We may wish to know, for example, how delinquency is related to social class background; whether an association exists between the number of years spent in full-time education and subsequent annual income; whether there is a link between personality and achievement. What, for example, is the relationship, if any, between membership of a public library and social class status? Is there a relationship between social class background and placement in different strata of the secondary school curriculum? Is there a relationship between gender and success or failure in 'first time' driving test results?

There are several simple measures of association readily available to the researcher to help her test these sorts of relationships. We have selected the most widely used ones here and set them out in Box 24.23.

Of these, the two most commonly used correlations are the Spearman rank order correlation for ordinal data and the Pearson product-moment correlation for interval and ratio data. At this point it is pertinent to say a few words about some of the terms used in Box 24.23 to describe the nature of variables. Cohen and Holliday (1982; 1996) provide worked examples of the appropriate use and limitations of the correlational techniques outlined in Box 24.23, together with other measures of association such as Kruskal's *gamma*, Somer's *d*, and Guttman's *lambda* (see http://www.routledge.com/textbooks/ 9780415368780 – Chapter 24, file 24.13.ppt and SPSS Manual 24.6).

Look at the words used at the top of Box 24.23 to explain the nature of variables in connection with the measure called the Pearson product moment, *r*. The variables, we learn, are 'continuous' and at the 'interval' or the 'ratio' scale of measurement.

A continuous variable is one that, theoretically at least, can take any value between two points on a scale. Weight, for example, is a continuous variable; so too is time, so also is height. Weight, time and height can take on any number of possible values between nought and infinity, the feasibility of measuring them across such a range being limited only by the variability of suitable measuring instruments.

Turning again to Box 24.23, we read in connection with the second measure shown there (rank order or Kendall's tau) that the two continuous variables are at the ordinal scale of measurement.

The variables involved in connection with the phi coefficient measure of association (halfway down Box 24.23) are described as 'true dichotomies' and at the nominal scale of measurement. Truly dichotomous variables (such as sex or driving test result) can take only two values (male or female; pass or fail).

To conclude our explanation of terminology, readers should note the use of the term 'discrete variable' in the description of the third correlation ratio (eta) in Box 24.23. We said earlier that a continuous variable can take on any value between two points on a scale. A discrete variable, however,

Box 24.23
Common measures of relationship

Measure	Nature of variables	Comment
Spearman's rho	Two ordinal variables	Relationship linear
Pearson product moment r	Two continuous variables; interval or ratio scale	Relationship linear
Rank order or Kendall's tau	Two continuous variables; ordinal scale	
Correlation ratio η (eta)	One variable continuous; other either continuous or discrete	Relationship nonlinear
Intraclass	One variable continuous other discrete; interval or ratio scale	Purpose: to determine within-group similarity
Biserial r_{bis} Point biserial $r_{pt\ bis}$	One variable continuous; other continuous but dichotomized, r_{bis} or true dichotomy $r_{pt\ bis}$	Index of item discrimination (used in item analysis)
Phi coefficient φ	Two true dichotomies; nominal or ordinal series	
Partial correlation $r_{12.3}$	Three or more continuous variables	Purpose: to determine relationship between two variables, with effect of third held constant
Multiple correlation $r_{1.234}$	Three or more continuous variables	Purpose: to predict one variable from a linear weighted combination of two or more independent variables
Kendall's coefficient of concordance (W)	Three or more continuous variables; ordinal series	Purpose: to determine the degree of (say, inter-rater) agreement

Source: Mouly 1978

can take on only numerals or values that are specific points on a scale. The number of players in a football team is a discrete variable. It is usually 11; it could be fewer than 11, but it could never be $7\frac{1}{4}$!

The percentage difference

The percentage difference is a simple asymmetric measure of association. An *asymmetric* measure is a measure of *one-way association*. That is to say, it estimates the extent to which one phenomenon implies the other but not vice versa. Gender, as we shall see shortly, may imply driving test success or failure. The association could never be the other way round! Measures that are concerned with the extent to which two phenomena imply each other are referred to as *symmetric* measures. Box 24.24 reports the percentage of public library members by their social class origin.

Box 24.24
Percentage of public library members by their social class origin

Public library membership	Social class status	
	Middle class	Working class
Member	86	37
Non-member	14	63
Total	100	100

What can we discover from the data set out in Box 24.24?

By comparing percentages in different columns of the same row, we can see that 49 per cent more middle-class persons are members of public libraries than working-class persons. By comparing percentages in different rows of the same columns we can see that 72 per cent more middle-class persons are members rather than non-members. The data suggest, do they not, an association between the social class status of individuals and their membership of public libraries.

A second way of making use of the data in Box 24.24 involves the computing of a *percentage ratio* (%R). Look, for example, at the data in the second row of Box 24.24. By dividing 63 by 14 (%R = 4.5) we can say that four and a half times as many working-class persons are not members of public libraries as are middle-class persons.

The *percentage difference* ranges from 0 per cent when there is complete independence between two phenomena to 100 per cent when there is complete association in the direction being examined. It is straightforward to calculate and simple to understand. Notice, however, that the percentage difference as we have defined it can be employed only when there are only two categories in the variable along which we percentage and only two categories in the variable in which we compare. In SPSS, using the 'Crosstabs' command can yield percentages, and we indicate this in the web site manual that accompanies this volume.

In connection with this issue, on the accompanying web site we discuss the phi coefficient, the correlation coefficient tetrachoric r (r_t), the contingency coefficient C, and combining independent significance tests of partial relations, see http://www.routledge.com/textbooks/9780415368780 – Chapter 24, file 24.4.doc.

Explaining correlations

In our discussion of the principal correlational techniques shown in Box 24.23, three are of special interest to us and these form the basis of much of the rest of the chapter. They are the Pearson product moment correlation coefficient, multiple correlation and partial correlation.

Correlational techniques are generally intended to answer three questions about two variables or two sets of data. First, 'Is there a relationship between the two variables (or sets of data)?' If the answer to this question is 'Yes', then two other questions follow: 'What is the direction of the relationship?' and 'What is the magnitude?'

Relationship in this context refers to any tendency for the two variables (or sets of data) to vary consistently. Pearson's product moment coefficient of correlation, one of the best known measures of association, is a statistical value ranging from -1.0 to $+1.0$ and expresses this relationship in quantitative form. The coefficient is represented by the symbol r.

Where the two variables (or sets of data) fluctuate in the same direction, i.e. as one increases so does the other, or as one decreases so does the other, a positive relationship is said to exist. Correlations reflecting this pattern are prefaced with a plus sign to indicate the positive nature of the relationship. Thus, $+1.0$ would indicate perfect positive correlation between two factors, as with the radius and diameter of a circle, and $+0.80$ a high positive correlation, as between academic achievement and intelligence, for example. Where the sign has been omitted, a plus sign is assumed.

A negative correlation or relationship, on the other hand, is to be found when an increase in one variable is accompanied by a decrease in the other variable. Negative correlations are prefaced with a minus sign. Thus, -1.0 would represent perfect negative correlation, as between the number of errors children make on a spelling test and their score on the test, and -0.30 a low negative correlation, as between absenteeism and intelligence, say. There is no other meaning to the signs used; they indicate nothing more than which pattern holds for any two variables (or sets of data).

Generally speaking, researchers tend to be more interested in the magnitude of an obtained correlation than they are in its direction. Correlational procedures have been developed so that no relationship whatever between two variables is represented by zero (or 0.00), as between body weight and intelligence, possibly. This means that people's performance on one variable is totally unrelated to their performance on a second variable. If they are high on one, for example, they are just as likely to be high or low on the other. Perfect correlations of $+1.00$ or -1.00 are rarely found and, as we shall see, most coefficients of correlation in social research are around +0.50 or less. The correlation coefficient may be seen then as an indication of the predictability of one variable given the other: it is an indication of covariation. The relationship between two variables can be examined visually by plotting the paired measurements on graph paper with each pair of observations being represented by a point. The resulting arrangement of points is known as a scatterplot and enables us to assess graphically the degree of relationship between the characteristics being measured. Box 24.25 gives some examples of scatterplots in the field of educational research (see http://www.routledge.com/textbooks/9780415368780 – Chapter 24, file 24.14.ppt).

While correlations are widely used in research, and they are straightforward to calculate and to interpret, the researcher must be aware of four caveats in undertaking correlational analysis:

- Do not assume that correlations imply causal relationships (i.e. simply because having large hands appears to correlate with having large feet does not imply that having large hands causes one to have large feet).
- There is a need to be alert to a Type I error – not supporting the null hypothesis when it is in fact true.
- There is a need to be alert to a Type II error – supporting the null hypothesis when it is in fact not true.
- Statistical significance must be accompanied by an indication of effect size.

In SPSS a typical printout of a correlation coefficient is given in Box 24.26.

In this fictitious example using 1,000 cases there are four points to note:

- The cells of data to the right of the cells containing the figure 1 are the same as the cells to the left of the cells containing the figure 1, i.e. there is a mirror image, and, if very many more variables were being correlated then, in fact, one would have to decide whether to look at only the variables to the right of the cell with the figure 1 (the perfect correlation, since

it is one variable being correlated with itself), or to look at the cells to the left of the figure 1.
- In each cell where one variable is being correlated with a different variable there are three figures: the top figure gives the correlation coefficient, the middle figure gives the significance level, and the lowest figure gives the sample size.
- SPSS marks with an asterisk those correlations which are statistically significant.
- All of the correlations are positive, since there are no negative coefficients given.

What these tables give us is the magnitude of the correlation (the coefficient), the direction of the correlation (positive and negative), and the significance level. The correlation coefficient can be taken as the effect size. The significance level (as mentioned earlier) is calculated automatically by SPSS, based on the coefficient and the sample size: the greater the sample size, the lower the coefficient of correlation has to be in order to be statistically significant, and, by contrast, the smaller the sample size, the greater the coefficient of correlation has to be in order to be statistically significant.

In reporting correlations one has to report the test used, the coefficient, the direction of the correlation (positive or negative), and the significance level (if considered appropriate). For example, one could write:

Using the Pearson-product moment correlation, a statistically significant correlation was found between students' attendance at school and their examination performance ($r = 0.87$, $\rho = 0.035$). Those students who attended school the most tended to have the best examination performance, and those who attended the least tended to have the lowest examination performance.

Alternatively, there may be occasions when it is important to report when a correlation has *not* been found, for example:

There was no statistically significant correlation found between the amount of time spent on homework and examination performance ($r = 0.37$, $\rho = 0.43$).

Box 24.25
Correlation scatterplots

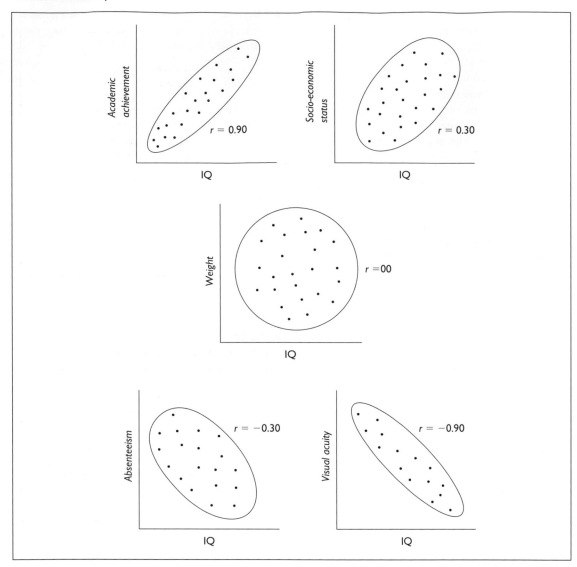

Source: Tuckman 1972

In both of these examples of reporting, exact significance levels have been given, assuming that SPSS has calculated these. An alternative way of reporting the significance levels (as appropriate) are: $\rho < 0.05$; $\rho < 0.01$; $\rho < 0.001$; $\rho = 0.05$; $\rho = 0.01$. In the case of statistical significance not having been found one could report this as $\rho > 0.05$ or $\rho = \text{NS}$.

Box 24.26
A Pearson product-moment correlation

		The attention given to teaching and learning at the school	How well students apply themselves to learning	Discussion and review by educators of the quality of teaching, learning and classroom practice
The attention given to teaching and learning at the school	Pearson correlation	1.000	0.060	0.066*
	Sig. (2-tailed)	.	0.058	0.036
	N	1000	1000	1000
How well students apply themselves to learning	Pearson correlation	0.060	1.000	0.585**
	Sig. (2-tailed)	0.058	.	0.000
	N	1000	1000	1000
Discussion and review by educators of the quality of teaching, learning and classroom practice	Pearson correlation	0.066*	0.585**	1.000
	Sig. (2-tailed)	0.036	0.000	.
	N	1000	1000	1000

* Correlation is significant at the 0.05 level (2-tailed).
** Correlation is significant at the 0.01 level (2-tailed).

Curvilinearity

The correlations discussed so far have assumed linearity, that is, the more we have of one property, the more (or less) we have of another property, in a direct positive or negative relationship. A straight line can be drawn through the points on the scatterplots (a regression line). However, linearity cannot always be assumed. Consider the case, for example, of stress: a little stress might enhance performance ('setting the adrenalin running') positively, whereas too much stress might lead to a downturn in performance. Where stress enhances performance there is a positive correlation, but when stress debilitates performance there is a negative correlation. The result is not a straight line of correlation (indicating linearity) but a curved line (indicating curvilinearity). This can be shown graphically (Box 24.27). It is assumed here, for the purposes of the example, that muscular strength can be measured on a single scale. It is clear from the graph that muscular strength increases from birth until fifty years, and thereafter it declines as muscles degenerate. There is a positive correlation between age and muscular

Box 24.27
A line diagram to indicate curvilinearity

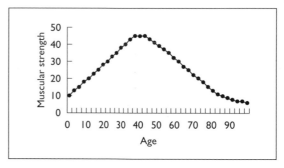

strength on the left-hand side of the graph and a negative correlation on the right-hand side of the graph, i.e. a curvilinear correlation can be observed.

Hopkins *et al.* (1996: 92) provide another example of curvilinearity: room temperature and comfort. Raising the temperature a little can make for greater comfort – a positive correlation – while raising it too greatly can make for discomfort – a negative correlation. Many correlational statistics assume linearity (e.g. the Pearson product-moment correlation). However, rather than using correlational statistics arbitrarily or blindly, the researcher will need to consider whether, in fact, linearity is a reasonable assumption to make, or whether a curvilinear relationship is more appropriate (in which case more sophisticated statistics will be needed, e.g. η ('eta') (Cohen and Holliday 1996: 84; Glass and Hopkins 1996, section 8.7; Fowler *et al.* 2000: 81–89) or mathematical procedures will need to be applied to transform non-linear relations into linear relations. Examples of curvilinear relationships might include:

- pressure from the principal and teacher performance
- pressure from the teacher and student achievement
- degree of challenge and student achievement
- assertiveness and success
- age and muscular strength
- age and physical control
- age and concentration
- age and sociability
- age and cognitive abilities.

Hopkins *et al.* (1996) suggest that the variable 'age' frequently has a curvilinear relationship with other variables, and also point out that poorly constructed tests can give the appearance of curvilinearity if the test is too easy (a 'ceiling effect' where most students score highly) or if it is too difficult, but that this curvilinearity is, in fact, spurious, as the test does not demonstrate sufficient item difficulty or discriminability (Hopkins *et al.* 1996: 92).

In planning correlational research, then, attention will need to be given to whether linearity or curvilinearity is to be assumed.

Coefficients of correlation

The coefficient of correlation, then, tells us something about the relations between two variables. Other measures exist, however, which allow us to specify relationships when more than two variables are involved. These are known as measures of 'multiple correlation' and 'partial correlation'.

Multiple correlation measures indicate the degree of association between three or more variables simultaneously. We may want to know, for example, the degree of association between delinquency, social class background and leisure facilities. Or we may be interested in finding out the relationship between academic achievement, intelligence and neuroticism. Multiple correlation, or 'regression' as it is sometimes called, indicates the degree of association between n variables. It is related not only to the correlations of the independent variable with the dependent variables, but also to the intercorrelations between the dependent variables.

Partial correlation aims at establishing the degree of association between two variables after the influence of a third has been controlled or partialled out. Guilford and Fruchter (1973) define a partial correlation between two variables as one which nullifies the effects of a third variable (or a number of variables) on the variables being correlated. They give the example of correlation between the height and weight of boys in a group whose age varies, where the correlation would be higher than the correlation between height and weight in a group comprised of boys of only the same age. Here the reason is clear – because some boys will be older they will be heavier and taller. Age, therefore, is a factor that increases the correlation between height and weight. Of course, even with age held constant, the correlation would still be positive and significant because, regardless of age, taller boys often tend to be heavier.

Consider, too, the relationship between success in basketball and previous experience in the game. Suppose, also, that the presence of a third factor, the height of the players, was known to have an important influence on the other two factors. The use of partial correlation techniques would enable a measure of the two primary variables to be achieved, freed from the influence of the secondary variable.

Correlational analysis is simple and involves collecting two or more scores on the same group of subjects and computing correlation coefficients.

Many useful studies have been based on this simple design. Those involving more complex relationships, however, utilize multiple and partial correlations in order to provide a clearer picture of the relationships being investigated.

One final point: it is important to stress again that correlations refer to measures of association and do not necessarily indicate causal relationships between variables. Correlation does not imply cause.

Interpreting the correlation coefficient

Once a correlation coefficient has been computed, there remains the problem of interpreting it. A question often asked in this connection is how large should the coefficient be for it to be meaningful. The question may be approached in three ways: by examining the strength of the relationship, by examining the statistical significance of the relationship and by examining the square of the correlation coefficient.

Inspection of the numerical value of a correlation coefficient will yield clear indication of the strength of the relationship between the variables in question. Low or near zero values indicate weak relationships, while those nearer to +1 or −1 suggest stronger relationships. Imagine, for instance, that a measure of a teacher's success in the classroom after five years in the profession is correlated with his or her final school experience grade as a student and that it was found that $r = +0.19$. Suppose now that the teacher's score on classroom success is correlated with a measure of need for professional achievement and that this yielded a correlation of 0.65. It could be concluded that there is a stronger relationship between success and professional achievement scores than between success and final student grade.

Where a correlation coefficient has been derived from a sample and one wishes to use it as a basis for inference about the parent population, the statistical significance of the obtained correlation must be considered. Statistical significance, when applied to a correlation coefficient, indicates whether or not the correlation is different from zero at a given level of confidence. As we have seen earlier, a statistically significant correlation is indicative of an actual relationship rather than one due entirely to chance. The level of statistical significance of a correlation is determined to a great extent by the number of cases upon which the correlation is based. Thus, the greater the number of cases, the smaller the correlation need be to be significant at a given level of confidence.

Exploratory relationship studies are generally interpreted with reference to their statistical significance, whereas prediction studies depend for their efficacy on the strength of the correlation coefficients. These need to be considerably higher than those found in exploratory relationship studies and for this reason rarely invoke the concept of significance.

The third approach to interpreting a coefficient is provided by examining the square of the coefficient of correlation, r^2. This shows the proportion of variance in one variable that can be attributed to its linear relationship with the second variable. In other words, it indicates the amount the two variables have in common. If, for example, two variables A and B have a correlation of 0.50, then $(0.50)^2$ or 0.25 of the variation shown by the B scores can be attributed to the tendency of B to vary linearly with A. Box 24.28 shows graphically the common variance between reading grade and arithmetic grade having a correlation of 0.65.

There are three cautions to be borne in mind when one is interpreting a correlation coefficient.

Box 24.28

Visualization of correlation of 0.65 between reading grade and arithmetic grade

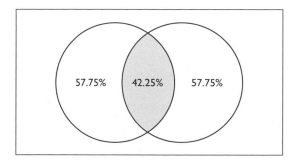

Source: Fox 1969

First, a coefficient is a simple number and must not be interpreted as a percentage. A correlation of 0.50, for instance, does not mean 50 per cent relationship between the variables. Further, a correlation of 0.50 does not indicate twice as much relationship as that shown by a correlation of 0.25. A correlation of 0.50 actually indicates more than twice the relationship shown by a correlation of 0.25. In fact, as coefficients approach $+1$ or -1, a difference in the absolute values of the coefficients becomes more important than the same numerical difference between lower correlations would be.

Second, a correlation does not necessarily imply a cause-and-effect relationship between two factors, as we have previously indicated. It should not therefore be interpreted as meaning that one factor is causing the scores on the other to be as they are. There are invariably other factors influencing both variables under consideration. Suspected cause-and-effect relationships would have to be confirmed by subsequent experimental study.

Third, a correlation coefficient is not to be interpreted in any absolute sense. A correlational value for a given sample of a population may not necessarily be the same as that found in another sample from the same population. Many factors influence the value of a given correlation coefficient and if researchers wish to extrapolate to the populations from which they drew their samples they will then have to test the significance of the correlation.

We now offer some general guidelines for interpreting correlation coefficients. They are based on Borg's (1963) analysis and assume that the correlations relate to 100 or more subjects.

Correlations ranging from 0.20 to 0.35

Correlations within this range show only very slight relationship between variables although they may be statistically significant. A correlation of 0.20 shows that only 4 per cent ($\{0.20 \times 0.20\} \times 100$) of the variance is common to the two measures. Whereas correlations at this level may have limited meaning in exploratory relationship research, they are of no value in either individual or group prediction studies.

Correlations ranging from 0.35 to 0.65

Within this range, correlations are statistically significant beyond the 1 per cent level. When correlations are around 0.40, crude group prediction may be possible. As Borg (1963) notes, correlations within this range are useful, however, when combined with other correlations in a multiple regression equation. Combining several correlations in this range can in some cases yield individual predictions that are correct within an acceptable margin of error. Correlations at this level used singly are of little use for individual prediction because they yield only a few more correct predictions than could be accomplished by guessing or by using some chance selection procedure.

Correlations ranging from 0.65 to 0.85

Correlations within this range make possible group predictions that are accurate enough for most purposes. Nearer the top of the range, group predictions can be made very accurately, usually predicting the proportion of successful candidates in selection problems within a very small margin of error. Near the top of this correlation range individual predictions can be made that are considerably more accurate than would occur if no such selection procedures were used.

Correlations over 0.85

Correlations as high as this indicate a close relationship between the two variables correlated. A correlation of 0.85 indicates that the measure used for prediction has about 72 per cent variance in common with the performance being predicted. Prediction studies in education very rarely yield correlations this high. When correlations at this level are obtained, however, they are very useful for either individual or group prediction.

Regression analysis

Regression analysis enables the researcher to predict 'the specific value of one variable when we know or assume values of the other variable(s)' (Cohen and Holliday 1996: 88). It is a way of modelling the relationship between variables. We concern ourselves here with simple linear regression and multiple regression (see http://www.routledge.com/textbooks/9780415368780 – Chapter 24, file SPSS Manual 24.7).

Simple linear regression

In simple linear regression the model includes one explanatory variable (the independent variable) and one explained variable (the dependent variable) (see http://www.routledge.com/textbooks/9780415368780 – Chapter 24, file 24.15.ppt). For example, we may wish to see the effect of hours of study on levels of achievement in an examination, to be able to see how much improvement will be made to an examination mark by a given number of hours of study. Hours of study is the independent variable and level of achievement is the dependent variable. Conventionally, as in the example in Box 24.29, one places the independent variable in the vertical axis and the dependent variable in the horizontal axis. In the example in Box 24.29, we have taken 50 cases of hours of study and student performance, and have constructed a scatterplot to show the distributions (SPSS performs this function at the click of two or three keys). We have also constructed a line of best fit (SPSS will do this easily) to indicate the relationship between the two variables. The line of best fit is the closest straight line that can be constructed to take account of variance in the scores, and strives to have the same number of cases above it and below it and making each point as close to the line as possible; for example, one can see that some scores are very close to the line and others are some distance away. There is a formula for its calculation, but we do not explore that here.

One can observe that the greater the number of hours spent in studying, generally the greater is the level of achievement. This is akin to correlation. The line of best fit indicates not only that there is a positive relationship, but also that

Box 24.29
A scatterplot with the regression line

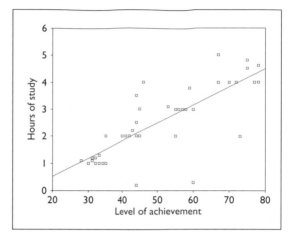

the relationship is strong (the slope of the line is quite steep). However, where regression departs from correlation is that regression provides an exact prediction of the value – the amount – of one variable when one knows the value of the other. One could read off the level of achievement, for example, if one were to study for two hours (43 marks out of 80) or for four hours (72 marks out of 80), of course, taking no account of variance. To help here scatterplots (e.g. in SPSS) can insert grid lines, for example (Box 24.30).

It is dangerous to predict *outside* the limits of the line; simple regression is to be used only to calculate values *within* the limits of the actual line, and not beyond it. One can observe, also, that though it is possible to construct a straight line of best fit (SPSS does this automatically), some of the data points lie close to the line and some lie a long way from the line; the distance of the data points from the line is termed the residuals, and this would have to be commented on in any analysis (there is a statistical calculation to address this but we do not go into it here).

Where the line strikes the vertical axis is named the *intercept*. We return to this later, but at this stage we note that the line does not go through the origin but starts a little way up the vertical

Box 24.30

A scatterplot with grid lines and regression line

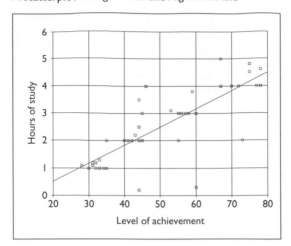

line. In fact this is all calculated automatically by SPSS.

Let us look at a typical SPSS output here (Box 24.31).

This table provides the R square. The R square tells us how much variance in the dependent variable is explained by the independent variable in the calculation. First, it gives us an R square value of 0.632, which indicates that 63.2 per cent of the variance is accounted for in the model, which is high. The adjusted R square is more accurate, and we advocate its use, as it automatically takes account of the number of independent variables. The adjusted R square is usually smaller than the unadjusted R square, as it also takes account of the fact that one is looking at

Box 24.31

A summary of the R, R square and adjusted R square in regression analysis

Model summary				
Model	R	R square	Adjusted R square	SE of the estimate
I	0.795[a]	0.632	0.625	9.200

a. Predictors: (Constant), Hours of study

a sample rather than the whole population. Here the adjusted R square is 0.625, and this, again, shows that, in the regression model that we have constructed, the independent variable accounts for 62.5 per sent of the variance in the dependent variable, which is high, i.e. our regression model is robust. Muijs (2004: 165) suggests that, for a goodness of fit with an adjusted R square:

<0.1:	poor fit
0.11–0.3:	modest fit
0.31–0.5:	moderate fit
>0.5:	strong fit

Second, SPSS then calculates the analysis of variance (ANOVA) (Box 24.32). At this stage we will not go into all of the calculations here (typically SPSS prints out far more than researchers may need; for a discussion of df (degrees of freedom) we refer readers to the earlier section). We go to the final column here, marked 'Sig.'; this is the significance level, and, because the significance is 0.000, we have a very statistically significant relationship (stronger than 0.001) between the independent variable (hours of study) and the dependent variable (level of achievement) (Box 24.32).

This tells us that it is useful to proceed with the analysis, as it contains important results. SPSS then gives us a table of coefficients, both unstandardized and standardized. We advise to opt for the standardized coefficients, the Beta weightings. The Beta weight (β) is the amount of standard deviation unit of change in the dependent variable for each standard deviation unit of change in the independent variable. In the example in Box 24.33 the Beta weighting is 0.795; this tell us that, for every standard deviation unit change in the independent variable (hours of study), the dependent variable (level of achievement) will rise by 0.795 (79.5 per cent) of one standard deviation unit, i.e. for every one unit rise in the independent variable there is just over three-quarters of a unit rise in the dependent variable. This also explains why the slope of the line of best fit is steep but not quite 45 degrees – each unit of one is worth only 79.5 per sent of a unit of the other (Box 24.33).

Box 24.32

Significance level in regression analysis

	ANOVA[b]					
Model		Sum of squares	df	Mean square	F	Sig.
I	Regression	6988.208	I	6988.208	82.573	0.000[a]
	Residual	4062.292	48	84.631		
	Total	11050.500	49			

a. Predictors: (Constant), Hours of study
b. Dependent variable: Level of achievement

Box 24.33

The beta coefficient in a regression analysis

	Coefficients[a]					
		Unstandardized coefficients		Standardized coefficients		
Model		B	SE	Beta	t	Sig.
I	(Constant)	26.322	2.982		8.828	0.000
	Hours of study	9.567	1.053	.795	9.087	0.000

a. Dependent variable: Level of achievement

Box 24.33 also indicates that the results are highly statistically significant (the 'Sig.' column (0.000) reports a significance level stronger than 0.001). Note also that Box 24.33 indicates a 'constant'; this is an indication of where the line of best fit strikes the vertical axis, the intercept; the constant is sometimes taken out of any subsequent analyses.

In reporting the example of regression one could use a form of words thus:

a scattergraph of the regression of hours of study on levels of achievement indicates a linear positive relationship between the two variables, with an adjusted R square of .625. A standardized beta coefficient of .795 is found for the variable 'hours of study', which is statistically significant ($\rho < 0.001$).

Multiple regression

In linear regression we were able to calculate the effect of one independent variable on one dependent variable. However, it is often useful to

be able to calculate the effects of two or more independent variables on a dependent variable. Multiple regression enables us to predict and weight the relationship between two or more *explanatory* – independent – variables and an *explained* – dependent – variable. We know from the previous example that the Beta weighting (β) gives us an indication of how many standard deviation units will be changed in the dependent variable for each standard deviation unit of change in each of the independent variables. Let us take a worked example. An examination mark may be the outcome of study time and intelligence, i.e. the formula is (see http://www.routledge.com/textbooks/ 9780415368780 – Chapter 24, file 24.16.ppt):

Examination mark $= \beta$ study time $+ \beta$ intelligence

Let us say that the β for study time is calculated by SPSS to be 0.65, and the β for intelligence is calculated to be 0.30. These are the relative weightings of the two independent variables. We wish to see how many marks in the examination a student will obtain who has an intelligence score of 110 and who studies for 30 hours per week. The formula becomes:

$$\text{Examination mark} = (0.65 \times 30) + (0.30 \times 110)$$

$$= 19.5 + 33 = 52.5$$

If the same student studies for 40 hours then the examination mark could be predicted to be:

$$\text{Examination mark} = (0.65 \times 40) + (0.30 \times 110)$$

$$= 26 + 33 = 59$$

This enables the researcher to see exactly the predicted effects of a particular independent variable on a dependent variable, when other independent variables are also present. In SPSS the constant is also calculated and this can be included in the analysis, to give the following, for example:

$$\text{Examination mark} = \text{constant} + \beta \text{ study time}$$

$$+ \beta \text{ intelligence}$$

Let us give an example with SPSS of more than two independent variables. Let us imagine that we wish to see how much improvement will be made to an examination mark by a given number of hours of study together with measured intelligence (for example, IQ) and level of interest in the subject studied. We know from the previous example that the Beta weighting (β) gives us an indication of how many standard deviation units will be changed in the dependent variable for each standard deviation unit of change in each of the independent variables. The equation is:

Level of achievement in the examination

$$= \text{constant} + \beta \text{ Hours of study} + \beta \text{ IQ}$$

$$+ \beta \text{ Level of interest in the subject.}$$

The constant is calculated automatically by SPSS. Each of the three independent variables – hours of study, IQ and level of interest in the subject – has its own Beta (β) weighting in relation to the dependent variable: level of achievement.

If we calculate the multiple regression using SPSS we obtain the results (using fictitious data on 50 students) shown in Box 24.34.

Box 24.34
A summary of the R, R square and adjusted R square in multiple regression analysis

Model summary				
Model	R	R square	Adjusted R square	SE of the estimate
I	0.988[a]	0.977	0.975	2.032

a. Predictors: (Constant), Level of interest in the subject, Intelligence, Hours of study

The adjusted R square is very high indeed (0.975), indicating that 97.5 per cent of the variance in the dependent variable is explained by the independent variables (Box 24.34). Similarly the analysis of variance is highly statistically significant (0.000), indicating that the relationship between the independent and dependent variables is very strong (Box 24.35).

The Beta (β) weighting of the three independent variables is given in the 'Standardized Coefficients' column (Box 24.36). The constant is given as 1.996.

It is important to note here that the Beta weightings for the three independent variables are calculated *relative to* each other rather than independent of each other. Hence we can say that, relative to each other:

- The independent variable 'hours of study' has the strongest positive effect on the level of achievement ($\beta = 0.920$), and that this is statistically significant (the column 'Sig.' indicates that the level of significance, at 0.000, is stronger than 0.001).
- The independent variable 'intelligence' has a negative effect on the level of achievement ($\beta = -0.062$) but that this is not statistically significant (at 0.644, $\rho > 0.05$).
- The independent variable 'level of interest in the subject' has a positive effect on the level of achievement ($\beta = 0.131$), but this is not statistically significant (at 0.395, $\rho > 0.05$).

Box 24.35
Significance level in multiple regression analysis

ANOVA[b]

Model		Sum of squares	df	Mean square	F	Sig.
I	Regression	7969.607	3	2656.536	643.116	0.000[a]
	Residual	190.013	46	4.131		
	Total	8159.620	49			

a. Predictors: (Constant), Level of interest in the subject, Intelligence, Hours of study
b. Dependent variable: Level of achievement

Box 24.36
The beta coefficients in a multiple regression analysis

Coefficients[a]

Model		Unstandardized coefficients		Standardized coefficients	t	Sig.
		B	SE	Beta		
I	(Constant)	21.304	10.675		1.996	0.052
	Hours of study	9.637	1.863	0.920	5.173	0.000
	Intelligence	−6.20E-02	0.133	−0.062	−0.466	0.644
	Level of interest in the subject	0.116	0.135	0.131	0.858	0.395

a. Dependent variable: Level of achievement

- The only independent variable that has a statistically significant effect on the level of achievement is 'hours of study'.

So, for example, with this knowledge, if we knew the hours of study, the IQ and the level of measured interest of a student, we could predict his or her expected level of achievement in the examination.

Multiple regression is useful in that it can take in a range of variables and enable us to calculate their relative weightings on a dependent variable. However, one has to be cautious: variables may interact with each other and may be intercorrelated (the issue of multicollinearity), for example Gorard (2001) suggests that

poverty and ethnicity are likely to have some correlation between themselves, so using both together means that we end up using their *common* variance twice. If collinearity is discovered (e.g. if correlation coefficients between variables are higher than .80) then one can either remove one of the variables or create a new variable that combines the previous two that were highly intercorrelated.

(Gorard 2001: 172)

Indeed SPSS will automatically remove variables where there is strong covariance (collinearity).[2]

In reporting multiple regression, in addition to presenting tables (often of SPSS output), one can use a form of words thus, for example:

Multiple regression was used, and the results include the adjusted R square (0.975), ANOVA ($\rho < 0.001$) and the standardized β coefficient of each component variable ($\beta = 0.920$, $\rho < 0.001$; $\beta = -0.062$, $\rho = 0.644$; $\beta = 0.131$, $\rho = 0.395$). One can observe that, relative to each other, 'hours of study' exerted the greatest influence on level of achievement, that 'level of interest' exerted a small and statistically insignificant influence on level of achievement, and that 'intelligence' exerted a negative but statistically insignificant influence on level of achievement.

In using regression techniques, one has to be faithful to the assumptions underpinning them. Gorard (2001: 213) sets these out as follows:

- The measurements are from a random sample (or at least a probability-based one).
- All variables used should be real numbers (or at least the dependent variable must be).
- There are no extreme outliers.
- All variables are measured without error.
- There is an approximate linear relationship between the dependent variable and the independent variables (both individually and grouped).
- The dependent variable is approximately normally distributed (or at least the next assumption is true).
- The residuals for the dependent variable (the differences between calculated and observed scores) are approximately normally distributed.
- The variance of each variable is consistent across the range of values for all other variables (or at least the next assumption is true).
- The residuals for the dependent variable at each value of the independent variables have equal and constant variance.
- The residuals are not correlated with the independent variables.
- The residuals for the dependent variable at each value of the independent variables have a mean of zero (or they are approximately linearly related to the dependent variable).
- No independent variable is a perfect linear combination of another (not perfect 'multicollinearity').
- For any two cases the correlation between the residuals should be zero (each case is independent of the others).

Although regression and multiple regression are most commonly used with interval and ratio data, more recently some procedures have been devised for undertaking regression analysis for ordinal data (SPSS Inc 2002). This is of immense value for calculating regression from rating scale data (see http://www.routledge.com/textbooks/ 9780415368780 – Chapter 24, file SPSS Manual 24.8).

Pallant (2001: 136) suggests that attention has to be given to the sample size in using multiple regression. She suggests that 15 cases for each independent variable are required, and that a formula can be applied to determine the minimum sample size required thus: sample size $\geq$ 50 + (8 × number of independent variables), i.e. for ten independent variables one would require a minimum sample size of 130 (i.e. 50 + 80).

Measures of difference between groups and means

Researchers will sometimes be interested to find whether there are differences between two or more groups of subsamples, answering questions such as: 'Is there a significant difference between the amount of homework done by boys and girls?'; 'Is there a significant difference between test scores from four similarly mixed-ability classes studying the same syllabus?'; 'Does school A differ significantly from school B in the stress level of its sixth form students?' Such questions require measures of difference. This section introduces measures of difference and how to calculate difference. The process commences with the null hypothesis, stating that 'there is no statistically significant difference between the two groups', or 'there is no statistically significant difference between the four groups', and, if this is not supported, then the alternative hypothesis is supported, namely, there is a statistically significant difference between the two (or more) groups'.

Before going very far one has to ascertain the following:

- The kind of data with which one is working, as this affects the choice of statistic used.
- The number of groups being compared, to discover whether there is a difference between them. Statistics are usually divided into those that measure differences between two groups and those that measure differences between more than two groups.

- Whether the groups are related or independent. Independent groups are entirely unrelated to each other, e.g. males and females completing an examination; related groups might be the same group voting on two or more variables or the same group voting at two different points in time (e.g. a pretest and a post-test).

Decisions on these matters will affect the choice of statistics used. Our discussion will proceed thus: first, we look at differences between two groups using parametric data; second, we look at differences between three or more groups using parametric data. Then we move to discussing non-parametric data: third, we look at differences between two groups using non-parametric data; fourth, we look at differences between three or more groups using non-parametric data. As in previous examples, we will be using SPSS to illustrate our points.

The t-test

The t-test is used to discover whether there are statistically significant differences between the means of two groups, using parametric data drawn from random samples with a normal distribution. It is used to compare two groups randomly assigned, for example on a pretest and a post-test in an experiment (see http://www.routledge.com/textbooks/9780415368780 – Chapter 24, file 24.17.ppt).

The t-test has two variants: the t-test for independent samples and the t-test for related (or 'paired') samples. The former assumes that the two groups are unrelated to each other; the latter assumes that it is the same group either voting on two variables or voting at two different points in time about the same variable. We will address the former of these first. The t-test assumes that one variable is categorical (e.g. males and females) and one is a continuous variable (e.g. marks on a test). The formula used calculates a statistic based on:

$$t = \frac{Sample\ one\ mean - sample\ two\ mean}{Standard\ error\ of\ the\ difference\ in\ means}$$

Let us imagine that we wish to discover whether there is a statistically significant difference between the leaders/senior management team of a group of randomly chosen schools and the teachers, concerning how well learners are cared for, guided and supported. The data are ratio, the participants having had to award a mark out of ten for their response, the higher the mark the greater is the care, guidance and support offered to the students. The t-test for two independent samples presents us with two tables in SPSS. First, it provides the average (mean) of the voting for each group: 8.37 for the leaders/SMT and 8.07 for the teachers, i.e. there is a difference of means between the two groups. Is this difference statistically significant, i.e. is the null hypothesis ('there is no statistically significant difference between the leaders/SMT and the teachers') supported or not supported? We commence with the null hypothesis ('there is no statistically significant difference between the two means') and then we set the level of significance (α) to use for supporting or not supporting the null hypothesis; for example we could say 'Let $\alpha = 0.05$'. Then the data are computed thus (Box 24.37).

In running the t-test SPSS gives us back what, at first glance, seems to be a morass of information. Much of this is superfluous for our purposes here. We will concern ourselves with the most important pieces of data for introductory purposes here: the Levene test and the significance level for a two-tailed test (Sig. 2-tailed) (Box 24.38).

The Levene test is a guide as to which row of the two to use ('equal variances assumed' and 'equal variances not assumed'). Look at the column 'Sig.' in the Levene test (0.004). If the probability value is statistically significant (as in this case (0.004)) then variances are *unequal* and researchers need to use the second row of data ('Equal variances not assumed'); if the probability value is not significant ($\rho > 0.05$) then equal variances *are* assumed and they use the first row of data ('Equal variances assumed'). Once researchers have decided which row to use then the Levene test has served its purpose and they can move on. For our commentary here the purpose of the Levene test is only there to determine which row to look at of the two presented.

Box 24.37
Means and standard deviations for a t-test

	Group statistics				
	Who are you	N	Mean	SD	SE mean
How well learners are cared for, guided and supported	Leader/SMT member	347	8.37	2.085	0.112
	Teachers	653	8.07	2.462	0.096

Box 24.38
The Levene test for equality of variances in a t-test

		Levene's test for equality of variances		t-test for equality of means					95 % confidence interval of the difference	
		F	Sig.	t	df	Sig. (2-tailed)	Mean difference	SE difference	Lower	Upper
How well learners are cared for, guided and supported	Equal variances assumed	8.344	0.004	1.92	998	0.055	0.30	0.155	0.006	0.603
	Equal variances not assumed			2.02	811.922	0.044	0.30	0.148	0.009	0.589

Having discovered which row to follow, in our example it is the second row, we go along to the column 'Sig. (2-tailed)'. This tells us that there is a statistically significant difference between the two groups – leaders/SMT and the teachers – because the significance level is 0.044 (i.e. $p < 0.05$). Hence we can say that the null hypothesis is not supported, that there is a statistically significant difference between the means of the two groups ($p = 0.044$), and that the mean of the leaders/SMT is statistically significantly higher (8.37) than the mean of the teachers (8.07), i.e. the leaders/SMT of the schools think more highly than the teachers in the schools that the learners are well cared for, guided and supported.

Look at Box 24.38 again, and at the column 'Sig. (2-tailed)'. Had equal variances been assumed (i.e.

if the Levene test had indicated that we should remain on the top row of data rather than the second row of data) then we would *not* have found a statistically significant difference between the two means ($p = 0.055$, i.e. $p > 0.05$). Hence it is sometimes important to know whether equal variances are to be assumed or not to be assumed.

In the example here we find that there *is* a statistically significant difference between means of the two groups, i.e. the leaders/SMT do not share the same perception as the teachers that the learners are well cared for, guided and supported, typically the leaders/SMT are more generous than the teachers. This is of research interest, e.g. to discover the reasons for, and impact of, the differences of perception. It could be, for example, that the leaders/SMT have a much rosier picture of the situation than the teachers, and that the teachers – the ones who have to work with the students on a close daily basis – are more in touch with the students and know that there are problems, a matter to which the senior managers may be turning a blind eye.

In reporting the t-test here the following form of words can be used:

The mean score of the leaders/SMT on the variable 'How well learners are cared for, guided and supported' (M = 8.37, SD = 2.085) is statistically significantly higher (t = 2.02, df = 811.922, two-tailed ($\rho = 0.044$) than those of teachers on the same variable (M = 8.07, SD = 2.462).

Let us take a second example. Here the leaders/SMT and teachers are voting on 'the

attention given to teaching and learning in the school', again awarding a mark out of 10, i.e. ratio data. The mean for the leaders/SMT is 5.53 and for the teachers it is 5.46. Are these means statistically significantly different (Boxes 24.39 and 24.40)?

If we examine the Levene test (Sig.) we find that equal variances *are* assumed ($\rho = 0.728$), i.e. we remain on the top row of the data output. Running along to the column headed 'Sig. (2-tailed)' we find that $\rho = 0.610$, i.e. there is no statistically significant difference between the means of the two groups, therefore the null hypothesis (there is no statistically significant difference between the means of the two groups) is supported. This should not dismay the researcher; finding or *not* finding a statistically significant difference is of equal value in research – a win-win situation.

Box 24.39

A t-test for leaders and teachers

Group statistics					
	Who are you	N	Mean	SD	SE mean
The attention given to teaching and learning at the school	Leaders/SMT member	347	5.53	2.114	0.113
	Teachers	653	5.46	2.145	0.084

Box 24.40

The Levene test for equality of variances between leaders and teachers

		Levene's test for equality of variances		t-test for equality of means					95 % confidence interval of the difference	
		F	Sig.	t	df	Sig. (2-tailed)	Mean difference	SE difference	Lower	Upper
The attention given to teaching and learning at the school	Equal variances assumed	0.121	0.728	0.510	998	0.610	0.07	0.142	−0.206	0.351
	Equal variances not assumed			0.513	714.630	0.608	0.07	0.141	−0.205	0.350

Here, for example, one can say that there is a shared perception between the leaders/SMT and the teachers on the attention given to teaching and learning in the school, even though it is that the attention given is poor (means of 5.53 and 5.46 respectively). The fact that there is a shared perception – that both parties see the same problem in the same way – offers a positive prospect for development and a shared vision, i.e. even though the picture is poor, nevertheless it is perhaps more positive than if there were very widely different perceptions.

In reporting the t-test here the following form of words can be used:

The mean score for the leaders/SMT on the variable 'The attention given to teaching and learning at the school' (M = 5.53, SD = 2.114) did not differ statistically significantly (t = 0.510, df = 998, two-tailed $p = 0.610$) from that of the teachers (M = 5.46, SD = 2.145).

The t-test for independent examples is a very widely used statistic, and we support its correct use very strongly.

Less frequently used is the t-test for a paired (related) sample, i.e. where the same group votes on two variables, or the same sample group is measured, or the same variable is measured at two points in time. Here two variables are paired, with marks awarded by the same group (Box 24.41).

Box 24.41
Means and standard deviations in a paired samples t-test

Paired samples statistics				
	Mean	N	SD	SE mean
Pair 1 The attention given to teaching and learning at the school	5.48	1,000	2.134	0.067
The quality of the lesson preparation	7.17	1,000	1.226	0.039

One can see here that we are looking to see if the mean of the 1,000 respondents who voted on 'the attention given to teaching and learning in the school' (mean = 5.48) is statistically significantly different from the mean of the same group voting on the variable 'the quality of the lesson preparation' (mean = 7.17) (Box 24.42).

Here we can move directly to the final column ('Sig. (2-tailed)') where we find that $p = 0.000$, i.e. $p < 0.001$, telling us that the null hypothesis is not supported, and that there is a statistically significant difference between the two means, even though it is the same group that is awarding the marks (see http://www.routledge.com/textbooks/9780415368780 – Chapter 24, file SPSS Manual 24.9).

The issue of testing the difference between two proportions is set out on the accompanying web site: see http://www.routledge.com/textbooks/9780415368780 – Chapter 24, file 24.5.doc).

Analysis of variance

The t-test is useful for examining differences between *two* groups of respondents, or the same group on either two variables or two occasions, using parametric data from a random sample and assuming that each datum value is independent of the others (see http://www.routledge.com/textbooks/9780415368780 – Chapter 24, file 24.18.ppt). However, in much educational research we may wish to investigate differences between *more than two* groups. For example, we may wish to look at the examination results of four regions or four kinds of schools. In this case the t-test will not suit our purposes, and we must turn to analysis of variance. Analysis of variance is premised on the same assumptions as t-tests, that is random sampling, a normal distribution of scores, and parametric data, and it can be used with three or more groups. There are several kinds of analysis of variance; here we introduce only the two most widely used versions: the one-way analysis of variance and the two-way analysis of variance. Analysis of variance, like the t-test, assumes that the independent variable(s) is/are categorical (e.g. teachers, students, parents,

Box 24.42

The paired samples t-test

		Paired samples test								
		Paired differences								
					95 % confidence interval of the difference					
		Mean	SD	SE mean	Lower	Upper	t	df	Sig. (2-tailed)	
Pair I	The attention given to teaching and learning at the school – the quality of the lesson preparation	−1.69	2.430	0.077	−1.84	−1.54	−21.936	999	0.000	

governors) and one is a continuous variable (e.g. marks on a test).

One-way analysis of variance

Let us imagine that we have four types of school: rural primary, rural secondary, urban primary and urban secondary. Let us imagine further that all of the schools in these categories have taken the same standardized test of mathematics, and the results have been given as a percentage thus (Box 24.43).

The table gives us the means, standard deviations, standard error, confidence intervals, and the minimum and maximum marks for each group. At this stage we are interested only in the means:

Rural primary: mean = 59.85 per cent
Rural secondary: mean = 60.44 per cent
Urban primary: mean = 50.64 per cent
Urban secondary: mean = 51.70 per cent

Are these means statistically significantly different? Analysis of variance will tell us whether they are. We commence with the null hypothesis ('there is no statistically significant difference between the four means') and then we set the level of significance (α) to use for supporting or not supporting the null hypothesis; for example

we could say 'Let $\alpha = 0.05$'. SPSS calculates the following (Box 24.44).

This tells us that, for three degrees of freedom (df), the F-ratio is 8.976. The F-ratio is the *between* group mean square (variance) divided by the *within* group mean square (variance), i.e.:

$$F = \frac{Between\ group\ variance}{Within\ group\ variance} = \frac{3981.040}{443.514} = 8.976$$

By looking at the final column ('Sig.') ANOVA tell us that there is a statistically significant difference between the means ($\rho = 0.000$). This does *not* mean that all the means are statistically significantly different from each other, but that some are. For example, it may be that the means for the rural primary and rural secondary schools (59.85 per cent and 60.44 per cent respectively) are not statistically significantly different, and that the means for the urban primary schools and urban secondary schools (50.64 per cent and 51.70 per cent respectively) are not statistically significantly different. However, it could be that there is a statistically significant difference between the scores of the rural (primary and secondary) and the urban (primary and secondary) schools. How can we find out which groups are different from each other?

There are several tests that can be employed here, though we will only concern ourselves with a very commonly used test: the Tukey honestly

Box 24.43

Descriptive statistics for analysis of variance

Descriptives

Standardized mathematics scores (percentages)

	N	Mean	SD	SE	95% confidence interval for mean Lower bound	Upper bound	Minimum	Maximum
Rural primary	134	59.85	21.061	1.819	56.25	63.45	30	100
Rural secondary	136	60.44	19.470	1.669	57.14	63.74	30	100
Urban primary	141	50.64	22.463	1.892	46.90	54.38	30	100
Urban secondary	194	51.70	21.077	1.513	48.72	54.69	30	100
Total	605	55.22	21.473	0.873	53.51	56.94	30	100

Box 24.44

SPSS output for one-way analysis of variance

ANOVA

Standardized mathematics scores (percentages)

	Sum of squares	df	Mean square	F	Sig.
Between groups	11943.119	3	3981.040	8.976	0.000
Within groups	266551.8	601	443.514		
Total	278494.9	604			

significant difference test, sometimes called the 'Tukey hsd' test, or simply (as in SPSS) the Tukey test. (Others include the Bonferroni and Scheffé test; they are more rigorous than the Tukey test and tend to be used less frequently.) The Tukey test groups together subsamples whose means are *not* statistically significantly different from each other and places them in a different group from a group whose means *are* statistically significantly different from the first group. Let us see what this means in our example of the mathematics results of four types of school (Box 24.45).

This table takes each type of school and compares it with the other three types, in order to see where there may be statistically significant differences between them. Here the rural primary school is first compared with the rural secondary school (row one of the left-hand column cell named 'Rural primary'), and no statistically

significant difference is found between them (Sig. = 0.996, i.e. $p > 0.05$). The rural primary school is then compared with the urban primary school and a statistically significant difference is found between them (Sig. = 0.002, i.e. $p < 0.05$). The rural primary school is then compared with the urban secondary school, and, again a statistically significant difference is found between them (Sig. = 0.003, i.e. $p < 0.05$). The next cell of the left-hand column commences with the rural secondary school, and this is compared with the rural primary school, and no statistically significant difference is found (Sig. = 0.996, i.e. $p > 0.05$). The rural secondary school is then compared to the urban primary school and a statistically significant difference is found between them (Sig. = 0.001, i.e. $p < 0.05$). The rural secondary school is then compared with the urban secondary school, and, again a statistically significant difference is found between them (Sig. = 0.001, i.e. $p < 0.05$). The

Box 24.45

The Tukey test

Multiple comparisons

Dependent variable: Standardized mathematics scores (percentages)

Tukey HSD

(I) Grouping of school	(J) Grouping of school	Mean difference (I–J)	SE	Sig.	95 % confidence interval	
					Lower bound	Upper bound
Rural primary	Rural secondary	−0.59	2.563	0.996	−7.19	6.01
	Urban primary	9.21*	2.541	0.002	2.67	15.76
	Urban secondary	8.15*	2.366	0.003	2.06	14.24
Rural secondary	Rural primary	0.59	2.563	0.996	−6.01	7.19
	Urban primary	9.80*	2.531	0.001	3.28	16.32
	Urban secondary	8.74*	2.355	0.001	2.67	14.81
Urban primary	Rural primary	−9.21*	2.541	0.002	−15.76	−2.67
	Rural secondary	−9.80*	2.531	0.001	−16.32	−3.28
	Urban secondary	−1.06	2.331	0.968	−7.07	4.94
Urban secondary	Rural primary	−8.15*	2.366	0.003	−14.24	−2.06
	Rural secondary	−8.74*	2.355	0.001	−14.81	−2.67
	Urban primary	1.06	2.331	0.968	−4.94	7.07

*. The mean difference is significant at the 0.05 level.

analysis is continued for the urban primary and the urban secondary school. One can see that the two types of rural school do *not* differ statistically significantly from each other, that the two types of urban school do *not* differ statistically significantly from each other, but that the rural and urban schools *do* differ statistically significantly from each other. We can see where the null hypothesis *is* supported and where it is *not* supported.

In fact the Tukey test in SPSS presents this very clearly (Box 24.46).

Here one group of similar means (i.e. those not statistically significantly different from each other: the urban primary and urban secondary) is placed together (the column labelled '1') and the other group of similar means (i.e. those not statistically significantly different from each other: the rural primary and rural secondary) is placed together (the column labelled '2'). SPSS automatically groups these and places them in ascending order (the group with the lowest means appears in the first column, and the group with the highest means is in the second column). So, one can see clearly

Box 24.46

Homogeneous groupings in the Tukey test

Standardized mathematics scores (percentages)

Tukey HSD[a,b]

Grouping of school	N	Subset for alpha = 0.05	
		1	2
Urban primary	141	50.64	
Urban secondary	194	51.70	
Rural primary	134		59.85
Rural secondary	136		60.44
Sig.		0.973	0.995

Means for groups in homogeneous subsets are displayed.

a. Uses Harmonic Mean Sample Size = 147.806.

b. The group sizes are unequal. The harmonic mean of the group sizes is used. Type I error levels are not guaranteed.

that the difference between the school lies *not* in the fact that some are primary and some are secondary, but that some are rural and some are urban, i.e. the differences relate to geographical location rather than age group in the school. The Tukey test helps us to locate exactly where the similarities and differences between groups lie. It places the means into homogeneous subgroups, so that we can see which means are close together but different from other groups of means.

Analysis of variance here tells us that there are or are not statistically significant differences between groups; the Tukey test indicates where these differences lie, if they exist. We advise using the two tests together. Of course, as with the t-test, it is sometimes equally important if we do *not* find a difference between groups as if we *do* find a difference. For example, if we were to find that there was no difference between four groups (parents, teachers, students and school governors/leaders) on a particular issue, say the move towards increased science teaching, then this would give us greater grounds for thinking that a proposed innovation – the introduction of increased science teaching – would stand a greater chance of success than if there had been statistically significant differences between the groups. Finding no difference can be as important as finding a difference.

In reporting analysis of variance and the Tukey test one could use a form of words thus:

Analysis of variance found that there was a statistically significant difference between rural and urban schools ($F = 8.976$, $\rho < 0.001$). The Tukey test found that the means for rural primary schools and rural secondary schools (59.85 and 60.44 respectively) were not statistically significantly different from each other, and that the means for urban primary schools and urban secondary schools (50.64 and 51.70 respectively) were not statistically significantly different from each other. The homogeneous subsets calculated by the Tukey test reveal two subsets in respect of the variable 'Standardized mathematics scores': (a) urban primary and urban secondary schools; (b) rural primary and rural secondary scores. The two subsets reveal that these two groups were distinctly and statistically significantly different from each other in respect of this variable. The means of the rural schools were statistically significantly higher than the means of the urban schools.

(See http://www.routledge.com/textbooks/ 9780415368780 – Chapter 24, file SPSS Manual 24.10.)

Two-way analysis of variance

The example of ANOVA above illustrates one-way analysis of variance, i.e. the difference between the means of three or more groups on a single independent variable. Additionally ANOVA can take into account more than one independent variable. Two-way analysis of variance is used 'to estimate the effect of two independent variables (factors) on a single variable' (Cohen and Holliday 1996: 277). Let us take the example of how examination performance in Science is affected by both age group and sex. Two-way ANOVA enables the researcher to examine not only the effect of each independent variable but also the interaction effects on each other of the two independent variables, i.e. how sex effects are influenced or modified when combined with age group effects. We may discover, for example, that age group has a differential effect on examination performance according to whether one is male or female, i.e. there is an interaction effect.

For two-way analysis of variance the researcher requires two independent categorical (nominal) variables (e.g. sex, age group) and one continuous dependent variable (e.g. performance on examinations). Two-way ANOVA enables one to calculate three effects. In the example here they are:

- Differences in examination performance by sex.
- Difference in examination performance by age group.
- The interaction of sex and age group on examination, e.g. is there a difference in the effects of age group on examination performance for males and females?

We will use SPSS to provide an example of this. SPSS first presents descriptive statistics, for example Box 24.47.

Box 24.47
Means and standard deviations in a two-way analysis of variance

Descriptive statistics

Dependent variable: Science

Sex	Age group	Mean	SD	N
Male	15–20	71.92	24.353	125
	21–25	63.33	31.459	111
	26–45	70.95	28.793	21
	46 and above	64.69	28.752	128
	Total	66.99	28.390	385
Female	15–20	70.33	25.768	182
	21–25	68.82	25.396	221
	26–45	69.59	28.059	49
	46 and above	61.66	28.464	163
	Total	67.43	26.731	615
Total	15–20	70.98	25.173	307
	21–25	66.99	27.646	332
	26–45	70.00	28.079	70
	46 and above	62.99	28.581	291
	Total	67.26	27.369	1000

Box 24.48
The Levene test of equality of variances in a two-way analysis of variance

Levene's test of equality of error variances[a]

Dependent variable: Science

F	df1	df2	Sig.
3.463	7	992	0.001

Tests the null hypothesis that the error variance of the dependent variable is equal across groups.
a. Design: Intercept+SEX+AGE GROUP +SEX*AGE GROUP

This simply presents the data, with means and standard deviations. Next SPSS calculates the Levene test for equality of error variances, degrees of freedom and significance levels (Box 24.48).

This test enables the researcher to know whether there is equality across the means. He or she needs to see if the significance level is greater than 0.05. The researcher is looking for a significance level *greater than* 0.05, i.e. *not*

statistically significant, which supports the null hypothesis that holds that there is no statistically significant difference between the means and variances across the groups (i.e. to support the assumptions of ANOVA). In our example this is not the case as the significance level is .001. This means that the researcher has to proceed with caution as equality of variances cannot be assumed, i.e. one of the assumptions of ANOVA is not present. SPSS provides her with important information, thus (Box 24.49).

Here one can see the three sets of independent variables listed (SEX, AGE GROUP, SEX*AGE GROUP). The column headed 'Sig.' shows that the significance levels for the three sets are, respectively: 0.956, 0.004 and 0.244. Hence one can see that sex does not have a statistically significant effect on Science examination performance. Age group does have a statistically significant effect on the performance in the Science examination ($\rho = 0.004$). The interaction effect of sex and age group does not have a statistically significant effect on performance, i.e. there is no difference in the effect on Science performance for males and females ($\rho = 0.244$). SPSS also computes the effect size (Partial Eta squared). For the important variable AGE GROUP this is given as 0.014, which shows that the effect size is very small indeed, suggesting that, even though statistical significance has been found, the actual difference in the mean values is very small.

As with one-way ANOVA, the Tukey test can be applied here to present the homogeneous groupings of the subsample means. SPSS can also present a graphic plot of the two sets of scores, which gives the researcher a ready understanding of the effects of the males and females across the four age groups in their Science examination (Box 24.50).

In reporting the results of the two-way analysis of variance one can use the following form of words:

A two-way between-groups analysis of variance was conducted to discover the impact of sex and age group on performance in a Science examination.

Box 24.49

Between-subject effects in two-way analysis of variance

Tests of between-subjects effects

Dependent variable: SCIENCE

Source	Type III sum of squares	df	Mean square	F	Sig.	Partial Eta squared	Noncent. parameter	Observed power[a]
Corrected model	13199.146[b]	7	1885.592	2.545	0.013	0.018	17.812	0.888
Intercept	2687996.888	1	2687996.9	3627.42	0.000	0.785	3627.421	1.000
SEX	2.218	1	2.218	0.003	0.956	0.000	0.003	0.050
AGE GROUP	10124.306	3	3374.769	4.554	0.004	0.014	13.663	0.887
SEX* AGE GROUP	3089.630	3	1029.877	1.390	0.244	0.004	4.169	0.371
Error	735093.254	992	741.021					
Total	5272200.000	1000						
Corrected total	748292.400	999						

a. Computed using alpha = 0.05
b. R squared = 0.018 (Adjusted R squared = 0.011)

Box 24.50

Graphic plots of two sets of scores on a dependent variable

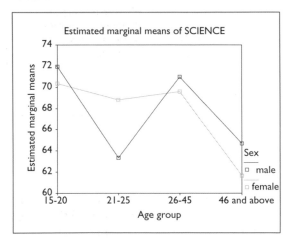

Subjects were divided into four groups by age: Group 1: 15–20 years; Group 2: 21–25 years; Group 3: 26–45 years; and Group 4: 46 years and above. There was a statistically significant main effect for age group ($F = 4.554$, $p = 0.004$), however the effect size was small (partial eta squared = 0.014). The main effect for sex ($F = 0.003$, $p = 0.956$) and the interaction effect ($F = 1.390$, $p = 0.244$) were not statistically significant.

The Mann-Whitney and Wilcoxon tests

The non-parametric equivalents of the t-test are the Mann-Whitney U test for two independent samples and the Wilcoxon test for two related samples, both for use with one categorical variable and a minimum of one ordinal variable. These enable us to see, for example, whether there are differences between males and females on a rating scale.

The Mann-Whitney test is based on ranks, 'comparing the number of times a score from one of the samples is ranked higher than a score from the other sample' (Bryman and Cramer 1990: 129) and hence overcomes the problem of low cell frequencies in the chi-square statistic (see http://www.routledge.com/textbooks/ 9780415368780 – Chapter 24, file 24.19.ppt). Let us take an example. Imagine that we have conducted a course evaluation, using five-point rating scales ('not at all', 'very little', 'a little', 'quite a lot', 'a very great deal'), and we wish to find if there is a statistically significant difference between the voting of males and females on the variable 'The course gave you opportunities to learn at your own pace'. We commence with the null hypothesis ('there is no statistically significant difference between the two means') and then we set the level of significance (α) to use for

Box 24.51

A cross-tabulation for a Mann-Whitney U test

Sex* The course gave you opportunities to learn at your own pace cross-tabulation

The course gave you opportunities to learn at your own pace

		Strongly Disagree	Disagree	Neither agree nor disagree	Agree	Strongly agree	Total
Male	Count	1	2	16	21	9	49
	% within sex	2.0%	4.1%	32.7%	42.9%	18.4%	100.0%
Female	Count	4	11	61	57	8	141
	% within sex	2.8%	7.8%	43.3%	40.4%	5.7%	100.0%
Total	Count	5	13	77	78	17	190
	% within sex	2.6%	6.8%	40.5%	41.1%	8.9%	100.0%

Box 24.52

SPSS output on rankings for the Mann-Whitney U test

Ranks

	Sex	N	Mean rank	Sum of ranks
The course gave you opportunities to learn at your own pace	Male	49	110.23	5401.50
	Female	141	90.38	12743.50
	Total	190		

Box 24.53

The Mann-Whitney U value and significance level in SPSS

Test statistics[a]

	The course gave you opportunities to learn at your own pace
Mann-Whitney U	2732.500
Wilcoxon W	12743.500
Z	−2.343
Asymp. sig. (2-tailed)	0.019

a. Grouping variable: Sex

supporting or not supporting the null hypothesis; for example we could say 'Let $\alpha = 0.05$'. A cross-tabulation might reveal the following (Box 24.51).

Are the differences between the two groups statistically significant? Using SPSS, the Mann-Whitney statistic indicates the following (Boxes 24.52 and 24.53).

Mann-Whitney using ranks (as in Box 24.52) yields a U-value of 2732.500 from the formula it uses for the calculation (SPSS does this automatically). The important information in Box 24.53 is the 'Asymp. sig. (2-tailed)', i.e. the statistical significance level of any difference found between the two groups (males and females). Here the significance level ($\rho = 0.019$, i.e. $\rho <$

0.05) indicates that the voting by males and females is statistically significantly different and that the null hypothesis is not supported. In the t-test and the Tukey test researchers could immediately find exactly where differences might lie between the groups (by looking at the means and the homogeneous subgroups respectively). Unfortunately the Mann-Whitney test does not enable the researcher to identify clearly where the differences lie between the two groups, so the researcher would need to go back to the cross-tabulation to identify where differences lie. In the example above, it appears that the males feel more strongly than the females that the course in question has afforded them the opportunity to learn at their own pace.

In reporting the Mann-Whitney test one could use a form of words such as the following:

> When the Mann-Whitney Wallis statistic was calculated to determine whether there was any statistically significant difference in the voting of the two groups (U = 2732.500, $\rho = 0.019$), a statistically significant difference was found between the males and females. A cross-tabulation found that males felt more strongly than the females that the course in question had afforded them the opportunity to learn at their own pace.

Ⓦ (See http://www.routledge.com/textbooks/ 9780415368780 – Chapter 24, file SPSS Manual 24.11.)

For two related samples (e.g. the same group voting for more than one item, or the same grouping voting at two points in time) the Wilcoxon test is applied, and the data are presented and analysed in the same way as the Mann-Whitney test. For example, in Boxes 24.54 and 24.55 are two variables ('The course was just right' and 'The lecturer was well prepared'), voted on by the same group. The frequencies are given. Is there a statistically significant difference in the voting?

As it is the same group voting on two variables, the sample is not independent, hence the Wilcoxon test is used. Using SPSS output, the data analysis shows that the voting of the group on the two variables is statistically significantly different (Boxes 24.56 and 24.57).

The reporting of the results of the Wilcoxon test can follow that of the Mann-Whitney test.

For both the Mann-Whitney and Wilcoxon tests, *not* finding a statistically significant difference between groups can be just as important as finding a statistically significant difference between them, as the former suggests that nominal characteristics of the sample make no statistically significant difference to the voting, i.e. the voting is consistent, regardless of particular features of the sample.

The Kruskal-Wallis and the Friedman tests

The non-parametric equivalents of analysis of variance are the Kruskal-Wallis test for three

Box 24.54
Frequencies and percentages of variable one in a Wilcoxon test

	The course was just right					
			Valid			
	Strongly disagree	Disagree	Neither agree nor disagree	Agree	Strongly agree	Total
Frequency	2	14	65	76	34	191
Valid percent	1.0	7.3	34.0	39.8	17.8	100.0

Box 24.55
Frequencies and percentages of variable two in a Wilcoxon test

	The lecturer was well prepared						
			Valid				
	Strongly disagree	Disagree	Neither agree nor disagree	Agree	Strongly agree	Total	Total
Frequency	3	5	25	85	72	190	191
Valid percent	1.6	2.6	13.2	44.7	37.9	100.0	

Box 24.56
Ranks and sums of ranks in a Wilcoxon test

		Ranks		
		N	Mean rank	Sum of ranks
The lecturer was well	Negative ranks	20[a]	50.30	1006.00
prepared – the course was	Positive ranks	89[b]	56.06	4989.00
just right	Ties	81[c]		
	Total	190		

a. the lecturer was well prepared < the course was just right
b. the lecturer was well prepared > the course was just right
c. the course was just right = the lecturer was well prepared

Box 24.57
Significance level in a Wilcoxon test

Test statistics[b]	
	The lecturer was well prepared – the course was just right
Z	−6.383[a]
Asymp. sig. (2-tailed)	0.000

a. Based on negative ranks
b. Wilcoxon Signed Ranks Test

or more independent samples and the Friedman test for three or more related samples, both for use with one categorical variable and one ordinal variable. These enable us to see, for example, whether there are differences between three or more groups (e.g. classes, schools, groups of teachers) on a rating scale (see http://www.routledge.com/textbooks/9780415368780 – Chapter 24, file 24.20.ppt).

These tests operate in a very similar way to the Mann-Whitney test, being based on rankings. Let us take an example. Teachers in different groups, according to the number of years that they have been teaching, have been asked to evaluate one aspect of a particular course that they have attended ('The teaching and learning tasks and activities consolidate learning through application'). One of the results is cross-tabulation

shown in Box 24.58. Are the groups of teachers statistically significantly different from each other? We commence with the null hypothesis ('there is no statistically significant difference between the four groups) and then we set the level of significance (α) to use for supporting or not supporting the null hypotheses; for example we could say 'Let $\alpha = 0.05$'.

Is the difference in the voting between the four groups statistically significantly different? The Kruskal-Wallis test calculates and presents the following in SPSS (Boxes 24.59 and 24.60).

The important figure to note here is the 0.009 ('Asymp. sig.') – the significance level. Because this is less than 0.05 we can conclude that the null hypothesis ('there is no statistically significant difference between the voting by the different groups of years in teaching') is not supported, and that the results vary according to the number of years in teaching of the voters. As with the Mann-Whitney test, the Kruskal-Wallis test tells us only that there *is* or *is not* a statistically significant difference, not *where* the difference lies. To find out where the difference lies, one has to return to the cross-tabulation and examine it. In the example here it appears that those teachers in the group which had been teaching from 16 to 18 years are the most positive about the aspect of the course in question.

In reporting the Kruskal-Wallis test one could use a form of words such as the following:

Box 24.58

Cross-tabulation for the Kruskal-Wallis test

Number of years teaching* the teaching and learning tasks and activities consolidate learning through application cross-tabulation							
				The teaching and learning tasks and activities consolidate learning through application			
			Disagree	Neither agree nor disagree	Agree	Strongly agree	Total
Number of years teaching	<16	Count		2	3		5
		% within number of years teaching		40.0%	60.0%		100.0%
	16–18	Count		29	52	14	95
		% within number of years teaching		30.5%	54.7%	14.7%	100.0%
	19–21	Count	6	40	34	7	87
		% within number of years teaching	6.9%	46.0%	39.1%	8.0%	100.0%
	>21	Count			2		2
		% within number of years teaching			100%		100.0%
Total		Count	6	71	91	21	189
		% within number of years teaching	3.2%	37.6%	48.1%	11.1%	100.0%

Box 24.59

Rankings for the Kruskal-Wallis test

Ranks			
	Number of years teaching	N	Mean rank
The teaching and learning tasks and activities consolidate learning through application	<16	5	90.60
	16–18	95	106.53
	19–21	87	82.02
	>21	2	123.00
	Total	189	

Box 24.60

Significance levels in a Kruskal-Wallis test

Test statistics[a,b]	
	The teaching and learning tasks and activities consolidate learning through application
Chi-square	11.595
df	3
Asymp. sig.	0.009

a. Kruskal-Wallis test

b. Grouping variable: Number of years teaching

When the Kruskal-Wallis statistic was calculated to determine whether there was any statistically significant difference in the voting of the four groups ($\chi^2 = 11.595$, $\rho = 0.009$), a statistically significant difference was found between the groups which had different years of teaching experience. A cross-tabulation found that those teachers in the group that had been teaching from 16 to 18 years were the most positive about the variable 'The teaching and learning tasks and activities consolidate learning through application'.

Box 24.61

Frequencies for variable one in the Friedman test

The course encouraged and stimulated your motivation and willingness to learn						
	Valid					
	Not at all	Very little	A little	Quite a lot	A very great deal	Total	Total
Frequency	1	13	64	79	32	189	191
Valid percent	0.5	6.9	33.9	41.8	16.9	100.0	

Box 24.62

Frequencies for variable two in the Friedman test

The course encouraged you to take responsibility for your own learning						
	Valid					
	Not at all	Very little	A little	Quite a lot	A very great deal	Total	Total
Frequency	1	9	64	85	30	189	191
Valid percent	0.5	4.8	33.9	45.0	15.9	100.0	

(See http://www.routledge.com/textbooks/ 9780415368780 – Chapter 24, file Manual 24.12.)

For more than two related samples (e.g. the same group voting for three or more items, or the same grouping voting at three points in time) the Friedman test is applied. For example, in Boxes 24.61 to 24.63 are three variables ('The course encouraged and stimulated your motivation and willingness to learn', 'The course encouraged you to take responsibility for your own learning' and 'The teaching and learning tasks and activities consolidate learning through application'), all of which are voted on by the same group. The frequencies are given. Is there a statistically significant difference between the groups in their voting?

The Friedman test reports the mean rank and then the significance level; in the examples here the SPSS output has been reproduced (Boxes 24.64 and 24.65).

Here one can see that, with a significance level of 0.838 (greater than 0.05), the voting by the same group on the three variables is not statistically significantly different, i.e. the null hypothesis is

supported. The reporting of the results of the Friedman test can follow that of the Kruskal-Wallis test.

For both the Kruskal-Wallis and the Friedman tests, as with the Mann-Whitney and Wilcoxon tests, *not* finding a statistically significant difference between groups can be just as important as finding a statistically significant difference between them, as the former suggests that nominal characteristics of the sample make no statistically significant difference to the voting, i.e. the voting is consistent, regardless of particular features of the sample.

The k-sample slippage test from Conover (1971), as an alternative to the Kruskal-Wallis test, is set out in the accompanying web site: see http://www.routledge.com/textbooks/ 9780415368780 – Chapter 24, file 24.6.doc.

Several data sets for use with SPSS are included on the accompanying web site, using fictitious data, thus:

- an SPSS data file on managing change: http://www.routledge.com/textbooks/ 9780415368780/, file 'data file on change'

Box 24.63

Frequencies for variable three in the Friedman test

The teaching and learning tasks and activities consolidate learning through application				
		Valid		
	Very little	A little	Quite a lot	A very great deal	Total
Frequency	6	71	92	22	191
Valid percent	3.1	37.2	48.2	11.5	100.0

Box 24.64

Rankings for the Friedman test

Ranks	
	Mean rank
The course encouraged and stimulated your motivation and willingness to learn	1.98
The course encouraged you to take responsibility for your own learning	2.03
The teaching and learning tasks and activities consolidate learning through application	1.99

Box 24.65

Significance level in the Friedman test

Test statistics[a]	
N	187
Chi-square	0.353
df	2
Asymp. sig.	0.838

a. Friedman Test

- an SPSS data file on organizational culture: http://www.routledge.com/textbooks/9780415368780/ file 'organizational culture data file'
- an SPSS data file on mathematics scores and related variables: http://www.routledge.com/textbooks/9780415368780/ file 'test results for mathematics'; the questionnaire that accompanies this file (in Word) is available at http://www.routledge.com/textbooks/9780415368780/, file 'SPSS questionnaire on mathematics'
- a Word file indicating all the SPSS files contained on the web site is available at: http://www.routledge.com/textbooks/9780415368780/, file 'SPSS FILES ON THE WEB SITE'.

25 Multidimensional measurement and factor analysis

Introduction

However limited our knowledge of astronomy, many of us have learned to pick out certain clusterings of stars from the infinity of those that crowd the Northern skies and to name them as the familiar Plough, Orion and the Great Bear. Few of us would identify constellations in the Southern Hemisphere that are instantly recognizable by those in Australia.

Our predilection for reducing the complexity of elements that constitute our lives to a more simple order doesn't stop at star gazing. In numerous ways, each and every one of us attempts to discern patterns or shapes in seemingly unconnected events in order to better grasp their significance for us in the conduct of our daily lives. The educational researcher is no exception.

As research into a particular aspect of human activity progresses, the variables being explored frequently turn out to be more complex than was first realized. Investigation into the relationship between teaching styles and pupil achievement is a case in point. Global distinctions between behaviour identified as progressive or traditional, informal or formal, are vague and woolly and have led inevitably to research findings that are at worse inconsistent, at best, inconclusive. In reality, epithets such as informal or formal in the context of teaching and learning relate to 'multidimensional concepts', that is, concepts made up of a number of variables. 'Multidimensional scaling', on the other hand, is a way of analysing judgements of similarity between such variables in order that the dimensionality of those judgements can be assessed (Bennett and Bowers 1977). As regards research into teaching

styles and pupil achievement, it has been suggested that multidimensional typologies of teacher behaviour should be developed. Such typologies, it is believed, would enable the researcher to group together similarities in teachers' judgements about specific aspects of their classroom organization and management, and their ways of motivating, assessing and instructing pupils.

Techniques for grouping such judgements are many and various. What they all have in common is that they are methods for 'determining the number and nature of the underlying variables among a large number of measures', a definition which Kerlinger (1970) uses to describe one of the best known grouping techniques, 'factor analysis'. We begin the chapter by illustrating elementary linkage analysis which can be undertaken by hand, and move to factor analysis, which is best left to the computer. Finally, we append a brief note on multilevel modelling and another about cluster analysis, the latter as a way of organizing people or groups rather than variables.

Elementary linkage analysis: an example

Elementary linkage analysis (McQuitty 1957) is one way of exploring the relationship between the teacher's personal constructs, that is, of assessing the dimensionality of the judgements that the teacher makes about his or her pupils. It seeks to identify and define the clusterings of certain variables within a set of variables. Like factor analysis, which we shortly illustrate, elementary linkage analysis searches for interrelated groups of correlation coefficients. The objective of the search is to identify 'types'. By type, McQuitty

(1957) refers to 'a category of people or other objects (personal constructs in our example) such that the members are internally self-contained in being like one another'.

Seven constructs were elicited from an infant school teacher who was invited to discuss the ways in which she saw the children in her class (see Chapter 20). She identified favourable and unfavourable constructs as follows: 'intelligent' (+), 'sociable' (+), 'verbally good' (+), 'well behaved' (+), 'aggressive' (−), 'noisy' (−) and 'clumsy' (−).

Four boys and six girls were then selected at random from the class register and the teacher was asked to place each child in rank order under each of the seven constructs, using rank position 1 to indicate the child most like the particular construct, and rank position 10, the child least like the particular construct. The teacher's rank ordering is set out in Box 25.1. Notice that on three constructs, the rankings have been reversed in order to maintain the consistency of Favourable 1, Unfavourable = 10.

Box 25.2 sets out the intercorrelations between the seven personal construct ratings shown in Box 25.1 (Spearman's *rho* is the method of correlation used in this example).

Elementary linkage analysis enables the researcher to cluster together similar groups of variables by hand.

Steps in elementary linkage analysis

1   In Box 25.2, underline the strongest, that is the highest, correlation coefficient in each column of the matrix. Ignore negative signs.
2   Identify the highest correlation coefficient in the entire matrix. The two variables having this correlation constitute the first two of Cluster 1.
3   Now identify all those variables which are most like the variables in Cluster 1. To do this, read along the rows of the variables which emerged in Step 2, selecting any of the coefficients which are underlined in the rows. Box 25.3 illustrates diagrammatically the ways in which these new cluster members

are related to the original pair which initially constituted Cluster 1.
4   Now identify any variables which are most like the variables elicited in Step 3. Repeat this procedure until no further variables are identified.
5   Excluding all those variables which belong within Cluster 1, repeat Steps 2 to 4 until all the variables have been accounted for.

Factor analysis

Factor analysis is a method of grouping together variables which have something in common. It is a process which enables the researcher to take a set of variables and reduce them to a smaller number of underlying factors which account for as many variables as possible. It detects structures and commonalities in the relationships between variables. Thus it enables researchers to identify where different variables in fact are addressing the same underlying concept. For example, one variable could measure somebody's height in centimetres; another variable could measure the same person's height in inches. The underlying factor that unites both variables is height; it is a latent factor that is indicated by the two variables.

Factor analysis can take two main forms: *exploratory factor analysis* and *confirmatory factor analysis*. The former refers to the use of factor analysis (principal components analysis in particular) to explore previously unknown groupings of variables, to seek underlying patterns, clusterings and groups. By contrast *confirmatory factor analysis* is more stringent, testing a found set of factors against a hypothesized model of groupings and relationships. This section introduces the most widely used form of factor analysis: principal components analysis. We refer the reader to further books on statistics for a fuller discussion of factor analysis and its variants.

The analysis here uses SPSS output, as it is the most commonly used way of undertaking principal components analysis by educational researchers.

As an example of factor analysis, one could have the following variables in a piece of educational research:

Box 25.1
Rank ordering of ten children on seven constructs

	INTELLIGENT		SOCIABLE
(favourable)	1 Heather	(favourable)	1 Caroline
	2 Richard		2 Richard
	3 Caroline		3 Sharon
	4 Tim		4 Jane
	5 Patrick		5 Tim
	6 Sharon		6 Janice
	7 Janice		7 Heather
	8 Jane		8 Patrick
	9 Alex		9 Karen
(unfavourable)	10 Karen	(unfavourable)	10 Alex

	AGGRESSIVE		NOISY
(unfavourable)	10 Alex	(unfavourable)	10 Alex
	9 Patrick		9 Patrick
	8 Tim		8 Karen
	7 Karen		7 Tim
	6 Richard		6 Caroline
	5 Caroline		5 Richard
	4 Heather		4 Heather
	3 Jane		3 Janice
	2 Sharon		2 Sharon
(favourable)	1 Janice	(favourable)	1 Jane

	VERBALLY GOOD		CLUMSY
(favourable)	1 Richard	(unfavourable)	10 Alex
	2 Caroline		9 Patrick
	3 Heather		8 Karen
	4 Janice		7 Tim
	5 Patrick		6 Richard
	6 Tim		5 Sharon
	7 Alex		4 Jane
	8 Sharon		3 Janice
	9 Jane		2 Caroline
(unfavourable)	10 Karen	(favourable)	1 Heather

continued

Box 25.1
Continued

WELL BEHAVED

(favourable)	1	Janice
	2	Jane
	3	Sharon
	4	Caroline
	5	Heather
	6	Richard
	7	Tim
	8	Karen
	9	Patrick
(unfavourable)	10	Alex

Source: Cohen 1977

Box 25.2
Intercorrelations between seven personal constructs

		(1)	(2)	(3)	(4)	(5)	(6)	(7)
Intelligent	(1)		53	−10	−16	83	−52	13
Sociable	(2)	53		−50	−59	44	−56	61
Aggressive	(3)	−10	−50		91	−07	79	−96
Noisy	(4)	−16	−59	91		−01	73	−93
Verbally good	(5)	83	44	−07	−01		−43	12
Clumsy	(6)	−52	−56	79	73	−43		−81
Well behaved (decimal points omitted)	(7)	13	61	−96	−93	12	−81	

Source: Cohen 1977

- student demotivation
- poor student concentration
- undue pressure on students
- narrowing effect on curriculum
- punishing the weaker students
- overemphasis on memorization
- testing only textbook knowledge.

These seven variables can be grouped together under the single overarching factor of 'negative effects of examinations'. Factor analysis, working through multiple correlations, is a method for grouping together several variables under one or more common factor(s).

To address factor analysis in more detail we provide a worked example. Consider the following variables concerning school effectiveness:

- the clarity of the direction that is set by the school leadership
- the ability of the leader to motivate and inspire the educators
- the drive and confidence of the leader

Box 25.3

The structuring of relationships among the seven personal constructs

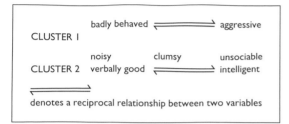

Source: Cohen 1977

- the consultation abilities or activities of the leader
- the example set by the leader
- the commitment of the leader to the school
- the versatility of the leader's styles
- the ability of the leader to communicate clear, individualized expectations
- the respect in which the leader is held by staff
- the staff's confidence in the senior management team
- the effectiveness of the teamwork of the SMT
- the extent to which the vision for the school impacts on practice
- educators given opportunities to take on leadership roles
- the creativity of the SMT
- problem-posing, problem-identifying and problem-solving capacity of the SMT
- the use of data to inform planning and school development
- valuing of professional development in the school
- staff consulted about key decisions
- the encouragement and support for innovativeness and creativity
- everybody is free to make suggestions to inform decision-making
- the school works in partnership with parents
- people take positive risks for the good of the school and its development
- staff voluntarily taking on coordination roles
- teamwork among school staff.

Here we have 24 different variables. The question here is, 'Are there any underlying groups of factors (latent variables) that can embrace several of these variables, or of which the several variables are elements or indicators?' Factor analysis will indicate whether there are. We offer a three-stage model for undertaking factor analysis. In what follows we distinguish *factors* from *variables*: a factor is an underlying or latent feature under which groups of variables are included; a variable is one of the elements that can be a member of an underlying factor. In our example here we have 24 variables and, as we shall see, 5 factors.

Stage 1

Let us imagine that we have gathered data from 1,000 teachers in several different schools, and we wish to see how the 24 variables above can be grouped, based on their voting (using ratio data by awarding marks out of ten for each of the variables). (This follows the rule that there should be more subjects in the sample than there are variables.) Bryman and Cramer (1990: 255) suggest that there should be at least 5 subjects per variable and a total of no fewer than 100 subjects in the total sample. This analysis will be based on SPSS processing and output, as Box 25.4.

Although Box 25.4 seems to contain a lot of complicated data, in fact most of this need not trouble us at all. SPSS has automatically found and reported 5 factors for us through sophisticated correlational analysis, and it presents data on these 5 factors (the first 5 rows of the chart, marked 'Component'). Box 25.4 takes the 24 variables (listed in order on the left-hand column (Component)) and then it provides three sets of readings: Eigenvalues, Extracted Sums of Squared Loadings, and Rotated Sums of Squared Loadings. Eigenvalues are measures of the variance between factors. We are interested only in those Eigenvalues that are greater than 1, since those that are smaller than 1 generally are not of interest to researchers as they account for less than the variation explained by a single variable. Indeed SPSS automatically filters out for us the Eigenvalues that are greater than 1, using the Kaiser criterion (in SPSS this is termed the Kaiser Normalization).

Box 25.4

Initial SPSS output for principal components analysis

				Total variance explained					
	Initial Eigenvalues			Extraction Sums of Squared Loadings			Rotation Sums of Squared Loadings		
Component	Total	% of variance	Cumulative %	Total	% of variance	Cumulative %	Total	% of variance	Cumulative %
1	9.343	38.930	38.930	9.343	38.930	38.930	4.037	16.820	16.820
2	1.424	5.931	44.862	1.424	5.931	44.862	2.810	11.706	28.527
3	1.339	5.580	50.442	1.339	5.580	50.442	2.779	11.578	40.105
4	1.220	5.085	55.526	1.220	5.085	55.526	2.733	11.386	51.491
5	1.085	4.520	60.047	1.085	4.520	60.047	2.053	8.556	60.047
6	0.918	3.825	63.872						
7	0.826	3.443	67.315						
8	0.723	3.013	70.329						
9	0.685	2.855	73.184						
10	0.658	2.743	75.927						
11	0.623	2.596	78.523						
12	0.562	2.342	80.864						
13	0.532	2.216	83.080						
14	0.512	2.132	85.213						
15	0.493	2.055	87.268						
16	0.466	1.942	89.210						
17	0.437	1.822	91.032						
18	0.396	1.650	92.682						
19	0.376	1.566	94.247						
20	0.364	1.517	95.764						
21	0.307	1.280	97.044						
22	0.271	1.129	98.174						
23	0.232	0.965	99.138						
24	0.207	0.862	100.000						

Extraction method: Principal components analysis

A scree plot can also be used at this stage, to identify and comment on factors (this is available at the click of a button in SPSS). A scree plot shows each factor on a chart, in descending order of magnitude. For researchers the scree plot becomes interesting where it flattens out (like the rubble that collects at the foot of a scree), as this indicates very clearly which factors account for a lot of the variance, and which account for little. In the scree plot here (Box 25.5) one can see that the scree flattens out considerably after the first factor, then it levels out a little for the next 4 factors, tailing downwards all the time. This suggests that the first factor is the significant factor in explaining the greatest amount of variance.

Indeed, in using the scree plot one perhaps has to look for the 'bend in the elbow' of the data (after factor one), and then regard those factors above the bend in the elbow as being worthy of inclusion, and those below the bend in the elbow as being relatively unimportant (Cattell 1966; Pallant 2001: 154). However, this is draconian, as it risks placing too much importance on those items above the bend in the elbow and too little importance on those below it. The scree plot adds little to the variance table presented in Box 25.4, though it does enable one to see at a glance which are the significant and less significant factors, or, indeed which factors to focus on (the ones before the scree levels off) and which to ignore.

Box 25.5
A scree plot

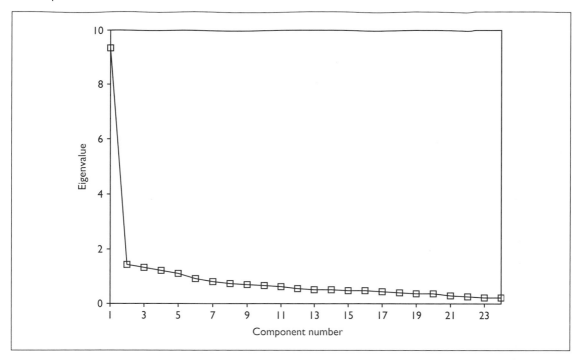

Next we turn to the columns labelled 'Extraction Sums of Squared Loadings'. The Extraction Sums of Squared Loadings contain two important pieces of information. First, in the column marked '% of variance' SPSS tells us how much variance is explained by each of the factors identified, in order from the greatest amount of variance to the least amount of variance. So, here the first factor accounts for 38.930 per cent of the variance in the total scenario – a very large amount – while the second factor identified accounts for only 5.931 per cent of the total variance, a much lower amount of explanatory power. Each factor is unrelated to the other, and so the amount of variance in each factor is unrelated to, or explained by, the other factors; they are independent of each other. By giving us how much variance in the total picture is explained by each factor we can see which factors possess the most and least explanatory power – the power to explain the total scenario of 24 variables. Second,

SPSS keeps a score of the cumulative amount of explanatory power of the 5 factors identified. In the column 'Cumulative' it tells us that in total 60.047 per cent of the total picture (of the 24 variables) is accounted for – explained – by the 5 factors identified. This is a moderate amount of explanatory power, and researchers would be happy with this.

However, the three columns under 'Extraction Sums of Squared Loadings' give us the initial, rather crude, unadjusted percentage of variance of the total picture explained by the 5 factors found. These are crude in the sense that the full potential of factor analysis has not been caught. What SPSS has done here is to plot the factors on a two-dimensional chart (which it does not present in the data output) to identify groupings of variables, the two dimensions being vertical and horizontal axes as in a conventional graph like a scattergraph. On such a two-dimensional chart some of the factors and variables could be plotted quite close to each other, such that discrimination between the factors would not be very clear. However, if we were to plot the factors and variables on a three-dimensional chart that includes not only horizontal and vertical axes but also *depth* by *rotating* the plotted points through 90 degrees, then the effect of this would be to bring closer together those variables that are similar to each other and to separate them more fully – in distance – from those variables that have no similarity to them, i.e. to render each group of variables (factors) more homogeneous and to separate more clearly one group of variables (factor) from another group of variables (factor). The process of rotation keeps together those variables that are closely interrelated and keeps them apart from those variables that are not closely related. This is represented in Box 25.6.

This distinguishes more clearly one factor from another than that undertaken in the Extraction Sums of Squared Loadings. Rotation is undertaken by *varimax rotation*. This maximizes the variance between factors and hence helps to distinguish them from each other. In SPSS the rotation is called *orthogonal* because the factors are unrelated to, and independent of, each other.

In the column 'Rotation Sums of Squared Loadings' the fuller power of factor analysis is tapped, in that the rotation of the variables from a two-dimensional to a three-dimensional chart has been undertaken, thereby identifying more clearly the groupings of variables into factors, and separating each factor from the other much more clearly. We advise researchers to use the Rotation Sums of Squared Loadings rather than the Extraction Sums of Squared Loadings. With the Rotation Sums of Squared Loadings the percentage of variance explained by each factor is altered, even though the total cumulative per cent (60.047 per cent) remains the same. For example, one can see that the first factor in the rotated solution no longer accounts for 38.930 per cent as in the Extraction Sums of Squared Loadings, but only 16.820 per cent of the variance, and that factors 2, 3 and 4, which each accounted for only just over 5 per cent of the variance in the Extraction Sums of Squared Loadings now each account for over 11 per cent of the variance, and that factor 5, which accounted for 4.520 per cent of the variance in the Extraction Sums of Squared Loadings now accounts for 8.556 per cent of the variance in the Rotated Sums of Squared Loadings.

By this stage we hope that the reader has been able to see that:

- Factor analysis brings variables together into homogeneous and distinct groups, each of which is a factor and each of which has an Eigenvalue of greater than 1.
- Factor analysis in SPSS indicates the amount of variance in the total scenario explained by each individual factor and all the factors together (the cumulative per cent).
- The Rotation Sums of Squared Loadings is preferable to the Extraction Sums of Squared Loadings.

We are ready to proceed to the second stage.

Stage 2

Stage 2 consists of presenting a matrix of all of the relevant data for the researcher to be able to identify which variables belong to which factor (Box 25.7). SPSS presents what at first sight is a bewildering set of data, but the reader is advised

Box 25.6
Three-dimensional rotation

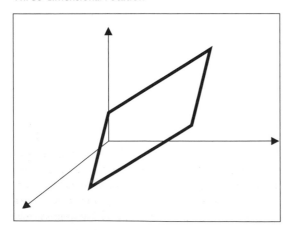

Box 25.7

The rotated components matrix in principal components analysis

Rotated component matrix[a]

	Component				
	1	2	3	4	5
The clarity of the direction that is set by the school leadership	0.559	0.133	7.552E-02	0.248	0.212
The ability of the leader to motivate and inspire the educators	0.743	0.142	0.176	9.058E-02	0.160
The drive and confidence of the leader	0.758	2.151E-02	0.122	2.796E-02	0.222
The consultation abilities/activities of the leader	0.548	0.342	0.208	0.278	0.160
The example set by the leader	0.572	0.239	0.126	0.319	0.209
The commitment of the leader to the school	0.513	0.290	0.252	0.329	0.137
The versatility of the leader's styles	0.284	0.332	0.377	0.285	5.668E-02
The ability of the leader to communicate clear, individualized expectations	0.449	0.246	0.303	0.351	0.205
The respect in which the leader is held by staff	0.184	7.988E-02	0.154	0.810	0.240
The staff's confidence in the SMT	0.180	0.121	7.859E-02	0.809	0.279
The effectiveness of the teamwork of the SMT	0.385	0.445	0.249	0.443	8.104E-02
The extent to which the vision for the school impacts on practice	0.413	0.341	0.305	0.379	0.113
Educators given opportunities to take on leadership roles	0.247	0.225	0.494	0.339	−2.66E-02
The creativity of the SMT	0.212	7.188E-02	0.822	−2.97E-03	0.189
Problem-posing, problem-identifying and problem-solving capacity of SMT	0.459	0.351	0.262	0.361	−3.21E-02
The use of data to inform planning and school development	0.690	0.167	0.188	5.158E-02	−3.79E-02
Valuing of professional development in the school	0.187	0.249	0.551	0.260	7.013E-02
Staff consulted about key decisions	0.148	6.670E-02	0.854	7.531E-02	0.167
The encouragement and support for innovativeness and creativity	0.143	5.187E-02	0.189	0.269	0.661
Everybody is free to make suggestions to inform decision-making	0.165	0.150	0.172	0.264	0.642
The school works in partnership with parents	0.222	0.804	8.173E-02	0.143	0.199
People take positive risks for the good of the school and its development	0.206	0.778	8.998E-02	0.181	2.635E-02
Staff voluntarily taking on coordination roles	0.195	0.210	2.681E-02	3.660E-02	0.779
Teamwork among school staff	0.114	0.642	0.220	−3.41E-02	0.277

Extraction method: Principal components analysis
Rotation method: Varimax with Kaiser Normalization
a. Rotation converged in six iterations.

to keep cool and to look at the data slowly, as, in fact, they are not complicated. SPSS often presents researchers with more data than they need, overwhelming the researcher with data. In fact the data in Box 25.7 are comparatively straightforward.

Across the top of the matrix in Box 25.7 we have a column for each of the 5 factors (1–5) that SPSS had found for us. The left-hand column prints the names of each of the 24 variables with which we are working. We can ignore those pieces of data which contain the letter 'E' (exponential), as these contain figures that are so small as to be able to be discarded. Look at the column labelled '1' (factor 1). Here we have a range of numbers that range from 0.114 for the variable 'Teamwork among school staff' to 0.758 for the variable 'The drive and confidence of the leader'. The researcher now has to use his or her professional judgement to decide what the 'cut-off' points should be for inclusion in the factor. Not all 24 variables will appear in factor 1, only those with high values (factor loadings – the amount that each variable contributes to the factor in question). The decision on which variables to include in factor 1 is not a statistical matter but a matter of professional judgement. Factor analysis is an art as well as a science. The researcher has to find those variables with the highest values (factor loadings) and include those in the factor. The variables chosen should not only have high values but also have values that are close to each other (homogeneous) and be some numerical distance away from the other variables. In the column labelled '1' we can see that there are 7 such variables, and we set these out in the example below. Other variables from the list are some numerical distance away from the variables selected (see below) and also seem to be conceptually unrelated to the seven variables identified for inclusion in the factor. The variables selected are high, close to each other and distant from the other variables. The lowest of these 7 values is 0.513; hence the researcher would report that 7 variables had been selected for inclusion in factor 1, and that the cut-off point was 0.51 (i.e. the lowest point, above which the variables have been selected). Having such a high cut-off point gives considerable power to the factor. Hence we have factor 1, which contains 7 variables.

Let us look at a second example, that of factor 2 (the column labelled '2'). Here we can identify 4 variables that have high values that are close to each other and yet some numerical distance away from the other variables (see example below). These 4 variables would constitute factor 2, with a reported cut-off point of 0.445. At first glance it may seem that 0.445 is low; however, recalling that the data in the example were derived from 1,000 teachers, 0.445

is still highly statistically significant, statistical significance being a combination of the coefficient *and* the sample size.

We repeat this analysis for all 5 factors, deciding the cut-off point, looking for homogeneous high values and numerical distance from other variables in the list.

Stage 3

By this time we have identified 5 factors. However, neither SPSS nor any other software package tells us what to name each factor. The researcher has to devise a name that describes the factor in question. This can be tricky, as it has to catch the issue that is addressed by all the variables that are included in the factor. We have undertaken this for all 5 factors, and we report this below, with the factor loadings for each variable reported in brackets.

Factor 1: Leadership skills in school management

Cut-off point: 0.51

Variables included:

- The drive and confidence of the leader (factor loading 0.758).
- The ability of the leader to motivate and inspire the educators (factor loading 0.743).
- The use of data to inform planning and school development (factor loading 0.690).
- The example set by the leader (factor loading 0.572).
- The clarity of the direction set by the school leadership (factor loading 0.559).
- The consultation abilities/activities of the leader (factor loading 0.548).
- The commitment of the leader to the school (factor loading 0.513).

Factor 2: Parent and teacher partnerships in school development

Cut-off point: 0.44

Variables included:

- The school works in partnership with parents (factor loading 0.804).
- People take positive risks for the good of the school and its development (factor loading 0.778).
- Teamwork among school staff (factor loading 0.642).
- The effectiveness of the teamwork of the SMT (factor loading 0.445).

Factor 3: Promoting staff development by creativity and consultation

Cut-off point: 0.55

Variables included:

- Staff consulted about key decisions (factor loading 0.854).
- The creativity of the SMT (factor loading 0.822).
- Valuing of professional development in the school (0.551).

Factor 4: Respect for, and confidence in, the senior management team

Cut-off point: 0.44

Variables included:

- The respect in which the leader is held by staff (factor loading 0.810).
- The staff's confidence in the SMT (factor loading 0.809).
- The effectiveness of the teamwork of the SMT (factor loading 0.443).

Factor 5: Encouraging staff development through participation in decision-making

Cut-off point 0.64

Variables included:

- Staff voluntarily taking on coordination roles (factor loading 0.779).
- The encouragement and support for innovativeness and creativity (factor loading 0.661).

- Everybody is free to make suggestions to inform decision-making (factor loading 0.642).

Each factor should usually contain a minimum of three variables, though this is a rule of thumb rather than a statistical necessity. Further, in the example here, though some of the variables included have considerably lower factor loadings than others in that factor (e.g. in factor 2: the effectiveness of the teamwork of the SMT (0.445)), nevertheless the conceptual similarity to the other variables in that factor, coupled with the fact that, with 1,000 teachers in the study, 0.445 is still highly statistically significant, combine to suggest that this still merits inclusion. As we mentioned earlier, factor analysis is an art as well as a science.

If one wished to suggest a more stringent level of exactitude then a higher cut-off point could be taken. In the example above, factor 1 could have a cut-off point of 0.74, thereby including only 2 variables in the factor; factor 2 could have a cut-off point of 0.77, thereby including only 2 variables in the factor; factor 3 could have a cut-off point of 0.82, thereby including only 2 variables in the factor; factor 4 could have a cut-off point of 0.80, thereby including only 2 variables in the factor; and factor 5 could have a cut-off point of 0.77, thereby including only 1 variable in the factor. The decision on where to place the cut-off point is a matter of professional judgement when reviewing the data.

In reporting factor analysis the above data would all be included, together with a short commentary, for example:

In order to obtain conceptually similar and significant clusters of issues of the variables, principal components analysis with varimax rotation and Kaiser Normalization were conducted. Eigenvalues equal to or greater than 1.00 were extracted. With regard to the 24 variables used, orthogonal rotation of the variables yielded 5 factors, accounting for 16.820, 11.706, 11.578, 11.386 and 8.556 per cent of the total variance respectively, a total of 60.047 per cent of the total variance explained. The factor loadings are presented in table such-and-such. To enhance the interpretability of the factors, only variables with factor loadings as follows were selected for inclusion in their respective factors: > 0.51 (factor 1), > 0.44 (factor 2), > 0.55 (factor 3), > 0.44 (factor 4), and > 0.64 (factor 5). The factors are named, respectively: *Leadership skills in school management; Parent and teacher partnerships in school development; Promoting staff development by creativity and consultation; Respect for, and confidence in, the senior management team;* and *Encouraging staff development through participation in decision-making.* (See http://www.routledge.com/textbooks/ 9780415368780 – Chapter 25, file SPSS Manual 25.1.)

Having presented the data for the factor analysis the researcher would then comment on what it showed, fitting the research that was being conducted.

Factor analysis is based on certain assumptions which should be maintained in order to serve fidelity to this technique, for example:

- The data must be interval and ratio.
- The sample size should be no fewer than around 150 persons.[1]
- There should be at least 5 cases for each variable (Pallant (2001: 153) suggests 10 cases for each variable).
- The relationships between the variables should be linear.
- Outliers should be removed.
- The data must be capable of being factored. To achieve this, several of the correlations should be of 0.3 or greater, the Bartlett test of sphericity (SPSS calculates this at the press of a button) should be significant at the 0.05 level or better, and the Kaiser-Meyer-Olkin measure of sampling adequacy (calculated automatically by SPSS) should be at 0.6 or above.

Factor analysis: an example

Factor analysis, we said earlier, is a way of determining the nature of underlying patterns among a large number of variables. It is particularly appropriate in research where investigators aim to impose an 'orderly simplification' (Child 1970)

upon a number of interrelated measures. We illustrate the use of factor analysis in a study of occupational stress among teachers (McCormick and Solman 1992).

Despite a decade or so of sustained research, the concept of occupational stress still causes difficulties for researchers intent upon obtaining objective measures in such fields as the physiological and the behavioural, because of the wide range of individual differences. Moreover, subjective measures such as self-reports, by their very nature, raise questions about the external validation of respondents' revelations. This latter difficulty notwithstanding, McCormick and Solman (1992) chose the methodology of self-report as the way into the problem, dichotomizing it into, first, the teacher's view of self, and second, the external world as it is seen to impinge upon the occupation of teaching. Stress, according to the researchers, is considered as 'an unpleasant and unwelcome emotion' whose negative effect for many is 'associated with illness of varying degree' (McCormick and Solman 1992). They began their study on the basis of the following premises:

- Occupational stress is an undesirable and negative response to occupational experiences.
- To be responsible for one's own occupational stress can indicate a personal failing.

Drawing on attribution theory, McCormick and Solman (1992) consider that the idea of blame is a key element in a framework for the exploration of occupational stress. The notion of blame for occupational stress, they assert, fits in well with tenets of attribution theory, particularly in terms of attribution of responsibility having a self-serving bias.[2] Taken in concert with organizational facets of schools, the researchers hypothesized that teachers would 'externalize responsibility for their stress increasingly to increasingly distant and identifiable domains' (McCormick and Solman 1992). Their selection of dependent and independent variables in the research followed directly from this major hypothesis.

McCormick and Solman (1992) developed a questionnaire instrument that included 32 items to do with occupational satisfaction. These were scored on a continuum ranging from 'strongly disagree' to 'strongly agree'. A further 38 items had to do with possible sources of occupational stress. Here, respondents rated the intensity of the stress they experienced when exposed to each source. Stress items were judged on a scale ranging from 'no stress' to 'extreme stress'. In yet another section of the questionnaire, respondents rated how responsible they felt certain nominated persons or institutions were for the occupational stress that they, the respondents, experienced. These entities included self, pupils, superiors, the Department of Education, the government and society itself. Finally, the teacher-participants were asked to complete a 14-item locus of control scale, giving a measure of internality/externality. 'Internals' are people who see outcomes as a function of what they themselves do; 'externals' see outcomes as a result of forces beyond their control. The items included in this lengthy questionnaire arose partly from statements about teacher stress used in earlier investigations, but mainly as a result of hunches about blame for occupational stress that the researchers derived from attribution theory. As Child (1970) observes:

In most instances, the factor analysis is preceded by a hunch as to the factors that might emerge. In fact, it would be difficult to conceive of a manageable analysis which started in an empty-headed fashion.... Even the 'let's see what happens' approach is pretty sure to have a hunch at the back of it somewhere. It is this testing and the generation of hypotheses which forms the principal concern of most factor analysts.

(Child 1970: 8)

The 90-plus-item inventory was completed by 387 teachers. Separate correlation matrices composed of the inter-correlations of the 32 items on the satisfaction scale, the 8 items in the persons/institutions responsibility measure and the 38 items on the stress scale were factor analysed.

The procedures followed by McCormick and Solman (1992), Principal Components, which were subsequently rotated, parallel those we have outlined earlier. (Readable accounts of factor analysis may be found in Child 1970; Kerlinger 1970.)

Box 25.8
Factor analysis of responsibility for stress items

Factor groupings of responsibility items with factor loadings and (rounded) percentages of teachers responding in the two most extreme categories of *much stress* and *extreme stress*.		
	Loading	Percentage
Factor 1: School structure		
Superiors	0.85	29
School organization	0.78	31
Peers	0.77	13
Factor 2: Bureaucratic authority		
Department of Education	0.89	70
Government	0.88	66
Factor 3: Teacher–student relationships		
Students	0.85	45
Society	0.60	60
Yourself	0.50	20

Source: McCormick and Solman 1992

In the factor analysis of the 8-item responsibility for stress measure, the researchers identified three factors. Box 25.8 shows those three factors with what are called their 'factor loadings'. As we have seen, these are like correlation coefficients, ranging from -1.0 to $+1.0$ and are interpreted similarly. That is to say they indicate the correlation between the person/institution responsibility items shown in Box 25.8, and the factors. Looking at factor 1, 'School structure', for example, it can be seen that in the 3 items loading there are, in descending order of weight, superiors (0.85), school organization (0.78) and peers (0.77). 'School structure' as a factor, the authors suggest, is easily identified and readily explained. But what of factor 3, 'Teacher–student relationships', which includes the variables students, society and yourself? McCormick and Solman (1992) proffer the following tentative interpretation:

An explanation for the inclusion of the variable 'yourself' in this factor is not readily at hand.

Clearly, the difference between the variable 'yourself' and the 'students' and 'society' variables is that only 20 per cent of these teachers rated themselves as very or extremely responsible for their own stress, compared to 45 per cent and 60 per cent respectively for the latter two. Possibly the degree of responsibility which teachers attribute to themselves for their occupational stress is associated with their perceptions of their part in controlling student behaviour. This would seem a reasonable explanation, but requiring further investigation.

(McCormick and Solman 1992)

Box 25.9 shows the factors derived from the analysis of the 38 occupational stress items. The 5 factors extracted were named: 'Student domain', 'External (to school) domain', 'Time demands', 'School domain' and 'Personal domain'. While a detailed discussion of the factors and their loadings is inappropriate here, we draw readers' attention to some interesting findings. Notice, for example, how the second factor, 'External (to school) domain', is consistent with the factoring of the responsibility for stress items reported in Box 25.8. That is to say, the variables to do with the government and the Department of Education have loaded on the same factor. The researchers venture this further elaboration of the point.

> when a teacher attributes occupational stress to the Department of Education, it is not as a member of the Department of Education, although such, in fact, is the case. In this context, the Department of Education is outside 'the system to which the teacher belongs', namely the school. A similar argument can be posed for the nebulous concept of Society. The Government is clearly a discrete political structure.

(McCormick and Solman 1992)

'School domain', factor 4 in Box 25.9, consists of items concerned with support from the school principal and colleagues as well as the general nurturing atmosphere of the school. Of particular interest here is that teachers report relatively low levels of stress for these items.

Box 25.10 reports the factor analysis of the 32 items to do with occupational satisfaction. Five

factors were extracted and named as 'Supervision', 'Income', 'External demands', 'Advancement' and 'School culture'. Again, space precludes a full outline of the results set out in Box 25.10. Notice, however, an apparent anomaly in the first factor, 'Supervision'. Responses to items to do with teachers' supervisors and recognition seem to indicate that in general, teachers are satisfied with their supervisors, but feel that they receive too little recognition.

Box 25.10 shows that 21 per cent of teacher-respondents agree or strongly agree that they receive too little recognition, yet 52 per cent agree or strongly agree that they do receive recognition from their immediate supervisors. McCormick and Solman (1992) offer the following explanation:

> The difference can be explained, in the first instance, by the degree or amount of recognition given. That is, immediate supervisors give recognition, but not enough. Another interpretation is that superiors other than the immediate supervisor do not give sufficient recognition for their work.

(McCormick and Solman 1992)

Here is a clear case for some form of respondent validation (see Chapter 6 and 11).

Having identified the underlying structures of occupational stress and occupational satisfaction, the researchers then went on to explore the relationships between stress and satisfaction by using a technique called 'canonical correlation analysis'. The technical details of this procedure are beyond the scope of this book. Interested readers are referred to Levine (1984), who suggests that 'the most acceptable approach to interpretation of canonical variates is the examination of the correlations of the original variables with the canonical variate' (Levine 1984). This is the procedure adopted by McCormick and Solman (1992).

From Box 25.11 we see that factors having high correlations with Canonical Variate 1 are Stress: Student domain (-0.82) and Satisfaction: External demands (0.72).

The researchers offer the following interpretation of this finding:

Box 25.9
Factor analysis of the occupational stress items

Factor groupings of stress items with factor loadings and (rounded) percentages of teachers responding to the two extremes of *much stress* and *extreme stress*

	Loading	Percentage
Factor 1: Student domain		
Poor work attitudes of students	0.79	49
Difficulty in motivating students	0.75	44
Having to deal with students who constantly misbehave	0.73	57
Inadequate discipline in the school	0.70	47
Maintaining discipline with difficult classes	0.64	55
Difficulty in setting and maintaining standards	0.63	26
Verbal abuse by students	0.62	39
Students coming to school without necessary equipment	0.56	23
Deterioration of society's control over children	0.49	55
Factor 2: External (to school) domain		
The Government's education policies	0.82	63
The relationship which the Department of Education has with its schools	0.80	55
Unrealistic demands from the Department of Education	0.78	63
The conviction that the education system is getting worse	0.66	49
Media criticism of teachers	0.64	52
Lack of respect in society for teachers	0.63	56
Having to implement departmental policies	0.59	38
Feeling of powerlessness	0.55	44
Factor 3: Time demands		
Insufficient time for personal matters	0.74	43
Just not enough time in the school day	0.74	51
Difficulty of doing a good job in the classroom because of other delegated responsibilities	0.73	43
Insufficient time for lesson preparation and marking	0.69	50
Excessive curriculum demands	0.67	49
Difficulty in covering the syllabus in the time available	0.61	37
Demanding nature of the job	0.58	64
Factor 4: School domain		
Lack of support from the principal	0.83	21
Not being appreciated by the principal	0.83	14
Principal's reluctance to make tough decisions	0.77	30
Lack of opportunity to participate in school decision-making	0.74	16
Lack of support from other colleagues	0.57	11

continued

Box 25.9
Continued

	Loading	Percentage
Lack of a supportive and friendly atmosphere	0.55	17
Things happen at school over which you have no control	0.41	36
Factor 5: Personal domain		
Personal failings	0.76	13
Feeling of not being suited to teaching	0.72	10
Having to teach a subject for which you are not trained	0.64	23

Source: McCormick and Solman 1992

Box 25.10
Factor analysis of the occupational satisfaction items

Factor groupings of satisfaction items with factor loadings and (rounded) percentages of teacher responses in the two positive extremes of 'strongly agree' and 'agree' for positive statements, or 'strongly disagree' and 'disagree' for statements of a negative nature; the latter items were reversed for analysis and are indicated by*

	Loading	Percentage
Factor 1: Supervision		
My immediate supervisor does not back me up*	0.83	70
I receive recognition from my immediate supervisor	0.80	52
My immediate supervisor is not willing to listen*	0.78	68
My immediate supervisor makes me feel uncomfortable*	0.78	66
My immediate supervisor treats everyone equitably	0.68	62
My superiors do not appreciate what a good job I do*	0.66	39
I receive too little recognition*	0.51	21
Factor 2: Income		
My income is less than I deserve*	0.80	10
I am well paid in proportion to my ability	0.78	8
My income from teaching is adequate	0.78	19
My pay compares well with other non-teaching jobs	0.66	6
Teachers' income is barely enough to live on*	0.56	24
Factor 3: External demands		
Teachers have an excessive workload*	0.72	5
Teachers are expected to do too many non-teaching tasks*	0.66	4
People expect too much of teachers*	0.56	4
There are too many changes in education*	0.53	10
I am satisfied with the Department of Education as an employer	0.44	12
People who aren't teachers do not understand the realities in schools*	0.34	1

Box 25.10
Continued

	Loading	Percentage
Factor 4: Advancement		
Teaching provides me with an opportunity to advance professionally	0.76	37
I am not getting ahead in my present position*	0.67	16
The Government is striving for a better education system	0.54	22
The Department of Education is concerned for teachers' welfare	0.52	6
Factor 5: School culture		
I am happy to be working at this particular school	0.77	73
Working conditions in my school are good	0.64	46
Teaching is very interesting work	0.60	78

Source: McCormick and Solman 1992

Box 25.11

Correlations between (dependent) stress and (independent) satisfaction factors and canonical variates

	Canonical variates		
	1	2	3
Stress factors			
Student domain	−0.82	−0.47	0.05
External (to school) domain	−0.15	−0.04	0.80
Time	−0.43	0.17	−0.52
School domain	−0.34	0.86	0.16
Personal domain	0.09	−0.05	−0.25
Satisfaction factors			
Supervision	0.23	−0.91	0.32
Income	0.45	0.13	0.12
External demands	0.72	0.33	0.28
Advancement	0.48	−0.04	−0.71
School culture	0.06	−0.28	−0.54

Source: adapted from McCormick and Solman 1992

[This] indicates that teachers perceive that 'non-teachers' or outsiders expect too much of them (*External demands*) and that stress results from poor student attitudes and behaviour (*Student domain*). One interpretation might be that for these teachers, high levels of stress attributable to the Student domain are associated with low levels of satisfaction in the context of demands from outside the school,

and vice versa. It may well be that, for some teachers, high demand in one of these is perceived as affecting their capacity to cope or deal with the demands of the other. Certainly, the teacher who is experiencing the urgency of a struggle with student behaviour in the classroom, is unlikely to think of the requirements of persons and agencies outside the school as important.

(McCormick and Solman 1992)

The outcomes of their factor analyses frequently puzzle researchers. Take, for example, one of the loadings on the third canonical variate. There, we see that the stress factor 'Time demands' correlates negatively (−0.52). One might have supposed, McCormick and Solman (1992) say, that stress attributable to the external domain would have correlated with the variate in the same direction. But this is not so. It correlates positively at 0.80. One possible explanation, they suggest, is that an increase in stress experienced because of time demands coincides with a lowering of stress attributable to the external domain, as time is expended in meeting demands from the external domain. The researchers concede, however, that this explanation would need more close examination before it could be accepted.

McCormick and Solman's (1992) questionnaire also elicited biographical data from the teacher-respondents in respect of sex, number of years teaching, type and location of school and position held in school. By rescoring the stress items on a scale ranging from 'No stress' (1) to 'Extreme stress' (5) and using the means of the factor scores, the researchers were able to explore associations between the degree of perceived occupational stress and the biographical data supplied by participants. Space precludes a full account of McCormick and Solman's (1992) findings. We illustrate some significant results in Box 25.12. In the *School domain* more stress was reported

by secondary school teachers than by their colleagues teaching younger pupils, not really a very surprising result, the researchers observe, given that infant/primary schools are generally much smaller than their secondary counterparts and that teachers are more likely to be part of a smaller, supportive group. In the domain of *Time demands*, females experienced more stress than males, a finding consistent with that of other research. In the *Personal domain*, a significant difference was found in respect of the school's location, the level of occupational stress increasing from the rural setting, through the country/city to the metropolitan area.

To conclude, factor analysis techniques are ideally suited to studies such as that of McCormick and Solman (1992) in which lengthy questionnaire-type data are elicited from a large number of participants and where researchers are concerned to explore underlying structures and relationships between dependent and independent variables.[3]

Inevitably, such tentative explorations raise as many questions as they answer.

Examples of studies using multidimensional scaling and cluster analysis

Forgas (1976) studied housewives' and students' perceptions of typical social episodes in their lives, the episodes having been elicited from the respective groups by means of a diary technique. Subjects were required to supply two adjectives to describe each of the social episodes they had recorded as having occurred during the previous 24 hours. From a pool of some 146 adjectives thus generated, 10 (together with their antonyms) were selected on the basis of their salience, their diversity of usage and their independence of one another. Next, 2 more scales from speculative taxonomies were added to give 12 unidimensional scales purporting to describe the underlying episode structures. These scales were used in the second part of the study to rate 25 social episodes in each group, the episodes being chosen as follows. An 'index of relatedness' was

Box 25.12
Biographical data and stress factors

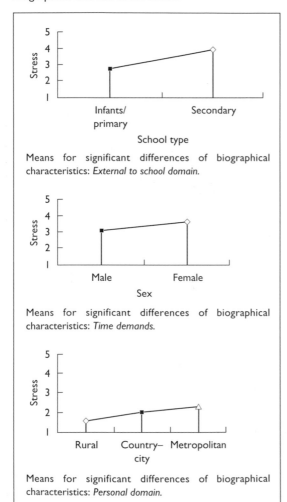

Means for significant differences of biographical characteristics: *External to school domain.*

Means for significant differences of biographical characteristics: *Time demands.*

Means for significant differences of biographical characteristics: *Personal domain.*

Source: McCormick and Solman 1992

computed on the basis of the number of times a pair of episodes was placed in the same category by respective housewife and student judges. Data were aggregated over the total number of subjects in each of the 2 groups. The 25 'top' social episodes in each group were retained. Forgas's (1976) analysis is based upon the ratings of 26 housewives and 25 students of their respective 25 episodes on each of the 12 unidimensional scales. Box 25.13 shows a three-dimensional configuration of 25 social episodes rated by the student group on 3 of the scales. For illustrative purposes some of

the social episodes numbered in Box 25.13 are identified by specific content.

In another study, Forgas (1978) examined the social environment of a university department consisting of tutors, students and secretarial staff, all of whom had interacted both inside and outside the department for at least 6 months prior to the research and thought of themselves as an intensive and cohesive social unit. Forgas's interest was in the relationship between two aspects of the social environment of the department – the perceived structure of the group and the perceptions that

Box 25.13
Students' perceptions of social episodes

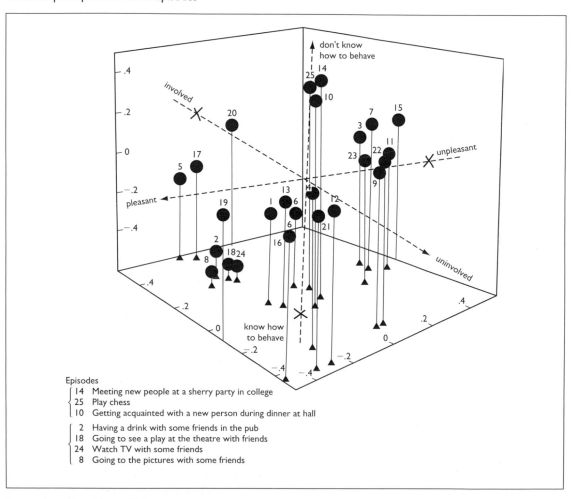

Episodes

{ 14   Meeting new people at a sherry party in college
  25   Play chess
  10   Getting acquainted with a new person during dinner at hall

{ 2   Having a drink with some friends in the pub
  18   Going to see a play at the theatre with friends
  24   Watch TV with some friends
  8   Going to the pictures with some friends

Source: adapted from Forgas 1976

were held of specific social episodes. Participants were required to rate the similarity between each possible pairing of group members on a scale ranging from '1 = extremely similar' to '9 = extremely dissimilar'. An individual differences multidimensional scaling procedure (INDSCAL) produced an optimal three-dimensional configuration of group structure accounting for 68 per cent of the variance, group members being differentiated along the dimensions of sociability, creativity and competence.

A semi-structured procedure requiring participants to list typical and characteristic interaction situations was used to identify a number of social episodes. These in turn were validated by participant observation of the ongoing activities of the department. The most commonly occurring social episodes (those mentioned by nine or more members) served as the stimuli in the second stage of the study. Bipolar scales similar to those reported by Forgas (1976) and elicited in like manner were used to obtain group members' judgements of social episodes.

An interesting finding reported by Forgas (1978) was that formal status differences exercised no significant effect upon the perception of the group by its members, the absence of differences being attributed to the strength of the department's cohesiveness and intimacy. In Forgas's analysis of the group's perceptions of social episodes, the INDSCAL scaling procedure produced an optimal four-dimensional solution accounting for 62 per cent of the variance, group members perceiving social episodes in terms of anxiety, involvement, evaluation and social-emotional versus task orientation. Box 25.14 illustrates how an average group member would see the characteristics of various social episodes in terms of the dimensions by which the group commonly judged them.

Finally we outline a classificatory system that has been developed to process materials elicited in a rather structured form of account gathering. Peevers and Secord's (1973) study of developmental changes in children's use of descriptive concepts of persons illustrates the application of quantitative techniques to the analysis of one form of account.

In individual interviews, children of varying ages were asked to describe three friends and one person whom they disliked, all four people being of the same sex as the interviewee. Interviews were tape-recorded and transcribed. A person-concept coding system was developed, the categories of which are illustrated in Box 25.15. Each person-description was divided into items, each item consisting of one discrete piece of information. Each item was then coded on each of four major dimensions. Detailed coding procedures are set out in Peevers and Secord (1973).

Tests of inter-judge agreement on descriptiveness, personal involvement and evaluative consistency in which two judges worked independently on the interview transcripts of 21 boys and girls aged between 5 and 16 years resulted in inter-judge agreement on those three dimensions of 87 per cent, 79 per cent and 97 per cent respectively.

Peevers and Secord (1973) also obtained evidence of the degree to which the participants themselves were consistent from one session to another in their use of concepts to describe other people. Children were reinterviewed between one week and one month after the first session on the pretext of problems with the original recordings. Indices of test-retest reliability were computed for each of the major coding dimensions. Separate correlation coefficients (Eta) were obtained for younger and older children in respect of their descriptive concepts of liked and disliked peers. Reliability coefficients are as set out in Box 25.16. Secord and Peevers (1974) conclude that their approach offers the possibility of an exciting line of inquiry into the depth of insight that individuals have into the personalities of their acquaintances. Their 'free commentary' method is a modification of the more structured interview, requiring the interviewer to probe for explanations of why a person behaves the way he or she does or why a person is the kind of person he or she is. Peevers and Secord (1973) found that older children in their sample readily volunteered this sort of information. Harré (1977b) observes that this approach could also be extended to elicit commentary upon children's friends and enemies

Box 25.14
Perception of social episodes

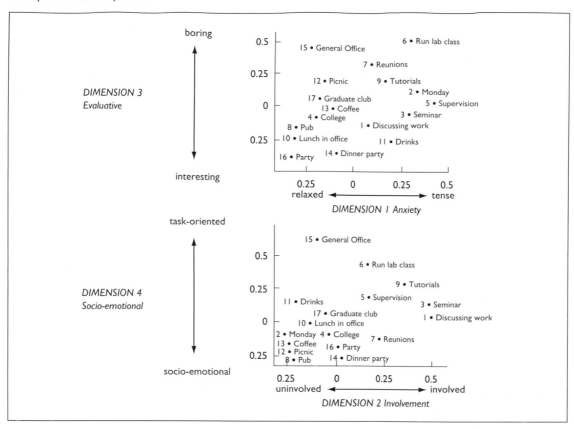

Source: adapted from Forgas 1978

and the ritual actions associated with the creation and maintenance of these categories.

Multidimensional data: some words on notation

The hypothetical data in Box 25.17 refer to a survey of voting behaviour in a sample of men and women in Britain. The outline that follows draws closely on an exposition by Whiteley (1983):

the row variable (sex) is represented by i
the column variable (voting preference) is represented by j
the layer variable (social class) is represented by k

The number in any one cell in Box 25.17 can be represented by the symbol n_{ijk} that is to say, the score in row category i, column category j, and layer category k, where:

$i = 1$ (men), 2 (women)

$j = 1$ (Conservative), 2 (Labour)

$k = 1$ (middle class), 2 (working class)

It follows therefore that the numbers in Box 25.17 can also be represented as in Box 25.18. Thus,

$n_{121} = 30$ (men, Labour, middle class)

and

$n_{212} = 40$ (women, Conservative, working class).

Box 25.15

Person concept coding system

Dimension	Levels of descriptiveness
Descriptiveness	1 *Undifferentiating*. . . (person not differentiated from his or her environment)
	2 *Simple differentiating*. . . (person differentiated in simple global terms)
	3 *Differentiating*. . . (person differentiated in specific characteristics)
	4 *Dispositional*. . . (person differentiated in terms of traits)
Personal involvement	*Degrees of involvement*
	1 *Egocentric*. . . (other person described in self-oriented terms)
	2 *Mutual*. . . (other person described in terms of his or her relationship to perceiver)
	3 *Other oriented*. . . (no personal involvement expressed by perceiver)
Evaluative consistency	*Amount of consistency*
	1 *Consistent*. . . (nothing favourable about 'disliked', nothing unfavourable about 'liked')
	2 *Inconsistent*. . . (some mixture of favourableness and unfavourableness)
Depth	*Levels of depth*
	Level 1 (includes all undifferentiated and simple differentiated descriptions)
	Level 2 (includes differentiated and some dispositional descriptions)
	Level 3 (includes explanation-type differentiated and dispositional descriptions)

Source: adapted from Peevers and Secord 1973

Three types of marginals can be obtained from Box 25.18 by:

1   Summing over two variables to give the marginal totals for the third. Thus:

n_{++k} = summing over sex and voting preference to give social class, for example:

$n_{111} + n_{121} + n_{211} + n_{221} = 230$ (middle class)

$n_{112} + n_{122} + n_{212} + n_{222} = 320$ (working class)

n_{+j+} = summing over sex and social class to give voting preference

n_{i++} = summing over voting preference and social class to give sex.

2   Summing over one variable to give the marginal totals for the second and third variables. Thus:

$n_{+11} = 180$ (middle-class Conservative)

$n_{+21} = 50$ (middle-class Labour)

$n_{+12} = 80$ (working-class Conservative)

$n_{+22} = 240$ (working-class Labour)

3   Summing over all three variables to give the grand total. Thus:

$$n_{+++} = 550 = N$$

Using the chi-square test in a three-way classification table

Whiteley (1983) shows how easy it is to extend the 2×2 chi-square test to the three-way case. The probability that an individual taken from the sample at random in Box 25.17 will be a woman is:

$$p_{2++} = \frac{n_{2++}}{n_{+++}} = \frac{270}{550} = 0.49$$

and the probability that a respondent's voting preference will be Labour is:

$$p_{+2+} = \frac{n_{+2+}}{n_{+++}} = \frac{290}{550} = 0.53$$

and the probability that a respondent will be working class is:

$$p_{++2} = \frac{n_{++2}}{n_{+++}} = \frac{320}{550} = 0.58$$

To determine the expected probability of an individual being a woman, Labour supporter and

Box 25.16

Reliability coefficients for peer descriptions

Dimension	Liked peers		Disliked peers	
	Younger subjects	Older subjects	Younger subjects	Older subjects
Descriptiveness	0.83	0.91	0.80	0.84
Personal involvement	0.76	0.80	0.84	0.77
Depth	0.65	0.71	0.65	0.75
Evaluative consistency	0.69	0.92	0.76	0.69

Source: Peevers and Secord 1973

Box 25.17

Sex, voting preference and social class: a three-way classification table

	Middle class		Working class	
	Conservative	Labour	Conservative	Labour
Men	80	30	40	130
Women	100	20	40	110

Source: adapted from Whiteley 1983

Box 25.18

Sex, voting preference and social class: a three-way notational classification

	Middle class		Working class	
	Conservative	Labour	Conservative	Labour
Men	n_{111}	n_{121}	n_{112}	n_{122}
Women	n_{211}	n_{221}	n_{212}	n_{222}

working class we assume that these variables are statistically independent (that is to say, there is no relationship between them) and simply apply the multiplication rule of probability theory:

$$p_{222} = (p_{2++})(p_{+2+})(p_{++2})$$

$$= (0.49)(0.53)(0.58) = 0.15$$

Box 25.19

Expected frequencies in sex, voting preference and social class

	Middle class		Working class	
	Conservative	Labour	Conservative	Labour
Men	55.4	61.7	77.0	85.9
Women	53.4	59.5	74.3	82.8

Source: adapted from Whiteley 1983

This can be expressed in terms of the expected frequency in cell n_{222} as:

$$N(p_{2++})(p_{+2+})(p_{++2}) = 550\,(0.49)(0.53)(0.58)$$

$$= 82.8$$

Similarly, the expected frequency in cell n_{112} is:

$$N(p_{1++})(p_{+1+})(p_{++2}) \text{ where :}$$

$$p_{1++} = \frac{n_{1++}}{n_{+++}} = \frac{280}{550} = 0.51$$

and

$$p_{+1+} = \frac{n_{+1+}}{n_{+++}} = \frac{260}{550} = 0.47$$

and

$$p_{++2} = \frac{n_{++2}}{n_{+++}} = \frac{320}{550} = 0.58$$

Thus $N(p_{1++})(p_{+1+})(p_{++2})$

$$= 550\,(0.51)(0.47)(0.58) = 77.0$$

Box 25.19 gives the expected frequencies for the data shown in Box 25.17.

With the observed frequencies and the expected frequencies to hand, chi-square is calculated in the usual way:

$$\chi^2 = \sum \frac{(O - E)^2}{E} = 159.41$$

Whiteley (1983) observes that degrees of freedom in a three-way contingency table is more complex than in a 2×2 classification. Essentially, however, degrees of freedom refer to the freedom with which the researcher is able to assign values to the cells, given fixed marginal totals. This can be computed by first determining the degrees of freedom for the marginals.

Each of the variables in our example (sex, voting preference and social class) contains two categories. It follows therefore that we have $(2 - 1)$ degrees of freedom for each of them, given that the marginal for each variable is fixed. Since the grand total of all the marginals (i.e. the sample size) is also fixed, it follows that one more degree of freedom is also lost. We subtract these fixed numbers from the total number of cells in our contingency table. In general therefore:

degrees of freedom (df) = the number of cells in the table -1 (for N) $-$ the number of cells fixed by the hypothesis being tested.

Thus, where r = rows, c = columns and l = layers:

$$df = rcl(r - 1) - (c - 1) - (1 - 1) - 1$$
$$= rcl - r - c - l + 2$$

that is to say $df = rcl - r - c - l + 2$ when we are testing the hypothesis of the mutual independence of the three variables.

In our example:

$$df = (2)(2)(2) - 2 - 2 - 2 + 2 = 4$$

From chi-square tables we see that the critical value of χ^2 with four degrees of freedom is 9.49 at $p = 0.05$. Our obtained value greatly exceeds that number. We reject the null hypothesis and conclude that sex, voting preference and social class are significantly interrelated.

Having rejected the null hypothesis with respect to the mutual independence of the three variables, the researcher's task now is to identify which variables cause the null hypothesis to be rejected. We cannot simply assume that because our chi-square test has given a significant result, it therefore follows that there are significant associations between all three variables. It may be the case, for example, that an association exists between two of the variables while the third is completely independent. What we need now is a test of 'partial independence'. Whiteley (1983) shows the following three such possible tests in respect of the data in Box 25.17. First, that sex is

independent of social class and voting preference:

$$(1)\ p_{ijk} = (p_i)(p_{jk})$$

Second, that voting preference is independent of sex and social class

$$(2)\ p_{ijk} = (p_j)(p_{ik})$$

Third, that social class is independent of sex and voting preference

$$(3)\ p_{ijk} = (p_k)(p_{ij})$$

The following example shows how to construct the expected frequencies for the first hypothesis. We can determine the probability of an individual being, say, woman, Labour, and working-class, assuming hypothesis (1), as follows:

$$p_{222} = (p_{2++})(p_{+22}) = \frac{(n_{2++})}{(N)}\frac{(n_{+22})}{(N)}$$

$$p_{222} = \frac{(270)}{(550)}\frac{(240)}{(550)} = 0.214$$

$$E_{222} = N(p_{2++})(p_{+22}) = 550\frac{(270)}{(550)}\frac{(240)}{(550)} = 117.8$$

That is to say, assuming that sex is independent of social class and voting preference, the expected number of female, working-class Labour supporters is 117.8.

When we calculate the expected frequencies for each of the cells in our contingency table in respect of our first hypothesis $(p_{ijk}) = (p_i)(p_{jk})$, we obtain the results shown in Box 25.20.

$$\chi^2 = \sum \frac{(O - E)^2}{E} = 5.71$$

Box 25.20
Expected frequencies assuming that sex is independent of social class and voting preference

	Middle class		Working class	
	Conservative	Labour	Conservative	Labour
Men	91.6	25.5	40.7	122.2
Women	88.4	24.5	39.3	117.8

Source: adapted from Whiteley 1983

Degrees of freedom is given by:

$$df = rcl - (cl - 1) - (r - 1) - 1$$
$$= rcl - cl - r + 1 = 8 - 4 - 2 + 1 = 3$$

Whiteley (1983) observes:

> Note that we are assuming c and l are interrelated so that once, say, p_{+11} is calculated, then P_{+12}, P_{+21} and P_{+22} are determined, so we have only 1 degree of freedom; that is to say, we lose $(cl - 1)$ degrees of freedom in calculating that relationship.
>
> (Whiteley 1983)

From chi-square tables we see that the critical value of χ^2 with three degrees of freedom is 7.81 at $p = 0.05$. Our obtained value is less than this. We therefore accept the null hypothesis and conclude that *there is no relationship between sex on the one hand and voting preference and social class on the other*.

Suppose now that instead of casting our data into a three-way classification as shown in Box 25.17, we had simply used a 2×2 contingency table and that we had sought to test the null hypothesis that *there is no relationship between sex and voting preference*. The data are shown in Box 25.21.

When we compute chi-square from the above data our obtained value is $\chi^2 = 4.48$. Degrees of freedom are given by $(r - 1)(c - 1) = (2 - 1)(2 - 1) = 1$.

From chi-square tables we see that the critical value of χ^2 with 1 degree of freedom is 3.84 at $p = 0.05$. Our obtained value exceeds this. We reject the null hypothesis and conclude that *sex is significantly associated with voting preference*.

But how can we explain the differing conclusions that we have arrived at in respect of the data in Boxes 25.17 and 25.21? These examples illustrate an important and general point, Whiteley (1983) observes. In the bivariate analysis (Box 25.21) we concluded that there was a significant relationship between sex and voting preference. In the multivariate analysis (Box 25.17) that relationship was found to be non-significant when we controlled for social class. The

Box 25.21
Sex and voting preference: a two-way classification table

	Conservative	Labour
Men	120	160
Women	140	130

Source: adapted from Whiteley 1983

lesson is plain: use a multivariate approach to the analysis of contingency tables wherever the data allow.

Multilevel modelling

Multilevel modelling (also known as multilevel regression) is a statistical method that recognizes that it is uncommon to be able to assign students in schools randomly to control and experimental groups, or indeed to conduct an experiment that requires an intervention with one group while maintaining a control group (Keeves and Sellin 1997: 394).

Typically in most schools, students are brought together in particular groupings for specified purposes and each group of students has its own different characteristics which renders it different from other groups. Multilevel modelling addresses the fact that, unless it can be shown that different groups of students are, in fact, alike, it is generally inappropriate to aggregate groups of students or data for the purposes of analysis. Multilevel models avoid the pitfalls of aggregation and the *ecological fallacy* (Plewis 1997: 35), i.e. making inferences about individual students and behaviour from aggregated data.

Data and variables exist at individual and group levels, indeed Keeves and Sellin (1997) break down analysis further into three main levels: between students over all groups, between groups, and between students within groups. One could extend the notion of levels, of course, to include individual, group, class, school, local, re-gional, national and international levels (Paterson and Goldstein 1991). This has been us- ing multilevel regression and hierarchical linear modelling. Multilevel models enable researchers to ask questions hitherto unanswered, e.g. about variability between and within schools, teach- ers and curricula (Plewis 1997: 34–5), in short about the *processes* of teaching and learning.[4] Useful overviews of multilevel modelling can be found in Goldstein (1987), Fitz-Gibbon (1997) and Keeves and Sellin (1997).

Multilevel analysis avoids statistical treatments associated with experimental methods (e.g. analysis of variance and covariance); rather it uses regression analysis and, in particular, multilevel regression. Regression analysis, argues Plewis (1997: 28), assumes *homoscedasticity* (where the residuals demonstrate equal scatter), that the residuals are independent of each other, and finally, that the residuals are normally distributed.

The whole field of multilevel modelling has proliferated rapidly since the early 1990s and is the basis of much research that is being undertaken on the 'value added' component of education and the comparison of schools in public 'league tables' of results (Fitz-Gibbon 1991; 1997). However, Fitz-Gibbon (1997: 42–4) provides important evidence to question the value of some forms of multilevel modelling. She demonstrates that residual gain analysis provides answers to questions about the value-added dimension of education which differ insubstantially from those answers that are given by multilevel modelling (the lowest correlation coefficient being 0.93 and 71.4 per cent of the correlations computed correlating between 0.98 and 1). The important point here is that residual gain analysis is a much more straightforward technique than multilevel modelling. Her work strikes at the heart of the need to use complex multilevel modelling to assess the 'value-added' component of education. In her work (Fitz-Gibbon 1997: 5) the value-added score – the difference between a statistically-predicted performance and the actual performance – can be computed using residual gain analysis rather than multilevel modelling.

Nonetheless, multilevel modelling now attracts worldwide interest.

Whereas ordinary regression models do not make allowances, for example, for different schools (Paterson and Goldstein 1991), multilevel regression can include school differences, and, in- deed other variables, for example: socio-economic status (Willms 1992), single and co-educational schools (Daly 1996; Daly and Shuttleworth 1997), location (Garner and Raudenbush 1991), size of school (Paterson 1991) and teaching styles (Zuzovsky and Aitkin 1991). Indeed Plewis (1991) indicates how multilevel modelling can be used in longitudinal studies, linking educational progress with curriculum coverage.

Cluster analysis

Whereas factor analysis and elementary linkage analysis enable the researcher to group together factors and variables, cluster analysis enables the researcher to group together similar and homogeneous subsamples of *people*. This is best approached through software packages such as SPSS, and we illustrate this here. SPSS creates a dendrogram of results, grouping and regrouping groups until all the variables are embraced.

For example, here is a simple cluster based on 20 cases (people). Imagine that their scores have been collected on an item concerning the variable 'the attention given to teaching and learning in the school'. One can see that, at the most general level there are two clusters (cluster one = persons 19, 20, 2, 13, 15, 9, 11, 18, 14, 16, 1, 10, 12, 5, 17; cluster two = persons 7, 8, 4, 3, 6). If one were to wish to have smaller clusters then three groupings could be found: cluster one: persons 19, 20, 2, 13, 15, 9, 11, 18; cluster two: persons 14, 16, 1, 10, 12, 5, 17; cluster three: persons 7, 8, 4, 3, 6 (Box 25.22).

Using this analysis enables the researcher to identify important groupings of people in a post-hoc analysis, i.e. not setting up the groupings and subgroupings at the stage of sample design, but *after* the data have been gathered. In the

Box 25.22
Cluster analysis

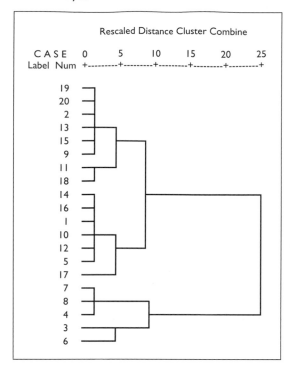

example of the two-group cluster here one could examine the characteristics of those participants who were clustered into groups one and two, and, for the three-group cluster, one could examine the characteristics of those participants who were clustered into groups one, two and three for the variable 'the attention given to teaching and learning in the school'.

Chapter 25

26 Choosing a statistical test

There are very many statistical tests available to the researcher. Which test one employs depends on several factors, for example:

- the purpose of the analysis (e.g. to describe or explore data, to test a hypothesis, to seek correlations, to identify the effects of one or more independent variables on a dependent variable, to identify differences between two or more groups; to look for underlying groupings of data, to report effect sizes)
- the kinds of data with which one is working (parametric and non-parametric)
- the scales of data being used (nominal, ordinal, interval, ratio)
- the number of groups in the sample
- the assumptions in the tests
- whether the samples are independent of each other or related to each other.

Researchers wishing to use statistics will need to ask questions such as:

- What statistics do I need to answer my research questions?
- Are the data parametric or non-parametric?
- How many groups are there (e.g. two, three or more)?
- Are the groups related or independent?
- What kind of test do I need (e.g. a difference test, a correlation, factor analysis, regression)?

We have addressed several of these points in the preceding chapters; those not addressed in previous chapters are addressed here. In this chapter we draw together the threads of the discussion of statistical analysis and address what, for many researchers, can be a nightmare: deciding which statistical tests to use. In the interests of clarity we have decided to use tables and graphic means of presenting the issues in this chapter (see http://www.routledge.com/textbooks/ 9780415368780 – Chapter 26, file 26.1.doc).

How many samples?

In addition to the scale of data being used (nominal, ordinal, interval, ratio), the *kind* of statistic that one calculates depends in part on, first, whether the samples are related to, or independent of, each other, and second, the number of samples in the test. With regard to the first point, as we have seen in previous chapters, different statistics are sometimes used when groups are related to each other and when they are independent of each other. Groups will be independent when they have no relationship to each other, e.g. in conducting a test to see if there is any difference between the voting of males and females on a particular item, say mathematics performance. The tests that one could use here are, for example: the chi-square test (for nominal data), the Mann-Whitney U test and Kruskal-Wallis (for ordinal data), and the t-test and analysis of variance (ANOVA) for interval and ratio data.

However, there are times when the groups might be related. For example, we may wish to measure the performance of the same group at two points in time – before and after a particular intervention – or we may wish to measure the voting of the same group on two different factors, say preference for mathematics and preference for music. Here it is not different groups that are being involved, but the same group on two occasions and the same two on two variables respectively. In this case different statistics would have to be used, for example the Wilcoxon test, the Friedman test, the t-test for paired samples, and the sign test. Let us give a frequently used example of an experiment (Box 26.1).

In preceding chapters we have indicated which tests are to be used with independent samples and which are to be used with related samples.

With regard to the number of samples in the test, there are statistical tests which are for single samples (one group only, e.g. a single class in school), for two samples (two groups, e.g. males and females in a school) and for three or more samples

Box 26.1

Identifying statistical tests for an experiment

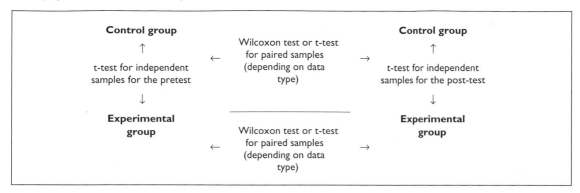

Box 26.2

Statistical tests to be used with different numbers of groups of samples

Scale of data	One sample	Two samples		More than two samples	
		Independent	Related	Independent	Related
Nominal	Binomial	Fisher exact test	McNemar	Chi-square (χ^2) k-samples test	Cochran Q
	Chi-square (χ^2) one-sample test	Chi-square (χ^2) two-samples test			
Ordinal	Kolmogorov-Smirnov one-sample test	Mann-Whitney U test	Wilcoxon matched pairs test	Kruskal-Wallis test	Friedman test
		Kolmogorov-Smirnov test	Sign test	Ordinal regression analysis	
		Wald-Wolfowitz			
		Spearman rho			
		Ordinal regression analysis			
Interval and ratio	t-test	t-test	t-test for paired samples	One-way ANOVA	Repeated measures ANOVA
		Pearson product moment correlation		Two-way ANOVA	
				Tukey hsd test	
				Scheffé test	

Box 26.3
Types of statistical tests for four scales of data

	Nominal	Ordinal	Interval and ratio
Measures of association	Tetrachoric correlation	Spearman's rho	Pearson product-moment correlation
	Point biserial correlation	Kendall rank order correlation	
	Phi coefficient	Kendall partial rank correlation	
	Cramer's V		
Measures of difference	Chi-square	Mann-Whitney U test	t-test for two independent samples
	McNemar	Kruskal-Wallis	t-test for two related samples
	Cochran Q	Wilcoxon matched pairs	One-way ANOVA
	Binomial test	Friedman two-way analysis of variance	Two-way ANOVA for more
		Wald-Wolfowitz test	Tukey hsd test
		Kolmogorov-Smirnov test	Scheffé test
Measures of linear relationship between independent and dependent variables		Ordinal regression analysis	Linear regression
			Multiple regression
Identifying underlying factors, data reduction			Factor analysis
			Elementary linkage analysis

(e.g. parents, teachers, students and administrative staff in a school). Tests which can be applied to a *single* group include the binomial test, the chi-square one-sample test, and the Kolmogorov-Smirnov one-sample test; tests which can be applied to *two* groups include the chi-square test, Mann-Whitney U test, the t-test, the Spearman and Pearson tests of correlation; tests which can be applied to *three or more* samples include the chi-square test, analysis of variance and the Tukey test. We set out some of these tests in Box 26.2. It is essential to use the correct test for the correct number of groups.

The statistical tests to be used also depend on the scales of data being treated (nominal – ratio) and the tasks which the researcher wishes to perform – the purpose of the analysis (e.g. to discover differences between groups, to look for degrees of association, to measure the effect of one or more independent variables on a dependent variable etc.). In preceding chapters we have described the different scales of data and the kinds of tests available for different purposes. In respect of these considerations, Box 26.3 summarizes some of the main tests here.

Chapter 26

Box 26.4

Choosing statistical tests for parametric and non-parametric data

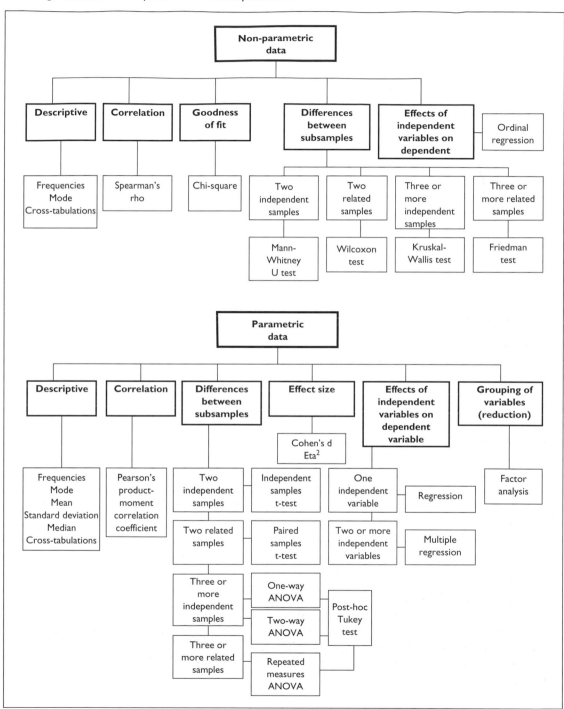

Box 26.5

Statistics available for different types of data

Data type	Legitimate statistics	Points to observe/questions/examples
Nominal	Mode (the score achieved by the greatest number of people)	Is there a clear 'front runner' that receives the highest score with low scoring on other categories, or is the modal score only narrowly leading the other categories? Are there two scores which are vying for the highest score – a bimodal score?
	Frequencies	Which are the highest/lowest frequencies? Is the distribution even across categories?
	Chi-square (a statistic that charts the difference between statistically expected and actual scores)	Are differences between scores caused by chance/accident or are they statistically significant, i.e. not simply caused by chance?
Ordinal	Mode	Which score on a rating scale is the most frequent?
	Median (the score gained by the middle person in a ranked group of people or, if there is an even number of cases, the score which is midway between the highest score obtained in the lower half of the cases and the lowest score obtained in the higher half of the cases).	What is the score of the middle person in a list of scores?
	Frequencies	Do responses tend to cluster around one or two categories of a rating scale? Are the responses skewed towards one end of a rating scale (e.g. 'strongly agree')? Do the responses pattern themselves consistently across the sample? Are the frequencies generally high or generally low (i.e. whether respondents tend to feel strongly about an issue)? Is there a clustering of responses around the central categories of a rating scale (the central tendency, respondents not wishing to appear to be too extreme)?
	Chi-square	Are the frequencies of one set of nominal variables (e.g. sex) significantly related to a set of ordinal variables?
	Spearman rank order correlation (a statistic to measure the degree of association between two ordinal variables)	Do the results from one rating scale correlate with the results from another rating scale? Do the rank order positions for one variable correlate with the rank order positions for another variable?
	Mann-Whitney U-test (a statistic to measure any significant difference between two independent samples)	Is there a significant difference in the results of a rating scale for two independent samples (e.g. males and females)?
	Kruskal-Wallis analysis of variance (a statistic to measure any significant differences between three or more independent samples)	Is there a significant difference between three or more nominal variables (e.g. membership of political parties) and the results of a rating scale?

continued

Box 26.5
continued

Interval and ratio	Mode Mean Frequencies Median Chi-square	What is the average score for this group?
	Standard deviation (a measure of the dispersal of scores)	Are the scores on a parametric test evenly distributed? Do scores cluster closely around the mean? Are scores widely spread around the mean? Are scores dispersed evenly? Are one or two extreme scores ('outliers') exerting a disproportionate influence on what are otherwise closely clustered scores?
	z-scores (a statistic to convert scores from different scales, i.e. with different means and standard deviations, to a common scale, i.e. with the same mean and standard deviation, enabling different scores to be compared fairly)	How do the scores obtained by students on a test which was marked out of 20 compare to the scores by the same students on a test which was marked out of 50?
	Pearson product-moment correlation (a statistic to measure the degree of association between two interval or ratio variables)	Is there a correlation between one set of interval data (e.g. test scores for one examination) and another set of interval data (e.g. test scores on another examination)?
	t-tests (a statistic to measure the difference between the means of one sample on two separate occasions or between two samples on one occasion)	Are the control and experimental groups matched in their mean scores on a parametric test? Is there a significant different between the pretest and post-test scores of a sample group?
	Analysis of variance (a statistic to ascertain whether two or more means differ significantly)	Are the differences in the means between test results of three groups statistically significant?

The type of tests used also vary according to whether one is working with parametric or non-parametric data. Boxes 26.4 and 26.5 draw together and present the kinds of statistical tests available, depending on whether one is using parametric or non-parametric data, together with the purpose of the analysis. Box 26.5 sets out the commonly used statistics for data types and purposes (Siegel 1956; Cohen and Holliday 1996; Hopkins *et al*. 1996).

Assumptions of tests

Statistical tests are based on certain assumptions. It is important to be aware of these assumptions and to operate fairly within them. Some of the more widely used tests have the following assumptions (Box 26.6).

The choice of which statistics to employ is not arbitrary, but dependent on purpose.

Box 26.6

Assumptions of statistical tests

Test	Assumptions
Mean	Data are normally distributed, with no outliers.
Mode	There are few values, and few scores, occurring which have a similar frequency.
Median	There are many ordinal values.
Chi-square	Data are categorical (nominal).
	Randomly sampled population.
	Mutually independent categories.
	Data are discrete (i.e. no decimal places between data points).
	80 per cent of all the cells in a cross-tabulation contain 5 or more cases.
Kolmogorov-Smirnov	The underlying distribution is continuous.
	Data are nominal.
t-test and analysis of variance	Population is normally distributed.
	Sample is selected randomly from the population.
	Each case is independent of the other.
	The groups to be compared are nominal, and the comparison is made using interval and ratio data.
	The sets of data to be compared are normally distributed (the bell-shaped Gaussian curve of distribution).
	The sets of scores have approximately equal variances, or the square of the standard deviation is known.
	The data are interval or ratio.
Wilcoxon test	The data are ordinal.
	The samples are related.
Mann-Whitney and Kruskal-Wallis	The groups to be compared are nominal, and the comparison is made using ordinal data.
	The populations from which the samples are drawn have similar distributions.
	Samples are drawn randomly.
	Samples are independent of each other.
Spearman rank order correlation	The data are ordinal.
Pearson correlation	The data are interval and ratio.
Regression (simple and multiple)	Assumptions underlying regression techniques:
	The data derive from a random or probability sample.
	The data are interval or ratio (unless ordinal regression is used).
	Outliers are removed.
	There is a linear relationship between the independent and dependent variables.
	The dependent variable is normally distributed (the bell-shaped Gaussian curve of distribution).
	The residuals for the dependent variable (the differences between calculated and observed scores) are approximately normally distributed.
	Collinearity is removed (where one independent variable is an exact or very close correlate of another).
Factor analysis	The data are interval or ratio.
	The data are normally distributed.
	Outliers have been removed.
	The sample size should not be less than 100–150 persons.
	There should be at least five cases for each variable.
	The relationships between the variables should be linear.
	The data must be capable of being factored.

Notes

I THE NATURE OF INQUIRY – SETTING THE FIELD

1 We are not here recommending, nor would we wish to encourage, exclusive dependence on rationally derived and scientifically provable knowledge for the conduct of education – even if this were possible. There is a rich fund of traditional and cultural wisdom in teaching (as in other spheres of life) which we would ignore to our detriment. What we are suggesting, however, is that total dependence on the latter has tended in the past to lead to an impasse: and that for further development and greater understanding to be achieved education must needs resort to the methods of science and research.

2 A classic statement opposing this particular view of science is that of Kuhn, T. S. (1962) *The Structure of Scientific Revolutions*. Chicago, IL: University of Chicago Press. Kuhn's book, acknowledged as an intellectual tour de force, makes the point that science is not the systematic accumulation of knowledge as presented in textbooks; that it is a far less rational exercise than generally imagined. In effect, it is 'a series of peaceful interludes punctuated by intellectually violent revolutions ... in each of which one conceptual world view is replaced by another.'

3 For a straightforward overview of the discussions here see Chalmers, A. F. (1982) *What Is This Thing Called Science?* (second edition). Milton Keynes: Open University Press.

4 The formulation of scientific method outlined earlier has come in for strong and sustained criticism. E. G. Mishler, for example, describes it as a 'storybook image of science', out of tune with the actual practices of working scientists who turn out to resemble craftpersons rather than logicians. By craftpersons, Mishler (1990) is at pains to stress that competence depends upon 'apprenticeship training, continued practice and experienced-based, contextual knowledge of the specific methods applicable to a phenomenon of interest rather than an abstract "logic of discovery" and application of formal "rules" ' (Mishler 1990). The knowledge base of scientific research, Mishler contends, is largely tacit and unexplicated; moreover, scientists learn it through a process of socialization into a 'particular form of life'. The discovery, testing and validation of findings is embedded in cultural and linguistic practices and experimental scientists proceed in pragmatic ways, learning from their errors and failures, adapting procedures to their local contexts, making decisions on the basis of their accumulated experiences. See, for example, Mishler, E. G. (1990) Validation in inquiry-guided research: the role of exemplars in narrative studies. *Harvard Educational Review*, 60 (4), 415–42.

5 See, for example, Rogers, C. R. (1969) *Freedom to Learn*. Columbus, OH: Merrill, and also Rogers, C. R. and Stevens, B. (1967) *Person to Person: The Problem of Being Human*. London: Souvenir.

6 Investigating social episodes involves analysing the accounts of what is happening from the points of view of the actors and the participant spectator(s)/investigator(s). This is said to yield three main kinds of interlocking material: images of the self and others, definitions of situations, and rules for the proper development of the action. See Harré, R. (1976) The constructive role of models. In L. Collins (ed.) *The Use of Models in the Social Sciences*. London: Tavistock.

7 See also Verma, G. K. and Beard, R. M. (1981) *What is Educational Research?* Aldershot: Gower, for further information on the nature of educational research and also a historical perspective on the subject.

2 THE ETHICS OF EDUCATIONAL AND SOCIAL RESEARCH

1 For example, Social Research Association (2003); American Sociological Association (1999); British Educational Research Association (2000); American Psychological Association (2002); British Sociological Association (2002); British Psychological

Society (2005). Comparable developments may be found in other fields of endeavour. For an examination of key ethical issues in medicine, business, and journalism together with reviews of common ethical themes across these areas, see Serafini, A. (ed.) (1989) *Ethics and Social Concern*. New York: Paragon House. The book also contains an account of principal ethical theories from Socrates to R. M. Hare.

2   US Dept of Health, Education and Welfare, Public Health Service and National Institute of Health (1971) *The Institutional Guide to D.H.E.W. Policy on Protecting Human Subjects*. DHEW Publication (NIH): 2 December, 72–102.

3   As regards judging researchers' behaviour, perhaps the only area of educational research where the term ethical absolute can be unequivocally applied and where subsequent judgement is unquestionable is that concerning researchers' relationship with their data. Should they choose to abuse their data for whatever reason, the behaviour is categorically wrong; no place here for moral relativism. For once a clear dichotomy is relevant: if there is such a thing as clearly ethical behaviour, such abuse is clearly unethical. It can take the form of, first, falsifying data to support a preconceived, often favoured, hypothesis; second, manipulating data, often statistically, for the same reason (or manipulating techniques used – deliberately including leading questions, for example); third, using data selectively, that is, ignoring or excluding the bits that don't fit one's hypothesis; and fourth, going beyond the data, in other words, arriving at conclusions not warranted by them (or over-interpreting them). But even malpractice as serious as these examples cannot be controlled by fiat: ethical injunctions would hardly be appropriate in this context, let alone enforceable. The only answer (in the absence of professional monitoring) is for the researcher to have a moral code that is 'rationally derived and intelligently applied', to use the words of the philosopher, R. S. Peters, and to be guided by it consistently. Moral competence, like other competencies, can be learned. One way of acquiring it is to bring interrogative reflection to bear on one's own code and practice, e.g. did I provide suitable feedback, in the right amounts, to the right audiences, at the right time? In sum, ethical behaviour depends on the concurrence of ethical thinking which in turn is based on fundamentally thought-out principles. Readers wishing to take the subject of data abuse further should read Peter Medawar's (1991) elegant and amusing essay, 'Scientific fraud', in D. Pike (ed.) *The Threat and the Glory: Reflections on Science and Scientists*. Oxford: Oxford University Press, and also Broad, W. and Wade, N. (1983) *Betrayers of Truth: Fraud and Deceit in the Halls of Science*. New York: Century.

5   SENSITIVE EDUCATIONAL RESEARCH

1   See also Walford (2001: 38) in his discussion of gaining access to UK public schools, where an early question that was put to him was 'Are you one of us?'

2   Walford (2001: 69) comments on the very negative attitudes of teachers to research on UK independent schools, the teachers feeling that researchers had been dishonest and had tricked them, looking only for salacious, sensational and negative data on the school (e.g. on bullying, drinking, drugs, gambling and homosexuality).

8   HISTORICAL AND DOCUMENTARY RESEARCH

1   By contrast, the historian of the modern period, i.e. the nineteenth and twentieth centuries, is more often faced in the initial stages with the problem of selecting from too much material, both at the stage of analysis and writing. Here the two most common criteria for such selection are the degree of significance to be attached to data, and the extent to which a specific detail may be considered typical of the whole.

2   However, historians themselves usually reject such a direct application of their work and rarely indulge in it on the grounds that no two events or contextual circumstances, separated geographically and temporally, can possibly be equated. As the popular sayings go, 'History never repeats itself' and so, 'The only thing we can learn from History is that we can learn nothing from History'.

3   Thomas, W. I. and Znaniecki, F. (1918) *The Polish Peasant in Europe and America*. Chicago, IL: University of Chicago Press. For a fuller discussion of the monumental work of Thomas and Znaniecki, see Plummer, K. (1983) *Documents of Life: An Introduction to the Problems and Literature of a Humanistic Method*. London: Allen & Unwin, especially Chapter 3, The Making of a Method. See also Madge, J. (1963) *The Origin of Scientific Sociology*. London: Tavistock. For a critique of Thomas and Znaniecki, see Riley, M. W. (1963) *Sociological Research 1: A Case Approach*. New York: Harcourt, Brace & World.

4   Sikes, P., Measor, L. and Woods, P. (1985) *Teacher Careers*. Lewes: Falmer. See also Smith, L. M. (1987) *Kensington Revisited*. Lewes: Falmer; Goodson, I. and Walker, R. (1988) Putting life into educational research. In R. R. Sherman and R. B. Webb (eds) *Qualitative Research in Education: Focus and Methods*. Lewes: Falmer; Acker, S. (1989) *Teachers,*

Gender and Careers. Lewes: Falmer; Blease, D. and Cohen, L. (1990) *Coping with Computers: An Ethnographic Study in Primary Classrooms.* London: Paul Chapman; Evetts, J. (1990) *Women in Primary Teaching.* London: Unwin Hyman; Goodson, I. (1990) *The Making of Curriculum.* Lewes: Falmer; Evetts, J. (1991) The experience of secondary headship selection: continuity and change. *Educational Studies,* 17 (3), 285–94; Sikes, P. and Troyna, B. (1991) True stories: a case study in the use of life histories in teacher education. *Educational Review,* 43 (1), 3–16; Winkley, D. (1995) *Diplomats and Detectives: LEA Advisers and Work.* London: Robert Royce.

9   SURVEYS, LONGITUDINAL, CROSS-SECTIONAL AND TREND STUDIES

1   There are several examples of surveys, including the following: Millan, R., Gallagher, M. and Ellis, R. (1993) Surveying adolescent worries: development of the 'Things I Worry About' scale. *Pastoral Care in Education,* 11 (1), 43–57; Boulton, M. J. (1997) Teachers' views on bullying: definitions, attitudes and abilities to cope. *British Journal of Educational Psychology,* 67, 223–33; Cline, T. and Ertubney, C. (1997) The impact of gender on primary teachers' evaluations of children's difficulties in school. *British Journal of Educational Psychology,* 67, 447–56; Dosanjh, J. S. and Ghuman, P. A. S. (1997) Asian parents and English education – 20 years on: a study of two generations. *Educational Studies,* 23 (3), 459–72; Foskett, N. H. and Hesketh, A. J. (1997) Constructing choice in continuous and parallel markets: institutional and school leavers' responses to the new post-16 marketplace. *Oxford Review of Education,* 23 (3), 299–319; Gallagher, T., McEwen, A. and Knip, D. (1997) Science education policy: a survey of the participation of sixth-form pupils in science and the subjects over a 10-year period, 1985–95. *Research Papers in Education,* 12 (2), 121–42; Jules, V. and Kutnick, P. (1997) Student perceptions of a good teacher: the gender perspective. *British Journal of Educational Psychology,* 67, 497–511; Borg, M. G. (1998) Secondary school teachers' perceptions of pupils' undesirable behaviours. *British Journal of Educational Psychology,* 68, 67–79; Papasolomoutos, C. and Christie, T. (1998) Using national surveys: a review of secondary analyses with special reference to schools. *Educational Research,* 40 (3), 295–310; Tatar, M. (1998) Teachers as significant others: gender differences in secondary school pupils' perceptions. *British Journal of Educational Psychology,* 68, 255–68; Terry, A. A. (1998) Teachers as targets

of bullying by their pupils: a study to investigate incidence. *British Journal of Educational Psychology,* 68, 255–68; Hall, K. and Nuttall, W. (1999) The *relative* importance of class size to infant teachers in England. *British Educational Research Journal,* 25 (2), 245–58; Rigby, K. (1999) Peer victimisation at school and the health of secondary school students. *British Journal of Educational Psychology,* 69, 95–104; Strand, S. (1999) Ethnic group, sex and economic disadvantage: associations with pupils' educational progress from Baseline to the end of Key Stage 1. *British Educational Research Journal,* 25 (2), 179–202.

Examples of different kinds of survey studies are as follows: Francis's (1992) 'true cohort' study of patterns of reading development, following a group of 54 young children for two years at six-monthly intervals; Blatchford's (1992) cohort, cross-sectional study of 133–175 children (two samples) and their attitudes to work at 11 years of age; a large-scale, cross-sectional study by Munn *et al.* (1990) into pupils' perceptions of effective disciplinarians, with a sample size of 543; a trend/prediction study of school building requirements by a government department (Department of Education and Science 1977), identifying building and improvement needs based on estimated pupil populations from births during the decade 1976–86; a survey study by Belson (1975) of 1,425 teenage boys' theft behaviour; a survey by Hannan and Newby (1992) of 787 student teachers (with a 46 per cent response rate) and their views on government proposals to increase the amount of time spent in schools during the training period.

2   Examples of longitudinal and cross-sectional studies include the following: Davies, J. and Brember, I (1997) Monitoring reading standards in year 6: a 7-year cross-sectional study. *British Educational Research Journal,* 23 (5), 615–22; Preisler, G. M. and Ahström, M. (1997) Sign language for hard of hearing children – a hindrance or a benefit for their development? *European Journal of Psychology of Education,* 12 (4), 465–77; Busato, V. V., Prins, F. J., Elshant, J. J. and Hamaker, C. (1998) Learning styles: a cross-sectional and longitudinal study in higher education. *British Journal of Educational Psychology,* 68, 427–41; Davenport, E. C. Jr, Davison, M. L., Kuang, H., Ding, S., Kin, S-K. and Kwak, N. (1998) High school mathematics course-taking by gender and ethnicity. *American Educational Research Journal,* 35 (3), 497–514; Davies, J. and Brember, I. (1998) Standards in reading at key stage 1 – a cross-sectional study. *Educational Research,* 40 (2), 153–60; Marsh, H. W. and Yeung, A. S. (1998) Longitudinal structural equation models of academic

self-concept and achievement: gender differences in the development of math and English constructs. *American Educational Research Journal*, 35 (4), 705–38; Noack, P. (1998) School achievement and adolescents' interactions with the fathers, mothers, and friends. *European Journal of Psychology of Education*, 13 (4), 503–13; Galton, M., Hargreaves, L, Comber, C., Wall, D. and Pell, T. (1999) Changes in patterns in teacher interaction in primary classrooms, 1976–1996. *British Educational Research Journal*, 25 (1), 23–37.

3   For further information on event-history analysis and hazard rates we refer readers to Allison (1984); Plewis (1985); Hakim (1987); Von Eye (1990); Rose and Sullivan (1993).

11   CASE STUDIES

1   For further examples of case studies see Woods, P. (1993) Managing marginality: teacher development through grounded life history. *British Educational Research Journal*, 19 (5), 447–88; Bates, I. and Dutson, J. (1995) A Bermuda triangle? A case study of the disappearance of competence-based vocational training policy in the context of practice. *British Journal of Education and Work*, 8 (2), 41–59; Jacklin, A. and Lacey, C. (1997) Gender integration in the infant classroom: a case study. *British Educational Research Journal*, 23 (5), 623–40.

12   *EX POST FACTO* RESEARCH

1   In Chapters 12 and 13 we adopt the symbols and conventions used in Campbell, D. T. and Stanley, J. C. (1963) *Experimental and Quasi-Experimental Designs for Research on Teaching*. Boston, MA: Houghton Mifflin. These are presented fully in Chapter 13.

2   For further information on logical fallacies, see Cohen, M. R. and Nagel, E. (1961) *An Introduction to Logic and Scientific Method*. London: Routledge & Kegan Paul. The example of the *post hoc, ergo propter hoc* fallacy given by the authors concerns sleeplessness, which may *follow* drinking coffee, but sleeplessness may not occur *because* coffee was drunk.

13   EXPERIMENTS, QUASI-EXPERIMENTS, SINGLE-CASE RESEARCH AND META-ANALYSIS

1   Questions have been raised about the authenticity of both definitions and explanations of the Hawthorne effect. See Diaper, G. (1990) The Hawthorne effect: a fresh examination. *Educational Studies*, 16 (3), 261–7.

2   Examples of experimental research can be seen in the following: Dugard, P. and Todman, J. (1995) Analysis of pre-test and post-test control group designs in educational research. *Educational Psychology*, 15 (2), 181–98; Bryant, P., Devine, M., Ledward, A. and Nunes, T. (1997) Spelling with apostrophes and understanding possession. *British Journal of Educational Psychology*, 67, 91–110; Hall, E., Hall, C. and Abaci, R. (1997) The effects of human relations training on reported teacher stress, pupil control ideology and locus of control. *British Journal of Educational Psychology*, 67, 483–96; Marcinkiewicz, H. R. and Clariana, R. B. (1997) The performance effects of headings within multi-choice tests. *British Journal of Educational Psychology*, 67, 111–17; Tones, K. (1997) Beyond the randomized controlled trial: a case for 'judicial review'. *Health Education Research*, 12 (2), i–iv; Alfassi, M. (1998) Reading for meaning: the efficacy of reciprocal teaching in fostering reading comprehension in high school students in remedial reading classes. *American Educational Research Journal*, 35 (2), 309–22; Bijstra, J. O. and Jackson, S. (1998) Social skills training with early adolescents: effects on social skills, well-being, self-esteem and coping. *European Journal of Psychology of Education*, 13 (4), 569–83; Cline, T., Proto, A., Raval, P. D. and Paolo, T. (1998) The effects of brief exposure and of classroom teaching on attitudes children express towards facial disfigurement in peers. *Educational Research*, 40 (1), 55–68; Didierjean, A. and Cauzinille-Marmèche, E. (1998) Reasoning by analogy: is it schema-mediated or case-based? *European Journal of Psychology of Education*, 13 (3), 385–98; Overett, S. and Donald, D. (1998) Paired reading: effects of a parental involvement programme in a disadvantaged community in South Africa. *British Journal of Educational Psychology*, 68, 347–56; Sainsbury, M., Whetton, C., Mason, K. and Schagen, I. (1998) Fallback in attainment on transfer at age 11: evidence from the summer literacy schools evaluation. *Educational Research*, 40 (1), 73–81; Littleton, K., Ashman, H., Light, P., Artis, J., Roberts, T. and Oosterwegel, A. (1999) Gender, task contexts, and children's performance on a computer-based task. *European Journal of Psychology of Education*, 14 (1), 129–39.

3   For a detailed discussion of the practical issues in educational experimentation, see Riecken and Boruch (1974); Bennett and Lumsdaine (1975); Evans (1978: Chapter 4).

4   An example of meta-analysis in educational research can be seen in Severiens, S. and ten Dam, G. (1998) A multilevel meta-analysis of gender differences in learning orientations. *British Journal of Educational Psychology*, 68, 595–618. The use of meta-analysis

is widespread, indeed the Cochrane Collaboration is a pioneer in this field, focusing on meta-analyses of randomized controlled trials (see Maynard and Chalmers 1997).

15 QUESTIONNAIRES

1 This is the approach used in Belbin's (1981) celebrated work on the types of personalities in a management team.

16 INTERVIEWS

1 Examples of interviews in educational research include the following: Ferris, J. and Gerber, R. (1996) Mature-age students' feelings of enjoying learning in a further education context. *European Journal of Psychology of Education*, 11 (1), 79–96; Carroll, S. and Walford, G. (1997) Parents' responses to the school quasi-market. *Research Papers in Education*, 12 (1), 3–26; Cullen, K. (1997) Headteacher appraisal: a view from the inside. *Research Papers in Education*, 12 (2), 177–204; Cicognani, C. (1998) Parents' educational styles and adolescent autonomy. *European Journal of Psychology of Education*, 13 (4), 485–502; Van Etten, S., Pressley, M., Freebern, G. and Echevarria, M. (1998) An interview study of college freshmen's beliefs about their academic motivation. *European Journal of Psychology of Education*, 13 (1), 105–30; Robinson, P. and Smithers, A. (1999) Should the sexes be separated for secondary education – comparisons of single-sex and co-educational schools? *Research Papers in Education*, 14 (1), 23–49.

17 ACCOUNTS

1 For an example of concept mapping in educational research see Lawless, L., Smee, P. and O'Shea, T. (1998) Using concept sorting and concept mapping in business and public administration, and education: an overview. *Educational Research*, 40 (2), 219–35.

2 For further examples of discourse analysis, see Ramsden, C. and Reason, D. (1997) Conversation – discourse analysis in library and information services. *Education for Information*, 15 (4), 283–95; Butzkamm, W. (1998) Code-switching in a bilingual history lesson: the mother tongue as a conversational lubricant. *Bilingual Education and Bilingualism*, 1 (2), 81–99; Mercer, N., Wegerif, R. and Dawes, L. (1999) Children's talk and the development of reasoning in the classroom. *British Educational Research Journal*, 25 (1), 95–111.

3 Cohen, L. (1993) *Racism Awareness Materials in Initial Teacher Training*. Report to the Leverhulme Trust, 11–19 New Fetter Lane, London, EC4A 1NR. The video scenarios are part of an inquiry

into pupils' perceptions of the behaviour of white teachers towards minority pupils in school. See Naylor, P. (1995) Adolescents' perceptions of teacher racism. Unpublished PhD dissertation, Loughborough University of Technology.

18 OBSERVATION

1 For an example of time-sampling, see Childs, G. (1997) A concurrent validity study of teachers' ratings for nominated 'problem' children. *British Journal of Educational Psychology*, 67, 457–74.

2 For an example of critical incidents, see Tripp, D. (1994) Teachers' lives, critical incidents and professional practice. *International Journal of Qualitative Studies in Education*, 7 (1), 65–72.

3 For an example of an observational study, see Sideris, G. (1998) Direct classroom observation. *Research in Education*, 59, 19–28.

20 PERSONAL CONSTRUCTS

1 See also the following applications of personal construct theory to research on teachers and teacher groups: Shapiro, B. L. (1990) A collaborative approach to help novice science teachers reflect on changes in their construction of the role of the science teacher. *Alberta Journal of Educational Research*, 36 (3), 203–22; Cole, A. L. (1991) Personal theories of teaching: development in the formative years. *Alberta Journal of Educational Research*, 37 (2), 119–32; Corporal, A. H. (1991) Repertory grid research into cognitions of prospective primary school teachers. *Teaching and Teacher Education*, 36, 315–29; Lehrer, R. and Franke, M. L. (1992) Applying personal construct psychology to the study of teachers' knowledge of fractions. *Journal for Research in Mathematical Education*, 23 (3), 223–41; Shaw, E. L. (1992) The influence of methods instruction on the beliefs of preservice elementary and secondary science teachers: preliminary comparative analyses. *School Science and Mathematics*, 92, 14–22.

2 For an example of personal constructs in educational research, see Morris, P. (1983) Teachers' perceptions of their pupils: a Hong Kong case study. *Research in Education*, 29, 81–6; Derry, S. J. and Potts, M. K. (1998) How tutors model students: a study of personal constructs in adaptive tutoring. *American Educational Research Journal*, 35 (1), 65–99.

21 ROLE-PLAYING

1 For an account of a wide range of role-play applications in psychotherapy, see Holmes, P.

and Karp, M. (1991) *Psychodrama: Inspiration and Technique*. London: Routledge.

24   QUANTITATIVE DATA ANALYSIS

1   Bynner and Stribley (1979: 242) present a useful table of alphas, which lists values of r_{ii} from 0.05 to 0.80 and the values of item numbers from 2 to 50. The values of alpha can then be interpolated. See Bynner, J. and Stribley, K. M. (eds.) (1979) *Social Research: Principles and Procedures*. London: Longman and the Open University Press, Table 19.1.

2   Muijs (2004) indicates that, in SPSS, one can find multicollinearity by looking at 'collinearity diagnostics' in the 'Statistics' command box, and in the collinearity statistics one should look at the 'Tolerance' column on the output. He indicates that values will vary from 0 to 1, and the higher the value the less is the collinearity, whereas a value close to 0 indicates that nearly all the variance in the variable is explained by the other variables in the model.

25   MULTIDIMENSIONAL MEASUREMENT AND FACTOR ANALYSIS

1   Robson, (1993) suggests that as few as 100 can be used.

2   Self-serving bias refers to our propensity to accept responsibility for our successes, but to deny responsibility for our failures.

3   For examples of research conducted using factor analysis, see McEneaney, J. E. and Sheridan, E. M. (1996) A survey-based component for programme assessment in undergraduate pre-service teacher education. *Research in Education*, 55, 49–61; Prosser, M. and Trigwell, K. (1997) Relations between perceptions of the teaching environment and approaches to teaching. *British Journal of Educational Psychology*, 67, 25–35; Vermunt, J. D. (1998) The regulation of constructive learning processes. *British Journal of Educational Psychology*, 68, 149–71; Andrews, P. and Hatch, G. (1999) A new look at secondary teachers' conception of mathematics and its teaching. *British Educational Research Journal*, 25 (2), 203–23; Valadines, N. (1999) Formal reasoning performance of higher secondary school students: theoretical and educational implications. *European Journal of Psychology of Education*, 14 (1), 109–17. For an example of research using cluster analysis see Seifert, T. L. (1997) Academic goals and emotions: results of a structural equation model and a cluster

analysis. *British Journal of Educational Psychology*, 67, 323–38. For examples of research using correlation coefficients, see Lamb, S., Bibby, P., Wood, D. and Leyden, G. (1997) Communication skills, educational achievement and biographic characteristics of children with moderate learning difficulties. *European Journal of Psychology of Education*, 12 (4), 401–14; Goossens, L., Marcoen, A., van Hees, S. and van de Woestlijne, O. (1998) Attachment style and loneliness in adolescence. *European Journal of Psychology of Education*, 13 (4), 529–42; Okagaki, L. and Frensch, P. A. (1998) Parenting and school achievement: a multiethnic perspective. *American Educational Research Journal*, 35 (1), 123–44.

4   Examples of multilevel modelling in educational research can be seen in the following: Fitz-Gibbon, C. T. (1991) Multilevel modelling in an indicator system. In S. W. Raudenbush and J. D. Willms (eds) *Schools, Classrooms and Pupils: International Studies of Schooling from a Multilevel Perspective*. San Diego, CA: Academic Press; Bell, J. F. (1996) Question choice in English literature examination. *Oxford Review of Education*, 23 (4), 447–58; Hill, P. W. and Rowe, K. J. (1996) Multilevel modelling in school effectiveness research. *School Effectiveness and School Improvement*, 7 (1), 1–34; Schagen, I. and Sainsbury, M. (1996) Multilevel analysis of the key stage 1 national curriculum data in 1995. *Oxford Review of Education*, 22 (3), 265–72; Croxford, L. (1997) Participation in science subjects: the effect of the Scottish curriculum framework. *Research Papers in Education*, 12 (1), 69–89; Thomas, S., Sammons, P., Mortimore, P. and Smees, R. (1997) Differential secondary school effectiveness: comparing the performance of different pupil groups. *British Educational Research Journal*, 23 (4), 351–69; Kivulu, J. M. and Rogers, W. T. (1998) A multilevel analysis of cultural experience and gender influences on causal attributions to perceived performance in mathematics. *British Journal of Educational Psychology*, 68, 25–37; McNiece, R. and Jolliffe, F. (1998) An investigation into regional differences in educational performance in the National Child Development Study. *Educational Research*, 40 (1), 13–30; Mooij, T. (1998) Pupil-class determinants of aggressive and victim behaviour in pupils. *British Journal of Educational Psychology*, 68, 373–85; Musch, J. and Bröder, A. (1999) Test anxiety versus academic skills: a comparison of two alternative models for predicting performance in a statistics exam. *British Journal of Educational Psychology*, 69, 105–16.

Bibliography

Acker, S. (1989) *Teachers, Gender and Careers*. Lewes: Falmer.

Acker, S. (1990) Teachers' culture in an English primary school: continuity and change. *British Journal of Sociology of Education*, 11 (3), 257–73.

Acton, H. B. (1975) Positivism. In J. O. Urmson (ed.) *The Concise Encyclopedia of Western Philosophy*. London: Hutchinson, 253–6.

Adams-Webber, J. R. (1970) Elicited versus provided constructs in repertory grid technique: a review. *British Journal of Medical Psychology*, 43, 349–54.

Adelman, C., Kemmis, S. and Jenkins, D. (1980) Rethinking case study: notes from the Second Cambridge Conference. In H. Simons (ed.) *Towards a Science of the Singular*. Norwich: Centre for Applied Research in Education, University of East Anglia, 45–61.

Adeyemi, M. B. (1992) The effects of a social studies course on the philosophical orientations of history and geography graduate students in Botswana. *Educational Studies*, 18 (2), 235–44.

Adler, P. A. and Adler, P. (1994) Observational techniques. In N. K. Denzin and Y. S. Lincoln (eds) *Handbook of Qualitative Research*. London: Sage, 377–92.

Agar, M. (1993) Speaking of ethnography. Cited in D. Silverman, *Interpreting Qualitative Data*. London: Sage.

Aiken, L. R. (2003) *Psychological Testing and Assessment* (eleventh edition). Boston, MA: Pearson Education.

Airasian, P. W. (2001) *Classroom Assessment: Concepts and Applications* (fourth edition). New York: McGraw-Hill.

Aitkin, M., Bennett, N. and Hesketh, J. (1981) Teaching styles and pupil progress: a re-analysis. *British Journal Educational Psychology*, 51 (2), 170–86.

Alban-Metcalf, R. J. (1997) Repertory Grid Technique. In J. P. Keeves (ed.) *Educational Research, Methodology and Measurement: An International Handbook* (second edition). Oxford: Elsevier Science, 315–18.

Alexander, P. C. and Neimeyer, G. J. (1989) Constructivism and family therapy. *International Journal of Personal Construct Psychology*, 2 (2), 111–21.

Alfassi, M. (1998) Reading for meaning: the efficacy of reciprocal teaching in fostering reading comprehension in high school students in remedial reading classes. *American Educational Research Journal*, 35 (2), 309–22.

Alkin, M. C., Daillak, R. and White, P. (1991) Does evaluation make a difference? In D. S. Anderson and B. J. Biddle (eds) *Knowledge for Policy: Improving Education through Research*. London: Falmer, 268–75.

Allison, P. (1984) Event history analysis: regression for longitudinal event data. *Sage University Papers: Quantitative Applications in the Social Sciences*, no. 46. Beverly Hills, CA: Sage.

Altricher, H. and Gstettner, P. (1993) Action research: a closed chapter in the history of German social science? *Educational Action Research*, 1 (3), 329–60.

Åm, O. (1994) *Back to Basics: Introduction to Systems Theory and Complexity*. http://www.stud.his.no/~onar/Ess/Back-to-Basics.html. Retrieved 10 June 2000.

American Educational Research Association (2000) *Ethical Standards of the American Educational Research Association*. http://www.aera.net/uploadedFiles/About_AERA/Ethical_Standards/EthicalStandards.pdf. Retrieved 15 May 2005.

American Psychological Association (1973) *Ethical Principles in the Conduct of Research with Human Subjects*. Ad Hoc Committee on Ethical Standards in Psychological Research. Washington, DC: American Psychological Association.

American Psychological Association (1994) *Publication Manual of the American Psychological Association* (fourth edition). Washington, DC: B. Thompson.

American Psychological Association (1999) *Standards for Educational and Psychological Testing* http://www.apa.org/science/standards/html. Retrieved 15 may 2005.

American Psychological Association (2001) *Publication Manual of the American Psychological Association* (fifth edition). Washington, DC: American Psychological Association.

American Psychological Association (2002) *Ethical Principles and Code of Conduct* http://www. apa.org/ethics/code2002.html. Retrieved 15 May 2005.

American Sociological Association (1999) *Code of Ethics and Policies and Procedures of the ASA Committee on Professional Ethics.* http://www. asanet.org/members/ecoderev.html. Retrieved 15 May 2005.

Anderson, D. S. and Biddle, B. J. (eds) (1991) *Knowledge for Policy: Improving Education through Research.* London: Falmer.

Anderson, G. and Arsenault, N. (1998) *Fundamentals of Educational Research* (second edition). London: RoutledgeFalmer.

Anderson, G. and Arsenault, N. (2001) *Fundamentals of Educational Research.* London: RoutledgeFalmer.

Andrews, P. and Hatch, G. (1999) A new look at secondary teachers' conception of mathematics and its teaching. *British Educational Research Journal,* 25 (2), 203–23.

Anfara, V. A., Brown, K. M. and Mangione, T. L. (2002) Qualitative analysis on stage: making the research process more public. *Educational Researcher* 31 (7), 28–38. http://35.8.171.42/ aera/pubs/er/pdf/vol31_07/AERA310706.pdf. Retrieved 29 October 2005.

Angoff, W. H. (1971) Scales, norms, and equivalent scores. In R. L. Thorndike (ed.) *Educational Measurement* (second edition). Washington, DC: American Council on Education, 508–600.

Antonsen, E. A. (1988) Treatment of a boy of twelve: help with handwriting, play therapy and discussion of problems. *Journal of Education Therapy,* 2 (1), 2–32.

Apple, M. (1990) *Ideology and Curriculum* (second edition). London: Routledge & Kegan Paul.

Applebee, A. N. (1976) The development of children's responses to repertory grids. *British Journal of Social and Clinical Psychology,* 15, 101–2.

Arditti, J. A. (2002) Doing family research at the jail: reflections of a prison widow. *The Qualitative Report,* 7 (4). http://www.nova.edu/ssss/QR/QR7-4/arditti.html. Retrieved 21 November 2003.

Argyle, M. (1978) Discussion chapter: an appraisal of the new approach to the study of social behaviour. In M. Brenner, P. Marsh and M. Brenner (eds) *The Social Contexts of Method.* London: Croom Helm, 237–55.

Argyris, C. (1990) *Overcoming Organizational Defenses – Facilitating Organizational Learning.* Boston, MA: Allyn & Bacon.

Arksey, H. and Knight, P. (1999) *Interviewing for Social Scientists.* London: Sage.

Arnold, P. and Atkins, J. (1991) The social and emotional adjustment of hearing-impaired children integrated in primary schools. *Educational Researcher,* 33 (3), 223-8.

Aronowitz, S. and Giroux, H. (1986) *Education Under Siege.* London: Routledge & Kegan Paul.

Aronson, E. and Carlsmith, J. M. (1969) Experimentation in social psychology. In G. Lindzey and E. Aronson (eds) *The Handbook of Social Psychology, Volume 2.* Reading, MA: Addison-Wesley, 1–79.

Aronson, E., Ellsworth, P. C., Carlsmith, J. M. and Gonzalez, M. H. (1990) *Methods of Research in Social Psychology.* New York: McGraw-Hill.

Arsenault, N. and Anderson, G. (1998) Qualitative research. In G. Anderson and N. Arsenault, *Fundamentals of Educational Research* (second edition). London: RoutledgeFalmer, 119–35.

Ary, D., Jacobs, L. C. and Razavieh, A. (1972) *Introduction to Research in Education.* New York: Holt, Rinehart & Winston.

Ashmore, M. (1989) *The Reflexive Thesis.* Chicago, IL: University of Chicago Press.

Atkinson, R. (1998) *The Life Interview.* London: Sage.

Axline, V. (1964) *Dibs: In Search of Self.* New York: Ballantine.

Bailey, K. D. (1978) *Methods of Social Research.* Basingstoke: Collier-Macmillan.

Bailey, K. D. (1994) *Methods of Social Research* (fourth edition). New York: The Free Press.

Baker, T. L. (1994) *Doing Social Research* (second edition). New York: McGraw-Hill.

Ball, S. J. (1981) *Beachside Comprehensive.* Cambridge: Cambridge University Press.

Ball, S. J. (1990) *Politics and Policy-Making in Education.* London: Routledge.

Ball, S. J. (1994a) *Education Reform: A Critical and Post-Structuralist Approach.* Buckingham: Open University Press.

Ball, S. J. (1994b) Political interviews and the politics of interviewing. In G. Walford (ed.) *Researching the Powerful in Education.* London: UCL Press, 96–115.

Bannister, D. (ed.) (1970) *Perspectives in Personal Construct Theory.* London: Academic Press.

Bannister, D. and Mair, J. M. M. (1968) *The Evaluation of Personal Constructs*. London: Academic Press.

Banuazizi, A. and Movahedi, A. (1975) Interpersonal dynamics in a simulated prison: a methodological analysis. *American Psychologist*, 30, 152–60.

Bargh, J. A., McKenna, K. Y. A. and Fitzsimons, G. M. (2002) Can you see the real me? Activation and expression of the 'true self' on the Internet. *Journal of Social Issues*, 58, 33–48.

Barker, C. D. and Johnson, G. (1998) Interview talk as professional practice. *Language and Education*, 12 (4), 229–42.

Barr Greenfield, T. (1975) Theory about organisations: a new perspective and its implications for schools. In M. G. Hughes (ed.) *Administering Education: International Challenge*. London: Athlone, 71–99.

Barratt, P. E. H. (1971) *Bases of Psychological Methods*. Sydney, NSW: John Wiley.

Bates, I. and Dutson, J. (1995) A Bermuda triangle? A case study of the disappearance of competence-based vocational training policy in the context of practice. *British Journal of Education and Work*, 8 (2), 41–59.

Batteson, C. and Ball, S. J. (1995) Autobiographies and interviews as means of 'access' to elite policy making in education. *British Journal of Educational Studies*, 43 (2), 201–16.

Bauman, R. (1986) *Story, Performance and Event*. Cambridge: Cambridge University Press.

Baumrind, D. (1964) Some thoughts on ethics of research. *American Psychologist*, 19, 421–3.

Beck, R. N. (1979) *Handbook in Social Philosophy*. New York: Macmillan.

Becker, H. (1968) Whose side are you on? *Social Problems*, 14, 239–47.

Becker, H. (1970) *Sociological Work*. Chicago, IL: Aldane.

Becker, H. S. and Geer, B. (1960) Participant observation: the analysis of qualitative field data. In R. Adams and J. Preiss (eds) *Human Organization Research: Field Relations and Techniques*. Homewood, IL: Dorsey.

Beer, M., Eisenstadt, R. A. and Spector, B. (1990) Why change programs don't produce change. *Harvard Business Review*, Nov./Dec. (68), 158–66.

Belbin, R.M. (1981) *Management Teams: Why They Succeed or Fail*. London: Heinemann.

Bell, J. (1991) *Doing your Research Project* (second edition). Milton Keynes: Open University Press.

Bell, J. (1999) *Doing your Research Project* (third edition). Milton Keynes: Open University Press.

Bell, J. F. (1996) Question choice in English literature examination. *Oxford Review of Education*, 23 (4), 447–58.

Belson, W. A. (1975) *Juvenile Theft: Causal Factors*. London: Harper & Row.

Belson, W. A. (1986) *Validity in Survey Research*. Aldershot: Gower.

Bennett, C. A. and Lumsdaine, A. A. (1975) *Evaluation and Experimentation*. New York: Academic Press.

Bennett, S. and Bowers, D. (1977) *An Introduction to Multivariate Techniques for Social and Behavioural Sciences*. London: Macmillan.

Bennett, S. N. (1976) *Teaching Styles and Pupil Progress*. Shepton Mallett, UK: Open Books.

Bennett, S. N., Desforges, C. and Wilkinson, E. (1984) *The Quality of Pupil Learning Experience*. London: Lawrence Erlbaum.

Berger, P. L. and Luckmann, T. (1967) *The Social Construction of Reality*. Harmondsworth: Penguin.

Bernstein, B. (1970) Education cannot compensate for society. *New Society*, February (387), 344–57.

Bernstein, B. (1971) On the classification and framing of educational knowledge. In M. F. D. Young (ed.) *Knowledge and Control*. Basingstoke: Collier-Macmillan, 47–69.

Bernstein, B. (1974) Sociology and the sociology of education: a brief account. In J. Rex (ed.) *Approaches to Sociology: An Introduction to Major Trends in British Sociology*. London: Routledge & Kegan Paul, 145–59.

Bernstein, B. (1975) Class and pedagogies: visible and invisible. In B. Bernstein, *Class, Codes and Control, Volume 3*. London: Routledge.

Bernstein, R. J. (1983) *Beyond Objectivism and Relativism*. Oxford: Blackwell.

Best, J. W. (1970) *Research in Education*. Englewood Cliffs, NJ: Prentice Hall.

Beynon, H. (1988) Regulating research: politics and decision-making in industrial organizations. In A. Bryman (ed.) *Doing Research in Organizations*. London: Routledge.

Bhadwal, S. C. and Panda, P. K. (1991) The effects of a package of some curricular strategies on the study habits of rural primary school students: a year long study. *Educational Studies*, 17 (3), 261–72.

Biddle, B. J. and Anderson, D. S. (1991) Social research and educational change. In D. S. Anderson and B. J. Biddle (eds) *Knowledge for Policy: Improving Education through Research*. London: Falmer, 1–20.

Bijstra, J. O. and Jackson, S. (1998) Social skills training with early adolescents: effects on social skills, well-being, self-esteem and coping. *European Journal of Psychology of Education*, 13 (4), 569–83.

Bimrose, J. and Bayne, R. (1995) A multicultural framework in counsellor training: a preliminary evaluation. *British Journal of Guidance and Counselling*, 23 (2), 259–65.

Binet, A. (1905) Méthode nouvelle pour le diagnostic de l'intelligence des anormaux. Cited in G. de Landsheere (1997) History of educational research. In J. P. Keeves (ed.) *Educational Research, Methodology, and Measurement: An International Handbook* (second edition). Oxford: Elsevier Science, 8–16.

Black, P. (1998) *Testing: Friend or Foe?*. London: Falmer.

Black, T. R. (1999) *Doing Quantitative in the Social Sciences*. London: Sage.

Blalock, H. Jnr. (1979) *Social Statistics* (second edition). New York: McGraw-Hill.

Blalock, H. M. (1991) Dilemmas of social research. In D. S. Anderson and B. J. Biddle (eds) *Knowledge for Policy: Improving Education through Research*. London: Falmer, 60–9.

Blatchford, P. (1992) Children's attitudes to work at 11 years. *Educational Studies*, 18 (1), 107–18.

Blease, D. and Cohen, L. (1990) *Coping with Computers: An Ethnographic Study in Primary Classrooms*. London: Paul Chapman.

Bliss, J., Monk, M. and Ogborn, J. (1983) *Qualitative Data Analysis for Educational Research*. London: Croom Helm.

Bloom, B. (ed.) (1956) *Taxonomy of Educational Objectives: Handbook 1: Cognitive Domain*. London: Longman.

Bloor, M. (1978) On the analysis of observational data: a discussion of the worth and uses of induction techniques and respondent validation. *Sociology*, 12 (3), 545–52.

Blumenfeld-Jones, D. (1995) Fidelity as a criterion for practising and evaluating narrative inquiry. *International Journal of Qualitative Studies in Education*, 8 (1), 25–33.

Blumer, H. (1969) *Symbolic Interactionism*. Englewood Cliffs, NJ: Prentice Hall.

Boas, F. (1943) Recent anthropology. *Science*, 98, 311–14.

Bogdan, R. G. and Biklen, S. K. (1992) *Qualitative Research for Education* (second edition). Boston, MA: Allyn & Bacon.

Bolton, G. M. and Heathcote, D. (1999) *So You Want to Use Role-Play? A New Approach in How to Plan*. Stoke on Trent, UK: Trentham Books.

Borg, M. G. (1998) Secondary school teachers' perceptions of pupils' undesirable behaviours. *British Journal of Educational Psychology*, 68, 67–79.

Borg, W. R. (1963) *Educational Research: An Introduction*. London: Longman.

Borg, W. R. (1981) *Applying Educational Research: A Practical Guide for Teachers*. New York: Longman.

Borg, W. R. and Gall, M. D. (1979) *Educational Research: An Introduction* (third edition). London: Longman.

Borg, W. R. and Gall, M. D. (1996) *Educational Research: An Introduction* (sixth edition). New York: Longman.

Borkowsky, F. T. (1970) The relationship of work quality in undergraduate music curricula to effectiveness in instrumental music teaching in the public schools. *Journal of Experimental Education*, 39, 14–19.

Borsboom, D., Mellenbergh, G. D. and van Heerden, J. (2004) The concept of validity. *Psychological Review*, 111 (4), 1061–71.

Boruch, R. F. (1997) *Randomized Experiments for Planning and Evaluation*. Applied Social Research Methods series, vol. 44. Thousand Oaks, CA: Sage.

Boruch, R. F. and Cecil, J. S. (1979) *Assuring the Confidentiality of Social Research Data*. Philadelphia, PA: University of Pennsylvania Press.

Boulton, M. J. (1992) Participation in playground activities at middle school. *Education Research*, 34 (3), 167–82.

Boulton, M. J. (1997) Teachers' views on bullying: definitions, attitudes and abilities to cope. *British Journal of Educational Psychology*, 67, 223–33.

Bowe, R., Ball, S. J. and Gold, A. (1992) *Reforming Education and Changing Schools*. London: Routledge.

Bowles, S. and Gintis, H. (1976) *Schooling in Capitalist America*. London: Routledge & Kegan Paul.

Bracht, G. H. and Glass, G. V. (1968) The external validity of experiments. *American Educational Research Journal*, 4 (5), 437–74.

Bradburn, N. M. and Berlew, D. E. (1961) *Economic Development and Cultural Change*. Chicago, IL: University of Chicago Press.

Bradburn, N. M. and Sudman, S. (1979) *Improving Interview Method and Questionnaire Design*. San Francisco, CA: Jossey-Bass.

Breakwell, G. M. (1990) *Interviewing*. London: Routledge and British Psychological Society.

Breakwell, G. M. (2000) Interviewing. In G. M. Breakwell, S. Hammond and C. Fife-Shaw (eds) (2000) *Research Methods in Psychology* (second edition). London: Sage 239–50.

Brenner, M., Brown, J. and Canter, D. (1985) *The Research Interview*. London: Academic Press.

Brenner, M. and Marsh, P. (eds) (1978) *The Social Contexts of Method*. London: Croom Helm.

British Educational Research Association (2000) *Ethical Guidelines*. http://www.bera.ac.uk. Retrieved 14 June 2000.

British Psychological Society (2005) *Code of Conduct, Ethical Principles and Guidelines*. http://www.bps.org.uk/document-download-area/document-download$.cfm?file_uuid= 6D0645CC-7E96-C67F-D75E2648E5580115 &ext=pdf. Retrieved 15 May 2005.

British Sociological Association (2002) *Statement of Ethical Practice for the British Sociological Association*. http://www.britsoc.co.uk/new_site/user_doc/ Statement%20of%20Ethical%20Practice.doc. Retrieved 15 May 2005.

Broad, W. and Wade N. (1983) *Betrayers of Truth: Fraud and Deceit in the Halls of Science*. New York: Century.

Brock-Utne, B. (1996) Reliability and validity in qualitative research within education in Africa. *International Review of Education*, 42 (6), 605–21.

Brown, J. and Sime, J. D. (1977) Accounts as general methodology. Paper presented to the British Psychological Society Conference, University of Exeter.

Brown, J. and Sime, J. D. (1981) A methodology of accounts. In M. Brenner (ed.) *Social Method and Social Life*. London: Academic Press.

Brown, R. and Herrnstein, R.J. (1975) *Psychology*. London: Methuen.

Bruner, J. (1986) *Actual Minds, Possible Worlds*. Cambridge, MA: Harvard University Press.

Bryant, P., Devine, M., Ledward, A., and Nunes, T. (1997) Spelling with apostrophes and understanding possession. *British Journal of Educational Psychology*, 67, 91–110.

Bryman, A. and Cramer, D. (1990) *Quantitative Data Analysis for Social Scientists*. London: Routledge.

Buhler, C. and Allen, M. (1972) *Introduction to Humanistic Psychology*. Monterey, CA: Brooks/Cole.

Bulmer, M. (ed.) (1982) *Social Research Ethics*. London: Macmillan.

Burgess, R. G. (ed.) (1989) *The Ethics of Educational Research*. Lewes: Falmer.

Burgess, R. G. (1993) Biting the hand that feeds you? Educational research for policy and practice. In R. G. Burgess (ed.) *Educational Research and Evaluation for Policy and Practice*. Lewes: Falmer, 1–18.

Burke, M., Noller, P. and Caird, D. (1992) Transition from probationer to educator: a repertory grid analysis. *International Journal of Personal Construct Psychology*, 5 (2), 159–82.

Burrell, G. and Morgan, G. (1979) *Sociological Paradigms and Organizational Analysis*. London: Heinemann Educational.

Busato, V. V., Prins, F. J., Elshant, J. J. and Hamaker, C. (1998) Learning styles: a cross-sectional and longitudinal study in higher education. *British Journal of Educational Psychology*, 68, 427–41.

Butt, T. (1995) What's wrong with laddering? *Changes*, 13, 81–7.

Butzkamm, W. (1998) Code-switching in a bilingual history lesson: the mother tongue as a conversational lubricant. *Bilingual Education and Bilingualism*, 1 (2), 81–99.

Bynner, J. and Stribley, K. M (eds) (1979) *Social Research: Principles and Procedures*. London: Longman and the Open University Press.

Calder, J. (1979) Introduction to applied sampling. *Research Methods in Education and the Social Sciences*. Block 3, part 4, DE304, Milton Keynes: Open University Press.

Callawaert, S. (1999) Philosophy of Education, Frankfurt critical theory, and the sociology of Pierre Bourdieu. In T. Popkewitz and L. Fendler (eds) *Critical Theories in Education: Changing Terrains of Knowledge and Politics*. London: Routledge, 117–44.

Campbell, D. T. and Fiske, D. W. (1959) Convergent and discriminant validation by the multitrait-multimethod matrix. *Psychological Bulletin*, 56, 81–105.

Campbell, D. T. and Stanley, J. (1963) *Experimental and Quasi-experimental Designs for Research on Teaching*. Boston, MA: Houghton Mifflin.

Campbell, D., Sanderson, R. E. and Laverty, S. G. (1964) Characteristics of a conditioned response in human subjects during extinction trials following a single traumatic conditioning trial. *Journal of Abnormal and Social Psychology*, 68, 627–39.

Cannell, C. F. and Kahn, R. L. (1968) Interviewing. In G. Lindzey and A. Aronson (eds) *The Handbook of Social Psychology, vol. 2: Research Methods*. New York: Addison-Wesley, 526–95.

Caplan, N. (1991) The use of social research knowledge at the national level. In D. S. Anderson and B. J. Biddle (eds) *Knowledge for Policy: Improving Education through Research*. London: Falmer, 193–202.

Capra, F. (1996) *The Web of Life*. New York: Anchor.

Bibliography

Capraro, R. M. and Capraro, M. (2002) Treatments of effect sizes and statistical significance tests in textbooks. *Educational and Psychological Measurement*, 62 (5), 771–82.

Carr, W. and Kemmis, S. (1986) *Becoming Critical*. Lewes: Falmer.

Carroll, S. and Walford, G. (1997) Parents' responses to the school quasi-market. *Research Papers in Education*, 12 (1), 3–26.

Carspecken, P. F. (1996) *Critical Ethnography in Educational Research*. London: Routledge.

Carspecken, P. F. and Apple, M. (1992) Critical qualitative research: theory, methodology, and practice. In M. LeCompte, W. L. Millroy and J. Preissle (eds) *The Handbook of Qualitative Research in Education*. London: Academic Press, 507–53.

Cartwright, D. (1991) Basic and applied social psychology. In D. S. Anderson and B. J. Biddle (eds) *Knowledge for Policy: Improving Education through Research*. London: Falmer, 23–31.

Carver, R. P. (1978) The case against significance testing. *Harvard Educational Review*, 48 (3), 378–99.

Cassell, J. (1993) The relationship of observer to observed when studying up. Cited in R. M. Lee, *Doing Research on Sensitive Topics*. London: Sage.

Cattell, R. B. (1966) The Scree test for the number of factors. *Multivariate Behavioral Research*, 1 (2), 245–76.

Cavan, S. (1977) Review of J. D. Douglas's (1976) *Investigative Social Research: Individual and Team Field Research*. *American Journal of Sociology*, 83 (3), 809–11.

Central Advisory Council for Education (1967) *Children and their Primary Schools*. London: HMSO.

Chalmers, A. F. (1982) *What Is This Thing Called Science?* (second edition). Milton Keynes: Open University Press.

Chambers, K. (2003) How often do you have sex: problem gambling as a sensitive issue. Paper presented at the Twelfth International Congress on Gambling and Risk Taking, Vancouver, BC.

Chelinsky, E. and Mulhauser, F. (1993) Educational evaluations for the US Congress: some reflections on recent experience. In R. G. Burgess (ed.) *Educational Research and Evaluation for Policy and Practice*. London: Falmer, 44–60.

Child, D. (1970) *The Essentials of Factor Analysis*. New York: Holt, Rinehart & Winston.

Childs, G. (1997) A concurrent validity study of teachers' ratings for nominated 'problem' children. *British Journal of Educational Psychology*, 67, 457–74.

Chomsky, N. (1959) Review of Skinner's *Verbal Behaviour*. *Language*, 35 (1), 26–58.

Cicognani, C. (1998) Parents' educational styles and adolescent autonomy. *European Journal of Psychology of Education*, 13 (4), 485–502.

Cicourel, A. V. (1964) *Method and Measurement in Sociology*. New York: The Free Press.

Clarke, A. and Dawson, R. (1999) *Evaluation Research*. London: Sage.

Cline, T. and Ertubney, C. (1997) The impact of gender on primary teachers' evaluations of children's difficulties in school. *British Journal of Educational Psychology*, 67, 447–56.

Cline, T., Proto, A., Raval, P. D. and Paolo T. (1998) The effects of brief exposure and of classroom teaching on attitudes children express towards facial disfigurement in peers. *Educational Research*, 40 (1), 55–68.

Cochrane, A. L. (1972) *Effectiveness and Efficiency: Random Reflections on Health Services*. London: Nuffield Provincial Hospitals Trust.

Coe, R. (2000) What is an effect size? Durham: CEM Centre, University of Durham: www.cemcentre.org/ebeuk/research/effectsize/ESbrief.htm. Retrieved 7 January 2005.

Coe, R., Fitz-Gibbon, C. T. and Tymms, P. (2000) *Promoting Evidence-Based Education: The Role of Practitioners*. Roundtable paper presented at the British Educational Research Association, University of Cardiff, 7–10 September.

Coffey, A., Holbrook, B. and Atkinson, P. (1996) Qualitative data analysis: technologies and representations. *Sociological Research Online*. http://www.socresonline.org.uk/socresonline/1/1/4.html. Retrieved 14 November 2000.

Cohen, D. K. and Garet, M. S. (1991) Reforming educational policy with applied social research. In D. S. Anderson and B. J. Biddle (eds) *Knowledge for Policy: Improving Education through Research*. London: Falmer, 123–40.

Cohen, J. (1988) *Statistical Power Analysis for the Behavioral Sciences*. Hillsdale, NJ: Erlbaum.

Cohen, J. and Stewart, I. (1995) *The Collapse of Chaos*. Harmondsworth: Penguin.

Cohen, L. (1977) *Educational Research in Classrooms and Schools: A Manual of Materials and Methods*. London: Harper & Row.

Cohen, L. (1993) *Racism Awareness Materials in Initial Teacher Training*. Report to the Leverhulme Trust, 11–19 New Fetter Lane, London, EC4A 1NR.

Cohen, L. and Holliday, M. (1979) *Statistics for Education and Physical Education*. London: Harper & Row.

Cohen, L. and Holliday, M. (1982) *Statistics for Social Scientists*. London: Harper & Row.

Cohen, L. and Holliday, M. (1996) *Practical Statistics for Students*. London: Paul Chapman.

Cohen, L. and Manion, L. (1994) *Research Methods in Education* (fourth edition). London: Routledge.

Cohen, L., Manion, L. and Morrison, K. R. B. (2004) *A Guide to Teaching Practice* (fifth edition). London: Routledge.

Cohen, M. R. and Nagel, E. (1961) *An Introduction to Logic and Scientific Method*. London: Routledge & Kegan Paul.

Cole, A. L. (1991) Personal theories of teaching: development in the formative years. *Alberta Journal of Educational Research*, 37 (2), 119–32.

Coleman, J. S. (1991) Social policy research and societal decision-making. In D. S. Anderson and B. J. Biddle (eds) *Knowledge for Policy: Improving Education through Research*. London: Falmer, 113–22.

Collins, J. S. and Duguid, P. (1989) Situated cognition and the culture of learning. *Educational Researcher*, 32, 32–42.

Connell, R. W., Ashenden, D. J., Kessler, S. and Doswett, G. W. (1996) Making the difference: schools, families and social division. Cited in B. Limerick, T. Burgess-Limerick and M. Grace, The politics of interviewing: power relations and accepting the gift. *International Journal of Qualitative Studies in Education*, 9 (4), 449–60.

Connelly, F. M. and Clandinin, D. J. (1997) Narrative inquiry. In J. P. Keeves (ed.) *Educational Research, Methodology, and Measurement: An International Handbook* (second edition). London: Elsevier Science, 81–6.

Connelly, F. M. and Clandinin, D. J.(1999) Narrative inquiry. In J. P. Keeves and G. Lakomski (eds) *Issues in Educational Research*. Oxford: Elsevier Science, 132–40.

Conover, N. J. (1971) *Practical Nonparametric Statistics*. New York: John Wiley.

Cook, T. D. (1991) Postpositivist criticisms, reform associations, and uncertainties about social research. In D. S. Anderson and B. J. Biddle (eds) *Knowledge for Policy: Improving Education through Research*. London: Falmer, 43–59.

Cook, T. D., Cooper, H., Cordray, D. S., Hartmann, H., Hedges, L. V., Light, R. J., Louis, T. A. and Mosteller, F. (1992) *Meta-analysis for Explanation*. New York: Russell Sage Foundation.

Cooke, R. A. and Lafferty, J. C. (1989) *The Organizational Culture Inventory*. Plymouth, MI: Human Synergistics International.

Cooley, C. H. (1902) *Human Nature and the Social Order*. New York: Charles Scribner.

Coomber, R. (1997) Using the Internet for survey research. *Sociological Research Online*, 2 (2). http://www.socresonline.org.uk/socresonline/2/2/2.html. Retrieved 14 November 2000.

Cooper, D. C. and Schindler, P. S. (2001) *Business Research Methods* (seventh edition). New York: McGraw-Hill.

Cooper, H. M. and Rosenthal, R. (1980) Statistical versus traditional procedures for summarizing research findings. *Psychological Bulletin*, 87, 442–9.

Cooper, M. (1976) An exact probability test for use with Likert scales. *Educational and Psychological Measurement*, 36, 647–55.

Corey, S. M. (1953) *Action Research to Improve School Practice*. New York: Teachers College, Columbia University.

Corporal, A. H. (1991) Repertory grid research into cognitions of prospective primary school teachers. *Teaching and Teacher Education*, 36, 315–29.

Coser, L. A. and Rosenberg, B. (1969) *Sociological Theory: A Book of Readings* (third edition). New York: Macmillan.

Coyle, A. (1995) Discourse analysis. In G. M. Breakwell, S. Hammond and C. Fife-Shaw (eds) *Research Methods in Psychology*. London: Sage, 243–58.

Cresswell, J. W. (1998) *Qualitative Inquiry and Research Design: Choosing among the Five Traditions*. Thousand Oaks, CA: Sage.

Cresswell, M. J. and Houston, J. G. (1991) Assessment of the national curriculum – some fundamental considerations. *Educational Review*, 43 (1), 63–78.

Cronbach, L. J. (1949) *Essentials of Psychological Testing* (first edition). New York: Harper & Row.

Cronbach, L. J. (1970) *Essentials of Psychological Testing* (third edition). New York: Harper & Row.

Crow, G. M. (1992) The principalship as a career: in need of a theory. *Educational Management and Administration*, 21 (2), 80–7.

Croxford, L. (1997) Participation in science subjects: the effect of the Scottish curriculum framework. *Research Papers in Education*, 12 (1), 69–89.

Cuff, E. G. and Payne, G. C. F. (eds) (1979) *Perspectives in Sociology*. London: Allen & Unwin.

Cullen, K. (1997) Headteacher appraisal: a view from the inside. *Research Papers in Education*, 12 (2), 177–204.

Cummings, L. (1985) Qualitative research in the infant classroom: a personal account. In R. Burgess (ed.) *Issues in Educational Research: Qualitative Methods*. Lewes: Falmer, 216–50.

Cunningham, G. K. (1998) *Assessment in the Classroom*. London: Falmer.

Curriculum Evaluation and Management Centre (2000) *A Culture of Evidence*. http://cem.dur.ac.uk/ebeuk/culture.htm. Retrieved 21 May 2001.

Curtis, B. (1978) Introduction to B. Curtis and W. Mays (eds) *Phenomenology and Education*. London: Methuen.

Daly, P. (1996) The effects of single-sex and co-educational secondary schooling on girls' achievement. *Research Papers in Education*, 11 (3), 289–306.

Daly, P. and Shuttleworth, I. (1997) Determinants of public examination entry and attainment in mathematics: evidence of gender and gender-type of school from the 1980s and 1990s in Northern Ireland. *Evaluation and Research in Education*, 11 (2), 91–101.

Davenport, E. C. Jr., Davison, M. L., Kuang, H., Ding, S., Kin, S-K. and Kwak, N. (1998) High school mathematics course-taking by gender and ethnicity. *American Educational Research Journal*, 35 (3), 497–514.

Davidson, J. (1970) *Outdoor Recreation Surveys: The Design and Use of Questionnaires for Site Surveys*. London: Countryside Commission.

Davie, R. (1972) The longitudinal approach. *Trends in Education*, 28, 8–13.

Davies, J. and Brember, I (1997) Monitoring reading standards in year 6: a 7-year cross-sectional study. *British Educational Research Journal*, 23 (5), 615–22.

Davies, J. and Brember, I. (1998) Standards in reading at key stage 1 – a cross-sectional study. *Educational Research*, 40 (2), 153–60.

Day, K. J. (1985) Perspectives on privacy: a sociological analysis. Unpublished PhD thesis, University of Edinburgh. Quoted in R. M. Lee (1993) *Doing Research on Sensitive Topics*. London: Sage.

De Laine, M. (2000) *Fieldwork, Participation and Practice*. London: Sage.

Deem, R. (1994) Researching the locally powerful: a study of school governance. In G. Walford (ed.) *Researching the Powerful in Education*. London: UCL Press, 151–71.

Delamont, S. (1976) *Interaction in the Classroom*. London: Methuen.

Delamont, S. (1981) All too familiar? A decade of classroom research. *Educational Analysis*, 3 (1), 69–83.

Delamont, S. (1992) *Fieldwork in Educational Settings: Methods, Pitfalls and Perspectives*. London: Falmer.

Denscombe, M. (1995) Explorations in group interviews: an evaluation of a reflexive and partisan approach. *British Educational Research Journal*, 21 (2), 131–48.

Denzin, N. (1970a) Strategies of multiple triangulation. In N. Denzin (ed.) *The Research Act in Sociology: A Theoretical Introduction to Sociological Method*. London: Butterworth, 297–313.

Denzin, N. K. (1970b) *The Research Act in Sociology: A Theoretical Introduction to Sociological Methods*. London: Butterworth.

Denzin, N. K. (1989) *The Research Act* (third edition). Englewood Cliffs, NJ: Prentice Hall.

Denzin, N. K. (1997) Triangulation in educational research. In J. P. Keeves (ed.) *Educational Research, Methodology and Measurement: An International Handbook* (second edition). Oxford: Elsevier Science, 318–22.

Denzin, N. K. (1999) Biographical research methods. In J. P. Keeves and G. Lakomski (eds) *Issues in Educational Research*. Oxford: Elsevier Science, 92–102.

Denzin, N. K. and Lincoln, Y. S. (eds) (1994) *Handbook of Qualitative Research*. Thousand Oaks, CA: Sage.

Department of Education and Science (1977) *A Study of School Buildings*. Annex 1. London: HMSO.

Derry, S. J. and Potts, M. K. (1998) How tutors model students: a study of personal constructs in adaptive tutoring. *American Educational Research Journal*, 35 (1), 65–99.

Deyle, D. L., Hess, G. and LeCompte, M. L. (1992) Approaching ethical issues for qualitative researchers in education. In M. LeCompte, W. L. Millroy and J. Preissle (eds) *The Handbook of Qualitative Research in Education*. London: Academic Press, 597–642.

Diaper, G. (1990) The Hawthorne effect: a fresh examination. *Educational Studies*, 16 (3), 261–7.

Dicker, R. and Gilbert, J. (1988) The role of the telephone in educational research. *British Educational Research Journal*, 14 (1), 65–72.

Didierjean, A. and Cauzinille-Marmèche, E. (1998) Reasoning by analogy: is it schema-mediated or case-based? *European Journal of Psychology of Education*, 13 (3), 385–98.

Diener, E. and Crandall, R. (1978) *Ethics in Social and Behavioral Research*. Chicago, IL: University of Chicago Press.

Dietz, S. M. (1977) An analysis of programming DRL schedules in educational settings. *Behaviour Research and Therapy*, 15, 103–11.

Dillman, D. A. (2001) Navigating the rapids of change: some observations on survey methodology in the early 21st century. Presidential address at the American Association for Public Opinion Research, St Petersburg, FL.

Dillman, D. A. and Bowker, D. K. (2000) The web questionnaire challenge to survey methodologists. In U.-D. Reips and M. Bosnjak (eds) *Dimensions of Internet Science*. Lengerich, Germany: Pabst Science. http://survey.sesrc.wsu.edu/dillman/zuma_paper_dillman_bowker.pdf. Retrieved 26 February 2005

Dillman, D. A., Tortora, R. D. and Bowker, D. (1998a) Influence of plain vs. fancy design in response rates for web surveys. Proceedings of Survey Methods Section, annual meeting of the American Statistical Association, Dallas, TX. http://survey.sesrc.wsu.edu/dillman.papers.htm. Retrieved 8 February 2005.

Dillman, D. A., Tortora, R. D. and Bowker, D. (1998b) Principles for constructing web surveys http://survey.sesrc.wsu.edu/dillman/papers/websurveyppr.pdf. Retrieved 8 February 2005.

Dillman, D. A., Carley-Baxter, L, and Jackson, A. (1999) Skip pattern compliance in three test forms: a theoretical and empirical evaluation. SESRC Technical Report #99–01. Social and Economic Sciences Research Center. Pullman, WA: Washington State University.

Dillman, D. A., Smyth, J. D., Christian, L. M. and Stern, M. J. (2003) Multiple answer questions in self-administered surveys: the use of check-all-that-apply and forced-choice question formats. Paper presented at the American Statistical Association, San Francisco, CA.

Dobbert, M. L. and Kurth-Schai, R. (1992) Systematic ethnography: toward an evolutionary science of education and culture. In M. LeCompte, W. L. Millroy and J. Preissle (eds) *The Handbook of Qualitative Research in Education*. London: Academic Press, 93–160.

Dochartaigh, N. O. (2002) *The Internet Research Handbook*. London: Sage.

Doll, W. E. Jr. (1993) *A Post-modern Perspective on Curriculum*. New York: Teachers College Press.

Dooley, D. (2001) *Social Research Methods* (fourth edition). Englewood Cliffs, NJ: Prentice Hall

Dosanjh, J. S. and Ghuman, P. A. S. (1997) Asian parents and English education – 20 years on: a study of two generations. *Educational Studies*, 23 (3), 459–72.

Douglas, J. D. (1973) *Understanding Everyday Life*. London: Routledge & Kegan Paul.

Douglas, J. D. (1976) *Investigative Social Research*. Beverly Hills, CA: Sage.

Douglas, J. W. B. (1976) The use and abuse of national cohorts. In M. D. Shipman (ed.) *The Organization and Impact of Social Research*. London: Routledge & Kegan Paul, 3–21.

Dugard, P. and Todman, J. (1995) Analysis of pre-test and post-test control group designs in educational research. *Educational Psychology*, 15 (2), 181–98.

Duncan, M. G. (1968) *A Dictionary of Sociology*. London: Routledge & Kegan Paul.

Duncombe, J. and Jessop, J. (2002) 'Doing rapport' and the ethics of 'faking friendship'. In M. Mauthner, M. Birch, J. Jessop and T. Miller (eds) *Ethics in Qualitative Research*. London: Sage, 107–22.

Dunham, R. B. and Smith, F. J. (1979) *Organizational Surveys: An Internal Assessment of Organizational Health*. Glenview, IL: Scott, Foreman.

Dunning, G. (1993) Managing the small primary school: the problem role of the teaching head. *Educational Management and Administration*, 21 (2), 79–89.

Durkheim, E. (1950) *The Rules of Sociological Method*. New York: The Free Press.

Durkheim, E. (1956) *Education and Sociology*. Glencoe, IL: Free Press.

Dyer, C. (1995) *Beginning Research in Psychology*. Oxford: Blackwell.

Eagleton, T. (1991) *Ideology*. London: Verso.

Ebbinghaus, H. (1897) Über eine neue methode zur Prüfung geistiger Fähigkeiten. Cited in G. de Landsheere (1997) History of educational research. In J. P. Keeves (ed.) *Educational Research, Methodology, and Measurement: An International Handbook* (second edition). Oxford: Elsevier Science, 8–16.

Ebbutt, D. (1985) Educational action research: some general concerns and specific quibbles. In R. Burgess (ed.) *Issues in Educational Research: Qualitative Methods*. Lewes: Falmer, 152–74.

Ebel, R. L. (1979) *Essentials of Educational Measurement* (third edition). Englewood Cliffs, NJ: Prentice Hall.

Eder, D. and Fingerson, L. (2003) Interviewing children and adolescents. In J. A. Holstein and J. F. Gubrium (eds) *Inside Interviewing: New Lenses, New Concerns.* Thousand Oaks, CA: Sage, 33–53.

Edwards, A. (1990) *Practitioner Research.* Study Guide No. 1. Lancaster: St Martin's College.

Edwards, A. D. (1976) *Language in Culture and Class.* London: Heinemann.

Edwards, A. D. (1980) Patterns of power and authority in classroom talk. In P. Woods (ed.) *Teacher Strategies: Explorations in the Sociology of the School.* London: Croom Helm, 237–53.

Edwards, A. D. and Westgate, D. P. G. (1987) *Investigating Classroom Talk.* Lewes: Falmer.

Edwards, D. (1991) Discourse and the development of understanding in the classroom. In O. Boyd-Barrett and E. Scanlon (eds), *Computers and Learning.* Wokingham: Addison-Wesley, 186–204.

Edwards, D. (1993) Concepts, memory and the organisation of pedagogic discourse: a case study. *International Journal of Educational Research,* 19 (3), 205–25.

Edwards, D. and Mercer, N. M. (1987) *Common Knowledge: The Development of Understanding in the Classroom.* London: Routledge & Kegan Paul.

Edwards, D. and Potter, J. (1993) Language and causation: a discursive action model of description and attribution. *Psychological Review,* 100 (1), 23–41.

Edwards, R. and Mauthner, M. (2002) Ethics and feminist research: theory and practice. In M. Mauthner, M. Birch, J. Jessop and T. Miller (eds) *Ethics in Qualitative Research.* London: Sage 14–31.

Eisenhart, M. A. and Howe, K. R. (1992) Validity in educational research. In M. D. LeCompte, W. L. Millroy and J. Preissle (eds) *The Handbook of Qualitative Studies in Education.* New York: Academic Press, 643–680.

Eisner, E. (1985) *The Art of Educational Evaluation.* Lewes: Falmer.

Eisner, E. (1991) *The Enlightened Eye: Qualitative Inquiry and the Enhancement of Educational Practice.* New York: Macmillan.

Ekehammar, B. and Magnusson, D. (1973) A method to study stressful situations. *Journal of Personality and Social Psychology,* 27 (2), 176–9.

Elliott, J. (1978) What is action-research in schools? *Journal of Curriculum Studies,* 10 (4), 355–7.

Elliott, J. (1991) *Action Research for Educational Change.* Buckingham: Open University Press.

Elliott, J. (2001) Making evidence-based practice educational. *British Educational Research Journal,* 27 (5), 555–574.

English, H. B. and English, A. C. (1958) *A Comprehensive Dictionary of Psychological and Psychoanalytic Terms.* London: Longman.

Entwistle, N. L. and Ramsden, P. (1983) *Understanding Student Learning.* Beckenham: Croom Helm.

Epting, F. R. (1988) Journeying into the personal constructs of children. *International Journal of Personal Construct Psychology,* 1 (1), 53–61.

Epting, F. R., Suchman, D. I. and Nickeson, K. J. (1971) An evaluation of elicitation procedures for personal constructs. *British Journal of Psychology,* 62, 513–17.

Erickson, F. (1973) What makes school ethnography 'ethnographic'? *Anthropology and Education Quarterly,* 4 (2), 10–19.

Erickson, F. E. (1992) Ethnographic microanalysis of interaction. In M. LeCompte, W. L. Millroy and J. Preissle (eds) *The Handbook of Qualitative Research in Education.* London: Academic Press, 201–26.

Erikson, K. T. (1967) A comment on disguised observation in sociology. *Social Problems,* 14, 366–73.

Evans, J. and Benefield, P. (2001) Systematic reviews of educational research: does the medical model fit? *British Educational Research Journal,* 27 (5), 527–41. Research Association Conference, University of Cardiff, 7–10 September.

Evans, K. M. (1978) *Planning Small Scale Research.* Windsor: NFER.

Everitt, B. S. (1977) *The Analysis of Contingency Tables.* London: Chapman & Hall.

Evetts, J. (1990) *Women in Primary Teaching.* London: Unwin Hyman.

Evetts, J. (1991) The experience of secondary headship selection: continuity and change. *Educational Studies,* 17 (3), 285–94.

Ewens, A. Howkins, E. and Badger, D. (2000) Evaluating interprofessional education from a community nurse and social work perspective. *Research in Post-Compulsory Education,* 5 (1), 5–20.

Eysenck, H. (1978) An exercise in mega-silliness. *American Psychologist,* 33, 517.

Ezzy, D. (2002) *Qualitative Analysis: Practice and Innovation.* London: Routledge.

Farberow, N. L. (ed.) (1963) *Taboo Topics.* New York: Atherton.

Fay, B. (1987) *Critical Social Science.* New York: Cornell University Press.

Feixas, G., Marti, J. and Villegas, M. (1989) Personal construct assessment of sports teams. *International Journal of Personal Construct Psychology,* 2 (1), 49–54.

Feldt, L. S. and Brennan, R. L. (1993) Reliability. In R. Linn (ed.) *Educational Measurement.* New York: Macmillan, 105–46.

Fendler, L. (1999) Making trouble: prediction, agency, critical intellectuals. In T. S. Popkewitz and L. Fendler (eds) *Critical Theories in Education: Changing Terrains of Knowledge and Politics*. London: Routledge, 169–88.

Ferris, J. and Gerber, R. (1996) Mature-age students' feelings of enjoying learning in a further education context. *European Journal of Psychology of Education*, 11 (1), 79–96.

Festinger, L. and Katz, D. (1966) *Research Methods in the Behavioral Sciences*. New York: Holt, Rinehart & Winston.

Fiedler, J. (1978) *Field Research: A Manual for Logistics and Management of Scientific Studies in Natural Settings*. London: Jossey-Bass.

Field, P. A. and Morse, J. M. (1989) *Nursing Research: The Application of Qualitative Methods*. London: Chapman and Hall.

Fielding, N. G. and Fielding, J. L. (1986) *Linking Data*. Beverly Hills, CA: Sage.

Fielding, N. G. and Lee, R. M. (1998) *Computer Analysis and Qualitative Research*. London: Sage.

Finch, J. (1985) Social policy and education: problems and possibilities of using qualitative research. In R. G. Burgess (ed.) *Issues in Educational Research: Qualitative Methods*. Lewes: Falmer, 109–28.

Fine, G. A. and Sandstrom, K. L. (1988) *Knowing Children: Participant Observation with Minors*. Qualitative Research Methods Series 15. Beverly Hills, CA: Sage.

Finn, C. E. (1991) What ails education research? In D. S. Anderson and B. J. Biddle (eds) *Knowledge for Policy: Improving Education through Research*. London: Falmer, 39–42.

Finnegan, R. (1996) Using documents. In R. Sapsford and V. Jupp (1996) (eds) *Data Collection and Analysis*. London: Sage and the Open University Press, 138–51.

Fisher, B., Russell, T. and McSweeney, P. (1991) Using personal constructs for course evaluation. *Journal of Further and Higher Education*, 15 (1), 44–57.

Fisher, R. A. (1941) *Statistical Methods for Research Workers*. Edinburgh: Oliver & Boyd.

Fitz, J. and Halpin, D. (1994) Ministers and mandarins: educational research in elite settings. In G. Walford (ed.) *Researching the Powerful in Education*. London: UCL Press, 32–50.

Fitz-Gibbon, C. T. (1984) Meta-analysis: an explanation. *British Educational Research Journal*, 10 (2), 135–44.

Fitz-Gibbon, C. T. (1985) The implications of meta-analysis for educational research. *British Educational Research Journal*, 11 (1), 45–9.

Fitz-Gibbon, C. T. (1991) Multilevel modelling in an indicator system. In S. W. Raudenbush and J. D. Willms (eds) *Schools, Classrooms and Pupils: International Studies of Schooling from a Multilevel Perspective*. San Diego, CA: Academic Press, 67–83.

Fitz-Gibbon, C. T. (1996) *Monitoring Education: Indicators, Quality and Effectiveness*. London: Cassell.

Fitz-Gibbon, C. T. (1997) *The Value Added National Project. Final Report*. London: School Curriculum and Assessment Authority.

Fitz-Gibbon, C. T. (1999) Education: high potential not yet realized. *Public Money and Management*, 19 (1), 33–9.

Flanagan, J. (1949) Critical requirements: a new approach to employee evaluation. Cited in E. C. Wragg, *An Introduction to Classroom Observation*. London: Routledge.

Flanders, N. (1970) *Analysing Teacher Behaviour*. Reading, MA: Addison-Wesley.

Flaugher, R. (1990) Item pools. In H. Wainer (ed.) *Computerized Adaptive Testing: A Primer*. Hillsdale, NJ: Erlbaum, 41–64.

Flick, U. (1998) *An Introduction to Qualitative Research*. London: Sage.

Flick, U. (2004) Design and process in qualitative research. In U. Flick, E. von Kardoff and I. Steinke (eds) *A Companion to Qualitative Research*. London: Sage, 146–52.

Flick, U., von Kardoff, E., and Steinke, I. (eds) (2004) *A Companion to Qualitative Research*. Translated by B. Jenner. London: Sage.

Floud, R. (1979) *An Introduction to Quantitative Methods for Historians* (second edition). London: Methuen.

Fogelman, K. (2002) Surveys and sampling. In M. Coleman and A. R. J. Briggs (eds) *Research Methods in Educational Leadership*. London: Paul Chapman.

Forgas, J. P. (1976) The perception of social episodes: categoric and dimensional representations in two different social milieux. *Journal of Personality and Social Psychology*, 34 (2), 199–209.

Forgas, J. P. (1978) Social episodes and social structure in an academic setting: the social environment of an intact group. *Journal of Experimental Social Psychology*, 14, 434–48.

Forward, J., Canter, R. and Kirsch, N. (1976) Role-enactment and deception methodologies. *American Psychologist*, 35, 595–604.

Foskett, N. H. and Hesketh, A. J. (1997) Constructing choice in continuous and parallel markets: institutional and school leavers' responses to the new post-16 marketplace. *Oxford Review of Education*, 23 (3), 299–319.

Foster, J. R. (1992) Eliciting personal constructs and articulating goals. *Journal of Career Development*, 18 (3), 175–85.

Foster, P. (1989) Change and adjustment in a Further Education College. In R. G. Burgess (ed.) *The Ethics of Educational Research*. Lewes: Falmer, 188–204.

Fournier, V. (1997) Graduates' construction systems and career development. *Human Relations*, 50, 363–91.

Fowler, J., Cohen, L. and Jarvis, P. (2000) *Practical Statistics for Field Biology*. Chichester: John Wiley.

Fox, D.J. (1969) *The Research Process in Education*. New York: Holt, Rinehart & Winston.

Francis, H. (1992) Patterns of reading development in the first school. *British Journal of Educational Psychology*, 62, 225–32.

Frankfort-Nachmias, C. and Nachmias, D. (1992) *Research Methods in the Social Sciences*. London: Edward Arnold.

Fransella, F. (1975) *Need to Change?* London: Methuen.

Fransella, F. (2004) *International Handbook of Personal Construct Psychology*. New York: John Wiley.

Fransella, F. (ed.) (2005) *The Essential Practitioner's Handbook of Personal Construct Psychology*. New York: John Wiley.

Fransella, F. and Bannister, D. (1977) *A Manual for Repertory Grid Technique*. London: Academic Press.

Frederiksen, J.R. and Collins, A. (1989) A systems approach to educational testing. *Educational Researcher*, 189, 27–32.

Freire, P. (1970) *Pedagogy of the Oppressed*. Harmondsworth: Penguin.

Frick, A., Bächtiger, M. T. and Reips, U.-D. (1999) Financial incentives, personal information and dropout rate in online studies. In U.-D. Reips and M. Bosnjak (eds) *Dimensions of Internet Science*. Lengerich, Germany: Pabst Science, 209–19.

Fricker, R. D. Jr. and Schonlau, M. (2002) Advantages and disadvantages of Internet-surveys: evidence from the literature. Washington, DC: Rand Organization. http://www.schonlau.net/publication/02fieldmethods.pdf. Retrieved 26 January 2005.

Frisbie, D. (1981) The relative difficulty ratio – a test and item index. *Educational and Psychological Measurement*, 41 (2), 333–9.

Fullan, M. (1999) *Change Forces* (second edition). London: Falmer.

Gadamer, H. G. (1975) *Truth and Method*. New York: Polity Press.

Gadd, D. (2004) Making sense of interviewee–interviewer dynamics in narratives about violence in intimate relationships. *International Journal of Social Research Methodology*, 7 (5), 383–401.

Gage, N. L. (1989) The paradigm wars and their aftermath. *Teachers College Record*, 91 (2), 135–50.

Gallagher, T., McEwen, A. and Knip, D. (1997) Science education policy: a survey of the participation of sixth-form pupils in science and the subjects over a 10-year period, 1985–95. *Research Papers in Education*, 12 (2), 121–42.

Galton, M. and Simon, B. (1980) *Inside the Primary Classroom*. London: Routledge.

Galton, M., Hargreaves, L, Comber, C., Wall, D. and Pell, T. (1999) Changes in patterns in teacher interaction in primary classrooms, 1976–1996. *British Educational Research Journal*, 25 (1), 23–37.

Gardner, G. (1978) *Social Surveys for Social Planners*. Milton Keynes: Open University Press.

Gardner, H. (1993) *Multiple Intelligences: The Theory in Practice*. New York: Basic Books.

Garfinkel, H. (1967) *Studies in Ethnomethodology*. Englewood Cliffs, NJ: Prentice Hall.

Garner, C. and Raudenbush, S. W. (1991) Neighbourhood effects in educational attainment: a multilevel analysis. *Sociology of Education*, 64 (4), 251–62.

Garrahan, P. and Stewart, P. (1992) *The Nissan Enigma: Flexibility at Work in a Local Economy*. London: Mansell.

Gaukroger, A. and Schwartz, L. (1997) A university and its region: student recruitment to Birmingham, 1945–75. *Oxford Review of Education*, 23 (2), 185–202.

Geertz, C. (1973a) *The Interpretation of Cultures*. New York: Basic Books.

Geertz, C. (1973b) Thick description: towards an interpretive theory of culture. In. C. Geertz (ed.) *The Interpretation of Cultures*. New York: Basic Books.

Geertz, C. (1974) From the native's point of view: on the nature of anthropological understanding. *Bulletin of the American Academy of Arts and Sciences*, 28 (1), 26–45.

Geuss, R. (1981) *The Idea of a Critical Theory*. London: Cambridge University Press.

Gewirtz, S. and Ozga, J. (1993) Sex, lies and audiotape: interviewing the education policy elite. Paper presented to the Economic and Research Council, 1988 Education Reform Act Research seminar. University of Warwick.

Gewirtz, S. and Ozga, J. (1994) Interviewing the education policy elite. In G. Walford (ed.) *Researching* the Powerful in Education. London: UCL Press, 186–203.

Gibbons, J. D. (1976) Nonparametric Methods for Quantitative Analysis. New York: Holt, Rinehart & Winston.

Gibson, R. (1985) Critical times for action research. Cambridge Journal of Education, 15 (1), 59–64.

Giddens, A. (ed.) (1975) Positivism and Sociology. London: Heinemann.

Giddens, A. (1976) New Rules of Sociological Method: A Positive Critique of Interpretative Sociologies. London: Hutchinson.

Giddens, A. (1979) Central Problems in Social Theory. London: Macmillan.

Giddens, A. (1984) The Constitution of Society. Cambridge: Polity Press.

Gilbert, N. and Troitzsch, K. G. (2005) Simulation for the Social Scientist (second edition). Maidenhead: Open University Press.

Gillies, V. and Alldred, P. (2002) The ethics of intention: research as a political tool. In M. Mauthner, M. Birch, J. Jessop and T. Miller (eds) Ethics in Qualitative Research. London: Sage, 32–52.

Ginsburg, G. P. (1978) Role playing and role performance in social psychological research. In M. Brenner, P. Marsh and M. Brenner (eds) The Social Contexts of Method. London: Croom Helm, 91–121.

Gipps, C. (1994) Beyond Testing: Towards a Theory of Educational Assessment. London: Falmer.

Giroux, H. (1989) Schooling for Democracy. London: Routledge.

Glaser, B. G. (1978) Theoretical Sensitivity: Advances in the Methodology of Grounded Theory. Mill Valley, CA: Sociology Press.

Glaser, B. G. (1996) Grounded theory: an interview with A. Lowe. Programme 8 of Doing a PhD in Business and Management. Glasgow: University of Sterling and Heriot-Watt University

Glaser, B. G. and Strauss, A. L. (1967) The Discovery of Grounded Theory. Chicago, IL: Aldane.

Glass, G. V. (1976) Primary, secondary and meta-analysis. Educational Research, 5, 3–8.

Glass, G. V. (1977) Integrating findings: the meta-analysis of research. Review of Research in Education, 5, 351–79.

Glass, G. V. and Hopkins, K. D. (1996) Statistical Methods in Education and Psychology (third edition). Boston, MA: Allyn & Bacon.

Glass, G. V. and Smith, M. L. (1978) Meta-Analysis of Research on the Relationship of Class-size and Achievement. San Francisco: Farwest Laboratory.

Glass, G. V. and Worthen, B. R. (1971) Evaluation and research: similarities and differences. Curriculum Theory Network, 3 (Fall), 149–65.

Glass, G. V., McGaw, B. and Smith, M.L. (1981) Meta-Analysis in Social Research. Beverly Hills, CA: Sage.

Gleick, J. (1987) Chaos. London: Abacus.

Goffman, E. (1968) Asylums. Harmondsworth: Penguin.

Golafshani, N. (2003) Understanding reliability and validity in qualitative research. The Qualitative Report, 8 (4), 597–607. http://www.nova.edu/ssss/QR/QR8-4/golafshani.pdf. Retrieved 29 October 2005.

Gold, R. L. (1958) Roles in sociological field observations. Social Forces, 36, 217–23.

Goldstein, H. (1987) Multilevel Modelling in Educational and Social Research. London: Charles Griffin.

Good, C. V. (1963) Introduction to Educational Research. New York: Appleton-Century-Crofts.

Goodson, I. (1983) The use of life histories in the study of teaching. In M. Hammersley (ed.) The Ethnography of Schooling. Driffield, UK: Nafferton, 129–54.

Goodson, I. (1990) The Making of Curriculum. Lewes: Falmer.

Goodson, I. and Walker, R. (1988) Putting life into educational research. In R. R. Sherman and R. B. Webb (eds) Qualitative Research in Education: Focus and Methods. Lewes: Falmer, 110–22.

Goossens, L., Marcoen, A., van Hees, S. and van de Woestlijne, O. (1998) Attachment style and loneliness in adolescence. European Journal of Psychology of Education, 13 (4), 529–42.

Gorard, S. (2001) Quantitative Methods in Educational Research: The Role of Numbers Made Easy. London: Continuum.

Gorard, S. (2003) Quantitative Methods in Social Science. London: Continuum.

Gorard, S. and Taylor, C. (2004) Combining Methods in Educational and Social Research. London: Open University Press.

Gorard, S., Taylor, C. and Fitz, J. (2002) Markets in public policy: the case of the United Kingdom Education Reform Act. International Studies in Sociology of Education, 12 (1), 23–42.

Gottschalk, L. (1951) Understanding History. New York: Alfred A. Knopf.

Graue, M. E. and Walsh, D. J. (1998) Studying Children in Context: Theories, Methods and Ethics. London: Sage.

Greig, A. D. and Taylor, J. (1998) Doing Research with Children. London: Sage.

Gronlund, N. (1981) *Measurement and Evaluation in Teaching* (fourth edition). New York: Collier-Macmillan.

Gronlund, N. (1985) *Stating Objectives for Classroom Instruction* (third edition). New York: Macmillan.

Gronlund, N. E. and Linn, R. L. (1990) *Measurement and Evaluation in Teaching* (sixth edition). New York: Macmillan.

Grundy, S. (1987) *Curriculum: Product or Praxis*. Lewes: Falmer.

Grundy, S. (1996) Towards empowering leadership: the importance of imagining. In O. Zuber-Skerritt (ed.) *New Directions in Action Research*. London: Falmer, 106–20.

Grundy, S. and Kemmis, S. (1988) Educational action research in Australia: the state of the art (an overview). In S. Kemmis and R. McTaggart (eds) *The Action Research Reader* (second edition). Geelong, Vic.: Deakin University Press, 83–97.

Guba, E. G. and Lincoln, Y. S. (1989) *Fourth Generation Evaluation*. Beverly Hills, CA: Sage.

Guilford, J. P. and Fruchter, B. (1973) *Fundamental Statistics in Psychology and Education*. New York: McGraw-Hill.

Habermas, J. (1970) Toward a theory of communicative competence. *Inquiry*, 13, 360–75.

Habermas, J. (1972) *Knowledge and Human Interests*, trans. J. Shapiro. London: Heinemann.

Habermas, J. (1974) *Theory and Practice*, trans. J. Viertel. London: Heinemann.

Habermas, J. (1976) *Legitimation Crisis*, trans. T. McCarthy. London: Heinemann

Habermas, J. (1979) *Communication and the Evolution of Society*. London: Heinemann.

Habermas, J. (1982) A reply to my critics. In J. Thompson and D. Held (eds) *Habermas: Critical Debates*. London: Macmillan, 219–83.

Habermas, J. (1984) *The Theory of Communicative Action. Volume One: Reason and the Rationalization of Society*, trans. T. McCarthy. Boston, MA: Beacon.

Habermas, J. (1987) *The Theory of Communicative Action. Volume Two: Lifeworld and System*, trans. T. McCarthy. Boston, MA: Beacon.

Habermas, J. (1988) *On the Logic of the Social Sciences*, trans. S. Nicholsen and J. Stark. Cambridge: Polity Press in association with Basil Blackwell.

Habermas, J. (1990) *Moral Consciousness and Communicative Action*, trans. C. Lenhardt and S. Nicholsen. Cambridge: Polity Press in association with Basil Blackwell.

Haig, B. D. (1997) Feminist research methodology. In J. P. Keeves (ed.) *Educational Research, Methodology, and Measurement: An International Handbook* (second edition). Oxford: Elsevier Science, 180–5.

Haig, B. (1999) Feminist research methodology. In J. P. Keeves and G. Lakomski (eds) *Issues in Educational Research*. Oxford: Elsevier Science, 222–31.

Hakim, C. (1987) *Research Design, Contemporary Social Research: 13*. London: Allen & Unwin.

Haladyna, T. M. (1997) *Writing Test Items to Evaluate Higher Order Thinking*. Needham Heights, MA: Allyn & Bacon.

Haladnya, T., Nolen, S. and Haas, N. (1991) Raising standardized achievement test scores and the origins of test score pollution. *Educational Researcher*, 20 (5), 2–7.

Hall, E., Hall, C. and Abaci, R. (1997) The effects of human relations training on reported teacher stress, pupil control ideology and locus of control. *British Journal of Educational Psychology*, 67, 483–96.

Hall, K. and Nuttall, W. (1999) The *relative* importance of class size to infant teachers in England. *British Educational Research Journal*, 25 (2), 245–58.

Hall, S. (1996) Reflexivity in emancipatory action research: illustrating the researcher's constitutiveness. In O. Zuber-Skerritt (ed.) *New Directions in Action Research*. London: Falmer.

Halsey, A. H. (ed.) (1972) *Educational Priority: Volume 1: E. P. A. Problems and Policies*. London: HMSO.

Hambleton, R. K. (1993) Principles and selected application of item response theory, in R. Linn (ed.) *Educational Measurement* (third edition). Phoenix, AZ: American Council on Education and the Oryx Press, 147–200.

Hamilton, V. L. (1976) Role-play and deception: a re-examination of the controversy. *Journal for the Theory of Social Behaviour*, 6, 233–50.

Hammersley, M. (1992) *What's Wrong with Ethnography?* London: Routledge.

Hammersley, M. (1993) *Social Research: Philosophy, Politics and Practice*. London: Sage in association with the Open University Press.

Hammersley, M. and Atkinson, P. (1983) *Ethnography: Principles in Practice*. London: Routledge.

Hampden-Turner, C. (1970) *Radical Man*. Cambridge, MA: Schenkman.

Haney, C., Ranks, C. and Zimbardo, P. (1973) Interpersonal dynamics in a simulated prison. *International Journal of Criminology and Penology*, 1, 69–97.

Hanna, G. S. (1993) *Better Teaching through Better Measurement*. Fort Worth, TX: Harcourt Brace Jovanovich.

Hannan, A. and Newby, M. (1992) Student teacher and headteacher views on current provision and proposals for the future of Initial Teacher Education for primary schools (mimeo). Rolle Faculty of Education, University of Plymouth.

Harlen, W. (ed.) (1994) *Enhancing Quality in Assessment*. London: Paul Chapman.

Harré, R. (1972) *The Philosophies of Science*. Oxford: Oxford University Press.

Harré, R. (1974) Some remarks on 'rule' as a scientific concept. In T. Mischel (ed.) *On Understanding Persons*. Oxford: Basil Blackwell, 143–84.

Harré, R. (1976) The constructive role of models. In L. Collins (ed.) *The Use of Models in the Social Sciences*. London: Tavistock, 16–43.

Harré, R. (1977a) The ethogenic approach: theory and practice. In L. Berkowitz (ed.) *Advances in Experimental Social Psychology*, Vol. 10. New York: Academic Press, 284–314.

Harré, R. (1977b) Friendship as an accomplishment. In S. Duck (ed.) *Theory and Practice in Interpersonal Attraction*. London: Academic Press, 339–54.

Harré, R. (1978) Accounts, actions and meanings – the practice of participatory psychology. In M. Brenner, P. Marsh and M. Brenner (eds) *The Social Contexts of Method*. London: Croom Helm, 44–66.

Harré, R. and Rosser, E. (1975) The rules of disorder. *The Times Educational Supplement*, 25 July.

Harré, R. and Secord, P. (1972) *The Explanation of Social Behaviour*. Oxford: Basil Blackwell.

Harris, N., Pearce, P. and Johnstone, S. (1992) *The Legal Context of Teaching*. London: Longman.

Harrison, R. and Stokes, H. (1992) *Diagnosing Organizational Culture*. San Francisco, CA: Jossey-Bass.

Hartley, S., Gerhardt-Powals, J., Jones, D., McCormack, C., Medley, D., Price, B., Reek, M. and Summers, M. (1997) *Evaluating Educational Materials on the Web*. University of Washington. http://staff.washington.edu/rells/pod97/evaluate.htm. Retrieved 1 May 2003.

Harvey, C. D. H. (1988) Telephone survey techniques. *Canadian Home Economics Journal*, 38 (1), 30–5.

Heath, S. B. (1982) Questioning at home and at school: a comparative study, in G. Spindler (ed.) *Doing the Ethnography of Schooling*. New York: Holt, Rinehart & Winston, 102–31.

Hedges, A. (1985) Group interviewing. In R. Walker (ed.) *Applied Qualitative Research*. Aldershot: Gower, 71–91.

Hedges, L. (1981) Distribution theory for Glass's estimator of effect size and related estimators. *Journal of Educational Statistics*, 6, 107–28.

Hedges, L. (1990) Directions for future methodology. In K. W. Wachter and M. L. Straf (eds) *The Future of Meta-analysis*. New York: Russell Sage Foundation. Cited in B. McGaw (1997) Meta-analysis. In J. P. Keeves (ed.) *Educational Research, Methodology, and Measurement: An International Handbook* (second edition). Oxford: Elsevier Science, 371–80.

Hedges, L. and Olkin, I. (1980) Vote-counting methods in research synthesis. *Psychological Bulletin*, 88 (2), 359–69.

Hedges, L. and Olkin, I. (1985) *Statistical Methods for Meta-analysis*. New York: Academic Press.

Held, D. (1980) *Introduction to Critical Theory*. Los Angeles, CA: University of California Press.

Hesse, M. (1982) Science and objectivity. In J. Thompson and D. Held (eds) *Habermas: Critical Debates*. London: Macmillan, 98–115.

Hewson, C., Yule, P., Laurent, D. and Vogel, C. (2003) *Internet Research Methods*. London: Sage.

Higgs, G., Webster, C. J. and White, S. D. (1997) The use of geographical information systems in assessing spatial and socio-economic impacts of parental choice. *Research Papers in Education*, 12 (1), 27–48.

Hildenbrand, B. (2004) Anselm Strauss. In U. Flick, E. von Kardoff and I. Steinke (eds) *A Companion to Qualitative Research*. London: Sage, 17–23.

Hill, J. E. and Kerber, A. (1967) *Models, Methods and Analytical Procedures in Educational Research*. Detroit, MI: Wayne State University Press.

Hill, P. W. and Rowe, K. J. (1996) Multilevel modelling in school effectiveness research. *School Effectiveness and School Improvement*, 7 (1), 1–34.

Hinkle, D. N. (1965) The change of personal constructs from the viewpoint of a theory of implications. Unpublished PhD thesis. Ohio State University.

Hitchcock, G. and Hughes, D. (1989) *Research and the Teacher*. London: Routledge.

Hitchcock, G. and Hughes, D. (1995) *Research and the Teacher* (second edition). London: Routledge.

Hockett, H.C. (1955) *The Critical Method in Historical Research and Writing*. London: Macmillan.

Hoinville, G. and Jowell, R. (1978) *Survey Research Practice*. London: Heinemann.

Holbrook, D. (1977) *Education, Nihilism and Survival*. London: Darton, Longman & Todd.

Holland, J. L. (1985) *Making Vocational Choices: A Theory of Vocational Personalities and Work Environments*. Englewood-Cliffs, NJ: Prentice-Hall.

Holly, P. (1984) *Action Research: A Cautionary Note*. Classroom Action Research Network, Bulletin no. 6. Cambridge: Cambridge Institute of Education.

Holly, P. and Whitehead, D. (1986) *Action Research in Schools: Getting It into Perspective*. Classroom Action Research Network.

Holmes, P. and Karp, M. (1991) *Psychodrama: Inspiration and Technique*. London: Routledge.

Holmes, R. M. (1998) *Fieldwork with Children*. London: Sage.

Holsti, O. R. (1968) Content analysis. In G. Lindzey and E. Aronson (eds) *The Handbook of Social Psychology. Volume 2: Research Methods*. Reading, MA: Addison-Wesley, 596–692.

Hopkins, D. (1985) *A Teacher's Guide to Classroom Research*. Milton Keynes: Open University Press.

Hopkins, K. D., Hopkins, B. R. and Glass, G. V. (1996) *Basic Statistics for the Behavioral Sciences* (third edition). Boston, MA: Allyn & Bacon.

Horkheimer, M. (1972) *Critical Theory: Selected Essays*, trans. M. Connell *et al.* New York: Herder and Herder.

Horowitz, I. L. and Katz, J. E. (1991) Brown vs Board of Education. In D. S. Anderson and B. J. Biddle (eds) *Knowledge for Policy: Improving Education through Research*. London: Falmer, 237–44.

Houghton, D. (1991) Mr Chong: a case study of a dependent learner of English for academic purposes. *System*, 19 (1–2), 75–90.

House, E. R. (1979) Technology versus craft: a ten-year perspective on innovation. *Journal of Curriculum Studies*, 11 (1), 1–15.

Howitt, D. and Cramer, D. (2005) *Introduction to Research Methods in Psychology*. Harlow: Pearson.

Hoyle, E. (1986) *The Politics of School Management*. Sevenoaks: Hodder & Stoughton.

Hudson, P. and Miller, C. (1997) The treasure hunt: strategies for obtaining maximum response to a postal survey. *Evaluation and Research in Education*, 11 (2), 102–12.

Hughes, J. A. (1976) *Sociological Analysis: Methods of Discovery*. Sunbury-on-Thames: Nelson and Sons.

Huizinga, J. (1949) *Homo Ludens*. London: Routledge & Kegan Paul, subsequently published by Paladin.

Hult, M. and Lennung, S. (1980) Towards a definition of action-research: a note and bibliography. *Journal of Management Studies*, 17 (2), 241–50.

Humphreys, L. (1970) *Tearoom Trade: A Study of Homosexual Encounters in Public Places*. London: Gerald Duckworth.

Humphreys, L. (1975) *Tearoom Trade: Impersonal Sex in Public Places* (enlarged edition). New York: Aldine.

Hunter, J. E. Schmidt, F. L. and Jackson, G. B. (1982) *Meta-analysis: Cumulating Research Findings across Studies*. Beverly Hills, CA: Sage.

Hurn, C. J. (1978) *The Limits and Possibilities of Schooling*. Boston, MA: Allyn & Bacon.

Hutchinson, B. and Whitehouse, P. (1986) Action research, professional competence and school organization. *British Educational Research Journal*, 12 (1), 85–94.

Hycner, R. H. (1985) Some guidelines for the phenomenological analysis of interview data. *Human Studies*, 8, 279–303.

Ions, E. (1977) *Against Behaviouralism: A Critique of Behavioural Science*. Oxford: Basil Blackwell.

Jacklin, A. and Lacey, C. (1997) Gender integration in the infant classroom: a case study. *British Educational Research Journal*, 23 (5), 623–40.

Jackson, D. and Marsden, D. (1962) *Education and the Working Class*. London: Routledge & Kegan Paul.

Jackson, G. B. (1980) Methods for integrative reviews. *Review of Educational Research*, 50, 438–60.

Jackson, P. W. (1968) *Life in Classrooms*. Eastbourne: Holt, Rinehart & Winston.

Jacob, E. (1987) Qualitative research traditions: a review. *Review of Educational Research*, 57 (1), 1–50.

James, M. (1993) Evaluation for policy: rationality and political reality: the paradigm case of PRAISE? In R. G. Burgess (ed.) *Educational Research and Evaluation for Policy and Practice*. London: Falmer.

Jayaratne, T. E. (1993) The value of quantitative methodology for feminist research. In M. Hammersley (ed.) *Social Research: Philosophy, Politics and Practice*. London: Sage in association with the Open University Press, 109–23.

Jayaratne, T. and Stewart, A. (1991) Quantitative and qualitative methods in the social sciences: current feminist issues and practical strategies. In M. Fonow and J. Cook (eds) *Beyond Methodology: Feminist Scholarship as Lived Research*. Bloomington, IN: Indiana University Press.

Jones, J. (1990) The role of the headteacher in staff development. *Educational Management and Administration*, 18 (1), 27–36.

Jones, N. (1999) The changing management agenda for primary heads. *International Journal of Public Sector Management*, 12 (4), 324–37.

Jones, S. (1987) The analysis of depth interviews. In R. Murphy and H. Torrance (eds) *Evaluating Education: Issues and Methods*. London: Paul Chapman, 263–77.

Jones, S. (ed.) (1999) *Doing Internet Research*. Thousand Oaks, CA: Sage.

Joy, G. T. (2003) A brief description of culturally valid knowledge. Personal communication. Sophia Junior College, Hakone-machi, Kanagawa-ken, Japan.

Jules, V. and Kutnick, P. (1997) Student perceptions of a good teacher: the gender perspective. *British Journal of Educational Psychology*, 67, 497–511.

Kamin, L. (1991) Some historical facts about IQ testing. In D. S. Anderson and B. J. Biddle (eds) *Knowledge for Policy: Improving Education through Research*. London: Falmer, 259–67.

Kaplan, A. (1973) *The Conduct of Inquiry*. Aylesbury: Intertext Books.

Karr, B. (1995) *Complexity Theory and Rhetorical Invention*. http://english.ttu.edu/courses/5361/papers/paper 1_karr_420.html. Retrieved 14 November 2000.

Kauffman, S. A. (1995) *At Home in the Universe: The Search for the Laws of Self-Organization and Complexity*. Harmondsworth: Penguin.

Kazdin, A. E. (1982) *Single-case Research Designs*. New York: Oxford University Press.

Keat, R. (1981) *The Politics of Social Theory*. Oxford: Basil Blackwell.

Keeves, J. P. (ed.) (1997a) *Educational Research, Methodology and Measurement: An International Handbook* (second edition). Oxford: Elsevier Science.

Keeves, J. P. (1997b) Longitudinal research methods. In J. P. Keeves (ed.) *Educational Research, Methodology and Measurement: An International Handbook* (second edition). Oxford: Elsevier Science, 138–49.

Keeves, J. P. and Sellin, N. (1997) Multilevel analysis. In J. P. Keeves (ed.) *Educational Research, Methodology and Measurement: An International Handbook* (second edition). Oxford: Elsevier Science, 394–403.

Kelle, U. (ed.) (1995) *Computer-Aided Qualitative Data Analysis*. London: Sage.

Kelle, U. (2004) Computer-assisted analysis of qualitative data. In U. Flick, E. V. Kardoff and I. Steinke (eds) *A Companion to Qualitative Research*, trans. B. Jenner. London: Sage, 276–293.

Kelle, U. and Laurie, H. (1995) Computer use in qualitative research and issues of validity. In U. Kelle (ed.) *Computer-Aided Qualitative Data Analysis*. London: Sage, 19–28.

Kelly, A. (1978) Feminism and research. *Women's Studies International Quarterly*, 1, 225–32.

Kelly, A. (1985) Action research: what is it and what can it do? In R. G. Burgess (ed.) *Issues in Educational Research: Qualitative Methods*. Lewes: Falmer, 129–51.

Kelly, A. (1986) The development of children's attitudes to science: a longitudinal study. *European Journal of Science Education*, 8, 399–412.

Kelly, A. (1987) *Science for Girls?* Milton Keynes: Open University Press.

Kelly, A. (1989a) Education or indoctrination? The ethics of school-based action research. In R. G. Burgess (ed.) *The Ethics of Educational Research*. Lewes: Falmer, 100–13.

Kelly, A. (1989b) *Getting the GIST: A Qualitative Study of the Effects of the Girls Into Science and Technology Project*. Manchester Sociology Occasional Papers, no. 22. Manchester: University of Manchester.

Kelly, A. and Smail, B. (1986) Sex stereotypes and attitudes to science among eleven-year-old children. *British Journal of Educational Psychology*, 56, 158–68.

Kelly G. A. (1955) *The Psychology of Personal Constructs*. New York: Norton.

Kelly, G. A. (1969) *Clinical Psychology and Personality: The Selected Papers of George Kelly*, edited by B. A. Maher. New York: John Wiley.

Kelman, H. C. (1967) Human use of human subjects. *Psychological Bulletin*, 67 (1), 1–11.

Kemmis, S. (1982) Seven principles for programme evaluation in curriculum development and innovation. *Journal of Curriculum Studies*, 14 (3), 221–40.

Kemmis, S. (1997) Action research. In J. P. Keeves (ed.) *Educational Research, Methodology, and Measurement: An International Handbook* (second edition). Oxford: Elsevier Science, 173–9.

Kemmis, S. and McTaggart, R. (eds) (1981) *The Action Research Planner* (first edition). Geelong, Vic.: Deakin University Press.

Kemmis, S. and McTaggart, R. (eds) (1988) *The Action Research Planner* (second edition). Geelong, Vic.: Deakin University Press.

Kemmis, S. and McTaggart, R. (1992) *The Action Research Planner* (third edition) Geelong, Vic.: Deakin University Press.

Kerlinger, F. N. (1970) *Foundations of Behavioral Research*. New York: Holt, Rinehart & Winston.

Kerlinger, F. N. (1986) *Foundations of Behavioral Research* (third edition). New York: Holt, Rinehart & Winston.

Kerlinger, F. N. (1991) Science and behavioural research. In D. S. Anderson and B. J. Biddle (eds)

Knowledge for Policy: Improving Education through Research. London: Falmer, 87–102.

Kgaile, A. P. and Morrison, K. R. B. (2006) Measuring and targeting internal conditions for school effectiveness in the Free State of South Africa. *Educational Management, Administration and Leadership,* 34 (1), 47–68.

Kierkegaard, S. (1974) *Concluding Unscientific Postscript.* Princeton, NJ: Princeton University Press.

Kimmel, A. J. (1988) *Ethics and Values in Applied Social Research.* Newbury Park, CA: Sage.

Kincheloe, J. L. (1991) *Teachers as Researchers: Qualitative Inquiry as a Path to Empowerment.* London: Falmer.

Kincheloe, J. L. (2003) *Teachers as Researchers: Qualitative Inquiry as a Path to Empowerment* (second edition). London: RoutledgeFalmer.

Kincheloe, J. and McLaren, P. (1994) Rethinking critical theory and qualitative research. In N. K. Denzin and Y. S. Lincoln (eds) *Handbook of Qualitative Research.* Beverly Hills, CA: Sage, 105–17.

King, J. A., Morris, L. L. and Fitz-Gibbon, C. T. (1987) *How to Assess Program Implementation.* Beverly Hills, CA: Sage.

King, R. (1979) *All Things Bright and Beautiful?* Chichester: John Wiley.

Kirk, J. and Miller, M. L. (1986) *Reliability and Validity in Qualitative Research.* Qualitative Research Methods Series no. 1. Beverly Hills, CA: Sage.

Kirk, R. E. (1999) *Statistics: An Introduction.* London: Harcourt Brace.

Kitwood, T. M. (1977) Values in adolescent life: towards a critical description, Unpublished PhD dissertation, School of Education, University of Bradford.

Kivulu, J. M. and Rogers, W. T. (1998) A multilevel analysis of cultural experience and gender influences on causal attributions to perceived performance in mathematics. *British Journal of Educational Psychology,* 68, 25–37.

Kline, P. (2000) *Handbook of Psychological Testing* (second edition). London: Routledge.

Kline, R. (2004) *Beyond Significance Testing.* Washington, DC: American Psychological Association.

Klockars, C. B. (1979) Dirty hands and deviant subjects. In C. B Klockars and F. O'Connor (eds) *Deviance and Decency: The Ethics of Research with Human Subjects.* Beverly Hills, CA: Sage.

Knott, J. and Wildavsky, A. (1991) If dissemination is the solution, what is the problem? In D. S. Anderson and B. J. Biddle (eds) *Knowledge for Policy: Improving Education through Research.* London: Falmer, 214–24.

Kogan, M. and Atkin, J. M. (1991) Special commissions and educational policy in the U.S.A. and U.K. In D. S. Anderson and B. J. Biddle (eds) *Knowledge for Policy: Improving Education through Research.* London: Falmer, 245–58.

Kohn, A. (2000) *The Case against Standardized Testing: Raising the Scores, Ruining the Schools.* Portsmouth, NH: Heinemann.

Kolakowski, L. (1978) *Main Currents of Marxism, Volume Three: The Breakdown,* trans. P. S. Falla. Oxford: Clarendon Press.

Krejcie, R. V. and Morgan, D. W. (1970) Determining sample size for research activities. *Educational and Psychological Measurement,* 30, 607–10.

Kremer-Hayon, L. (1991) Personal constructs of elementary school principals in relation to teachers. *Research in Education,* 43, 15–21.

Krippendorp, K. (2004) *Content Analysis: An Introduction to its Methodology.* Thousand Oaks, CA: Sage.

Krosnick, J. A. (1999) Survey research. *Annual Review of Psychology,* 50, 537–67.

Krosnick, J. A. and Alwin, D. F. (1987) An evaluation of a cognitive theory of response-order effects in survey measurement. *Public Opinion Quarterly,* 51, 201–19.

Krueger, R. A. (1988) *Focus Groups: A Practical Guide for Applied Research.* Beverly Hills, CA: Sage.

Kuhn, T. S. (1962) *The Structure of Scientific Revolutions.* Chicago, IL: University of Chicago Press.

Kvale, S. (1996) *Interviews.* London: Sage.

Labov, W. (1969) The logic of non-standard English. In N. Keddie (ed.) *Tinker, Tailor . . . the Myth of Cultural Deprivation.* Harmondsworth: Penguin, 21–66.

Laing, R. D. (1967) *The Politics of Experience and the Bird of Paradise.* Harmondsworth: Penguin.

Lakatos, I. (1970) Falsification and the methodology of scientific research programmes. In I. Lakatos and A. Musgrave (eds) *Criticism and the Growth of Knowledge.* Cambridge: Cambridge University Press, 91–195.

Lakomski, G. (1999) Critical theory. In J. P. Keeves and G. Lakomski (eds) *Issues in Educational Research.* Oxford: Elsevier Science, 174–83.

Lamb, S., Bibby, P., Wood, D. and Leyden, G. (1997) Communication skills, educational achievement and biographic characteristics of children with moderate learning difficulties. *European Journal of Psychology of Education,* 12 (4), 401–14.

Lansing, J. B., Ginsberg, G. P. and Braaten, K. (1961) *An Investigation of Response Error.* Urbana-Champaign,

IL: Bureau of Economic and Business Research, University of Illinois.

Lather, P. (1986) Research as praxis. *Harvard Educational Review*, 56, 257–77.

Lather, P. (1991) *Getting Smart: Feminist Research and Pedagogy within the Post Modern*. New York: Routledge.

Laudan, L. (1990) *Science and Relativism*. Chicago, IL: University of Chicago Press.

Lave, J. and Kvale, S. (1995) What is anthropological research? An interview with Jean Lave by Steiner Kvale. *International Journal of Qualitative Studies in Education*, 8 (3), 219–28.

Lawless, L., Smee, P. and O'Shea, T. (1998) Using concept sorting and concept mapping in business and public administration, and education: an overview. *Educational Research*, 40 (2), 219–35.

Layder, D. (1994) *Understanding Social Theory*. London: Sage.

Lazarsfeld, P. (1940) 'Panel' studies. *Public Opinion Quarterly*, 4 (1), 122–8.

Lazarsfeld, P. P. and Barton, A. (1951) Qualitative measurement in the social sciences: classification, typologies and indices. In D. P. Lerner and H. D. Lasswell (eds) *The Policy Sciences*. Stanford, CA: Stanford University Press, 155–92.

LeCompte, M. and Preissle, J. (1993) *Ethnography and Qualitative Design in Educational Research* (second edition). London: Academic Press.

LeCompte, M., Millroy, W. L. and Preissle, J. (eds) (1992) *The Handbook of Qualitative Research in Education*. London: Academic Press.

Lee, R. M. (1993) *Doing Research on Sensitive Topics*. London: Sage.

Lee, R. M. and Renzetti, C. M. (1993) The problems of researching sensitive topics: an overview and introduction. In C. Renzetti and R. M. Lee (eds) *Researching Sensitive Topics*. London: Sage.

Leech, N. L. and Onwuegbuzie, A. J. (2004) A proposed fourth measure of significance: The role of economic significance in educational research. *Evaluation and Research in Education*, 18 (3), 179–98.

Lehrer, R. and Franke, M. L. (1992) Applying personal construct psychology to the study of teachers' knowledge of fractions. *Journal for Research in Mathematical Education*, 23 (3), 223–41.

Leistyna, P., Woodrum, A. and Sherblom, S. A. (1996) *Breaking Free*. Cambridge, MA: Harvard Educational Review.

Lemke, J. (2001) *Toward Systemic Educational Change: Questions from a Complex Systems Perspective*. Cambridge, MA: New England Complex Systems Institute. http://www.necsi.org/events/cxedk16_3.html. Retrieved 10 November 2001.

Levačić, R. and Glatter, R. (2000) Really good ideas: developing evidence-informed policy and practice in educational leadership and management. *Educational Management and Administration*, 29 (1), 5–25.

Levin, H. M. (1991) Why isn't educational research more useful? In D. S. Anderson and B. J. Biddle (eds) *Knowledge for Policy: Improving Education through Research*. London: Falmer, 70–8.

Levine, M. (1984) *Canonical Analysis and Factor Comparisons*. Beverly Hills, CA: Sage.

Lewin, K. (1946) Action research and minority problems. *Journal of Social Issues*, 2 (4), 34–46.

Lewin, K. (1948) *Resolving Social Conflicts*. New York: Harper.

Lewin, K. (1952) *Field Theory in Social Science*. London: Tavistock.

Lewin, R. (1993) *Complexity: Life on the Edge of Chaos*. London: Phoenix.

Lewis, A. (1992) Group child interviews as a research tool, *British Educational Research Journal*, 18 (4), 413–21.

Lewis, D. (1974) *Assessment in Education*. London: University of London Press.

Lewis-Beck, M. S. (ed.) (1993) *Experimental Design and Methods*. London: Toppan with the cooperation of Sage.

Liebling, H. and Shah, S. (2001) Researching sensitive topics: investigations of the sexual abuse of women in Uganda and girls in Tanzania. *Law, Social Justice and Global Development*. http://elj.warwick.ac.uk/global/issue/2001-1/liebling.html. Retrieved 21 November 2003.

Lietz, P. (1997) Cross-sectional research methods. In J. B. Keeves (ed.) *Educational Research, Methodology and Measurement*. Oxford: Elsevier Science, 119–26.

Lietz, P. and Keeves, J. P. (1997) Cross-sectional research methods. In J. P. Keeves (ed.) *Educational Research, Methodology and Measurement: An International Handbook* (second edition). Oxford: Elsevier Science, 138–49.

Light, R. J. and Smith, P. V. (1971) Accumulating evidence: procedures for resolving contradictions among different research studies. *Harvard Educational Review*, 41, 429–71.

Likert, R. (1932) A *Technique for the Measurement of Attitudes*. New York: Columbia University Press.

Limerick, B., Burgess-Limerick, T. and Grace, M. (1996) The politics of interviewing: power relations and accepting the gift. *International Journal of Qualitative Studies in Education*, 9 (4), 449–60.

Lin, N. (1976) *Foundations of Social Research*. New York: McGraw-Hill.

Lincoln, Y. S. and Guba, E. (1985) *Naturalistic Inquiry*. Beverly Hills, CA: Sage.

Lincoln, Y. S. and Guba, E. G. (1986) But is it rigorous? Trustworthiness and authenticity in naturalistic inquiry. In D. D. Williams (ed.) *Naturalistic Evaluation*. San Francisco, CA: Jossey-Bass, 73–84.

Linn, R.L. (ed.) (1993) *Educational Measurement* (third edition). Phoenix, AZ: American Council on Education and the Oryx Press.

Lipsey, M. W. (1992) Juvenile delinquency treatment: a meta-analytic inquiry into the variability of effects. In T. D. Cook, H. Cooper, D. S. Cordray, H. Hartmann, L. V. Hedges, R. J. Light, T. A. Louis and F. Mosteller (eds) *Meta-analysis for Explanation*. New York: Russell Sage Foundation.

Lissack, M. R. (2000) *Complexity Metaphors and the Management of a Knowledge Based Enterprise: An Exploration of Discovery*. http://lissack.com/writings/proposal.htm. Retrieved 10 November 2001.

Littleton, K., Ashman, H., Light, P., Artis, J., Roberts, T. and Oosterwegel, A. (1999) Gender, task contexts, and children's performance on a computer-based task. *European Journal of Psychology of Education*, 14 (1), 129–39.

Loevinger, J. (1957) Objective tests as instruments of psychological theory. *Psychological Review*, 72, 143–55.

Loewenthal, K. M. (2001) *An Introduction to Psychological Tests and Scales*. Hove: Psychology Press.

Lofland, J. (1970) Interactionist imagery and analytic interrupts. In T. Shibutani (ed.) *Human Nature and Collective Behaviour: Papers in Honour of Herbert Blumer*. Englewood Cliffs, NJ: Prentice-Hall, 35–45.

Lofland, J. (1971) *Analysing Social Settings*. Belmont, CA: Wadsworth.

Lonkila, M. (1995) Grounded theory as an emerging paradigm for computer-assisted qualitative data analysis. In U. Kelle (ed.) *Computer-Aided Qualitative Data Analysis*. London: Sage, 41–51.

MacDonald, B. (1987) *Research and Action in the Context of Policing*. Paper commissioned by the Police Federation. Norwich: Centre for Applied Research in Education, University of East Anglia.

MacDonald, G. (1997) Social work: beyond control? In A. Maynard and I. Chalmers (eds) *Non-random Reflections on Health Service Research*. London: BMJ Publishing Group, 122–46.

McClelland, D. C., Atkinson, J. W., Clark, R. A. and Lowell, E. L. (1953) *The Achievement Motive*. New York: Appleton-Century-Crofts.

McCormick, J. and Solman, R. (1992) Teachers' attributions of responsibility for occupational stress and satisfaction: an organisational perspective. *Educational Studies*, 18 (2), 201–22.

McCormick, R. and James, M. (1988) *Curriculum Evaluation in Schools* (second edition). London: Croom Helm.

McEneaney, J. E. and Sheridan, E. M. (1996) A survey-based component for programme assessment in undergraduate pre-service teacher education. *Research in Education*, 55, 49–61.

McGaw, B. (1997) Meta-analysis. In J. P. Keeves (ed.) *Educational Research, Methodology and Measurement: An International Handbook* (second edition). Oxford: Elsevier Science, 371–80.

McHugh, J. D. (1994) The Lords' will be done: interviewing the powerful in education. In G. Walford (ed.) *Researching the Powerful in Education*. London: UCL Press, 51–66.

McIntyre, D. and Macleod, G. (1978) The characteristics and uses of systematic classroom observation. In R. McAleese and D. Hamilton (eds) *Understanding Classroom Life*. Windsor: NFER, 102–31.

McKernan, J. (1991) *Curriculum Action Research*. London: Kogan Page.

McLaren, P. (1995) *Critical Pedagogy and Predatory Culture*. London: Routledge.

McLoughlin, T. (2002) The use of repertory grid analysis in studying students' conceptual frameworks in science. Paper presented at the European Conference on Educational Research, University of Lisbon, 11–14 September.

McNiece, R. and Jolliffe, F. (1998) An investigation into regional differences in educational performance in the National Child Development Study. *Educational Research*, 40 (1), 13–30.

McNiff, J. (1988) *Action Research: Principles and Practice*. London: Macmillan.

McNiff, J., with Whitehead, J. (2002) *Action Research: Principles and Practice* (second edition). London: RoutledgeFalmer.

McNiff, J., Lomax, P. and Whitehead, J. (1996) *You and your Action Research Project*. London: Routledge in association with Hyde Publications, Bournemouth.

McQuitty, L. L. (1957) Elementary linkage analysis for isolating orthogonal and oblique types and typal relevancies. *Educational and Psychological Measurement*, 17, 207–29.

McTaggart, R. (1996) Issues for participatory action researchers. In O. Zuber-Skerritt (ed.) *New Directions in Action Research*. London: Falmer, 243–55.

Madge, J. (1963) *The Origin of Scientific Sociology*. London: Tavistock.

Madge, J. (1965) *The Tools of Social Science*. London: Longman.

Mager, R. F. (1962) *Preparing Instructional Objectives*. Belmont, CA: Fearon.

Magnusson, D. (1971) An analysis of situational dimensions. *Perceptual and Motor Skills*, 32, 851–67.

Malinowski, B. (1922) *Argonauts of the Western Pacific: An Account of Native Enterprise and Adventure in the Archipelagoes of Melanesian New Guinea*. New York: Dutton.

Mannheim, K. (1936) *Ideology and Utopia*. London: Routledge & Kegan Paul.

Marcinkiewicz, H. R. and Clariana, R. B. (1997) The performance effects of headings within multi-choice tests. *British Journal of Educational Psychology*, 67, 111–17.

Marris, P. and Rein, M. (1967) *Dilemmas of Social Reform: Poverty and Community Action in the United States*. London: Routledge & Kegan Paul.

Marsh, H. W. and Yeung, A. S. (1998) Longitudinal structural equation models of academic self-concept and achievement: gender differences in the development of math and English constructs. *American Educational Research Journal*, 35 (4), 705–38.

Maslow, A. H. (1954) *Motivation and Personality*. New York: Harper & Row.

Mason, J. (2002) *Qualitative Researching* (second edition). London: Sage.

Mason, M., Mason, B. and Quayle, T. (1992) Illuminating English: how explicit language teaching improved public examination results in a comprehensive school. *Educational Studies*, 18 (3), 341–54.

Masschelein, J. (1991) The relevance of Habermas's communicative turn. *Studies in Philosophy and Education*, 11 (2), 95–111.

Mastrangelo, A., Eddy, E. R. and Lorenzet, S. J. (2004) The importance of personal and professional leadership. *Leadership and Organization Development Journal*, 25 (5–6), 435–51.

Mauthner, M., Birch, M., Jessop, J. and Miller, T. (eds) (2002) *Ethics in Qualitative Research*. London: Sage.

Maxwell, J. A. (1992) Understanding and validity in qualitative research. *Harvard Educational Review*, 62 (3), 279–300.

Mayall, B. (1999) Children and childhood. In S. Hood, B. Mayall and S. Oliver (eds) *Critical Issues in Social Research: Power and Prejudice*. Philadelphia, PA: Open University Press, 10–24.

Maynard, A. and Chalmers, I. (eds) (1997) *Non-random Reflections on Health Service Research*. London: BMJ Publishing Group.

Mayring, P. (2004) Qualitative content analysis. In U. Flick, E. von Kardoff and I. Steinke (eds) *A Companion to Qualitative Research*. London: Sage.

Mead, G. H. (ed. Charles Morris) (1934) *Mind, Self and Society*. Chicago, IL: University of Chicago Press.

Medawar, P. B. (1972) *The Hope of Progress*. London: Methuen.

Medawar, P. B. (1981) *Advice to a Young Scientist*. London: Pan.

Medawar, P. B. (1991) Scientific fraud. In D. Pike (ed.) *The Threat and the Glory: Reflections on Science and Scientists*. Oxford: Oxford University Press, 64–70.

Megarry, J. (1978) Retrospect and prospect. In R. McAleese (ed.) *Perspectives on Academic Gaming and Simulation 3: Training and Professional Education*. London: Kogan Page, 187–207.

Mehrens, W. and Kaminski, J. (1989) Methods for improving standardized test scores: fruitful, fruitless or fraudulent? *Educational Measurement: Issues and Practice*, 8 (1), 14–22.

Meinefeld, W. (2004) Hypotheses and prior knowledge in qualitative research. In U. Flick, E. von Kardoff and I. Steinke (eds) *A Companion to Qualitative Research*. London: Sage, 153–8.

Melrose, M. J. (1996) Got a philosophical match? Does it matter? In O. Zuber-Skerritt (ed.) *New Directions in Action Research*. London: Falmer.

Menzel, H. (1978) Meaning – who needs it? In M. Brenner, P. Marsh and M. Brenner (eds) *The Social Contexts of Method*. London: Croom Helm, 140–71.

Mercer, N., Wegerif, R. and Dawes, L. (1999) Children's talk and the development of reasoning in the classroom. *British Educational Research Journal*, 25 (1), 95–111.

Merriam, S. B. (1988) *Case Study Research in Education*. San Francisco, CA: Jossey Bass.

620 BIBLIOGRAPHY

Merry, U. (1998) *Organizational Lifespan LO17822.* http://www.learning-org.com/98.04/0206.html. Retrieved 14 November 2000.

Merton, R. K. (1949) *Social Theory and Social Structure.* Glencoe, IL: The Free Press.

Merton, R. K. (1967) *On Theoretical Sociology.* New York: The Free Press.

Merton, R. K. and Kendall, P. L. (1946) The focused interview. *American Journal of Sociology*, 51, 541–57.

Merton, R. K., Fiske, M. and Kendall, P. L. (1956) *The Focused Interview.* Glencoe, IL: The Free Press.

Messick, S. (1993) Validity. In R. Linn (ed.) *Educational Measurement* (third edition). Phoenix, AZ: American Council on Education and the Oryx Press, 13–103.

Michaels, M. (1995) The chaos network on-line. *The Chaos Network*, http://www.prairienet.org/business.ptech. Retrieved 14 November 2000.

Mickelson, R. A. (1994) A feminist approach to researching the powerful in education. In G. Walford (ed.) *Researching the Powerful in Education.* London: UCL Press, 132–50.

Miedama, S. and Wardekker, W. L. (1999) Emergent identity versus consistent identity: possibilities for a postmodern repoliticization of critical pedagogy. In T. Popkewitz and L. Fendler (eds) *Critical Theories in Education: Changing Terrains of Knowledge and Politics.* London: Routledge, 67–83.

Mies, M. (1993) Towards a methodology for feminist research. In M. Hammersley (ed.) *Social Research: Philosophy, Politics and Practice.* London: Sage in association with the Open University Press, 64–82.

Miles, M. and Huberman, M. (1984) *Qualitative Data Analysis.* Beverly Hills, CA: Sage.

Miles, M. and Huberman, M. (1994) *Qualitative Data Analysis* (second edition). Beverly Hills, CA: Sage.

Milgram, S. (1963) Behavioral study of obedience. *Journal of Abnormal and Social Psychology*, 67, 371–8.

Milgram, S. (1974) *Obedience to Authority.* New York: Harper & Row.

Millan, R., Gallagher, M. and Ellis, R. (1993) Surveying adolescent worries: development of the 'Things I Worry About' scale. *Pastoral Care in Education*, 11 (1), 43–57.

Miller, C. (1995) In-depth interviewing by telephone: some practical considerations. *Evaluation and Research in Education*, 9 (1), 29–38.

Miller, P. V. and Cannell, C. F. (1997) Interviewing for social research. In J. P. Keeves (ed.) *Educational Research, Methodology and Measurement:* *An International Handbook* (second edition). Oxford: Elsevier Science, 361–70.

Miller, R. L. (1999) *Researching Life Stories and Family Histories.* London: Sage.

Miller, T. and Bell, L. (2002) Consenting to what? Issues of access, gatekeeping and 'informed consent'. In M. Mauthner, M. Birch, J. Jessop and T. Miller (eds) *Ethics in Qualitative Research.* London: Sage, 53–69.

Millmann, J. and Greene, J. (1993) The specification and development of tests of achievement and ability. In R. Linn (ed.) *Educational Measurement* (third edition). Phoenix, AZ: American Council on Education and the Oryx Press, 147–200.

Mishler, E. G. (1986) *Research Interviewing: Context and Narrative.* Cambridge, MA: Harvard University Press.

Mishler, E. G. (1990) Validation in inquiry-guided research: the role of exemplars in narrative studies. *Harvard Educational Review*, 60 (4), 415–42.

Mishler, E. G. (1991) Representing discourse: the rhetoric of transcription. *Journal of Narrative and Life History*, 1, 225–80.

Mitchell, M. and Jolley, J. (1988) *Research Design Explained.* New York: Holt, Rinehart & Winston.

Mitchell, R. G. (1993) *Secrecy in Fieldwork.* London: Sage.

Mixon, D. (1972) Instead of deception. *Journal for the Theory of Social Behaviour*, 2, 146–77.

Mixon, D. (1974) If you won't deceive, what can you do? In N. Armistead (ed.) *Reconstructing Social Psychology.* Harmondsworth: Penguin, 72–85.

Monge, D. and Contractor, N. (2003) *Theories of Communication Networks.* Oxford: Oxford University Press.

Mooij, T. (1998) Pupil-class determinants of aggressive and victim behaviour in pupils. *British Journal of Educational Psychology*, 68, 373–85.

Morgan, C. (1999) Personal communication. University of Bath, Department of Education.

Morgan, C. (2005) Cultural validity. Personal communication. University of Bath, Department of Education.

Morgan, D. L. (1988) *Focus Groups as Qualitative Research.* Beverly Hills, CA: Sage.

Morris, L. L., Fitz-Gibbon, C. T. and Lindheim, E. (1987) *How to Measure Performance and Use Tests.* Beverly Hills, CA: Sage.

Morris, P. (1983) Teachers' perceptions of their pupils: a Hong Kong case study. *Research in Education*, 29, 81–6.

Morrison, K. R. B. (1993) *Planning and Accomplishing School-Centred Evaluation.* Dereham, UK: Peter Francis.

Morrison, K. R. B. (1995a) Habermas and the school curriculum. Unpublished PhD thesis, School of Education, University of Durham.

Morrison, K. R. B. (1995b) Dewey, Habermas and reflective practice. *Curriculum*, 16 (2), 82–94.

Morrison, K. R. B. (1996a) Developing reflective practice in higher degree students through a learning journal. *Studies in Higher Education*, 21 (3), 317–32.

Morrison, K. R. B. (1996b) Structuralism, postmodernity and the discourses of control, *Curriculum*, 17 (3), 164–77.

Morrison, K. R. B. (1996c) Why present school inspections are unethical. *Forum*, 38 (3), 79–80.

Morrison, K. R. B. (1997) Researching the need for multicultural perspectives in counsellor training: a critique of Bimrose and Bayne. *British Journal of Guidance and Counselling*, 25 (1), 135–42.

Morrison, K. R. B. (1998) *Management Theories for Educational Change*. London: Paul Chapman.

Morrison, K. R. B. (2001a) The open society and education in Macau. Public *sapientia* lecture presented at the Inter-University Institute of Macau, October.

Morrison, K. R. B. (2001b) Randomised controlled trials for evidence-based education: some problems in judging 'what works'. *Evaluation and Research in Education*, 15 (2), 69–83.

Morrison, K. R. B. (2002a) *School Leadership and Complexity Theory*. London: RoutledgeFalmer.

Morrison, K. R. B. (2002b) Education for the open, democratic society in Macau. Paper presented to the Catholic Teachers' Association, Macau, April.

Morrison, K. R. B. (2003) Complexity theory and curriculum reforms in Hong Kong. *Pedagogy, Culture and Society*, 22 (2), 279–302.

Morrison, K. R. B. (2005a) Schooling for conformity in Macau. Conference paper for the conference 'Implementation and Rethinking of Educational Reforms in Mainland China, Taiwan, Hong Kong and Macau'. University of Macau, 29 May.

Morrison, K. R. B. (2005b) Improving teaching and learning in higher education: metaphors and models for partnership consultancy. *Evaluation and Research in Education*, 17 (1), 31–44.

Morrison, K. R. B. (2006) Sensitive educational research in small states and territories: the case of Macau. *Compare*, 36 (2), 249–64.

Morrison, K. R. B and Tang, F. H. (2002) Testing to destruction: a problem in a small state. *Assessment in Education: Principles, Policy and Practice*, 9 (3), 289–317.

Morse, J. M. (1994) Design in funded qualitative research. In N. Denzin and Y. S. Lincoln (eds) *Handbook of Qualitative Research*. Thousand Oaks, CA: Sage, 220–35.

Mortimore, P., Sammons, P., Stoll, L., Lewis, D. and Ecob, R. (1988) *School Matters: The Junior Years*. London: Open Books.

Moser, C. and Kalton, G. (1977) *Survey Methods in Social Investigation*. London: Heinemann.

Mouly, G. J. (1978) *Educational Research: The Art and Science of Investigation*. Boston, MA: Allyn & Bacon.

Moyles, J. (2002) Observation as a research tool. In M. Coleman and A. J. Briggs (eds) *Research Methods in Educational Leadership*. London: Paul Chapman, 172–91.

Muijs, D. (2004) *Doing Quantitative Research in Education with SPSS*. London: Sage.

Munn, P., Johnstone, M. and Holligan, C. (1990) Pupils' perceptions of effective disciplinarians. *British Educational Research Journal*, 16 (2), 191–8.

Murphy, J., John, M. and Brown, H. (eds) (1984) *Dialogues and Debates in Social Psychology*. London: Erlbaum.

Musch, J. and Bröder, A. (1999) Test anxiety versus academic skills: a comparison of two alternative models for predicting performance in a statistics exam. *British Journal of Educational Psychology*, 69, 105–16.

Nash, R. (1976) *Classrooms Observed*. London: Routledge & Kegan Paul.

National Education Association of the United States: Association for Supervision and Curriculum Development (1959) *Learning about Learning from Action Research*. Washington, DC: National Education Association of the United States.

Naylor, P. (1995) Adolescents' perceptions of teacher racism. Unpublished PhD dissertation, Loughborough University of Technology.

Neal, S. (1995) Researching powerful people from a feminist and anti-racist perspective: a note on gender, collusion and marginality. *British Educational Research Journal*, 21 (4), 517–31.

Nedelsky, L. (1954) Absolute grading standards for objective tests. *Educational and Psychological Measurement*, 14, 3–19.

Neimeyer, G. J. (1992) Personal constructs in career counselling and development. *Journal of Career Development*, 18 (3), 163–73.

Nesfield-Cookson, B. (1987) *William Blake: Prophet of Universal Brotherhood*. London: Crucible.

Nias, J. (1989) *Primary Teachers Talking*. London: Routledge.

Nias, J. (1991) Primary teachers talking: a reflexive account of longitudinal research. In G. Walford (ed.) *Doing Educational Research*. London: Routledge, 147–65.

Nisbet, J. and Watt, J. (1984) Case study. In J. Bell, T. Bush, A. Fox, J. Goodey and S. Goulding (eds) *Conducting Small-Scale Investigations in Educational Management*. London: Harper & Row, 79–92.

Nixon, J. (ed.) (1981) *A Teacher's Guide to Action Research*. London: Grant McIntyre.

Noack, P. (1998) School achievement and adolescents' interactions with their fathers, mothers, and friends. *European Journal of Psychology of Education*, 13 (4), 503–13.

Noah, H. J. and Eckstein, M. A. (1988) Trade-offs in examination policies: an international comparative perspective. In P. Broadfoot, R. Murphy and H. Torrance (eds) *Changing Educational Assessment*. London: Routledge, 84–97.

Noffke, S. E. and Zeichner, K. M. (1987) Action research and teacher thinking. Paper presented at the annual meeting of the American Educational Research Association, Washington, DC.

Norris, N. (1990) *Understanding Educational Evaluation*. London: Kogan Page.

Nuttall, D. (1987) The validity of assessments. *European Journal of Psychology of Education*, 11 (2), 109–18.

Oakley, A. (1981) Interviewing women: a contradiction in terms. In H. Roberts (ed.) *Doing Feminist Research*. London: Routledge & Kegan Paul, 30–61.

Oakley, A. (1998) Gender, methodology and people's ways of knowing. *Sociology*, 34 (4), 707–31.

Oja, S. N. and Smulyan, L. (1989) *Collaborative Action Research: A Developmental Approach*. Lewes: Falmer.

Okagaki, L. and Frensch, P. A. (1998) Parenting and school achievement: a multiethnic perspective. *American Educational Research Journal*, 35 (1), 123–44.

Oldroyd, D. (1986) *The Arch of Knowledge: An Introductory Study of the History of the Philosophy and Methodology of Science*. New York: Methuen.

Olejnik, S. and Algina J. (2000) Measures of effect size for comparative studies: applications, interpretations, and limitations. *Contemporary Educational Psychology*, 25, 241–86.

O'Neill, B. and McMahon, H. (1990) *Opening New Windows with Bubble Dialogue*. Language Development and Hypermedia Research Group, Faculty of Education, University of Ulster at Coleraine.

Oppenheim, A. N. (1966) *Questionnaire Design and Attitude Measurement*. London: Heinemann.

Oppenheim, A. N. (1992) *Questionnaire Design, Interviewing and Attitude Measurement*. London: Pinter.

Osborne, J. I. (1977) College of education students' perceptions of the teaching situation. Unpublished MEd dissertation, University of Liverpool.

Osgood, C. E., Suci, G. S. and Tannenbaum, P. H. (1957) *The Measurement of Meaning*. Urbana, IL: University of Illinois.

Overett, S. and Donald, D. (1998) Paired reading: effects of a parental involvement programme in a disadvantaged community in South Africa. *British Journal of Educational Psychology*, 68, 347–56.

Pallant, J. (2001) *SPSS Survival Manual*. Maidenhead: Open University Press and McGraw-Hill Education.

Palys, T. S. (1978) Simulation methods and social psychology. *Journal for the Theory of Social Behaviour*, 8, 341–68.

Papasolomoutos, C. and Christie, T. (1998) Using national surveys: a review of secondary analyses with special reference to schools. *Educational Research*, 40 (3), 295–310.

Parker, H. J. (1974) *View from the Boys*. Newton Abbot: David & Charles.

Parker, I. (1992) *Discourse Dynamics: Critical Analysis for Social and Individual Psychology*. London: Routledge.

Parlett, M. and Hamilton, D. (1976) Evaluation as illumination. In D. Tawney (ed.) *Curriculum Evaluation Today: Trends and Implications*. London: Macmillan, 84–101.

Parsons, E., Chalkley, B. and Jones, A. (1996) The role of Geographic Information Systems in the study of parental choice and secondary school catchments. *Evaluation and Research in Education*, 10 (1), 23–34.

Parsons, J. M., Graham, N. and Honess, T. (1983) A teacher's implicit model of how children learn. *British Educational Research Journal*, 9 (1), 91–101.

Parsons, M. and Lyons, G. (1979) An alternative approach to enquiry in educational management. *Educational Management and Administration*, 8 (1), 75–84.

Paterson, L. (1991) An introduction to multilevel modelling. In S. W. Raudenbush and J. Willms (eds) *Schools, Classrooms and Pupils: International Studies of Schooling from a Multilevel Perspective*. San Diego, CA: Academic Press, 13–24.

Paterson, L. and Goldstein, H. (1991) New statistical methods for analysing social structures: an introduction of multilevel models. *British Educational Research Journal*, 17 (4), 387–93.

Patrick, J. (1973) *A Glasgow Gang Observed*. London: Eyre Methuen.

Patton, M. Q. (1980) *Qualitative Evaluation Methods*. Beverly Hills, CA: Sage.

Patton, M. Q. (1990) *Qualitative Evaluation and Research Methods* (second edition). London: Sage.

Pawson, R. and Tilley, N. (1993) OXO, Tide brand X and new improved evaluation. Paper presented at the British Sociological Association Annual Conference, University of Essex.

Payne, G., Dingwall, R., Payne, J. and Carter, M. (1980) *Sociology and Social Research*. London: Routledge & Kegan Paul.

Peak, D. and Frame, M. (1994) *Chaos under Control: The Art and Science of Complexity*. New York: W. H. Freeman.

Peevers, B. H. and Secord, P. F. (1973) Developmental changes in attribution of descriptive concepts to persons. *Journal of Personality and Social Psychology*, 27 (1), 120–8.

Peters, T. (1989) *Thriving on Chaos*. London: Pan.

Phillips, R. (1998) Some methodological and ethical dilemmas in élite-based research. *British Educational Research Journal*, 24 (1), 5–20.

Pike, D. (ed.) (1991) *The Threat and the Glory: Reflections on Science and Scientists*. Oxford: Oxford University Press.

Pilliner, A. (1973) *Experiment in Educational Research*. E 341. Milton Keynes: Open University Press.

Pitman, M. A. and Maxwell, J. A. (1992) Qualitative approaches to evaluation: models and methods. In M. LeCompte, W. L. Millroy and J. Preissle (eds) *The Handbook of Qualitative Research in Education*. London: Academic Press, 729–70.

Platt, J. (1981) Evidence and proof in documentary research: some specific problems of documentary research. *Sociological Review*, 29 (1), 31–52.

Plewis, I. (1985) *Analysing Change: Measurement and Explanation Using Longitudinal Data*. Chichester: John Wiley.

Plewis, I. (1991) Using multilevel models to link educational progress with curriculum coverage. In S. W. Raudenbush and J. Willms (eds) *Schools, Classrooms and Pupils: International Studies of Schooling from a Multilevel Perspective*. San Diego, CA: Academic Press, 53–65.

Plewis, I. (1997) *Statistics in Education*. London: Arnold.

Plummer, K. (1983) *Documents of Life: An Introduction to the Problems and Literature of a Humanistic Method*. London: Allen & Unwin.

Pollard, A. (1985) *The Social World of the Primary School*. Eastbourne: Holt, Rinehart & Winston.

Pope, M. L. and Keen, T. R. (1981) *Personal Construct Psychology and Education*. London: Academic Press.

Popper, K. (1968) *The Logic of Scientific Discovery* (second edition). London: Hutchinson.

Potter, J. and Wetherall, M. (1987) *Discourse and Social Psychology: Beyond Attitudes and Behaviour*. London: Sage.

Prein, G., Kelle, U. and Bird, K. (1995) An overview of software. In U. Kelle (ed.) *Computer-Aided Qualitative Data Analysis*. London: Sage.

Preisler, G. M. and Ahström, M. (1997) Sign language for hard of hearing children – a hindrance or a benefit for their development? *European Journal of Psychology of Education*, 12 (4), 465–77.

Pring, R. (1984) The problems of confidentiality. In M. Skilbeck (ed.) *Evaluating the Curriculum in the Eighties*. Sevenoaks: Hodder & Stoughton, 38–44.

Prior, L. (2003) *Using Documents in Social Research*. London: Sage.

Prosser, M. and Trigwell, K. (1997) Relations between perceptions of the teaching environment and approaches to teaching. *British Journal of Educational Psychology*, 67, 25–35.

Punch, K. F. (2003) *Survey Research: The Basics*. London: Sage.

Quantz, R. A. (1992) On critical ethnography (with some postmodern considerations). In M. LeCompte, W. L. Millroy and J. Preissle (eds) *The Handbook of Qualitative Research in Education*. London: Academic Press, 447–506.

Raffe, D., Bundell, I. and Bibby, J. (1989) Ethics and tactics: issues arising from an educational survey. In R. G. Burgess (ed.) *The Ethics of Educational Research*. Lewes: Falmer, 13–30.

Ramsden, C. and Reason, D. (1997) Conversation – discourse analysis in library and information services. *Education for Information*, 15 (4), 283–95.

Rapoport, R. N. (1970) Three dilemmas in action research. *Human Relations*, 23 (6), 499–513.

Rasmussen, D. M. (1990) *Reading Habermas*. Oxford: Basil Blackwell.

Ravenette, A. T. (1977) Personal construct theory: an approach to the psychological investigation of children and young people. In D. Bannister (ed.) *New Perspectives in Personal Construct Theory*. London: Academic Press, 251–80.

Redline, C. D., Dillman, D. A., Carley-Baxter, L. and Creecy, R. (2002) Factors that influence reading and comprehension in self-administered questionnaires. Paper presented at the Workshop on Item-Nonresponse and Data Quality, Basle, Switzerland, 10 October.

Reips, U.-D. (2002a) Internet-based psychological experimenting: five dos and don'ts. *Social Science Computer Review*, 20 (3), 241–9.

Reips, U.-D. (2002b) Standards for Internet-based experimenting. *Experimental Psychology*, 49 (4), 243–56.

Renzetti, C. M. and Lee, R. M. (1993) *Researching Sensitive Topics*. London: Sage.

Rex, J. (ed.) (1974) *Approaches to Sociology: An Introduction to Major Trends in British Sociology*. London: Routledge & Kegan Paul.

Reynolds, P. D. (1979) *Ethical Dilemmas and Social Science Research*. San Francisco, CA: Jossey-Bass.

Ribbens, J. and Edwards, R. (1997) *Feminist Dilemmas in Qualitative Research: Public Knowledge and Private Lives*. London: Sage.

Rice, J. M. (1897) The futility of the spelling grind. Cited in G. de Landsheere (1997) History of educational research. In J. P. Keeves (ed.) *Educational Research, Methodology, and Measurement: An International Handbook* (second edition). Oxford: Elsevier Science, 8–16.

Richardson, J. T. E. (1996) Measures of effect size. *Behavior Research Methods Instruments and Computers*, 28, 12–22.

Ridgway, J. (1998) *The Modeling of Systems and Macro-Systemic Change: Lessons for Evaluation from Epidemiology and Ecology*. Research Monograph 8. University of Wisconsin-Madison, WI: National Institute for Science Education.

Riecken, H. W. and Boruch, R. F. (1974) *Social Explanation: A Method for Planning and Evaluating Social Intervention*. New York: Academic Press.

Rigby, K. (1999) Peer victimisation at school and the health of secondary school students. *British Journal of Educational Psychology*, 69, 95–104.

Riley, M. W. (1963) *Sociological Research 1: A Case Approach*. New York: Harcourt, Brace & World.

Robinson, B. (1982) *Tutoring by Telephone: A Handbook*. Milton Keynes: Open University Press.

Robinson, P. and Smithers, A. (1999) Should the sexes be separated for secondary education – comparisons of single-sex and co-educational schools? *Research Papers in Education*, 14 (1), 23–49.

Robson, C. (1993) *Real World Research*. Oxford: Blackwell.

Robson, C. (2002) *Real World Research* (second edition). Oxford: Blackwell.

Robson, J. and Collier, K. (1991) Designing "Sugar 'n' Spice" – An anti-sexist simulation. *Simulation/Games for Learning*, 21 (3), 213–19.

Roderick, R. (1986) *Habermas and the Foundations of Critical Theory*. London: Macmillan.

Rodrigues, D. and Rodrigues, R. (2000) *The Research Paper and the World Wide Web*. Englewood Cliffs, NJ: Prentice Hall.

Rogers, C. R. (1942) *Counselling and Psychotherapy*. Boston, MA: Houghton Mifflin.

Rogers, C. R. (1945) The non-directive method as a technique for social research. *American Journal of Sociology*, 50, 279–83.

Rogers, C. R. (1969) *Freedom to Learn*. Columbus, OH: Merrill.

Rogers, C. R. and Stevens, B. (1967) *Person to Person: The Problem of Being Human*. London: Souvenir.

Rogers, V. M. and Atwood, R. K. (1974) Can we put ourselves in their place? *Yearbook of the National Council for Social Studies*, 44, 80–111.

Roman, L. G. and Apple, M. (1990) Is Naturalism a move away from positivism? Materialist and feminist approaches to subjectivity in ethnographic research. In E. Eisner and A. Peshkin (eds) *Qualitative Inquiry in Education: The Continuing Debate*. New York: Teachers College Press, 38–73.

Rose, D. and Sullivan, O. (1993) *Introducing Data Analysis for Social Scientists*. Buckingham: Open University Press.

Rosenthal, R. (1991) *Meta-analysis Procedures for Social Research*. Beverly Hills, CA: Sage.

Rosier, M. J. (1997) Survey research methods. In J. P. Keeves (ed.) *Educational Research, Methodology and Measurement: An International Handbook* (second edition). Oxford: Elsevier Science, 154–62.

Ross, K. N. and Rust, K. (1997) Sampling in survey research. In J. P. Keeves (ed.) *Educational Research, Methodology and Measurement: An International Handbook* (second edition). Oxford: Elsevier Science, 427–38.

Ross, K. N. and Wilson, M. (1997) Sampling error in survey research. In J. P. Keeves (ed.) *Educational Research, Methodology and Measurement: An International Handbook* (second edition). Oxford: Elsevier Science, 663–70.

Roszak, T. (1970) *The Making of a Counter Culture*. London: Faber & Faber.

Roszak, T. (1972) *Where the Wasteland Ends*. London: Faber & Faber.

Rozeboom, W. W. (1997) Good science is abductive, not hypothetico-deductive. In L. L. Harlow, S. A.

Muliak and J. H. Steiger (eds) *What if There Were No Significance Tests?* Mahwah, NJ: Erlbaum, 335–92.

Roztocki, N. and Lahri, N. A. (2002) Is the applicability of web-based surveys for academic research limited to the field of information technology? Proceedings of the Thirty-sixth Hawaii International Conference on System Sciences. http://csdl.computer.org/comp/proceedings/hicss/2003/1874/08/187480262a.pdf. Retrieved 26 February 2005.

Ruane, J. M. (2005) *Essentials of Research Methods: A Guide to Social Science Research.* Oxford: Blackwell.

Ruddock, J. (1981) *Evaluation: A Consideration of Principles and Methods.* Manchester Monographs 10. Manchester: University of Manchester.

Ruspini, E. (2002) *Introduction to Longitudinal Research.* London: Routledge.

Ryle, A. (1975) *Frames and Cages: The Repertory Grid Approach to Human Understanding.* Brighton: Sussex University Press.

Sacks, H. (1992) *Lectures on Conversation,* edited G. Jefferson. Oxford: Basil Blackwell.

Sacks, P. (1999) *Standardized Minds.* Cambridge, MA: Perseus.

Sagor, R. (2005) *The Action Research Guidebook: A Four-Step Process for Educators and Teams.* Thousand Oaks, CA: Corwin.

Sainsbury, M., Whetton, C., Mason, K. and Schagen, I. (1998) Fallback in attainment on transfer at age 11: evidence from the summer literacy schools evaluation. *Educational Research,* 40 (1), 73–81.

Salmon, P. (1969) Differential conforming of the developmental process. *British Journal of Social and Clinical Psychology,* 8, 22–31.

Sanday, A. (1993) The relationship between educational research and evaluation and the role of the local education authority. In R. G. Burgess (ed.) *Educational Research and Evaluation for Policy and Practice.* London: Falmer, 32–43.

Santonus, M. (1998) *Simple, Yet Complex.* http://www.cio.com/archive/enterprise/041598_qanda_content.html. Retrieved 10 November 2000.

Sapsford, R. (1999) *Survey Research.* London: Sage.

Schagen, I. and Sainsbury, M. (1996) Multilevel analysis of the key stage 1 national curriculum data in 1995. *Oxford Review of Education,* 22 (3), 265–72.

Schatzman, L. and Strauss, A. L. (1973) *Field Research: Strategies for a Natural Sociology.* Englewood Cliffs, NJ: Prentice Hall.

Scheurich, J. J. (1995) A postmodernist critique of research interviewing. *Qualitative Studies in Education,* 8 (3), 239–52.

Scheurich, J. J. (1996) The masks of validity: a deconstructive investigation. *International Journal of Qualitative Studies in Education,* 9 (1), 49–60.

Schofield, J. W. (1990). Generalizability in qualitative research. In E. Eisner and A. Peshkin (eds) *Qualitative Inquiry in Education.* New York: Teachers College Press, 201–32.

Schofield, W. (1996) Survey sampling. In R. Sapsford and V. Jupp (1996) (eds) *Data Collection and Analysis.* London: Sage and the Open University Press, 25–55.

Schön, D. (1983) *The Reflective Practitioner: How Professionals Think in Action.* London: Temple Smith.

Schön, D. (1987) *Educating the Reflective Practitioner.* San Francisco, CA Jossey-Bass.

Schutz, A. (1962) *Collected Papers.* The Hague: Nijhoff.

Schwarz, S. and Reips, U.-D. (2001) CGI versus Javascript: a web experiment on the reversed hindsight bias. In U.-D. Reips and M. Bosnjak (eds) *Dimensions of Internet Science.* Lengerich, Germany: Pabst Science, 75–90.

Scott, J. (1990) *A Matter of Record.* Cambridge: Polity Press.

Scott, S. (1985) Feminist research and qualitative methods: a discussion of some of the issues. In R. G. Burgess (ed.) *Issues in Educational Research: Qualitative Methods.* Lewes: Falmer, 67–85.

Sears, R., Maccoby, E. and Levin, H. (1957) *Patterns of Child Rearing.* Palo Alto, CA: Stanford University Press.

Sears, R. R., Rau, L. and Alpert, R. (1965) *Identification and Child Rearing.* Stanford, CA: Stanford University Press.

Secord, P. F. and Peevers, B. H. (1974) The development and attribution of person concepts. In T. Mischel (ed.) *On Understanding Persons.* Oxford: Basil Blackwell.

Seidel, J. and Kelle, U. (1995) Different functions of coding in the analysis of textual data. In U. Kelle (ed.) *Computer-aided Qualitative Data Analysis: Theory, Methods and Practice.* London: Sage, 52–61.

Seifert, T. L. (1997) Academic goals and emotions: results of a structural equation model and a cluster analysis. *British Journal of Educational Psychology,* 67, 323–38.

Selleck, R. W. J. (1991) The Manchester Statistical Society and the foundation of social science research. In D. S. Anderson and B. J. Biddle (eds) *Knowledge for Policy: Improving Education through Research*. London: Falmer, 291–304.

Sellitz, C., Wrightsman, L. S. and Cook, S. W. (1976) *Research Methods in Social Relations*. New York: Holt, Rinehart & Winston.

Senge, P., Cambron-McCabe, N., Lucas, T., Smith, B., Dutton, J. and Kleiner, A. (2000) *Schools that Learn*. London: Nicholas Brealey.

Serafini, A. (ed.) (1989) *Ethics and Social Concern*. New York: Paragon House.

Severiens, S. and ten Dam, G. (1998) A multilevel meta-analysis of gender differences in learning orientations. *British Journal of Educational Psychology*, 68, 595–618.

Shapiro, B. L. (1990) A collaborative approach to help novice science teachers reflect on changes in their construction of the role of the science teacher. *Alberta Journal of Educational Research*, 36 (3), 203–22.

Shaughnessy, J. J., Zechmeister, E. B. and Zechmeister, J. S. (2003) *Research Methods in Psychology* (sixth edition). New York: McGraw-Hill.

Shavelson, R. J. and Berliner, D. C. (1991) Erosion of the education research infrastructure: a reply to Finn. In D. S. Anderson and B. J. Biddle (eds) *Knowledge for Policy: Improving Education through Research*. London: Falmer, 79–84.

Shaw, E. L. (1992) The influence of methods instruction on the beliefs of preservice elementary and secondary science teachers: preliminary comparative analyses. *School Science and Mathematics*, 92, 14–22.

Shuy, R. W. (2003) In-person versus telephone interviewing. In J. A. Holstein and J. F. Gubrium (eds) *Inside Interviewing: New Lenses, New Concerns*. Thousand Oaks, CA: Sage, 173–193.

Sideris, G. (1998) Direct classroom observation. *Research in Education*, 59, 19–28.

Sieber, J. E. (1992) *Planning Ethically Responsible Research: A Guide for Students and Internal Review Boards*. Beverly Hills, CA: Sage.

Sieber, J. E. and Stanley, B. (1988) Ethical and professional dimensions of socially sensitive research. *American Psychologist*, 43, 49–55.

Siegel, H. (1987) *Relativism Refuted*. Dordrecht, Netherlands: D. Reidel.

Siegel, S. (1956) *Nonparametric Statistics for the Behavioral Sciences*. New York: McGraw-Hill.

Sikes, P. and Troyna, B. (1991) True stories: a case study in the use of life histories in teacher education. *Educational Review*, 43 (1), 3–16.

Sikes, P., Measor, L. and Woods, P. (1985) *Teacher Careers*. Lewes: Falmer.

Silverman, D. (1985) *Qualitative Methodology and Sociology: Describing the Social World*. Brookfield, VT: Gower.

Silverman, D. (1993) *Interpreting Qualitative Data*. London: Sage.

Simon, H. A. (1996) *The Sciences of the Artificial* (third edition). Cambridge, MA: The MIT Press.

Simon, J. L. (1978) *Basic Research Methods in Social Science*. New York: Random House.

Simons, H. (1982) Conversation piece: the practice of interviewing in case study research. In R. McCormick (ed.) *Calling Education to Account*. London: Heinemann, 239–46.

Simons, H. (1989) *Getting to Know School in a Democracy*. London: Falmer.

Simons, H. (1996) The paradox of case study. *Cambridge Journal of Education*, 26 (2), 225–40.

Simons, H. (2000) Damned if you do, damned if you don't: ethical and political dilemmas in education. In H. Simons and R. Usher (eds) *Situated Ethics in Educational Research*. London: RoutledgeFalmer, 39–55.

Simons, H. and Usher, R. (2000) Introduction: ethics in the practice of research. In H. Simons and R. Usher (eds) *Situated Ethics in Educational Research*. London: RoutledgeFalmer, 1–11.

Simons, H. and Usher, R. (eds) (2000) *Situated Ethics in Educational Research*. London: RoutledgeFalmer.

Slavin, R. E. (1984a) Meta-analysis in education: how has it been used? *Educational Researcher* (American Educational Research Association), 13 (8), 6–15

Slavin, R. E. (1984b) A rejoinder to Carlberg et al. *Educational Researcher* (American Educational Research Association), 13 (8), 24–7.

Smith, H. W. (1975) *Strategies of Social Research: The Methodological Imagination*. London: Prentice Hall.

Smith, H. W. (1991) *Strategies of Social Research* (third edition). Orlando, FL: Holt, Rinehart & Winston.

Smith, L. M. (1987) *Kensington Revisited*. Lewes: Falmer.

Smith, M. and Leigh, B. (1997) Virtual subjects: using the Internet as an alternative source of subjects and research environment. *Behavior Research Methods, Instruments and Computers*, 29, 496–505.

Smith, M. L. and Glass, G. V. (1977) Meta-analysis of psychotherapy outcome studies. *American Psychologist*, 32, 752–60.

Smith, M. L. and Glass, G. V. (1987) *Research and Evaluation in Education and the Social Sciences*. Englewood Cliffs, NJ: Prentice-Hall.

Smith, S. and Leach, C. (1972) A hierarchical measure of cognitive complexity. *British Journal of Psychology*, 63 (4), 561–8.

Smyth, J. (1989) Developing and sustaining critical reflection in teacher education. *Journal of Teacher Education*, 40 (2), 2–9.

Smyth, J. D., Dillman, D. A., Christian, L. M. and Stern, M. J. (2004) How visual grouping influences answers to Internet surveys. Paper presented at the American Association for Public Opinion Research, Phoenix, AZ.

Social and Community Planning Research (1972) *Questionnaire Design Manual No. 5*. Available from 16 Duncan Terrace, London, N1 8BZ.

Social Research Association (2003) *Ethical Guidelines*. http://www.the-sra.org.uk/ethics03.pdf. Retrieved 15 May 2005.

Social Sciences and Humanities Research Council of Canada (1981) *Ethical Guidelines for the Institutional Review Committee for Research with Human Subjects*.

Solomon, D. J. (2001) Conducting web-based surveys ERIC Digest. ED458291 ERIC Clearinghouse on Assessment and Evaluation, College Park, MD. http://www.ericdigests.org/2002–2/surveys.htm. Retrieved 14 April 2004.

Solomon, R. L. (1949) An extension of control group design. *Psychological Bulletin*, 46, 137–50.

Somekh, B. (1995) The contribution of action research to development in social endeavours: a position paper on action research methodology. *British Educational Research Journal*, 21 (3), 339–55.

Southgate, V., Arnold, H. and Johnson, S. (1981) *Extending Beginning Reading*. London: Heinemann Educational Books for the Schools Council.

Spector, P. E. (1993) Research designs. In M. L. Lewis-Beck (ed.) *Experimental Design and Methods*. International Handbook of Quantitative Applications in the Social Sciences, Volume 3. London: Sage, 1–74.

Spencer, J. R. and Flin, R. (1990) *The Evidence of Children*. London: Blackstone.

Spindler, G. (ed.) (1982) *Doing the Ethnography of Schooling*. New York: Holt, Rinehart & Winston.

Spindler, G. and Spindler, L. (1992) Cultural process and ethnography: an anthropological perspective. In M. LeCompte, W. L. Millroy and J. Preissle (eds) *The Handbook of Qualitative Research in Education*. London: Academic Press, 53–92.

Spradley, J. P. (1979) *The Ethnographic Interview*. New York: Holt, Rinehart & Winston.

Spradley, J. P. (1980) *Participant Observation*. New York: Holt, Rinehart & Winston.

Stables, A. (1990) Differences between pupils from mixed and single-sex schools in their enjoyment of school subjects and in their attitude to science in school. *Educational Review*, 42 (3), 221–30.

Stacey, J. (1988). Can there be a feminist ethnography? *Women's Studies International Forum*, 11 (1), 21–7.

Stake, R. E. (1978) The case study method in social inquiry. *Educational Researcher*, 7 (2), 5–8.

Stake, R. E. (1994) Case studies. In N. K. Denzin and Y. S. Lincoln (eds) *Handbook of Qualitative Research*. London: Sage, 236–47.

Stake, R. E. (1995) *The Art of Case Study Research*. Thousand Oaks, CA: Sage.

Stenbacka, C. (2001) Qualitative research requires quality concepts of its own. *Management Decision*, 39 (7), 551–5.

Stenhouse, L. (1975) *An Introduction to Curriculum Research and Development*. London: Heinemann.

Stenhouse, L. (1979) What is action research? (mimeo). Norwich: Classroom Action Research Network.

Stenhouse, L. (1985) Case study methods. In T. Husen and T. N. Postlethwaite (eds) *International Encyclopaedia of Education* (first edition). Oxford: Pergamon, 640–6.

Stewart, I. (1990) *Does God Play Dice?* Harmondsworth: Penguin.

Stewart, J. and Yalonis, C. (2001) Internet-based surveys and sampling issues. Communique Partners. http://www.communiquepartners.com/white_papers/sampling_issues_and_the_internet_briefing_paper.pdf. Retrieved 26 January 2005.

Stewart, M. (2001) *The Co-Evolving Organization*. Rutland, UK: Decomplexity Associates. http://www.decomplexity.com/Coevolving%20Organization%20VU.pdf. Retrieved 14 November 2001.

Stiggins, R. J. (2001) *Student-Involved Classroom Assessment* (third edition). Upper Saddle River, NJ: Merrill Prentice Hall.

Stillar, G. F. (1998) *Analysing Everyday Texts: Discourses, Rhetoric, and Social Perspectives*. London: Sage.

Strand, S. (1999) Ethnic group, sex and economic disadvantage: associations with pupils' educational progress from Baseline to the end of Key Stage 1. *British Educational Research Journal*, 25 (2), 179–202.

Strauss, A. L. (1987) *Qualitative Analysis for Social Scientists*. Cambridge: Cambridge University Press.

Strauss, A. and Corbin, J. (1990) *Basics of Qualitative Research: Grounded Theory Procedures and Techniques*. Newbury Park, CA: Sage.

Strauss, A. L. and Corbin, J. (1994) Grounded theory methodology: an overview. In N. Denzin and Y. Lincoln (eds) *Handbook of Qualitative Research*. Thousand Oaks, CA: Sage, 273–85.

Strike, K. A. (1990) The ethics of educational evaluation. In J. Millman and L. Darling-Hammond (eds) *A New Handbook of Teacher Evaluation*. Newbury Park, CA: Corwin, 356–73.

Stronach, I. and Morris, B. (1994) Polemical notes on educational evaluation in an age of 'policy hysteria'. *Evaluation and Research in Education*, 8 (1–2), 5–19.

Stubbs, M. and Delamont, S. (eds) (1976) *Explorations in Classroom Observation*. Chichester: John Wiley.

Sturman, A. (1997) Case study methods. In J. P. Keeves (ed.) *Educational Research, Methodology and Measurement: An International Handbook* (second edition). Oxford: Elsevier Science, 61–6.

Sturman, A. (1999) Case study methods. In J. P. Keeves and G. Lakomski (eds) *Issues in Educational Research*. Oxford: Elsevier Science, 103–12.

Sudman, S. and Bradburn, N. M. (1982) *Asking Questions: A Practical Guide to Questionnaire Design*. San Francisco, CA: Jossey-Bass.

Sutherland, G. (1969) The study of the history of education. *History*, 54 (180).

Swantz, M. (1996) A personal position paper on participatory research: personal quest for living knowledge. *Qualitative Inquiry*, 2 (1), 120–36.

Sykes, W. and Hoinville, G. (1985) *Telephone Interviewing on a Survey of Social Attitudes*. London: Social and Community Planning Research.

Task Group on Assessment and Testing (1988) *National Curriculum: Testing and Assessment: A Report*. London: HMSO.

Tatar, M. (1998) Teachers as significant others: gender differences in secondary school pupils' perceptions. *British Journal of Educational Psychology*, 68, 255–68.

Taylor, J. L. and Walford, R. (1972) *Simulation in the Classroom*. Harmondsworth: Penguin.

Terry, A. A. (1998) Teachers as targets of bullying by their pupils: a study to investigate incidence. *British Journal of Educational Psychology*, 68, 255–68.

Tesch, R. (1990) *Qualitative Research: Analysis Types and Software Tools*. London: Falmer.

Thapar-Björket, S. and Henry, M. (2004) Reassessing the research relationship: location, position and power in fieldwork accounts. *International Journal of Social Research Methodology*, 7 (5), 363–81.

Thissen, D. (1990) Reliability and measurement precision. In H. Wainer (ed.) *Computer Adaptive Testing: A Primer*. Hillsdale, NJ: Erlbaum, 161–86.

Thody, A. (1997) Lies, damned lies – and storytelling. *Educational Management and Administration*, 25 (3), 325–38.

Thomas, G. and Pring, R. (2004) *Evidence-Based Practice in Education*. Maidenhead: Open University Press.

Thomas, J. B. (1992) Birmingham University and teacher training: day training college to department of education. *History of Education*, 21 (3), 307–21.

Thomas, L. F. (1978) A personal construct approach to learning in education, training and therapy. In F. Fransella (ed.) *Personal Construct Psychology*. London: Academic Press, 45–58.

Thomas, P. (1991) Research models: insiders, gadflies, limestone. In D. S. Anderson and B. J. Biddle (eds) *Knowledge for Policy: Improving Education through Research*. London: Falmer, 225–33.

Thomas, S., Sammons, P., Mortimore, P. and Smees, R. (1997) Differential secondary school effectiveness: comparing the performance of different pupil groups. *British Educational Research Journal*, 23 (4), 351–69.

Thomas, W. I. (1923) *The Unadjusted Girl*. Boston, MA: Little Brown.

Thomas, W. I. (1928) *The Child in America*. New York: Knopf.

Thomas, W. I. and Znaniecki, F. (1918) *The Polish Peasant in Europe and America*. Chicago, IL: University of Chicago Press.

Thompson, B. (1994) Guidelines for authors. *Educational and Psychological Measurement*, 54, 837–47.

Thompson, B. (1996) AERA editorial policies regarding statistical significance testing: three suggested reforms. *Educational Researcher*, 25 (2), 26–30.

Thompson, B. (1998) In praise of brilliance: where that praise really belongs. *American Psychologist*, 53, 799–800.

Thompson, B. (2001) Significance, effect sizes, stepwise methods, and other issues: strong arguments more the field. *Journal of Experimental Education*, 70, 80–93.

Thompson, B. (2002) What future quantitative social science research could look like: confidence intervals for effect sizes. *Educational Researcher*, April, 25–32.

Thompson, B. and Snyder, P. A. (1997) Statistical significance testing practices in the *Journal of Experimental Education*, 66, 75–83.

Thorne, B. (1994) *Gender Play: Girls and Boys in School.* New Brunswick, NJ: Rutgers University Press.

Thurstone, L. L. and Chave, E. J. (1929) *The Measurement of Attitudes.* Chicago, IL: University of Chicago Press.

Ticehurst, G. W. and Veal, A. J. (2000) *Business Research Methods.* Frechs Forest, NSW: Pearson.

Tombari, M. and Borich, G. (1999) *Authentic Assessment in the Classroom.* Englewood Cliffs, NJ: Prentice Hall.

Tones, K. (1997) Beyond the randomized controlled trial: a case for 'judicial review'. *Health Education Research,* 12 (2), i–iv.

Torres, C. A. (1992) Participatory action research and popular education in Latin America. *International Journal of Qualitative Studies in Education,* 5 (1), 51–62.

Travers, R. M. W. (1969) *An Introduction to Educational Research.* London: Collier-Macmillan.

Tripp, D. H. (1985) Case study generalisation: an agenda for action. *British Educational Research Journal,* 11 (1), 33–43.

Tripp, D. H. (1994) Teachers' lives, critical incidents and professional practice. *International Journal of Qualitative Studies in Education,* 7 (1), 65–72.

Troyna, B. and Hatcher, R. (1992) *Racism in Children's Lives: A Study in Mainly White Primary Schools.* London: Routledge.

Tuckman, B. W. (1972) *Conducting Educational Research.* New York: Harcourt Brace Jovanovich.

Tweddle, S., Avis, P., Wright, J. and Waller, T. (1998) Towards evaluating web sites. *British Journal of Educational Technology,* 29 (3), 267–70.

Tyler, R. (1949) *Basic Principles of Curriculum and Instruction.* Chicago, IL: University of Chicago Press.

Tymms, P. (1996) Theories, models and simulations: school effectiveness at an impasse. In J. Gray, D. Reynolds, C. T. Fitz-Gibbon and D. Jesson (eds) *Merging Traditions: The Future of Research on School Effectiveness and School Improvement.* London: Cassell, 121–35.

Tymms, P. B. (1999) *Baseline Assessment and Monitoring in the Primary Schools.* London: David Fulton.

UNESCO (1996) *Learning: The Treasure Within.* Paris: UNESCO.

US Dept of Health, Education and Welfare, Public Health Service and National Institute of Health (1971) *The Institutional Guide to D.H.E.W. Policy on Protecting Human Subjects,* DHEW Publication (NIH): 2 December, 72–102.

Usher, P. (1996) Feminist approaches to research. In D. Scott and R. Usher (eds) *Understanding Educational Research.* London: Routledge, 120–42.

Usher, R. and Scott, D. (1996) Afterword: the politics of educational research. In D. Scott and R. Usher (eds) *Understanding Educational Research.* London: Routledge, 175–80.

Valadines, N. (1999) Formal reasoning performance of higher secondary school students: theoretical and educational implications. *European Journal of Psychology of Education,* 14 (1), 109–17.

Van Etten, S., Pressley, M., Freebern, G. and Echevarria, M. (1998) An interview study of college freshmen's beliefs about their academic motivation. *European Journal of Psychology of Education,* 13 (1), 105–30.

Van Ments, M. (1978) Role-playing: playing a part or a mirror to meaning? *Sagset Journal,* 8 (3), 83–92.

Van Ments, M. (1983) *The Effective Use of Role-Play: A Handbook for Teachers and Trainers.* London: Croom Helm.

Van Meter, K. M. (2000) Sensitive topics – sensitive questions: overview of the sociological research literature. *Bulletin de Methodologie Sociologique,* 68 (October), 59–78.

Vasta, R. (1979) *Studying Children: An Introduction to Research Methods.* San Francisco, CA: W. H. Freeman.

Verma, G. K. and Mallick, K. (1999) *Researching Education: Perspectives and Techniques.* London: Falmer.

Verma, G. K. and Beard, R. M. (1981) *What is Educational Research?* Aldershot: Gower.

Vermunt, J. D. (1998) The regulation of constructive learning processes. *British Journal of Educational Psychology,* 68, 149–71.

Virtual Surveys Limited (2003) *How to Do Online Research.* Virtual Surveys Limited. http://www.virtualsurveys.com/papers/paper_3.asp. Retrieved 6 January 2003.

Von Eye, A. (1990) *Statistical Methods in Longitudinal Research.* New York: Academic Press.

Vulliamy, G. (1990) The potential of qualitative educational research in developing countries. In G. Vulliamy, K. Lewin and D. Stephens (1990) *Doing Educational Research in Developing Countries: Qualitative Strategies.* London: Falmer, 7–25.

Vulliamy, G., Lewin, K. and Stephens, D. (1990) *Doing Educational Research in Developing Countries: Qualitative Strategies.* London: Falmer.

Wainer, H. (ed.) (1990) *Computerized Adaptive Testing: A Primer.* Hillsdale, NJ: Erlbaum.

Wainer, H. and Mislevy, R. J. (1990) Item response theory, item calibration and proficiency estimation.

In H. Wainer (ed.) *Computerized Adaptive Testing: A Primer*. Hillsdale, NJ: Erlbaum, 65–102.

Waldrop, M. M. (1992) *Complexity: The Emerging Science at the Edge of Order and Chaos*. Harmondsworth: Penguin.

Walford, G. (1994a) A new focus on the powerful. In G. Walford (ed.) *Researching the Powerful in Education*. London: UCL Press, 2–11.

Walford, G. (1994b) Ethics and power in a study of pressure group politics. In G. Walford (ed.) *Researching the Powerful in Education*. London: UCL Press, 81–93.

Walford, G. (1994c) Reflections on researching the powerful. In G. Walford (ed.) *Researching the Powerful in Education*. London: UCL Press, 222–31.

Walford, G. (ed.) (1994d) *Researching the Powerful in Education*. London: UCL Press.

Walford, G. (2001) *Doing Qualitative Educational Research: A Personal Guide to the Research Process*. London: Continuum.

Walker, R. (1980) Making sense and losing meaning: problems of selection in doing case study. In H. Simons (ed.) *Towards a Science of the Singular*. Norwich: Centre for Applied Research in Education, University of East Anglia, 222–35.

Walker R. and Adelman, C. (1976) *Strawberries*. In M. Stubbs and S. Delamont (eds) *Explorations in Classroom Research*. London: Wiley, 133–50.

Wardekker, W. L. and Miedama, S. (1997) Critical pedagogy: an evaluation and a direction for reformulation. *Curriculum Inquiry*, 27 (1), 45–61.

Warnock, M. (1970) *Existentialism*. London: Oxford University Press.

Watt, J. H. (1997) Using the Internet for quantitative survey research. *Quirk's Marketing Research Review*, July, http://www.swiftinteractive.com.white1.asp. Retrieved 6 January 2003.

Watts, M. and Ebbutt, D. (1987) More than the sum of the parts: research methods in group interviewing. *British Educational Research Journal*, 13 (1), 25–34.

Webb, G. (1996) Becoming critical of action research for development. In O. Zuber-Skerritt (ed.) *New Directions in Action Research*. London: Falmer, 137–61.

Webb, L. M., Walker, K. L. and Bollis, T. S. (2004) Feminist pedagogy in the teaching of research methods. *International Journal of Social Research Methodology*, 7 (5), 415–28.

Weber, R. P. (1990) *Basic Content Analysis* (second edition). Thousand Oaks, CA: Sage.

Wedeen, P., Winter, J. and Broadfoot, P. (2002) *Assessment: What's in it for Schools?* London: RoutledgeFalmer.

Weems, G. H., Onwuegbuzie, A. J. and Lustig, D. (2003) Profiles of respondents who respond inconsistently to positively- and negatively-worded items on rating scales. *Evaluation and Research in Education*, 17 (1), 45–60.

Weisberg, H. F., Krosnick, J. A. and Bowen, B. D. (1996) *An Introduction to Survey Research, Polling, and Data Analysis* (third edition). Thousand Oaks, CA: Sage.

Weiskopf, R. and Laske, S. (1996) Emancipatory action research: a critical alternative to personnel development or a new way of patronising people? In O. Zuber-Skerritt (ed.) *New Directions in Action Research*. London: Falmer, 121–36.

Weiss, C. (1991a) The many meanings of research utilization. In D. S. Anderson and B. J. Biddle (eds) *Knowledge for Policy: Improving Education through Research*. London: Falmer, 173–82.

Weiss, C. (1991b) Knowledge creep and decision accretion. In D. S. Anderson and B. J. Biddle (eds) *Knowledge for Policy: Improving Education through Research*. London: Falmer, 183–92.

Wheatley, M. (1999) *Leadership and the New Science: Discovering Order in a Chaotic World* (second edition). San Francisco, CA: Berrett-Koehler.

Whitehead, J. (1985) An analysis of an individual's educational development: the basis for personally oriented action research. In M. Shipman (ed.) *Educational Research: Principles, Policies and Practices*. Lewes: Falmer, 97–108.

Whiteley, P. (1983) The analysis of contingency tables. In D. McKay, N. Schofield and P. Whiteley (eds) *Data Analysis and the Social Sciences*. London: Frances Pinter, 72–119.

Whitty, G. and Edwards, A. D. (1994) Researching Thatcherite policy. In G. Walford (ed.) *Researching the Powerful in Education*. London: UCL Press, 14–31.

Whyte, J. (1986) *Girls Into Science and Technology: The Story of a Project*. London: Routledge & Kegan Paul.

Whyte, W. F. (1949) *Street Corner Society: The Social Structure of an Italian Slum* (second edition). Chicago, IL: University of Chicago Press.

Whyte, W. F. (1955) *Street Corner Society: The Social Structure of an Italian Slum* (enlarged edition). Chicago, IL: University of Chicago Press.

Whyte, W. F. (1982) Interviewing in field research. In R. Burgess (ed.) *Field Research: A Sourcebook and Field Manual*. London: Allen & Unwin, 111–22.

Whyte, W. F. (1993) *Street Corner Society: The Social Structure of an Italian Slum* (fourth edition). Chicago, IL: University of Chicago Press.

Wickens, P. (1987) *The Road to Nissan: Flexibility, Quality, Teamwork.* London: Macmillan.

Wiggins, G. (1998) *Educative Assessment.* San Francisco, CA: Jossey-Bass.

Wilcox, R. R. (1997) Simulation as a research technique. In J. P. Keeves (ed.) *Educational Research, Methodology and Measurement: An International Handbook* (second edition). Oxford: Elsevier Science, 150–4.

Wild, P., Scivier, J. E. and Richardson, S. J. (1992) Evaluating information technology-supported local management of schools: the user acceptability audit. *Educational Management and Administration*, 20 (1), 40–8.

Wiles, J. and Bondi, J.C. (1984) *Curriculum Development: A Guide to Practice* (second edition). Columbus, OH: Merrill.

Wiliam, D. (1996) Standards in examinations: a matter of trust. *The Curriculum Journal*, 7 (3), 293–306.

Wilkinson, J. (2000) Direct observation. In G. M. Breakwell, S. Hammond and C. Fife-Shaw (eds) *Research Methods in Psychology* (second edition). London: Sage, 224–238.

Wilkinson, L. and the Task Force on Statistical Inference, APA Board of Scientific Affairs (1999) Statistical methods in psychology journals: guidelines and explanations. *American Psychologist*, 54, 594–604.

Willis, P. E. (1977) *Learning to Labour.* Farnborough, UK: Saxon House.

Willms, J. D. (1992) Pride or prejudice? Opportunity structure and the effects of Catholic schools in Scotland. In A. Yogev (ed.) *International Perspectives on Education and Society: A Research and Policy Annual*, Volume 2. Greenwich, CT: JAI Press.

Wilson, M. (1996) Asking questions. In R. Sapsford and V. Jupp (eds) *Data Collection and Analysis.* London: Sage and the Open University Press, 94–120.

Wilson, N. and McLean, S. (1994) *Questionnaire Design: A Practical Introduction.* Newtown Abbey, Co. Antrim: University of Ulster Press.

Wineburg, S. S. (1991) The self-fulfilment of the self-fulfilling prophecy. In D. S. Anderson and B. J. Biddle (eds) *Knowledge for Policy: Improving Education through Research.* London: Falmer, 276–90.

Winkley, D. (1995) *Diplomats and Detectives: LEA Advisers and Work.* London: Robert Royce.

Winter, G. (2000) A comparative discussion of the notion of 'validity' in qualitative and quantitative research. *The Qualitative Report*, 4 (3–4), March. www.nova.edu/sss/QR/QR4–3/winter.html. Retrieved 29 October 2005.

Winter, R. (1982) Dilemma analysis: a contribution to methodology for action research. *Cambridge Journal of Education*, 12 (3), 161–74.

Winter, R. (1996) Some principles and procedures for the conduct of action research. In O. Zuber-Skerritt (ed.) *New Directions in Action Research.* London: Falmer.

Witmer, D. F., Colman, R. W. and Katzman, S. L. (1999) From paper-and-pencil to screen-and-keyboard: toward a methodology for survey research on the Internet. In S. Jones (ed.) *Doing Internet Research.* Thousand Oaks, CA: Sage, 145–61.

Witte, J. C., Amoroso, L. M. and Howard, P. E. N. (1999) *Method and Representation in Internet–based Survey Tools: Mobility, Community, and Cultural Identity in Survey2000.* Evanston, IL: Department of Sociology, Northwestern University.

Wittgenstein, L. (1974) *Tractatus Logico-Philosophicus*, trans. D. Pears and B. McGuiness. London: Routledge & Kegan Paul.

Wolcott, H. F. (1973) *The Man in the Principal's Office.* New York: Holt, Rinehart & Winston.

Wolcott, H. F. (1992) Posturing in qualitative research. In M. LeCompte, W. L. Millroy and J. Preissle (eds) *The Handbook of Qualitative Research in Education.* London: Academic Press, 3–52.

Wolf, F. M. (1986) *Meta-analysis: Quantitative Methods for Research Synthesis.* Newbury Park, CA: Sage.

Wolf, R. M. (1994) The validity and reliability of outcome measure. In A. C. Tuijnman and T. N. Postlethwaite (eds) *Monitoring the Standards of Education.* Oxford: Pergamon, 121–32.

Wolff, S. (2004) Ways into the field and their variants. In U. Flick, E. von Kardoff and I. Steinke (eds) *A Companion to Qualitative Research.* London: Sage, 195–202.

Wood, P. (1995) Meta-analysis. In G. M. Breakwell, S. Hammond and C. Fife-Shaw (eds) *Research Methods in Psychology.* London: Sage, 396–99.

Woods, P. (1979) *The Divided School.* London: Routledge & Kegan Paul.

Woods, P. (1983) *Sociology and the School.* London: Routledge & Kegan Paul.

Woods, P. (1986) *Inside Schools: Ethnography in Educational Research.* London: Routledge & Kegan Paul.

Woods, P. (1989) *Working for Teacher Development.* Dereham, UK: Peter Francis.

Woods, P. (1992) Symbolic interactionism: theory and method. In M. LeCompte, W. L. Millroy and J. Preissle (eds) *The Handbook of Qualitative Research in Education*. London: Academic Press, 337–404.

Woods, P. (1993) Managing marginality: teacher development through grounded life history. *British Educational Research Journal*, 19 (5), 447–88.

Wooldridge, M. and Jennings, N. R. (1995) Intelligent agents: theory and practice. *Knowledge Engineering Review*, 10 (2), 115–52.

Worrall, L. (ed.) (1990) *Geographic Information Systems: Developments and Applications*. London: Belhaven Press.

Wragg, E. C. (1994) *An Introduction to Classroom Observation*. London: Routledge.

Wragg, E. C. (2002) Interviewing. In M. Coleman and A. R. J. Briggs (eds) *Research Methods in Educational Leadership*. London: Paul Chapman, 143–58.

Wright, D. B. (2003) Making friends with your data: improving how statistics are conducted and reported. *British Journal of Educational Psychology*, 73, 123–36.

Yan, S. U. (2005) Development in infants and its implications for parenting education: a review and case study. Unpublished MSc dissertation. Macau, People's Republic of China: School of Arts, Letters and Sciences, Macau Inter-University Institute.

Yin, R. K. (1984) *Case Study Research: Design and Methods*. Beverly Hills, CA: Sage.

Yorke, D. M (1978) Repertory grids in educational research: some methodological considerations. *British Educational Research Journal*, 4 (2), 63–74.

Young, J. (1971) *The Drugtakers*. London: Paladin.

Youngblood, M. (1997) *Life at the Edge of Chaos*. Dallas, TX: Perceval.

Youngman, M. B. (1984) Designing questionnaires. In J. Bell, T. Bush, A. Fox, J. Goodey and S. Goulding (eds) *Conducting Small-Scale Investigations in Educational Management*. London: Harper & Row, 156–76.

Zechmeister, E. B. and Shaughnessy, J. J. (1992) *A Practical Introduction to Research Methods in Psychology*. New York: McGraw-Hill.

Zimbardo, P. C. (1984) On the ethics of intervention in human psychological research with specific reference to the 'Stanford Prison Experiment'. In J. Murphy, M. John and H. Brown (eds) *Dialogues and Debates in Social Psychology*. London: Erlbaum in association with the Open University Press.

Znaniecki, F. (1934) *The Method of Sociology*. New York: Farrar & Rinehart.

Zuber-Skerritt, O. (1996a) Introduction. In O. Zuber-Skerritt (ed.) *New Directions in Action Research*. London: Falmer, 3–9.

Zuber-Skerritt, O. (1996b) Emancipatory action research for organisational change and management development. In O. Zuber-Skerritt (ed.) *New Direct-ions in Action Research*. London: Falmer, 83–105.

Zuzovsky, R. and Aitkin, M. (1991) Curriculum change and science achievement in Israel elementary schools. In S. W. Raudenbush and J. Willms (eds) *Schools, Classrooms and Pupils: International Studies of Schooling from a Multilevel Perspective*. San Diego, CA: Academic Press, 25–36.

INDEX